D0596998

THE WORLD ALMANAC
WHO'S WHO
of FILM

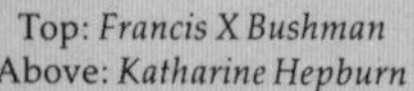

Top: *Francis X Bushman*
Above: *Katharine Hepburn*

Top: *Mae West*
Above: *Richard Gere*

# Foreword by Douglas Fairbanks Jr

World Almanac
An Imprint of Pharos Books
New York, New York

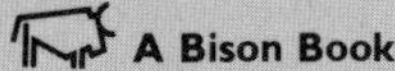

First published in 1987.



Distributed in the United States by Ballantine Books, a division of Random
House, Inc., and in Canada by Random House Canada Ltd.

Library of Congress Catalog Card Number 87-50075
Pharos Books ISBN 0-88687-308-8
Ballantine Books ISBN 0-345-34884-2

Printed in the United States of America

World Almanac
An Imprint of Pharos Books
A Scripps Howard Company
200 Park Avenue
New York, NY 10166

10 9 8 7 6 5 4 3 2 1

# The Dream Makers

*by Douglas Fairbanks Junior*

It's only a footnote in the history books now, but Hollywood, for the record was once a fig tree ranch before it was sectioned off into streets and lots. The town was founded in 1886 by a certain Horace Henderson Wilcox, a Methodist, a prohibitionist and a land developer from Topeka, Kansas, whose wife Diada named it Hollywood after a friend's summer house in Illinois. The town's first mayor was a retired meat packer, by the way, who banned 'the driving of more than two thousand sheep, goats or hogs through the city streets at any time unless accompanied by eight competent men.'

Within only a few decades, of course, it would become what film reviewer Vincent Canby has called 'the greatest dream factory in the history of the world,' but not before that uncanny formula was arrived at of making the dream out of wooden facades, celluloid, let's-pretend tears and even the occasional – and competent – sheep or goat. The early artisans who crafted the dream were engaged in what my father, being one of them, liked to call 'exaggeration apropos.' Film, to him, was a retelling of some aspect of our daily lives in such a heightened and dramatic way that real life became dream-like and therefore, I suppose, all the more palatable and compelling.

What is a motion picture or a movie or a film? By whatever name it goes by, it is probably best summed up as an inexpensive provider of amusement, elevated to an art form. But the making of a film is an enormous exercise in collaboration. Sometimes films can be dominated by the forceful personality of one producer, director or star, but even in those instances the contributions of other talent must be recognized. The industry's craftsmen and artisans were, in addition to its writers, some of the most important and least-appreciated contributors to this great art form.

But the movie-going public has always preferred learning more about the great film stars, which is understandable. Even though my family and I were long-time occupiers of the movie goldfish bowl, I myself have done my own fair share of star-gazing, helped, of course, by luckily being able to know many of the more celebrated ones personally. As a youth I remember first being goggle-eyed to behold the great shadows of the screen coming to life before me in the flesh. In the case of my father, he was a natural exception, and was, to me, very much the same man 'in person' as he appeared in films – dynamic, quick-witted and a fine athlete. But it is true that the theatrical world has always included a number of surprising personalities. For instance, one of its most venerated stars, Gloria Swanson, gave the appearance of glamour beyond all approachability, but was known by her friends off-screen to be in fact, one of the most down-to-earth, witty and amusing of women. John Barrymore was another superb contradiction of his image. On screen he could, when he chose, look almost saint-like, but in person it was well known that he could be outrageously shocking, although at the same time humorous and clever. They were a couple of prime examples of the 'flesh-and-blood' people behind the 'legend' labels. They were successful because in addition to the luck of opportunity, each of them possessed a special talent or quality that could be projected right through the film itself, out into the audience where our emotions could be pitched to great heights or lows – by the deft gesture or the well-spoken line – and where we were made to believe the unbelievable.

Hollywood today is a state of mind. The decline of the major producing studios over the years, due in part to independent competition, has meant the imaginary city limits now know no outer boundaries and the dream has taken us as far away as distant galaxies and as close to home as last night's nightmare. Its more celebrated citizens are those people who have refined a unique formula of story-telling for the millions. Now the stories of their own lives – summarized here – make for important, and even compelling, reading. Their accomplishments are proof that the call to competence made by the first 'mayor' of Hollywood – long after the sheep have been driven from the streets and the city has grown to engulf the globe – has still been upheld, fulfilled, exceeded.

# A

## ABBOTT, Bud (1895-1974) and COSTELLO, Lou (1906-1959)

William Abbott, known as Bud, was the snide straight man of the long-standing cross-talking vaudeville team. Costello was the pudgy funnyman. Abbott, born in Asbury Park, New Jersey, was the bully who left the dirty work to his partner, never believed his tall but true stories of crooks and monsters, and usually avoided the pie in the face. Costello, born Louis Cristillo in Patterson, New Jersey, began as a stunt man, and was the zanier part of the duo. The two teamed up in the early 1930s and honed their act in vaudeville and burlesque, on Broadway and radio before going to Hollywood. Their first film, and the only one in which they had supporting roles, was *One Night in the Tropics* (40). At the time, Universal Studios was in desperate financial difficulties, and it was Abbott and Costello who saved them from bankruptcy with *Buck Privates* (41), an immensely popular film that also featured The Andrews Sisters, the female singing trio that was to appear with the two comedians in several more films. The management of Universal knew a good thing when they saw it and immediately Abbott and Costello appeared in *In the Navy*, *Hold That Ghost*, *Keep 'Em Flying* and *Ride 'Em Cowboy* – all made in 1941. All of their more than 30 films relied on the same basic characterizations and the same broad, slapstick humor. Yet throughout the 1940s and early 1950s the team was consistently among Hollywood's top box-office draws. Along the way, they also went into science-fiction (*Abbott and Costello Go to Mars*, 53) and back in time (*The Naughty Nineties*, 45) in which their classic routine, 'Who's On First?' was featured. Their personal lives were marred by tragedy and the friction between the pair finally exploded in 1956 when they split. Costello made one film on his own, *The Thirty-Foot Bride of Candy Rock* (59), but it was not a success at the box-office.

**Selected Films:** *One Night in the Tropics* (40), *Buck Privates* (41), *In the Navy* (41), *Keep 'Em Flying* (41), *Ride 'Em Cowboy* (41), *Hold That Ghost* (41), *Who Done It?* (42), *The Naughty Nineties* (45), *The Wistful Widow of Wagon Gap* (47), *Abbott and Costello Meet Frankenstein* (48), *Jack and the Beanstalk* (52), *Abbott and Costello Go to Mars* (53), *Dance With Me Henry* (55), *The Thirty-Foot Bride of Candy Rock* (59 – Costello only).

## ABBOTT, John (1905- )

Born in London, Abbott began his acting career on the stage and also made several films in his native England including *Mademoiselle Docteur* (37), before moving to California. He made his Hollywood debut in *The Shanghai Gesture* (41). Best known for his intensely staring eyes Abbott was frequently cast in rather eccentric roles.

**Selected Films:** *Mademoiselle Docteur* (37), *The Shanghai Gesture* (41), *Mrs Miniver* (42), *Jane Eyre* (43), *Deception* (46), *The Woman in White* (48), *The Merry Widow* (52), *Gigi* (58), *Gambit* (66), *The Black Bird* (75), *Slapstick of Another Kind* (84).

## ABEL, Walter (1898-1987)

A character actor who became a familiar and reliable presence in Hollywood movies over four decades, Walter Abel was born in St Paul, Minnesota, where as a schoolboy he gained a reputation as a comic actor. He went to New York City to study at the American Academy of Dramatic Arts and by 1924 was playing serious, if minor, roles on Broadway. He also appeared in several silent films including *Out of a Clear Sky* (18) and *The North Wind's Malice* (20). He was signed up by Paramount and made his sound film debut in *Liliom* (34) but his first notable part was D'Artagnan in *The Three Musketeers* (35). From then on Abel appeared regularly in films, and although he occasionally got interesting roles, he usually played the somewhat harried or fidgety relative or friend of the leads.

**Selected Films:** *Out of a Clear Sky* (18), *The North Wind's Malice* (20), *Liliom* (34), *The Three Musketeers* (35), *Fury* (36), *Men With Wings* (38), *Arise My Love* (40), *Beyond the Blue Horizon* (42), *Star Spangled Rhythm* (42), *Holiday Inn* (42), *Mr Skeffington* (44), *Kiss and Tell* (45), *The Kid from Brooklyn* (46), *13 Rue Madeleine* (46), *Dream Girl* (48), *The Steel Jungle* (56), *Raintree County* (57), *Mirage* (65), *The Ultimate Solution of Grace Quigley* (84).

*Lou Costello and Bud Abbott in* Rio Rita *(42).*

## ABRAHAM, F Murray (1940- )

Born in Pittsburgh, Pennsylvania, he appeared in television commercials, in Shakespeare in New York's Central Park, and on the Broadway stage. He divides his time between his acting career and his work as a professor of theater at Brooklyn College. Abraham's greatest role was undoubtedly as the jealous composer, Antonio Salieri, in *Amadeus* (84), for which he won the Golden Globe Award and the Academy Award for Best Actor.
**Selected Films:** *Serpico* (73), *The Sunshine Boys* (75), *The Ritz* (76), *All the President's Men* (76), *The Big Fix* (78), *Scarface* (83), *Amadeus* (84), *The Name of the Rose* (86).

*F Murray Abraham in* Amadeus *(84).*

## ADAIR, Jean (1872-1953)

Jean Adair, born in Hamilton, Ontario, spent most of her acting career on the stage, but did appear now and then in films, mostly in old-lady roles. Among these was the classic film version of *Arsenic and Old Lace* (44), in which she played one of the homicidal aunts.
**Selected Films:** *In the Name of the Law* (22), *Advice to the Lovelorn* (33), *Arsenic and Old Lace* (44), *Something in the Wind* (46), *Living in a Big Way* (47).

## ADAMS, Edie (1929- )

Born Elizabeth Edith Enke in Kingston, Pennsylvania, Edie Adams studied music at Juilliard and acting at the Columbia School of Drama and went on to a career on Broadway (*Li'l Abner*) and television, most notably as a singer and comedienne with her husband Ernie Kovacs. Her film work, mostly secondary roles in movies such as *The Apartment* (60) displayed her talent for effervescent, mock-sexy comedy.
**Selected Films:** *The Apartment* (60), *Lover Come Back* (61), *It's a Mad Mad Mad Mad World* (63), *Love With the Proper Stranger* (64), *The Honey Pot* (67), *Racquet* (79), *Box Office* (82).

## ADAMS, Julie (1926- )

The soft and vulnerable quality of Julie (originally Betty May, and then Julia) Adams, born in Waterloo, Iowa, made her the ideal object of villains and monsters in second-feature movies from the 1940s – *The Dalton Gang* (49) – into the 1950s – *The Creature From the Black Lagoon* (54) – and through the 1970s – *McQ* (74). She is married to actor Ray Danton.
**Selected Films:** *The Dalton Gang* (49), *Bright Victory* (51), *Mississippi Gambler* (53), *The Creature From the Black Lagoon* (54), *Slaughter on Tenth Avenue* (57), *Valley of Mystery* (67), *McQ* (74), *Killer Force* (76), *The Fifth Floor* (80), *Champions* (84).

## ADAMS, Nick (1931-1968)

Nicholas Adamschock was born in Nanticoke, Pennsylvania. As Nick Adams, the young actor found early success playing leads and supporting parts as troubled-youths, making his debut in *Somebody Loves Me* (52). Despite an intensive career during the 1950s and 1960s that included supporting roles in *Picnic* (55) and *Rebel Without a Cause* (55), Adams never quite seemed to take off in films. He remained an also-ran as a movie rebel, and died of a drug overdose.
**Selected Films:** *Somebody Loves Me* (52), *Mister Roberts* (55), *Picnic* (55), *Rebel Without a Cause* (55), *No Time for Sergeants* (58), *Hell is for Heroes (62)*, *Die Monster Die!* (65), *Mission Mars* (68).

## ADDAMS, Dawn (1930-1985)

Born in Felixstowe, England, Dawn Addams went

to Hollywood in 1950. Though quite intelligent and reasonably capable as an actress, her main stock in trade was her physical appearance. She has been in some two dozen movies made in America and abroad. Most of them are unmemorable except for a leading role in Charlie Chaplin's *A King in New York* (57).
**Selected Films:** *Night into Morning* (51), *The Robe* (53), *Khyber Patrol* (54), *A King in New York* (57), *The Two Faces of Dr Jekyll* (60), *The Black Tulip* (64), *Vault of Horror* (73).

## ADDY, Wesley (1912- )

Born in Omaha, Nebraska, Wesley Addy spent many years on the stage before going into films, where he was often associated with the work of director Robert Aldrich, in films like *Kiss Me Deadly* (55) and *Whatever Happened to Baby Jane?* (62). More recently he has worked with James Ivory and Ismail Merchant, appearing in their productions of Henry James' *The Europeans* (79) and *The Bostonians* (84). He is married to actress Celeste Holm.
**Selected Films:** *The First Legion* (51), *Kiss Me Deadly* (55), *The Big Knife* (55), *Whatever Happened to Baby Jane?* (62), *Seconds* (66), *Network* (76), *The Europeans* (79), *The Verdict* (82), *The Bostonians* (84).

## ADLER, Luther (1903-1985)

Born into a noted Yiddish theatrical family in New York, the brother of Jay and Stella Adler, Luther Adler made his stage debut at the age of five. Most of his acting career was spent on the stage, but occasionally he brought his heavy features and powerful gift for character roles to films. Adler's first movie was *Lancer Spy* (37), and over the next four decades he appeared in some two dozen films including *The Desert Fox* (51), *The Brotherhood* (68), and *The Man in the Glass Booth* (75). He was married to actress Sylvia Sidney from 1938 to 1945.
**Selected Films:** *Lancer Spy* (37), *The Loves of Carmen* (48), *House of Strangers* (49), *The Magic Face* (51), *The Desert Fox* (51), *The Miami Story* (54), *The Last Angry Man* (59), *The Brotherhood* (68), *The Man in the Glass Booth* (75), *Voyage of the Damned* (76), *Absence of Malice* (81).

## ADLER, Stella (1895- )

The sister of Luther and Jay Adler and a member of a prominent Yiddish stage family, Stella Adler spent most of her career as one of the most notable acting teachers in her native New York. She made only three films.
**Selected Films:** *Love on Toast* (38), *Shadow of the Thin Man* (41), *My Girl Tisa* (48).

## ADORÉE, Renée (1898-1933)

Born Jeanne de la Fonte, in Lille, Renée Adorée began her performing career in her native France as a child bareback rider in a circus. After a stint in the chorus of the Folies-Bergères, she made her first Hollywood picture, *The Strongest*, in 1920. Her role as Melisande, opposite John Gilbert in *The Big Parade* (25) rocketed her to stardom. After a series of silents that included *La Bohème* (26) and *The Show* (27), she failed to make a successful change to sound. She died soon after of tuberculosis.
**Selected Films:** *The Strongest* (20), *Monte Cristo* (22), *The Bandolero* (24), *The Big Parade* (25), *Parisian Nights* (25), *La Bohème* (26), *The Show* (27), *The Mating Call* (28), *Hollywood Revue of 1929* (29), *Call of the Flesh* (30).

## ADRIAN, Iris (1913- )

Born Iris Adrian Hotsetter in Los Angeles, Iris Adrian started her career as a dancer in the Ziegfeld Follies. She appeared in over 100 Hollywood films from the 1930s to the 1980s, becoming familiar to moviegoers as a wisecracking blonde, chorus girl, or gangster's moll in productions such as *The G-String Murders* (42). Her later films included work for Disney in *That Darn Cat* (65).
**Selected Films:** *Paramount on Parade* (30), *Gold Diggers of 1937* (36), *Road to Zanzibar* (41), *The G-String Murders* (42), *The Stork Club* (45), *Blue Hawaii* (61), *That Darn Cat* (65), *The Love Bug* (68), *The Odd Couple* (68), *The Shaggy D.A.* (76), *Herbie Goes Bananas* (80).

## ADRIAN, Max (1903-1973)

Max Adrian, born Max Bor in Enniskillen, Ireland, first established his high-camp character acting on the British stage. Though his style was a bit overwhelming onscreen, he did make an occasional movie, stretching from *The Primrose Path* (34), to *The Boy Friend* (71). He also appeared in *Uncle Vanya*, a film of Laurence Olivier's 1963 production which was not released until 1977.
**Selected Films:** *The Primrose Path* (34), *Macushla* (37), *Kipps* (41), *Henry V* (45), *The Pickwick Papers* (52), *Dr Terror's House of Horrors* (65), *The Boy Friend* (71), *Uncle Vanya* (77).

## AGAR, John (1921- )

John Agar was born in Chicago and entered the movies after military service in World War II, cutting a handsome figure in John Ford classics such as *Fort Apache* (48) and *She Wore a Yellow Ribbon* (49). But Agar failed to develop into a strong screen personality and soon settled into leads in B movies including *Revenge of the Creature* (55) and *Frontier Gun* (58). He was married to Shirley Temple (1945-1949).
**Selected Films:** *Fort Apache* (48), *She Wore a Yellow Ribbon* (49), *Sands of Iwo Jima* (49), *Revenge of the Creature* (55), *The Mole People* (56), *Frontier Gun* (58), *Cavalry Command* (65), *King Kong* (76).

*Renée Adorée starred with John Gilbert in* The Big Parade *(25).*

## AGUTTER, Jenny (1952- )

Trained as a ballet dancer in her native England, Agutter, born in Taunton, made her film debut at the age of 12 in *East of Sudan* (64). She played a teenager confronting an Australian bushman in Nicholas Roeg's *Walkabout* (70). Her later films were mostly popular thrillers and horror movies such as *The Eagle Has Landed* (77) and *An American Werewolf in London* (81).
**Selected Films:** *East of Sudan* (64), *Star!* (68), *Walkabout* (70), *The Railway Children* (70), *Logan's Run* (76), *The Eagle Has Landed* (77), *Equus* (77), *The Riddle of the Sands* (79), *An American Werewolf in London* (81), *Secret Places* (85).

## AHERNE, Brian (1902-1986)

Beginning as a child actor on the British stage, Brian Aherne, born in King's Norton, grew up to be everyone's image of the proper English gentleman. He broke off his early theatrical career to study architecture, then returned to acting. His silent films include *The Eleventh Commandment* (24) and *Safety First* (26). Moving easily into talkies, he went to Hollywood in 1933 and established his screen image with a series of romantic leads in films such as *The Great Garrick* (37) and *Smilin' Through* (41). Roles out of his usual character included the Emperor Maximilian in *Juarez* (39). Aherne was married to actress Joan Fontaine from 1939 to 1943. Among his later films were Alfred Hitchcock's *I Confess* (53) and *The Swan* (56), the latter his first comic role. His autobiography, *A Proper Job*, appeared in 1980.
**Selected Films:** *The Eleventh Commandment* (24), *King of the Castle* (25), *Safety First* (26), *A Woman Redeemed* (27), *Shooting Stars* (28), *I Was A Spy* (33), *The Constant Nymph* (34), *Beloved Enemy* (36), *The Great Garrick* (37), *Juarez* (39), *The Lady in Question* (40), *Smilin' Through* (41), *My Sister Eileen* (42), *A Night to Remember* (43), *I Confess* (53), *Prince Valiant* (54), *The Swan* (56), *Rosie* (67).

## AHN, Philip (1911-1978)

Born in Los Angeles of Korean background, Philip Ahn specialized in Oriental roles, from the Yellow-Peril type to the mandarin and comic parts, in films such as *Charlie Chan in Honolulu* (38), *Dragon Seed* (44), and *Love is a Many Splendored Thing* (55).
**Selected Films:** *The General Died at Dawn* (36), *Charlie Chan in Honolulu* (38), *Dragon Seed* (44), *China Sky* (45), *Love is a Many Splendoured Thing* (55), *Around the World in 80 Days* (56), *One-Eyed Jacks* (61), *Voodoo Heartbeat* (75).

## AIELLO, Danny (1935- )

Italian-American character actor Aiello appeared on Broadway before making his film debut in the late 1970s. Mostly cast as working-class Italians and crooks, his best-known roles to date are in two Woody Allen movies as Monk in *The Purple Rose of Cairo* (85) and as a mobster in *Radio Days* (87).
**Selected Films:** *Blood Brothers* (79), *Hide in Plain Sight* (80), *Fort Apache, the Bronx* (80), *Once Upon a Time in America* (84), *The Protectors* (85), *The Purple Rose of Cairo* (85), *Radio Days* (87).

## AIMÉE, Anouk (1932- )

Beautiful enough to be a popular romantic leading lady, known in her native France simply as Anouk, Aimée did not have the usual outgoing and glamorous persona of a great star. Rather she was feline and enigmatic, with the result that only a few directors knew how to utilize her well – she appeared in a few classic films for directors such as Federico Fellini and Claude Lelouch, and otherwise in a good many forgettable ones. Born Françoise Sorya, she made her film debut in her native Paris at 14. Anouk came to fame with a role written for her in *The Lovers of Verona* (49). It was only after years of indifferent films that she blossomed again in Federico Fellini's *La Dolce Vita* (60) and *8½* (63). Her greatest acclaim and an Oscar nomination came for her role in Lelouch's arch-

romance *A Man and A Woman* (66). She was married to actor Albert Finney from 1970 to 1978.
**Selected Films:** *La Maison sous la Mer* (47), *The Lovers of Verona* (49), *The Golden Salamander* (50), *Le Rideau Cramoisi* (51), *Les Mauvaises Recontres* (55), *Pot-Bouille* (56), *La Dolce Vita* (60), *Sodom and Gomorrah* (61), *8½* (63), *A Man and A Woman* (66), *Justine* (69), *The Model Shop* (69), *The Appointment* (69), *Mon Premier Amour* (78), *The Tragedy of a Ridiculous Man* (81), *General of the Dead Army* (83), *A Man and A Woman: 20 Years Later* (86).

## AKINS, Claude (1918- )

Born in Nelson, Georgia, Claude Akins grew up with the features and air of a solidly-built, somewhat dense good-ole-boy, which initially led to casting as a heavy in films such as *From Here to Eternity* (53) and *The Defiant Ones* (58). Later, these same features led to roles as a working-class hero and his lead in the TV series *Movin' On*. As bad guy and good, he has been busy in films and television for three decades.

*Aimée and Trintignant in* A Man and A Woman *(66).*

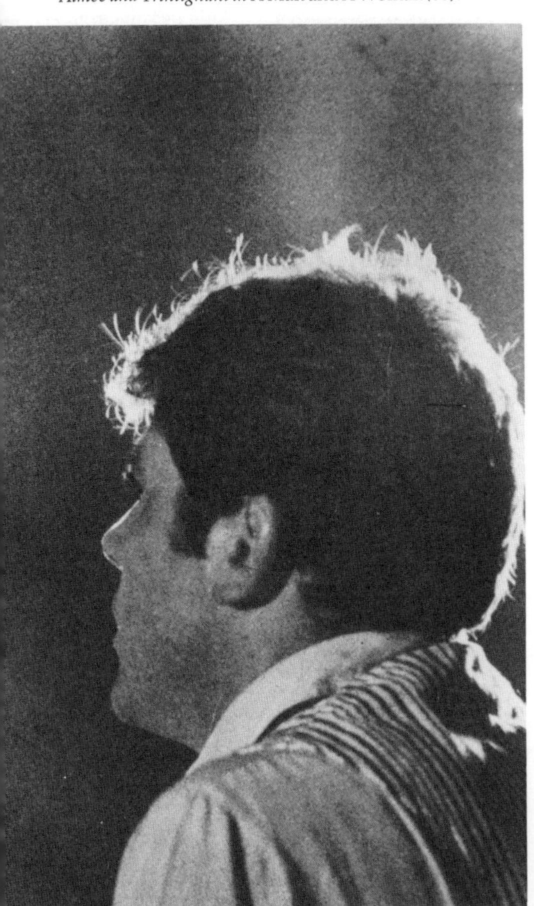

**Selected Films:** *From Here to Eternity* (53), *The Caine Mutiny* (54), *The Sea Chase* (55), *The Defiant Ones* (58), *Rio Bravo* (59), *Porgy and Bess* (59), *The Great Bank Robbery* (69), *Battle for the Planet of the Apes* (73), *Tentacles* (77).

## ALBERGHETTI, Anna Maria (1936- )

Born into a musical family in Pesaro, Italy, Alberghetti was headed for a career in opera, and made her singing debut at Carnegie Hall at 14. But her delicate beauty led instead to roles on Broadway and in movies. Her first film was *The Medium* (51) based on Gian-Carlo Menotti's opera. Thereafter she appeared in popular films, the last being Jerry Lewis's *Cinderfella* (60).
**Selected Films:** *The Medium* (51), *Here Comes the Groom* (51), *The Stars Are Singing* (53), *The Last Command* (55), *Cinderfella* (60).

## ALBERT, Eddie (1908- )

Born Edward Albert Heimberger in Rock Island, Illinois, this character actor has been playing honest men, nice guys and best friends for almost 50 years, seldom getting the girl but sometimes taking on a meaty role, in a career that has covered radio, stage, screen and television. Albert attended the University of Minnesota and then became a circus trapeze artist. In his film debut, he almost stole the show in *Brother Rat* (38), playing the star pitcher for the baseball team at a small military college. Later he received Academy Award nominations for *Roman Holiday* (53) and *The Heartbreak Kid* (72). He also co-starred with Eva Gabor in the successful TV series *Green Acres*. In 1945 he married the Mexican-American actress Margo.
**Selected Films:** *Brother Rat* (38), *On Your Toes* (39), *Four Wives* (39), *Eagle Squadron* (42), *Smash Up* (47), *Time Out of Mind* (47), *The Fuller Brush Girl* (50), *You're in the Navy Now* (51), *Carrie* (52), *Roman Holiday* (53), *Oklahoma!* (55), *I'll Cry Tomorrow* (55), *Attack!* (56), *The Teahouse of the August Moon* (56), *The Sun Also Rises* (57), *Beloved Infidel* (59), *The Longest Day* (62), *The Hearbreak Kid* (72), *The Longest Yard* (74), *The Devil's Rain* (75), *Yes Giorgio* (82), *Dreamscape* (84), *Head Office* (86).

## ALBERTSON, Frank (1909-1964)

Born in Fergus Falls, Minnesota, Frank Albertson began in films as an extra and prop boy in 1922, and was a light leading man in early talkies such as *Blue Skies* (29). Thereafter he appeared in dozens of movies including *Room Service* (38) and *The Last Hurrah* (58), as a respected character actor.
**Selected Films:** *The Farmer's Daughter* (28), *Blue Skies* (29), *A Connecticut Yankee* (31), *Ah Wilderness* (35), *The Plainsman* (37), *Room Service* (38), *Wake Island* (42), *It's a Wonderful Life* (46), *The Last Hurrah* (58), *Psycho* (60), *Bye Bye Birdie* (63).

## ALBERTSON, Jack (1907-1981)

Starting as a straight man in burlesque, Jack Albertson, born in Lynn, Massachusetts began his long film career with *Miracle on 34th Street* (47). He went on to play 'old-cuss' character roles in films such as *The Subject Was Roses* (68), for which he won a supporting-actor Academy Award. On television he received an Emmy award for the lead in *Chico and the Man.*

**Selected Films:** *Miracle on 34th Street* (47), *Top Banana* (54), *The Harder They Fall* (56), *The Subject Was Roses* (68), *Willie Wonka and the Chocolate Factory* (71), *The Poseidon Adventure* (72), *Dead and Buried* (81).

## ALBERTSON, Mabel (1901-1982)

Mabel Albertson, like her brother, Jack was born in Lynn, Massachusetts and spent most of her career as a character actress in comedies, often cast as a wisecracking old lady or gossipy neighbor. Her film career began with *Mutiny on the Blackhawk* (39).

**Selected Films:** *Mutiny on the Blackhawk* (39), *She's Back on Broadway* (53), *The Long Hot Summer* (58), *The Gazebo* (60), *Barefoot in the Park* (67), *On a Clear Day You Can See Forever* (70), *What's Up Doc?* (72).

## ALBRIGHT, Hardie (1903-1975)

A bright and thoughtful man who toured with Eva Le Gallienne and George Arliss as a young actor, Albright (originally Hardy Albrecht) born in Charleroi, Pennsylvania, spent most of his Hollywood years in some 50 minor films of the 1930s and 1940s. Perhaps his most notable effort was *Three Cornered Moon* (33). He later taught at UCLA and wrote textbooks on theater.

**Selected Films:** *Young Sinners* (31), *Jewel Robbery* (32), *Three Cornered Moon* (33), *White Heat* (34), *Granny Get Your Gun* (40), *Angel on My Shoulder* (46).

## ALBRIGHT, Lola (1925- )

Born in Akron, Ohio, Albright was a model before making her movie debut in *The Pirate* (48). Her stylish-but-tough screen image in the Stanwyck mode was best seen in *Champion* (49). Besides her many films of the 1950s and 1960s which included the role of an ex-stripper in *A Cold Wind in August* (61), she appeared in the TV series *Peter Gunn.*

**Selected Films:** *The Pirate* (48), *Champion* (49), *Arctic Flight* (52), *The Tender Trap* (56), *A Cold Wind in August* (61), *Lord Love a Duck* (66), *The Impossible Years* (68), *Delta County USA* (77).

## ALDA, Alan (1936- )

Born in New York City, the son of actor Robert Alda, this deceptively bland star is a real screen talent, projecting the quiet charm of low-key dignity. His private life has also endeared him to his fans, for he is an intelligent, decent, compassionate man with solid values. He made his film debuted at the age of 27 in *Gone Are the Days* (63), the film version of the stage play *Purlie Victorious*, with Ossie Davis and Ruby Dee. Alda continue making movies, but it was television that catapulted him to fame. He played Captain Benjamin Franklin 'Hawkeye' Pierce in the revered television series *M*A*S*H.* When he returned to films, he chose his roles wisely, making *Same Time Next Year* (78) with Ellen Burstyn and *The Seduction of Joe Tynan* (79) with Meryl Streep. His biggest success came in *The Four Seasons* (81), a witty movie about middle-aged marriage, which he wrote, directed and starred in.

**Selected Films:** *Gone Are the Days* (63), *Paper Lion* (68), *The Moonshine War* (70), *The Mephisto Waltz* (71), *To Kill a Clown* (72), *Same Time Next Year* (78), *California Suite* (78), *The Seduction of Joe Tynan* (79), *The Four Seasons* (81), *Sweet Liberty* (86).

## ALDA, Robert (1914-1986)

Born Alfonso Giuseppe Giovanni Roberto D'Abruzzo in New York City, Alda became a professional singer while he was attending New York University. His two greatest roles were as Sky Masterson in Broadway's *Guys and Dolls* (50) and as George Gershwin in the film *Rhapsody in Blue* (45).

**Selected Films:** *Rhapsody in Blue* (45), *Cloak and Dagger* (46), *April Showers* (48), *Imitation of Life* (59), *The Girl Who Knew Too Much* (68), *Every Girl Should Have One* (78).

## ALEXANDER, Ben (1911-1969)

Born Nicholas Benton Alexander in Goldfield, Nevada, Ben Alexander appeared as a young child in silent films directed by Cecil B De Mille and D W Griffith, progressing to supporting roles in sound pictures such as *All Quiet on the Western Front* (30). After years of obscurity he re-emerged as Jack Webb's sidekick on the TV series *Dragnet.*

**Selected Films:** *Each Pearl a Tear* (16), *Hearts of the World* (18), *Flaming Love* (25), *All Quiet on the Western Front* (30), *Stage Mother* (33), *Western Gold* (37), *Criminals Within* (41), *Dragnet* (54), *Pay the Devil* (57).

## ALEXANDER, Jane (1939- )

Born Jane Quigley in Boston and educated at Sarah Lawrence and the University of Edinburgh, Jane Alexander established herself as a major presence playing leading roles on the stage before her film debut as Jack Johnson's white mistress in *The Great White Hope* (70). She continued to concentrate on stage work, but still found acclaim in supporting movie roles, including a brief but striking appearance in *All the President's Men* (76). She also gave a fine portraval of Eleanor Roosevelt in the TV film *Eleanor and Franklin* (76).

**Selected Films:** *The Great White Hope* (70), *A Gunfight* (71), *The New Centurions* (72), *All the President's Men* (76), *The Betsy* (78), *Kramer Vs Kramer* (79), *Brubaker* (80), *Night Crossing* (82), *Testament* (83), *City Heat* (84), *Sweet Country* (87).

## ALEXANDER, John (1897-1982)

Alexander was born in Newport, Kentucky and began acting with a Shakespearean company. After success as the mad uncle, Teddy Brewster, in both the stage and film versions of *Arsenic and Old Lace* (44), he established an amiable film personality in a series of secondary roles.
**Selected Films:** *The Petrified Forest* (36), *Arsenic and Old Lace* (44), *A Tree Grows in Brooklyn* (45), *The Marrying Kind* (52), *One Foot in Hell* (60).

## ALLBRITTON, Louise (1920-1979)

Born in Oklahoma City, Oklahoma, Allbritton made her screen debut with *Not a Ladies Man* (42) and was received well enough to be featured in two more films that year. A vivacious blonde she starred in Universal comedies of the 1940s such as *The Egg and I* (47). She was married to news commentator Charles Collingwood.
**Selected Films:** *Not a Ladies Man* (42), *A Date with an Angel* (42), *Son of Dracula* (43), *The Egg and I* (47), *Sitting Pretty* (48), *The Great Manhunt* (50).

*George Burns and Gracie Allen in* A Damsel in Distress *(37).*

## ALLEN, Corey (1934- )

Born in Cleveland, Ohio, actor Corey Allen gained instant recognition as James Dean's antagonist in *Rebel Without a Cause* (55), but as so often with Hollywood careers, he was then typecast in a series of similar roles as a nasty character – a sort of Marlon Brando who had gone to Harvard. By the 1970s, Allen moved on to writing and directing films.
**Selected Films:** *The Mad Magician* (54), *Night of the Hunter* (55), *Rebel Without a Cause* (55), *Party Girl* (58), *Private Property* (60), *Sweet Bird of Youth* (62), *The Chapman Report* (62).

## ALLEN, Debbie (1953- )

Allen, born in Houston, Texas, first appeared on the Broadway stage in the 1970s. Her musicals include *Raisin* and revivals of *West Side Story* and *Sweet Charity*. The black performer is best-known as the dance teacher on the TV series *Fame*. She is the sister of actress Phylicia Raschad.
**Selected Films:** *Ragtime* (81), *JoJo Dancer, Your Life is Calling* (86).

## ALLEN, Gracie (1905-1964)

For more than 30 years the funniest thing about George Burns was his wife. It was said that she could make a door funny; she always made the implausible plausible. She was born Grace Ethel Cecile Rosalie Allen in San Francisco, and in typical fashion claimed, 'I'm not sure of the order, but together they should spell Grace.' She began performing in vaudeville at the age of three, but later decided to become a secretary. When she was 17, she met Burns and they formed a comedy team, with Burns doing most of the writing and Allen getting most of the laughs. They were married three years later. For years they had one of the top comedy shows on radio, taking time out to appear in films including many short subjects. In the 1950s they did a television series that ended when Allen retired in 1958.
**Selected Films:** *College Humor* (33), *We're Not Dressing* (34), *College Holiday* (36), *A Damsel in Distress* (37), *The Gracie Allen Murder Case* (39), *Mr and Mrs North* (42), *Two Girls and a Sailor* (44).

## ALLEN, Rex (1922- )

Born in Wilcox, Arizona, Allen enjoyed a career as a singing cowboy on radio and in rodeos before appearing and singing in Republic B-movies such as *Under Mexicali Stars* (50). In the 1960s and 1970s, his voice was heard on the soundtrack of animated films for Walt Disney and others. Allen also starred in the TV series *Frontier Doctor*.
**Selected Films:** *Under Mexicali Stars* (50), *Arizona Cowboy* (50), *The Old Overland Trail* (53), *Shadows of Tombstone* (58), *For the Love of Mike* (60).

## ALLEN, Steve (1921- )

Steve Allen was born to a vaudeville family in New York and developed a multifaceted career as songwriter, prose writer, and topflight radio and TV performer – usually, but not always, as a comedian. His screen appearances were rare, but included the title role in *The Benny Goodman Story* (56). He is married to actress Jayne Meadows.
**Selected Films:** *Down Memory Lane* (49), *I'll Get By* (50), *The Benny Goodman Story* (56), *College Confidential* (60), *The Comic* (69).

## ALLEN, Woody (1935- )

Allen has been described as a 98-pound weakling with a Superman brain, and he certainly is a comic genius – being America's most original movie actor, writer and director rolled into one. On screen, he is the epitome of the modern bungler tormented by self-doubt, neuroses and unswervable lusts. Born Allen Stewart Konigsberg in Brooklyn, New York, he attended New York University and the City College of New York. While he was still in his teens, he was on the writing staff of the celebrated television program *Your Show of Shows*, coming up with gags for such luminaries as Sid Caesar, Imogene Coca, Carl Reiner and Howard Morris. In 1961 he began appearing in Greenwich Village cafes as a standup comedian, and soon he was a popular television talk-show guest and night club funnyman. Allen co-wrote and appeared in *What's New, Pussycat?* (65), his first film. He dubbed an English sound track on to a Japanese movie and came up with *What's Up, Tiger Lily?* (67), and with his wife of the time, Louise Lasser, scored a hit with *Bananas* (71). *Play It Again, Sam* (72), based on his own hit play, with Diane Keaton, was the plaintive cry of a man who never got the girl and a tribute to Humphrey Bogart, who usually did. Allen continued to make movies filled with gags and one-liners until *The Front* (76), a film about blacklisted writers during the Red Scare, but it was *Annie Hall* (77), also with Keaton, which represented a major change for him. It was a humorous picture with a serious side, and it won the Academy Award for Best Picture and Allen won Oscars for Best Director and Co-writer. *Zelig* (83), with Mia Farrow, used old black and white film footage with novel and brilliant results. Most recently, with *Purple Rose of Cairo* (85) and *Radio Days* (87), he has remained behind the camera, writing and directing. He also did the narration for *Radio Days*.
**Selected Films:** *What's New, Pussycat?* (65), *Casino Royale* (67), *Take the Money and Run* (69), *Bananas* (71), *Everything You Always Wanted to Know About Sex (But Were Afraid to Ask)* (72), *Play It Again, Sam* (72), *Sleeper* (73), *Love and Death* (76), *The Front* (76), *Annie Hall* (77), *Manhattan* (79), *Stardust Memories* (80), *A Midsummer Night's Sex Comedy* (82), *Zelig* (83), *Broadway Danny Rose* (84), *Hannah and Her Sisters* (86).

## ALLGOOD, Sara (1883-1950)

In her native Dublin, Allgood appeared at the famed Abbey Theatre for some years, and in one of her first films repeated her stage lead in *Juno and the Paycock* (30). Arriving to Hollywood in 1940, she played motherly Irish characters in most of her films, which included *Jane Eyre* (44).
**Selected Films:** *Blackmail* (29), *That Hamilton Woman* (41), *How Green Was My Valley* (41), *Between Two Worlds* (44), *The Lodger* (44), *Jane Eyre* (44), *The Spiral Staircase* (46), *One Touch of Venus* (48), *Cheaper by the Dozen* (50).

## ALLWYN, Astrid (1909-1978)

Born in South Manchester, Connecticut, Astrid Allwyn appeared in the 1930s and 1940s as a leggy blonde in mostly B movies. As lead or supporting player, she was cast usually as a seductress and the 'other woman.'
**Selected Films:** *Lady With a Past* (32), *Beggars in Ermine* (34), *Way Down East* (35), *Dimples* (36), *Mr Smith Goes to Washington* (39), *The Lone Wolf Strikes* (40), *Hit Parade of 1943* (43).

## ALLYSON, June (1917- )

She was usually seen in the role of the pretty, peppy girl next door, but sometimes she was allowed to play spiteful or nasty characters, and she did them quite well. She could play a tomboy or a tease, and she was always ready with a smile or a tear. Born Ella Geisman in Lucerne, New York, she started out making two-reelers in 1937, then became a Broadway show girl and dancer in the chorus. Five years later she was back in Hollywood to appear in feature films, beginning with *Best Foot Forward* (43), in which she won the hearts of America with her singing, dancing and acting. She was married to actor Dick Powell from 1945 until his death in 1963. The husky-voiced star had her own television series in the 1950s.

**Selected Films:** *Best Foot Forward* (43), *Girl Crazy* (43), *Thousands Cheer* (43), *Two Girls and a Sailor* (44), *Music for Millions* (45), *Two Sisters from Boston* (46), *Till the Clouds Roll By* (46), *Good News* (47), *The Three Musketeers* (48), *Words and Music* (48), *Little Women* (49), *The Stratton Story* (49), *Battle Circus* (53), *The Glenn Miller Story* (54), *Executive Suite* (54), *Strategic Air Command* (55), *The Shrike (55)*, *Interlude* (57), *They Only Kill Their Masters* (72), *Blackout* (78).

Left: *Woody Allen and Diane Keaton in* Manhattan (79).
Below: *June Allyson with Peter Lawford, Kathryn Grayson, Lauritz Melchior and Jimmy Durante* – Two Sisters from Boston *(46).*

*Don Ameche with Betty Grable and Chris Pin-Martin in* Down Argentine Way *(40).*

## AMECHE, Don (1908- )

Born Dominic Felix Amici in Kenosha, Wisconsin, this pleasant and gifted light comedian and romantic lead of stage, screen and radio began his career on stage and on the radio. He once was the announcer of the popular *First Nighter* dramatic series on the airwaves. His first film was *Sins of Man* (36), but he became a star in his second picture, *Ramona* (36), in which he played an outcast American Indian opposite Loretta Young as an aristocratic Spanish girl. Ameche appeared in many musicals, often with Alice Faye, and in several biographical films, including *The Story of Alexander Graham Bell* (39). It was this last film that started the joke about Don Ameche inventing the telephone. During his career he has also played in several light bubbling comedies as well as taking on an occasional serious role. Hollywood finally awarded this grand old trouper an Academy Award as Best Supporting Actor for his work in *Cocoon* (85).

**Selected Films:** *Sins of Man (36), Ramona* (36), *One in a Million* (37), *You Can't Have Everything* (37), *In Old Chicago* (38), *Alexander's Ragtime Band* (38), *The Three Musketeers* (39), *Midnight* (39), *The Story of Alexander Graham Bell* (39), *Swanee River* (39), *Lillian Russell* (40), *Four Sons* (40), *Down Argentine Way* (40), *That Night in Rio* (41), *Moon Over Miami* (41), *Heaven Can Wait* (43), *Happy Land* (43), *Greenwich Village* (44), *Sleep My Love* (48), *A Fever in the Blood* (61), *The Boatniks* (70), *Trading Places* (83), *Cocoon* (85), *Harry and the Hendersons* (87).

## AMES, Leon (1903- )

Born Leon Wycoff to a Russian immigrant family in Indiana, Ames became a familiar movie father figure, usually playing harrassed or kindly parents. He appeared in a number of classics including *Murders in the Rue Morgue* (32), *Thirty Seconds Over Tokyo* (44), and *The Postman Always Rings Twice* (46). In later years he worked in several TV series including *Mister Ed.*

**Selected Films:** *The Count of Monte Cristo* (34), *Stowaway* (36), *Meet Me in St Louis* (44), *Little Women* (49), *From the Terrace* (60), *Hammersmith is Out* (72), *Testament* (83), *Jake Speed* (86), *Peggy Sue Got Married* (86).

## ANDERSON, Eddie 'Rochester' (1905-1977)

He of the inimitable rasping voice, bulging eyes, and sardonic ripostes, black comedian 'Rochester' Anderson, born in Oakland, California, was a fixture on radio and television as Jack Benny's butler. On his own, however, he played leads and supporting roles in a number of films including *The Green Pastures* (36), *Gone With the Wind* (39) and *Cabin in the Sky* (43).

**Selected Films:** *What Price Hollywood* (30), *The Green Pastures* (36), *You Can't Take It With You* (38), *Gone With the Wind* (39), *Cabin in the Sky* (43), *Brewster's Millions* (45), *It's a Mad Mad Mad Mad World* (63).

## ANDERSON, G M (1882-1971)

Born Max Aronson in Little Rock, Arkansas, as 'Broncho Billy' Anderson, this cowboy actor became one of the screen's first stars. He was an unsuccessful vaudeville performer who drifted

into films in *The Great Train Robbery* (03). Later he co-founded the Essanay Company and made nearly 400 one-reel westerns with himself as star. Anderson was given a special Academy Award in 1957 'for his contributions to the development of motion pictures.'
**Selected Films:** *The Great Train Robbery* (03), *Raffles, the American Cracksman* (05), *The Bandit Makes Good* (07), *Broncho Billy's Redemption* (10), *Broncho Billy's Marriage* (15), *The Bounty Killer* (65).

## ANDERSON, Judith (1898- )

Fiery passion always seemed to rage under her icily controlled exterior. When Alfred Hitchcock cast her as Mrs Danvers, the evil housekeeper in *Rebecca* (40), screen history was made. She was born Frances Margaret Anderson in Adelaide, Australia, and became one of the great luminaries of the theater, often appearing in Shakespearean plays. In 1960 she was named Dame Commander of the British Empire.
**Selected Films:** *Blood Money* (33), *Rebecca* (40), *King's Row* (42), *Laura* (44), *And Then There Were None* (45), *The Diary of a Chambermaid* (45), *Specter of the Rose* (46), *The Strange Love of Martha Ivers* (47), *Pursued* (47), *Tycoon* (47), *The Furies* (50), *Salome* (53), *Cat on a Hot Tin Roof* (58), *Macbeth* (63), *A Man Called Horse* (70), *Star Trek III: The Search for Spock* (84).

## ANDERSON, Mary (1920- )

Born in Birmingham, Alabama, Mary Anderson was one of the of actresses in Hollywood during the 1940s and 1950s who could play almost any part in about any kind of movie, without making too much impression. She appeared first in *Gone With the Wind* (39), as Maybelle Merriweather, otherwise most notably in *The Song of Bernadette* (44).
**Selected Films:** *Gone With the Wind* (39), *Lifeboat* (43), *The Song of Bernadette* (44), *To Each His Own* (46), *I the Jury* (53), *Jet Over the Atlantic* (60).

## ANDERSON, Richard (1926- )

With his overall versatility, Anderson, born in Long Branch, New Jersey, was a much-used supporting actor in films after 1949 including *Forbidden Planet* (56), *Paths of Glory* (57) and *The Long Hot Summer* (58).
**Selected Films:** *Twelve O'Clock High* (49), *Escape From Fort Bravo* (54), *Forbidden Planet* (56), *Paths of Glory* (57), *The Long Hot Summer* (58), *Compulsion* (59), *Seconds* (66), *Tora! Tora! Tora!* (70), *Sharks* (79).

## ANDERSON, Warner (1911-1976)

Brooklyn-born Anderson first appeared in war movies such as *Destination Tokyo* (43). He showed an attractive and reliable, if rather colorless, screen personality in later films including *Destination Moon* (50) and *Detective Story* (51). Perhaps his best-known role was one of the detectives on the TV series *The Line-Up*.
**Selected Films:** *Destination Tokyo* (43), *Objective Burma* (45), *Command Decision* (48), *Destination Moon* (50), *Detective Story* (51), *The Caine Mutiny* (54), *The Blackboard Jungle* (55), *Rio Conchos* (64).

## ANDERSSON, Bibi (1935- )

Born in Stockholm, Bibi Andersson was educated in her native Sweden at the Kungliga Dramatiska Teatern, which counts among its alumni Greta Garbo and Ingrid Bergman. Discovered at 19 by director Ingmar Bergman, she appeared in his *Smiles of a Summer Night* (55) and went on to become part of the extraordinary stable of performers assembled by that brilliant director. Andersson often portrayed flirtatious girls in her younger years with Bergman, as in *Wild Strawberries* (57). Later she tended to play middle-class women with neurotic undercurrents, as in *A Passion* (70). Perhaps her greatest role was in Bergman's searing *Persona* (66), in which Andersson had virtually the only speaking part (her costar Liv Ullmann was mute throughout); she played an unimaginative nurse driven to nervous breakdown by her patient's silence. Andersson has also appeared internationally in a variety of films, including thrillers like *The Kremlin Letter* (69).
**Selected Films:** *Smiles of a Summer Night* (55), *The Seventh Seal* (56), *Wild Strawberries* (57), *The Devil's Eye* (61), *My Sister My Love* (66), *Persona* (66), *The Kremlin Letter* (69), *A Passion* (70), *Cries and Whispers* (72), *I Never Promised You a Rose Garden* (77), *Airport 79 – the Concorde* (79), *Exposed* (83).

## ANDERSSON, Harriet (1932- )

First trained as a dancer, Swedish actress Harriet Andersson, born in Stockholm, (no relation to Bibi) was discovered at 20 by Ingmar Bergman, who wrote *Summer With Monika* (52) for her. Becoming part of Ingmar Bergman's company, she proved both brilliant and versatile in roles ranging from the naive young wife in *Sawdust and Tinsel* (53), to the servant in *Smiles of a Summer Night* (55), the crazed visionary of *Through a Glass Darkly* (62), and the dying sister in *Cries and Whispers* (72).
**Selected Films:** *Summer With Monika* (52), *Sawdust and Tinsel* (53), *A Lesson in Love* (54), *Smiles of a Summer Night* (55), *Siska* (62), *Through a Glass Darkly* (62), *Cries and Whispers* (72), *Hempa's Bar* (77), *Fanny and Alexander* (83).

## ANDES, Keith (1920- )

After radio and stage work, Andes, born in Ocean City, New Jersey, played light leads and supporting roles in minor films of the 1950s on. He costarred in the TV series *Glynis*.
**Selected Films:** *The Farmer's Daughter* (47), *Blackbeard the Pirate* (52), *Back From Eternity* (56), *Tora! Tora! Tora!* (70).

**ANDRESS, Ursula** (1936- )

This dazzling blonde sex symbol was born in Bern, Switzerland. She got her career start in Rome and came to the public's attention in the first James Bond movie, *Dr No* (62). At one time she was married to John Derek, and now she makes most of her films in Italy.
**Selected Films:** *The Loves of Casanova* (54), *Dr No* (62), *Four for Texas* (63), *She* (64), *What's New, Pussycat?* (65), *The Tenth Victim* (65), *The Blue Max* (66), *Casino Royale* (67), *The Lives and Times of Scaramouche* (76), *The Clash of the Titans* (81), *Red Bells* (82).

**ANDREWS, Anthony** (1948- )

Born in London, Anthony Andrews has spent most of his career as a romantic lead in TV dramas such as *The Scarlet Pimpernel* (82). He also played Lord Sebastian Flyte in the acclaimed TV adaptation of *Brideshead Revisited* (81).
**Selected Films:** *Take Me High* (74), *Percy's Progress* (75), *Operation Daybreak* (76), *Under the Volcano* (84), *The Holcroft Covenant* (85), *The Second Victory* (87).

**ANDREWS, Dana** (1909- )

Andrews was a solid leading man and fine supporting actor in many important films, but his career peaked in the 1940s, and then his hard and immobile features limited him in middle age. Born Carver Daniel Andrews in Collins, Mississippi, he began his film career in *The Westerner* (40), which starred Gary Cooper and Walter Brennan. He gained some notice playing youthful roles in *Tobacco Road* (41) and *Swamp Water* (41). His portrayal of the young man about to be lynched in *The Ox Bow Incident* (43) was sensational, and *Laura* (44) and *A Walk in the Sun* (45) were outstanding vehicles for him. He also was excellent in *The Best Years of Our Lives* (46) as the discharged officer who can't readjust to working in a drug store, and he was also fine in one of the most intelligent monster movies of all time – *Night of the Demon* (57).
**Selected Films:** *The Westerner* (40), *Tobacco Road* (41), *Swamp Water* (41), *Berlin Correspondent* (42), *The Ox Bow Incident* (43), *The Purple Heart* (44), *Laura* (44), *State Fair* (45), *A Walk in the Sun* (45), *The Best Years of Our Lives* (46), *Boomerang* (47), *The Iron Curtain* (48), *My Foolish Heart* (50), *Elephant Walk* (53), *Night of the Demon* (57), *Crack in the World* (65), *In Harm's Way* (65), *Airport 1975* (74), *The Pilot* (81), *Prince Jack* (85).

**ANDREWS, Edward** (1914-1985)

Round of face and bespectacled, Andrews, born in Griffen, Georgia, was able to mold his features to roles ranging from the amicable through the henpecked to the malevolent, in films such as *Tea and Sympathy* (57), *Elmer Gantry* (60) and *Tora! Tora! Tora!* (70). He also enjoyed a long and successful career on stage.
**Selected Films:** *The Harder They Fall* (56), *Tea and Sympathy* (57), *Elmer Gantry* (60), *The Absent-Minded Professor* (62), *Youngblood Hawke* (64), *Tora! Tora! Tora* (70), *The Photographer* (75), *Sixteen Candles* (84), *Gremlins* (84).

**ANDREWS, Harry** (1911- )

The distinguished-looking British character actor, born in Tonbridge, Kent, who often plays sergeant-majors or other no-nonsense characters began his stage career in 1933, often appearing in Shakespearean roles. He then turned to films and made his screen debut in *The Red Beret* (1952).
**Selected Films:** *The Red Beret* (52), *A Hill in Korea* (56), *Alexander the Great* (56), *Moby Dick* (56), *Saint Joan* (57), *Ice Cold in Alex* (58), *The Devil's Disciple* (59), *The Hill* (65), *The Deadly Affair* (66), *Theatre of Blood* (73), *Equus* (77), *Superman* (78), *Hawk the Slayer* (80).

**ANDREWS, Julie** (1935- )

Born Julia Elizabeth Wells in Walton, England, Andrews began singing on stage when she was a little girl. Andrews became a star when she was cast as Eliza Doolittle in *My Fair Lady* on Broadway. Audrey Hepburn got the role in the 1964 screen version, but it was Andrews who won the Oscar that year in her first screen appearance in *Mary Poppins* (64). She proved that she could act in

*Ursula Andress in* Dr No *(62).*

a straight role in *The Americanization of Emily* (64), holding her own against actors of caliber such as James Garner, Melvyn Douglas and James Coburn. She starred in *The Sound of Music* (65) one of Hollywood's most successful and popular films. By this time she was number one at the box office. But her film career began to falter. Shedding the sugar coating, she altered her whole screen personality and recouped her career in the late 1970s by appearing in a contemporary series of comedies directed by her husband Blake Edwards, even baring her breasts in *S.O.B.* (81).
**Selected Films:** *Mary Poppins* (64), *The Americanization of Emily* (64), *The Sound of Music* (65), *Torn Curtain* (66), *Hawaii* (66), *Thoroughly Modern Millie* (67), *Star!* (68), *Darling Lili* (69), *The Tamarind Seed (74), 10* (79), *S.O.B.* (81), *Victor Victoria* (82), *That's Life* (86), *Duet for One* (87).

## ANDREWS SISTERS, The

The three sisters from Minneapolis, Minnesota, Laverne (1913-1967), Maxine (1918- ) and Patty (1920- ) Andrews began singing together when their mother urged them to warble so that they would stop squabbling. That was in 1927, and for ten lean years they toured professional show business singing their close harmony. Then, in 1937 they recorded 'Nice Work if You Can Get It,' which was popular, but it was the flip side of the record, a catchy tune incorporating the Yiddish phrase, 'Bei Mir Bist Du Schön,' that became the real hit. It earned the sisters a gold record and made them stars. But they were not rich, having been paid a flat $50 for the recording. They went on to record other hits, such as 'Three Little Fishes,' 'Rum And Coca-Cola,' 'Apple Blossom Time' and 'The Beer Barrel Polka.' Then Hollywood beckoned. Their first film was *Argentine Nights* (40), but they became stars when they appeared with Abbott and Costello in *Buck Privates* (41). After several movies, the sisters, whose personalities never really blended like their music, broke up the act in the 1950s. In 1974, the two surviving sisters, Maxine and Patty, were reunited in a Broadway musical, *Over Here!*
**Selected Films:** *Argentine Nights* (40), *Buck Privates* (41), *In the Navy* (41), *Hold That Ghost* (41), *Private Buckaroo* (42), *How's About It?* (43), *Follow the Boys* (44), *Hollywood Canteen* (44), *Her Lucky Night* (45), *The Road to Rio* (47).

## ANDREWS, Tige (ca 1923- )

Born Tiger Androwaous in the United States to Lebanese parents, Tige Andrews was a perennial supporting player, usually a good-natured heavy, on film and television from the 1950s on. His movies include *Mister Roberts* (55) and *The Last Tycoon* (76); his TV series include *The Mod Squad.*
**Selected Films:** *Mister Roberts* (55), *The Wings of Eagles* (57), *China Doll* (58), *A Private Affair* (59), *The Last Tycoon* (76).

## ANGEL, Heather (1909-1986)

The delicate features and considerable stage and film experience of British-born Heather Angel took her to Hollywood in 1933, where she starred in *Berkeley Square* (33) and *The Mystery of Edwin Drood* (35). However, soon she found herself stuck in B movies such as the 'Bulldog Drummond' series. She later turned to supporting roles in TV series like *Peyton Place*. Her second husband was actor/director Henry Wilcoxon.
**Selected Films:** *City of Song* (30), *Berkeley Square* (33), *Orient Express* (33), *The Informer* (35), *The Mystery of Edwin Drood* (35), *Suspicion* (41), *Lifeboat* (43), *Premature Burial* (62).

## ANGELI, Pier (1932-1971)

The sister of actress Marisa Pavan, Pier Angeli was born Anna Maria Pierangeli in Cagliari, Sardinia, and made two films there including the sensitive *Tomorrow is Too Late* (49). After her first American film, *Teresa* (51) she reigned for several years as one of Hollywood's top gamine actresses in films such as *The Silver Chalice* (55). A period of emotional trouble followed and her career declined. After a series of forgettable films she died of a drug overdose at 39.
**Selected Films:** *Tomorrow is Too Late* (49), *Teresa* (51), *The Flame and the Flesh* (54), *The Silver Chalice* (55), *Somebody Up There Likes Me* (56), *The Vintage* (57), *Sodom and Gomorrah* (61), *Shadow of Evil* (64), *Octaman* (72).

## ANKERS, Evelyn (1918-1985)

Born to British parents in Valparaiso, Chile, Ankers acted in England before going to Hollywood. She is best known to moviegoers with her attractive features frozen in fear, having graced horror movies like *The Wolf Man* (41), *The Mad Ghoul* (43) and *Son of Dracula* (43). Her specialized talents earned her the title, 'The Screamer.' She was married to actor Richard Denning.
**Selected Films:** *Hold That Ghost* (41), *The Wolf Man* (41), *The Ghost of Frankenstein* (42), *The Mad Ghoul* (43), *Son of Dracula* (43), *Tarzan's Magic Fountain* (49), *The Empty Room* (56), *No Greater Love* (60).

## ANNABELLA (1909- )

Born Suzanne Charpentier near Paris, Annabella became a popular leading actress in French films during her twenties. Among her credits there are the classics *Sur les toits de Paris* (30) and *Le Million* (31). She went on to make films in England and America including *Suez* (38) with Tyrone Power, but never gained great popularity. She was married to Power from 1939 to 1948 and retired to France in the early 1950s.
**Selected Films:** *Napoleon* (26), *Sur les Toits de Paris* (30), *Le Million* (31), *Le Quatorze Juillet* (33), *Suez* (38), *Hôtel du Nord* (38), *13 Rue Madeleine* (46), *Dernier Amour* (48).

## ANN-MARGRET (1941- )

Born Ann-Margret Olsson in Valsjobyn, Sweden, this gorgeous performer has worked on stage and in cabaret, television and movies. Her family moved to the United States in 1946 and settled in Illinois. She was discovered by George Burns singing and dancing in a night club and started her career in lightweight films such as *The Pleasure Seekers* (64) and *Kitten With a Whip* (64), causing the critic Pauline Kael to write that 'she comes through dirty, no matter what she plays.' Early in her career, she was voted 'least promising actress' by the student body at Harvard University, but went on to prove them wrong with her two Academy Award nominations for *Carnal Knowledge* (71) and *Tommy* (75). Ann-Margret has been married to Roger Smith, the former star of the TV series *77 Sunset Strip*, since 1967, and she has become a fine actress.

**Selected Films:** *Pocketful of Miracles* (61), *State Fair* (62), *Bye Bye Birdie* (62), *Viva Las Vegas* (64), *Kitten With a Whip* (64), *The Pleasure Seekers* (64), *Bus Riley's Back in Town* (65), *Once a Thief* (65), *The Cincinnati Kid* (65), *Made in Paris* (66), *The Swinger* (66), *Stagecoach* (66), *Murderers' Row* (66), *The Tiger and the Pussycat* (67), *Mr Kinky* (68), *C C and Co* (70), *Carnal Knowledge* (71), *R P M* (71), *The Train Robbers* (73), *The Outside Man* (73), *Tommy* (75), *The Cheap Detective* (78), *The Return of the Soldier* (82), *Twice in a Lifetime* (85), *52 Pickup* (86).

*Fatty Arbuckle and Mabel Normand co-starred in several two-reelers.*

## ANSARA, Michael (1922- )

Born in Lowell, Massachusetts, Ansara turned to films after a few years on stage. His swarthy features and muscled figure led naturally to shirtless roles, most often as an Indian, in films such as *The Lone Ranger* (58), *The Comancheros* (62), and *Guns of the Magnificent Seven* (69). In the 1950s he starred in the TV series *Broken Arrow*. He was married to actress Barbara Eden.
**Selected Films:** *Action in Arabia,* (44), *The Robe* (53), *The Ten Commandments* (56), *The Lone Ranger* (58), *The Comancheros* (62), *Guns of the Magnificent Seven* (69), *The Bears and I* (74), *Assassination* (87).

## ANSPACH, Susan (1939- )

Susan Anspach was born in New York and studied at the Catholic University of America in Washington, DC. Most of her work has been concentrated in the theater, but she has appeared in a few good-to-excellent films including *Five Easy Pieces* (70), and *Nashville* (75).
**Selected Films:** *The Landlord* (70), *Five Easy Pieces* (70), *Play It Again Sam* (72), *Nashville* (75), *The Big Fix* (78), *Montenegro* (81), *Misunderstood* (84).

## AQUANETTA (1920- )

Though she was American-born (her real name was Burnu Davenport) the features and style of Aquanetta seemed to lend themselves best to stories of the Mysterious East, as in *Arabian Nights* (42), and of Darkest Africa, as in *Tarzan and the Leopard Woman* (46). Her heyday was the exotic adventure films of the 1940s.
**Selected Films:** *Arabian Nights* (42), *Jungle Captive* (43), *Jungle Woman* (44), *Dead Man's Eyes* (44), *Tarzan and the Leopard Woman* (46), *Lost Continent* (51).

## ARBUCKLE, Roscoe (1887-1933)

'Fatty' Arbuckle was the grown-up fat boy of America's silent movie days. He was a gentle buffoon, a sensitive actor whose baby face and 325-pound body made him one of Hollywood's favorite early funny men. He was born in Smith Center, Kansas, where he sang, danced and even collected tickets in a nickelodeon. After a stint in vaudeville, he began appearing in one- and two-reel films in 1907, and in 1913, Mack Sennett made him a Keystone Kop. Arbuckle and Mabel Normand co-starred in a series of classic comedies heavy on verve and low on subtlety. He formed his own production company in 1917, and gave newcomer Buster Keaton his first break. Arbuckle wrote his own material and directed his own films. He then moved to Famous Players, who paid him a staggering sum of $7000 a week. But in September 1921, Virginia Rappe, a bit player, collapsed at a party and died a few days later. Arbuckle was charged with manslaughter, but was acquitted. The acquittal didn't matter to the public because they had decided that Arbuckle was guilty. The studios imposed a rigid self-censorship, and Arbuckle's movies were banned and withdrawn. His wife, Minta Durfee, insisted on his innocence. Keaton offered him a directing job and Marion Davies let him direct her under the name of William B Goodrich. He also directed Eddie Cantor's first films. But the strain destroyed him. He lost his comic gifts and became moody and difficult to work with. An attempt to make an acting tour of Europe in 1932 was a failure, and he died the next year.
**Selected Films:** *Fatty and Mabel's Simple Life* (15), *Mabel and Fatty's Married Life* (16), *Fatty's Flirtation* (16), *Fickle Fatty's Fall* (17), *His Wedding Night* (17), *The Life of the Party* (20), *The Round-up* (20), *A Travelling Salesman* (21), *Gasoline Gus* (21), *Brewster's Millions* (21).

## ARCHER, John (1915- )

John Archer was born Ralph Bowman in Osceola, Nebraska and got into films by winning a talent contest. From the late 1930s to the 1970s he was a familiar face as the lead in B movies like *Gangs Inc.* (41) and *Rodeo* (53), with occasional supporting roles in major features including *Destination Moon* (50). He was married to actress Marjorie Lord.
**Selected Films:** *Flaming Frontier* (38), *King of the Zombies* (41), *Gangs Inc* (41), *Guadalcanal Diary* (43), *White Heat* (49), *Destination Moon* (50), *Rodeo* (53), *She Devil* (57), *Blue Hawaii* (62), *How To Frame a Figg* (71).

## ARDEN, Eve (1912- )

Born in Mill Valley, California, Eve Arden (originally Eunice Quedens) came to film from the Ziegfeld Follies. She was tall and attractive, but lacked a typical leading-lady face. What she had instead was a succinct and inimitable voice and a gift for wisecracking. Thus, in three or so films a year in the 1930s and 1940s she tended to play the leading lady's sardonic friend in movies such as *Stage Door* (37), *Mildred Pierce* (45) (which won her a nomination for best supporting-actress), and *Tea for Two* (50). (Her barbs were apparently as good in real life as onscreen: outtakes survive of Arden's ad libs cracking up actor Ronald Reagan.) However, her greatest role began in 1948 and lasted for ten years on radio and then television when she played *Our Miss Brooks,* a whole generation's favorite high school teacher. Throughout her teaching tenure, Arden continued to appear now and then in films. Returning to the screen after a decade's absence in 1975, she appeared in *The Strongest Man in the World* (75) and *Grease* (78).
**Selected Films:** *Stage Door* (37), *Cover Girl* (44), *Mildred Pierce* (45), *The Voice of the Turtle* (47), *Tea for Two* (50), *Three Husbands* (50), *Anatomy of a Murder* (59), *The Dark at the Top of the Stairs* (60), *The Strongest Man in the World* (75), *Grease* (78), *Grease II* (82).

*Alan Arkin played a Soviet submarine officer in* The Russians Are Coming, The Russians Are Coming *(66).*

## ARKIN, Alan (1934- )

Alan Arkin was born in New York City and studied at Los Angeles City College. His first effort in show business was as a folk singer, one of the group The Tarriers. His gift for comedy gained attention when he worked with the famed Second City troupe in Chicago. That led to successful Broadway appearances and soon to his first film – *The Russians Are Coming, The Russians Are Coming* (66), a comedy in which he played the mate of a Soviet sub aground on an island off the American coast. That film set Arkin's particular film character, which tends to broad and often loud comedy – as in *The Last of the Red Hot Lovers* (72) – but with a certain intimation of intelligence and competence: he plays bumblers, but there is more to them than the bumbling. Arkin has also done straight roles, most notably the chilling killer in *Wait Until Dark* (67) and the wistful deaf-mute in *The Heart is a Lonely Hunter* (68). He tried his hand as a director with *Little Murders* (71).

**Selected Films:** *The Russians Are Coming, The Russians Are Coming* (66), *Wait Until Dark* (67), *The Heart is a Lonely Hunter* (68), *Inspector Clouseau* (68), *Popi* (69), *Catch 22* (70), *The Last of the Red Hot Lovers* (72), *Freebie and the Bean* (74), *Rafferty and the Gold Dust Twins* (75), *The Seven Per Cent Solution* (76), *The In-Laws* (79), *The Return of Captain Invincible* (83), *Big Trouble* (86).

## ARLEN, Richard (1900-1976)

This rugged American leading man was born Cornelius Van Mattimore in Charlottesville, Virginia. He began his career as an extra and was later to become the durable hero of scores of B pictures, making the shift from silent to talking pictures with no trouble. He was truly one of the screen's more familiar faces, and his brawny body was the envy of every male movie fan.

**Selected Films:** *In the Name of Love* (25), *Wings* (27), *The Four Feathers* (28), *The Virginian* (29), *Touchdown* (31), *College Humor* (33), *Call of the Yukon* (38), *When My Baby Smiles at Me* (48), *The Best Man* (64), *Sex and the College Man* (70), *Won Ton Ton, The Dog Who Saved Hollywood* (75), *A Whale of a Tale* (76).

## ARLETTY (1898- )

Arletty, born Leonie Bathiat, in Courbevoie, came to films in her native France by way of modelling and the music hall, making her screen debut in *Un Chien Qui Rapporte* (31). Her beauty and her world-weary air took her through a number of pictures in the 1930s, but it was not until she joined director Marcel Carné and screenwriter Jacques Prévert

that she became the eternal Arletty of the haunting eyes and the Mona Lisa smile. The four films she made with Carné are all classics – *Hôtel du Nord* (38), *Le Jour Se Leve* (39), *Les Visiteurs du Soir* (42), and the incomparable *Les Enfants du Paradis* (44), in which she played the romantic obsession of mime Jean-Louis Barrault. The latter film was made at the end of the German occupation and after the war she was imprisoned briefly as a collaborator, the result of an affair with a German officer. Though she had hit her peak with Carné, Arletty worked steadily over the next decades, including an appearance in *The Longest Day* (62).
**Selected Films:** *Un Chien Qui Rapporte* (31), *La Guerre de Valses* (33), *Les Perles de la Couronne* (37), *Hôtel du Nord* (38), *Le Jour Se Leve* (39), *Fric-Frac* (39), *Les Visiteurs du Soir* (42), *Les Enfants du Paradis* (44), *L'Amour Madame* (51), *No Exit* (54), *The Longest Day* (62), *Les Volets Fermés* (72).

## ARLISS, George (1868-1946)

Born George Augustus Andrews, this distinguished British stage actor of the old school, made his stage debut at the age of 18 in his native London. In 1902 he came to the United States on tour and stayed to perform on Broadway for years. Turning to movies in his fifties, he astonished himself and almost everyone else by becoming a star both in Britain and the United States. On stage he had played kings and statesmen, and continued these roles in pictures, making a silent version of *Disraeli* (21) and a sound version (29), which won him an Academy Award. He was famous for years playing kings, statesmen, rajahs, eccentric millionaires and an occasional unconvincing hobo. He retired in 1937 and returned to England.
**Selected Films:** *The Devil* (21), *The Green Goddess* (23), *Disraeli (21)*, *Disraeli* (29), *The Green Goddess* (30), *Old English* (30), *Alexander Hamilton* (31), *The Man Who Played God* (32), *Voltaire* (33), *The House of Rothschild* (34), *Cardinal Richelieu* (35), *Dr Syn* (37).

## ARMENDARIZ, Pedro (1912-1963)

Born in Churubusco, Mexico, Pedro Armendariz worked briefly on the stage before entering films. In a short time he became Mexico's top star, appearing in many movies including *Simon Bolivar* (41). It was with his role in the celebrated *Maria Candelaria* (43) that Armendariz attracted worldwide attention with his virile and expansive screen personality. From that point he was destined for Hollywood, and appeared in the John Ford classics *The Fugitive* (47) and *Fort Apache* (48). He worked with Luis Buñuel in *The Brute* (*El Bruto*) (52), and throughout the 1950s appeared in films internationally. His final appearance was in the James Bond thriller *From Russia With Love* (63). That same year he committed suicide after learning he had cancer.
**Selected Films:** *El Indio* (38), *La Reina del Rio* (39), *Simon Bolivar* (41), *Guadalajara* (42), *Maria Candelaria* (43), *El Corsaro Negro* (44), *The Fugitive* (47), *Fort Apache* (48), *We Were Strangers* (49), *El Bruto* (52), *The Conqueror* (56), *The Wonderful Country* (59), *From Russia With Love* (63).

## ARMETTA, Henry (1888-1945)

At the age of 14 Armetta, born in Palermo, Sicily, stowed away on a boat leaving Italy for the United States. After several years of menial jobs he found work in the theater. His first film was *My Cousin* (18). Before long he had settled into character parts, usually excitable Italians, and played in silents and later in talkies.
**Selected Films:** *My Cousin* (18), *The Silent Command* (23), *Strangers May Kiss* (31), *Poor Little Rich Girl* (36), *The Big Store* (41), *Anchors Aweigh* (45), *A Bell for Adano* (45).

## ARMSTRONG, Robert (1890-1973)

Born Donald Robert Armstrong, in Saginaw, Michigan, this tough American character actor played cops, tough guys, sheriffs, trail bosses or shady investigators in countless films. Probably the most famous role of his career, however, was as producer Carl Denham in *King Kong* (33), the man responsible for bringing the giant ape to New York.
**Selected Films:** *The Silent Voice* (15), *The Main Event* (27), *The Most Dangerous Game* (32), *King Kong* (33), *Son of Kong* (33), *My Favorite Spy* (42), *Mighty Joe Young* (49), *For Those Who Think Young* (63).

## ARNAZ, Desi (1917-1986)

Born Desiderio Alberto Arnaz y De Acha in Santiago, Cuba, Arnaz came to the United States as a teenager and eventually formed a popular Cuban-style band. While working on his first film, *Too Many Girls* (40), he met and soon married co-star Lucille Ball. After making a few movies in the 1940s, Arnaz and Ball developed their classic TV sit-com *I Love Lucy*, which ran from 1950 until 1961 – by which time the two were divorced, and Arnaz was bought out of their successful production company Desilu by his former wife.
**Selected Films:** *Too Many Girls* (40), *Father Takes a Wife* (41), *Bataan* (43), *Holiday in Havana* (49), *The Long Long Trailer* (54), *The Escape Artist* (82).

## ARNAZ, Desi Jr (1953- )

The existence of Desi Arnaz Jr was hinted on television before his birth, when his mother Lucille Ball's pregnancy became part of the *I Love Lucy* TV show. Arnaz also worked on his mother's solo TV program for some years before going into film and further television work.
**Selected Films:** *Red Sky at Morning* (70), *Billy Two Hats* (74), *A Wedding* (79), *The House of Long Shadows* (83).

## ARNESS, James (1923- )

James Arness was born James Aurness in Minneapolis, Minnesota, and fought in Europe during World War II. After the war he worked in little theater for a couple of years before discovery by Hollywood, and made his film debut in *The Farmer's Daughter* (47). Arness went on to make several movies as a supporting actor, but his film career never quite took off, due partly to his competent but rather expressionless acting style and his height – his 6-foot 6-inch frame tended to tower unsettlingly over both leading ladies and men. One of his few lead roles was as the monster in *The Thing* (52). In 1955 Arness found his greatest success with the TV series *Gunsmoke* as Marshal Matt Dillon. He later starred in the TV series *How the West Was Won*. Arness is the brother of actor Peter Graves.
**Selected Films:** *The Farmer's Daughter* (47), *Battleground* (49), *Horizons West* (52), *The Thing* (52), *Hondo* (53), *Them* (54), *The Sea Chase* (55).

## ARNO, Sig (1895-1975)

Born Siegfried Aron in Hamburg, Germany, Arno was a noted stage and screen actor there before fleeing the Nazis in 1933. Making his Hollywood debut in *The Star Maker* (38), he went on to play character and comedy roles, usually as an amusing foreigner, in a great many films including Charlie Chaplin's *The Great Dictator* (40) and *The Palm Beach Story* (42).
**Selected Films:** *Manon Lescaut* (26), *Pandora's Box* (28), *The Star Maker* (38), *The Great Dictator* (40), *The Mummy's Hand* (40), *The Palm Beach Story* (42), *Song to Remember* (45), *On Moonlight Bay* (51), *The Great Diamond Robbery* (53).

## ARNOLD, Edward (1890-1956)

Edward Arnold was born Gunther Schneider to German immigrant parents in New York City and made his first appearances onstage in amateur theatricals on the Lower East Side. Moving to the professional stage, he became a respected actor in leading and supporting roles. He made his film debut in 1916 and played the lead in dozens of film Westerns, before resuming his stage career. In 1932 Arnold returned to the screen in several movies including *Okay, America* (32), and began a career that eventually amounted to some 150 movies. A fleshy and unremarkable-looking man, he nonetheless became a popular star for decades with his dynamic portrayals of a wide variety of character roles – politicians, judges, detectives, fathers and villains. His many notable roles included parts in Frank Capra's *You Can't Take It With You* (38) and in *All That Money Can Buy* (41) in which he played Daniel Webster.
**Selected Films:** *Okay, America* (32), *I'm No Angel* (33), *Crime and Punishment* (35), *Meet Nero Wolfe* (36), *Come and Get It* (36), *The Toast of New York* (37), *You Can't Take It With You* (38), *Meet John Doe* (41), *All That Money Can Buy* (41), *Eyes in the Night* (42), *Kismet* (44), *Three Wise Fools* (46), *Dear Ruth* (47), *Annie Get Your Gun* (50), *Miami Exposé* (56).

## ARQUETTE, Rosanna (1959- )

Born to a theatrical family in New York (granddaughter of Cliff Arquette, TV's 'Charley Weaver'), Arquette spent her youth traveling and, in her words, 'Waking up in Woodstock and dancing naked.' By the late 1970s she was playing troubled teenagers in dismal TV movies. In 1982 she found acclaim as Gary Gilmore's girlfriend in the TV production of *The Executioner's Song*. That led to her first starring role onscreen, as an honor student who takes up with a handsome dumb rake in John Sayles' *Baby, It's You* (83). After that came a flurry of top billings in popular – but often thoughtful and low-budget as well – films, including the superhit *Desperately Seeking Susan* (85) (the presence of rock singer Madonna as co-star had much to do with its success, to Arquette's manifest annoyance). Arquette's screen image tends to combine a certain elfin sensuality with a rather spacey persona. In *Nobody's Fool* (86), it was generally agreed that her superlative performance saved an otherwise forgettable movie.
**Selected Films:** *Baby It's You* (83), *Desperately Seeking Susan* (85), *After Hours* (85), *Silverado* (85), *Eight Million Ways to Die* (86), *Nobody's Fool* (86).

## ARTHUR, Beatrice (1923- )

Born in New York, tall, comedienne Beatrice Arthur (originally Bernice Frankel) is best known for her title role in the TV series *Maude* and her role in *The Golden Girls*. Among her occasional films was *Mame* (73) in which she reprised the part of Vera Charles which she originated on Broadway.
**Selected Films:** *That Kind of Woman* (58), *Lovers and Other Strangers* (69), *Mame* (73), *The History of the World – Part One* (81).

## ARTHUR, Jean (1905- )

If Jean Arthur never attained the giddy heights of certain sexier Hollywood stars, she ended up with the enviable reputation of an actress whose presence guaranteed quality. Born Gladys Greene in New York City, she was something of a tomboy in her youth. As a teenager she modeled for Howard Chandler Christy, a popular artist, and this led to some minor roles in the New York theater. In 1923 she made her first movie, John Ford's *Cameo Kirby*, and she continued to play small roles in two-reel comedies and Westerns. Her first leading part was in *Warming Up* (28) and she went on to make several films, including two Dr Fu Manchu mysteries. Unsatisfied with her Hollywood career, Arthur returned to the New York theater in 1932 and for three years she acted in several lightweight plays. In 1934, she signed with Columbia Pictures and re-launched her film

*Peggy Ashcroft with Robert Donat in* The Thirty-Nine Steps *(35).*

career with *Whirlpool*. It was not until John Ford's *The Whole Town's Talking* (35) that she finally found a part appropriate to her appearance and voice. For as a petite 5 foot 4 inch brunette, Jean Arthur was not intended to be a 'sex goddess,' while her voice – variously described as 'husky,' 'squeaky,' 'wistful,' or 'sort of lilting' – was at first thought to be a liability in the early days of talkies. From then on, Arthur tended to be cast as a spunky, no-nonsense, but ultimately lovable young woman with a mind, and usually a job, of her own. Her real breakthrough came when she starred opposite Gary Cooper in Frank Capra's *Mr Deeds Goes to Town* (36), and from then on her credits read like a catalog of film classics, including *You Can't Take It With You* (38), *Mr Smith Goes to Washington* (39), *The Talk of the Town* (42) and *A Foreign Affair* (48). Her last major role was in *Shane* (53), but she appeared in occasional theater and television productions and in 1966 had her own TV comedy series, *The Jean Arthur Show*. She also headed the theater department at Vassar College for some years. Long married to Frank J Ross, Jr, a Hollywood producer, Arthur was an extremely shy and private person, shunning the limelight off the screen, but her portrayals continue to glow whenever her films are shown.

**Selected Films:** *Cameo Kirby* (23), *Warming Up* (28), *Whirlpool* (34), *The Whole Town's Talking* (35), *Adventure in Manhattan* (36), *Mr Deeds Goes to Town* (36), *The Plainsman* (36), *History Is Made at Night* (37), *Easy Living* (37), *You Can't Take It With You* (38), *Mr Smith Goes To Washington* (39), *Only Angels Have Wings* (39), *Arizona* (40), *The Talk of the Town* (42), *The More the Merrier* (43), *The Impatient Years* (44), *A Foreign Affair* (48), *Shane* (53).

## ASHCROFT, Peggy (1907- )

Edith Margaret Emily Ashcroft was born in Croydon, England and had a thorough British dramatic training. By the 1930s she was a leading Shakespearean actress, and as such, made her American stage debut in 1937. She became Dame Commander of the British Empire in 1956. Her film appearances have been sporadic, but include both English and American productions including a supporting role in Hitchcock's classic *The Thirty-Nine Steps* (35), a few films in the 1940s and 1950s and some roles in notable, if not particularly commercial, pictures of the 1970s including *Sunday Bloody Sunday* (71). She won the Academy Award for Best Supporting Actress for her performance as Mrs Moore in *Passage to India* (84). She also appeared in several British TV series including *The Jewel in the Crown*.

**Selected Films:** *The Wandering Jew* (33), *The Thirty-Nine Steps* (35), *Rhodes of Africa* (36), *Quiet Wedding* (40), *The Nun's Story* (58), *Secret Ceremony* (68), *Sunday Bloody Sunday* (71), *Joseph Andrews* (77), *Passage to India* (84).

## ASHLEY, Elizabeth (1939- )

Elizabeth Ashley was born Elizabeth Cole in Ocala, Florida, and made a considerable splash in her first role on Broadway, winning a Tony for her performance in *Take Her, She's Mine* (61-62). Her versatility and her cool but intense acting style took her very far very fast. She made her film debut in *The Carpetbaggers* (64), starred in the hit stage comedy *Barefoot in the Park* (63), and appeared in the movies *Ship of Fools* (65) and *The Third Day* (65). At that point personal difficulties intervened and sent her into retirement for five years, but in 1970 she returned to the Broadway stage to acclaim in *Cat on a Hot Tin Roof*. Since then her films have included *Rancho de Luxe* (75) and *Coma* (78).
**Selected Films:** *The Carpetbaggers* (64), *Ship of Fools* (65), *The Third Day* (65), *Marriage of a Young Stockbroker* (71), *Paperback Hero* (75), *92 in the Shade* (75), *Rancho de Luxe* (75), *The Great Scout and Cathouse Thursday* (76), *Coma* (78), *Windows* (80), *Split Image* (82).

## ASNER, Edward (1929- )

Born in Kansas City, Kansas, Asner began acting in college and went on to the professional stage including work with Shakespearean companies. In later life he said of himself, 'I really wanted to be an adventurer, to lay pipeline in South America or be a cabin boy . . . but I didn't have the guts.' However, he *looked* like he had the guts, with his burly figure and robust features, and thus he tended to be cast as a heavy – though his obvious intelligence often tempered the roughness of his characters. His first film was *The Satan Bug* (65). Though he appeared in a few more minor films of the late 1960s, he first gained wide fame on television playing Lou Grant, the flinty-but-goodhearted editor on *The Mary Tyler Moore Show* and *Lou Grant*. He won an Emmy for his role in the TV drama *Roots* in 1977; in the same year he played Huey Long in the TV movie *The Life and Assassination of the Kingfish*. As President of the Screen Actors' Guild in the early 1980s, Asner's militant leadership of a TV actors' strike was controversial and perhaps led to the cancellation of the TV series *Lou Grant*. While continuing to appear in occasional theater and TV movies, Asner was actively involved in social and political issues during the 1980s.
**Selected Films:** *The Satan Bug* (65), *El Dorado* (66), *The Venetian Affair* (67), *Gunn* (67), *The Todd Killings* (70), *The Skin Game* (71), *Gus* (76), *Fort Apache the Bronx* (82), *Daniel* (83), *O'Hara's Wife* (84).

## ASTAIRE, Fred (1899- )

The studio report on Astaire's first screen test read, 'Can't act. Can't sing. Can dance a little.' Astaire, modest, with a boyish charm, was possibly one of the best dancers who ever lived – an elegant perfectionist, graceful and professional from the tip of his top hat to the soles of his feet. Born Frederick Austerlitz in Omaha, Nebraska, he and his sister Adele were brought to New York by their mother to study dancing while they were still children. They toured the vaudeville circuits and debuted on Broadway in 1917, becoming popular stars. They were big hits in London, too, before Adele retired to marry Lord Charles Cavendish. Astaire appeared on screen in *Dancing Lady* (33) opposite Joan Crawford, but his big film break came when he danced with Ginger Rogers in *Flying Down to Rio* (33). She gave him sex, he gave her class, so the saying goes. They made ten films together which landed them in the box-office top ten. *Top Hat* (35) and *Swing Time* (36) are arguably the two best musicals Hollywood ever produced. After the Astaire and Rogers team broke up, Astaire made movies with stars like Eleanor Powell, Rita Hayworth, Judy Garland and Cyd Charisse, retiring periodically but always being wooed back. *Holiday Inn* (42), with Bing Crosby, was a sign that Astaire was getting older. He could still dance up a storm, but he was no longer the major male lead in every film. When Gene Kelly broke his ankle Astaire got the lead in MGM's *Easter Parade* (49), opposite Judy Garland. At MGM his dances tended toward the balletic, rather than the tap dancing he had featured at RKO, but movie musicals had changed, too, becoming big, splashy, full-color events. In 1949 Astaire was given a special Academy Award for his work in musicals, which he went right on making well into the 1950s. In 1959 he began playing straight dramatic roles in films, appearing in movies as late as the 1980s in *Ghost Story* (81).
**Selected Films:** *Dancing Lady* (33), *Flying Down to Rio* (33), *The Gay Divorcee* (34), *Roberta* (35), *Top Hat* (35), *Follow the Fleet* (36), *Swing Time* (36), *Shall We Dance? (37), A Damsel in Distress* (37), *Carefree* (38), *The Story of Vernon and Irene Castle* (39), *You'll Never Get Rich* (41), *Holiday Inn* (42), *Blue Skies* (46), *Easter Parade* (49), *The Barkleys of Broadway* (48), *Royal Wedding* (51), *The Band Wagon* (53), *Daddy Longlegs* (5), *Funny Face* (57), *Silk Stockings* (57), *On the Beach* (59), *Finian's Rainbow* (68), *The Towering Inferno* (75), *Ghost Story* (81).

## ASTHER, Nils (1897-1981)

Born in Malmö and trained for the stage in his native Sweden where he began his movie career, in Hollywood Asther played romantic leads in dozens of silents such as *Our Dancing Daughters* (28). After the change to talkies, he maintained his suave screen image for some three decades, including an appearance in Frank Capra's *The Bitter Tea of General Yen* (33) as a Chinese warlord.
**Selected Films:** *Topsy and Eva* (27), *Our Dancing Daughters* (28), *The Single Standard* (29), *The Bitter Tea of General Yen* (33), *Abdul the Damned* (35), *Dr Kildare's Wedding Day* (41), *Son of Lassie* (45), *That Man from Tangier* (53), *Gudrun* (63).

*Fred Astaire and Ginger Rogers in* Swing Time *(36).*

*Humphrey Bogart, Sydney Greenstreet, Peter Lorre, Mary Astor in* The Maltese Falcon *(41).*

## ASTIN, John (1930- )

Born in Baltimore, Maryland, Astin pursued work on the stage before gravitating to film and TV as a character comedian. His first movie appearance was in *West Side Story* (61), and he turned up in other comedies including *That Touch of Mink* (62), and *Viva Max!* (69). His TV work included the role of Gomez on *The Addams Family*. He is married to actress Patty Duke.
**Selected Films:** *West Side Story* (61), *That Touch of Mink* (62), *The Wheeler Dealers* (63), *Candy* (68), *Viva Max!* (69), *Freaky Friday* (77), *National Lampoon's European Vacation* (85).

## ASTOR, Mary (1906- )

Astor was born Lucille Vasconcellos Langehanke in Quincy, Illinois and was famous for her antics off screen as well as her characterizations of nasty women on screen. Opposite Humphrey Bogart in *The Maltese Falcon* (41) she was enticingly wicked. Astor was a silent film star before the age of 20. Four marriages, a custody battle, alcoholism, a suicide attempt, revelations from her personal diary in court and much publicized affairs with John Barrymore and George S Kaufman made her a prime subject of Hollywood gossip columnists. She won an Academy Award for Best Supporting Actress in the Bette Davis vehicle *The Great Lie* (1941), and is the author of an autobiography and several novels.
**Selected Films:** *The Beggar Maid* (21), *Beau Brummel* (24), *Don Q, Son of Zorro* (25), *Don Juan* (25), *Holiday* (30), *The Lost Squadron* (32), *Red Dust* (32), *Dodsworth* (36), *The Prisoner of Zenda* (37), *Midnight* (39), *Turnabout* (40), *The Great Lie* (41), *The Maltese Falcon* (41), *The Palm Beach Story* (42), *Meet Me in St Louis* (44), *Act of Violence* (49), *Little Women* (49), *Return to Peyton Place* (61), *Hush ... Hush Sweet Charlotte* (64).

## ATES, Roscoe (1892-1962)

Cured of stuttering in his childhood, Ates, born in Grange, Mississippi, revived his affliction for a generation of comic film roles, many of them as a sidekick to leading cowboys.
**Selected Films:** *South Sea Rose* (29), *Cimarron* (30), *Alice in Wonderland* (33), *Gone with the Wind* (39), *The Palm Beach Story* (42), *The Stranger Wore a Gun* (53), *The Errand Boy* (61).

## ATHERTON, William (1947- )

In his teens, Connecticut-born Atherton appeared professionally at New Haven's famed Long Wharf Theatre. His sensitive approach to roles took him through several successful stage leads. After his first film, *The New Centurions* (72), he played the lead in *The Day of the Locust* (74).
**Selected Films:** *The New Centurions* (72), *Class of '44* (73), *The Day of the Locust* (74), *The Sugarland Express* (74), *The Hindenburg* (75), *Looking for Mr Goodbar* (77), *No Mercy* (86).

## ATTENBOROUGH, Richard (1923- )

Attenborough, that splendid character actor, was born in Cambridge, England. He made his professional stage debut in 1941 and played a coward in

the Noel Coward film, *In Which We Serve* (42). Typecast as a coward for some time, he broke out of the mold and went on to play character roles and leads in both British and American movies. In the late 1950s, he began producing and directing motion pictures. His directing debut was *Oh What a Lovely War!* (69). He won a British Film Academy Award as Best Actor for *Guns at Batasi* (64) and was knighted in 1976. Sir Richard won an Academy Award for Best Director for *Gandhi* (82). He also directed *A Bridge Too Far* (77), *Magic* (78) and *A Chorus Line* (85).
**Selected Films:** *In Which We Serve* (42), *Brighton Rock* (47), *The Guinea Pig* (49), *Private's Progress* (55), *The Man Upstairs* (58), *The Angry Silence* (59), *The Great Escape* (63), *Seance on a Wet Afternoon* (64), *Guns at Batasi* (64), *The Flight of the Phoenix* (65), *The Sand Pebbles* (66), *Doctor Doolittle* (67), *Loot* (71), *Conduct Unbecoming* (76), *The Human Factor* (79).

## ATWILL, Lionel (1885-1946)

Lionel Alfred William Atwill is probably best remembered for his performance as the wooden-armed police chief in *Son of Frankenstein* (39) and his other monster movie roles. But this character actor born in Croydon, England, was a veteran of the London stage and Broadway before he came to Hollywood to play Teutonic villains, mad doctors and city officials.
**Selected Films:** *For Sale* (18), *Dr X* (32), *The Mystery of the Wax Museum* (33), *Murders in the Zoo* (33), *Nana* (34), *The Devil is a Woman* (35), *Captain Blood* (35), *Son of Frankenstein* (39), *The Three Musketeers* (39), *The Hound of the Baskervilles* (39), *Man Made Monster* (41), *To Be or Not to Be* (42), *House of Dracula* (45), *Genius at Work* (46).

*Richard Attenborough in* 10 Rillington Place *(70).*

## AUBERJONOIS, René (1940- )

Auberjonois was born in New York and by his twenties had established himself as a competant character actor. His intense eyes and beakish nose lent themselves to parts both serious and comic, including supporting roles in *M*A*S*H* (70), *Brewster McCloud* (71), and *The Eyes of Laura Mars* (78).
**Selected Films:** *Petulia* (68), *M*A*S*H* (70), *McCabe and Mrs Miller* (71), *Brewster McCloud* (71), *Images* (72), *Pete 'n Tillie* (72), *King Kong* (76), *The Eyes of Laura Mars* (78), *Where The Buffalo Roam* (80).

## AUDRAN, Stéphane (1939- )

Born in Versailles, France, Audran began her film career in *Kill or Cure* (58). In 1964 she married director Claude Chabrol and became his favorite leading lady in films such as *Violette Noziere* (78), for which she won a French César. Her air of cool sophistication with unexpected emotional undercurrents made her much in demand internationally; she has made dozens of films including Luis Buñuel's *The Discreet Charm of the Bourgeoisie* (72), as well as *The Big Red One* (80).
**Selected Films:** *Kill or Cure* (58), *Bluebeard* (63), *Les Biches* (68), *La Femme Infidèle* (69), *Le Boucher* (70), *The Discreet Charm of the Bourgeoisie* (72), *Dead Pigeon on Beethoven Street* (73), *And Then There Were None* (74), *Violette Noziere* (78), *The Big Red One* (80), *Coup de Torchon* (82), *Eagle's Wing* (83), *Les Plouffe* (85).

## AUER, Mischa (1905-1967)

Born Mischa Ounskowsky in St Petersburg, Russia, Mischa Auer arrived in the United States in 1920 and first acted on the stage. He made his screen debut in *Something Always Happens* (28) and for several years played minor and mostly villainous roles. In *My Man Godfrey* (36), his goggly eyes and fractured English revealed their comic possibilities, and Auer turned these gifts to good use in dozens of roles thereafter.
**Selected Films:** *Something Always Happens* (28), *My Man Godfrey* (36), *100 Men and a Girl* (37), *You Can't Take It With You* (38), *Destry Rides Again* (39), *Hellzapoppin* (41), *Twin Beds* (42), *Lady in the Dark* (44), *Confidential Report* (55), *Drop Dead Darling* (66).

## AUMONT, Jean-Pierre (1909- )

Born Jean-Pierre Salomons in Paris, Jean-Pierre Aumont made his acting debut in 1930 on the French stage. He first found acclaim as the lead in Cocteau's play *La Machine Infernale* (34); by then he had made several films including *Jean de la Lune* (32). Tall, blond, blue-eyed, and charming, Aumont was to become the archetypal Continental leading man for decades in films around the world. After appearing in Carné's classic *Hôtel du Nord*

(38), Aumont fought with the Free French during World War II, and won the Legion of Honor. He made several films during the war as well, including two in the United States, *Cross of Lorraine* (42) and *Assignment in Brittany* (43). His film career has stretched unbroken into the 1980s, including *Lili* (53), *The Devil at Four O'Clock* (61) and *Nana* (83). His autobiography, *Sun and Shadow*, appeared in 1977. He was married to actress Maria Montez from 1943 to her death in 1951. Since 1956, he has been married to actress Marisa Pavan.
**Selected Films:** *Jean de la Lune* (32), *Taras Bulba* (36), *Bizarre Bizarre* (37), *Hôtel du Nord* (38), *Three Hours* (39), *Cross of Lorraine* (42), *Assignment in Brittany* (43), *The First Gentleman* (48), *Charge of the Lancers* (53), *Lili* (53), *John Paul Jones* (59), *The Devil at Four O'Clock* (61), *Castle Keep* (69), *Day for Night* (74), *Mahogany* (75), *Seven Suspects for Murder* (77), *Nana* (83), *Sweet Country* (87).

## AUTRY, Gene (1907- )

Autry's gigantic success in films stemmed from his being the first successful 'singing cowboy.' He and his studio producers invented the formula for a new type of cowboy hero for children – one who paused during his action-packed adventures to sing songs and play a guitar. His breakthrough with this formula in the 1930s was a revolution in B westerns that propelled him into the top ten of Hollywood movie stars with box office appeal. Roy Rogers and many others imitated Autry, but he was the original and his career in movies, radio, television, recording and personal shows flourished until the 1960s. He had nine million-seller record hits, more than any of his imitators. Born Orvon Autry in Tioga, Texas, he became a railroad telegrapher in Oklahoma. Will Rogers happened to stop at the station while Autry was singing to himself and strumming his guitar one dull evening. Rogers encouraged the young man and a Columbia records scout soon signed him to a contract. Radio stardom on *The National Barn Dance* soon followed, then the movies. Autry's mellow singing voice and his famous horse, Champion, made him a superstar all over the world. When he wound up his performing career, Autry went on to be an even bigger success as a businessman.
**Selected Films:** *Springtime in the Rockies* (37), *Under Western Stars (38)*, *South of the Border* (39), *Back in the Saddle* (41), *Down Mexico Way* (41), *Goldtown Ghost Riders* (53), *Silent Treatment* (68).

*Dan Aykroyd in* Ghostbusters *(84).*

## AVALON, Frankie (1939- )

Avalon was born Francis Avallone in Philadelphia and by his late teens was a famous rock 'n' roll singer in an era when that was a ticket to a movie career. First appearing onscreen in action features such as *The Alamo* (60) and *Voyage to the Bottom of the Sea* (61), he settled into being a staple star of beach-and-bikini epics such as *Beach Party* (63), and *How to Stuff a Wild Bikini* (65). He made a nostalgic screen comeback as himself in *Grease* (78).
**Selected Films:** *Jamboree* (57), *The Alamo* (60), *Voyage to the Bottom of the Sea* (61), *Panic in the Year Zero!* (62), *Beach Party* (63), *Operation Bikini* (63), *How to Stuff a Wild Bikini* (65), *Skidoo* (68), *The Take* (74), *Grease* (78), *Back to the Beach* (87).

## AYKROYD, Dan (1954- )

This writer and comedian was born in Ottawa, Canada. Early on he joined the famous improvisational troupe Second City in Toronto. Soon he was working closely with the comedian John Belushi and the rest of the madcap gang on the hit television program, *Saturday Night Live* in New York. He then went on to films, and was the co-writer and one of the stars in the blockbuster hit comedy *Ghostbusters* (84).
**Selected Films:** *The Blues Brothers* (80), *Trading Places* (83), *Ghostbusters* (84), *Spies Like Us* (85).

## AYLMER, Felix (1889-1979)

Felix Edward Aylmer Jones was born in Corsham, England, and first appeared on the stage in 1911. He soon became one of the most durable and distinguished stage actors of his time. His screen career, beginning with *Escape* (30), was nearly as long and as successful. He usually appeared in supporting character roles such as clerics, businessmen and professors. He was knighted in 1965.
**Selected Films:** *Escape* (30), *The Wandering Jew* (33), *Victoria the Great* (37), *Mr Emmanuel* (44), *Hamlet* (48), *Quo Vadis* (51), *Ivanhoe* (52), *Separate Tables* (58), *Becket* (64), *Hostile Witness* (68).

## AYRES, Agnes (1896-1940)

Born Agnes Hintle in Carbondale, Illinois, Ayres appeared in a bit part in her first movie in 1915 and went on to become one of the great stars of the silents. The most noted of her dozens of romantic leads were opposite Rudolph Valentino in *The Sheik* (21) and *The Son of the Sheik* (26). Her career failed to survive the coming of sound.
**Selected Films:** *The Sacred Silence* (19), *Forbidden Fruit* (19), *The Sheik* (21), *The Ordeal* (22), *The Ten Commandments* (23), *The Son of the Sheik* (26), *Eve's Love Letters* (29).

## AYRES, Lew (1908- )

Born in Minneapolis, Minnesota, Lewis Ayer changed his name and became an immediate success in his first picture – *The Kiss* (29), which starred Greta Garbo. He was a boyish leading man and he occasionally was able to prove himself to be a comfortable and friendly actor. *All Quiet on the Western Front* (30), in which he played a young German soldier of World War I, made him a star. He starred in the *Doctor Kildare* film series with Lionel Barrymore, but his film career suffered when he became a conscientious objector during World War II, although he did volunteer for hazardous ambulance duty. He was married to Ginger Rogers from 1934 to 1941.
**Selected Films:** *The Kiss* (29), *All Quiet on the Western Front* (30), *The Spirit of Notre Dame* (31), *State Fair* (33), *Last Train from Madrid* (37), *Holiday* (38), *Young Dr Kildare* (38), *Calling Dr Kildare* (39), *The Dark Mirror* (46), *Johnny Belinda* (48), *Advise and Consent* (61), *The Carpetbaggers* (64), *Battle for the Planet of the Apes* (73), *Damien – Omen II* (78), *Letter from Frank* (79).

## AZNAVOUR, Charles (1924- )

Born Shahnour Aznävurjan in Paris to Armenian parents, Aznavour grew up to be a multitalented entertainer – singer, songwriter, composer, and screen actor. After establishing himself as a popular singer, he began his prolific film career with *La Tête contre les Murs* (58). Most of his films have been French, but he has appeared occasionally in American films such as *The Adventurers* (70).
**Selected Films:** *La Tête contre les Murs* (58), *The Testament of Orpheus* (59), *Shoot the Piano Player* (60), *High Infidelity* (64), *Cloportes* (65), *Un Beau Monstre* (70), *The Adventurers* (70), *And Then There Were None* (74), *The Tin Drum* (79), *Edith and Marcel* (84).

# B

## BACALL, Lauren (1924- )

Born Betty Jean Perske in New York City, Bacall attended the American Academy of Dramatic Arts and became a model. Director Howard Hawks saw her picture on the cover of *Harper's Bazaar* magazine and signed her to a seven-year contract. Nicknamed 'The Look,' she made her screen debut with Humphrey Bogart in *To Have and Have Not* (44). In the film, the husky-voiced Bacall gave Bogart a riveting glance through arched eyebrows that became her trademark – 'If you want anything, just whistle' – and a new screen goddess was born. The chemistry of Bacall-Bogart was magic at the box office. They were married in 1945 and made three successive movies – *The Big Sleep* (46), *Dark Passage* (47) and *Key Largo* (48). The gutsiness of the women she played applied privately as well – she was suspended 12 times by Warner Bros. because of casting quarrels, and she bought out her contract in 1950. Her finesse in comedy was showcased in *How to Marry a Millionaire* (53), in which she deftly stole scenes from Marilyn Monroe and Betty Grable. Bogart's death from cancer in 1957 left Bacall adrift. In 1961 she married actor Jason Robards Jr, but they divorced in 1969. Bacall's best film of that era was *Harper* (66). She became the toast of Broadway in *Cactus Flower* (67) and *Applause* (70), a musical adaptation of the movie *All About Eve* (50), which had starred Bette Davis. In the latter role, she won a Tony Award as Best Actress in a Musical. Back in films, she was one of the stars of *Murder on the Orient Express* (74), and her most recent Broadway show, *Woman of the Year*, was a smash hit.
**Selected Films:** *To Have and Have Not* (44), *The Big Sleep* (46), *Dark Passage* (47), *Key Largo* (48), *Young Man with a Horn* (50), *How to Marry a Millionaire* (53), *The Cobweb* (55), *Blood Alley* (55), *Designing Woman* (57), *Harper* (66), *Murder on the Orient Express* (74), *The Shootist* (76), *Health* (79), *The Fan* (81).

## BACCALONI, Salvatore (1900-1969)

Salvatore Baccaloni was born in Rome and became a noted operatic bass famed for comedy roles such as Dr Bartolo in *The Barber of Seville* and Dr Dulcamara in *L'Elisir d'Amore*. His film career was a sidelight, involving comedy roles in movies of the 1950s and 1960s.
**Selected Films:** *Full of Life* (56), *Merry Andrew* (58), *Rock a Bye Baby* (59), *Fanny* (61), *The Pigeon That Took Rome* (62).

## BACKUS, Jim (1913- )

This burly character comedian was born in Cleveland, Ohio, and has long worked in vaudeville, radio, films, television and the stage. He appeared in *The Pied Piper* (42), but his first important movie was *The Great Lover* (49), which starred Bob Hope as a Scout leader. Possibly his greatest fame was as the voice of the nearsighted Mr Magoo in the UPA cartoons of the 1950s. He has also done extensive work in television, most notably as the husband of Joan Davis in *I Married Joan*, and as the millionaire

on *Gilligan's Island.*
**Selected Films:** *The Pied Piper* (42), *The Great Lover* (49), *Pat and Mike* (52), *Androcles and the Lion* (53), *Rebel without a Cause* (55), *Man of a Thousand Faces* (57), *It's a Mad Mad Mad Mad World* (63), *Billie* (65), *Pete's Dragon* (77), *There Goes the Bride* (80), *Slapstick of Another Kind* (84).

## BACON, Kevin (1958- )

Philadelphia-born Bacon studied drama and appeared on Broadway before making his screen debut in *Animal House* (78). He has since appeared in a number of popular films of the 1980s, including *Diner* (81).
**Selected Films:** *Animal House* (78), *Friday the 13th* (80), *Diner* (82), *Footloose* (84), *Quicksilver* (85).

## BACON, Lloyd (1890-1955)

Born in San Jose, California, Bacon first appeared before the camera in the silent era, as a supporting player for Chaplin in the classics, *The Tramp* (15) and *The Floorwalker* (16). Later Bacon directed comedies for Mack Sennett and then moved into talkies to become one of the most prolific directors in history. As director, his movies ranged from comic to serious, the quality from forgettable to classic. Among his more memorable efforts were several musicals choreographed by Busby Berkeley, including *Gold Diggers of 1937* (36).
**Selected Films:** *The Tramp* (15), *The Champion* (15), *The Bank* (15), *The Floorwalker* (16), *The Rink* (16). (As a director): *The Singing Fool* (28), *Forty-Second Street* (33), *Wonder Bar* (34), *Devil Dogs of the Air* (35), *Gold Diggers of 1937* (36), *Brother Orchid* (40), *Action in the North Atlantic* (43), *Call Me Mister* (51), *She Couldn't Say No* (54).

## BADDELEY, Hermione (1906-1986)

Born in Broseley, England, Hermione Baddeley came to films via the usual British route of the stage, making her debut at the age of 12. Her first film part was in *The Guns of Loos* (28). She went on to a long and active career in both stage and films. For her role in *Room at the Top* (59) Baddeley received an Oscar nomination. In the mid-1970s she appeared on the TV series *Maude.*
**Selected Films:** *The Guns of Loos* (28), *Kipps* (41), *Quartet* (48), *Tom Brown's Schooldays* (51), *Room at the Top* (59), *The Unsinkable Molly Brown* (64), *Mary Poppins* (64), *The Happiest Millionaire* (67), *Up the Front* (72), *The Black Windmill* (74), *There Goes the Bride* (80).

## BAGGOTT, King (1874-1948)

Tall, handsome, and powerful, Baggott born in St Louis, Missouri, became one of the first movie actors to be known by name. After virile leading roles in dozens of adventure films such as *Ivanhoe* (12) and *The Corsican Brothers* (15), he turned to direction (*Tumbleweeds* [25]) then returned to acting in character parts into the 1940s.
**Selected Films:** *The Scarlet Letter* (11), *Ivanhoe* (12), *Dr Jekyll and Mr Hyde* (13), *The Corsican Brothers* (15), *Going Straight* (22), *Romance in the Rain* (34), *Come Live With Me* (41).

## BAILEY, Pearl (1918- )

Bailey was born in Newport News, Virginia and began singing and dancing with bands in her teens. By the 1940s she was performing on Broadway, cementing her reputation as one of the great popular vocalists of that era. Her films were occasional, usually singing roles in musicals.
**Selected Films:** *Variety Girl* (47), *Carmen Jones* (54), *Porgy and Bess* (59), *The Landlord* (69), *Norman, Is That You?* (76).

## BAINTER, Fay (1892-1968)

Born in Los Angeles, Bainter made her Broadway debut in 1912 and her film debut in *This Side of Heaven* (34). In 1938 she was nominated for both a leading and supporting Oscar, winning the latter for her role in *Jezebel.* She appeared regularly in films into the 1960s, usually cast in sympathetic matronly roles.
**Selected Films:** *This Side of Heaven* (34), *Quality Street* (37), *Jezebel* (38), *White Banners* (38), *Our Town* (40), *The Human Comedy* (43), *Dark Waters* (44), *State Fair* (45), *The Secret Life of Walter Mitty* (47), *The Children's Hour* (62).

## BAKER, Carroll (1931- )

Born in Johnstown, Pennsylvania, Baker gave a sensational performance as the thumb-sucking child-wife in *Baby Doll* (56), and Hollywood began grooming her as the new Marilyn Monroe. She tried to vary her sex-symbol status by playing roles of melodramatic intensity, but she never really caught on with American audiences. Discouraged, she moved to Europe and has appeared in Italian and Spanish movies and on the London stage.
**Selected Films:** *Easy to Love* (53), *Giant* (56), *Baby Doll* (56), *The Miracle* (59), *The Carpetbaggers* (64), *Harlow* (65), *Captain Apache* (71), *The Devil Has Seven Faces* (77), *Star 80* (83), *Native Son* (86).

## BAKER, Diane (1938- )

Diane Baker was born in Hollywood, the daughter of a stage actress. She made an auspicious screen debut as Margot, the older sister, in Otto Preminger's *The Diary of Anne Frank* (59) and appeared in two more films that year, including *Journey to the Center of the Earth.* Given her delicate, attractive features of the cool and conventional rather than sultry variety, Baker tended to be cast in demure parts in action dramas such as *Mirage* (65), and Alfred Hitchcock's *Marnie* (64). In the 1970s she appeared mostly in TV movies

including *A Tree Grows in Brooklyn* (74).
**Selected Films:** *The Diary of Anne Frank* (59), *Journey to the Center of the Earth* (59), *Nine Hours to Rama* (63), *The Prize* (63), *Marnie* (64), *Mirage* (65), *Krakatoa, East of Java* (68), *The Horse in the Gray Flannel Suit* (68), *Baker's Hawk* (76), *The Pilot* (79).

## BAKER, Joe Don (1943- )

The rough-hewn features and husky form of Baker, born in Groesbeck, Texas, which match his blunt acting style, led him to starring and supporting roles, in crime and adventure movies of the less subtle sort. His most popular role was as the avenging sheriff Buford Pusser in *Walking Tall* (72).
**Selected Films:** *Cool Hand Luke* (67), *Guns of the Magnificent Seven* (69), *Junior Bonner* (72), *Walking Tall* (72), *Charley Varrick* (73), *Framed* (75), *Speedtrap* (78), *The Natural* (84), *Fletch* (85).

## BAKER, Kenny (1912-1985)

Born in Monrovia, California, Baker was a popular crooner of the 1930s and 1940s who appeared in movie musicals of that era, including *King of Burlesque* (36). In the film of *The Mikado* (39) he played Nanki-Poo.
**Selected Films:** *Metropolitan* (35), *King of Burlesque* (36), *The King and the Chorus Girl* (37), *52nd Street* (39), *The Mikado* (39), *Silver Skates* (43), *The Harvey Girls* (46), *Calendar Girl* (47), *Amadeus* (84).

## BAKER, Stanley (1927-1976)

Born in Glamorgan, Wales, this virile actor rose

*Carroll Baker and Eli Wallach in* Baby Doll *(56).*

from character roles to stardom, projecting honesty or villainy with equal ease. During the 1960s Baker produced many of his own films. He was knighted just a month before his death from cancer at age 49.
**Selected Films:** *Undercover* (41), *The Cruel Sea* (53), *Hell Below Zero* (54), *Richard III* (56), *Campbell's Kingdom* (57), *Hell Drivers* (57), *The Criminal* (60), *The Guns of Navarone* (61), *Zulu* (63), *Accident* (67), *Innocent Bystanders* (72), *Zorro* (75).

## BALL, Lucille (1911- )

Ball was born in Celeron, New York, and at the age of 15 she took off for New York, then went to Hollywood to be a bit player, appearing in dozens of films, including being one of the fabulous Goldwyn Girls. She spent four years appearing in such trivia as *Bottoms Up* (34) and *Carnival* (35), the latter being her first billed role. Movie patrons first really noticed her in *Follow the Fleet* (37), which starred Ginger Rogers and Fred Astaire. Ball divided her time between movies and radio for a while, appearing on Phil Baker's show and the *Jack Haley Wonder Show*, and starring in *My Favorite Husband*. She married Cuban band leader Desi Arnaz in 1940, a marriage that lasted 20 years. She is currently married to actor Gary Morton, whom she wed in 1961. Ball's career was doing well, but only when she switched to television in 1951 in *I Love Lucy* did she become America's favorite comedienne – one of the great female clowns – at the age of 40. She returned to Broadway to star in *Wildcat* in 1960. Ball returned to television in 1986

in her fifth different program. She also was the guiding hand of the very successful Desilu Production Company.
**Selected Films:** *Bottoms Up* (34), *Carnival* (35), *Roberta* (35), *Top Hat* (35), *Follow the Fleet* (37), *Stage Door* (37), *Having a Wonderful Time* (38), *The Affairs of Annabel* (38), *Room Service* (38), *Five Came Back* (39), *Too Many Girls* (40), *Look Who's Laughing* (41), *The Big Street* (42), *Du Barry Was a Lady* (43), *Best Foot Forward* (43), *Without Love* (45), *The Ziegfeld Follies* (46), *Easy to Wed* (46), *Her Husband's Affairs* (47), *Sorrowful Jones* (49), *The Fuller Brush Girl* (50), *The Long Long Trailer* (54), *The Facts of Life* (60), *Yours Mine and Ours* (68), *Mame* (73).

## BALSAM, Martin (1919- )

Martin Balsam was born in New York and learned his craft at the Actor's Studio. After a good deal of stage experience he made his film debut in the classic *On the Waterfront* (54). From that point on he was a fixture of American feature films and television for decades. Balsam is a self-contained and understated character actor rather than a star type – the sort one immediately recognizes onscreen but whose name may not come to mind. Among his notable appearances was as the determined but doomed detective of Alfred Hitchcock's *Psycho* (60). In 1965 he won an Oscar as best supporting-actor for *A Thousand Clowns*; the same year he received a Tony for his stage performance in *You Know I Can't Hear You When the Water's Running*. In the 1970s and 1980s he was most often seen in TV movies including *Miles to Go Before I Sleep* and *Raid on Entebbe*.
**Selected Films:** *On the Waterfront* (54), *Twelve Angry Men* (57), *Psycho* (60), *Breakfast at Tiffany's* (61), *The Carpetbaggers* (64), *Seven Days in May* (64), *A Thousand Clowns* (65), *Hombre* (67), *Tora! Tora! Tora!* (70), *Little Big Man* (70), *Catch-22* (70), *The Anderson Tapes* (71), *Summer Wishes Winter Dreams* (73), *The Taking of Pelham 123* (74), *Murder on the Orient Express* (74), *All the President's Men* (76), *Two Minute Warning* (76), *The Sentinel* (77), *Cuba* (79), *The Salamander* (83), *St Elmo's Fire* (85).

## BANCROFT, Anne (1931- )

Anne Bancroft has never looked or acted quite like the usual feminine movie star: beautiful but not particularly glamorous, commanding onscreen but also warm and believable, she was once dubbed 'a female Brando.' Accordingly, it took Hollywood some years to figure out what to do with her. Bancroft was born Anna Maria Louise Italiano in the Bronx and began acting and dancing onstage at age four. While studying in New York at the American Academy of Dramatic Arts and the Actors Studio, she began appearing on TV in 1950 and made her movie debut in *Don't Bother to Knock* (52). For the next five years she was squandered in second features. Finally she left Hollywood for Broadway and there scored two triumphs in a row,

winning a Tony in 1958 for her lead opposite Henry Fonda in *Two for the Seesaw* and another Tony the following year, plus a New York Drama Critics Award, for her unforgettable Annie Sullivan in *The Miracle Worker*. (Preparing for that role as Helen Keller's teacher, she masked herself with tape – to get a sense of blindness – and learned sign language.) She played the role of Sullivan in the screen version of *The Miracle Worker* (62) and for it won that year's best-actress Academy Award. There followed a string of memorable roles, among them as a woman obsessed with having children in *The Pumpkin Eater* (64) and Mrs. Robinson, who seduces Dustin Hoffman in *The Graduate* (68). More recently, Bancroft starred with Shirley MacLaine in the popular film *The Turning Point* (77), both of them playing aging and combative dancers. In 1964 she married comic and film-maker Mel Brooks; they starred together in his 1983 remake of *To Be or Not To Be*.
**Selected Films:** *Don't Bother to Knock* (52), *Treasure of the Golden Condor* (53), *Demetrius and the Gladiators* (54), *The Restless Breed* (57), *The Miracle Worker* (62), *The Pumpkin Eater* (64), *The Slender Thread* (65), *The Graduate* (68), *Young Winston* (72), *The Prisoner of Second Avenue* (74), *Silent Movie* (76), *The Hindenberg* (77), *The Turning Point* (77), *The Elephant Man* (80), *To Be Or Not To Be* (83), *Garbo Talks* (84), *Agnes of God* (85), *'night Mother* (86), *84 Charing Cross Road* (87).

*Anne Bancroft as Annie Sullivan in* The Miracle Worker *(62), with Pattie Duke as Helen Keller.*

## BANCROFT, George (1882-1956)

George Bancroft was born in Philadelphia and began his performing career in minstrel shows. Moving on to Broadway, he appeared for years in musicals and dramas before making a belated film debut in *The Journey's End* (21). His burly form and menacing air made Bancroft a natural for villains, gangsters, and the like and he was cast in these roles in dozens of movies during the 1920s and 1930s, including James Cruze's *The Pony Express* (25), Josef von Sternberg's *Underworld* (27), and John Ford's *Stagecoach* (39). Though Bancroft appeared in these and a few other first-rate films, most of his work was in action dramas, in which he occasionally alternated villains with tough-but-goodhearted roles. In 1942 he retired from films to his ranch.

**Selected Films:** *The Journey's End* (21), *Driven* (21), *The Pony Express* (25), *Code of the West* (25), *Old Ironsides* (26), *White Gold* (27), *Underworld* (27), *The Docks of New York* (28), *Thunderbolt* (29), *Paramount on Parade* (30), *Scandal Sheet* (31), *Blood Money* (34), *Mr Deeds Goes to Town* (36), *Submarine Patrol* (38), *Angels With Dirty Faces* (38), *Stagecoach* (39), *Young Tom Edison* (40), *Green Hell* (40), *Whistling in Dixie* (42).

## BANKHEAD, Tallulah (1902-1968)

Bankhead was born in Huntsville, Alabama, the daughter of a United States senator. More people remember her for her presence than her performances, however. They remember that she called everyone 'dahling' because she had difficulty remembering names. She had a deep seductive voice, a searing sense of humor and she had a habit of taking off her clothes in public. She titillated Broadway and London in the 1920s by her extravagant performances on stage and off, and later frittered away her talent by living too dangerously. She could outtalk, outsmoke (four packs of cigarettes a day) and outdrink anybody. Bankhead was a first-rate actress – she won the New York Drama Critic's Circle Award for her performance in Lillian Hellman's *The Little Foxes* in 1939, and won it again in 1942 in Thornton Wilder's *The Skin of Our Teeth.* Although much of what else she did was mediocre, she gave memorable performances on stage in *A Streetcar Named Desire, Private Lives* and *The Milk Train Doesn't Stop Here Anymore.* Her work in movies was spotty. It seemed that films never really managed to contain her. Except for a magnificent performance in Alfred Hitchcock's *Lifeboat* (43), her motion pictures were lackluster.

**Selected Films:** *When Men Betray* (18), *Tarnished Lady* (31), *The Devil and the Deep* (32), *Stage Door Canteen* (43), *Lifeboat* (43), *A Royal Scandal* (45), *Main Street to Broadway* (53), *Die! Die! My Darling* (65).

## BANKS, Leslie (1890-1952)

Leslie Banks was born in West Derby, England and attended Oxford. In his early twenties he began acting on the British stage and quickly made a name for himself as one of the distinguished actors of his generation. Having made some tentative efforts in silent film, he went to Hollywood in the 1930s and made his first successful movie as the deranged Zaroff in *The Most Dangerous Game* (32). Having thus shown his movie possibilities, Banks returned to England for most of the rest of his career, alternating stage appearances with character roles in films major and minor, including Hitchcock's *The Man Who Knew Too Much* (34), *Sanders of the River* (35), and *Twenty-One Days* (39). In 1944 Banks played the Chorus in Laurence Olivier's brilliant Shakespearean film *Henry V.*

**Selected Films:** *The Most Dangerous Game* (32), *The Fire-Raisers* (33), *The Man Who Knew Too Much* (34), *Transatlantic Tunnel* (35), *Sanders of the River* (35), *Wings of the Morning* (37), *Troopship* (37), *Twenty-One Days* (39), *Busman's Honeymoon* (40), *Ships With Wings* (41), *48 Hours* (42), *Henry V* (45), *The Small Back Room* (49), *Madeleine* (50), *Your Witness* (50).

## BANKY, Vilma (1902- )

Vilma Banky was born Vilma Konsics near Budapest in Hungary. Her first films were made in her native country, her debut being *Im letzen Augenblick* (20). For the next few years she made films in Austria and Hungary including *Hotel Potemkin* (24) and *Das Bildis* (25). Then Samuel Goldwyn, taken by her ethereal beauty, brought her back to Hollywood. Billed as 'The Hungarian Rhapsody,' Banky starred in some of the most successful films of the late silent era, beginning with *The Dark Angel* (25) and including *Son of the Sheik* (26), *The Winning of Barbara Worth* (26), and finally *A Lady to Love* (30). Her co-stars were actors of the caliber of Ronald Colman, Gary Cooper, Rudolph Valentino and silent screen idol Rod La Rocque whom she married in 1927. However, the coming of sound spelled doom for Banky, since she barely spoke English. Her career crashed as meteorically as it once had risen. Banky's last film, made at age 31 in Germany, was *The Rebel* (33).

**Selected Films:** *Im letzen Augenblick* (20), *Galathea* (21), *Hotel Potemkin* (24), *Das Bildnis* (25), *The Dark Angel* (25), *The Eagle* (25), *Son of the Sheik* (26), *The Winning of Barbara Worth* (26), *The Night of Love* (27), *The Magic Flame* (27), *The Awakening* (28), *A Lady to Love* (30), *The Rebel* (33).

## BANNEN, Ian (1928- )

Ian Bannen was born in Airdrie, Scotland and educated in England. His acting career began before he was twenty, and he established a reputation on the stage before his first film, *Private's Progress* (55). He went on to be one of those British actors whose main allegiance remains the stage, but whose solid skills and imposing presence grace the occasional film. In Bannen's case, his movies have been American, British, and sometimes Italian, including *The Hill* (65), *Doomwatch* (72), and *Gandhi* (82). In 1965 he received an Oscar nomination for his supporting role in *The Flight of the Phoenix*.

**Selected Films:** *Private's Progress* (55), *A Tale of Two Cities* (58), *Suspect* (60), *Psyche 59* (64), *Rotten to the Core* (65), *The Hill* (65), *The Flight of the Phoenix* (65), *Penelope* (66), *The Sailor From Gibraltar* (67), *Lock Up Your Daughters* (69), *Too Late the Hero* (70), *The Deserter* (71), *Doomwatch* (72), *The Offense* (73), *The Driver's Seat* (74), *The Voyage* (74), *Bite the Bullet* (75), *From Beyond the Grave* (75), *Sweeney* (77), *Eye of the Needle* (81), *Night Crossing* (82), *Gandhi* (82), *Gorky Park* (83), *The Prodigal* (84), *Defense of the Realm* (86).

## BANNER, John (1910-1973)

Born in Vienna, Banner came to Hollywood as a veteran of the German stage and found a career in comic roles, often in the dubious vein of the comic Nazi – as in his sergeant Schultz in the TV series *Hogan's Heroes* – or otherwise excitable foreigners.

**Selected Films:** *Once Upon a Honeymoon* (42), *My Girl Tisa* (48), *The Juggler* (53), *The Blue Angel* (59), *The Yellow Canary* (63), *The Wicked Dreams of Paula Schultz* (68).

## BARA, Theda (1890-1955)

Born Theodosia Goodman in Cincinnati, Ohio, Bara became the epitome of Hollywood studio hype. She was given her new name and billed as the daughter of an Eastern potentate whose name was an anagram for 'Arab death.' She was called a 'vamp' because of her absurdly vampirish, man-hungry screen personality. In *A Fool There Was*

*Theda Bara – the archetypal vamp of the silent screen.*

(16), she supposedly hissed to her lover, 'Kiss me, my fool!' She wore indigo makeup, kept skulls and ravens, and met reporters while caressing a snake. Bara was the embodiment of female sexuality run amok. Most of her films were made in a mere four years. In 1919, her popularity waning, she left Hollywood for Broadway. For six years she tried to become a successful stage actress, but the publicity that had rocketed her to stardom turned into overkill. Returning to Hollywood in 1925, she was forced to accept parts burlesquing her former glories. She soon retired.
**Selected Films:** *The Two Orphans* (15), *A Fool There Was* (16), *Sin* (16), *Carmen* (16), *Cleopatra* (17), *When A Woman Sins* (18), *Her Greatest Love* (21), *The Hunchback of Notre Dame* (23), *The Dancer of Paris* (26).

## BARBEAU, Adrienne (1945-     )

Born in Sacramento, California, Barbeau spent much of the 1970s working in made-for-TV movies such as *Red Alert* (77) and *The Disappearance of Flight 401* (79). In the 1980s she starred in several horror movies for John Carpenter and other directors.
**Selected Films:** *The Fog* (80), *Escape from New York* (81), *The Swamp Thing* (82), *Creep Show* (82), *Back to School* (86).

## BARBIER, George (1865-1945)

Born in Philadelphia, Barbier left theological studies for the stage, becoming a popular Broadway actor in the first decades of the century. His first film was the silent *Monsieur Beaucaire* (24). However it was in talkies that Barbier blossomed, becoming a familiar figure in dozens of films of the 1930s and 1940s, usually in roles of blustering but goodhearted fathers and businessmen.
**Selected Films:** *Monsieur Beaucaire* (24), *Million Dollar Legs* (32), *Tillie and Gus* (34), *The Merry Widow* (34), *On the Avenue* (37), *Little Miss Broadway* (38), *The Man Who Came to Dinner* (41), *Song of the Islands* (42), *Yankee Doodle Dandy* (42), *Her Lucky Night* (45).

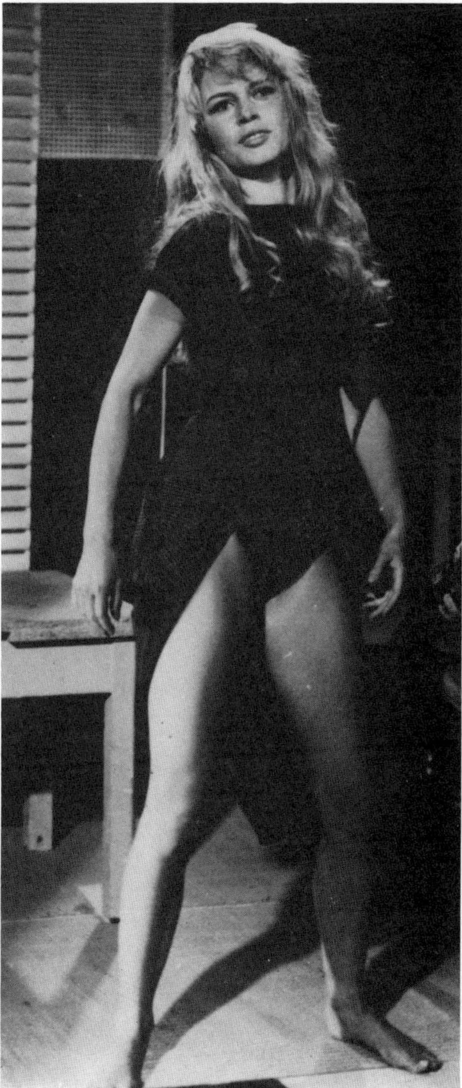

*Brigitte Bardot in* And God Created Woman *(56).*

## BARDOT, Brigitte (1933-     )

Bardot was born Camille Javal in Paris, France. She was a top model when, in 1950, an *Elle* magazine cover photo brought her to the attention of French film assistant director Roger Vadim. It was he, whom she married in 1952, who is credited with her development as an actress. Their marriage lasted until 1957. She began with a series of supporting roles in French movies, pouting her famous pout and flashing her famous smile. 'The Sex Kitten' had a small part in *Act of Love* (54), with Kirk Douglas, and appeared in *Doctor at Sea* (55) enticing Dirk Bogarde. She created a sensation in her first starring role in *The Light Across the Street* (55). *And God Created Woman* (56), Vadim's first effort as a director (he also wrote the script), allowed Bardot's child-woman appeal full scope and the movie became an enormous international success. From then on the world could not get enough of Bardot's public and private life. She set the style for bikinis and put the beaches of southern France on the map. Gossip columnists around the world wrote about her affairs, her moods, her tastes. In 1960 Simone de Beauvoir wrote a treatise about her and 'The Lolita Syndrome.' Teenage Bardot types, aping her clothes and hair, were everywhere, especially on the beaches. Many members of their parents' generation attacked Bardot as if she alone were responsible for the sexual revolution. At last, her

performance in *The Truth* (61) brought her critical recognition. Today Bardot's fame still glitters. Although retired from films, she has appeared on television and has been an active supporter of many worthy causes, most especially the preservation of endangered animal species. According to her, she is 'now spending my life trying to erase the Bardot legend.'
**Selected Films:** *Act of Love* (54), *Doctor at Sea* (55), *The Light Across the Street* (55), *Helen of Troy* (55), *And God Created Woman* (56), *Heaven Fell That Night* (57), *Une Parisienne* (57), *En Cas de Malheur* (57), *Please Mr Balzac* (57), *The Devil Is a Woman* (58), *Mam'zelle Pigalle* (58), *Babette Goes to War* (59), *Please Not Now* (61), *The Truth* (61), *Vie Privée* (61), *Love on a Pillow* (62), *Contempt* (64), *Dear Brigitte* (65), *Viva Maria* (65), *Masculin Feminin* (67), *Two Weeks in September* (67), *Shalako* (68), *The Novices* (70), *The Legend of Frenchy King* (72), *Don Juan* (73).

## BARI, Lynn (1915- )

Born Marjorie Fisher, Lynn Bari was the stepdaughter of a minister in Roanoke, Virginia, where she received the most of her dramatic training, appearing in school plays. By the age of 20 the pert and beautiful Bari had been discovered by Hollywood and graced the chorus of *Dancing Lady* (33). She soon graduated to leads and supporting roles, most often in routine productions such as *The Return of the Cisco Kid* (39). Often cast as the 'other woman,' Bari was appearing in over a half dozen films a year in the late 1930s and early 1940s. Among her better-known efforts are *Sun Valley Serenade* (41), *Orchestra Wives* (42), and *The Bridge of San Luis Rey* (44). In the 1950s she worked in TV and touring stage productions.
**Selected Films:** *Dancing Lady* (33), *Pigskin Parade* (36), *Wee Willie Winkie* (37), *Meet the Girls* (38), *The Return of the Cisco Kid* (39), *Kit Carson* (40), *Sun Valley Serenade* (41), *Blood and Sand* (41), *Moon Over Her Shoulder* (41), *Orchestra Wives* (42), *The Bridge of San Luis Rey* (44), *Tampico* (44), *Shock* (45), *Margie* (46), *I'd Climb the Highest Mountain* (51), *Has Anybody Seen My Gal?* (52), *Francis Joins the WACS* (54), *Abbott and Costello Meet the Keystone Cops* (55), *The Women of Pitcairn Island* (56), *Trauma* (64), *The Young Runaways* (68).

## BARKER, Lex (1919-1973)

Alexander Barker was born to a wealthy family in Rye, New York, and graduated from Princeton. His granite features and virile air took him to Hollyood, where he became the tenth Tarzan for five films starting with *Tarzan's Magic Fountain* (49). Thereafter Barker tended to appear in routine Westerns and adventure movies in America and Europe, though he did turn up in Federico Fellini's classic *La Dolce Vita* (60). Married five times, his wives included Lana Turner and Arlene Dahl.
**Selected Films:** *Doll Face* (45), *The Farmer's Daughter* (47), *Tarzan's Magic Fountain* (49), *Tarzan and the Slave Girl* (50), *Tarzan's Peril* (51), *Tarzan's Savage Fury* (52), *Away All Boats* (56), *La Dolce Vita* (60), *The Return of Dr. Mabuse* (61), *Woman Times Seven* (67).

## BARNES, Binnie (1905-1983)

Born Gitelle Barnes in London, England, she was a chorus girl before making her first screen appearances in English two-reel comedies. Her first successful feature appearance was in *Night in Montmartre* (31), and she found acclaim and Hollywood attention with the role of Katherine Howard in *The Private Life of Henry VIII* (33). Thereafter mostly working in the United States, she tended to be cast in supporting parts as an acerbic wisecracker, though she also played an occasional lead.
**Selected Films:** *Night in Montmartre* (31), *Love Lies* (31), *The Private Life of Henry VIII* (33), *Diamond Jim* (35), *The Last of the Mohicans* (35), *Three Smart Girls* (37), *The Three Musketeers* (39), *Up in Mabel's Room* (44), *It's in the Bag* (45), *Fugitive Lady* (51), *The Trouble with Angels* (66), *Forty Carats* (72).

## BARNES, Joanna (1934- )

Barnes was born in Boston and graduated from Smith College. She is primarily a journalist and novelist, but her stylish good looks have brought her a few supporting film roles.
**Selected Films:** *Violent Road* (58), *Home Before Dark* (58), *Auntie Mame* (58), *Tarzan the Ape Man* (59), *Spartacus* (60), *The Parent Trap* (61), *Don't Make Waves* (67), *B.S. I Love You* (71).

## BARNETT, Vince (1902-1977)

Pittsburgh-born Barnett was an airmail pilot before gravitating to Broadway and film. The bald actor became a staple in movies of the 1930s and 1940s, usually playing comic gangster types or patsies.
**Selected Films:** *All Quiet on the Western Front* (30), *Scarface* (32), *I Cover the Waterfront* (35), *A Star is Born* (37), *The Killers* (46), *Brute Force* (47), *The Human Jungle* (54).

## BARRAT, Robert (1891-1970)

Beginning his acting career on Broadway, New York-born Barrat went into films to become a versatile character actor in mostly minor features from the 1930s to the 1950s. Tall and strong, he played both Western heavies and assertive heroes (he was twice cast as General Douglas MacArthur). Appearing in some 150 movies, he made 19 films in 1934 alone.
**Selected Films:** *Mayor of Hell* (33), *Captain Blood* (35), *The Charge of the Light Brigade* (36), *The Last of the Mohicans* (36), *The Life of Emile Zola* (37), *Union Pacific* (39), *Northwest Passage* (40), *Riders of the Purple Sage* (41), *They Were Expendable* (45), *Son of Ali Baba* (52), *Tall Man Riding* (55).

## BARRAULT, Jean-Louis (1910- )

From his 20s, Jean-Louis Barrault was one of the most distinguished of French actors and theater directors; in addition, one critic observed of his immortal performance as Baptiste in *Les Enfant du Paradis* that it was the first time the film role of a mime had been played by a mime of genius. Barrault was born in Vésinet, France, and studied art in his childhood. Given a scholarship as a theatrical student, the impoverished youth slept for a time in the wings of the Théâtre de L'Atelier; meanwhile, he studied mime as well as drama. In 1931 Barrault made his Paris stage debut in a production of *Volpone*. Four years later he directed his first play and first appeared onscreen, in *Les Beaux Jours* (34). Despite his slight and graceful figure, he made a fine murderer as Kramps in the Marcel Carné/Jacques Prévert farce *Drôle de Dame* (37), known in English as *Bizarre Bizarre*. After several other movie roles, Barrault came to Carné and Prévert with an idea for a film about a historical figure, the nineteenth century mime Baptiste Debureau. The result was *Les Enfants du Paradis* (44) (*Children of Paradise*), in which Baptiste loves and loses the courtesan Garance in one of the most brilliant and romantic films of all time. Barrault also worked during World War II in the Comédie-Française; after the war he and his wife Madeleine Renaud formed their own theatrical company. Despite his wide involvement with the stage, Barrault appeared in a few films during the 1950s and 1960s; among them were a supporting role in Max Ophuls' *La Ronde* (50) and two American outings – *The Longest Day* (62) and *Chappaqua* (67). Barrault was appointed by the government as director of the Théâtre de France in 1959, but his support for rioting students in 1968 got him fired. A major figure in the French theater for much of his life, he will likely be remembered by the world above all as the indomitable, tragic figure in white in *Les Enfants du Paradis*.

**Selected Films:** *Les Beaux Jours* (34), *Mademoiselle Docteur* (36), *The Life and Loves of Beethoven* (36), *Bizarre Bizarre* (37), *Le Puritain* (38), *Les Enfants du Paradis* (44), *Blind Desire* (45), *D'Homme à Hommes* (48), *La Ronde* (50), *Royal Affairs in Versailles* (54), *Le Testament du Docteur Cordelier* (59), *Le Dialogue des Carmelites* (60), *The Longest Day* (62), *Chappaqua* (67), *La Nuit de Varennes* (82).

## BARRIE, Mona (1909- )

Born Mona Smith and educated in her native London, Barrie worked on the British stage before going to Hollywood in 1933. Her sculptured beauty tended to type her in decorous ladylike roles, most of them second leads in minor films from the 1930s into the 1950s.

**Selected Films:** *Sleepers East* (33), *Carolina* (34), *Charlie Chan in London* (34), *Love on the Run* (36), *Never Give a Sucker an Even Break* (41), *Cairo* (42), *I Cover Big Town* (47), *Plunder of the Sun* (53).

## BARRIE, Wendy (1912-1978)

Wendy Barrie was born Margaret Jenkins in Hong Kong and educated in England and Switzerland. She made her debut on the British stage in 1930 and in 1932 appeared in three films – *Wedding Rehearsal*, *It's a Boy*, and Alexander Korda's *The Private Life of Henry VIII* (33), as Jane Seymour. That film won Barrie acclaim and took her to Hollwood. However, as has happened with a number of bright and attractive talents of both sexes, Hollywood proceeded to waste Barrie in mostly routine pictures such as *Love on a Bet* (36), *The Gay Falcon* (41), and *Women in War* (42). Finally she turned to television, hosting one of the early talk shows, and later had a syndicated radio show.

**Selected Films:** *Wedding Rehearsal* (32), *It's a Boy* (32), *The Private Life of Henry VIII* (33), *A Feather in Her Hat* (35), *Love on a Bet* (36), *Wings Over Honolulu* (37), *Dead End* (37), *I Am the Law* (38), *The Saint Strikes Back* (39), *Daytime Wife* (39), *The Hound of the Baskervilles* (39), *Men Against the Sky* (40), *The Gay Falcon* (41), *Women in War* (42), *Forever and a Day* (43), *It Should Happen to You* (54), *The Moving Finger* (63).

## BARRY, Donald (1912-1980)

Don 'Red' Barry never had red hair. The 'Red' was added to his billing to take advantage of his popularity as Red Ryder, a role he played in *The Adventures of Red Ryder*, a B western serial made in 1940 and 1941. Born Donald Barry d'Acosta in Houston, Texas, this rugged actor arrived in Hollywood in 1936, after a good deal of stage experience, and became an instant hit in second feature westerns. Later he switched to supporting roles in movies and on television and turned his back on the horse operas. Small in stature, he projected a certain feistiness that some have compared with James Cagney.

**Selected Films:** *This Day and Age* (33), *Night Waitress* (36), *The Crowd Roars* (38), *Calling All Marines* (39), *Remember Pearl Harbor* (42), *The Chicago Kid* (45), *The Dalton Gang* (49), *Jesse James' Women* (53), *I'll Cry Tomorrow* (55), *Walk on the Wild Side* (62), *Fort Utah* (66), *Bandolero* (68), *Shalako* (68), *Rio Lobo* (70), *Orca* (77), *Back Roads* (81).

## BARRY, Gene (1921- )

Born Eugene Klass in New York City, Gene Barry appeared on the stage before going into films in the 1950s. Handsome and debonaire on the one hand, limited in expressive range on the other, he largely appeared in minor adventure films and costume dramas including *The Atomic City* (52) and *China Gate* (57). Among his more substantial films have been leading and supporting parts in *War of the Worlds* (53), *Red Garters* (54), and *Thunder Road* (58). His best-known roles were on television as the dandyish lead in the series *Bat Masterson* and his later lead in *Burke's Law*. His made-for-TV

movies include *Istanbul Express* and *The Devil and Miss Sarah*. In the 1970s Barry put together his own production company, with his son Michael as director.
**Selected Films:** *The Atomic City* (52), *The Girls of Pleasure Island* (53), *War of the Worlds* (53), *Those Redheads of Seattle* (53), *Red Garters* (54), *Alaska Seas* (54), *Naked Alibi* (54), *Soldier of Fortune* (55), *Back From Eternity* (56), *China Gate* (57), *Thunder Road* (58), *Maroc 7* (67), *Subterfuge* (69), *The Second Coming of Suzanne* (74), *Guyana – The Crime of the Century* (79).

## BARRYMORE, Diana (1921-1960)

Born in New York, the daughter of John Barrymore and thus part of the most distinguished American acting family, Diana Barrymore failed to establish a solid career, appearing in only a few minor films. Her autobiography, *Too Much Too Soon*, detailed her struggle with alcohol and was made into a film in 1958, starring Errol Flynn as John Barrymore.
**Selected Films:** *Eagle Squadron* (42), *Between Us Girls* (42), *Nightmare* (42), *Frontier Badmen* (43), *Fired Wife* (43), *Ladies Courageous* (44).

## BARRYMORE, Ethel (1879-1959)

Born in Philadelphia, Pennsylvania, Ethel May Barrymore was the daughter of the actor Maurice Barrymore (Herbert Blythe) and the actress Georgiana Drew. She was the sister of John and Lionel Barrymore, the brilliant actors. Barrymore later said, 'We became actors not because we wanted to go on the stage, but because it was the thing we could do best.' She made her stage debut at the age of 14 in a New York production of *The Rivals*. Known for her imperious beauty, her elegant, husky voice (one critic called her Ethel Barrytone), and her command of the stage, she was the first lady of the American theater for 40 years, and one of her most famous roles was Miss Moffat in *The Corn Is Green* (42). Barrymore appeared in films primarily from 1914 to 1919 and later came back in the 1940s when she established herself as the image of the gracious and spirited elderly woman. In 1932 she appeared with her brothers in *Rasputin and the Empress* and won an Academy Award for Best Supporting Actress for *None But the Lonely Heart* (44).
**Selected Films:** *The Nightingale* (14), *The Final Judgment* (15), *Kiss of Hate* (16), *Life's Whirlpool* (17), *Rasputin and the Empress* (32), *None But the Lonely Heart* (44), *The Spiral Staircase* (46), *The Farmer's Daughter* (47), *Moss Rose* (47), *Portrait of Jennie* (49), *Kind Lady* (51), *Deadline* (52), *Young at Heart* (54), *Johnny Trouble* (57).

## BARRYMORE, John (1882-1942)

John Barrymore was everything a great stage and screen legend should be – glamorous, debonair, gallant, gifted and even tragic. Although he was a major force in the American theater, by the time he reached Hollywood, life had begun to catch up with him. Still, he was the matinee idol with 'The Great Profile,' and became a romantic movie star of the 1920s and 1930s, but later squandered his talents in inferior comedies caricaturing his own alcoholism and debauchery. He had a great personality and a splendid if misguided talent. He did, however, leave some fine films to remember him by. The youngest of the 'fabulous Barrymores,' America's first family of the stage and screen, he was born in Philadelphia, Pennsylvania, the son of stage actors Maurice Barrymore (Herbert Blythe) and Georgiana Drew, and the brother of Lionel and Ethel Barrymore. He began working as a cartoonist but theater tradition won out and Barrymore became a leading light comedian and Shakespearean actor, the Broadway idol of his time. He began making movies in 1913, appearing in *Are You a Mason?*, and went on to romantic dramas, comedies and swashbucklers. Although audiences adored him as the great lover, a role he excelled at off screen as well as on, there were few limits to his range. He was paid vast sums for his movies, but he kept returning to the stage. Hollywood took him on any terms because in one of the first box office polls ever conducted, Barrymore came in at the top, ahead of Harold Lloyd, Gloria Swanson and Rin-Tin-Tin. But he did not sustain this position. In fact, many critics accused him of hamming it up on screen. Barrymore's beautiful voice guaranteed that he would survive the coming of talking pictures, but alcohol was taking its toll and he suffered acute memory lapses. Still, he and Greta Garbo were enormously successful in *Grand Hotel* (32). *A Bill of Divorcement* (32), with Katharine Hepburn, the sparkling *Dinner at Eight* (33), *Twentieth Century* (34) and *Midnight* (39) proved that he still had the old magic. Toward the end of his film career, he began to parody himself, playing aging actors dreaming of the past. It is ironic that he was later portrayed by Errol Flynn, himself notorious for his roguish life style, in the movie version of *Too Much Too Soon* (58), based on his daughter Diana's autobiography.
**Selected Films:** *Are You a Mason?* (13), *Raffles* (17), *Dr Jekyll and Mr Hyde* (20), *Sherlock Holmes* (22), *Beau Brummell* (24), *The Sea Beast* (26), *Don Juan* (26), *The Beloved Rogue* (27), *Tempest* (28), *Show of Shows* (29), *Moby Dick* (30), *Svengali* (31), *Arsène Lupin* (32), *Grand Hotel* (32), *A Bill of Divorcement* (32), *Rasputin and the Empress* (32), *Topaze* (33), *Reunion in Vienna* (33), *Dinner at Eight* (33), *Counsellor at Law* (33), *Twentieth Century* (34), *Romeo and Juliet* (36), *Maytime* (37), *Midnight* (39), *Playmates* (42).

*John Barrymore, Ralph Morgan, Ethel Barrymore, Tad Alexander, Lionel Barrymore –* Rasputin and the Empress *(32).*

## BARRYMORE, John Jr (1932- )

Son of the distinguished stage and screen actor John Barrymore, John Jr, like his sister Diana, had a troubled life and tenuous career, though he did make a number of films – most of them mediocre. In between bouts with stimulants and the law, Barrymore born in Beverly Hills, California, was usually cast as a weakling in his films, which included appearances in *The Sundowners* (60)and *The Christine Keeler Affair* (64). In 1958, in search of a new image, he changed his name to John Drew Barrymore. Most of his films since have been Italian costume cheapies. After a period of reclusion in the late 1960s he returned to occasional work on film and TV. Child actress Drew Barrymore is his daughter.

**Selected Films:** *High Lonesome* (50), *The Big Night* (51), *High School Confidential* (58), *The Sundowners* (60), *The Trojan Horse* (61), *The Christine Keeler Affair* (64), *This Savage Land* (66).

## BARRYMORE, Lionel (1878-1954)

Unlike his siblings, Ethel and John, this member of the great first family of actors devoted almost all of his acting career to the movies, including directing several pictures. From the early 1930s he was a famous and well-beloved member of the MGM stock company, often playing churlish millionaires and sentimental grandfather figures. From 1938 until the end of his career, terrible arthritis and a couple of falls forced him to do all his performing in a wheelchair. Born in Philadelphia, Pennsylvania, the eldest son of actors Maurice Barrymore (Herbert Blythe) and Georgiana Drew, he was the first Barrymore to appear in motion pictures, making his debut in *Friends* (09) – the first of scores of roles he played as he went from leading roles to character parts over the years. Some of the films that he directed were: *Madame X* (29), *The Rogue Song* (30), and *Ten Cents a Dance* (31). Barrymore won an Academy Award for *A Free Soul* (31), but is probably best remembered for playing Dr Gillespie in the *Doctor Kildare* series of films – the kindly yet stern mentor of the callow Kildare, who, in the beginning, was played by Lew Ayres. He also played Judge Hardy in the original Andy Hardy movie, *A Family Affair* (37), opposite Mickey Rooney.

**Selected Films:** *Friends* (09), *The New York Hat* (12), *The Copperhead* (20), *The Bells* (26), *Sadie Thompson* (28), *Alias Jimmy Valentine* (29), *A Free Soul* (31), *Mata Hari* (31), *The Man I Killed* (32), *Arsène Lupin* (32), *Grand Hotel* (32), *Rasputin and the Empress* (32), *Dinner at Eight* (33), *Treasure Island* (34), *David Copperfield* (34), *The Little Colonel* (35), *Ah Wilderness* (35), *The Devil Doll* (36), *Camille* (37), *A Family Affair* (37), *You Can't Take It With You* (38), *Young Dr Kildare* (38), *On Borrowed Time* (39), *Calling Dr Gillespie* (42), *Three Wise Fools* (46), *It's a Wonderful Life* (46), *Duel in the Sun* (46), *Key Largo* (48), *Main Street to Broadway* (53).

## BARTHELMESS, Richard (1895-1963)

Barthelmess was discovered by the great actress Alla Nazimova. Lillian Gish thought that his face was the most beautiful of any man who had ever been before the camera. D W Griffith thought that he would make a perfect hero, and used him memorably. He was born in New York City and was in amateur theater productions at Trinity College. Beginning his film career directly out of college with *The Hope Chest* (19), he was immensely popular throughout the silent screen era. His best film role was the country boy in *Tol'able David* (21), and it was in that year that he formed his own production company. Despite the fact that the advent of sound made his innocent image seem old-fashioned, he was nominated for an Academy Award in the first year that the Oscar was given, 1927-1928. The nomination was for his work on two films, *The Patent Leather Kid* (27) and *The Noose* (28). Barthelmess later turned to character roles before retiring from films in the 1940s.

**Selected Films:** *The Hope Chest* (19), *Broken Blossoms* (19), *The Love Flower* (20), *Way Down East* (20), *Tol'able David* (21), *The Enchanted Cottage* (24), *The Patent Leather Kid* (27), *The Noose* (28), *The Dawn Patrol* (30), *Cabin in the Cotton* (32), *A Modern Hero* (34), *Only Angels Have Wings* (39), *The Spoilers* (42).

## BARTHOLOMEW, Freddie (1924- )

Born Frederick Llewellyn in London, England, this curly-haired, well-bred child actor became a Hollywood star playing the boy hero in movie versions of great adventure novels, delighting elderly aunts and children alike all over the world. Bartholomew was raised by his aunt, Millicent Bartholomew, and was performing on stage at the age of three. When he was six, he appeared in his first movie, the British *Fascination* (30). After appearing in another British film, *Lily Christine* (32), he made his first American movie in 1935, giving a masterful and heart-wrenching performance as the young *David Copperfield.* The public loved his English accent and his well-bred manners. He went on to play in several movies, and was at his best in adventure classics. In 1937 he was the focus of two legal battles. One was an attempt by his parents to get him away from his aunt, and the other involved his aunt's attempt to get him away from MGM. He wound up with his aunt and MGM until his career hit the skids during World War II – the movie public was not interested in sweet little boys anymore. Bartholomew left show business and moved into advertising.

**Selected Films:** *Fascination* (30), *Lily Christine* (32), *David Copperfield* (35), *Anna Karenina* (35), *Little Lord Fauntleroy* (36), *The Devil Is a Sissy* (36), *Lloyds of London* (36), *Captains Courageous* (37), *Kidnapped* (38), *Lord Jeff* (38), *The Swiss Family Robinson* (40), *Tom Brown's Schooldays* (40), *The Town Went Wild* (44), *St Benny the Dip* (51).

*Kim Basinger.*

## BARTOK, Eva (1926- )

Born Eva Szöke in Kecskemet, Hungary, Bartok was a well-known stage actress in her native country when producer Alexander Paal brought her to London to be his wife and appear in his movie *A Tale of Five Cities* (51). Bartok thereafter divorced Paal (she subsequently married actor Curt Jurgens) and went on to an international career as an amiable Hungarian leading lady in minor films.
**Selected Films:** *A Tale of Five Cities* (51), *The Crimson Pirate* (52), *Front Page Story* (54), *Ten Thousand Bedrooms* (57), *Beyond the Curtain* (60), *Blood and Black Lace* (64).

## BARTON, James (1890-1962)

Born in Glouster City, New Jersey, Barton worked his way through vaudeville, burlesque and Broadway, finally making his silent film debut in *Why Women Remarry* (23). His first talkie was *Captain Hurricane* (35). Thereafter Barton tended to appear in character roles, usually of the grizzled variety; perhaps the most notable was his performance as Kit Carson in William Saroyan's *The Time of Your Life* (48).
**Selected Films:** *Why Women Remarry* (23), *Captain Hurricane* (35), *Shepherd of the Hills* (41), *The Time of Your Life* (48), *The Daughter of Rosie O'Grady* (50), *Here Comes the Groom* (51), *The Naked Hills* (57), *The Misfits* (61).

## BARYSHNIKOV, Mikhail (1948- )

Baryshnikov born in Riga, Latvia, was one of the most celebrated stars of the Leningrad Kirov Ballet in the Soviet Union when he defected to the West in 1974. His film debut was in *The Turning Point* (77), in which he played the dancer who has an affair with Shirley MacLaine's daughter. He is today the director of American Ballet Theatre.
**Selected Films:** *The Turning Point* (77), *White Nights* (85), *Giselle* (87)

## BASEHART, Richard (1914-1984)

Richard Basehart was born in Zanesville, Ohio, the son of a newspaper editor. After working in radio he turned to the stage, making his Broadway debut in 1938. In 1945 his lead in *The Hasty Heart* earned Basehart both the New York Drama Critics Award and the attention of Hollywood. His first film appearance was in *Cry Wolf* (47). From that point on, Basehart was a familiar face in films ranging from the mediocre to the excellent, including *He Walked by Night* (48) and Federico Fellini's classic *La Strada* (54). Somehow, though, Basehart never became the superstar one might have expected from his early successes, perhaps because his acting, while sensitive and versatile, was also distant and a bit subdued – an example being his performance as Ishmael in John Huston's *Moby Dick* (56). Basehart's later work was mostly for television, including his lead in the series *Voyage to the Bottom of the Sea* and made-for-TV movies such as *City Beneath the Sea*, and *Knight Rider*.
**Selected Films:** *Cry Wolf* (47), *He Walked by Night* (48), *The Black Book* (49), *Fourteen Hours* (51), *La Strada* (59), *Il Bidone* (55), *Moby Dick* (58), *The Brothers Karamazov* (58), *Hitler* (63), *The Satan Bug* (65), *The Island of Dr. Moreau* (77), *Being There* (79).

## BASINGER, Kim (1954- )

Born in Athens, Georgia, of Cherokee ancestry Basinger was a model before breaking into movies in 1982. After some decorative parts, including *Never Say Never Again* (83), Basinger made a sustained effort to be seen as more than a sizzling and hauntingly beautiful blonde, and that effort culminated in her intense starring role as a compulsive masochist in *9½ Weeks* (85). Though the movie was much criticized for its story, Basinger seemed to come out of it with increased respect for her ability.
**Selected Films:** *Mother Lode* (82), *Never Say Never Again (83)*, *The Natural* (84), *9½ Weeks* (85), *No Mercy* (86).

*Alan Bates and Anthony Quinn in* Zorba the Greek *(64).*

## BASS, Alfie (1920- )

Born in London, the diminutive Bass has worked on the stage and screen for decades, usually comedies, in Cockney and/or Jewish character parts. His more notable film appearances include *The Lavender Hill Mob* (51), *Alfie* (66), and Roman Polanski's *The Fearless Vampire Killers (67).*
**Selected Films:** *The Lavender Hill Mob* (51), *The Bespoke Overcoat* (55), *A Funny Thing Happened on the Way to the Forum* (66), *Alfie* (66), *The Fearless Vampire Killers (67), The Magnificent Seven Deadly Sins* (72), *Moonraker* (79).

## BASSERMAN, Albert (1867-1952)

Basserman was born in Mannheim, and had a long and distinguished career on the stage and screen in his native Germany before fleeing the Nazis in 1933. From 1939 on he worked in Hollywood, usually playing sympethetic, wise European gentlemen. His best-known films include *Foreign Correspondent* (40), *The Shanghai Gesture* (41), *The Moon and Sixpence* (42), and *The Red Shoes* (48).
**Selected Films:** *Der Andere* (13), *Lucrecia Borgia* (22), *Inquest* (31), *Foreign Correspondent* (40), *The Shanghai Gesture* (41), *The Moon and Sixpence* (42), *Madame Curie* (44), *Rhapsody in Blue* (45), *Escape Me Never* (47), *The Red Shoes* (48).

## BATES, Alan (1934- )

Born in Allestree, England, Bates began his film career in *The Entertainer* (59), which starred Laurence Olivier. He developed into a solid stage and screen actor who tended to play thoughtful criminals with soft personalities. It wasn't until the 1970s that he really became a star in such movies as *A Day in the Death of Joe Egg* (71) and *Butley* (73).
**Selected Films:** *The Entertainer* (59), *A Kind of Loving* (62), *Whistle Down the Wind* (62), *The Caretaker* (63), *Zorba the Greek* (64), *Georgy Girl* (66), *Far From the Madding Crowd* (67), *The Fixer* (68), *Women in Love* (69), *A Day in the Death of Joe Egg* (71), *Butley* (73), *An Unmarried Woman* (77), *The Rose* (78), *Nijinsky* (79), *The Return of the Soldier* (82), *Britannia Hospital* (82), *Duet for One* (87).

## BATES, Florence (1888-1954)

Florence Bates was born Florence Rabe in San Antonio, Texas, and for most of her adult life was a businesswoman and lawyer. In her mid-forties she was bitten by the acting bug and began to study at the school of the Pasadena Playhouse. Several years later, Hollywood discovered this unlikely figure. She was first seen on screen in *The Man in Blue* (37). In 1940 she made her most famous film, appearing as the insensitive American who has hired Joan Fontaine as a companion in Alfred Hitchcock's *Rebecca*. Bates went on to other

matronly roles, ranging from the sympathetic to the monstrous, in films including *The Moon and Sixpence* (42) and *I Remember Mama* (48).
**Selected Films:** *The Man in Blue* (37), *Rebecca* (40), *Calling All Husbands* (40), *Kitty Foyle* (40), *The Chocolate Soldier* (41), *Strange Alibi* (41), *The Devil and Miss Jones* (41), *The Moon and Sixpence* (42), *His Butler's Sister* (43), *Mister Big* (43), *Heaven Can Wait* (43), *Mr Lucky* (43), *Since You Went Away* (44), *Kismet* (44), *Tonight and Every Night* (45), *The Diary of a Chambermaid* (46), *The High Window* (47), *A Letter to Three Wives* (48), *I Remember Mama* (48), *On the Town* (49), *Lullaby of Broadway* (51), *Les Miserables* (52), *Main Street to Broadway* (53).

## BAUR, Harry (1880-1943)

Baur, born in Montrouge, first came to fame on the stage in his native France. His film debut was the title role in *Shylock* (10) and other silent films followed. With the advent of sound, Baur became one of the most popular stars in French cinema. He played the title roles in *Rothschild* (34), and *Rasputin* (38), and the part of Jean Valjean in *Les Misérables* (34). Having lost his Jewish wife to the Nazis during the Occupation, Baur was himself arrested by the Germans as a spy and died after interrogation.
**Selected Films:** *Shylock* (10), *La Voyante* (23), *Les Cinq Gentlemen maudits* (31), *The Three Musketeers* (33), *Les Misérables* (34), *Rothschild* (34), *Crime and Punishment* (35), *Taras Bulba* (36), *Rasputin* (38), *Symphonie eines Lebens* (42).

## BAXTER, Alan (1908-1976)

Born in East Cleveland, Ohio, Baxter began his film career with *Mary Burns, Fugitive* (35). The strong-featured, rather chilly-eyed actor became a perennial in Hollywood – a star in Bs, supporting player in As, and finally character parts.
**Selected Films:** *Mary Burns, Fugitive* (35), *The Trail of the Lonesome Pine* (36), *Each Dawn I Die* (39), *The Lone Wolf Strikes* (40), *Abe Lincoln in Illinois* (40), *Santa Fe Trail* (40), *Saboteur* (42), *The Human Comedy* (43), *The True Story of Jesse James* (57), *Judgement at Nuremburg* (61), *Willard* (71).

## BAXTER, Ann (1923-1985)

Baxter was born in Michigan City, Indiana, and was the granddaughter of architect Frank Lloyd Wright. She became a competent stage actress and in the beginning of her movie career was pretty much typecast as the shy and innocent girl next door, making her film debut in *Twenty Mule Team* (40) at the age of 17, appearing with Wallace Beery and Marjorie Rambeau – a minor western picture. Her big break came in *The Magnificent Ambersons* (42). She proved to be equally at home in the role of a schemer, and is remembered for her fine performance in *All About Eve* (50). She won an Oscar for Best Supporting Actress for her role as a dipsomaniac in *The Razor's Edge* (46), but her career declined in the 1960s when she married and moved to Australia.
**Selected Films:** *Twenty Mule Team* (40), *Charley's Aunt* (41), *The Magnificent Ambersons* (42), *Five Graves to Cairo* (43), *The Eve of St Mark* (44), *Guest in the House* (45), *The Razor's Edge* (46), *All About Eve* (50), *The Spoilers* (55), *The Late Liz* (71), *Jane Austen in Manhattan* (80).

## BAXTER, Stanley (1926- )

Stanley Baxter born in Glasgow, brought his Scottish brogue and his rubber features to comedy roles in stage, television, and occasional movies.
**Selected Films:** *Wee Geordie* (55), *Very Important Person* (61), *Crooks Anonymous* (62), *The Fast Lady* (63), *And Father Came Too* (63), *Joey Boy* (65).

## BAXTER, Warner (1889-1951)

Warner Baxter was born in Columbus, Ohio, and grew up in San Francisco. After trying various jobs he gravitated to acting, becoming a leading man in stock companies. His first films were minor silents, starting with *Her Own Money* (14). Baxter found acclaim with his first sound film, playing the Cisco Kid – for the first of three times – in *In Old Arizona* (29). For this role he received an Academy Award. Baxter went on to be an elegant leading man in romantic films of the 1930s including *Daddy Long Legs* (31), *Forty-Second Street* (33), and *Penthouse* (34). In the early 1940s Baxter had a nervous breakdown. On recovery he played leads in Bs, including several of the 'Crime Doctor' series.
**Selected Films:** *The Love Charm* (21), *The Female* (24), *The Awful Truth* (25), *The Great Gatsby* (26), *Drums of the Desert* (27), *Ramona* (28), *In Old Arizona* (29), *Romance of the Rio Grande* (29), *The Cisco Kid* (31), *Daddy Long Legs* (31), *The Squaw Man* (31), *Six Hours to Live* (32), *Man About Town* (32), *Forty-Second Street* (33), *Dangerously Yours* (34), *Broadway Bill* (34), *One More Spring* (35), *Prisoner of Shark Island* (36), *Slave Ship* (37), *Kidnapped* (38), *The Return of the Cisco Kid* (39), *Crime Doctor* (43), *The Crime Doctor's Gamble* (47), *State Penitentiary* (50).

## BEAL, John (1909- )

Born James Alexander Bliedung in Joplin, Missouri, Beal found his first and greatest success playing clean-cut young men in films of the 1930s such as *The Little Minister* (34), and *The Cat and the Canary* (39). Thereafter Beal appeared in minor films and TV roles into the 1980s.
**Selected Films:** *Another Language* (33), *The Little Minister* (34), *Les Misérables* (35), *Laddie* (35), *The Man Who Found Himself* (37), *The Cat and the Canary* (39), *Edge of Darkness* (43), *Alimony* (49), *The Vampire* (57), *The Sound and the Fury* (59), *Ten Who Dared* (60), *The House That Cried Murder* (73), *Amityville 3D* (83).

*Sting and Jennifer Beals in* The Bride *(85).*

## BEALS, Jennifer (1965- )

Chicago-born Beals was just another freshman at Yale when she found herself cast in the lead role of a movie about a young woman who wanted to be a serious dancer. The result, *Flashdance* (83), was one of the biggest hits of the year. Meanwhile Beals returned to Yale, coming back to the screen in 1985 to co-star with Sting in *The Bride*.
**Selected Films:** *Flashdance* (83), *The Bride* (85).

## BEATTY, Ned (1937- )

Beatty, born in Louisville, Kentucky, grew up looking the part of the beer-bellied Southern good ol' boy, but his character roles in films have ranged far wider than that. After experience in stock theater he made an impressive debut in *Deliverance* (72). His roles since have ranged from a suburban husband in *Nashville* (76), to a demonic chairman of the board in *Network* (76) (for which he got an Oscar nomination), to the dopy sidekick of the villain in *Superman* (79). Beatty has also appeared in a number of TV movies including *Friendly Fire*.
**Selected Films:** *Deliverance* (72), *The Life and Times of Judge Roy Bean* (72), *White Lightning* (73), *Nashville* (75), *Network*, (76), *Exorcist II: The Heretic* (77), *Superman* (79), *Wise Blood* (79), *Superman II* (81), *The Toy* (82), *Touched* (83), *Back to School* (86), *Restless Natives* (86).

## BEATTY, Warren (1937- )

One of Hollywood's more complex talents, Beatty is an innovative director and producer, and he is more than a competent actor, specializing in psychological maladjustment. He was born Warren Beaty in Richmond, Virginia. He was a gifted athlete and actor whose sister, Shirley Maclean Beaty was an aspiring dancer (she would change her name to Shirley Maclaine). Beatty attended Northwestern University for a year, then moved to New York to study acting with Stella Adler. He appeared in William Inge's *A Loss of Roses* on Broadway, then broke into movies co-starring opposite Natalie Wood in *Splendor in the Grass* (61). A series of less than memorable films followed, until Beatty produced and starred in *Bonnie and Clyde* (67), with Faye Dunaway, a movie that introduced a new level of violence to the screen. He was nominated for Best Actor for the picture. *McCabe and Mrs Miller* (71), with Julie Christie, got some notice, as did *Shampoo* (75), also with Christie, which Beatty starred in, co-authored and produced. Feminists labeled the latter film sexist, which Beatty denied. Even more popular was the delightful comedy *Heaven Can Wait* (78), a remake of *Here Comes Mr Jordan* (41). Beatty and Elaine May co-authored the script and Beatty played the part originated by Robert

Montgomery, as the football hero sent to heaven by mistake and returned to earth. The movie was nominated for the Academy Award as Best Picture, and Beatty himself received two Oscar nominations – Best Director (in collaboration) and Best Actor. He won an Academy Award at last as Best Director for *Reds* (82). *Reds* was an elaborate production and Beatty oversaw each detail. It told the story of American radical John Reed. Beatty's costar was Diane Keaton.
**Selected Films:** *Splendor in the Grass* (61), *The Roman Spring of Mrs Stone* (61), *All Fall Down* (62), *Lilith* (65), *Mickey One* (65), *Promise Her Anything* (66), *Kaleidoscope* (66), *Bonnie and Clyde* (67), *The Only Game in Town* (69), *McCabe and Mrs Miller* (71), *$* (72), *The Parallax View* (74), *Shampoo* (75), *The Fortune* (75), *Heaven Can Wait* (78), *Reds* (82), *Ishtar* (87).

## BEAUMONT, Hugh (1909-1983)

Beaumont, born in Lawrence, Kansas, spent most of his movie career as a leading man in B pictures of the 1940s and 1950s such as *Objective Burma* (45) and *The Mole People* (57). He also played detective Michael Shayne in several mysteries. His best-known role was as the father in the TV series *Leave It to Beaver.*
**Selected Films:** *South of Panama* (41), *The Seventh Victim* (43), *The Blue Dahlia* (46), *Objective Burma* (45), *The Mississippi Gambler* (53), *The Mole People* (57), *The Human Duplicators* (65).

## BEAVERS, Louise (1902-1962)

Black actress Beavers, born in Cincinnati, Ohio, went to Hollywood as the maid of silent screen star Leatrice Joy. Usually cast as a maid or mammy, she was in scores of Hollywood features including *Imitation of Life* (35).
**Selected Films:** *Gold Diggers* (23), *Uncle Tom's Cabin* (27), *She Done Him Wrong* (33), *Imitation of Life* (35), *Shadow of the Thin Man* (41), *Du Barry Was a Lady* (43), *Mr Blandings Builds His Dream House* (48), *Tammy and the Bachelor* (57), *The Facts of Life* (61).

## BECKETT, Scotty (1929-1968)

As a child, Beckett was a regular in the *Our Gang* series, and graduated to teenage roles in films such as *The Jolson Story* (46). He failed to maintain his career as an adult, however, and died early – apparently a suicide.
**Selected Films:** *Gallant Lady* (33), *Anthony Adverse* (36), *Conquest* (38), *The Bluebird* (40), *King's Row* (42), *The Jolson Story* (46), *Corky of Gasoline Alley* (51), *Three for Jamie Dawn* (56).

## BEDELIA, Bonnie (1946-    )

Born in New York and educated at Hunter College, Bedelia began playing screen leads and supporting roles in the late 1960s. Among her films of the

*Faye Dunaway and Warren Beatty in* Bonnie and Clyde *(67).*

1970s were *Lovers and Other Strangers* (70) and *The Big Fix* (78).
**Selected Films:** *The Gypsy Moths* (69), *They Shoot Horses, Don't They?* (70), *Lovers and Other Strangers* (70), *The Big Fix* (78), *Heart Like a Wheel* (83), *The Boy Who Could Fly* (86).

## BEDOYA, Alfonso (1904-1957)

After establishing a film career in his native Mexico, Bedoya born in Vicam, Sonora, brought his beaming features and steel-band smile to embody the cliché Mexican in American films, beginning with his unforgettable debut as the grinning murderous bandit leader in John Huston's *The Treasure of the Sierra Madre* (48).
**Selected Films:** *The Treasure of the Sierra Madre* (48), *Streets of Laredo* (49), *The Black Rose* (50), *The Stranger Wore a Gun* (53), *The Big Country* (57).

## BEERY, Noah (1884-1946)

Beery was the screen's most celebrated villain and scoundrel in the silent era and became a character actor in the talkies. Beery was born in Kansas City, Missouri. He was the half-brother of actor Wallace Beery and the father of actor Noah Beery Jr. He began acting on stage in 1900 and made his first appearance in 1918 in *The Mormon Maid*. He became the man that audiences loved to hate in such pictures as *The Mark of Zorro* (20), *The Sea Wolf* (20) and as the cruel Sergeant Lejaune in *Beau Geste* (26). He also appeared in many Zane Grey westerns.
**Selected Films:** *The Mormon Maid* (18), *The Mark of Zorro* (20), *The Sea Wolf* (20), *Tol'able David* (21), *The Spoilers* (22), *Beau Geste* (26), *Don Juan* (26), *Tol'able David* (30), *She Done Him Wrong* (33), *The Girl of the Golden West* (38), *This Man's Navy* (45).

## BEERY, Noah Jr (1913- )

This American character actor is the son of movie villain Noah Beery and the nephew of Wallace Beery. Born in New York City, he appeared in the silent movie *The Mark of Zorro* (20), at the age of seven, with his father and Douglas Fairbanks and continued to perform with his father on stage. He later started playing country cousins in films, including westerns starring Johnny Mack Brown and Buck Jones, marrying Jones' daughter Maxine in 1940. Later he had lead roles in several low-budget movies, but is probably best known for his television performances as a regular character in *Circus Boy*, *Custer* and *The Rockford Files*, in which he costarred with James Garner.
**Selected Films:** *The Mark of Zorro* (20), *Heroes of the West* (26), *The Road Back* (37), *Only Angels Have Wings* (39), *Of Mice and Men* (40), *Riders of Death Valley* (41), *Gung Ho* (44), *Red River* (48), *Destination Moon* (50), *Inherit the Wind* (60), *The Seven Faces of Dr Lao* (64), *Little Fauss and Big Halsy* (70), *Walking Tall* (73), *The Best Little Whorehouse in Texas* (82).

## BEERY, Wallace (1889-1949)

Beery had a rubbery face and a gravelly voice, yet he became a popular movie star in the talkies. Born in Kansas City, Missouri, he was the half-brother of Noah Beery and the uncle of Noah Beery Jr. This character actor started out with the circus and switched to Broadway musical comedies before going to Hollywood, where he became a long-time member of the MGM family. In 1913 he began his film career as a grotesque female impersonator in comedies. In 1916 he married screen actress Gloria Swanson, his co-star in a series of Mack Sennett comedies, divorcing her two years later. He played chiefly tough guys and villains until the advent of sound. It was then that he finally found his persona – a tough, ugly, slow-thinking and easy-going personality. He and Marie Dressler became one of Hollywood's memorable movie couples. Beery appeared in several screen classics, receiving an Academy Award for Best Actor for his work in *The Champ* (31). His portrayal of an ex-heavyweight boxing champion on the skids with Jackie Cooper as his loyal son made the films such a ferocious hit with the public that Beery moved into the top ten list of box office draws and remained a major money-maker for some years.
**Selected Films:** *Teddy at the Throttle* (16), *Robin Hood* (22), *Richard the Lion-Hearted* (23), *The Lost World* (24), *Beggars of Life* (28), *The Big House* (30), *Min and Bill* (30), *The Champ* (31), *Grand Hotel* (32), *Dinner at Eight* (33), *Tugboat Annie* (33), *The Bowery* (33), *Viva Villa* (34), *Treasure Island* (34), *The Mighty Barnum* (34), *Ah, Wilderness* (35), *A Message to Garcia* (36), *Slave Ship* (37), *Stablemates* (38), *Stand Up and Fight* (39), *Twenty Mule Team* (40), *Barbary Coast Gent* (44), *Bad Bascomb* (46), *A Date with Judy* (48), *Big Jack* (49).

## BEGLEY, Ed (1901-1970)

Ed Begley was born into a family of Irish immigrants in Hartford, Connecticut. After running away from home at 11 he joined a carnival and later the US Navy. A radio announcer in the early 1930s, he went on to dramatic roles on radio and stage; his Broadway debut was in 1943. Soon Begley became a popular stage figure. Among his roles was Joe Keller in the original production of Arthur Miller's *All My Sons*. In the same year as that production, Begley made his film debut in *Boomerang* (47). Over the next 20-odd years he was to appear in 35 movies, the more notable ones including *Patterns* (56), *Twelve Angry Men* (57), and *Sweet Bird of Youth* (62). His role as Boss Finley in the latter film earned Begley a supporting actor Oscar. He tended to be cast as blusterers, sometimes criminals or corrupt businessmen, sometimes lighter roles as fathers or uncles. Throughout his film career, Begley kept up an active schedule of radio and stage performances.
**Selected Films:** *Boomerang* (47), *Sorry, Wrong Number* (48), *The Great Gatsby* (49), *On Dangerous*

*Ground* (51), *What Price Glory* (52), *Patterns* (56), *Twelve Angry Men* (57), *Odds Against Tomorrow* (59), *Sweet Bird of Youth* (62), *The Unsinkable Molly Brown* (64), *Billion Dollar Brain* (67), *Hang 'Em High* (68), *The Dunwich Horror (70).*

## BEL GEDDES, Barbara (1922- )

Born in New York City, the daughter of stage designer and architect Norman Bel Geddes, Barbara made her first stage appearance in summer stock as a teenager. A year later, in 1941, she made her Broadway debut in *Out of the Frying Pan*. From the 1940s through the 1960s, Bel Geddes appeared regularly on the stage, including roles in *Cat on a Hot Tin Roof* (55) and *Mary Mary* (61). In 1945 she won a New York Drama Critics Award for her performance in *Deep Are the Roots*. Her film debut was in *The Long Night* (47), but thereafter Bel Geddes graced only occasional films. Most of her screen appearances were in placid supporting roles, such as Jimmy Stewart's wry, reliable friend in Alfred Hitchcock's *Vertigo* (58). Of her performance as the artistic daughter Katrin in *I Remember Mama* (48), critic James Agee wrote "Barbara Bel Geddes has little to do except register gentle, clear emotions, but she does it exceedingly well and even manages not to make it monotonous" – a description that would apply to much of her screen career. She received a supporting-actress Oscar nomination for that role. Recent appearances have included a part in the prime-time TV soap *Dallas*.

**Selected Films:** *The Long Night* (47), *I Remember Mama* (48), *Caught* (49), *Panic in the Streets* (50), *Fourteen Hours* (51), *Vertigo* (58), *The Five Pennies* (59), *Five Branded Women* (59), *By Love Possessed* (61), *Summertree* (71), *The Todd Killings* (71).

Above: *Wallace Beery, Joseph Schildkraut* – Viva Villa *(34).*

Below: *Harry Belafonte, Dorothy Dandridge* – Carmen Jones *(55).*

## BELAFONTE, Harry (1927- )

Harry Belafonte was born in New York City and grew up in impoverished circumstances in his father's native Jamaica. After a stint in the Navy, he made a living in unskilled jobs while pursuing at New York's Dramatic Workshop his dream of a show-business career. In the early 1950s Belafonte's handsome features and mellow-but-strong voice brought him fame as a popular singer. One of the main figures of the Calypso rage, his hits included 'The Banana Boat Song.' Belafonte's first film appearance was in *Bright Road* (53). Remaining active as a singer through the 1960s, Belafonte made a number of television appearances but only occasional films. In later years he wound down his

singing and acting careers, tending to work as a producer and promoter.
**Selected Films:** *Bright Road* (53), *Carmen Jones* (55), *Island in the Sun* (57), *The World the Flesh and the Devil* (59), *Odds Against Tomorrow* (59), *The Angel Levine* (70), *Buck and the Preacher* (72), *Uptown Saturday Night* (74).

## BELASCO, Leon (1902- )

Born in Odessa, Russia, Belasco was a bandleader before becoming the perennial Hollywood Slav, playing a flustered ethnic in dozens of films – mostly in small parts as nervous balletmasters, waiters, and the like.
**Selected Films:** *The Best People* (26), *Topper Takes a Trip* (39), *The Mummy's Hand* (40), *Never Give a Sucker an Even Break* (41), *Road to Morocco* (42), *Pin-Up Girl* (44), *Can-Can* (60), *Superdad* (74).

*Ralph Bellamy in* The Court Martial of Billy Mitchell *(55).*

## BELL, Rex (1905-1962)

Chicago-born Bell (originally George Beldam) was a football star in college and first brought his muscular frame and handsome features to the screen in silents. He found his greatest popularity as a cowboy star in the 1930s and 1940s. Married to actress Clara Bow, Bell left Hollywood for a political career in Nevada.
**Selected Films:** *The Cowboy Kid* (28), *Forgotten Women* (31), *The Man from Arizona* (32), *Rainbow Ranch* (33), *Saddle Aces* (35), *Stormy Trails* (36), *Dawn on the Great Divide* (42), *The Misfits* (61).

## BELLAMY, Madge (1900- )

Bellamy, born in Hillsboro, Texas, made her film debut in *The Riddle Woman* (20). She soon became a popular leading lady in silents, usually cast in sweet and genteel roles in mostly routine films, though she did have leads in a few first-rate productions including *Lorna Doone* (22) and John Ford's *The Iron Horse* (24).
**Selected Films:** *The Call of the North* (21), *Lorna Doone* (22), *The Iron Horse* (24), *Wings of Youth* (25), *Silk Legs* (27), *Charlie Chan in London* (34).

## BELLAMY, Ralph (1904- )

Bellamy, a versatile stage and screen actor, was born in Chicago, Illinois. Beginning his film career in 1931 in *The Secret Six*, appearing with such luminaries as Wallace Beery, Jean Harlow and Johnny Mack Brown, he quickly became type-cast as the soft-voiced, serious-looking, simple-minded rich man who never got the girl. After a few years, he played the title role in the *Ellery Queen* mystery movies. It wasn't until 1960 that the movie audiences realized what a fine actor he was when he appeared as President Franklin D Roosevelt in *Sunrise at Campobello*, turning in a stunning performance as the patrician politician who was struck down by polio and, through force of will, came back to lead the country through World War II.
**Selected Films:** *The Secret Six* (31), *Rebecca of Sunnybrook Farm* (32), *The Awful Truth* (37), *Boy Meets Girl* (38), *Blind Alley* (39), *His Girl Friday* (40), *Ellery Queen, Master Detective* (40), *Guest in the House* (44), *Sunrise at Campobello* (60), *Rosemary's Baby* (67), *Oh, God!* (77), *Trading Places* (83).

## BELMONDO, Jean-Paul (1933- )

Sexy, charming and appealingly homely, this French leading man was born in Neuilly-sur-Seine, France – a suburb of Paris. After studying drama at the Paris Conservatory and appearing on stage, he had supporting roles in films at first, such as in *Dimanche . . . Nous Volerons* (56), until he skyrocketed to fame in *Breathless* (59). He soon symbolized the New Wave antihero and young rebel to international audiences, and by age 30 he

was president of the French actors' union and had published an autobiography. Talent and skill have kept him at the top ever since, and Belmondo has worked with nearly every famous French movie director, including Jean-Luc Godard, François Truffaut, Alain Resnais and Louis Malle.
**Selected Films:** *Dimanche ... Nous Volerons* (56), *Breathless* (59), *Two Women* (61), *Cartouche* (62), *A Monkey in Winter* (62), *That Man from Rio* (64), *Is Paris Burning?* (66), *The Mississippi Mermaid* (69), *Scoundrel in White* (72), *Stavisky* (74), *Le Professionnel* (81).

## BELUSHI, Jim (1954- )

Illinois-reared Belushi studied drama in college and arrived on TV in the late 1970s, when his older brother John was already a comedy star. His film career began with supporting roles.
**Selected Films:** *The Man with One Red Shoe* (85), *About Last Night* (86), *Jumpin' Jack Flash* (86), *Little Shop of Horrors* (86).

## BELUSHI, John (1949-1982)

Belushi was born in Chicago, Illinois. A member of the Second City improvisational troupe, he first became known to the American public with his hilarious performances on television's *Saturday Night Live*. His first film, *Animal House* (78), was one of the most successful comedies of the era. Later, he and Dan Aykroyd teamed up in a full-length feature taken from some of their skits on *Saturday Night Live* and appeared as *The Blues Brothers* (79). His subsequent movies were only marginally successful. Belushi's death from a drug overdose prompted a national outcry against drugs in the entertainment industry.
**Selected Films:** *Animal House* (78), *Going South* (78), *1941* (79), *The Blues Brothers* (79), *Continental Divide* (81), *Neighbors* (81).

*John Belushi in* Animal House *(78).*

## BENCHLEY, Robert (1889-1945)

Born in Worcester, Massachusetts, Benchley worked his way through the ranks as a journalist to become one of the nation's favorite magazine humorists and a major writer at *The New Yorker*. His best-known film appearances were in a series of shorts made between 1928 and 1945, in which he lectured gamely and hilariously on such subjects as *The Sex Life of the Polyp* (28), *The Romance of Digestion* (37), *The Courtship of a Newt* (38) and *How to Sleep* (35) which won an Oscar. Benchley also appeared in a number of features, usually as a bumbling *bon vivant*.
**Selected Films:** *Headline Shooter* (33), *How to Sleep* (35) *Foreign Correspondent* (40), *I Married a Witch* (42), *It's in the Bag* (45), *The Road to Utopia* (45).

## BENDIX, William (1906-1964)

Though destined to play louts and working-class heroes, William Bendix was born in New York City, the son of a conductor at the Metropolitan Opera. After various jobs including a stint playing minor league baseball, Bendix plunged into theater work, making his 1939 Broadway debut in William Saroyan's *The Time of Your Life*. The first of his many movies was *Woman of the Year* (42). Two years later he played a memorable lead in the film version of O'Neill's *The Hairy Ape* (44). Given his gravelly voice and his face – which he described as 'about as handsome as a mud fence' – Bendix was usually typed as a dense, though often good-hearted, working man. Among his notable film appearances were in Hitchcock's *Lifeboat* (43), *A Bell for Adano* (45), and the lead in *The Babe Ruth Story* (48). In 1949 he starred as factory-worker Chester A Riley in the film *The Life of Riley*. He had been appearing in the radio serial of that name since 1944, and continued the role on TV.
**Selected Films:** *Woman of the Year* (42), *The Glass Key* (42), *Lifeboat* (43), *Guadalcanal Diary* (43), *The Hairy Ape* (44), *A Bell for Adano* (45), *Two Years Before the Mast* (46), *The Babe Ruth Story* (48), *The Big Steal* (49), *The Life of Riley* (49), *Detective Story* (51), *Boy's Night Out* (62), *Young Fury* (65).

## BENJAMIN, Richard (1938- )

Born in New York City, Richard Benjamin appeared as a juvenile in two films of the 1950s, *Thunder Over the Plains* (53) and *Crime Wave* (54). After a stage career he returned to the screen as the lead in the film of Philip Roth's novel *Goodbye Columbus* (69). Again playing a young Jewish neurotic, Benjamin also starred in the film of Roth's *Portnoy's Complaint* (72). Most of Benjamin's other movie parts have been supporting roles in routine comedies such as *House Calls* (78). His screen image is vague, neither romantic nor emphatically funny. In 1961 he married actress Paula Prentiss, his costar in the TV series *He and She*. In 1982 Benjamin made a successful debut as a

feature director with *My Favorite Year*.
**Selected Films:** *Thunder Over the Plains* (53), *Crime Wave* (54), *Goodbye Columbus* (69), *Catch 22* (70); *Diary of a Mad Housewife* (70), *Marriage of a Young Stockbroker* (71), *Portnoy's Complaint* (72), *The Last of Sheila* (73), *Westworld* (73), *The Sunshine Boys* (76), *House Calls* (78), *The Last Married Couple in America* (80), *Saturday the 14th* (81).

## BENNETT, Bruce (1909- )

Bruce Bennett was born Herman Brix in Tacoma, Washington. As a young man he was an Olympic shot-putter, and his athletic build and incisive features brought him to Hollywood in 1934, where he first appeared – still as Herman Brix – in *Student Tour* (34). There followed a lead in a serial, *The New Adventures of Tarzan* (35), later re-released as the feature *Tarzan and the Green Goddess* (38). After various other appearances in serials and thrillers, Brix changed his name in 1940 to Bruce Bennett, traded his loincloth for an army uniform, and played leads and supporting roles as a granite-jawed soldier in World War II movies such as *Atlantic Convoy* (42). Bennett also appeared in films of the later 1940s often as a second lead and/or 'other man.' Perhaps his most memorable role was Cody in Huston's classic *The Treasure of the Sierra Madre* (48). In the 1950s Bennett's movie career wound down to minor thrillers such as *The Alligator People* (59), and he finally retired to enter real estate.
**Selected Films:** *Student Tour* (34), *Danger Patrol* (37), *Tarzan and the Green Goddess* (38), *The Man With Nine Lives* (40), *Atlantic Convoy* (42), *Sahara* (43), *Mildred Pierce* (45), *Dark Passage* (47), *The Treasure of the Sierra Madre* (48), *The Last Outpost* (51), *Strategic Air Command* (55), *The Alligator People* (59), *The Fiend of Dope Island* (61), *Deadhead Miles* (72), *Hero's Return* (80).

## BENNETT, Constance (1904-1965)

Born in New York City, daughter of matinee idol Richard Bennett, sister of movie actresses Barbara and Joan Bennett, Constance lived a glamorous life that included, but was not limited to, being a movie star. She first appeared in films as a teenager, playing leading roles in a number of silents including *The Goose Hangs High* (25). For a few years in the 1920s she was married to a railroad heir and retired from acting, but after a divorce she returned to films in *This Thing Called Love* (29). Thereafter, Bennett had an unbroken film career into the 1950s, usually playing glamorous and sophisticated women in everything from comedies – where she was a deft wisecracker – to weepies. Among her notable appearances were in *Moulin Rouge* (33), *Topper* (37), (as the ghostly Marion Kerby), and *Two-Faced Woman* (41). After *It Should Happen to You* (54), Bennett turned to the legitimate stage for some years. She died shortly after making a film comeback in *Madame X* (66) which was released after her death.
**Selected Films:** *Reckless Youth* (22), *Cytherea* (24), *The Goose Hangs High* (25), *This Thing Called Love* (29), *Rich People* (30), *Three Faces East* (30), *What Price Hollywood?* (32), *Moulin Rouge* (33), *Affairs of Cellini* (34), *Topper* (37), *Merrily We Live* (38), *Escape to Glory* (40), *Two-Faced Woman* (41), *The Unsuspected* (47), *It Should Happen to You* (53), Madame X (65).

## BENNETT, Joan (1910- )

Bennett was born in Palisades, New Jersey, and was the sister of actresses Constance and Barbara Bennett. She was a popular and attractive leading lady in films of the 1930s and 1940s, playing everything from ambitious and mercenary women to motherly types, beginning with *The Valley of Decision* (15), at the age of five. Her film career really began in 1928, when she appeared in *Power*, and lasted for over thirty years. She began as a blonde, but her career was given new impetus when she dyed her hair black in the 1940s and audiences noticed how much she looked like the beautiful Hedy Lamarr. In the 1960s she starred in the popular Gothic TV soap opera, *Dark Shadows*, and continued making made-for-television features well into the 1970s.
**Selected Films:** *The Valley of Decision* (15), *Power* (28), *Bulldog Drummond* (29), *Disraeli* (29), *Moby Dick* (30), *Little Women* (33), *Private Worlds* (35), *The Man in the Iron Mask* (39), *The Housekeeper's Daughter* (39), *Man Hunt* (41), *The Woman in the Window* (44), *Scarlet Street* (45), *The Macomber Affair* (47), *Father of the Bride* (50), *We're No Angels* (55), *Desire in the Dust* (60), *House of Dark Shadows* (70).

## BENNY, Jack (1894-1974)

Benny was a comedian's comedian – the master of timing who was successful in letting his co-stars share the laughs. This celebrated funny man was a star in vaudeville, radio, movies and television. Born Benjamin Kubelsky in Waukegan, Illinois (a town that named a school after him), his inimitable reproachful look, his pretense of stinginess and his much maligned violin playing were among the trademarks which kept him popular for 40 years. He was a graduate of burlesque, and later married his radio leading lady, Mary Livingstone, who was born Sadye Marks. Although films were possibly his least successful medium, and he often joked about this, his performance in *To Be or Not To Be* (42) was so touchingly funny that Mel Brooks reprised the film in 1983. His first picture was *Hollywood Revue of 1929* (29), and he went on to score comedy triumphs in such films as *Charley's Aunt* (41) and *George Washington Slept Here* (42). At the time of his death, he was set to co-star with lifelong friend George Burns, in *The Sunshine Boys*, Neil Simon's comedy, released in 1975 with Burns and Walter Matthau.

**Selected Films:** *Hollywood Revue of 1929* (29), *Broadway Melody of 1936* (35), *The Big Broadcast of 1937* (36), *Buck Benny Rides Again* (39), *Charley's Aunt* (41), *To Be or Not To Be* (42), *George Washington Slept Here* (42), *The Meanest Man in the World* (43), *It's in the Bag* (45), *The Horn Blows at Midnight* (45), *A Guide for the Married Man* (67).

## BENSON, Robby (1957- )

Born in Dallas, Texas, the son of playwright Jerry Segal and actress Ann Benson, Robby grew up in New York and began his acting career at the age of five. His screen debut came at 16 in *Jory* (72). Since then he has appeared in nearly 20 films in a variety of roles, among them as a hoodlum in *Walk Proud* (79), a troubled Hasidic kid in *The Chosen* (82), and an Indian track runner in *Running Brave* (83). Meanwhile, he has acted in theater productions ranging from *The Rothschilds* to *The Pirates of Penzance*. In 1977, Benson co-wrote *One on One* with his father and starred in the film. However, despite the wide range of his films and their healthy box-office, critical response to most of Benson's movies has ranged from lukewarm to savage. The reviews tended to the latter for his big role as Paul Newman's son in the Newman-directed *Harry and Son* (85). Benson has tried hard to escape from the cute-teenager image that has pursued him into adulthood.
**Selected Films:** *Jory* (72), *Jeremy* (73), *The Godfather – Part II* (74), *Ode to Billy Joe* (76), *The End* (78), *Tribute* (80), *The Chosen* (82), *Running Brave* (83), *Harry and Son* (85), *City Limits* (85).

## BERENGER, Tom (1950- )

Born in Chicago, Illinois, Berenger did a good deal of theater work and appeared in a TV soap opera before making his film debut with a small role in *The Sentinel* (77). After several minor films like *Butch and Sundance: the Early Days* (79) and a major role in *The Big Chill* (83), Berenger found acclaim and earned an Academy Award nomination for Best Supporting Actor playing somewhat against type as the physically and spiritually scarred Sergeant Barnes in *Platoon* (86).
**Selected Films:** *The Sentinel* (77), *Looking for Mr Goodbar* (77), *In Praise of Older Women* (79), *The Big Chill* (84), *Firstborn* (84), *Rustler's Rhapsody* (85), *Platoon* (86).

## BERESFORD, Harry (1864-1944)

British-born Harry Beresford moved to the United States to become a familiar face in movies from the 1920s on. An all-purpose supporting actor, he was seen in everything from comedies to thrillers.
**Selected Films:** *The Quarterback* (26), *Charles Chan Carries On* (31), *Dr X* (32), *The Sign of the Cross* (32), *Cleopatra* (34), *Seven Keys to Baldpate* (35), *David Copperfield* (35), *The Prince and the Pauper* (37).

*Candice Bergen in* Rich and Famous *(81).*

## BERGEN, Candice (1946- )

This stylish leading lady was born in Beverly Hills, California, the daughter of Edgar Bergen, the celebrated radio, television and film ventriloquist, and later lamented that she had seemed to grow up with his famous dummies, Charlie McCarthy and Mortimer Snerd. She was a model before appearing in her first film, *The Group* (66), in which she held her own against formidable competition, such as Joan Hackett and Elizabeth Hartman. In 1979, she received an Oscar nomination for Best Supporting Actress for her work in *Starting Over*. A beautiful, talented actress and also an accomplished photographer, she is married to director Louis Malle.
**Selected Films:** *The Group* (66), *The Sand Pebbles* (66), *The Magus* (68), *Getting Straight* (70), *Carnal Knowledge* (71), *The Wind and the Lion* (76), *The Cassandra Crossing* (76), *Starting Over* (79), *Rich and Famous* (81), *Gandhi* (82), *Stick* (86).

## BERGEN, Polly (1930- )

Born in Knoxville, Tennessee, Nellie Burgin changed her name to Polly Bergen and followed two careers as a singer and actress more or less concurrently, from the early 1950s on. Her singing and her television appearances have been the more visible part of her career, but she has appeared in film roles both light and dramatic.
**Selected Films:** *At War with the Army* (50), *Warpath* (51), *Arena* (53), *Escape from Fort Bravo* (54), *Cape Fear* (62), *Move Over Darling* (63), *A Guide for the Married Man* (67), *Murder on Flight 502* (75), *The Million Dollar Face* (81).

## BERGER, Helmut (1944- )

Born in Salzburg, Austria, Berger was a bit player in Italian movies when he was discovered by director Luchino Visconti, who gave him the lead

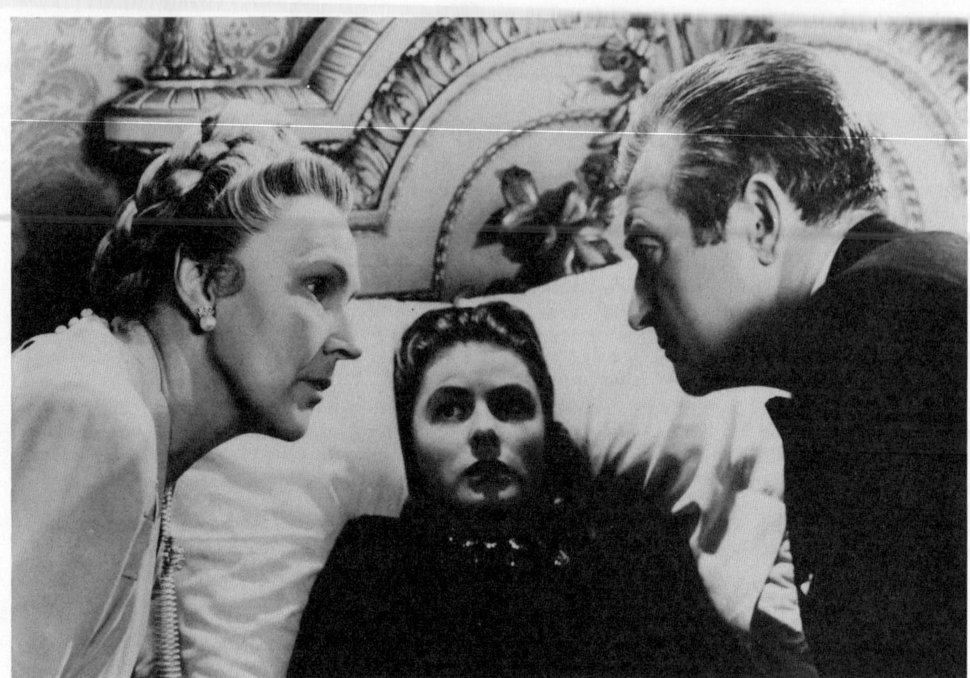

*Ingrid Bergman (c) with Leopoldine Konstantin and Claude Rains in* Notorious *(46).*

in *The Damned* (69). With his good looks and considerable acting skill, Berger went on to playing leads, often somewhat twisted individuals, in international films.
**Selected Films:** *The Damned* (69), *Un Beau Monstre* (70), *The Garden of the Finzi-Continis* (71), *Ash Wednesday* (73), *The Romantic Englishwoman* (75), *Madam Kitty* (77).

## BERGER, Senta (1941- )

Born in Vienna, Berger trained for the ballet before starting her film career at 16. Beautiful and sensuous, she has appeared internationally in numerous popular romantic and adventure films.
**Selected Films:** *The Journey* (58), *The Good Soldier Schweik* (60), *The Victors* (63), *Major Dundee* (65), *The Ambushers* (67), *De Sade* (69), *Ludwig* (72), *The Scarlet Letter* (72), *Cross of Iron* (77).

## BERGMAN, Ingrid (1915-1982)

Bergman had a natural beauty and a warm smile that allowed her to outshine all of Hollywood's female stars. Born in Stockholm, Sweden, she was raised by her photographer father and other relatives after the early death of her mother. Her father wanted her to be a performing artist and he encouraged her to follow her own path in life. He also helped give her a deep inner confidence. From other relatives, she received her passion for order, discipline and hard work. In 1933 she enrolled in the Royal Theatre of Dramatic Art in Stockholm, but switched to films instead and quickly became a well-known screen actress in her native land. Married to Petter Lindstrom, she made *Intermezzo* in Sweden in 1936, a few months before the birth of her daughter, Pia. Bergman was brought to Hollywood by David O Selznick to co-star with Leslie Howard in the American version of that film, which was released in 1939. The movie was an enormous success, and Bergman became a Hollywood star overnight. Bergman's wholesome freshness and sincerity made her the perfect choice for a new kind of star. She seemed to embody the best of European womanhood and culture at a time when the Nazis were plunging Europe into darkness. Thus, Bergman was cast in a series of important films, most notably *Casablanca* (42), opposite Humphrey Bogart. She won her first Academy Award for her work with Charles Boyer in *Gaslight* (44). In 1946 she was the top female Hollywood money earner. Also in 1946, she appeared on Broadway in Maxwell Anderson's play *Joan of Lorraine*, and her interpretation of Joan of Arc won her a Tony Award. The film version (48), in which she also starred, was less successful. Her image changed when she was making a film with director Roberto Rossellini – *Stromboli* (50). She left her husband to live with Rossellini, bearing him a son two months before they were married. American moviegoers would not forgive her. She was even called 'Hollywood's apostle of degradation' on the floor of the United States Senate. The marriage was annulled in 1958.

With the passage of time, the public's view of Bergman changed and she was welcomed back to America. She won an Academy Award for *Anastasia* (56), which was Hollywood's way of making amends, since the picture was far from outstanding. An Oscar for Best Supporting Actress and a British Film Academy Award went to her for *Murder on the Orient Express* (74). She continued to work in films and on television until her death from cancer.

**Selected Films:** *Munkbrogreven* (34), *Intermezzo* (39), *Adam Had Four Sons* (41), *Dr Jekyll and Mr Hyde* (41), *Casablanca* (42), *For Whom the Bell Tolls* (43), *Gaslight* (44), *The Bells of St Mary's* (45), *Spellbound* (45), *Saratoga Trunk* (45), *Notorious* (46), *Arch of Triumph* (48), *Joan of Arc* (48), *Stromboli* (50), *Anastasia* (56), *Indiscreet* (58), *The Inn of the Sixth Happiness* (58), *The Visit* (64), *The Yellow Rolls Royce* (64), *Cactus Flower* (69), *Murder on the Orient Express* (74), *A Matter of Time* (76), *Autumn Sonata* (78).

## BERGNER, Elisabeth (1898-1986)

Elisabeth Bergner was born Elizabeth Ettel in Drohobycz, Poland and received her dramatic training in Vienna. After her European stage debut in 1919 she appeared to great acclaim around the world. (She was one of the favorite actresses of the legendary German stage director Max Reinhardt.) After her first film, *Der Evangelimann* (23), Bergner went on to become a popular gamine-type lead in German silents and talkies, most of them directed by Paul Czinner, whom Bergner married in 1933. Fleeing the Nazis the year of their marriage, the couple lived in London and occasionally in the United States for the rest of their careers. Critic Alexander Woolcott called Bergner 'probably the ablest actress living today.' Her performance in *Escape Me Never* (35) earned her an Oscar nomination. She made only one film in the United States, *Paris Calling* (41). From the 1940s on Bergner was less active, but did appear in occasional stage and screen roles. Her later screen appearances included a return to German films.

**Selected Films:** *Der Evangelimann* (23), *Liebe* (27), *Der Traumende Mund* (32), *Catherine the Great* (34), *Escape Me Never* (35), *As You Like It* (36), *A Stolen Life* (39), *Paris Calling* (41), *Die Glückliche Jahre der Thorwalds* (62), *Whitsun Holiday* (79), *Society Limited* (81).

## BERLE, Milton (1908-      )

Milton Berle was born Mendel Berlinger in New York City. From early childhood he was cutting up onstage and in front of the camera for Biograph and other studios, and touring in vaudeville – one of the last generation of comedians to be trained in that unforgiving school. Making his New York stage debut at 12, Berle appeared in various productions such as *The Ziegfeld Follies*. His film work began as early as 1914 in the serial *Perils of Pauline*, and included juvenile roles in a number of silents. His film career never quite took off, however, despite several tries in the 1930s and 1940s – one of

*Terry-Thomas and Milton Berle in* It's A Mad Mad Mad Mad World *(63).*

them, *Always Leave Them Laughing* (49), was based on the first of his two autobiographies. In 1948 Berle found his niche in TV: for the next eight years he was called 'Uncle Miltie' and 'Mr Television,' his gooney smile, drag routines, and broad unsubtle comedy helping to cinch the triumph – and the intellectual level – of the new medium. In his later movie appearances, which included *It's a Mad Mad Mad Mad World* (63), and several minor comedies, he played various roles but all were essentially the character named Milton Berle.
**Selected Films:** *The Mark of Zorro* (20), *New Faces of 1937* (37), *Sun Valley Serenade* (41), *Margin for Error* (43), *Always Leave Them Laughing* (49), *It's a Mad Mad Mad Mad World* (63), *The Loved One* (65), *Lepke* (75), *The Muppet Movie* (80).

## BERLINGER, Warren (1937- )

Brooklyn-born Berlinger played chubby adolescents and naive youths in films from the 1950s on, including *The Wackiest Ship in the Army* (61), *Thunder Alley* (67) and *The Long Goodbye* (73).
**Selected Films:** *Teenage Rebel* (56), *Three Brave Men* (57), *Platinum High School* (60), *The Wackiest Ship in the Army* (61), *Spinout* (66), *Thunder Alley* (67), *The Long Goodbye* (73), *Harry and Walter Go to New York* (76), *The World According to Garp* (82).

## BERNARDI, Herschel (1923-1986)

Born in New York City, Bernardi spent the bulk of his career on the stage. His appearances on Broadway include the role of Tevye in *Fiddler on the Roof*. Having made two Yiddish films in the 1930s the burly, balding Bernardi went on to occasional film roles, often as a heavy.
**Selected Films:** *Green Fields* (37), *Miss Susie Slagle's* (46), *The Savage Eye* (60), *Irma La Douce* (63), *Love With the Proper Stranger* (64), *The Front* (76).

## BERNHARDT, Sarah (1844-1923)

Born in Paris, the French actress Bernhardt was one of the legendary figures of stage history, with a career that stretched over many decades. Her attitude toward film was ambiguous – she hated her first two appearances, *Hamlet's Duel* (00) and *Tosca* (08), but still continued to preserve many of her great roles including the notable *La Dame aux Camélias* (11) on celluloid. She died while working on *La Voyante* (23).
**Selected Films:** *Tosca* (08), *La Dame aux Camélias* (11), *Queen Elizabeth* (12), *Adrienne Lecouvreur* (13), *Mothers of France* (17), *La Voyante* (23).

## BESSER, Joe: See STOOGES, The Three

## BEST, Edna (1900-1974)

Born in Hove, Sussex, Best came to America in 1939 after considerable success on the stage including *The Constant Nymph* in her native Britain. In her first Hollywood films she played romantic leads, later settling into sympathetic maternal roles. She was married to actor Herbert Marshall from 1928 to 1940.
**Selected Films:** *Tilly of Bloomsbury* (21), *Tilly of Bloomsbury* (30), *Michael and Mary* (32), *The Man Who Knew Too Much* (34), *South Riding* (38), *Intermezzo* (39), *The Swiss Family Robinson* (40), *The Ghost and Mrs Muir* (48).

## BEST, Willie (1916-1962)

Black actor Best was born in Mississippi and got into films in the 1930s. For some years known as 'Sleep 'n Eat,' he played lazy and frightened men in dozens of movies, in an era when the film image of blacks was lamentably stereotyped and demeaning.
**Selected Films:** *Feet First* (30), *The Monster Walks* (32), *The Littlest Rebel* (35), *Ghost Breakers* (40), *High Sierra* (41), *Cabin in the Sky* (43), *South of Caliente* (51).

## BEY, Turhan (1920- )

The handsome, dapper Bey whose real name was Turhan Selahattin Sahultavy was born in Vienna to a Turkish father and a Czech mother. After studying acting in California he appeared as both heavy and hero in exotic-adventure films of the 1940s. His career ended with the decline of that genre.
**Selected Films:** *Footsteps in the Dark* (41), *Drums of the Congo* (42), *Arabian Nights* (42), *Ali Baba and the Forty Thieves* (43), *Sudan* (45), *Song of India* (49), *Prisoners of the Casbah* (53).

## BEYMER, Richard (1939- )

Born in Avoca, Iowa, Beymer entered films at age 14, a promising juvenile lead in productions including *The Diary of Anne Frank* (59) and *West Side Story* (61). However, his career never quite took off, and his appearances declined in the 1960s. In 1974 he produced, directed, and shot a feature, *The Innerview*.
**Selected Films:** *So Big* (52), *Johnny Tremain* (57), *The Diary of Anne Frank* (59), *High Time* (60), *West Side Story* (61), *Hemingway's Adventures of a Young Man* (62), *The Stripper* (62), *Cross Country* (83).

## BICKFORD, Charles (1889-1967)

Charles Bickford was born in Cambridge, Massachusetts, and graduated from MIT. After working as a civil engineer and a sailor, he got into show business by way of burlesque. In 1919 he made his Broadway debut and stayed there until the coming of sound films attracted him to Hollywood. His first film, C B DeMille's *Dynamite* (29), was almost his last because Bickford punched out the director. However, the two became friends, and Bickford soon shot to stardom as Garbo's lover in *Anna*

*Natalie Wood and Richard Beymer* – West Side Story *(61).*

*Christie* (30). Thereafter, he would be a fixture in Hollywood virtually until his death. After a few years as a romantic lead, Bickford settled into the character roles that suited his craggy and intense features. Sometimes a villain, he more often played likeable fathers, businessmen, captains, and such; in all roles, he was an actor who commanded attention onscreen. Though he never won an Academy Award, Bickford was nominated for three supporting roles – in *The Song of Bernadette* (43), *The Farmer's Daughter* (47) and *Johnny Belinda* (48). In later years he did TV work, including the series *The Virginian*. His autobiography, *Bulls, Balls, Bicycles, and Actors*, was published in 1965.
**Selected Films:** *Dynamite* (29), *Anna Christie* (30), *Thunder Below* (32), *The Littlest Rebel* (35), *Of Mice and Men* (40), *The Song of Bernadette* (43), *Duel in the Sun* (46), *The Farmer's Daughter* (47), *Brute Force* (47), *Johnny Belinda* (48), *A Star is Born* (54), *The Big Country* (58), *A Big Hand for the Little Lady* (66).

## BIKEL, Theodore (1924- )

Born in Vienna, Theodore Bikel emigrated to Israel as a teenager and first appeared on the stage in Tel Aviv. After studying drama at the Royal Academy of Dramatic Art in England, he worked on the London stage before coming to New York in 1955. Bikel made the first of his many supporting appearances in film as a German naval officer in John Huston's *The African Queen* (52). For the rest of his screen career, the heavyset but handsome Bikel has played character roles of varying nationalities, like the Russian submarine captain in *The Russians Are Coming, The Russians Are Coming* (66). Concurrently with his acting career, Bikel has been a distinguished folk singer and guitarist whose popularity has been steady since the 1950s.
**Selected Films:** *The African Queen* (52), *Melba* (53), *The Divided Heart* (54), *The Pride and the Passion* (57), *Fraulein* (58), *The Defiant Ones* (58), *My Fair Lady* (64), *The Russians Are Coming, The Russians Are Coming* (68), *My Side of the Mountain* (69), *The Little Ark* (71), *Prince Jack* (85).

## BILL, Tony (1940- )

Bill, born in San Diego, California, played light romantic roles in movies of the 1960s into the 1970s. Moving behind the scenes, he produced several films including *The Sting* (73) and *Hearts of the West* (75). He made his directorial debut with *My Bodyguard* (80).
**Selected Films:** *Come Blow Your Horn* (63), *None But the Brave* (65), *Ice Station Zebra* (68), *Shampoo* (75).

## BING, Herman (1889-1947)

Born in Frankfurt, Germany, Bing was an assistant to German director F W Murnau and accompanied him to Hollywood. Bing appeared in comic roles frequently as an effusive and excitable character.
**Selected Films:** *Married in Hollywood* (29), *Dinner at Eight* (33), *The Merry Widow* (34), *Call of the Wild* (35), *Rose Marie* (36), *Maytime* (37), *Night and Day* (46).

## BISHOP, Julie (1914- )

Born Jacqueline Wells Brown in Denver, Colorado, Bishop made silent films in childhood as Jacqueline Wells and went on to comedies and then leads in B-pictures during the 1930s. In the 1940s she reemerged as Julie Bishop, with a more glamorous image, but was still mostly relegated to second features, before retiring in the 1950s.
**Selected Films:** *Maytime* (23), *Captain Blood* (24), *Alice in Wonderland* (33), *Highway Patrol* (38), *Lady Gangster* (42), *Sands of Iwo Jima* (49), *The Big Land* (57).

## BISSELL, Whit (1914-1981)

This character actor, born in New York City, has been known to play anything from attorneys to garage attendants. He has also had his share of horror movie roles, most notably playing the mad scientists in *I Was a Teen-age Frankenstein* (57), with Gary Conway, and *I Was a Teen-age Werewolf* (57), with Michael Landon.
**Selected Films:** *Holy Matrimony* (43), *Another Part of the Forest* (47), *I Was a Teen-age Frankenstein* (57), *I Was a Teen-age Werewolf* (57), *Hud* (63), *The Time Machine* (64), *Airport* (70), *Soylent Green* (73), *Casey's Shadow* (78).

## BISSET, Jacqueline (1944- )

Born Winifred Bisset in Weybridge, England, Bisset began her career as a model, and had bit parts in British films such as *The Knack* (64) and *Arrivederci Baby* (65) before she was summoned to Hollywood. In the United States, she was groomed for a stardom that has never quite been realized.
**Selected Films:** *The Knack* (64), *Arrivederci Baby* (65), *Two For the Road* (67), *Bullitt* (68), *Airport* (70), *The Mephisto Waltz* (71), *Murder on the Orient Express* (74), *Who is Killing the Great Chefs of Europe?* (78), *Rich and Famous* (81), *Class* (83).

## BIXBY, Bill (1934- )

Born in San Francisco, Bixby was a model before becoming a light lead in mostly minor films of the 1960s and 1970s. His TV work included *My Favorite Martian* and *The Hulk*.
**Selected Films:** *Irma La Douce* (63), *Under the Yum Yum Tree* (63), *Clambake* (67), *Speedway* (68), *The Kentucky Fried Movie* (77).

## BLACK, Karen (1942- )

Karen Black was born Karen Zeigler in Park Ridge, Illinois, and began her acting career off Broadway, while studying with Lee Strasberg at the Actor's Studio. She made an impressive Broadway debut in the short-lived *The Playroom* in 1965, and two years later first appeared onscreen in *You're a Big Boy Now* (67). Her attractive but unusual features and her earthy sensuality tended to land her in sexual, as opposed to sexy, roles: an addicted whore in *Easy Rider* (69), a dumb but goodhearted waitress and Jack Nicholson's bedmate in *Five Easy Pieces* (70) (for which she received an Oscar nomination), a loose woman in the Nicholson-directed *Drive, He Said* (71), and so on. Despite often playing less-than-bright types, Black has shown a strong screen presence and an underlying intelligence as an actress. Her performance as a country singer in Robert Altman's *Nashville* (75) is an example of that quality.
**Selected Films:** *You're a Big Boy Now* (67), *Easy Rider* (69), *Five Easy Pieces* (70), *Drive, He Said* (71), *Portnoy's Complaint* (72), *Rhinoceros* (73), *The Day of the Locust* (75), *Nashville* (75), *Family Plot* (76), *In Praise of Older Women* (79), *Come Back to the Five and Dime, Jimmy Dean, Jimmy Dean* (82), *Bad Manners* (84), *Invaders from Mars* (86).

## BLACKMAN, Honor (1926- )

Honor Blackman was born in London and began her film career with *Fame is the Spur* (47). During the 1940s and 1950s she played mostly decorous leads in minor British movies. Her career surged, however, when she showed up in various leather outfits as a judo expert in the memorable British TV action series *The Avengers* (60-63). In 1964 Blackman made a splash as Pussy Galore in the James Bond thriller *Goldfinger*. Blackman continued to appear mostly in thrillers and shockers through the 1970s.
**Selected Films:** *Fame is the Spur* (47), *So Long at the Fair* (50), *A Night to Remember* (58), *Goldfinger* (64), *The Virgin and the Gypsy* (70), *To the Devil a Daughter* (75), *The Cat and the Canary* (78).

## BLACKMER, Sidney (1895-1973)

Born in Salisbury, North Carolina, Blackmer appeared in silent films from 1914 on, but found his first acting success on Broadway; his later stage appearances included roles in *Come Back Little Sheba* and *Sweet Bird of Youth*. Busy as he was on the stage, Blackmer still found time to appear in over 100 movies, in a wide variety of roles from suave heavies and sympathetic characters to more robust roles – he played Teddy Roosevelt more than a dozen times on film and stage.
**Selected Films:** *The Perils of Pauline* (14), *Little Caesar* (31), *The Little Colonel* (35), *This is My Affair* (37), *Heidi* (37), *Love Crazy* (41), *My Girl Tisa* (48), *The High and the Mighty* (54), *High Society* (56), *Rosemary's Baby* (68).

## BLADES, Rubén (1948- )

Panama-born singer and songwriter Blades is one of the primary figures in the Latin music called *salsa*; he developed his highly politicized song style while studying and practicing law in Panama (he recently earned a Harvard doctorate in international law). In 1985 Blades starred in the *salsa-*

based movie *Crossover Dreams*; it was generally agreed that his presence and music saved an otherwise slight film.
**Selected Films:** *Crossover Dreams* (85), *Critical Condition* (87).

## BLAINE, Vivian (1921- )

Born Vivienne Stapleton in Newark, New Jersey, Vivian Blaine started her singing career with bands and in nightclubs during the 1930s. She went on to be a vivacious presence in light films and musicals of the 1940s including *Thru Different Eyes* (42), *State Fair* (45), and *Three Little Girls in Blue* (46). Her biggest successes came on the Broadway musical stage, most notably as Miss Adelaide in the 1950 production of *Guys and Dolls*; a role she repeated in the 1955 film version. Her film career continued into the 1980s, including occasional TV movies such as *Portrait of a Centerfold*.
**Selected Films:** *Girl Trouble* (42), *Jitterbugs* (43), *Doll Face* (45), *State Fair* (45), *Skirts Ahoy* (52), *Guys and Dolls* (55), *Public Pigeon Number One* (57), *The Dark* (78), *Parasite* (82), *I'm Going to be Famous* (83).

## BLAIR, Betsy (1923- )

Born Elizabeth Boger in New York City, Blair worked on the stage before her first film appearance in *The Guilt of Janet Ames* (47). Mostly a second lead in films, often as shy or nervous types, she gained considerable acclaim and received an Oscar nomination for her leading role in *Marty* (55). Her later films were mostly European.
**Selected Films:** *The Snake Pit* (48), *Another Part of the Forest* (48), *Mystery Street* (50), *Marty* (55), *The Halliday Brand* (57), *The Dauphins* (60), *Marry Me! Marry Me!* (68), *A Delicate Balance* (73).

## BLAIR, Janet (1921- )

Janet Blair was born Martha Janet Lafferty in Altoona, Pennsylvania. She started her show-business career singing with bands, and that led to her first film role in *Three Girls About Town* (41). Blair proved to be a vivacious and attractive screen presence in such films as *Broadway* (42) and *My Sister Eileen* (42) (in the latter she played the title role). These films were the peak of her success, however; in the later 1940s Blair largely appeared in B-movies. In the 1950s she turned to stage roles, touring with a very successful production of *South Pacific*. Blair continued to appear in the occasional film, among them the British horror picture *Burn, Witch, Burn!* (62). For one season she co-starred with Henry Fonda in the TV series *The Smith Family*.
**Selected Films:** *Three Girls About Town* (41), *Blondie Goes to College* (42), *My Sister Eileen* (42), *Once Upon a Time* (44), *Tonight and Every Night* (45), *Tars and Spars* (46), *The Fabulous Dorseys* (47), *The Fuller Brush Man* (48), *The Black Arrow* (48), *Public Pigeon Number One* (57), *The One and Only Genuine Original Family Band* (68), *Won Ton Ton, The Dog Who Saved Hollywood* (75).

## BLAIR, Linda (1959- )

Born in St Louis, Missouri, Blair made a spectacular debut in films as the possessed child in *The Exorcist* (74). Once she could no longer play children's parts, her career went downhill, complicated by drug problems.
**Selected Films:** *The Exorcist* (74), *Airport 75* (75), *The Exorcist II: The Heretic* (77), *Hell Night* (81), *Night Patrol* (84).

## BLAKE, Robert (1933- )

Michael Gubitosi, born in Nutley, New Jersey, was in front of a camera almost as soon as he was able to find his mark on a sound stage. As Bobby Blake, he appeared in the *Our Gang* shorts in the 1930s and 1940s, played Little Beaver in *Red Ryder* Westerns, and was a Mexican youth in *The Treasure of the Sierra Madre* (48). After a hiatus he returned to films in 1957, now Robert Blake, and scored a success as a killer in *In Cold Blood* (67). His image as a feisty bantam brought him offbeat roles in movies and in his popular TV series *Baretta*.
**Selected Films:** *Andy Hardy's Double Life* (43), *The Horn Blows at Midnight* (45), *The Treasure of the Sierra Madre* (48), *Pork Chop Hill* (60), *In Cold Blood* (67), *Tell Them Willie Boy is Here* (69), *Electra Glide in Blue* (73), *Second Hand Hearts* (80)

## BLAKELY, Colin (1930-1987)

Born in Bangor, Northern Ireland, Blakely has spent much of his career on the stage, and didn't make a film until he was 30. His character roles include Watson in *The Private Life of Sherlock Holmes* (70).
**Selected Films:** *Saturday Night and Sunday Morning* (60), *The Informers* (63), *A Man for All Seasons* (66), *The Day the Fish Came Out* (67), *Decline and Fall* (68), *Murder on the Orient Express* (74), *Equus* (77), *The Dogs of War* (80), *Loophole* (86).

## BLONDELL, Joan (1909-1979)

Born in New York City, Blondell played reporters, gold-diggers and dizzy friends of the heroine in countless comedies and musicals of the 1930s. She was one of the most popular supporting actresses, and beginning in 1929, she appeared in 32 pictures in a period of 27 months. She spent most of the 1950s on stage, and then returned to films in character parts. Blondell appeared in *Gold Diggers of 1933* (33) with Dick Powell, and they went on to set the record for the number of times a team co-starred in musical films – ten different movies. One of her greatest roles was not in a musical, but rather in a drama, *A Tree Grows in Brooklyn* (45).
**Selected Films:** *Sinner's Holiday* (30), *Public Enemy* (31), *Gold Diggers of 1933* (33), *Dames* (34), *Three*

*Men on a Horse* (36), *Stand-In* (37), *A Tree Grows in Brooklyn* (44), *Nightmare Alley* (47), *The Cincinnati Kid* (65), *Support Your Local Gunfighter* (71), *Grease* (78), *The Champ* (79).

## BLOOM, Claire (1931- )

Claire Bloom is one of those stars who radiates something beyond beauty; there is a great thoughtfulness in all her roles as well as masterful skill as an actress. Charlie Chaplin, who directed her first screen success in *Limelight*, said of her, 'Claire has distinction, enormous range, and underneath her sadness there is a bubbling humor, so unexpected, so wistful.' Born Claire Blume in London, Bloom lived in the United States for a time; she returned to England in 1943 already determined to be a Shakespearean actress. At age 15 she worked with the Oxford Repertory Theater and soon was playing Shakespeare at Stratford-on-Avon. Her film debut came with *The Blind Goddess* (48). In 1952 Bloom found fame as the young ballet dancer Terry, whom Charlie Chaplin saves from suicide in *Limelight*. Also that year Bloom joined the Old Vic stage company. In 1956 she held her own as Lady Anne opposite Laurence Olivier in his personal *tour de force*, *Richard III*. For the rest of her career Bloom has appeared regularly in the theater and in films both substantial and workaday, in both starring and supporting roles. Her notable film performances include Tony Richardson's *Look Back in Anger* (59), in *The Haunting* (63) and *The Spy Who Came in from the Cold* (65). In 1957 she married actor Rod Steiger; their marriage ended in 1969, the year they appeared together in *The Illustrated Man*. Bloom's lead opposite Anthony Hopkins in the film of Ibsen's *A Doll's House* (73) reaffirmed what Chaplin had said of her two decades before.
**Selected Films:** *The Blind Goddess* (48), *Innocents in Paris* (52), *Limelight* (52), *Alexander the Great* (56), *Richard III* (56), *The Brothers Karamazov* (58), *The Buccaneer* (59), *Look Back in Anger* (59), *The Chapman Report* (61), *The Haunting* (63), *The Spy Who Came in from the Cold* (65), *High Infidelity* (65), *Charly* (68), *The Illustrated Man* (69), *A Doll's House* (73), *Islands in the Stream* (77), *Clash of the Titans* (81), *Déjà Vu* (85).

## BLORE, Eric (1887-1959)

London-born Blore worked on the stage in Australia and London before his first film, *A Night Out and a Day In* (20). Alternating between stage and screen roles in America, he was most often typecast in film as an eccentric or as a sharp-tongued butler, the latter notably in Preston Sturges's *Sullivan's Travels* (41).
**Selected Films:** *The Great Gatsby* (26), *The Gay Divorcee* (34), *Top Hat* (35), *It's Love I'm After* (37), *Sullivan's Travels* (41), *The Lady Eve* (41), *The Moon and Sixpence* (42), *Abie's Irish Rose* (46), *Fancy Pants* (50), *Bowery to Bagdad* (55).

## BLUE, Ben (1901-1975)

Born in Montreal, Blue came to film from vaudeville, where he perfected his sad-faced, rubber-limbed comic style. Beginning in shorts for Hal Roach among others, Blue had a long screen career in usually small but memorable roles.
**Selected Films:** *The Arcadians* (27), *College Rhythm* (34), *For Me and My Gal* (42), *Easy to Wed* (46), *The Russians Are Coming, The Russians Are Coming* (66), *Where Were You When the Lights Went Out?* (68).

## BLUE, Monte (1890-1963)

Born in Indianapolis, Indiana, the powerfully-built Blue was a lumberjack and cowboy before beginning his film career with D W Griffith, with whom he had a bit part in *The Birth of a Nation* (15). Blue went on to appear in over 200 films, most of them action pictures; into the 1950s his parts ranged from leads to character roles to bit parts.
**Selected Films:** *The Birth of a Nation* (15), *Intolerance* (16), *Orphans of the Storm* (22), *White Shadows of the South Seas* (28), *Lives of a Bengal Lancer* (34), *The Mask of Dimitrios* (44), *Apache* (54).

## BLYTH, Ann (1928- )

Ann Blyth was born in Mt Kisco, New York, and studied voice as a child. After three years as a juvenile singer with an opera company, she made her Broadway debut at 13 and her film debut at 15 – in *Chip off the Old Block*, the first of her four films in 1944. The next year she appeared as Joan Crawford's vindictive daughter in *Mildred Pierce*, for which Blyth received an Oscar nomination. She brought her delicately beautiful features and diminutive form to starring roles in a variety of pictures in the 1940s and 1950s, ranging from adventure films (*Thunder on the Hill* [51]) to dramas (*Another Part of the Forest* [48]) to musicals (*Rose Marie* [54]). After appearing in *The Helen Morgan Story* (57), Blyth retired from the screen, occasionally appearing on stage in operettas and musicals.
**Selected Films:** *Babes on Swing Street* (44), *Mildred Pierce* (45), *Swell Guy* (46), *Brute Force* (47), *Mr Peabody and the Mermaid* (48), *Once More My Darling* (49), *The Great Caruso* (51), *One Minute to Zero* (52), *Rose Marie* (54), *The Student Prince* (54), *Kismet* (55), *The Buster Keaton Story* (57), *The Helen Morgan Story* (57).

## BOGARDE, Dirk (1920- )

Elegant, handsome and gifted Dirk Bogarde has consistently turned in first-rate performances in films, even when presented with weak material. Born Derek Van Den Bogaerde in London, England, his Dutch-born father was the art director for the London *Times*. Bogarde began working as a scenic designer and commercial artist, but he really wanted to act, and he made his stage debut in a small suburban London theater in 1939. Only

Dirk Bogarde, Donald Sinden and Kenneth More in Doctor in the House *(53).*

after he returned from his World War II service did his theatrical career begin in earnest. A stage play, *Power Without Glory*, won him a movie contract with Rank Studios and he made a string of pictures. One of them, *The Blue Lamp* (50), was the most successful British film of the year. Critics praised his performance in *Hunted* (52), a thriller. Then came Bogarde's first big hit, *Doctor in the House* (53), the first of a series of irreverant 'Doctor' comedies. Hollywood beckoned, but Bogarde resisted. Later he would appear in both American and international films, but in the mid- through late 1950s he was distinctly a British star, the number-one box office draw. In 1957 *Picturegoer* magazine voted him the year's best actor. In the 1960s Bogarde began receiving the kind of roles he needed to display his subtlety and sensitivity as an actor. In *Victim* (61), he played a gay character, a courageous move on the part of a major star at a time when the subject of homosexuality was still taboo on screen. His performance as the decadent valet in *The Servant* (63) won him a British Film Academy Award as Best Actor. He won a second for *Darling* (65), with Julie Christie. His performance as a dying composer obsessed with a young boy in *Death in Venice* (71) was a *tour de force*. In the early 1970s Bogarde moved to Italy and then to France, in part because he felt that he wasn't being offered the kind of roles he craved in Britain. He was by then an international star and highly respected. One of his finest performances of that time was in Alain Resnais' complex *Providence* (77).

**Selected Films:** *Esther Waters* (47), *Quartet* (48), *The Blue Lamp* (50), *Hunted* (52), *Doctor in the House* (53), *The Sea Shall Not Have Them* (54), *The Sleeping Tiger* (54), *Cast a Dark Shadow* (55), *The Spanish Gardener* (56), *Campbell's Kingdom* (58), *A Tale of Two Cities* (58), *Song Without End* (60), *Victim* (61), *The Servant* (63), *King and Country* (64), *Darling* (65), *The Damned* (69), *Death in Venice* (71), *The Night Porter* (74), *A Bridge Too Far* (77), *Providence* (77), *Despair* (78).

*Humphrey Bogart and Lauren Bacall in* The Big Sleep *(46).*

## BOGART, Humphrey (1899-1957)

'Bogey' is a cult hero to almost everybody; he was simply one of the best film actors America ever produced. He was born Humphrey DeForest Bogart in New York City, the son of a prominent doctor and a famous illustrator. Although Bogart would one day play the common man to perfection, he was given a classic education – Trinity School in upper Manhattan and Phillips Academy in Andover, Massachusetts – but Bogart never finished prep school. Instead he joined the Navy, where he received an injury to his lip which may have accounted for his distinctive lisp. After his service, he became a stage manager and then turned to acting, appearing in several Broadway farces. In 1930 he tried films, appearing in five unmemorable movies, and returned to New York. His big break came when he played Duke Mantee, the escaped killer, in Robert E Sherwood's 1934 Broadway play, *The Petrified Forest*. When the film version was being planned, the star, Leslie Howard (who had also starred in the play), demanded that Bogart be given his old role rather than having Edward G Robinson play Mantee. The movie was also successful and Bogart had become a Hollywood star. Bogart played mostly gangster roles for the next few years in such films as *Dead End* (37) and *San Quentin* (37). It wasn't until he began working with screen writer and director John Huston that movie history was made. Bogart turned from bad guy to good guy – but a cynical good guy, not a saint. Beginning with *High Sierra* (41), he moved on to *The Maltese Falcon* (41), a masterpiece. *Casablanca* (42), with Ingrid Bergman, was absolutely the ultimate Hollywood movie of World War II. Then there were *To Have and Have Not* (43), *The Big Sleep* (46) and *The Treasure of the Sierra Madre* (48). On the set of *To Have and Have Not* he met a gorgeous young actress/model named Lauren Bacall and later married her. She was his fourth wife. Bogart and his third wife, Mayo Methot, had been notorious in Hollywood for their fights and were known as 'the battling Bogarts,' but his marriage to Bacall was immensely successful – lasting until his death. Bogart finally won a much-deserved Academy Award for Best Actor for his work in *The African Queen* (51) opposite Katharine Hepburn.

**Selected Films:** *Broadway's Like That* (30), *Up the River* (30), *Bad Sister (30)*, *Body and Soul* (31), *The Petrified Forest* (36), *Bullets or Ballots* (36), *China Clipper* (36), *Kid Galahad* (37), *San Quentin* (37), *Dead End* (37), *The Amazing Dr Clitterhouse* (38), *Angels With Dirty Faces* (38), *Virginia City* (40), *High Sierra* (41), *The Maltese Falcon* (41), *Casablanca* (42), *Action in the North Atlantic* (43), *Sahara* (43), *To Have and Have Not* (44), *The Big Sleep* (46), *Dark Passage* (47), *The Treasure of the Sierra Madre* (48), *Key Largo* (48), *Knock on Any Door* (49), *The African Queen* (51), *Beat the Devil* (54), *The Caine Mutiny* (54), *The Desperate Hours* (55), *The Harder They Fall* (56).

## BOLAND, Mary (1880-1965)

The daughter of an actor, Mary Boland was born in Philadelphia and attended a convent school in Detroit. As a teenager she began acting in stock companies and by 1905 was working on Broadway. For some time Boland was noted for her tragic roles, both on stage and in silent films beginning with *The Edge of the Abyss* (15). However, in the 1920s she switched to comedy and went on to dozens of roles as a scatterbrained wife and mother, most memorably in movies with Charlie Ruggles, including *Ruggles of Red Gap* (35).
**Selected Films:** *The Edge of the Abyss* (15), *His Temporary Wife* (18), *Trouble in Paradise* (32), *Mama Loves Papa* (33), *Down to Their Last Yacht* (34), *Ruggles of Red Gap* (35), *People Will Talk* (36), *Mama Runs Wild* (37), *There Goes the Groom* (37), *The Women* (39), *Pride and Prejudice* (40), *In Our Time* (44), *Julia Misbehaves* (48), *Guilty Bystander* (50).

## BOLES, John (1895-1969)

Born in Greenville, Texas, Boles was a pre-med student, an espionage agent during World War I, an operetta singer and Broadway star before making his first silent film, *So This Is Marriage* (24). His career blossomed in talkies, and during the 1930s he was an elegant leading man in musicals, romantic movies, and dramas.
**Selected Films:** *So This Is Marriage* (24), *The Loves of Sunya* (27), *The Desert Song* (29), *Rio Rita* (29), *The King of Jazz* (30), *Back Street* (32), *Only Yesterday* (33), *Redheads on Parade* (35), *The Littlest Rebel* (35), *Stella Dallas* (37), *Thousands Cheer* (43), *Babes in Bagdad* (52).

## BOLGER, Ray (1904-1987)

This rubber-legged eccentric dancer, singer, actor and comedian appeared in many musicals on stage and screen. Born in Boston, Massachusetts, Raymond Wallace Bolger was already a Broadway musical comedy star when he made his first picture, *The Great Ziegfeld* (36). During his long career he made too few movies, but he will always be remembered as the scarecrow in *The Wizard of Oz* (39).
**Selected Films:** *The Great Ziegfeld* (36), *Rosalie* (37), *The Wizard of Oz* (39), *Sunny* (41), *The Harvey Girls* (46), *Look for the Silver Lining* (49), *Where's Charley?* (52), *Babes in Toyland* (60), *The Daydreamer* (66), *The Runner Stumbles* (79), *That's Dancing* (84).

## BOLOGNA, Joseph (1936- )

Born in Brooklyn, Joe Bologna attended Brown University and served in the Marines before beginning to produce and direct TV commercials in the 1960s. Then, with his wife Renee Taylor, Bologna wrote the sex farce *Lovers and Other Strangers*, which was a hit on Broadway and also successful in the 1969 screen version. In 1971 he co-wrote and starred in the comedy set in Brooklyn *Made for Each Other*. Since then Bologna has had no screenwriting credits but has appeared regularly as an actor in comedies, most of them offbeat in one direction or another; they range from his starring role in the flop *The Big Bus* (76) to a supporting role in the hit *My Favorite Year* (82).
**Selected Films:** *Made for Each Other* (71), *Cops and Robbers* (73), *The Big Bus* (76), *Chapter Two* (79), *My Favorite Year* (82), *Blame It on Rio* (84), *The Woman in Red* (84), *Transylvania 6-5000* (85).

## BOND, Ward (1903-1960)

Born in Denver, Ward Bond was picked off the University of Southern California football team, along with his teammate Marion Morrison, to be in a movie called *Salute* (29), one of the first efforts of John Ford. Ford went on to become one of the great film directors, Morrison went on to become John Wayne, and Bond went on to play supporting roles in a great many movies by John Ford and others. (The three men remained close friends.) Bond was rugged of face and sturdy of frame; his roles ranged from heavies to sympathetic lawmen and sidekicks. Most of his films were Westerns, where his bluff and stolid screen presence worked best; they included the Ford classics *My Darling Clementine* (46), *Fort Apache* (48), *The Searchers* (56), and *Rio Bravo* (59). In his last years Bond finally had a leading role, starring in the popular TV series *Wagon Train*.
**Selected Films:** *The Big Trail* (30), *You Only Live Once* (37), *Gone With the Wind* (39), *The Grapes of Wrath* (40), *Tobacco Road* (41), *They Were Expendable* (45), *My Darling Clementine* (46), *Fort Apache* (48), *Wagonmaster* (50), *The Quiet Man* (52), *The Searchers* (56), *Wings of Eagles* (57), *The Halliday Brand* (57), *Rio Bravo* (59).

*Gary Cooper and Ward Bond in* Sergeant York *(41).*

## BONDI, Beulah (1892-1981)

Chicago-born Bondi spent over two decades in stock and repertory companies before making her Broadway debut in 1925. By the time of her screen debut in *Street Scene* (31), she was nearly fifty and one of the most distinguished actresses of the American stage. Nonetheless, she had a film career that lasted over 30 years, involving a wide variety of mature roles in dozens of films including *Our Town* (40) and *It's a Wonderful Life* (46). She received two Oscar nominations, for her roles in *The Gorgeous Hussy* (36) and *Of Human Hearts* (38). In 1977 she won an Emmy for her role in the TV series *The Waltons*.
**Selected Films:** *Street Scene* (31), *The Invisible Ray* (36), *The Gorgeous Hussy* (36), *Make Way for Tomorrow* (37), *Of Human Hearts* (38), *Mr Smith Goes to Washington* (39), *Our Town* (40), *One Foot in Heaven* (41), *Our Hearts Were Young and Gay* (44), *The Southerner* (45), *It's a Wonderful Life* (46), *The Life of Riley* (49), *Track of the Cat* (54), *Tammy Tell Me True* (61), *Tammy and the Doctor* (63).

## BONHAM-CARTER, Helena (1967- )

A dark-haired English beauty who looks wise beyond her years, Bonham-Carter starred in two popular romantic films of 1986.
**Selected Films:** *Lady Jane* (86), *Room With a View* (86).

## BOONE, Pat (1934- )

Born Charles Boone in Jacksonville, Florida, in the later 1950s Pat Boone became a major pop singer – his clean-cut and soft-spoken image making him a sort of anti-Elvis in the business. Boone's singing success brought him film roles, usually youthful romantic leads in movies like *April Love* (57). But his personality proved too bland for the screen and his work for religious causes finally edged out his show business career.
**Selected Films:** *April Love* (57), *Bernardine* (57), *Journey to the Center of the Earth* (59), *State Fair* (62), *The Greatest Story Ever Told* (65), *The Cross and the Switchblade* (70).

## BOONE, Richard (1916-1981)

Born in Los Angeles, Richard Boone experimented with various jobs, including writing, prizefighting, and the Navy before settling on an acting career. After studying with the Actors' Studio in New York, he made his Broadway debut in 1947 in *Medea*; in 1951 came his first film, *The Halls of Montezuma*. Boone's elusive screen image kept him from being typecast, but perhaps kept him from major stardom as well. He was craggy and commanding, but also articulate and intelligent. Thus Boone mostly played supporting roles, sometimes villains and sometimes tough-but-good sorts, in films including *The Robe* (53), *The Alamo* (60) (as Sam Houston), *Rio Conchos* (64), and *The Kremlin Letter* (70). He made his greatest impression on TV with his starring roles in the series *Medic*, *Have Gun Will Travel*, and *The Richard Boone Show*.
**Selected Films:** *The Halls of Montezuma* (51), *The Desert Fox* (51), *The Robe* (53), *Beneath the Twelve-Mile Reef* (53), *Dragnet* (54), *Man Without a Star* (55), *Away All Boats* (56) *The Alamo* (60), *Rio Conchos* (60), *The War Lord* (65), *Hombre* (67), *The Arrangement* (69), *The Kremlin Letter* (70), *The Shootist* (76), *Winter Kills* (79).

## BOOTH, James (1930- )

Born David Geeves Booth, in Croydon, Booth came to films after considerable stage experience in his native Britain. A flexible actor, he has played both good and bad guys, in both leading and supporting roles, in films British and international.
**Selected Films:** *The Trials of Oscar Wilde* (60), *Zulu* (64), *Robbery* (67), *Revenge* (71), *Airport 77* (77), *The Jazz Singer* (80), *Pray for Death* (85), *Avenging Force* (86).

## BOOTH, Shirley (1907- )

Born Thelma Ford in New York City, Booth began her long and distinguished Broadway career at age 12. She won praise for her starring role in *Come Back, Little Sheba* (50), and made her film debut in the 1952 film version of the play for which she won an Academy Award. In the early 1960s she starred in the popular TV series *Hazel*.
**Selected Films:** *Come Back, Little Sheba* (52), *Main Street to Broadway* (53), *Hot Spell* (58), *The Matchmaker* (59).

## BORG, Veda Ann (1915-1973)

Born in Boston, Borg was a model before making her film debut in *Three Cheers for Love* (36). The blonde actress went on to be a fixture of B-movies for years, usually as a hard-boiled gangster's moll, friend of the female lead, or fallen woman.
**Selected Films:** *Three Cheers for Love* (36), *Alcatraz Island* (37), *The Pittsburgh Kid* (41), *Mildred Pierce* (45), *Forgotten Women* (49), *Guys and Dolls* (55), *The Alamo* (60).

## BORGNINE, Ernest (1917- )

Born Ermes Borgnino in Hamden, Connecticut, Borgnine's broad frame and broad face made him a forceful character actor who was typecast as a villain in films. He spent part of his childhood in Milan, Italy, and joined the United States Navy in 1935, taking up acting after his discharge. He has often returned to Italy to make films. In *From Here to Eternity* (53) he played the evil sadistic sergeant in the army stockade. In *Bad Day at Black Rock* (54) he was a murderer. Then came *Marty* (55), in

Ben Johnson, Warren Oates, William Holden and Ernest Borgnine in The Wild Bunch (69).

which he played the title role as a lonely sensitive Bronx butcher who didn't hope to find love, but did. Borgnine won the Academy Award for Best Actor in the film, as well as the British Film Academy Award, which brought him better roles, both in movies and on television. For a brief time he was married to Ethel Merman.
**Selected Films:** *China Corsair* (51), *From Here to Eternity* (53), *Demetrius and the Gladiators* (54), *Vera Cruz* (54), *Bad Day at Black Rock* (54), *Marty* (55), *The Catered Affair* (56), *The Vikings* (58), *Pay or Die* (60), *Barabbas* (62), *McHale's Navy* (64), *The Flight of the Phoenix* (65), *The Dirty Dozen* (67), *Ice Station Zebra* (68), *The Wild Bunch* (69), *Willard* (71), *The Poseidon Adventure* (72), *Escape from New York* (81).

## BOSLEY, Tom (1927-     )

Born in Chicago, the rotund and agreeable Bosley has worked regularly in film, TV, and stage since the 1960s, mostly in supporting comic roles. Bosley won a Tony for his lead in the Broadway musical *Fiorello!* and was a familiar face on the TV series *The Debbie Reynolds Show* and *Happy Days.*
**Selected Films:** *The Street with No Name* (46), *The World of Henry Orient* (64), *Love with the Proper Stranger* (64), *Divorce American Style* (67), *The Secret War of Harry Frigg* (67), *Gus* (76).

## BOSWORTH, Hobart (1867-1943)

Born in Marietta, Ohio, Bosworth joined the theater as a teenager and made his Broadway debut in 1902. His long film career began in 1909 with *In the Sultan's Power;* he went on to be an all-purpose figure in Hollywood – a leading man for over a decade, thereafter a writer, director or producer (he was all three on *The Sea Wolf* [13]), and finally a character actor in mostly minor films into the 1940s.
**Selected Films:** *In the Sultan's Power* (09), *Oliver Twist* (16), *Vanity Fair* (23), *The Big Parade* (25), *Mammy* (30), *The Crusades* (35), *Sin Town* (42).

## BOTTOMS, Joseph (1954-     )

Born in Santa Barbara, California, the brother of actors Sam and Timothy Bottoms, Joseph acted in community theater before making his onscreen debut in *The Dove* (74). He has since played youthful roles in mostly routine films and on TV, the latter including the miniseries *Holocaust.*
**Selected Films:** *The Dove* (74), *Crime and Passion* (76), *The Black Hole* (79), *Cloud Dancer* (80), *King of the Mountain* (81), *Blind Date* (84).

## BOTTOMS, Timothy (1950-     )

Born in Santa Barbara, California, Timothy is the oldest of the three Bottoms brothers (the others being Sam and Joseph) who all started their film careers as juvenile leads. After much TV work, Timothy starred in two successful 1971 films, Dalton Trumbo's *Johnny Got His Gun* and Peter Bogdanovich's *The Last Picture Show.* After *The Paper Chase* (73) his career largely languished in less notable pictures.
**Selected Films:** *Johnny Got His Gun* (71), *The Last Picture Show* (71), *The Paper Chase* (73), *The Crazy World of Julius Vrooder* (74), *Rollercoaster* (77), *Hurricane* (79), *Invaders from Mars* (86).

## BOURVIL (1917-1970)

Born André Raimbourg on a French farm near Petrot-Vicqumare, Bourvil came to films by way of the music hall. His diminutive figure and long nose appeared in mostly comic roles in many French films beginning with *La Ferme du Pendu* (45). In 1956 he won acclaim for a serious role in *Four Bags Full*.
**Selected Films:** *La Ferme du Pendu* (45), *Mr Peek-A-Boo* (51), *The Three Musketeers* (53), *La Traversée du Paris* (56), *Four Bags Full* (56), *The Longest Day* (62), *The Sucker* (66), *Don't Look Now* (67), *The Red Circle* (70).

## BOW, Clara (1905-1965)

The first female screen stars were Lillian and Dorothy Gish and Mary Pickford – young, meek, uncomplaining and, most of all, childlike. Then came Clara Bow – the most famous flapper of the jazz age. She was the 'It Girl' ('It' meaning sex appeal). And with her red hair, expressive eyes, coquettish ways and on-screen energy, she helped make movies popular in the 1920s. Bow's bobbed hair, bow lips, bangles and beads became the emblem of the emancipated woman. She lived the wild exuberant life of the Roaring Twenties off screen as well as on, and that, in the prudish America of the time, was to prove her downfall. In sordid biographies, readers could read about her alleged sexual appetites, but in the 1920s she had two things going for her: movies without sound tracks and a kewpie-doll sex appeal. Bow was born in Brooklyn, New York, where her father was a sometime waiter at Coney Island and her mother was a mentally unstable semi-invalid. At 16 Bow escaped poverty by winning a fan magazine beauty contest. When the New York film studios didn't pan out for her, she went to Hollywood, where she was nicknamed 'The Brooklyn Bonfire.' As was then common she turned out movies by the score – 14 releases in 1925 alone. She was popular, but *Mantrap* (26), her first smash hit, made her a legendary star. Bow started making big money, though never what she was worth. *It* (27) captured the imagination of her generation and shop girls and waitresses aped her style. *Rough House Rosie* (27), *The Wild Party* (29) and *Dangerous Curves* (29) only increased her popularity. Bow's list of admirers included a rising star – Gary Cooper. In 1928 a national poll declared Clara Bow America's most popular female movie star. But by 1930 she was the focus of scandals involving adultery and gambling. Revelations in court about drink, drugs and men turned the public and the press against her; her sizzling career turned to ashes. Bow married cowboy star Rex Bell in 1931. He later became lieutenant governor of Nevada, but by then she was in and out of rest homes, suffering from chronic insomnia and recurring breakdowns.
**Selected Films:** *Down to the Sea in Ships* (23), *Black Oxen* (24), *Kiss Me Again* (25), *Dancing Mothers* (26), *Mantrap* (26), *It* (27), *Rough House Rosie* (27), *Wings* (27), *Get Your Man* (27), *Ladies of the Mob* (28), *The Fleet's In* (28), *The Wild Party* (29), *Dangerous Curves* (29), *Her Wedding Night* (30), *Call Her Savage* (32), *Hoopla* (33).

## BOWIE, David (1947- )

Bowie was born David Robert Jones in London, England. He began his professional career as a bizarrely-decorated British pop singer, then he went on to give remarkably touching performances in such films as *Just a Gigolo* (78).
**Selected Films:** *The Man Who Fell to Earth* (76), *Just a Gigolo* (78), *The Hunger* (83), *Merry Christmas Mr Lawrence* (83), *Labyrinth* (86).

## BOWMAN, Lee (1910-1979)

Born in Cincinnati, Ohio, Lee Bowman attended the American Academy of Dramatic Arts and began his stage and radio career in the 1930s. He turned to film in 1937, making several movies that year including *I Met Him in Paris* (37). His suave and elegant screen image typed him in light romantic leads through the 1930s and 1940s. Bowman was never a major star, and most of his films were routine. Perhaps his most notable film was *Smash-Up* (47) co-starring Susan Hayward. In the early 1950s Bowman starred in the short-lived TV series *Ellery Queen*. In later life he coached Republican politicians and businessmen, improving their media image.
**Selected Films:** *Three Men in White* (36), *I Met Him In Paris* (37), *Love Affair* (39), *Cover Girl* (44), *Tonight and Every Night* (45), *Smash Up* (47), *Double Barrel Miracle* (55), *Youngblood Hawke* (64).

## BOYD, Stephen (1928-1977)

Born William Millar in Belfast, Northern Ireland, Stephen Boyd began his show-business career as a child, working on stage in Britain, Canada, and the United States – without, however, any notable success. His break into films came in 1955, with the British-made *An Alligator Named Daisy*. A handsome and virile man, Boyd went on to regular film work, which peaked with his memorable performance as the villainous Messala in William Wyler's *Ben Hur* (59). For several years thereafter, Boyd tended to be cast in epics Biblical and otherwise, including *The Fall of the Roman Empire* (64), *Genghis Khan* (64), *Fantastic Voyage* (66), and *The Bible* (66). During the 1970s his career declined to TV movies and cheap European films before he died of a heart attack.
**Selected Films:** *An Alligator Named Daisy* (55), *A Hill in Korea* (56), *The Man Who Never Was* (56), *Island in the Sun* (57), *The Bravados* (58), *Ben Hur* (59), *Imperial Venus* (63), *The Fall of the Roman Empire* (64), *Genghis Khan* (64), *Fantastic Voyage* (66), *The Bible* (66), *The Oscar* (66), *Slaves* (69), *The Man Called Noon* (73), *Kill, Kill, Kill* (74), *Impossible*

*Love* (75), *Left Hand of the Law* (76), *The Devil Has Seven Faces* (77).

## BOYD, William (1895-1972)

Born in poverty in Cambridge, Ohio, Boyd worked at menial jobs until he broke into the movies in *Why Change Your Wife?* (19). He became an unassuming leading man, featured in a number of comedies and swashbuckling adventure films in the silent era, including some for Cecil B De Mille. Boyd's well-modulated voice helped him make the transition to sound films and he continued to star. He was known for his high living, drinking and gambling around Hollywood and his popularity was declining, when he turned everything around in 1935 by signing a six-picture deal to play the cowboy, Hopalong Cassidy, based on the character in the Clarence E Mulford novels. It was a role he would play for the rest of his life. Hoppy, of course, didn't smoke, drink or swear on screen (and, after the first picture, he didn't limp), and hardly ever kissed the heroine. Boyd insisted on minimizing the violence in Cassidy films and the later television programs. Hopalong Cassidy, dressed in black and riding his white horse, Topper, was an enormous hero to millions of youngsters for many years, and Boyd bought the rights to the character. The advent of television killed the B westerns in the 1950s, but Boyd was one star who prospered. He took his role as Hoppy to television and became a hero to a new generation of children. He later sold his William Boyd Enterprises for $8 million – a successful end to a fabulous career.
**Selected Films:** *Why Change Your Wife?* (19), *The Temple of Venus* (23), *Changing Husbands* (24), *The Volga Boatman* (26), *The King of Kings* (27), *Two Arabian Nights* (27), *Skyscraper* (28), *The Leatherneck* (29), *The Benson Murder Case* (30), *The Spoilers* (30), *The Painted Desert* (31), *Lucky Devils* (33), *Port of Lost Dreams* (34), *Hopalong Cassidy* (35), *The Greatest Show on Earth* (52).

## BOYER, Charles (1897-1978)

Boyer was a gentlemanly French romantic actor in international films who first went to Hollywood in 1929, and later gained a reputation as the screen's 'great lover.' American audiences found him exotic, romantic and possessed of Gallic charm. Born in Figeac, France, Boyer made his film and stage debuts in Paris in 1920 and was chiefly a French matinee idol until returning to America in 1934. In the 1930s and 1940s, he played opposite Hollywood's greatest beauties – stars like Ingrid Bergman and Hedy Lamarr. In 1942 he won a special Academy Award for establishing the French Research Foundation. Despite his film triumphs, his personal life was tinged with tragedy. Boyer's only child committed suicide in 1965. In 1978 Boyer also committed suicide after the death of his wife, Patricia Paterson.

*Charles Boyer and Hedy Lamarr in* Algiers *(38).*

**Selected Films:** *L'Homme du Large* (20), *Chantelouve (21), L'Esclave* (23), *La Ronde Infernale* (27), *La Barcarolle d'Amour* (28), *The Magnificent Lie* (31), *Red-Headed Woman* (32), *Caravan* (34), *The Garden of Allah* (36), *Mayerling* (37), *Tovarich* (37), *Conquest* (37), *History Is Made at Night* (37), *Algiers* (38), *Love Affair* (39), *All This and Heaven Too* (40), *Back Street* (41), *Hold Back the Dawn* (41), *Gaslight* (44), *Cluny Brown (46), Arch of Triumph* (48), *The Happy Time* (52), *Fanny* (62), *How to Steal a Million* (66), *Is Paris Burning?* (66), *Barefoot in the Park* (68), *The Madwoman of Chaillot* (69), *Stavisky* (74), *A Matter of Time* (76).

## BOYLE, Peter (1933-     )

Born in Philadelphia, Peter Boyle had a unique background for an actor – he was for a time a monk in the order of the Christian Brothers. Leaving the cloister for more secular endeavors, he came to New York to find stage work off-Broadway, then appeared with Chicago's famed Second City improvisational-comedy troupe. Boyle started in films with *The Virgin President* (68); for most of his ensuing career he has tended to appear in offbeat movies, including *Diary of a Mad Housewife* (70) and *The Candidate* (72). His first big success was as a bigoted redneck in *Joe* (70). Boyle's burly figure and tough features suited that and other working-class parts admirably, but he managed to avoid being typecast – other sorts of parts included the monster in Mel Brooks' *Young Frankenstein* (74) and Senator Joseph McCarthy in the TV movie *Tail Gunner Joe*. Boyle continued his appearances in offbeat films like *Outland* (81).
**Selected Films:** *The Virgin President* (68), *Medium Cool* (69), *Diary of a Mad Housewife* (70), *Joe* (70), *T R Baskin* (71), *The Friends of Eddie Coyle* (72), *The Candidate* (72), *Steelyard Blues* (73), *Slither* (73), *Young Frankenstein* (74), *Taxi Driver* (76), *Superman* (78), *Where the Buffalo Roam* (80), *Outland* (81), *Yellowbeard* (83), *Turk 182* (85).

## BRACKEN, Eddie (1920- )

Born in Queens, New York, Eddie Bracken was a trouper on vaudeville and nightclub circuits by age 10. His film career started with a stint in the *Our Gang* shorts of the 1930s. Beginning with *Too Many Girls* (40), Bracken was a popular juvenile actor in light comedies and musicals of the time including *The Fleet's In* (42).He reached his zenith in two comedies by the brilliant director Preston Sturges – *The Miracle of Morgan's Creek* (43) and *Hail the Conquering Hero* (44). These two films immortalized the cracked voice and anxious bumbling of Bracken. His film career continued through the 1940s with films such as *Hold that Blonde* (45) and *Duffy's Tavern* (45). In the 1950s interest in his broad comedy style declined, and Bracken retired from films to successful stage work. Later efforts included producing and lending his inimitable voice to sound tracks.

**Selected Films:** *Too Many Girls* (40), *Life With Henry* (41), *The Fleet's In* (42), *Happy Go Lucky* (43), *The Miracle of Morgan's Creek* (43), *Hail the Conquering Hero* (44), *Hold That Blonde* (45), *Duffy's Tavern* (45), *The Girl From Jones Beach* (49), *About Face* (52), *A Slight Case of Larceny* (53), *A Summer Sunday* (62), *National Lampoon's Vacation* (83).

## BRADY, Alice (1892-1939)

New York-born Brady began her stage career singing in operettas, later going on to dramatic appearances on Broadway. Her first film roles were romantic leads in silents, beginning with *As Ye Sow* (14). With the coming of sound she played a variety of character roles in both comedies and dramas, often cast as a society matron or housewife. She won the Oscar for best supporting-actress for her performance in *In Old Chicago* (38).

**Selected Films:** *As Ye Sow* (14), *La Bohème* (16), *The Snow Bride* (23), *When Ladies Meet* (33), *The Gay Divorcee* (34), *My Man Godfrey* (36), *Three Smart Girls* (37), *In Old Chicago* (38), *Young Mr Lincoln* (39).

## BRAND, Neville (1921- )

Born in Kewanee, Illinois, Brand spent a decade in the Army and came out of World War II the fourth most-decorated-soldier of the war. His film career began with *D.O.A.* (49). Brand's rough features, burly figure, and aggressive air most often had him cast as a gangster – he played Al Capone in *The George Raft Story* (61).

**Selected Films:** *D.O.A.* (49), *Halls of Montezuma* (51), *Stalag 17* (53), *Riot in Cell Block 11* (54), *The George Raft Story* (61), *Birdman of Alcatraz* (62), *Seven From Heaven* (78), *Without Warning* (80), *Evils of the Night* (85).

## BRANDAUER, Klaus Maria (1945- )

Brandauer was a celebrated leading man in German and Austrian theater before finding equal acclaim onscreen playing complex, troubling title roles in the German films *Mephisto* (81) (which won him the Best Actor award at Cannes) and *Colonel Redl* (85). He has also been featured in English-speaking parts, including the philandering Baron Bror Blixen in *Out of Africa* (85). For that role, Brandauer received a supporting-actor Oscar nomination.

**Selected Films:** *Mephisto* (81), *Never Say Never Again* (83), *Colonel Redl* (85), *Out of Africa* (85), *The Lightship* (86), *Streets of Gold* (86).

## BRANDO, Marlon (1924- )

Brando was born in Omaha, Nebraska, where his father sold cattle feed and his mother was a talented amateur actress. Later, when the family moved to Illinois, 'Bud' Brando became a rebellious and undisciplined boy and his father sent him to military school. When he was expelled, he headed for New York, where he became an acting pupil of Stella Adler at the Actors' Studio. Brando was to become the first American 'Stanislavsky Method' actor to make an impression in films. In 1944 Brando made his Broadway debut in John Van Druten's *I Remember Mama.* Two years later he appeared in *Truckline Cafe* and was voted 'Broadway's Most Promising Actor.' After a couple of more plays, he played the role that would catapult him into stardom – that of Stanley Kowalski in

Tennessee Williams' *A Streetcar Named Desire*. He played the brutal Kowalski with equal brilliance in the movie version in 1951. One of a group of young actors from New York who transformed Hollywood, he emerged as the image of nonconformity and individuality at a time when nonconformity was rare. *On the Waterfront* (54) brought him an Academy Award as Best Actor after three successive nominations. He also received the Cannes Film Festival Prize and his third British Film Academy Award. He had received the British Awards for his roles in *Viva Zapata* (52) and as Mark Antony in *Julius Caesar* (53). In the 1960s Brando's movies were not up to his achievements during the previous decade. A stormy personal life, including three marriages, added to his image as a temperamental artist. Directors found him difficult to work with and his own attempts at producing and directing films via a company he founded led to financial disaster. Brando then made a brilliant comeback as Don Vito Corleone in *The Godfather* (72), winning an Academy Award for Best Actor which he refused to accept. He created a stir in the bold and sexually explicit *Last Tango in Paris* (72), and he was the cruel Commander Kurtz in *Apocalypse Now* (79). Lesser roles in the 1970s still made money and for the most part Brando preferred to spend his time in Tahiti away from stage or film.
**Selected Films:** *The Men* (50), *A Streetcar Named Desire* (51), *Viva Zapata* (52), *Julius Caesar* (53), *The Wild One* (53), *On the Waterfront* (54), *Desirée* (54), *Guys and Dolls* (55), *The Teahouse of the August Moon* (56), *Sayonara* (57), *The Young Lions* (58), *One Eyed Jacks* (60), *Mutiny on the Bounty* (62), *The Ugly American* (63), *The Chase* (66), *Reflections in a Golden Eye* (67), *The Nightcomers* (71), *The Godfather* (72), *Last Tango in Paris* (72), *Superman: The Movie* (78), *Apocalypse Now* (79).

## **BRASSELLE, Keefe** (1923-1981)

Keefe Brasselle was born in Elyria, Ohio, the son of a Hollywood hairdresser. His early life included various efforts in night clubs and vaudeville and a stint in the Air Force. In 1944 he broke into films in *Janie* and, having the looks of a leading man, was groomed for stardom. Instead, Brasselle ended up largely a light leading man in B's and a supporting actor in A's. His most notable appearance was the title role in *The Eddie Cantor Story* (53). After retiring from films in the late 1950s, Brasselle became a CBS television producer under his mentor James Aubrey. The results were several failed series including *The Baileys of Balboa*. Given the boot by TV, Brasselle took his revenge on the industry with two *romans a clef* – *The Cannibals* and *The Barracudas*. In 1977 he made a screen comeback in *If You Don't Stop It You'll Go Blind*.
**Selected Films:** *Janie* (44), *River Gang* (45), *Not Wanted* (48), *A Place in the Sun* (51), *Skirts Ahoy* (52), *The Eddie Cantor Story* (53), *Battle Stations* (56), *West of Suez* (57), *If You Don't Stop It You'll Go Blind* (77).

## **BRAZZI, Rossano** (1916-     )

Born in Bologna, Italy, Brazzi left law studies – after his parents were killed by the Fascists – for work on the stage. His darkly handsome features first appeared on the screen in *Ritorno* (39), and he soon became a favorite romantic lead in Italian cinema. He went to Hollywood after the war, his first role there being in *Little Women* (49). In 1954 he hit his stride as a Hollywood-style Latin lover in *The Barefoot Contessa*. Another memorable romantic part was Emile de Becque in the film of *South Pacific* (58). After nearly two decades commuting between Italy and the United States, Brazzi settled again in his native country, where he appeared in films and occasionally directed them.
**Selected Films:** *Ritorno* (39), *The Story of Tosca* (40), *The Merry Chase* (45), *Little Women* (49), *Flesh and Desire* (53), *The Barefoot Contessa* (54), *Summertime* (55), *Legend of the Lost* (57), *South Pacific* (58), *A Certain Smile* (58), *Dark Purpose* (64), *The Bobo* (67), *Woman Times Seven* (67), *Krakatoa – East of Java* (68), *The Adventurers* (70), *The White Telephone* (76), *The Final Conflict* (81), *Final Justice* (85).

*Vivien Leigh and Marlon Brando in* A Streetcar Named Desire *(51).*

## BREMER, Lucille (1923-        )

MGM picked Bremer born in Amsterdam, New York, out of a Broadway chorus line and groomed her for the studio's star stable. However, after a few films including *Yolanda and the Thief* (45) and *Ziegfeld Follies* (46) in which the attractive redhead danced with Fred Astaire, her career fizzled, and she retired.

**Selected Films:** *Meet Me in St Louis* (44), *Yolanda and the Thief* (45), *Till the Clouds Roll By* (46), *Ziegfeld Follies* (46), *Dark Delusion* (47), *Adventures of Casanova* (48), *Behind Locked Doors* (48).

## BRENDEL, El (1890-1964)

Philadelphia-born Brendel came to films from vaudeville and Broadway. He played mostly comic roles in dozens of movies, his speciality being a phony but amusing Swedish accent. Now and then he occasionally played a lead, among them *Olsen's Big Moment* (33).

**Selected Films:** *You Never Know Women* (26), *Wings* (27), *Sunny Side Up* (29), *Olsen's Big Moment* (33), *If I Had My Way* (40), *The Beautiful Blonde From Bashful Bend* (49), *The She-Creature* (56).

## BRENNAN, Eileen (1935-        )

Born in Los Angeles, Brennan has been a brassy leading lady in various theater and TV roles since the 1960s, often working with Peter Bogdanovich. Brennan appeared with Goldie Hawn in *Private Benjamin* (80) and went on to the TV series based on the film – but the series was cancelled in part because of Brennan's injury in an automobile accident.

**Selected Films:** *Divorce, American Style* (67), *The Last Picture Show* (71), *Daisy Miller* (74), *At Long Last Love* (75), *Murder By Death* (76), *The Cheap Detective* (78), *Private Benjamin* (80), *Clue* (85).

## BRENNAN, Walter (1894-1974)

Although he became well known for his western movie roles, Brennan was born in Swampscott, Massachusetts. Appearing first in vaudeville, he went to Hollywood in 1923 and found work as an extra and a stuntman. From there he moved into supporting roles, beginning to play toothless old men while he was still in his thirties, and he was still a star in his seventies, best remembered as a countrified wit, but he also played villains and city slickers. Brennan was the first actor to win three Academy Awards for Best Supporting Actor. His first Oscar came for his work in *Come and Get It* (36), based on the Edna Ferber book about life in the lumbering country of Wisconsin. The second came for *Kentucky* (38), about rival horse-breeding families in the bluegrass country. The third was for *The Westerner* (40), in which he played Judge Roy Bean. He also starred in four television series, including *The Real McCoys.*

**Selected Films:** *Tearin' Into Trouble* (27), *The Long Long Trail* (29), *King of Jazz* (30), *Law and Order* (32), *Northern Frontier* (35), *Barbary Coast* (35), *Seven Keys to Baldpate* (35), *Come and Get It* (36), *The Adventures of Tom Sawyer* (38), *Kentucky* (38), *Stanley and Livingstone* (39), *The Westerner* (40), *Meet John Doe* (41), *Sergeant York* (41), *To Have and Have Not* (44), *My Darling Clementine* (46), *The Far Country* (54), *Bad Day at Black Rock* (55), *Rio Bravo* (59), *Support Your Local Sheriff* (69), *Smoke in the Wind* (71).

*Gary Cooper and Walter Brennan in* The Westerner *(40).*

## BRENT, Evelyn (1899-1975)

Born Elizabeth Mary Riggs in Tampa, Florida and reared in Brooklyn, Brent played bit parts in film before moving up to leads in 1916. She became a star of the sultry sort in the 1920s, her most notable leads being in Von Sternberg's *Underworld* (27) and *The Last Command* (28). In the sound era her parts declined largely to small roles and B adventure movies. Brent retired in the late 1940s.

**Selected Films:** *The Lure of Heart's Desire* (16), *Raffles the Amateur Cracksman* (17), *Silk Stocking Sal* (24), *Underworld* (27), *The Last Command* (28), *Broadway* (29), *Hopalong Cassidy Returns* (36), *The Seventh Victim* (43), *Stage Struck* (48), *Again, Pioneers* (50).

## BRENT, George (1904-1979)

Brent was born George Brent Nolan in Dublin, Ireland. A stage actor there, he was forced to flee his country because of his political activities during The Troubles. He came to America and continued his acting career in the theater. Hollywood discovered this suave, attractive, romantic leading man with the pencil-thin moustache, and, after years as a tough hero, he was changed into a light leading man who was very effective, especially when he was playing against strong leading ladies such as Bette Davis and Myrna Loy. Brent's film career began with *Under Suspicion* (30), and spanned some 20 years. He appeared opposite some of Hollywood's most famous leading ladies and was married six times. His wives included Ruth Chatterton and Ann Sheridan.

**Selected Films:** *Under Suspicion* (30), *So Big* (32), *Forty-Second Street* (33), *Stamboul Quest* (34), *The Painted Veil* (34), *Front Page Woman* (35), *Jezebel* (38), *The Old Maid* (39), *Dark Victory* (39), *The Rains Came* (39), *The Fighting 69th* (40), *The Great Lie* (41), *The Affairs of Susan* (45), *The Spiral Staircase* (45), *Born Again* (78).

## BRENT, Romney (1902-1976)

Born Romulo Larralde in Saltillo, Mexico, the son of a diplomat, Brent had a multi-faceted show business career: he appeared in numerous major stage productions, directed several, and wrote plays and a musical, *Nymph Errant* with Cole Porter. Meanwhile, Brent appeared as a supporting player in a number of British and American films.

**Selected Films:** *East Meets West* (36), *Dinner at the Ritz* (37), *The Adventures of Don Juan* (48), *Don't Go Near the Water* (57), *The Sign of Zorro* (58).

## BRESSART, Felix (1890-1949)

Bressart, born in Eydtkuhem, East Prussia, had an active film and stage career in his native Germany before fleeing the Nazis in 1933. Arriving in the United States in 1937, he began an even more active life as a supporting character actor and comedian in numerous Hollywood films. In his unique persona he usually played amiable foreigners, most notably with Garbo in *Ninotchka* (39).

**Selected Films:** *Liebe im Kuhstall* (28), *Drei von der Tankstelle* (31), *Der Wahre Jakob* (31), *Swanee River* (39), *Ninotchka* (39), *Ziegfeld Girl* (40), *To Be or Not to Be* (42), *The Thrill of Brazil* (46), *Portrait of Jennie* (48), *One False Step* (49).

## BRIAN, David (1914- )

New York-born Brian Davis was a song and dance man before his name change and stage and film career. His movie debut was in *Flamingo Road* (49) with Joan Crawford. A strong screen presence, he played both second leads and villains in films from the 1950s to the 1970s. Among his TV appearances was his lead in the series *Mr District Attorney* (54-55).

**Selected Films:** *Flamingo Road* (49), *Intruder in the Dust* (49), *The High and the Mighty* (54), *A Pocketful of Miracles* (61), *How the West Was Won* (62), *The Seven Minutes* (71).

## BRIDGES, Beau (1941- )

Beau Bridges was born in Los Angeles, the son of actor Lloyd Bridges. In his youth Beau had a few child roles in films, including *Force of Evil* (48) and *The Red Pony* (49), but was more interested in a career in basketball, at which he excelled in school. However, Bridges' size kept him out of professional sports, and he returned to films in 1961 with *The Explosive Generation* (61). From that point on, his film career slowly gathered momentum. His screen image has most often been all-American, an example being his role as a goodhearted-hick husband to Sally Field in *Norma Rae* (79). Bridges has also appeared in several costume movies such as *Swashbuckler* (76). He has been active in TV, his work including the series *Ensign O'Toole* (62-64) and made-for-TV movies *The President's Mistress* (78), and *The Runner Stumbles* (79).

**Selected Films:** *Force of Evil* (48), *The Red Pony* (49), *The Explosive Generation* (61), *Gaily, Gaily* (69), *The Landlord* (70), *Hammersmith is Out* (72), *The Other Side of the Mountain* (75), *One Summer Love* (76), *Two Minute Warning* (76), *Greased Lightning* (77), *Norma Rae* (79), *Love Child* (82), *Night Crossing* (82), *Heart Like a Wheel* (83).

## BRIDGES, Jeff (1949- )

The son of Lloyd Bridges and younger brother of Beau Bridges, Jeff was born in Los Angeles and, unlike his brother Beau, did not make a serious effort to find another career as an adult. Jeff's adult film debut was in *Halls of Anger* (70). The next year he received an Academy Award nomination for

his role as a troubled youth in Peter Bogdanovich's *The Last Picture Show*. Often typecast as a troubled youth, Bridges has a screen image at once forceful and a bit elusive; thus he is likely to be seen in offbeat films such as the quirky *Cutter's Way* (81). He also starred in the computer-sci-fi Disney film *Tron* (82).
**Selected Films:** *Halls of Anger* (70), *The Last Picture Show* (71), *Fat City* (71), *Bad Company* (72), *The Last American Hero* (73), *Lolly-Madonna XXX* (73), *The Iceman Cometh* (73), *Thunderbolt and Lightfoot* (74), *Rancho de Luxe* (75), *Hearts of the West* (75), *King Kong* (76), *Somebody Killed her Husband* (79), *Winter Kills* (79), *Heaven's Gate* (80), *Cutter's Way* (81), *Tron* (82), *Kiss Me Goodbye* (82), *Jagged Edge* (85), *Eight Million Ways to Die* (86), *The Morning After* (87).

## BRIDGES, Lloyd (1913- )

Lloyd Bridges is one of those perennial leading men whose screen careers never reached the heights but who is nonetheless stamped indelibly on the American consciousness. In his case, the nation habitually pictures him in scuba gear, the result of his starring role in the TV series *Sea Hunt*. Bridges was born in San Leandro, California, and got his first acting experience in stock companies. By the late 1930s he had made it to Broadway and, in 1941, was signed to a movie contract at Columbia. After *Here Comes Mr Jordan* (41), the studio typed the handsome blond actor as a tough leading man and occasional heavy in second features like *The Heat's On* (43). Finally Bridges left the studio and struck out on his own: slowly he began to appear in better pictures, among them *Home of the Brave* (49). It was in *High Noon* (52) that he first found acclaim with his supporting role as a hotheaded but ultimately cowardly deputy who is of little use to Gary Cooper's Sheriff Kane. Bridges was one of the actors who preserved their screen careers by testifying against colleagues during the witch hunts of the 1950s. After his TV success with *Sea Hunt*, Bridges starred in several other series into the 1970s, but none caught the public as well as his skindiving days. He also played character roles in a number of major made-for-TV productions including *Roots* (77) and *Grace Kelly* (82). Not least among his contributions to the industry – along with his wife, actress Dorothy Simpson – are two notable actor sons, Beau and Jeff Bridges.
**Selected Films:** *The Lone Wolf Takes a Chance* (41), *Here Comes Mr Jordan* (41), *The Heat's On* (43), *The Master Race* (44), *Ramrod* (47), *Home of the Brave* (49), *Rocketship XM* (50), *Try and Get Me* (51), *High Noon* (52), *The Tall Texan* (53), *The Rainmaker* (56), *The Goddess* (58), *Around the World Under the Sea* (66), *Running Wild* (73), *Airplane!* (80), *Airplane II* (82).

## BRIMLEY, Wilford ( - )

Utah-born Wilford Brimley arrived in movies rather late but memorably in the 1970s, playing strong character roles in popular films including *The Electric Horseman* (79) and *Absence of Malice* (81). Since then he has co-starred in *The Thing* (82) and played retiree Ben Luckett in *Cocoon* (85). He has recently been seen in the TV series *Our House* (86-7).
**Selected Films:** *The Electric Horseman* (79), *The China Syndrome* (79), *Absence of Malice* (81), *The Thing* (82), *Tender Mercies* (83), *High Road to China* (83), *Country* (84), *Cocoon* (85).

## BRITT, May (1933- )

Maybritt Wilkens, born in Lindingo, Sweden, was discovered by producer Carlo Ponti, who launched her career as a sexy blonde supporting actress in Italian productions. She went on to appear in several big-budget American movies including *The Young Lions* (58), but retired upon marrying Sammy Davis, Jr. After their divorce she returned to film in the 1970s.
**Selected Films:** *Le Infideli* (52), *War and Peace* (56), *The Young Lions* (58), *The Blue Angel* (59), *Murder Inc.* (60), *The Veil* (77).

## BRITTON, Barbara (1919-1980)

Born in Long Beach, California, Barbara Brantingham Czukor went directly from college theatricals to the Hollywood screen. She brought her wholesome beauty to minor pictures in the 1940s and 1950s, then retired to stage and TV work, including the series *Mr and Mrs North*. She also became a spokesperson for Revlon products.
**Selected Films:** *Secrets of the Wastelands* (41), *So Proudly We Hail* (43), *Till We Meet Again* (44), *The Virginian* (46), *I Shot Jesse James* (49), *Bwana Devil* (53), *The Spoilers* (56).

## BRODERICK, Helen (1891-1959)

Born in Philadelphia, Broderick spent most of her career as a comedienne in vaudeville and Broadway musicals. Her wry face and nimble wisecracking appeared in a number of screen comedies in the 1930s. She was the mother of actor Broderick Crawford.
**Selected Films:** *High Speed* (24), *Top Hat* (35), *Swing Time* (36), *The Road to Reno* (38), *No No Nanette* (40), *Stage Door Canteen* (43), *Because of Him* (46).

## BRODERICK, Matthew (1961- )

Matthew Broderick, the son of stage actor James Broderick, is one of the juvenile stars who first appeared in youth-oriented films of the 1980s, most notably as a computer whiz who nearly blows up the world in *War Games* (83).
**Selected Films:** *Max Dugan Returns* (83), *War Games* (84), *Ladyhawke* (85), *1918* (85), *Ferris Bueller's Day Off* (86), *Project X* (87).

*Matthew Broderick and Ally Sheedy in* War Games *(83).*

## BRONSON, Charles (1922- )

Bronson was born Charles Buchinsky in Scooptown, Pennsylvania, the son of a coal miner. He first appeared in *You're in the Navy Now* (51) in a small part. He knocked around Hollywood for years, and this somber-looking, deep-featured character actor kept playing a variety of small roles ranging from Russians to American Indians. Indeed, one of his first important roles was as Vincent Price's assistant in *House of Wax* (53), in which he played a mute and therefore had no lines. For years, B movies were the best he could get, and then suddenly, when he was 50 years old, he zoomed to stardom as an antihero, first in Europe and then in the United States. He is married to actress Jill Ireland.

**Selected Films:** *You're in the Navy Now* (51), *Pat and Mike* (52), *House of Wax* (53), *The Magnificent Seven* (60), *The Great Escape* (63), *The Dirty Dozen* (67), *Death Wish* (74), *Hard Times* (75), *From Ten to Midnight (82)*, *The Evil Men Do* (84), *Murphy's Law* (86), *Act of Vengeance* (86), *Assassination* (87).

*Charles Bronson in* Death Wish *(74).*

## BROOK, Clive (1887-1974)

Born Clifford Brook in London, Clive Brook worked in insurance and journalism and fought in World War I before starting his film career in British silents with *A Debt of Honor* (19). The smoothly handsome Brook was soon a popular leading man of the gentlemanly, stiff-upper-lip sort – though now and then he played a villain, for variety. Brook arrived in Hollywood in 1924 and with the coming of sound became even more popular. His dozens of films ranged from the routine to the first-rate, the latter including leads in two Von Sternberg classics, *Underworld* (27) and *Shanghai Express* (32). He also played Sherlock Holmes in two films. Returning to his native Britain in 1935, Brook more or less wound up his movie career by appearing in, directing, and producing *On Approval* (45). After nearly two decades of occasional stage and TV appearances, he returned briefly to the screen in *The List of Adrian Messenger* (63). He was married to actress Mildred Evelyn; two of their children, Faith and Lyndon Brook, are also screen performers.

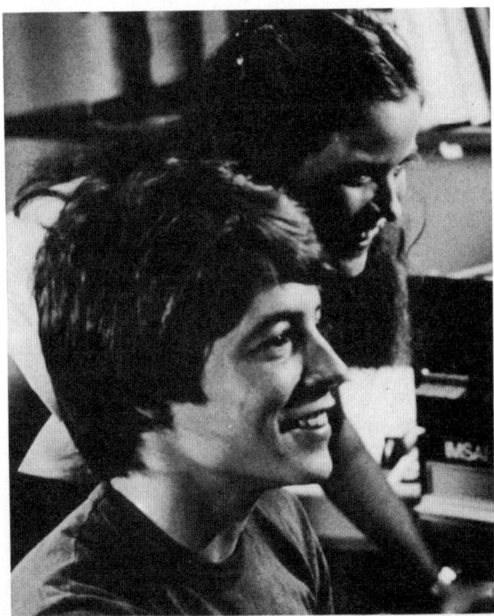

**Selected Films:** *A Debt of Honor* (19), *The Mirage* (24), *Underworld* (27), *The Devil Dancer* (27), *The Four Feathers* (29), *The Return of Sherlock Holmes* (29), *Scandal Sheet* (31), *Sherlock Holmes* (32), *Shanghai Express* (32), *Cavalcade* (33), *For Love of a Queen* (35), *Convoy* (40), *On Approval* (45), *The List of Adrian Messenger* (63).

## BROOKE, Walter (1915-1986)

Brooke was born in New York City and earned his first acting credits in Shakespearean roles, going on to radio and TV.

**Selected Films:** *Executive Suite* (54), *The Graduate* (67), *Lawman* (70), *Damien: Omen II* (78), *North Dallas Forty* (79).

## BROOKS, Louise (1906-1985)

This leading lady of the 1920s was an intelligent woman and a fine actress. Brooks was born in Cherryvale, Kansas, and was primarily a dancer until her film debut in 1925. Her striking good looks and distinctive brunette bob created the image that she was just another bubble-headed flapper, but her performances in *A Girl in Every Port* (28) and *Beggars of Life* (28) proved that she had real acting talent. Brooks went to Germany, where she came into her own, making her best films under the direction of G W Pabst, but upon her return to Hollywood she was unwilling or unable to tolerate life in the movie capital. Eventually she abandoned show business completely, becoming a recluse. In the 1950s she was rediscovered by movie buffs and she began to write critically acclaimed articles on motion pictures, as well as an

interesting autobiography *Lulu in Hollywood*. One critic wrote of her: 'Not one woman exerted more magic, not one had her genius of interpretation.'
**Selected Films:** *The Street of Forgotten Men* (25), *The American Venus* (26), *Love 'Em and Leave 'Em* (27), *A Girl in Every Port* (28), *Beggars of Life* (28), *Pandora's Box* (29), *Diary of a Lost Girl* (30), *It Pays to Advertise* (31), *Overland Stage Raiders* (38).

## BROOKS, Mel (1926- )

A talented comedian, Brooks is most famous as a producer, director and scriptwriter, but he often appears in his own movies. He won an Oscar for his screenplay of the 1968 film, *The Producers*, which was a hilarious Broadway send-up starring Zero Mostel. Gene Wilder, also in the film, was nominated for an Academy Award as Best Supporting Actor. Brooks didn't appear at all in his finest creation, *Young Frankenstein* (75), an homage to old horror movies, which he wrote, produced and co-directed. The movie starred Wilder, again, in the title role. Born Melvin Kaminsky in Brooklyn, New York, Brooks got his start in the 1950s writing television comedy, chiefly for Sid Caesar, the star of *Your Show of Shows*. A standup comedian himself, Brooks appeared in Broadway musicals, then in the 1960s, he created the hilarious and popular television series, *Get Smart!*. He also found time to ad lib with Carl Reiner on two comedy record albums about the 2000 Year Old Man. Brooks specializes in broad, often vulgar, humor and slapstick. He is married to gifted actress Anne Bancroft.
**Selected Films:** *The Twelve Chairs* (70), *Blazing Saddles* (74), *Silent Movie* (76), *High Anxiety* (77), *The History of the World – Part I* (81), *To Be or Not To Be* (83), *Space Balls* (87).

## BROPHY, Edward S (1895-1960)

New York-born Brophy first appeared in films opposite Norma Talmadge in the silent *Yes or No* (20). For the rest of his long career, Brophy was a supporting character actor, variously appearing as crooks, dumb cops, valets, and the like. Near the end of his life he had a notable part as a corrupt politician in *The Last Hurrah* (58).
**Selected Films:** *Free and Easy* (30), *Flesh* (32), *The Thin Man* (34), *Mad Love* (35), *A Slight Case of Murder* (37), *The Falcon in San Francisco* (45), *Wonder Man* (45), *The Last Hurrah* (58).

## BROWN, Bryan (1947- )

Part of the film renaissance in his native Australia, Brown has appeared in several Australian films including *Breaker Morant* (79).He also starred in the made-for-TV films *A Town Like Alice* and *The Thorn Birds*. He is married to actress Rachel Ward.
**Selected Films:** *Breaker Morant* (79), *Newsfront* (79), *Winter of Our Dreams* (81), *Far East* (82), *F/X* (86), *Tai-Pan* (86), *Rebel* (86), *The Good Wife* (87).

*Joe E Brown in* Sally *(30).*

## BROWN, Joe E (1892-1973)

Born in Holgate, Ohio, Joe E Brown was working as a circus acrobat before he was ten. He continued his apprenticeship in show business with minor league baseball, burlesque, and vaudeville before making his Broadway debut in 1918. A decade later he appeared in his first film, *Crooks Can't Win* (28). From the 1930s into the 1940s Brown's inimitable wall-to-wall smile, rubber features, and unsubtle slapstick made him one of the most popular comedians on the screen (few of his low-budget features have worn well, however). Occasionally Brown had supporting roles in more substantial films, including his memorable appearance in Max Reinhardt's *A Midsummer Night's Dream* (35). His later film appearances were sporadic, often involving a more or less special-guest role like Cap'n Andy in *Show Boat* (51), his cameo in *Around the World in Eighty Days* (56), and his randy millionaire in *Some Like it Hot* (59). His autobiography, *Laughter is a Wonderful Thing*, appeared in 1959.
**Selected Films:** *Crooks Can't Win* (28), *Hold Everything* (30), *You Said a Mouthful* (32), *Alibi Ike* (35), *A Midsummer Night's Dream* (35), *Wide Open Faces* (38), *Pin Up Girl* (44), *Show Boat* (51), *Around the World in Eighty Days* (56), *Some Like It Hot* (59), *It's a Mad Mad Mad Mad World* (63), *The Graveside Story* (63).

## BROWN, Johnny Mack (1904-1974)

Johnny Mack Brown, born in Dothan, Alabama, first came to public attention as an all-American halfback for the University of Alabama. After college an actor friend persuaded Brown to pass up pro football offers for a try at Hollywood. Within a couple of years the muscular and ruggedly handsome Brown was a leading man playing opposite Garbo and Mary Pickford. In 1930 he appeared in the title role of King Vidor's *Billy the Kid*. There-

after, Brown was largely typecast in Westerns, his popularity as a cowboy rising as the budgets of his films declined. He appeared in some 200 movies from the 1930s on, most of them routine Westerns for Republic and Monogram, among others. He retired in 1953 but returned to the screen for an occasional nostalgic appearance.
**Selected Films:** *The Bugle Call* (26), *Our Dancing Daughters* (28), *Billy the Kid* (30), *The Last Flight* (31), *Flames* (32), *Belle of the Nineties* (34), *Wells Fargo* (38), *Ride 'Em Cowboy* (41), *Triggerman* (48), *Canyon Ambush* (53), *The Bounty Killer* (65), *Apache Uprising* (66).

## BROWN, Pamela (1917-1975)

Born in London and trained for the stage in her native Britain, Brown played her first lead in *Romeo and Juliet* at 19. After establishing a distinguished reputation in Britain, she made her Broadway debut in 1947. Her film roles were sporadic but memorable, as in her brief appearance as Jane Shore in Olivier's *Richard III*. Brown won an Emmy for her role in the TV movie *Victoria Regina*.
**Selected Films:** *One of Our Aircraft is Missing* (42), *I Know Where I'm Going* (45), *Tales of Hoffman* (51), *Richard III* (56), *Becket* (64), *A Funny Thing Happened on the Way to the Forum* (66), *Lady Caroline Lamb* (72).

## BROWN, Tom (1913- )

Born in New York, Brown came from an early radio and stage career to make his first silent films at 11. In the 1930s his smooth features were most often seen in wholesome juvenile roles such as kid brothers and college students. Brown fought in World War II and in Korea, finally becoming a lieutenant colonel, and meanwhile struggled to maintain his screen career and develop a tougher image. Much of his later work was in television.
**Selected Films:** *The Hoosier Schoolmaster* (24), *Tom Brown of Culver* (32), *Freckles* (35), *Maytime* (37), *Sargeant Madden* (39), *The Quiet Gun* (57), *The Choppers* (61).

## BROWNE, Roscoe Lee (1925- )

Multi-talented black character actor Browne was born in Woodbury, New Jersey, and was a track star, salesman, and teacher before taking up acting. Onscreen he has mostly played supporting roles, often unsympathetic parts. He is also a published poet and fiction writer.
**Selected Films:** *The Connection* (62), *The Comedians* (67), *Topaz* (69), *Cisco Pike* (71), *Superfly Two* (73), *Logan's Run* (76), *Nothing Personal* (80), *Legal Eagles* (86).

## BRUCE, Nigel (1895-1953)

Born in Ensenada, Mexico – while his English parents were on vacation – William Nigel Bruce started his adult life adventurously for one destined to be a second fiddle in movies: he fought in World War I and was seriously wounded. After the war he gravitated to the stage, appearing on both sides of the Atlantic, before making his English film debut in *Red Aces* (29). In 1934 Bruce arrived in Hollywood, where, given his well-upholstered form and inimitable accent, he was usually typecast as a bumbling Englishman of the Colonel Blimp variety, a phlegmatic supporting player in action films; his movies of the earlier 1930s included *Treasure Island* (34) and *The Charge of the Light Brigade* (36). In the later 1930s he found his immortality as the partner of Basil Rathbone in the Sherlock Holmes movies. Bruce became the popular image of Dr Watson, both on film and on radio. In his later career, Bruce appeared in Chaplin's nostalgic *Limelight* (53).
**Selected Films:** *Red Aces* (29), *The Squeaker* (31), *Springtime for Henry* (34), *Coming Out Party* (34), *Treasure Island* (34), *The Scarlet Pimpernel* (35), *The Charge of the Light Brigade* (36), *Kidnapped* (38), *The Hound of the Baskervilles* (39), *Rebecca* (40), *The Bluebird* (40), *Sherlock Holmes and the Voice of Terror* (42), *Sherlock Holmes Faces Death* (44), *House of Fear* (45), *Limelight* (53), *Bwana Devil* (53), *World for Ransom* (54).

## BRUCE, Virginia (1910-1982)

Born Helen Virginia Briggs in Minneapolis, Minnesota, Virginia Bruce went to Los Angeles to attend college but instead found her way into the movies. Working up from bit parts in the late 1920s, the liquid-eyed blonde seemed headed for a top position in the MGM stable of stars. However, she never quite made the turn into major leads,

*Virginia Bruce and John Gilbert in* Downstairs *(32).*

Deborah Kerr and Yul Brynner in The King and I (56).

despite some meaty parts, including the title role in the Monogram film of *Jane Eyre* (34). From 1932 to 1934 Bruce was married to romantic star John Gilbert, in the late 1930s to director J Walter Ruben. By the 1940s her career had settled down mostly to leads in B movies; in the next decade her film career declined. She made a notable final appearance in *Strangers When We Meet* (60).

**Selected Films:** *Woman Trap* (29), *Lilies of the Field* (30), *Hell Divers* (31), *Kongo* (32), *Downstairs* (32), *The Mighty Barnum* (34), *Jane Eyre* (34), *Metropolitan* (35), *The Great Ziegfeld* (36), *Born to Dance* (36), *There Goes My Heart* (38), *Let Freedom Ring* (39), *Pardon My Sarong* (42), *Action in Arabia* (44), *Night Has a Thousand Eyes* (48), *The Reluctant Bride* (52), *Strangers When We Meet* (60).

## BRYNNER, Yul (1915-1985)

This bald-headed international star was born Youl Bryner on Sakhalin, an island east of Siberia and north of Japan, according to legend. But it was also alleged that he was born in Switzerland, and he himself often claimed to be of gypsy blood. He was, however, surely American by adoption. He was a success on Broadway, most notably for his work as the king in *The King and I*, a role he re-created in the film version of the Rodgers and Hammerstein musical in 1956. His baldness and his odd accent made it difficult to cast him in other movies. He was married to actress Virginia Gilmore from 1944 to 1960.

**Selected Films:** *Port of New York* (49), *The King and I* (56), *Anastasia* (56), *The Brothers Karamazov* (58), *The Magnificent Seven* (60), *Taras Bulba* (62), *Invitation to a Gunfighter* (64), *Westworld* (73), *Futureworld* (76).

## BUCHANAN, Edgar (1903-1979)

Born in Humansville, Missouri, William Edgar Buchanan attended college in Oregon and practiced dentistry, before boredom drove him to try a Hollywood career. He broke into films in the late 1930s and from that point went on to appear in about 100 movies from the 1940s into the 1970s. Most of his work was in Westerns, where he was a perennial all-purpose supporting character – variously a heavy, a judge, a sidekick, a crooked sheriff, a grizzled old cuss. Even his villains were not without their charm and often were rather likeable. Most of the productions in which Buchanan appeared were fairly routine Westerns, but he did appear in the classic *Shane* (53). He began TV work in the early 1950s with the *Hopalong Cassidy* series; later he had a long tenure as a co-star in the TV series *Petticoat Junction*.

**Selected Films:** *My Son Is Guilty* (39), *The Richest Man in Town* (41), *The Desperadoes* (42), *Buffalo Bill* (44), *Abilene Town* (46), *The Black Arrow* (48), *The Great Missouri Raid* (51), *Shane* (53), *Day of the Badman* (57), *Cimarron* (61), *McLintock* (63), *The Rounders* (65), *Angel in My Pocket* (69), *Benji* (75).

## BUCHANAN, Jack (1891-1957)

Buchanan, born in Glasgow, was a debonair British entertainer, a memorable song-and-dance man of stage and screen in the 1920s and 1930s. He was good-looking, long-legged and had a nasal voice that delighted his audiences. Buchanan also appeared on Broadway and in several Hollywood films, most notably *The Band Wagon* (53).

**Selected Films:** *Auld Lang Syne* (17), *Bulldog Drummond's Third Round* (25), *Happy Landing* (25), *Monte Carlo* (30), *Yes, Mr Brown* (32), *Brewster's Millions* (33), *The Gang's All Here* (39), *The Band Wagon* (53), *The Diary of Major Thompson* (56).

## BUCHHOLZ, Horst (1932- )

Horst Buchholz was born in Berlin, Germany, and as a child worked in radio and on stage, gradually working up to his film debut in *Marianne de ma Jeunesse* (55). Two years later he made an international reputation with his title role as a charming young confidence man in the German film of Thomas Mann's novel, *The Confessions of Felix Krull* (57). This success soon brought Buchholz to Hollywood; his American film debut was as a determined hanger-on in *The Magnificent Seven* (60). (Americans were apparently undisturbed by his being a cowboy with a slight but unmistakable German accent). The wiry and intense Buchholz went on to be a leading man in international pictures – most of them routine – through the 1970s, his films including *One Two Three* (61), *Marco the Magnificent* (65, in which he played Marco Polo), and *The Great Waltz* (72, as Johann Strauss, Jr). In 1977 Buchholz appeared in the made-for-TV docudrama *Raid on Entebbe*.
**Selected Films:** *Emil and the Detectives* (54), *Himmel Ohne Sterne* (55), *The Confessions of Felix Krull* (57), *Resurrection* (58), *Tiger Bay* (59), *The Magnificent Seven* (60), *One, Two, Three* (61), *Fanny* (61), *Nine Hours to Rama* (63), *That Man in Istanbul* (66), *The Pilot* (79), *Code Name: Emerald* (85).

## BUJOLD, Genevieve (1942- )

For a star of girlish form and no consistently striking screen personality or mannerisms, Genevieve Bujold has nonetheless maintained her place in the limelight for some two decades. She was born to a working-class French Canadian family of Montreal and worked her way through drama school by ushering in a movie house. Her first stage appearance was in a Canadian production of *The Barber of Seville*; for a time she appeared in French-language dramatic roles. Her first film exposure came in her early twenties, in the internationally-produced *The Adolescents* (64). It was during a visit to Europe that Bujold's big break came – she was cast as a one-night-stand of Yves Montand in Alain Resnais' *La guerre est finie* (66). Though her part was not large, Bujold's fragile beauty and kittenish personality were among the most memorable aspects of that film. She next played a supporting role as a gently demented girl in the cult comedy *King of Hearts* (66). With the role of Anne Boleyn in *Ann of the Thousand Days* (70), Bujold emerged as a major star. Having established herself as an actress of great versatility, she went on to film roles ranging from Cassandra in *The Trojan Women* (71), to the adventurous heroines of *Swashbuckler* (76) and *Coma* (78). For several years Bujold was married to the Canadian director Paul Almond, and appeared in several of his movies, including *Isabel* (68). Bujold has kept much of her delicacy of features as she ages, but like all actresses determined to keep working and keep growing, she has experimented with new kinds of roles, like the lonely radio host in *Choose Me* (85).
**Selected Films:** *The Adolescents* (64), *La guerre est finie* (66), *King of Hearts* (66), *The Thief of Paris* (67), *Isabel* (68), *Anne of the Thousand Days* (70), *The Trojan Women* (71), *Journey* (72), *Earthquake* (74), *Obsession* (76), *Swashbuckler* (76), *Another Man, Another Chance* (77), *Coma* (78), *Murder By Decree* (79), *Final Assignment* (80), *Monsignor* (81), *Choose Me* (85).

## BULL, Peter (1912-1984)

Born in London, the portly character actor acted onstage before his screen debut in the later 1930s. In films to the last year of his life, he usually played blustering and aggressive foreign roles, among the most familiar being his arrogant captain in *The African Queen* (51) and his hulking Russian ambassador in *Dr Strangelove* (63). He wrote several books, two of them concerning his passion for collecting Teddy bears.
**Selected Films:** *Sabotage* (37), *Oliver Twist* (48), *The African Queen* (51), *Tom Jones* (63), *Dr Strangelove* (63), *Joseph Andrews* (77), *Yellowbeard* (83).

## BUNNY, John (1863-1915)

Born in New York, Bunny ran away as a child to join a minstrel show. After years of work on the stage, he came to films in 1910 and quickly became

*John Bunny.*

the first and one of the greatest of silent-film comedians. His expansive style and bulbous figure (he weighed over 300 pounds) were seen in over 200 comedy shorts between 1910 and his death in 1915, usually with Flora Finch as his wife and visual foil (she was quite skinny). Now and then Bunny appeared in supporting roles in dramatic films such as *Vanity Fair* (11) and *The Pickwick Papers* (13).
**Selected Films:** *In Neighboring Kingdoms* (10), *Subduing Mrs Nag* (11), *Vanity Fair* (11), *Cure for Pokeritis* (12), *Bunny at the Derby* (12), *The Pickwick Papers* (13), *Bunny's Dilemma* (13), *The Honeymooners* (15), *Bunny in Bunnyland* (15).

## BUONO, Victor (1938-1982)

Buono born in San Diego, California, worked in amateur theatricals and on TV – including a stint on *The Untouchables* – before making his film debut in *What Ever Happened to Baby Jane?* (62); for which he received an Academy Award nomination. He went on to be a familiar character actor in movies and TV of the 1960s and 1970s. One of his few leads was in *The Strangler* (64).
**Selected Films:** *What Ever Happened to Baby Jane?* (62), *The Strangler* (64), *The Greatest Story Ever Told* (65), *Hush . . . Hush Sweet Charlotte* (65), *The Silencers* (66), *Beneath the Planet of the Apes* (69), *The Mad Butcher* (72), *Arnold* (75), *The Evil* (78), *The Man with Bogart's Face* (80).

## BURKE, Billie (1885-1970)

Billie Burke was born Mary William Ethelbert Appleton Burke in Washington, DC, the daughter of a Barnum and Bailey circus clown named Billy Burke, whose name she later adopted. After an education in Britain and France, Billie made her stage debut in London. Her first Broadway appearance was in the 1907 *My Wife*; with that role Burke began a glittering Broadway career as a beautiful romantic lead. Among her admirers were Enrico Caruso, Mark Twain, and producer Florenz Ziegfeld, whom she married in 1914. Burke's screen debut came in *Peggy* (16). She played leads in a number of silents before going back to the stage in 1921. A decade later she picked up her movie career again after Ziegfeld had gone bust. As an inimitably scatterbrained comedienne, Burke graced the screen for nearly three decades, in films including *A Bill of Divorcement* (32), *Dinner at Eight* (33), *Topper* (as Henrietta) (37), *The Wizard of Oz* (39) (as Glinda the Good), and *The Man Who Came to Dinner* (41). In 1936 Burke coached Myrna Loy to play Billie Burke for the film *The Great Ziegfeld*. Burke summed up her long and ebullient stage and film career in two autobiographies, *With a Feather on My Nose* (49) and *With Powder on My Nose* (59).
**Selected Films:** *Peggy* (16), *Eve's Daughter* (18), *The Frisky Mrs Johnson* (21), *A Bill of Divorcement* (32), *Dinner at Eight* (33), *Becky Sharp* (35), *A Feather in Her Hat* (35), *Parnell* (36), *Topper* (37), *Merrily We Live* (38), *The Young in Heart* (38), *The Wizard of Oz* (39), *Topper Returns* (41), *The Man Who Came To Dinner* (41), *Girl Trouble* (42), *Father of the Bride* (50), *The Young Philadelphians* (59), *Pepe* (60).

## BURNETT, Carol (1934- )

Burnett, complete with her overbite, whooping laugh, body English, booming voice and comic talents, is everybody's favorite performer. Born in San Antonio, Texas, she had a sad childhood. Both her parents were alcoholic, and she lived across the hall from them with her grandmother in a one-room apartment. She had ambitions to become a newspaper reporter until she got her first laugh in a high school play and went to UCLA as a drama student, where she appeared in *Annie Get Your Gun*. She went to New York and worked as a hat check girl and performed in industrial shows. After appearing in small revues, she was a hit in a night club show and on television with the song 'I Made a Fool of Myself Over John Foster Dulles.' The song got her on *The Jack Paar Show* and led to a job as a regular on *The Garry Moore Show* in 1959. She went on to star for many years on her own television variety show and to make movies in her spare time, often demonstrating a rare dramatic talent.
**Selected Films:** *Who's Been Sleeping in My Bed?* (63), *Pete 'n Tillie* (72), *The Front Page* (74), *The Four Seasons* (81), *Annie* (82).

## BURNETTE, Smiley (1911-1967)

Born in Summurn, Illinois, Lester Alvin Burnette got into stage and radio work singing with his buddy Gene Autry, and followed Autry into films. From 1934 on Burnette was Autry's comic sidekick in dozens of movies. Burnette also sidekicked Alan Lane, among other cowboy leads, appearing in over 200 Westerns in all, many of them featuring his own songs and singing. After a long retirement from the screen, Burnette appeared as a railroad engineer in the TV series *Petticoat Junction*.
**Selected Films:** *In Old Santa Fe* (34), *The Phantom Empire* (35), *Tumblin' Tumbleweeds* (35), *Under Western Stars* (38), *South of the Border* (39), *Down Mexico Way* (41), *Laramie* (49), *Winning of the West* (53).

## BURNS, George (1896- )

George Burns was born Nathan Birnbaum in New York City and as a child began his career in vaudeville. He was a relatively minor performer until 1925, when he met Gracie Allen, who soon became his wife. As a comedy team, Burns and Allen rose to the top of vaudeville with their inimitable back-and-forth style: she the scatterbrained schemer, he her foil, a dry, ironic smile hovering over the inevitable cigar. After several shorts, Burns and Allen made their feature film debut with *The Big*

*Broadcast* (32), and through the 1930s appeared in a number of mostly unmemorable screen comedies. During the 1940s their film career languished until they began their classic TV series in 1950 which lasted until Gracie retired in 1957. Burns did some solo TV work until Gracie died in 1964 which seemed an appropriate time to wind up his show-business career. Then in 1975 Burns suddenly re-appeared in the role of an old vaudevillian in the film *The Sunshine Boys*, for which he won an Oscar. Two years later he was an oddly satisfying deity in the title role of *Oh God*. In his eighties Burns found himself with one of the more active careers in the business, encompassing reviews, stage, and movies. His own comment on his unprecedented resurrection was typical: 'Retirement at 65 is ridiculous. When I was 65 I still had pimples.'
**Selected Films:** *The Big Broadcast* (32), *International House* (33), *Here Comes Cookie* (35), *A Damsel in Distress* (37), *Honolulu* (39), *The Sunshine Boys* (75), *Oh God* (77), *Sergeant Pepper's Lonely Hearts Club Band* (78), *Two of a Kind* (79), *Oh God Book Three* (83), *Oh God! You Devil* (84).

## BURR, Raymond (1917- )

Given his intense and ominous eyes and hulking figure, it is not surprising that Hollywood for years typed Raymond Burr as a heavy; in the end, though, the public would know him best as a good guy in two long-running TV crime series. Burr was born in New Westminster, British Columbia, and got into show business by way of the theater and radio, during which time he developed his distinctively commanding voice. Moving into films in 1946, he appeared as a villain in a number of films over the next decade, most of them second features including two forgettable simian epics, *Bride of the Gorilla* (51) and *Gorilla at Large* (54). In 1954 came perhaps the best of his film roles, as the harassed husband who murders his wife under the scrutiny of Jimmy Stewart in Hitchcock's *Rear Window*. So shambling and bearlike is Burr in that role that those who know his later heroic image scarcely recognize him; he nonetheless manages to make his character somewhat pitiable. His most famous screen role came in the classic Japanese-made monster picture *Godzilla* (55), in which Burr's sad-eyed and magnetic presence managed single-handedly to raise the film a notch above the routine. The next year he began his eight years of winning cases as lawyer Perry Mason. Then in 1967 he settled his large frame into a wheelchair for a seven-year run as *Ironside*.
**Selected Films:** *Without Reservations* (46), *Code of the West* (47), *Pitfall* (48), *Walk a Crooked Mile* (48), *Love Happy* (49), *A Place in the Sun* (51), *FBI Girl* (51), *Bride of the Gorilla* (51), *Tarzan and the She Devil* (53), *Rear Window* (54), *Gorilla at Large* (54), *Godzilla* (55), *P.J.* (68), *Tomorrow Never Comes* (78), *Out of the Blue* (80), *Godzilla 85* (85).

## BURSTYN, Ellen (1932- )

Ellen Burstyn – the last of her several stage names – was born Edna Gillooly in Detroit, Michigan. She began her career at the age of 18 – she was model Edna Rae, dancer Keri Flynn, unsuccessful actress Erica Dean, and, in 1957, Broadway actress Ellen McRae. She stuck with that name through several years of movie and TV work, including *The Doctors* series in the 1960s. Her first film roles were in 1964, including *Goodbye Charlie*; she went on to appearances in several forgettable films of the late 1960s. While studying at the Actors' Studio, changing her stage name to Ellen Burstyn – and becoming apparently too old for leading roles. However, after a long struggle, she gained success and received an Academy Award nomination for her role in *The Last Picture Show* (71). Nominated again for *The Exorcist* (73), Burstyn finally won an Oscar for her memorable portrayal of a small-time waitress who wanted to be a nightclub singer in *Alice Doesn't Live Here Anymore* (75), a film she produced as well (besides playing the title role, she had packaged the entire production herself). In that same year she won a Tony for her Broadway lead in *Same Time Next Year*; playing the same role in the 1978 screen version of the play, she received another Oscar nomination.
**Selected Films:** *Goodbye Charlie* (64), *Tropic of Cancer* (69), *Alex in Wonderland* (70), *The Last Picture Show* (71), *The King of Marvin Gardens* (72), *The Exorcist* (73), *Harry and Tonto* (74), *Alice Doesn't Live Here Anymore* (75), *Providence* (77), *Same Time Next Year* (78), *Resurrection* (80), *The Ambassador* (84), *Twice in a Lifetime* (85), *Act of Vengeance* (86).

*Raymond Burr in* Rear Window *(54).*

## BURTON, Richard (1925-1984)

Born Richard Jenkins in Pontrhydfen, in South Wales, Burton had a reputation as a fine actor that was primarily based on his stage, not his film, career. He was a son of a coal miner who won a scholarship to Oxford University. He became a leading actor whose dark brooding good looks and magnificent voice did not bring him immediate film success. But Shakespearean roles and the 1960 Broadway musical *Camelot* kept him in the public eye. Stardom came with the movie *Cleopatra* (62), a vehicle for Elizabeth Taylor, with Burton playing Mark Anthony. Burton and Taylor's steamy off-screen romance led to the discarding of spouses and a remarriage to each other. They were hot news and they made big money. They divorced in 1976, only to remarry and redivorce. One of the films that they made together, *Who's Afraid of Virginia Woolf?* (66), was a *tour de force* for both of them, but Burton went on to star in ever-more-inferior films until his death.

**Selected Films:** *The Last Days of Dolwyn* (48), *My Cousin Rachel* (52), *The Robe* (53), *The Rains of Ranchipur* (55), *Alexander the Great* (56), *Sea Wife* (57), *Look Back in Anger* (59), *Ice Palace* (60), *Cleopatra* (62), *The VIPs* (63), *Becket* (64), *The Night of the Iguana* (64), *The Spy Who Came in from the Cold* (65), *Who's Afraid of Virginia Woolf?* (66), *The Taming of the Shrew* (67), *The Comedians* (67), *Anne of the Thousand Days* (70), *Exorcist II: The Heretic* (77), *Equus* (77), *1984* (84).

## BUSCH, Mae (1897-1946)

Born in Melbourne, Australia, Busch grew up in the United States and went in to films in her teens, appearing in many silents, including Erich von Stroheim's *Foolish Wives* (22). Later, her cynical air made her a fine foil for Laurel and Hardy in many of their two-reel comedies.

**Selected Films:** *The Cowboy Socialist* (12), *Foolish Wives* (22), *Married Flirts* (24), *The Unholy Three* (25), *While the City Sleeps* (28), *Come Clean* (31), *Sucker Money* (33), *The Private Life of Oliver the Eighth* (34), *The Bohemian Girl* (36), *Ziegfeld Girl* (40), *Masquerade in Mexico* (46).

## BUSHMAN, Francis X (1883-1966)

Bushman was born in Norfolk, Virginia, and began acting while he was still a child. He was a heavily-built leading actor of the silent era who had once been a sculptor's model. Bushman's strong body and handsome face paved the way to stardom in Hollywood, where he was known as 'the handsomest man in the world.' He started making films in 1912 and moviegoers, particularly female ones, went mad over him. Bushman worked fiendishly, playing romantic roles in scores of films, but when fans discovered that he had secretly married actress Beverly Bayne, they

*Richard Burton with Clint Eastwood, Mary Ure, Ingrid Pitt and Patrick Wymark* – Where Eagles Dare *(69).*

deserted him in droves. His career wasn't over, however, and his most famous role came as the Roman Messala in *Ben Hur* (26). He returned to the stage and later played bit parts in some small films of the 1960s.
**Selected Films:** *The Magic Wand* (12), *One Wonderful Night* (14), *Graustark* (15), *Romeo and Juliet* (15), *Ben Hur* (26), *The Lady in Ermine* (27), *Hollywood Boulevard* (36), *Sabrina* (54), *The Story of Mankind* (57), *The Ghost in the Invisible Bikini* (66).

## BUTTERWORTH, Charles (1896-1946)

Born in South Bend, Indiana, Butterworth passed through careers in law and journalism before gravitating to the stage. Starting in films in 1930, the balding Butterworth tended to play supporting roles as wimpy, sometimes drunken upper-crust bachelors.
**Selected Films:** *The Life of the Party* (30), *Love Me Tonight* (32), *Bulldog Drummond Strikes Back* (34), *Ruggles of Red Gap* (34), *Magnificent Obsession* (35), *The Boys from Syracuse* (40), *Follow the Boys* (44).

## BUTTONS, Red (1918- )

Born Aaron Chwatt in New York, Buttons as a teenager was a singing bellboy (where his uniform gave him his stage name); he went on to be a comedian in vaudeville and the Catskill 'borscht circuit' before arriving on Broadway. After a short-lived 1953 TV show he landed a role in the movie *Sayonara* (57), for which he won a supporting-actor Oscar.
**Selected Films:** *Winged Victory* (44), *Sayonara* (57), *The Longest Day* (62), *They Shoot Horses, Don't They* (69), *The Poseidon Adventure* (72), *When Time Ran Out* (80).

## BYINGTON, Spring (1893-1971)

Byington, born in Colorado Springs, Colorado, turned to films in 1933 after a long stage career. She was to play supporting roles in over 100 movies, appearing as various sorts of high-spirited, usually dizzy, and likeable women – as in *You Can't Take It With You* (38), for which she received an Oscar nomination. Her TV work in the 1950s and 1960s, included *December Bride* and *Laramie*.
**Selected Films:** *Little Women* (33), *Ah Wilderness* (35), *The Adventures of Tom Sawyer* (38), *You Can't Take It With You* (38), *The Devil and Miss Jones* (41), *Rings on Her Fingers* (42), *Heaven Can Wait* (43), *In the Good Old Summertime* (49), *Please Don't Eat the Daisies* (60).

## CAAN, James (1939- )

Born James Cahn in New York City, Caan began his film career in *Irma La Douce* (63), with Jack Lemmon and Shirley MacLaine. He has played sailors, athletes, suburbanites and gangsters in his career, almost always with a smile on his face. Caan gave a memorable performance as Brian Piccolo in the made-for-television movie *Brian's Song* (71), with a sensitive portrayal of the dying professional football player. His riveting performance as the violent Sonny Corleone in *The Godfather* (72) made him one of the hottest properties in Hollywood, although he never has achieved the sort of stardom he seemed destined for. In recent years he has tried to soften the gangster image and has effectively directed a film, *Hide in Plain Sight* (80).
**Selected Films:** *Irma La Douce* (63), *Lady in a Cage* (64), *El Dorado* (67), *The Rain People* (69), *Rabbit Run* (70), *The Godfather* (72), *Cinderella Liberty* (73), *The Gambler* (75), *Funny Lady* (75), *The Killer Elite* (75), *Rollerball* (75), *A Bridge Too Far* (77), *Comes a Horseman* (78), *Thief* (81), *Gardens of Stone* (87).

*James Caan in* The Killer Elite *(75).*

## CABOT, Bruce (1904-1972)

Bruce Cabot was born Etienne Jacques de Bujac in Carlsbad, New Mexico, the grandson of a French diplomat. In his youth he wandered through jobs ranging from cowboy to boxer before he cornered David O Selznick at a Hollywood party and talked the producer into giving him a screen test. It was successful, and Cabot soon made his mark by rescuing Fay Wray from the attentions of a big ape in *King Kong* (33). That role, plus his solid, square-jawed looks, type-cast Cabot in action and adventure films, in which he appeared during the 1930s in leads and supporting roles, as heroes and heavies, in first and second features; these included *Fury* (36), and *Dodge City* (39). After service in the Air Corps during World War II, Cabot re-

turned to acting; his later career included work in several films alongside John Wayne, among them *The Comancheros* (61). By no means a subtle actor or the handsomest man on the screen, Cabot nonetheless maintained an unbroken career of nearly 40 years.
**Selected Films:** *Roadhouse Murder* (32), *King Kong* (33), *Fury* (36), *Dodge City* (39), *Wild Bill Hickok Rides* (42), *Fancy Pants* (50), *The Quiet American* (58), *The Comancheros* (61), *Hatari* (62), *Cat Ballou* (65), *Diamonds are Forever* (71).

## CABOT, Sebastian (1918-1977)

Born in London, Cabot began working on radio, stage, and screen in his native Britain before coming to America. The portly, usually bearded character actor played both sympathetic and villainous roles in films including *Ivanhoe* (52) and *Kismet* (55). During the 1960s he was a popular figure in the TV series *Checkmate* and *A Family Affair*.
**Selected Films:** *Secret Agent* (36), *Dick Barton Strikes Back* (48), *Ivanhoe* (52), *Romeo and Juliet* (54), *Kismet* (55), *The Time Machine* (60), *The Family Jewels* (65).

## CAESAR, Adolph (1934-1986)

For years, American character actor Caesar was a staple member of the Negro Ensemble Company. In 1982 he shot into stage stardom with a stunning performance as the self-hating black sergeant of *A Soldier's Play*. He played the same role in the 1985 screen version, called *A Soldier's Story*, and was nominated for an Oscar.
**Selected Films:** *A Soldier's Story* (85), *The Color Purple* (85), *Club Paradise* (86).

## CAESAR, Sid (1922- )

Few players have fallen as far as did Sid Caesar after his early successes, and still fewer have climbed back from personal disaster with his determination. Born in Yonkers, New York, Caesar appeared in a couple of films of the 1940s. In the early 1950s, after starring in a Broadway review, Caesar joined the young medium of television, and the result was *Your Show of Shows* and its successors, in which Caesar and his writers and costars brought live TV comedy to a level it has never equalled (sketches from these programs were released in 1974 as the feature *Ten From Your Show of Shows*). But by 1952 Caesar was drinking and popping pills at an extraordinary rate and by 1958 was out of TV and virtually out of work. His name brought him a few movie roles in the 1960s and 1970s, most notably in *It's a Mad Mad Mad Mad World* (63). In 1979, he wrote a biography appropriately called *Where Have I Been?*
**Selected Films:** *Tars and Spars* (45), *The Guilt of Janet Ames* (47), *Its a Mad Mad Mad Mad World* (63), *A Guide for the Married Man* (67), *Airport* (75), *Silent Movie* (76), *The Cheap Detective* (78), *History of the World – Part One* (81).

## CAGE, Nicolas (1964- )

Born Nicholas Coppola in Long Beach, California, the nephew of director Francis Coppola, Cage made an engaging screen debut in *Valley Girl* (83). Since then he has been a regular part of the Hollywood 'Brat Pack,' often seen in Coppola films – *Rumble Fish* (83), *Cotton Club* (84), and as Charlie in *Peggy Sue Got Married* (86). Perhaps Cage's most striking role was as the intense Al in *Birdy* (84).
**Selected Films:** *Valley Girl* (83), *Rumble Fish* (83), *Racing with the Moon* (84), *Birdy* (84), *Cotton Club* (84), *The Boy in Blue* (86), *Peggy Sue Got Married* (86), *Raising Arizona* (87), *Moonstruck* (87).

## CAGNEY, James (1899-1986)

Cagney was America's favorite tough guy, a pugnacious little Irish terrier, a whirlwind of energy on screen. Dapper and defiant, Cagney, with his high-pitched rat-a-tat voice and wary eyes, was a Hollywood legend. He was born in New York City, and he attended Columbia University until a lack of money forced him to leave. After working as a waiter and a racker in a pool room, he broke into vaudeville as a female impersonator. He was a chorus boy, did cabaret with his wife, June Vernon, and eventually made it to Broadway. Films followed and in *The Public Enemy* (31), Cagney lit up the screen by shoving a grapefruit into Mae Clark's face. He made a series of cheap, quick, but popular, tough guy pictures, fighting Warner Bros. to receive the salary he deserved. Cagney proved the depth and sensitivity of his talent when he played Bottom in *A Midsummer Night's Dream* (35), receiving critical acclaim. In *Angels with Dirty Faces* (38), he was cast with another fine actor who played gangsters, Humphrey Bogart. Cagney was ready for a career change and so he tried romance, difficult because he wasn't the Hollywood stereotyped leading man – tall, dark and handsome. Witty, with a masterful sense of timing, he turned to comedy. Although these metamorphoses made money, his popularity was ensured when, drawing on his vaudeville and musical comedy background, he played George M Cohan in *Yankee Doodle Dandy* (42). He had been a song-and-dance man from the beginning, and his first film, *Sinner's Holiday* (30), featured him in that role. He was naturally graceful – even as a gangster he had had the lithe grace that was as distinctive as his fast, clipped speech. Even in his many tough guy roles, the dancer side of him was always there. It surfaced again when he was in *Footlight Parade* (33) as a producer of musicals, in which he got to do some dancing. *Yankee Doodle Dandy* brought Cagney an Academy Award as Best Actor. His sister, actress Jean Cagney, appeared with him in this film and others. In the 1950s, although Cagney tried directing, he continued to act, playing Lon Chaney in *Man of a Thousand Faces* (57), and

showing a deft comedy touch in the hilarious *One, Two, Three* (61). Retiring from the screen while still a star in 1961, he received the American Film Institute's Life Achievement Award in a televised ceremony in 1974, and then came back to do *Ragtime* (81). Highly respected until his death, James Cagney was the grand old man of American films.
**Selected Films:** *Sinner's Holiday* (30), *The Public Enemy (31), The Crowd Roars* (32), *Footlight Parade* (33), *Lady Killer* (33), *Here Comes the Navy* (34), *Devil Dogs of the Air* (35), *A Midsummer Night's Dream* (35), *Ceiling Zero* (35), *Angels with Dirty Faces* (38), *The Roaring Twenties* (39), *The Fighting 69th* (40), *Strawberry Blonde* (41), *Yankee Doodle Dandy* (42), *13 Rue Madeleine* (46), *The Time of Your Life* (48), *White Heat* (49), *Come Fill the Cup* (51), *A Lion Is in the Streets* (53), *Love Me or Leave Me* (55), *Mister Roberts* (55), *Man of a Thousand Faces* (57), *Shake Hands with the Devil* (59), *One, Two, Three* (61), *Ragtime* (81).

## CAINE, Michael (1933- )

Caine was born Maurice Micklewhite Jr in London, England, and became a believable hero and light romantic lead, due in part to his unabashed Cockney charm and mild manner. His father was a fish market porter and his mother a cleaning woman. Caine dropped out of school at the age of 15, and appeared in amateur theatrical productions while working as a laborer. Caine saw action in Korea with the Royal Fusiliers. He broke into British television and from there to films, making a good impression in *Zulu* (63), in which he played an upper-class British officer for a change, and *Alfie* (66) for which he received an Oscar nomination. Caine (who had taken his new name because of his liking for the movie *The Caine Mutiny* [54]) has since become one of the hardest-working stars in the movie industry, with six films released in 1986 alone including *Hannah and Her Sisters* for which he won the Academy Award as Best Supporting Actor.
**Selected Films:** *A Hill in Korea* (56), *How to Murder a Rich Uncle* (56), *The Key* (58), *The Wrong Arm of the Law* (62), *Zulu* (63), *The Ipcress File* (65), *Alfie* (66), *The Wrong Box* (66), *Gambit* (66), *Hurry Sundown* (67), *The Magus* (68), *Get Carter* (71), *Sleuth* (73), *The Man Who Would Be King* (76), *The Eagle Has Landed* (76), *A Bridge Too Far* (77), *California Suite* (78), *Dressed to Kill* (80), *Educating Rita* (83), *The Holcroft Covenant* (85), *Sweet Liberty (86), Mona Lisa* (86), *Half Moon Street* (86), *Hannah and Her Sisters* (86).

## CALHERN, Louis (1895-1956)

Born Carl Henry Vogt in New York City, Louis Calhern was to pursue an active career on both

*Stanley Baker and Michael Caine in* Zulu *(64).*

stage and screen for over three decades, though his film work really blossomed only in the later years of his life. He was most often a romantic leading man in silents of the 1920s. Moving easily into talkies, he played leads and supporting roles in films through the 1930s and 1940s, the more notable among them being *Duck Soup* (33), *The Life of Emile Zola* (37), and *The Red Pony* (49). In the 1950s Calhern became a powerful character actor in MGM films, the best of his career, his roles including Buffalo Bill in *Annie Get Your Gun* (50), Oliver Wendell Holmes in *The Magnificent Yankee* (50), and the title role in *Julius Caesar* (53). He died on the job, during the filming of *The Teahouse of the August Moon*. His wives included actresses Ilka Chase and Natalie Schafer.
**Selected Films:** *The Blot* (21), *Blonde Crazy* (31), *Duck Soup* (33), *The Count of Monte Cristo* (34), *The Last Days of Pompeii* (35), *The Life of Emile Zola* (37), *Heaven Can Wait* (43), *Notorious* (46), *The Red Pony* (49), *Annie Get Your Gun* (50), *The Asphalt Jungle* (50), *The Magnificent Yankee* (50), *The Prisoner of Zenda* (52), *Julius Caesar* (53), *The Blackboard Jungle* (55), *High Society* (56).

## CALHOUN, Rory (1922- )

Born Francis Timothy Durgin in Los Angeles, California, Calhoun drifted through various laboring jobs including cowboy and lumberjack before meeting Alan Ladd and beginning a successful film career with *Something for the Boys* (44). In his earliest movie he called himself Frank McCown. A natural for Westerns, in which he was to spend most of his career, Calhoun was handsome in a rugged sort of way, sat on a horse well, had the appropriately stolid acting style, and was entirely likeable onscreen. For some two decades Calhoun was popular in mostly middle-level Westerns. His films, not all Westerns, included *With a Song in My Heart* (52), *How to Marry a Millionaire* (53), and *The Spoilers* (55). In the late 1950s Calhoun starred in the TV series *The Texan*.
**Selected Films:** *Something for the Boys* (44), *Miraculous Journey* (48), *I'd Climb the Highest Mountain* (51), *With a Song in My Heart* (52), *How to Marry a Millionaire* (53), *Treasure of Pancho Villa* (55), *The Spoilers* (55), *Raw Edge* (56), *The Big Caper* (57), *The Colossus of Rhodes* (60), *Apache Uprising* (65), *Finger on the Trigger* (67), *Night of the Lepus* (72), *The Main Event* (79), *The Circle of Crime* (82).

## CALLEIA, Joseph (1897-1975)

Born on Malta, Calleia came to films after an operatic career. He brought his dark and somewhat sinister looks to mostly villainous roles, though they were sometimes tinged with comedy. His appearances included a masked wooer of Mae West in *My Little Chickadee* (40) and Orson Welles' *Touch of Evil* (58).
**Selected Films:** *His Woman* (31), *Algiers* (38), *Golden Boy* (39), *My Little Chickadee* (40), *The Glass Key* (42), *For Whom the Bell Tolls* (43), *Gilda* (46), *Treasure of Pancho Villa* (55), *The Littlest Outlaw* (56), *Touch of Evil* (58), *The Alamo* (60), *Johnny Cool* (63).

## CALVERT, Phyllis (1915- )

Born Phyllis Bickle in London, Calvert began her career on the stage and in the 1940s became a popular film leading lady in her native Britain. She went to Hollywood in 1947 for *Time Out of Mind;* thereafter she played intermittent movie leads and supporting roles, usually sympathetic parts, on both sides of the Atlantic. In the early 1970s she starred in the British TV series *Kate*.
**Selected Films:** *Kipps* (41), *The Man in Grey* (43), *Madonna of the Seven Moons* (44), *Time Out of Mind* (47), *My Own True Love* (48), *Mandy* (52), *Oh, What a Lovely War* (69), *The Walking Stick* (70).

## CALVET, Corinne (1925- )

Paris-born Calvet whose real last name was Dibos started in French films in 1945 and came to America to be a leading lady during the 1950s, her films including *When Willie Comes Marching Home* (50) and *So This Is Paris* (55). Her career slowed down in the 1960s.
**Selected Films:** *La Part de l'Ombre* (45), *Rope of Sand* (49), *When Willie Comes Marching Home* (50), *So This is Paris* (55), *Bluebeard's Ten Honeymoons* (60), *Hemingway's Adventures of a Young Man* (62), *Apache Uprising* (65), *Too Hot to Handle* (76).

## CAMERON, Rod (1910-1983)

Born in Calgary, Alberta, Cameron was a movie stunt man named Nathan Cox before playing leading roles of his own. In the 1940s and 1950s he starred in dozens of B-movie Westerns and action films and appeared frequently on TV, including in the series *State Trooper*.
**Selected Films:** *Christmas in July* (40), *Northwest Mounted Police* (40), *Wake Island* (42), *Gung Ho* (43), *Panhandle* (49), *San Antone* (53), *The Bounty Killer* (65), *The Last Movie* (71), *Evel Knievel* (71), *Jessie's Girls* (76).

## CANDY, John (1950- )

Canadian-born Candy began his career where many comics of his generation did – with the Second City troupes in Chicago and Toronto. His rotund figure turned up in Hollywood films in the late 1970s. After supporting roles in several popular movies including *Stripes* (81) and *Splash* (84), he played a starring role in *Summer Rental* (85).
**Selected Films:** *The Blues Brothers* (80), *Stripes* (81), *National Lampoon's Vacation* (83), *Splash* (84), *Brewster's Millions* (85), *Summer Rental* (85), *Little Shop of Horrors* (86), *Spaceballs* (87).

## CANNON, Dyan (1938- )

Born Samille Friesen in Tacoma, Washington, Cannon acted on TV before making her film debut in the late 1950s. For a decade she was seen often in major roles of trendy films, usually playing sexy and somewhat flaky parts. These include *Bob & Carol & Ted & Alice* (69), *Such Good Friends* (72), and *Heaven Can Wait* (78). At one time married to Cary Grant, Cannon is the mother of his only child. She has also directed.
**Selected Films:** *The Rise and Fall of Legs Diamond* (59), *Bob & Carol & Ted & Alice* (69), *Such Good Friends* (72), *The Last of Sheila* (73), *Revenge of the Pink Panther* (77), *Heaven Can Wait* (78), *Deathtrap* (82).

## CANOVA, Judy (1916-1983)

Best-remembered for her hillbilly humor and strident yodelling, comedienne Judy (Juliet) Canova was born in Jacksonville, Florida, and played in vaudeville and on Broadway. She first appeared in film in Busby Berkeley's *In Caliente* (35). Also successful in radio, she returned to the screen in 1976 for her last film, *Cannonball.*
**Selected Films:** *In Caliente* (35), *Artists and Models* (37), *Joan of Ozark* (42), *Untamed Heiress* (54), *The Adventures of Huckleberry Finn* (60), *Cannonball* (76).

## CANTINFLAS (1911- )

Born Mario Moreno Reyes in Mexico City, Cantinflas prepared for his career in films by performing as a song-and-dance man in tent shows, then moved on to wider popularity as a circus clown and acrobat. He next mastered the art of bullring clown, a demanding profession in which the performer must not only amuse the crowd but distract the bull when the serious bullfighter gets into difficulty, often literally clowning on the brink of disaster. In 1936 he began appearing in Mexican films with *No te engañes Corazón* and clowned through a series of unambitious local comedies which nevertheless made him immensely popular throughout the Spanish-speaking world, where he became known as the Spanish Charlie Chaplin. His Hollywood break came in 1956, when he played Passepartout in Mike Todd's sumptuous *Around the World in 80 Days,* a role which greatly enhanced his reputation. *Pepe* (60), another major production, was made to exploit his rising international star, but failed critically and commercially, proving conclusively, at least as far as Hollywood was concerned, that his popularity in the Spanish world was not translatable.
**Selected Films:** *No Te engañes Corazón* (36), *Romeo and Juliet* (43), *Gran Hotel* (44), *El Mago* (49), *Around the World in 80 Days* (56), *Pepe* (60), *El Ministro y Yo* (76), *El Patrullero 777* (78).

## CANTOR, Eddie (1892-1964)

Born Edward Israel Iskowitz in New York, he was famous for his rolling eyes, volatile movements and unique high-pitched singing voice. Cantor was a star of burlesque, vaudeville, theater, movies and radio, who had begun his show business career as a singing waiter in New York's Coney Island Amusement Park. He starred in the *Ziegfeld Follies,* and two of his Broadway successes, *Kid Boots* and *Whoopee,* were made into films in which he starred in 1926 and 1930, respectively. He went on to become a big Hollywood star in the 1930s. For years he had one of the most popular radio programs, and made a thing about discovering new talent, among them Bobby Breen and Eddie Fisher. He was given a Special Academy Award in 1956 for his 'distinguished service to the film industry.' Married for 48 years to the former Ida Tobias, he had his theme song, 'Ida,' written in her honor.
**Selected Films:** *Kid Boots* (26), *Whoopee* (30), *The Kid from Spain* (32), *Roman Scandals* (33), *Kid Millions* (34), *Strike Me Pink* (35), *Forty Little Mothers* (40), *Show Business* (44), *If You Knew Susie* (48), *The Story of Will Rogers* (52).

## CAPSHAW, Kate (1954- )

Texas-born Capshaw was a schoolteacher before acting on TV (including the soap *The Edge of Night*) and in the theater. In films since the 1980s, she is best-known as the spunky sidekick of Harrison Ford in *Indiana Jones and the Temple of Doom* (84).
**Selected Films:** *Best Defense* (84), *Dreamscape* (84), *Indiana Jones and the Temple of Doom* (84), *Power* (84), *Windy City* (85), *Spacecamp* (86).

*Eddie Cantor and Lyda Roberti*–The Kid from Spain *(32).*

## CAPUCINE (1933-     )

Born Germaine Lefebvre in Toulon, France, Capucine came to America in the late 1950s and translated the lean, classic beauty that had made her one of France's top models into leading roles in several international films.
**Selected Films:** *Song Without End* (60), *North to Alaska* (60), *A Walk on the Wild Side* (62), *The Pink Panther* (63), *What's New Pussycat?* (65), *Satyricon* (69), *Curse of the Pink Panther* (83).

## CARDINALE, Claudia (1936-     )

Originally intended to be Italy's answer to Brigitte Bardot as well as a replacement for Gina Lollobrigida and Sophia Loren, both recently lost to Hollywood, Claudia Cardinale, born in Tunis, burst upon the international scene in 1957 when she won 'the most beautiful Italian girl in Tunisia' contest and attended the Venice Film Festival as part of her prize. If she never quite attained the heights of Bardot at her peak or achieved the popularity of Lollobrigida and Loren, she nevertheless established herself as an international star by the early 1960s. While Bardot's films are really memorable only because she appeared in them, Cardinale – equally a world-class beauty – has lasted far longer and starred in a much better class of films under the distinguished directions of such masters as Luchino Visconti, Federico Fellini, Mauro Bolognini, Luigi Comencini, Sergio Leone, Blake Edwards, and Richard Brooks. She made her film debut with a small role in *Goha* (57), a Tunisian production, and made her first mark in *Big Deal on Madonna Street* (58). A role as the fiancée of the oldest brother in *Rocco and His Brothers* (60) heralded an association with Visconti that lasted through *The Leopard* (63), with Burt Lancaster and Alain Delon; *Sandra* (65), and *Conversation Piece* (76), in which she plays Burt Lancaster's wife. Comencini starred her in *La Ragazza di Bube* (64), and Fellini had her portray herself in *8½* (63) as a stimulus for Marcello Mastroianni's exotic fantasies. Her beauty was essential to the plot of *The Pink Panther* (63) with David Niven and Robert Wagner, and especially so in *The Professionals* (66). She is still much in demand for Italian, American, French and English productions, with a box-office appeal as strong as ever.
**Selected Films:** *Goha* (57), *Big Deal on Madonna Street* (58), *Persons Unknown* (58), *Upstairs and Downstairs* (59), *Rocco and His Brothers* (60), *The Love Makers* (61), *The Leopard* (63), *8½* (63), *The Pink Panther* (63), *La Ragazza di Bube* (64), *Circus World* (64), *The Magnificent Cuckold* (64), *Blindfold* (65), *Sandra* (65), *The Professionals* (66), *The Queens* (67), *Once Upon a Time in the West* (69), *A Fine Pair* (69), *Popsy Pop* (70), *Days of Fury* (73), *Midnight Pleasures* (76), *Conversation Piece* (76), *Escape to Athena* (78), *The Salamander* (80), *Fitzcarraldo* (82), *Next Summer* (86).

## CAREY, Harry (1878-1947)

Although born Henry De Witt Carey II in New York City, his forte turned out to be westerns and action pictures. This leading man of silent screen westerns later became a character actor in quiet dependable roles. Often appearing on the screen as 'Cheyenne Harry,' he became a dependable and reliable actor. Carey did some of his most memorable work in films directed by John Ford.
**Selected Films:** *Ridin' the Trail* (11), *The Outcasts of Poker Flat* (19), *Trader Horn* (30), *Barbary Coast* (35), *Kid Galahad* (37), *Mr Smith Goes to Washington* (39), *The Spoilers* (42), *Duel in the Sun* (46), *Red River* (48).

## CAREY, Harry Jr (1921-     )

This actor, the son of Harry Carey, followed in his father's footsteps and was seen mostly in westerns. But they include some of the classics of the genre.
**Selected Films:** *Rolling Home* (46), *Pursued* (47), *Red River* (48), *So Dear to My Heart* (49), *Rio Grande* (50), *The Long Gray Line* (55), *The Searchers* (56), *Rio Bravo* (59), *The Great Imposter* (61), *Nickelodeon* (76), *The Long Riders* (80), *The Whales of August* (87).

## CAREY, MacDonald (1913-     )

Usually the sympathetic mild-mannered-to-bland leading man in routine romantic productions of the forties and fifties, Edward MacDonald Carey was born in Sioux City, Iowa, and brought radio and stage experience to a Hollywood career which began in 1942, and suffered a four-year hiatus, when he was in the Marines. Since 1965 he has starred in TV's soap opera 'Days of Our Lives.'
**Selected Films:** *Dr Broadway* (42), *Wake Island* (42), *Dream Girl* (47), *My Wife's Best Friend* (52), *Stranger at My Door* (56), *Tammy and the Doctor* (63), *End of the World* (77), *American Gigolo* (80).

## CARIOU, Len (1939-     )

Cariou, born in Winnipeg, Manitoba, made his New York stage debut in the late 1960s and went on to a distinguished career in the theater. He became assistant director of the Tyrone Guthrie Theatre in 1972 and won a Tony for his title role in the innovative musical *Sweeney Todd* (79). His film appearances have been infrequent.
**Selected Films:** *A Little Night Music* (78), *The Four Seasons* (81).

## CARLSON, Richard (1912-1977)

Born in Albert Lea, Minnesota, after several Broadway appearances Carlson made his film debut in *The Young in Heart* (38). He played numerous leading roles in B pictures in the 1940s and supporting roles in major productions through the 1960s.
**Selected Films:** *The Young in Heart* (38), *The Ghost*

*Breakers* (40), *No, No, Nanette* (40), *The Little Foxes* (41), *King Solomon's Mines* (50), *The Creature from the Black Lagoon* (54), *Kid Rodelo* (65), *The Power* (68), *The Valley of Gwangi* (69).

## CARMICHAEL, Hoagy (1899-1981)

Born Hoaglund Howard Carmichael in Bloomington, Indiana, he was a law student at Indiana University before he discovered that he preferred a career in show business. He had played the piano at campus parties and even composed his best-known song there – 'Stardust' – as well as importing jazz musicians to play at dances, among them Bix Biederbecke. He became a song writer and lyricist full time, later winning an Academy Award for the Best Song in a Movie – 'In the Cool, Cool, Cool of the Evening' from *Here Comes the Groom* (51). His relaxed delivery of lines led to a career as a slow-speaking actor in light supporting roles that often involved his singing at the piano. He later was a regular on the *Laramie* television series from 1959 to 1962.
**Selected Films:** *To Have and Have Not* (44), *Canyon Passage* (46), *The Best Years of Our Lives* (46), *Young Man with a Horn* (50), *Belles on Their Toes* (52), *Timberjack* (55).

## CARMICHAEL, Ian (1920- )

This delightful actor, light comedian and leading man was born in Hull, England. Carmichael was educated at Scarborough College and appeared on stage in 1939 as a robot in *RUR*, Karel Capek's play about the future. He also appeared in revues. Carmichael is at his best playing bumbling upper-class fools and his nervous delicacy helped make *Private's Progress* (55) one of the finest comedies of the era. He also starred as Lord Peter Wimsey, the hero of Dorothy L Sayers mystery novels, in a series of television programs shown in Britain and America, and as P G Wodehouse's Bertie Wooster.
**Selected Films:** *Bond Street* (48), *Meet Mr Lucifer* (54), *Storm Over the Nile* (55), *Simon and Laura* (55), *Private's Progress* (55), *Brothers in Law* (57), *Lucky Jim* (57), *I'm All Right, Jack* (59), *Light Up the Sky* (60), *Heavens Above* (63), *Smashing Time* (67), *The Lady Vanishes* (79).

## CARNEY, Art (1918- )

Forever remembered as Ed Norton the sewer worker in Jackie Gleason's TV comedy series *The Honeymooners,* Arthur William Matthew Carney had already put in journeyman time with comic greats such as Fred Allen, Edgar Bergen, and Bert Lahr. Born in Mount Vernon, New York, Carney started as a comedian with a dance band, a career interrupted by World War II; a wound suffered at Omaha Beach left him with a slight limp. On his return he built a reputation on Broadway as a dramatic as well as a comic actor, and gained wide popularity on TV. His Broadway credits include *The Rope Dancers, The Prisoner of Second Avenue,* and *The Odd Couple*, a successful production he left in 1960 for a short stay at a psychiatric hospital. Carney won an Academy Award for his portrayal of a 72-year-old man in *Harry and Tonto* (74), and has earned several Emmys for his TV performances.
**Selected Films:** *Pot O' Gold* (41), *The Yellow Rolls Royce* (64), *A Guide for the Married Man* (67), *Harry and Tonto* (74), *Won Ton Ton, The Dog Who Saved Hollywood* (76), *The Late Show* (77), *Scot Joplin* (77), *Movie Movie* (78), *Steel* (79), *Roadie* (80), *St Helens* (81), *Take This Job and Shove It* (81).

## CARNOVSKY, Morris (1897- )

The son of a St Louis grocer, Carnovsky distinguished himself on Broadway and in the Jewish theater, making his film debut in *The Life of Emile Zola* (37). His many appearances in character roles between 1943 and 1951 ended when he was blacklisted after refusing to testify before the House Un-American Activities Committee.
**Selected Films:** *The Life of Emile Zola* (37), *Tovarich* (37), *Edge of Darkness* (43), *Address Unknown* (44), *Rhapsody in Blue* (45), *Dead Reckoning* (47), *Cyrano de Bergerac* (50), *A View From the Bridge* (62), *The Gambler* (74).

## CAROL, Martine (1922-1967)

Martine (Marie-Louise de Maryse Mourer), born in Biarritz, France, is best-remembered for her seminude scenes and inviting sexuality, as exemplified in Richard Pottier's *Caroline Cherie* (50). She was the French screen's leading sex symbol and box-office attraction in the early fifties, pre-dating Brigitte Bardot. She made her film debut in *Les Inconnus dans la maison* (42), and first starred in *Voyage Surprise* (48).
**Selected Films:** *Les Inconnus dans la maison* (42), *Voyage Surprise* (48), *Caroline Cherie* (50), *Lucrezia Borgia* (52), *The Bed* (53), *Nana* (55), *Lola Montes* (55), *Hell is Empty* (66).

## CARON, Leslie (1931- )

Born in Boulogne, France, this dancer and actress became a star in American musicals thanks to Gene Kelly, who discovered her in the *Ballets des Champs Elysées*. She was the one whom he picked to co-star with him in *An American in Paris* (51) – her first film. Caron scored an enormous personal triumph in the musical *Lili* (53), winning a British Film Academy Award. Later she turned effectively to serious dramatic roles, winning another BFA Award for *The L-Shaped Room* (62).
**Selected Films:** *An American in Paris* (51), *The Story of Three Loves* (53), *Lili* (53), *Daddy Long Legs* (55), *Gigi* (58), *The Doctor's Dilemma* (58), *Fanny* (61), *The L-Shaped Room* (62), *Father Goose* (64), *Is Paris Burning?* (66), *The Man Who Loved Women* (77), *Chanel Solitaire* (81), *Contract* (82).

## CARRADINE, David (1936- )

Son of actor John Carradine and a native of Hollywood, lean, sad-eyed David Carradine, born John Arthur Carradine, made his film debut in 1964. In 1965 he appeared on Broadway in *The Royal Hunt of the Sun*, and the following year played Shane in an unsuccessful TV show of the same name. After a succession of supporting film roles in which he often played a villainous or ruthless character, Carradine achieved international fame as the star of the TV series *Kung Fu*. Leading roles followed, culminating in his portrayal of Woody Guthrie in *Bound for Glory* (76), for which his abilities as a singer and songwriter made him admirably well-suited; and as the male lead opposite Liv Ullmann in Ingmar Bergman's *The Serpent's Egg* (77). He is the half-brother of Keith and Robert Carradine.
**Selected Films:** *Taggart* (64), *Bus Riley's Back in Town* (6 ), *The Violent Ones* (67), *Young Billy Young* (69), *Macho Callahan* (71), *Boxcar Bertha* (72), *Death Race 200* (75), *Bound for Glory* (76), *Cannonball* (76), *The Serpent's Egg* (77), *The Silent Flute* (78), *The Long Riders* (80), *Safari 3000* (82), *The Winged Serpent* (84), *Sweet Revenge* (87).

## CARRADINE, John (1906- )

Born Richmond Reed Carradine in New York City, he started his career doing Shakespearean readings on Hollywood Boulevard in the late 1920s. His tall, gaunt figure and deep, full voice attracted the attention of Cecil B DeMille, who used him as an off-screen voice in some pictures. His first film was a remake of *Tol'able David* (30), and he acted under the name of John Peter Richmond until 1935. Carradine's most notable film role was in *The Grapes of Wrath* (40), and he has appeared in more than 200 movies, many of them horror films, in which he often played a mad doctor. Although he has rarely played a leading role in any horror film, he has probably appeared in more of them than any other actor, and his face, figure and voice are instantly recognizable to fans of the genre. He has also appeared frequently on stage and on television.
**Selected Films:** *Tol'able David* (30), *The Sign of the Cross* (32), *Cleopatra* (34), *Bride of Frankenstein* (35), *The Prisoner of Shark Island* (36), *The Garden of Allah* (36), *Winterset* (36), *Captains Courageous* (36), *Alexander's Ragtime Band* (38), *Jesse James* (39), *Drums Along the Mohawk* (39), *Five Came Back* (39), *Stagecoach* (39), *The Grapes of Wrath* (40), *The Black Swan* (42), *Bluebeard* (44), *House of Frankenstein* (45), *The Egyptian* (54), *The Ten Commandments* (56), *The Last Hurrah* (58), *The Man Who Shot Liberty Valance* (62), *Cheyenne Autumn* (64), *Billy the Kid Versus Dracula* (66), *Bigfoot* (69), *The Seven Minutes* (71), *Won Ton Ton The Dog Who Saved Hollywood* (75), *The Shootist* (76), *The Howling* (82), *The House of Long Shadows* (83), *Peggy Sue Got Married* (86).

*John Carradine with Louise Platt* – Stagecoach *(39).*

## CARRADINE, Keith (1950- )

Half-brother of David, brother of Robert and son of John Carradine, and born in San Mateo, California, Keith Carradine began his career in *A Gunfight* (70). This led to leading roles in the 1970s notably in *Nashville* (75), in which his songwriting and singing ability earned him an Academy Award for the song 'I'm Easy.'
**Selected Films:** *A Gunfight* (70), *McCabe and Mrs Miller* (71), *Nashville* (75), *Welcome to LA* (77), *Pretty Baby* (77), *The Duellists* (77), *The Long Riders* (80), *Southern Comfort* (81), *Backfire* (87).

## CARRILLO, Leo (1880-1961)

Born in Los Angeles, a Spanish Californian of wealthy landowning ancestry, Carrillo was one of Hollywood's busiest character actors of the 1930s and 1940s, usually portraying an amiable Latin, speaking comically fractured English. After retiring from the screen, he immortalized himself on TV as Pancho, the sidekick in *The Cisco Kid*.
**Selected Films:** *Mr Antonio* (29), *Viva Villa!* (34), *Manhattan Melodrama* (35), *The Gay Desperado* (36), *History is Made at Night* (37), *Phantom of the Opera* (43), *Pancho Villa Returns* (50).

## CARROLL, John (1906-1979)

Born Julian La Faye in New Orleans, Carroll was blessed with a good singing voice, but not too much personality. He made his film debut in *Marianne* (29) and was playing leads for RKO by 1935. He was a leading man in many light MGM productions of the early 1940s.
**Selected Films:** *Marianne* (29), *Devil-May-Care* (29), *Hi, Gaucho!* (35), *Rose of the Rio Grande* (38), *Rio Rita* (42), *Plunderers of Painted Flats* (59).

*Gary Cooper, Akim Tamiroff, Madeleine Carroll* – The General Died at Dawn (36).

## CARROLL, Leo G (1892-1972)

Best-remembered for his heavy-browed expression and impeccable diction, Carroll was born in Weedon, England, of Irish parents and made his debut as an actor in 1911. The next year he made his debuts on both the London and New York stages, and for many years commuted between Broadway and London. His Hollywood career began in 1934 with *What Every Woman Knows*. Once based in Hollywood he distinguished himself in numerous character roles in American films (but continued to perform on stage and in occasional British films), often as a doctor, judge, or teacher, and frequently as an extremely shy and timid Englishman. American audiences will particularly remember his portrayal of Cosmo Topper in the TV series *Topper*; and of Mr Waverly in TV series *The Man from U.N.C.L.E.*

**Selected Films:** *What Every Woman Knows* (34), *Sadie McKee* (34), *Outcast Lady* (34), *Stamboul Quest* (34), *The Barretts of Wimpole Street* (34), *Clive of India* (35), *London by Night* (37), *A Christmas Carol* (38), *Wuthering Heights* (39), *Rebecca* (40), *Scotland Yard* (41), *The House on 92nd Street* (45), *Spellbound* (45), *Forever Amber* (47), *Strangers on a Train* (51), *North by Northwest* (59), *The Prize* (63), *One Spy Too Many* (66), *From Nashville With Music* (69).

## CARROLL, Madeleine (1906- )

One of the first of the English leading ladies to make a career in Hollywood, blonde, ladylike Carroll (born Marie-Madeleine Bernadette O'Carroll, in West Bromwich, England), had the beauty, fragility, and air of well-bred bravery to make her the perfect storybook heroine. She taught French and modeled hats briefly before making her West End stage debut in 1927, and first appeared in films the following year in *The Guns of Loos*. More film and stage offers followed (she acted on the Engish stage until 1935), and by the early 1930s she was established as the biggest female star in British films. Her first Hollywood production, John Ford's *The World Moves On* (34) was a flop, but her cinematic career was secured when Alfred Hitchcock used her brilliantly in *The 39 Steps* (35) and *The Secret Agent* (36). She is still remembered as the first of his 'blondes,' and the sleek persona she displayed in his films was developed to advantage in Hollywood. She was married to actor Sterling Hayden.

**Selected Films:** *The Guns of Loos* (28), *Young Woodley* (30), *I Was a Spy* (33), *The World Moves On* (34), *The 39 Steps* (35), *The General Died at Dawn* (36), *The Secret Agent* (36), *The Prisoner of Zenda* (37), *My Favorite Blonde* (42), *The Fan* (49).

## CARROLL, Nancy (1905-1965)

Warmly remembered for her flowing red hair and cupid-bow mouth, the vivacious Carroll (born Ann LaHiff in New York City) moved from Broadway musicals to the screen in *Ladies Must Dress* (27). She became an immensely popular leading lady of early talkies, starring in musicals and light comedies throughout the 1930s.
**Selected Films:** *Ladies Must Dress* (27), *Abie's Irish Rose* (28), *The Shopworn Angel* (29), *Laughter* (30), *There Goes My Heart* (38).

## CARSON, Jack (1910-1963)

Carson played scores of memorable supporting roles ranging from nagging fools in comedies and musicals to cowardly bullies in Westerns, and was often the con artist who proved dumber than the mark he was trying to take. Born John Elmer Carson in Carmen, Manitoba, the beefy Canadian moved from vaudeville to the screen in 1937, making his film debut in *You Only Live Once*. His weight gave a pathetic quality to his characterizations of bullies and buffoons, and the amazing flexibility of his facial expressions was famous throughout the industry. Carson appeared in a series of Doris Day musicals in the 1940s and his TV appearances included *Three Men On A Horse* One of his four wives was the actress Lola Albright.
**Selected Films:** *You Only Live Once* (37), *Stage Door* (37), *Too Many Wives* (37), *The Toast of New York* (37), *The Saint in New York* (37), *Crashing Hollywood* (38), *The Law of the Underworld* (38), *Maid's Night Out* (38), *The Kid From Texas* (38), *Mr Smith Goes to Washington* (39), *The Strawberry Blonde* (41), *Make Your Own Bed* (44), *Roughly Speaking* (45), *Mildred Pierce* (45), *April Showers* (48), *Red Garters* (54), *A Star is Born* (54), *Cat on a Hot Tin Roof* (58), *King of the Roaring Twenties* (61).

## CARUSO, Anthony (c. 1915- )

Cast as a mobster in his first film, *Johnny Apollo* (40), which starred Tyrone Power, American-born Caruso has been busy in Hollywood ever since playing Italian gangsters and unsavory, unpleasant or menacing Mexicans, Latins and Arabs.
**Selected Films:** *Johnny Apollo* (40), *Sunday Punch* (42), *Wild Harvest* (47), *Bride of Vengeance* (49), *The Asphalt Jungle* (50), *The Iron Mistress* (52), *Baby Face Nelson* (57), *Young Dillinger* (65), *Mean Johnny Barrows* (76).

## CASSAVETES, John (1929- )

Cassavetes was born in New York City, and this slight, intense, gifted actor played a wide variety of parts before he became an experimental director of interesting and controversial films, often starring his wife, Gena Rowlands. As an actor he started in gritty, low-budget melodramas, and delivered impressive performances in *Edge of the City* (57) and *Rosemary's Baby* (68).
**Selected Films:** *Taxi* (54), *The Night Holds Terror* (55), *Crime in the Streets* (56), *Edge of the City* (57), *The Killers* (64), *The Dirty Dozen* (67), *Rosemary's Baby* (68), *Capone* (75), *Brass Target* (78), *Whose Life Is It Anyway?* (81), *Tempest* (82), *Marvin and Tige* (83).

## CASSEL, Jean-Pierre (1932- )

Paris-born Cassel (Jean-Pierre Crochon), played minor French stage and TV roles until 1956, when he was discovered by Gene Kelly while on location in Paris. He soon established himself as a leading man in comedies and romantic farces in French and international films.
**Selected Films:** *Les Jeux de L'Amour* (60), *Candide* (60), *Seven Capital Sins* (62), *Those Magnificent Men in Their Flying Machines* (65), *Is Paris Burning?* (66), *The Discreet Charm of the Bourgeoisie* (72), *The Three Musketeers* (74), *Murder On the Orient Express* (74).

## CATLETT, Walter (1889-1960)

Experience as a stage and vaudeville comedian prepared Catlett, who entered films in the mid-twenties, for innumerable supporting roles as a flustered, inept, scatterbrained crook or minor official, usually comical and often bespectacled.
**Selected Films:** *Second Youth* (24), *Rain* (32), *Mr Deeds Goes to Town* (36), *Bringing Up Baby* (38), *It Started with Eve* (41), *Ghost Catchers* (44), *Look for the Silver Lining* (49), *Friendly Persuasion* (56).

*John Cassavetes, Mia Farrow* – Rosemary's Baby *(68).*

## CAULFIELD, Joan (1922- )

Former model Beatrice Joan Caulfield, from Orange, New Jersey, played ingenues on Broadway before breaking into films in the mid-1940s as a demure leading lady. She retired from the screen in 1950, but has since appeared in occasional films and on TV more often.
**Selected Films:** *Duffy's Tavern* (45), *Monsieur Beaucaire* (46), *Blue Skies* (46), *Dear Ruth* (47), *The Petty Girl* (50), *The Rains of Ranchipur* (55), *Red Tomahawk* (67), *Pony Express Rider* (76).

## CHAKIRIS, George (1933- )

A dancer and singer from Norwood, Ohio, Chakiris made his debut singing in the chorus of *Song of Love* (47), danced in *Brigadoon* (54), and debuted as a dramatic actor in *Under Fire* (57). His portrayal of Bernardo in *West Side Story* (61) earned him an Academy Award for best supporting actor.
**Selected Films:** *Song of Love* (47), *Brigadoon* (54), *Under Fire* (57), *West Side Story* (61), *Diamond Head* (63), *Is Paris Burning?* (66), *The Big Cube* (69), *Why Not Stay for Breakfast?* (80).

## CHAMBERLAIN, Richard (1935- )

A native of Beverly Hills, California, educated at Pomona College, George Richard Chamberlain made his film debut in *The Secret of the Purple Reef* (60), but established himself as a star of great popularity in the title role of the long-playing TV series *Dr Kildare*. The great success of this show proved both a blessing and a curse to the blond, boyish-looking, almost too-pretty Chamberlain, providing him with an image that has been hard to shake, but at the same time enabling him to establish himself as a serious international performer. He has tackled 'Hamlet' and other ambitious roles on the British stage, and has shown himself to advantage as Tchaikovsky in *The Music Lovers* (70) and as Byron in *Lady Caroline Lamb* (72). Notable TV appearances include leading roles in the mini-series *Shogun* and *The Thorn Birds*.
**Selected Films:** *The Secret of the Purple Reef* (60), *A Thunder of Drums* (62), *Twilight of Honor* (63), *Petulia* (68), *The Madwoman of Chaillot* (69), *The Music Lovers* (70), *Julius Caesar* (70), *Lady Caroline Lamb* (72), *The Three Musketeers* (74), *The Towering Inferno* (75), *The Slipper and the Rose* (76), *The Last Wave* (78), *Swarm* (78), *Murder by Phone* (82), *King Solomon's Mines* (86).

## CHAMPION, Marge (1923- ) and Gower (1921-1980)

Gower Champion was born in Geneva, Illinois and Marge Belcher was born in Los Angeles, California. While in her teens she posed for the figure of Snow White for the Disney studios. In the late 1940s they married and formed a dance act – billing themselves as Gower and Jean (Campion) – and played in supper clubs all over the country. They appeared together in Hollywood musicals in the early 1950s, most notably *Show Boat* (51). After their divorce, Gower went on to become a skillful director of both films and Broadway musicals, and Marge became a character actress.
**Selected Films:** *The Story of Vernon and Irene Castle* (39, Marge only), *Till the Clouds Roll By* (46, Gower only), *Mr Music* (50), *Show Boat* (51), *Lovely to Look At* (52), *Give a Girl a Break* (53), *Jupiter's Darling* (55), *Three for the Show* (55), *The Swimmer* (67, Marge only), *The Party* (68, Marge only).

## CHANDLER, Jeff (1918-1961)

Although he made his screen debut as a gangstger in *Johnny O'Clock* (47), the prematurely gray-haired Chandler (born Ira Grossel in Brooklyn) found a more fitting home for his growling voice and rugged good looks as the great Apache chief Cochise in three films, *Broken Arrow* (50), *Battle at Apache Pass* (52) and, briefly, in *Taza, Son of Cochise* (54). Especially as Cochise in *Broken Arrow*, for which he received an Academy Award nomination, Chandler was almost always the classic hero – naive, strong, honest, noble; he invested the most tenuous of his exotic films with a simple earnestness. Starting his screen career after work in radio dramas following service in World War II, he was a particular favorite with female audiences, despite a heavy concentration of roles in macho Westerns and action productions, portrayals of Indians and other exotics with few romantic leads. His early death from blood poisoning at the age of 42 left many with the feeling that his promise as an actor had yet to be fulfilled.
**Selected Films:** *Johnny O'Clock* (47), *Roses are Red* (47), *Mr Belvedere Goes to College* (49), *Two Flags West* (50), *Broken Arrow* (50), *Iron Man* (51), *Battle of Apache Pass* (52), *The Great Sioux Uprising* (53), *Taza, Son of Cochise* (54), *Away All Boats* (56), *Jeanne Eagles* (57), *The Plunderers* (60), *Merrill's Marauders* (61).

## CHANEY, Lon (1883-1930)

Chaney was born Alonzo Chaney and was called 'The Man of a Thousand Faces.' Director Tod Browning praised him by saying 'He was the hardest working person in the studio.' Certainly few actors have suffered as much physically for their craft as did Chaney. He had his arms strapped tightly to his body to play the part of an armless knife thrower. In order to look like a vampire he wore a set of false teeth so enormous that he was in constant pain, and placed metal rings inside his eyelids to give himself a staring look. Chaney was born in Colorado Springs, Colorado, of deaf-mute parents, and his efforts to communicate with them were probably the reason that he became so skilled as a pantomimist in the silent film era. He started in the theater early because his brother owned

*Lon Chaney as* The Phantom of the Opera *(25), with Mary Philbin.*

one. For years he toured as a comic song-and-dance man before trying to make it in the new movie industry, but success was not immediate. Chaney played scores of minor parts, usually cast as the villain. His first major success came with *The Miracle Man* (19), in which he played a bogus cripple. After that he played a long series of grotesque characters mixed in with a few straight parts. His makeup artistry was so inventive that he often played two parts in one film. It was this skill that gave rise to the joke, 'Don't step on that spider, it might be Lon Chaney.' His greatest suc cess was in the title role in *The Hunchback of Notre Dame* (24), but the film he is most remembered for is *The Phantom of the Opera* (25). There were several changes of directors during the filming of that movie and, as as result, parts of it really don't make sense – yet it is one of the two or three horror classics of the silent era and Chaney's phantom makeup is instantly recognizable. It is hard to evaluate Chaney as an actor under all that makeup, for the prints of many of his non-horror films have been lost, but Victor Sjöström, a great Swedish director of the silent era, called him 'without question one of the most marvelous actors in the history of stage or screen.' Chaney died of throat cancer after completing his first talkie, *The Unholy Three* (30), just before he was to take on the role of Dracula.

**Selected Films:** *Where the Forest Ends* (14), *That Devil Bateese* (18), *The Kaiser, Beast of Berlin* (18), *The Miracle Man* (19), *Treasure Island* (20), *The Penalty* (21), *A Blind Bargain* (22), *The Hunchback of Notre Dame* (24), *He Who Gets Slapped* (24), *The Phantom of the Opera* (25), *The Unholy Three* (25), *The Black Bird* (26), *The Road to Mandalay* (26), *Tell It to the Marines* (26), *London after Midnight* (27), *West of Zanzibar* (28), *Where East Is East* (29), *The Unholy Three* (30).

## CHANEY, Lon Jr (1905-1973)

Born Creighton Chaney, this massive character actor usually played his father's type of role in progressively inferior films, although he was outstanding as the idiot Lennie in *Of Mice and Men* (39) and as the arthritic coward in *High Noon* (52).

His most notable horror film characterization was that of *The Wolf Man* (41), and he also took his turn playing the Frankenstein monster, the Mummy, and even Dracula.
**Selected Films:** *Bird of Paradise* (32), *Jesse James* (39), *Of Mice and Men* (39), *One Million BC* (40), *Man-Made Monster* (41), *The Wolf Man* (41), *The Ghost of Frankenstein* (42), *The Mummy's Tomb* (42), *Son of Dracula* (43), *Abbot and Costello Meet Frankenstein* (48), *High Noon* (52), *A Lion Is in the Streets* (53), *The Defiant Ones* (58), *Buckskin* (68), *Blood of Frankenstein* (70).

## CHANNING, Stockard (1944- )

New York-born Channing began acting in college; after stage work, she made her way into TV and then film bits before starring in *The Fortune* (75). However, that did not lead to screen stardom. Channing's roles have remained occasional, probably the best-known being the high school kid in *Grease* (78) which she played as best she could in her mid-thirties. She has starred in several short-running TV series including the *Stockard Channing Show* and in 1985 won a Tony for her Broadway performance in *Joe Egg*.
**Selected Films:** *The Hospital* (71), *The Fortune* (75), *The Big Bus* (76), *Grease* (78), *The Fish that Saved Pittsburgh* (79), *Without a Trace* (83), *The Men's Club* (86), *Heartburn* (86).

## CHAPLIN, Charles (1889-1977)

Sir Charles Spencer Chaplin was a legendary figure in his own lifetime despite a comparatively limited output. He was a great artist whose character 'Charlie the Tramp' was a superb blend of pathos and humor. The tramp became the little man that everyone could identify with and love. Born in London to a family of music hall entertainers, Chaplin's childhood was Dickensian in its poverty and tragedy. At 17 he joined the Fred Karno Company and toured Britain. Arriving in America with the troupe in 1912, Chaplin started making movies for Mack Sennett in 1913, churning out 35 in his first year, evolving the tramp character as he went along. A funny walk, a bowler hat, a pair of baggy pants, a silly moustache and a cane became his trademarks. He left Sennett and the Keystone Company to make movies for both Essanay and Mutual – all of them two-reelers. Searching for ways to increase his artistic freedom and gain control of the profits from his films, he helped form United Artists (with Mary Pickford, Douglas Fairbanks and D W Griffith) in 1919. By then Chaplin was an international movie star whose *The Kid* (20) was an enormous box office smash. Conservatives attacked Chaplin for not fighting in World War I, for his left-wing politics, for his refusal to become an American citizen and for his fondness for teen-age girls. A bitter divorce case involving Chaplin and his second wife, Lolita MacMurray (whose stage name was Lita Grey), the mother of his sons, Charles Chaplin Jr and Sidney Chaplin, and a paternity suit inflamed his critics. Essentially a balletic mime, he resisted sound as long as he could. *City Lights* (31), with a score composed and conducted by Chaplin, and *Modern Times* (36), with his third wife Paulette Goddard, are basically silent movies. Though there are great moments in Chaplins's later films, the use of sound reveals the flaws, chiefly his tendency to become excessively sentimental. *A Countess from Hong Kong* (66), directed by Chaplin, appeared dated upon release. In 1943 Chaplin married playwright Eugene O'Neill's young daughter, Oona. The marriage was a happy one and the couple had eight children, including the actress Geraldine Chaplin. The family moved to Switzerland during the Red-baiting McCarthy era, but in 1971 Chaplin returned to the United States in triumph to receive a special Academy Award. His first Academy Award had been for *The Circus* (28). A British subject until his death, he was knighted in 1975.
**Selected Films:** *Kid Auto Races at Venice* (13), *Making a Living* (14), *Tillie's Punctured Romance* (14), *The Tramp* (15), *The Adventurer* (16), *The Cure* (16), *The Immigrant* (17), *Shoulder Arms* (18), *The Kid* (20), *The Gold Rush* (24), *The Circus* (28), *City Lights* (31), *Modern Times* (36), *The Great Dictator* (40), *Monsieur Verdoux* (47), *Limelight* (52), *A King in New York* (57), *A Countess from Hong Kong* (66).

*Charlie Chaplin in* Shoulder Arms *(18).*

## CHAPLIN, Geraldine (1944- )

Daughter of Sir Charles Chaplin and first of his children by his fourth wife Oona O'Neill (daughter of playwright Eugene O'Neill), Geraldine Chaplin made her screen debut at the age of 8 in her father's *Limelight* (52) and has since gone on to become a star in her own right. Born on 31 July 1944 in Santa Monica, California, Chaplin was sent to be educated in Swiss schools and began her adult professional career as a dancer in England's Royal Ballet. She was hailed as one of the promising new talents of 1965 for her performance as Tonya, the beautiful, devoted wife of Omar Sharif in David Lean's *Dr Zhivago* (65), and has continued to play leads in international films ever since. Stage work includes apearances in a Broadway revival of *The Little Foxes*.

**Selected Films:** *Limelight* (52), *Dr Zhivago* (65), *A Countess from Hong Kong* (66), *Stranger in the House* (67), *I Killed Rasputin* (68), *The Hawaiians* (70), *Innocent Bystanders* (72), *The Three Musketeers* (74), *Nashville* (75), *Buffalo Bill and the Indians* (76), *Roseland* (77), *Welcome to L A* (77), *A Wedding* (78), *Remember My Name* (78), *The Mirror Crack'd* (80), *Les uns et les autres* (80), *Voyage en Douce* (81), *Bolero* (82).

## CHAPMAN, Graham (1939- )

A graduate of Cambridge University, who trained as a doctor Chapman is a member of Monty Python, an ensemble of British comedians whose esoteric nonsense and satirical routines have made the group a legend in its own time and exercised considerable influence on comedy of the last two decades, particularly on TV.

**Selected Films:** *Monty Python and the Holy Grail* (75), *The Odd Job* (78), *The Life of Brian* (79), *Yellowbeard* (83).

## CHARISSE, Cyd (1912- )

Born Tula Ellice Finklea in Amarillo, Texas, this stylish, long-legged dancer joined the Ballet Russe de Monte Carlo at the age of 13. She took the name Cyd from her baby brother's efforts to say 'sister,' and got her last name from her ballet teacher, Nico Charisse, to whom she was married from 1939 to 1947. At the outbreak of World War II she began her Hollywood film career, appearing in *Mission to Moscow* (43). Her first important role came in 1952, dancing opposite Gene Kelly, in *Singin' in the Rain*. Charisse married singer Tony Martin in 1948, and they often toured together in a night club act.

**Selected Films:** *Mission to Moscow* (43), *The Harvey Girls* (46), *Till the Clouds Roll By* (46), *The Unfinished Dance* (47), *On an Island with You* (48), *Words and Music* (48), *Singin' in the Rain* (52), *The Band Wagon* (53), *Brigadoon* (54), *It's Always Fair Weather* (55), *Invitation to the Dance* (57), *Silk Stockings* (57), *Two Weeks in Another Town* (62), *Warlords of Atlantis* (78).

## CHASE, Chevy (1943- )

Born Cornelius Crane Chase in New York, Chase attended Bard College and pursued graduate studies at Columbia and MIT. Meanwhile, he and two friends collaborated on some hip and raunchy comedy sketches that made their way from underground TV to off-Broadway and finally to the screen, under the name *The Groove Tube* (74); Chase appeared in all versions. That led to his tenure as writer and Not Ready for Prime Time Player on TV's classic comedy show *Saturday Night Live* during the 1970s. Chase made his film debut co-starring with Goldie Hawn in *Foul Play* (78). It was the beginning of a steady output of movies for Chase, none of which elicited much enthusiasm from critics and none of them substantial hits; Chase seems so far unable to find the right screen vehicles for the satiric persona that dominated *Saturday Night Live*.

**Selected Films:** *The Groove Tube* (74), *Foul Play* (78), *O Heavenly Dog* (80), *Under the Rainbow* (81), *National Lampoon's Vacation* (83), *Deal of the Century* (83), *Fletch* (85), *National Lampoon's European Vacation* (85), *Spies Like Us* (86), *The Three Amigos* (86).

## CHATTERTON, Ruth (1893-1961)

A success on Broadway at 20, Chatterton made her screen debut in *Sins of the Fathers* (28), and had a popular Hollywood career over the next decade playing dignified, sometimes tense or misguided leading ladies. Married to actors Ralph Forbes (1924-1932) and George Brent (1932-34), she also published several successful novels in the 1950s.

**Selected Films:** *Sins of the Fathers* (28), *Madame X* (29), *The Lady of Scandal* (30), *Paramount on Parade* (30), *The Crash* (32), *Female* (33), *Girl's Dormitory* (36), *Dodsworth* (36), *The Rat* (38), *A Royal Divorce* (38).

## CHER (1946- )

Born Cherilyn Sarkisian in El Centro, California, for years this tall brunette was half of the 'Sonny and Cher' pop singing team, sharing the billing with husband Sonny Bono. They appeared together on their own television variety show, and the public began to realize that she was not the overdressed hippie that she seemed to be. Her sense of humor was excellent and her rapport with her audiences was electric. After her divorce from her second husband Greg Allman of the Allman Brothers, she went into the movies. In *Silkwood* (83), she played Meryl Streep's roommate and her touching portrayal of an unhappy Southern woman earned her an Academy Award nomination for Best Supporting Actress.

**Selected Films:** *Come Back to the Five and Dime, Jimmy Dean, Jimmy Dean* (82), *Silkwood* (83), *Mask* (85), *Moonstruck* (87), *The Witches of Eastwick* (87).

## CHERKASSOV, Nikolai (1903-1966)

Born in St Petersburg, Cherkassov was a musician and dancer before joining the Leningrad Pushkin Theater. Best known for epic, heroic roles, including the title role in Sergei Eisenstein's *Alexander Nevsky* (38) and *Ivan the Terrible* (42 and 44), Cherkassov made his screen debut in *The Tsar's Poet* (27). In the late 1930s he was also a deputy of the Supreme Soviet. His autobiography *Notes of a Soviet Actor* was published in 1957.
**Selected Films:** *The Tsar's Poet* (27), *Baltic Deputy* (36), *Peter the Great* (37), *Alexander Nevsky* (38), *Ivan the Terrible* (42, 44), *The First Front* (49), *Ivan Pavlov* (50), *Mussorgsky* (51), *Rimsky-Korsakov* (54), *Don Quixote* (57).

## CHEVALIER, Maurice (1888-1972)

This inimitable French singing entertainer, born in Paris, was a cabaret and music hall star before he became famous in Paris revues. He made several films in France before going to Hollywood in the 1930s, where he quickly became one of the most popular musical stars with his familiar image – a rakishly tilted straw hat and a protruding lower lip. He became a major Hollywood heartthrob in such films as *The Love Parade* (30), *Love Me Tonight* (32) and *The Merry Widow* (34). Chevalier returned to Europe in the 1940s, and his popularity declined during the war years, when he was suspected – incorrectly – of being a Nazi collaborator. He then re-emerged as an international star in the 1950s when he made *Gigi* (58) and *Can Can* (59). In 1958 he received a Special Academy Award 'for his contributions to the world of entertainment for more than half a century.'
**Selected Films:** *Par habitude* (24), *Innocents in Paris* (29), *The Love Parade* (30), *The Smiling Lieutenant* (31), *One Hour With You* (32), *Love Me Tonight* (32), *The Merry Widow* (34), *Folies Bergère* (35), *Paris 1900* (46), *Love in the Afternoon* (57), *Gigi* (58), *Can Can* (59), *Fanny* (61), *Monkeys, Go Home!* (67).

## CHONG, Rae Dawn (1961- )

Born in California, the daughter of comedian Tommy Chong, Rae Dawn made her screen debut wearing a coating of mud in the caveman epic *Quest for Fire* (82). The delicately beautiful black actress has gone on to effective supporting roles in offbeat films like *Choose Me* (84) as well as mainstream ones like *The Color Purple* (85).
**Selected Films:** *Quest for Fire* (82), *Choose Me* (84), *Commando* (85), *The Color Purple* (85), *Soul Man* (86), *Skip Tracer* (87).

## CHRISTIE, Julie (1941- )

This lovely British actress was born in Assam, India, and was educated in England and studied art in Paris. From 1957 to 1960, she was with the Frinton-on-the-Sea Repertory Company in England. Her film debut was in *Crooks Anonymous* in 1962. In 1965 she appeared in *Darling*, for which she won the Academy Award as Best Actress for her portrayal of a self-centered model who has a negative impact on other people's lives. After *Darling*, critics were unimpressed with most of her films, although *Doctor Zhivago* (65), *McCabe and Mrs Miller* (71) and *Shampoo* (75) were box office successes. Although she possesses great range and skill as an actress, she has rarely been given parts which allowed her to display much more than her beauty, and she has been accused of being careless with her career.
**Selected Films:** *Crooks Anonymous* (62), *Billy Liar* (63), *Darling* (65), *Doctor Zhivago* (65), *Fahrenheit 451* (66), *Far from the Madding Crowd* (67), *Petulia* (68), *McCabe and Mrs Miller* (71), *Don't Look Now* (74), *Shampoo* (75), *Nashville* (75), *Heaven Can Wait* (78), *The Return of the Soldier* (82), *Heat and Dust* (83), *Miss Mary* (86).

*Maurice Chevalier in* Gigi *(58).*

## CIANNELLI, Eduardo (1887-1969)

Born on the island of Ischia in Italy, Ciannelli moved from a career in medicine to opera and then to musical comedies on Broadway after World War I, establishing himself as a serious actor in the play *Winterset*, a part he repeated on the screen in 1936. His sharply-defined features lent themselves to many roles as a villain, but he played sympathetic roles as well.
**Selected Films:** *Reunion in Vienna* (33), *Winterset* (36), *Gunga Din* (39), *The Mask of Dimitrios* (44), *Houseboat (58)*, *The Brotherhood (68)*, *The Secret of Santa Vittoria* (69).

## CLAIRE, Ina (1892-1985)

Born Ina Fagan in Washington, DC, Claire started

in vaudeville in her teens and made her screen debut in 1915. In the 1920s she became an expert and much-loved Broadway comedienne and remained more a theater than a screen actress. Nonetheless, she played a number of turns as sophisticates in film comedies, most memorably her catty Russian grand duchess in *Ninotchka* (39). She was married to John Gilbert from 1929 to 1931.
**Selected Films:** *Wild Goose Chase* (15), *The Awful Truth* (29), *The Royal Family at Broadway* (31), *The Greeks Had a Name for Them* (32), *Ninotchka* (39), *Claudia* (43).

## CLARK, Dane (1913- )

The diminutive Clark (born Bernard Zanville in Brooklyn) made his Broadway debut in 1934 and broke into films in 1942. He played many leads in the forties as a brooding tough guy in the style of John Garfield. His recent appearances are almost exclusively on TV.
**Selected Films:** *Destination Tokyo* (43), *God is My Co-Pilot* (45), *Moonrise* (49), *The Toughest Man Alive* (55), *Outlaw's Son* (57), *The McMasters* (70), *Days in My Father's House* (75).

## CLARK, Fred (1914-1968)

A native of Lincoln, California, this bald, dour character comedian played numerous roles, often as an inept villain or short-tempered businessman, after he moved from the Broadway stage to the screen in *The Unsuspected* (47). His TV roles included several seasons with Burns and Allen.
**Selected Films:** *The Unsuspected* (47), *Sunset Boulevard* (50), *Don't Go Near the Water* (57), *Bells Are Ringing* (60), *Skidoo* (68).

## CLARK, Petula (1932- )

After achieving fame as a child singer in her native England during World War II, Clark, born in Epsom, began playing a series of saccharine child roles in British films at the age of 11. She became immensely popular as a popular singer with such hits as 'Downtown' in the 1960s and returned to the screen (and to TV) in lavish musicals.
**Selected Films:** *Medal for the General* (44), *Here Come the Huggetts* (48), *The Card* (52), *Goodbye Mr Chips* (69), *Never Never Land* (81).

## CLARK, Susan (1940- )

Born in Sarnia, Ontario, Clark studied at London's Royal Academy of Dramatic Art. She has played many leading roles since her screen debut in *Banning* (67). Active in TV, she starred in the biographies *Babe* and *Amelia Earheart*, and the series *McNaughton's Daughter* and *Webster* .
**Selected Films:** *Banning* (67), *Madigan* (68), *Coogan's Bluff* (68), *The Skin Game* (71), *Showdown* (73), *Airport 75* (74), *Night Moves* (75), *Murder by Decree* (78), *Nobody's Perfekt* (81).

*Jill Clayburgh* – An Unmarried Woman *(78)*.

## CLAYBURGH, Jill (1945- )

Clayburgh was born to a wealthy family in New York City and achieved success on the Broadway stage before turning to films. She is an outstanding comedienne, as she proved in *Silver Streak* (76), opposite Gene Wilder and Richard Prior, but she is most noted for her strong dramatic work in such films as *An Unmarried Woman* (78) and *I'm Dancing As Fast As I Can* (82). Clayburgh was nominated for an Academy Award as Best Actress for *An Unmarried Woman*, as a betrayed wife who has an affair with an artist (Alan Bates). She was nominated again for *Starting Over* (79).
**Selected Films:** *The Wedding Party* (66), *Portnoy's Complaint* (72), *The Terminal Man* (74), *Gable and Lombard* (76), *Silver Streak* (76), *Semi-Tough* (77), *An Unmarried Woman* (78), *Starting Over* (79), *First Monday in October* (81), *I'm Dancing As Fast As I Can* (82), *Where Are the Children* (86).

## CLEESE, John (1939- )

A member of the legendary and widely-imitated British satirical comedy troupe Monty Python, Cleese, educated at Cambridge University, also starred in the TV series *Fawlty Towers*.
**Selected Films:** *Interlude* (68), *The Best House in London* (68), *And Now for Something Completely Different* (71), *The Love Bug* (72), *The Life of Brian* (79), *Time Bandits* (80), *Monty Python and the Meaning of Life* (83), *Clockwise* (86).

## CLIFF, Jimmy (1946- )

Jamaican singer-songwriter Cliff is one of the major figures in reggae music, has hit songs including the classic 'You Can Get It if You Really

Want.' He starred in the successful Jamaican reggae film *The Harder They Come* (72).
**Selected Films:** *The Harder They Come* (72), *Club Paradise* (86).

## CLIFT, Montgomery (1920-1966)

Born Edward Clift in Omaha, Nebraska, he was one of the most promising young stars of the 1950s – handsome, talented and serious about his work. But he was tragically unhappy. Marilyn Monroe once said about him, 'He's the only person I know worse off than me.' He played in summer stock at the age of 14 and soon made his way to Broadway. He made his film debut in *The Search* (48), a poignant story of an American soldier (Clift) caring for a boy who was a concentration camp survivor in postwar Berlin, and Clift received an Academy Award nomination as Best Actor. He later received nominations for *A Place in the Sun* (51), *From Here to Eternity* (53) and a nomination as Best Supporting Actor for *Judgment at Nuremberg* (61). Clift was a leading man who generally played introspective, sensitive heroes, and his movies were generally well received, even after an automobile accident in 1957 scarred his face, somewhat disfiguring him. Off screen, his drinking, drug use and concealed homosexuality took a heavy toll, and he died of a heart attack at the age of 45.
**Selected Films:** *The Search* (48), *Red River* (48), *The Heiress* (49), *A Place in the Sun* (49), *I Confess* (53), *From Here to Eternity* (53), *Indiscretion of an American Wife* (54), *Raintree County* (57), *The Young Lions* (58), *Lonelyhearts* (59), *Suddenly Last Summer* (59), *Wild River* (60), *The Misfits* (60), *Judgment at Nuremberg* (61), *Freud* (63), *The Defector* (66).

## CLIVE, Colin (1898-1937)

Born Colin Clive Greig in St Malo, France, to British parents, he became a leading man who looked older than his years. He arrived in Hollywood in 1930, to repeat his stage success in *Journey's End*. Then James Whale picked him for the title role in *Frankenstein* (31). Clive repeated the role in *Bride of Frankenstein* (35), and appeared in another horror film, *Mad Love* (35). Despite his fine work in other movies, he is best remembered as the mad scientist.
**Selected Films:** *Journey's End* (30), *Frankenstein* (31), *Looking Forward* (33), *Jane Eyre* (34), *Clive of India* (35), *Bride of Frankenstein* (35), *The Girl from Tenth Avenue* (35), *Mad Love* (35), *History is Made at Night* (37), *The Woman I Love* (37).

*Montgomery Clift (c) in* I Confess *(53).*

## CLIVE, E E (1879-1940)

Born in Monmouthshire, Wales, Clive moved from the London stage to the American stage in 1912 and began his Hollywood career in 1933, when he made his debut in *The Invisible Man*. Clive played numerous dour but frequently likeable butlers, statesmen, town officials and stern Englishmen.
**Selected Films:** *The Invisible Man* (33), *Charlie Chan in London* (34), *The Bride of Frankenstein* (35), *The Charge of the Light Brigade* (36), *Bulldog Drummond Comes Back* (37), *Personal Property* (37), *Pride and Prejudice* (40), *Foreign Correspondent* (40).

## CLOSE, Glenn (1947- )

Born in Greenwich, Connecticut, Close made her professional stage debut at New York's Phoenix Theatre and went on to several Broadway productions including the musical *Barnum* and her Tony-winning role in *The Real Thing* (84). Since making her screen debut in *The World According to Garp* (82), she has been a sensitive and intelligent presence in several films of the decade.
**Selected Films:** *The World According to Garp* (82), *The Big Chill* (83), *The Natural* (84), *The Stone Boy* (84), *Jagged Edge* (85), *Maxie* (85), *Fatal Attraction* (87).

## COBB, Lee J (1911-1976)

Born Leo Jacoby in New York City, this powerful character actor was best known for his stage roles. He created the character Willy Loman on Broadway in Arthur Miller's *Death of a Salesman*. In Hollywood he usually played brooding or menacing character parts. Cobb received an Academy Award nomination for Best Supporting Actor for his role as the mob boss in *On the Waterfront* (54). Later he was nominated for Best Supporting Actor for *The Brothers Karamazov* (58).
**Selected Films:** *North of the Rio Grande* (37), *Golden Boy* (39), *The Moon is Down* (43), *The Song of Bernadette* (43), *Anna and the King of Siam* (46), *The Dark Past* (48), *On the Waterfront* (54), *The Man in the Gray Flannel Suit* (46), *Twelve Angry Men* (57), *The Brothers Karamazov* (58), *Exodus* (60), *Come Blow Your Horn* (63), *The Exorcist* (73), *That Lucky Touch* (75).

## COBURN, Charles (1877-1961)

A distinguished star of the American stage for many years, Coburn did not begin his film career until he was 56. Remembered as a crusty but warm-hearted gentleman of the old school, Coburn became a beloved international film star after he was 60 when he received an Academy Award for his supporting role in *The More the Merrier* (43). He also received nominations for Best Supporting Actor in *The Devil and Miss Jones* (41) and *The Green Years* (46). Born Charles Douville Coburn in Savannah, Georgia, he began his theater career at the age of 14 as a program boy at a Savannah theater. He made his Broadway debut in 1901, and in 1906 organized the Coburn Shakespeare Players with his wife, resisting all film offers until *Boss Tweed* (33). He then molded himself into a delightful and exemplary screen character actor.
**Selected Films:** *Boss Tweed* (33), *Of Human Hearts* (38), *Bachelor Mother* (39), *Edison the Man* (40), *The Lady Eve* (41), *The Devil and Miss Jones* (41), *Heaven Can Wait* (43), *The More the Merrier* (43), *Knickerbocker Holiday* (44), *The Green Years* (46), *Monkey Business* (52), *Has Anybody Seen My Gal?* (52), *The Remarkable Mr Pennypacker* (59), *Pepe* (60).

## COBURN, James (1928- )

Born in Laurel, Nebraska, Coburn started in supporting roles and later moved on to leads. Tall, rangy and sinister-looking, with lithe movements and an easy grin, he has often played tough guys and villains in action films, although he achieved his greatest success in movies as *Our Man Flint* (66), a comic spoof of the James Bond pictures.
**Selected Films:** *Ride Lonesome* (59), *The Magnificent Seven* (60), *The Great Escape* (63), *Charade* (63), *The Americanization of Emily* (64), *Major Dundee* (65), *Our Man Flint* (66), *The President's Analyst* (67), *The Last of Sheila* (73), *Hard Times* (75), *Looker* (81), *Death of a Soldier* (86).

## COLBERT, Claudette (1905- )

With her warm, sensual voice, the petite apple-cheeked Colbert (born Lily Claudette Chauchoin in Paris) was one of Hollywood's favorite stars. During the 1940s she was also its highest paid female star. Playing the gamut of Hollywood's concepts of women, she was at her best in comedy. She moved from Paris to New York when she was six years old, and later studied to be a fashion designer. But instead she became an ingénue on Broadway, making her debut in 1923 in *The Wild Westcotts*. Her film career took off in the sound era, and she could do it all – Cecil B De Mille epics, sophisticated light comedy, three-handkerchief weepies. Her first big film role was in *The Smiling Lieutenant* (31), with Maurice Chevalier. She exhibited a lot of sex appeal in de Mille's *The Sign of the Cross* (32) and *Cleopatra* (34). Her blockbuster was *It Happened One Night* (34) opposite Clark Gable, for which she won the Academy Award as Best Actress. This picture set the tone for a number of sparkling movies. She was always a polished and spunky match for her leading men and from Gable to Gary Cooper, they were Hollywood's elite romantic heroes. Colbert refused to play the parts usually offered to older actresses, and retired from films, turning to Broadway, where she played opposite such leading men as Rex Harrison.
**Selected Films:** *For the Love of Mike* (28), *The Smiling Lieutenant* (31), *The Sign of the Cross* (32), *Three Cornered Moon* (33), *It Happened One Night*

(34), *Cleopatra* (34), *Imitation of Life* (34), *Under Two Flags* (36), *Maid of Salem* (37), *Tovarich (37)*, *Bluebeard's Eighth Wife* (38), *Zaza* (39), *Midnight* (39), *Drums Along the Mohawk* (39), *Boom Town* (40), *Arise My Love* (40), *The Palm Beach Story* (42), *So Proudly We Hail* (43), *Since You Went Away* (44), *The Egg and I (47)*, *Three Came Home* (50), *Parrish* (61).

## COLE, George (1925- )

Born in London, Cole made his first stage appearance in England in 1939, and his debut in British films as a cockney child evacuee in *Cottage to Let* (41). His many leading comedy roles in British, American, and international films usually featured him as a confused and silly young man.
**Selected Films:** *Cottage to Let* (41), *Henry V* (44), *Quartet* (48), *Top Secret* (51), *The Green Man* (57), *Cleopatra* (63), *The Blue Bird* (76), *The Bounder* (81).

## COLEMAN, Nancy (1917- )

Radio and stage experience, including a Broadway debut in 1941, earned Coleman, born in Everett, Washington, lead and second lead roles in Warner Bros. films of the forties.
**Selected Films:** *King's Row* (42), *Dangerously They Live* (42), *The Gay Sisters* (42), *Edge of Darkness* (43), *Devotion* (45), *Violence* (47), *Mourning Becomes Electra* (48), *That Man From Tangier* (53), *Slaves* (68).

*Clark Gable and Claudette Colbert in* It Happened One Night *(34).*

*Joan Collins in* Empire of the Ants *(77).*

## COLLIER, Constance (1878-1955)

After distinguishing herself on both the British and the American stage, first as a chorus girl and then as a dramatic actress, Collier, born Laura Constance Hardie in Windsor, England, made her film debut in *Intolerance* (16). In later years she played eccentric or caustic grandes dames in Hollywood productions.
**Selected Films:** *Bleak House* (20), *Our Betters* (33), *Dinner at Eight* (33), *Stage Door* (37), *Kitty* (46), *An Ideal Husband* (48), *Whirlpool* (50).

## COLLINS, Joan (1933- )

She was born in London, where her father was a theatrical agent and a partner of Lew (later Lord) Grade, one of England's most successful impresarios. Collins always wanted to act, and spent two years at the Royal Academy of Dramatic Art, making her debut on the London stage in 1946 in Ibsen's *A Doll's House*. Her film career began at J Arthur Rank Studios, where she usually played the part of a sexy juvenile delinquent. She was signed by 20th Century-Fox in Hollywood in the mid-1950s, and immediately began appearing in major films. She had the title role of Evelyn Nesbit *The Girl in the Red Velvet Swing* (55). After her big start, her career did begin to wind down, but she did keep busy, both in the United States and in Britain, although many of her films, such as *The Stud* (78) and *The Bitch* (79), were less than high-class. Then came the television series *Dynasty*, and Collin's career was reborn. She is probably a bigger sex symbol today, in her fifties, than she was when she started in pictures in 1952. She was married to actor Anthony Newley.
**Selected Films:** *I Believe in You* (52), *Cosh Boy* (53), *Land of the Pharaohs* (55), *The Virgin Queen* (5), *The Girl in the Red Velvet Swing* (55), *Island in the Sun* (57), *Sea Wife* (57), *Rally Round the Flag Boys* (58), *Warning Shot* (66), *Quest for Love* (71), *The Stud* (78), *The Bitch* (79), *Game for Vultures* (79), *Sunburn* (79).

## COLLINS, Ray (1890-1965)

A native of Sacramento, California and on the stage from the age of six, Collins moved from Broadway to radio and Orson Welles's Mercury Theater. His screen career began with Welles's first Hollywood films, and he remained in Hollywood to play many kindly uncles and political bosses. He played Lt Tragg in the TV series *Perry Mason*.
**Selected Films:** *The Grapes of Wrath* (40), *Citizen Kane* (41), *The Magnificent Ambersons* (42), *The Desperate Hours* (55), *I'll Give My Life (61).*

## COLMAN, Ronald (1891-1958)

Distinguished, aristocratic and dignified, Colman was a romantic hero that women sighed over for nearly three decades. Born in Richmond, England and orphaned at 16, he got a job with the British Steamship Company. He was wounded in World War I, and upon returning to England he decided to become an actor. In 1918 he starred in a play called *Damaged Goods* and this led to films. He played bit parts until he got the lead in *The Black Spider* (20), but there was a slump in the British movie industry at the time and he opted for Hollywood, where he was discovered by Lillian Gish, who picked him as her co-star in *The White Sister* (23). One of the most popular of all silent screen actors, Colman achieved even greater success when cast with Vilma Banky in *The Dark Angel* (25). With the coming of sound, Banky's career collapsed, but Colman carried on. He was blessed with a beautiful and distinctive voice. Unlike many silent screen stars, he understood instinctively that talkies required a less melodramatic style of acting, and he set the tone for acting techniques with sound in movies such as *Arrowsmith* (31). Opposite such stars as Myrna Loy, Loretta Young and Rosalind Russell, he remained a heartthrob. He was the definitive Sidney Carton in *A Tale of Two Cities* (35) and masterful in *Lost Horizon* (37), as he was when he played the dual role in *The Prisoner of Zenda* (37). Colman was unusual in his ability to retain his independence in the Hollywood of the 1930s. While many actors were virtually owned by their studios, he moved around, eventually freelancing, choosing only plum roles. In the 1940s his career began to ebb, but he was still impressive, *Random Harvest* (42), with Greer Garson, was a gem, and he won an Academy Award for Best Actor for *A Double Life* (47). He appeared on radio and television regularly with his second wife, British actress Benita Hume, in a series called *The Halls of Ivy*, about the president of a small college.
**Selected Films:** *The Toilers* (19), *The Black Spider* (20), *The White Sister* (23), *The Dark Angel* (25), *Beau Geste* (26), *The Winning of Barbara Worth* (26), *Bulldog Drummond* (29), *Raffles* (30), *Arrowsmith* (31), *Clive of India* (35), *A Tale of Two Cities* (35), *Lost Horizon* (37), *The Prisoner of Zenda* (37), *If I Were King* (38), *The Light that Failed* (39), *The Talk of the Town* (42), *Random Harvest* (42), *The Late George Apley* (47), *A Double Life (47)*, *Champagne for Caesar* (50), *The Story of Mankind* (57).

*Ronald Colman with May McAvoy* – Lady Windermere's Fan *(25).*

## COLONNA, Jerry (1904-1986)

Born Gerardo Luigi Colonna in Boston, Massachusetts, this bulging-eyed, mustachioed comic with a high-pitched voice began his professional career in 1917 by playing the drums in his own jazz band. After a stint as staff trombonist for CBS radio, he went to Hollywood, where he switched to comedy. After working in night clubs and musical revues, he signed a contract with Bob Hope in 1938 and became a fixture on Hope's radio show. Colonna made several pictures that showcased his zany style, some of them with Hope.
**Selected Films:** *52nd Street* (37), *College Swing* (38), *Naughty But Nice* (39), *Comin' Round the Mountain* (40), *The Road to Singapore* (40), *Ice Capades* (41), *Star Spangled Rhythm* (42), *Atlantic City* (44), *It's In the Bag* (45), *The Road to Rio* (47), *Meet Me in Las Vegas (56)*, *Andy Hardy Comes Home* (58), *The Road to Hong Kong* (61).

## CONKLIN, Chester (1888-1971)

Work in vaudeville and as a circus clown prepared Conklin, born in Oskaloosa, Iowa, for his career as a silent slapstick comedian, beginning with a role as a Keystone Cop in 1913. This fumbling or mischievous fellow with the walrus mustache appeared in Chaplin's first film, *Making a Living* (14), and in many short comedies. His career continued well into the sound era.
**Selected Films:** *Making a Living* (14), *Greed* (24), *Gentlemen Prefer Blondes* (28), *Modern Times* (36), *Big Hand for a Little Lady* (66).

## CONNERY, Sean (1930- )

In the early 1960s, Connery (born Thomas Connery in Edinburgh, Scotland), although a relative unknown, was given one of the most sought-after roles in filmdom, that of Ian Fleming's superspy, James Bond, possibly because he didn't demand as high a salary as other bigger names who were under consideration. At first the decision looked like a mistake, for the initial Bond film, *Dr No* (62), opened to poor reviews, critics saying that the stolid Connery was miscast as the suave Agent 007. The public disagreed and *Dr No* became a huge commercial success. It was followed by an even better Bond film, *From Russia with Love* (63), and another and another, each being more commercially successful than the last. Connery as James Bond had become an international phenomenon, but he was increasingly unhappy with his identification as the secret agent. Connery tried other roles and in 1971 announced that he was giving up the Bond part forever. However, he was persuaded to come back in *Never Say Never Again* (83) as a middle-aged Bond, and once again he was a box office smash. As a young man, Connery had held a wide variety of menial jobs, from being a life guard to modeling swimming trunks, before going into the theater. He landed a part as a chorus boy in the London production of *South Pacific*, and after that he got small parts in movies and somewhat better parts on British television. His career, however, was undistinguished until he took the Bond role. Although he is a serious and competent actor, Connery has shown no inclination to do classical or experimental films. In his best non-Bond parts he has delivered solid performances in action films and thrillers such as *The Anderson Tapes* (71), *The Man Who Would Be King* (76) and *Outland* (81). In 1986 he astonished audiences with his brilliant performance as a balding medieval monk turned detective in *The Name of the Rose*.
**Selected Films:** *No Road Back* (55), *Darby O'Gill and the Little People* (59), *The Longest Day* (62), *Dr No* (62), *From Russia with Love* (63), *Marnie* (64), *Goldfinger* (64), *The Hill* (65), *Thunderball* (65), *You Only Live Twice* (67), *Shalako* (68), *The Molly Maguires* (69), *The Anderson Tapes* (71), *Diamonds Are Forever* (71), *Zardoz* (74), *Murder on the Orient Express (74)*, *The Wind and the Lion* (75), *The Man Who Would Be King* (76), *Robin and Marian* (76), *A Bridge Too Far* (77), *Time Bandits* (80), *Outland* (81), *Never Say Never Again* (83), *The Name of the Rose* (86), *The Untouchables* (87).

*Sean Connery as James Bond.*

## CONNOLLY, Walter (1887-1940)

A native of Cincinnati, this distinguished stage actor refused film offers for years. Eventually Connolly made his film debut in 1932 and played many memorable character parts, often leads, in his seven years in Hollywood, the grumpy millionaire and the irate editor personified.
**Selected Films:** *No More Orchids* (32), *It Happened One Night* (34), *Father Brown Detective* (35), *Soak the Rich* (36), *Nothing Sacred* (37), *Fifth Avenue Girl* (39), *The Great Victor Herbert* (39).

## CONNORS, Chuck (1921- )

After playing major-league baseball for several years, Brooklyn-born Kevin Joseph Connors began playing bit roles in films in the 1950s and moved on to tough-guy leads in B films, where his thin smile was equally suitable to heroism or villainy. His success in TV's *The Rifleman* series made him a film star, primarily in westerns and action productions.
**Selected Films:** *Pat and Mike* (52), *Geronimo* (62), *Pancho Villa* (71), *Soylent Green* (73), *Airplane 2: The Sequel* (82), *The Vals* (85).

## CONNORS, Mike (1925- )

Formerly known as Touch Connors, tall, masculine, California-born Krekor Ohanian entered films in the early 1950s and progressed from supporting to lead roles, mostly as an action hero in undistinguished productions. He starred in the TV series *Tightrope* and *Mannix*.
**Selected Films:** *Sudden Fear* (52), *Five Guns West* (55), *Suicide Battalion* (58), *Good Neighbor* (64), *Harlow* (65), *Stagecoach* (66), *Avalanche Express* (79).

## CONREID, Hans (1917-1982)

Best-remembered for his lead in *The 5000 Fingers of Dr T* (53), Baltimore-born Conreid moved from radio to film in *Dramatic School* (37). His facility with foreign accents and trademark clipped diction earned the tall actor many eccentric comedy roles, although he also played sinister parts, particularly Nazis during World War II.
**Selected Films:** *Dramatic School* (37), *Crazy Horse* (43), *My Friend Irma* (49), *The 5000 Fingers of Dr T* (53), *Bus Stop* (56), *The Patsy* (64), *The Brothers O'Toole* (73), *Oh God Book II* (80).

## CONTE, Richard (1914-1975)

Often cast as a world-weary war hero or sympathetic gangster, Italian-American Conte, born Nicolas Peter Conte in Jersey City, got his start when Elia Kazan discovered him working as a performing waiter. His first film, *Heaven With a Barbed Wire Fence* (40) was followed by a contract with 20th Century-Fox and many leading roles. He also directed the film *Operation Cross Eagles* (69).
**Selected Films:** *Heaven With a Barbed Wire Fence* (40), *Guadalcanal Diary* (43), *The Purple Heart* (44), *A Walk in the Sun* (46), *I'll Cry Tomorrow* (55), *Circus World* (64), *The Godfather* (72).

## CONTI, Tom (1946- )

Born in Glasgow, Conti appeared in repertory in his native Scotland before going to England to pursue his stage career. He made his film debut in *Galileo* (75) and has since appeared occasionally onscreen, most notably with his tour de force as a drunken poet in the title role of *Reuben, Reuben* (83) which earned him an Oscar nomination. Conti has continued his theater work, winning a Tony for his role in *Whose Life is it Anyway?* (79).
**Selected Films:** *Galileo* (75), *The Duellists* (78), *Reuben, Reuben* (83), *Merry Christmas Mr Lawrence* (83), *American Dreamer* (84), *Saving Grace* (86), *Gospel According to Vic* (87).

## CONWAY, Tom (1904-1967)

Born Thomas Sanders in St Petersburg, Russia of British parents, Conway went to Hollywood in 1940 after stage experience in England and achieved considerable success in the 1940s as a suave leading man especially in 'the Falcon' series which he inherited from his brother George.
**Selected Films:** *Sky Murder* (40), *Mrs Miniver* (43), *The Falcon's Brother* (42), *Cat People* (42), *The Falcon Out West* (44), *Park Plaza 505* (53), *The She-Creature* (56), *Twelve to the Moon* (60), *What a Way to Go!* (64).

## COOGAN, Jackie (1914-1984)

Coogan was born in Los Angeles, California, and became a childhood superstar at the age of seven when he appeared with Charlie Chaplin in *The Kid* (21) as a street-wise orphan being raised by the little tramp. Coogan earned a fortune as a youth, but he never saw the money. The resulting scandal gave rise to the 'Coogan Law' protecting child actors. He was briefly married to Betty Grable and later played heavies in films and comic parts on television, ending his career as the comic ghoul, Uncle Fester, on the series *The Addams Family* in the 1960s.
**Selected Films:** *Skinner's Baby* (16), *The Kid* (21), *Peck's Bad Boy* (21), *Oliver Twist* (22), *A Boy of Flanders* (24), *Tom Sawyer* (30), *Huckleberry Finn* (31), *College Swing* (38), *High School Confidential* (58), *Marlowe* (69), *Cahill – US Marshal* (73), *The Escape Artist* (81).

## COOK, Elisha, Jr (1902- )

Best-remembered as the shifty-eyed 'gunsel' Wilmer in *The Maltese Falcon* (41), the diminutive Cook, born in San Francisco, Hollywood's 'lightest heavy,' moved from the stage to the screen in *Her*

*Unborn Child* (29), and was typecast in numerous films as a coward, a neurotic, a fall guy, or a small-time villain.
**Selected Films:** *Her Unborn Child* (29), *Pigskin Parade* (36), *Submarine Patrol* (38), *I Wake Up Screaming* (41), *The Maltese Falcon* (41), *Phantom Lady* (44), *Dark Waters* (44), *The Big Sleep* (46), *Shane* (53), *The Killing* (56), *The Black Bird* (75), *Hammett* (82).

## COOK, Peter (1937- )

The sharp features and dry humor of British comic Cook, who was born in Torquay, first gained attention in the stage revue *Beyond the Fringe* in the 1960s. He has since appeared in films occasionally, most notably in the offbeat comedy *Bedazzled* (67) which he co-wrote, and in which he played the Devil. In 1981 he worked in the TV series *The Two of Us.*
**Selected Films:** *The Wrong Box* (66), *Bedazzled* (67), *A Dandy in Aspic* (68), *The Hound of the Baskervilles* (77), *Yellowbeard* (83), *Supergirl* (84).

*Gary Cooper in* For Whom the Bell Tolls *(43).*

## COOPER, Gary (1901-1961)

To millions of people throughout the world, Gary Cooper was the epitome of the natural American. It is ironic that Cooper's parents were both English, and had settled in Helena, Montana, not long before the birth of their child. Young Frank James Cooper grew up in a bi-cultural world: he learned to ride and work as a hand on his father's ranch, but he also attended a English private school from 1910 to 1917. He went to Grinnell College for three years and studied journalism, hoping for a career as a cartoonist. After attempts at that profession in Montana and Chicago failed, he went to Los Angeles and began to work as an extra in 'horse operas.' He changed his name to Gary, when a friend suggested that the Indiana city's name sounded 'romantic.' Cooper's first big break came in *The Winning of Barbara Worth* (26) and he then played opposite Clara Bow in *It* (27). In 1929, he starred in *The Virginian,* an early talkie, which was the prototype Western and the beginning of Cooper's enduring persona as the straight-shooting man of few words. In one form or another, this was Cooper's basic role: the anti-hero as ultimate hero. Sometimes he played the part in a war setting: *A Farewell to Arms* (32) and *Sergeant York* (41), a role for which he won his first Oscar. The real Alvin York had made Cooper's acceptance of the lead a condition of his releasing his life story to the movies. Sometimes Cooper played the individualist who defies the Establishment as in *Mr Deeds Goes to Town* (36) or *Meet John Doe* (41) or as an athlete – Lou Gehrig in *Pride of the Yankees* (42). He also played the role in Westerns, from *The Virginian* (29) to *High Noon* (52), the film which won Cooper his second Oscar as the marshal who reluctantly went forth to kill those who threaten society. Cooper also starred in several sophisticated comedies, including *Design for Living* (34) and *Ball of Fire* (41). He once admitted, 'I recognize my limitations . . . I never tried Shakespeare.' He was least convincing as the intense intellectual in *The Fountainhead* (49), and ironically his final film, *The Naked Edge* (61), had him playing his only 'bad guy.' Cooper was a great film star, one who conveyed genuine integrity through a natural talent.
**Selected Films:** *Blind Justice* (23), *The Winning of Barbara Worth* (26), *It* (27), *Wings* (27), *Lilac Time* (28), *The Virginian* (29), *Morocco* (30), *The Devil and the Deep* (32), *A Farewell to Arms* (32), *Design for Living* (34), *The Lives of a Bengal Lancer* (35), *Mr Deeds Goes to Town* (36), *The Plainsman* (37), *The Adventures of Marco Polo* (38), *The Cowboy and the Lady* (38), *Beau Geste* (39), *The Westerner* (40), *Sergeant York* (41), *Meet John Doe* (41), *Ball of Fire* (41), *Pride of the Yankees* (42), *For Whom the Bell Tolls* (43), *Saratoga Trunk* (45), *The Fountainhead* (49), *High Noon* (52), *The Court Martial of Billy Mitchell* (55), *Friendly Persuasion* (56), *Love in the Afternoon* (57), *Ten North Frederick* (58), *They Came to Cordura* (59), *The Naked Edge* (61).

## COOPER, Gladys (1888-1971)

This distinguished, aristocratic British stage actress born Gladys Constance Cooper, in Lewisham, whose youthful beauty made her World War I's leading pinup, made her screen debut in 1913. Her film career did not develop until she moved to Hollywood in 1940, where she played many dignified but gracious character roles. She was created a Dame in 1967.
**Selected Films:** *The Eleventh Commandment* (13), *The Bohemian Girl* (22), *Rebecca* (40), *Now Voyager* (42), *The Song of Bernadette* (43), *The Bishop's Wife* (47), *Separate Tables (58), My Fair Lady* (64), *The Happiest Millionaire* (67).

## COOPER, Jackie (1921- )

Famous 'little tough guy' and one of Hollywood's most popular child stars ever, John Cooper Jr, born in Los Angeles, began his professional career at the age of 3, acting in Bobby Clark and Lloyd Hamilton comedies, and later appeared in eight indelible *Our Gang* shorts (27-28). He reached full-blown stardom in *Skippy* (31), for which he received an Academy Award nomination as best actor; his uncle Norman Taurog received an Oscar for his direction of the film. Cooper attracted considerable attention the same year for his role in *The Champ* (31), and starred in a succession of 1930s tear-jerkers. Collaboration with Beery also produced *The Bowery* (33) and *Treasure Island* (34). His roles thinned considerably in the 1940s and after World War II Cooper tried B films, Broadway, and stock before starring in the highly successful TV series *The People's Choice* and *Hennessy* and establishing himself as a powerful TV executive.
**Selected Films:** *Sunny Side Up* (29), *Skippy* (31), *The Champ* (31), *When a Feller Needs a Friend* (32), *Divorce in the Family* (32), *The Bowery* (33), *Treasure Island* (34), *Peck's Bad Boy* (34), *Dinky* (35), *Tough Guy* (36), *Gangster's Boy* (38), *Seventeen* (40), *French Leave* (48), *Chosen Survivors* (74), *Superman* (78), *Superman III* (83).

## COOPER, Melville (1896-1973)

Best-remembered for his roles as a butler, Cooper, born in Birmingham, England, was a British character actor, often comic, of astonishing versatility. In Hollywood from 1936, he specialized in portraying upper-class fools, such as pompous Mr Collins in *Pride and Prejudice* (40).
**Selected Films:** *The Calendar* (31), *The Scarlet Pimpernel* (34), *The Adventures of Robin Hood* (38), *Rebecca* (40), *Pride and Prejudice* (40), *Murder Over New York* (40), *Heartbeat* (46), *Moonfleet* (55), *From the Earth to the Moon* (58).

## COREY, Jeff (1914- )

A former New York City sewing machine salesman who switched to the stage in the mid-thirties, the gaunt Corey established himself as a supporting actor in the forties playing winos, gangsters, farmers, cops, and junkies. He played Wild Bill Hickok in *Little Big Man* (71).
**Selected Films:** *All That Money Can Buy* (41), *My Friend Flicka* (43), *The Killers* (46), *Rawhide* (51), *Seconds* (66), *Little Big Man* (71), *Battle Beyond the Stars* (80).

## COREY, Wendell (1914-1968)

The son of a Congregational minister in Dracut, Massachusetts, Corey began acting in amateur productions and made his professional debut in 1935. By 1942 he was acting on Broadway, and in 1945, after his stage success in *Dream Girl*, he was signed to a film contract by producer Hal Wallis. For two decades he played many leads, usually solid, dependable types, sometimes sceptical or cynical, occasionally unsympathetic. Versatile and dependable as an actor, he was rarely used to his full extent, perhaps because he lacked the screen idol's looks and charisma. Corey was a president of the Academy of Motion Picture Arts and Sciences and a director of the Screen Actors Guild. He was elected to the Santa Monica city council in 1965, but failed in higher political aspirations when he lost his bid to become the Republican nominee for a congressional seat in 1966.
**Selected Films:** *Desert Fury* (47), *Man-Eater of Kumaon* (48), *Any Number Can Play* (49), *The Great Missiouri Raid* (50), *The Wild Blue Yonder* (51), *My Man and I* (52), *Hell's Half Acre* (54), *Rear Window* (54), *The Big Knife* (55), *The Killer is Loose* (56), *The Light in the Forest* (59), *Red Tomahawk* (67), *The Astro-Zombies* (68), *Buckskin* (68).

## CORT, Bud (1950- )

Seen to advantage in *Harold and Maude* (72), Cort is an American actor with a seeming speciality in portraying youths in mental or emotional difficulty.
**Selected Films:** *M*A*S*H* (70), *Brewster McCloud* (70), *Harold and Maude* (72), *Why Shoot the Teacher?* (77), *Hitler's Son* (78), *Die Laughing* (80), *She Dances Alone* (82), *Invaders from Mars* (86).

## CORTEZ, Ricardo (1899-1977)

Tall, dark, and handsome with classic bedroom eyes, Cortez, born Jacob Krantz (or Kranze) in Vienna, was groomed by Paramount in the twenties as a Latin lover in the style of Valentino. He played opposite Greta Garbo in her first Hollywood film, *The Torrent* (26), and many similar leading roles. With the advent of sound, Cortez was more often cast as a villain.
**Selected Films:** *Pony Express* (24), *The Torrent* (26), *The Sorrows of Satan* (27), *Ten Cents a Dance* (31), *The Maltese Falcon* (31), *Wonder Bar* (34), *The Inner Circle* (46), *The Last Hurrah* (58).

## COSBY, Bill (1938- )

Philadelphia-born Cosby first came to fame as a stand-up comedian, but he was still more successful on TV from the 1960s series *I Spy* (for which he won three Emmys in a row) to his celebrated series of the 1980s, in which he plays the father of a middle-class black family. His films have been occasional and largely forgettable.
**Selected Films:** *Hickey and Boggs* (72), *Uptown Saturday Night* (74), *Mother, Jugs, and Speed* (76), *California Suite* (79).

## COSTELLO, Dolores (1905-1979)

A gentle blonde beauty who was the image of the

delicate silent screen heroine, Costello, born in Pittsburgh, Pennsylvania, was the daughter of a matinee and early screen idol Maurice Costello. She leaped to stardom when she appeared in *The Sea Beast* (25), opposite John Barrymore whom she married in 1928. They were divorced in 1935.
**Selected Films:** *Lawful Larceny* (23), *The Sea Beast* (25), *When a Man Loves* (27), *Noah's Ark* (29), *Little Lord Fauntleroy* (36), *The Magnificent Ambersons* (42), *This is the Army* (43).

## COSTELLO, Lou (1906-1959)

See **ABBOTT, Bud**

## COTTEN, Joseph (1905- )

This tall, quiet leading man with the resonant voice and Southern sophistication became a popular Broadway and Hollywood performer. Born in Petersburg, Virginia, Cotten wrote drama reviews for the *Miami Herald* until he became assistant stage manager for David Belasco in New York in 1930. Later, he joined Orson Welles' Mercury Theatre, leaving it to appear opposite Katharine Hepburn in *The Philadelphia Story* on Broadway. Welles cast Cotten in some of his major films, including *Citizen Kane* (41) and *The Magnificent Ambersons* (42). Cotten also made movies for major directors Alfred Hitchcock and Carol Reed, and shone in romantic films such as *Portrait of Jennie* (48), which earned him a Best Actor Award at the Venice Film Festival.
**Selected Films:** *Citizen Kane* (41), *The Magnificent Ambersons* (42), *Journey Into Fear* (42), *Shadow of a Doubt* (43), *Gaslight* (44), *I'll Be Seeing You* (45), *Duel in the Sun* (46), *The Farmer's Daughter* (47), *Portrait of Jennie* (48), *The Third Man* (49), *Niagara* (52), *The Bottom of the Bottle* (55), *Hush ... Hush, Sweet Charlotte* (65), *The Oscar* (66), *Petulia* (68), *The Abominable Dr Phibes* (71), *Tora! Tora! Tora!* (71), *Soylent Green* (73), *Airport 77* (77), *Screamers* (81).

## COULOURIS, George (1903- )

Best-remembered as a villain, Coulouris, born in Manchester, England, moved from the British stage to Broadway and made his Hollywood debut in *Christopher Bean* (33). He has appeared in numerous character roles in British and American films.
**Selected Films:** *Christopher Bean* (33), *All This and Heaven Too* (40), *Citizen Kane* (41), *Watch on the Rhine* (43), *An Outcast of the Islands* (51), *Doctor in the House* (54), *Arabesque* (66), *Murder on the Orient Express* (76), *The Long Good Friday* (80).

*Joseph Cotten, Orson Welles and Erskine Sanford in* Citizen Kane *(41).*

## COURTENAY, Tom (1937- )

Tom Courtenay is an actor whose screen career never really took off, but whose performances nonetheless linger in the mind with a certain resonance: he is more famous and respected than his screen credits might indicate. Born in Hull, England, Courtenay trained at the Royal Academy of Dramatic Art and made his stage debut with the Old Vic in 1960. In 1961 he followed Albert Finney in the title role of the stage comedy *Billy Liar*, who is a sort of British Walter Mitty; Courtenay also played the role in the 1963 screen version of the play and the same year triumphed in a dramatic role – the lead in Tony Richardson's *The Loneliness of the Long Distance Runner*. There followed strong roles in the grim POW film *King Rat* (65) and in *Dr Zhivago* (65). For the latter he received an Academy Award nomination. But after 1971 Courtenay's screen career mysteriously dissolved; while appearing regularly in the theater, he has returned to the screen only once, repeating his stage role opposite Albert Finney in *The Dresser* (83).

**Selected Films:** *Billy Liar* (63), *The Loneliness of the Long Distance Runner* (65), *King Rat* (65), *Operation Crossbow* (65), *Dr Zhivago* (65), *The Night of the Generals* (66), *A Dandy in Aspic* (68), *Otley* (69), *One Day in the Life of Ivan Denisovitch* (71), *Catch Me a Spy* (71), *The Dresser* (83).

## COWAN, Jerome (1897-1972)

A native New Yorker, Cowan of the pencil-thin mustache became well-known for his many diversified character roles, particularly of urbane sophisticates. His screen debut in *Beloved Enemy* (36), followed a career in vaudeville, stock, and Broadway. His TV work includes *The Tab Hunter Show* and *Tycoon*.

**Selected Films:** *Beloved Enemy* (36), *The Maltese Falcon* (41), *Crime by Night* (43), *Find the Blackmailer* (44), *Blondie's Holiday* (47), *June Bride* (48), *The West Point Story* (50), *The Gnome-Mobile* (67), *The Comic* (69).

## COWARD, Noël (1899-1973)

A playwright, screenwriter, composer, novelist, director and producer as well as an actor, Sir Noel was one of the bright lights of international show business of the 1920s and 1930s, and achieved, through his persona as the ultimate sophisticate, the status of one of the best-known entertainment celebrities of the twentieth century. Born in Teddington, England, Coward was on stage from the age of 12, and soon became a controversial catalyst of the British theater. Three of his successful plays had been made into silent films by 1931. His first screen appearance – he appeared in only eleven films – was as a minor player in D W Griffith's *Hearts of the World* (18). His performance as a publisher in *The Scoundrel* (35) elevated the film to cult status in New York. In his next screen appearance, in 1942, he portrayed a gallant naval commander in *In Which We Serve*, a patriotic film he wrote, produced, and directed, and which earned him a special Academy Award. He was knighted in 1970.

**Selected Films:** *Hearts of the World* (18), *The Scoundrel* (35), *In Which We Serve* (42), *The Astonished Heart* (49), *Around the World in 80 Days* (55), *Our Man in Havana* (59), *Surprise Package* (60), *Paris When it Sizzles* (63), *Bunny Lake Is Missing* (65), *Boom!* (68), *The Italian Job* (69).

## CRABBE, Buster (1907-1983)

Winner of a gold medal in swimming at the 1932 Olympics, Clarence Lindon Crabbe, born in Oakland, California, rose to stardom in B action productions, Westerns, and adventure serials. His portrayals of Flash Gordon and Buck Rogers made him a household name with young audiences.

**Selected Films:** *Good News* (30), *The Most Dangerous Game* (32), *King of the Jungle* (33), *Tarzan the Fearless* (33), *Flash Gordon's Trip to Mars* (38), *Buck Rogers* (39), *Arizona Raiders* (65), *Swim Team* (79).

## CRAIN, Jeanne (1925- )

Glamorous as well as girlish, Jeanne Crain was Hollywood's personification of sweetness and light, one of the prettiest decorations of 1940s costume films, her trim figure and delicate features carrying her into starring roles through the 1950s. Born in Barstow, California, at the age of 16 she won the competition for Miss Long Beach of 1941, began modeling, and was named 'Camera Girl of 1942.' Hollywood could not long ignore her charms, and in 1943 she made her film debut in *The Gang's All Here*, the first of many films she made for 20th Century Fox. She rose to stardom with her performance in Henry Hathaway's *Home in Indiana* (44), playing opposite June Haver and several

*Sir Noel Coward.*

horses. She usually played the girl-next-door and the best of her films during this era were period family comedies such as *State Fair* (45) and *Cheaper by the Dozen* (50). One of her more memorable performances was in the delightful *Margie* (46), in which she plays mother and daughter. Its very funny falling-knickers sequence undoubtedly contributed to her first nomination for an Academy Award. Her other Academy Award nomination came for her performance in Elia Kazan's *Pinky* (49), a dated if well-meaning film about a black girl trying to pass for white. Her role in *The Gift of the Magi* episode in *O Henry's Full House* (52) was a similar attempt to transcend merely decorative parts, and was also well-received. But for the most part she was limited to sweet prettiness, as in her excellent performance opposite Cary Grant in *People Will Talk* (51). After she left Fox in 1953 her career lost momentum, although under King Vidor's direction in *Man Without a Star* (55) she hinted at a new sexiness and sophistication that was never exploited. Married since 1943, Crain has had seven children. She continued to appear in occasional films into the seventies, notably in *Skyjacked* (72).

**Selected Films:** *The Gang's All Here* (43), *In the Meantime Darling* (44), *Home in Indiana* (44), *Winged Victory* (44), *Leave Her to Heaven* (45), *State Fair* (45), *Centennial Summer* (46), *Margie* (46), *Apartment for Peggy* (48), *You Were Meant for Me* (48), *Pinky* (49), *A Letter to Three Wives* (49), *Cheaper by the Dozen* (50), *People Will Talk* (51), *O'Henry's Full House* (52), *Dangerous Crossing* (53), *Duel in the Jungle* (54), *Gentleman Marry Brunettes* (55), *Man Without a Star* (55), *The Fastest Gun Alive* (56), *The Joker is Wild* (57), *Madison Avenue* (61), *Pontius Pilate* (61), *The Night God Screamed* (71), *Skyjacked* (72).

## CRAVAT, Nick (1911- )

A diminutive American actor who was formerly Burt Lancaster's circus partner, the agile, acrobatic Cravat broke into films with Lancaster in the early 1950s, and remained to play many character roles.

**Selected Films:** *The Flame and the Arrow* (51), *The Crimson Pirate* (52), *King Richard and the Crusaders* (54), *Three-Ring Circus* (55), *Davy Crockett* (57), *Run Silent, Run Deep* (59), *Ulzana's Raid* (72), *The Island of Dr Moreau* (77).

## CRAVEN, Frank (1875-1945)

Veteran Broadway stage actor and playwright, Craven, who was born in Boston, went to Hollywood to work as a screen-writer and ended up in films. His kindly pipe-smoking philosopher in *Our Town* (40), a reprise of his Broadway role, the stage manager, was typical of many character parts he played.

**Selected Films:** *We Americans* (28), *The Very Idea* (29), *Barbary Coast* (35), *The Richest Man in Town* (41), *Three Different Eyes* (42), *My Best Gal* (44), *Colonel Effingham's Raid* (45).

## CRAWFORD, Broderick (1911-1986)

Big, fast-talking, with a kicked-in looking face, Broderick Crawford personified the Hollywood tough guy. But despite such major successes as an Academy Award for his portrayal of Willie Stark in *All the King's Men* (49), he is probably best known as Chief Dan Matthews of TV's *Highway Patrol* (55-58), a role in which his character, leaning against a patrol car and barking into a radio microphone, forever established the sign-off phrase '10-4' as part of the American language. Crawford was born in Philadelphia, Pennsylvania, into the theatrical family of vaudevillian Lester Crawford and famed stage and film comedienne Helen Broderick. He made his stage debut in London in 1932, and after his Broadway debut in 1935 was signed by Sam Goldwyn, beginning a series of supporting roles as gangster and knockabout comedian in minor Hollywood productions with *Woman Chases Man* (37). He worked as a stevedore and a merchant seaman between engagements. Crawford, whose nose was broken six times, attracted considerable notice for his Broadway portrayal of Lennie in *Of Mice and Men* (37), but continued to play unimportant thugs and loud-mouth gangsters, detectives, and cowboys in routine films until after the war, when his blustery style landed him his role in *All the King's Men*. After his portrayal of a demagogue governor modeled after Louisiana's Huey Long, he scored the following year with a more refined version of the same belligerent persona, this time a crooked tycoon, in *Born Yesterday* (50). He had further success in *The Mob* (51), but Hollywood never again offered him any outstanding roles and Crawford returned to more ordinary parts as the tough detective or villain in routine films. His brilliant portrayal of a con-man down on his luck in Fellini's *Il Bidone* (55), filmed in Italy, was his last great film. He spent most of the sixties playing in low-budget western and adventure epics in Italy and Spain, but Crawford performed well in *Embassy* (72) and was at the top of his form as J Edgar in *The Private Files of J Edgar Hoover* (78). Off screen Crawford's life included three marriages and a long-time battle with the bottle. TV familiarity blunted his appeal, but he continued working, mostly in routine films, until a stroke disabled him about a year before his death.

**Selected Films:** *Woman Chases Man* (37), *The Real Glory* (39), *When the Daltons Rode* (40), *Tight Shoes* (41), *Butch Minds the Baby* (42), *Broadway* (42), *Sin Town* (42), *The Runaround* (46), *Anna Lucasta* (49), *All the King's Men* (49), *Born Yesterday* (50), *The Mob* (51), *Lone Star* (52), *Human Desire* (54), *Il Bidone* (55), *Convicts Four* (62), *Kid Rodelo* (65), *The Texican* (66), *Red Tomahawk* (66), *Embassy* (72), *Terror in the Wax Museum* (73), *Smashing the Crime Syndicate* (73), *The Private Files of J Edgar Hoover* (78), *A Little Romance* (79), *Liar's Moon* (82).

*Joan Crawford and John Garfield in* Humoresque *(46).*

## **CRAWFORD, Joan** (1906-1977)

Crawford was often the movie star the audiences loved to hate. A star whose career began with silents, she was the epitome of the glamorous Hollywood leading lady. Her films chronicle her hard work and ambition as much as her talent, which did not really flourish until she had been in films for nearly 20 years. Crawford proved immensely durable in Hollywood. Hers was a rags to riches story and it took toughness, shrewdness and a formidable single-mindedness to make it happen. The story of her life reads like a B movie. Born Lucille le Sueur in San Antonio, Texas, her parents were separated before she was born and her mother married a vaudeville theater manager. They divorced in 1915, but by then Crawford was hooked – on dancing. She worked as a laundress, waitress and shopgirl, but life got better after she won a Charleston contest. Calling herself Billie Cassin, she danced her way into clubs. A stint in the chorus line of a Broadway show – *Innocent Eyes* – led to her screen debut as Norma Shearer's stand-in in *Lady of the Night* (25). After a series of mediocre silents, MGM sponsored a contest for her in a fan magazine, hoping to give her a new name. The winner came up with 'Joan Crawford.' She became a symbol of the Jazz Age in *Our Dancing Daughters* (28), and she became a star and took over the image of 'Number One Flapper' from Clara Bow. Her first talkie was *Hollywood Revue of 1929* (29), and her first dramatic role was in *Paid* the following year. Like Bette Davis at Warner Bros, Crawford hounded her studio (MGM) for substantial parts. And it was those parts that always pulled her out of a box office slump – *The Women* (39), *A Woman's Face* (41) and *Mildred Pierce* (45), for which she won an Oscar. In the 1940s MGM thought that she was box office poison, but she became a star at Warner Bros. playing in women's pictures, mostly soap opera stuff ignored by the critics. She became the personification of the career girl and the repressed older woman, and it was said that woman fans loved to see her suffering in mink. Crawford later worked again at MGM and at other studios, struggling to remain at the top. Columnist Hedda Hopper said of her, 'She spends 24 hours a day keeping her name in the pupil of the public eye.' She played aging femme fatales in the 1950s, and in the 1960s, with rival Bette Davis, she appeared in *What Ever Happened to Baby Jane?* (62), a psychological drama. She kept working as long as she was offered roles. Crawford was married four times: to Douglas Fairbanks Jr, Franchot Tone, Philip Terry and Alfred Steel, the board chairman of Pepsi Cola. After Steel's death, she became an active member of the company. *Mommie Dearest*, a 1978 biography by her daughter Christina, made her sound like a fiend, but Crawford was one of Hollywood's most glittering stars

for over four decades.
**Selected Films:** *Pretty Ladies* (25), *The Taxi Dancer* (27), *Rose Marie* (28), *Our Dancing Daughters* (28), *Paid* (29), *Hollywood Revue of 1929* (29), *Laughing Sinners* (31), *Grand Hotel* (32), *Rain* (32), *Dancing Lady* (33), *The Gorgeous Hussy* (36), *The Women* (39), *Strange Cargo* (40), *Susan and God* (40), *A Woman's Face* (41), *Mildred Pierce* (45), *Humoresque* (46), *Possessed* (47), *Harriet Craig* (50), *Sudden Fear* (52), *Johnny Guitar* (54), *The Story of Esther Costello* (57), *What Ever Happened to Baby Jane?* (62), *Trog* (70).

## CRAWFORD, Michael (1942- )

Born Michael Dumble-Smith in England, Crawford had a career as a child actor which included films and BBC radio as well as London and New York stage appearances before he established himself as a spirited comic lead.
**Selected Films:** *Soap Box Derby* (50), *Blow Your Own Trumpet* (54), *The War Lover* (62), *The Knack* (65), *A Funny Thing Happened on the Way to the Forum* (66), *The Jokers* (66), *How I Won the War* (67), *Hello Dolly!* (69), *Alice's Adventures in Wonderland* (72), *Condorman* (81).

## CREGAR, Laird (1916-1944)

During a screen career that lasted only five years, Philadelphia-born Samuel Laird Cregar emerged as a first-rate character actor who could play a wide variety of roles. His best known role was Jack the Ripper in *The Lodger* (44).
**Selected Films:** *Granny Get Your Gun* (40), *Charley's Aunt* (41), *I Wake Up Screaming* (41), *Ten Gentlemen From West Point* (42), *The Black Swan* (42), *Heaven Can Wait* (43), *The Lodger* (44), *Hangover Square* (44).

## CRENNA, Richard (1926- )

Around 1950, a poll was taken to find the most popular boy characters on radio and Richard Crenna was to be the winner, most famously the crack-voiced highschool kid of *Our Miss Brooks* (which he also played on TV). Born in Los Angeles, Crenna moved over to TV after much experience in radio comedy. Since the 1950s he has appeared in several series including *The Real McCoys*, *Slattery's People*, *All's Fair*, and *It Takes Two*. Meanwhile he worked in occasional films, but his screen career did not take off until he was cast against type as a killer in *Wait Until Dark* (67). A good many straight parts have followed, including a lead in *Marooned* (69); among his recent roles have been a ruthless businessman and murder victim in *Body Heat* (81) and costarring in *Table for Five* (83).
**Selected Films:** *Red Skies of Montana* (52), *John Goldfarb Please Come Home* (65), *The Sand Pebbles* (66), *Wait Until Dark* (67), *Star!* (68), *Marooned* (69), *Red Sky at Morning* (71), *Breakheart Pass* (76), *Body Heat* (81), *First Blood* (82), *Table for Five* (83), *The Flamingo Kid* (84).

## CRISP, Donald (1880-1974)

Born in Aberfeldy, Scotland, Crisp began his career in the motion picture industry in 1906, became a director of silent films (including some work with Buster Keaton on *The Navigator*), and from 1930 concentrated on acting, playing hundreds of usually stern character roles. Millions know him from the *Lassie* series of movies (42-45) and his Academy Award winning performance in *How Green was My Valley* (41).
**Selected Films:** *The Birth of a Nation* (15), *The Black Pirate* (26), *The Dawn Patrol* (38), *Brother Orchid* (40), *How Green Was My Valley* (41), *Lassie Come Home* (43), *The Uninvited* (44), *National Velvet* (44), *The Long Grey Line* (54), *The Last Hurrah* (58), *Pollyanna* (60), *Spencer's Mountain* (63).

## CRONYN, Hume (1911- )

Although his career in films has always been secondary to his distinguished career on the stage, since the 1940s Cronyn has proved his versatility in a wide range of supporting roles, often as an 'ordinary' person in an unusual situation who reveals previously untapped resources of pathos, fancy, or evil. Born Hume Cronyn Blake in London, Ontario, the son of a prominent politician, Cronyn made his stage debut at the age of 19 with the Montreal Repertory Theatre. He moved to Broadway in 1934, where he soon established himself not only as an outstanding actor, but as a skillful director. In 1942 he married Jessica Tandy, with whom he performed in many plays, and the following year made his screen debut in *Shadow of a Doubt*. His impressive screen writing credits include Alfred Hitchcock's *Rope* (48) and *Under Capricorn* (49).
**Selected Films:** *Shadow of a Doubt* (43), *Phantom of the Opera* (43), *The Cross of Lorraine* (43), *The Seventh Cross* (44), *Lifeboat* (44), *The Sailor Takes a Wife* (45), *The Green Years* (46), *The Postman Always Rings Twice* (46), *Brute Force* (47), *People Will Talk* (51), *Crowded Paradise* (56), *Sunrise at Campobello* (60), *Cleopatra* (63), *Hamlet* (64), *The Parallax View* (74), *Rollover* (80), *Honky Tonk Freeway* (81), *Cocoon* (85).

## CROSBY, Bing (1904-1977)

Born Harry Lillis Crosby in Tacoma, Washington, he was Mr Nice Guy personified, a crooner, an amiable and relaxed singer and light comedian whose warbling style made him a superstar. He took the name Bing from a comic strip character. While at Gonzaga University in Spokane, Washington, he began singing and playing drums with a small combo. By 1926 he had made it to the Paul Whiteman Band as part of a trio called 'Paul Whiteman's Rhythm Boys.' Going solo, Crosby began making records and doing Mack Sennett shorts, but his real break came with radio. In 1931 he starred in his own show and his theme song,

*Dorothy Lamour with Bing Crosby and Bob Hope in* The Road to Zanzibar *(41).*

'When the Blue of the Night (Meets the Gold of the Day),' swept America. His records set sales records – sales were in the millions. His on-screen records won him a spot in the box office top ten by 1934. In 1945 he was number one. Crosby's films were bits of fluff filled with song. In the 1940s he and comedian Bop Hope made a series of 'Road' pictures with Dorothy Lamour which were immensely popular and irresistably entertaining. Crosby also made movies on his own, combining humor and sentimentality. *Holiday Inn* (42), with the song 'White Christmas,' is a classic. In *Going My Way* (44), he played a singing priest, winning an Academy Award for Best Actor. He was a priest again in *The Bells of St Mary's* (45), with Ingrid Bergman as a nun, and after that the aura of friendly neighborhood priest seemed to cling to him. Actually Crosby was considerably more worldly and complex than he appeared. He proved his abilities as a serious actor in *The Country Girl* (54), with Grace Kelly, playing the part of an aging alcoholic. In 1930 Crosby had married singer Dixie Lee, and the couple had four sons. It was a stormy marriage and she died an alcoholic in 1953. Crosby married a young actress named Kathryn Grant in 1957 who bore him three children. One is actress Mary Frances Crosby. In his day, Bing was one of the most widely-loved stars in the world.

**Selected Films:** *King of Jazz* (30), *The Big Broadcast* (32), *College Humor* (33), *We're Not Dressing* (34), *Mississippi* (35), *Anything Goes* (36), *Pennies From Heaven* (36), *Sing You Sinners* (38), *The Road to Singapore* (40), *The Road to Zanzibar* (41), *Holiday Inn* (42), *The Road to Morocco* (42), *Going My Way* (44), *The Road to Utopia* (45), *The Bells of St Mary's* (45), *Blue Skies* (46), *The Road to Rio* (47), *The Emperor Waltz* (48), *A Connecticut Yankee in King Arthur's Court* (49), *Mr Music* (50), *The Road to Bali* (52), *The Country Girl (54)*, *High Society* (56), *The Road to Hong Kong* (62), *Stagecoach* (66), *That's Entertainment* (74).

## CROTHERS, Scatman (1910-1986)

Born Benjamin Sherman Crothers in Terre Haute, Indiana, he took the nickname 'Scatman' when a radio director said that he needed a snappier name, and Crothers rechristened himself after the scat singing technique at which he was proficient. He began his show business career at the age of 14 as a singer, drummer and guitarist in local speakeasies. In the mid-1930s he toured with his own band throughout the Midwest, and when they got a booking in Los Angeles, he began to appear on a local TV show called *Dixie Showboat*. His first movie break was in *Meet Me at the Fair* (52), which starred Dan Dailey. Crothers was perhaps best known for his television work, appearing in many dramas and miniseries, plus having a regular spot as Louie the garbage collector on the situation comedy series, *Chico and the Man*.

**Selected Films:** *Meet Me at the Fair* (52), *Hello, Dolly!* (69), *One Flew Over the Cuckoo's Nest* (75), *The Shootist* (76), *Broncho Billy* (80), *The Shining* (80), *Twilight Zone: The Movie* (83).

## CRUISE, Tom (1962- )

Catapulted to stardom along with co-star Rebecca De Mornay by the surprisingly successful film *Risky Business* (83), Cruise, born in Syracuse, New York, is emerging as a leading man for the eighties: clean-cut but sexy, strong but vulnerable, cool, knowledgeable, and mildly self-mocking – 'Superman in miniature.'

**Selected Films:** *Endless Love* (81), *Taps* (81), *Losin' It* (83), *The Outsiders* (83), *Risky Business* (83), *All the Right Moves* (83), *Top Gun* (86), *Legend* (86), *The Color of Money* (86).

## CRYSTAL, Billy (1945- )

Born in Long Beach, New York, the son of a jazz promoter, Crystal came to fame as a comedian in the 1980s, appearing often in guest roles on TV shows and series like *Soap*; in 1985-6 he relaunched his career on TV's *Saturday Night Live* comedy show. His screen appearances have been few to date.

**Selected Films:** *Rabbit Test* (78), *Running Scared* (86), *Whereabouts* (87).

## CUMMINGS, Constance (1910- )

Born Constance Halverstadt in Seattle, Washington, Cummings began acting onstage in her teens and arrived in Hollywood from Broadway in the early 1930s. Her smoothly beautiful features graced a number of minor films until, unhappy with her roles, she turned to the stage and then moved to England, where she appeared in occasional films into the 1960s.

**Selected Films:** *The Criminal Code* (31), *Busman's Honeymoon* (40), *Blithe Spirit* (45), *In the Cool of the Day* (63).

## CUMMINGS, Robert (1908- )

Unforgettable as the star of TV's long-running sitcom *The Bob Cummings Show*, the ever-youthful Cummings delivered on TV essentially the same persona that had made him a favorite light leading man in romantic Hollywood comedies of the forties. But Cummings was never limited to the affable bumbler, as his dramatic effectiveness in such films as *Dial M for Murder* (54) amply illustrates. Born Clarence Robert Orville Cummings in Joplin, Missouri, Cummings forged a British accent and an English identity as Blade Stanhope Conway to help him break onto Broadway in 1931. He posed as Texan Brice Hutchens to ease his way into films in *The Virginia Judge* (35), but reclaimed his own name for his forties leads. His TV series *My Living Doll* (64) was also a success. Cummings is a champion of health foods and vitamins, and has written a nutritional work, *How To Stay Young and Vital*.

**Selected Films:** *Sons of the Desert* (33), *The Virginia Judge* (35), *Forgotten Faces* (36), *Last Train from Madrid* (37), *Rio* (39), *Spring Parade* (40), *King's Row* (41), *Moon Over Miami* (41), *It Started with Eve* (41), *Saboteur* (42), *The Bride Wore Boots* (46), *The Accused* (48), *For Heaven's Sake* (50), *Dial M for Murder* (54), *My Geisha* (62), *The Carpetbaggers* (64), *Stagecoach* (66), *Five Golden Dragons* (67).

## CURRIE, Finlay (1878-1968)

A native of Edinburgh and veteran of stage and music hall, Currie (born Finlay Jefferson) is memorable for his Scottish burr, flowing gray hair, and comfortable girth. He received an Academy Award nomination for his portrayal of Magwitch in David Lean's *Great Expectations* (46).

**Selected Films:** *The Old Man* (31), *The Case of the Frightened Lady* (32), *Great Expectations* (46), *Sleeping Car to Trieste* (48), *Whiskey Galore* (49), *The History of Mr Polly* (49), *The Mudlark* (51), *People Will Talk* (52), *Ben Hur* (59), *Bunny Lake is Missing* (65).

## CURTIS, Alan (1909-1953)

Dark and handsome, Curtis was a male model before breaking into films in 1936. Born Harold Neberroth in Chicago, Curtis played many romantic leads and sometimes villains in B films of the forties.

**Selected Films:** *Walking on Air* (36), *Winterset* (36), *Mannequin* (38), *Hollywood Cavalcade* (39), *High Sierra* (41), *New Wine* (41), *Hitler's Madman* (43), *Gung Ho!* (43), *Phantom Lady* (44), *See My Lawyer* (45), *Renegade Girl* (46), *The Masked Pirate* (50).

## CURTIS, Jamie Lee (1958- )

The daughter of actor Tony Curtis and actress Janet Leigh, Curtis was born in Los Angeles and thus far in her career has apparently specialized in horror films. Her TV appearances include *Operation Petticoat.*

**Selected Films:** *Halloween* (79), *Prom Night* (80), *Terror Train* (80), *The Fog* (80), *Halloween II* (81), *Road Games* (81), *My Love Letters* (83), *Trading Places* (83), *Perfect* (85), *Amazing Grace and Chuck* (87).

## CURTIS, Tony (1925- )

Curtis was a teen idol in the 1950s, a good-looking, curly-haired, juvenile delinquent type who made young girls swoon. But he proved that he had staying power and later turned in several sensitive performances in important films. He was born Bernard Schwartz in The Bronx, New York, the son of an immigrant tailor from Hungary. Curtis spent his early years in poverty and joined a street gang at the age of 11. A neighborhood settlement house rescued him from his potential life of crime and taught him a love of the theater. He served in the Navy during World War II and when he returned to New York he studied at the City College of New York and took acting classes at the Dramatic Workshop. Next he toured the Catskill Mountains 'Borscht Circuit,' a time-honored training ground for young comedians and actors. Off-Broadway followed, and then he got a lucky break. Universal Studios signed him in 1949, decided that he was right for stardom, and put real muscle into promoting him. He was one of the last movie actors to make a career aided by the Hollywood studio buildup. Despite his Bronx accent, Curtis played swashbuckling roles, wowing the girls as *The Prince Who Was a Thief* (51), an Arabian Nights dream fantasy. That same year Curtis married Hollywood star Janet Leigh. Divorced in 1962, they are the parents of up-and-coming actress Jamie Lee Curtis. Curtis was an admirer of Cary Grant and hoped to emulate his career. But to become a star of that rank, Curtis had to shed his bobby-soxer following without taking a fall at the box office. Although he never became a second Cary Grant, when he teamed up with Burt Lancaster to do *The Sweet Smell of Success* (57), he won critical recognition for the first time, and was excellent as the unctious fawning press agent. *The Defiant Ones* (58) won him an Oscar nomination. He was also excellent as a musician in drag pursuing Marilyn Monroe in *Some Like It Hot* (59). Since then Curtis has done serious roles and light comedies as well as worked in television. In 1977 he became an author, publishing his first novel, *Kid Andrew Cody and Julie Sparrow.*

**Selected Films:** *Criss Cross* (49), *City Across the River* (49), *The Prince Who Was a Thief* (51), *Houdini* (53), *The Black Shield of Falworth* (54), *Trapeze* (56), *The Sweet Smell of Success* (57), *The Vikings* (58), *Kings Go Forth* (58), *The Defiant Ones* (58), *Some Like It Hot* (59), *Operation Petticoat* (59), *Spartacus* (60), *The Great Imposter* (60), *Taras Bulba* (62), *Captain Newman MD* (63), *The Great Race* (65), *The Boston Strangler* (68), *The Last Tycoon* (76), *Sextette* (78), *The Mirror Crack'd* (80), *Brainwaves* (82)

*Jack Lemmon and Tony Curtis in* Some Like It Hot *(59).*

## CUSACK, Cyril (1910- )

Born in Durban, South Africa and raised in Ireland, the diminutive Cusack made his film debut at the age of 7, in *Knocknagow* (18) and joined the Abbey Theatre for 14 years in 1932. His film appearances, regular since the 1940s, are mainly supporting roles because of his size. His daughters Sinead and Sorcha are both actresses.
**Selected Films:** *Knocknagow* (18), *Odd Man Out* (47), *The Man Who Never Was* (56), *Jacqueline* (56), *Waltz of the Toreadors* (62), *Fahrenheit 451* (66), *The Homecoming* (73), *Juggernaut* (74), *Tristan and Isolt* (79), *True Confessions* (81), *Little Dorrit* (87).

## CUSACK, John (1967- )

Born in Chicago and raised in Evanston, Illinois, Cusack began studying acting as a child and made his film debut in *Class* (83). After roles in two more midwestern productions he landed the comedic lead in *The Sure Thing* (84).
**Selected Films:** *Class* (83), *Sixteen Candles* (83), *Grandview, U.S.A* (83), *The Sure Thing* (84), *The Journey of Natty Gann* (85), *Greetings From Nantucket* (86), *Stand By Me* (86), *One Crazy Summer* (86), *Hot Pursuit* (87).

## CUSHING, Peter (1913- )

This distinguished actor was born in Surrey, England, and has solid experience on stage, screen and television. His slightly fussy manner at first confined him to mild roles, but then he was discovered by Hammer Films in England and starred in many of their horror pictures, in which he dealt firmly with monsters of all kinds. Often teamed with Christopher Lee in those films, he played Dr Frankenstein to Lee's Monster, an archaeologist to Lee's Mummy and Dr Van Helsing to Lee's Dracula. He has also played in science-fiction movies, most notably in *Star Wars* (77).
**Selected Films:** *The Man in the Iron Mask* (39), *Hamlet* (47), *Moulin Rouge* (53), *The Curse of Frankenstein* (57), *Dracula* (58), *The Revenge of Frankenstein* (58), *The Hound of the Baskervilles* (59), *The Mummy* (59), *Brides of Dracula* (60), *Cash on Demand* (63), *Dr Terror's House of Horrors* (65), *Frankenstein Created Woman* (67), *The Vampire Lovers* (70), *Dracula AD 1972* (72), *Tales from the Crypt* (72), *Madhouse* (74), *Star Wars* (77), *An Arabian Adventure* (79), *Black Jack* (81), *House of the Long Shadows* (82), *Top Secret* (84).

*Peter Cushing in* The Satanic Rites of Dracula *(73).*

## DA SILVA, Howard (1909-1986)

The tough-looking Da Silva moved from character roles of suspicious heavies to leads in the late 1940s. Born Harold Silverblatt, in Cleveland, Ohio, he had experience as a steel worker and on Broadway, where he played Jud in the musical *Oklahoma!* (43). He was blacklisted during the 1950s.
**Selected Films:** *Abe Lincoln in Illinois* (39), *The Sea Wolf* (41), *The Lost Weekend* (45), *The Great Gatsby* (49), *M* (51), *David and Lisa* (63), *1776* (72), *Mommie Dearest* (81).

## DAHL, Arlene (1924- )

A ravishing redhead born in Minneapolis, Minnesota, whose leading Hollywood roles are noteworthy more for their decorative quality than for any display of acting, the glamorous Dahl broke into films in 1947 with modeling and Broadway experience. She has been a successful beauty columnist.
**Selected Films:** *Life With Father* (47), *My Wild Irish Rose* (47), *Ambush* (49), *Journey to the Center of the Earth* (59), *Land Raiders* (69), *Du blé en liasses* (70).

## DAILEY, Dan (1914-1978)

This lanky actor-singer-dancer was born in New York, and began his career in vaudeville and cabaret acts. He had leading roles in many popular Hollywood musicals during the 1940s and 1950s, most notably in *Mother Wore Tights* (47), *Give My Regards to Broadway* (48) and *It's Always Fair Weather* (55), in which he held his own against dancers like Gene Kelly, Michael Kidd, Cyd Charisse and Dolores Gray.
**Selected Films:** *The Mortal Storm* (40), *Mother Wore Tights* (47), *Give My Regards to Broadway* (48), *My Blue Heaven* (50), *It's Always Fair Weather* (55), *The Best Things in Life Are Free* (56), *Pepe* (60), *The Private Files of J Edgar Hoover* (77).

## DALTON, Timothy (1944- )

Born in Wales, the tall, saturnine Dalton is an established leading man on the British stage and in occasional films, especially period pieces. In 1987 he became the fourth actor to play James Bond.
**Selected Films:** *The Lion in Winter* (68), *Wuthering Heights* (70), *Mary Queen of Scots* (71), *Lady Caroline Lamb* (72), *Agatha* (79), *Flash Gordon* (80), *Chanel Solitaire* (81), *The Doctor and the Devils* (85), *The Living Daylights* (87).

## DANDRIDGE, Dorothy (1923-1965)

Born in Cleveland, Ohio, Dandridge broke into films in *A Day at the Races* (37). In the late 1950s the dancer and singer became one of the first blacks to achieve star status in film. Financial reverses probably contributed to her death from an overdose.
**Selected Films:** *A Day at the Races* (37), *Lady from Louisiana* (41), *Bright Road* (52), *Carmen Jones* (54), *Island in the Sun* (57), *Porgy and Bess* (59), *Tamango* (59), *Moment of Danger* (60).

## D'ANGELO, Beverly (1952- )

Ohio-born D'Angelo was an animation cartoonist and rock singer before making her film debut in *The Sentinel* (77). She has since played off-beat roles in films including *National Lampoon's Vacation* (83).
**Selected Films:** *The Sentinel* (77), *Every Which Way But Loose* (78), *Hair* (79), *Coal Miner's Daughter* (80), *Honky Tonk Freeway* (81), *National Lampoon's Vacation* (83), *Slow Burn* (86), *Big Trouble* (86).

## DANGERFIELD, Rodney (1921- )

Born Jacob Coehn on Long Island, Dangerfield began doing standup comedy in his teens. Later, after some years of retirement, he returned with his trademark line 'I don't get no respect' to fame on TV and in nightclubs. Having made a few relatively tentative appearances in movies he scored a hit in 1986, starring in *Back to School*.
**Selected Films:** *The Projectionist* (71), *Caddyshack* (80), *Easy Money* (83), *Back to School* (86).

## DANIELL, Henry (1894-1963)

London-born Charles Henry Daniell came to Hollywood via the British and Broadway stage. Suave, cutting, cold-eyed, Daniell usually played upper-crust or authoritarian roles. He was a popular villain in scores of character roles in the 1930s, 1940s and 1950s.
**Selected Films:** *Jealousy* (29), *Camille* (36), *The Sea Hawk* (40), *The Philadelphia Story* (40), *The Great Dictator* (40), *Sherlock Holmes in Washington* (43), *The Suspect* (44), *The Body Snatcher* (45), *The Prodigal* (55), *The Chapman Report* (62), *My Fair Lady* (64).

## DANIELS, Bebe (1901-1971)

One of Paramount's most popular leading ladies of the silent era, Virginia Daniels, often cast in impish, light leads, came from a theatrical family and made her screen debut at 7 in the short *The Common Enemy* (10). After marrying Ben Lyon in 1931, she and her husband starred on British radio.
**Selected Films:** *Male and Female* (19), *Rio Rita* (29), *The Maltese Falcon* (31), *Forty-Second Street* (33), *Life with the Lyons* (53), *The Lyons in Paris* (55).

## DANIELS, Jeff (1955- )

Georgia-born Daniels pursued a stage apprenticeship at New York's Circle Repertory Theatre and appeared often on TV before making his screen debut in *Ragtime* (81). After a major role as Flap Horton in *Terms of Endearment* (83), his wholesome good looks were used to advantage in Woody Allen's *The Purple Rose of Cairo* (85), where Daniels engagingly played a double role as an ingenuous character who steps off a movie screen and the disingenuous real-life actor.
**Selected Films:** *Ragtime* (81), *Terms of Endearment* (83), *Marie* (85), *The Purple Rose of Cairo* (85), *Heartburn* (86), *Something Wild* (86), *Radio Days* (87).

## DANNER, Blythe (1945- )

A native of Philadelphia, Danner made her mark as a young actress of the seventies on stage, TV, and films, receiving a Tony Award for her Broadway performance in *Butterflies are Free*. Her work also includes many made-for-TV films and the series *Adam's Rib*. Her films are infrequent.
**Selected Films:** *1776* (72), *Lovin' Molly* (74), *Futureworld* (76), *The Great Santini* (79), *Man, Woman and Child* (83), *Brighton Beach Memoirs* (87).

## DANSON, Ted (1947- )

California-born Danson is most familiar as the tavern owner in the TV series *Cheers*. He has appeared in only a few films since his debut in *The Onion Field* (79).
**Selected Films:** *The Onion Field* (79), *Body Heat* (81), *Creepshow* (83), *A Fine Mess* (86), *Just Between Friends* (86).

## DANTINE, Helmut (1917-1982)

Born in Vienna, the lean, handsome Dantine arrived in California in 1938 and made his film debut in *International Squadron* (41). Ironically he specialized in Nazi roles during the 1940s, and in the late 1950s became a ranking executive with Schenck Enterprises.
**Selected Films:** *International Squadron* (41), *Mrs Miniver* (41), *Casablanca* (43), *Passage to Marseilles* (44), *Hotel Berlin* (45), *Whispering City* (48), *Call Me Madam* (53), *War and Peace* (56), *Operation Crossbow* (65), *The Killer Elite* (75).

## DARBY, Kim (1948- )

Born Deborah Zerby to parent performers the 'Dancing Zerbies,' in Hollywood, Kim Darby began in show business early and appeared in the TV series *Mr Novak* and *Run for Your Life*. She made her film debut in *Bye, Bye Birdie* (63), and has been seen frequently in made-for-television films. She is best known for her performance in *True Grit* (69).
**Selected Films:** *Bye, Bye Birdie* (63), *The Restless Ones* (65), *True Grit* (69), *The Strawberry Statement* (70), *The Grissom Gang* (71), *The One and Only* (78), *Better Off Dead* (85).

## DARNELL, Linda (1921-1965)

One of Hollywood's most popular stars of the 1940s, the sultry, wide-eyed Darnell was never more than a decorative actress, but she performed her role so well that she carved herself a niche as one of the premier sirens of the era. Born Monetta Eloyse Darnell in Dallas, Texas, she was entered by her stage mother into beauty and talent contests when she was eleven years old. At sixteen she won an RKO screen test, and two years later she was signed by Fox, where she made her debut in *Hotel for Women* (39). Her early roles emphasized the virginal side of her exotic beauty and gemlike complexion; under the direction of Otto Preminger, for whom she did her best work *Fallen Angel* (45), *Forever Amber* (47), and *The 13th Letter* (51), she became an exquisite temptress. Darnell worked only intermittantly during the 1950s. She died in a fire that started while she was watching her film *Star Dust* (40) on TV.
**Selected Films:** *Hotel for Women* (39), *Star Dust* (40), *Brigham Young* (40), *The Mark of Zorro* (40), *Rise and Shine* (41), *The Song of Bernadette* (43), *It Happened Tomorrow* (44), *Fallen Angel* (45), *Forever Amber* (47), *Unfaithfully Yours* (48), *No Way Out* (50), *Two Flags West* (50), *The 13th Letter* (51), *Second Chance* (53), *Zero Hour* (57), *Black Spurs* (65).

## DARRIEUX, Danielle (1917- )

A fine actress, stunningly beautiful and always elegant, Darrieux began her long career as the personification of French femininity with an adolescent role in *Le Bal* (31). Born in Bordeaux, she was studying cello in Paris when her mother had her audition for the part. At the age of 19, playing opposite Charles Boyer in *Mayerling* (36), she became an international star. Of all her films, her greatest were those directed by Max Ophuls: *La Ronde* (50), *Le Plaisir* (51), and *Madame de ...* (53). In the last of these she gave perhaps her greatest performance as a romantic but knowing woman with impenetrable charm who loses the greatest love of her life over a pair of earrings. She made an excellent American film with Douglas Fairbanks in 1938, *The Rage of Paris*. Still active, she appeared in the Broadway musical *Coco* in 1970.
**Selected Films:** *Le Bal* (31), *Mayerling* (36) *The Rage of Paris* (38), *Battements de Coeur* (39), *Occupe-Toi d'Amelie* (49), *La Ronde* (50), *Le Plaisir* (51), *Five Fingers* (52), *Madame de ...* (53), *Le Rouge et le Noir* (54), *24 Heures de la Vie d'une Femme* (68), *Le Cavaleur* (79), *Scene of the Crime* (86).

## DARRO(W), Frankie (1917-1976)

The son of circus performers, Darro, born Frank Johnson in Chicago, debuted in film at six and moved on to roles as Depression-era tough kids. His diminutive stature made him perfect for leads as jockeys and punks in many second features.
**Selected Films:** *So Big* (24), *The Circus Kid* (28), *Wild Boys of the Road* (33), *Broadway Bill* (34), *No Greater Glory* (34), *Racing Blood* (37), *Laughing at Danger* (40), *Trouble Makers* (48), *Across the Wide Missouri* (51), *Operation Petticoat* (59), *Hook, Line and Sinker* (69).

## DARWELL, Jane (1880-1967)

Best-rememberd for her warm, maternal roles, as exemplified by Ma Joad in *The Grapes of Wrath* (40), for which she received an Academy Award, Darwell, was born Pattie Woodward, in Palmyra, Missouri, and began her film career in *The Capture of Aguinaldo* (13).
**Selected Films:** *The Capture of Aguinaldo* (13), *Rose of the Rancho* (14), *Tom Sawyer* (30), *Slave Ship* (37), *The Grapes of Wrath* (40), *All That Money Can Buy* (41), *Captain Tugboat Annie* (46), *Wagonmaster* (50), *The Last Hurrah* (58), *Mary Poppins* (64).

## DAUPHINE, Claude (1903-1978)

Born Claude Legrand in Corbeil, France, into a family of French performers, Dauphine began as a set designer, moved to the stage, and made his film debut in 1930. The dapper actor played sophisticated, cosmopolitan leads and supporting roles in American, French and British films.
**Selected Films:** *Langrevin Père et Fils* (30), *Entrée des Artists* (38), *Battements de Coeur* (39), *English Without Tears* (44), *Le Plaisir* (51), *The Quiet American* (58), *Lady L* (65), *Rosebud* (75), *Madame Rosa* (77), *Le Point de Mire* (77).

## DAVENPORT, Harry (1866-1949)

Born into a family of actors in New York City, after a distinguished stage career and a few insignificant silent films Davenport established himself in the talkies in hundreds of character roles, especially as everybody's good old gramps – cheerful, chucklesome, good-natured and benevolent.
**Selected Films:** *Father and the Boy* (15), *Her Unborn Child* (29), *The Life of Emile Zola* (37), *You Can't Take It With You* (38), *The Hunchback of Notre Dame* (39), *King's Row* (41), *Son of Fury* (42), *The Ox Bow Incident* (43), *Meet Me in St Louis* (44), *The Enchanted Forest* (45), *That Forsyte Woman* (49), *Riding High* (50).

## DAVENPORT, Nigel (1928- )

On the British stage beginning in the early 1950s, Davenport, a native of Shelford, Cambridge, made his film debut in *Look Back in Anger* (59), and has played numerous leads and supporting roles of a virile, urbane nature.

**Selected Films:** *Peeping Tom* (59), *Where the Spies Are* (66), *A Man for All Seasons* (67), *The Virgin Soldiers* (69), *Living Free* (72), *Zulu Dawn* (79), *Chariots of Fire* (80), *Nighthawks* (81).

## DAVIES, Marion (1897-1961)

Born Marion Douras in Brooklyn, she was really a gifted comedienne, but never seemed to get a good role, although she enjoyed moderate success from 1917 to 1937, when she retired. She was the long-time mistress of newspaper tsar William Randolph Hearst, who used his publications empire to try to make her a star, and even formed Cosmpolitan Studios to film her pictures. The costume dramas that Hearst favored buried her bubbly talent and probably destroyed her career.

**Selected Films:** *Runaway Romany* (17), *Cecilia of the Pink Roses* (18), *The Belle of New York* (19), *When Knighthood Was in Flower* (22), *Beverly of Graustark* (26), *Quality Street* (27), *Show People* (28), *Polly of the Circus* (32), *Page Miss Glory* (35), *Cain and Mabel* (36), *Ever Since Eve* (37).

## DAVIS, Bette (1908- )

In her more than 80 films during her career, Davis was often the flinty, acid-tongued woman who could speak words as though she were spitting nails. Her toe-to-toe combat in the front offices of Hollywood film companies made her a force to be reckoned with as well. She was born Ruth-Elizabeth Davis in Lowell, Massachusetts, and began acting in summer stock productions with the Provincetown Players. She was short, with a high-pitched voice, and wasn't the sort to win beauty contests. Carl Laemmle, the head of Universal Studios, described her as having 'as much sex appeal as Slim Summerville.' Only by fighting like a tiger did Davis win the recognition she deserved. She made her Broadway debut in a trifle called *Broken Dishes* in 1929, and by 1930 she was in Hollywood, making her first film, *Bad Sister* (31), playing the good sister. Her performance went unnoticed. Not a classic beauty, she was the electrifying bitch in *Of Human Bondage* (34) and *Dangerous* (35), which won her an Academy Award for Best Actress, and also made her a box-office attraction with clout. Davis' confrontations with the front office of Warner Bros. led to 16 suspensions without pay. Women in particular flocked to Davis films and she appeared in a series of vehicles tailored specifically for her. Audiences liked her best when she was bright and bitchy, but she was also effective in weepy soaps. *Jezebel* (38), won her a second Academy Award. In the late 1940s Davis' career took a dive but she again fought back, appearing with fourth husband Gary Merrill in *All About Eve* (50), possibly her best film, playing a character based on Tallulah Bankhead. The movie took an Oscar for Best Picture and put Davis back on top. When her career bagan to falter again, she appeared on Broadway in *The Night of the Iguana* (61), by Tennessee Williams, and took out trade advertisements announcing her availability for films. She accepted work in horror pictures and on television. She later referred to

*Bette Davis and Edward G Robinson in* Kid Galahad *(37).*

herself during this era as 'Boris Karloff in skirts.' However, *What Ever Happened to Baby Jane?* (62), with Joan Crawford, was a huge success. A real pro, Davis continued acting, and in 1977 was the first woman to receive the American Film Institute Life Achievement Award.
**Selected Films:** *Bad Sister* (31), *The Man Who Played God* (32), *Cabin in the Cotton* (32), *Twenty Thousand Years in Sing Sing* (32), *Jimmy the Gent* (34), *Of Human Bondage* (34), *Bordertown* (34), *Front Page Woman* (35), *Dangerous* (35), *The Petrified Forest* (36), *Marked Woman* (37), *Kid Galahad* (37), *Jezebel* (38), *Dark Victory* (39), *Juarez* (39), *The Old Maid* (39), *The Private Lives of Elizabeth and Essex* (39), *All This and Heaven Too* (40), *The Letter* (40), *The Great Lie* (41), *The Little Foxes* (41), *The Man Who Came to Dinner* (41), *Now Voyager* (42), *Watch on the Rhine* (43), *Old Acquaintance* (43), *Mr Skeffington* (43), *The Corn Is Green* (45), *All About Eve* (50), *The Catered Affair* (56), *A Pocketful of Miracles* (61), *What Ever Happened to Baby Jane?* (62), *Hush ... Hush Sweet Charlotte* (65), *The Nanny* (65), *The Anniversary* (67), *Burnt Offerings* (76), *Death On the Nile* (78), *The Whales of August* (87).

## DAVIS, Brad (1949- )

American actor Davis first starred as Billy, in *Midnight Express* (77). He appeared in the TV mini-series *Roots* and as the lead role in Rainer Werner Fassbinder's screen adaptation of Jean Genet's novel *Querelle* (83).
**Selected Films:** *Midnight Express* (77), *A Small Circle of Friends* (80), *Chariots of Fire* (81), *Querelle* (83).

## DAVIS, Joan (1907-1961)

Known to millions as Joan in the TV series *I Married Joan*, the rubber-faced comedienne born Madonna Davis in St Paul, Minnesota, began performing as a child and made her first feature film in 1935. Her slapstick style brightened many musicals of the 1930s and 1940s.
**Selected Films:** *Millions in the Air* (35), *Thin Ice* (37), *Hold That Coed* (38), *Hold That Ghost* (41), *Show Business* (44), *George White's Scandals* (45), *Harem Girl* (53).

## DAVIS, Judy (1956- )

Born in Perth, Australia, Davis was a rock singer before gravitating to acting. After stage experience she made a stunning debut starring as the feminist heroine in the Australian film *My Brilliant Career* (79), for which she won a British Film Academy Best Actress award. Her movie work since has been occasional, but she did star in *A Passage to India* (84), a role which earned her an Academy Award nomination for Best Actress.
**Selected Films:** *My Brilliant Career* (79), *The Winter of our Dreams* (81), *Heatwave* (82), *Who Dares Wins* (82), *A Passage to India* (84), *Kangaroo* (87).

## DAVIS, Nancy (1923- )

Born Anne Frances Robbins in New York, Davis was leading lady of a few 1950s films. She is best known for marrying one of her leading men, Ronald Reagan, in 1952.
**Selected Films:** *Shadow on the Wall* (50), *The Doctor and the Girl* (50), *Night Into Morning* (51), *It's a Big Country* (53), *Donovan's Brain* (53), *Crash Landing* (57), *Hellcats of the Navy* (57).

## DAVIS, Ossie (1917- )

A black American actor, producer, director, playwright and screenwriter of powerful presence, Davis made his way from Cogdell, Georgia to the screen via Broadway in 1950. His stage triumphs include *Purlie Victorious* (61), which he wrote and starred in. He is married to actress Ruby Dee.
**Selected Films:** *No Way Out* (50), *The Joe Louis Story* (53), *Gone Are the Days!* (63), *Slaves* (69), *Let's Do It Again* (75), *Hot Stuff* (79).

## DAVIS, Sammy Jr (1925- )

Dynamism and energy are the stock in trade of this one-eyed black singer, dancer, actor and all-round entertainer. Born in New York, he was performing in vaudeville before he was three. Primarily a night club performer, he has appeared in several pictures as a member of 'The Rat Pack,' which included his friends Frank Sinatra, Dean Martin, Joey Bishop and Peter Lawford. On the other hand, he has shown great sensitivity as an actor in the few pictures in which he was given a straight part, most notably in *Anna Lucasta* (58), and he was wonderful as Sportin' Life in *Porgy and Bess* (59).
**Selected Films:** *Anna Lucasta* (58), *Porgy and Bess* (59), *Ocean's Eleven* (60), *Sergeants Three* (62), *Robin and the Seven Hoods* (64), *The Threepenny Opera* (65), *Sweet Charity* (68), *Stop the World – I Want to Get Off* (78), *The Cannonball Run* (81), *The Cannonball Run II* (82).

## DAY, Doris (1924- )

Born Doris Kappelhoff in Cincinnati, Ohio, she started off as a dance band singer, and while she was with the Les Brown Orchestra, her rendition of 'Sentimental Journey' took the country by storm – it was a superb recording and she was magnificently nostalgic, but also it was recorded at the end of World War II, and had a special meaning for almost everyone. Signed to a film contract, she rocketed to movie stardom overnight in her first picture, the musical *Romance on the High Seas* (48). With her short blonde hair, freckles and sunny smile, she became a symbol of the lighthearted 1950s films. Although she was primarily a singer, she also became known for her non-musical dramatic and comedy roles. During her career she sang two songs that received Academy Awards – 'Secret Love' in *Calamity Jane* (53) and 'Que Sera

Sera' in *The Man Who Knew Too Much* (56). It looked as though she had the world on a string until at the death of her third husband, Marty Melcher, in 1968, it was revealed that he had either mismanaged her career or embezzled all her money. She recouped her fortunes with *The Doris Day Show* on television and by suing her former lawyer, but her film career was over. She had starred with the best of them – Kirk Douglas, Gordon MacRae, Howard Keel, Frank Sinatra, James Cagney, James Stewart, John Raitt, Rock Hudson, David Niven, Jimmy Durante, Cary Grant and Clark Gable.
**Selected Films:** *Romance on the High Seas* (48), *Young Man with a Horn* (50), *Storm Warning* (50), *On Moonlight Bay* (50), *Calamity Jane* (53), *Young at Heart* (55), *Love Me or Leave Me* (55), *The Man Who Knew Too Much* (56), *The Pajama Game* (57), *Teacher's Pet* (58), *Pillow Talk* (59), *Please Don't Eat the Daisies* (60), *That Touch of Mink* (62), *Billy Rose's Jumbo* (62), *Send Me No Flowers* (64), *With Six You Get Egg Roll* (68).

*Doris Day in* Lullaby of Broadway *(51).*

## DAY, Josette (1914-1978)

Born Josette Dagory in Paris, Day first appeared in film at the age of five. After dancing in the Paris Opera she returned to the screen in the early thirties and played leads in many French films, including the role of Beauty in Cocteau's *La Belle et la Bête* (45).
**Selected Films:** *La Pochard* (19), *Allo Berlin . . . Ici Paris* (32), *La Fille du Puisatier* (40), *La Belle et la Bête* (45), *Les Parents Terribles* (48), *Four Day's Leave* (49).

## DAY, Laraine (1917- )

Born in Roosevelt, Utah, Day appeared with the Long Beach Players and made her screen debut in *Stella Dallas* (37). She played many leads, notably as Nurse Mary Lamont in the 'Dr Kildare' series. From 1947-1960 she was married to baseball player-manager Leo Durocher.
**Selected Films:** *Stella Dallas* (37), *Young Doctor Kildare* (39), *Foreign Correspondent* (40), *The Trial of Mary Dugan* (41), *The Locket* (46), *The Third Voice* (60), *House of Dracula's Daughter* (70).

## DEAN, James (1931-1955)

A cult figure to the young of the 1950s and a cult figure still today, Dean was the symbol of vulnerability, sensitivity and doomed rebellion. Born in Marion, Indiana, he moved to California with his parents when he was five. He was eight when, after the death of his mother, he returned to Indiana. In high school he participated in both athletics and drama, but he was on the short side for basketball. Jimmy (he was always called Jimmy or James, never Jim) attended Santa Monica Junior College in California and the University of California at Los Angeles. He studied acting with

*James Dean in* Giant *(56).*

James Whitmore, did some commercials and had bit parts in films. Dean went to New York in 1952, where he worked at a variety of odd jobs, getting his first big break with a role in *See the Jaguar* on Broadway. Classes at the Actors' Studio, the American homeland of the Stanislavsky Method, and roles on television followed. Despite his slight build and far-from-perfect features, Dean had charisma and he was soon noticed. He was cast in *The Immoralist* on Broadway in 1954, and after that moved to Hollywood and a meteoric rise to fame. He played the bad son whom the audience adored and identified with in *East of Eden* (55), winning an Academy Award nomination. *Rebel Without a Cause* (55) became the theme film of the affluent but apolitical 1950s generation. He was appealing as the poor cowboy who makes a killing in oil but remains a tortured soul in *Giant* (56), released shortly after his death. On 30 September 1955 Dean died in a car crash when driving his new Porsche to an auto race. The response to his death was astonishing. His funeral was a major event. Nothing like it had occurred since the death of Rudolph Valentino in the 1920s. James Dean fan clubs sprouted across America; many of the members refused to accept their hero's death. The 'Jimmy Dean Look' – short-sleeved shirt, blue jeans, partially unzipped jacket – became the uniform of teen-age boys everywhere. Books, poems and plays were written about Dean, and his home town in Indiana was invaded by kids. He epitomized their idea of loneliness, rejection and victimization by an unfeeling adult world.
**Selected Films:** *Has Anybody Seen My Gal?* (51), *Sailor Beware* (51), *Fixed Bayonets* (52), *Trouble Along the Way* (53), *East of Eden* (55), *Rebel Without a Cause* (55), *Giant* (56).

## DE CARLO, Yvonne (1922- )

Born Peggy Yvonne Middleton in Vancouver, Canada, De Carlo began dancing as a child, graduated to nightclubs, and in 1942 was hired by Paramount to play opposite men in screen tests. After she was cast in the title role of *Salome – Where She Danced* (45) followed by the *Song of Scheherezade* (47) and *Slave Girl* (47), she became one of Hollywood's favorite adventuresses, the image of the exotic Arabian Night temptress. Curiously enough, when she wasn't performing in exotic easterns she was usually playing leads in westerns, often as a dance hall girl. Although she was rarely asked to use it, she had considerable acting ability, with a flair for comedy. She starred in the TV series *The Munsters*.
**Selected Films:** *This Gun For Hire* (41), *Salome – Where She Danced* (45), *Brute Force* (47), *Song of Scheherazade* (47), *Slave Girl* (47), *Black Bart* (48), *Casbah* (48), *Criss Cross* (49), *The Desert Hawk* (50), *Hotel Sahara* (51), *Scarlet Angel* (52), *The Ten Commandments* (56), *Band of Angels* (57), *Timbuktu* (58), *McClintock!* (63), *Law of the Lawless* (64), *Munster Go Home* (66), *Hostile Guns* (67), *The Power* (68), *The Delta Factor* (70), *The Seven Minutes* (71), *Guyana: Crime of the Century* (80), *Liar's Moon* (82), *American Gothic* (87).

## DE CORDOVA, Arturo (1908-1973)

Popular in Mexican films since 1936, De Cordova was born Arturo Garcia in Merida, Yucatan, Mexico. His classic grin and flashing eyes made him a perfect Latin lover for Hollywood films in the 1940s, after which he returned to leads in Spanish lauguage films.
**Selected Films:** *Celos* (36), *For Whom the Bell Tolls* (43), *Frenchman's Creek* (44), *The Flame* (47), *New Orleans* (47), *The Adventures of Casanova* (48), *Kill Him for Me* (53), *Cena di Matrimonio* (62).

## DE CORSIA, Ted (1904-1973)

De Corsia, a native of New York City, is best remembered as a mean, ugly villainous character, often with leadership ability. He brought extensive vaudeville and radio experience to his many screen character roles which began in the late 1940s.
**Selected Films:** *The Lady From Shanghai* (47), *The Naked City* (48), *The Enforcer* (51), *Twenty Thousand Leagues Under the Sea* (54), *The Killing* (56), *From the Terrace* (60), *Nevada Smith* (66), *Five Card Stud* (68), *The Delta Factor* (70).

## DEE, Frances (1907- )

After beginning as an extra in 1929, Dee, born Jean Frances Dee in Pasadena, played opposite Maurice Chevalier in her first speaking role in 1931. She played many lovely leading ladies into the 1950s. She married actor Joel McCrea in 1933.
**Selected Films:** *Words and Music* (29), *Playboy of Paris* (31), *An American Tragedy* (31), *King of the Jungle* (33), *Little Women* (33), *If I Were King* (38), *Happy Land* (43), *The Private Affairs of Bel Ami* (48), *Mr Scoutmaster* (53), *Gypsy Colt* (54).

## DEE, Ruby (1923- )

Born Ruby Ann Wallace in Cleveland, Dee made an auspicious Broadway debut in 1946 in *Anna Lucasta*, and broke into films in the 1950s. She married Ossie Davis in 1948 and has been active in racial and humanitarian causes with him.
**Selected Films:** *No Way Out* (50), *The Jackie Robinson Story* (50), *Tall Target* (51), *Edge of the City* (57), *A Raisin in the Sun* (61), *Black Girl* (72), *Cat People* (82).

## DEE, Sandra (1942- )

A former model, the petite Dee, born Alexandra Zuck in Bayonne, New Jersey, broke into films in her teens and played the glamorous nymphet in many teen-oriented productions. She was married to singer Bobby Darin from 1960 to 1967.

**Selected Films:** *Until They Sail* (57), *Gidget* (59), *Imitation of Life* (59), *A Summer Place* (59), *Tammy Tell Me True* (61), *Tammy and the Doctor* (63), *You've Got to be Kidding* (67), *Rosie* (68), *The Dunwich Horror* (70), *Ad Est di Marsa Matruh* (71).

## DEFORE, Don (1917- )

Remembered as a regular on the TV series *Ozzie and Harriet* and *Hazel*, Defore, born in Cedar Rapids, Iowa, moved from Broadway roles to dozens of second leads and occasional leads in 1940s and 1950s films. He usually portrayed the good guy or gullible westerner.
**Selected Films:** *We Go Fast* (41), *A Guy Named Joe* (43), *Thirty Seconds Over Tokyo* (44), *Ramrod* (47), *Dark City* (50), *Battle Hymn* (57), *The Facts of Life* (61), *Carnauba* (81).

## DE HAVEN, Gloria (1924- )

Born in Los Angeles, the daughter of California vaudeville performers, De Haven first appeared on screen as an extra in *Modern Times* (36). A band vocalist in the 1930s, she was featured in many MGM musicals of the 1940s.
**Selected Films:** *Modern Times* (36), *The Great Dictator* (40), *Susan and God* (40), *Best Foot Forward* (43), *Two Girls and a Sailor* (44), *Yes Sir, That's My Baby* (49), *The Girl Rush* (55), *Evening in Byzantium* (78).

## DE HAVILLAND, Olivia (1916- )

There was fire under the sweetness in de Havilland. Born in Tokyo, Japan, the sister of actress Joan Fontaine, she was famous for her bitter feud with her sister, and it became a Hollywood legend. She began in Hollywood films as a teenager, scoring a coup in her first film, *A Midsummer Night's Dream* (35), but she soon became just another leading lady in comedy, romance and costume pictures, and was especially noted for playing the helpless heroine in Errol Flynn swashbucklers. Although their on-screen personalities meshed well, she yearned for better roles. De Havilland got them, thanks in part to winning a law suit against Warner Bros. after her success as a loan-out to David O Selznick, who cast her as Melanie in *Gone With the Wind* (39). She had proven herself to be an actress, and later won Academy Awards for Best Actress for *To Each His Own* (46) and *The Heiress* (49). In addition, she was nominated for Oscars as Best supporting Actress in *Gone With the Wind*. Best Actress for *Hold Back the Dawn* (41) and Best Actress in *The Snake Pit* (48). In 1955 she married Pierre Galante, editor of *Paris Match* magazine, and moved to France.
**Selected Films:** *A Midsummer Night's Dream* (35), *Captain Blood* (35), *Anthony Adverse* (36), *The Charge of the Light Brigade* (36), *The Adventures of*

*Olivia de Havilland, Leslie Howard, Vivien Leigh in* Gone With the Wind *(39).*

*Robin Hood* (38), *Gone With the Wind* (39), *Strawberry Blonde* (41), *Hold Back the Dawn* (41), *They Died with Their Boots On* (41), *The Male Animal* (42), *Devotion* (46), *The Dark Mirror* (46), *To Each His Own* (46), *The Snake Pit* (47), *The Heiress* (49), *My Cousin Rachel* (52), *Hush . . . Hush, Sweet Charlotte* (65), *Airport 77* (77), *The Swarm* (78).

## DEHNER, John (1915- )

A former animator for Walt Disney, this New York City native, born John Forkum, made his film debut in 1945, He usually portrays a sympathetic wise guy or a cruel villain.
**Selected Films:** *Captain Eddie* (45), *Barbary Pirate* (49), *Scaramouche* (52), *Apache* (54), *Carousel* (56), *Timbuktu* (59), *The Chapman Report* (62), *Youngblood Hawke* (64), *Stiletto* (69), *Support Your Local Gunfighter* (71), *The Boys from Brazil* (78).

## DEKKER, Albert (1904-1968)

Born Albert van Dekker in Brooklyn, the large-framed Dutch-American character actor was established on Broadway by 1927 and made his screen debut ten years later in *The Great Garrick*. He is especially known for his villainous roles, as in *Dr Cyclops* (40).
**Selected Films:** *The Great Garrick* (37), *The Last Warning* (38), *Extortion* (38), *Strange Cargo* (40), *Dr Cyclops* (40), *Among the Living* (41), *Yokel Boy* (42), *The Killers* (46), *Destination Murder* (50), *East of Eden* (55), *The Wonderful Country* (59), *The Wild Bunch* (69).

## DELEVANTI, Cyril (1887-1975)

Born in England, Delevanti brought considerable stage experience to his film career. He is best remembered for the many roles in which he played aged gentlemen.
**Selected Films:** *Mary Poppins* (64), *Night of the Iguana* (64), *The Greatest Story Ever Told* (65), *Counterpoint* (67), *The Killing of Sister George* (68), *Bedknobs and Broomsticks* (71), *Black Eye* (73).

## DELON, Alain (1935- )

Handsome, romantic-looking and sexy, Delon appears chiefly in French and Italian suspense films. He was born in Sceaux, France, was expelled from Catholic schools and served as a parachutist in Indochina during the siege of Dien Bien Phu. Delon first broke into films because of his good looks, but worked hard to overcome being type-cast as a 'pretty boy,' even forming his own production company, Adel, in 1964. He was the focus of a major scandal in 1968 involving drugs, sex and the murder of his bodyguard. He was later cleared, but his friendships with gangsters only added to his image as an aggressive and exciting screen personality.
**Selected Films:** *Quand la femme s'en mêle* (57), *Plein Soleil* (59), *Rocco and His Brothers* (60), *Eclipse* (61), *The Leopard* (62), *The Black Tulip* (64), *The Yellow Rolls Royce* (64), *Is Paris Burning?* (66), *Texas Across the River* (66), *Samurai* (67), *Borsalino* (70), *Scorpio* (72), *Mr Klein* (76), *Airport 79 – The Concorde* (79), *The Cache* (83).

## DEL RIO, Dolores (1905-1983)

A hauntingly beautiful and popular leading lady of the 1920s and 1930s, Del Rio, born Dolores Asunsolo in Durango, Mexico, abandoned Hollywood in 1943 for a more rewarding career in her native Mexico. She returned to Hollywood for occasional roles through the 1960s.
**Selected Films:** *Joanna* (25), *What Price Glory?* (26), *The Loves of Carmen* (27), *Evangeline* (29), *The Dove* (31), *Madame du Barry* (34), *Journey into Fear* (42), *The Fugitive* (47), *Cheyenne Autumn* (64), *The Children of Sanchez* (78).

## DE LUISE, Dom (1933- )

On screen from the mid-1960s, the rotund, balding Brooklyn-born De Luise first made his mark as a comedian in the 1950s on TV's *The Garry Moore Show*. He has appeared in films by Mel Brooks.
**Selected Films:** *Fail Safe* (64), *The Glass Bottom Boat* (65), *The Twelve Chairs* (70), *Blazing Saddles* (73), *Silent Movie* (76), *The Muppet Movie* (79), *Fatso* (80), *The Last Married Couple in America* (80), *The Best Little Whorehouse in Texas* (82), *Haunted Honeymoon* (86).

## DEMAREST, William (1892-1983)

His character roles made the versatile Demarest, born in St Paul, Minnesota, instantly recognizable to many who never knew his name. Vaudeville experience preceded his screen debut in 1927. He also appeared in the TV series *My Three Sons*.
**Selected Films:** *The Jazz Singer* (27), *Mr Smith Goes to Washington* (39), *Sullivan's Travel's* (41), *The Miracle of Morgan's Creek* (43), *Hail the Conquering Hero* (43), *The Jolson Story* (46), *The First Legion* (51), *Son of Flubber* (63), *That Darn Cat* (65), *Won Ton Ton, The Dog Who Saved Hollywood* (76).

## DE MORNAY, Rebecca (1963- )

Young American actress De Mornay was educated in Switzerland and made her screen debut with a bit part in *One from the Heart* (82). Since getting attention as a call girl in *Risky Business* (83) her career has taken off.
**Selected Films:** *One from the Heart* (82), *Risky Business* (83), *The Trip to Bountiful* (85), *Runaway Train* (85), *The Slugger's Wife* (85).

## DENEUVE, Cathérine (1943- )

In her screen persona the exquisitely beautiful Deneuve has somehow combined an icy in-

Eddie Albert and Catherine Deneuve in Hustle (75).

nocence with an intense sexuality. She has often been compared to Greta Garbo for her ability to reflect the emotions and fantasies of her public, and has been called cinema's greatest cool blonde – a nun on the way to a brothel. Daughter of actor Maurice Dorléac and younger sister of Françoise Dorléac, the young Parisienne took the maiden name of her mother – also an actress – when she made her screen debut at 13. She became well-known for her performance in *The Umbrellas of Cherbourg* (64) and internationally famous for her performance in Luis Bunuel's *Belle de Jour* (67), in which she plays an affluent, proper bourgeois housewife who moonlights as a whore while her husband is at work. She is a girl obsessed by sex in Polanki's *Repulsion* (65), a virgin who seduces the hero in *Benjamin* (68), a call girl and Burt Reynolds's mistress in *Hustle* (75). In her private life she has also gone her own way. She has a child by Roger Vadim (whom she refused to marry) and a child by Marcello Mastroianni; her only marriage, to photographer David Bailey, ended in divorce.

**Selected Films:** *Les Collégians* (56), *Les Portes Claquent* (60), *Vice and Virtue* (62), *The Umbrellas of Cherbourg* (64), *Repulsion* (66), *Belle de Jour* (67), *Benjamin* (68), *Mississippi Mermaid* (69), *Tristana* (70), *Peau d'Ane* (70), *Dirty Money* (72), *Hustle* (75), *Ils Sont Grands ces Petits* (79), *Le Dernier Metro* (80), *The Hunger* (83), *Scene of the Crime* (86).

## DE NIRO, Robert (1943- )

Power and strength define this actor who frequently chooses roles of artistic merit over commercial success. De Niro was born and raised in New York City where he studied with Stella Adler and Lee Strasberg, major forces in American theater. Off-Broadway roles, touring companies and films followed. De Niro first came to critical attention with his moving performance as a not-too-bright dying baseball catcher in *Bang the Drum Slowly* (73), opposite Michael Moriarty. He played a small time hood in the violent world of *Mean Streets* (73). *The Godfather, Part II* (74) won him an Academy Award for Best Supporting Actor, and he received another for *Raging Bull* (80), this time as Best Actor. He was also nominated as Best Actor for *The Deer Hunter* (78). Brilliant in all his films, De Niro is one of the modern Hollywood's most outstanding talents.

**Selected Films:** *Hi Mom* (71), *Bang the Drum Slowly* (73), *Mean Streets* (73), *The Godfather, Part II* (74), *Taxi Driver* (76), *The Last Tycoon* (76), *1900* (76), *The Deer Hunter* (78), *Raging Bull* (80), *True Confessions* (81), *The King of Comedy* (83), *Brazil* (85), *The Mission* (86), *Angel Heart* (87), *The Untouchables* (87).

## DENNEHY, Brian (1940- )

Brian Dennehy was born in Bridgeport, Connecticut, educated at Columbia University and did a tour in Vietnam with the Marine Corps. After leaving the service he studied acting with teachers in New York and broke into film and TV in the later 1970s. A hefty character actor, he has worked most often on television, including the made-for-TV movies *A Real American Hero* and *Rumor of War*, and the series *Big Shamus Little Shamus*. Meanwhile, Dennehy has played supporting roles in a number of popular films. These include the football comedy *Semi-Tough* (77), the Rambo film *First*

*Blood* (78), as well as *Cocoon* (85) and *Silverado* (85).
**Selected Films:** *Semi-Tough* (77), *Looking for Mr Goodbar* (77), *Foul Play* (78), *First Blood* (78), *Little Miss Marker* (80), *Gorky Park* (83), *River Rat* (84), *Silverado* (85), *Cocoon* (85), *Legal Eagles* (86), *F/X* (86), *Hard Cover* (87).

## DENNIS, Sandy (1937- )

Off-Broadway and Broadway roles led Dennis, born in Hastings, Nebraska, to her screen debut in a supporting role in *Splendor in the Grass* (61). Her first substantial screen role in *Who's Afraid of Virginia Woolf?* (66) earned her an Academy Award for best supporting actress.
**Selected Films:** *Splendor in the Grass (61), Who's Afraid of Virginia Woolf* (66), *Up the Down Staircase* (67), *The Fox* (68), *A Touch of Love* (69), *Nasty Habits* (76), *The Four Seasons* (81), *Come Back to the Five and Dime, Jimmy Dean, Jimmy Dean* (82).

## DENNY, Reginald (1891-1967)

On stage from childhood, Reginald Leigh Daymore born in Richmond, England, made his film debut in 1912, then returned to Hollywood in 1919 for leading roles in many comedy adventure films. With the advent of sound he switched to playing amiable if silly Englishman.
**Selected Films:** *The Oakdale Affair* (19), *The Leather Pushers* (22), *Skinner's Dress Suit* (25), *Madame Satan* (30), *Of Human Bondage* (34), *Bulldog Drummond's Peril* (38), *Rebecca* (40), *Mr Blandings Builds His Dream House* (48), *Bengal Brigade* (54), *Cat Ballou* (65), *Batman* (66).

## DEPARDIEU, Gerard (1948- )

Strong performances are the speciality of this husky, forceful, offbeat actor. Born in Chateauroux, France, he became a star of theater, television and films in his native country, making his movie debut in the early 1970s and rapidly rising to stardom. He starred in *Nathalie Granger* (72), and later appeared in the controversial *Le Camion* (77). Admired widely by critics, he has worked with some of Europe's greatest directors, such as Bernardo Bertolucci, François Truffaut and Alain Resnais. Depardieu has been called 'the thinking man's lug' and there are few actors of his generation who can equal his popularity in Europe today.
**Selected Films:** *Nathalie Granger* (72), *Going Places* (74), *Stavisky* (74), *Maltresse* (75), *Baxter – Vera Baxter* (77), *Le Camion* (77), *Violant* (77), *Get Out Your Handkerchiefs* (78), *Lou Lou* (79), *Mon Oncle d'Amerique* (80), *The Last Metro* (80), *The Return of Martin Guerre* (83), *Police* (86), *Menage* (86), *One Woman or Two* (87).

## DEREK, Bo (1956- )

Derek was born Mary Cathleen Collins in Long Beach, California. The wife and latest protogée of actor and director John Derek, she made a tremendous impression in *10* (79). Although she is generally acknowledged to be one of the most beautiful women in the movies, her subsequent films have not been successful.
**Selected Films:** *And Once Upon a Time* (75), *10* (79), *A Change of Seasons* (80), *Tarzan the Ape Man* (81), *Bolero* (84), *A Knight of Love* (87).

## DEREK, John (1926- )

A handsome leading man whose roles were mainly in costume adventures, Derek was born Derek Harris in Hollywood. Now a producer/director, he has been married to Ursula Andress, Linda Evans and Bo Derek.
**Selected Films:** *I'll Be Seeing You* (45), *Knock on Any Door* (49), *All the Kings Men* (49), *Rogues of Sherwood Forest* (50), *Prince of Players* (55), *Exodus* (60), *Fantasies* (81).

## DE RITA, Joe: See: STOOGES, The Three

## DERN, Bruce (1936- )

Although Dern is first to admit that he's played 'more psychotics and freaks and dopers than anyone,' he has played other roles with ability, and his talents clearly belie typecasting. Even the unfortunate characters he often portrays are exceptional, because their evil is usually obsessional, open to understanding and empathy. Born in Winnetka, Illinois, outside Chicago, Dern was educated at Choate and dropped out of the University of Pennsylvania for the Actors' Studio and off-Broadway productions, breaking into films with *Wild River* (60). His portrayal of a hillbilly psycho in an episode of the TV series *Alfred Hitchcock Presents* was so convincing the he began being cast in the roles which have become his hallmark. Dern was nominated for an Academy Award for his role in *Coming Home* (78), in which he played a Vietnam veteran married to Jane Fonda who threatens her life and then kills himself.
**Selected Films:** *Wild River* (60), *Marnie* (64), *The Trip* (67), *Transplant* (70), *Silent Running* (72), *The King of Marvin Gardens* (72), *The Cowboys* (72), *The Great Gatsby* (74), *Family Plot* (75), *Smile* (75), *Black Sunday* (76), *Coming Home* (78), *Tattoo* (71), *That Championship Season* (82), *On the Edge* (86), *The Big Town* (87).

## DERN, Laura (1967- )

Reared in California, the daughter of movie star Bruce Dern and TV star Diane Ladd, Laura made her screen debut at age 7 in *Alice Doesn't Live Here Anymore* (75). Since then the lanky blonde has played a variety of teenager parts while managing to avoid teen-oriented movies.
**Selected Films:** *Alice Doesn't Live Here Anymore* (75), *Mask* (85), *Smooth Talk* (86), *Blue Velvet* (86).

## DE SICA, Vittorio (1901-1974)

Born in Naples to a struggling middle-class family, Vittorio De Sica found his way into films in 1918. A few years later he made his stage debut. Before long the strikingly handsome youth was a stage and screen idol all over Italy. Through the 1920s and 1930s he played suave leading men in light comic roles. During World War II, De Sica turned to directing. After a few minor comedies he began directing amateur actors in the neorealist dramas that made him famous worldwide. Two of these, *Shoeshine* (46) and *Bicycle Thieves* (48) won Academy Awards as best foreign films and are still remembered as some of the most compelling in screen history. His three part film, *Yesterday, Today and Tomorrow* (64), also won an Oscar. Meanwhile, De Sica paid the bills by continuing to act, including roles in *Madame De* (52), *A Farewell to Arms* (58), and *The Amorous Adventures of Moll Flanders* (65). As an actor he appeared in some 150 films, most of them forgettable. After nearly a decade of eclipse as a director, De Sica made a triumphant comeback, and won another Oscar for *The Garden of the Finzi-Continis* (72).
**Selected Films: (as an actor)** *The Clemenceau Affair* (18), *Passa l'Amore* (33), *Bread, Love, and Dreams* (54), *Il Generale della Rovere* (59), *The Angel Wore Red* (60), *Andy Warhol's Dracula* (74), *We All Loved Each Other So Much* (75).

## DEVINE, Andy (1905-1977)

Comic relief in innumerable westerns, the hefty gravel-voiced Devine, born Jeremiah Schwartz, in Flagstaff, Arizona, broke into silent films in the twenties. He also played Guy Madison's sidekick in the TV series *Wild Bill Hickok*.
**Selected Films:** *We Americans* (28), *Law and Order* (32), *Stagecoach* (39), *The Vigilantes Return* (47), *The Red Badge of Courage* (51), *Pete Kelly's Blues* (55), *Two Rode Together* (61), *The Ballad of Josie* (68), *A Whale of a Tale* (77).

## DEVITO, Danny (1945-     )

DeVito born in New Jersey, studied at the American Academy of Dramatic Arts and worked in the theater before making his screen debut in *One Flew Over the Cuckoo's Nest* (75). He starred as the dispatcher Louie DePalma in the TV series *Taxi*. De Vito is married to actress Rhea Perlman.
**Selected Films:** *One Flew Over the Cuckoo's Nest* (75), *Goin' South* (78), *Terms of Endearment* (83), *Romancing the Stone* (84), *The Jewel of the Nile* (85), *Head Office* (86), *Ruthless People* (86), *Wise Guys* (86), *Tin Men* (87).

## DEWHURST, Colleen (1926-     )

Though she has concentrated on the theater and appeared in relatively few films, Colleen Dewhurst has been widely known for a good many years as one of the finest actresses of her generation, a reputation that is due not only to her manifest skill but also to her compelling screen presence. Born the daughter of a hockey player in Montreal, Dewhurst dropped out of college and worked in various menial jobs before turning to acting. She entered the American Academy of Dramatic Arts in New York and made her Broadway debut in the early 1950s. Over the years she has found acclaim in plays including *Desire Under the Elms*, *All the Way Home*, and *A Moon for the Misbegotten*; for the latter two she won Tonys and otherwise garnered several Obies from off-Broadway productions. Her movie work started with a supporting role in *The Nun's Story* (59). Most of her roles have been character parts behind more glamorous stars. Her few minutes onscreen as Annie's mother in Woody Allen's *Annie Hall* (77) show how much authority Dewhurst can wield in a short time with her gravelly voice and hard-used face. She has done a good deal of TV work, mostly in specials and made-for-TV movies, the latter including *Silent Victory* (79) and *Studs Lonigan* (79). Her private life includes two marriages and two divorces to and from actor George C Scott.
**Selected Films:** *The Nun's Story* (59), *Man on a String* (60), *A Fine Madness* (63), *The Last Run* (71), *McQ* (74), *Annie Hall* (77), *Ice Castles* (78), *When a Stranger Calls* (79), *Tribute* (80), *The Dead Zone* (83), *The Boy Who Could Fly* (86).

## DE WILDE, Brandon (1942-1972)

Born in Brooklyn, De Wilde made his stage debut to great acclaim at the age of seven in *Member of the Wedding* and his screen debut in the film version in 1952.
**Selected Films:** *Member of the Wedding* (52), *Shane* (53), *Goodbye My Lady* (56), *Night Passage* (57), *Blue Denim* (59), *Hud* (63), *In Harm's Way* (65), *The Calloways* (65), *The Deserter* (70), *Wild in the Sky* (72).

## DEXTER, Anthony (1919-     )

Great publicity surrounded stage actor Dexter's film debut in the title role of *Valentino* (51). Since then Dexter, born Walter Fleischmann, in Fleischmann, Nebraska, has played leads in low-budget action and science fiction features.
**Selected Films:** *Valentino* (51), *The Brigand* (52), *Captain John Smith and Pocohontas* (53), *Captain Kidd and the Slave Girl* (54), *Fire Maidens from Outer Space* (54), *Black Pirates* (54), *He Laughed Last* (56), *Twelve to the Moon* (59), *Thoroughly Modern Millie* (67).

## DICKINSON, Angie (1931-     )

Success in a beauty contest brought Angeline Brown of Kulm, North Dakota, into film in 1954, and she played her first lead in *Rio Bravo* (59). Later Dickinson starred in the TV series *Police Woman*

She has been married to football star Gene Dickinson and composer Burt Bacharach.
**Selected Films:** *Lucky Me* (54), *China Gate* (57), *Ocean's Eleven* (60), *The Art of Love* (65), *Point Blank* (67), *Pretty Maids All in a Row* (71), *Labyrinth* (79), *Dressed to Kill* (80), *Death Hunt* (81).

## DIETRICH, Marlene (1901- )

Dietrich's fascination today is exactly what it was when she began making films over 50 years ago: she is beautiful, aloof, sophisticated, demanding, generous and world-weary. Born in Berlin, Germany, as Maria Magdalene von Losch, she had a middle-class upbringing appropriate to the daughter of an officer in the Royal Prussian Police, but her ambition to become a concert violinist was torpedoed when she suffered a wrist injury. Dietrich went on tour performing in a revue, and then left the chorus for Max Reinhardt's famous theater school. In 1924 she married Rudolf Sieber, a movie production assistant, and in 1925 she had her only child, a daughter, Maria, who as an adult had a brief acting career under the name Maria Riva. She went on to make several films in Germany, where she was a well-known theater actress, beginning with *The Tragedy of Love* (24). The director Josef von Sternberg cast her as the sexy vamp. Lola Lola, in *The Blue Angel* (30), in which she outshone the presumed star, Emil Jannings. The film made her an international star, and she came to Hollywood where she was a huge success. Under von Sternberg's direction, Dietrich changed her image and became exotically, lyrically blonde, an object of mystery on the screen. *Desire* (36) was a romantic comedy, but it was followed by other films that were not so popular. It was *Destry Rides Again* (39), in which she sang 'See What the Boys in the Back Room Will Have,' that really established her as a major star. In the film she was sexy, playful, accessible. An anti-Nazi, she refused to return to Germany, defying Hitler's orders, and her motion pictures were banned in that country. In 1939 she became an American citizen, but despite all this, Dietrich remained an outsider in Hollywood, intrinsically cosmopolitan with strong ties to Europe and with a pantheon of friends who were noted intellectuals and international celebrities. During World War II she endured many hardships entertaining Allied troops, and was widely admired for it, being awarded both the US Medal of Freedom and the French Legion of Honor for her front-line work. After the war she launched a new career as a night club and cabaret performer, and a recording star known for her distinctive lisp and throaty voice. At the same times, movies such as *Stage Fright* (50) and *Witness for the Prosecution* (58) kept her film career alive. A loving retrospective of her career entitled *Marlene*, produced by Maximilian Schell, was released in 1986.
**Selected Films:** *The Tragedy of Love* (23), *Manon Lescaut* (26), *The Blue Angel* (30), *Morocco* (30), *Dishonored* (31), *Shanghai Express* (32), *Blonde Venus* (32), *The Scarlet Empress* (34), *The Devil Is a Woman* (35), *Desire* (36), *The Garden of Allah* (36), *Destry Rides Again* (39), *The Flame of New Orleans* (41), *The Spoilers* (42), *Kismet* (44), *Golden Earrings* (47), *A Foreign Affair* (48), *Stage Fright* (50), *No Highway in the Sky* (50), *Rancho Notorious* (52), *Witness for the Prosecution* (58), *Touch of Evil* (58), *Judgement at Nuremberg* (61), *Just a Gigolo* (78).

*Emil Jannings and Marlene Dietrich in* The Blue Angel *(30).*

## DIFFRING, Anton (1918- )

Stage work in Canada and the United States prefaced Diffring's debut in British films in 1950. Born in Koblenz, Germany, he often portrays a Nazi or other villainous type, sometimes the protagonist in a horror film.
**Selected Films:** *State Secret* (50), *Albert RN* (53), *The Colditz Story* (55), *I Am a Camera* (56), *The Man Who Could Cheat Death* (59), *Circus of Horrors* (60), *The Double Man* (67), *Counterpoint* (67), *Zeppelin* (71), *Operation Daybreak* (76), *Valentino* (77), *Escape to Victory* (81).

## DIGGES, Dudley (1879-1947)

A veteran of the Abbey Theatre in Dublin, Digges displayed great versatility in the numerous solid character parts he played in Hollywood in the 1930s.
**Selected Films:** *Condemned* (29), *Upper Underworld* (30), *The Maltese Falcon* (31), *The Hatchet Man* (32), *Roar of the Dragon* (32), *The Emperor Jones* (33), *What Every Woman Knows* (34), *Mutiny on the Bounty* (35), *The General Died at Dawn* (36), *The Light That Failed* (39), *Raffles* (40), *The Searching Wind* (46).

## DILLMAN, Bradford (1930- )

San Francisco native Dillman began his acting career and enjoyed considerable success on Broadway in 1956 in *Long Day's Journey Into Night*, before his film debut in 1958. Lean, sensitive, and intelligent, he is also a frequent performer in TV movies and series. He is married to actress Suzy Parker.
**Selected Films:** *A Certain Smile* (58), *Compulsion* (59), *Frances of Assisi* (61), *The Bridge at Remagen* (69), *Brother John* (71), *The Iceman Cometh* (73), *The Lincoln Conspiracy* (77), *Piranha* (78), *Sudden Impact* (83).

## DILLON, Matt (1964- )

Born in New Rochelle, New York, Dillon was discovered by talent scouts while still in junior high school and given the second lead in the movie *Over the Edge* (79). Due to its violence, that film was not released for two years, but in the meantime Dillon had made his way to stardom with roles in teenage films like *Little Darlings* (80) and *My Bodyguard* (80). He has since held on to his status as a teen heartthrob while expanding his acting range with the comedy and drama.
**Selected Films:** *Over the Edge* (79), *Little Darlings* (80), *My Bodyguard* (80), *Tex* (82), *The Outsiders* (83), *Rumble Fish* (83), *Flamingo Kid* (84), *Target* (85), *Rebel* (86), *Native Son* (86).

## DINEHART, Alan (1886-1944)

As exemplified in *The Cat's Paw* (34), Dinehart's many supporting roles in the 1930s and 1940s often saw him playing a businessman of questionable morality.
**Selected Films:** *The Brat* (31), *Rackety Rax* (32), *Cross Country Cruise* (34), *Jimmy the Gent* (34), *The Cat's Paw* (34), *Dante's Inferno* (35), *Charlie Chan at the Race Track* (36), *Step Lively Jeeves* (37), *Girl Trouble* (42), *Moon Over Las Vegas* (44), *Oh What a Night* (44).

## DINGLE, Charles (1887-1956)

A fifty-year veteran of stage, screen, radio, and TV, Dingle made a great impression in *The Little Foxes* (41), his second film. He played everything from Shakespearean actors to judges and comedians, but was most often a cheerful, respectable and thoroughly wicked villain.
**Selected Films:** *One Third of a Nation* (33), *The Little Foxes* (41), *The Talk of the Town* (42), *Edge of Darkness* (43), *Sister Kenny* (46), *State of the Union* (48), *The Court Martial of Billy Mitchell* (55).

## DIX, Richard (1894-1949)

Born Ernest Brimmer in St Paul, Minnesota, Dix epitomized the strong, silent type and was an extremely popular leading man during the 1920s. Despite early success in talkies, Dix drifted into B action pictures.
**Selected Films:** *One of the Finest* (19), *Dangerous Curves Ahead* (21), *The Vanishing American* (25), *Seven Keys to Baldpate* (29), *Cimarron* (31), *The Arizonian* (35), *Cherokee Strip* (40), *The Kansan* (43), *Mark of the Whistler* (44), *The Thirteenth Hour* (47).

## DONAHUE, Troy (1936- )

Readily identifiable from his roles in the TV series *Hawaiian Eye* and *Surfside Six*, Donahue, born Merle Johnson in New York City, got his start in film in 1957 and established himself as a leading hero of the 1960s. He was briefly married to actress Suzanne Pleshette.
**Selected Films:** *Man Afraid* (57), *This Happy Feeling* (58), *A Summer Place* (59), *Parrish* (61), *Rocket to the Moon* (67), *The Godfather Part II* (75), *Tin Man* (82).

## DONALD, James (1917- )

A native of Aberdeen, Scotland, Donald began playing supporting roles on the British stage in 1935 and made his film debut in *The Missing Million* (41). He usually plays men of introspection or conscience. He continues to perform on stage, but is also active on TV and in the movies.
**Selected Films:** *The Missing Million* (41), *In Which We Serve* (42), *White Corridors* (51), *Lust for Life* (56), *The Bridge on the River Kwai* (57), *The Great Escape* (63), *The Royal Hunt of the Sun* (69), *Conduct Unbecoming* (75), *The Big Sleep* (78).

*Robert Donat in* The Thirty-Nine Steps *(35).*

## DONALDSON, Ted (1933- )

American child actor Donaldson played kids in films of the 1940s and 1950s, most notably *A Tree Grows in Brooklyn* (45) and a series beginning with *For the Love of Rusty* (47).
**Selected Films:** *Once Upon a Time* (44), *A Tree Grows in Brooklyn* (45), *The Decision of Christopher Blake* (48), *Phone Call from a Stranger* (52).

## DONAT, Robert (1905-1958)

Popular and widely admired, this dashing and gifted British actor with his inimitably melodious voice was born in Manchester, England. He studied elocution as a child to rid himself of a stutter, and by the age of 16 he had made his stage debut. Donat played Sheakespearean and classical roles, becoming a film actor in 1930. He could have gone to Hollywood, but hated it, and his home base was always England. He first came to worldwide attention for his starring role opposite Madeleine Carroll in the Alfred Hitchcock thriller, *The Thirty-Nine Steps* (35), and showed his versatility in a comedy role in *The Ghost Goes West* (36). But it was in *Goodbye Mr Chips* (39) that he won the hearts of the world. Donat was superb as Mr Chipping, the public school classics master in the screen adaptation of James Hilton's novel, a shy man who devotes his life to 'his boys,' only coming out of his shell when he met Greer Garson. Donat aged on screen from 25 to 83, and won the Academy Award for Best Actor. He was always plagued by severe insecurities and a debilitating case of asthma, yet he created some of film's finest roles. Donat continued working until his death at the early age of 53.
**Selected Films:** *Men of Tomorrow* (32), *The Private Life of Henry VIII* (33), *The Count of Monte Cristo* (34), *The Thirty-Nine Steps* (35), *The Ghost Goes West* (36), *The Citadel* (38), *Goodbye Mr Chips* (39), *The Young Mr Pitt* (42), *The Adventures of Tartu* (43), *The Winslow Boy* (48), *The Magic Box* (50), *The Inn of the Sixth Happiness* (58).

## DONATH, Ludwig (1900-1967)

Born in Vienna, Austria, Donath distinguished himself on the Berlin stage in the late 1920s but left Germany after the Nazi rise to power. He played a variety of character roles in Hollywood, particularly in anti-Nazi films. He was blacklisted during the 1950s.
**Selected Films:** *Lady From Chungking* (42), *The Strange Death of Adolf Hitler* (43), *The Hitler Gang* (44), *The Jolson Story* (46), *The Great Caruso* (51), *Sins of Jezebel* (53), *Torn Curtain* (66).

## DONLEVY, Brian (1889-1972)

Known for his villainous roles, Donlevy was born Grosson Brian Donlevy, in Portadown, Ireland, the son of a whiskey distiller, and moved to the United States when still a child. He joined Pershing's Mexican Expedition while still a teenager, and later lied about his age to serve as a World War I pilot in the Lafayette Escadrille. After the war he modeled shirts and began acting with a walk-on part on Broadway in 1924, beginning small parts in film about the same time. Before long he was playing leads, finding his place in Hollywood at first as a villain – as exemplified in his portrayal of the sadistic sergeant in *Beau Geste* (39) – but also as a tough guy with a heart of gold – as in *An American Romance* (44) – and at shades of fast-talking toughness and naive honesty inbetween. Later in his long career he slipped from leads to B pictures and character roles, but never performed in these without a certain distinction.
**Selected Films:** *Damaged Hearts* (24), *Mother's Boy* (28), *Barbary Coast* (35), *Jesse James* (39), *Beau Geste* (39), *Destry Rides Again* (39), *The Great McGinty* (40), *The Glass Key* (42), *An American Romance* (44), *Shakedown* (50), *The Quatermass Experiment* (55), *Cowboy* (58), *The Errand Boy* (61), *The Curse of the Fly* (65), *Rogue's Gallery* (67), *Pit Stop* (69).

## DONNELL, Jeff (1921- )

This spunky actress from South Windham, Maine, specialized in playing a teenager or the friend of

the heroine in many routine screen comedies of the 1940s. She now plays mothers. She was married to actor Aldo Ray from 1954 to 1956.
**Selected Films:** *My Sister Eileen* (42), *A Night to Remember* (43), *Three Is a Family* (44), *The Fuller Brush Girl* (50), *My Man Godfrey* (57), *Gidget Goes Hawaiian* (61), *The Iron Maiden* (62), *Stand Up and Be Counted* (72).

## DONNELLY, Ruth (1896-1982)

Broadway roles led to a 1927 screen debut and scores of character roles for Donnelly. Though born in Trenton, New Jersey, she specialized in Irish dialect parts, and sometimes played a shrew, a fast-talker, or friend to the heroine. Later she turned to maternal roles.
**Selected Films:** *Rubber Heels* (27), *Transatlantic* (31), *Wonder Bar* (34), *Mr Deeds Goes to Town* (36), *A Slight Case of Murder* (38), *Holiday* (38), *The Snake Pit* (48), *The Way to the Gold* (57).

## DONOVAN, King (1919-1987)

Seen to advantage in the immortal *Invasion of the Body Snatchers* (56) and other tales of horror, in his career as a general purpose actor Donovan has included guest star appearances on such TV series as *The Bob Cummings Show* and *Please Don't Eat the Daisies*.
**Selected Films:** *Cargo to Capetown* (50), *The Beast from Twenty Thousand Fathoms* (53), *The Invasion of the Body Snatchers* (56), *The Hanging Tree* (59).

## DORAN, Ann (1914- )

Often a friend of the heroine, Doran, born in Amarillo, Texas, has been one of the busiest character actresses in Hollywood since the mid-1930s, appearing in over 200 films as well as on TV.
**Selected Films:** *Charlie Chan in London* (34), *Palm Springs Penitentiary* (38), *Blondie* (38), *Mr Smith Goes to Washington* (39), *The More the Merrier* (43), *The Snake Pit* (48), *Rebel without a Cause* (55), *Rosie* (67), *The Hired Hand* (71), *First Monday in October* (81).

## DORLEAC, Françoise (1941-1967)

Born in Paris, the sister of actress Catherine Deneuve, Dorleac acted onstage before making her screen debut in 1959. A charming actress and an elegant beauty, she starred in a number of popular films, notably opposite Belmondo in *That Man from Rio* (64), before she was killed in a car crash.
**Selected Films:** *Mensonges* (59), *The Man from Rio* (64), *Genghis Khan* (65), *Where the Spies Are* (65), *Cul de Sac* (66), *Billion Dollar Brain* (67).

## DORN, Philip (1905-1975)

A popular matinee idol and film actor in Europe by the beginning of World War II, the handsome Dorn, born Hein Van Der Niet in Scheveningen, Holland (stage name Frits Van Dongen) played leads in Hollywood during the forties, often as a refugee or Continental lover.
**Selected Films:** *Ski Patrol* (40), *Escape* (40), *Ziegfeld Girl* (41), *Random Harvest* (42), *Passage to Marseilles* (44), *I Remember Mama* (48), *Salto Mortale* (53).

## DORS, Diana (1931-1984)

Born Diana Fluck in Swindon, England, she was often called Britain's answer to Marilyn Monroe. This blonde bombshell played goodtime girls from the mid-1940s on, but her bosomy sex symbol fame hurt her career, and she was seldom given parts that allowed her to use her considerable acting talents.
**Selected Films:** *The Shop at Sly Corner* (46), *Oliver Twist* (78), *It's A Grand Life* (53), *A Kid for Two Farthings* (55), *Yield to the Night* (56), *Hannie Caulder* (71), *Theatre of Blood* (73), *Steaming* (released 86).

## D'ORSAY, Fifi (1904-1983)

Born Yvonne Lussier in Montreal, D'Orsay moved from vaudeville to film in 1929, appearing opposite Will Rogers in *They Had to See Paris*. She was a leading lady in Hollywood during the early thirties, often typecast as a French sex symbol.
**Selected Films:** *They Had to See Paris* (29), *Hot for Paris* (30), *Just Imagine* (31), *Going Hollywood* (33), *Wonder Bar* (34), *Wild and Wonderful* (63), *The Art of Love* (65), *Assignment to Kill* (68).

## DOTRICE, Roy (1923- )

British character actor Dotrice has worked largely on the stage, but has apeared in occasional supporting roles of films since the 1960s.
**Selected Films:** *The Heroes of Telemark* (65), *A Twist of Sand* (68), *Lock Up Your Daughters* (69), *Nicholas and Alexandra* (71), *Amadeus* (84).

## DOUGLAS, Kirk (1916- )

Douglas was born Issur Danielovitch Demsky in Amsterdam, New York, to Russian Jewish parents who had come to the United States in 1910. After high school he hitch-hiked to Canton, New York, and convinced the dean of St Lawrence University to admit him on a loan. After college, he talked his way into the American Academy of Dramatic Art in New York, supporting himself by working as a waiter, a professional wrestler, an usher and a belllman. After his Broadway debut in 1941 he joined the Navy, returning to Broadway after World War II. He was seen by producer Hal Wallis and invited to Hollywood. At first he played weaklings and gangsters. In his first picture, *The Strange Love of Martha Ivers* (46), opposite Barbara Stanwyck, he was a weak man dominated by women. In *A Letter to Three Wives* (48), he was an intellectual school teacher. It wasn't until

*Kirk Douglas and Lana Turner*–The Bad and The Beautiful *(52).*

*Champion* (49), in which he played a driven, sexy, immoral prizefighter, that the Douglas intensity was put on display. It made him a star. He turned down flashier films to make *Young Man with a Horn* (50), the life story of trumpet player Bix Beiderbecke. Along with Burt Lancaster and Tony Curtis, he was rapidly establishing himself as one of the new postwar breed of masculine movie idols, successors to John Garfield. In 1954, while he was making *Act of Love*, he met studio publicist Anne Buydens, who became his second wife and mother of two sons, Peter and Eric. Douglas' other sons, Michael and Joel, were from a former marriage. In 1955, Douglas formed his own production company, which gave him more freedom to produce the pictures he wanted to appear in, such as *Paths of Glory* (57), a truly significant film that might not have been made without his help, and *The Vikings* (58), with Tony Curtis and Ernest Borgnine. Despite his movie success, Douglas retained an interest in the Broadway stage, and in 1963 he appeared in *One Flew Over the Cuckoo's Nest*, based on the novel by Ken Kesey. When he failed to get the backing he needed to produce it as a film, he passed the play on to his son Michael, a television and film actor. Douglas continues to be a forceful presence in the film industry.

**Selected Films:** *The Strange Love of Martha Ivers* (46), *A Letter to Three Wives* (48), *Champion* (49), *Young Man with a Horn* (50), *The Glass Menagerie* (51), *Ace in the Hole* (51), *The Bad and the Beautiful* (52), *Act of Love* (54), *Man Without a Star* (55), *Lust for Life* (56), *Gunfight at the O K Corral* (57), *Paths of Glory* (57), *The Vikings* (58), *Spartacus* (60), *Town Without Pity* (61), *Lonely Are the Brave* (62), *Seven Days in May* (64), *In Harm's Way* (65), *The Heroes of Telemark* (65), *Cast a Giant Shadow* (66), *The Brotherhood* (68), *The Arrangement* (69), *There was a Crooked Man* (70), *The Fury* (78), *The Final Countdown* (80), *The Man from Snowy River* (81), *Tough Guys* (86).

## DOUGLAS, Melvyn (1901-1981)

This suave, polished actor was a leading man first, in the 1930s and 1940s, most at home in a dinner jacket with a lovely lady on his arm. He later became a character actor, but he was always superb. Born Melvyn Edouard Hesselberg in Macon, Georgia, he made his Broadway debut in 1928. He then went to Hollywood, appearing opposite Greta Garbo in *As You Desire Me* (32). Debonair and intelligent, Douglas costarred with other great female stars, including Joan Crawford, Marlene Dietrich, Claudette Colbert, Irene Dunne and Myrna Loy. After he began appearing in character roles, the public found out just how good an actor he was. In 1963 he won the Academy Award for Best Supporting Actor in *Hud*, as an aging rancher and father of Paul Newman, who played the title role. He won another Oscar for Best Supporting Actor for *Being There* (79), in which he played a millionaire. Along the way, he was nominated for Best Actor for *I Never Sang for My Father* (70), perhaps his best performance, as a selfish and domineering father who sabotages his son's efforts to be closer to him. He did stage and television, winning both a Tony and an Emmy Award. His second wife was actress and politician Helen Gahagan.

**Selected Films:** *Tonight or Never* (31), *As You Desire Me* (32), *The Old Dark House* (32), *Dangerous Corner* (34), *Theodora Goes Wild* (36), *Captains Courageous* (37), *That Certain Age* (38), *Ninotchka* (39), *A Woman's Face* (41), *Mr Blandings Builds His Dream House* (48), *Hud* (63), *The Americanization of Emily* (64), *Hotel* (67), *I Never Sang for My Father* (70), *The Candidate* (72), *The Seduction of Joe Tynan* (79), *Being There* (79), *Ghost Story* (81).

## DOUGLAS, Michael (1945- )

The son of actor Kirk Douglas and born in New Brunswick, New Jersey, Michael inherited some of his father's craggy features but not quite the superstar quality. Nonetheless, Michael Douglas is involved in the industry from producing to acting. He starred in a number of popular and not so popular films including *Summertree* (71), *Coma* (78), and *Running* (79). He also co-produced the multiple-Oscar-winning *One Flew Over the Cuckoo's Nest* (75) and produced and acted in *The China Syndrome* (79). Recently he co-starred with Kathleen Turner in the jungle adventure *Romancing the Stone* (84).
**Selected Films:** *Hail Hero!* (69), *Summer Tree* (71), *Napoleon and Samantha* (72), *Coma* (78), *China Syndrome* (79), *Running* (79), *It's My Turn* (80), *Romancing the Stone* (84), *Jewel of the Nile* (85), *A Chorus Line* (86), *Fatal Attraction* (87).

## DOUGLAS, Paul (1907-1959)

After leaving college Douglas became a professional football player and a radio sportscaster before he made his debut on Broadway in 1935. He returned to radio, then starred for over 1000 performances in one of Broadway's longest-running shows, *Born Yesterday*. Middle-aged by the time he made his screen debut in *A Letter to Three Wives* (48), Douglas's appealing gruffness and unexpected sense of comedy proved he could be an effective comedy lead, sometimes cantankerous and sometimes foolish, the image of the irascible tycoon in *The Solid Gold Cadillac* (56), and an American businessman who proved comically deflatable in *The Maggie* (54). Born in Philadelphia and educated at Yale, Douglas died of a heart attack at the age of 52.
**Selected Films:** *A Letter to Three Wives* (48), *It Happens Every Spring* (49), *Everybody Does It* (49), *Panic in the Street* (50), *Fourteen Hours* (51), *Clash by Night* (52), *Green Fire* (54), *The Maggie* (54), *The Solid Gold Cadillac* (56), *This Could Be the Night* (57), *Beau James* (57), *Fortunella* (58), *The Mating Game* (59).

## DOVE, Billie (1900- )

Dove (born Lillian Bohney in New York City) was a spectacular beauty who began her career as a Ziegfeld showgirl and became one of the silent screen's loveliest and most popular stars. Billed as 'The American Beauty,' she appeared with Douglas Fairbanks in the early color film, *The Black Pirate* (26). She could not adapt to sound pictures at first, but later reappeared in her sixties in supporting character roles.
**Selected Films:** *Beyond the Rainbow* (22), *Polly of the Follies* (22), *The Black Pirate* (26), *Painted Angel* (30), *Blondie of the Follies* (32), *Diamond Head* (62).

## DOWLING, Constance (1923-1969)

American actress Dowling played major roles in films of the 1940s including *Knickerbocker Holiday* (44) and the Danny Kaye vehicle *Up in Arms* (44). She was the sister of actress Doris Dowling.
**Selected Films:** *Knickerbocker Holiday* (44), *Up in Arms* (44), *The Flame* (47), *Gog* (54).

## DOWLING, Doris (1921— )

While her sister Constance played leading roles, Doris held down character parts in Hollywood films of the 1940s and 1950s. After appearing in some Italian films including the classic *Bitter Rice* (48), she returned to the US and in the 1960s appeared in the TV series *My Living Doll*.
**Selected Films:** *The Lost Weekend* (45), *The Blue Dahlia* (46), *Bitter Rice* (48), *Running Target* (58).

## DOWN, Lesley Anne (1954- )

Delicately beautiful, Down is best known from the British TV series, *Upstairs, Downstairs*. The London-born actress went on to films but her movie career has not matched her television fame.
**Selected Films:** *All the Right Noises* (69), *The Pink Panther Strikes Again* (76), *A Little Night Music* (77), *The Betsy* (78), *The Great Train Robbery* (79), *Hanover Street* (79), *Sphinx* (81).

## DOWNS, Johnny (1913- )

A child actor in the *Our Gang* series, Brooklyn-born Downs returned to the screen after vaudeville and Broadway experience to dance his way through leads in musicals and light romances, especially those with a college setting.
**Selected Films:** *Valley of the Giants* (27), *The Crowd* (28), *College Scandal* (35), *College Holiday* (38), *Hold That Co-Ed* (38), *All-American Co-Ed* (41), *The Right to Love* (45), *Cruising Down the River* (53).

## DRAKE, Charles (1914- )

Specializing as a dull nice guy in second leads, Drake, born Charles Ruppert in New York City, was a salesman and acted in little theaters before he broke into films in the late 1930s.
*Selected Films: Career* (39), *Dive Bomber* (41), *The Man Who Came to Dinner* (42), *Air Force* (43), *You Came Along* (44), *Whistle Stop* (46), *Gunsmoke* (52), *The Price of Fear* (56), *Dear Heart* (64), *The Swimmer* (68), *The Seven Minutes* (71).

## DRAKE, Dona (1920- )

Small and fiery, a former band vocalist and dancer who called herself Rita Rio, Drake, born Rita Novella in Mexico City, appeared in second leads and leads in Hollywood productions of the 1940s and 1950s.
**Selected Films:** *Aloma of the South Seas* (41), *The Road to Morocco* (42), *Let's Face It* (43), *The House of Tao Ling* (47), *The Fortunes of Captain Blood* (50), *Valentino* (51), *Princess of the Nile* (54).

## DRAKE, Tom (1918-1982)

Born Alfred Alderice in Brooklyn, this young actor worked in stock and on Broadway before making his film debut in *The Howards of Virginia* (40) as Richard Aldene. After a return to New York, Drake joined the MGM studio. After playing opposite Judy Garland in *Meet Me in St Louis* (44), it is as 'The Boy Next Door' in many films of the 1940s that Drake is best remembered.
**Selected Films:** *The Howards of Virginia* (40), *Two Girls and a Sailor* (44), *Meet Me in St Louis* (44), *The Green Years* (46), *Master of Lassie* (48), *Sudden Danger* (55), *Raintree County* (57), *The Sandpiper* (65), *Red Tomahawk* (67), *The Spectre of Edgar Allan Poe* (72), *Savage Abduction* (75).

## DRESSER, Louise (1878-1965)

Vaudeville and Broadway experience prepared Dresser, born Louise Kerlin, in Evansville, Indiana, for dramatic character leads and supporting roles in silent films and talkies. She played Catherine the Great opposite Valentino in *The Eagle* (25) and co-starred with Will Rogers in several films.
**Selected Films:** *The Glory of Clementine* (22), *Prodigal Daughters* (23), *The Eagle* (25), *Not Quite Decent* (27), *Mammy* (22), *State Fair* (33), *Doctor Bull* (33), *The Scarlet Empress* (34), *The County Chairman* (35), *Maid of Salem* (37).

## DRESSLER, Marie (1869-1934)

Born Leila Marie Koerber in Coburg, Ontario, Dressler put the lie to the notion that a woman had to be young and beautiful to be a star. She was an experienced light opera singer and actress at age 20. By 1892 she was on Broadway and was a vaudeville star a decade later. As a character actress she became the heavyweight star of silent film comedy and later a leading lady in MGM comedy-dramas in the early 1930s. She was fat and homely, but possessed a great natural comic talent. Dressler made her screen debut with Charlie Chaplin in *Tillie's Punctured Romance* (14), following this up with other silent films, but real stardom came with talkies. *Anna Christie* (30), with Greta Garbo, proved her to be a fine serious actress, and she won an Academy Award for Best Actress for *Min and Bill* (30), in which she was cast with Wallace Beery, as two waterfront characters. She was also nominated as Best Actress for *Emma* (32).
**Selected Films:** *Tillie's Punctured Romance* (14), *The Joy Girl* (27), *Bringing Up Father* (28), *Anna Christie* (30), *Min and Bill* (30), *Emma* (32), *Prosperity* (32), *Tugboat Annie* (33), *Dinner at Eight* (33), *The Late Christopher Bean* (33).

## DREW, Ellen (1915- )

Daughter of a barber in Kansas City, Missouri, Drew, born Terry Ray, won a beauty contest and got work in Hollywood in 1936. She was a vivacious light leading lady of the 1940s.
**Selected Films:** *College Holiday* (36), *Murder Goes to College* (37), *The Buccaneer* (38), *Geronimo* (39), *Christmas in July* (40), *Our Wife* (41), *The Imposter* (44), *China Sky* (45), *Johnny O'Clock* (47), *The Great Missouri Raid* (50), *Outlaw's Son* (57).

## DREYFUSS, Richard (1947- )

Born in Brooklyn, New York, this energetic, likeable and boyish-charming leading man appeared in some of the most popular films of the 1970s, although sometimes, as in *Jaws* (75) and *Close Encounters of the Third Kind* (77), he was overshadowed by the special effects. He won the Oscar for Best Actor in *The Goodbye Girl* (77).
**Selected Films:** *Hello Down There* (68), *The Graduate* (67), *American Graffiti* (73), *The Apprenticeship of Duddy Kravitz* (74), *Jaws* (75), *Close Encounters of the Third Kind* (77), *The Goodbye Girl* (77), *The Big Fix* (78), *The Competition* (80), *Whose Life Is It Anyway?* (81), *Down and Out in Beverly Hills* (86), *Tin Men* (87).

*Richard Dreyfuss in* The Goodbye Girl *(77).*

## DRISCOLL, Bobby (1937-1968)

Recipient of a special Academy Award for his performance in *The Window* (49), child actor Driscoll was signed by Walt Disney for several memorable productions. He was unable to find film work in his teens, took to drugs, and died an anonymous death in New York.
**Selected Films:** *Lost Angel* (43), *Song of the South* (46), *The Window* (49), *Treasure Island* (50), *The Happy Time* (52), *The Scarlet Coat* (55), *The Party Crashers* (58).

## DRU, Joanne (1923- )

Best remembered as the female lead in such classic westerns as *Red River* (48), *She Wore a Yellow Ribbon* (49), and *Wagonmaster* (50), former model and showgirl Dru, born Joanne la Coque, in Logan, West Virginia, played leads in the 1940s and 1950s. She was married to actors Dick Haymes, who brought her to Hollywood, and John Ireland.
**Selected Films:** *Abie's Irish Rose* (46), *Red River* (48), *She Wore a Yellow Ribbon* (49), *All the King's Men* (49), *Wagonmaster* (50), *Thunder Bay* (53), *The Light in the Forest* (58), *September Storm* (60), *Sylvia* (65), *Supersnooper* (80).

## DRURY, James (1934- )

Readily identifiable as the star of the TV series *The Virginian*, Drury played second leads in Hollywood productions before establishing himself in the popular TV series. A motorcycle accident in the 1970s put a temporary end to his career.
**Selected Films:** *Forbidden Planet* (56), *Love Me Tender* (56), *Bernardine* (57), *Pollyanna* (60), *Ride the High Country* (62), *The Young Warriors* (65).

## DUFF, Howard (1917- )

Duff was radio's original Sam Spade before he began a movie career in which he played the tough hero or cop – as exemplified in *The Naked City* (48). A native of Bremerton, Washington, Duff studied drama and played with the Seattle Repertory Playhouse, but his film debut had to wait until the end of his military service in 1947. Strong supporting roles in some major productions led the good-looking Duff to leading roles in many B action films. He appeared with his wife Ida Lupino in the TV series *Mr Adams and Eve*, and also in the TV series *Dante*, *The Felony Squad* and *Flamingo Road*.
**Selected Films:** *Brute Force* (47), *All My Sons* (48), *The Naked City* (48), *Red Canyon* (49), *Calamity Jane and Sam Bass* (49), *Woman in Hiding* (50), *Shakedown* (50), *Steel Town* (51), *Models Inc* (52), *Women's Prison* (54), *Flame of the Islands* (56), *While the City Sleeps* (56), *Boy's Night Out* (62), *Sardanapalus the Great* (63), *Panic in the City* (68), *The Late Show* (77), *A Wedding* (78), *Kramer vs Kramer* (79), *Double Negative* (80), *Oh God Book II* (80).

## DUGAN, Tom (1889-1955)

American actor Dugan played comic supporting roles in films from the 1920s into the 1950s, among them *To Be or Not To Be* (42) and *The Lemon Drop Kid* (51).
**Selected Films:** *Sharp Shooters* (27), *Doctor X* (29), *Four Daughters* (38), *To Be or Not To Be* (42), *Bataan* (43), *Take Me Out to the Ball Game* (49), *The Lemon Drop Kid* (51).

## DUGGAN, Andrew (1923- )

On screen since 1956, when he made his film debut in *Patterns*, Duggan has usually played resolute characters. His extensive TV work has included appearances in the series *Twelve O'Clock High*, *Lancer*, and the mini-series *The Winds of War*.
**Selected Films:** *Patterns* (56), *The Domino Kid* (57), *The Bravados* (58), *Westbound* (59), *Merrill's Marauders* (62), *The Secret War of Harry Frigg* (68), *The Bears and I* (74), *The Private Files of J Edgar Hoover* (78).

## DUKE, Patty (1946- )

Born in Elmhurst, New York, Duke became a star overnight before she reached her teens when she appeared as the young Helen Keller in Broadway's *The Miracle Worker* (59). Her reprise of the role in the 1962 movie *The Miracle Worker* made her the youngest person ever to receive an Academy Award for best supporting actress. Her popularity broadened through her TV series *The Patty Duke Show*, and although she has appeared in innumerable TV movies and occasional films, she has yet to discover the adult persona that is a truly suitable vehicle for her talent. Since her marriage to comic actor John Astin in 1972, Patty Duke is also billed as Patty Duke Astin.
**Selected Films:** *I'll Cry Tomorrow* (55), *Somebody Up There Likes Me* (56), *Country Music Holiday* (57), *My Goddess* (58), *Happy Anniversary* (59), *4-D Man* (59), *The Miracle Worker* (62), *Billie* (65), *Valley of the Dolls* (67), *Me Natalie* (69), *You'll Like My Mother* (72), *The Swarm* (78), *Hard Feelings* (82).

## DULLEA, Keir (1936- )

After an impressive debut performance as a disturbed delinquent in *The Hoodlum Priest* (61) and his portrayal of another disturbed youth in *David and Lisa* (63), the sensitive, intense Dullea, born in Cleveland, Ohio, has gone on to play a number of leads in the same vein.
**Selected Films:** *The Hoodlum Priest* (61), *David and Lisa* (63), *Mail Order Bride* (64), *Madame X* (66), *2001: A Space Odyssey* (69), *Paperback Hero* (73), *Leopard in the Snow* (78), *Brain Waves* (83), *2010* (84).

## DUMBRILLE, Douglas (1890-1974)

Often cast as a suave villain, corrupt entrepreneur

or politician, Dumbrille played over 200 character roles in Hollywood after he left his native Hamilton, Ontario.
**Selected Films:** *His Woman* (31), *Mr Deeds Goes to Town* (36), *A Day at the Races* (37), *The Big Store* (41), *Road to Utopia* (46), *The Ten Commandments* (56), *The Buccaneer* (58), *Shock Treatment* (63).

## DUMONT, Margaret (1889-1965)

Born Margaret Baker in Brooklyn, Dumont played in Marx Brothers stage comedies and later appeared in seven Marx Brothers films as the stuffy, stately foil for their absurd antics. She also appeared with W C Fields, Jack Benny, and many other comedians.
**Selected Films:** *A Tale of Two Cities* (17), *The Cocoanuts* (29), *Animal Crackers* (30), *Duck Soup* (33), *A Night at the Opera* (35), *A Day at the Races* (37), *At the Circus* (39), *The Big Store* (41), *The Horn Blows at Midnight* (45), *Auntie Mame* (58), *What a Way to Go!* (64).

## DUNAWAY, Faye (1941- )

High cheekbones, green eyes and chic style make Dunaway one of Hollywood's loveliest leading ladies – besides, she can act. Born in Bascom, Florida, she appeared in *Hogan's Goat* off-Broadway, then went to Hollywood, making three pictures in 1967 alone, rising from unknown to star in a matter of months, especially thanks to *Bonnie and Clyde* that year. Dunaway has appeared in a variety of films – *Little Big Man* (70) was a western; *Chinatown* (74) was a tough guy detective story; *Three Days of the Condor* (75) was a suspense movie. She won an Academy Award for Best Actress for *Network* (76), in which she played an icy television executive for whom success means more than sex. She had previously been nominated as Best Actress for her work as the gangster's moll in *Bonnie and Clyde*, and as the troubled rich girl in *Chinatown*. She was chosen to play Joan Crawford in *Mommie Dearest* (81), achieving an uncanny physical resemblance to the late star and giving a stunning performance.
**Selected Films:** *Hurry Sundown* (67), *Bonnie and Clyde* (67), *The Thomas Crown Affair* (68), *The Arrangment* (69), *Little Big Man* (70), *Oklahoma Crude* (73), *The Three Musketeers* (73), *Chinatown* (74), *The Four Musketeers* (74), *The Towering Inferno* (74), *Three Days of the Condor* (75), *Voyage of the Damned* (76), *Network* (76), *The Eyes of Laura Mars* (78), *The Champ* (79), *Mommie Dearest* (81), *Supergirl* (84), *Barfly* (87).

## DUNCAN, Sandy (1946- )

Born in Henderson, Texas, the tomboyish Duncan has performed on stage and on TV, and has been the light leading lady in a few films.
**Selected Films:** *$1,000,000 Duck* (71), *Star Spangled Girl* (71), *The Cat From Outer Space* (78).

## DUNN, Emma (1875-1966)

Housekeepers and matronly roles were among the many character parts this fine British character actress (born in Cheshire) played in Hollywood films of the 1930s and 1940s. She played Dr Kildare's mother.
**Selected Films:** *Old Lady 31* (20), *Pied Piper Malone* (23), *Side Street* (29), *Bad Sister* (31), *Mr Deeds Goes to Town* (36), *Son of Frankenstein* (39), *The Great Dictator* (40), *Dr Kildare's Wedding Day* (41), *Life With Father* (47), *The Woman in White* (48).

## DUNN, James (1905-1967)

Born in New York City, Dunn played genial leading men in B features of the 1930s and 1940s and received an Academy Award for his supporting role in *A Tree Grows in Brooklyn* (45). The remainder of his career often found him in low-budget westerns.
**Selected Films:** *Bad Girl* (31), *Over the Hill* (31), *Bright Eyes* (34), *Bad Boy* (35), *A Tree Grows in Brooklyn* (45), *Mysterious Crossing* (47), *Killer McCoy* (48), *The Golden Gloves Story* (50), *The Bramble Bush* (60), *The Oscar* (66).

## DUNN, Michael (1935-1973)

A dwarf actor who managed to push his career beyond the obvious freak roles, Dunn, born Gary Neil Miller in Shattuck, Oklahoma, made an impression on Broadway and was nominated for an Academy Award for his debut in *Ship of Fools* (65).
**Selected Films:** *Ship of Fools* (65), *You're a Big Boy Now* (67), *Madigan* (68), *Boom!* (68), *Justine* (69), *Murders in the Rue Morgue* (71), *The Mutations* (74), *The Abdication* (74).

## DUNNE, Griffin (1956- )

The son of novelist Dominick Dunne, Griffin grew up in California and came to screen acting by way of screen producing. He co-produced as well as starred in Martin Scorcese's *After Hours* (85), playing a bewildered Yuppie.
**Selected Films:** *An American Werewolf in London* (81), *Johnny Dangerously* (84), *Almost You* (85), *After Hours* (85).

## DUNNE, Irene (1901- )

Born in Louisville, Kentucky, this highly competent actress had originally hoped for a career as a singer with the Metropolitan Opera Company but became a luminary of musical comedy instead, touring in *Show Boat* in 1929. Her film career, begun in 1930 with *Leathernecking*, an innocuous musical, lasted for more than two decades. Primarily she was cast in sensible, well-bred roles, but she also appeared in romances, musicals, comedies and melodramas, with co-stars such as Melvyn Douglas and Cary Grant. She played her

parts with great control and dignity. Dunne retired in the 1950s to devote herself to Republican Party politics.
**Selected Films:** *Leathernecking* (30), *Cimmaron* (31), *Back Street* (32), *Symphony of Six Million* (32), *Ann Vickers* (33), *Roberta* (35), *Magnificent Obsession* (35), *Show Boat* (36), *Theodora Goes Wild* (36), *The Awful Truth* (37), *Love Affair* (39), *My Favorite Wife* (40), *The White Cliffs of Dover* (44), *Anna and the King of Siam* (46), *Life With Father* (47), *I Remember Mama* (48), *The Mudlark* (51), *It Grows on Trees* (52).

## DUNNOCK, Mildred (1904- )

A veteran of the Broadway stage, Dunnock, born in Baltimore, Maryland, made her film debut with Bette Davis in *The Corn is Green* (45), the film version of a play in which she was featured. She specialized in motherly roles.
**Selected Films:** *The Corn is Green* (45), *Kiss of Death* (47), *Death of a Salesman* (51), *Baby Doll* (56), *Sweet Bird of Youth* (62), *The Spiral Staircase* (75), *One Summer Love* (76).

## DUPREZ, June (1918- )

The dark-haired London-born leading lady of British and Hollywood films, Duprez frequently played exotic roles, as in *The Four Feathers* (39), and *The Thief of Bagdad* (41).
**Selected Films:** *The Crimson Circle* (36), *The Spy in Black* (38), *The Four Feathers* (39), *The Thief of Bagdad* (41), *None But the Lonely Heart* (44), *The Brighton Strangler* (45), *And Then There Were None* (45), *Calcutta* (46), *That Brennan Girl* (47).

## DURANTE, Jimmy (1893-1980)

A beloved comedian, born in New York City, well-known for his enormous nose, Durante's immortal career saw his hoarse singing, malapropisms and buffoonery featured in vaudeville, night clubs, Broadway, films, radio, and TV.
**Selected Films:** *Roadhouse Nights* (30), *What! No Beer?* (33), *Carnival* (35), *You're In the Army Now* (40), *The Man Who Came to Dinner* (41), *Two Sisters From Boston* (46), *Billy Rose's Jumbo* (62), *It's a Mad Mad Mad Mad World* (63).

## DURBIN, Deanna (1921- )

Born Edna Mae Durbin in Winnipeg, Manitoba, Canada, she was a teenage star in the days when that meant a wholesome sweetness. A peppery, bubbly and attractive young girl with a precocious singing voice, she was signed by MGM when she was 14. When her contract lapsed Durbin moved to Universal and won instant worldwide success as a classical teenage singing star. Indeed, she saved the studio from bankruptcy with *Three Smart Girls* (36). The whole world seemed to love her and she became an enormous box office success at home and abroad. In 1938 she shared a Special Academy Award with Mickey Rooney 'for their significant contribution in bringing to the screen the spirit and the personification of youth.' Her career faltered after about ten years when weight problems, added to a change in musical fashions, brought about her premature retirement in 1948, after which she moved to France and married.
**Selected Films:** *Every Sunday* (36), *Three Smart Girls* (36), *One Hundred Men and a Girl* (37), *Mad About Music* (38), *That Certain Age* (38), *It Started With Eve* (41), *Can't Help Singing* (44), *Up in Central Park* (47), *For the Love of Mary* (48).

*Deanna Durbin in* One Hundred Men and A Girl *(37).*

## DURNING, Charles (1933- )

Born in Highland Falls, New York, Charles Durning made his way to Broadway, where he appeared in a number of successful productions including *The Andersonville Trial* and *That Championship Season*. In films from the mid-1960s, he has become one of the busier character actors in Hollywood. His burly figure and working-man looks tend to type him as a cop; he starred in that capacity in *The Choirboys* (77). Durning has been seen in supporting roles of some of the biggest hits of the 1970s and 1980s, including *The Sting* (73), *Dog Day Afternoon* (75), and *Tootsie* (82). In 1982 as

the governor he virtually stole *The Best Little Whorehouse in Texas* from stars Burt Reynolds and Dolly Parton. Durning has also been busy on the television, where his roles include the miniseries *Captains and Kings* and the TV movie *Studs Lonigan*.
**Selected Films:** *Harvey Middleman, Fireman* (65), *Sisters* (72), *The Sting* (73), *Dog Day Afternoon* (75), *The Hindenburg* (75), *Harry and Walter Go to New York* (76), *The Choirboys* (77), *The Greek Tycoon* (78), *The Fury* (78), *The Muppet Movie* (79), *True Confessions* (81), *Tootsie* (82), *The Best Little Whorehouse in Texas* (82), *To Be or Not To Be* (83), *Mass Appeal* (84), *Stick* (85), *Tough Guys* (86).

## DURYEA, Dan (1907-1968)

Usually typecast as a whining, sneering villain who was often strangely attractive to women, Duryea, born in White Plains, New York, made his film debut as Leo in *The Little Foxes* (41), a role he had played on Broadway. He appeared in many TV dramas.
**Selected Films:** *The Little Foxes* (41). *Ball of Fire* (41), *The Woman in the Window* (44), *Black Angel* (46), *Another Part of the Forest* (48), *Criss Cross* (49), *Chicago Calling* (51), *The Flight of the Phoenix* (65), *The Bamboo Saucer* (68).

## DUVALL, Robert (1931- )

Some actors are showy and some actors quietly immerse themselves in the characters they play. Duvall, born in San Diego, California, falls into the latter category. He made a fine film debut as the mysterious neighbor, Boo Radley, in *To Kill a Mockingbird* (63). Duvall continued to excell, but other actors seemed to grab the Oscars and the headlines until *The Great Santini* (79) allowed him to shine. At last Hollywood gave Duvall his due by presenting him with the Academy Award for Best Actor for his performance as a country-western singer in *Tender Mercies* (83). This award was probably given for his previous work, also. He had been nominated as Best Supporting Actor for his work as the family lawyer in *The Godfather* (72) and for playing the crazed army officer in *Apocalypse Now* (72), as well as for Best Actor as the brutally macho flier in *The Great Santini*.
**Selected Films:** *To Kill a Mockingbird* (63), *Captain Newman MD* (64), *The Chase* (65), *Bullitt* (68), *True Grit* (69), *M*A*S*H* (70), *The Godfather* (72), *The Great Northfield Minnesota Raid* (72), *Apocalypse Now* (72), *The Godfather, Part II* (74), *Network* (76), *The Seven Percent Solution* (76), *The Eagle Has Landed* (77), *The Betsy* (78), *Apocalypse Now* (79), *The Great Santini* (79), *True Confessions* (81), *Tender Mercies* (83), *The Lightship* (86).

*Robert Duvall in* The Great Santini *(79).*

## DUVALL, Shelly (1949- )

Tall and toothy, the Texas lawyer's daughter from Houston was discovered at a Houston party and made her film and acting debut in *Brewster McCloud* (70). Duvall has since established herself as a slightly offbeat character actress.
**Selected Films:** *McCabe and Mrs Miller* (71), *Thieves Like Us* (74), *Nashville* (75), *Buffalo Bill and the Indians* (76), *Three Women* (72), *Annie Hall* (77), *The Shining* (79), *Popeye* (80), *Time Bandits* (81).

## DVORAK, Ann (1912-1979)

Born Anna McKim into a New York City theatrical family, Dvorak entered films as a child in silents. She established herself as an adult playing intelligent and sensitive dramatic leading roles opposite Spencer Tracy in *Sky Devils* (32) and Paul Muni in *Scarface* (32).
**Selected Films:** *The Hollywood Revue of 1929* (29), *Sky Devils* (32), *Scarface* (32), *Housewife* (34), *G-Men* (35), *Racing Lady* (37), *Cafe Hostess* (40), *The Long Night* (47), *The Secret of Convict Lake* (51).

# E

## EASTWOOD, Clint (1930- )

Although his films have usually been scorned by critics, Eastwood may legitimately lay claim to the title of the world's most popular movie star. While other stars have had successful and unsuccessful pictures, there are millions throughout the world who will go to see *any* Eastwood film. Born in San Francisco, California, he was more interested in athletics than in acting, but since he was photogenic and had moved to Los Angeles, California, he was able to pick up bit parts, usually in low-budget films. His Hollywood career was going nowhere when, in 1958, he was picked for the

second lead – that of cattle drive ramrod Rowdy Yates – in a television western series called *Rawhide*. *Rawhide* was a success and it brought him modest fame and a steady income. It also brought him to the attention of Italian movie director Sergio Leone. Eastwood owes his superstar status to that discovery. Italian film companies were making a killing on cheaply produced westerns, dubbed 'Spaghetti Westerns.' These films usually used a European cast and an American actor (although never a high-priced star) playing the lead. That was the role that Eastwood filled. He appeared in *A Fistful of Dollars* (64), one of the first Spaghetti Westerns. He was paid only $15,000 for his work and the film didn't appear in the United States until two years later. But he quickly followed up with two more of those westerns and the public went wild over them. Eastwood played the deadliest, most cold-blooded, most unkempt cowboy heros ever seen on screen. His thin-lipped, unemotional style was perfect for the scruffy brutal hero of those violent films. After these three movies, Eastwod became an established star who could pick any role he wished. He created the character of 'Dirty Harry' Callahan, a San Francisco cop who regularly takes the law into his own hands, and played him in a successful series of pictures. In recent years he has also successfully tried his hand at comedy, appearing in such movies as *Every Which Way But Loose* (70), *Any Which Way You Can* (80) and *City Heat* (85). Eastwood has also effectively directed several of his own films and one movie in which he did not appear, *Breezy* (73). He has tightly managed his career, producing many of his own films with an

*Clint Eastwood in* Hang 'Em High *(68).*

efficiency and economy rare in Hollywood, and practically every one of his pictures has been a big money maker. Today he lives in Carmel, California, and in 1986 he was elected mayor of that community.

**Selected Films:** *Revenge of the Creature* (55), *Francis in the Navy* (55), *Ambush at Cimarron Pass* (58), *A Fistful of Dollars* (64), *For a Few Dollars More* (65), *The Good, the Bad and the Ugly* (66), *Hang 'Em High* (68), *Coogan's Bluff* (68), *Where Eagles Dare* (69), *Two Mules for Sister Sarah* (70), *Play Misty for Me* (71), *Dirty Harry* (71), *Magnum Force* (73), *The Outlaw Josie Wales* (76), *Every Which Way But Loose* (78), *Escape from Alcatraz* (79), *Any Which Way You Can* (80), *Sudden Impact* (84), *Tightrope* (84), *City Heat* (84), *Pale Rider* (85), *Heartbreak Ridge* (86).

## EBSEN, Buddy (1908- )

Immortalized as the head of the clan in TV's *Beverly Hillbillies* and also starring in *Barnaby Jones*, Christian Rudolf Ebsen, born in Belville, Illinois, trained in his father's dance studio and performed in vaudeville before appearing in supporting roles and musicals of the 1930s. Originally cast as the Tin Woodman in *The Wizard of Oz* (39), Ebsen developed an allergic reaction to the make up and lost the part to Jack Haley.

**Selected Films:** *Broadway Melody of 1936* (35), *Captain January* (36), *Born to Dance* (36), *Sing Your Worries Away* (42), *Davy Crockett* (55), *Attack* (56), *The Interns* (62), *The One and Only Genuine Original Family Band* (68).

## EDDY, Nelson (1901-1967)

Born in Providence, Rhode Island, Eddy began his career as a boy soprano. After his voice changed, he sang with a Gilbert and Sullivan opera troupe and the Philadelphia Civic Opera Company, financing his music studies by working as a newspaper reporter. In 1931 he went to Hollywood, where he made four pictures before making it as a star, when in 1935 he appeared with Jeanette MacDonald in the first of their several musical comedies together – *Naughty Marietta*. He was blond. He sang baritone. And the film made more money for the studio than had any musical up to that time. Considering everything, especially Eddy's lack of screen experience, the venture had been a risky one, but it paid handsome dividends. Eddy was almost hopelessly wooden, but the two charmed audiences as a team because their voices blended to near perfection. 'The Singing Sweethearts' worked together for seven years. Eddy went on to go it alone in such musicals as *Balalaika* (39) and *Knickerbocker Holiday* (44). He became enormously popular on radio and on concert tours.
**Selected Films:** *Broadway to Hollywood* (31), *Naughty Marietta* (35), *Rose Marie* (36), *Maytime* (37), *Rosalie* (37), *The Girl of the Golden West* (38), *Sweethearts* (38), *Balalaika* (39), *New Moon* (40), *Bitter Sweet* (40), *The Chocolate Soldier* (41), *I Married an Angel* (43), *Knickerbocker Holiday* (44), *Northwest Outpost* (47).

## EDEN, Barbara (1934- )

A few decorative leads in films led Eden, born Barbara Huffman in Tucson, Arizona, to greater popularity and renown in the TV series *How to Marry a Millionaire* and *I Dream of Jeannie*. She was married to actor Michael Ansara from 1958 to 1973.
**Selected Films:** *Back From Eternity* (56), *The Wayward Girl* (57), *Voyage to the Bottom of the Sea* (61), *The Brass Bottle* (64), *Harper Valley PTA* (78).

## EDWARDS, Anthony (1962- )

A blond six-footer from Santa Barbara, California, Edwards made his film debut in the teen exploitation film *Fast Times at Ridgemont High* (82). He has been seen by millions since as an amiable misfit in *Revenge of the Nerds* (84), and as a sexually frustrated teenager in *Gotcha!* (85).
**Selected Films:** *Fast Times at Ridgemont High* (82), *Heart Like a Wheel* (83), *Revenge of the Nerds* (84), *Gotcha!* (85), *The Sure Thing* (85), *Top Gun* (86).

## EDWARDS, Cliff (1895-1971)

Known to millions as the off-screen voice of Disney's Jiminy Cricket in *Pinocchio* (40), 'Ukelele Ike' Edwards born in Hannibal, Missouri, was a vaudeville and Broadway headliner before getting into pictures. He introduced the song 'Singing in the Rain' in *The Hollywood Revue of 1929* (29).
**Selected Films:** *The Hollywood Revue of 1929* (29), *Hell Divers* (31), *Fast Life* (32), *Flying Devils* (33), *Red Salute* (35), *Bad Guy* (39), *The Monster and the Girl* (41), *The Avenging Rider* (53).

## EDWARDS, Vince (1928- )

Born Vincent Edward Zoimo in New York City, the intense, tough, sincere Edwards, who also sings, made his Broadway debut in the musical *High Button Shoes* (47). His success as TV's *Ben Casey* considerably boosted his career.
**Selected Films:** *Mr Universe* (51), *Sailor Beware* (52), *Hiawatha* (52), *Rogue Cop* (54), *Murder by Contract* (59), *The Victors* (63), *Hammerhead* (68), *The Devil's Brigade* (68), *The Mad Bomber* (72), *Evening in Byzantium* (79), *Space Raiders* (83), *Sno-Line* (85).

## EGAN, Richard (1921-1987)

Tall, rugged and virile, San Francisco-born Egan was once touted as the likely successor to Clark Gable. He played leads in many westerns and action melodramas, and was recently seen mostly on TV and in touring plays.
**Selected Films:** *The Damned Don't Cry* (50), *Undercover Girl* (50), *Split Second* (53), *Love Me Tender* (56), *These Thousand Hills* (58), *Pollyanna* (60), *The 300 Spartans* (62), *The Destructors* (66), *The Big Cube* (69), *The Sweet Creek County War* (79).

## EGGAR, Samantha (1939- )

A convent education and Shakespearean stage roles preceded London-born Victoria Samantha Eggar's leap to international stardom for her performance in *The Collector* (65), which earned her the Best Actress Award at the Cannes Film Festival. She continues to play leads in international productions.
**Selected Films:** *The Wild and the Willing* (62), *Psyche 59* (63), *The Collector* (65), *Doctor Dolittle* (67), *The Molly Maguires* (69), *The Dead Are Alive* (72), *The Seven-Per-Cent Solution* (76), *The Brood* (79), *Curtains* (81).

## EILERS, Sally (1908-1978)

At her peak considered one of Hollywood's most beautiful leading ladies, Dorothea Sallye Eilers, born in New York City, played her first major role in Mack Sennet's *The Goodbye Kiss* (28) and starred opposite James Dunn in *Bad Girl* (31). Her career failed to flourish after the 1930s. She was married to western star Hoot Gibson.
**Selected Films:** *Slightly Used* (27), *Dry Martini* (28), *The Goodbye Kiss* (28), *The Crowd* (28), *Dough Boys* (30), *Quick Millions* (31), *Bad Girl* (31), *State Fair* (33), *Alias Mary Dow* (35), *Danger Patrol* (37), *Full Confession* (39), *Strange Illusion* (45), *Coroner Creek* (48), *Stage to Tucson* (51).

*Marcello Mastroianni and Anita Ekberg in* La Dolce Vita *(61).*

## EKBERG, Anita (1931- )

The classic statuesque blonde, born in Malmö, came to the United States as Miss Sweden 1951 and made her screen debut in Hollywood in 1953. She got her best parts in Italy, however, in King Vidor's *War and Peace* (56), in Federico Fellini's *La Dolce Vita* (59), and in *Boccaccio '70* (61).
**Selected Films:** *The Golden Blade* (53), *War and Peace* (56), *Interpol* (57), *La Dolce Vita* (59), *The Mongols* (60), *Boccaccio '70* (61), *Four for Texas* (63), *Way Way Out* (66), *The Divorcee* (70), *The Clowns* (70), *Gold of the Amazon Women* (79).

## EKLAND, Britt (1942- )

A former model and wife of Peter Sellers from 1963 to 1968, pert, blonde, sexy Stockholm native Britt-Marie Eklund played leads in international productions of the 1960s and 1970s.
**Selected Films:** *Short is the Summer* (62), *After the Fox* (66), *The Bobo* (67), *The Night They Raided Minsky's* (68), *Stiletto* (69), *Percy* (71), *Get Carter* (71), *Asylum* (72), *The Ultimate Thrill* (74), *Casanova & Co.* (77), *King Solomon's Treasure* (77), *Satan's Mistress* (82).

## ELAM, Jack (1916- )

Laconic, swarthy and lean, since 1950, Elam, born in Phoenix, Arizona, has supplied black comic relief and villainous behavior in westerns and gangster dramas. He starred in the TV series *The Dakotas.*
**Selected Films:** *The Sundowners* (50), *Rawhide* (51), *Vera Cruz* (54), *Gunfight at the O.K. Corral* (57), *Edge of Eternity* (59), *The Way West* (67), *Rio Lobo* (70), *Grayeagle* (77), *The Norsemen* (78), *Jinxed* (82).

## ELDRIDGE, Florence (1901- )

On stage since the age of 17, Brooklyn-born Eldridge (Florence McKechnie) was one of Broadway's greatest, receiving the New York Drama Critics Award for her performance in *Long Day's Journey Into Night.* Her films often co-starred husband Fredric March.
**Selected Films:** *Six Cylinder Love* (23), *The Matrimonial Bed* (30), *Les Misérables* (35), *Mary of Scotland* (36), *An Act of Murder* (48), *Another Part of the Forest* (48), *Inherit the Wind* (60).

## ELLIOTT, Denholm (1922- )

London-born Elliott came to acting after three years in a Nazi POW camp during World War II. Following stage experience he made his screen debut in 1949; since then he has played character roles in films great and small, for the most part as various well-mannered and somewhat hapless Englishmen. The variety of his films has been wide; they include the war adventure *The Cruel Sea* (53), the gritty POW story *King Rat* (65), the comedy *The Night They Raided Minsky's* (68), and the Ibsen classic *A Doll's House* (73). As he ages, his earnest features and affable manner have found their way into steadily stronger and more intriguing roles; including the role of the father to the lovestruck young man of *A Room With a View* (86) which brought him an Academy Award nomination. For a time Elliott was married to actress Virginia McKenna.
**Selected Films:** *Dear Mr Prohack* (49), *The Cruel Sea* (53), *Nothing But the Best* (64), *King Rat* (65), *Alfie* (66), *Here We Go Round the Mulberry Bush* (67), *The Night They Raided Minsky's* (68), *A Doll's House* (73), *The Apprenticeship of Duddy Kravitz* (75), *The Boys from Brazil* (78), *Bad Timing* (80), *Raiders of the Lost Ark* (81), *Trading Places* (83), *The Razor's Edge* (84), *A Room With a View* (86), *Defense of the Realm* (87).

## ELLIOTT, Sam (1944- )

Since playing supporting roles in several films of the 1970s and starring in the fluffy teen film *Lifeguard* (76), California-born Elliott has largely been seen in made-for-TV movies including *Evel Knievel* and *The Shadow Riders.*
**Selected Films:** *The Games* (70), *Frogs* (72), *Molly and Lawless John* (72), *Lifeguard* (76), *The Legacy* (79), *Mask* (85).

## ELLIOTT, William (1903-1965)

Born Gordon Nance, 'Wild Bill' Elliott is remembered as one of the better actors among the western movie stars, and they were generally of better quality than most. Born in Pattonsburg, Missouri, he began riding horses when he was five years old and became a champion rodeo rider while in his teens. After studying acting at the Pasadena Playhouse, he changed his name to Gordon Elliott and entered the movie industry in 1925. Elliott spent many years playing small parts before gaining recognition in a Columbia Pictures serial, *The Great Adventures of Wild Bill Hickok* (38). Changing his name to Bill Elliott, he became a fixture of many B westerns from then on. Elliott

*Denholm Elliott in* Bad Timing *(80).*

played a strong, low-keyed cowboy and his trademark was the way he wore his two guns reversed in his holsters. He succeeded Donald 'Red' Barry as Red Ryder in the serials of that name, and made a number of good cowboy films until his career was ended when television wiped out the B western in the 1950s.
**Selected Films:** *The Private Life of Helen of Troy* (27), *The Great Divide* (31), *Wonder Bar* (34), *False Evidence* (40), *The Fabulous Texan* (48), *Hellfire* (49), *The Longhorn* (51), *Chain of Evidence* (57).

## ELLIS, Patricia (1916-1970)

Born Patricia Gene O'Brian in Birmingham, Michigan, Ellis worked on the stage before making her screen debut in 1932, then played the tall, blonde lead in films before retiring in 1940.
**Selected Films:** *Three on a Match* (33), *42nd Street* (33), *Easy in Love* (34), *Boulder Dam* (36), *Step Lively Jeeves* (37), *Block-Heads* (38), *Back Door to Heaven* (39), *Fugitive at Large* (39).

## ELLISON, James (1910- )

Best known as Buffalo Bill in *The Plainsman* (36), with Jean Arthur and Gary Cooper, the handsome, genial Ellison (James Ellison Smith, born in Guthrie Center, Iowa) played many routine second leads, specializing in westerns. He played Johnny Nelson in the *Hopalong Cassidy* series of 1935-37. He retired from the movies in the 1950s.
**Selected Films:** *The Play Girl* (32), *The Plainsman* (36), *The Barrier* (37), *Fifth Avenue Girl* (39), *Ice Capades* (41), *Charley's Aunt* (41), *Last of the Wild Horses* (48), *Lone Star Lawman* (50), *Dead Man's Trail* (52), *Ghost Town* (56).

## ELSOM, Isobel (1893-1981)

After stage work and starring roles in early British romantic films, Elsom, born Isobel Reed in Cambridge, England, appeared in the Broadway hit *Ladies in Retirement* (39). She repeated her role for MGM in 1941 and remained in Hollywood to play innumerable *grandes dames.*
**Selected Films:** *Milestones* (16), *The Wandering Jew* (23), *Stranglehold* (30), *Ladies in Retirement* (41), *Of Human Bondage* (46), *Desirée* (54), *My Fair Lady* (64), *The Pleasure Seekers* (65).

## ELWES, Cary (1963- )

Blond and boyishly handsome, the young English actor Elwes made his film debut in *Another Country* (84).
**Selected Films:** *Another Country* (84), *Lady Jane* (86).

## EMERSON, Faye (1917-1983)

Her cool beauty made Emerson, born in Elizabeth, Louisiana, a natural for socialite leads and supporting roles during the 1930s. Married to Franklin D Roosevelt's son Elliot, then to bandleader Skitch Henderson, she was a successful TV personality during the 1950s.
**Selected Films:** *Blues in the Night* (41), *The Mask of Dimitrios* (44), *Hotel Berlin* (45), *Her Kind of Man* (46), *Nobody Lives Forever* (46), *Guilty Bystander* (50), *A Face in the Crowd* (57).

## EMERSON, Hope (1897-1960)

A six-foot-two 230-pound woman who made her debut on Broadway as an Amazon in *Lysistrata,* sang in opera and also put in time in vaudeville and nightclubs, Emerson, born in Hawarden, Iowa, played many memorable Hollywood character parts from a circus strongwoman in *Adam's Rib* (49) to a sadistic prison matron in *Caged* (50). She also appeared in several television series.
**Selected Films:** *Smiling Faces* (32), *Cry of the City* (48), *Adam's Rib* (49), *Caged* (50), *Casanova's Big Night* (54), *Rock-a-Bye Baby* (59).

## EMERY, John (1905-1964)

Suave, handsome, with a deep, resonant voice, New York City's Emery distinguished himself on the Broadway stage before appearing on screen. He was married to Tallulah Bankhead.
**Selected Films:** *The Road Back* (37), *Here Comes Mr Jordan* (41), *The Woman in White* (48), *Double Crossbones* (51), *The Mad Magician* (54), *Ten North Frederick* (57), *Youngblood Hawke* (64).

## EMHARDT, Robert (1916- )

Once an understudy for Sydney Greenstreet, since the early 1950s the short, portly Emhardt, a native of Indianapolis, has played many characters on stage and television as well as impressive, usually sinister roles on the screen.
**Selected Films:** *The Iron Mistress* (52), *3:10 to Yuma* (57), *The Badlands* (58), *Underworld USA* (60), *Kid Galahad* (62), *The Group* (66), *Lawman* (71), *It's Alive* (74), *Alex and the Gypsy* (76), *Seniors* (78).

## ERDMAN, Richard (1925- )

A native of Enid, Oklahoma, the freckle-faced Erdman began playing callow youths in the mid-1940s. By the end of the 1950s he was also active as a director, especially for TV, where his credits include *The Dick Van Dyke Show*.
**Selected Films:** *Thunder Across the Pacific* (44), *Objective Burma* (45), *The Men* (50), *Cry Danger* (51), *The Blue Gardenia* (53), *Saddle the Wind* (58), *The Brass Bottle* (64), *Heidi's Song* (82).

## ERICKSON, Leif (1911-1986)

A former singer and musician, Erickson, born William Anderson in Alameda, California, broke into films in *Wanderer of the Wasteland* (35) and played routine second leads. He was married to actress Frances Farmer (36-42).
**Selected Films:** *Wanderer of the Wasteland* (35), *College Holiday* (36), *Ride a Crooked Mile* (38), *Eagle Squadron* (42), *Sorry, Wrong Number* (48), *Show Boat* (51), *On the Waterfront* (54), *Tea and Sympathy* (57), *The Carpetbaggers* (64), *Winter Hawk* (75), *Twilight's Last Gleaming* (76).

## ERICSON, John (1927- )

Born Joseph Meibes in Dusseldorf, Germany, the good-looking Ericson made both his Broadway debut in *Stalag 17* and his screen debut in *Teresa* in 1951, and has continued playing Hollywood leads.
**Selected Films:** *Teresa* (51), *Rhapsody* (54), *The Student Prince* (54), *Bad Day at Black Rock* (54), *Forty Guns* (57), *Day of the Badman* (58), *Pretty Boy Floyd* (59), *Under Ten Flags* (60), *The Seven Faces of Dr Lao* (64), *Operation Bluebook* (67), *Bedknobs and Broomsticks* (71), *Hustle Squad* (76), *Crash* (77).

## ERROL, Leon (1881-1951)

Best remembered for the numerous two-reelers in which he played a bald, nervous, henpecked little man, the gifted, rubber-legged comedian, born in Sydney, Australia, moved from vaudeville and the stage into films in 1924.
**Selected Films:** *Yolanda* (24), *The Lunatic at Large* (27), *Finn and Hattie* (31), *Alice in Wonderland* (33), *Princess O'Hara* (35), *Mexican Spitfire* (40), *Higher and Higher* (43), *Mama Loves Papa* (45), *The Noose Hangs High* (48), *Footlight Varieties* (51),

## ERWIN, Stuart (1902-1967)

Nominated for an Academy Award for his supporting role in *Pigskin Parade* (36), the character comedian born in Squaw Valley, California, often played the hero's bumbling but faithful friend. He co-starred with wife June Collyer in the TV series *The Trouble With Father*, later known as *The Stu Erwin Show*.
**Selected Films:** *Mother Knows Best* (28), *Sweetie* (29), *Men Without Women* (30), *Dude Ranch* (31), *Palooka* (34), *Pigskin Parade* (36), *Our Town* (40), *The Great Mike* (34), *Main Street* (53), *Son of Flubber* (64), *The Misadventures of Merlin Jones* (64).

## ESMOND, Carl (1905- )

Born Willy Eichberger in Vienna, the good-looking, elegant Esmond left his stage career in his native Austria to take refuge from the Nazis in London in 1933. He started a film career in England, then moved to Hollywood in 1938. His speciality is suave villainy. Ironically he is often cast as a Nazi officer.
**Selected Films:** *Evensong* (33), *Dawn Patrol* (38), *Ministry of Fear* (44), *Address Unknown* (44), *The Catman of Paris* (46), *The Desert Hawk* (50), *The Racers* (55), *Hitler* (62), *Agent for H.A.R.M.* (66).

## ESTEVEZ, Emilio (1962- )

The son of actor Martin Sheen, Estevez was born in New York and grew up in California. He began acting in amateur theatricals in childhood and wrote a play which was produced in his high school with Estevez in the lead and his friend Sean Penn directing. His screen debut came in *Tex* (82); two years later he had his first hit, starring as teenager Otto, who moves slightly stunned through the bizarre landscape of *Repo Man*. His next role, also in a hit, was very different – Andy, a jock in his teen movie *The Breakfast Club* (85). Estevez has since starred in a film based on his own screenplay, *That Was Then . . . This is Now* (85).
**Selected Films:** *Tex* (82), *The Outsiders* (83), *Repo Man* (84), *The Breakfast Club* (85), *St. Elmo's Fire* (85), *That Was Then . . . This Is Now* (85), *Maximum Overdrive* (86), *Wisdom* (87).

*Emilio Estevez in* Repo Man *(84).*

## EVANS, Dale (1912- )

Wife of Roy Rogers since 1947 and co-star of TV's *The Roy Rogers Show*, singer and actress Evans, born Frances Octavia Smith, left her native Uvalde, Texas and began appearing on screen in Hollywood in the early 1940s.
**Selected Films:** *The East Side Kids* (40), *Orchestra Wives* (42), *Swing Your Partner* (43), *The Yellow Rose of Texas* (45), *Helldorado* (46), *My Pal Trigger* (46), *Apache Rose* (47), *Trigger Jr* (51), *Pals of the Golden West* (51).

## EVANS, Edith (1888-1976)

Famous for her performances of the classics on the London and Broadway stage, Dame Edith, born in London, also distinguished herself in her memorable if infrequent film roles. She was created a Dame in 1976.
**Selected Films:** *A Welsh Singer* (15), *East is East* (16), *The Queen of Spades* (48), *The Last Days of Dolwyn* (48), *The Importance of Being Earnest* (51), *Look Back In Anger* (59), *Tom Jones* (63), *The Chalk Garden* (64), *The Whisperers* (67), *The Madwoman of Chaillot* (69), *Scrooge* (70), *The Slipper and The Rose* (76).

*Dame Edith Evans in* Scrooge *(70).*

## EVANS, Madge (1909-1981)

A child star who began in silent films at the age of five, New York-born Evans made the transition to pretty leading lady on Broadway and also played leads in light, unremarkable romantic films of the 1930s. She retired from films when she married playwright Sidney Kingsley.
**Selected Films:** *The Sign of the Cross* (14), *Zaza* (15), *The Burglar* (16), *True Blue* (18), *Classmates* (24), *Lovers Courageous* (30), *Hallelujah I'm a Bum* (33), *David Copperfield* (34), *The Thirteenth Chair* (37), *Army Girl* (38).

## EVANS, Maurice (1901- )

Curiously enough, the eloquent Evans, whose distinguished career on stage includes exemplary interpretations of Shaw and Shakespeare, has found more work consistent with his stature on TV than he has on screen. Born in Dorchester, England, Evans began his professional career as a boy singer and cut his dramatic teeth on productions of his amateur playwright father's adaptations of Thomas Hardy novels. He first appeared on the London stage in 1927, and two years later attracted attention for his performance in *Journey's End*, joining the Old Vic in 1934. The following year found him beginning his long career on Broadway. He became an American citizen in 1941 and served with the rank of major in charge of entertainment for the Central Pacific theater. His more worthy screen roles include his portrayal of Caesar in *Androcles and the Lion* (53) and Macbeth in *Macbeth*.
**Selected Films:** *White Cargo* (30), *Raise the Roof* (30), *Should a Doctor Tell* (30), *Wedding Rehearsal* (32), *Heart Song* (33), *Scrooge* (35), *Kind Lady* (51), *The Story of Gilbert and Sullivan* (53), *Androcles and the Lion* (53), *The War Lord* (65), *Jack of Diamonds* (67), *Planet of the Apes* (68), *Rosemary's Baby* (68), *Terror in the Wax Museum* (73).

## EVERETT, Chad (1936- )

Dark and handsome, Everett, born Ray Cramton in South Bend, Indiana, played leads in routine Hollywood productions of the 1960s. Television work includes the series *Medical Center*.
**Selected Films:** *Claudelle Inglish* (61), *The Chapman Report* (62), *Get Yourself a College Girl* (64), *The Singing Nun* (65), *Johnny Tiger* (66), *First to Fight* (67), *The Last Challenge* (67), *The Impossible Years* (68), *Airplane II* (83).

## EWELL, Tom (1909- )

A comic actor with a particular knack for exposing the weaknesses of the ordinary man, Ewell made a screen debut of considerable impact in *Adam's Rib* (49). Ewell was born S Yewell Tompkins in Owensboro, Kentucky, and began acting at the University of Wisconsin. He made his professional stage debut in 1928 and worked at Macy's as a salesman before breaking onto Broadway in 1934. By the time of his screen debut he had carved a stable niche for himself as a stage actor. Among his Broadway triumphs was *The Seven Year Itch* (52). He starred in the 1955 screen version of the play opposite Marilyn Monroe, characteristically as a man dealing with common weaknesses. *The Tom Ewell Show* had only a brief run on TV, but he

proved more durable in *Baretta* with Robert Blake.
**Selected Films:** *Adam's Rib* (49), *A Life of Her Own* (50), *An American Guerilla in the Philippines* (50), *Mr Music* (51), *Up Front* (51), *Finders Keepers* (52), *Lost in Alaska* (52), *The Lieutenant Wore Skirts* (55), *The Seven Year Itch* (55), *The Girl Can't Help It* (56), *Tender is the Night* (61), *State Fair* (62), *To Find a Man* (72), *The Great Gatsby* (74).

## EYTHE, William (1918-1957)

His career cut short by alcohol and hepatitis, Eythe, born in Mars, Pennsylvania, was a leading man in Hollywood films of the 1940s. He also produced, acted and directed for the stage.
**Selected Films:** *The Ox-Bow Incident* (42), *The Song of Bernadette* (43), *The Eve of St Mark* (44), *Wing and a Prayer* (44), *The House on 92nd Street* (45), *Meet Me at Dawn* (47), *Customs Agent* (50).

# F

## FABARES, Shelley (1942- )

The niece of actress Nanette Fabray, Fabares, born in Santa Monica, California, played juvenile leads in the early 1960s and leads in occasional films since. Her television appearances include a continuing role on *One Day at a Time*.
**Selected Films:** *Never Say Goodbye* (56), *Summer Love* (58), *Ride the Wild Surf* (64), *Happy Girl* (65), *Hold On* (66), *Spinout* (66), *Hot Pursuit (87).*

## FABIAN (1942- )

A major rock-and-roll idol of the 1950s, the singer, born Fabian Forte Bonapare, in Philadelphia has played film leads since *Hound-Dog Man* (59), often in teen-oriented productions. Since 1970 he has been billed as Fabian Forte.
**Selected Films:** *Hound Dog Man* (59), *North to Alaska* (60), *Mr Hobbs Takes a Vacation* (62), *Ride the Wild Surf* (64), *(64), Dear Brigitte* (65), *The Wild Racers* (68), *A Bullet for Pretty Boy* (70), *Lovin' Man* (72), *Disco Fever* (78), *Crisis in Mid-Air* (79).

## FABRAY, Nanette (1920- )

On the screen at the age of seven as Baby Nan in *Our Gang* shorts, Fabray, born in San Diego, California, made her name as an adult singer and comedy actress with starring roles in Broadway musical comedies. She returned to the screen for occasional supporting roles in 1939. She costarred with Sid Caesar on the TV series *Caesar's Hour*.
**Selected Films:** *The Private Lives of Elizabeth and Essex* (39), *The Band Wagon* (53), *The Happy Ending* (69), *The Cockeyed Cowboys of Calico County* (70), *Harper Valley PTA* (78), *Amy* (81).

*Douglas Fairbanks in* The Private Life of Don Juan *(34).*

## FAIRBANKS, Douglas (1883-1939)

Born Douglas Elton Ulman, Fairbanks began his film career in *The Lamb* in 1915 and, for a while, played the All-American boy, but after his marriage to Mary Pickford, in 1920, he changed his persona – becoming the acrobatic, zestful, ever-smiling, strong, handsome, indestructable American swashbuckler of the silent screen, sporting a new moustache and new sophistication. Fairbanks grew up in Denver, Colorado, moving to New York in 1900. He made his Broadway debut in 1902, moving effortlessly upward in his career until he married Anna Beth Sully, a soap company heiress, and quit the theater. In 1909, Douglas Fairbanks Jr, who would become an actor himself one day, was born. The soap company went broke and Fairbanks went back to the stage, becoming a star. In 1915, ever the adventurer, he decided to leave the theater and make movies. Under the guidance of D W Griffith, Fairbanks became a star instantly, playing in tongue-in-cheek social comedies. His success was rivaled only by Charlie Chaplin and Mary Pickford, 'America's Sweetheart.' In 1916 he established his own company, the Douglas Fairbanks Film Corporation. During a World War I Liberty Bond tour, Fairbanks met Mary Pickford. They fell in love and were married in 1920 after divorcing their respective spouses. So popular were they that the divorces were forgiven by a normally prudish public and they became the closest thing to a royal couple that America would ever know. They moved into their Hollywood mansion, Pickfair, a magnet for celebrities. Doug and Mary, as they were lovingly called by their fans, formed United Artists with Chaplin and Griffith in 1919, giving them control of their vast movie earnings. Fairbanks' career zoomed higher in the 1920s when most of his famous costume adventure pictures were made. He swashbuckled his way through such classics as *The Mark of Zorro* (20), *The Three Musketeers* (21) and *Robin Hood* (21). He carried off daredevil feats half naked until he was well past 40. It was his age, not his voice, which hurt Fairbanks when the talkies came. *The Taming of the Shrew* (29), with Pickford, was not a success, and as their careers dimmed, so did their marriage. They were divorced in 1936 and Fairbanks married Lady Sylvia Ashley, retiring from films. In 1939 he received a posthumous Special Academy Award 'recognizing the unique and outstanding contribution of the first President of the Academy to the international development of the motion picture.'

**Selected Films:** *The Lamb* (15), *Double Trouble* (15), *Reggie Mixes In* (16), *Manhattan Madness* (16), *Wild and Woolly* (17), *A Modern Musketeer* (18), *His Majesty, the American* (19), *The Mark of Zorro* (20), *The Three Musketeers* (21), *Robin Hood* (21), *The Thief of Baghdad* (23), *Don Q, Son of Zorro* (25), *The Black Pirate* (26), *The Taming of the Shrew* (29), *Reaching for the Moon* (30), *Around the World in Eighty Minutes* (31), *Mr Robinson Crusoe* (32), *The Private Life of Don Juan* (34).

## FAIRBANKS, Douglas Jr (1909- )

The son of Douglas Fairbanks, he was born in New York City, and later became an attractive leading man in American movies. He was of a more conventional debonair mold than his father, and in his films he spent as much time in drawing rooms as he did on castle battlements, but he seemed to be at home in any situation. His first wife was superstar Joan Crawford. For many years he lived in London, England, and in 1949 he was knighted for 'furthering Anglo-American amity.'

**Selected Films:** *Party Girl* (20), *Stella Dallas* (25), *The Jazz Age* (29), *The Dawn Patrol* (30), *Outward Bound* (30), *Little Caesar* (30), *Morning Glory* (33), *Catherine the Great* (34), *The Prisoner of Zenda* (37), *The Young in Heart* (38), *Gunga Din* (39), *The Corsican Brothers* (41), *Sinbad the Sailor* (47), *State Secret* (50), *Ghost Story* (81).

## FALK, Peter (1927- )

One-eyed actor Falk has turned his handicap into an advantage. His squinty, fast-talking style makes him adept at playing detectives, gangsters and working-class men. Born in New York City, he was a highly respected off-Broadway stage actor before making his first film, *Wild Across the Everglades* (58). Probably most famous for his success on the television detective series, *Columbo*, he has also been a success in films.

**Selected Films:** *Wild Across the Everglades* (58), *Murder, Inc* (60), *Pocketful of Miracles* (61), *The Balcony* (63), *The Great Race* (65), *Luv* (67), *Anzio* (68), *Murder by Death* (76), *The In-Laws* (79), *All the Marbles* (82), *Big Trouble* (86).

*Alan Arkin and Peter Falk in* The In-Laws *(79).*

## FARENTINO, James (1938- )

Primarily a leading man on TV, Farentino is also a leading man on stage and in occasional films. Born in Brooklyn, he is married to actress and singer Michele Lee.
**Selected Films:** *Violent Midnight* (63), *Psychomania* (63), *Ensign Pulver* (64), *The War Lord* (65), *Banning* (67), *Me Natalie* (69), *The Story of a Woman* (70), *Jesus of Nazareth* (78), *Dead and Buried* (81).

## FARMER, Frances (1914-1970)

Talented and beautiful, Seattle-born Farmer was for a time a sensation, touted as the next big star, but she had problems with Hollywood's values, alcohol, and her health. After her screen debut in 1936 she defied the studios to work with the Group Theatre of New York. She was married to actor Leif Erickson from 1936 to 1942. Her autobiography *Will There Ever Be a Morning?* was published posthumously.
**Selected Films:** *Too Many Parents* (36), *Border Flight* (36), *Rhythm on the Range* (36), *Come and Get It* (36), *Among the Living* (41), *The Party Crashers* (58).

## FARNUM, Dustin (1870-1929)

Best remembered for his cowboy roles, Farnum, born in Hampton Beach, New Hampshire, became a star playing the title role in *The Squaw Man* (13), Cecil B De Mille's first film. Vaudeville work with his brother William Farnum preceded his screen career.
**Selected Films:** *The Squaw Man* (13), *Soldiers of Fortune* (13), *The Virginian* (14), *Captain Courtesy* (15), *The Iron Strain* (16), *Davey Crockett* (16), *The Scarlet Pimpernel* (17), *The Corsican Brothers* (19), *A Man's Fight* (19), *The Devil Within* (21), *The Flaming Frontier* (26).

## FARNUM, William (1876-1953)

A leading man of the silent screen who commanded one of the highest salaries of his day, the Boston-born Farnum, who had made his stage debut at the age of 12, rose to stardom in his first film, *The Spoilers* (14). He was the brother of Dustin Farnum.
**Selected Films:** *The Spoilers* (14), *Samson* (15), *A Man of Sorrow* (16), *Les Miserables* (17), *The Lone Star Ranger* (19), *If I Were King* (20), *A Stage Romance* (22), *A Man Who Fights Alone* (24), *The Crusades* (35), *The Spoilers* (42), *Samson and Delilah* (49), *Jack and the Beanstalk* (52).

## FARR, Felicia (1932- )

Stage experience preceded Farr's appearance as leading lady in a few Hollywood productions, mostly westerns. Born in Westchester County, New York, she is married to actor Jack Lemmon.
**Selected Films:** *Timetable* (56), *Jubal* (56), *Reprisal!* (56), *3:10 to Yuma* (57), *Onionhead* (57), *Hell Bent for Leather* (60), *Kiss Me Stupid* (64), *The Venetian Affair* (67), *Kotch* (71), *Charley Varrick* (73).

## FARRAR, David (1908- )

The tall, handsome, virile Englishman, born in Forest Gate, went on stage in 1932 and made his film debut in *Return of the Stranger* (37). Farrar peaked as a leading man in the late 1940s. His career was not enhanced when he went to Hollywood and was cast in villainous roles.
**Selected Films:** *Return of the Stranger* (37), *Danny Boy* (42), *Black Narcissus* (47), *Mr Perrin and Mr Traill* (48), *The Small Black Room* (48), *Lost* (56), *The 300 Spartans* (62).

## FARRAR, Geraldine (1882-1967)

An American opera star who sang with Berlin's Royal Opera at the age of 19, then at the Metropolitan Opera in New York from 1906 to 1922, the talented and beautiful soprano became a silent film star under Samuel Goldwyn, and made several films with Cecil B De Mille. She was married to silent screen star Lou Tellegen.
**Selected Films:** *Carmen* (15), *Maria Rosa* (16), *Joan the Woman* (16), *The Woman God Forgot* (17), *The Flame of the Desert* (19), *The Riddle Woman* (21).

## FARRELL, Charles (1901- )

After stage experience and a film debut in *The Cheat* (23), the gentlemanly Farrell, born in Onset Bay, Massachusetts, co-starred with Janet Gaynor in *Seventh Heaven* (27). He and Gaynor became the most popular screen lovers of the period. His later TV work includes *My Little Margie* and *The Charlie Farrell Show*.
**Selected Films:** *The Cheat* (23), *The Ten Commandments* (23), *Old Ironsides* (26), *Seventh Heaven* (27), *Street Angel* (28), *Fighting Youth* (35), *The Deadly Game* (42).

## FARRELL, Glenda (1904-1971)

Born in Enid, Oklahoma, Farrell played in stock and on Broadway before her film debut in *Lucky Boy* (29). She is best remembered as a leading lady and wisecracking comedienne in light films of the 1930s including the Torchy Blane series. She returned to stage, screen and TV in character roles in the 1950s.
**Selected Films:** *Lucky Boy* (29), *Little Caesar* (30), *Life Begins* (32), *I Am a Fugitive From a Chain Gang* (32), *Gold Diggers of 1935* (35), *Torchy Blane in Chinatown* (39), *Johnny Eager* (41), *Girls in the Night* (52), *Kissin' Cousins* (64), *Tiger By the Tail* (70).

## FARROW, Mia (1945- )

Frail and delicately beautiful, Farrow, who was born Maria Farrow in Los Angeles, California, is

*Tyrone Power and Alice Faye in* Alexander's Ragtime Band *(38).*

the daughter of actress Maureen O'Sullivan and director John Farrow, the ex-wife of Frank Sinatra and André Previn and the companion of Woody Allen with whom she seems to do her best work. At her best in *Rosemary's Baby* (68), she was very good as a Mafia moll in *Broadway Danny Rose* (84).
**Selected Films:** *Guns at Batasi* (64), *A Dandy in Aspic* (67), *Rosemary's Baby* (68), *See No Evil* (71), *The Great Gatsby* (73), *Death on the Nile* (78), *A Midsummer Night's Sex Comedy* (82), *Zelig* (83), *Broadway Danny Rose* (84), *Supergirl* (84), *The Purple Rose of Cairo* (85), *Hannah and Her Sisters* (86), *Radio Days* (87).

## FAWCETT, Farah (1947- )

A starring role in the TV series *Charlie's Angels* and record-breaking sales of her bathing suit poster made her a household word in 1977. Since her first lead in 1978, Fawcett, born in Corpus Christi, Texas, has been striving for legitimacy as an actress in such productions as the off-Broadway hit (and later movie) *Extremities*. She was married to actor Lee Majors and was billed in the early 1970s as Farrah Fawcett-Majors.
**Selected Films:** *Love is a Funny Thing* (69), *Myra Breckinridge* (70), *Logan's Run* (76), *Somebody Killed Her Husband* (78), *The Cannonball Run* (81), *Extremities* (85).

## FAYE, Alice (1915- )

She was Hollywood's leading star of musicals in the 1930s and early 1940s. Born Ann Leppert in New York, Faye was blonde and pretty with a charming contralto voice. A professional performer from the age of 14, she was plucked from a Broadway chorus line by singer and band leader Rudy Vallee to sing with his orchestra and appear on his radio show. She came to 20th Century-Fox with Vallee for a minor part in *George White's Scandals* (34), but when star Lilian Harvey walked off the set, Faye took over the role. She became a fixture in Fox musicals for the next ten years, starring in such major films as *Alexander's Ragtime Band* (38), *Lillian Russell* (40) and *Tin Pan Alley* (40). Her feuds with Darryl F Zanuck, then head of Fox, were legendary. Threatening to ruin her career, he banned her radio appearances. But Faye was a sensitive, vulnerable and lovely talent and audiences always adored her. Married first to singer Tony Martin, she married bandleader Phil Harris in 1941.
**Selected Films:** *George White's Scandals* (34), *In Old Chicago* (38), *Alexander's Ragtime Band* (38), *Rose of Washington Square* (39), *Lillian Russell* (40), *Tin Pan Alley* (40), *That Night in Rio* (41), *Hello, Frisco, Hello* (43), *The Gang's All Here* (43), *Fallen Angel* (45), *State Fair* (62), *The Magic of Lassie* (78).

## FAYLEN, Frank (1907-1985)

His best role, as the sadistic male nurse Bim in *The Lost Weekend* (45), is representative of the wide range of character roles Faylen, born Frank Ruf in St Louis, Missouri, to vaudevillian parents, played after he moved from stage to screen in 1936. He played Dobie's father in the TV series *The Many Loves of Dobie Gillis.*
**Selected Films:** *Thanks a Million* (35), *Bullets or Ballots* (36), *The Grapes of Wrath* (40), *The Lost Weekend* (45), *Away All Boats* (56), *North to Alaska* (60), *Funny Girl* (68).

## FAZENDA, Louise (1895-1962)

In films since 1913, Fazenda, born in Lafayette, Indiana, evolved into an enormously popular comedienne with Mack Sennett and later proved herself a gifted character actress. She was married to producer Hal Wallis.
**Selected Films:** *The Cheese Special* (13), *Stark Mad* (15), *The Judge* (16), *The Kitchen Lady* (18), *It's a Boy* (20), *The Beautiful and Damned* (22), *Main Street* (23), *Noah's Ark* (29), *No No Nanette* (30), *Wonder Bar* (34), *Swing Your Lady* (38), *The Old Maid* (39).

## FELD, Fritz (1900- )

A native of Berlin, Feld worked in films and for Max Reinhardt in Germany before arriving in Hollywood in 1923. A dapper versatile actor, he was the co-founder of the Hollywood Playhouse and played innumerable eccentric waiters and temperamental hotel clerks and film directors. His comedic trademark is a popping sound achieved with hand and mouth.
**Selected Films:** *Der Golem und die Tänzerin* (17), *Broadway* (29), *At the Circus* (39), *World Premiere* (41), *Phantom of the Opera* (43), *My Girl Tisa* (48), *Full House* (52), *Barefoot in the Park* (67), *Silent Movie* (77), *History of the World – Part One* (81).

## FELDMAN, Marty (1933-1982)

The diminutive, pop-eyed London-born comedian began writing for British TV in the late 1950s before moving into TV acting himself. He made his film debut in 1969 and achieved great popularity via Mel Brooks's *Young Frankenstein* (74) and *Silent Movie* (76).
**Selected Films:** *The Bed-Sitting Room* (69), *Every Home Should Have One* (70), *Young Frankenstein* (74), *The Adventures of Sherlock Holmes' Smarter Brother* (75), *Silent Movie* (76), *The Last Remake of Beau Geste* (77), *In God We Trust* (79), *Yellowbeard* (83).

## FELL, Norman (1924- )

Easily identifiable by his sad eyes, Fell has established a solid career for himself as a character actor. His extensive TV work includes roles in the series *The Man From U.N.C.L.E.* and *Three's Company.*
**Selected Films:** *Ocean's 11* (51), *Pork Chop Hill* (59), *It It's Tuesday This Must Be Belgium* (69), *The Stone Killer* (73), *Guardian of the Wilderness* (76), *On the Right Track* (81), *Paternity* (81).

## FELLOWS, Edith (1923- )

Boston-born Fellows was a child and teenage star of the 1930s and early 1940s, often in roles in which she was trying but nice. She retired from film in her early twenties, but has since done some stage and TV work.
**Selected Films:** *Madame X* (29), *Daddy Long Legs* (31), *Emma* (32), *Riders of Death Valley* (32), *Jane Eyre* (34), *Pennies From Heaven* (36), *The Five Little Peppers* (39), *Nobody's Children* (40), *Girls' Town* (42), *Her First Romance* (47).

## FERNANDEL (1903-1971)

The man who, after Maurice Chevalier, would epitomize the Frenchman onscreen for over 30 years, was born Fernand Joseph Désiré Contandin in Marseilles, France, to the family of a music-hall player. After various jobs he finally gravitated to the stage as a comic singer in vaudeville and music halls. His stock-in trade then, as always, were his long face, his inimitable grin (which looked like a cartoon horse's grin), and his gift for playing likeable dumb clucks with pluck. Following his screen debut in 1930, Fernandel appeared in Renoir's *On Purge Bébé* (31). In 1934 he made the first of several

films with the director Marcel Pagnol, *Angèle*, and was otherwise seen in some of the best French movies of the decade – *Un Carnet de Bal* (37), *Fric Frac* (39), and *La Fille du Puisatier* (40). After several minor films in the 1940s, Fernandel returned to form in the 1950s with his 'Don Camillo' series, in which he was a somewhat dotty priest whose enemy is the Communist mayor of the town. An American favorite since the 1930s, Fernandel appeared in only a couple of films in the US including *Paris Holiday* (58) with Bob Hope.
**Selected Films:** *Le blanc et le noir* (30), *On Purge Bébé* (31), *Angèle* (34), *Un Carnet de Bal* (37), *Harvest* (37), *Fric-Frac* (39), *La Fille du Puisatier* (40), *The Red Inn* (51), *The Little World of Don Camillo* (52), *The Sheep Has Five Legs* (54), *Around the World in 80 Days* (56), *Paris Holiday* (58), *En avant le musique* (62), *Le voyage du père* (66), *Heureux qui comme Ulysse* (70).

## FERRER, José (1909-     )

A distinguished stage actor with a magical voice, considered one of the finest on the stage, Jose Ferrer has himself remarked, 'My entire film career has been dominated by *Cyrano de Bergerac* and *Moulin Rouge*. I have learned to live with the situation, but I regret the form my career has taken.' But while consistent screen success has eluded Ferrer – in 1961 he stated 'For three years there has been no call for my services as a film actor' – his prestige has remained deservedly high. Ferrer was born Jose Vincente Ferrer Otero y Cintron in Santurce, Puerto Rico, on 8 January 1909. His family moved to the United States when he was six years old, and while at Princeton studying architecture Ferrer discovered the theater, acting at the Triangle Club with James Stewart and Joshua Logan. He began working as an assistant stage manager for Joshua Logan in 1935, making his Broadway debut that year in a walk-on part in *A Slight Case of Murder*. He was soon playing featured roles, appearing opposite Uta Hagen, his first of four wives, in summer stock in 1938. By 1946, when he played the title role in *Cyrano de Bergerac* on Broadway, he was also a respected stage director. After his film debut as the Dauphin opposite Ingrid Bergman in *Joan of Arc* (48) Ferrer was cast in flamboyant or foreign roles, as a murdering hypnotist in *Whirlpool* (49) and a South American dictator in *Crisis* (50). His theatrical style was perfectly suited to *Cyrano de Bergerac* (50), which earned him the Best Actor Academy Award and international fame. His powerful portrayal of Toulouse-Lautrec in *Moulin Rouge* (52) earned him another Academy Award nomination. In 1955 Ferrer began his screen directing career with *The Shrike*; during the mid-1950s he also made several successful recordings with his third wife, singer Rosemary Clooney. His films as director and actor-director were good but not sensational, and after a remake of *State Fair* (62) Ferrer concentrated on stage and character acting, Hollywood usually typing him as a swarthy foreigner. He played the Turkish Bey in *Lawrence of Arabia* (62). While continuing stage and film work, including producing, he has also done much TV work, specializing in made-for-TV movies.
**Selected Films:** *Joan of Arc* (48), *Whirlpool* (49), *Crisis* (50), *Cyrano de Bergerac* (50), *Moulin Rouge* (52), *The Caine Mutiny* (54), *Cockleshell Heroes* (56), *The Great Man* (56), *I Accuse* (58), *Lawrence of Arabia* (62), *Nine Hours to Rama* (63), *Ship of Fools* (65), *Order to Kill* (75), *A Midsummer Night's Sex Comedy* (82), *Blood Tide* (82), *The Being* (83), *Dune* (84), *Seduced* (85).

*Mala Powers and Jose Ferrer in* Cyrano de Bergerac *(50).*

## FERRER, Mel (1917-     )

Typically the lean, sensitive leading man, as exemplified in his portrayal of the lame puppeteer in *Lili* (53), the multi-talented Ferrer, who has written, produced and directed as well as acted in films, has sometimes carried his reserved screen persona to the point of woodenness. Born Melchior Gaston Ferrer to affluent parents in Elberon, New Jersey, he attended prep school but dropped out of Princeton to act in summer stock, making his Broadway debut as a dancer in 1938 and his New York acting debut in 1940. When polio interrupted his career he worked for a while with great success writing and producing for radio. He directed his first film, *The Girl of the Limberlost*, in 1945, and returned to Broadway the

same year, acting in the first of many films, *Lost Boundaries*, in 1949. In 1954 he married Audrey Hepburn, whom he directed in *Green Mansions* (59). He produced *Wait Until Dark* for Hepburn in 1967, and shortly after they were divorced in 1968, he suffered a heart attack which has somewhat limited his activity. He has worked primarily in Europe since 1960.
**Selected Films:** *Lost Boundaries* (49), *Scaramouche* (52), *Lili* (53), *War and Peace* (56), *The Vintage* (57), *Blood and Roses* (61), *El Greco* (65), *Every Day's A Holiday* (67), *Brannigan* (75), *The Fifth Floor* (80).

## FETCHIT, Stepin (1898-1985)

Tall and lanky, slow-moving, slow-talking and funny Stepin Fetchit, born Lincoln Perry in Key West, Florida, was the stereotypical Jim Crow black comedian in the white world of 1930s American cinema. He took his stage name, it is said, from a winning racehorse.
**Selected Films:** *In Old Kentucky* (29), *Stand Up and Cheer* (33), *Steamboat Round the Bend* (35), *On the Avenue* (37), *Elephants Never Forget* (39), *Bend of the River* (52), *The Sun Shines Bright* (53), *Amazing Grace* (74), *Won Ton Ton, the Dog Who Saved Hollywood* (76).

## FEUILLÈRE, Edwige (1907- )

Kown as the first lady of French cinema, Feuillère, born Caroline Vivette Edwige Cunati in Vésoul, France, has also had a distinguished career on stage, including work with the Comédie Française. She usually plays the elegant femme fatale.
**Selected Films:** *Le Cordon Bleu* (30), *La Perle* (31), *Topaze* (32), *Feu!* (37), *L'Emigrante* (39), *L'Idiot* (46), *L'Aigle a Deux Tetes* (47), *Olivia* (50), *Le Blé en Herbe* (53), *Crime Doesn't Pay* (62), *Let's Make Love* (68), *Clair de Terre* (70).

## FIELD, Betty (1918-1973)

A popular Broadway ingenue in the late 1930s, Field, born in Boston, made her screen debut in a repeat of her Broadway role in *What a Life!* (39). In 1940s films she usually played neurotic characters, in the 1950s slatternly mothers.
**Selected Films:** *What a Life!* (39), *Of Mice and Men* (39), *Seventeen* (40), *King's Row* (42), *Flesh and Fantasy* (43), *The Southerner* (45), *The Great Gatsby* (49), *Bus Stop* (56), *Bird Man of Alcatraz* (62), *Seven Women* (65), *Coogan's Bluff* (68).

## FIELD, Sally (1946- )

The success Sally Field enjoyed as the cute, wholesome, button-nosed star of the TV series *Gidget* and *The Flying Nun* was, as it always is for a young performer, disturbing as well as affirming. Field herself often describes the conflict in screen image that has been her lot as a fight between Cinderella and Scarlett O'Hara. But however her career is viewed, there can no longer be any doubt that she is a first-rate talent with credits to match. Field was born on 6 November 1946 in Pasadena, California. Her mother Margaret Field (Maggie Mahoney) played leads in several films of the late forties and early fifties, and her stepfather is actor Jock Mahoney. Field began playing the title role in *Gidget* when she was 19 years old; while playing Sister Bertrille in *The Flying Nun* she attended classes at Lee Strasberg's Actors Studio. Her film debut in *The Way West* (67) was followed by several movies made for TV, culminating in the four-hour *Sybil* (76) which earned her an Emmy for her portrayal of a mentally disturbed woman with 16 personalities. *Sybil* not only helped her distance herself from her all-American-girl image, it also attracted the attention of Martin Ritt, who eventually directed her in *Norma Rae* (79). Her first feature after *Sybil*, however, was with Burt Reynolds in *Smokey and the Bandit* (77), in which she plays a runaway bride. The film owed much of its great box-office success to the highly-publicized romance between Reynolds and Field. By the time she completed *Hooper* (78) and *Smokey and the Bandit II* (80) with Reynolds, Field was back in the public eye, now perceived as a tough but vulnerable young cookie. Greater popularity and critical recognition came for her title role in Ritt's *Norma Rae*, for which she received the Academy Award for best actress, the Cannes Festival Award, and several other awards. Further distancing herself from her *Flying Nun* Image as well as from her more recent image of a gutsy little crusader, Field played prostitute Amy Post in Ritt's *Back Roads* (81). She received a second Academy Award for her performance in *Places of the Heart* (84), in which she portrays a depression-era widow who steps out of her accepted place to save her farm. Field has been married twice, to Steve Craig in 1968, with whom she had two sons; and to producer Alan Greisman, in 1984.
**Selected Films:** *The Way West* (67), *Stay Hungry* (76), *Smokey and the Bandit* (77), *Heroes* (77), *The End* (78), *Beyond the Poseidon Adventure* (79), *Norma Rae* (79), *Smokey and the Bandit II* (80), *Absence of Malice* (81), *Kiss Me Goodbye* (82), *Places in the Heart* (84), *Murphy's Romance* (85), *Punchline* (87).

## FIELDS, Gracie (1898-1979)

Singer, actress and comedienne, Fields was born Gracie Stansfield in Rochdale, Lancashire, England, and became a music hall entertainer at the age of 13. During the 1930s she became Britain's highest-paid actress, a major box office draw on screen and on stage, and so popular on radio that Parliament once adjourned early so that members could listen to one of her broadcasts. Her bold spirit and Lancashire humor buoyed audiences during the dreary years of the Great Depression. Fields came to the United States when her second husband, Italian-born Monty Banks, was declared

an alien by the British Government during World War II. She was a success in Hollywood, especially when playing opposite Monty Woolley, retiring from films after the war. Fields returned to Europe and was created a Dame Commander of the Order of the British Empire in 1979.
**Selected Films:** *Sally in Our Alley* (31), *Looking at the Bright Side* (32), *Love, Life and Laughter* (33), *Sing As We Go* (34), *Keep Smiling* (38), *Stage Door Canteen* (43), *Holy Matrimony* (43), *Molly and Me* (45), *Paris Underground* (45).

## FIELDS, W C (1879-1946)

Born William Claude Dunkinfield in Philadelphia, Pennsylvania, Fields had a tragic childhood. The son of a poor Cockney immigrant, he ran away from home at the age of 11, surviving by his wits, but he dreamed of being a great juggler and it was this skill that allowed him to break into show business. After a hard life as a tramp juggler, at the age of 20 he was a comic star in vaudeville, giving a command performance at Buckingham Palace in London while on a European tour. He had a long string of successes in the *Ziegfeld Follies* and *George White's Scandals,* and in 1923 was the star of a hit Broadway musical, *Poppy,* retitled for the screen as *Sally of the Sawdust* (25). Fields had been making moves since 1915 and most of them were more popular with the critics than with the public. But by late silent era he had achieved a modest following of devoted fans. It was sound that brought him to his full flowering as a screen personality. Many of his routines were made up as he went along. Once he sold a story line for $25,000 that was written on the back of an envelope. This red-nosed, gravel-voiced, bottle-hitting misogynist became a great comic genius around whose intolerance and eccentric habits many legends have been built. Fields usually played the world's greatest drinker (a role he upheld off-screen as well), the all-time cynic and misanthrope, henpecked past endurance, persecuted by authorites of every stripe. He fought back by bragging, griping, avoiding his enemies, speaking harsly to children and weakly abandoning himself to pointless fits of temper. When all else failed he resorted to telling lies and making oily compliments. Under pseudonyms such as Otis J Cribblecoblis and Mahatma Kane Jeeves, Fields wrote many of his own film scripts. He became a cult hero as early as the 1930s because of his legendary fears and odd behavior. He shone not only in his classic film comedies, but also when he stepped out of character to play Humpty Dumpty in *Alice in Wonderland* (33) or Mr Micawber in *David Copperfield* (34). In *My Little Chickadee* (40) he appeared with another comic genius, Mae West. Not only have his films survived but today his reputation is greater than it was even at the peak of his long and succesful career.
**Selected Films:** *Pool Sharks* (15), *Sally of the Sawdust* (25), *It's the Old Army Game* (26), *So's Your Old Man* (26), *Two Flaming Youths* (27), *Tillie's Punctured Romance* (27), *The Golf Specialist* (30), *Million Dollar Legs* (32), *If I Had a Million* (32), *The Dentist* (32), *The Fatal Glass of Beer* (32), *Tillie and Gus* (33), *Alice in Wonderland* (33), *Mrs Wiggs of the Cabbage Patch* (34), *It's a Gift* (34), *David Copperfield* (34), *Poppy* (36), *You Can't Cheat an Honest Man* (39), *My Little Chickadee* (40), *The Bank Dick,* (40), *Never Give a Sucker an Even Break* (41), *Sensations of 1945* (45).

*W C Fields in* The Bank Dick *(40).*

## FINCH, Jon (1941- )

The British leading man made his screen debut in 1970 in *The Fearless Vampire Lovers* and played the title role in Roman Polanski's screen version of *Macbeth* (71).
**Selected Films:** *The Fearless Vampire Lovers* (70), *Macbeth* (71), *Horror of Frankenstein* (71), *Sunday, Bloody Sunday* (71), *Frenzy* (72), *Lady Caroline Lamb* (72), *The Final Programme* (73), *Diagnosis: Murder* (74), *A Faithful Wife* (75), *The Man with the Green Cross* (76), *Death on the Nile* (78). *The Threat* (81).

## FINCH, Peter (1916-1977)

Born William Mitchell in London, England, this thoughtful-looking actor migrated to Australia, where he became that country's leading radio actor. He returned home in 1949 and his handsome rugged-looking appearance let him become a respected stage and film actor, the protégé of Laurence Olivier. He received British Film Academy Awards for his work in *A Town Like Alice* (56), *No Love for Johnnie* (61) and *Sunday, Bloody Sunday* (71). This international star made his last film, *Network,* in 1976. The Academy Award for Best Actor that year was won by Finch for his performance as a crazed television commentator.

*Peter Finch, Murray Head, Glenda Jackson* – Sunday Bloody Sunday *(71)*.

Finch died while on a publicity tour and became the first actor to win the Award posthumously.
**Selected Films:** *Dad and Dave Come to Town* (37), *The Power and the Glory* (45), *Eureka Stockade* (49), *Elephant Walk* (54), *Simon and Laura* (55), *The Battle of the River Plate* (56), *A Town Like Alice* (56), *The Nun's Story* (59), *The Trials of Oscar Wilde* (60), *No Love for Johnnie* (61), *The Girl With Green Eyes* (64), *The Flight of the Phoenix* (65), *Far From the Madding Crowd* (67), *Sunday, Bloody Sunday* (71), *England Made Me* (72), *Network* (76).

## FINE, Larry: See STOOGES, The Three

## FINLAY, Frank (1926- )

Nominated for an Academy Award for his potrayal of Iago in the National Theatre of Great Britain's film version of *Othello* (65), Finlay, born in Farnsworth, is primarily known for his British stage and TV work, but has been impressive in film appearances since the 1960s.
**Selected Films:** *Life for Ruth* (62), *The Informers* (63), *Othello* (65), *Robbery* (67), *Inspector Clouseau* (68), *Cromwell* (69), *Sitting Target* (72), *The Three Musketeers* (74), *Murder by Decree* (79), *Enigma* (82), *Nineteen Nineteen* (86)

## FINLAYSON, James (1877-1953)

Stage actor Finlayson, born in Falkirk, Scotland, arrived in Hollywood in 1916 and stayed on to become one of the silent screen's most memorable comic villains. Famous for his exaggerated double takes, the bald, mustached Finlayson was an explosive foil for Laurel and Hardy.
**Selected Films:** *Married Life* (20), *A Small Town Idol* (21), *Ladies' Night in a Turkish Bath* (28), *Dawn Patrol* (30), *Big Business* (30), *Way Out West* (37), *Royal Wedding* (51).

## FINNEY, Albert (1936- )

Finney has been called the second Olivier. An illustrious stage actor and brilliant film star, he comes as close as anyone to deserving that title. Born in Salford, England, the son of a bookie, Finney was encouraged by his headmaster at a grammar school to apply for a scholarship at the Royal Academy of Dramatic Art. After completing his studies, he made his stage debut with the Birmingham Reperatory Theatre and for the next ten years did chiefly Shakespearean roles. Fame came with *Billy Liar*, on stage, and with *Saturday Night and Sunday Morning* (60), on screen. He was virile and sensitive as a working-class youth trapped by the circumstances of his life, and the film was a huge success. So was *Tom Jones* (63), a bawdy, energetic romp. Significantly, although the film made Finney a millionaire and won him a Best Actor Award at the Venice Film Festival, he did not abandon the stage. On the contrary, he turned down lucrative movie contracts and flashy roles so that he could continue in the theater. His most successful play of this era was *Luther*, performed in Britain and America. In 1965 Finney

formed his own production company for films, plays and television, which did not prevent him from spending two seasons with Britain's National Theatre, enhancing his reputation as one of the best actors of his generation. Although his movies of this period were not blockbusters, he was always good – as a psychotic murderer in the remake of the Robert Montgomery 1940s classic *Night Must Fall* (63), and as the self-absorbed husband in *Two for the Road* (67), co-starring Audrey Hepburn. In 1970, Finney, once married to actress Jane Wenham, was married a second time to French film star Anouk Aimée. In the years that followed, he tackled the premiere roles of the theater, such as Tamburlaine, Hamlet and Macbeth. Finney also showed exceptional range on screen in a rather eccentric choice of roles. He has played Scrooge, Hercule Poirot, Daddy Warbucks, oddballs and neurotics. There is simply very little that Albert Finney cannot do.
**Selected Films:** *The Entertainer* (59), *Saturday Night and Sunday Morning* (60), *Tom Jones* (63), *The Victors* (63), *Night Must Fall* (63), *Two for the Road* (67), *Charlie Bubbles* (68), *The Picasso Summer* (69), *Scrooge* (70), *Gumshoe* (71), *Alpha Beta* (73), *Murder on the Orient Express* (74), *The Duellists* (77), *Wolfen* (81), *Shoot the Moon* (82), *Annie* (82), *The Dresser* (83), *Under the Volcano* (84), *Loophole* (86).

*Albert Finney* – Under the Volcano *(84)*.

## **FISHER, Carrie** (1956- )

Carrie Fisher's portryal of Princess Leia in the phenomenally popular *Star Wars* (77) has earned her a permanent place in American film folklore. Born in Los Angeles to actress Debbie Reynolds and singer Eddie Fisher, she began performing in her mother's night club act at the age of 12 and dropped out of school at 15 to devote herself to show business. 'I always wanted to do what my mother did – get all dressed up, shoot people, fall in the mud. I never considered anything else.' She made her debut on Broadway in a chorus line in 1973 and in film as a nymphet who seduces Warren Beatty in *Shampoo* (75). Her leading role in *Star Wars* followed eighteen months of acting and speech training in London. Fisher was briefly married to songwriter and singer Paul Simon.
**Selected Films:** *Shampoo* (75), *Mr Mike's Mondo Video* (75), *Star Wars* (77), *I Want to Hold Your Hand* (78), *Wise Blood* (79), *The Empire Strikes Back* (80), *The Blues Brothers* (80), *Under the Rainbow* (81), *Return of the Jedi* (83), *The Man With One Red Shoe* (85), *Hannah and Her Sisters* (86).

## **FITZGERALD, Barry** (1888-1961)

Hollywood's Irishman-in-residence for many years, Barry Fitzgerald played the movie Irishman with such whimsical, irascible, scene-stealing charm that he eventually achieved star status. Born William Joseph Shields in Dublin, Fitzgerald worked with the Abbey Theatre before making his film debut in Alfred Hitchcock's *Juno and the Paycock* (30). A visit to America with the Abbey Players led him to many Broadway appearances, and in 1936 John Ford invited him to Hollywood to repeat his stage role in *The Plough and the Stars.* This American screen debut proved to be the first of innumerable Irish-ethnic dialect roles that Fitzgerald played with such skill that he is still remembered as one of Hollywood's finest character actors. His role was the older priest in *Going My Way* (44), won him an Academy Award for Best Supporting Actor. He was the brother of Arthur Shields, who was also a character actor.
**Selected Films:** *Juno and the Paycock* (30), *The Plough and the Stars* (36), *Ebb Tide* (37), *Bringing Up Baby* (38), *The Dawn Patrol* (38), *The Long Voyage Home* (40), *How Green Was My Valley* (41), *Going My Way* (44), *And Then There Were None* (45), *The Naked City* (48), *Union Station* (50), *The Quiet Man* (52), *Rooney* (58), *Broth of a Boy* (59).

## **FITZGERALD, Geraldine** (1914- )

Fitzgerald began acting in her native Dublin, Ireland, at the Gate Theatre, where she met Orson Welles. After making her debut in British films in 1943, she acted for Welles in New York, then went to Hollywood, where lackluster roles squelched her film career. She made a successful comeback in the 1960s on stage and as a folk singer.
**Selected Films:** *Blind Justice* (34), *Wuthering Heights* (39), *Wilson* (44), *Ten North Frederick* (58), *The Pawnbroker* (65), *Rachel, Rachel* (68), *Harry and Tonto* (74), *Arthur* (80), *Poltergeist II* (86).

## **FIX, Paul** (1901-1983)

In Hollywood from the early 1920s, Paul Fix Morrison, born in Dobbs Ferry, New York, portrayed innumerable good-guy and bad-guy sheriffs, doctors, ranchers and criminals, usually in westerns and gangster films. He was the sheriff in the TV series *The Rifleman.*
**Selected Films:** *The Adventuress* (20), *Hoodoo Ranch* (26), *The First Kiss* (28), *Souls at Sea* (37), *The Ghost Breakers* (40), *Dakota* (45), *Giant* (56), *To Kill a Mockingbird* (63), *Zabriskie Point* (70), *Grayeagle* (77), *Wanda Nevada* (80).

## **FLEMING, Rhonda** (1923- )

A beautiful, photogenic redhead who delighted cinematographers, Fleming, born Marilyn Louis to show business parents in Los Angeles, moved gracefully into bad-girl leads in the 1940s and 1950s soon after graduating from Beverley Hills High School.
**Selected Films:** *When Strangers Marry* (43), *Spellbound* (45), *Abilene Town* (46), *Cry Danger* (50), *The Redhead and the Cowboy* (51), *Slightly Scarlet* (56), *Gun Glory* (57), *The Crowded Sky* (60), *The Patsy* (64), *Won Ton Ton, The Dog Who Saved Hollywood* (75), *The Nude Bomb* (80).

## **FLETCHER, Bramwell** (1904- )

Born in Bradford, England, Fletcher made his Shakespearean stage debut in 1927 and his British film debut in 1928. He worked on Broadway and played light leads and supporting roles in 1930s films before retiring from the screen in 1943. He continues to perform on the stage and on TV.
**Selected Films:** *Chick* (28), *Raffles* (30), *Svengali* (31), *The Mummy* (32), *Only Yesterday* (33), *The Scarlet Pimpernel* (34), *Random Harvest* (42), *White Cargo* (42), *The Immortal Sergeant* (42).

## **FLETCHER, Louise** (1934- )

Best remembered for her Academy Award-winning portrayal of the heartless Nurse Ratched in the screen adaptation of Ken Kesey's best-selling novel *One Flew Over the Cuckoo's Nest* (75), Louise Fletcher was born in Birmingham, Alabama, to parents who were totally deaf; her father was an Episcopalian minister. She studied acting with Jeff Corey in Los Angeles while supporting herself as a secretary and appeared in episodes of 1950s and 1960s TV series such as *Wagon Train* and *The Untouchables*, then retired in 1964 to give birth to her second child. Her comeback performance in Robert Altman's *Thieves Like Us* (74) convinced Milos Forman to approach her for her part in *One Flew Over the Cuckoo's Nest.*
**Selected Films:** *Thieves Like Us* (74), *One Flew Over the Cuckoo's Nest* (75), *Russian Roulette* (75), *Exorcist II: The Heretic* (77), *The Cheap Detective* (78), *The Lady in Red* (79), *Natural Enemies* (79), *The Magician of Lublin* (79), *The Lucky Star* (80), *Strange Behavior* (81), *Brainstorm* (83), *Invaders from Mars* (86), *Nobody's Fool* (86).

## **FLIPPEN, Jay C** (1898-1971)

A native of Little Rock, Arkansas, Flippen began his stage career in 1916 and had achieved star billing on Broadway in 1926. He usually played tough but nice characters on the screen – a sheriff, a cop, or a sergeant – and was often in westerns.
**Selected Films:** *Marie Galante* (34), *Brute Force* (47), *Intrigue* (48), *The Wild One* (53), *Oklahoma!* (55), *The Killing* (56), *Cat Ballou* (65), *Hellfighters* (68), *The Seven Minutes* (71).

## **FLYNN, Errol** (1909-1959)

Colorful, witty and charming, Flynn – the dashing hero of some of Hollywood's finest adventure films, a talented comedian and a more than competent actor – was usually underrated by the critics. But fans and critics alike agreed that he had few peers when it came to off-screen escapades. Born in Hobart, Tasmania, the son of a distinguished marine biologist, Flynn was sent to various schools. He was expelled from each. At 15 he became a clerk with a shipping company in Sydney, Australia, and at 16 entered government service in New Guinea. Finding life tame, Flynn set off on a sailing adventure, which he later wrote about in the first of his autobiographies, *Beam Ends* (34). His schemes also included searching for gold and managing a plantation. Then it was off to England to become an actor and later a contract with Warner Bros., which brought him to Hollywood in 1935. That same year he married actress Lili Damita. He also became a major star, thanks to *Captain Blood* (35). He made a series of costume pictures with Olivia De Havilland, which were immensely popular. Female fans adored him for his wry cynicism, good body and muscular legs that looked great in tights. Much-publicized barroom brawls, and three marriages and scores of flamboyant affairs helped build the Errol Flynn 'Don Juan' legend. In 1942 he was the center of a notorious statutory rape case involving two teenage girls who claimed he had had his way with them on his yacht. Although Flynn was acquitted, uttering many amusing comments along the way, the case hurt his career. So did being declared 4F during World War II, even though he suffered from a heart defect, tuberculosis and recurring malaria. In the late 1940s he began using drugs, which, added to his alcoholism, began to take a toll on his looks. His career took a plunge and he lost all his money in ill-conceived film production ventures. When Flynn died at age 50 his body was old beyond his years. Still, the thundering good times of his romping youth shine through in movies like *The Adventures of Robin Hood* (38).
**Selected Films:** *In the Wake of the Bounty* (33),

*Errol Flynn* – The Adventures of Robin Hood *(38).*

*Murder at Monte Carlo* (34), *Captain Blood* (35), *The Charge of the Light Brigade* (36), *The Prince and the Pauper* (37), *The Adventures of Robin Hood* (38), *The Dawn Patrol* (38), *Dodge City* (39), *The Sea Hawk* (40), *They Died with Their Boots On* (41), *Gentleman Jim* (42), *Objective Burma* (45), *Cry Wolf* (46), *That Forsyte Woman* (49), *Kim* (51), *Mara Maru* (52), *The Master of Ballantrae* (53), *The Sun Also Rises* (57), *Too Much Too Soon* (58), *Roots of Heaven* (58), *Cuban Rebel Girls* (59).

## FOCH, Nina (1924- )

Born Nina Fock in Leyden, Holland, and raised in New York City, the cool, blonde Foch made her Broadway debut in 1947. She played aloof, sophisticated ladies on the screen. Her directing credits include associate director of George Stevens' *The Diary of Anne Frank.*

**Selected Films:** *The Return of the Vampire* (43), *Cry of the Werewolf* (44), *My Name is Julia Cross* (45), *An American in Paris* (51), *Executive Suite* (54), *Spartacus* (60), *Salty* (73), *Mahogany* (76), *Jennifer* (78).

## FONDA, Henry (1905-1983)

On the stage and on the screen, Fonda began playing gauche young fellows and graduated to roles of amiable wisdom. By the time he died, he had attained mythic proportions in America, the result of a long career spent playing characters embodying the values of the Midwestern prairie which was his home. Honesty, sincerity, quiet decency and reason rather than passion seemed to echo in his flat, unaccented voice. He was not the kind of hero to inspire awe, but rather one an audience could like. Born in Grand Island, Nebraska, Fonda was an office boy at an Omaha credit company when he began acting. He later became a member of the University Players Company where he worked with the first of his five wives, the actress Margaret Sullavan. By 1934 he was a respected Broadway peformer. Movies followed, and the shy, unassuming Fonda shot to stardom within a year. The versatile actor appeared in westerns, comedies and melodramas until the greatest role in his career came along, that of Tom Joad in *The Grapes of Wrath* (40). His private life, however, was not as rosy as his career prospects. In 1936 Fonda married socialite Frances Seymour Brokaw, who committed suicide in a rest home in 1950. The couple had two children, Jane and Peter, who were later to become actors in their own right. Fonda joined the Navy during World War II, and when he returned from service, his acting reflected a new maturity. He longed for the stage and in 1948 had an enormous success in the title role of *Mister Roberts.* He repeated his triumph in the film version of the play in 1955. From then on his career alternated between screen and theater. Films such as *Twelve Angry Men* (57), for which he won a British Film Academy Award, *Advise and Consent* (61) and *The Best Man* (64) reflected his preference for scripts with political and social content. He also appeared on television, his least favorite medium. In 1978 Fonda won the Life Achievement Award of the American Film Institute. Then, thanks to a film in which he co-starred opposite Katharine Hepburn and his daughter Jane, *On Golden Pond* (82), in which he scored a major acting triumph, he at last was given a much-deserved Academy Award for Best Actor. Fonda died soon after.

**Selected Films:** *The Farmer Takes a Wife* (35), *Way Down East* (35), *The Trail of the Lonesome Pine* (36), *The Moon's Our Home* (36), *You Only Live Once* (37), *Slim* (37), *Jezebel* (38), *Blockade* (38), *Jesse James* (39), *Young Mr Lincoln* (39), *Drums Along the Mohawk* (39), *The Grapes of Wrath* (40), *Chad Hanna* (40), *The Lady Eve* (41), *The Male Animal* (42), *The Ox Bow Incident* (43), *My Darling Clementine* (46), *Fort Apache* (48), *Mister Roberts* (55), *The Wrong Man* (56), *War and Peace* (56), *Twelve Angry Men* (57), *Stage Struck* (57), *Advise and Consent* (61), *The Longest Day* (62), *The Best Man* (64), *Fail Safe* (64), *Welcome to Hard Times* (67), *Madigan* (68), *Midway* (76), *Rollercoaster* (77), *On Golden Pond* (82).

Below: *Jane Fonda, Jon Voight* – Coming Home *(78).*
Right: *Henry Fonda in* The Grapes of Wrath *(40).*

## FONDA, Jane (1937- )

Born in New York City, the daughter of Henry Fonda, she started life among the privileged. Her childhood was marked by tragedy when her mother, Frances Brokaw, committed suicide in a rest home in 1950. She showed little interest in acting as a child, and while attending Vassar College, she decided to go to Paris to study art. Upon her return, she dabbled in modeling, making the cover of *Vogue* magazine twice. Lee Strasberg of the Actors Studio persuaded her to become an actress, and she later starred with her father in an Omaha production of *The Country Girl* in 1955. In 1960, family friend Joshua Logan gave her a big part in her first film, *Tall Story*, which he directed. That film and her next, *Walk on the Wild Side* (61) were critically praised. Not so *In the Cool of the Day* (63), for which the *Harvard Lampoon* gave her the Worst Actress Award. Then she emerged as a sexpot when she made *La Ronde* (64) for Roger Vadim, the ex-husband of Brigitte Bardot. They were married and he turned her into another Bardot in *Barbarella* (68). She was cute in *Cat Ballou* (65), but there was no way to guess the changes that were about to take place in her life and career. She became a star in her own right, a political presence, an accomplished actress and one of the most famous women in America. Fonda became deeply involved in radical, and later feminist, politics during the Vietnam War. As her ability as an actress coalesced and her marriage to Vadim crumbled, she became outspoken – often strident – as an anti-war critic and civil rights exponent. With actor Donald Sutherland she formed the Anti-War Troupe, touring military camps despite Pentagon opposition. Nicknamed 'Hanoi Jane,' she became a symbol of the riotous 1960s to her detractors. Still she continued her activities despite the risk of destroying her career. Divorced from Vadim, she married a political militant, Tom Hayden. Fonda's career not only survived but prospered. She won Academy Awards for Best Actress in *Klute* (71) and *Coming Home* (78). Although she has appeared in movies with light comic appeal, she refuses to make films which run counter to her political views. Perhaps Fonda's finest moment came when in tribute to her father she produced and appeared in *On Golden Pond* (82).

**Selected Films:** *Tall Story* (60), *Walk on the Wild Side* (61), *Period of Adjustment* (62), *In the Cool of the Day* (63), *Sunday in New York* (63), *La Ronde* (64), *Cat Ballou* (65), *Barefoot in the Park* (67), *Barbarella* (68), *They Shoot Horses Don't They?* (69), *Klute* (71), *A Doll's House* (74), *Fun with Dick and Jane* (77), *Julia* (77), *Coming Home* (78), *California Suite* (78), *Comes a Horseman* (79), *The China Syndrome* (79), *9 to 5* (80), *On Golden Pond* (82), *Agnes of God* (85), *The Morning After* (87).

## FONDA, Peter (1939- )

Son of Henry and brother of Jane, Peter Fonda, born in New York City, has made a distinctive career of his own as actor, producer, and director. He produced, co-wrote and starred in the highly successful *Easy Rider* (69).

**Selected Films:** *Tammy and the Doctor* (63), *Lilith* (64), *The Wild Angels* (66), *The Trip* (67), *Easy Rider* (69), *The Hired Hand* (71), *Dirty Mary Crazy Larry* (74), *Futureworld* (76), *High-Ballin'* (78), *Wanda Nevada* (79), *Split Image* (82), *Certain Fury* (85).

## FONG, Benson (1916-1987)

California-born character actor Fong has made his features his meal ticket, playing Orientals in supporting roles of some 200 films since the 1940s, including several in the Charlie Chan series.
**Selected Films:** *Thirty Seconds Over Tokyo* (44), *Boston Blackie's Chinese Adventure* (49), *Flower Drum Song* (62), *Our Man Flint* (66), *The Love Bug* (69), *Jinxed* (82).

## FONTAINE, Joan (1917- )

Fontaine was born Joan De Havilland in Tokyo, Japan, to British parents and moved to America as a child. Her first pseudonym, used primarily on stage, was Joan Burfield. A year younger than her sister, Olivia de Havilland, Fontaine began her film career playing mousy ladylike types and moved on to sophisticated glamorous roles. It took years for her to achieve a success equal to her sister's and their sibling feud was notorious. Probably her finest moment came when she played the innocent heroine in Alfred Hitchcock's brilliant *Rebecca* (40), opposite Laurence Olivier, which earned her an Academy Award nomination as Best Actress. She won the Oscar for Best Actress the following year, for her work in another Hitchcock film, *Suspicion*, with Cary Grant. The fact that her sister was nominated that year for her role in *Hold Back the Dawn*, considering their fierce rivalry, either real or publicity inspired, added interest to this particular competition. She was nominated again as Best Actress for her portrayal of a teenager in *The Constant Nymph* (43), with Charles Boyer. She was married to actor Brian Aherne from 1939 to 1945.
**Selected Films:** *No More Ladies* (35), *Quality Street* (37), *A Damsel in Distress* (38), *Gunga Din* (39), *The Women* (39), *Rebecca* (40), *Suspicion* (41), *The Constant Nymph* (43), *Jane Eyre* (43), *Frenchman's Creek* (44), *The Affairs of Susan* (45), *From This Day Forward* (46), *Letter from an Unknown Woman* (48), *Ivanhoe* (52), *Island in the Sun* (56), *A Certain Smile* (58), *Tender is the Night* (61), *Voyage to the Bottom of the Sea* (61), *The Witches* (66).

## FONTANNE, Lynn (1887-1983)

The celebrated stage actress born in Woodford, England, formed with her husband, Alfred Lunt, one of the greatest teams the American theater has ever seen, but neither as a team nor as individuals did they make much of a mark in films.
**Selected Films:** *The Man Who Found Himself* (25), *Second Youth* (26), *The Guardsman* (32), *Stage Door Canteen* (43).

## FORAN, Dick (1910-1979)

Born John Foran in Flemington, New Jersey, the husky Foran began in show business as a singer. He made his screen debut in 1934, therafter becoming the singing hero of several westerns and playing leads and supporting roles in innumerable dramatic productions.
**Selected Films:** *Stand Up and Cheer* (34), *Moonlight on the Prairie* (35), *The Petrified Forest* (36), *The Mummy's Hand* (40), *Fort Apache* (48), *Chicago Confidential* (57), *Taggart* (64), *Brighty of Grand Canyon* (67).

*Cary Grant and Joan Fontaine in* Suspicion *(41).*

## FORBES, Mary (1883-1974)

Best remembered for her many roles as a haughty lady of society, the London-born Forbes began acting on stage as a child, played on Broadway, and played scores of character roles in Hollywood.
**Selected Films:** *Women Who Win* (19), *The Child Thou Gavest Me* (21), *Sunny Side Up* (29), *A Farewell to Arms* (32), *The Awful Truth* (37), *The Adventures of Sherlock Holmes* (40), *The Picture of Dorian Gray* (44), *The Ten Commandments* (56).

## FORBES, Ralph (1902-1951)

Son of Mary Forbes, Ralph Taylor took his mother's stage name and made his debut in British films in 1921. Arriving in Hollywood in 1926, Forbes was a popular leading man in silent films of the late 1920s and early talkies.
**Selected Films:** *The Fifth Form at St Dominic's* (21), *Comin' Through the Rye* (22), *Beau Geste* (26), *Mr Wu* (27), *The Latest From Paris* (28), *Bachelor Father* (31), *Romeo and Juliet* (36), *Frenchmen's Creek* (44).

Harrison Ford in Witness (85) with Lucas Haas.

## FORD, Glenn (1916- )

Born Gwyllyn Ford in Quebec, Canada, he got his start playing juveniles on stage in California where his boyish good looks soon won him a movie contract. A stint with the Marines in World War II interrupted his career, and when he came back from service, he radiated integrity and determination in his roles and continued his stardom into tortured middle-age roles. A solid, steady actor, even though he played opposite Rita Hayworth in steamy 1940s films, he appeared in comedies, thrillers, westerns and dramas, and by the late 1950s his popularity was assured. His low-key style allowed him to make adjustments in his roles as the years passed. He was married to actress Eleanor Powell from 1943 to 1959.
**Selected Films:** *Heaven with a Barbed Wire Fence* (39), *So Ends Our Night* (41), *The Adventures of Martin Eden* (42), *Gilda* (46), *The Big Heat* (53), *The Blackboard Jungle* (55), *The Fastest Gun Alive* (56), *The Teahouse of the August Moon* (56), *3:10 to Yuma* (57), *Don't Go Near the Water* (57), *The Sheepman* (58), *The Four Horsemen of the Apocalypse* (62), *The Courtship of Eddie's Father* (63), *Superman* (78), *The Visitor* (79), *Happy Birthday to Me* (81).

## FORD, Harrison (1942- )

Born in Chicago, Illinois, Ford began his motion picture career as a juvenile lead in the late 1960s. He later became a leading star of action films that are strong on special effects. He played Han Solo, a spaceship commander in the *Star Wars* series and Indiana Jones in Steven Spielberg's adventure movies. Ford has also played in some serious films, notably *Witness* (85) for which he received an Academy Award nomination.
**Selected Films:** *Dead Heat on a Merry Go Round* (66), *American Graffiti* (73), *Star Wars* (77), *Heroes* (77), *Force Ten from Navarone* (78), *Hanover Street* (79), *The Frisco Kid* (79), *The Empire Strikes Back* (80), *Raiders of the Lost Ark* (81), *Blade Runner* (82), *Return of the Jedi* (83), *Indiana Jones and the Temple of Doom* (84), *Witness* (85), *The Mosquito Coast* (86).

## FORD, Paul (1901-1976)

The sad jowls framing as mournful a face made character actor Ford (Paul Ford Weaver, born in Baltimore, Maryland) a natural for success as the agitated colonel in Broadway's *The Teahouse of the August Moon* (53) a role he repeated in the 1956 film version. He played the harassed colonel in the *Sergeant Bilko* TV series.
**Selected Films:** *The House on 92nd Street* (45), *Perfect Strangers* (50), *The Teahouse of the August Moon* (53), *The Matchmaker* (58), *The Music Man* (62), *Never Too Late* (65), *The Comedians* (67), *Lola* (73).

## FORD, Wallace (1897-1966)

Born Samuel Grundy in Batton, England, and raised in a London orphanage, Wallace was in vaudeville at the age of eleven and soon reached the legitimate stage. Leads on Broadway preceded his move to Hollywood in 1930, where he soon settled into character roles.

**Selected Films:** *Swellhead* (30), *Possessed* (31), *Freaks* (32), *The Informer* (35), *A Son Comes Home* (36), *The Mummy's Hand* (40), *The Green Years* (46), *Harvey* (50), *Johnny Concho* (56), *Warlock* (59), *A Patch of Blue* (65).

## FORREST, Sally (1928- )

Born Katharine Scully Feeney in San Diego, California, Forrest taught dance in high school, entered films as a dancer in 1946, and played leads in routine films of the early 1950s.
**Selected Films:** *Till the Clouds Roll By* (47), *Not Wanted* (49), *Mr Belvedere Goes to College* (49), *Mystery Street* (50), *Valentino* (51), *Hard Fast and Beautiful* (51), *The Strip* (51), *Son of Sinbad* (55), *While the City Sleeps* (56), *Ride the High Iron* (57).

## FORREST, Steve (1924- )

Star of the TV series *S.W.A.T.*, Forrest, born in Huntsville, Texas, turned to films in the early 1950s after stage and radio experience and has played mostly leading roles. Born William Forrest Andrews, he is the younger brother of Dana Andrews.
**Selected Films:** *The Bad and the Beautiful* (52), *Dream Wife* (53), *Phantom of the Rue Morgue* (54), *Rogue Cop* (54), *Heller in Pink Tights* (60), *Rascal* (69), *North Dallas Forty* (79). *Mommie Dearest* (81), *Spies Like Us* (86).

## FORSYTH, Rosemary (1944- )

Modeling and TV preceded Montreal-born Forsyth's film debut in *Shenandoah* (65). The five-foot-nine actress has continued to play screen and TV leads.
**Selected Films:** *Shenandoah* (65), *The War Lord* (65), *Texas Across the River* (66), *Where It's At* (69), *Whatever Happened to Aunt Alice?* (69), *Some Kind of a Nut* (69), *How Do I Love Thee?* (70), *One Little Indian* (73), *Black Eye* (74), *Gray Lady Down* (78).

## FORSYTHE, John (1918- )

Tall, handsome, and smooth, John Forsythe became a popular star of the long-running TV series *Bachelor Father*. Born John Freund in Penns Grove, New Jersey, Forsythe played college baseball and worked as a radio broadcaster for the Brooklyn Dodgers before securing minor parts on Broadway. He made his film debut in a supporting role in *Destination Tokyo* (43) and in 1947 began working in what was to become his primary medium, TV. Equally at ease with comedy and drama, Forsythe took over Henry Fonda's Broadway role in *Mister Roberts* in the early fifties, and also starred in Broadway's *The Teahouse of the August Moon* (53). He starred in TV's *The John Forsythe Show* and was the voice in *Charlie's Angels*, and then went on to attain perhaps his greatest popularity as the star of the TV series, *Dynasty*.
**Selected Films:** *Destination Tokyo* (43), *The Captive City* (52), *The Glass Web* (53), *It Happens Every Thursday* (53), *Escape From Fort Bravo* (53), *The Ambassador's Daughter* (56), *The Trouble with Harry* (56), *Kitten With a Whip* (64), *Madame X* (66), *In Cold Blood* (67), *Topaz* (69), *And Justice for All* (79).

## FOSTER, Jodie (1962- )

Performing professionally since the age of three, the attractive, versatile Foster, born in The Bronx, New York, was twelve years old when she played the drug-addicted teenage hooker Iris in *Taxi Driver* (76). It was this role that led to John Hinckley Jr's obsession with Ms Foster and it was to impress her that he tried to assassinate President Reagan in 1981.
**Selected Films:** *Kansas City Bomber* (72), *Tom Sawyer* (73), *One Little Indian* (73), *Alice Doesn't Live Here Anymore* (74), *Bugsy Malone* (76), *Taxi Driver* (76), *The Little Girl Who Lives Down the Lane* (76), *Foxes* (80), *O'Hara's Wife* (82).

## FOSTER, Preston (1901-1970)

Big, dashing and handsome, the burly six-foot-two 200-pound Foster played innumerable two-fisted heroes and occasionally villains in leading roles in the 1930s. Born in Ocean City, New Jersey, the young Foster was something of an adventurer, working at everything from clerk to professional wrestler before getting his start in show business as a singer with Philadelphia's Pennsylvania Grand Opera Company. By the late 1920s he was working on Broadway, and in 1930 he made his film debut in *Nothing But the Truth*. By 1936 he was bickering with Carole Lombard in *Love Before Breakfast*. His TV work includes the series *Waterfront* and *Gunslinger*. His busy career continued well into the 1960s.
**Selected Films:** *Nothing But the Truth* (30), *Life Begins* (31), *The Last Mile* (32), *Wharf Angel* (34), *The Informer* (35), *The Last Days of Pompeii* (35), *Annie Oakley* (36), *Love Before Breakfast* (36), *The Plough and the Stars* (37), *The Outcasts of Poker Flat* (37), *First Lady* (37), *News is Made at Night* (38), *Geronimo* (39), *Missing Evidence* (39), *Moon Over Burma* (4), *North West Mounted Police* (40), *Unfinished Business* (41), *Secret Agent of Japan* (42), *Thunder Birds* (42), *My Friend Flicka* (43), *Ramrod* (47), *Tomahawk* (49), *I the Jury* (55), *The Time Travellers* (65), *Chubasco* (68).

## FOSTER, Susanna (1924- )

A child opera singer from Chicago who made her film debut with MGM at the age of 15, Foster, born Suzan Larsen, starred in *The Phantom of the Opera* (43) and was heroine of several 1940s films.
**Selected Films:** *The Great Victor Herbert* (39), *There's Magic in Music* (41), *Glamour Boy* (41), *Top Man* (43), *The Phantom of the Opera* (43), *The Climax* (44), *This Is the Life* (44), *Frisco Sal* (45), *That Night with You* (45).

## FOWLEY, Douglas (1911- )

Memorable as the hysterical director in *Singin' in the Rain* (52), Fowley, born and reared in New York's Greenwich village, prepared for his many screen roles as a nervous or comic villain or gangster with stage work as a singer and comedian.

**Selected Films:** *Mad Game* (33), *Let's Talk it Over* (34), *Charlie Chan on Broadway* (37), *Dodge City* (39), *Jiterbugs* (43), *Criminal Lawyer* (51), *Singin' in the Rain* (52), *Barabbas* (62), *The White Buffalo* (77).

## FOX, Edward (1937- )

Fox, born into a British theatrical family in London, is the brother of actor James Fox. On screen he has been extremely effective in villainous roles such as that of the cold-blooded assassin in *The Day of the Jackal* (73). His best role was as Edward VIII in the British television miniseries *Edward and Mrs Simpson*(78).

**Selected Films:** *The Mind Benders* (63), *The Naked Runner* (67), *Oh What a Lovely War* (69), *The Battle of Britain* (69), *The Go-Between* (71), *The Day of the Jackal* (73), *The Duellists* (77), *A Bridge Too Far* (77), *Force 10 From Navarone* (79), *The Mirror Crack'd* (80), *Gandhi* (82), *The Shooting Party* (84).

*Edward Fox* – A Bridge Too Far *(77).*

## FOX, James (1939- )

Born in London into a theatrical family (brother of Edward Fox), Fox appeared in films as a child and returned in the early sixties to play leads, usually portraying a refined weakling most memorably in *The Servant* (63). After 1973 he devoted most of his energies to religion.

**Selected Films:** *The Magnet* (50), *The Loneliness of the Long Distance Runner* (62), *The Servant* (63), *Those Magnificent Men in their Flying Machines* (65), *King Rat* (65), *Isadora* (68), *Performance* (70), *No Longer Alone* (78), *Runners* (83), *A Passage to India* (84).

## FOX, Michael J (1961- )

Funny, cute, vulnerable and equally adept at electric guitar and skateboard, Michael J Fox indisputably established himself as the world's favorite movie teenager in *Back to the Future* (85). Born in Edmonton, Albert, Canada on 9 June 1961, the fourth of five children to a Canadian army officer and his wife, Fox grew up on a series of military bases and landed a starring role in the hit Canadian TV show *Leo and Me* at the age of 15. His five-foot-four stature helped make him an ideal choice to play the pompous if endearing Alex P Keaton in TV's *Family Ties*. He filmed the role of Marty McFly in *Back to the Future* at night, after full days on the *Family Ties* set.

**Selected Films:** *Back to the Future* (85), *Teen Wolf* (85), *Light of Day* (87), *Private Affairs* (87).

## FOY, Eddie Jr (1905-1983)

Son of the famous vaudeville comedian Eddie Foy Sr, whom he portrayed in several films, Foy, born in New Rochelle, New York, began in vaudeville as one of The Seven Little Foys, making his Broadway debut in 1929 and beginning in films the same year.

**Selected Films:** *Queen of the Night Clubs* (29). *Turn Off the Moon* (37), *Frontier Marshal* (39), *Fugitive From Justice* (40), *Yankee Doodle Dandy* (42), *The Farmer Takes a Wife* (53), *The Pajama Game* (57), *Bells Are Ringing* (60), *Thirty is a Dangerous Age, Cynthia* (68).

## FRANCEN, Victor (1888-1977)

Most familiar as a top Nazi or ambitious villain in Hollywood spy dramas of World War II vintage, Francen, born in Tirlemont, Belgium, was a member of the Comédie-Française and a star of French cinema in the 1930s.

**Selected Films:** *Crépuscle d'Epuvante* (21), *La Doute* (24), *Aprés l'Amour* (31), *J'Accuse* (38), *La Fin du Jour* (39), *Tales of Manhattan* (42), *Madame Curie* (43), *Mission to Moscow* (43), *The Conspirators* (44), *A Farewell to Arms* (58), *Top Crack* (66).

## FRANCIOSA, Anthony (Tony) (1928- )

Born Anthony Papaleo in New York, Franciosa began his theatrical career in small parts on Broadway and received critical praise for his performance in *A Hatful of Rain* (55), which caught the attention of Hollywood. After making his film debut in *A Face in the Crowd* (57), he repeated his stage role in the screen version of *A Hatful of Rain* (57), and for it was nominated for an Oscar. Despite his intense image onscreen, Franciosa's ensuing movies were variable and often forgettable; he was a strong member of a strong cast (including Orson Welles and Paul Newman) in *The Long Hot Summer* (58) but in the next year starred in the dismal *The*

*Naked Maja* (59). Most of his films of the 1960s were disappointing. Paul Newman, Joanne Woodward, and Franciosa together were unable to save *The Drowning Pool* (77).Since the late-60s his TV series *The Name of the Game*, has been syndicated on television. For several years he was married to actress Shelley Winters.
**Selected Films:** *A Face in the Crowd* (57), *This Could Be the Night* (57), *A Hatful of Rain* (57), *Wild is the Wind* (58), *The Long Hot Summer* (58), *The Naked Maja* (59), *The Story on Page One* (59), *Rio Conchos* (64), *The Swinger* (66), *Across 110th Street* (72), *The Drowning Pool* (77), *Death Wish II* (82).

## FRANCIS, Anne (1930- )

Blonde and good-looking, a former model as well as a child radio personality, Francis, born in Ossining, New York, moved from bit parts to leads in films of the 1950s. Frequently seen on TV, she starred in her own series, *Honey West*.
**Selected Films:** *This Time for Keeps* (47), *Summer Holiday* (48), *So Young, So Bad* (50), *Elopement* (52), *Susan Slept Here* (54), *The Blackboard Jungle* (55), *Forbidden Planet* (56), *Funny Girl* (68), *Pancho Villa* (71), *Born Again* (78).

## FRANCIS, Kay (1899-1968)

One of Hollywood's highest-paid stars of the thirties, the ladylike Francis, born Katherine Gibbs in Oklahoma City, usually played stylish, serious-faced brunettes in melodramas and comedies. She played Florence Nightingale in *The White Angel* (36).
**Selected Films:** *Gentlemen of the Press* (29), *The Cocoanuts* (29), *Dangerous Curves* (29), *Street of Chance* (30), *One Way Passage* (32), *Trouble in Paradise* (32), *Stranded* (34), *The White Angel* (36), *First Lady* (37), *Charley's Aunt* (41), *Wife Wanted* (46).

## FRANCISCUS, James (1934- )

Born in Clayton, Missouri, Franciscus played leads in Hollywood and European films before and during his more familiar roles in such TV series as *Naked City*, *Mr Novak*, *Longstreet*, and *Hunter*.
**Selected Films:** *Four Boys and a Gun* (56), *The Mugger* (58), *I Passed for White* (60), *The Outsider* (61), *Youngblood Hawke* (64), *Marooned* (69), *Cat O'Nine Tails* (71), *The Amazing Dobermans* (76), *When Time Ran Out* (80), *The Great White* (82).

## FRANKLIN, Pamela (1950- )

Franklin was born in Tokyo, Japan, to English parents and studied ballet before her debut in British films in 1961. Her juvenile roles of the 1960s gradually gave way to ingenue leads.
**Selected Films:** *The Innocents* (61), *The Lion* (62), *A Tiger Walks* (64), *The Third Secret* (64), *The Nanny* (65), *Our Mother's House* (67), *The Prime of Miss Jean Brodie* (69), *The Food of the Gods* (76).

## FRANZ, Arthur (1920- )

A native of Perth Amboy, New Jersey, Franz worked on stage and in radio prior to his film debut in *Jungle Patrol* (48). Film work includes leads and second leads, mainly in action pictures, and many character parts.
**Selected Films:** *Jungle Patrol* (48), *Roseanna McCoy* (49), *Sands of Iwo Jima* (50), *Abbott and Costello Meet the Invisible Man* (51), *The Caine Mutiny* (54), *The Atomic Submarine* (60), *Alvarez Kelly* (66), *Sisters of Death* (76), *That Championship Season* (82).

## FRANZ, Eduard (1902-1983)

Born in Milwaukee, Wisconsin, Franz appeared regularly on Broadway from the late 1920s and also played many character roles in films and on TV, often as a foreign dignitary or intellectual.
**Selected Films:** *Killer at Large* (47), *The Iron Curtain* (48), *The Scar* (48), *Francis* (50), *The Jazz Singer* (52), *Dream Wife* (53), *The Ten Commandments* (56), *The Story of Ruth* (60), *The President's Analyst* (67), *Johnny Got His Gun* (71).

## FRAWLEY, William (1887-1966)

A regular on the TV series *I Love Lucy*, the stocky Frawley, a native of Burlington, Iowa, was a cigar-chewing vaudeville comedian. His many films appearances which began in silent short films feature Frawley as a gruff taxi driver, bumbling cop, or comic gangster.
**Selected Films:** *Lord Loveland Discovers America* (16), *Surrender* (31), *Moonlight and Pretzels* (33), *Alibi Ike* (35), *One Night in the Tropics* (40), *Roxie Hart* (42), *Gentleman Jim* (42), *The Babe Ruth Story* (48), *Rancho Notorious* (52), *Safe at Home!* (62).

## FRAZEE, Jane (1918-1985)

Leading lady of many minor musicals and light westerns of the forties, the vivacious Frazee (born Mary Jane Frehse in Duluth, Minnesota) began singing and dancing with her sister Ruth at the age of six. She performed in vaudeville, nightclubs and radio before reaching Hollywood.
**Selected Films:** *Melody and Moonlight* (40), *Moonlight in Hawaii* (41), *Moonlight in Havana* (42), *Kansas City Kitty* (44), *Swing and Sway* (44), *Calendar Girl* (47), *Incident* (48), *Rhythm Inn* (51).

## FREDERICK, Pauline (1883-1938)

A popular leading lady on Broadway, the Boston-born Frederick (Beatrice Pauline Libbey) starred in many Hollywood silent films and moved to character roles when the talkies came in, often as an overbearing mother.
**Selected Films:** *The Eternal City* (15), *Bella Donna* (15), *Lydia Gilmore* (16), *Sleeping Fires* (17), *Resurrection* (18), *Married Flirts* (24), *The Sacred Flame* (29), *Ramona* (36), *Thank You, Mr Moto* (37).

## FREEMAN, Al Jr (1934- )

Black American actor Freeman appeared in a number of movies of the 1960s and 1970s, including a starring role in the film version of LeRoi Jones' play *Dutchman* (67) and a supporting part in the war movie *Castle Keep* (69). In 1971 he directed and appeared in *A Fable*. He also appeared in the TV miniseries *Roots*.
**Selected Films:** *Black Like Me* (64), *Dutchman* (67), *The Detective* (68), *Finian's Rainbow* (68), *Castle Keep* (69), *The Lost Man* (70), *A Fable* (71).

## FREEMAN, Mona (1926- )

Born in Baltimore, Maryland, Freeman was an extremely popular movie teenager of the 1940s, sometimes troubled, sometimes bright-eyed, but less successful as an adult leading lady of the 1950s.
**Selected Films:** *National Velvet* (44), *Our Hearts Were Young and Gay* (44), *Till We Meet Again* (44), *Junior Miss* (45), *That Brennan Girl* (46), *Dear Ruth* (47), *Dear Wife* (49), *Angel Face* (52), *The World Was His Jury* (58).

## FRESNAY, Pierre (1897-1975)

The French actor made both his screen debut and his debut with the Comédie-Française in 1915. It was not until the early thirties, beginning with his lead in *Marius* (31), after he had already distinguished himself on stage, that Fresnay became a film star as well.
**Selected Films:** *France d'abord* (15), *L'Essor* (21), *Marius* (31), *Rocambole* (34), *Fanny* (32), *César* (34), *La Grande Illusion* (37), *Monsier Vincent* (47), *God Needs Men* (50), *Les Vieux de la Vieille* (60).

## FRÖBE, Gert (1913- )

Best remembered in the title role of *Goldfinger* (64), Fröbe, born in Planitz-Swickau, Germany, played many impressive character roles beginning with *The Berliner* (48) before turning to villainous or heavy roles in international productions.
**Selected Films:** *The Berliner* (48), *Salto Mortale* (52), *He Who Must Die* (56), *The Girl Rosemarie* (58), *The Longest Day* (62), *Die Dreigroschenoper* (63), *Goldfinger* (64), *Those Magnificent Men in their Flying Machines* (65), *Is Paris Burning?* (66), *Ludwig* (72), *Bloodline* (79), *Le Coup de Parapluie* (80).

## FRYE, Dwight (1899-1943)

Frye was an American actor who seemed to corner the market in crazed hunchbacks and nutty assistants to mad scientists in horror films. He played Renfield, the real-estate-agent-turned-vampire in *Dracula* (30), staying in his cell and eating flies, and Igor, the hunchback assistant in *Frankenstein* (31), helping the good doctor make his monster.
**Selected Films:** *The Night Bird* (27), *Dracula* (30), *Frankenstein* (31), *The Vampire Bat* (33), *Bride of Frankenstein* (35), *Frankenstein Meets the Wolf Man* (43).

## FUNICELLO, Annette (1942- )

Known to millions simply as 'Annette' for her part in Walt Disney's *The Mickey Mouse Club*, Funicello, born in Utica, New York, moved from juvenile success to leading lady roles in action pictures, frequently for the Disney studios.
**Selected Films:** *Johnny Tremain* (57), *The Shaggy Dog* (61), *Babes in Toyland* (61), *The Misadventures of Merlin Jones* (63), *Bikini Beach* (64), *The Monkey's Uncle* (65), *Back to the Beach* (87).

# G

## GABEL, Martin (1912-1986)

A versatile character actor who also directed on stage and screen, the balding, plump Gabel, born in Philadelphia, began acting on Broadway in 1933 and appeared with Orson Welles' Mercury Theater. Most of his work has been on stage; he was married to actress Arlene Francis.
**Selected Films:** *14 Hours* (51), *Deadline USA* (52), *The Thief* (52), *Marnie* (64), *Divorce American Style* (67), *The Front Page* (75), *The First Deadly Sin* (80).

*Gert Frobe in* Is Paris Burning? *(66).*

## GABIN, Jean (1904-1976)

Born Alexis Moncourge in Villette, a suburb of Paris, France, this versatile actor began his career as an extra and later a dancer with the Folies Bergère, then became a cabaret entertainer. He made his film debut in *Chacun sa Chance* (30), and within a few years he was an established star, the 'tragic hero of contemporary cinema,' according to Andre Bazin. His stocky virility and world-weary features kept him a star for over 40 years. Early on, although he was adept at many types of characters, at this stage of his career Gabin generally played courageous anti-heroes and loners. He came to the United States during World War II, returning to France in 1950. He and actor-comedian Fernandel formed their own production company in 1963. By the time of his death, Gabin was revered in France and admired worldwide.

**Selected Films:** *Chacun sa Chance* (30), *Maria Chapdelaine* (34), *La Belle Equipe* (36), *Pépé le Moko* (37), *La Grande Illusion* (37), *Quai des Brumes* (38), *La Bête Humaine* (38), *Le Jour se Lève* (39), *Moontide* (42), *Victor* (51), *Touchez Pas au Grisbi* (54), *Can Can* (55), *Maigret Sets a Trap* (58), *A Monkey in Winter* (62), *The Tattooed Man* (68), *Le Chat* (72), *L'Année Saint* (76).

## GABLE, Clark (1901-1960)

Known as the 'King' of Hollywood, Gable's popularity spanned nearly 30 years, and his impudent grin won female hearts all over the world. He was box office gold, a big handsome man with a small moustache. He was masculine without being brutal, a man who exuded sexual confidence, yet was comfortable trading wise-cracks with co-stars like Myrna Loy and Jean Harlow. Throughout the 1930s and a large part of the 1940s, Gable was in a class by himself. The only complaint that his female co-stars ever had was that his breath was occasionally bad. Gable was born William Gable in Cadiz, Ohio. His mother died when he was a baby and his father was an oil driller. Gable spent his youth working in hard-hat jobs and trying to get into the theater. His first wife, drama coach Josephine Dillon, got him his start in movies in the 1920s, but he didn't catch on in silent pictures. Stage work followed, including a stint on Broadway, then screen tests and supporting roles, usually as a gangster, starting with *The Painted Desert* (30). He finally achieved stardom in MGM's *A Free Soul* (31), as Ace Willfong the gangster who pushes Norma Shearer around. A well-publicized affair with Joan Crawford, his co-star in *Possessed* (32), seemed to further his career, as did the joyous romping with Jean Harlow in *Red Dust* (32). But it took *It Happened One Night* (34) to win Gable an Academy Award as Best Actor. That film, of course, swept the Oscars. It won the Academy Award as Best Picture, co-star Claudette Colbert won for Best Actress, Frank Capra won for Best Director, Robert Riskin won for Best Writing

*Clark Gable in* Gone With the Wind *(39).*

Adaptation. The part was, as it turned out, a Cinderella story. It was MGM boss Louis B Mayer's way of punishing Gable for asking for a raise. To humble the rising star, Mayer loaned him out to struggling Columbia Pictures to make a silly little film that nobody would go to see. Gable began turning out one popular film after another, with only one box office disaster in the 1930s – *Parnell* (37). Gable married the talented and beautiful Carole Lombard in 1939, and it turned out to be one of the great real-life Hollywood love stories. That was the year he made movie history as Rhett Butler in *Gone With the Wind* (39), setting a new standard for virility. All America was sure that he was the only one who could play the anti-hero in that film based on the best-selling novel, and America was right. Tragedy struck in 1942 when Lombard died in a plane crash while returning from a War Bond Drive. Deep in mourning, Gable joined the Army Air Corps. He returned to the screen in *Adventure* (45) with Greer Garson, and the Hollywood flacks trumpeted 'Gable's back and Garson's got him.' He was still popular, but by the 1950s MGM and other big studios were in trouble. Gable freelanced successfully, giving an especially fine performance in his last film, *The Misfits* (61), opposite Marilyn Monroe. He insisted on doing his own stunts, including breaking a horse, and the strain proved to be too much. He died of a heart attack in November of 1960, and his first and only child, John, was born to his fifth wife Kay shortly after his death.

**Selected Films:** *The Painted Desert* (30), *Dance Fools Dance* (31), *A Free Soul* (31), *Susan Lennox* (31), *Possessed* (32), *Polly of the Circus* (32), *Red Dust* (32), *Strange Interlude* (32), *Dancing Lady* (33), *It Happened One Night* (34), *Manhattan Melodrama* (34), *Mutiny on the Bounty* (35), *Call of the Wild* (35), *China Seas* (35), *San Francisco* (36), *Wife vs Secretary* (36), *Parnell* (37), *Saratoga* (37), *Test Pilot* (38),

Greta Garbo and Rex O'Malley in Camille (36).

*Idiot's Delight* (39), *Gone With the Wind* (39), *Strange Cargo* (40), *Boom Town* (40), *Honky Tonk* (41), *Adventure* (45), *The Hucksters* (47), *Command Decision* (48), *To Please a Lady* (50), *Across the Wide Missouri* (51), *Mogambo* (53), *The Tall Men* (55), *Teacher's Pet* (58), *It Started in Naples* (59), *The Misfits* (61).

## GABOR, Eva (1921- )

Youngest of the glamorous Hungarian Gabor sisters, Eva Gabor, born in Budapest, began appearing in Hollywood films in the early forties but achieved stardom on Broadway in *The Happy Time* (50) and national popularity in the TV comedy series *Green Acres*.
**Selected Films:** *Pacific Blackouts* (41) *Forced Landing* (41), *A Royal Scandal* (45), *The Wife of Monte Cristo* (46), *Paris Model* (53), *Gigi* (58), *Youngblood Hawke* (64), *The Pricess Academy* (87).

## GABOR, Zsa Zsa (1919- )

The exotic Zsa Zsa, older sister of Eva was born in Sari Gabor in Budapest, made her stage debut in Vienna at the age of 15 and was Miss Hungary of 1936. She is as famous for her jewels and serial husbands as for her mostly decorative film roles.
**Selected Films:** *Lovely to Look At* (52), *Lili* (53), *Moulin Rouge* (53), *Arreviderci Baby* (68), *Up the Front* (72), *Every Girl Should Have One* (78).

## GALLAGHER, Skeets (1891-1955)

Born in Terre Haute, Indiana, Richard Gallagher was a long-time vaudeville song-and-dance man before making his cheerful mark in supporting roles and occasional leads in early talkies.
**Selected Films:** *The Daring Years* (23), *New York* (27), *Alex the Great* (28), *The Racket* (28), *It Pays to Advertise* (31), *Merrily We Go to Hell* (32), *Easy Millions* (33), *Riptide* (34), *Polo Joe* (36), *Espionage* (37), *Idiot's Delight* (39), *The Duke of Chicago* (50), *Three for Bedroom C* (52).

## GARBO, Greta (1905- )

Hollywood has spawned no myth greater than the myth of Garbo. Paradoxically sensual and spiritual, the beautiful and sensitive Garbo was the most magnetic actress in the history of the movies. Born Greta Louisa Gustafson in Stockholm, Sweden, she grew up in poverty but was able to attend the Royal Dramatic Theatre School on a scholarship. There director Mauritz Stiller discovered her, made her his protégée and turned the photogenic actress into a Swedish film star, even refusing an offer from MGM unless Garbo, too, was given a contract. Big and clumsy off-screen, with large feet, the unconventionally lovely Garbo was not MGM studio boss Louis B Mayer's idea of a sex symbol, but when her first film for the studio, *The Torrent* (26), was a huge success, he saw the light and she received top promotion. A typical Garbo film had her acting outside the prescribed social code – and suffering for it. In *Anna Karenina* (35), for example, she was forsaken by the man for whom she abandoned her family and threw herself beneath a train. Stories of miserable love affairs were her speciality in the 1930s, and she played them all with sob-inducing flair. The moody and elusive or just plain clever Garbo got more publicity than any other star by simply running away from it. 'I vant to be alone' was a life-long credo that made journalists and fans maniacally curious. She also got an enormous salary from MGM. She often appeared with John Gilbert and gossip columnists were quick to call them lovers. Garbo's success went beyond anything that the film world had ever known. Women everywhere copied her. She mingled with celebrities and aristocrats as she chose. Although she never married, her name was linked with Gilbert, director Rouben Mamoulian, symphony conductor Leopold Stokowski and nutrition expert Gaylord Hauser. But since 'The Swedish Sphinx' kept her private life truly private, these romances may be only rumors. Garbo made the transition to sound easily, making some of her best films during the talkie era, most notably *Ninotchka* (39), which offered her a rare chance to show off her comic talents. In the early 1940s, when some of her box office appeal had faded and a new wind of puritanism was sweeping Hollywood, she simply retired. But her legend grew stronger and today, well over 40 years since her last movie was released, she remains the most famous star in the world. In 1954 she was awarded a special Academy Award 'for her unforgettable screen performances.'

**Selected Films:** *Peter the Tramp* (22), *The Story of Gösta Berling* (24), *Joyless Street* (25), *The Torrent* (26), *The Temptress* (26), *Flesh and the Devil* (27), *Love* (27), *The Mysterious Lady* (27), *The Divine Woman* (28), *The Kiss* (29), *A Woman of Affairs* (29), *Wild Orchids* (29), *The Single Standard* (29), *Anna Christie* (30), *Romance* (30), *Inspiration* (31), *Susan Lennox* (31), *Mata Hari* (31), *Grand Hotel* (32), *As You Desire Me* (32), *Queen Christina* (33), *The Painted Veil* (34), *Anna Karenina* (35), *Camille* (36), *Conquest* (37), *Ninotchka* (39), *Two-Faced Woman* (41).

## GARDENIA, Vincent (1922-     )

Born Vincent Scognamiglio in Naples and raised in America, Gardenia made his mark as a comic character actor on stage in the mid-1950s. He received a Tony Award for his performance in Broadway's *The Prisoner of Second Avenue* and was nominated for an Academy Award for his work in *Bang the Drum Slowly* (73).

**Selected Films:** *Cop Hater* (58), *The Hustler* (61), *Bang the Drum Slowly* (73), *Death Wish* (74), *Heaven Can Wait* (78), *Little Shop of Horrors* (86).

## GARDINER, Reginald (1903-1980)

Handsome, suave and silly, the ultimate pompous ass, Gardiner, born in Wimbledon, England, had logged considerable British stage and film experience prior to his Hollywood debut in *Born to Dance* (36).

**Selected Films:** *The Lovelorn Lady* (32), *Just Smith* (33), *Borrow a Million* (34), *Born to Dance* (36), *Sweethearts* (39), *The Great Dictator* (40), *The Man Who Came to Dinner* (41), *Ain't Misbehaving* (55), *Back Street* (61), *Do Not Disturb* (65), *Sergeant Deadhead* (66).

## GARDNER, Ava (1922-     )

One has only to look at a picture of Gardner at the height of her beauty to understand why she was Hollywood's leading sex symbol and glamour queen between the end of World War II and the reign of Marilyn Monroe. She was exotically gorgeous and steamingly sensual. Born in Smithfield, North Carolina, she was one of six children of a poor tenant farmer. Dreaming only of a job as a secretary, Gardner paid a visit to her married sister in New York – a visit that transformed her life. Her brother-in-law was a photographer and a picture that he took of her reached the MGM casting office, winning her a screen test. After seeing the test, an MGM executive allegedly said, 'She can't act; she didn't talk; she's sensational.' As a product of the Hollywood studio factory that manufactured starlets like gumdrops, Gardner had to do what the studio handed her, which did nothing to improve her acting ability. What got attention for her was her marriage to Mickey Rooney in 1942, then at the top of his career. That marriage lasted a little over a year, as did her next marriage to band leader Artie Shaw in 1945. Her popularity gained momentum, mainly because the publicity department ground out pictures of her looking sultry, glamorous and a little bit wicked. It wasn't until *The Killers* (46), that audiences really zoomed in on Gardner's erotic charisma. Her acting talent was also showcased in

*Ava Gardner in* Mogambo *(53).*

*Show Boat* (51), in which she was an exquisitely ravaged Julie. She was angry that her voice was dubbed on the sound track, although the movie's record album with her voice on it was a success. In 1951 she married Frank Sinatra, after a headline-making scandal over their affair and his divorce from his first wife. By this time she was demonstrating that she was not just another pretty face. She was outstanding in *The Snows of Kilimanjaro* (52) and *The Barefoot Contessa* (54). *Mogambo* (53), with Clark Gable, a remake of *Red Dust* (32), which had also starred Gable opposite Jean Harlow, earned Gardner an Academy Award nomination for her portrayal of a wise-cracking showgirl. Her stormy and highly visible romance with Sinatra ended in divorce in 1957. After the divorce she spent a lot of time abroad, and the columnists had a field day over her fondness for matadors and her lavish life amidst the rich and famous. When she did make films she was hauntingly lovely, and she got critical praise for her work in *On the Beach* (59) and *Seven Days in May* (64). Her finest performance may have been in *The Night of the Iguana* (64) as an earthy hotel owner – a bawdy, passionate woman of ebbing beauty – which she played with venom and understanding.

**Selected Films:** *We Were Dancing* (42), *Swing Fever* (44), *The Killers* (46), *The Hucksters* (47), *One Touch of Venus* (48), *Show Boat* (51), *Pandora and the Flying Dutchman* (51), *The Snows of Kilimanjaro* (52), *Mogambo* (53), *The Barefoot Contessa* (54), *The Sun Also Rises* (57), *The Naked Maja* (59), *On the Beach* (59), *Seven Days in May* (64), *The Night of the Iguana* (64), *Mayerling* (68), *The Life and Times of Judge Roy Bean* (72), *Earthquake* (74), *The Cassandra Crossing* (77), *The Kidnapping of the President* (80), *Priest of Love* (81).

## GARFIELD, John (1913-1952)

Garfield excelled as the defiant young man trying to rise from poverty through charm and brute strength yet who is vulnerable beneath the facade. He was usually cast in aggressive or embittered roles. Born Julius Garfinkle, he was the product of a brawling slum area in New York City, the personification of the street-wise rebel hero he often portrayed on film. He first appeared as a star in New York's leftish Group Theater, and then went to Hollywood. He appeared in the definitive version of *The Postman Always Rings Twice* (46) and received acclaim for his role as a boxer in *Body and Soul* (47). Garfield was superb in his very first featured role in *Four Daughters* (38), for which he received a nomination for the Academy Award for Best Supporting Actor. He was nominated as Best Actor in 1947 for *Body and Soul*. Garfield was blacklisted in the 1950s for refusing to give a government committee the names of friends who had been Communists. He died of a heart attack shortly afterwards.

**Selected Films:** *Four Daughters* (38), *They Made Me a Criminal* (39), *Castle on the Hudson* (40), *The Sea Wolf* (41), *Destination Tokyo* (44), *Pride of the Marines* (45), *The Postman Always Rings Twice* (46), *Humoresque* (46), *Body and Soul* (47), *Gentleman's Agreement* (47), *Force of Evil* (49), *The Breaking Point* (50), *He Ran All the Way* (51).

## GARGAN, William (1905-1979)

Usually seen in 'good guy' roles, the Brooklyn-born Gargan acted on Broadway before playing leads and second leads in Hollywood films. He was nominated for an Oscar for his performance in *They Knew What They Wanted* (40) and starred in the TV series *Martin Kane, Private Eye*. He retired from films after a cancer operation.
**Selected Films:** *Mother's Darling* (17), *The Misleading Lady* (32), *Rain* (32), *The Animal Kingdom* (32), *Black Fury* (35), *The Housekeeper's Daughter* (39), *They Knew What They Wanted* (40), *The Bells of St Mary's* (45), *Miracle in the Rain* (56), *The Rawhide Years* (56).

## GARLAND, Beverly (1926- )

A pretty Californian who played leads in films of the 1950s, often as a tough dame, Garland, born Beverly Fessenden in Santa Cruz, has had great success on TV, notably in the series *My Three Sons*. She has played character roles in films since the late 1960s.
**Selected Films:** *DOA* (49), *The Glass Web* (53), *The Miami Story* (54), *The Alligator People* (59), *Twice Told Tales* (63), *Pretty Poison* (68), *Airport 1975* (74), *Sixth and Main* (77), *It's My Turn* (80).

## GARLAND, Judy (1922-1969)

When Garland sang 'You Made Me Love You' in *Broadway Melody of 1938* (37), it was impossible to believe that the mature, succulent voice belonged to a 14-year-old. She had a great voice – stirring, soulful and wistful. She had lots of nervous energy and a streak of vulnerability. She could dance and she could act. 'The little girl with the great big voice' was born Francis Gumm into a vaudeville family in Grand Rapids, Minnesota, and made her stage debut at age three, part of the Gumm Sisters Kiddie Act with her two older sisters. When the act broke up, Garland, guided by her ambitious mother, continued to sing on her own, and made her way to Hollywood. She had an MGM contract by the age of 13. It was as Dorothy in *The Wizard of Oz* (39) that she really shone. Already a veteran of several films, she became a star at 17, receiving a special Academy Award for the Best Juvenile Performer of the year. She went on to star with Mickey Rooney in a string of movies showing the rosy side of teenage life. Although Garland's career was blooming, her personal life started to go downhill. To combat her fatigue and to help her keep her weight down, M-G-M moguls had her put on pills. She was to have a drug problem all the rest of her life, later complicated by alcohol. During the 1940s she made some of MGM's greatest musicals, such as *For Me and My Gal* (42), *Meet Me in St Louis* (44), *The Harvey Girls* (46) and *Easter Parade* (48). She married director Vincente Minnelli, and their daughter Liza grew up to become a star in her own right. Garland later married Sid Luft, and they had a daughter, Lorna, who also exhibited musical talent. By the end of the 1940s, she had acquired a reputation for unreliability because of her alleged dependence on pills, and abandoned or was fired from several pictures. Luft arranged an engagement for her at the London Palladium when her film career faltered, and the show was a great success; she then took it to New York's Palace Theater, where it was the beginning of her comeback. In 1954 she made *A Star Is Born* with James Mason, and it was her finest dramatic performance. The film, which is a classic today, became a smash hit. Though Garland continued to make fine films and give great concerts, her private troubles proved overwhelming. Her marriage to Luft fell apart and there was an ugly custody battle over their two children. But in another comeback, she received an Oscar nomination for her role in *Judgment at Nuremberg* (60). There were two more marriages for Garland, suicide attempts, a tour that didn't go well. Still, she seemed on her way back when she died of an overdose of sleeping pills, leaving a million dollars in debts. Despite her demons, if not because of them, she was still a draw even in death – 20,000 people mobbed her funeral.
**Selected Films:** *Pigskin Parade* (36), *Broadway Melody of 1938* (37), *Thoroughbreds Don't Cry* (38), *Everybody Sing* (38), *Love Finds Andy Hardy* (38), *The Wizard of Oz* (39), *Babes in Arms* (39), *Strike Up the Band* (40), *Ziegfeld Girl* (41), *For Me and My Gal* (42), *Girl Crazy* (42), *Meet Me in St Louis* (44), *The Clock* (45), *The Harvey Girls* (46), *The Pirate* (47), *Easter Parade* (48), *In the Good Old Summertime* (49), *Summer Stock* (50), *A Star Is Born* (54), *Judgment at Nuremberg* (60), *A Child Is Waiting* (62), *I Could Go on Singing* (63).

## GARNER, James (1928- )

By the mid-1960s one of Hollywood's most popular and highest-paid leading men, the amiable, good-looking James Garner was introduced to acting when a childhood friend offered him a nonspeaking role in the 1954 Broadway production of *The Caine Mutiny Court-Martial*. Born James Baumgarner in Norman, Oklahoma, Garner dropped out of high school and joined the merchant marine at the age of 16. He was wounded in Korea, and after his discharge knocked about at a variety of jobs before he discovered acting. He made his film debut in a small role in *Toward the Unknown* (56), but established himself as a star in the popular TV western series *Maverick*. His first starring role in films was in *Darby's Rangers* (58). A series of films in 1963 including *The Great Escape*, two pictures with Doris Day and *The Wheeler Dealers* with Lee Remick secured his place as a film star. In the 1970s his easy-going, good-natured, ostensibly cowardly persona seemed to be out of fashion, but his popularity has remained immense via such TV series as *The Rockford Files*.
**Selected Films:** *Toward the Unknown* (56), *Darby's*

*Judy Garland and Mickey Rooney in* Babes in Arms *(39).*

*Rangers* (58), *Cash McCall* (59), *The Wheeler Dealers* (63), *The Thrill of It All* (63), *The Great Escape* (63), *The Americanization of Emily* (64), *36 Hours* (64), *Support Your Local Sheriff* (69), *The Skin Game* (71), *Health* (79), *Victor/Victoria* (82), *Murphy's Romance* (86).

## GARNER, Peggy Ann (1931-1984)

Promoted by a stage-mother, Garner, born in Canton, Ohio, won an Academy Award as 'outstanding child performer of 1945' for her role in *A Tree Grows in Brooklyn* (45). After stage and TV work she settled into real estate in the 1970s. She was married to actor Albert Salmi from 1956 to 1963.
**Selected Films:** *Little Miss Thoroughbred* (38), *In Name Only* (39), *The Pied Piper* (42), *Jane Eyre* (44), *A Tree Grows in Brooklyn* (45), *Bomba the Jungle Boy* (49), *The Black Forest* (54), *The Cat* (67), *A Wedding* (78).

## GARR, Teri (1952- )

San Francisco's Teri Garr established herself as a leading lady in such landmark productions as *Close Encounters of the Third Kind* (77) and *Tootsie* (82).
**Selected Films:** *Young Frankenstein* (74), *The Conversation* (74), *Won Ton Ton, The Dog Who Saved Hollywood* (76), *Oh God!* (77), *Close Encounters of the Third Kind* (77), *The Black Stallion* (79), *Honky Tonk Freeway* (81), *One From the Heart* (82), *Tootsie* (82), *The Black Stallion Returns* (83), *Mr Mom* (83), *Firstborn* (84), *After Hours* (85), *Miracles* (86).

## GARRETT, Betty (1919- )

The bright and bouncy Garrett, born in St Joseph, Missouri, made her stage debut in 1938 with the Mercury Theater, danced with Martha Graham and sang on Broadway. Her film career suffered when her husband Larry Parks was blacklisted. She later played Archie Bunker's neighbor in the TV series *All in the Family*.
**Selected Films:** *Big City* (48), *Words and Music* (48), *Take Me Out to the Ball Game* (48), *Neptune's Daughter* (49), *On the Town* (49), *My Sister Eileen* (55), *The Shadow on the Window* (57).

## GARSON, Greer (1908- )

Born in County Down in Northern Ireland, this lovely, red-haired leading lady first appeared on the stage. She had class, and her forte was playing strong but gracious and elegant women. After appearing in her first film, *Remember?* (39), she was cast as Mrs Chipping opposite Robert Donat in *Goodbye, Mr Chips* (39) and was so impressive that she was called to Hollywood, where her gentle aristocratic good looks enabled her to reign as a star for years. She was nominated for the Academy Award as Best Actress for *Chips*, and again in 1941 for *Blossoms in the Dust*. She finally won the Oscar for Best Actress in *Mrs Miniver* (42), in which she played a brave English housewife who held her family together during the Blitz of World War II. In 1943 she received another Best Actress nomination for her role as *Madame Curie*, the biopic of the Nobel Prize-winning woman scientist, and in 1944 came another one in the title role of *Mrs Parkington*. In 1945 she received another nomination for her role as an Irish parlormaid who makes it big in Pittsburgh society in *The Valley of Decision*, and in 1960 she was nominated yet again for her role as Eleanor Roosevelt in *Sunrise at Campobello*, with Ralph Bellamy as FDR.
**Selected Films:** *Remember?* (39), *Goodbye, Mr Chips* (39), *Pride and Prejudice* (40), *Blossoms in the Dust* (41), *Mrs Miniver* (42), *Random Harvest* (42), *Madame Curie* (43), *Mrs Parkington* (44), *The Valley of Decision* (45), *Julia Misbehaves* (48), *That Forsyte Woman* (49), *The Miniver Story* (50), *Julius Caesar* (53), *Sunrise at Campobello* (60), *Pepe* (60), *The Singing Nun* (66), *The Happiest Millionaire* (67).

## GASSMAN, Vittorio (1922- )

While his international reputation as an actor rests upon only a handful of films and his critical reputation, due to a tendency to overact in his earlier work, has had its ups and downs, Vittorio Gassman, one of Italy's great matinee idols, has never been less than a commercial success, and his major international films, such as *Bitter Rice* (49) and *Big Deal on Madonna Street* (58) have been profoundly influential. Son of an Austrian father and an Italian mother, Gassman was born on 1 September 1922 in the northern Italian port city of Genoa. After briefly toying with law studies he enrolled at

*Greer Garson and Walter Pidgeon in* Mrs Miniver *(42).*

Rome's National Academy of Dramatic Art. By the time of his film debut in *Preludio d'Amore* (46) he had performed in 40-odd plays, and stage work, grounded in Shakespearean and other classical roles, has remained an important part of his career. The first film which attracted international attention for the good-looking actor was *Bitter Rice* (49), in which he co-starred with the voluptuous Silvana Mangano. After another international success with Mangano in *Anna* (51), Gassman was enticed to Hollywood where both his marriage to Shelley Winters and his contract with MGM, which resulted in four credible but less than sensational films, soon fizzled out. He returned to Italy to play Anatole in Vidor's *War and Peace* (56), started his own stage company, and with *Big Deal on Madonna Street* (58), in which he played a slap-happy ex-boxer involved in an incompetent robbery, began a new and highly successful phase of his screen career as a comedic actor. His acting and co-directing in a movie called *Kean* (57), about the famous English actor, enhanced his reputation for overacting; but in the 1960s he was successful with incisive satirical-political comedy. In 1975 under the direction of Dino Risi, with whom he has worked on 15 films, Gassman won the Best Actor Award at the Cannes Film Festival, playing a blind thief forced to rely on senses other than sight in *Scent of a Woman*. Similar whimsical roles and vehicles have gained Gassman a renewed popularity, both at home and internationally. Recent American work includes performances in Robert Altman's *A Wedding* (78) and *Quintet* (79) and in Burt Reynolds' *Sharkey's Machine* (81).
**Selected Films:** *Preludio d'Amore* (46), *Bitter Rice* (49), *Anna* (51), *The Glass Wall* (53), *Sombrero* (53), *War and Peace* (56), *Rhapsody* (54), *Kean* (57), *Big Deal on Madonna Street* (58), *The Love Specialist* (60), *Barabbas* (62), *Woman Times Seven* (67), *Scent of A Woman* (75), *The Prophet* (76), *A Wedding* (78), *Quintet* (79), *The Nude Bomb* (80), *Sharkey's Machine* (81), *Tempest* (82), *Benvenuta* (84), *Life Is a Bed of Roses* (84).

## GATES, Larry (1915- )

Most often appearing as a small town merchant or solid middle-aged type, Gates played numerous character roles in the 1950s and 1960s.
**Selected Films:** *Has Anybody Seen My Gal?* (52), *Invasion of the Body Snatchers* (56), *Cat on a Hot Tin Roof* (58), *The Hoodlum Priest* (62), *Toys in the Attic* (63), *The Sand Pebbles* (67), *Airport* (69).

## GAVIN, John (1928- )

Born in Los Angeles, Gavin has played leads in Hollywood since the mid-1950s. A former president of the Screen Actors Guild, Gavin, born Jack Golenor, has worked on Broadway and starred in such TV series as *Destry* and *Convoy*. He is now US Ambassador to Mexico.
**Selected Films:** *Behind the High Wall* (56), *Quantez* (57), *A Time to Live and a Time to Die* (58), *Psycho* (60), *Romanoff and Juliet* (61), *Thoroughly Modern Millie* (67), *Jennifer* (78), *Heidi* (79).

## GAXTON, William (1893-1963)

Born Arturo Gaxiola in San Francisco, Gaxton was chiefly an entertainer on stage and in vaudeville. He appeared in a few 1930s and 1940s films of the frothier type.
**Selected Films:** *Stepping Along* (26), *It's the Old Army Game* (26), *Fifty Million Frenchmen* (31), *Silent Partners* (32), *Their Big Moment* (34), *Something to Shout About* (42), *Best Foot Forward* (43), *Tropicana* (44), *Diamond Horseshoe* (45).

## GAYNOR, Janet (1906-1984)

Wide-eyed, wistful and waif-like, the five-foot-nothing 96-pound Janet Gaynor displayed neither an abundance of charisma nor exceptional acting ability, but her charming innocence produced such wonderful results in the hands of skillful directors that she became one of the most popular and highest-paid stars of the early 1930s. Born Laura Gainor in Philadelphia, she graduated from a San Francisco high school and moved to Los Angeles, where she worked as an extra and appeared in comedy shorts and westerns before landing her first substantial role in *The Johnstown Flood* (26). Minor stardom in John Ford's *The Blue Eagle* (26) quickly blossomed under heavy Fox promotion and Gaynor won the first Academy Award ever given for best actress for her performances in *Sunrise* (27), *Seventh Heaven* (27) and *Street Angel* (28). *Sunrise* marked the first of twelve films co-starring Charles Farrell that propelled her to immense popularity as half of 'America's Favorite Lovebirds.' She is probably best remembered today for her performance as Esther Blodgett in *A Star is Born* (37). Gaynor retired from films in 1938 and has appeared in only one film since, *Bernadine* (57). She was married to the costume designer (Gilbert) Adrian from 1939 until his death.
**Selected Films:** *The Johnstown Flood* (26), *The Blue Eagle* (26), *Sunrise* (27), *Seventh Heaven* (27), *Street Angel* (27), *Two Girls Wanted* (27), *Four Devils* (29), *Sunny Side Up* (29), *Daddy Long Legs* (31), *State Fair* (33), *Change of Heart* (34), *The Farmer Takes a Wife* (35), *A Star is Born* (37), *Three Loves has Nancy* (38), *The Young in Heart* (38), *Bernadine* (57).

## GAYNOR, Mitzi (1930- )

Although Gaynor was born Francesca Mitzi von Gerber in Chicago, Illinois, this charming actress, dancer and singer, the daughter of a ballerina, was a descendant of Hungarian aristocrats. By the age of 12 she was member of the corps de ballet of the Los Angeles Civil Light Opera. Gaynor began her film career in musicals, beginning with *My Blue Heaven* (50), but her bright, perky style was often better than the material she was given, and her

movies did not always fare well at the box office. Dropped by 20th Century-Fox in 1954, she married agent Jack Bean, who helped her recoup her movie career, but performing live was her speciality.
**Selected Films:** *My Blue Heaven* (50), *Golden Girl* (51), *The I Don't Care Girl* (53), *Down Among The Sheltering Palms* (53), *There's No Business Like Show Business* (54), *Anything Goes* (56), *Les Girls* (57), *South Pacific* (58), *Surprise Package* (60), *For Love or Money* (63), *For the First Time* (69).

## GAZZARA, Ben (1930- )

Intense, brooding and always promising a rebellious explosion of pent-up hostility, Ben Gazzara burst upon the Broadway stage in the mid-1950s with starring roles in *Cat on a Hot Tin Roof* and *A Hatful of Rain*. Born Biago Anthony Gazzara to Sicilian immigrants and reared on New York's tough Lower East Side, Gazzara gladly left off engineering studies when a scholarship enabled him to pursue his dream of an acting career. Work with the Actors Guild preceded his Broadway triumphs, and in his first two film roles, as a sadistic cadet in *The Strange One* (57) and as a rape suspect in *Anatomy of a Murder* (59), Gazzara continued to show great promise. Most of his film work since then has been insignificant, however, perhaps a casualty of his busy TV career; but it is his successes in such TV series as *Arrest and Trial* and *Run for Your Life* that have gained him his widest popularity.
**Selected Films:** *The Strange One* (57), *Anatomy of a Murder* (59), *The Young Doctors* (61), *Convicts 4* (62), *The Captured City* (62), *A Rage to Live* (65), *The Bridge at Remagen* (69), *Husbands* (70), *Capone* (75), *Saint Jack* (79), *Inchon* (81), *Tales of Ordinary Madness* (83), *The Girl from Trieste* (83).

## GEDRICK, Jason (1965- )

Born and raised in Chicago, the boyish-looking Gedrick made his film debut with a small part in *Bad Boys* (83). His combination of ingenuousness and self-confidence won him the lead as the nice high school kid who steals a fighter-jet to rescue his pilot father in *Iron Eagle* (86).
**Selected Films:** *Bad Boys* (83), *Risky Business* (83), *Zoo Gang* (84), *Massive Retaliation* (84), *The Heavenly Kid* (85), *Iron Eagle* (86).

## GEER, Will (1902-1978)

Well-known for his role in the long-running TV series *The Waltons*, Geer, born William Ghere in Frankfort, Indiana, made occasional screen appearances before settling into a Hollywood career as a character actor in 1948. Blacklisted during the 1950s, he returned to the screen in the 1960s.
**Selected Films:** *The Misleading Lady* (32), *Deep Waters* (48), *Broken Arrow* (50), *Advise and Consent* (61), *Seconds* (66), *Jeremiah Johnson* (72), *The Billion Dollar Hobo* (78), *The Mafu Cage* (78).

## GEESON, Judy (1948- )

On stage at the age of nine and on TV at twelve, Geeson, born in Arundel, England, made her screen debut in *Wings of Mystery* (63) and began her film career playing sexy teenagers.
**Selected Films:** *Wings of Mystery* (63), *To Sir with Love* (67), *Berserk!* (67), *Here We Go Round the Mulberry Bush* (67), *Prudence and the Pill* (68), *Two Gentlemen Sharing* (69), *The Executioner* (69), *Doomwatch* (72), *Brannigan* (75), *Carry on England* (76), *The Eagle Has Landed* (76), *Dominique* (78).

## GÉLIN, Daniel (1921- )

Drama studies at the Paris Conservatoire preceded Gélin's entry into films at the beginning of the 1940s and his rise to prominence as a leading man in French cinema. Born in Angers, he usually plays sensitive, intelligent, worldly characters.
**Selected Films:** *Miquette* (40), *Her First Affair* (41), *Rendez-Vous de Juillet* (49), *Édouard et Caroline* (50), *La Ronde* (50), *Charmants Garçons* (57), *Carthage in Flames* (60), *Black Sun* (66), *Le Souffle de Coeur* (70), *L'Honorable Société* (78).

## GENN, Leo (1905-1978)

Born in London and educated to be a barrister, Genn gradually abandoned his profession in favor of acting. Stage triumphs led to intelligent, personable and bland supporting roles and character leads on both sides of the Atlantic.
**Selected Films:** *Immortal Gentleman* (35), *Dream Doctor* (36), *Jump for Glory* (37), *Contraband* (40), *Henry V* (44), *Green for Danger* (46), *The Snake Pit* (48), *Quo Vadis* (51), *Connecting Rooms* (69), *The Martyr* (75), *Escape to Nowhere* (75).

## GEORGE, Chief Dan (1899-1982)

A Canadian Indian actor who began in films in his seventies and often played American Indians, Chief George had one of his finest parts in *Little Big Man* (70), starring Dustin Hoffman.
**Selected Films:** *Smith!* (69), *Little Big Man* (70), *Alien Thunder* (73), *Harry and Tonto* (74), *The Bears and I* (74), *The Outlaw Josey Wales* (76), *Shadow of the Hawk* (76), *Americathon* (79).

## GEORGE, Gladys (1900-1954)

A daughter of actors and a veteran of vaudeville and stage comedy, the blonde, vivacious George, born in Patton, Maine, played leads and second leads in Hollywood melodramas of the 1930s and 1940s. She played character roles toward the end of her career.
**Selected Films:** *Red Hot Dollars* (19), *The House That Jazz Built* (21), *Valiant is the Word for Carrie* (36), *Madame X* (37), *The Roaring Twenties* (39), *The Maltese Falcon* (41), *Flamingo Road* (49), *It Happens Every Thursday* (54).

## GEORGE, Linda Day (1944- )

The American actress of the 1970s got her start as Linda Day in the long-running TV series *Petticoat Junction*. Most of her work has been on television. She was married to TV and film actor Christopher George (1929-1983).
**Selected Films:** *Chisum* (71), *The Junkman* (82), *Mortuary* (83).

## GEORGE, Susan (1950- )

Usually typed in leads that exploit her youthful sexuality, George was born in London to performers and made her film debut at the age of four. She worked extensively on British TV before beginning mature leads on both sides of the Atlantic in the late sixties.
**Selected Films:** *Come Fly With Me* (62), *Billion Dollar Brain* (67), *Lola* (68), *Straw Dogs* (71), *Mandingo* (75), *Tomorrow Never Comes* (78), *Enter the Ninja* (81), *Venom* (82).

## GERAY, Steven (1899-1973)

Born Stefan Gyergyay in Uzhgorod, Czechoslovakia and a former member of the Hungarian National Theater, Geray appeared in European films before arriving in Hollywood in 1941. He often played mild-mannered little men, sometimes menacing foreigners.
**Selected Films:** *Dance Band* (34), *Inspector Hornleigh* (39), *Man at Large* (41), *The Moon and Sixpence* (42), *The Mask of Dimitrios* (44), *So Dark the Night* (46), *Gilda* (46), *All About Eve* (50), *Call Me Madam* (53), *Daddy Long Legs* (55), *Count Your Blessings* (59), *Ship of Fools* (65), *The Swinger* (66).

## GERE, Richard (1949- )

Born in Philadelphia, Pennsylvania, Gere dropped out of college to try to make it on Broadway, but he got his first real break in the London production of the musical *Grease*. On the strength of that performance, he did a season with the Young Vic Company, a rare opportunity for an American actor. Gere has always been serious about the theater, and in 1980 he left Hollywood to go to Broadway to star in *Bent* – a depressing and uncommercial play about homosexuals in Nazi death camps. This was a major risk, particularly for a sex symbol, but Gere received fine notices. Touted as one of Hollywood's new sex symbols, yet also regarded as an actor of impressive talent, Gere scored a major film success in *An Officer and a Gentleman* (82). Yet aside from this movie, his career has been more promise than fulfillment.
**Selected Films:** *Report to the Commissioner* (75), *Baby Blue Marine* (76), *Looking for Mr Goodbar* (77), *Days of Heaven* (78), *Bloodbrothers* (78), *American Gigolo* (79), *An Officer and a Gentleman* (82), *Breathless* (83), *Beyond the Limits* (83), *The Cotton Club* (84), *King David* (85), *Power* (86), *No Mercy* (86).

## GHOSTLEY, Alice (1926- )

Born in Eve, Missouri and educated at the University of Oklahoma, Ghostley brought experience as a revue comedienne to her film character roles. She was a regular on *The Jackie Gleason Show* and received a Tony Award for her supporting role in the Broadway production *The Sign in Sidney Brustein's Window* (65).
**Selected Films:** *New Faces* (54), *To Kill a Mockingbird* (63), *My Six Loves* (63), *The Graduate* (67), *Viva Max* (69), *Ace Eli and Rodger of the Skies* (72), *Gator* (76), *Record City* (77), *Rabbit Test* (78), *Grease* (78).

## GIANNINI, Giancarlo (1942- )

Although he has occasionally appeared in films by other directors, the sad-eyed Giancarlo Giannini's award-winning career is based almost entirely upon his appearances as the protagonist in the films of Lina Wertmuller. Born in La Spezia, Italy, on 1 August 1942, Giannini studied at the Rome Academy of Drama and met Wertmuller when he appeared in her play *Two and Two Are No Longer Four*. After Wertmuller's second film, in 1965, Giannini became a partner in her production company, Liberty Films, and began to star in most of her pictures. Her dominant theme is the little man, and Giannini was ideal as the Chaplinesque guy caught up in a system he can neither comprehend nor successfully navigate. In 1972 he starred in *The Seduction of Mimi*, which won Wertmuller the best director award at Cannes, and he triumphed personally when he won best actor at Cannes for his role in *Love and Anarchy* (73). In the internationally acclaimed *Seven Beauties* (76) Giannini played Pasqualino, a concentration camp prisoner caught in a desperate struggle to survive; and he also starred with Candice Bergen in Wertmuller's first American-backed film, *A Nightful of Rain* (77).
**Selected Films:** *Rita the Mosquito* (66), *Anzio* (68), *The Secret of Santa Vittoria* (69), *The Pizza Triangle* (70), *The Seduction of Mimi* (72), *The Sensual Man* (73), *Love and Anarchy* (73), *Swept Away* (74), *Seven Beauties* (76), *A Nightful of Rain* (77), *Travels with Anita* (79), *Suffer or Die* (79), *American Dreamer* (84), *Saving Grace* (86).

## GIBSON, Edward 'Hoot' (1892-1962)

'Hoot' Gibson was one of the biggest cowboy heroes in the 1920s, ranking just behind William S Hart and Tom Mix. Born in Takama, Nebraska, a former drifter, a champion rodeo rider and a very good movie stuntman, Gibson became a star in 1919. Billed as 'The Smiling Whirlwind,' he appeared in a two-reel series of films directed by the young John Ford. Moving on, he became an even bigger star with an immense following, earning himself huge amounts of money. He spent the money as fast as he made it, on women, fast cars, motorcycles and airplanes. Gibson's breezy personality and flair for light comedy gave him an appealing screen personality. His movies were packed with action but light on violence, with Gibson usually capturing the villains without shooting at them. He also smiled a lot – unusual for a cowboy hero. Gibson was never successful in the sound era. His popularity waned in the 1930s and his career ended in the early 1940s. One of his four wives was actress Sally Eilers.

**Selected Films:** *His Only Son* (12), *The Hazards of Helen* (15), *The Cactus Kid* (19), *The Denver Dude* (22), *Surefire* (24), *Galloping Fury* (27), *Points West* (29), *Spirit of the West* (32), *Powdersmoke Range* (33), *Sunset Range* (35), *The Marshal's Daughter* (53), *The Horse Soldiers* (59), *Ocean's Eleven* (61).

## GIBSON, Mel (1956- )

One of the most bankable products of Australia's budding film industry, dark-haired, blue-eyed Mel Gibson has been received internationally as a major new star to rank with the greatest of Hollywood's male sex symbols. But contrary to publicity efforts which compare him to Errol Flynn, his appeal, as the image of Australian reserve and courage, is closer to that of James Dean or Marlon Brando. Born the sixth of eleven children in Peekskill, New York, at the age of 12 Gibson moved with his family to Sydney, Australia when his father decided to leave the States to prevent his older sons from being drafted and sent to Vietnam (Gibson is still an American citizen). After high school Gibson was accepted at Australia's National Institute of Dramatic Art. His film debut was in the low budget abomination *Summer City* (77), but his performance landed him the title role in *Mad Max* (79), the first of the action-adventure films with which he has become identified and Australia's biggest commercial success to that date. Gibson won Australia's best actor and 'Sammy' awards for his portrayal of a retarded young man in *Tim* (79); he was again named Australia's best actor for his work in *Gallipoli* (81), which together with *The Year of Living Dangerously* (83) brought him international stardom. He has combined film work with appearances on the Australian stage, sometimes in Shakespeare, notably in his highly successful *Death of a Salesman*. Gibson lives in Sydney with his wife and four children.

**Selected Films:** *Summer City* (77), *Mad Max* (79), *Tim* (79), *Attack Force Z* (80), *Gallipoli* (81), *Road Warrior (Mad Max II)* (82), *The Year of Living Dangerously* (83), *The Bounty* (84), *Mrs Soffel* (84), *The River* (85), *Mad Max Beyond Thunderdome* (85), *Lethal Weapon* (87).

## GIELGUD, John (1904- )

Sir John Gielgud is known primarily for his illustrious stage career, but this great Shakespearean actor first began appearing in films in the silent, era. Critics often accused the London-born actor, descended from the great acting family, the Terrys on his mothers' side, of looking uncomfortable in movies, in contrast to his colleague Laurence Olivier, who seemed to move with ease in both stage and screen appearances. Yet from early on, Gielgud turned in some excellent screen performances. He was outstanding in *Julius Caesar* (53), playing the role of Cassius, and he proved that he had a rare gift for comedy playing the valet-butler in *Arthur* (81) a role which won him an Academy Award. Amazingly, he seems to have improved with age. Now in even small roles on screen, he steals the picture with regularity and has brought many a gleaming moment to television productions as well. He was knighted in 1953.

*Sir John Gielgud in* The Elephant Man *(80).*

**Selected Films:** *Who Is the Man?* (24), *Insult* (32), *Secret Agent* (36), *The Prime Minister* (40), *Julius Caesar* (53), *Richard III* (56), *The Barretts of Wimpole Street* (57), *Saint Joan* (57), *Becket* (64), The Loved One (65), *The Charge of the Light Brigade* (68), *The Shoes of the Fisherman* (68), *Julius Caesar* (70), *Lost Horizon* (73), *QB VII* (73), *Luther* (74), *Murder on the Orient Express* (74), *Providence* (77), *Murder by Decree* (79), *The Elephant Man* (80), *Arthur* (81), *Chariots of Fire* (81), *Gandhi* (82), *The Shooting Party* (84).

## GIFFORD, Frances (1920- )

After playing brave Nyoka, heroine of the serial *Jungle Girl* (41), Gifford, born in Long Beach, California, went on to play leads throughout the 1940s.

An automobile accident halted her career.
**Selected Films:** *Woman Chases Man* (37), *Mr Smith Goes to Washington* (39), *Hold That Woman* (40), *Border Vigilantes* (41), *Tarzan Triumphs* (43), *She Went to the Races* (45), *Luxury Liner* (48), *Riding High* (50), *Sky Commando* (53).

## GILBERT, Billy (1893-1971)

A comedian who elevated the sneeze to an art form, Gilbert was the voice of Sneezy in Walt Disney's *Snow White and the Seven Dwarfs* (38). He worked with Laurel and Hardy, The Three Stooges, and the Marx Brothers, and was Herring in Charlie Chaplin's *The Great Dictator* (40). A huge man, Gilbert often played excitable foreigners, but was born in Louisville, Kentucky.
**Selected Films:** *Bubbles of Trouble* (16), *Noisy Neighbors* (29), *Sutter's Gold* (37), *The Great Dictator* (40), *His Girl Friday* (40), *Bride of Vengeance* (49), *Five Weeks in a Balloon* (62).

## GILBERT, John (1895-1936)

Handsome dark-haired men with passionate eyes were all the rage in the silent era, and no one, not even Rudolph Valentino, eclipsed Gilbert (born John Pringle) on the screen. This fine actor was born into a show business family in Logan, Utah. From an early age he dreamed of becoming a movie star and in 1916 he broke into films as an extra, using the name Jack Gilbert. He was soon seen in leads and featured roles although chiefly as 'the other man' or an unsympathetic character, because it was generally believed that his Latin-type looks gave him a slightly villainous air. During this phase of his career, Gilbert often co-wrote scripts for the films he appeared in. By the early 1920s he was playing dashing heroes in movies such as *Monte Cristo* (22) and *Arabian Love* (22). From 1921 on he was John Gilbert, emerging, once he went to MGM, as an extraordinarily popular star. He played a wide range of roles. Gilbert was in the circus drama *He Who Gets Slapped* (24) with Lon Chaney. In *The Snob* (24) he played a despicable cad. He made a remarkable silent version of *The Merry Widow* (25). King Vidor directed him in *The Big Parade* (25), a brilliant movie about World War I, which grossed a fortune. Over the years Gilbert appeared with some of the most famous leading ladies of silent films, including Renée Adorée, Billy Dove, Barbara La Marr, Mae Murray, Lillian Gish and Norma Shearer. His reputation as a great lover was established through the movies he made with Greta Garbo, beginning with *Flesh and the Devil* (27). Rumors of their affair, real or studio-created, fanned the fires and upped the box office take. Gilbert's career went sour during the sound era, presumably because he had a high squeaky voice. But although his voice might have lacked authority, it was adequate and could, with training, have been improved. Gilbert was a victim of changing fashions. He simply couldn't adapt to the low-key style of the talkies and he tragically died, an alcoholic, at the age of 41. He had been married to three actresses, Leatrice Joy, Ina Claire and Virginia Bruce.
**Selected Films:** *Hell's Hinges* (16), *Happiness* (16), *The Devil Dodger* (17), *The Mask* (18), *White Heather* (19), *The White Circle* (20), *Ladies Must Live* (21), *Monte Cristo* (22), *Arabian Love* (22), *Cameo Kirby* (23), *He Who Gets Slapped* (24), *The Snob* (24), *The Merry Widow* (25), *The Big Parade* (25), *La Bohème* (26), *Flesh and the Devil* (27), *Love* (27), *A Woman of Affairs* (29), *Desert Nights* (29), *His Glorious Night* (29), *Redemption* (30), *Gentleman's Fate* (31), *Queen Christina* (33), *The Captain Hates the Sea* (35).

## GILBERT, Melissa (1964- )

Born to a theatrical family in Los Angeles, Gilbert made her first appearance at age 3 in a TV commercial. Since then she has worked in a number of TV series of the 1970s and 1980s including *Gunsmoke* and *Love Boat*. She was a regular on *Little House on the Prairie*.
**Selected Films:** *Sylvester* (85).

## GILFORD, Jack (1907- )

A veteran vaudevillian, Gilford, born Jacob Gellman in New York City, has played many comic character roles on stage, TV, and in films. He received an Academy Award nomination for his supporting role in *Save the Tiger* (72).
**Selected Films:** *Hey Rookie* (44), *Main Street to Broadway* (53), *A Funny Thing Happened on the Way to the Forum* (66), *Catch-22* (70), *Save the Tiger* (72), *Wholly Moses* (80), *Caveman* (81), *Cocoon* (85).

## GILLIAM, Terry (1940- )

Best known as a member of the British comedy troupe Monty Python, whose films he has sometimes animated, written and directed as well as acted in, Gilliam is a native of Minneapolis, Minnesota. He worked with other members of the incipient troupe on the childrens' TV show *Do Not Adjust Your Set* before Monty Python took off in 1969. He also directed the film *Brazil* (85).
**Selected Films:** *And Now for Something Completely Different* (71), *Monty Python and the Holy Grail* (75), *Monty Python's The Life of Brian* (79), *Time Bandits* (81), *Monty Python's The Meaning of Life* (83).

## GILLINGWATER, Claude (1870-1939)

Born in Lauseanna, Missouri, Gillingwater was a veteran stage actor who made his film debut in *Little Lord Fauntleroy* (21) and stayed on to play innumerable irascible old men.
**Selected Films:** *Little Lord Fauntleroy* (21), *My Boy* (22), *Dulcy* (23), *Souls for Sale* (24), *Cheaper to Marry* (25), *For Wives Only* (26), *The Gorilla* (27), *Daddy Long Legs* (31), *A Tale of Two Cities* (36), *Conquest* (37), *Café Society* (39).

## GILLIS, Ann (1927- )

A minor child star of the 1930s and early 1940s who appealed more to children than adults and often played the brat, Gillis, born Alma O'Connor in Little Rock, Arkansas, was unsuccessful in making the transition to adult star.

**Selected Films:** *The Garden of Allah* (36), *Off to the Races* (37), *The Adventures of Tom Sawyer* (38), *Beau Geste* (39), *Little Men* (40), *Nice Girl* (41), *In Society* (44), *Big Town After Dark* (47), *2001: A Space Odyssey* (68).

## GINGOLD, Hermione (1897-1987)

On stage at 11, the London-born Gingold became a popular revue comedienne on both sides of the Atlantic. Her memorable film appearances usually saw her portraying outlandish or grotesque characters.

**Selected Films:** *Someone at the Door* (36), *Meet Mr Penny* (39), *The Butler's Dilemma* (43), *The Pickwick Papers* (52), *Around the World in Eighty Days* (56), *Bell Book and Candle* (58), *Gigi* (58), *The Music Man* (61), *A Little Night Music* (77).

## GISH, Dorothy (1898-1968)

Gish was born Dorothy de Guiche in Springfield, Ohio. She began her screen career as a child actress, as did her sister, Lillian, in D W Griffith films. Although Lillian is more famous today as a dramatic actress, during the silent era Dorothy was a major star in her own right. A talented light comedienne and pantomimist, Gish made many movies, beginning with *An Unseen Enemy* (12). Although the Gish sisters appeared together frequently at the beginning of their careers, later they generally went their separate ways. Dorothy Gish made her last silents in London, then appeared primarily on stage. She remained close to her sister all her life.

**Selected Films:** *An Unseen Enemy* (12), *The Sisters* (14), *Susan Rocks the Boat* (16), *Hearts of the World* (18), *Battling Jane* (18), *Remodeling Her Husband* (20), *Orphans of the Storm* (22), *Romola* (24), *Nell Gwyn* (26), *Madame Pompadour* (27), *Our Hearts Were Young and Gay* (44), *The Whistle at Eaton Falls* (51), *The Cardinal* (63).

## GISH, Lillian (1896- )

Gish is a superb actress who has often been compared to Sarah Bernhardt, and is able to convey power and strength on screen despite her fragile appearance. Early in her career, she was, according to actress and critic Louise Brooks, 'a shining symbol of purity,' an image that created problems for her when Victorian sentimental standards faded in the late 1920s. She was the queen of the silent silver screen and drew critical praise throughout her career. She was born Lillian de Guiche in Springfield, Ohio, and made stage appearances as 'Baby Lillian' with her mother and sister Dorothy from the age of five. In 1912, when the family was living in New York, she was introduced to D W Griffith through an old friend, Gladys Smith, who became known as Mary Pickford, and began appearing in his films that same day. Griffith admired her talent and intelligence and she, in turn, admired his genius. Together they created some of the classics of the silent era, She played either good girls who were rewarded, as in *Orphans of the Storm* (22), or bad girls who repented, as in *Way Down East* (20). The innocent young woman she played in *Birth of a Nation* (15) was equally memorable. Gish learned everything there was to know about film technique, directing her sister Dorothy in *Remodeling Her Husband* (20), and insisting on full script and production control when she made movies for minor companies. Joining MGM in 1925, Gish chose King Vidor and Victor Sjöström as her directors. Even though she turned in a masterful performance in *The Scarlet Letter* (26), and the movie was great commercial success, the growing popularity of Greta Garbo allowed MGM to rid themselves of the independent well-paid Gish, and she went to United Artists for a brief time. Sound was no problem for this actress who had an excellent stage-trained voice, but changing fashions were catching up with her. No longer a box office draw, she decided to leave Hollywood and return to the theater rather than continue her film career. Her stage roles were more varied than her film parts had been, ranging from Marguerite Gautier in *Camille* to the nurse in *Romeo and Juliet*. She also was in *Hamlet* with John Gielgud. From the 1940s Gish did character parts in films and appeared on television and lectured

*Lillian Gish in* The Scarlet Letter *(26) with Lars Hanson.*

widely. In 1946 she was nominated for the Academy Award for Best Supporting Actress for her role as Lionel Barrymore's consumptive wife in *Duel in the Sun*. And in 1970 she was given a Special Academy Award 'for superlative artistry and for distinguished contribution to the progress of motion pictures.'
**Selected Films:** *An Unseen Enemy* (13), *The Madonna of the Storm* (13), *The Birth of a Nation* (15), *The Lily and the Rose* (15), *An Innocent Magdalene* (15), *Intolerance* (16), *Broken Blossoms* (18), *True Heart Susie* (20), *Way Down East* (20), *Orphans of the Storm* (22), *The White Sister* (23), *Romola* (24), *La Bohème* (26), *The Scarlet Letter* (26), *Annie Laurie* (27), *The Wind* (28), *His Double Life* (34), *The Commandos Strike at Dawn* (43), *Miss Susie Slagle's* (46), *Duel in the Sun* (46), *Portrait of Jennie* (48), *The Cobweb* (55), *The Night of the Hunter* (55), *Orders to Kill* (58), *Follow Me Boys* (66), *The Comedians* (67), *A Wedding* (78), *Sweet Liberty* (86), *The Whales of August* (87).

## GLEASON, Jackie (1916-1987)

Through such vehicles as the TV comedy series *The Honeymooners* and *The Jackie Gleason Show* Brooklyn's Gleason became one of TV's leading personalities. The big man also played dramatic roles, but never scored consistently in films either before or after his TV success.
**Selected Films:** *Navy Blues* (41), *The Desert Hawk* (50), *The Hustler* (61), *Soldier in the Rain* (63), *Skidoo* (68), *Mr Billioun* (77), *Smokey and the Bandit* (77), *The Sting II* (82), *The Toy* (83), *Nothing in Common* (86).

## GLEASON, James (1886-1959)

Also a screenwriter and playwright, Gleason, born in New York City, played an outstanding gallery of hard-boiled, acidly comic, tough-talking character roles that included big-city cops, detectives, fight managers, politicians, reporters, gamblers, crooks, marine sergeants and navy non-coms. He was married to actress Lucille Gleason.
**Selected Films:** *Polly of the Follies* (22), *The Count of Ten* (28), *Oh Yeah!* (30), *Orders is Orders* (33), *Forty Naughty Girls* (37), *Here Comes Mr Jordan* (41), *Once Upon a Time* (44), *Suddenly* (54), *The Last Hurrah* (58).

## GLEASON, Lucille (1886-1947)

A talented character actress, Gleason, born Lucille Webster in Pasadena, California, was married to James Gleason, with whom she often appeared. Their son Russell Gleason (1908-1945) appeared in films in leads, second leads, and supporting roles until his accidental death.
**Selected Films:** *The Shannons of Broadway* (29), *Nice Woman* (32), *Beloved* (33), *Klondike Annie* (36), *First Lady* (37), *The Higgins Family* (38), *Lucky Partners* (40), *The Clock* (45).

## GLENN, Scott (1939- )

Born in Pittsburgh, Pennsylvania, Glenn was a journalist and off-Broadway stage actor before making his screen debut in *The Baby Maker* (70). Since then he has regularly played major roles in big films, most notably Alan Shepard in *The Right Stuff* (83) and the laconic Emmett in *Silverado* (85).
**Selected Films:** *The Baby Maker* 70), *Apocalypse Now* (79), *Urban Cowboy* (80), *The Right Stuff* (83), *The River* (84), *Silverado* (85), *Wild Geese II* (85).

## GLOVER, Danny (1948- )

Glover was born in San Francisco, California, where he still lives with his wife, Asake, a jazz vocalist, and their daughter. He attended San Francisco State University and from there became a stage actor, turning to films later.
**Selected Films:** *The Color Purple* (85), *Silverado* (85), *Witness* (85), *Places in the Heart* (85), *Lethal Weapon* (87).

## GLOVER, Julian (1935- )

A thoroughly professional British actor who studied at the Royal Academy of Dramatic Art, Glover played his first major film role in *Tom Jones* (63). He is primarily seen on stage and TV.
**Selected Films:** *Tom Jones* (63), *Girl with Green Eyes* (64), *I Was Happy Here* (66), *Alfred the Great* (69), *The Adding Machine* (69), *Wuthering Heights* (70), *Nicholas and Alexandra* (71), *Juggernaut* (75), *The Brute* (77), *For Your Eyes Only* (81).

## GODDARD, Paulette (1911- )

Goddard, born Marion Levy in Great Neck, New York, could be a fine comedienne or a sexy siren. She was as witty and intelligent as she was beautiful. A Ziegfeld Girl at age 14, she decided to try Hollywood and became a Goldwyn Girl. She married Charlie Chaplin and appeared in two of his films, *Modern Times* (36) and *The Great Dictator* (40). In the meantime she was busy achieving stardom on her own with co-stars like Bob Hope and Ray Milland. By the 1940s she was a top star, a favorite of Cecil B De Mille, but her career took a dip in the 1950s. After divorcing Chaplin she married actor Burgess Meredith, then author Erich Maria Remarque, and lived elegantly in Europe.
**Selected Films:** *The Locked Door* (29), *The Girl Habit* (31), *The Kid from Spain* (32), *Kid Millions* (34), *Modern Times* (36), *The Young in Heart* (38), *The Women* (39), *The Cat and the Canary* (39), *The Ghost Breakers* (40), *The Great Dictator* (40), *Northwest Mounted Police* (40), *Nothing But the Truth* (41), *Reap the Wild Wind* (42), *So Proudly We Hail* (43), *Kitty* (45), *The Diary of a Chambermaid* (46), *Unconquered* (47), *Suddenly It's Spring* (47), *On Our Merry Way* (48), *Anna Lucasta* (49), *The Stranger Came Home* (54), *Time of Indifference* (66).

## GOLDBERG, Whoopi (1949- )

Catapulted into the national spotlight by her outstanding performance as the female lead in Steven Spielberg's film version of Alice Walker's best-selling novel *The Color Purple* (85), New York City-born black actress/comedienne Whoopi Goldberg had already received considerable critical acclaim for her one-woman show 'Whoopi Goldberg,' produced by Mike Nichols, which opened on Broadway at the beginning of the 1984-1985 season.

**Selected Films:** *The Color Purple* (85), *Jumpin' Jack Flash* (86), *Burglar* (87).

## GOLDBLUM, Jeff (1953- )

Born in Pittsburgh, Pennsylvania, Goldblum, a tall, lean, sharp-featured, goggle-eyed actor, began studying acting immediately after high school. He landed his first role on stage because he was tall, and played a guard in Joe Papp's New York production of *Two Gentlemen of Verona,* later playing in the comic revue *El Grande de Coca Cola*. In the latter he was seen by film director Robert Altman, who offered him a part in *California Split* (74) and another in *Nashville* (75). Goldblum went on to play in comedies, science-fiction films, horror movies and dramas, and is fast becoming one of the most capable actors in Hollywood.

**Selected Films:** *California Split* (74), *Nashville* (75), *Invasion of the Body Snatchers* (78), *The Big Chill* (83), *Into the Night* (84), *Silverado* (85), *Transylvania 6-5000* (85), *The Fly* (86), *Beyond Therapy* (87).

## GOMEZ, Thomas (1905-1971)

The heavyset Gomez, a native of New York City, spent years on the stage, including seven with Lunt and Fontanne before making his film debut in *Sherlock Holmes and the Voice of Terror* (42). In films he often played the villain or detective.

**Selected Films:** *Sherlock Holmes and the Voice of Terror* (42), *Arabian Nights* (42), *Phantom Lady* (44), *Ride the Pink Horse* (47), *Force of Evil* (48), *Macao* (52), *Summer and Smoke* (61), *Beneath the Planet of the Apes* (70).

## GOODWIN, Bill (1910-1958)

A former radio announcer and later much on TV, Goodwin, a native of San Francisco, began in films in the early 1940s and played many genial, dependable types in routine productions.

**Selected Films:** *Let's Make Music* (41), *Wake Island* (42), *So Proudly We Hail* (43), *Bathing Beauty* (44), *Incendiary Blonde* (45), *The Jolson Story* (46), *Heaven Only Knows* (47), *Mickey* (48), *Jolson Sings Again* (49), *Tea for Two* (50), *The Big Beat* (58).

## GORCEY, Leo (1915-1969)

Moving with the original Broadway production of *Dead End* (35) to the 1937 film version starring Humphrey Bogart, the diminutive Gorcey, born in New York City, maintained his tough, fast-talking but not unkindly punk persona through scores of second feature productions including the *East Side Kids* and *The Bowery Boys* series.

**Selected Films:** *Dead End* (37), *Mannequin* (38), *Crime School* (38), *Angels With Dirty Faces* (38), *Mr Wise Guy* (42), *Bowery Bombshell* (46), *Bowery to Bagdad* (55), *It's a Mad Mad Mad Mad World* (63), *The Phynx* (69).

## GORDON, Gale (1905- )

Best known for his TV appearances on such comedy series as *Our Miss Brooks* and *The Lucy Show*, Gordon, born Gaylord Aldrich in New York City, also amused film audiences with his plump, fussy persona.

**Selected Films:** *Here We Go Again* (42), *A Woman of Distinction* (50), *Don't Give Up the Ship* (59), *Visit to a Small Planet* (60), *Sergeant Deadhead* (65), *Speedway* (68).

## GORDON, Mary (1882-1963)

Best remembered as Mrs Hudson, housekeeper for Sherlock Holmes, a role she played to perfection in many films as well as in the radio series, Gordon was born Mary Gilmour in Scotland and played many character roles in Hollywood after she arrived in America in the mid-1920s.

**Selected Films:** *The Home Maker* (25), *Naughty Nannette* (27), *The Bride of Frankenstein* (35), *Sherlock Holmes Faces Death* (43), *West of Wyoming* (50).

## GORDON, Ruth (1896-1985)

By the time she received an Academy Award for best supporting role in *Rosemary's Baby* (68), as a Manhattan witch, Ruth Gordon had already logged an impressive record of stage and film appearances, and had also authored and co-authored (with her second husband Garson Kanin) several successful plays and screenplays. Born Ruth Gordon Jones on 30 October 1896 in Wollaston, Massachusetts, Gordon actually first appeared in film in bit parts in *Camille* (15) and *Wheel of Life* (16) while trying to find roles on Broadway. By the time she returned to the screen as Mary Todd Lincoln in *Abe Lincoln in Illinois* (40) she was established on the stage as an actress equally adept at drama and comedy. Although her career has remained centered on the stage, she appeared in films intermittently in a wide variety of roles. Her notable credits as a writer include *Double Life* (48) and *Adam's Rib* (49).

**Selected Films:** *Camille* (15), *Wheel of Life* (16), *Abe Lincoln in Illinois* (40), *Two-Faced Woman* (41), *Edge of Darkness* (43), *Inside Daisy Clover* (66), *Rosemary's Baby* (68), *Harold and Maude* (72), *Boardwalk* (78), *Every Which Way But Loose* (78), *My Bodyguard* (80), *Any Which Way You Can* (80), *Smokey and the Bandit II* (80).

*Elliott Gould and JoAnn Pflug in* M*A*S*H *(70).*

## GORING, Marius (1912- )

Born at Newport on the Isle of Wight, Goring first appeared on stage at the age of 13 and was a veteran of the Old Vic and Sadler's Welles. He made his screen debut in *Consider Your Verdict* (36) and supplemented his impressive stage career with leads and character roles in films, often as a neurotic or effete aristocrat.
**Selected Films:** *Consider Your Verdict* (36), *Rembrandt* (36), *The Case of the Frightened Lady* (38), *A Matter of Life and Death* (45), *The Red Shoes* (48), *Ill Met by Moonlight* (57), *Exodus* (60), *Zeppelin* (71), *The Little Girl in Blue Velvet* (78).

## GOSSETT, Lou Jr (1936- )

Lou Gossett's Emmy award-winning performance in the TV mini-series *Roots* brought him wide critical acclaim, but it was not until his portrayal of a tough drill instructor in *An Officer and a Gentleman* (82), a role not originally intended for a black performer, that the lanky actor attracted national attention. Gossett was born on 27 May 1936 in New York City. Following a high school leg injury he substituted acting for basketball and appeared on Broadway in the lead of *Take a Giant Step* (53), for which he won the Donaldson Award as Best Newcomer of the Year. After much work on TV and stage he made his film debut in a reprise of his Broadway role in *A Raisin in the Sun* (61). He portrayed a cuckold in *The Landlord* (70) and co-starred with James Garner in *The Skin Game* (71), showing the charming side of his usually intense persona. He won the Academy Award for Best Supporting Actor for his highly acclaimed performance in *An Officer and a Gentleman.*
**Selected Films:** *A Raisin in the Sun* (61), *The Landlord* (70), *The Skin Game* (71), *The River Niger* (72), *The White Dawn* (74), *The Choirboys* (77), *Don't Look Back* (81), *An Officer and a Gentleman* (82), *Enemy Mine* (85), *Iron Eagle* (86), *Firewalker* (87).

## GOUGH, Michael (1917- )

Born in Malaya to British parents, Gough made his first stage appearance in 1936 and his film debut in *Blanche Fury* (46). Tall and gaunt, he often plays sinister or homicidal characters.
**Selected Films:** *Blanche Fury* (46), *Anna Karenina* (48), *The Man in the White Suit* (51), *Richard III* (5), *The Horror of Dracula* (57), *Horrors of the Black Museum* (58), *The Horse's Mouth* (59), *The Phantom of the Opera* (62), *Women in Love* (69), *The Boys From Brazil* (78), *The Dresser* (83), *Memed, My Hawk* (87).

## GOULD, Elliott (1938- )

Gould's very unhandsomeness made him a star of the early 1970s. He is the ex-husband of superstar Barbra Streisand and was born Elliott Goldstein in Brooklyn, New York. He became a Broadway leading man, an out-of-work stage actor, a Hollywood hot property and a performer in search of good scripts. If he were cast in the right movie, the roller coaster could start up again, but at present he works in television situation comedies. Along the way, he was very good in particular films, virtually stealing *Bob & Carol & Ted & Alice* (69) from Natalie Wood, Robert Culp and Dyan Cannon, and *M*A*S*H* (70) from Donald Sutherland.
**Selected Films:** *The Confession* (66), *The Night They Raided Minsky's* (68), *Bob & Carol & Ted & Alice* (69), *M*A*S*H* (70), *Getting Straight* (70), *Little Murders* (71), *The Long Goodbye* (72), *Nashville* (74), *A Bridge Too Far* (77), *The Devil and Max Devlin* (81).

## GRABLE, Betty (1916-1973)

World War II GIs loved Grable for her lovely legs, and made her their favorite pin-up. Three million photographs of her, scattered around the world at assorted war fronts attested to that. 'My legs made me,' she said, admitting that she had little voice and below-average dancing skills. All the same, she was one of Hollywood's most popular musical comedy stars in the 1940s. Her forty-plus films grossed millions of dollars, her characters were fun and she took war-weary minds off their troubles. Grable was Technicolor's brightest blondes in some of Hollywood's most famous musicals. She was just right for her era, a fantasy version of the kind of girl that could be found in a diner or working a shift in a war plant. She was born Elizabeth Grasle in St Louis, Missouri. By nature an easy-going sort, she was pushed into her career by her ferocious stage mother, who provided dancing and saxophone lessons. Grable later said, 'It's good she pushed me, because I'm basically a lazy person.' By the age of 12 she was in Hollywood, trying to break into movies. She had bits in films while still in her early teens, occasionally appearing under the name Frances Dean. A series of leads in B pictures followed. Grable married Jackie Coogan in 1937 and his success boosted her career. They divorced in 1940, the year that she caught the eye of Darryl F Zanuck at 20th Century-Fox. She had just scored a big success on Broadway in *Du Barry Was a Lady*. When she replaced Alice Faye in *Down Argentine Way* (40), audiences sat up and took notice. Although Grable was good in light comedies, stardom came in films such as *Song of the Islands* (42), *Coney Island* (43), and *Sweet Rosie O'Grady* (43). She frequently co-starred with Dan Dailey in lavishly costumed musicals set in a bygone era. Grable became Hollywood's highest-paid star – box office magic. Her legs were insured with Lloyd's of London for a million dollars. In 1943 she married trumpet-playing band leader Harry James, but they were divorced in 1965. Critical recognition came with *Mother Wore Tights* (47), and Grable continued to be popular in movies until the mid-1950s when movie musicals went into a decline. She continued to have a loyal following who came out to see her in night clubs and in plays, especially when she appeared on Broadway in the role made famous by Carol Channing in *Hello Dolly!*. She died of lung cancer at the age of 56.

**Selected Films:** *Let's Go Places* (30), *Whoopee* (30), *Kiki* (31), *The Kid from Spain* (32), *Cavalcade* (33), *The Gay Divorcee* (34), *Collegiate* (35), *Follow the Fleet* (36), *Pigskin Parade* (36), *College Swing* (38), *Million Dollar Legs* (39), *Down Argentine Way* (40),

*Betty Grable with John Payne in* The Dolly Sisters *(45).*

*Tin Pan Alley* (40), *Moon Over Miami* (41), *A Yank in the RAF* (41), *I Wake Up Screaming* (41), *Footlight Serenade* (42), *Song of the Islands* (42), *Springtime in the Rockies* (42), *Coney Island* (43), *Sweet Rosie O'Grady* (43), *Four Jills in a Jeep* (44), *Pin-Up Girl* (44), *The Dolly Sisters* (45), *The Shocking Miss Pilgrim* (47), *Mother Wore Tights* (47), *When My Baby Smiles at Me* (48), *Wabash Avenue* (50), *My Blue Heaven* (50), *How to Marry a Millionaire* (53), *How to Be Very Very Popular* (53).

## GRAHAME, Gloria (1925-1981)

Cheap slut, blonde floozie, femme fatale or unfaithful wife, the sultry Gloria Grahame brought to the Hollywood stereotype of the bad girl a sensuality and depth of characterization rarely seen in practitioners of the persona. Born Gloria Grahame Hallward on 28 November 1925 in Los Angeles, Grahame began acting at the age of nine with the Pasadena Community Playhouse and appeared in Hollywood High productions. She made her Broadway debut as Gloria Hallward in 1943, and her film debut – as a bad girl – in *Blonde Fever* (44). After playing a delightful small town tart in *It's A Wonderful Life* (46) she revealed, as a pathetic cafe hostess in *Crossfire* (47), the pouting lips and seductive presence she brought to fruition to make her reputation opposite Humphrey Bogart in *In a Lonely Place* (50). She received an Academy Award as supporting actress for being an unfaithful wife to Dick Powell in *The Bad and the Beautiful* (52). Never truly exploited was her comedic talent, brilliantly displayed in *Oklahoma!* (55) – as Ado Annie the girl who 'cain't say no'. Grahame did little film work in the 1960s but returned triumphantly in *Head Over Heels* (79) and *Melvin and Howard* (80).
**Selected Films:** *Blonde Fever* (44), *It's A Wonderful Life* (46), *Crossfire* (47), *A Woman's Secret* (48), *Sudden Fear* (52), *The Bad and the Beautiful* (52), *The Greatest Show on Earth* (52), *The Big Heat* (54), *The Cobweb* (55), *Oklahoma!* (55), *Odds Against Tomorrow* (59), *Ride Beyond Vengeance* (66), *Tarot* (73), *Head Over Heels* (79), *Melvin and Howard* (80), *The Nesting* (81).

## GRANGER, Farley (1925- )

Although Farley Granger's period as a major film star was limited to the years between 1948 and 1955, the brevity of his ascendency was less a reflection on his talent than on the paucity of starring roles for his particular screen persona – a combination of vulnerable pretty-boy freshness with weakness and guilt. Born in San Jose, California on 1 July 1925, Granger was signed by Sam Goldwyn while still a student at North Hollywood High and made his film debut in *North Star* (43). After one more propaganda film, *The Purple Heart* (44), he went into the army. On his return he began the series of films for which he is best known. In Alfred Hitchcock's *Rope* (48) he played a thrill-killer; in *They Live By Night* (48) a weak-willed newly-wed coerced into criminality; and in *Strangers on a Train* (51), another Hitchcock vehicle, he is perfect as a weak socialite tennis pro almost maneuvered into a murder pact. After a superb performance as a cowardly, betraying lover in Visconti's *Senso* (54) he returned to Hollywood for two more films, then forsook the screen for stage and TV, returning to the screen in the late 1960s chiefly in obscure European films.
**Selected Films:** *North Star* (43), *The Purple Heart* (44), *Rope* (48), *They Live By Night* (48), *Side Street* (49), *Strangers on a Train* (51), *The Story of Three Loves* (53), *Senso* (54), *Naked Street* (55), *The Girl in the Red Velvet Swing* (55), *Rogue's Gallery* (68), *The Man Called Noon* (73), *Arnold* (75), *The Image Maker* (86).

*Stewart Granger in* Green Fire *(54).*

## GRANGER, Stewart (1913- )

Tall, athletic and masculine, Stewart Granger was – with James Mason – one of Britain's top romantic leads of the 1940s before he came to Hollywood to star in swashbucklers. Born James Lablanche Stewart on 6 May 1913 in London, Granger got his start in British films as an extra in 1933, gained more acting experience with various stage companies, then returned to the screen in his first leading role in *So This is London* (39). By then he had changed his name to Granger to avoid confusion with the American actor James Stewart. Enticed by his box-office success, Hollywood beckoned, and in 1949 Granger arrived in America with his second wife Jean Simmons to sign with MGM. He achieved international stardom through such high-budget adventure films as *King Solomon's Mines* (50), the first of his American pictures, and *Scaramouche* (52), but steadfastly disparaged his talent and his vehicles. During the

1960s he appeared in Italian and German westerns, but since the 1970s he has accepted starring roles on American TV, notably as Sherlock Holmes in *The Hound of the Baskervilles*.

**Selected Films:** *A Southern Maid* (33), *So This is London* (39), *The Man in Grey* (43), *Waterloo Road* (44), *Man of Evil* (44), *Caesar and Cleopatra* (45), *Captain Boycott* (47), *King Solomon's Mines* (50), *Scaramouche* (52), *The Prisoner of Zenda* (52), *Beau Brummel* (54), *Moonfleet* (55), *Bhowani Junction* (56), *Sodom and Gomorrah* (62), *The Secret Invasion* (64), *The Last Safari* (67), *The Wild Geese* (77).

## GRANT, Cary (1904-1986)

Grant, the extraordinarily handsome British-born movie star, was one of the most famous screen personalities in the world. He played light romantic comic leads seemingly forever, and appeared, at least from a distance, to lead a charmed life. Actually his early life was anything but charmed. Born Archibald Leach in Bristol, England, into poverty, he ran away from home in his early teens. Joining a traveling acrobatic troupe he came to New York on a tour in 1920. Grant scraped along at the lowest level in vaudeville, returning to England in 1923 where he appeared in musical comedies. An accomplished song and dance man, he returned to New York and had a modest success on Broadway. Hollywood beckoned, and when he decided to leave his up-and-coming vaudeville troupe, he was replaced by an unknown song-and-dance man – James Cagney. In the movie capital, Grant got off to a good start in supporting roles and was given a real boost by Mae West, who cast him as her co-star in *She Done Him Wrong* (33). Soon he rivaled Gary Cooper in popularity, but it wasn't until the late 1930s, beginning with *The Awful Truth* (37), with Irene Dunne, that his gifts for screwball comedy flowered on the screen. By the 1940s, Grant was the established master of roles requiring a sophisticated man-about-town. What set him apart from other actors of the genre, besides his unique voice with its tinge of Bristol accent, was his air of not taking himself too seriously. He always appeared slightly embarrassed in love scenes, and despite his self-assurance, was never a snob. When other leading men of his generation had to turn to aging character roles, Grant still looked young and handsome. He was still in top form in *North by Northwest* (59), at the age of 55, and *Charade* (63), at the age of 59. Witty and urbane off-screen as well as on, Grant once said, 'I play myself to perfection.' Among his ex-wives were heiress Barbara Hutton and actresses Betsy Drake and Dyan Cannon, mother of his only child, a daughter born when he was past 60. In 1969 Grant received a special Academy Award 'for his unique mastery of the art of screen acting with the respect and affection of his colleagues.'

**Selected Films:** *This Is the Night* (32), *Blonde Venus* (33), *She Done Him Wrong* (33), *The Eagle and the Hawk* (33), *I'm No Angel* (33), *Sylvia Scarlett* (35), *The Awful Truth* (37), *Topper* (37), *Bringing Up Baby* (38), *Holiday* (38), *Gunga Din* (39), *Only Angels Have Wings* (39), *My Favorite Wife* (40), *His Girl Friday* (40), *The Philadelphia Story* (40), *Penny Serenade* (41), *Suspicion* (41), *Destination Tokyo* (43), *Mr Lucky* (43), *Arsenic and Old Lace* (44), *Night and Day* (45), *Notorious* (46), *The Bachelor and the Bobby Soxer* (47), *The Bishop's Wife* (48), *Mr Blandings Builds His Dream House* (48), *I Was a Male War Bride* (49), *Room for One More* (52), *To Catch a Thief* (55), *The Pride and the Passion* (57), *An Affair to Remember* (57), *Indiscreet* (58), *Houseboat* (58), *North by Northwest* (59), *Operation Petticoat* (59), *That Touch of Mink* (62), *Charade* (63), *Father Goose* (64), *Walk, Don't Run* (66).

*Cary Grant in* The Philadelphia Story (40).

## GRANT, Kathryn (1933-     )

Born Olive Grandstaff in Houston, Texas, Grant began winning beauty contests at the age of 14. She played leading roles in films of the 1950s, and retired soon after her marriage to Bing Crosby in 1957. During the 1970s she hosted a San Francisco TV talk show.

**Selected Films:** *Arrowhead* (53), *Forever Female* (54), *Cell 2455, Death Row* (55), *Mister Cory* (56), *The Brothers Rico* (57), *The Seventh Voyage of Sinbad* (58), *The Big Circus* (59).

## GRANT, Lee (1926-     )

Lyova Haskell Rosenthal was born in New York City to an actress-model mother, and made her stage debut at the age of four. After high school she was offered the ingenue role in the Broadway production of *Detective Story* (49), for which she

received the Critics Circle Award. She was named best actress at Cannes and received an Oscar nomination for the film version. Immediately afterwards Grant was blacklisted for refusing to testify against her then-husband, writer Arnold Manoff. She remained active on the stage, returning in the 1960s to play memorable leads and character parts on TV and film. She received an Emmy for her acting in TV's *Peyton Place*, an Oscar nomination for *The Landlord* (70), and an Oscar as Best Supporting Actress for her role as the philandering wife Felicia in *Shampoo* (75). The only Hollywood actress of her generation to move successfully into directing her credits began with *The Stronger* (76) and include *Tell Me a Riddle* (80) and *What Sex Am I?* (85).
**Selected Films:** *Detective Story* (51), *Storm Fear* (55), *Terror in the City* (65), *In the Heat of the Night* (67), *The Landlord* (70), *Plaza Suite* (71), *Portnoy's Complaint* (72), *Shampoo* (75), *Voyage of the Damned* (76), *Little Miss Marker* (80), *Visiting Hours* (82), *Teachers* (84).

## GRANVILLE, Bonita (1923- )

Born to Chicago entertainers, Granville was on stage at the age of 3 and played mischievous or vicious children in 1930s films. Routine adult roles ended with her marriage to a Texas oilman; she now produces.
**Selected Films:** *Westward Passage* (32), *Silver Dollar* (32), *Cavalcade* (33), *Ah Wilderness!* (35), *These Three* (36), *Maid of Salem* (37), *Nancy Drew, Detective* (38), *Hitler's Children* (43), *Love Laughs at Andy Hardy* (46), *The Lone Ranger* (56), *The Magic of Lassie* (78).

## GRAPEWIN, Charlie (1869-1956)

Born in Xenia, Ohio, Grapewin was almost always called 'Pop' or something like it in 100-odd film character roles including Grandpa Joad in *The Grapes of Wrath* (40) and Jeeter Lester in *Tobacco Road* (41). Grapewin's glossary of grizzled old men also includes Inspector Queen, father of Ellery.
**Selected Films:** *Above the Limit* (02), *The Shannons of Broadway* (29), *Only Saps Work* (30), *Judge Priest* (34), *Captains Courageous* (37), *The Wizard of Oz* (39), *The Grapes of Wrath* (40), *Tobacco Road* (41), *Gunfighters* (47), *When I Grow Up* (51).

## GRAVES, Peter (1925- )

Best known as the star of the TV series *Mission Impossible*, Graves, born Peter Aurness in Minneapolis, Minnesota, is the brother of actor James Arness. He made his film debut in *Rogue River* (50), and his film credits include *Stalag 17* (53).
**Selected Films:** *Rogue River* (50), *Fort Defiance* (52), *Stalag 17* (53), *Beneath the 12-Mile Reef* (53), *Wolf Larsen* (59), *A Rage to Live* (65), *Sidecar Racers* (75), *Spree* (78), *Airplane* (80), *Savannah Smiles* (82).

## GRAVET, Fernand (1904-1970)

Also known as Fernand Garvey, the debonair Gravet, born Fernand Mertens to actors Georges Mertens and Fernande Depernay in Brussells, Belgium, was a popular Continental leading man for decades. He began appearing in occasional Hollywood productions in 1933.
**Selected Films:** *Monsieur Beulemeister* (13), *Cherie* (30), *Bitter Sweet* (33), *The Great Waltz* (38), *Pamela* (44), *La Ronde* (50), *How to Steal a Million* (66), *The Madwoman of Chaillot* (69), *L'Explosion* (71).

## GRAY, Colleen (1922- )

Born Doris Jensen in Staplehurst, Nebraska, Gray cut her teeth playing in little theaters before moving to Hollywood in the 1940s. She was usually seen in westerns, crime melodramas, and action films.
**Selected Films:** *State Fair* (45), *Kiss of Death* (47), *Red River* (48), *Sand* (49), *Riding High* (50), *The Sleeping City* (51), *Arrow in the Dust* (54), *The Killing* (56), *Johnny Rocco* (58), *P J* (68), *The Late Liz* (71)

## GRAY, Dolores (1924- )

Long on stage as a singer and dancer – she played in *Annie Get Your Gun* in London – the statuesque American appeared in films during the 1950s when Hollywood was relying heavily on Broadway for vehicles.
**Selected Films:** *It's Always Fair Weather* (54), *Kismet* (55), *The Opposite Sex* (56), *Designing Woman* (57).

## GRAY, Gilda (1901-1959)

Primarily a dancer with stage and vaudeville experience, Gray was born Marianna Michalska in Krakow, Poland. She arrived in the United States when she was seven years old and starred in several Hollywood silent productions; she is credited with having invented the shimmy.
**Selected Films:** *Lawful Larceny* (23), *Aloma of the South Seas* (26), *Cabaret* (28), *The Devil Dancer* (28), *Piccadilly* (29), *Rose Marie* (36).

## GRAYSON, Kathryn (1922- )

Born Zelma Hedrick in Winston-Salem, North Carolina, she was to become one of the best lyric sopranos in Hollywood, and often appeared in film versions of top Broadway musicals, although she also did straight roles. Her first appearance in films was in the title role of *Andy Hardy's Private Secretary* (40).
**Selected Films:** *Andy Hardy's Private Secretary* (40), *Andy Hardy's Spring Fever* (41), *Rio Rita* (42), *Thousands Cheer* (43), *Anchors Aweigh* (45), *Till the Clouds Roll By* (46), *The Kissing Bandit* (48), *Show Boat* (51), *Kiss Me Kate* (53), *The Vagabond King* (55), *That's Entertainment II* (76).

## GREEN, Kerri (1967- )

A native of Fort Lee, New Jersey, Green skipped summer camp in 1984 to go for auditions that landed her a debut role in the successful *Goonies* (85). Her perky, wide-eyed, red-haired-and-freckled appeal has won her subsequent roles.
**Selected Films:** *Goonies* (85), *Summer Rental* (85), *Lucas* (86).

## GREEN, Mitzi (1920-1969)

Born Elizabeth Keno, in The Bronx, to vaudevillian parents and billed as 'Little Mitzi,' Green began in films at the age of nine and starred in such early talkies as *Tom Sawyer* (30) and *Little Orphan Annie* (32). She retired from films at the age of 14, returning in the 1950s to play supporting roles before dying of cancer at 48.
**Selected Films:** *The Marriage Playground* (29), *Honey* (30), *Tom Sawyer* (30), *Little Orphan Annie* (32), *Transatlantic Merry-Go-Round* (34), *Walk With Music* (40), *Bloodhounds of Broadway* (52).

## GREEN, Nigel (1924-1972)

A native of Pretoria, South Africa, Green logged stage and TV experience before playing many character parts and dominant, forceful roles in British and a few Hollywood films.
**Selected Films:** *The Sea Shall Not Have Them* (54), *Reach for the Sky* (56), *Sword of Sherwood Forest* (60), *Jason and the Argonauts* (63), *Zulu* (64), *The Ipcress File* (65), *The Face of Fu Manchu* (65), *Deadlier Than the Male* (66), *Tobruk* (67), *The Ruling Class* (71), *Gawain and the Green Knight* (73).

## GREENE, Lorne (1915- )

Formerly one of Canada's top radio newscasters, the Ottawa-born Greene worked on Broadway, in Hollywood, and in American TV in the early 1950s before starring as patriarch Ben Cartwright in the long-running TV series *Bonanza*.
**Selected Films:** *The Silver Chalice* (54), *Tight Spot* (55), *Autumn Leaves* (56), *Peyton Place* (57), *The Hard Man* (57), *The Gift of Love* (58), *The Buccaneer* (58), *Earthquake* (74), *Klondike Fever* (79).

## GREENE, Richard (1914-1985)

Tall and good-looking, Greene, born in Plymouth, England into a theatrical family, acted briefly on stage before he was imported to Hollywood at the age of twenty to play romantic and swashbuckling leads. He continued to play lightweight leads from 1938. He also starred in British TV series *Robin Hood*. Greene was married to actress Patricia Medina from 1941 to 1951.
**Selected Films:** *Four Men and a Prayer* (38), *The Hound of the Baskervilles* (39), *Flying Fortress* (42), *The Fan* (49), *Captain Scarlett* (53), *Dangerous Island* (67), *Tales from the Crypt* (71).

## GREENSTREET, Sydney (1879-1954)

Usually sinister and always fat, Greenstreet, born in Sandwich, became one of Hollywood's most memorable villians. A stage actor, he didn't appear on screen until *The Maltese Falcon* (41), when he was 61 years old. He became a major star of the 1940s, and in his best films he was teamed with Humphrey Bogart and/or Peter Lorre.
**Selected Films:** *The Maltese Falcon* (41), *They Died with Their Boots On* (41), *Across the Pacific* (42), *Casablanca* (42), *Between Two Worlds* (44), *The Mask of Dimitrios* (44), *Three Strangers* (46), *The Hucksters* (47), *The Woman in White* (48), *Flamingo Road* (49), *Malaya* (50).

## GREENWOOD, Charlotte (1890-1978)

Well-known for her eccentric dancing, this tall, energetic Philadelphia-born comedienne was one of Broadway's favorites and appeared in silent films. She returned to play comic leads and supporting roles in musicals.
**Selected Films:** *Jane* (15), *Baby Mine* (27), *So Long Letty* (30), *Palmy Days* (32), *Down Argentine Way* (40), *Moon Over Miami* (41), *Springtime in the Rockies* (43), *Home in Indiana* (47), *Oklahoma* (56), *The Opposite Sex* (56)

## GREENWOOD, Joan (1921-1987)

Graceful and sophisticated, with a husky, velvety voice, the petite Joan Greenwood combined exaggeration and restraint, innuendo and sincerity, into a unique style of playful eroticism which is at once the reason for her enduring fame and, for its very subtlety, the reason she never gained wider popularity. Born on 4 March 1921 in London, the daughter of artist Sydney Earnshaw Greenwood, she attended the Royal Academy of Dramatic Art and made her stage debut in London in 1938. Her first film was *John Smith Wakes Up* (40); stage work continued, including Ophelia in *Hamlet* (44). Her roles in *Whisky Galore* (49) and *Kind Hearts and Coronets* (49), in which she plays the hero's mistress with consummate wit, gave her international popularity. She was perfect as Gwendolyn in *The Importance of Being Earnest* (52), but ultimately neither Britain nor Hollywood could supply leads to satisfy her distinctive style, and beginning in the mid-1950s she worked chiefly on the stage in England, playing leads in *Hedda Gabler* and *The Understanding*.
**Selected Films:** *John Smith Wakes Up* (40), *The Gentle Sex* (42), *The October Man* (47), *Saraband for Dead Lovers* (48), *Whisky Galore* (49), *Kind Hearts and Coronets* (49), *The Importance of Being Earnest* (52), *Father Brown* (54), *Tom Jones* (63), *Girl Stroke Boy* (71), *The Water Babies* (78), *Little Dorrit* (87).

## GREER, Dabbs (1917- )

Memorable as Schuyler, one of the inmate ring-

*Joan Greenwood and Dennis Price* – Kind Hearts and Coronets *(49).*

leaders in the classic prison film *Riot in Cell Block 11* (54), Greer, a native of Fairview, Missouri, has played numerous character roles since his debut in *The Black Book* (48). His TV credits include *The Little House on the Prairie.*
**Selected Films:** *The Black Book* (48), *House of Wax* (53), *Riot in Cell Block 11* (54), *Invasion of the Body Snatchers* (56), *The Vampire* (57), *Shenandoah* (65), *Cheyenne Social Club* (70), *Rage* (72).

## GREER, Jane (1924- )

A professional model at the age of 12 and a nightclub singer in high school, Washington, DC's Bettejane Greer signed with Howard Hughes and married Rudy Vallee. She made her film debut in *Pan Americana* (45) and played cool, deep-voiced leads into the 1950s.
**Selected Films:** *Pan Americana* (45), *Dick Tracy* (45), *They Won't Believe Me* (47), *Out of the Past* (47), *The Big Steal* (49), *Run for the Sun* (56), *Man of a Thousand Faces* (57), *Billie* (65), *The Outfit* (73).

## GREGORY, James (1911- )

Forsaking Wall Street for Broadway, Gregory, born in New Rochelle, New York, made his film debut in the late 1940s and has been much seen in Hollywood productions and on TV as a heavy, often a tough customer or a veteran cop.
**Selected Films:** *The Naked City* (48), *The Frogmen* (51), *Al Capone* (59), *The Manchurian Candidate* (62), *The Silencers* (66), *The Main Event* (79).

## GREGSON, John (1919-1975)

A star of British comedies and action features of the 1950s, the mild-mannered, dependable Gregson, born in Liverpool, played character roles in international productions later in his career. Much seen on British TV, he starred in the Scotland Yard TV series *Gideon's Way.*
**Selected Films:** *Saraband for Dead Lovers* (48), *Whisky Galore* (49), *Treasure Island* (50), *The Lavender Hill Mob* (51), *The Brave Don't Cry* (51), *Genevieve* (53), *Jaqueline* (56), *Rooney* (57), *The Captain's Table* (58), *Live Now Pay Later* (62), *Fright* (71), *The Tiger Lily* (75).

## GRENFELL, Joyce (1910-1979)

A British comedienne on the London stage with her own monologues since 1939, Grenfell, born Joyce Phipps, in London, made her first film in the early 1940s. She toured internationally with her one-woman show in the late 1950s and 1960s.
**Selected Films:** *The Demi-Paradise* (42), *The Happiest Days of Your Life* (49), *Laughter in Paradise* (51), *Genevieve* (53), *The Pure Hell of St Trinians* (60), *The Americanization of Emily* (64), *The Yellow Rolls-Royce* (64).

## GREY, Joel (1932- )

Son of comedian Mickey Katz, Grey, born Joel Katz in Cleveland, was on stage as a child and achieved stardom in 1966 in Broadway's *Cabaret.* He received a Tony Award for his Master of Ceremonies in that production and won an Academy Award for the same role in the 1972 film version.
**Selected Films:** *About Face* (52), *Calypso Heat Wave*

(57), *Come September* (71), *Cabaret* (72), *Man on a Swing* (74), *The Seven-Per-Cent Solution* (76), *Remo Williams: The Adventure Begins* (85).

## GREY, Nan (1918- )

The blonde Houston native, born Eschal Miller, played leads and second leads in the 1930s, usually in routine productions. She was married to singer Frankie Laine in 1950.
**Selected Films:** *The Firebird* (34), *Babbit* (34), *Sutter's Gold* (36), *Dracula's Daughter* (36), *Three Smart Girls Grow Up* (38), *Tower of London* (39), *The Invisible Man Returns* (40), *Margie* (40), *Under Age* (41), *Sandy is a Lady* (41).

## GREY, Virginia (1917- )

Los Angeles-born daughter of silent comedy director Ray Grey, Grey made her film debut as Little Eva in *Uncle Tom's Cabin* (27). She was an attractive blonde adult leading lady in numerous routine pictures of the 1930s and 1940s, and played second leads in major productions.
**Selected Films:** *Uncle Tom's Cabin* (27), *The Michigan Kid* (28), *Misbehaving Ladies* (31), *Dames* (34), *Test Pilot* (38), *Idaho* (43), *Unconquered* (47), *Target Earth* (54), *Back Street* (61), *Rosie* (67), *Airport* (70).

## GRIER, Pam (1949- )

A voluptuous black American actress, Grier established herself as a leading lady playing heroines in black exploitation films of the 1970s.
**Selected Films:** *Beyond the Valley of the Dolls* (70), *The Big Doll House* (71), *The Big Bird Cage* (72), *Twilight People* (72), *Blacula* (72), *Coffy* (74), *Black Mama White Mama* (74), *The Arena* (74), *Foxy Brown* (74), *Sheba Baby* (75), *Drum* (76), *Fort Apache – the Bronx* (78), *Something Wicked This Way Comes* (83), *Stand Alone* (86).

## GRIFFITH, Andy (1926- )

Everybody's favorite country boy, Griffith was born in Mount Airy, North Carolina and studied to be a preacher. He achieved success on Broadway in *No Time for Sergeants* in 1955, and made his film debut in *A Face in the Crowd* (57). Personal appearances and TV work, especially *The Andy Griffith Show*, account for most of his great popularity.
**Selected Films:** *A Face in the Crowd* (57), *No Time for Sergeants* (58), *Hearts of the West* (75), *Rustlers' Rhapsody* (85).

## GRIFFITH, Corinne (1898-1979)

Known as the 'Orchid Lady' for her delicate beauty, Griffith, born in Texarkana, Texas, was billed as 'the world's most beautiful woman' and was in great popular demand through the end of the silent era. Some of her novels, including *Papa's Delicate Condition*, were adapted to the screen.
**Selected Films:** *The Last Man* (16), *Thin Ice* (19), *The Yellow Girl* (22), *Infatuation* (25), *The Divine Lady* (29), *Back Pay* (30), *Lily Christine* (32).

## GRIFFITH, Hugh (1912-1980)

Winner of an Academy Award for his role as Sheik Ilderim in *Ben Hur* (59), the flamboyant Griffith, born in Marian Glas, on the island of Anglesey, North Wales, was a bank clerk before he took to the stage in 1939. His first film was *Neutral Port* (40).
**Selected Films:** *Neutral Port* (40), *The Last Days of Dolwyn* (48), *The Beggar's Opera* (52), *The Titfield Thunderbolt* (53), *Lucky Jim* (57), *Exodus* (61), *Tom Jones* (63), *Oliver!* (68), *Wuthering Heights* (70), *Luther* (73), *The Hound of the Baskervilles* (78).

## GRIZZARD, George (1925- )

Primarily a stage actor, Grizzard, born in Roanoke Rapids, North Carolina, usually plays underhanded characters in films. Much seen on TV, he won an Emmy Award for his supporting role in the 1980 production *The Oldest Living Graduate*.
**Selected Films:** *From the Terrace* (60), *Advise and Consent* (62), *Warning Shot* (67), *Happy Birthday, Wanda Jane* (71), *Comes a Horseman* (78), *Firepower* (79), *Seems Like Old Times* (80), *Wrong is Right* (82).

## GRODIN, Charles (1935- )

A native of Pittsburgh, Grodin attracted considerable attention as the protagonist in Elaine May's *The Heartbreak Kid* (72), although most of his roles as a leading man have been of a more wholesome nature. Grodin studied acting with Lee Strasberg and Uta Hagen.
**Selected Films:** *Rosemary's Baby* (68), *Sex and the College Girl* (70), *Catch-22* (70), *The Heartbreak Kid* (72), *King Kong* (76), *Heaven Can Wait* (78), *The Great Muppet Caper* (81), *The Incredible Shrinking Woman* (81), *The Lonely Guy* (84), *Woman in Red* (84), *Last Resort* (86), *Ishtar* (87).

## GUARDINO, Harry (1925- )

Seen more on stage and TV than in films, where he is equally at home in comedy and drama, Brooklyn-born Guardino plays a variety of tough-guy leads and character roles.
**Selected Films:** *Flesh and Fury* (52), *Houseboat* (58), *Pork Chop Hill* (59), *King of Kings* (61), *Hell is for Heroes* (62), *Madigan* (68), *Dirty Harry* (71), *Al Capone* (75), *The Enforcer* (76), *Rollercoaster* (77), *Any Which Way You Can* (80).

## GUILFOYLE, Paul (1902-1961)

Often appearing as a villain or weakling and coming to a bad end (James Cagney stuffs him into an automobile trunk in *White Heat* [49]), Guilfoyle, born in Jersey City, New Jersey, moved from the

*Richard Burton, James Earl Jones, Alec Guinness, Elizabeth Taylor and Peter Ustinov in* The Comedians *(67).*

stage to the screen in the mid-1930s. His directing credits include *Captain Scarface* (53), *A Life at Stake* (54), and *Tess of the Storm Country* (60).
**Selected Films:** *Special Agent* (36), *Time to Kill* (42), *White Heat* (49), *Julius Caesar* (53), *Chief Crazy Horse* (54), *Valley of Fury* (55).

## GUINNESS, Alec (1914- )

When it comes to film technique, versatility and an artistic instinct for the understated, no actor can rival Guinness. Born in London, this foremost British actor made his screen debut in 1933 in *Evensong*, and was not seen on the screen again for years. His next role was as Herbert Pocket in *Great Expectations* (46), in David Lean's adaptation of Charles Dickens' novel. Discovered by John Gielgud, Guinness went to the Old Vic Company, eventually appearing in leading roles. In 1941 he joined the Royal Navy and after the war returned to the stage. For the most part he continued his career in the theater right through his years as a major screen attraction and beyond. An extraordinary Fagin in *Oliver Twist* (48), he played eight different characters in *Kind Hearts and Coronets* (49), won a Picturegoer Gold Medal as Disraeli in *The Mudlark* (50) and appeared in two of Ealing Studios' best comedies, *The Lavender Hill Mob* (51) and *The Man in the White Suit* (51). In 1951 Guinness became Britain's top box office star and number five in the world. He didn't stop making great pictures, charming the public as a mild priest turned sleuth in *Father Brown* (54) and as a mad mastermind undone by a sweet old lady in *The Ladykillers* (55). *The Bridge on the River Kwai* (57) won him a British Film Academy Award as well as an Oscar for Best Actor. Guinness, the master of disguise, has played everything from an Arab king to Adolf Hitler. He was knighted in 1959 for his achievements, but he was on the threshold of difficult years, when the critics took to sniping at him. Still he had his triumphs. He won a Venice Film Festival Award for *The Horse's Mouth* (58), for which he wrote the screenplay. He was an excellent King Faisal in *Lawrence of Arabia* (62), magnificent in *Tunes of Glory* (60) and he was a hit on Broadway in *Dylan* in 1964. Guinness outlasted the sniping, maintaining his reputation through a series of fine supporting roles in films, further serious stage performances and superb appearances on television.
**Selected Films:** *Evensong* (33), *Great Expectations* (46), *Oliver Twist* (48), *Kind Hearts and Coronets* (49), *The Mudlark* (50), *The Lavender Hill Mob* (51), *The Man in the White Suit* (51), *The Card* (52), *The Captain's Paradise* (52), *Father Brown* (54), *The Ladykillers* (55), *The Bridge on the River Kwai* (57), *The Horse's Mouth* (58), *Our Man in Havana* (59), *Tunes of Glory* (60), *Lawrence of Arabia* (62), *Doctor Zhivago* (66), *Hotel Paradiso* (66), *The Comedians* (67), *Scrooge* (70), *Murder by Death* (76), *Star Wars* (77), *Lovesick* (83), *Return of the Jedi* (83), *A Passage to India* (84), *Little Dorrit* (87).

## GUNN, Moses (1929-     )

A native of St Louis, Missouri, Gunn, a black character actor, began on stage in 1962 and in films two years later. He specializes in powerful if somewhat stylized characterizations.
**Selected Films:** *Nothing but a Man* (64), *What's So Bad About Feeling Good?* (68), *The Great White Hope* (70), *WUSA* (70), *The Wild Rovers* (71), *Shaft* (72), *The Hot Rock* (72), *Rollerball* (75), *Ragtime* (81), *Amityville II* (82), *Certain Fury* (85), *Heartbreak Ridge* (86).

## GURIE, Sigrid (1911-1969)

Born Sigrid Gurie Haukelid in Brooklyn and reared in Norway and Belgium, Gurie returned to America as an adult and became Sam Goldwyn's 'Siren of the Fjords,' playing exotic Hollywood leads with modest success from the late 1930s until her retirement in 1948.
**Selected Films:** *The Adventures of Marco Polo* (38), *Algiers* (38), *The Forgotten Woman* (39), *Rio* (40), *Three Faces West* (40), *A Voice in the Wind* (44), *Sword of the Avenger* (48), *Sofia* (48).

## GUTTENBERG, Steve (1958-     )

A Brooklyn-born graduate of the High School for the Performing Arts and Julliard, Guttenberg studied acting with Lee Strasberg and Uta Hagen, making his film debut in *The Chicken Chronicles* (77).
**Selected Films:** *The Chicken Chronicles* (77), *Rollercoaster* (77), *The Boys from Brazil* (79), *Players* (79), *Diner* (82), *Police Academy* (84), *Police Academy II* (85), *Cocoon* (85), *Bad Medicine* (85), *Police Academy III: Back in Training* (86), *Short Circuit* (86), *The Bedroom Window* (87).

## GWENN, Edmund (1875-1959)

Born in Glamorgan, this veteran Welsh actor began his stage career in the early 1900s where he was much admired by playwright George Bernard Shaw. Although Gwenn made his debut in British films in 1916 in *The Real Thing at Last*, it was in Hollywood during the 1940s that he became a star. The stocky, elfin Gwenn played lovable avuncular characters, receiving an Academy Award for Best Supporting Actor for his performance as Kris Kringle in *Miracle on 34th Street* (47). He was also splendid in Alfred Hitchcock's *The Trouble with Harry* (55), at the ripe age of 80.
**Selected Films:** *The Real Thing at Last* (16), *The Skin Game* (20), *The Skin Game* (32), *The Good Companions* (33), *Sylvia Scarlett* (35), *Anthony Adverse* (36), *Pride and Prejudice* (40), *Foreign Correspondent* (40), *Charlie's Aunt* (41), *Lassie Come Home* (43), *Between Two Worlds* (44), *Miracle on 34th Street* (47), *Green Dolphin Street* (47), *Apartment for Peggy* (48), *Mister 880* (50), *The Student Prince* (54), *The Trouble with Harry* (55), *Calabuch* (57).

## HAAS, Hugo (1901-1968)

Born in Brno, Haas fled the Nazis after establishing himself in films in his native Czechoslovakia. He appeared in supporting character parts through the 1940s, then produced, directed, acted in, and often wrote a number of lesser melodramas during the 1950s.
**Selected Films:** *Skeleton on Horseback* (39), *A Bell for Adano* (45), *My Girl Tisa* (48), *King Solomon's Mines* (50), *Thy Neighbor's Wife* (53), *Born to be Loved* (59), *Paradise Alley* (62).

## HACKETT, Buddy (1924-     )

Rotund, Brooklyn-born Hackett (originally Leonard Hacker) developed his inimitable wise-guy comic style in the Catskill 'borscht circuit,' and working in nightclubs and television. Most of his films were made in the 1960s, including *The Music Man* (62) and *The Love Bug* (69).
**Selected Films:** *Walking My Baby Back Home* (53), *God's Little Acre* (58), *The Music Man* (62), *It's a Mad Mad Mad Mad World* (63), *Muscle Beach Party* (64), *The Love Bug* (69), *The Good Guys and The Bad Guys* (69).

## HACKETT, Joan (1934-1983)

Born in New York, Hackett was a model before studying acting and making a name on Broadway. After her first film appearance in *The Group* (66), she went on to play leads, often non-glamorous roles, in films into the 1980s. At the end of her career, she was seen in a number of made-for-TV movies.
**Selected Films:** *The Group* (66), *Support Your Local Sheriff* (69), *The Last of Sheila* (73), *The Terminal Man* (74), *Mackintosh and T J* (75), *One Trick Pony* (80), *The Escape Artist* (82).

## HACKMAN, Gene (1930-     )

An American actor who unexpectedly became a star in the early 1970s, Hackman can play a villain or a saint. Either way, he is one of the finest character actors in Hollywood. Although not handsome or charismatic enough to draw audiences in on the strength of his name alone, he has been turning in fine performances in films for over 25 years, beginning with *Mad Dog Coll* (61). Born in San Bernadino, California, Hackman quit high school to join the Marines, then drifted from one small town to another until deciding to become an actor when he was in his thirties. Success came with *Bonnie and Clyde* (67) and he won an Academy Award for Best Actor in the role of the eccentric New York detective Popeye Doyle in *The French Connection* (71).

**Selected Films:** *Mad Dog Coll* (61), *Lilith* (64), *Hawaii* (66), *Bonnie and Clyde* (67), *Downhill Racer* (69), *I Never Sang for My Father* (69), *The Gypsy Moths* (69), *The French Connection* (71), *The Poseidon Adventure* (72), *The Conversation* (74), *Young Frankenstein* (74), *Bite the Bullet* (75), *The French Connection II* (75), *Lucky Lady* (75), *A Bridge Too Far* (77), *Superman* (78), *Superman II* (80), *Reds* (82), *Under Fire* (83), *Target* (85), *Hoosiers* (86), *Twice in a Lifetime* (86), *Power* (86), *Kid Gloves* (87).

## HADEN, Sara (1897-1981)

Born in Galveston, Texas the daughter of an actress, Haden began stage work in childhood and had an extensive Broadway career before coming to Hollywood in the 1930s as a character actress. Usually cast as a plain spinster, she was best known in her role as Andy Hardy's Aunt Milly.
**Selected Films:** *Spitfire* (34), *Magnificent Obsession* (35), *Out West With the Hardys* (38), *Life Begins for Andy Hardy* (41), *Woman of the Year* (42), *The Big Cat* (49), *Andy Hardy Comes Home* (58).

## HADLEY, Reed (1911-1974)

Born Reed Herring in Petrolia, Texas, Hadley came from stage and radio (where he played Red Ryder) to play leads and second leads in B movies from the late 1930s to the 1950s. His lanky form and steely-handsome features were also seen on the early TV series *Racket Squad* and *Public Defender*.
**Selected Films:** *Female Fugitive* (38), *The Bank Dick* (41), *Guadalcanal Diary* (43), *Captain from Castile* (49), *Highway Dragnet* (54), *The St Valentine's Day Massacre* (68).

*Gene Hackman in* The Conversation *(74).*

## HAGEN, Jean (1923-1977)

New York-born Jean Ver Hagen came to films by way of Broadway, making her screen debut in *Adam's Rib* (49). Thereafter her screen career was spotty despite her manifest talents, though she did make notable appearances in John Huston's *The Asphalt Jungle* (50) and the musical *Singin' in the Rain* (52). She played Danny Thomas's wife in the TV series *Make Room for Daddy*.
**Selected Films:** *Adam's Rib* (49), *The Asphalt Jungle* (50), *Carbine Williams* (52), *Singin' in the Rain* (52), *The Big Knife* (55), *Sunrise at Campobello* (60), *Panic in the Year Zero* (62), *Dead Ringer* (64).

## HAGMAN, Larry (1930- )

The son of Broadway star Mary Martin, Hagman was born in Weatherford, Texas and went into stage musical comedy himself. His film appearances have been occasional, mostly light leading parts. He is best known for his roles in the TV series *I Dream of Jeannie* and *Dallas*.
**Selected Films:** *Ensign Pulver* (64), *Fail Safe* (64), *The Group* (66), *Mother, Jugs, and Speed* (76), *The Eagle Has Landed* (76), *Crash* (77).

## HAIGH, Kenneth (1929- )

Coming to films after extensive stage work in his native Britain (where he played the original lead in *Look Back in Anger*), Haigh largely tended to play angry-young-men roles in movies such as *Man at the Top* (73) and *The Bitch* (79). He also appeared in the TV series *Man at the Top*.
**Selected Films:** *My Teenage Daughter* (56), *High Flight* (56), *Saint Joan* (57), *Cleopatra* (63), *A Hard Day's Night* (64), *Eagle in a Cage* (71), *Man at the Top* (73), *The Bitch* (79).

## HALE, Alan (1892-1950)

Born Rufus Alan McKahan in Washington, DC, Hale had a brief career in opera before making his screen debut in *The Cowboy and the Lady* (11). A muscular, jovial giant of a man, Hale starred in silents – and directed some – before making the transition to talkies. From the 1930s to the year of his death, he was a perennial supporting character actor in dozens of films. He played Little John in three movies, the most notable of them *The Adventures of Robin Hood* (38).
**Selected Films:** *The Cowboy and the Lady* (11), *Martin Chuzzlewit* (14), *The Four Horsemen of the Apocalypse* (21), *Robin Hood* (22), *It Happened One Night* (34), *The Last Days of Pompeii* (35), *Stella Dallas* (37), *The Adventures of Robin Hood* (38), *The Man in the Iron Mask* (40), *Strawberry Blonde* (41), *Desperate Journey* (42), *My Wild Irish Rose* (47), *My Girl Tisa* (49), *Rogues of Sherwood Forest* (50).

## HALE, Alan Jr (1918- )

The son of Alan Hale, and like his father originally named Alan McKahan, Hale took up his father's trade of character actor in movies as a teenager. He grew up to look almost exactly like his dad and to play similar roles in the movies. He also appeared in the TV series *Casey Jones* and *Gilligan's Island*.
**Selected Films:** *Wild Boys of the Road* (33), *To the Shores of Tripoli* (42), *The Gunfighter* (50), *Rogue Cop* (54), *The Killer is Loose* (56), *Advance to the Rear* (63), *The Great Monkey Rip-Off* (79).

## HALE, Barbara (1922- )

Born in Dekalb, Illinois, Hale went from modelling to roles in mostly minor Hollywood productions of the 1940s and 1950s. She is best remembered for her role as Della Street, secretary to Perry Mason in the long-running TV series. She is married to actor Bill Williams, and is the mother of actor William Katt.
**Selected Films:** *The Seventh Victim* (43), *Lady Luck* (46), *Jolson Sings Again* (49), *Lorna Doone* (51), *Unchained* (54), *Airport* (69), *Big Wednesday* (78).

## HALE, Creighton (1882-1965)

Born Patrick Fitzgerald in Cork, Ireland, Hale came to the United States in 1913 and made his film debut soon after. Like many screen actors, the dashing Hale was a leading man first and character actor later – he starred in silent features of the 1920s such as *The Marriage Circle* (24) and *The Cat and the Canary* (27), but in talkies played supporting roles, sometimes as a meek and comic little man.
**Selected Films:** *The Million Dollar Mystery* (14), *Way Down East* (20), *Trilby* (23), *The Marriage Circle* (24), *The Cat and the Canary* (27), *Annie Laurie* (27), *Hollywood Boulevard* (36), *The Gorilla Man* (42), *Beyond the Forest* (49).

## HALE, Jonathan (1892-1966)

Canadian-born Hale (originally Jonathan Hatley) was a diplomat before turning to films in the 1930s. Appearing in some 200 movies, he was usually cast in supporting roles as an excitable businessman, among them Mr Dithers in the *Blondie* series.
**Selected Films:** *Lightning Strikes Twice* (34), *Her Jungle Love* (39), *The Steel Trap* (52), *Jaguar* (58).

## HALEY, Jack (1899-1979)

Jack Haley was born John Joseph Haley in Boston, the son of a seaman, and after trying life as an electrician went into show business as a vaudeville musical comedian. After a few years he moved to Broadway revues and light comedy. He began in films in the 1920s, and through the 1930s appeared in various light movies, among them *Poor Little Rich Girl* (36) and *Alexander's Ragtime Band* (38). In 1938 Haley found his immortality as the Tin Man – with a Boston accent – who secured his heart through the efforts of Dorothy in *The Wizard of Oz*. Haley's later film career ground to a halt in the 1940s with a string of routine movies. After a long retirement, he reappeared on the screen briefly in his producer-director son's (Jack Haley Jr) movie *Norwood* (70).
**Selected Films:** *Broadway Madness* (27), *Follow Thru* (30), *Poor Little Rich Girl* (36), *Rebecca of Sunnybrook Farm* (38), *Alexander's Ragtime Band* (38), *Hold That Co-Ed* (38), *The Wizard of Oz* (39), *Moon over Miami* (41), *Beyond the Blue Horizon* (42), *Scared Stiff* (44), *People are Funny* (45), *Make Mine Laughs* (49), *Norwood* (70).

## HALL, Huntz (1920- )

Born in New York, Hall appeared in his teens in the stage and screen versions of *Dead End* (37). Before long, Hall was cast as Dippy or Satch in a series of movies about the gang first called the Dead End Kids, then the East Side Kids, and finally the Bowery Boys. The movies, all low-budget comedies, ran from the 1940s into the 1950s. He later worked on TV and in occasional films.
**Selected Films:** *Dead End* (37), *Angels With Dirty Faces* (38), *Spooks Run Wild* (41), *Bowery Bombshell* (46), *Ghost Chasers* (51), *Dig That Uranium* (56), *Spook Chasers* (57), *The Love Bug Rides Again* (73), *Valentino* (77), *The Escape Artist* (81).

## HALL, Jon (1913-1979)

Born Charles Hall Locher in Fresno, California, Hall began his film career in the mid-1930s and for a few years after making a splash in *The Hurricane* (37), was a beefy and handsome lead in loincloth roles. However, his career slowly eroded into B-adventure movies, and he found his greatest fame in the 1950s TV series *Ramar of the Jungle*.
**Selected Films:** *Charlie Chan in Shanghai* (35), *The Hurricane* (37), *South of Pago Pago* (40), *Arabian Nights* (42), *Sudan* (45), *Last Train from Bombay* (52), *The Beach Girls and the Monster* (65).

## HALL, Porter (1888-1953)

Clifford Porter Hall was born in Cincinnati, Ohio, and began his career in minor stage work before turning to films in the 1930s. Noted for his wry features, Hall appeared in numberless character parts into the 1950s, most often as a shifty little guy. He was in several Preston Sturges comedies including *Sullivan's Travels* (41).
**Selected Films:** *The Thin Man* (34), *The Petrified Forest* (36), *The General Died at Dawn* (36), *Sullivan's Travels* (41), *The Miracle of Morgan's Creek* (44), *Ace in the Hole* (51), *Vice Squad* (53).

## HALL, Thurston (1883-1958)

Boston-born Hall first appeared in silent films as a leading man. His roles included Marc Antony to

*Haley, Lahr, Garland, Bolger* – The Wizard of Oz *(39).*

Theda Bara's *Cleopatra* (18). After leaving film for Broadway for some years, he returned to play character roles, often as a disgruntled boss, in hundreds of movies and in the TV series *Topper*.
**Selected Films:** *The Squaw Man* (19), *Professor Beware* (38), *The Great McGinty* (40), *Brewster's Millions* (45), *The Secret Life of Walter Mitty* (47), *Affair in Reno* (56).

## HALLIDAY, John (1880-1947)

Born in Brooklyn, New York, the dapper Halliday worked on Broadway before starting in films in the 1920s. He was an elegant lead and second lead in movies of the 1930s including *Hollywood Boulevard* (36) and *The Philadelphia Story* (40).
**Selected Films:** *The Woman Gives* (20), *Fifty Million Frenchmen* (31), *Perfect Understanding* (33), *Peter Ibbetson* (35), *Hollywood Boulevard* (36), *Desire* (36), *That Certain Age* (39), *The Philadelphia Story* (40), *Lydia* (41).

## HALOP, Billy (1920-1976)

Born in New York, Halop was one of the original Dead End Kids in the 1937 play and film *Dead End*. He went on to appear in several of the gang's comedies, then left in search of stardom. That didn't happen and Halop descended to bit parts and alcoholism. Making a comeback in later years, he appeared on the TV series *All in the Family*.
**Selected Films:** *Angels with Dirty Faces* (38), *Hell's Kitchen (39)*, *Mob Town* (41), *Gas House Kids* (46), *Air Strike* (55), *Fitzwilly* (66).

## HAMILL, Mark (1952- )

Born in Oakland, California, Hamill made his TV debut on *The Bill Cosby Show* while studying acting in college. For several years he was relegated to routine film and TV work, until George Lucas cast Hamill as Luke Skywalker, the boyish hero of *Star Wars* (77). Despite the effects of age and of a serious auto accident, Hamill starred in two sequels of Lucas's space epic, observing, 'I'm waiting for my body to catch up with my age.'
**Selected Films:** *Star Wars* (77), *Corvette Summer* (78), *The Big Red One* (79), *The Empire Strikes Back* 80), *Return of the Jedi* (83).

## HAMILTON, George (1939- )

Born in Memphis, Tennessee, George Hamilton made his film debut in *Crime and Punishment USA* (59), but first caught attention as an effeminate youth in *Home From the Hill* (60). The early 1960s was the busiest period of Hamilton's career, with leads and supporting roles in a number of films including *By Love Possessed* (61), *The Victors* (63), and *Act One* (63) (in which he played Moss Hart). Meanwhile, Hamilton's playboy behavior generated a good deal of publicity, which increased when he courted the President's daughter, Lynda Bird Johnson. Hamilton developed the image of a 1930s-style screen glamour boy, affecting a cape and jet-set friends. Hamilton has never been a notably subtle actor, which has led to smaller-budget pictures. Besides doing much TV work, Hamilton has in the last decade starred in screen comedies – the Dracula parody, *Love at First Bite* (79), and *Zorro, the Gay Blade* (81).
**Selected Films:** *Crime and Punishment USA* (59), *Home from the Hill* (60), *All the Fine Young Cannibals* (60), *By Love Possessed* (61), *The Light in the Piazza* (62), *The Victors* (63), *Act One* (63), *Viva Maria* (65), *The Long Ride Home* (67), *The Man Who Loved Cat Dancing* (73), *The Magnificent Hustle* (77), *Love at First Bite* (79), *Zorro, the Gay Blade* (81).

## HAMILTON, Margaret (1902-1985)

Born in Cleveland, Ohio, Hamilton came to Hollywood in the early 1930s and with her inimitably pinched features was typecast in character roles as spinsters and servants, sometimes nice and sometimes nasty. Her immortality is secured by her unforgettable performance as the Wicked Witch of the West in *The Wizard of Oz* (39). Subsequently, she appeared in films and plays and TV commercials into the 1970s.
**Selected Films:** *Another Language* (33), *Way Down East* (35), *The Wizard of Oz* (39), *Invisible Woman* (41), *State of the Union* (48), *People Will Talk* (51), *Rosie* (67), *Brewster McCloud* (71), *Letters From Frank* (79).

## HAMILTON, Murray (1923-1986)

One of those supporting actors whose face you often recognize and whose name you often don't, Hamilton has played general-purpose roles in many movies from the 1950s on.
**Selected Films:** *Bright Victory* (50), *No Time for Sergeants* (58), *The Graduate* (67), *The Way We Were* (73), *The Amityville Horror* (79), *Brubaker* (80).

## HAMILTON, Neil (1899-1984)

A former model born in Lynn, Massachusetts, James Neil Hamilton became a major silent star in movies by D W Griffith and others, including *The White Rose* (23) and *Beau Geste* (26). Moving to character roles in talkies, he appeared now and then into the 1960s and played Commissioner Gordon in the TV series *Batman*.
**Selected Films:** *The Beloved Imposter* (18), *The White Rose* (23), *America* (24), *Isn't Life Wonderful?* (25), *Beau Geste* (26), *The Great Gatsby* (27), *The Dawn Patrol* (30), *Tarzan the Ape Man* (32), *The Little Shepherd of Kingdom Come* (61), *Madame X* (66), *Which Way to the Front?* (70).

## HAMMOND, Kay (1909-1980)

Born Dorothy Standing, the daughter of the English actor Sir Guy Standing, Hammond began her theatrical career in her native London. She worked in Hollywood from the late 1920s on, but also on stage. She played occasional leads in film in the United States and England, including the roles of Mary Lincoln in *Abraham Lincoln* (30) and Elvira, the ghostly wife in *Blithe Spirit* (45). She was married to the actor-manager John Clements and the actor John Standing is her son.
**Selected Films:** *Her Private Affair* (29), *Abraham Lincoln* (30), *Two on A Doorstep* (36), *Blithe Spirit* (45), *Call of the Blood* (48), *Five Golden Hours* (61).

## HAMPDEN, Walter (1879-1955)

Brooklyn-born, Harvard-educated Hampden had a distinguished career on the American stage in Shakespearean and other classical roles. His film appearances were infrequent and in supporting parts, but his career lasted from the silent era into the 1950s.
**Selected Films:** *The Dragon's Claw* (15), *The Hunchback of Notre Dame* (39), *They Died with Their Boots On* (41), *All About Eve* (50), *The Silver Chalice* (54), *The Prodigal* (55), *The Vagabond King* (56).

## HAMPSHIRE, Susan (1938- )

Hampshire was born in London, England. This charming, talented actress has been on stage since childhood and made her screen debut at the age of six. She began appearing in films again in 1959 in *Upstairs and Downstairs*. A demure actress, she is best known for her role as Fleur in the British television series *The Forsyte Saga*. She was also in *The Pallisers*.
**Selected Films:** *The Woman in the Hall* (47), *Upstairs and Downstairs* (59), *The Three Lives of Thomasina* (63), *Paris in the Month of August* (66), *A Time for Loving* (72), *Living Free* (72), *The Lonely Woman* (76), *Bang!* (77).

## HAMPTON, Hope (1899-1982)

Hope Hampton was one of the dewy-eyed heroines of the silent screen who appeared in mostly forgotten films. Her career did not survive the coming of sound.
**Selected Films:** *The Bait* (21), *The Gold Diggers* (23), *The Truth About Women* (24), *Lover's Island* (25), *The Unfair Sex* (26).

## HANEY, Carol (1929-1964)

An American-born dancer with Broadway experience who was often associated with Gene Kelly, Haney appeared in film musicals of the 1950s.
**Selected Films:** *Kiss Me Kate* (53), *Invitation to the Dance* (54), *The Pajama Game* (57).

## HANKS, Tom (1957- )

After a California childhood, Hanks began his acting career with Shakespearean walk-ons. His break came when he secured a role in the TV series *Bosom Buddies*. He has been playing wry young men since, most notably in the 1984 hit *Splash*, where he was the love object of a mermaid; that film paved the way to a busy slate of starring roles.
**Selected Films:** *Splash* (84), *Bachelor Party* (84), *Volunteers* (85), *The Man With One Red Shoe* (85), *The Money Pit* (86), *Nothing in Common* (86), *Everytime We Say Goodbye* (86), *Punchline* (87).

## HANNAH, Daryl (1961- )

Hannah studied drama while growing up in Chicago and made her screen debut at 17 with a bit part in *The Fury* (78). She first attracted notice in

*Blade Runner* (82). Her films have ranged from flops like *The Clan of the Cave Bear* (85) to hits like *Splash* (84), in which she played an amorous mermaid.
**Selected Films:** *The Fury* (78), *Blade Runner* (82), *Summer Lovers* (82), *The Pope of Greenwich Village* (84), *Reckless* (84), *Splash* (84), *The Clan of the Cave Bear* (85), *Legal Eagles* (86), *Roxane* (87).

## HARDING, Ann (1902-1981)

Born Dorothy Gatley at Fort Sam Houston in San Antonio, Texas, Harding made her film debut in 1929, after a successful Broadway career. The gentle-faced blonde, frequently typecast as a long-suffering patrician, received an Academy Award nomination for the role of Linda Seton in *Holiday* (30). She continued to work on stage throughout her film career. Harding retired from acting in 1965.
**Selected Films:** *Paris Bound* (29), *Holiday* (30), *The Animal Kingdom* (32), *Biography of a Batchelor Girl* (35), *Love from a Stranger* (37), *Mission to Moscow* (43), *The Magnificent Yankee* (51), *The Man in the Gray Flannel Suit* (56).

## HARDWICKE, Cedric (1893-1964)

This distinguished British stage and screen actor, admired both in Britain and America, was born in Rye, England, and made his London stage debut in 1912. Although he too frequently allowed his talents to be squandered on inferior material, he had a distinguished career in theater and films and for this was knighted in 1934. Settling in Hollywood in the late 1930s, Hardwicke played villains and Nazis until, after the war, he alternated between stage and screen.
**Selected Films:** *Nelson* (26), *Dreyfus* (31), *Nell Gwynn* (34), *Becky Sharp* (35), *King Solomon's Mines* (37), *On Borrowed Time* (39), *Stanley and Livingstone* (39), *Tom Brown's School Days* (40), *Victory* (40), *The Commandos Strike at Dawn* (42), *The Moon Is Down* (43), *Ivy* (47), *Nicholas Nickleby* (47), *I Remember Mama* (48), *The Winslow Boy* (48), *Rope* (48), *The Desert Fox* (51), *Richard III* (55), *The Ten Commandments* (56), *Baby Face Nelson* (57), *The Pumpkin Eater* (64).

## HARDY, Oliver: See LAUREL, Stanley

## HARLOW, Jean (1911-1937)

She was a star with sass. She was tough, flamboyant and had a sense of humor that, in her prime, was, tragically, seldom reported in the media. Harlow was the shimmering light of the silver screen, a wise-cracking sexy woman with radiant platinum blonde hair who made brunette vamps obsolete overnight. She was America's answer to exotic European screen goddesses. In the arms of men like Clark Gable and Franchot Tone she was as bold as brass. Born Harlean Carpenter in Kansas City, Missouri, this dentist's daughter married a wealthy young businessman when she was 16. They moved to Beverly Hills, California, and she began in minor film roles, first appearing in *Moran of the Marines* (28). Hanging around the Paramount lot, she was discovered by millionaire playboy and film maker Howard Hughes. It was 1930 and the era of talking pictures had arrived. Hughes was looking for a new kind of female star, one who could handle dialogue, whose style was modern, for *Hell's Angels* (30), which he was reconstructing from a silent to a sound picture. He found what he wanted in Harlow, and she was an immediate sensation. It was her style rather than her acting ability that brought Harlow success. With her bleached platinum blonde hair and a lusty, slim body, she portrayed three-dimensional women who liked sex at a time when this was unusual. Her natural comic talent and saucy vulgar charm emerged after she signed with MGM in 1932. In 1932 she made *Red Dust* with Clark Gable, who became her lifelong friend. She stole *Dinner at Eight* (33) from a cast of veterans, spoofing blonde sexpots as they wouldn't be spoofed again until Marilyn Monroe hit the screen with her own brand of good-natured self-parody. *Bombshell* (33) may have been her best film, in which she gleefully satirized her sex-driven image. Harlow's private life belied her cheery movie image. Divorced from her first

*Jean Harlow.*

husband in 1932, she married MGM executive Paul Bern, who committed suicide several months later, leaving behind a note which presumably hinted at impotence. Despite enormous adverse publicity, Harlow's career was unhurt. A third unhappy marriage followed and she was engaged to actor William Powell when work began on *Saratoga* (37), her last picture. While filming it, Harlow became ill. Hospitalized and treated for uremic poisoning, she died of a cerebral edema. She was 26 years old. MGM released *Saratoga* anyway, with a double filling in for Harlow in some scenes – shot from the back – and audiences went to see it in droves. Harlow's death robbed the silver screen of much of its glow, and her humor and glamor were sorely missed.
**Selected Films:** *Moran of the Marines* (28), *Double Whoopee* (29), *The Saturday Night Kid* (29), *The Love Parade* (30), *Hell's Angels* (30), *The Secret Six* (31), *The Iron Man* (31), *The Public Enemy* (31), *Goldie* (31), *Platinum Blonde* (31), *Three Wise Girls* (32), *Red Headed Woman* (32), *Red Dust* (32), *Dinner at Eight* (33), *Hold Your Man* (33), *Bombshell* (33), *The Girl from Missouri* (34), *Reckless* (35), *China Seas* (35), *Wife vs Secretary* (35), *Suzy* (36), *Libeled Lady* (36), *Personal Property* (37), *Saratoga* (37).

## HARPER, Valerie (1940- )

Born in Suffern, New York, Harper was a dancer at Radio City before finding success on TV as Mary Tyler Moore's amiable friend; she later starred in the spinoff series, *Rhoda*. Her movies have been few, mainly supporting roles in films including *Freebie and the Bean* (74).
**Selected Films:** *The Ones in Between* (72), *Freebie and the Bean* (74), *The Last Married Couple in America* (79), *Blame It On Rio* (83).

## HARRIS, Barbara (1936- )

Born Barbara Markowitz in Evanston, Illinois, Harris came up through Chicago's Second City troupe to success off and on Broadway. The attractive and intelligent actress's film appearances have been few, beginning with *A Thousand Clowns* (65) and including Hitchcock's final film, *Family Plot* (76). She received an Academy Award nomination for best actress for *Who is Harry Kellerman and Why Is He Saying These Terrible Things About Me?* (71).
**Selected Films:** *Oh Dad, Poor Dad . . ., Mama's Hung You in the Closet and I'm Feeling So Sad* (67), *The War Between Men and Women* (72), *Nashville* (75), *The Seduction of Joe Tynan* (79), *Second Hand Hearts* (80), *Peggy Sue Got Married* (86).

## HARRIS, Ed (1950- )

New Jersey-born Harris acted a good deal onstage before coming to the screen (Sam Shepard's play *Fool for Love* was written for him). His first screen role was as a killer in the Charles Bronson thriller *Borderline*(80). For some years, his air of simmering violence tended to get Harris cast in supporting parts as psychopaths and the like. His best-known role to date is as John Glenn – with a certain crazed look in the eye – in *The Right Stuff* (83). Harris is married to actress Amy Madigan.
**Selected Films:** *Borderline* (80), *Knightriders* (81), *Creepshow* (82), *Under Fire* (83), *The Right Stuff* (83), *Swing Shift* (84), *Places in the Heart* (84), *Alamo Bay* (85), *Walker* (87).

## HARRIS, Julie (1925- )

A noted drama teacher once said that there are some actors with whom you simply cannot share a stage because you will be ignored as though you were invisible. Harris is such an actress, a tiny woman with a presence so riveting that members of the audience can look at no one but her. In her 40 years as an actress she has won five Tonys for her work on the Broadway stage and was nominated for an Academy Award for Best Actress for her astonishing work in *The Member of the Wedding* (52), in which she played a 12-year-old girl, although she was herself 27. Harris was born in Grosse Point Park, Michigan. She studied at the Yale University School of the Theater and New York's Actors Studio. Her Broadway debut was in a short-lived play, *It's a Gift*. *The Member of the Wedding* was her first film, and she went on to perform stunningly in such blockbusters as *East of Eden* (55) and *The Haunting* (63).
**Selected Films:** *The Member of the Wedding* (52), *East of Eden* (55), *I Am a Camera* (56), *Requiem for a Heavyweight* (62) *The Haunting* (63), *Harper* (66), *Reflections in a Golden Eye* (67), *The Hiding Place* (75), *Voyage of the Damned* (76), *The Bell Jar* (79).

## HARRIS, Phil (1904- )

Born in Linton, Indiana, Harris got into show business as a drummer and bandleader. It was in the latter capacity that he first appeared in films; later the genial Harris acted in light films and on radio with his wife Alice Faye.
**Selected Films:** *Melody Cruise* (33), *Man About Town* (39), *I Love a Bandleader* (45), *Here Comes the Groom* (51), *The High and the Mighty* (54), *The Wheeler Dealers* (63), *The Cool Ones* (67).

## HARRIS, Richard (1932- )

Night club battles and on-set brawls have marked the colorful career of this talented actor. Harris has always drawn much of his charisma and strength from his earthy pugnaciousness, and his rugged 'man's man' image. Born in Limerick, Ireland, he attended the London Academy of Music and Dramatic Art, making his stage debut in 1956 and his movie debut in *Alive and Kicking* (58). Although trained as a classical actor, stardom came to him as a rugby-playing rebel in *This Sporting Life* (63). Besides films, he scored a major triumph as Richard Burton's replacement in the stage version

*Franco Nero, Richard Harris, Vanessa Redgrave* – Camelot *(64).*

of *Camelot*. He also played King Arthur in the film version of that musical, and in a successful stage revival which was televised.

**Selected Films:** *Alive and Kicking* (58), *The Wreck of the Mary Deare* (59), *The Guns of Navarone* (61), *Mutiny on the Bounty* (62), *This Sporting Life* (63), *The Red Desert* (64), *Camelot* (65), *The Molly Maguires* (69), *A Man Called Horse* (69), *Cromwell* (70), *Robin and Marian* (75), *The Cassandra Crossing* (77), *The Wild Geese* (78), *Tarzan the Ape Man* (81).

## HARRISON, Rex (1908- )

Born Reginald Carey in Huyton, England, Harrison went on to a distinguished career on stage and screen. Cool and debonair, he adds a unique diamond-sharp edge to sophisticated comedy, and has appeared in such movie classics as *Major Barbara* (40), with Wendy Hiller, and *Blithe Spirit* (45), with Margaret Rutherford. Harrison was nominated for an Academy Award for Best Actor for his role as Julius Caesar in *Cleopatra* (63), and won the Oscar the next year for his delightful portrayal of Professor Henry Higgins in *My Fair Lady* – a role he had made his own both on Broadway and in the movies. He has also played a Siamese potentate in *Anna and the King of Siam* (46), a supernatural sea captain in *The Ghost and Mrs Muir* (47), Saladin in *King Richard and the Crusaders* (54), a Roman emperor in *Cleopatra*, a pope in *The Agony and the Ecstacy* (65) and a man who could talk to animals in *Doctor Doolittle* (67). Three of his wives were actresses, Lilli Palmer, Kay Kendall and Rachel Roberts.

**Selected Films:** *The Great Game* (30), *School for Scandal* (30), *Men Are Not Gods* (36), *St Martin's Lane* (38), *The Citadel* (38), *Night Train to Munich* (40), *Major Barbara* (40), *Blithe Spirit* (45), *The Rake's Progress* (46), *Anna and the King of Siam* (46), *The Ghost and Mrs Muir* (47), *The Foxes of Harrow* (47), *Unfaithfully Yours* (48), *The Four Poster* (52), *King Richard and the Crusaders* (54), *The Constant Husband* (55), *The Reluctant Debutante* (58), *Midnight Lace* (60), *Cleopatra* (63), *My Fair Lady* (64), *The Agony and the Ecstacy* (65), *Doctor Doolittle* (67), *Staircase* (69), *The Fifth Musketeer* (77), *Shalimar* (78).

## HARRON, Robert (Bobby) (1894-1920)

Born in New York, Harron was a messenger boy for a movie studio when he caught the attention of D W Griffith. Harron went on to play juvenile leads and supporting roles in many classic films by Griffith and others, including *The Birth of a Nation* (15) and *Intolerance* (16). He died at the peak of his career in a handgun accident.
**Selected Films:** *Dr Sinkum* (07), *Enoch Arden* (11), *Man's Genesis* (12), *The Birth of a Nation* (15), *Intolerance* (16), *Hearts of the World* (18), *True Heart Susie* (19), *Coincidence* (21).

## HART, William S (1870-1946)

Hart was one of the giants in the history of western movies. He took the Western from the short one- and two-reelers of Broncho Billy Anderson and made it into full-length stories that depicted the Old West with realism and poetic feeling. He made silent westerns that appealed to adults as well as children and he made them in his own way, putting his personal vision into each one. Acting as director and sometimes writer as well as a star, Hart made films that achieved immense popularity and made him one of the most famous of movie stars. He was born in Newburgh, New York, but spent much of his early years in the West, which he loved. At the age of 19 Hart moved to New York City, where he became such a prominent Shakespearean actor that it was rumored that the initial 'S' in his name stood for Shakespeare. It actually stood for his middle name, Surrey. During the 1890s Hart began appearing in western dramas on Broadway, such as *The Squaw Man, The Virginian* and *The Trail of the Lonesome Pine*. In 1914 Hart started making movies for his friend, producer and director Thomas H Ince. A villain in two-reelers, he soon became a star and went on to become a superstar. He had known real cowboys and Indians in his youth and his vivid memories of the West made him approach westerns from a new angle. Insisting on realism and careful reconstructions of sets and costumes, Hart westerns were strong on plot and character. He created the villain turned hero, the man who starts out as evil but who is redeemed at the end of the film by a virtuous act. Unlike most of his contemporaries, Hart refused to romanticize and prettify the West. The towns in his films were dusty and filled with shacks, and Hart was serious and unsmiling riding his pinto pony Fritz. Instead of being glamorous adventure films, his movies had the feel of a documentary. There was nothing like them before and there has never really been anything quite like them since. Hart's popularity dwindled when action heroes strong on stunts, such as Tom Mix and Buck Jones, caught the public's fancy. In 1925 Hart sued United Artists because he felt the studio had mishandled the distribution of his last film, *Tumbleweeds* (25). He won his case, and although the movie turned out to be a critical and commercial success, Hart retired and wrote western novels. His influence on the western film cannot be exaggerated.
**Selected Films:** *The Fugitive* (13), *The Disciple* (15), *The Captive God* (16), *The Return of Draw Egan* (16), *Hell's Hinges* (17), *Blue Blazes Rawden* (18), *Wagon Tracks* (18), *Sand* (20), *White Oak* (21), *Travellin' On* (22), *Wild Bill Hickok* (23), *Tumbleweeds (25).*

*William S Hart –* Tumbleweeds *(25).*

## HARTLEY, Mariette (1941- )

New York-born Hartley made her film debut with a supporting role in Sam Peckinpah's *Ride the High Country* (62). Since then she has appeared occasionally in movies and often in TV series, among them *The Incredible Hulk*, and in some wry commercials for Polaroid with James Garner. In 1986 she became an anchor on a morning network news program.
**Selected Films:** *Ride the High Country* (62), *Marnie* (64), *Marooned* (69), *Improper Channels* (81), *O'Hara's Wife* (83).

## HARVEY, Laurence (1928-1973)

Harvey was born Larushka Mischa Skikne in Lithuania, but he was raised in South Africa. He then moved to England to study acting and worked his way slowly from British B pictures to top Hollywood productions. His first film was *House of Darkness* (48). In 1959 he was nominated for an Academy Award for Best Actor for his work in *Room at the Top*, which co-starred Simone Signoret as his mistress. Although sometimes he was

accused of being cold and uninspiring, he created several memorable screen roles and was a success as *Henry V* at the Old Vic. He died of cancer at the age of 45.
**Selected Films:** *House of Darkness* (48), *Cairo Road* (49), *The Black Rose* (50), *I Believe in You* (52), *Romeo and Juliet* (54), *King Richard and the Crusaders* (54), *I Am a Camera* (55), *Storm Over the Nile* (56), *Room at the Top* (59), *Expresso Bongo* (59), *The Alamo* (60), *Butterfield 8* (60), *Summer and Smoke* (61), *Walk on the Wild Side* (62), *The Manchurian Candidate* (63), *Of Human Bondage* (64), *Darling* (65), *A Dandy in Aspic* (67), *The Magic Christian* (70), *Night Watch* (73).

## HASSO, Signe (1910- )

Born in Stockholm, Hasso's stage career began in her native Sweden and she made her first films there using her real name, Signe Lars. She went to Hollywood in the early 1940s and for a decade or so played cool, strong leading roles. Her career continued in Sweden and the United States with occasional appearances into the 1970s.
**Selected Films:** *House of Silence* (33), *Journey for Margaret* (42), *Heaven Can Wait* (43), *The House on 92nd Street* (45), *To the Ends of the Earth* (48), *Crisis* (50), *Picture Mommy Dead* (66), *The Black Bird* (75), *I Never Promised You a Rose Garden* (77).

*Kim Novak, Laurence Harvey* – Of Human Bondage *(64).*

## HATFIELD, Hurd (1918- )

Born in New York, Hatfield studied drama in England and came to films from Broadway. After playing the lead in *The Picture of Dorian Gray* (45), the darkly handsome actor seemed primed for stardom, but his film roles remained occasional and he spent most of his career on the stage.
**Selected Films:** *Dragon Seed* (44), *The Picture of Dorian Gray* (45), *The Diary of a Chambermaid* (46), *Joan of Arc* (48), *The Left Handed Gun* (58), *King of Kings* (61), *El Cid* (61), *The Boston Strangler* (68), *Von Richthofen and Brown* (71), *Crimes of the Heart* (86).

## HATTON, Raymond (1887-1971)

Hatton, born in Red Oak, Iowa, came to films from the stage and appeared in silents for Cecil B De Mille and others. In the 1920s he made several successful comedies with Wallace Beery. Thereafter he played the sidekick of stars like Johnny Mack Brown, Buck Jones and others, in hundreds of westerns.
**Selected Films:** *The Circus Man* (14), *Oliver Twist* (16), *The Hunchback of Notre Dame* (23), *Behind the Front* (26), *The Squaw Man* (31), *Black Gold* (47), *Shake, Rattle, and Rock* (56), *In Cold Blood* (67).

## HAUER, Rutger (1944- )

Born in Amsterdam, Holland, Hauer starred in the Dutch film *Soldier of Orange* (77), before moving to the United States. His blond and rather exotic good looks get him cast as villains and psychopaths.
**Selected Films:** *Soldier of Orange* (77), *Blade Runner* (82), *Eureka* (83), *Ladyhawke* (85), *The Hitcher* (86), *Wanted Dead or Alive* (87).

## HAVER, June (1926- )

Born June Stovenour in Rock Island, Illinois, Haver was a singer before moving to Hollywood, where she starred mostly in musicals of the 1940s. Retiring in the early 1950s, she was briefly a novice nun before marrying Fred MacMurray.
**Selected Films:** *The Gang's All Here* (43), *The Dolly Sisters* (45), *Scudda Hoo, Scudda Hay* (48), *Look for the Silver Lining* (49), *I'll Get By* (50), *The Girl Next Door* (53).

## HAVOC, June (1916- )

Born Ellen Hovick in Seattle, Washington, the younger sister of high-class stripper Gypsy Rose Lee, Havoc was a child vaudeville performer and movie bit player. She also still holds a record for marathon dancing in 1933. After success in Broadway's *Pal Joey* she moved to Hollywood in 1941. Despite a good launching, the blonde beauty appeared mostly in routine productions.
**Selected Films:** *Four Jacks and a Jill* (42), *Brewster's Millions* (45), *Gentleman's Agreement* (47), *Once a Thief* (50), *The Private Files of J Edgar Hoover* (78), *Can't Stop the Music* (80).

## HAWKINS, Jack (1910-1973)

Hawkins, the strong and dominant British actor, was born in London and began his theater career at the age of 13. He made his film debut in *Birds of Prey* (30) at the age of 20. But he had to wait until middle age before becoming an international star. His first wife was the noted British-born stage actress Jessica Tandy. A prolific performer, Hawkins was dynamic in either leads or character roles, generally playing tough decisive men of action who retained their charm and sense of humor. In 1966 he lost his voice following an operation for cancer of the larynx and his subsequent minor appearances in films were dubbed.
**Selected Films:** *Birds of Prey* (30), *The Lodger* (32), *Peg of Old Drury* (35), *The Fallen Idol* (48), *State Secret* (50), *Angels One Five* (52), *The Cruel Sea* (52), *The Bridge on the River Kwai* (58), *The League of Gentlemen* (59), *Ben Hur* (59), *Lawrence of Arabia* (62), *Rampage* (63), *Zulu* (64), *Shalako* (68), *Nicholas and Alexandra* (71), *Theatre of Blood* (73), *Tales That Witness Madness* (73).

*Goldie Hawn in* Private Benjamin *(80).*

## HAWN, Goldie (1945- )

Although she often plays dumb blondes, Hawn isn't one, having emerged after her start on television's *Laugh-In* as a fine comedienne, a sensitive actress and a clever producer. Born in Washington, DC, she had made only one film, the forgettable Disney effort, *The One and Only Genuine Original Family Band* (68) before appearing in *Cactus Flower* (69). No one thought that she would be able to match and almost outshine such established talents as Ingrid Bergman and Walter Matthau as an infatuated young woman, but she did, and won the Academy Award for Best Supporting Actress. She was nominated as Best Actress for her work in *Private Benjamin* (80) – her biggest hit so far.
**Selected Films:** *The One and Only Genuine Original Family Band* (68), *Cactus Flower* (69), *There's a Girl in My Soup* (70), *Butterflies Are Free* (72), *$* (72), *The Sugarland Express* (73), *Shampoo* (75), *The Duchess and the Dirtwater Fox* (76), *Foul Play* (78), *Private Benjamin* (80), *Best Friends* (82), *Swing Shift* (83), *Protocol* (84), *Wild Cats* (86).

## HAYAKAWA, Sessue (1889-1973)

Born Kitaro Hayakawa in Chiba, Sessue Hayakawa began acting on the stage in his native Japan. In the early years of the century he came to the United States to study at the University of Chicago, after which he returned to Japan and formed a theater company that toured America and caught the attention of moviemakers. In 1914 Hayakawa and his wife starred in *The Typhoon.* His darkly intense image and acting style which

was notably realistic for the time, made him an overnight sensation. But Hollywood seemed unprepared for an Oriental romantic leading man at that time. In 1915 he was cast as a villain in Cecil B De Mille's *The Cheat*, and for the rest of his extensive career in silents Hayakawa tended to play such Yellow Peril roles. His American movie appearances declined after 1923. In the next three decades he appeared sporadically, including in the 1949 Bogart film *Tokyo Joe*. Finally in 1957 Hayakawa made a much-heralded comeback as a Japanese prison camp commander in *The Bridge on the River Kwai*. The role earned him an Oscar nomination for Best Supporting Actor, and over the next few years he appeared in several American movies.
**Selected Films:** *The Typhoon* (14), *The Cheat* (15), *The Ambassador's Envoy* (15), *The Tong Man* (19), *Daughter of the Dragon* (29), *Macao* (39), *Tokyo Joe* (49), *The Bridge on the River Kwai* (57), *The Geisha Boy* (59), *The Swiss Family Robinson* (60), *The Big Wave* (62), *The Daydreamer* (66).

## HAYDEN, Russell (1912-1981)

A native of Chico, California, Hayden emerged from working behind the camera to appear in mostly Westerns from the mid-1930s to the early 1950s. Best-known as Hopalong Cassidy's sidekick, Lucky, Hayden later produced TV westerns. His real name was Pate Lucid.
**Selected Films:** *Hills of Old Wyoming* (37), *'Neath Canadian Skies* (46), *Silver City* (49), *Valley of Fire* (51).

## HAYDEN, Sterling (1917-1986)

Born Sterling Walter Relyea in Montclair, New Jersey, Sterling Hayden ran away to sea at 15. Earning his captain's ticket at 22, the handsome and rangy Hayden turned to films soon after appearing in *Virginia* (41) and in the same year finding acclaim in the lead of *Bahama Passage*. Thereafter, and billed for a time as 'The Beautiful Blonde Viking God,' Hayden was a staple in Hollywood, though for the duration of his career he thought very little of his acting ability or of acting in general, rarely took his films seriously, and escaped to the sea every chance he got. Nonetheless, besides appearing in a number of routine westerns and adventure movies, Hayden made his mark in several solid roles in notable pictures; among them were his crook in John Huston's *The Asphalt Jungle* (50) and, most memorably, his role as the demented General Jack D Ripper in Stanley Kubrick's *Dr Strangelove* (63). In his films, Hayden had a unique screen image – taciturn, tough, but also enigmatic. In private life he was not always as uncompromising as he was onscreen – he cooperated with the House of Un-American Activities Committee in the early 1950s, denouncing former colleagues as Communists. (Soon after, he played the lead as a gunfighter in Nicolas Ray's offbeat film *Johnny Guitar* (54), a fable of mob rule that symbolized the Red scare.) Hayden published two books, the autobiography *Wanderer* (63), in which he repented his House testimony, and the 1978 novel *Voyage*. He was married to actress Madeleine Carroll from 1942 to 1946.
**Selected Films:** *Virginia* (41), *Bahama Passage* (41), *El Paso* (49), *The Asphalt Jungle* (50), *The Golden Hawk* (52), *Prince Valiant* (54), *Johnny Guitar* (54), *The Last Command* (55), *Dr Strangelove* (63), *Hard Contract* (69), *The Godfather* (72), *1900* (76), *Winter Kills* (79), *Lighthouse of Chaos* (83).

## HAYDN, Richard (1905-1985)

After starring in musical revues in his native Britain, Haydn brought his inimitable adenoidal voice and antic personality to mostly small parts in Hollywood. He also directed several films including *Dear Wife* (50).
**Selected Films:** *Ball of Fire* (41), *Cluny Brown* (46), *The Green Years* (46), *Sitting Pretty* (47), *Jupiter's Darling* (55), *The Lost World* (60), *The Sound of Music* (65), *Young Frankenstein* (74).

## HAYES, Gabby (1885-1969)

Born in Wellesville, New York, George Hayes played in vaudeville before going into silent films in the 1920s. For a while he was typed as a villain, then became the bewhiskered old geezer who was the sidekick of Hopalong Cassidy and Roy Rogers.
**Selected Films:** *Why Women Marry* (23), *The Rainbow Man* (29), *Tumbling Tumbleweeds* (35), *Mr Deeds Goes to Town* (36), *Hopalong Rides Again* (38), *Tall in the Saddle* (44), *Pals of the Golden West* (51).

## HAYES, Helen (1900- )

Born Helen Hayes Brown in Washington, DC, she is truly 'the first lady of the American theater' and even had a New York theater named after her. She made her stage debut at the age of five in Washington, and her Broadway debut at the age of nine. Her first film was made when she was ten. Having grown up in theaters and films, she has seldom left them. Her career is marked as much by achievement as by longevity. Her first talking picture, *The Sin of Madelon Claudet* (31) won her an Academy Award for Best Actress, and she won the Drama League of New York Medal for her tour de force performance in *Victoria Regina* in 1935. Hayes won a Tony for *Time Remembered* in 1958, and another Oscar in 1970 for *Airport*, clearly a show of respect for past performances rather than an acknowledgment of any special merit for her appearance in that film. Hayes is the widow of writer Charles MacArthur and mother of actor James MacArthur.
**Selected Films:** *Jean and the Calico Doll* (10), *The Weavers of Life* (17), *The Sin of Madelon Claudet* (31), *Arrowsmith* (31), *A Farewell to Arms* (32), *The White Sister* (33), *What Every Woman Knows* (34), *Stage Door Canteen* (43), *Anastasia* (56), *Airport* (70), *Candleshoe* (77).

## HAYMES, Dick (1916-1980)

Dick Haymes was born Richard Benjamin Haymes in Buenos Aires, Argentina, to a American family, and grew up around the world – the confusion of his background and citizenship a source of later troubles. He got into show business by way of radio announcing and singing with bands, by the 1940s becoming one of the most popular vocalists of the time. That led to screen roles, the first being *Irish Eyes Are Smiling* (44) (he had previously done screen bit parts). There followed musical roles in a number of big-budget films including *State Fair* (45) and *One Touch of Venus* (48), but Haymes never managed to make himself into a strong screen performer. He was married several times (including to actresses Joanne Dru and Rita Hayworth) and had spats with the authorities, the latter due to his avoiding the World War II draft by registering as an alien. In 1953 Haymes was denied resident status. Though he returned finally to the United States, his film and singing career had already peaked.
**Selected Films:** *Dramatic School* (38), *Du Barry was a Lady* (43), *Irish Eyes Are Smiling* (44), *Four Jills in a Jeep* (44), *Diamond Horseshoe* (45), *State Fair* (45), *The Shocking Miss Pilgrim* (47), *One Touch of Venus* (48), *All Ashore* (53).

## HAYWARD, Louis (1909-1985)

Born Seafield Grant in Johannesburg, South Africa, Hayward acted on the London stage before moving to Broadway and then on to Hollywood. For some two decades the elegant-featured Hayward was a familiar leading man in mostly adventure films, many of them swashbucklers – he played the Count of Monte Cristo (twice), D'Artagnan, and similar roles. He also starred in some TV series, among them *The Survivors*. His first wife was actress Ida Lupino.
**Selected Films:** *Self-Made Lady* (32), *Anthony Adverse* (36), *The Man in the Iron Mask* (39), *The Black Arrow* (48), *Captain Blood* (50), *Royal African Rifles* (53), *The Search for Bridey Murphy* (56), *Chuka* (67), *Terror in the Wax Museum* (73).

## HAYWARD, Susan (1918-1975)

This beautiful husky-voiced, red-haired actress was born Edythe Marrener in Brooklyn, New York. She was an actress who dignified any movie she was in, even the flops, of which there were many. She became a model whose photograph came to the attention of Hollywood producers, and her first role was a bit part in *Hollywood Hotel* (37). It was in *The Hairy Ape* (44) that she established herself as a star. A serious actress, she found her niche playing tough, aggressive women, often those on the skids. She played an alcoholic in *Smash-Up* (47), a Southern belle in *Tap Roots* (48) and Bathsheba in *David and Bathsheba* (51). When she made *With a Song in My Heart* (52), her box office standing was

*Susan Hayward in* Back Street *(61).*

at its peak. She was nominated for an Academy Award for Best Actress for *I'll Cry Tomorrow* (55), playing the role of singer Lillian Roth and her battle with alcohol. She won the Oscar for best actress in *I Want to Live* (58), playing a call girl convicted of murder and sentenced to be executed. In 1955 a court case involving her ex-husband, Jess Barker, over the custody of their twin sons, led to Hayward's attempted suicide. She died of a brain tumor when she was only 56.
**Selected Films:** *Hollywood Hotel* (37), *Beau Geste* (39), *Adam Had Four Sons* (41), *Reap the Wild Wind* (42), *Jack London* (43), *And Now Tomorrow* (44), *The Hairy Ape* (44), *Smash-Up* (47), *Tap Roots* (48), *Tulsa* (49), *My Foolish Heart* (49), *House of Strangers* (49), *I Can Get It for You Wholesale* (51), *David and Bathsheba* (51), *With a Song in My Heart* (52), *The Snows of Kilimanjaro* (52), *I'll Cry Tomorrow* (55), *Top Secret Affair* (57), *I Want to Live* (58), *The Marriage-Go-Round* (60), *Back Street* (61), *The Honey Pot* (67), *Valley of the Dolls* (67), *The Revengers* (72).

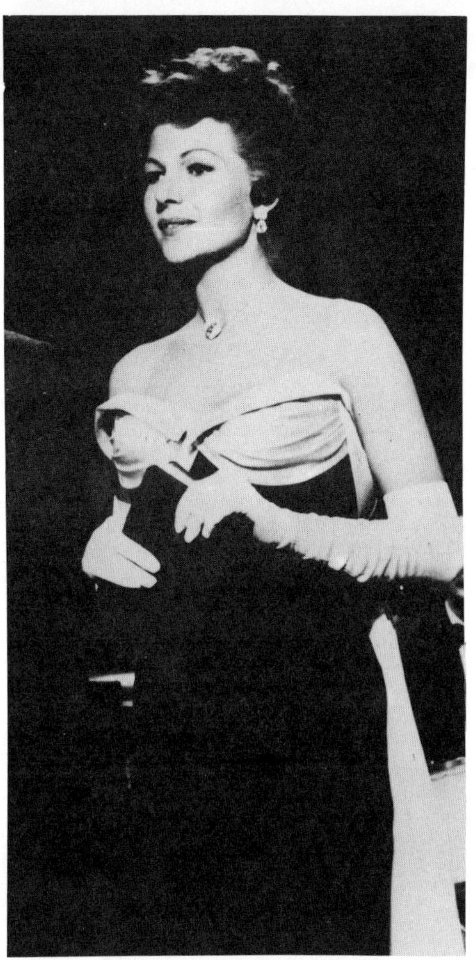

*Rita Hayworth in* Pal Joey *(57).*

## HAYWORTH, Rita (1918-1987)

Hayworth was the love goddess of the 1940s, so glamorous, seductive and beautiful that even the camera fell in love with her. Shy and inhibited in private life, she came alive before the camera and it repaid her, making her a lovely vision in black and white and a blaze of ruby glory in Technicolor. She was born Margarita Carmen Cansino in Brooklyn, the daughter of Eduardo Cansino, a well-known Latin dancer, and she began her dancing career when she was a mere six years old. A teenager when she began dancing in films, her naturally dark hair and Spanish background led her to being stereotyped at first as a sultry señorita. She slimmed down, took acting lessons, changed her name and her hairline and shed her old persona. A series of B pictures led to *Only Angels Have Wings* (39) and *The Strawbery Blonde* (41), where she appeared for the first time (ironically, because the film was shot in black and white) with red hair. Soon Hayworth was Columbia Picture's top star, a versatile performer who could play 'good girls' and temptresses, appear in straight romantic films and, despite dubbed singing, dance her way through a musical very nicely. During World War II the servicemen loved her. Off screen, she married Hollywood's genius producer, director, actor, Orson Welles. The couple had one child, a daughter, Rebecca. Welles and Hayworth were divorced in 1945. In 1948 she met Aly Khan, Europe's reigning playboy and the son of the fabulously wealthy Aga Khan. By then Hayworth was one of the world's most desirable women, having made *Gilda* (46), co-starring with Glenn Ford, the smash hit movie which took Hollywood out of the wholesome era forever. The romance of Rita and Aly made headline news. But Aly remained a playboy and the marriage ended in 1951. The couple had one daughter, Yasmin. Hayworth went back to making movies. Her star quality still shone but problems surfaced. She began forgetting her lines and uncharacteristically showed up late on the set. Two unhappy marriages followed. Some blamed her troubles on alcoholism but it turned out that she was a victim of Alzheimer's Disease, which results in premature aging. However, nothing can ever diminish the glamorous image of Rita Hayworth on film.

**Selected Films:** *Dante's Inferno* (35), *Under the Pampas Moon* (35), *Human Cargo* (36), *Only Angels Have Wings* (39), *The Lady in Question* (40), *The Strawberry Blonde* (41), *Blood and Sand* (41), *You'll Never Get Rich* (41), *My Gal Sal* (42), *You Were Never Lovelier* (42), *Cover Girl* (44), *Tonight and Every Night* (45), *Gilda* (46), *Down to Earth* (47), *The Lady from Shanghai* (48), *The Loves of Carmen* (48), *Miss Sadie Thompson* (53), *Fire Down Below* (57), *Pal Joey* (57), *Separate Tables* (58), *They Came to Cordura* (59), *Circus World* (64), *The Money Trap* (66), *The Rover* (68), *The Road to Salina* (70), *The Wrath of God* (72).

## HEALY, Ted (1886-1937)

A bluff vaudevillian usually equipped with a cigar, Healy created the Three Stooges and appeared in a few films.

**Selected Films:** *Soup to Nuts* (30), *The Band Plays On* (34), *Mad Love* (35), *Hollywood Hotel* (37).

## HECKART, Eileen (1919- )

Born in Columbus, Ohio, Heckart has spent most of her career on Broadway and other stage work. Tall and slender, she has appeared occasionally and memorably as a character actress in films, winning an Academy Award for Best Supporting Actress for her role in *Butterflies Are Free* (72). Her TV movies include *FDR: The Last Year.*

**Selected Films:** *The Bad Seed* (56), *Bus Stop* (56), *Heller in Pink Tights* (60), *Up the Down Staircase* (68), *Butterflies Are Free* (72), *Burnt Offerings* (77), *Heartbreak Ridge* (86).

## HEDISON, David (1926- )

David Hedison, born Ara Heditsian and known for a while as Al Hedison, has been a leading man and supporting player in film and TV since the 1950s. Among his TV appearances were in the series *Voyage to the Bottom of the Sea*.
**Selected Films:** *The Enemy Below* (57), *The Fly* (58), *The Lost World* (60), *The Greatest Story Ever Told* (65), *Live and Let Die* (73), *North Sea Hijack* (80).

## HEDREN, Tippi (1935- )

Born in Lafayette, Minnesota, Elizabeth Hedren was a model before being discovered by Alfred Hitchcock, who groomed her as another of his cool blonde leading ladies in the Grace Kelly tradition. She starred in *The Birds* (63), but while making *Marnie* (64), Hedren fell out with Hitchcock, to the considerable detriment of the latter film. Her movie appearances thereafter were infrequent. She is the mother of actress Melanie Griffith.
**Selected Films:** *The Petty Girl* (50), *The Birds* (63), *Marnie* (64), *A Countess From Hong Kong* (66), *Tiger by the Tail* (68), *The Harrad Experiment* (73), *Roar* (82).

## HEFLIN, Van (1910-1971)

Born Emmett Evan Heflin in Walters, Oklahoma, Van Heflin took a job on a seagoing freighter after high school, then gravitated to acting in the late 1920s. After an abortive Broadway career he earned acting degrees in his home state and at Yale and returned to Broadway, where he played for two years with Katharine Hepburn and Joseph Cotten in *The Philadelphia Story*. By that point Heflin had already made some movies, including his film debut, *A Woman Rebels* (36), with Katharine Hepburn. His career took off in the early 1940s in films such as *Santa Fe Trail* (40) and *Johnny Eager* (41); for the latter he won the Academy Award for Best Supporting Actor for his role as a boozy scholar. After a few outings as a romantic lead, Heflin settled into supporting roles; as he said of himself: 'I've never played the same part twice, and no one has ever said "This is a Heflin character" like they've said about Cary Grant and Clark Gable . . . I'm a character actor, always have been.' His stolid, purposeful, and usually sympathetic image was seen to best advantage in his role as a brave rancher in the classic Western *Shane* (53). Never a major star, Heflin nonetheless proved durable both on screen and stage, and he rarely appeared in an unsuccessful film.
**Selected Films:** *A Woman Rebels* (36), *The Outcasts of Poker Flat* (37), *Santa Fe Trail* (40), *Johnny Eager* (41), *Kid Glove Killer* (42), *Presenting Lily Mars* (43), *Green Dolphin Street* (47), *The Three Musketeers* (48), *The Prowler* (51), *Shane* (53), *Battle Cry* (57), *Patterns* (56), *10 to Yuma* (57), *They Came to Codura* (59), *The Greatest Story Ever Told* (65), *Airport* (69).

## HEGGIE, O P (1879-1936)

Born in Scotland, Heggie was a familiar stage character actor before moving to Hollywood to play similar roles in films of the 1930s. Among his most famous roles was that of the blind hermit in *Bride of Frankenstein* (35).
**Selected Films:** *The Mysterious Dr Fu Manchu* (29), *Smiling Through* (32), *The Count of Monte Cristo* (34), *Bride of Frankenstein* (35), *Prisoner of Shark Island* (36).

## HELM, Brigitte (1906- )

Born Gisele Eve Schittenhelm in Berlin, Germany, the beautiful Helm made her film debut in one of the classic films, Fritz Lang's *Metropolis* (26). That film, however, was also the peak of her career. After a dozen or so movies in Europe and England, her career did not continue through the 1930s.
**Selected Films:** *Metropolis* (26), *The Loves of Jeanne Ney* (27), *Countess of Monto Cristo* (31), *L'Atlantide* (31), *The Blue Danube* (34), *Ein idealer Batte* (35).

## HELPMANN, Robert (1909-1986)

Helpmann born in Mount Gambier, Australia, was a ballet dancer, who turned to choreography, then became a stage and screen actor. He combined all three roles in the classic ballet movie *The Red Shoes* (48). In the dance film *Don Quixote* (73) he played the title role and co-directed. He was knighted in 1950.
**Selected Films:** *One of Our Aircraft Is Missing* (42), *Henry V* (44), *The Red Shoes* (48), *Tales of Hoffman* (50), *Chitty Chitty Bang Bang* (68), *Alice's Adventures in Wonderland* (72), *Don Quixote* (73), *The Mango Tree* (77), *Patrick* (78).

## HEMINGWAY, Margaux (1955- )

Granddaughter of writer Ernest Hemingway, Margaux was a popular fashion model before making a much-ballyhooed but ultimately rather floppy film debut in the thriller *Lipstick* (76). More promisingly, the film introduced her sister Mariel. She has made few screen appearances since.
**Selected Films:** *Lipstick* (76), *Killer Fish* (80), *They Call Me Bruce* (82).

## HEMINGWAY, Mariel (1961- )

Hemingway, the granddaughter of writer Ernest Hemingway, was born in Ketchum, Idaho. Her film career began when she played a child rape victim in a B movie called *Lipstick* (76) that starred her older sister Margaux. Woody Allen spotted this 15-year-old in the film and cast her as his teenage girlfriend in *Manhattan* (79), for which she received an Academy Award nomination.
**Selected Films:** *Lipstick* (76), *Manhattan* (79), *Personal Best* (82), *Star 80* (83), *Mean Season* (85), *Creator* (85).

## HEMMINGS, David (1941- )

Hemmings' slight build and expressive eyes give him a distinctive appearance. Born in Guildford, England, he began his career as a boy soprano, later turning to night clubs, stage and television. After appearing in many B pictures in England, he became a leading man who suddenly seemed to have the acceptable image for the late 1960s. He became a star with *Blow Up* (66). In addition to playing leads in movies, he also directs and writes novels. He was married to actress Gayle Hunnicutt.

**Selected Films:** *The Rainbow Jacket* (54), *No Trees in the Street* (59), *Live It Up* (63), *Blow Up* (66), *Camelot* (67), *The Charge of the Light Brigade* (68), *Barbarella* (68), *The Love Machine* (71), *Islands in the Stream* (77), *Just a Gigolo* (78), *Murder by Decree* (79), *Man, Woman and Child* (82).

## HENDRIX, Wanda (1928-1981)

Born in Jacksonville, Florida, Dixie Wanda Hendrix made a splash as a teenager in *Confidential Agent* (45). After a promising start, though, the dark-haired, wide-featured beauty was relegated to leads in routine action pictures. She was briefly married to Audie Murphy.

**Selected Films:** *Confidential Agent* (45), *Ride the Pink Horse* (47), *Prince of Foxes* (49), *The Highwayman* (52), *The Black Dakotas* (54), *Stage to Thunder Rock* (64), *The Oval Portrait* (74).

## HENIE, Sonja (1910-1969)

The dimpled blonde from Oslo, Norway, with the beautiful smile and the great athletic ability was an Olympic figure skating champion. She won the gold medal in women's single figure skating at the Winter Olympics in 1928, 1932 and 1936. Following the 1936 meet, she went to Hollywood, to make her first movie, *One in a Million* (36). Henie appeared in light musicals in the 1930s and 1940s designed to show off her skills on the ice.

**Selected Films:** *Syv Dager for Elisabeth* (27), *One in a Million* (36), *Thin Ice* (37), *Happy Landing* (38), *My Lucky Star* (38), *Second Fiddle* (39), *Sun Valley Serenade* (41), *Iceland* (42), *Wintertime* (43), *The Countess of Monte Cristo* (48), *Hello London* (58).

## HENREID, Paul (1908- )

Born Paul von Hernreid in Trieste, which was then part of Austria, the gallant, handsome and cosmopolitan actor fled to Britain with the rise of Hitler. He then went to Hollywood where his immobile good looks made him a suitable leading man opposite a number of strong-willed women, for example Bette Davis in *Now Voyager* (42). His most famous movie was *Casablanca* (42), in which he played Ingrid Bergman's husband, the anti-Nazi leader Victor Lazlo. In the 1950s he began directing TV shows, and films, including *Dead Ringer* (64).

*David Hemmings in* Blow-Up *(67).*

**Selected Films:** *Hohe Schule* (34), *Goodbye, Mr Chips* (39), *Night Train to Munich* (40), *Now Voyager* (42), *Casablanca* (42), *Devotion* (46), *Song of Love* (47), *Holiday for Lovers* (59), *Operation Crossbow* (65), *Exorcist II: The Heretic* (77).

## HENRY, Buck (1930- )

Born Buck Zuckerman in New York, Henry came to films by way of playwriting, improvisational theater, and writing for TV comedy shows. Working on the script and in the cast of the offbeat movie *The Troublemaker* (64), Henry made himself a name as a comic screenwriter and acerbic actor. He received an Oscar nomination for co-writing the script of *Heaven Can Wait* (78).

**Selected Films:** *The Troublemaker* (64), *The Graduate* (67), *Catch-22* (70), *The Man Who Fell to Earth* (76), *Gloria* (80).

## HENRY, William (1918- )

Born in Los Angeles, Henry played movie bit parts as a child, then juvenile roles. With his strong and agreeable features and stolid acting style, he settled into leads in dozens of B movies and occasional supporting roles in A pictures.

**Selected Films:** *Lord Jim* (26), *Tarzan Escapes* (36), *Sweater Girl* (42), *Mr Roberts* (55), *The Man Who Shot Liberty Valance* (62), *Taggart* (64).

*Audrey Hepburn in* Breakfast at Tiffanys *(61) with George Peppard.*

## HEPBURN, Audrey (1929-        )

Born Audrey Hepburn-Ruston near Brussels, Belgium, of Dutch-Irish parentage, she had a refined image almost from the beginning of her career. Hepburn had played only minor movie and stage roles until she got her big break at the age of 22 when she starred in the Broadway play *Gigi*. This brought her to the attention of director William Wyler, who gave her the lead in the film, *Roman Holiday* (53), opposite Gregory Peck. She won the Academy Award for Best Actress in this, her first starring vehicle, at the age of 24. The film also gained her enormous popularity. In an age when the screen was dominated by bosomy sex goddesses, Hepburn, the elegant elfin gamine, was different. Her enduring charm is that she has always seemed proper without being stiff, spunky without being spoiled. Her reed-slim, high-fashion face and figure, and her breathy, upper-class accent have contributed to her appeal. Hepburn is best known for light comedy, but she also excells in more serious roles. She was the perfect Natasha in an otherwise overstuffed 1956 version of *War and Peace*. She was beautifully introspective in *The Nun's Story* (59). She was magnificent as a blind woman beset by hoodlums in *Wait Until Dark* (67). Somehow, however, she never seemed to attain the superstar status for which she once seemed destined. She lives mainly in Europe and, although she is still lovely, she had made few films since the late 1960s. She was married to actor Mel Ferrer from 1954 to 1968.

**Selected Films:** *Nederland in 7 Lessen* (48), *One Wild Oat* (51), *The Lavender Hill Mob* (51), *Roman Holiday* (53), *Sabrina* (54), *War and Peace* (56), *Funny Face* (57), *Love in the Afternoon* (57), *The Nun's Story* (59), *Green Mansions* (59), *Breakfast at Tiffany's* (61), *The Children's Hour* (62), *Charade* (63), *My Fair Lady* (64), *How to Steal a Million* (66), *Two for the Road* (67), *Wait Until Dark* (67), *Robin and Marian* (76), *Bloodline* (79), *They All Laughed* (81).

## HEPBURN, Katharine (1907-        )

Hepburn may well be the most respected actress ever to emerge from Hollywood because she has never confused her movie star image with her strong individualism. This highly-charged and well-bred woman has always done exactly what she wanted to do, and has never been accused of reticence or vulgarity. Her box-office fortunes have run the gamut from A to Z, but her ego has never flagged. Hepburn's iron-clad sense of worth and work began in her native Hartford, Connecticut, where her physician father and feminist mother imbued her with the sense to break rules that are stupid. Educated at Bryn Mawr, she took her upperclass voice first to Broadway and then to Hollywood, where she wore oxfords and trousers and no makeup, in a era where carefully applied

*Tracy and Hepburn* – Woman of the Year *(42).*

allure was an actress' stock in trade. She was an instant success in *A Bill of Divorcement* (32), which she nearly stole from the great John Barrymore. Several popular movies followed, including *Morning Glory* (33) for which she won her first Academy Award, as did a stint on Broadway in *The Lake*, which failed badly. By the late 1930s, Hepburn was declared to be box-office poison, partly because of her sharp manner and her refusal to let up on her insistence for good roles. She hit her stride as a screwball comedienne in *Bringing Up Baby* (38) with Cary Grant. She starred on Broadway in *The Philadelphia Story* in 1939, and early decided that she wanted to do it on the screen. But knowing that the Hollywood bigwigs would resist casting her in it, she had the foresight to buy up the movie rights to the play. The film version won an Academy Award nomination for her as well as the New York Film Critics' Award. She also owned the screen rights for *Woman of the Year* (42), the first of several very successful films with Spencer Tracy. A popular couple on screen, they were devoted to each other off-screen as well. Columnists kept mum about the affair, although they hadn't hesitated to link Hepburn to billionaire Howard Hughes in the 1930s. Tracy and Hepburn also starred in *Sea of Grass* (47), *State of the Union* (48), *Adam's Rib* (49), *Pat and Mike* (52), and *Desk Set* (57). Their final film, completed shortly before Tracy's death, was *Guess Who's Coming to Dinner* (67). Hepburn and Humphrey Bogart scored a triumph with *The African Queen* (51). It was one of her better spinster characterizations, a part in which she also excelled. She won the Best Actress Award at the Cannes Film Festival for her fine performance as the hopelessly drug-addicted mother in *Long Day's Journey into Night* (62). Another triumph on Broadway in *Coco*, several critically acclaimed television performances and further films enhanced her legendary status. Opposite the dying Henry Fonda in *On Golden Pond* (82), Hepburn proved she still had that touch of greatness after over 50 years of making films. Along the way, she picked up a record four Oscars for Best Actress in *Morning Glory* (33), *Guess Who's Coming to Dinner* (67), *The Lion in Winter* (68) and *On Golden Pond* (82).

**Selected Films:** *A Bill of Divorcement* (32), *Morning Glory* (33), *Little Women* (33), *The Little Minister* (34), *Alice Adams* (35), *Sylvia Scarlett* (35), *Mary of Scotland* (36), *Stage Door* (37), *Bringing Up Baby* (38), *Holiday* (38), *The Philadelphia Story* (40), *Woman of the Year* (42), *Dragon Seed* (44), *Sea of Grass* (47), *State of the Union* (48), *Adam's Rib* (49), *The African Queen* (51), *Pat and Mike* (52), *Summer Madness* (55), *The Rainmaker* (56), *Desk Set* (57), *Suddenly Last Summer* (59), *Long Day's Journey into Night* (62), *Guess Who's Coming to Dinner* (62), *The Lion in Winter* (68), *The Madwoman of Chaillot* (69), *The Trojan Women* (73), *A Delicate Balance* (73), *Rooster Cogburn* (75), *On Golden Pond* (82), *The Ultimate Solution of Grace Quigley* (85).

## HERBERT, Hugh (1887-1952)

Born in Binghampton, New York, Herbert was a comedian in vaudeville and on stage before coming to films in the late 1920s. In dozens of screen comedies into the 1950s, he played supporting parts.
**Selected Films:** *Husbands for Rent* (27), *Wonder Bar* (34), *Sh! The Octopus* (37), *Gold Diggers in Paris* (38), *Hellzapoppin* (41), *Kismet* (44), *Havana Rose* (51).

## HERNANDEZ, Juano (1896-1970)

Born in San Juan, Puerto Rico, Hernandez was a boxer and circus performer before acting on stage and in film. One of the first black actors to play strong and often sympathetic roles, he made an impressive screen debut as the man who is almost lynched in *Intruder in the Dust* (48).
**Selected Films:** *Intruder in the Dust* (48), *Young Man with a Horn* (50), *Kiss Me Deadly* (55), *The Pawnbroker* (64), *The Reivers* (69), *They Call Me Mister Tibbs* (70).

## HERSHEY, Barbara (1948- )

Born Barbara Herzstein in Hollywood, California, she was a regular on *The Monroes*, a television series, while she was a teenager. She seemed to be on her way to being a star in *Last Summer* (69). In 1972 she changed her name to Barbara Seagull, but has since been billed again as Hershey.
**Selected Films:** *With Six You Get Eggroll* (68), *Last Summer* (69), *The Liberation of L B Jones* (70), *The Pursuit of Happiness* (71), *Dealing* (72), *The Last Hard Men* (76), *The Stunt Man* (78), *The Entity* (82), *The Right Stuff* (83), *Hannah and Her Sisters* (86), *Hoosiers* (86), *Tin Men* (87).

## HERSHOLT, Jean (1886-1956)

Hersholt, born in Copenhagen, Denmark, was a stage actor in all the Scandiniavian countries before moving to Hollywood in 1914. He was a character actor for the next four decades, specializing in kindly doctors and similar roles, including the 'Dr. Christian' radio and movie series. A kindly man in real as well as reel life, he helped found the Motion Picture Country Home and Hospital. In his lifetime, he received two special Academy Awards, for services to the industry. Today, he is best rememberd for the Special Oscar – the Jean Hersholt Humanitarian Award – named after him.
**Selected Films:** *The Disciple* (15), *Greed* (25), *Grand Hotel* (32), *Heidi* (37), *Stage Door Canteen* (43), *Run for Cover* (55).

## HERVEY, Irene (1910- )

Born Irene Herwick in Los Angeles, Hervey began her film career in the mid-1930s. After a substantial role in *The Stranger's Return* (33), the dimpled and amiable actress was groomed to be an MGM star. When her contract was dropped she ended up at Universal, gradually relegated to second features. From the mid-1950s she was active on television.
**Selected Films:** *The Strangers Return* (33), *The Count of Monte Cristo* (34), *Say It in French* (38), *Destry Rides Again* (39), *The Boys From Syracuse* (40), *Chicago Deadline* (49), *Going Steady* (59), *Cactus Flower* (69), *Play Misty For Me* (71).

## HESTON, Charlton (1923- )

Tall, muscular and strong-jawed, Heston looks every inch the hero that he has played throughout most of his film career. He has played Moses, John the Baptist, Michelangelo, Ben Hur, El Cid, Mark Anthony, Andrew Jackson and General 'Chinese' Gordon, among others. Although he has starred in some of the most popular films ever made, he is often overshadowed by hordes of spear-waving extras and spectacular special effects. Heston was born John Charlton Carter in Evanston, Illinois, and was a speech major at Northwestern University. He began his professional career as a radio actor in Chicago, and after a stint in the Air Force, he spent years playing small roles, then bigger ones, on stage, television and in movies. Cecil B De Mille chose him to play the circus manager in *The Greatest Show on Earth* (52), a hug box office success. His real breakthrough to stardom came in another De Mille epic, *The Ten Commandments* (56), in which he played Moses. De Mille said that Heston had been chosen because he looked like Michelangelo's statue of the Biblical leader. The movie was an enormous financial success. Still another grand scale success was *Ben Hur* (59), a remake of the old silent film, which earned Heston an Academy Award for Best Actor. Some of his better performances have come in smaller pictures, notably *Touch of Evil* (58), directed by Orson Welles, who also appeared in the movie, where Heston effectively played a Mexican detective in a seedy little town, without benefit of lavish sets or a cast of thousands. The popularity of the Heston epics declined sharply during the 1960s, but he did score one notable box office triumph in *Planet of the Apes* (68) and one of its sequels, *Beneath the Planet of the Apes* (69). The 1970s saw Heston regaining his popularity with other science-fiction films such as *The Omega Man* (71), and some disaster movies such as *Earthquake* (74). Off screen he has been active in the politics of Hollywood, having served terms as president of the Screen Actors' Guild. In 1977 he won the Academy's Jean Hersholt Humanitarian Award.
**Selected Films:** *Dark City* (50), *The Greatest Show on Earth* (52), *Ruby Gentry* (52), *The President's Lady* (52), *The Naked Jungle* (54), *The Private War of Major Benson* (55), *The Ten Commandments* (56), *Touch of Evil* (58), *The Big Country* (58), *The Buccaneer* (58), *The Wreck of the Mary Deare* (59), *Ben Hur* (59), *El Cid* (61), *Diamond Head* (62),*55 Days at Peking* (63), *Major Dundee* (65), *The Agony and the Ecstacy* (65),

*Charlton Heston as* Ben Hur *(59).*

*The War Lord* (65), *Khartoum* (66), *Planet of the Apes* (67), *Will Penny* (68), *Beneath the Planet of the Apes* (69), *The Hawaiians* (70), *The Omega Man* (71), *Call of the Wild* (72), *Soylent Green* (73), *Earthquake* (74), *Airport 75* (74), *Two Minute Warning* (76), *The Awakening* (80), *Mother Lode* (82).

## HEYDT, Louis Jean (1905-1960)

Born in Montclair, New Jersey, Heydt began his theatrical career on the stage. A character actor, he was usually cast as a shifty guy in films of the 1930s to the 1950s.
**Selected Films:** *Make Way for Tomorrow* (37), *Test Pilot* (38), *Gone With the Wind* (39), *Gung Ho!* (43), *They Were Expendable* (45), *The Big Sleep* (46), *Rawhide* (51), *The Man Who Died Twice* (58).

## HICKMAN, Darryl (1931- )

Hickman was born in Hollywood and made his film debut at seven. Effecting a smooth transition from child to juvenile to character roles, he ended up producing TV soaps in the 1970s. In 1976 he made a screen comeback in *Network*.
**Selected Films:** *If I Were King* (38), *The Grapes of Wrath* (40), *Meet Me in St Louis* (44), *Boys' Ranch* (45), *Rhapsody in Blue* (45), *Submarine Command* (51), *Tea and Sympathy* (56), *Network* (76).

## HICKMAN, Dwayne (1934- )

Born in Los Angeles, Hickman followed his older brother Darryl into show business, beginning in films as a child. After appearing in the popular 1950s TV series *The Bob Cummings Show* and *Dobie Gillis*, he had a brief film career in several bikini epics, then retired.
**Selected Films:** *Captain Eddie* (45), *Rally 'Round the Flag, Boys!* (59),*Cat Ballou* (65), *Dr Goldfoot and the Bikini Machine* (65), *Doctor You've Got to Be Kidding* (67).

## HILL, Arthur (1922- )

Hill, born in Melfort, Saskatchewan, has had a distinguished stage career in England and on Broadway, winning a Tony in 1962. His film appearances have been sporadic but often memorable. From 1971 to 1974 he appeared in the TV series *Owen Marshall: Counselor at Law*.
**Selected Films:** *Miss Pilgrim's Progress* (49), *The Ugly American* (63), *Harper* (66), *Petulia* (68), *The Andromeda Strain* (70), *A Bridge Too Far* (77), *The Amateur* (82).

## HILLER, Wendy (1912- )

Born in Stockport, in England, Hiller was a sensation on the London stage at the age of 18 in *Love on the Dole*. Her first major film triumph came in 1938 when she played Eliza Doolittle opposite Leslie Howard's Professor Henry Higgins in George Bernard Shaw's *Pygmalion*. Hiller won an Academy Award for Best Supporting Actress for her moving portrayal of a lonely woman who runs an English guest house in *Separate Tables* (58). Throughout her career, she has chosen her film roles with wisdom and care. Hiller was created a Dame in 1975.
**Selected Films:** *Lancashire Lad* (37), *Pygamalion* (38), *Major Barbara* (40), *I Know Where I'm Going* (45), *Something of Value* (57), *Separate Tables* (58), *Sons and Lovers* (60), *Toys in the Attic* (63), *A Man for All Seasons* (66), *Murder on the Orient Express* (74), *Voyage of the Damned* (76), *The Elephant Man* (81), *Making Love* (82).

## HILLERMAN, John (1931- )

Appearing mostly in comedies, Hillerman brought a dapper image to movies starting in the 1970s. His TV work includes appearances on *The Betty White Show* and *Magnum, PI*.
**Selected Films:** *Paper Moon* (73), *At Long Last Love* (76), *The Day of the Locust* (76), *Lucky Lady* (77), *History of the World – Part One* (81).

## HILLIARD, Harriet (1914- )

Born Peggy Lou Snyder in Des Moines, Iowa, Hilliard sang with the band of Ozzie Nelson before marrying him. After a film career in mostly B musicals and action pictures, in 1952 she and Ozzie teamed up to create TV's *The Adventures of Ozzie and Harriet*.
**Selected Films:** *Follow the Fleet* (36), *Cocoanut Grove* (38), *Confessions of Boston Blackie* (41), *Gals Inc.* (43), *Here Come the Nelsons* (52).

## HINDS, Samuel S (1875-1948)

Born in Brooklyn, Hinds was a lawyer and amateur actor 35 years before his film debut. In dozens of movies he played shifty lawyers and sympathetic fathers. He is best known as the father in the *Doctor Kildare* movie series.
**Selected Films:** *The Crime of the Century* (33), *You Can't Take It With You* (38), *Destry Rides Again* (39), *The Boy with Green Hair* (48), *The Bribe* (49).

## HINES, Gregory (1946- )

New York-born Hines began tap dancing at age three and in childhood toured in a nightclub act with his father and brother. By the late 1970s he was dancing in all-black Broadway musicals like *Eubie* and *Sophisticated Ladies*. His screen debut in *Wolfen* (81) was followed by roles that demonstrated that he could act as well as dance, most notably with Mikael Baryshnikov in *White Nights* (85).
**Selected Films:** *History of the World Part One* (81), *Deal of the Century* (83), *White Nights* (85), *The Cotton Club* (85), *Running Scared* (86).

## HINGLE, Pat (1923- )

Born in Denver, Colorado, Hingle was a laborer before coming to acting, and maintains the hefty figure of a working man. He has been a familiar character actor in films since *On the Waterfront* (54).
**Selected Films:** *On the Waterfront* (54), *The Ugly American* (63), *Hang 'Em High* (68), *Norwood* (69), *Running Wild* (73), *Norma Rae* (79), *Maximum Overdrive* (86).

## HIRSCH, Judd (1935- )

New York-born Hirsch studied physics in college but then turned to acting, arriving on Broadway in 1966. After a fine performance in the play *Hot l Baltimore,* the actor found character roles on TV and in movies. Though nominated for a supporting-actor Oscar for his performance as the psychiatrist in *Ordinary People* (80), Hirsch remains best known for his crusty Alex in the TV series *Taxi*.
**Selected Films:** *Serpico* (74), *Ordinary People* (80), *Without a Trace* (83), *The Goodbye People* (84), *Teachers* (84).

## HOBBES, Halliwell (1877-1962)

Born in Stratford-on-Avon, Hobbes moved to Hollywood after long stage experience in his native Britain, where he made his theatrical debut in 1898. From the early years of the sound era into the 1950s he played Hollywood-Englishmen, running the social gamut from butlers to their aristocratic employers.
**Selected Films:** *Jealousy* (29), *Charley's Aunt* (30), *The Masquerader* (33), *Dracula's Daughter* (36), *Sherlock Holmes Faces Death* (43), *Miracle in the Rain* (56).

## HOBSON, Valerie (1917- )

Hobson was born in Larne, Ireland, and began appearing in British films in her teens. In Hollywood in the 1930s, she starred in several horror movies including *The Bride of Frankenstein* (35) before returning to England for many roles as an upper-class woman. She was later married to politician John Profumo, a central figure in the Christine Keeler scandal. She retired from films in 1954.
**Selected Films:** *Eyes of Fate* (33), *The Werewolf of London* (35), *The Bride of Frankenstein* (35), *This Man is News* (38), *Contraband* (40), *Great Expectations* (46), *Kind Hearts and Coronets* (49), *Knave of Hearts* (54).

## HODIAK, John (1914-1955)

Born in Pittsburgh, Pennsylvania, to a Polish-Ukrainian family, Hodiak came to movies via radio during World War II (the hypertension that finally killed him kept him out of the Army). He made a good start, bringing his somber and sensitive features to meaty roles in Alfred Hitchcock's *Lifeboat* (44) and *A Bell for Adano* (45). However, with the end of the war and the return of flashier leading men, Hodiak was increasingly relegated to routine productions. He died suddenly two years after a much-praised Broadway role in *The Caine Mutiny Court Martial*. He was married to actress Anne Baxter from 1946 to 1953.
**Selected Films:** *A Stranger in Town* (43), *Lifeboat* (44), *Sunday Dinner for a Soldier* (44), *A Bell for Adano* (45), *Command Decision* (48), *The Miniver Story* (50), *The Conquest of Cochise* (53), *On the Threshold of Space* (56).

## HOFFMAN, Dustin (1937- )

Talent and brains have made Hoffman a superstar, bold in his choice of roles and willing to take chances. Born in Los Angeles, California, he dropped out of Santa Monica City College to become an actor. He went to New York and for years he worked at odd jobs, did bit parts on television and did summer stock. In 1965 he had made it as far as Off-Broadway, then his luck changed. Hoffman was chosen by director Mike Nichols to play a young man floudering in a cynical world in his film *The Graduate* (67). This was not Hoffman's first movie, since he had done a couple of unmemorable minor roles. Despite having won an Obie Award for his Off-Broadway work, he was certainly an unknown, but *The Graduate* made him a star. He proved that he wasn't a flash in the pan in *Midnight Cowboy* (69), playing the sad, grotesque Ratso brilliantly. Essentially a character actor, Hoffman opted for versatility and challenging roles rather than for personality and charisma in most of his following films. In *Little Big Man* (70) he aged on screen from adolescence to over 100 years old. He was deliberately ugly and eccentric

in *Papillon* (73), and he worked hard to catch the strange contradictions of comedian Lenny Bruce in *Lenny* (74). Shifting times never caught Hoffman unaware. He was excellent as Carl Bernstein, the reporter who helped to break the Watergate story, in *All the President's Men* (76), and he was quick to sense the rise of a new non-macho male image, deftly playing a father who learns to nurture his son in *Kramer vs Kramer* (79). The movie at last earned Hoffman a much-deserved Academy Award for Best Actor. Then came his sensitive subtle performance as a man pretending to be a woman in the extraordinarily popular *Tootsie* (82), a *tour de force* for him, since the film never descended into a cheap drag show. Hoffman gave a masterful performance as Willie Loman on Broadway in *Death of a Salesman* in 1984.

**Selected Films:** *Madigan's Millions* (66), *The Tiger Makes Out* (67), *The Graduate* (67), *Midnight Cowboy* (69), *John and Mary* (69), *Little Big Man* (70), *Who Is Harry Kellerman, and Why Is He Saying Those Terrible Things About Me?* (71), *Alfredo, Alfredo* (72), *Straw Dogs* (72), *Papillon* (73), *Lenny* (74), *All the President's Men* (76), *Marathon Man* (76), *Straight Time* (78), *Agatha* (79), *Kramer vs Kramer* (79), *Tootsie* (82), *Ishtar* (87).

## HOLBROOK, Hal (1925- )

Hal Holbrook was born Harold Rowe Holbrook Jr in Cleveland, Ohio. Abandoned by his parents when he was two, he was raised by relatives and first appeared on stage at age 17. After war service Holbrook worked in nightclubs and then in TV soap operas. His first and greatest stage success – and still the role for which he is best known – was his stunning impersonation: *Mark Twain Tonight*, which Holbrook has brought to the stage some 2000 times around the world since its off-Broadway premiere. Primarily a stage actor, Holbrook's film career has been sporadic. His character roles have included 'Deep Throat' in *All the President's Men* (76), Alan Campbell in *Julia* (77), and Father Malone in *The Fog* (80). His TV work includes the series *The Bold Ones* and the movies *That Certain Summer* and *The Legend of the Golden Gun*.

*Dustin Hoffman and Jane Alexander in* Kramer vs Kramer *(79).*

**Selected Films:** *The Group* (66), *Wild in the Streets* (68), *Magnum Force* (73), *All the President's Men* (76), *Julia* (77), *Capricorn One* (79), *The Fog* (80), (80), *Creepshow* (82), *The Star Chamber* (82).

## HOLDEN, Fay (1894-1973)

Born Fay Hammerton in Birmingham, England, Holden had a stage career there before moving to Hollywood in the mid-1930s. Usually cast in warm maternal roles, she was best known as Andy Hardy's impossibly swell mom.

**Selected Films:** *I Married a Doctor* (36), *Bulldog Drummond Escapes* (37), *Judge Hardy's Children* (38), *Andy Hardy's Double Life* (43), *Samson and Delilah* (49), *Andy Hardy Comes Home* (58).

## HOLDEN, Gloria (1908- )

London-born Holden came from work on the stage and as a model to appear in Hollywood films from the 1930s to the 1950s. The darkly attractive,

*Judy Holliday and William Holden in* Born Yesterday *(50).*

slightly exotic-looking actress's most famous picture was her first – the title role in *Dracula's Daughter* (36).
**Selected Films:** *Dracula's Daughter* (36), *The Life of Emile Zola* (37), *The Corsican Brothers* (41), *The Eddy Duchin Story* (57), *This Happy Feeling* (58).

## HOLDEN, William (1918-1981)

Holden's clean-cut good looks were far from dazzling and his low-key restrained acting style wasn't charismatic, so it was sometimes easy to forget that he was a consummate film actor. Although there were times when the public took him for granted, a mere presence in many fine movies, Holden was on the top ten box office list from 1954 to 1958 and was the top drawer in 1956. He was also rewarded for his steady stream of reliably good performances with an enormous income. By the end of his life he was a resident of Geneva, Switzerland, and was involved in multimillion dollar business enterprises and was co-owner of the vast Mount Kenya Safari Club. He was by then an ardent conservationist and environmentalist. Born William Franklin Beedle Jr in O'Fallon, Illinois, he was spotted by a movie talent scout while acting at Pasadena Junior College, and became a star in his first picture, *Golden Boy* (39). After that he played nice guys in a whole series of films, although he did show an unsuspected flair for comedy in *Dear Ruth* (47). Then came four important pictures that broke his mold. He played a psychotic killer in *The Dark Past* (49), an almost creepy gigolo in *Sunset Boulevard* (50) with Gloria Swanson, Judy Holliday's tutor in the comedy *Born Yesterday* (50), and the unheroic hero of *Stalag 17* (53), which won him an Academy Award for Best Actor. Holden was the drifter and Kim Novak the beauty queen in the very popular *Picnic* (55), which allowed him a rare shot at being sexy. *The Bridge on the River Kwai* (57) was an artistic triumph for Holden and his percentage of the box office receipts alone set him up with a tidy annual income for life. Further good movies followed. Holden's personal life had its share of problems. His marriage to actress Brenda Marshall ended in 1970, about the time that their son, Scott Holden, began making movies. Holden's bouts with alcohol were common knowledge in Hollywood. But he was a man of integrity, as films such as *Network* (76), *S.O.B.* (81) and *The Earthling* (81) show.
**Selected Films:** *Golden Boy* (39), *I Wanted Wings* (41), *Dear Ruth* (47), *Rachel and the Stranger* (48), *The Dark Past* (49), *Sunset Boulevard* (50), *Born Yesterday* (50), *Stalag 17* (53), *Executive Suite* (54), *The Country Girl* (54), *Love Is a Many-Splendored Thing* (55), *Picnic* (55), *The Bridge on the River Kwai* (57), *The Counterfeit Traitor* (62), *The Wild Bunch* (69), *The Towering Inferno* (74), *Network* (76), *Fedora* (78), *S.O.B.* (81), *The Earthling* (81).

## HOLLIDAY, Judy (1922-1965)

Holliday was just about the funniest film actress of her time, and the public was robbed when she died at the age of 42. Born Judith Tuvim in New York City, she was a small night club revue star, often appearing with Betty Comden and Adolph Green. She made her film debut in *Greenwich*

*Village* (44), and shot to fame in the 1950s as slightly daft in some well-scripted comedies. Despite an IQ of 172, she continued with her naive roles, winning an Academy Award for Best Actress in 1950 for her work in *Born Yesterday*. She had played the role on Broadway, and another of her stage roles was as the star of *Bells Are Ringing*, a comedy in which she also starred on screen in 1960. Holliday had a mastectomy at the age of 37 and did one more stage comedy, *Hot Spot*, which never made it to Broadway, before her death from cancer.
**Selected Films:** *Greenwich Village* (44), *Something for the Boys* (44), *Winged Victory* (44), *Adam's Rib* (49), *Born Yesterday* (50), *The Marrying Kind* (52), *It Should Happen to You* (53), *Phffft* (54), *The Solid Gold Cadillac* (56), *Full of Life* (56), *Bells Are Ringing* (60).

## HOLLIMAN, Earl (1928- )

Born in Delhi, Louisiana, Holliman arrived in Hollywood in the early 1950s to play supporting roles, frequently in westerns. He was most often cast as a slightly dumb character, ranging from Southern good ole boys to villains. He co-starred in the TV series *Police Woman*.
**Selected Films:** *Pony Soldier* (52), *Scared Stiff* (53), *The Bridges at Toko-Ri* (54), *Forbidden Planet* (56), *Giant* (56), *Visit to a Small Planet* (60), *Summer and Smoke* (61), *The Sons of Katie Elder* (65), *The Biscuit Eater* (72), *Sharkey's Machine* (81).

## HOLLOWAY, Stanley (1890-1982)

Born in London, England, Holloway was a music hall performer who also appeared on the legitimate stage. In 1921 he began playing comic roles in films, beginning with *The Rotters*. He gave a memorable performance as Mr Crummles in *Nicholas Nickleby* (47) and in the brilliantly funny *The Lavender Hill Mob* (51). And he was magnificent as the grave digger in *Hamlet* (48). But he is most famous for his dynamic performance as Alfred P Doolittle, Eliza's dustman father, in both the stage and screen versions of the musical *My Fair Lady* (64). In 1962 Holloway did a television series, *Our Man Higgins*.
**Selected Films:** *The Rotters* (21), *The Co-Optimists* (30), *Squibs* (35), *The Vicar of Bray* (36), *Salute John Citizen* (42), *Champagne Charlie* (44), *This Happy Breed* (44), *Brief Encounter* (45), *Nicholas Nickleby* (47), *Hamlet* (48), *The Lavender Hill Mob* (51), *The Titfield Thunderbolt* (52), *The Beggar's Opera* (53), *No Love for Johnnie* (61), *My Fair Lady* (64), *The Private Life of Sherlock Holmes* (70), *Journey into Fear* (76).

## HOLLOWAY, Sterling (1905- )

Born in Cedartown, Georgia, Holloway aimed for a serious theater career before his cracked voice and goofy features landed him inescapably in comedy. In some 40 movies over some 50 years, he played a succession of hayseeds, delivery boys and soda jerks. He also had supporting roles in the TV series *The Life of Riley* and *The Baileys of Balboa* and provided voices for many Disney cartoons.
**Selected Films:** *Casey at the Bat* (27), *Alice in Wonderland* (33), *The Bluebird* (40), *The Beautiful Blonde from Bashful Bend* (49), *Batman* (66), *Thunder and Lightning* (77).

## HOLM, Celeste (1919- )

Born into a comfortable artistic family in New York, Celeste Holm studied acting in college and made her Broadway debut at 19. She was the original Ado Annie, the girl who 'cain't say no,' in *Oklahoma!* Making her film debut in 1946, she won a supporting-actress Oscar the next year for her role in *Gentleman's Agreement* (47). Holm went on to be cast most often in wisecracking roles, to which she brought her considerable beauty and also a cool but entirely likeable intelligence. Among her memorable parts was the wise and witty friend of Bette Davis in *All About Eve* (50); for that role and for one in *Come to the Stable* (49), Holm received supporting-actress Oscar nominations. Among other notable appearances was as Frank Sinatra's sidekick in *High Society* (56), in which they sang the duet 'Who Wants to be a Millionaire.' Holm's later career included a good deal of TV roles, among them the series *Nancy* and the TV movies *Death Cruise* and *Captains and the Kings*. She is married to actor Wesley Addy.
**Selected Films:** *Three Little Girls in Blue* (46), *Gentleman's Agreement* (47), *The Snake Pit* (48), *Come to the Stable* (49), *All About Eve* (50), *Champagne for Caesar* (50), *High Society* (56), *Doctor, You've Got to be Kidding* (67), *Tom Sawyer* (73), *The Private Files of J Edgar Hoover* (78).

## HOLM, Ian (1932- )

Born Ian Cuthbert in Goodmayes, England, Holm had an extensive stage career there before turning to movies in the late 1960s. The authoritative-looking and versatile actor won British Academy Awards for his roles in *The Bofors Gun* (68) and *Chariots of Fire* (81).
**Selected Films:** *The Fixer* (68), *The Bofors Gun* (68), *Nicolas and Alexandra* (71), *Juggernaut* (75), *Alien* (79), *Time Bandits* (81), *Chariots of Fire* (81), *Return of the Soldier* (82), *Dreamchild* (85), *Wetherby* (85)

## HOLT, Jack (1888-1951)

Charles John Holt II was born in Winchester, Virginia and began in silents as a stuntman and soon became a popular hero of the strong-jawed and two-fisted ilk. Later moving from action to romantic leads – the latter mostly in B's – he finally appeared in some 90 features. His children include screen actor Tim Holt.
**Selected Films:** *A Cigarette – That's All* (15), *The Little American* (17), *Held by the Enemy* (20), *Dirigible* (31), *The Littlest Rebel* (35), *They Were Expendable* (45), *Across the Wide Missouri* (51).

## HOLT, Tim (1919-1973)

Holt, born Charles John Holt III, was the son of actor Jack Holt, who had a long career playing heroes and villains in westerns. While the father rarely got beyond supporting parts, the son became a western star. Holt graduated from Culver Military Academy in Indiana with top grades before taking up his film career. His first adult picture was *History Is Made at Night* (37). His first western was *The Law West of Tombstone* (38); a year later he had a good role in John Ford's classic *Stagecoach* (39), which made John Wayne a star. Holt went on to appear in many other better-than-average westerns and also gave a fine performance in Orson Welles' *The Magnificent Ambersons* (42). He became a B-29 bombardier in World War II, winning many decorations for bravery in Pacific action. In 1948 he gave his best performance in *The Treasure of the Sierra Madre* with Humphrey Bogart and Walter Huston. Holt ended his movie career in 1952 and became a rancher in Oklahoma. He did occasional radio and television work after that, and was also in the construction business for a while before his death.

**Selected Films:** *The Vanishing Pioneer* (28), *History is Made at Night* (37), *The Law West of Tombstone* (38), *Stagecoach* (39), *The Swiss Family Robinson* (40), *The Magnificent Ambersons* (42), *Hitler's Children* (42), *My Darling Clementine* (46), *The Treasure of the Sierra Madre* (48), *The Mysterious Desperado* (49), *His Kind of Woman* (51), *The Monster that Challenged the World* (57), *This Stuff'll Kill Ya!* (71).

## HOMIER, Skip (1929- )

Born in Chicago, George Homier made his film debut at 14 in *Tomorrow the World* (44) repeating his stage success as a young Nazi. His screen career lasted through the 1970s, his appearances growing through juvenile roles and hoods to grownup supporting parts in mostly routine films.

**Selected Films:** *Tomorrow the World* (44), *Boys' Ranch* (46), *Fixed Bayonets* (51), *Beachhead* (54), *Comanche Station* (60), *Starbird and Sweet William* (76), *The Greatest* (77).

## HOMOLKA, Oscar (1898-1978)

Vienna-born Homolka acted widely on stage and screen in Europe before his Hollywood career began in the mid-1930s. From then on he appeared in character roles in over 80 films as both good guys and bad (he received an Oscar nomination for his Uncle Chris in *I Remember Mama* [48]). His rough, Slavic-looking features often typed him as a scheming Russian.

**Selected Films:** *Die Abenteuer eines Zehnmarkscheines* (26), *Dreyfus* (30), *Rhodes of Africa* (36), *Sabotage* (36), *Hostages* (43), *I Remember Mama* (48), *War and Peace* (56), *Funeral in Berlin* (66), *The Tamarind Seed* (74).

## HOPE, Bob (1903- )

Although born Leslie Townes Hope in London, England, this legendary comedian was to become the world's favorite wisecracking funny man and a major name in entertainment for over 50 years. After a brief fling in professional boxing (where he was billed as Packy East), Hope spent years in American vaudeville and musical comedy – his most notable Broadway role being in *Roberta* (33), after he had been discovered by producer Max Gordon doing a comedy vaudeville act at New York's Palace Theater. He then won the national attention as a radio comedian. His first picture was *The Big Broadcast of 1938* (38) – a variety show film – and it was discovered that his humor transferred well to the screen. In 1939, he was still given second billing with Martha Raye in *Never Say Die*, but then he starred in the comedy/mystery movie, *The Cat and the Canary* (39), with Paulette Goddard. Hope's film popularity became permanently established when he teamed up with Bing Crosby and Dorothy Lamour in a series of 'Road' pictures which began with *The Road to Singapore* (40). Those films included *The Road to Zanzibar* (40), *The Road to Morocco* (42), *The Road to Utopia* (45), *The Road to Rio* (47), *The Road to Bali* (52) and *The Road to Hong Kong* (61). In all of them, Hope was the brash yet cowardly smart aleck, manipulated by Crosby, and always losing Lamour to him. During World War II, he began what was to become a life-long habit – extensive traveling to entertain American troops in the field. For all those trips, as well as other charitable ventures, Hope has been awarded Special Academy Awards in 1940, 1944 and 1952. Until the mid-1950s, Hope was among the top box office draws, and he continues to work on stage, in television and in the occasional movie.

**Selected Films:** *The Big Broadcast of 1938* (38), *College Swing* (38), *Thanks for the Memory* (38), *Never Say Die* (39), *The Cat and the Canary* (39), *The Road to Singapore* (40), *The Ghost Breakers* (40), *The Road to Zanzibar* (40), *Caught in the Draft* (41), *Nothing but the Truth* (41), *Louisiana Purchase* (41), *My Favorite Blonde* (42), *The Road to Morocco* (42), *They Got Me Covered* (42), *The Road to Utopia* (45), *Monsieur Beaucaire* (46), *My Favorite Brunette* (47), *The Road to Rio* (47), *The Paleface* (48), *Sorrowful Jones* (48), *Fancy Pants* (50), *The Lemon Drop Kid* (51), *My Favorite Spy* (51), *The Road to Bali* (52), *The Seven Little Foys* (54), *That Certain Feeling* (56), *Beau James* (57), *The Road to Hong Kong* (61), *I'll Take Sweden* (65), *Cancel My Reservation* (62), *The Muppet Movie* (79).

## HOPKINS, Anthony (1937- )

Born in Port Talbot, Wales, Anthony Hopkins was a concert pianist before he discovered his gift for acting while at the Welsh College of Music and Drama. His stage work led him to the Old Vic, where he was once understudy for Lawrence Olivier. Hopkins' first film was *The Lion in Winter*

(68), where he made an impressive debut as Richard the Lion-Hearted. His ensuing movie career has alternated with stage and TV work. His films include *A Doll's House* (73), *A Bridge Too Far* (77), and *The Elephant Man* (80). In his roles he tends to be, despite his stocky and imposing figure, an understated and intelligent presence. His TV appearances have been frequent, including the made-for-TV movies *QB VII*, *Victory at Entebbe*, and *The Hunchback of Notre Dame*.
**Selected Films:** *The Lion in Winter* (68), *Hamlet* (69), *Young Winston* (72), *A Doll's House* (73), *Juggernaut* (74), *Audrey Rose* (77), *A Bridge Too Far* (77), *Magic* (78), *International Velvet* (78), *The Elephant Man* (80), *The Good Father* (87), *84 Charing Cross Road* (87).

## HOPKINS, Bo (1942-     )

Born in Greenwood, South Carolina, Hopkins made his film debut in San Peckinpah's *The Wild Bunch* (69); from that point he has most often been seen as a tough macho type in action movies. He has also appeared on the TV series *Dynasty*.
**Selected Films:** *The Wild Bunch* (69), *Monte Walsh* (70), *American Graffiti* (73), *The Day of the Locust* (75), *Midnight Express* (78), *The Fifth Floor* (80).

## HOPKINS, Miriam (1902-1972)

Born Ellen Hopkins in Savannah, Georgia, Miriam Hopkins was a chorus girl before acting on the Broadway stage in the 1920s. She went to Hollywood in 1930 to make *Fast and Loose* and during the next decade was a leading lady in popular films including *Dr Jekyll and Mr Hyde* (32). Director Ernst Lubitsch first showed the sharp-featured blonde's acid style to advantage in three films – *The Smiling Lieutenant* (31), *Trouble in Paradise* (32), and *Design for Living* (33). She also played the title role in *Becky Sharp* (35); in that movie and in *The Old Maid* (39) with Bette Davis, Hopkins tended to play roles of surface sweetness concealing a rather nasty nature. A reported feud with Davis led to Hopkins leaving films for some years; during that time she appeared on Broadway. She returned to the screen for supporting roles including one in *The Heiress* (49) and appeared occasionally into the 1960s.
**Selected Films:** *Fast and Loose* (30), *The Smiling Lieutenant* (31), *Dancers in the Dark* (32), *Dr Jekyll and Mr Hyde* (32), *Trouble in Paradise* (32), *Design for Living* (33), *Becky Sharp* (35), *These Three* (36), *The Old Maid* (39), *Lady with Red Hair* (41), *Old Acquaintance* (43), *The Heiress* (49), *Carrie* (52), *The Children's Hour* (62), *The Chase* (66).

## HOPPER, Dennis (1935-     )

Born in Dodge City, Kansas, Dennis Hopper began his acting career in juvenile roles in the TV series *Medic*. His friendship with James Dean landed Hopper supporting parts in *Rebel Without a Cause* (55) and *Giant* (56). Hopper lost roles due to his rebelliousness; but in the mid-1960s he turned

*Miriam Hopkins and Bette Davis in* The Old Maid *(39).*

that unconventionality to good use in films exploiting the counterculture – including *The Trip* (67), which was written by Jack Nicholson and starred Peter Fonda. Those three then played the leads in the blockbuster *Easy Rider* (69), which Hopper directed, co-wrote, and starred in as a befuddled and archetypal hippie motorcyclist. That success led to Hollywood giving him his own company and complete freedom as writer, director, and actor; the result, *The Last Movie* (71), won the Best Picture award at the Venice film festival, but was otherwise panned as self-indulgent. Hopper turned to occasional acting including his supporting role in *Apocalypse Now* (79). His return to directing with *Out of the Blue* (80) did not salvage his career but his performance in *Hoosiers* (86) brought him an Academy Award nomination for Best Supporting Actor.
**Selected Films:** *Johnny Guitar* (54), *Rebel Without a Cause* (55), *Giant* (56), *The Story of Mankind* (57), *The Sons of Katie Elder* (65), *Cool Hand Luke* (67), *The Trip* (67), *Easy Rider* (69), *The Last Movie* (71), *Mad Dog Moran* (76), *The American Friend* (77), *Apocalypse Now* (79), *Out of the Blue* (80), *The Osterman Weekend* (83), *Hoosiers* (86), *Blue Velvet* (86), *River's Edge* (87).

## HOPPER, Hedda (1890-1966)

Born Elda Furry in Hollidaysburg, Pennsylvania, Hopper began acting in vampish roles in silents of the 'teens, later becoming a character actress. In the late 1930s she began her long career as a Hollywood gossip columnist, but continued to appear occasionally in films (sometimes as herself).
**Selected Films:** *Battle of Hearts* (16), *Sherlock Holmes* (22), *Holiday* (30), *Topper* (37), *Sunset Boulevard* (50), *The Oscar* (66).

## HOPPER, William (1915-1969)

Hopper was born in New York, the son of movie matinee idol DeWolf Hopper and his wife, then-actress, later-columnist Hedda Hopper. He began appearing in leads and supporting roles in films in the 1930s and is best remembered as the stalwart detective Paul Drake in the *Perry Mason* TV series.
**Selected Films:** *Footloose Heiress* (37), *Track of the Cat* (54), *Rebel Without a Cause* (55), *The Bad Seed* (56), *Twenty Million Miles to Earth* (57).

## HORDERN, Michael (1911- )

Besides a distinguished stage career in his native Britain, Hordern, born in Berkhamstead, has made a speciality of playing world-weary officials or officers in some 35 films on both sides of the Atlantic. He was knighted in 1982.
**Selected Films:** *The Girl, in the News* (39), *The Spanish Gardener* (56), *El Cid* (61), *A Funny Thing Happened on the Way to the Forum* (66), *Anne of the Thousand Days* (70), *England Made Me* (72), *The Slipper and the Rose* (76), *Joseph Andrews* (76), *Gandhi* (82), *The Missionary* (82), *Yellowbeard* (83).

## HORNBY, Leslie, See: TWIGGY

## HORNE, Lena (1917- )

After establishing herself as one of the most exciting nightclub singers of her time, the sultry and lovely Horne, born in Brooklyn, became the first black actress signed to a Hollywood studio contract. However, for years she was relegated to small musical appearances that were cut for showing in the South; an exception was her part in the all-black *Cabin in the Sky* (43). Her friendship with Paul Robeson got Horne blacklisted for some years, after which she returned to the screen in a dramatic role with *Death of a Gunfighter* (69).
**Selected Films:** *The Duke is Tops* (38), *Panama Hattie* (42), *Cabin in the Sky* (43), *Stormy Weather* (43), *Ziegfeld Follies* (46), *Till the Clouds Roll By* (46), *Death of a Gunfighter* (69), *The Wiz* (78).

## HORTON, Edward Everett (1886-1970)

Horton was the master of the double take, a lanky comedian who twittered his nervous way through many an embarrassing situation. He added a bright spot to every movie he was in for decades. Horton was born in Brooklyn, New York, and made his theater debut in 1908 while a student at Columbia University. He moved from singing in the chorus on stage to playing leads and character parts in 150 films, beginning in the early 1920s. He played Fred Astaire's pal in 1930s movie musicals.
**Selected Films:** *Leave It to Me* (20), *Too Much Business* (22), *Ruggles of Red Gap* (22), *The Sap* (29), *Holiday* (30), *Trouble in Paradise* (32), *The Gay Divorcee* (35), *Top Hat* (35), *Lost Horizon* (37), *Bluebeard's Eighth Wife* (38), *Holiday* (38), *Here Comes Mr Jordan* (41), *Down to Earth* (47), *Pocketful of Miracles* (61), *Cold Turkey* (70).

## HORTON, Robert (1924- )

After playing in several minor films of the 1950s, the rangy and handsome Horton, born in Los Angeles, found fame with TV leads in *Wagon Train* and *A Man Called Shenandoah*.
**Selected Films:** *The Tanks are Coming* (51), *Prisoner of War* (54), *The Dangerous Days of Kiowa Jones* (66), *The Green Slime* (69).

## HOSKINS, Bob (1942- )

British-born Hoskins was a steeplejack before getting into acting in his twenties. After working with the Royal Shakespeare Company, he came to the screen in the mid-1970s. He has played both supporting roles and leads, among them the mobster Harold Shand in *The Long Good Friday* (81). He received a nomination for Best Actor for his role in *Mona Lisa* (86).
**Selected Films:** *Royal Flash* (75), *The Long Good Friday* (81), *Beyond the Limit* (83), *The Cotton Club* (85), *Brazil* (85), *Sweet Liberty* (86), *Mona Lisa* (86).

## HOUSEMAN, John (1902- )

Born Jacques Haussman in Bucharest, Rumania, the English-educated Houseman is one of the major theatrical figures of the century. As a stage and film writer and producer he was closely associated with Orson Welles in the Mercury Theater and in creating *Citizen Kane* (41). After years of Hollywood producing, Houseman emerged as a popular actor in his seventies, winning a supporting-actor Oscar for *The Paper Chase* (73).
**Selected Films:** *Seven Days in May* (64), *The Paper Chase* (73), *Three Days of the Condor* (75), *The Cheap Detective* (78), *Murder by Phone* (82).

## HOUSTON, Donald (1923- )

Houston, born in Tonypandy, Wales, made his film debut in *The Blue Lagoon* (49). After some years as a leading man, the stocky blond actor played character roles in a number of mostly routine productions.
**Selected Films:** *The Blue Lagoon* (49), *A Run for Your Money* (49), *Doctor in the House* (54), *Room at the Top* (58), *Where Eagles Dare* (68), *Tales that Witness Madness* (73), *The Sea Wolves* (80).

## HOWARD Jerome 'Curly': See: STOOGES, The Three

## HOWARD, John (1913- )

Born in Cleveland, Ohio, John Cox came to films in

1935. Stolid and handsome, he was mostly relegated to leads in series such as Bulldog Drummond. Howard played occasional character roles in major productions; memorable among them was the role of Katharine Hepburn's stuffy fiancé in *The Philadelphia Story* (40).
**Selected Films:** *Annapolis Farewell* (35), *Lost Horizon* (37), *The Philadelphia Story* (40), *The Mad Doctor* (41), *Experiment Alcatraz* (51), *The High and the Mighty* (54), *The Destructors* (68), *Buck and the Preacher* (71).

## HOWARD, Ken (1944-    )

Born in El Centro, California, the hulkily handsome Howard came to films in the 1970s. He has worked much on TV in movies and series, including *Adam's Rib* and *The White Shadow*. His film appearances have been occasional.
**Selected Films:** *Tell Me That You Love Me, Junie Moon* (70), *Such Good Friends* (71), *1776* (72), *Second Thoughts* (83).

## HOWARD, Leslie (1890-1943)

Sensitive, intellectual, with a dreamy air, Howard was America's ideal as the model Englishman. Actually, his parents were Hungarian immigrants to England (his real name was Leslie Stainer) and London was his birthplace almost by chance. Still, there is no arguing with his deep attachment to Great Britain. He was to become a major force in the British film industry as a director and producer as well as an actor. Howard abandoned the comforts of Hollywood to live in London during World War II, where he was actively engaged in the war effort. He attended Dulwich College and took up acting only because he had been shell-shocked in World War I and acting was recommended to him as a form of therapy. Blond, blue-eyed and utterly charming, he rapidly established himself as a leading man on both sides of the Atlantic. Howard became a movie star when Warner Bros. cast him in the movie version of his hit play, *Outward Bound* (30), a fascinating drama about a shipload of passengers who slowly come to realize that they are dead. Beginning with Norma Shearer in *A Free Soul* (31), he appeared opposite many of Hollywood's most glamorous leading ladies, wooing them skilfully on screen and off. Despite his delicate appearance, his look of being a poet in need of mothering, Howard's conquests were the talk of Hollywood, as was his business acumen. Actor David Niven once described him as being 'about as naive as General Motors.' He generally considered Hollywood movies rather silly, but he worked wonders playing even the most cardboard of characters. He shone in *Berkeley Square* (33), a haunting story of a man sent back in time to the eighteenth century, in *Of Human Bondage* (34) co-starring Bette Davis, and in *The Scarlet Pimpernel* (35), a costume drama that brought Howard a Picturegoer Gold Medal. The chemistry was right opposite brassy Joan Blondell in *Stand-In* (37), and his performance as Henry Higgins in *Pygmalion* (38), which he co-directed, was brilliant. Howard played Ashley Wilkes in *Gone with the Wind* (39) only under pressure, and he far preferred *Intermezzo* (39), which he co-produced, co-starring with Ingrid Bergman. Howard went on making fine films until 1943 when, while flying back to London from a secret mission in Lisbon, his plane was shot down by the Nazis.
**Selected Films:** *The Happy Warrior* (17), *Outward Bound* (30), *A Free Soul* (31), *Five and Ten* (31), *Devotion* (31), *Service for Ladies* (32), *Smilin' Through* (32), *The Animal Kingdom* (32), *Captured* (33), *Berkeley Square* (33), *Of Human Bondage* (34), *British Agent* (34), *The Scarlet Pimpernel* (35), *The Petrified Forest* (36), *Romeo and Juliet* (36), *Stand-In* (37), *Pygmalion* (38), *Gone with the Wind* (39), *Intermezzo* (39), *The 49th Parallel* (41), *The First of the Few* (42).

## HOWARD, Moe:

See STOOGES, The Three

## HOWARD, Ron (1953-    )

Born in Duncan, Oklahoma, Howard first appeared onstage at age two. He went on to juvenile parts in films and in TV's *The Andy Griffith Show* (as Opie). Thereafter the seemingly ageless actor impersonated a teenager nearly into his 30s on the series *Happy Days*. His most notable screen role was in *American Graffiti* (73). Turning to directing, he has made good-natured hits such as *Splash* (84), and *Cocoon* (85).
**Selected Films:** *The Journey* (59), *The Music Man* (62), *American Graffiti* (73), *The Shootist* (76), *More American Graffiti* (79).

## HOWARD, Shemp:

See STOOGES, The Three

## HOWARD, Trevor (1916-    )

Howard is not one of the glamorous stars, yet he is a total perfectionist who is invariably good and at times flawless. His performance in *Brief Encounter* (46), opposite Celia Johnson, places him in the first rank of movie actors. Born in Cliftonville, England, Howard was educated at Clifton College and made his London stage debut in 1934 while studying at the Royal Academy of Dramatic Art. After he was invalided out of the Royal Artillery in 1943 he played Captain Plume in *The Recruiting Officer*. Next he starred in *A Soldier for Christmas*. Appearing in the cast was actress Helen Cherry, who became his wife. Howard made his film debut in *The Way Ahead* (44) and quickly established a reputation as a polished actor of understated style, who could be cynical or gentle, able to express

*Trevor Howard and John Mills in* Ryan's Daughter *(70).*

anguish behind a bleak stare. Although he began his movie career playing romantic leads, he moved on to heroic roles and character parts. *I See a Dark Stranger* (46) was a tension-packed thriller. Howard was the other man in the sparkling romance, *The Passionate Friends* (48) and he helped make *The Third Man* (49) a superb spy picture. Howard devoted an increasing amount of his time and energy to movies from the late 1940s on. From the mid-1950s he was seen frequently in American as well as British films, developing into an actor of international stature. *The Key* (58), with William Holden and Sophia Loren, brought him a British Film Award, and *Sons and Lovers* (60) an Academy Award nomination. As Captain Bligh he stole *Mutiny on the Bounty* (62) away from Marlon Brando. He was magnificent as a fiery general in *The Charge of the Light Brigade* (68), as a priest in *Ryan's Daughter* (70) and as the man describing Glenda Jackson as the poet in *Stevie* (77). He has also performed on television, notably when reunited with Celia Johnson in *Staying On*.
**Selected Films:** *The Way Ahead* (44), *Brief Encounter* (46), *I See a Dark Stranger* (46), *Green for Danger* (46), *They Made Me a Fugitive* (47), *The Passionate Friends* (48), *The Third Man* (49), *An Outcast of the Islands* (52), *The Heart of the Matter* (53), *The Key* (58), *Roots of Heaven* (59), *Sons and Lovers* (60), *Mutiny on the Bounty* (62), *The Charge of the Light Brigade* (68), *Ryan's Daughter* (70), *The Night Visitor* (71), *11 Harrowhouse* (74), *Stevie* (77), *The Missionary* (82), *Foreign Body* (86), *Dust* (86).

## HOWELL, C Thomas (1967- )

After being a junior rodeo circuit champion, Howell made his screen debut as a teenager in *E.T. The Extra-Terrestrial* (82). He started in show business when he was four years old in a television series, *Little People*.
**Selected Films:** *E.T. The Extra-Terrestrial* (82), *The Outsiders* (83), *Tank* (84), *Grandview USA* (84), *Red Dawn* (84), *Secret Admirer* (85), *The Hitcher* (86).

## HOYT, John (1905- )

Yale-educated Hoyt came to films in the 1940s from stage and nightclub work. He was most known for his roles as Nazi officers and elegant criminals.
**Selected Films:** *OSS* (46), *Rommel, The Desert Fox* (51), *When Worlds Collide* (52), *Julius Caesar* (53), *The Blackboard Jungle* (55), *Duel at Diablo* (66).

## HUBBARD, John (1914- )

The genial and suave features of Hubbard appeared largely in a number of light leading roles from the late 1930s on, including several Hal Roach comedies.
**Selected Films:** *The Housekeeper's Daughter* (39), *Turnabout* (40), *Gunfight at Comanche Creek* (63), *Duel at Diablo* (66), *Herbie Rides Again* (73).

## HUBER, Harold (1904-1959)

American-born Huber left a law practice for a career as a character actor in film. He was most often seen as a sly or unintelligent man on one side or another of the law.
**Selected Films:** *The Bowery* (33), *The Thin Man* (34), *San Francisco* (36), *Kit Carson* (40), *Let's Dance* (50).

## HUDSON, Rochelle (1914-1972)

After studio grooming and a number of roles as an ingénue in popular films of the 1930s, Oklahoma City native Hudson landed in more hard-boiled parts in B pictures. After some 75 films that thinned out after the early 1940s, she retired from acting when her health failed.
**Selected Films:** *Fanny Foley Herself* (31), *She Done Him Wrong* (33), *Poppy* (36), *Meet Boston Blackie* (41), *Rebel Without a Cause* (55), *Strait-Jacket* (65), *Dr Terror's Gallery of Horrors* (67).

## HUDSON, Rock (1925-1985)

Persistence was the key ingredient in the success of this big handsome leading man who began his career as a male sex object and matured into a solid competent actor. Born Roy Scherer in Winnetka, Illinois, Hudson had no formal acting training when he began appearing in films, starting with *Fighter Squadon* (48), but he learned on the job and by the mid-1950s was a top star, having moved from western to sob stories to sophisticated comedies. He earned an Oscar nomination for *Giant* (56). In the 1960s he often co-starred with Doris Day. In the 1970s he starred in a hit television show, *McMillan and Wife*. Hudson died tragically of AIDS, the first prominent actor to succumb to this disease.
**Selected Films:** *Fighter Squadron* (48), *Winchester 73* (50), *Bend of the River* (52), *Magnificent Obsession* (53), *One Desire* (55), *All That Heaven Allows* (55), *Giant* (56), *Written on the Wind* (56), *Something of Value* (57), *The Tarnished Angels* (57), *Pillow Talk* (59), *Lover Come Back* (61), *Seconds* (66), *Pretty Maids All in a Row* (71), *The Mirror Crack'd* (80).

## HUGHES, Barnard (1915- )

American-born Hughes lent his absorbing features and incisive voice to character roles in film, TV, and stage (the latter including his Broadway triumph in *Da* in the 1970s). He played an acerbic physician in the TV series *Doc* and starred in *The Callahans*.
**Selected Films:** *Midnight Cowboy* (69), *Where's Poppa?* (71), *The Hospital* (72), *Sisters* (73), *Oh God!* (77), *Where Are the Children?* (86).

## HUGHES, Mary Beth (1919- )

Born in Alton, Illinois, blonde and pretty Hughes began her film career after repertory work in college and the stage. Despite a good role opposite John Barrymore in *The Great Profile* (40) and a few other films, she mostly appeared in B pictures of the 1940s, usually as a loose woman or gangster's moll.
**Selected Films:** *These Glamour Girls* (39), *The Great Profile* (40), *Dressed to Kill* (41), *The Ox-Bow Incident* (43), *Caged Fury* (47), *Gun Battle at Monterey* (57), *How's Your Love Life?* (77).

*Rock Hudson*

## HULL, Henry (1890-1977)

This versatile American character actor was born in Louisville, Kentucky, and appeared on stage, in films and on television for over 40 years, generally playing older men. He did star in a horror film, *The Werewolf of London* (35), as the first 'wolf man,' but he did not like the makeup and was unwilling to return to the role.
**Selected Films:** *The Man Who Came Back* (16), *The Volunteer* (17), *The Hoosier Schoolmaster* (24), *Great Expectations* (34), *The Werewolf of London* (35), *Yellow Jack* (38), *Boys' Town* (38), *Jesse James* (39), *High Sierra* (40), *Lifeboat* (43), *Mourning Becomes Electra* (47), *The Great Gatsby* (49), *Inferno* (53), *Covenant with Death* (67).

## HULL, Josephine (1884-1957)

Born in Newton, Massachusetts, Hull had been on the stage for decades when she first came to film in the early 1930s. She appeared in only a few movies, but two were classic: *Arsenic and Old Lace* (44) and *Harvey* (50). The latter role won Hull an Oscar for Best Supporting Actress.
**Selected Films:** *After Tomorrow* (32), *Careless Lady* (32), *Arsenic and Old Lace* (44), *Harvey* (50), *The Lady From Texas* (51).

## HULL, Warren (1903-1974)

Born in Gasport, New York, Hull's career began in operetta. He later appeared in film cheapies such as the *Green Hornet* and *Mandrake the Magician* serials. At the same time, he pursued radio and later TV announcing; he ended being best known as host of the TV quiz show *Strike it Rich*.
**Selected Films:** *Miss Pacific Fleet* (35), *The Walking Dead* (36), *The Green Hornet Strikes Again* (40), *The Spider Returns* (41).

## HUME, Benita (1906-1967)

After acting on the stage in her native England, Hume began her film career in the mid-1920s. Beautiful and talented though she was, she was relegated to decorous roles in minor pictures. In 1938 she married Ronald Colman and retired from the screen. She later appeared with Colman in the TV series *The Halls of Ivy*. After Colman's death in 1958, she married actor George Sanders.
**Selected Films:** *The Happy Ending* (25), *The Constant Nymph* (28), *The Garden Murder Case* (36), *Peck's Bad Boy with the Circus* (39).

## HUNNICUTT, Arthur (1911-1979)

Hunnicutt was born in Gravelly, Arkansas, and spent most of his career on the stage, but appeared often in films from the 1940s on. He usually played a slow-speaking farmer.
**Selected Films:** *Northwest Passage* (40), *Wildcat* (42), *The Red Badge of Courage* (51), *The Last Command* (56), *The Kettles in the Ozarks* (56), *Cat Ballou* (65), *Harry and Tonto* (74), *Winter Hawk* (75).

## HUNNICUTT, Gayle (1942- )

Born in Fort Worth, Texas, Hunnicutt made her screen debut in *The Wild Angels* (66) and for the next decade played leads in a number of popular films. She was married to actor David Hemmings from 1968 to 1974. From the late 1970s she appeared mostly in made-for-TV movies.
**Selected Films:** *The Widl Angels* (66), *P.J.* (68), *Eye of the Cat* (69), *Scorpio* (72), *The Spiral Staircase* (75), *Once in Paris* (78).

## HUNT, Linda (1947- )

Hunt is tiny, only four feet nine inches, and weighs barely 80 pounds, and her face is old beyond its years. But she created a sensation playing Billy Kwan, a Chinese-Australian dwarf, in *The Year of Living Dangerously* (82), and received an Oscar for Best Supporting Actress for the part. Prior to that she had played only one part in a film and had appeared primarily Off-Broadway.
**Selected Films:** *Popeye* (80), *The Year of Living Dangerously* (82), *The Bostonians* (84), *Dune* (84), *Silverado* (85), *Waiting for the Moon* (87).

## HUNT, Marsha (1917- )

Chicago-born Marcia Hunt was a model in the mid-1930s before changing the spelling of her name and beginning her film career. For a while she was cast in good-natured supporting roles such as bridesmaids and coeds. In the 1940s she broke into leads, notably with Van Heflin in *Kid Glove Killer* (42). Blacklisted during the 1950s, she returned to character roles with *Blue Denim* (59) and in the TV series *Peck's Bad Girl*.
**Selected Films:** *The Virginia Judge* (35), *The Hardys Ride High* (38), *Kid Glove Killer* (42), *Lost Angel* (43), *The Happy Time* (52), *Blue Denim* (59), *The Plunderers* (60), *Johnny Got His Gun* (71), *Rich and Famous* (81).

## HUNT, Martita (1900-1969)

Though born in Argentina, Hunt spent the greater amount of her career on the stage in Britain. Starting in the early 1930s, she brought her strong features to character roles, frequently spinsters in a number of films, most memorably as Miss Havisham in *Great Expectations* (46).
**Selected Films:** *Service for Ladies* (32), *I Was a Spy* (33), *The Man in Grey* (43), *Grerat Expectations* (46), *Treasure Hunt* (52), *Paradise Lagoon* (57), *Brides of Dracula* (60), *Becket* (63), *Bunny Lake Is Missing* (65), *The Best House in London* (68).

## HUNTER, Glen (1897-1945)

Hunter was a popular leading man in the latter days of the silents. His appearances included *Smilin' Through* (22) and *Merton of the Movies* (24). His career declined with the coming of sound, though he did appear in *For Beauty's Sake* (41).
**Selected Films:** *The Case of Becky* (21), *Smilin' Through* (22), *Puritan Passions* (23), *Merton of the Movies* (24), *The Pinch Hitter* (25), *For Beauty's Sake* (41).

## HUNTER, Ian (1900-1975)

Hunter, born in Kenilworth, South Africa, came to silent filmsfrom the stage. From the 1930s to the 1960s his mild features and genial manner type cast him as a decent, self-sacrificing man in supporting roles, an example being his King Richard in *The Adventures of Robin Hood* (38).
**Selected Films:** *Mr Oddy* (22), *A Midsummer Night's Dream* (35), *52nd Street* (38), *The Adventures of Robin Hood* (38), *Strange Cargo* (40), *Dr Jekyll and Mr Hyde* (41), *Edward My Son* (49), *Appointment in London* (53), *Guns of Darkness* (63).

## HUNTER, Jeffrey (1927-1969)

Born Henry McKinnies in New Orleans, Hunter trained as an actor at UCLA and made his film debut in *A Date with Judy* (48). The boyishly handsome and piercing-eyed actor quickly became a

popular leading man and something of a teen heart-throb (along with then-wife Barbara Rush). In the 1950s he mostly appeared in action pictures, notably in John Ford's *The Searchers* (56). In 1961 Hunter was cast radically against type as Jesus in *King of Kings*, for which he garnered more snickers than approval.
**Selected Films:** *A Date with Judy* (48), *Call Me Mister* (51), *The Searchers* (56), *Hell to Eternity* (60), *King of Kings* (61), *The Longest Day* (62), *Custer of the West* (66), *Make Love Not War* (69).

## HUNTER, Kim (1922- )

Kim Hunter was born Janet Cole in Detroit, Michigan, and began appearing on the stage in her teens. After studies at the Actors Studio, she made her film debut in the 1943 thriller *The Seventh Victim*. Two years later she found success as David Niven's love interest in *Stairway to Heaven* (45). For several years Hunter's career languished, but she scored a triumph as passion-ruled Stella Kowalski, after whom Marlon Brando keened unforgettably in *A Streetcar Named Desire* (51); the role won Hunter a supporting-actress Academy Award. However, her career soon suffered a second and far worse setback when she was vaguely branded as subversive during the witch hunts of the early 1950s. After over a decade of infrequent screen appearances, Hunter played a lady simian in three *Planet of the Apes* movies.
**Selected Films:** *The Seventh Victim* (43), *When Strangers Marry* (44), *Stairway to Heaven* (45), *A Streetcar Named Desire* (51), *Lilith* (64), *Planet of the Apes* (67), *Beneath the Planet of the Apes* (70), *Escape from the Planet of the Apes* (71), *Dark August* (79).

## HUNTER, Tab (1931- )

Tab Hunter was born Arthur Gelien in New York City and at the age of 15 joined the Coast Guard by claiming he was 18. When he actually reached the latter age, he made, with no previous acting experience, his film debut in *The Lawless* (50). By the mid-1950s the handsome, athletic Hunter was simply 'Tab,' the guy the teenage girls yearned for and the boys wanted to look like. Given his negligible dramatic skills and his impressive chest, Hunter was destined for sand-and-surf epics such as *Operation Bikini* (63), but in earlier years his sheer box-office draw landed him roles in big-budget action pictures like the 1955 films *Battle Cry* and *The Sea Chase*, and the 1958 musical *Damn Yankees*. Hunter's career slowed as he passed thirty, but he continued to appear mostly for nostalgia value in films ranging from the offbeat comedy *The Loved One* (65) to *Grease II* (82).
**Selected Films:** *The Lawless* (50), *Gun Belt* (53), *Battle Cry* (55), *Damn Yankees* (58), *That Kind of Woman* (59), *Operation Bikini* (63), *Ride the Wild Surf* (64), *The Loved One* (65), *Birds Do It* (66), *Judge Roy Bean* (72), *Polyester* (81), *Grease II* (82).

## HUPPERT, Isobel (1955- )

Huppert was born in Paris, France, and was trained in a music conservatory in Versailles. She broke into French films in *Faustine* (71), and won the Best Actress Award at the Cannes Film Festival for *Violette Nozier* in 1978.
**Selected Films:** *Faustine* (71), *Cesar and Rosalie* (72), *La Judge et l'Assissin* (76), *The Indians Are Still Far Away* (77), *Violette Nozier* (78), *Les Soeurs Brontë* (79), *Every Man for Himself* (80), *Loulou* (80), *Heaven's Gate* (80), *Les Ailes de la Colombe* (81), *Passion* (82), *La Truite* (82), *The Bedroom Window* (87).

## HURST, Paul (1889-1953)

Hurst began in films as a director in the silent days. After his first role in *The Red Raiders* (27), he went on to small character roles as crooks, cops, bartenders, and the like, in some 90 movies.
**Selected Films:** *The Red Riders* (27), *Tugboat Annie* (32), *Gone With the Wind* (39), *Yellow Sky* (49), *The Sun Shines Bright* (53).

## HURT, John (1940- )

Born in Chesterfield, England, this slightly-built highly-talented, offbeat and versatile actor received critical acclaim as the monstrously deformed but sympathetic character in *The Elephant Man* (80). He received praise again for his appearances in two remarkable television productions, *I, Claudius* (as Caligula) and *The Naked Civil Servant*.
**Selected Films:** *The Wild and the Willing* (62), *A Man for All Seasons* (66), *10 Rillington Place* (71), *Midnight Express* (78), *Alien* (79), *The Elephant Man* (80), *Night Crossing* (81), *Champions* (82), *1984* (84), *Jake Speed* (86), *From the Hip* (87).

## HURT, Mary Beth (1948- )

Hurt was born Mary Supinger in Marshalltown, Iowa, and was trained at the New York University School of Arts. She made her stage debut in 1973 in a New York Shakespeare Festival production, and worked on Broadway in *More Than You Deserve*, *Trelawny of the Wells* and *Father's Day*. Hurt switched to films with her finer performance in Woody Allen's *Interiors* (78). She was married to actor William Hurt.
**Selected Films:** *Interiors* (78), *Head Over Heels* (79), *Change of Season* (80), *The World According to Garp* (82), *D.A.R.Y.L.* (85), *Compromising Positions* (85).

## HURT, William (1950- )

William Hurt was born in Washington, DC, the stepson of Time-Life founder Henry Luce III. For some time Hurt was a theological student, but then gravitated to acting, which he studied at the Juilliard School in New York. After wide and successful stage experience – he has been most associated with the Circle Rep in New York – Hurt made a striking film debut in the Ken Russell/Paddy Chayevsky reincarnation-cum-werewolf film *Altered States* (80). Hurt returned to the screen the next year as a dumb stud lawyer in *Body Heat*. In another hit, *The Big Chill* (83), Hurt refined a screen image as an intelligent, sensitive, and obscurely damaged character – for all the hunkiness of his form. In *Kiss of the Spider Woman* (85), Hurt gave a virtuoso performance as a pathetic but indomitable homosexual in a South American prison; the role won Hurt a best-actor Oscar and a rare reputation as not only a major star but a formidable actor was well.

**Selected Films:** *Altered States* (80), *Body Heat* (81), *The Big Chill* (83), *Kiss of the Spider Woman* (85), *Children of a Lesser God* (86).

## HUSSEY, Olivia (1951- )

Born in Buenos Aires, Argentina, but raised in England, Hussey made a considerable splash at 17 as Juliet in Franco Zefferelli's *Romeo and Juliet* (68), but her ensuing film appearances have been intermittent. Her TV-movie work has included *Jesus of Nazareth*.

**Selected Films:** *The Battle of the Villa Fiorita* (65), *Romeo and Juliet* (68), *Lost Horizon* (73), *Death on the Nile* (78), *The Man with Bogart's Face* (80), *Turkey Shoot* (81).

## HUSSEY, Ruth (1914- )

After methodical dramatic training and stage experience, Hussey (born Ruth O'Rourke in Providence, Rhode Island) came to films to find herself underutilized. However, after some years of minor leads – usually as a sophisticate – she received an Oscar nomination for her supporting role as Jimmy Stewart's sidekick in *The Philadelphia Story* (40). She later concentrated on her stage career.

**Selected Films:** *Madame X* (37), *Spring Madness* (38), *Fast and Furious* (39), *The Philadelphia Story* (40), *HM Pulham Esq.* (41), *The Uninvited* (44), *Stars and Stripes Forever* (52), *The Facts of Life* (60).

## HUSTON, Anjelica (1952- )

Born in Ireland the daughter of director John Huston, Anjelica appeared at 16 in *A Walk With Love and Death* (69), an unsuccessful film of her father's. After a desultory movie career, she gained acclaim (and an Oscar) as a gangster's daughter in *Prizzi's Honor* (85), this time a very successful John Huston production.

**Selected Films:** *A Walk With Love and Death* (69), *Sinful Davey* (69), *Swashbuckler* (76), *Prizzi's Honor* (85), *The Dead* (87), *Gardens of Stone* (87).

## HUSTON, John (1906- )

Born in Nevada, Missouri, the son of actor and vaudeville hoofer Walter Huston, John Huston came to movies by the roundabout route of being – in rough order – a boxer, teenage actor, Mexican cavalry officer, playwright, movie bit player, journalist, and bum. In the late 1930s Huston rearrived in Hollywood to write screenplays and in 1941 wrote and directed *The Maltese Falcon*, which made Huston a major director. His directing career from then on was steady, but almost as erratic as his former life, ranging from masterpieces like *The Treasure of the Sierra Madre* (50) to bombs like *The Bible* (66). In both those films Huston appeared onscreen, in the latter playing Noah. Starting in the 1970s, Huston brought his battered features and velvety-but-ominous drawl to a number of acting roles, perhaps the most notable being his wily and incestuous villain in Roman Polanski's *Chinatown* (74). As an actor, Huston is limited in range but nonetheless is a powerful screen presence.

**Selected Films:** *The Shakedown* (28), *The Treasure of the Sierre Madre* (63), *The Cardinal* (63), *The Bible* (66), *Casino Royale* (67), *De Sade* (69), *Myra Breckinridge* (70), *Battle for the Planet of the Apes* (74), *Chinatown* (74), *The Wind and the Lion* (75), *Winter Kills* (79), *Under the Volcano* (84).

## HUSTON, Walter (1884-1950)

This distinguished American character actor of stage and screen came to films when he was already in his mid-forties, with a long career of vaudeville and serious drama behind him. Born Walter Houghston in Toronto, Ontario, Canada, he had originally studied engineering before he joined a road show. After the birth of his son, director-to-be John Huston, he went back to engineering, but he returned to the stage in a few years. Even in small roles he could outshine the greatest stars. Huston was the best performer in *Rain* (32), although the star was the formidable Joan Crawford. He was more memorable than Bogart in *The Treasure of the Sierra Madre* (48), a part which awarded him a long overdue Oscar. He ended his career playing a roguish and eccentric characters, and also played bit parts in his son John's first two movies, as Captain Jacoby in *The Maltese Falcon* (41) and as a bartender in *In This Our Life* (42).

**Selected Films:** *Gentlemen of the Press* (29), *The Virginian* (29), *Abraham Lincoln* (30), *The Criminal Code* (31), *Law and Order* (32), *Rain* (32), *The Prize fighter and the Lady* (33), *The Tunnel* (35), *Dodsworth* (36), *All That Money Can Buy* (41), *The Maltese Falcon* (41), *In This Our LIfe* (42), *The Shanghai Gesture* (42), *The Outlaw* (43), *And Then There Were None* (45), *Duel in the Sun* (47), *The Treasure of the Sierre Madre* (48), *The Furies* (50).

## HUTCHINSON, Josephine (1898- )

Seattle-born Hutchinson came to the stage and film bit parts as a child and spent most of her career

on the stage. In her occasional films she tended to play good-hearted maternal roles, such as Widow Douglas in *The Adventures of Huckleberry Finn* (60).
**Selected Films:** *The Little Princess* (17), *Happiness Ahead* (34), *Son of Frankenstein* (39), *Cass Timberlane* (47), *Ruby Gentry* (52), *North by Northwest* (59), *The Adventures of Huckleberry Finn* (60), *Baby, the Rain Must Fall* (65), *Rabbit Run* (70).

## HUTTON, Betty (1921- )

Born Betty Jane Thornburg in Battle Creek, Michigan, this blonde and bouncy leading lady appeared in many musical films during the 1940s and also proved herself to be an excellent light comedienne. Her best musical performance was as Annie Oakley in *Annie Get Your Gun* (50), and her finest straight role was in the Preston Sturges comedy *The Miracle of Morgan's Creek* (44).
**Selected Films:** *The Fleet's In* (42), *Star Spangled Rhythm* (42), *The Miracle of Morgan's Creek* (44), *And the Angels Sing* (44), *Here Come the Waves* (44), *Incendiary Blonde* (45), *The Perils of Pauline* (47), *Dream Girl* (48), *Annie Get Your Gun* (50), *The Greatest Show on Earth* (52), *Spring Reunion* (57).

## HUTTON, Jim (1934-1979)

Born in Binghamton, New York, the gangly and affable Hutton was called 'the new Jimmy Stewart,' but his career remained as modest as his manner. He mostly appeared in light films, several co-starring Paula Prentiss. The most popular was probably *Where the Boys Are* (60).
**Selected Films:** *A Time to Love and a Time to Die* (58), *Where the Boys Are* (60), *The Honeymoon Machine* (62), *Period of Adjustment* (62), *The Hallelujah Trail* (65), *Walk, Don't Run* (66), *The Green Berets* (68), *Psychic Killer* (75).

*Betty Hutton in* Annie Get Your Gun *(50).*

## HUTTON, Lauren (1943- )

Born in Charleston, South Carolina, the stunningly-beautiful Hutton was a top New York model before moving into films in the late 1960s. At first a sort of ambulatory set decoration, she has become reasonably adept at light roles, but has remained largely in routine productions.
**Selected Films:** *Paper Lion* (68), *Little Fauss and Big Halsy* (71), *Welcome to LA* (77), *A Wedding* (78), *American Gigolo* (80), *Zorro, the Gay Blade* (81), *Once Bitten* (85).

## HUTTON, Robert (1920- )

Born Robert Bruce Winne in Kingston, New York, the earnest-looking Hutton played leads in mostly minor productions from the 1940s on. His later roles were often in horror movies; he wrote some films in the 1970s.
**Selected Films:** *Destination Tokyo* (44), *The Steel Helmet* (51), *Invisible Invaders* (58), *The Slime People* (62), *They Came from Beyond Space* (68), *Cry of the Banshee* (70), *Tales from the Crypt* (72).

## HUTTON, Tim (1960- )

The son of the actor, Jim Hutton, Hutton toured in a stage production with his father during high school. He made an impressive screen debut as a suicidal teenager in *Ordinary People* (80) – for which he won a supporting actor Oscar – and has since become one of the busiest of the young Hollywood stars known as the 'brat pack.' He has also appeared often in TV movies, among them *Friendly Fire*. He is married to actress Debra Winger.
**Selected Films:** *Ordinary People* (80), *Taps* (81), *Daniel* (83), *Iceman* (84), *The Falcon and the Snowman* (85), *Destiny* (87).

## HYAMS, Leila (1905-1977)

New York-born Hyams had an active career in silents and talkies for just over a decade. Usually cast as a vivacious ingenue type, she retired in 1936 after leads in a number of popular films including several famous horror classics.
**Selected Films:** *Sandra* (24), *The Wizard* (27), *The Big House* (30), *Freaks* (32), *Island of Lost Souls* (32), *Ruggles of Red Gap* (35), *Yellow Dust* (36).

## HYDE-WHITE, Wilfrid (1903- )

Though he did not make his screen debut until his mid-thirties, Wilfrid Hyde-White, born in Bourton-on-the-Water, England, was destined to spend the better part of five decades in movies. On the whole, he has played Englishmen whose surface gentility conceals a mischevious or larcenous or sinister soul. Among the roles that made him a virtual institution were a hypocritical school headmaster in *The Browning Version* (51), a British

Council functionary in *The Third Man* (49), and Colonel Pickering in *My Fair Lady* (64). In recent years Hyde-White has appeared in a number of TV roles, including the series *The Associates* and the TV movies *A Brand New Life* and *The Great Houdini*.
**Selected Films:** *Rembrandt* (36), *Elephant Boy* (37), *The Third Man* (44), *The Winslow Boy* (48), *The Mudlark* (50), *The Browning Version* (51), *See How They Run* (55), *North-West Frontier* (59), *Let's Make Love* (60), *My Fair Lady* (64), *Ten Little Indians* (66), *Chamber of Horrors* (66), *The Magic Christian* (70), *The Cat and the Canary* (78), *Oh God! Book Two* (80), *The Toy* (82), *Fanny Hill* (83).

## HYER, Martha (1929- )

Born in Fort Worth, Texas, the attractive blonde made her film debut in 1946. Thereafter she was cast as nice-girl leads and other-woman supporting parts in mostly routine productions. Hyer received an Oscar nomination for her supporting role in *Some Came Running* (59). She was married to producer Hal B Wallis.
**Selected Films:** *The Locket* (46), *Abbott and Costello Go to Mars* (52), *Riders to the Stars* (54), *Battle Hymn* (56), *Some Came Running* (59), *The Carpetbaggers* (64), *Massacre at Fort Grant* (68), *The Tyrant* (71).

## HYMER, Warren (1906-1948)

After a stage career, Hymer was usually cast in supporting roles as a dumb crook in minor crime movies.
**Selected Films:** *Up the River* (30), *Twenty Thousand Years in Sing Sing* (32), *Destry Rides Again* (39), *Baby Face Morgan* (42), *Joe Palooka Champ* (46).

# I

## IDLE, Eric (1943- )

A member of the wildly inventive British comedy troupe inexplicably called Monty Python's Flying Circus, Idle, educated at Cambridge University, moved with the group from TV madness into their equally outrageous movies. As did the other Pythons, Idle played multiple roles in each film.
**Selected Films:** *Monty Python and the Holy Grail* (75), *The Life of Brian* (79), *Monty Python's The Meaning of Life* (83).

## INESCORT, Frieda (1900-1976)

Born in Edinburgh, Scotland, the aristocratic-featured Inescort was Lady Astor's secretary before turning to acting in 1922. Not surprisingly, she was typed in upper-class roles in mostly minor films of the 1930s through the 1950s.
**Selected Films:** *If You Could Only Cook* (35), *Woman Doctor* (39), *Pride and Prejudice* (40), *The Return of the Vampire* (43), *Foxfire* (55), *The Crowded Sky* (60).

## INGELS, Marty (1936- )

Brooklyn-born Ingels was a nightclub and TV entertainer who occasionally played comic roles in films. He later became an agent for talent, including his wife Shirley Jones.
**Selected Films:** *The Ladies' Man* (61), *A Guide for the Married Man* (67), *If It's Tuesday, This must Be Belgium* (69), *How to Seduce a Woman* (74).

## INGRAM, Rex (1894-1969)

The career of the brilliant and talented Rex Ingram is a survey of the status of black actors in Hollywood. Born in Cairo, Illinois, a Phi Beta Kappa scholar and a doctor, Ingram went into films instead of practicing medicine. In Hollywood he was long relegated to stereotyped native and black roles. However, in 1936 Ingram found acclaim in the role of De Lawd in *The Green Pastures* (36). Thereafter he refused to play the more demeaning roles, which in those days were virtually all that were available to blacks. Nonetheless, his film career remained extensive – he was a memorable Jim in *Huckleberry Finn* (39), a genie in *The Thief of Bagdad* (40), and a standout in the all-black *Cabin in the Sky* (43) in which he complemented his role as De Lawd by playing Lucifer. During these years Ingram also worked extensively on the stage. As the status of blacks in films inched higher, so did Ingram's roles and their frequency improved.
**Selected Films:** *Tarzan of the Apes* (18), *The Sign of the Cross* (32), *King Kong* (33), *The Emperor Jones* (33), *The Green Pastures* (36), *Huckleberry Finn* (39), *The Thief of Bagdad* (40), *Cabin in the Sky* (43), *Sahara* (43), *King Solomon's Mines* (50), *Congo Crossing* (56), *The Ten Commandments* (56), *God's Little Acre* (58), *Watusi* (59), *Elmer Gantry* (60), *Your Cheating Heart* (64), *Hurry Sundown* (67), *Journey to Shiloh* (68).

## IRELAND, Jill (1936- )

London-born Ireland was a ballet dancer before starting in films in the mid-1950s. She mostly played leads and supporting roles in adventure movies before and after moving to Hollywood with her first husband David McCallum. After her 1968 marriage to action hero Charles Bronson, she co-starred in several of his films.
**Selected Films:** *Oh Rosalinda!* (55), *Hell Drivers* (57), *Carry on Nurse* (59), *Villa Rides* (68), *The Mechanic* (72), *Death Wish II* (82), *Assassination* (87).

## IRELAND, John (1914- )

Born in Vancouver, British Columbia, Ireland played Shakespeare on Broadway before moving to Hollywood in the mid-1940s. For over a decade he was an introspective, sometimes cynical actor largely in popular adventure movies, and received a supporting-actor Oscar nomination for his role in *All the King's Men* (49). In the 1960s, however,

Ireland's films declined to low-budget action pictures and horror movies. He was married to actress Joanne Dru from 1949 to 1956.
**Selected Films:** *A Walk in the Sun* (45), *I Shot Jesse James* (49), *All The King's Men* (49), *The Good Die Young* (54), *Gunfight at the OK Corral* (57), *Spartacus* (60), *The Fall of the Roman Empire* (64), *The House of the Seven Corpses* (73), *Delta Fox* (76), *Incubus* (81).

## IRONS, Jeremy (1948-      )

An uncommonly handsome and fine low-key actor, Irons was born in Cowes, on the Isle of Wight, off the coast of England. He has appeared on stage, winning critical acclaim, and he made an impression in the television production of *Brideshead Revisited*, as Charles Ryder. Recent film appearances have added luster to his career.
**Selected Films:** *Nijinsky* (80), *The French Lieutenant's Woman* (81), *Moonlighting* (82), *Betrayal* (83), *Swann in Love* (84), *The Mission* (86).

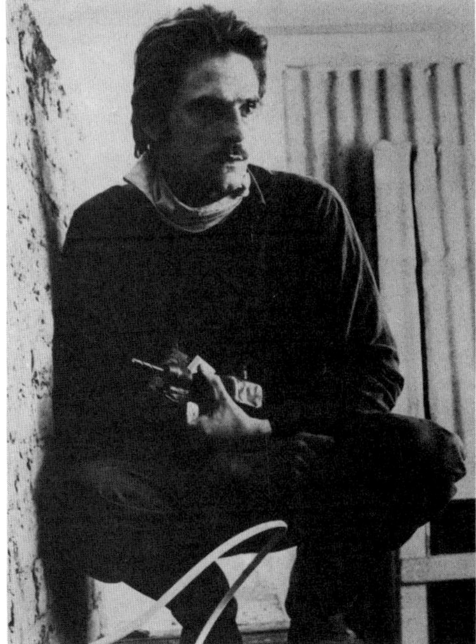

*Jeremy Irons in* Moonlighting *(82).*

## IVES, Burl (1909-      )

Burl Ives was born Burle Icle Ivanhoe in Hunt Township, Illinois. After working as a laborer and pro football player, the burly Ives became one of the most successful American folksingers of the century, his mellow voice familiar to a generation of listeners. After a Broadway musical role in the 1938 *The Boys From Syracuse*, Ives made his screen debut singing in *Smoky* (46). It was a few years before Hollywood discovered that Ives without guitar was a powerful screen presence. In a series of films in the 1950s, he proved he could handle dramatic roles in memorable fashion – he played Sam Hamilton in *East of Eden* (55), Ephraim Cabot in *Desire Under the Elms*, and Big Daddy in Tennessee Williams' *Cat on a Hot Tin Roof* (57). In 1958 Ives received a supporting-actor Oscar for his role in *The Big Country*.
**Selected Films:** *Smoky* (46), *So Dear to My Heart* (49), *East of Eden* (55), *Cat on a Hot Tin Roof* (57), *Desire Under the Elm* (58), *Wind Across the Everglades* (58), *The Big Country* (58), *Our Man in Havana* (59), *The Brass Bottle* (64), *Baker's Hawk* (76), *Just You and Me, Kid* (79).

## IVEY, Judith (1951-      )

Texas-born Ivey attended Illinois State University before going on to Broadway where she won two Tonys as a featured actress – in *Steaming* (85) and *Hurleyburly* (85). Her slightly wacky persona has only begun to enliven films.
**Selected Films:** *The Lonely Guy* (84), *Harry & Son* (84), *The Woman in Red* (84), *Compromising Positions* (85), *Steaming* (85), *Brighton Beach Memoirs* (87).

# J

## JACKSON, Anne (1925-      )

Born in Allegheny, Pennsylvania, Jackson studied at New York's Actor's Studio and began appearing in the theater in the mid-1940s. While remaining mainly a stage actress – and a much respected one – she has appeared in occasional films since the 1950s, usually playing eccentric roles. She is married to actor Eli Wallach.
**Selected Films:** *So Young, So Bad* (50), *Tall Story* (60), *The Secret Life of an American Wife* (68), *The Bell Jar* (79), *The Shining* (80).

## JACKSON, Glenda (1936-      )

Cool strength and keen intelligence are the hallmarks of Jackson's performances. As critic Stanley Kauffman once wrote of her, 'She is not an actress in order to be loved but in order to act.' Born in Liverpool, England, she spent years supporting herself with odd jobs and struggling to find acting roles. She joined the Royal Shakespeare Company in 1964, and her luck changed when she appeared in Peter Brook's London stage production of what was commonly called *Marat/Sade*, but whose real title was *The Persecution and Assassination of Jean-Paul Marat as Performed by the Inmates of the Asylum of Charenton under the Direction of the Marquis de Sade*, turning in an unforgettable performance as Charlotte Corday, which she repeated on Broadway. The play established Jackson as a serious actress, and she went on to films, winning the New York Film Critics Award and the Academy Award for Best Actress for *Women in*

*Glenda Jackson and Jennie Linden in* Women in Love *(70).*

*Love* (70), based on the novel by D H Lawrence. She won the Oscar again for *A Touch of Class* (73). Critics also praised her work in *Sunday Bloody Sunday* (71) and *Stevie* (78). This tall, angular actress has a range that rivals the best in the business. The embodiment of her talent for wit, romance and brittle genius was the role of Queen Elizabeth I in the BBC production of *Elizabeth R*, a tour de force performance. Despite exceptional talent, however, Jackson sometimes squanders her gifts in unworthy films.
**Selected Films:** *Marat/Sade* (66), *Negatives* (68), *Women in Love* (70), *The Music Lovers* (70), *Sunday, Bloody Sunday* (71), *Mary Queen of Scots* (71), *A Touch of Class* (72), *The Maids* (73), *The Romantic Englishwoman* (75), *Hedda* (76), *The Incredible Sarah* (76), *Nasty Habits* (76), *House Calls* (77), *Stevie* (78), *Health* (79), *Hopscotch* (80), *Turtle Diary* (86), *Beyond Therapy* (87).

## JACKSON, Gordon (1923- )

Born in Glasgow, Scotland, Jackson began appearing in films in the early 1940s. A character actor, he has played a wide variety of roles, often as a put-upon man. He is best known as the butler with the gentle voice and longsuffering air in the TV series *Upstairs Downstairs*.
**Selected Films:** *The Foreman Went to France* (42), *Whisky Galore* (48), *Tunes of Glory* (60), *The Ipcress File* (65), *The Prime of Miss Jean Brodie* (69), *Kidnapped* (71), *The Shooting Party* (84).

## JACKSON, Kate (1949- )

Jackson, born in Birmingham, Alabama, studied drama and worked as a model before getting her break on the TV series *Dark Shadows*. She later became the most ordinary of the stars of TV's *Charlie's Angels* and starred as a mother and sometimes spy on *Scarecrow and Mrs King*. Her movie roles have been occasional.
**Selected Films:** *Limbo* (70), *Night of Dark Shadows* (71), *Thunder and Lightning* (77), *Dirty Tricks* (81), *Making Love* (82).

## JACKSON, Thomas (1886-1967)

After some years in the theater, New York-born Jackson originated the role of Detective Dan McCord in the 1920s show *Broadway* and went on to appear in the same role in the 1929 screen version. He stayed in Hollywood to appear in minor roles, often as a cop, for the next 35 years.
**Selected Films:** *Broadway* (29), *Little Caesar* (30), *Hollywood Boulevard* (36), *The Big Sleep* (46), *Attack of the Fifty Foot Woman* (58), *Synanon* (65).

## JACOBI, Derek (1938- )

Jacobi, born in London, has alternated roles in film and TV since the early 1970s. He is perhaps best-known for his TV work, most notably in the title role of *I, Claudius*. Among his other TV-movie appearances were the title role in *The Hunchback of Notre Dame* and as Hitler in *Inside the Third Reich*.
**Selected Films:** *The Day of the Jackal* (73), *The Odessa File* (74), *The Medusa Touch* (77), *Enigma* (82), *Little Dorrit* (87).

## JACOBSON, Ulla (1929-1982)

Born in Göteborg, Sweden, Jacobsson came to film in her native country from theater work. After finding acclaim with her role in *One Summer of Happiness* (51), she appeared in films internationally into the 1970s, among them Ingmar Bergman's elegant comedy of *Smiles of a Summer Night* (55).
**Selected Films:** *One Summer of Happiness* (51), *Smiles of a Summer Night* (55), *Crime and Punishment* (56), *Zulu* (64), *Fox and His Friends* (75).

## JACOBY, Scott (1956- )

Chicago-born Jacoby arrived in films in the early 1970s and through the decade played juvenile leads in a number of largely routine films.
**Selected Films:** *Baxter* (72), *Love and the Midnight Auto Supply* (77), *The Little Girl Who Lives Down the Lane* (77).

## JAECKEL, Richard (1926- )

Born in Long Beach, New York, the baby-faced Jaeckel was a mailboy at Fox before making his film debut in *Guadalcanal Diary* (43). Since then he has been seen mostly in war movies, often as a frightened youth. Jaeckel has done serious roles and received a supporting-actor Oscar nomination for *Sometimes a Great Notion* (71).

**Selected Films:** *Guadalcanal Diary* (43), *Sands of Iwo Jima* (49), *Come Back Little Sheba* (52), *Town Without Pity* (61), *The Dirty Dozen* (67), *Sometimes a Great Notion* (71), *The Dark (79)*, *Herbie Goes Bananas* (80), *All the Marbles* (81).

## JAFFE, Sam (1893-1984)

Born in New York, Sam Jaffe was a teacher before starting his stage career in 1915. He entered films in the mid-1930s, among his early roles was Russia's Grand Duke Peter in *The Scarlet Empress* (34). With his striking and unconventional features – notably a hawklike nose and wild shock of hair – and his impressive screen personality, Jaffe tended to appear in character parts as wise and/or spiritual men. That image led to his most famous part, as the Grand Lama in *Lost Horizon* (37); a later example was Simonides in *Ben Hur* (59). Jaffe had the title role in *Gunga Din* (39). Playing somewhat against type, he co-starred as the burglary kingpin Doc Riedenschneider in John Huston's *The Asphalt Jungle* (50). In the last decades of his life Jaffe appeared often on TV, most memorably as wise old Dr Zorba in the *Ben Casey* series.
**Selected Films:** *We Live Again* (34), *The Scarlet Empress* (34), *Lost Horizon* (37), *Gunga Din* (39), *Stage Door Canteen* (43), *Gentleman's Agreement* (47), *The Asphalt Jungle* (50), *The Day the Earth Stood Still* (51), *The Barbarian and the Geisha* (58), *Ben Hur* (59), *Guns for San Sebastian* (68), *Bedknobs and Broomsticks* (71), *Battle Beyond the Stars* (80).

## JAGGER, Dean (1903- )

Dean Jagger was born Dean Jeffries in Lima, Ohio, and in his youth found his way to vaudeville and stage touring companies. He first appeared in films in the late 1920s. After several years of minor parts in minor films like *College Rhythm* (34), he left Hollywood to appear on Broadway. Having made a name for himself on the stage, Jagger returned to movies and to better parts, among them the title role in *Brigham Young* (40). Soon the sturdy, strong-featured Jagger was a popular favorite in leads and supporting roles, playing heroes and heavies, his range encompassing everything from action films like *The Omaha Trail* (42) to biblical epics such as *The Robe* (53). He received a supporting-actor Academy Award for his performance as Major Stovall in *Twelve O'Clock High* (49). Jagger appeared in films regularly through the 1970s. In the 1960s he worked often on TV, including the *Mr Novak* series.
**Selected Films:** *The Woman from Hell* (29), *College Rhythm* (34), *People Will Talk* (35), *Revolt of the Zombies* (36), *Brigham Young* (40), *The Omaha Trail* (42), *The North Star* (43), *Twelve O'Clock High* (49), *Warpath* (51), *The Robe* (53), *White Christmas* (54), *The Proud Rebel* (58), *First to Fight* (67), *The Kremlin Letter* (70), *Alligator* (80).

*Emil Jannings, Marlene Dietrich* – The Blue Angel *(30).*

## JANIS, Conrad (1926- )

Janis began his career playing teenagers in films of the 1940s including *Snafu* (45) and *Margie* (46). His screen appearances since then have been sporadic, but he has worked on TV including the series *Mork and Mindy*.
**Selected Films:** *Snafu* (45), *Margie* (46), *The High Window* (46), *Beyond Glory* (48), *Keep it Cool* (58), *The Duchess and the Dirtwater Fox* (76), *Roseland* (77), *Oh God! Book Two* (80).

## JANNINGS, Emil (1886-1950)

Before the talkies, Jannings had a peerless international reputation. He was born Theodor Friedrich Emil Janenz in Rorshach, Switzerland to a German mother and an American father. Jannings was raised in Gorlitz, Germany, leaving home at the age of 16 to become a sailor. But it was the stage, not the sea, which would become his true love and he became an actor at 18. In 1906 he joined Max Reinhardt's famous theater considered by many to be the finest in the world at the time, and by the time he made his film debut in 1914, appearing in *Im Banne der Leidenschaft*, he was a widely admired actor. Although he would emerge as a major force in the brilliantly experimental film industry of Germany in the 1920s, ultimately abandoning the stage altogether, Jannings' techniques remained theatrical rather than cinematic. Seen today, many of his highly praised performances seem overdone and overblown. Jannings found the ideal director in Ernst Lubitsch, an old theater chum. They built their great movie careers together when, beginning in 1919, Jannings, a strong, heavy-set, powerful man, played a series of historical characters on screen, including Henry

VIII in *Anne Boleyn* (20) and Peter the Great in *Peter the Great* (24). These were remarkably well received, as was his *Othello* (23) and his Mephistopheles in *Faust* (26). Jannings went to Hollywood in 1927 and in the first Academy Awards, he was voted Best Actor for his performances in two films – *The Way of All Flesh* (27) and *The Last Command* (28). In Hollywood Jannings generally played tragic characters, respectable citizens humiliated and destroyed by the cruelty of society and their own weaknesses. He had played such roles in Germany, too, with remarkable force and characterization and would do so again in the brilliant *The Blue Angel* (30), the German film that made a star of Marlene Dietrich. Unfortunately, despite his remarkable performance, the movie did not enhance Jannings' career in America, and, partly because of his thick German accent, he never made a successful transition to talking pictures in Hollywood. In 1933 Jannings, a strong supporter of the Nazis, began making anti-British propaganda films in Germany and in 1938 he was appointed as the head of Tobis, a large film company. In 1941 he was made an 'Artist of the State,' but with the defeat of Hitler his career came to an end.
**Selected Films:** *Im Banne der Leidenschaft* (14), *The Brothers Karamazov* (18), *Madame Dubarry* (19), *Anne Boleyn* (20), *Danton* (21), *Othello* (23), *Peter the Great* (24), *Quo Vadis* (24), *The Last Laugh* (24), *Tartuffe* (25), *Faust* (26), *Variety* (26), *The Way of All Flesh* (27), *The Last Command* (28), *The Patriot* (28), *The Sins of the Fathers* (29), *The Blue Angel* (30), *Robert Koch* (39), *Die Entlassing* (42), *Where Is Herr Belling?* (45).

## JANSSEN, David (1930-1980)

Born David Meyer in Naponee, Nebraska, Janssen began acting at an early age, appearing as a child in several films made during World War II. As an adult he was seen regularly in action pictures. His handsome and rather gloomy features were most familiar from TV series including *Richard Diamond, The Fugitive* and *Harry O.*
**Selected Films:** *It's a Pleasure* (45), *Yankee Buccaneer* (52), *Hell to Eternity* (60), *King of the Roaring Twenties* (61), *The Green Berets* (68), *Once is Not Enough* (75), *Two Minute Warning* (76), *Inchon!* (80).

## JARMAN, Claude Jr (1934- )

With no previous acting experience, Jarman,born in Nashville, was taken straight from his fifth-grade class in Tennessee to star as Jody in *The Yearling* (46), for which he received a special Academy Award. After playing kids for a few years more – notably in *Intruder in the Dust* (49) – he retired at 17. After a failed comeback attempt, Jarman became a show-business producer.
**Selected Films:** *The Yearling* (46), *High Barbaree* (47), *The Sun Comes Up* (49), *Intruder in the Dust* (49), *Rio Grande* (50), *Fair Wind to Java* (53), *The Great Locomotive Chase* (56).

## JAYSTON, Michael (1936- )

Born Michael James in Britain, Jayston has concentrated on theater work in his native country. His film appearances have been occasional; they include *Nicholas and Alexandra* (71), and the TV series *Tinker Tailor Soldier Spy* and *Smiley's People.*
**Selected Films:** *Cromwell* (70), *Nicholas and Alexandra* (71), *Follow Me* (72), *Alice's Adventures in Wonderland* (72), *Tales that Witness Madness* (73), *The Internecine Project* (74).

## JEAN, Gloria (1928- )

Born Gloria Jean Schoonover in Buffalo, Gloria Jean was singing on radio at the age of three and on the New York stage at 11. Making her film debut in *The Under-Pup* (39), she was groomed by Universal to be a successor to child star Deanna Durbin. Jean appeared in some 21 movies in the 1940s, including W C Fields' *Never Give a Sucker an Even Break* (41), and her voice and sweet features earned her a following. However, most of her outings remained second features and she failed to make the transition to adult roles. She retired in the 1960s.
**Selected Films:** *The Under-Pup* (39), *A Little Bit of Heaven* (40), *Never Give a Sucker an Even Break* (41), *Moonlight in Vermont* (43), *Copacabana* (47), *The Ladies' Man* (61), *The Madcaps* (63).

## JEANMAIRE, Zizi (Renée) (1924- )

Paris-born Jeanmaire studied ballet in her youth and grew up to be a prima ballerina. In the 1950s she appeared in a few films, most notably in *Hans Christian Andersen* (52).
**Selected Films:** *Hans Christian Andersen* (52), *Anything Goes* (56), *Folies-Bergère* (56), *Black Tights* (60).

## JEANS, Isabel (1891-1985)

Born in London, Jeans made her British stage debut in 1909 and appeared occasionally in films, making her debut in *The Profligate* (17). She began playing leads and progressed to character parts, as in *Gigi* (58). She was married to Claude Rains at one time.
**Selected Films:** *The Profligate* (17), *The Rat* (25), *Tovarich* (38), *Suspicion* (41), *Gigi* (58), *A Breath of Scandal* (60), *Heavens Above* (63).

## JEFFREYS, Anne (1923- )

Born Anne Carmichael in North Carolina, Jeffreys came to movies from the operatic and Broadway stage. Most of her screen appearances were second-feature leads during the 1940s. Later, she and husband Robert Sterling played the fun-loving ghosts in the mid-1950s TV series *Topper* and then starred in *Love That Jill.*
**Selected Films:** *I Married an Angel* (42), *Step Lively* (44), *Riff-Raff* (47), *Return of the Badmen* (48), *Panic in the City* (68).

## JEFFRIES, Lionel (1926- )

British-born Jeffries came to film as a character comedian. Thin and bald, he usually plays a stiff and bumbling Englishman, an example being his Inspector Parker in *The Wrong Arm of the Law* (63). He began directing films with *The Railway Children* (71).
**Selected Films:** *Stage Fright* (50), *Law and Disorder* (57), *The Trials of Oscar Wilde* (60), *The Wrong Arm of the Law* (63), *Camelot* (67), *Chitty Chitty Bang Bang* (68), *Royal Flash* (75), *Better Late Than Never* (81), *Menage à Trois* (82).

## JENKINS, Allen (1900-1974)

Born Alfred McGonegal in New York, Jenkins came to films from extensive Broadway experience. From the early 1930s on he was one of the most beloved bozos of the screen and variously cast as crooks, taxi drivers, fight managers, and the like. His roles were once described as 'illiterate, illogical, but illuminating mugs.' He finally appeared in over 200 pictures.
**Selected Films:** *The Girl Habit* (31), *I Am a Fugitive from a Chain Gang* (31), *Dead End* (37), *A Slight Case of Murder* (38), *Destry Rides Again* (39), *Wonder Man* (45), *Pillow Talk* (59), *The Front Page* (74).

## JENKINS, Jackie 'Butch' (1937- )

Born in Los Angeles, Butch Jenkins was discovered by an MGM talent scout while playing on the beach and made his film debut as Mickey Rooney's brother in *The Human Comedy* (43). The freckly, gap-toothed youngster appeared in ten more pictures of the 1940s, among them as Elizabeth Taylor's brother in *National Velvet* (44). He retired when he developed an intractable stutter.
**Selected Films:** *The Human Comedy* (43), *National Velvet* (44), *Our Vines Have Tender Grapes* (45), *Boys' Ranch* (46), *My Brother Talks to Horses* (46), *Summer Holiday* (48).

## JENKS, Frank (1902-1962)

Born in Iowa, Jenks came to the movies in the early 1930s after working in vaudeville. For some two decades he usually played minor comic roles as cops, stooges, and other Runyonesque characters.
**Selected Films:** *College Humor* (33), *Dancing on a Dime* (40), *Rogue's Gallery* (45), *The She-Creature* (56), *The Amazing Colossal Man* (57).

## JERGENS, Adele (1922- )

Brooklyn-born Jergens was a model and chorus girl when she was named *Miss World's Fairest* at the 1939 New York World's Fair. The celebrity took her to Broadway and then to Hollywood. In the 1940s and 1950s the platinum blonde appeared in dozens of second features, usually as a showgirl or gangster's moll.
**Selected Films:** *A Thousand and One Nights* (44), *Blonde Dynamite* (50), *Girls in Prison* (56), *The Lonesome Trail* (58).

## JESSEL, George (1898-1981)

New York-born Jessel started his stage career at 9 and had appeared extensively in vaudeville when he made his screeen debut in the 1910s. Though he appeared in a number of films, the screen was the lesser part of his 60 years in show business. After starring on Broadway in *The Jazz Singer*, Jessel turned down the screen part – it went to Al Jolson, and the rest was history. Besides playing occasional supporting roles in films over the decades, Jessel also produced a number of screen musicals for Fox. Noted as an after-dinner and graveside speaker, he was dubbed 'The Toastmaster General of the United States.'
**Selected Films:** *Widow at the Races* (11), *Love, Live and Laugh* (29), *Stage Door Canteen* (43), *Four Jills in a Jeep* (44), *The Busy Body* (67).

## JEWELL, Isabel (1910-1972)

Jewell, born in Shoshone, Wyoming, appeared in stock and on Broadway before making her film debut repeating her stage role in *Blessed Event* (32). For most of her ensuing career, the small platinum blonde was cast as one of Hollywood's resident hussys, playing molls in mostly minor productions. However, she also had some supporting roles in first-rate films, among them the prostitute in *Lost Horizon* (37). After some character roles, Jewell's career coasted to a halt in the 1950s.
**Selected Films:** *Blessed Event* (32), *A Tale of Two Cities* (35), *Lost Horizon* (37), *Gone With the Wind* (39), *The Story of Molly X* (48), *Bernardine* (57).

## JOHANN, Zita (1904- )

Born near Temesvar, Hungary, Johann came to America as a child and began acting in her teens. She was an established star on Broadway when she made her screen debut in D W Griffith's last film, *The Struggle* (31). Johann's movie career was short and largely unsatisfactory, but she is remembered as the Princess Anankha, beloved of the title character in *The Mummy* (32).
**Selected Films:** *The Struggle* (31), *Tiger Shark* (32), *The Mummy* (32), *Luxury Liner* (33), *The Man Who Dared* (33), *Grand Canary* (34).

## JOHNS, Glynis (1923- )

Born in Pretoria, South Africa the daughter of actor Mervyn Johns, Glynis began on the British stage in her teens and soon made her screen debut as a giggly schoolgirl in *South Riding* (36). After her success in *Miranda* (48) (in which she played a mermaid), the exuberant air, impish and sensual features of Johns – and her inimitable husky voice – made her a popular star in films through the

*Timothy Bottoms, Ben Johnson*–The Last Picture Show *(71).*

1960s, most successfully in comedies. Noted for her theater work as well, she won a Tony for her role in *A Little Night Music* (73). She also starred in the TV series *Glynis.*
**Selected Films:** *49th Parallel* (41), *Perfect Strangers* (45), *The Card* (52), *The Court Jester* (56), *The Chapman Report* (62), *Mary Poppins* (64), *Vault of Horror* (73).

## JOHNS, Mervyn (1899- )

Born in Wales, Johns had a long career as a character actor on stage and screen. He usually played sympathetic roles, like Bob Cratchit in *A Christmas Carol* (51) and Captain Peleg in *Moby Dick* (56). He is the father of actress Glynis Johns.
**Selected Films:** *Lady in Danger* (34), *Next of Kin* (41), *Pink String and Sealing Wax* (45), *Dead of Night* (45), *Romeo and Juliet* (54), *The Day of the Triffids* (63), *The Confessional* (77), *Game for Vultures* (79).

## JOHNSON, Arte (1934- )

Diminutive, Chicago-born Johnson came to fame as a comedian on the TV comedy series *Laugh-In.* He appeared in occasional screen supporting roles starting in 1950s.
**Selected Films:** *Miracle in the Rain* (56), *The Subterraneans* (60), *The President's Analyst* (67), *Charge of the Model Ts* (77), *Love at First Bite* (79).

## JOHNSON, Ben (1919- )

Born in Foreaker, Oklahoma, Johnson was talked into leaving his Oklahoma ranch to appear in films by Howard Hughes, who used him in *The Outlaw* (43), and for many years this fine character actor became a staple figure in top westerns and a standard in John Ford pictures, appearing in as many sagebrush sagas as John Wayne. He was a top-notch stuntman and supporting actor, both as a villain and a hero, in many of the best westerns made. He played a villain in *Shane* (53); he doubled for Henry Fonda in *Fort Apache* (48) and for William Holden in *Horse Soldiers* (59). He was a featured actor with Wayne in *She Wore a Yellow Ribbon* (49), *Rio Grande* (50) and many other films. In 1971 Johnson finally got the recognition he deserved, winning the Academy Award for Best Supporting Actor for his role as the philosophical pool hall owner in *The Last Picture Show.*
**Selected Films:** *The Outlaw* (43), *Three Godfathers* (49), *Mighty Joe Young* (49), *She Wore a Yellow Ribbon* (49), *Wagonmaster* (50), *Rio Grande* (50), *Fort Defiance* (51), *Shane* (53), *One Eyed Jacks* (61), *Major Dundee* (65), *Will Penny* (67), *The Wild Bunch* (69), *The Last Picture Show* (71), *Junior Bonner* (72), *The Sugarland Express* (73), *The Town that Dreaded Sundown* (77), *The Hunter* (80).

## JOHNSON, Celia (1908-1982)

Celia Johnson was born in Richmond, England, and studied at the Royal Academy of Dramatic Art.

She made her dramatic debut in George Bernard Shaw's *Major Barbara.* Her first acclaim onstage came for her appearances in the early 1930s in *Debonair* and *Wind and the Rain.* From that point she went on to become one of the most distinguished stage actresses of her time. She also became one of those fine players who concentrate on the stage and make only occasional but memorable appearances onscreen. In movies, Johnson tended to play restrained, well-bred roles, as in her lead in *Brief Encounter* (45), for which she won a New York Films Critics Award. She also had starring roles in two films of Noel Coward plays, *In Which We Serve* (42), and *This Happy Breed* (44). After resuming her stage career for most of the 1960s, Johnson returned to the screen to play a headmistress in *The Prime of Miss Jean Brodie* (69). In the 1970s she appeared in several made-for-TV movies including *Les Misérables.*
**Selected Films:** *In Which We Serve* (42), *Dear Octopus* (42), *This Happy Breed* (44), *Brief Encounter* (45), *I Believe In You* (51), *The Holly and the Ivy* (52), *A Kid for Two Farthings* (55), *The Good Companions* (57), *The Prime of Miss Jean Brodie* (68), *The Hostage Tower* (80).

## JOHNSON, Chic (1891-1962)

Chicago-born Harold Johnson was a ragtime pianist when in 1914 he joined Ole Olsen to make up a vaudeville comedy team. After considerable success on the stage, Olsen and Johnson began appearing in movies in the early 1930s; their biggest splash came when they brought their engagingly beserk Broadway hit *Hellzapoppin* to the screen in 1941.
**Selected Films:** *Oh Sailor Behave!* (30), *Fifty Million Frenchmen* (31), *Country Gentlemen* (36), *Helzapoppin* (41), *Ghost Catchers* (44), *See My Lawyer* (45).

## JOHNSON, Kay (1904-1975)

Cecil B DeMille brought the New York actress, born Catherine Townsend in Mount Vernon, from Broadway to star in his first sound film, *Dynamite* (29). For a decade she was often seen in leads, but never became a major star. Later she played character roles before her career finished in the 1940s.
**Selected Films:** *Dynamite* (29), *The Ship from Shanghai* (30), *Of Human Bondage* (34), *White Banners* (38), *The Adventures of Mark Twain* (44).

## JOHNSON, Richard (1927- )

Born in Upminster, Johnson made his stage debut in his native Britain in the mid-1940s, and has maintained a long association with the Royal Shakespeare Company. The handsome and intense actor has appeared in movie leads and supporting parts since the early 1950s, ranging from routine productions to roles such as Creon in *Oedipus the King* (68) and Cassius in *Julius Caesar* (70). He was briefly married to actress Kim Novak.
**Selected Films:** *Captain Horatio Hornblower* (51), *The Haunting* (63), *The Pumpkin Eater* (64), *Khartoum* (66), *Oedipus the King* (68), *Julius Caesar* (70), *Aces High* (76), *The Monster Club* (80).

## JOHNSON, Rita (1912-1965)

Rita McSean was born in Worcester, Massachusetts and worked her way up from radio to Broadway to movies, making her screen debut with *London By Night* (37). For the next decade she played occasional leads and often 'other women,' mostly in B movies. After moving to more sympathetic parts, Johnson was injured by a freak accident in 1948. Returning to the screen after recovering, she appeared in minor roles until her death at 53.
**Selected Films:** *London By Night* (37), *Man-Proof* (38), *Edison the Man* (40), *My Friend Flicka* (43), *The Big Clock* (48), *Susan Slept Here* (54), *Emergency Hospital* (56), *All Mine to Give* (57).

## JOHNSON, Van (1916- )

Blue-eyed, freckled, red-haired and cute as he could be, Van Johnson came to movies as an object of teenage passion and never quite grew out of it, though fans of later years are most likely to remember him in uniform for his several World War II pictures. Born Charles Van Johnson in Newport, Rhode Island, Johnson entered show business by way of Broadway chorus lines. Soon Hollywood took notice and he turned up in bits and small roles in several pictures of 1942 including *Murder in the Big House.* In the talent vacuum created by the departure of many stars to war, Johnson graduated to friend-of-the-leading-man parts and leads, among them with Spencer Tracy in *A Guy Named Joe* (43) and in *Thirty Seconds Over Tokyo* (44). He also shone in a dramatic role in the screen version of Saroyan's *The Human Comedy* (43). All the same, Johnson remained an actor who looked all too good and whose dramatic range was all too narrow; he was sometimes called 'The Voiceless Sinatra.' Thus, both during and after the war he was most likely to be seen in light romantic films such as *In the Good Old Summertime* (49). His career declined through the 1950s as the former glamour boy began to age. One of the last of his strong dramatic parts was as Lieutenant Steve Maryk, who leads the mutiny and is ambiguously acquitted in Edward Dmytryk's *The Caine Mutiny* (54). In the 1960s Johnson worked sporadically in movies, among them *Divorce, American Style* (67). In the 1970s he was mainly seen in made-for-TV productions such as *Rich Man, Poor Man,* while appearing on the dinner-theater circuit. His cameo performance in Woody Allen's *The Purple Rose of Cairo* (85) placed Johnson in a night-club crowd, a nostalgic return to the tuxedoed roles of his youth.
**Selected Films:** *Too Many Girls* (40), *Murder in the*

Big House (42), *Dr Gillespie's New Assistant* (42), *A Guy Named Joe* (43), *The Human Comedy* (43), *The White Cliffs of Dover* (44), *Thirty Seconds Over Tokyo* (44), *No Leave, No Love* (45), *State of the Union* (48), *Command Decision* (48), *The Good Old Summertime* (49), *Battleground* (50), *The Caine Mutiny* (54), *Brigadoon* (55), *Miracle in the Rain* (56), *Wives and Lovers* (63), *Divorce, American Style* (67), *Yours, Mine and Ours* (68), *The Kidnapping of the President* (80), *The Purple Rose of Cairo* (85).

## JOLSON, Al (1886-1950)

Energy and dynamism made Al Jolson a superstar in every branch of show business. He was a legend in vaudeville, on Broadway, in movies and in radio. Although his career occasionally declined, he was never out, rising to the top again even in old age. He is considered by some to be the greatest and most popular entertainer in American history. Born Asa Yoelson in St Petersburg, Russia, Jolson came to the United States as a child. He began singing in a synagogue where his father was cantor, but he ran away from home to join a circus. By 1906 he was singing in blackface in a minstrel show and by 1909 was a major attraction at New York's Winter Garden Theater, electrifying audiences with his mere presence. In 1923 D W Griffith signed Jolson to star in *Mammy's Boy*, but the film was never completed; three years later he sang in an experimental short feature. Then came movie history. George Jessel had appeared in *The Jazz Singer* on Broadway, the story of a Jewish boy who didn't want to be a cantor and wound up a huge success in vaudeville. Warner Bros. decided to make the film version of the play into the first real talkie. Jessel demanded too high a salary, so Jolson got the role. The sound consisted mostly of background music, but Jolson sang and spoke a few sentences, including the immortal words, 'You ain't heard nothin' yet.' Movies were never the same again. Jolson appeared in more films, including *The Singing Fool* (28), a part-talkie that grossed more money than any movie until *Gone with the Wind* (39). Gradually his popularity declined as fashions changed, but he recouped his success by singing for the troops during World War II. A romanticized version of his life, *The Jolson Story* (46), starring Larry Parks, was an immense hit, as was the sequel, *Jolson Sings Again* (49), in which Jolson appeared briefly. In both pictures Jolson dubbed the singing. The films rejuvenated his radio and recording career. Married four times, Jolson's third wife was singer/dancer/movie star Ruby Keeler. He died of a heart attack shortly after entertaining US troops in Korea.

**Selected Films:** *The Jazz Singer* (27), *The Singing Fool* (28), *Sonny Boy* (29), *Say It with Songs* (29), *Mammy* (30), *Hallelujah I'm a Bum* (33), *Wonder Bar* (34), *Go into Your Dance* (35), *The Singing Kid* (36), *Rose of Washington Square* (39), *Swanee River* (39), *Rhapsody in Blue* (45), *Jolson Sings Again* (49).

*Al Jolson in* The Jazz Singer *(27).*

## JONES, Allan (1907- )

Born in Old Forge, Pennsylvania, Allan Jones studied singing in college and overseas. By the 1930s he had become a popular Broadway musical star, his roles including operettas like *The Student Prince*. Besides a steady career in recordings and nightclubs, Jones began appearing in films, making a considerable success at the time (and earning groans in later times) as a singer and inadvertantly parodistic love interest in two classic Marx Brothers comedies – *A Night at the Opera* (35) and *A Day at the Races* (37). His most popular roles were in musicals such as *Show Boat* (36), in which he sang to Irene Dunne, and *The Firefly* (37), where his leading lady was Jeanette MacDonald (in the latter he sang 'Donkey Serenade,' thereafter his theme song). Jones's screen popularity declined with the decline of romantic musical comedies in the 1940s, but he occasionally showed up in movies into the 1960s. At one time married to actress Irene Hervey, their son was singer Jack Jones.

**Selected Films:** *Reckless* (35), *A Night at the Opera* (35), *Show Boat* (36), *Rose Marie* (36), *The Firefly* (37), *A Day at the Races* (37), *The Great Victor Herbert* (39), *The Boys from Syracuse* (40), *Moonlight in Havana* (42), *Sing a Jingle* (44), *Honeymoon Ahead* (45), *Stage to Thunder Rock* (67).

## JONES, Barry (1893-1981)

Besides a long stage career that began in 1921 in his native Britain, Jones played character roles in

many movies beginning with Bluntschli in *Arms and the Man* (31). Usually playing rather wimpy parts, he starred against type as a mad scientist in *Seven Days to Noon* (50).
**Selected Films:** *Arms and the Man* (31), *Squadron Leader X* (42), *Seven Days to Noon* (50), *Brigadoon* (55), *The Safecracker* (58), *A Study in Terror* (66).

## JONES, Buck (1889-1942)

Born Charles Gebhart in Vincennes, Indiana, Jones was a youngster when his family moved to Oklahoma. He learned ranch life and became a top rodeo rider and then joined the army. He later appeared as a trick rider with the Ringling Brothers Circus before getting his start in the movies as a bit player and stuntman. Fox Studios built him up as a rival to their biggest star, Tom Mix, to keep Mix in line. Jones then launched himself on a spectacular career as a B western star, becoming one of a handful of great stars in the 1920s and 1930s. He was a better-than-average cowboy actor who developed a huge following, especially among youngsters at Saturday matinees. He always appeared astride his white horse, Silver. He was still acting in 1942, although he was not the big star he had been earlier. In that year, he was killed in the Cocoanut Grove night club fire in Boston, Massachusetts, which took nearly 500 lives. Jones died a hero's death, going back into the fire to save other people.
**Selected Films:** *Blood Will Tell* (17), *Straight from the Shoulder* (20), *Skid Proof* (23), *Riders of the Purple Sage* (26), *The Flying Horseman* (27), *The Lone Rider* (30), *Border Law* (32), *The California Trail* (33), *Boss Rider of Gun Creek* (36), Unmarried (39), *Riders of Death Valley* (41), *Riders of the West* (42).

## JONES, Carolyn (1933-1983)

Jones, born in Amarillo, Texas, came to films from the stage. Dark-eyed and unconventionally beautiful, she appeared in a few supporting roles before making a splash as a wacky Bohemian in *The Bachelor Party* (57); her seven minutes on the screen got her an Oscar nomination. From then on she was usually typed in offbeat roles, including her Morticia in the TV series *The Addams Family.*
**Selected Films:** *The Road to Bali* (52), *The Bachelor Party* (57), *Marjorie Morningstar* (58), *A Hole in the Head* (59), *How the West Was Won* (62), *Good Luck, Miss Wyckoff* (79).

## JONES, Christopher (1941- )

American-born Jones appeared in leads and supporting roles in a number of popular films of the later 1960s including *Wild in the Streets* (68) and David Lean's *Ryan's Daughter* (70). He also starred in the TV series *The Legend of Jesse James.*
**Selected Films:** *Chubasco* (67), *Wild in the Streets* (68), *The Looking Glass War* (69), *Three in the Attic* (69), *Ryan's Daughter* (70).

## JONES, Dean (1933- )

Born in Morgan City, Alabama, Jones was a blues singer before making his film debut in *Gaby* (56). Mostly he has played easygoing light leads, many of them for Disney including *That Darn Cat* (65). A more recent and more dramatic role was as Charles Colson in *Born Again* (78).
**Selected Films:** *Gaby* (56), *Tea and Sympathy* (56), *Under the Yum Yum Tree* (64), *That Darn Cat* (65), *The Ugly Dachshund* (66), *The Love Bug* (69), *The Shaggy DA* (76), *Born Again* (78).

## JONES, Henry (1912- )

Born in Philadelphia, Jones has been a familiar character actor on screen and TV since the early 1950s, often playing the quirky guy next door – as in the TV series *Phyllis.* He lends himself equally well to comic and to bad-guy roles.
**Selected Films:** *This Is the Army* (43), *The Lady Says No* (51), *The Bad Seed* (56), *Vertigo* (58), *Never Too Late* (65), *Support Your Local Sheriff* (69), *Pete 'n' Tillie* (72), *Nine to Five* (80), *Deathtrap* (82).

## JONES, James Earl (1931- )

Jones born in Arkabutla, Mississipi, studied drama in college and made his Broadway debut in 1957, soon becoming one of the most distinguished black actors of the American stage. After several supporting roles in films, Jones took his stage lead to the screen in *The Great White Hope* (70), which earned him an Oscar nomination. Among his wide- ranging screen and TV roles since, he provided the ominous voice of Darth Vader in the *Star Wars* series.
**Selected Films:** *The Great White Hope* (70), *Claudine* (74), *The Bingo Long Traveling All Stars and Motor Kings* (76), *Exorcist II* (77), *Conan the Barbarian* (82), *Soul Man* (86), *Gardens of Stone* (87).

## JONES, Jennifer (1919- )

Born Phyllis Isley in Tulsa, Oklahoma, Jones was an intense leading lady who could be ethereal or sensual as the role required. Married first to actor Robert Walker, then to producer David O Selznick, who carefully guided her career, she won an Academy Award for Best Actress for her performance as a French peasant girl who saw visions of the Virgin Mary in *The Song of Bernadette* (43). The movie was publicized as being Jones' film debut, ignoring the B pictures she had made using her real name beginning in 1939.
**Selected Films:** *Dick Tracy's G Men* (39), *The Song of Bernadette* (43), *Since You Went Away* (44), *Cluny Brown* (46), *Duel in the Sun* (46), *Portrait of Jennie* (48), *Ruby Gentry* (52), *Beat the Devil* (54), *Love Is a Many-Splendored Thing* (55), *The Man in the Gray Flannel Suit* (56), *The Barretts of Wimpole Street* (57), *A Farewell to Arms* (58), *Tender Is the Night* (61), *The Towering Inferno* (74), *Patricia* (80).

*Shirley Jones and Robert Preston* – The Music Man *(62).*

## JONES, L Q (1936- )

Born J E McQueen, Jones came to films in the late 1960s and over the next few years appeared in several popular movies including *The Wild Bunch* (69), and *Mother, Jugs and Speed* (76).
**Selected Films:** *The Wild Bunch* (69), *The Ballad of Cable Hogue* (70), *The Hunting Party* (71), *The Brotherhood of Satan* (71), *Mother, Jugs and Speed* (76).

## JONES, Marcia Mae (1924- )

Los Angeles-born Jones made her movie debut at the age of 2 in *Mannequin* (26). In the 1930s she was one of the popular child stars of the era. Although she was no Shirley Temple in looks or charm, she showed real depth in a serious part in *These Three* (36). After some attempts at grown-up roles she retired for many years, coming back (sometimes as Marsha Jones) to screen and TV work in the 1970s.
**Selected Films:** *Mannequin* (26), *King of Jazz* (31), *These Three* (36), *Heidi* (37), *The Adventures of Tom Sawyer* (38), *Secrets of a Co-Ed* (42), *Arson, Inc.* (49), *Chicago Calling* (52), *The Way We Were* (73).

## JONES, Shirley (1934- )

Born in Smithton, Pennsylvania, Shirley Jones got a starring role in musical comedy on her first try with an agent – the part of Laurie in a touring company of *Oklahoma!*. She played the same role on screen in 1955. The next year she co-starred with Gordon MacRae again in another Rodgers and Hammerstein musical, *Carousel*. After several similar efforts on stage and screen, Jones seemed headed for typecasting as a sweet young thing, but she broke out of that mold with her role as a prostitute in *Elmer Gantry* (60) – for which she won a supporting-actress Academy Award. Thereafter her stage and screen parts ranged satisfactorily from the wholesome to the serious. She continued to star in musicals, among them *The Music Man* (62). In the early 1970s Jones was the mother of *The Partridge Family* and one of the TV family was played by her stepson David Cassidy, son of actor Jack Cassidy. Her role in the TV movie *Silent Night, Lonely Night* earned Jones an Emmy nomination.
**Selected Films:** *Oklahoma!* (55), *Carousel* (56), *April Love* (57), *Pepe* (60), *Elmer Gantry* (60), *The Music Man* (62), *Dark Purpose* (64), *The Happy Ending* (70), *Beyond the Poseidon Adventure* (79).

## JONES, Tommy Lee (1946- )

Jones, born in San Saba, Texas, appeared in the 1970s as a strong-featured young leading man both on screen and TV. Among his roles were as a cop and secret psycho who menaces Faye Dunaway in

*The Eyes of Laura Mars* (78). He also starred in the TV movie *The Amazing Howard Hughes.*
**Selected Films:** *Love Story* (70), *Rolling Thunder* (77), *The Betsy* (78), *The Eyes of Laura Mars* (78), *Coal Miner's Daughter* (80), *Nate and Hayes* (83), *Black Moon Rising* (86).

## JORDAN, Bobby (1923-1965)

One of the original Dead End Kids in the slum drama *Dead End* (37), Jordan moved with Huntz Hall and Leo Gorcey into the low-budget 'Bowery Boys' series of the 1940s and 1950s. He also appeared in minor roles on his own.
**Selected Films:** *Dead End* (37), *Angels With Dirty Faces* (38), *That Gang of Mine* (40), *Bowery Champs* (44), *Hard Boiled Mahoney* (47), *This Man is Armed* (56).

## JORDAN, Richard (1938- )

New York-born Jordan attended Harvard and played Shakespeare onstage before breaking into films in the 1970s. While working on the TV mini-series *Captains and the Kings* he met actress Blair Brown, with whom he had a child.
**Selected Films:** *Lawman* (70), *The Friends of Eddie Coyle* (73), *Logan's Run* (76), *Interiors* (78), *Raise the Titanic!* (80).

## JORY, Victor (1902-1982)

Victor Jory was born in Dawson City, Alaska, and attended the University of California. The tough and determined air that finally he displayed in movies was not a pose; he was a boxing and wrestling champ during a Coast Guard stint. After drama studies at the Pasadena Playhouse and stage experience beginning in the late 1920s, Jory entered films with *Sailor's Luck* (32). Given his robust physique, saturnine features, and lugubrious voice, he was usually typed in supporting or bit parts as a heavy. He did, however, have the lead in a few films of the 1930s including *Escape from Devil's Island* (35), and he was Fairy King, Oberon, in *A Midsummer Night's Dream* (35) and Injun Joe in *The Adventures of Tom Sawyer* (38). Through his decades of movie work, Jory maintained an active stage career as well; his play *Five Who Were Mad* was produced on Broadway. He remained one of everybody's favorite bad guys in movies until the end of his life.
**Selected Films:** *Sailor's Luck* (32), *A Midsummer Night's Dream* (35), *Escape from Devil's Island* (35), *The Adventures of Tom Sawyer (38)*, *Gone With the Wind* (39), *Canadian Pacific* (49), *Valley of the Kings* (54), *The Miracle Worker* (62), *Papillon* (73), *The Mountain Men* (80).

## JOSLYN, Allyn (1905-1981)

Born in Milford, Pennsylvania, Joslyn appeared on Broadway before making his film debut in 1937. He usually played pompous rich guys. Joslyn also did much radio and TV work, including the TV series *The Addams Family.*
**Selected Films:** *They Won't Forget* (37), *Heaven Can Wait* (43), *It Shouldn't Happen to a Dog* (47), *The Fastest Gun Alive* (56), *The Brothers O'Toole* (73).

## JOURDAN, Louis (1919- )

Jourdan, born Louis Gendice in Marseilles, pursued dramatic studies in Paris before appearing on the stage. Before long his dashing, dark-eyed good looks brought him to screen romantic roles that made him a great favorite in France; the first of these was *Le Corsaire* (39). However, this phase of his career came to an abrupt end when Jourdan refused to make propaganda films for the Nazis during the occupation; for the duration of the war he was associated with the French Underground. After the war David O Selznick brought Jourdan to Hollywood, where he appeared in Hitchcock's *The Paradine Case* (48) and, memorably, as the obsession of Joan Fontaine in Max Ophul's *Letter From an Unknown Woman* (48). From that point on, Jourdan was an international star, though one who was perhaps too good-looking for his own good: despite determined efforts, he has never quite escaped from his Continental-lover image. His later roles have included several made-for-TV swashbucklers such as *The Count of Monte Cristo.*
**Selected Films:** *Le Corsaire* (39), *L'Arlesienne* (42), *Letter From an Unknown Woman* (48), *The Paradine Case* (48), *Madame Bovary* (49), *Three Coins in the Fountain* (54), *Gigi* (58), *Can-Can* (60), *A Flea in Her Ear* (68), *Silver Bears* (77), *Octopussy* (83).

*Leslie Caron, Louis Jourdan in* Gigi *(58).*

## JOUVET, Louis (1887-1951)

Originally a druggist, Louis Jouvet, born in Corzan, France, pursued dreams of a stage career despite initial rejections from the Paris Conservatoire. Finally he became a theater administrator – which he would remain for much of his life – and made his acting debut in 1910. By the end of the next decade Jouvet had proved himself one of the finest actors in France, had fought in World War I, and had brought his repertory troupe to New York to considerable acclaim. Jouvet made his film debut in *Shylock* (13), but he did not try movies again until 1933, when he played the lead in *Topaze*. He became a forceful and memorable figure in French films. Among his roles were The Baron in *The Lower Depths* (36) and Mosca in *Volpone* (40). After leaving the country during World War II, Jouvet returned to stage and film work in France; the quality of his films declined, but his obsession with the stage persisted – he said that he made films only to secure money for his stage companies.
**Selected Films:** *Shylock* (13), *Topaze* (33), *La Kermesse Héroïque* (35), *The Lower Depths* (36), *Un Carnet de Bal* (37), *Hôtel du Nord* (38), *Volpone* (40), *Quai des Orfèvres* (47), *Une Histoire d'Amour* (51).

## JOY, Leatrice (1899-1985)

Born Leatrice Joy Zeidler in New Orleans, Joy started in films as an extra in 1915. Within three years she had developed into one of the great stars of the era. Usually she played a sophisticated and fashionable female. Joy's career declined with the coming of sound, but she continued to appear in films occasionally. She was married to actor John Gilbert.
**Selected Films:** *The Folly of Revenge* (16), *You Can't Fool Your Wife* (23), *The Ten Commandments* (23), *A Most Immoral Lady* (29), *First Love* (39), *Love Nest* (52).

*Leatrice Joy.*

*Raul Julia and William Hurt in* Kiss of the Spider Woman *(85).*

## JOYCE, Alice (1889-1955)

Joyce, born in Kansas City, Missouri, was a model before she began appearing in films around 1910. It was some years before she played leads, but from *The Courage of Silence* (17) she was a charming and very popular leading lady, adept at tear-jerkers like *Stella Dallas* (25). Called 'The Madonna of the Screen' in her heyday, Joyce saw her career evaporate with the coming of sound.
**Selected Films:** *The Engineer's Sweetheart* (10), *The Courage of Silence* (17), *Cousin Kate* (21), *The Green Goddess* (23), *Stella Dallas* (25), *Beau Geste* (26), *Song of My Heart* (38).

## JOYCE, Brenda (1918- )

Born Betty Leabo in Kansas City, Missouri, Joyce grew up with a fresh-faced, lithe beauty that led her first to modelling and then to the screen. Rather wooden in acting but highly decorative in presence, Joyce usually played the heroine in assorted Bs. She did play Jane in several Tarzan movies with Johnny Weissmuller and Lex Barker.
**Selected Films:** *The Rains Came* (39), *The Enchanted Forest* (46), *Tarzan's Magic Fountain* (49).

## JUDGE, Arline (1912-1974)

Born in Bridgeport, Connecticut, Judge was appearing in a nightclub when she was discovered by a director. Making her debut in *Are These Our Children?* (31), she played girlish roles for a while,

and then more mature leads in Bs. Judge was known for her rapid changes of husband (final total: 7) as much as for her acting.
**Selected Films:** *Are These Our Children?* (31), *Girl Crazy* (32), *King of Burlesque* (36), *The Lady is Willing* (42), *Two Nights in Brooklyn* (49).

## JULIA, Raul (1940- )

Born to a prosperous family in Puerto Rico, Julia began acting in school plays. Coming to New York in 1964, the young man found work off- and then on Broadway, where his roles have ranged from Shakespeare and Harold Pinter to the musical *Nine*. Following his screen debut in *Panic in Needle Park* (71), Julia has worked his movie roles around a busy theater schedule; he is best-known for his touching and memorable performance as a jailed revolutionary in *Kiss of the Spider Woman* (85).
**Selected Films:** *Panic in Needle Park* (71), *The Organization Man (71), The Gumball Rally* (76). *One From the Heart* (82), *Kiss of the Spider Woman* (85), *Compromising Positions* (85), *The Morning After* (87).

## JURADO, Katy (1927- )

Born Maria Jurado Garcia in Guadalahara, Jurado acted in films in her native Mexico before making her Hollywood debut in *The Bullfighter and the Lady* (51). Next year came her most famous role as the fiery señorita who taunts Lloyd Bridges in *High Noon* (52). Jurado continued to be a striking presence in films and received a supporting-actress Oscar nomination for *Broken Lance* (54). She was married to actor Ernest Borgnine from 1959 to 1963.
**Selected Films:** *No Maturas* (43), *The Bullfighter and the Lady* (51), *High Noon* (52), *Broken Lance* (54), *One-Eyed Jacks* (59), *Barabbas* (61), *Pat Garrett and Billy the Kid* (72), *The Children of Sanchez* (78).

## JURGENS, Curt (1912-1982)

Born in Munich, Germany, Jurgens came to acting from journalism, making his stage and screen debut in *The Royal Waltz* (35). For nearly a decade he was a popular figure in German cinema where he was billed as Curd Jürgens, but then in 1944 the Nazis declared Jurgens ideologically suspect and sent him to a concentration camp. After the war besides acting in movies, he began to direct with *Prämien auf den Tod* (50), and thereafter was apt to be found in credits for acting, directing, or screenwriting (though the latter were never as successful as his acting). After *The Devil's General* (55) Jurgens was known internationally. From then to the end of his life he played in dozens of films, most often as an urbane villain, not infrequently a Nazi. Among his later films were *The Threepenny Opera* (63) and *The Spy Who Loved Me* (77). Despite his nearly 100 movies he considered himself mainly a stage actor.
**Selected Films:** *The Royal Waltz* (35), *Operette* (40), *Orient Express* (54), *The Devil's General* (55), *Me and the Colonel* (57), *Inn of the Sixth Happiness* (58), *I Aim at the Stars* (59), *The Longest Day* (62), *The Threepenny Opera* (63), *The Assassination Bureau* (68), *The Spy Who Loved Me* (77), *Just a Gigolo* (80).

## JUSTICE, James Robertson (1905-1975)

Justice once observed, 'No one is more surprised than I to find myself acting for a living.' Among his other endeavors were being a naturalist and journalist, racing cars, and teaching falconry to the British Royal Family. A PhD, Justice, born in Wigtown, Scotland, also served as an honorary rector of the University of Edinburgh. The bearded gentleman acted in quite a few films including a turn as Henry VIII in *The Sword and the Rose* (53), and the crusty surgeon Sir Lancelot Spratt in the series that began with *Doctor in the House* (54).
**Selected Films:** *Champagne Charlie* (44), *Scott of the Antarctic* (48), *Whisky Galore* (49), *Rob Roy* (53), *The Sword and the Rose* (53), *Doctor in the House* (54), *Moby Dick* (56), *Campbell's Kingdom* (57), *The Guns of Navarone* (61), *Some Will, Some Won't* (70).

## JUSTIN, John (1917- )

Born John Ledsman in London, Justin has acted on the stage in his native Britain for most of his career. Though he made a notable start in movies as the star of *The Thief of Bagdad* (40), his ensuing movie appearances have been intermittent.
**Selected Films:** *Dark Journey* (37), *The Thief of Bagdad* (40), *Journey Together* (45), *King of the Khyber Rifles* (53), *The Golden Salamander* (62), *Savage Messiah* (72), *The Big Sleep* (78), *Trenchcoat* (83).

# K

## KAHN, Madeline (1942-     )

Boston-born Kahn grew up in New York and attended Hofstra University, where she studied voice and majored in speech therapy. After a few years of singing in revues she appeared on Broadway, in the Richard Rodgers musical *Two By Two* (70). Kahn made her screen debut in Peter Bogdanovich's *What's Up, Doc?* (72). The next year she made a splash in his *Paper Moon*, where her role as tartish Trixie Delight earned her an Oscar nomination. With her next role, as the Dietrich-gone-to-seed barroom singer Lili Von Shtupp in Mel Brooks' *Blazing Saddles* (74), Kahn received another Oscar nomination and the public realized she was one of the more memorable and offbeat comediennes of her time. Continuing her fruitful association with Brooks, she appeared in *Young Frankenstein* (74), *High Anxiety* (77), and *History of the World Part One* (81). In 1983 she starred in the TV series *Oh Madeline*.
**Selected Films:** *What's Up, Doc?* (72), *Paper Moon* (73), *Blazing Saddles* (74), *Young Frankenstein* (74), *The Adventures of Sherlock Holmes' Smarter Brother* (75), *High Anxiety* (77), *Wholly Moses* (80), *History of the World Part One* (81), *Yellowbeard* (83), *City Heat* (84), *Clue* (85).

## KAMINSKA, Ida (1899-1980)

Born in Odessa, Russia, Kaminska emigrated to Poland and became a famous figure of the Polish stage. Her film roles were infrequent, but she appeared in movies from Polish silents to the American production, *The Angel Levine* (70). She is best known for her supporting part in the touching Czech film *The Shop on Main Street* (66), for which she received an Oscar nomination.
**Selected Films:** *A Vilna Legend* (24), *Without a Home* (36), *The Shop on Main Street* (66), *The Angel Levine* (70).

*Madeline Kahn in* Young Frankenstein *(74).*

## KANE, Carol (1952-     )

Born in Cleveland, Ohio, the daughter of an architect, Carol Kane began acting on the stage at 14 and made her first film appearance at 18 in *Is This Trip Really Necessary?* (70). The next year she had a brief but memorable role as Art Garfunkel's hippie ladyfriend and mentor in Mike Nichols' *Carnal Knowledge* (71). In 1975 Kane played her first big role as a delicate but determined young wife in the nostalgic movie about Jewish emigrés, *Hester Street*. The role earned her an Oscar nomination. For several years her wide-eyed and unconventional features were seen in leads and supporting roles in some of the better films of the decade, including *Dog Day Afternoon* (75) and *Annie Hall* (77). She also appeared on the stage, and on television, in the series *Taxi*.
**Selected Films:** *Is This Trip Necessary?* (70), *Carnal Knowledge* (71), *The Last Detail* (73), *Hester Street* (75), *Dog Day Afternoon* (75), *Harry and Walter Go to New York* (76), *Valentino* (77), *Annie Hall* (77), *When a Stranger Calls* (79), *Norman Loves Rose* (82), *Transylvania 6-5000* (85), *Jumpin' Jack Flash* (86).

## KANE, Helen (1904-1966)

Born Helen Schroeder in The Bronx, Kane appeared in vaudeville in her teens and moved to Broadway in 1927. It was the next year that in the musical *Good Boy* she defined the flapper era with her squeaky, boop-boop-a-doop rendition of the song 'I Wanna Be Loved by You.' She made a few movies at that time. Years later, she was a character in the film *Three Little Words* (50). In it Kane dubbed her famous song to be lip-synched by Debbie Reynolds.
**Selected Films:** *Pointed Heels* (29), *Dangerous Nan McGrew* (29), *Heads Up* (30).

## KAPLAN, Marvin (1924-     )

Born in Brooklyn, Kaplan studied drama at USC and in a stage performance caught the eye of Katherine Hepburn, who got him a part in *Adam's Rib* (49). With his owlish looks and archetypal Brooklyn accent, Kaplan became a familiar comic actor. Among his TV work has been a role in the series *Alice*.
**Selected Films:** *Adam's Rib* (49), *I Can Get It for You Wholesale* (51), *It's a Mad Mad Mad Mad World* (63), *The Great Race* (65).

## KARLOFF, Boris (1887-1969)

Born William Henry Pratt in Dulwich, England, Karloff was the reigning king of horror during the 1930s, and for decades his face and voice were instantly recognizable as symbols of terror, although in his later years it was often mock terror. Karloff was an actor of sensitivity and skill, yet because of his identification with the horror genre, he was rarely given a chance to appear in other

Zita Johann as the reincarnation of his beloved, and Boris Karloff as the undead Imhotep, in The Mummy (32).

types of films. He left England for Canada, took up acting and landed a position with a touring stock company. He proved to be a quick study, and would play as many as a hundred roles a year. Like other touring actors, Karloff faced hard times because of competition from the growing film industry. In 1918 he went to Hollywood, where he struggled for years, working his way up from extra to bit part and occasional featured role. Because of his sinister appearance, he usually got the part of a villain. His wonderfully well-developed voice was a great asset when sound came in. Karloff was picked by director James Whale for the part of the monster in *Frankenstein* (31). Since he was an average-sized man, he was given a padded costume and big boots to make him look larger, plus a sensational makeup job by Hollywood's makeup wizard, Jack Pierce, which allowed the audience to see his expression. *Frankenstein* was a sensation and it made Karloff a star. He was always identified with the role of the monster, although he played it only three times. He also created the character of the Mummy in *The Mummy* (32). Karloff played Indians, Orientals, gangsters and mad scientists – an impressive number of mad scientists. Even when the quality of the films in which he appeared declined, he always gave a thoroughly professional performance. *Targets* (68), a quickie, was one of his last films and one of his best. Karloff never abandoned the stage. He was enormously successful as Captain Hook in *Peter Pan*, but his best role was in the stage version of *Arsenic and Old Lace*, where he played a madman who killed every time somebody told him he looked like Boris Karloff.

**Selected Films:** *His Majesty the American* (19), *The Prisoner* (23), *Frankenstein* (31), *Scarface* (32), *The Old Dark House* (32), *The Mask of Fu Manchu* (32), *The Mummy* (32), *The Lost Patrol* (34), *The Black Cat* (34), *Bride of Frankenstein* (35), *The Black Room* (35), *Son of Frankenstein* (39), *Tower of London* (39), *The Ape* (40), *House of Frankenstein* (44), *The Body Snatcher* (45), *Isle of the Dead* (45), *Tap Roots* (48), *The Black Castle* (52), *Corridors of Blood* (58), *The Raven* (63), *Black Sabbath* (64), *Targets* (68), *House of Evil* (70).

## KARNS, Roscoe (1893-1970)

Karns, born in San Bernadino, California, started in the theater in his teens and appeared in a few silents of the 1920s. With the coming of sound he became a familiar character actor, usually playing newspaper reporters, and hard-boiled salesmen. In the late 1950s he appeared with Jackie Cooper in the TV series *Hennessey*.

**Selected Films:** *The Life of the Party* (20), *Beggars of Life* (28), *The Front Page* (30), *Twentieth Century* (34), *It Happened One Night* (34), *His Girl Friday* (40), *Onionhead* (58), *Man's Favorite Sport* (64).

## KARRAS, Alex (1935- )

Born in Gary, Indiana, Alex Karras played football at the University of Iowa and was a tackle for the Detroit Lions when he retired from sports. He worked in several TV movies in the 1970s including *The 500 Pound Jerk* (73), then appeared in Mel Brooks' *Blazing Saddles* (74). In 1982 the burly Karras was cast in the unlikely role of a gay valet in *Victor/Victoria*. He is married to actress Susan Clark, his costar in the TV series *Webster*.

**Selected Films:** *Blazing Saddles* (74), *When Time Ran Out* (80), *Nobody's Perfekt* (81), *Victor/Victoria* (82).

## KASZNAR, Kurt (1913-1979)

Born Kurt Servischer in Vienna, Austria, Kaznar was a prominent actor in Germany when he came to the United States in the mid-1930s. Soon he was appearing on Broadway and stuck with stage work until his movie debut in *The Light Touch* (52). From then on the hefty actor occasionally appeared in leads and supporting roles in films, often playing eccentric and enthusiastic characters.
**Selected Films:** *The Light Touch* (52), *Lili* (53), *My Sister Eileen* (55), *A Farewell to Arms* (58), *Casino Royale* (67).

## KAYE, Danny (1913-1987)

Born David Daniel Kaminsky in Brooklyn, New York, he started singing and dancing for audiences while he was still in school. After making several unpromising two-reelers in the 1930s, he went back to New York to act on the stage. It was his show-stopping patter song, 'Tchaikowsky,' which he sang in Kurt Weill's Broadway musical, *Lady in the Dark*, that got him a real movie contract. His first film for Goldwyn, *Up in Arms* (44), was an instant success, and Kaye was a star – a likeable comedian whose trademark was the fast patter song, often sung with a foreign accent, even with fake foreign phrases. This movie was followed by several similar, and nearly as successful, films, but then there were contract disputes and a poor choice of scripts. *Hans Christian Andersen* (52) was a big hit, although critics thought it excessively sentimental, and purists wondered where Hollywood ever got the idea that Andersen was a shoemaker. *White Christmas* (54), opposite Bing Crosby, was another box office success, but not an overwhelming one. In his last years he was best known for his charity work, especially his work with children all over the world while representing UNICEF. In 1954 Kaye was given a Special Academy Award 'for his unique talents and his service to the American people.' And in 1981 he was given the Academy's Jean Hersholt Humanitarian Award.

*Danny Kaye in* The Kid From Brooklyn *(46).*

**Selected Films:** *Up in Arms* (44), *Wonder Man* (45), *The Kid from Brooklyn* (46), *The Secret Life of Walter Mitty* (47), *A Song Is Born* (48), *The Inspector General* (49), *Hans Christian Andersen* (52), *Knock on Wood* (53), *White Christmas* (54), *The Court Jester* (56), *Me and the Colonel* (57), *Merry Andrew* (58), *The Five Pennies* (59), *The Man from the Diner's Club* (63), *The Madwoman of Chaillot* (69).

## KAYE, Stubby (1918- )

Born in New York, Kaye got into show business by way of a radio amateur hour in 1939. After vaudeville experience, the short round Kaye played the classic role of Nicely-Nicely Johnson in the 1950 Broadway production of *Guys and Dolls*, singing 'A Fugue for Tinhorns' in his inimitable brassy voice. Bringing that role to the screen version in 1955, he has alternated film and stage work since.
**Selected Films:** *Taxi* (53), *Guys and Dolls* (55), *Li'l Abner* (59), *Cat Ballou* (65), *Sweet Charity* (69), *Six Pack Annie* (75).

## KEACH, Stacy (1941- )

Born in Savannah, Georgia, Stacy Keach was once told by an agent to forget leading roles because he had a harelip that resisted surgery; fortunately, Keach ignored the advice. After drama studies at Yale and in London, he found acclaim in the off-Broadway satire *MacBird!* and won a Tony on Broadway for *Indians*. Keach made his movie debut as a drunken drifter in *The Heart is a Lonely Hunter* (68). Over the next decade he appeared in a number of films including leading roles in *Doc* (71) and *Luther* (72). In the range of his performances the solid and strong-featured Keach is nicely versatile, handling everything from his role as Martin Luther to tough-guy parts such as his Frank James in *The Long Riders* (80). In 1983 he began appearing in the title role of the TV series *Mike Hammer*. The show and his career came to an abrupt halt when Keach was arrested and imprisoned in England for cocaine possession. After some months in prison, a contrite and chastened Keach emerged in 1986 to restart his career – and the *Mike Hammer* show.
**Selected Films:** *The Heart Is a Lonely Hunter* (68), *End of the Road* (68), *Brewster McCloud* (70), *Doc* (71), *Luther* (72), *Fat City* (72), *Conduct Unbecoming* (75), *Gray Lady Down* (78), *The Long Riders* (80), *Butterfly* (82), *That Championship Season* (82).

## KEATING, Larry (1897-1963)

Born in St Paul, Minnesota, Keating came to show business early and worked long in theater, radio, movies, and later in TV. Most often he played a businessman or a neighbor, as he did on *The Burns and Allen* TV show.
**Selected Films:** *Song of the Sarong* (45), *When Worlds Collide* (51), *Daddy Long Legs* (55), *Boys' Night Out* (62), *The Incredible Mr Limpet* (64).

*Buster Keaton in* The General *(26).*

## KEATON, Buster (1895-1966)

Keaton was an accomplished acrobat when he was little more than a baby, a genuine genius, one of America's greatest silent film comedians – the unsmiling but game little fellow who always came out on top no matter what the odds. He was born Joseph Francis Keaton in Piqua, Kansas, to parents who performed in medicine shows. They later moved to vaudeville, and during his childhood Keaton learned all there is to know about comedy, from timing to pratfalls. He became a vaudeville star himself and then abandoned the stage to make a series of comic two-reelers with Fatty Arbuckle. He then co-wrote, co-directed and starred in shorts on his own. His screen persona was that of a handsome, dignified and infinitely resourceful young man whose deadpan 'stone face' showed emotion with brilliant subtlety. His lithe acrobatic body expressed whirlwind motion and activity with complete originality as he was caught in the clutches of machinery or dogged by confusion and misunderstandings. Keaton was a bridegroom trying to put together a portable home in *One Week* (20). *The Playhouse* (22) was dreamy and surrealistic with amazing photographic illusions. *The Boat* (22), which pulled down everything around it, had hints of black fatalism behind the humor. In 1923, Keaton began making feature-length comedies. *Sherlock Junior* (24) about a movie projectionist lost between reality and the dreams on the screen; *The General* (27), a Civil War story; and *Our Hospitality* (23) are among his greatest longer films. It was after Keaton gave up his own studio that his troubles began. A trusting soul, he was devoured by studio bosses, lost control of his movies and was hit by sound films. His marriage to Natalie Talmadge dissolved and he began to drink heavily. For years a neglected artist, Keaton survived in movies as an actor, assistant director and gag writer. Beginning with a series of live appearances in Paris, France, his reputation was fully restored. Keaton won a Special Academy Award in 1959 'for his unique talents which brought immortal comedies to the screen,' and in 1965, shortly before he died of cancer, he received the greatest ovation ever given at the Venice Film Festival.

**Selected Films:** *The Butcher Boy* (17), *Good Night Nurse* (18), *The Hayseed* (19), *The Saphead* (20), *One Week* (20), *The Playhouse* (22), *The Boat* (22), *The Paleface* (22), *Cops* (22), *The Balloonatics* (22), *Our Hospitality* (23), *Sherlock Junior* (24), *The Navigator* (24), *The General* (27), *The Cameraman* (28), *Spite Marriage* (29), *Doughboys* (30), *The Jones Family in Hollywood* (39), *Quick Millions* (39), *San Diego I Love You* (44), *You're My Everything* (49), *The Loveable Cheat* (50), *Sunset Boulevard* (50), *Limelight* (52), *Around the World in Eighty Days* (56), *It's a Mad Mad Mad Mad World* (63), *Railrodder* (65), *Film* (65), *A Funny Thing Happened on the Way to the Forum* (66).

## KEATON, Diane (1949- )

Born Diane Hall in Los Angeles, California, Keaton moved to New York to study acting, appearing in the Broadway musical *Hair*. She then worked with Woody Allen, becoming a film star under his direction. She won an Academy Award for Best Actress in Allen's *Annie Hall* (77), playing the title role. In 1981 she was nominated for Best Actress for her fine work as Louise Bryant, the lover and fellow radical of John Reed, in *Reds*.

**Selected Films:** *Lovers and Other Strangers* (70), *The Godfather* (72), *Play It Again Sam* (72), *Looking for Mr Goodbar* (77), *Annie Hall* (77), *Manhattan* (79), *Reds* (81), *Shoot the Moon* (82), *The Little Drummer Girl* (84), *Crimes of the Heart* (86), *Radio Days* (87), *Baby Boom* (87).

## KEATON, Michael (1952- )

American actor Keaton played puckish comic roles in several screen hits of the 1980s including the flaky-but-vulnerable party animal in *Night Shift* (82), and Teri Garr's househusband in *Mr Mom* (83).

**Selected Films:** *Night Shift* (82), *Mr Mom* (83), *Johnny Dangerously* (84), *Touch and Go* (86).

## KEDROVA, Lila (1918- )

Born in Leningrad, Russia, Kedrova emigrated to France as a child and began her stage and screen career in Europe. Her first English-language film role is still her best-known – as Madame Hortense in *Zorba the Greek* (64), for which Kedrova won an Oscar as best supporting-actress. She has appeared in films internationally since.

**Selected Films:** *Zorba the Greek* (64), *Torn Curtain* (66), *The Kremlin Letter* (69), *March or Die* (77), *Tell Me a Riddle* (80).

## KEEL, Howard (1917- )

Keel was born Harold Leek in Gillespie, Illinois. Beginning his film career in a British movie, *The*

*Small Voice* (48), he skyrocketed to fame in his next picture, *Annie Get Your Gun* (50), the film version of the immensely successful Irving Berlin Broadway musical. Keel played Frank Butler, the sharpshooter who captivates Annie Oakley, played by Betty Hutton. He immediately became cast as the stalwart baritone who played the lead in many big Hollywood musicals, including *Show Boat* (51), *Kiss Me Kate* (53) and *Seven Brides for Seven Brothers* (54). His career faltered when musicals went out of style, but he continued to turn in solid performances in dramatic roles, such as in *The Day of the Triffids* (63).
**Selected Films:** *The Small Voice* (48), *Annie Get Your Gun* (50), *Pagan Love Song* (50), *Show Boat* (51), *Lovely to Look At* (52), *Calamity Jane* (53), *Kiss Me Kate* (53), *Rose Marie* (54), *Seven Brides for Seven Brothers* (54), *Deep in My Heart* (54), *Jupiter's Darling* (54), *Kismet* (55), *The Big Fisherman* (59), *The Day of the Triffids* (63), *Arizona Bushwhackers* (68).

## KEELER, Ruby (1909- )

Keeler was the perfect ingenue in musicals, a petite singer and dancer, a pert little thing with big eyes and a winning smile whose funny cracked voice and baby face endeared her to audiences. She was at her best in musicals opposite fellow innocent Dick Powell, with whom she appeared in seven films, and when she was guided by the genius movie dance choreographer Busby Berkeley. Born Ethel Keeler in Halifax, Nova Scotia, Canada, she came to New York as a child. Although her family was poor, she took dancing lessons and made it into chorus lines on Broadway at the age of 14. Night clubs followed, and soon she was a featured attraction in Broadway musicals. Then Florenz Ziegfeld spotted her, offering her a solid role in the stage production of *Whoopee*, which starred Eddie Cantor. Al Jolson met Keeler when she went to the West Coast for a brief stage engagement. They were married in 1928, she left *Whoopee*, and although she got star billing in *Show Girl* on Broadway in 1929, she went west with her husband, quitting the show. During the 1930s she appeared in some of the best and most popular musicals ever made in that great age of musicals. *42nd Street* (33) cast her as the kid plucked from the chorus to save the show. It is one of the film classics of all time and decades later was re-created as a colorful musical spoof, running for years on Broadway. More froth followed with Berkeley's wonderful geometrically-patterned displays of girls forming a backdrop to the simple plots and tuneful songs of Keeler's movies. She was good opposite James Cagney in *Footlight Parade* (33) and the film grossed a fortune. She made one movie with Jolson, *Go Into Your Dance* (35). In 1937 she left Warner Bros. reluctantly in Jolson's wake after he quarreled with the top brass. Despite her popularity and four-figure salary, Keeler was always modest about her talents. After her divorce from Jolson in 1940, she pursued her movie career halfheartedly for a while. Then she married a real estate broker and had four children. In 1970 she appeared in a very successful revival of the 1925 musical, *No, No, Nanette*, on Broadway.
**Selected Films:** *42nd Street* (33), *Gold Diggers of 1933* (33), *Footlight Parade* (33), *Dames* (34), *Flirtation Walk* (35), *Go Into Your Dance* (35), *Shipmates Forever* (35), *Colleen* (36), *Ready Willing and Able* (37), *Sweetheart of the Campus* (41), *The Phynx* (70).

## KEITEL, Harvey (1947- )

Brooklyn-born Keitel turned to acting after a stint in the Marines, and studied at New York's Actors Studio. His first film appearance was in Martin Scorsese's college thesis project in 1968. Five years later, Keitel made a memorable commercial screen debut in Scorsese's *Mean Streets* (73). In most of his ensuing films Keitel has played supporting roles as a tough of some sort, like the vicious pimp in *Taxi Driver* (76). He also played an engaging Tom Paine in the French film *La Nuit de Varennes* (83).
**Selected Films:** *Mean Streets* (73), *Alice Doesn't Live Here Anymore* (75), *Buffalo Bill and the Indians* (76), *Taxi Driver* (76), *Bad Timing* (80), *The Border* (81), *Deathwish* (82), *Order of Death* (83), *La Nuit de Varennes* (83), *The Men's Club* (86), *Wise Guys* (86).

## KEITH, Brian (1921- )

Born Robert Brian Keith in Bayonne, New Jersey the son of character actor Robert Keith, Keith worked in movies and the theater from the age of three, but his career did not develop until after he served in the Marines in World War II. Keith has appeared regularly in film and TV character parts since the early 1950s. At first he often played a villain, but later switched to the crusty-but-goodhearted roles for which he is best known, an example being Teddy Roosevelt in *The Wind and the Lion* (76). In the 1960s and 1970s he starred in several TV series including *Family Affair*.
**Selected Films:** *Pied Piper Malone* (24), *Arrowhead* (52), *The Young Philadelphians* (59), *The Russians Are Coming, the Russians are Coming* (66), *The Yakuza* (75), *The Wind and the Lion* (76), *Sharkey's Machine* (81), *Death Before Dishonor* (87).

## KEITH, Ian (1899-1960)

Born Keith Ross in Boston, Massachusetts, Keith came early to acting and was a Broadway star in his twenties. He appeared extensively in later silent movies and then occasionally in sound films into the 1950s, meanwhile concentrating on his theater career. Developing into a character actor, he played de Rochefort in *The Three Musketeers* (36) and Rameses I in *The Ten Commandments* (56).
**Selected Films:** *Manhandled* (24), *My Son* (25), *Abraham Lincoln* (31), *Queen Christina* (33), *The Three Musketeers* (36), *The Sea Hawk* (40), *Nightmare Alley* (47), *Prince of Players* (55), *The Ten Commandments* (56).

## KELLAWAY, Cecil (1891-1973)

Cecil Kellaway received an Academy Award nomination for his role as a leprechaun in *The Luck of the Irish* (48), a part ideally in character. Kellaway spent his screen career embodying rotund, twinkly-eyed, roguish old men in dozens of movies. He was not Irish, however: Kellaway was born in Capetown, South Africa and got his start in stage and films in Australia. Coming to Hollywood in 1939, he appeared that year in *Wuthering Heights* and *Intermezzo*. Though Kellaway played the lead in *The Good Fellows* (43), he was usually to be found backing up the stars in popular movies for four decades – among them *The Postman Always Rings Twice* (46), *Harvey* (50), *Fitzwilly* (67), and, his last movie, *Getting Straight* (70).
**Selected Films:** *The Hayseeds* (33), *Wuthering Heights* (39), *Intermezzo* (39), *My Heart Belongs to Daddy* (42), *The Good Fellows* (43), *Kitty* (45), *The Postman Always Rings Twice* (46), *The Luck of the Irish* (48), *Harvey* (50), *The Beast from 20,000 Fathoms* (53), *The Shaggy Dog* (59), *Guess Who's Coming to Dinner?* (67), *Fitzwilly* (67), *Getting Straight* (70).

## KELLERMAN, Annette (1888-1975)

Australian-born Kellerman made her name as a champion swimmer and diver, the beauty of her face and form getting her dubbed, 'The Diving Venus.' Coming to stage and then film in the first decade of the century, she swam her way through roles in her pioneering and then-scandalous one-piece bathing suit. She also appeared nude in films such as *A Daughter of the Gods* (16). In 1952 a film biography of Kellerman, *Million Dollar Mermaid*, starred Esther Williams.
**Selected Films:** *Neptune's Daughter* (14), *A Daughter of the Gods* (16), *Queen of the Sea* (18), *What Women Love* (20), *Venus of the South Seas* (24).

## KELLERMAN, Sally (1937- )

Kellerman was born in Long Beach, California, and for years only small parts fell her way until she hit stardom as Major Margaret 'Hot Lips' Houlihan, an Army nurse, in *M*A*S*H* (70), for which she received an Academy Award nomination for Best Supporting Actress. The tall blonde Kellerman can play either comic or dramatic roles deftly.
**Selected Films:** *Reform School Girl* (57), *The Third Day* (65), *The Boston Strangler* (68), *M*A*S*H* (70), *Brewster McCloud* (70), *Last of the Red Hot Lovers* (72), *Slither* (73), *Welcome to LA* (77), *A Little Romance* (79), *Melvin and Howard* (80), *Moving Violations* (85), *That's Life!* (86).

## KELLY, Gene (1912- )

Born Eugene Curran Kelly in Pittsburgh, Pennsylvania, Kelly has a dance style that is strong, masculine, open, expansive and even earthy. As a choreographer, he revolutionized movie musicals during the 1940s and 1950s, creating dance sequences that told a story and that formed an integral part of the whole film, a big change from the 1930s when movie musicals featured more song-and-dance men and lines of pretty chorus girls in filmed revues. Charming, a more than competent actor and a director besides, Kelly was one of the main reasons that MGM became Hollywood's showplace for the making of musicals. He started studying dance as a child, and was in the chorus of *Leave It to Me* on Broadway in 1938. Two years later he choreographed *Billy Rose's Diamond Horseshoe*, starred in *Pal Joey* in 1941 playing a no-good heel, and choreographed another Broadway hit, *Best Foot Forward*. He was well established as a major Broadway talent, and his next step was Hollywood. Kelly made his debut on screen in *For Me and My Gal* (42) with Judy Garland. Audiences soon fell in love with the man with the husky pleasant singing voice, and although the popular Kelly never achieved Fred Astaire's elegance, he was a master entertainer. Verve and style marked his performance opposite Rita Hayworth in *Cover Girl* (44), and he received an Academy Award nomination for Best Actor in *Anchors Aweigh* (45), delighting fans by dancing with a cartoon mouse – Jerry, of the *Tom and Jerry* short subjects. He and Vera-Ellen made the screen sizzle dancing 'Slaughter on Tenth Avenue' in *Words and Music* (48). It is still a classic, as is *An American in Paris* (51), with its 20-minute ballet danced to George Gershwin's music. *On the Town* (49), shot on location in New York, broke new ground, and Kelly made the best movie musical ever when he did *Singin' in the Rain* (52). His *Invitation to the Dance* (56), a musical without dialogue, won the Grand Prize at the West Berlin Film Festival. Kelly has also appeared in non-musical films and on television. In 1951 he received a Special Academy Award in honor of his versatility 'and specifically for his brilliant achievements in the art of choreography on film.'
**Selected Films:** *For Me and My Gal* (42), *The Cross of Lorraine* (43), *Cover Girl* (44), *Christmas Holiday* (44), *Anchors Aweigh* (45), *Ziegfeld Follies* (46), *The Pirate* (48), *The Three Musketeers* (48), *Words and Music* (48), *Take Me Out to the Ball Game* (49), *On the Town* (49), *Summer Stock* (50), *An American in Paris* (51), *Singin' in the Rain* (52), *Brigadoon* (54), *Invitation to the Dance* (56), *Les Girls* (57), *Marjorie Morningstar* (58), *Inherit the Wind* (60), *What a Way to Go!* (64), *Forty Carats* (73), *That's Entertainment, Part II* (76), *Xanadu* (80).

## KELLY, Grace (1928-1982)

Cool, blonde and beautiful, Kelly was fire under ice. Alfred Hitchcock used her to perfection in his thrillers and she showed a flair for serious acting which won her an Academy Award for Best Actress for her work in *The Country Girl* (54), in which she played a bitter but determined loving

wife trying to deal with an alcoholic husband. Later, as Princess Grace of Monaco, she was a widely admired celebrity. Born into a wealthy Philadelphia family, Kelly became a model during her student days at New York's American Academy of Dramatic Arts. She made her Broadway debut in 1949 in a revival of Strindberg's *The Father*. Kelly began her movie career in the early 1950s and landed her first big film role opposite Gary Cooper in *High Noon* (52). At the height of her stardom she married Prince Rainier III of Monaco in a fairy-tale wedding and retired from the screen. The world was stunned when she died in a car crash at the age of 54.
**Selected Films:** *Fourteen Hours* (51), *High Noon* (52), *Mogambo* (53), *Dial M for Murder* (54), *Rear Window* (54), *The Country Girl* (54), *Green Fire* (54), *The Bridges at Toko-Ri* (55), *To Catch a Thief* (55), *The Swan* (56), *High Society* (56).

## KELLY, Jack (1927- )

Born in Astoria, New York, the younger brother of actress Nancy Kelly, Jack began his movie career in the early 1950s. Besides occasional appearances in routine action movies, he starred in the TV series *King's Row* and *Maverick*.
**Selected Films:** *Where Danger Lives* (51), *To Hell and Back* (56), *Forbidden Planet* (56), *Young Billy Young* (69).

## KELLY, Nancy (1921- )

Kelly, born in Lowell, Massachusetts, got into films at the age of four and by eight had appeared in over 50 silents. After taking a break from movies to work in radio, she returned to films at 17 in *Submarine Patrol* (38) and became a leading lady mostly in Bs. Developing into a character actress in the 1950s, she won a Tony for her stage role as the mother in *The Bad Seed*. Repeating the part in the 1956 movie Kelly earned an Oscar nomination. She was married briefly to Edmond O'Brien.
**Selected Films:** *Untamed Lady* (26), *Tailspin* (38), *Jesse James* (39), *Tarzan's Desert Mystery* (43), *Song of the Sarong* (45), *The Bad Seed* (56), *Crowded Paradise* (56).

Grace Kelly.

## KELLY, Patsy (1910-1981)

Brooklyn-born Kelly sang and danced her way onto Broadway in her twenties and made her Hollywood debut in 1933. After playing in a number of short comedies, Kelly entered features as a funny fat girl, sometimes a friend of the heroine, often a maid. After languishing for years she won a Tony as one of the old dancing girls in the 1971 stage revival of *No No Nanette*.
**Selected Films:** *Going Hollywood* (33), *Pigskin Parade* (36), *Broadway Limited* (41), *Please Don't Eat the Daisies* (60), *Rosemary's Baby* (68), *The North Avenue Irregulars* (79).

## KELLY, Paul (1899-1956)

Born in Brooklyn, Kelly began acting on stage and the silent screen as a child. His career was interrupted in 1927 when he killed the husband of actress Dorothy MacKaye. After two years in jail for manslaughter, he married MacKaye and returned to movies. The steely-looking actor, well regarded on the Broadway stage, mostly starred in B movies of the 1930s through the 1950s.
**Selected Films:** *A Good Little Devil* (08), *Anne of Green Gables* (20), *Slide Kelly Slide* (27), *Side Streets* (34), *The Roaring Twenties* (39), *Flying Tigers* (42), *Crossfire* (47), *The High and the Mighty* (54), *Bailout at 43,000 Feet* (57).

## KELLY, Paula (1943- )

Florida-born black American actress and dancer Kelly was a graceful presence in screen musicals and dramas from the late 1960s.
**Selected Films:** *Sweet Charity* (69), *The Andromeda Strain* (70), *Trouble Man* (72), *Soylent Green* (73), *Uptown Saturday Night* (74), *Drum* (76), *Jojo Dancer, Your Life is Calling* (86).

## KELLY, Tommy (1928- )

A classic cute kid, Tommy Kelly was picked by David O Selznick to play the title role in the 1938 production of *The Adventures of Tom Sawyer*, but after that his film career vanished.
**Selected Films:** *The Adventures of Tom Sawyer* (38), *Peck's Bad Boy at the Circus* (38).

## KELTON, Pert (1907-1968)

Born to a vaudeville family near Great Falls, Montana, Kelton was onstage from early child-

hood and made her Broadway debut in 1925. Moving to films in the early days of talkies, she played a comic tart in a good many movies of the 1930s. After a long retirement she returned to character parts playing Mrs Paroo in *The Music Man* (62).
**Selected Films:** *Sally* (29), *The Bowery* (33), *Cain and Mabel* (36), *The Music Man* (62), *Love and Kisses* (65), *The Comic* (69).

## KEMP, Jeremy (1934- )

Kemp, born Edmund Walker near Chesterfield, England, appeared early in theater in his native Britain, joining the Old Vic in 1958. His film and television work has been occasional, the former including *A Bridge Too Far* (77), the latter including the British series *Z-Cars* and the TV movie *The Winds of War*.
**Selected Films:** *Dr Terror's House of Horrors* (65), *Darling Lili* (70), *The Seven Per Cent Solution* (76), *The Prisoner of Zenda* (79), *The Return of the Soldier* (82).

*Gene Kelly with* Les Girls *(57) Mitzi Gaynor, Kay Kendall and Taina Elg.*

## KENDALL, Kay (1926-1959)

Born Justine McCarthy in Withernsea, England, Kendall began dancing in music halls in her native Britain in her teens, then moved to minor parts in movies in the mid-1940s. In *Genevieve* (53) she proved herself one of the most vivacious and charming comediennes of her time. Over the next six years she made some memorable movies and married Rex Harrison. Kendall died of leukemia soon after finishing *Once More, With Feeling* (59).
**Selected Films:** *Fiddlers Three* (44), *London Town* (46), *Genevieve* (53), *Doctor in the House* (54), *Simon and Laura* (55), *The Reluctant Debutante* (58), *Once More, With Feeling* (59).

## KENDALL, Suzy (1944- )

Born Frieda Harrison in Belper, England, Kendall came from the fashion industry to movies. From the mid-1960s she played leads in mostly minor films of various countries. For a time she was married to comedian Dudley Moore.
**Selected Films:** *The Liquidator* (66), *To Sir With Love* (67), *Up the Junction* (68), *Tales that Witness Madness* (73), *Spasmo* (75), *Adventures of a Private Eye* (77).

## KENNEDY, Arthur (1914- )

John Arthur Kennedy was born in Worcester, Massachusetts, and began performing on the stage in the mid-1930s. James Cagney, impressed by the young actor, brought Kennedy to Hollywood to play his brother in *City for Conquest* (40). After several more films including *High Sierra* (41), Kennedy served in the Air Force and then returned to an active movie career. Between 1947 and 1949 he triumphed on Broadway in two Arthur Miller plays – *All My Sons* and *Death of a Salesman* (he won a Tony in the latter for his role as Biff). Though major stardom eluded him, Kennedy played leads and supporting parts in many notable movies through the 1960s, in an impressive variety of roles from sympathetic to villainous. He received four Oscar nominations in the 1950s – for *Bright Victory* (51), *Trial* (55), *Peyton Place* (57), and *Some Came Running* (59), but in the 1970s his pictures declined to European and South American cheapies.
**Selected Films:** *City for Conquest* (40), *High Sierra* (41), *Air Force* (43), *Devotion* (46), *The Glass Menagerie* (50), *Bright Victory* (51), *Rancho Notorious* (52), *Trial* (55), *Peyton Place* (57), *Some Came Running* (59), *Elmer Gantry* (60), *Lawrence of Arabia* (62), *Fantastic Voyage* (66), *The Tempter* (76), *The Humanoids* (79).

## KENNEDY, Douglas (1915-1973)

Born in New York, Kennedy came to films in 1940. For a while he used the name Keith Douglas. Over the next two decades he appeared in a great many action pictures, sometimes as a supporting actor, sometimes as a lead in B movies, finally as a heavy and character actor.
**Selected Films:** *The Way of All Flesh* (40), *Dark Passage* (47), *Chain Gang* (50), *The Amazing Transparent Man* (59), *The Destructors* (68).

## KENNEDY, Edgar (1890-1948)

He was the master of the slow burn in movies for over 30 years. Born in Monterey, California, this bald, explosive comedian started out in vaudeville. His film debut was in *Tillie's Punctured Romance* (15), which featured Charlie Chaplin and Marie Dressler. Kennedy went on to play one of

Mack Sennett's Keystone Kops, and then came in demand for supporting roles, starring in innumerable two-reelers. Until he died, he was one of Hollywood's instantly recognizable faces, and he never failed to make audiences laugh. The actor Tom Kennedy was his older brother.
**Selected Films:** *Tillie's Punctured Romance* (15), *The Leather Pushers* (22), *Midnight Patrol* (31), *Duck Soup* (33), *King Kelly of the USA* (34), *Captain Tugboat Annie* (46), *My Dream is Used* (49).

## KENNEDY, George (1925- )

New York-born George Kennedy started off on the stage at age two and by the well-seasoned age of seven was a disc jockey. His dramatic career was shelved when he joined the army during World War II and stayed there for 16 years. By the end of his hitch, however, Kennedy had connected with show-business again as an adviser in matters military for Phil Silvers' TV show. Leaving the service to take a crack at Hollywood, he made his screen debut in *The Little Shepherd of Kingdom Come* (61). The tall and burly Kennedy was usually typed as a bad guy in the 1960s – he menaced Joan Crawford in *Strait Jacket* (64), Audrey Hepburn and Cary Grant in *Charade* (64), and played a brawling convict in *Cool Hand Luke* (67). The latter role earned Kennedy a supporting-actor Oscar. Gradually he moved from mean-and-brawny to more sympathetic roles, including the sheriff in *Tick . . . Tick . . . Tick . . .* (70). Kennedy worked occasionally in TV, including the series *The Blue Knight*.
**Selected Films:** *The Little Shepherd of Kingdom Come* (61), *Charade* (64), *Strait Jacket* (64), *Shenandoah* (65), *The Flight of the Phoenix* (65), *The Dirty Dozen* (67), *Cool Hand Luke* (67), *The Boston Strangler* (68), *Airport* (69), *Tick . . . Tick . . . Tick . . .* (70), *Lost Horizon* (73), *The Eiger Sanction* (75), *Modern Romance* (81), *Creepshow* (87).

## KENNEDY, Merna (1908-1944)

Born in Kankakee, Illinois, Kennedy appeared onstage from the age of 9. She was discovered by Charlie Chaplin who starred her in *The Circus* (26). Kennedy made a couple of dozen films over the next six years before her marriage to director Busby Berkeley. They were divorced the next year, and her screen career dissolved. She died of a heart attack at age 35.
**Selected Films:** *The Circus* (26), *Broadway* (30), *Laughter in Hell* (32), *Arizona to Broadway* (33), *I Like It That Way* (34).

## KENNEDY, Tom (1884-1965)

Born in New York, the older brother of actor Edgar Kennedy, Tom was an amateur boxer before coming to films in 1915. For some years a beefy, smashed-nose Keystone Kop for Mack Sennett, he played mostly dumb mugs in over 100 features and a good many shorts over the next fifty years.
**Selected Films:** *The Village Blacksmith* (16), *Fireman Save My Child* (27), *Tillie's Punctured Romance* (28), *She Done Him Wrong* (33), *Bringing Up Father* (40), *It's a Mad Mad Mad Mad World* (63), *The Bounty Killers* (65).

## KENYON, Doris (1897-1979)

Born in Syracuse, New York, Kenyon began her dramatic career on film and stage at 18. She was a favorite leading lady of the Broadway stage and the silent screen through the 1920s and then moved easily into talkies. Among her last roles was Queen Anne in *The Man in the Iron Mask* (39).
**Selected Films:** *The Rack* (15), *The Pawn of Fate* (16), *The Hidden Hand* (17), *The Ruling Passion* (22), *Monsieur Beaucaire* (24), *Alexander Hamilton* (31), *The Man in the Iron Mask* (39).

## KERR, Deborah (1921- )

Born Deborah Kerr-Trimmer in Helensburgh, Scotland, she took a long time to prove that she was more than just another long-suffering British lady in films. She began her career as a ballet dancer – a member of the Sadlers' Wells *corps de ballet* – in 1938. Her film debut was in *Major Barbara* (40), and she went on to star in a series of British films in which she was properly prim. After several stage and film roles in London, she went to Hollywood, playing a variety of movies. Her leading men were stars such as Clark Gable, Spencer Tracy and Cary Grant. It wasn't until *Black Narcissus* (46) that she got the credit for being the heavyweight actress that she is, and she won the New York Film Critics' Award for it. But she continued to play the long-suffering heroine in such films as *The Hucksters* (47), *If Winter Comes* (48), *King Solomon's Mines* (50) and *Quo Vadis* (51). She fought for the role of the promiscuous army wife in *From Here to Eternity* (53), for which she received an Oscar nomination. Kerr made her Broadway debut to great praise in *Tea and Sympathy* (56), and again became a Hollywood hit in the movie version of the play in 1956. She was brilliant in *The Night of the Iguana* (64) as a neurotic spinster. *The King and I* (56), in which she played the tutor, Anna Leonowens, of the King of Siam's children, was probably her most popular movie.
**Selected Films:** *Major Barbara* (40), *Love on the Dole* (41), *Hatter's Castle* (41), *The Life and Death of Colonel Blimp* (43), *Perfect Strangers* (45), *I See a Dark Stranger* (45), *Black Narcissus* (46), *The Hucksters* (47), *If Winter Comes* (48), *Edward My Son* (49), *King Solomon's Mines* (50), *Quo Vadis* (51), *Dream Wife* (53), *From Here to Eternity* (53), *The King and I* (56), *Tea and Sympathy* (56), *Heaven Knows, Mr Allison* (56), *An Affair to Remember* (57), *Separate Tables* (58), *The Sundowners* (60), *The Innocents* (61), *The Chalk Garden* (63), *The Night of the Iguana* (64), *Prudence and the Pill* (68), *The Arrangement* (69), *The Assam Garden* (86).

## KERR, John (1931- )

Born in New York, Kerr made it to Broadway at an early age and soon began appearing in movies. His most notable role was as a sensitive young man in *Tea and Sympathy* (56). After he played Lt Cable in *South Pacific* (58), his appearances were infrequent as he pursued a career as a lawyer.
**Selected Films:** *The Cobweb* (55), *Tea and Sympathy* (56), *Gaby* (56), *South Pacific* (58), *The Pit and the Pendulum* (61), *Seven Women from Hell* (62).

## KERRIGAN, J M (1885-1964)

Dublin-born Kerrigan was one of the staples of the famed Abbey Players when he became interested in movies. After directing one of the first Irish films, *O'Neil of the Glen* (16), he set out for Broadway and Hollywood and spent the rest of his career as a resident Irishman in America. Among his characteristic roles was the groom in *Black Beauty* (46).
**Selected Films:** *Little Old New York* (23), *Song O' My Heart* (30), *The Informer* (35), *Gone With the Wind* (39), *Abie's Irish Rose* (46), *Black Beauty* (46), *The Fastest Gun Alive* (56).

## KEYES, Evelyn (1919- )

Born in Port Arthur, Texas, Keyes worked as a nightclub dancer while trying to establish herself in movies. After some minor film roles in 1938, she was cast as Suellen O'Hara in *Gone With the Wind* (39). She was a leading lady in films into the 1950s, notable among them *Here Comes Mr Jordan* (41). She was married four times, her husbands included John Huston and bandleader Artie Shaw. Though she usually played nice girls, her 1977 autobiography, *Scarlett O'Hara's Young Sister*, revealed her naughtier side.
**Selected Films:** *The Buccaneer* (38), *Gone With the Wind* (39), *Here Comes Mr Jordan* (41), *Nine Girls* (44), *The Jolson Story* (46), *The Prowler* (51), *The Seven Year Itch* (54), *Around the World in Eighty Days* (56), *Across 110th Street* (72).

## KIBBEE, Guy (1882-1956)

Kibbee, born in El Paso, Texas, started on Mississippi riverboats. After years of theater work he finally made his Broadway debut in 1930. Soon he was in films, and over some two decades appeared in dozens of movies. Usually his round features and rotund figure lent themselves to supporting roles as sly, flustery, or blustery types; not infrequently, however, Kibbee played leads, as in his empty-headed businessman in the title role of *Babbitt* (34).
**Selected Films:** *Stolen Heaven* (31), *42nd Street* (33), *Babbitt* (34), *Dames* (34), *Captain Blood* (35), *Little Lord Fauntleroy* (36), *Mr Smith Goes to Washington* (39), *Our Town* (40), *Fort Apache* (48), *Three Godfathers* (49).

## KIDDER, Margot (1948- )

Margot Kidder was born in Yellow Knife, British Columbia, Canada, and attended the University of British Columbia. She made her screen debut at 19 in *Gaily, Gaily* (69) and went on to alternate movie and TV roles into the 1980s. With her unconventional beauty and engaging screen presence, she has most often been cast as strong, sensual, and sincere women, as in her leading role with Robert Redford in *The Great Waldo Pepper* (75). Her most famous part has been as a gutsy and entirely believable fantasy character – she played reporter Lois Lane in the first two *Superman* movies, with Christopher Reeve. Recent efforts have included a starring role in the mediocre but very popular *The Amityville Horror* (79). Her made-for-TV movies include *Honky Tonk*.
**Selected Films:** *Gaily, Gaily* (69), *Quackser Fortune Has a Cousin in the Bronx* (70), *Sisters* (73), *Gravy Train* (74), *The Great Waldo Pepper* (75), *The Reincarnation of Peter Proud* (75), *92 in the Shade* (75), *Superman* (78), *The Amityville Horror* (79), *Superman II* (80), *Willie and Phil* (80), *Heartaches* (82), *Trenchcoat* (83), *Little Treasure* (85).

## KIEL, Richard (1939- )

Born in Redford, Michigan, the 7 foot 2 inches Kiel was a nightclub bouncer before getting into films in the 1960s. He is most known as the toothy villain Jaws in the James Bond pictures *The Spy Who Loved Me* (77), and *Moonraker* (79).
**Selected Films:** *The Phantom Planet* (61), *The Human Duplicators* (65), *The Spy Who Loved Me* (77), *Moonraker* (79), *So Fine* (81), *Hysterical* (83).

## KIEPURA, Jan (1902-1966)

Jan Kiepura, born in Sosnowiec, Poland, was a leading tenor in European opera houses in his early twenties and made his screen debut in *Farewell to Love* (31). For two decades he made occasional musical movies, mostly in Europe, often co-starring with his wife Marta Eggerth.
**Selected Films:** *Farewell to Love* (31), *My Song for You* (31), *Be Mine Tonight* (32), *Give Us This Night* (36), *Her Wonderful Lie* (50), *Land of Smiles* (52).

## KILBRIDE, Percy (1888-1964)

Born in San Francisco, Kilbride spent years on the stage before making his movie debut in the early 1930s. Over a decade later, having demonstrated his gift for portraying wily hayseeds, he teamed up with Marjorie Main in *The Egg and I* (47). The success of that film led to the duo's resolutely lowbrow and highly successful series featuring 'Ma and Pa Kettle,' in which they played the farming couple in various locales.
**Selected Films:** *White Woman* (33), *Knickerbocker Holiday* (44), *The Egg and I* (47), *Ma and Pa Kettle* (49), *Ma and Pa Kettle at Waikiki* (55).

## KILBURN, Terry (1926- )

London-born Kilburn got into show business in America through radio. After his superlative performance as Tiny Tim in *A Christmas Carol* (38), he went on to a number of child roles, playing four different children in *Goodbye, Mr Chips* (39). His movie roles thinned out as he aged and Kilburn turned to the stage and directing.
**Selected Films:** *A Christmas Carol* (38), *Goodbye, Mr Chips* (39), *The Swiss Family Robinson* (40), *National Velvet* (45), *Only the Valiant* (51), *Lolita* (62).

## KILEY, Richard (1922- )

Born in Chicago, Kiley was on radio before making his film debut in 1951. He continued to play heavies in minor productions. He later starred on Broadway, notably in *Man of La Mancha*. More recently he has appeared in several TV movies, including *Angel on My Shoulder*.
**Selected Films:** *The Mob* (51), *The Blackboard Jungle* (55), *Pendulum* (69), *Looking for Mr Goodbar* (77), *Endless Love* (81).

## KILIAN, Victor (1897-1979)

Born in Jersey City, New Jersey, Kilian worked his way through vaudeville, stock, and Broadway before arriving in films. Tall and tough-looking, he usually played villains in movies of the 1930s and 1940s. After concentrating on the stage for years, he made a comeback on the TV series *Mary Hartman, Mary Hartman*.
**Selected Films:** *The Wiser Sex* (32), *Dr Cyclops* (39), *Spellbound* (45), *Gentleman's Agreement* (47), *The Tall Target* (51).

## KILKER, Henry (1847-1947)

American-born Kilker came to movies from the stage. From the 1910s through the 1940s he played supporting roles in a great many films, often cast as a lawyer or unpleasant dad.
**Selected Films:** *The Bigger Man* (15). *Imitation of Life* (34), *Mad Love* (35), *Romeo and Juliet* (36), *Holiday* (38), *The Secret Life of Walter Mitty* (47).

## KING, Alan (1924- )

Born Irwin Kniberg in Brooklyn, King came up through the Catskills 'Borcht Circuit' as a comedian and by the 1950s was cracking jokes in nightclubs around the country. His film appearances have been occasional.
**Selected Films:** *Hit the Deck* (55), *Miracle in the Rain* (56), *Bye Bye Braverman* (68), *The Anderson Tapes* (71), *Author! Author!* (82), *Cat's Eyes* (85).

## KING, Andrea (1915- )

Born Georgette Barry in Paris, France, King came to the United States in her youth and acted in theater before coming to films in the mid-1940s. She played leads and second leads, usually as a scheming woman, in mostly minor films into the 1970s. Later she turned to character roles and worked a good deal in TV.
**Selected Films:** *The Very Thought of You* (44), *The Man I Love* (46), *The Lemon Drop Kid* (51), *Darby's Rangers* (58), *Daddy's Gone A Hunting* (69), *Blackenstein* (73).

## KING, Dennis (1897-1971)

Born Dennis Pratt, in Coventry, King was a matinee idol in his native Britain as a young man. He also played Shakespearean roles and sang in operettas in Britain and the United States. He made only a few films, including the operetta *The Vagabond King* (30).
**Selected Films:** *Paramount on Parade* (30), *The Vagabond King* (30), *Fra Diavolo* (31), *Between Two Worlds* (37), *Some Kind of Nut* (69).

## KING, Perry (1948- )

King, born in Alliance, Ohio, studied at the Yale Drama School and made his film debut in *The Possession of Joel Delaney* (71). He has since played leads and supporting roles in films ranging from *Mandingo* (75) to the *A Different Story* (78). King has also appeared in TV series including *Hawaii Five-O, Cannon* and *Riptide*.
**Selected Films:** *The Possession of Joel Delaney* (71), *The Lords of Flatbush* (74), *The Wild Party* (75), *Mandingo* (75), *Lipstick* (76), *The Choirboys* (77), *A Different Story* (78), *Search and Destroy* (81), *Class of 1984* (82).

## KING, Walter Woolf (1899-1984)

King was a popular figure in Broadway musical comedy when he made his film debut with the Marx Brother's *A Night at the Opera* (35). Despite his background he was usually typed as a bad guy, appearing in movies into the 1950s.
**Selected Films:** *A Night at the Opera* (35), *Call It a Day* (37), *Balaika* (39), *The Marx Brothers Go West* (41), *Today I Hang* (42), *Kathy O'*, (58).

## KINGSLEY, Ben (1943- )

Kingsley emerged from nowhere, sweeping all before him in *Gandhi* (81), winning an Academy Award as Best Actor for his stunning debut in films in the title role of the picture. His portrayal of Mahatma Gandhi was little short of miraculous. Born Krisha Bahnji in Yorkshire, England, Kingsley's father was an Indian physician and his mother was an English model. His love of Shakespeare led him to an acting career. He was spotted by actor/director Richard Attenborough when he appeared on stage in *Nicholas Nickleby*, and was invited to test for the lead in *Gandhi*. Kingsley had done classical and Shakespearean roles as well as

television work. Following his tour de force in the role of Gandhi, he showed his versatility by appearing in *Betrayal* (82), a Harold Pinter drama.
**Selected Films:** *Gandhi* (81), *Betrayal* (82), *Turtle Diary* (86), *Harem* (86).

## KINNEAR, Roy (1934- )

Born in Britain, the rotund Kinnear has appeared in broadly comic character roles in movies from the 1960s, among them the Beatles film *Help!* (66) and Disney's *Herbie Goes to Monte Carlo* (77).
**Selected Films:** *Sparrows Can't Sing* (62), *Help* (66), *A Funny Thing Happened on the Way to the Forum* (67), *Willy Wonka and the Chocolate Factory* (71), *The Three Musketeers* (73), *The Last Remake of Beau Geste* (77), *Herbie Goes to Monte Carlo* (77), *Hawk the Slayer* (80), *The Boys in Blue* (82).

## KINSKEY, Leonid (1903- )

Born in St Petersburg, Russia, Kinskey began his career as a mimer. He came to America in the 1930s and soon gravitated to films, where he usually played an excitable foreigner. His debut role was the revolutionary in *Trouble in Paradise* (32).
**Selected Films:** *Trouble in Paradise* (32), *Duck Soup* (33), *Algiers* (38), *Down Argentine Way* (40), *Casablanca* (43), *Monsieur Beaucaire* (46), *The Man With the Golden Arm* (55).

## KINSKI, Klaus (1926- )

Born Claus Gunther Nakszynsk in Danzig in present Poland, Kinski acted in theater in Germany before coming to films in the late 1940s. His imposing and rather sinister persona lent itself to character roles in international films of the 1950s and 1960s, among them *Dr Zhivago* (65) and *For a Few Dollars More* (65). In 1972 Kinski starred as a demented Spanish conqueror in Werner Herzog's *Aguirre: the Wrath of God*, and thereafter played leads as crazed or monstrous figures including his vampire in Werner Herzog's *Nosferatu* (79). He is the father of actress Nastassia Kinski.
**Selected Films:** *Morituri* (48), *Ludwig II* (54), *Dr Zhivago* (65), *For a Few Dollars More* (65), *Circus of Fear* (67), *Aguirre: Wrath of God* (72), *Nosferatu* (79), *Fitzcarraldo* (82), *The Little Drummer Girl* (84).

## KINSKI, Nastassia (1959- )

The daughter of German actor Klaus Kinski, the delicately-beautiful Nastassia was born in Berlin and made her film debut at 16 in *To the Devil a Daughter* (76). She came to the attention of director Roman Polanski, who liked her type and with whom she had a much publicized liaison. The artistic fruit of their relationship was Polanski's romantic film of Thomas Hardy's *Tess* (80), which established Kinski as a sensuous star. Her next film was a remake of the 1940s horror film, *Cat People* (82). Kinski's films since include Wim Wender's *Paris, Texas* (84) and *Revolution* (85).
**Selected Films:** *To the Devil a Daughter* (76), *Tess* (80), *One from the Heart* (82), *Cat People* (82), *The Little Drummer Girl* (84), *Paris, Texas* (84), *Revolution* (85), *Spring Symphony* (86), *Harem* (86).

## KIRK, Phyllis (1926- )

Born Phyllis Kirkegaard in Syracuse, New York, Kirk was a model before making her film debut in 1950. Over the next decade she played leads in mostly minor movies such as Jerry Lewis's *The Sad Sack* (57), but was best known for her role as Nora Charles to Peter Lawford's Nick in the TV series *The Thin Man*.
**Selected Films:** *Our Very Own* (50), *House of Wax* (53), *The Sad Sack* (57), *City After Midnight* (59).

## KIRK, Tommy (1941- )

Kirk, born in Louisville, Kentucky, was a child star in Disney movies beginning with the dog story *Old Yeller* (57). Later he turned to surfing epics such as *How to Stuff a Wild Bikini* (65).
**Selected Films:** *Old Yeller* (57), *The Shaggy Dog* (59), *The Swiss Family Robinson* (60), *Son of Flubber* (63), *How to Stuff a Wild Bikini* (57), *Downhill Racer* (69), *My Name is Legend* (76).

## KITT, Eartha (1928- )

Born to a black sharecropper's family in North, South Carolina, Kitt studied dancing in New York and found acclaim singing in nightlubs in Paris. She returned to America in the early 1950s to become one of the most popular singers of the day. Her film appearances include the 1954 film of the Broadway revue *New Faces*.
**Selected Films:** *New Faces* (54), *St Louis Blues* (57), *Anna Lucasta* (58), *Synanon* (65), *Friday Foster* (75), *All By Myself* (82).

## KJELLIN, Alf (1920- )

Born in Lund, Sweden, and trained for the stage, Kjellin played leads in a number of films in his native country before making an international success in *Frenzy* (44). Moving to Hollywood, he starred under the name Christopher Kent in Vincente Minnelli's *Madame Bovary* (49), then he returned to his real name. The handsome and sturdy actor's later films were mostly routine action pictures. He later directed.
**Selected Films:** *John Ericsson, the Victor at Hampton Roads* (37), *Frenzy* (44), *Madame Bovary* (49), *My Six Convicts* (52), *Ship of Fools* (65), *Ice Station Zebra* (68), *The McMasters* (70).

## KLEIN-ROGGE, Rudolf (1888-1955)

Born in Cologne, Germany, Klein-Rogge appeared in some of the classic films of the German Expressionist era. A favorite of director Fritz Lang, he

played the title role in three of Lang's 'Dr Mabuse' films and appeared in *Metropolis* (26). After Lang had fled the country, Klein-Rogge married Lang's ex-wife and encouraged her to work for the Nazis.
**Selected Films:** *Morphium* (19), *Dr Mabuse* (22), *Siegfrid* (24), *Metropolis* (26), *The Testament of Dr Mabuse* (33), *Madame Bovary* (37), *Hochzeit auf Barenhof* (42).

## KLEMPERER, Werner (1919- )

Born in Cologne, Germany, Klemperer fled the Nazis and came to the United States with his father, legendary conductor Otto Klemperer. Werner grew up to play a disconcertingly lovable Commandant Klink in the Nazi-POW camp TV series *Hogan's Heroes*, which ran through the late 1960s. Otherwise Klemperer played Germans funny and unfunny in films of the 1950s and 1960s, among them Adolf Eichmann in *Operation Eichmann* (61).
**Selected Films:** *Death of a Scoundrel* (56), *Judgement at Nuremberg* (61), *Operation Eichmann* (61), *Youngblood Hawke* (64), *Ship of Fools* (65).

## KLINE, Kevin (1947- )

Kline was born in St Louis, Missouri, and was educated at Indiana University and the Juilliard School in New York City. He performed in classics when he was a member of John Houseman's Acting Company, then switched to a musical on Broadway, *On the Twentieth Century*. In the early 1980s he started his movie career.
**Selected Films:** *Sophie's Choice* (82), *The Big Chill* (83), *The Pirates of Penzance* (83), *Silverado* (85).

## KLUGMAN, Jack (1922- )

Born in Philadelphia, Klugman grew up with the face and the skill to handle both heavies and good guys in acting roles. Coming to film from the stage during the 1950s, he was a solid character actor in films such as *Twelve Angry Men* (57) and *Days of Wine and Roses* (63). However, he is best known for his Emmy-winning role as Oscar Madison in the TV series *The Odd Couple*. He also appeared in the *Quincy* series and in many commercials.
**Selected Films:** *Timetable* (56), *Twelve Angry Men* (57), *Days of Wine and Roses* (63), *Act One* (63), *Goodbye Columbus* (69), *Two-Minute Warning* (76).

## KNAPP, Evalyn (1908-1981)

Born in Kansas City, Missouri, Knapp was a B movie blonde in a number of pictures of the 1930s and 1940s, including a revival of the old *Perils of Pauline* serial in 1934.
**Selected Films:** *Sinner's Holiday* (30), *Fifty Million Frenchmen* (31), *Fireman, Save My Child* (32), *Laughing Irish Eyes* (36), *Two Weeks to Live* (43).

## KNEF, Hildegarde see NEFF

## KNIGHT, Fuzzy (1901-1976)

Born John Forrest Knight in Fairmont, West Virginia, Knight was first a nightclub musician and came to films in musical shorts of the early 1930s. The role of Ragtime Kelly in Mae West's *She Done Him Wrong* (33) established Knight as a comic supporting actor. He soon landed in the stuttering-old-cuss roles that made him one of the most famous of comic western sidekicks; he played alongside Johnny Mack Brown, Tex Ritter and others through the 1950s. He also played some non-Western character parts.
**Selected Films:** *Hell's Highway* (32), *She Done Him Wrong* (33), *The Trail of the Lonesome Pine* (36), *The Egg and I* (47), *Topeka* (54), *Hostile Guns* (67).

## KNIGHT, Shirley (1937- )

Born in Wichita, Kansas, Knight went straight from drama studies into movies with *Five Gates to Hell* (59). Within two years she received supporting-actress Oscar nominations for her roles in *The Dark at the Top of the Stairs* (60) and *Sweet Bird of Youth* (62). In the 1960s, disillusion with Hollywood led Knight to concentrate on stage and TV roles, with distinguished success. Her film appearances since have been sporadic.
**Selected Films:** *Five Gates to Hell* (59), *The Dark at the Top of the Stairs* (60), *Sweet Bird of Youth* (62), *The Group* (66), *Petulia* (71), *Endless Love* (81).

## KNOTTS, Don (1924- )

Born in Morgantown, West Virginia, Knotts came to TV in the 1950s as a regular on the Steve Allen variety show. His character there as a skinny, jittery wimp was to endure throughout his career as deputy Barney Fife on the *Andy Griffith Show* and in subsequent unsubtle movies.
**Selected Films:** *No Time for Sergeants* (58), *The Incredible Mr Limpet* (64), *The Ghost and Mr Chicken* (66), *The Love God?* (69), *The Apple Dumpling Gang* (75), *The Private Eyes* (81).

## KNOWLES, Patric (1911- )

Born Reginald Knowles in Horsforth, he appeared on stage and screen in his native Britain before coming to Hollywood in 1936, where he scored a hit as a romantic lead alongside Errol Flynn in *The Charge of the Light Brigade* (36). From then on, Knowles was a lead and second lead in dozens of movies.
**Selected Films:** *Irish Hearts* (34), *The Charge of the Light Brigade* (36), *The Adventures of Robin Hood* (38), *The Wolf Man* (41), *Monsieur Beaucaire* (46), *Mutiny* (52), *Auntie Mame* (59), *In Enemy Country* (67), *Chisum* (70), *Terror in the Wax Museum* (73).

## KNOX, Alexander (1907- )

Knox, born in Strathroy, Ontario, came to Holly-

wood in the early 1940s and earned acclaim and an Oscar nomination with his title role as the great President in *Wilson* (44). The mild-featured actor went on to distinguished character leads and supporting parts in dozens of films into the 1980s, and also wrote several books and plays.
**Selected Films:** *The Gaunt Stranger* (38), *The Sea Wolf* (40), *Wilson* (44), *The Judge Steps Out* (49), *The Vikings* (58), *The Longest Day* (62), *Nicholas and Alexandra* (71), *Gorky Park* (83).

## KNOX, Elyse (1917- )

Born in Hartford, Connecticut, the daughter of the World War II Secretary of the Navy, Knox took her blonde beauty from modelling to the movies. She starred in a number of routine films in the 1940s, while married to football great Tom Harmon.
**Selected Films:** *Lillian Russell* (40), *The Mummy's Tomb* (42), *Joe Palooka – Champ* (46), *There's a Girl in My Heart* (50).

## KOHNER, Susan (1936- )

Born to a show-business family in Los Angeles, Kohner had a brief but intense Hollywood career. Her role in *Imitation of Life* (59) earned Kohner a supporting-actress Oscar nomination. She retired after a 1964 marriage.
**Selected Films:** *To Hell and Back* (55), *Imitation of Life* (59), *All the Fine Young Canibals* (60), *By Love Possessed* (61), *Freud* (62).

## KOLB, Clarence (1874-1964)

Born in Cleveland, Ohio, Kolb appeared briefly in early silents after long experience in vaudeville. Returning to movies in the mid-1930s, he had a long career as a character actor, often playing crusty businessmen. He appeared much on TV as well, notably in the series *My Little Margie*.
**Selected Films:** *Glory* (17), *Wells Fargo* (37), *Hellzapoppin* (42), *Adam's Rib* (49), *Man of a Thousand Faces* (57).

## KORMAN, Harvey (1927- )

Chicago-born Korman came from Broadway to establish himself as a TV comedian on the Danny Kaye and Carol Burnett shows. His movie work has been occasional light supporting parts. He frequently appears in Mel Brooks' films.
**Selected Films:** *Living Venus* (61), *Lord Love a Duck* (66), *Blazing Saddles* (74), *High Anxiety* (78), *Americathon* (79), *The Longshot* (86).

## KORVIN, Charles (1907- )

Born Geza Korvin Karpathi in Czechoslovakia, Korvin was a director and cinematographer in Europe before coming to Hollywood in the mid-1940s. Appearing often on stage and TV, he played leads and supporting roles in occasional films.
**Selected Films:** *Enter Arsene Lupin* (44), *Lydia Bailey* (52), *Ship of Fools* (65), *The Man Who Had Power Over Women* (70), *Inside Out* (75).

## KOSCINA, Sylva (1935- )

A native of Zagreb, Yugoslavia, Koscina came to films as a steamy leading lady in Italian spectaculars of the 1960s such as *Hercules Unchained* (60). She developed into a competent leading actress and comedienne in international films.
**Selected Films:** *Il Ferroviere* (56), *Hercules Unchained* (60), *Jessica* (62), *Juliet of the Spirits* (65), *A Lovely Way to Die* (68), *Hornet's Nest* (70), *The Student Connection* (74), *Sunday Lovers* (80).

## KOSLECK, Martin (1907- )

Born Nicolai Yoshkin in Barkotzen, Pomerania, Kosleck had wide acting experience in Europe before coming to Hollywood in 1932. He specialized in playing sinister characters.
**Selected Films:** *Confessions of a Nazi Spy* (39), *Foreign Correspondent* (40), *The Hitler Gang* (44), *The Mummy's Curse* (45), *Hitler* (61), *The Flesh Eaters* (67), *Which Way to the Front?* (70).

## KOTTO, Yaphet (1937- )

Born in New York, black actor Kotto has pursued an active career on both stage and screen. In movies he usually plays aggressive leads and supporting roles. He also produced and directed *Time Limit* (72).
**Selected Films:** *Nothing But a Man* (64), *The Thomas Crown Affair* (68), *Live and Let Die* (73), *Drum* (76), *Alien* (79), *Brubaker* (80), *The Star Chamber* (83), *Pretty Kill* (87).

## KOVACK, Nancy (1935- )

American actress Nancy Kovack came to movies from the stage and appeared in routine productions of the 1960s, including *The Silencers* (66) with Dean Martin, and the sci-fi film *Marooned* (69).
**Selected Films:** *Strangers When We Meet* (60), *Diary of a Madman* (62), *The Silencers* (66), *Tarzan and the Valley of Gold* (66), *Marooned* (69).

## KOVACS, Ernie (1919-1962)

So celebrated has Ernie Kovacs been – long after his death – as the great innovative genius of TV, that his ten film appearances have been nearly forgotten. Making his movie debut in *Operation Mad Ball* (57), the mustachioed, cigar-brandishing Kovacs, born in Trenton, New Jersey, was on his way to establishing his uniquely strange persona onscreen when he was killed in a auto accident. He was married to actress Edie Adams.
**Selected Films:** *Operation Mad Ball* (57), *Bell, Book, and Candle* (58), *Our Man in Havana* (59), *Pepe* (60), *Sail a Crooked Ship* (62).

## KRAUSS, Werner (1884-1959)

Krauss had a distinguished stage career in his native Germany before becoming one of the major figures in the German expressionist film. Among his more than 100 silent appearances were the title role in the legendary *The Cabinet of Dr Caligari* (19). Later Krauss appeared in Nazi-sponsored productions including the virulently anti-Semitic *Jud Süss* (40).
**Selected Films:** *Die Pagode* (14), *Tales of Hoffman* (16), *The Cabinet of Dr Caligari* (19), *The Brothers Karamazov* (20), *Nathan the Wise* (23), *Waxworks* (24), *Tartuffe* (26), *Robert Koch* (39), *Jud Süss* (40), *Paracelsus* (43), *Sohn ohne Heimat* (55).

## KREUGER, Kurt (1917-     )

Born in Michenberg, Germany, and educated in England and America, the blond and Teutonic Kreuger came to films in the early 1940s, playing smooth Nazis and occasional romantic leads. By the 1960s he was appearing in supporting parts.
**Selected Films:** *Sahara* (43), *Madame Pimpernel* (45), *Unfaithfully Yours* (48), *The St Valentine's Day Massacre* (67).

## KRISTEL, Sylvia (1952-     )

A native of Utrecht in the Netherlands, Kristel was a model and beauty-contest winner before starting in films. In 1973 she played the title role in *Emmanuelle*. Her slim figure and gamine looks compensate somewhat for her limitations as an actress.
**Selected Films:** *Because of the Cats* (72), *Emmanuelle* (73), *Emmanuelle II* (75), *The Fifth Musketeer* (77), *The Nude Bomb* (80), *Private Lessons* (81), *Lady Chatterley's Lover* (82).

## KRISTOFFERSON, Kris (1936-     )

Born in Brownsville, Texas, Kristofferson is the son of a retired Air Force major general who became manager of air operations for Aramco in Saudi Arabia. As a youth he endured the typical pattern of military families of living in many locations, but the family settled in California, where he pursued literature and athletics at Pomona College. He sent entries to an *Atlantic Monthly* short story contest and won first and third places as well as two honorable mentions. Awarded a Rhodes Scholarship, he went to Oxford University in England after graduating from Pomona in 1958. While at Oxford he attempted novel writing and songwriting. Signed by Tommy Steel's manager, he became Kris Carson, but had lackluster results as a performer. So after receiving an Oxford degree, he joined the US Army and served in Germany. After five years of service, and just before he was to begin teaching at West Point, he took a vacation to Nashville, Tennessee, and decided to become a country singer. He earned his living at odd jobs until his songs began to get notices, especially 'Me and Bobby McGee.' Soon top popular singers were standing in line to sing his tunes, and he became a country artist on his own. Eventually Hollywood beckoned, and it turned out that his low-key acting style was pleasant and warm. With his beard and rugged appearance, he projected a sexuality that created sparks when he appeared opposite strong leading ladies, such as Barbra Streisand and Jane Fonda.
**Selected Films:** *The Last Movie* (71), *Cisco Pike* (72), *Pat Garrett and Billy the Kid* (73), *Bring Me the Head of Alfredo Garcia* (74), *Alice Doesn't Live Here Anymore* (75), *The Sailor Who Fell from Grace with the Sea* (76), *A Star is Born* (76), *Vigilante Force* (76), *Semi-Tough* (78), *Convoy* (78), *Rollover* (81), *Flashpoint* (84), *Songwriter* (84).

## KRUGER, Alma (1872-1960)

Born in Pittsburgh, Pennsylvania, Kruger was a leading Shakespearean actress in her early career. After some years of retirement and a return to acting via radio, she became a familiar character actress of the 1930s and 1940s. Usually playing sympathetic older women, Kruger was the head nurse in the *Dr Kildare* movies.
**Selected Films:** *These Three* (36), *Marie Antoinette* (38), *The Secret of Dr Kildare* (39), *Saboteur* (42), *Forever Amber* (47).

## KRÜGER, Hardy (1928-     )

Born Eberhardt Krüger in Berlin, Kruger began in films and on stage in his teens, making his movie debut in *Junge Adler* (44). Following his popularity in Germany, the blond and handsome actor became an international star in the 1950s, playing leading and supporting roles in action films including *Hatari* (62), *The Flight of the Phoenix* (65) and *A Bridge Too Far* (77). Kruger has also directed TV documentaries.
**Selected Films:** *Junge Adler* (44), *Insel Ohne Moral* (50), *Solange* (53), *Alibi* (55), *Bachelor of Hearts* (58), *The Rest is Silence* (59), *Sundays and Cybèle* (62), *Hatari* (62), *The Flight of the Phoenix* (65), *The Defectors* (66), *The Red Tent* (70), *Paper Tiger* (75), *Barry Lyndon* (75), *A Bridge Too Far* (77), *The Wild Geese* (78).

## KRUGER, Otto (1885-1974)

Born in Toledo, Ohio, Kruger was a Broadway matinee idol in the 1920s. In the next decade he plunged into films. His wavy hair, trim mustache, and suave manner became a Hollywood trademark for three decades. While occasionally playing romantic leads, Kruger was more often cast as an elegant cad.
**Selected Films:** *Under the Red Robe* (23), *The Intruder* (32), *Chained* (34), *Dracula's Daughter* (36), *Saboteur* (42), *Duel in the Sun* (46), *High Noon* (52), *Sex and the Single Girl* (64).

## KULP, Nancy (1919- )

Nancy Kulp was born in Harrisburg, Pennsylvania and has appeared in character roles in a number of movies including the classic Western *Shane* (53) and Disney's *The Parent Trap* (61). However, she is most known for her TV work, including the long-running series *The Beverly Hillbillies*. In the 1980s, she ran unsuccessfully for Congress.
**Selected Films:** *The Model and the Marriage Broker* (52), *Shane* (53), *Five Gates to Hell* (59), *The Parent Trap* (61), *The Patsy* (64).

## KWAN, Nancy (1938- )

Born to Chinese/Scottish parents in Hong Kong, Kwan was a dancer before she was discovered by Hollywood. She made her debut in the *The World of Suzie Wong* (60). Despite that lead and another in the musical *Flower Drum Song* (61), she was thereafter relegated to minor films.
**Selected Films:** *The World of Suzie Wong* (60), *Flower Drum Song* (61), *Fate Is the Hunter* (64), *Arrivederci, Baby!* (66), *The McMasters* (70), *Night Creature* (78), *Angkor* (81).

## KYO, Machiko (1924- )

Born in Osaka, Japan, Kyo was a dancer when she was discovered by Japanese filmmakers. Among her first efforts was the female lead in Kurosawa's classic *Rashomon* (50), and from that point on she was a star in the cinema of her native country. Her only American film was *The Teahouse of the August Moon* (56).
**Selected Films:** *Final Laugh* (49), *Rashomon* (50), *Gate of Hell* (53), *Ugetsu* (53), *Street of Shame* (56), *The Teahouse of the August Moon* (56), *Odd Obsession* (59), *Buddha* (63), *Thousand Cranes* (69).

## KYSER, Kay (1897-1985)

Born in Rocky Mount, North Carolina, Kyser came to fame as a bandleader with his classic radio show 'Kay Kyser's Kollege of Musical Knowledge' in the 1930s. In his radio heyday he and his band were featured in several routine movie musicals.
**Selected Films:** *That's Right, You're Wrong* (39), *Playmates* (41), *Around the World* (43), *Swing Fever* (44), *Carolina Blues* (44).

# L

## La MARR, Barbara (1896-1926)

Born Rheatha Watson in Richmond, Virginia, La Marr was a dancer before making her film debut in 1920. With *Cinderella of the Hills* (21) she became one of the romantic stars of the silent era, generally considered the most beautiful woman on the screen. Her roles included the lead opposite Ramon Novarro in *The Prisoner of Zenda* (22). Her meteoric career proved too much for La Marr. A slide into scandal and excess was climaxed by her death from a drug overdose in 1926.
**Selected Films:** *Flame of Youth* (20), *Cinderella of the Hills* (21), *The Three Musketeers* (21), *The Prisoner of Zenda* (22), *The Eternal City* (23), *The White Moth* (24), *The Heart of a Siren* (25), *The Girl from Montmatre* (26).

## La PLANCHE, Rosemary (1923-1979)

American actress La Planche was a leading lady in a number of routine productions of the 1930s and 1940s.
**Selected Films:** *Mad About Music* (38), *The Falcon in Danger* (43), *Prairie Chickens* (43), *Devil Bat's Daughter* (46).

## La PLANTE, Laura (1904- )

Born in St Louis, Missouri, La Plante started in films in her teens, and by the 1920s was a major star. She was usually cast in wholesome parts in Westerns, later in comedies and dramas including the role of Magnolia in *Show Boat* (29). She retired in the 1930s, returning for a couple of character roles.
**Selected Films:** *The Old Swimmin' Hole* (21), *The Cat and the Canary* (27), *Show Boat* (29), *King of Jazz* (30), *Little Mister Jim* (46), *Spring Reunion* (57).

## La ROCQUE, Rod (1896-1969)

Chicago-born La Rocque was a circus performer before making his film debut in 1917. Within a few years the handsome, dashing actor had become one of the prime heartthrobs of the silent era. The occasion of his marriage to screen goddess Vilma Banky was one of the biggest spectacles in Hollywood history. La Rocque made the transition to sound, but his career declined in the 1940s. He later became a Hollywood real estate tycoon.
**Selected Films:** *The Snow Man (14)*, *Efficiency Edgar's Courtship* (17), *Stolen Kiss* (20), *The Ten Commandments* (23), *Resurrection* (27), *SOS Iceberg* (33), *The Hunchback of Notre Dame* (40), *Meet John Doe* (41).

## La RUE, Jack (1903-1984)

Born Gaspare Biondolillo in New York, La Rue entered sound films after a Broadway career in the early 1930s. With his memorably mean features and menacing air, he became a familiar Hollywood villain for two decades. He later went into business but returned to the screen now and then.
**Selected Films:** *Virtue* (32), *The Story of Temple Drake* (33), Lady Killer (34), *Captains Courageous* (37), *Road to Utopia* (46), *Ride the Man Down* (53), *Won Ton Ton, the Dog Who Saved Hollywood* (76).

*Alan Ladd in* China *(43).*

## LADD, Alan (1913-1964)

No one ever said that this unsmiling, pint-sized, tough guy was a great actor, but he was just the kind of hero that was wanted in the 1940s. Born in Hot Springs, Arkansas, he had icy good looks and a fine resonant voice, although he exhibited a total lack of expression, and he became one of Hollywood's top stars. His star potential was recognized by Sue Carol, a former actress turned agent, who married him and devoted herself to his career. After a series of small parts, Ladd turned in a highly effective performance as the cold-eyed killer in *This Gun for Hire* (42). His co-star was the diminutive Veronica Lake, and the two soon became a recognized team. Ladd's most successful performance, both critically and at the box office, was in the title role of *Shane* (53), a western in which he played an enigmatic gunman who helps a farmer's family. Ladd was a sensitive and insecure man, and by the 1960s his drinking had become a severe problem. He died at the age of 51 apparently from a lethal combination of alcohol and sedatives.

**Selected Films:** *Once in a Lifetime* (32), *Citizen Kane* (41), *This Gun for Hire* (42), *The Glass Key* (42), *China* (43), *The Blue Dahlia* (46), *Two Years Before the Mast* (46), *The Great Gatsby* (49), *Chicago Deadline* (49), *Shane* (53), *The McConnell* Story (55), *Boy on a Dolphin* (57), *The Proud Rebel* (58), *The Carpetbaggers* (64).

## LADD, Cheryl (1951- )

Born Cheryl Stoppelmoore in Huron, South Dakota, Ladd came to her best-known TV role by way of commercials, bit parts, and the low-budget thriller *Satan's School for Girls* (73). Since her big success as one of *Charlie's Angels*, she has been a frequent guest star on television.

**Selected Films:** *Satan's School for Girls* (73), *Purple Hearts* (84).

## LADD, Diane (1932- )

Born in Meridian, Mississippi, Ladd acted onstage before coming to films in the early 1960s. For over a decade she was relegated to routine films, before receiving critical acclaim as the hard-bitten waitress Flo in Martin Scorse's *Alice Doesn't Live Here Anymore* (75). For a time Ladd was married to actor Bruce Dern.

**Selected Films:** *Something Wild* (61), *The Reivers* (69), *Chinatown* (74), *Alice Doesn't Live Here Anymore* (75), *Something Wicked This Way Comes* (83), *Black Widow* (87).

## LAHR, Bert (1895-1967)

Bert Lahr was born Irving Lahrheim in New York and learned his craft in the exacting school of vaudeville and burlesque. From that experience came his unique comic persona – the wildly prancing gestures, goggly eyes, lisping delivery and mock-operatic singing style which made Lahr a lifelong star in stage and nightclub work. However, it did not translate well to the more intimate medium of the screen. Thus all but one of his films were rather routine; these included his debut in *Faint Heart* (31), and such films as *Josette* (38), *Always Leave Them Laughing* (49), and *The Night They Raided Minsky's* (68). The exception in his film career, of course, was his immortal Cowardly Lion in *The Wizard of Oz* (39), a part for which his extravagant style seemed precisely fated: every detail of his performance, from his pseudoheroic snarling to his shadowboxing, was unforgettable. Of his screen career, Lahr later ruefully observed, 'I was typecast as a lion, and there aren't all that many parts for lions.' In 1966 the aged comedian found one of his greatest successes in a serious Broadway role as one of the two tramps in Samuel Beckett's *Waiting for Godot*. John Lahr memorialized his father in the 1975 *Notes on a Cowardly Lion*.

**Selected Films:** *Faint Heart* (31), *Love and Hisses* (37), *Josette* (38), *The Wizard of Oz* (39), *Ship Ahoy* (42), *Always Leave Them Laughing* (49), *Rose Marie* (54), *The Second Greatest Sex* (56), *The Night They Raided Minsky's* (68).

## LAHTI, Christine (1950- )

Lahti grew up in a Detroit suburb and studied drama at the University of Michigan. Her first big break came in a supporting role in *Swing Shift* (1984), for which she received an Academy Award nomination. She has a reputation for stealing scenes from big stars – from Goldie Hawn in *Swing Shift* and from Mary Tyler Moore in *Just Between Friends* (86).

**Selected Films:** *Swing Shift* (84), *Stacking* (85), *Just Between Friends* (86).

## LAINE, Frankie (1913- )

Born Frank Paul Lo Vecchio in Chicago, Illinois, Laine struggled for years to get into show business and by the late 1940s had become a popular nightclub and recording singer. His film work was mostly in minor musicals of the 1950s; he is better-

known for singing several popular title songs.
**Selected Films:** *When You're Smiling* (50), *Sunny Side of the Street* (51), *Rainbow 'Round My Shoulder* (52), *He Laughed Last* (56).

## LAKE, Arthur (1905-1987)

Born Arthur Silverlake in Corbin, Kentucky, to a vaudeville family, Lake appeared onstage as a kid and in films at 12. For some years he played adolescents, as in *Harold Teen* (28). Then, with his youthful and longsuffering air, he became the definitive Dagwood Bumstead (to Penny Singleton's Blondie) in 28 movies and on radio and TV. His Dagwoods lasted into the 1950s.
**Selected Films:** *Jack and the Beanstalk* (17), *Harold Teen* (28), *Topper* (37), *Blondie* (38), *Three is a Family* (44), *Beware of Blondie* (50).

## LAKE, Veronica (1919-1973)

Lake was famous for her 'peek-a-boo' hair style and her cool determined screen manner. Born Constance Ockleman in Brooklyn, she made her first films as Constance Keane, changing her name to Veronica Lake in 1941, when she made her big splash with her long blonde hair obscuring one eye in *I Wanted Wings*, with William Holden and Ray Milland. Her rise to fame in the 1940s was meteoric, but by the 1950s, alcoholism had destroyed her career. She was discovered working as a barmaid in New York in the early 1960s and managed to pick up some stage and film work before her death.
**Selected Films:** *All Women Have Secrets* (39), *Forty Little Mothers* (40), *I Wanted Wings* (41), *Sullivan's Travels* (41), *This Gun for Hire* (42), *The Glass Key* (42), *I Married a Witch* (42), *So Proudly We Hail* (43), *Miss Susie Slagle's* (45), *The Blue Dahlia* (46), *Saigon* (48), *Slattery's Hurricane* (49), *Flesh Feast* (70).

## LAMARR, Hedy (1913- )

Dark-haired and exquisitely beautiful, Lamarr, born Hedwig Kiesler in Vienna, Austria, was coldly mysterious on screen, an exotic glamour queen. Her father was a wealthy bank director and her mother was a concert pianist who abandoned her career to care for her only child. Lamarr lived in a big house, traveled to Paris, to Switzerland, to Ireland. She had private tutors, ballet lessons and piano lessons, and was sent to the finest of private schools. In 1929 she managed to break into Austrian films and her parents let her go to Max Reinhardt's famous theater school. She did plays, more films and then came the movie which would bring her notoriety for the rest of her life – *Symphonie er Liebe/Extase* (33), or, as it was called in English, *Ecstacy*. In it she appeared nude and there was also another scene in which the camera focused on her face while she was supposed to be making passionate love. It was a sensation for those prudish times. Later Lamarr married Austrian munition maker Fritz Mandl, who tried unsuccessfully to buy up all the copies of the film. In 1937 she divorced Mandl and persuaded Louis B Mayer to give her an MGM contract. *Algiers* (38), with Charles Boyer, made Lamarr a star, and a series of movies of varying quality followed. In all of them she looked ravishing. Her biggest success was in *Samson and Delilah* (49), opposite Victor Mature, a lavish costume picture. Despite a colorful life, several rich husbands and a high salary in her heyday, Lamarr made the headlines in the 1960s because of her severe financial problems.
**Selected Films:** *Geld auf der Strasse* (30), *Ecstacy* (33), *Algiers* (38), *Lady of the Tropics* (39), *I Take This Woman* (40), *Boom Town* (40), *Comrade X* (40), *Ziegfeld Girl* (41), *Tortilla Flat* (42), *White Cargo* (42), *Her Highness and the Bellboy* (45), *Let's Live a Little* (48), *Samson and Delilah* (49), *My Favorite Spy* (51), *The Female Animal* (57).

## LAMAS, Fernando (1915-1982)

Born in Buenos Aires, Argentina, Lamas was a veteran actor in Spanish-language films when he made his Hollywood debut in *Rich, Young and Pretty* (51). For several years MGM groomed him as a Latin lover type, but despite leads in *The Merry Widow* (52) and *Rose Marie* (54), Lamas never quite caught on. He later starred in various low-budget films and worked often on stage and TV. He was married to actress Arlene Dahl from 1954 to 1960 and to Esther Williams from 1967 until his death.
**Selected Films:** *Rich, Young and Pretty* (31), *Frontera Sur* (42), *The Merry Widow* (52), *Sangaree* (53), *Rose Marie* (54), *The Girl Rush* (55), *The Lost World* (60), *The Violent Ones* (67), *The Cheap Detective* (78).

*Hedy Lamarr in* Lady of the Tropics *(39).*

## LAMB, Gil (1906- )

The agile features of American comic Lamb were familiar in supporting parts of 1940s musicals. He made occasional appearances into the 1960s.
**Selected Films:** *The Fleet's In* (42), *Rainbow Island* (44), *Humphrey Takes a Chance* (50), *Blackbeard's Ghost* (67).

## LAMBERT, Jack (1920- )

Lambert brought his home-grown Yonkers accent and sinister looks to gangster roles in mostly crime dramas of the 1940s into the 1960s. (He is not to be confused with the older Scottish character actor of the same name.)
**Selected Films:** *The Cross of Lorraine* (43), *The Killers* (46), *Scared Stiff* (53), *Kiss Me Deadly* (55), *The George Raft Story* (61), *Four for Texas* (63).

## LAMOUR, Dorothy (1914- )

A number of film stars are remembered in a typical role in a typical costume – John Wayne in cowboy gear, Charles Laughton as Captain Bligh – which is often a too-limited view of the range of their roles. Not so with Dorothy Lamour: she is invariably imagined as a pretty native girl in a sarong, which she indeed played often as not in her screen roles and sometimes in her personal appearances as well. Lamour was born Mary Kaumeyer and as a teenager was named Miss New Orleans in her hometown. Soon thereafter she was singing with bands and by the mid-1930s had her own radio show in Los Angeles. From there it was a short step to Hollywood, where she was renamed with the French word for love. Her first screen role typecast Lamour once and for all: she and Ray Milland, both youthful and fresh-faced, starred together in the South-Seas yarn *The Jungle Princess* (36). Perhaps her finest performance as a native girl with long dark hair and skimpy sarong was the next year, with Jon Hall in Ford's *The Hurricane* (37). Now and then, as in the urban-glamour film *Man About Town* (39), Lamour wore regular American attire, but in the following year she reverted to type as the invariable exotic lass in *The Road to Singapore* (40), the first of the Hope/Crosby 'Road' pictures (in which Lamour lampooned her image). During the war she was often on the road for the betterment of US servicemens' morale. By the late 1940s her image and her screen career were wearing thin. Notable among her few films in the 1950s was in De Mille's *The Greatest Show on Earth* (53). However, she did appear throughout the 1960s, most nostalgically, in *The Road to Hong Kong* (62). Of all the stars who have been rigidly typecast, Lamour seemed to wear her rather skimpy yoke the lightest and to enjoy it most.
**Selected Films:** *The Jungle Princess* (36), *The Hurricane* (37), *Last Train from Madrid* (37), *The Big Broadcast of 1938* (38), *Tropic Holiday* (38), *Man About Town* (39), *The Road to Singapore* (40), *Johnny Apollo* (40), *Aloma of the South Seas* (41), *Road to Utopia* (45), *The Girl from Manhattan* (48), *The Greatest Show on Earth* (53), *The Road to Hong Kong* (62), *Pajama Party* (64), *Won Ton Ton, The Dog Who Saved Hollywood* (75), *Creepshow* (87).

## LANCASTER, Burt (1913- )

This athletic leading leading man was born in New York City and began his show business career as a circus acrobat, and during World War II acted and danced in soldier shows. His fine physique and radiant smile made him a star in adventure films of the 1950s, but later he became a distinguished actor because he took control of his own career and never allowed himself to be trapped in typical leading parts. Lancaster is intelligent, extremely hard working and has turned in fine performances in a number of roles on screen. A good performance in a Broadway flop got him a movie contract, and a lucky break got him a starring role in *The Killers* (46), a strong adaptation of the Ernest Hemingway short story that belatedly achieved popularity. Lancaster's range is impressive. In 1952 he starred in (and produced) *The Crimson Pirate*, a rousing spoof of swashbucklers, where he spent much of his time shirtless, climbing around the rigging of a ship. That same year he played an alcoholic husband in *Come Back Little Sheba* opposite Shirley Booth, an adaptation of the William Inge Broadway hit about an unhappy marriage. In 1953 he starred in *From Here to Eternity* and his on the beach love scene with Deborah Kerr remains one of the most sensual and memorable in film history. He was frightening as a vicious gossip columnist in *Sweet Smell of Success* (57), and overpowering as the crooked evangelist in *Elmer Gantry* (60), a film which earned him the Academy Award for Best Actor. *Gantry* was one of Lancaster's favorite films; another was *The Leopard* (63), a long, slow film about an aristocratic Italian family. It was filmed in Italy and was a smash hit throughout Europe, but American audiences were shown a chopped up, badly dubbed version and

*Burt Lancaster in* Elmer Gantry *(60).*

the picture was a flop. In 1984 the original version was given a selected release in the United States. Those who saw it hailed Lancaster's performance as masterful. The late 1960s and 1970s were a barren period for him, but his subtle and touching portrayal of an aging gambler in *Atlantic City* (80) led some critics to comment that his career as a character actor may have just been starting. He proved them right with his triumphal performance teamed with his old co-star Kirk Douglas in *Tough Guys* (86), in which they played a pair of aging train robbers.
**Selected Films:** *The Killers* (46), *I Walk Alone* (47), *Brute Force* (47), *Sorry, Wrong Number* (48), *All My Sons* (48), *Rope of Sand* (49), *Mister 880* (50), *The Flame and the Arrow* (50), *Ten Tall Men* (50), *Jim Thorpe, All-American* (51), *The Crimson Pirate* (52), *Come Back Little Sheba* (52), *From Here to Eternity* (53), *Vera Cruz* (54), *The Kentuckian* (55), *The Rose Tattoo* (55), *Trapeze* (56), *Gunfight at the OK Corral* (57), *Sweet Smell of Success* (57), *Separate Tables* (58), *Elmer Gantry* (60), *Birdman of Alcatraz* (62), *The Leopard* (63), *Seven Days in May* (64), *The Professionals* (66), *The Swimmer* (67), *Airport* (69), *Lawman* (70), *The Midnight Man* (74), *1900* (76), *The Cassandra Crossing* (77), *The Island of Dr Moreau* (77), *Zulu Dawn* (79), *Atlantic City* (80), *Local Hero* (82), *Little Treasure* (85), *Tough Guys* (86).

## LANCHESTER, Elsa (1902-1986)

Born Elizabeth Sullivan in London, England, this character actress was prominent on the English stage and screen. When her husband, actor Charles Laughton, was lured to Hollywood in the early 1930s, she came with him, and landed a part in *Bride of Frankenstein* (35). Although she appeared only briefly on screen as the female monster (and as Mary Shelley in the prologue), her performance was a memorable one. That same year she also appeared in *David Copperfield*, and went on to play in countless movies.
**Selected Films:** *Bluebottles* (28), *The Private Life of Henry VIII* (32), *Bride of Frankenstein* (35), *David Copperfield* (35), *The Ghost Goes West* (36), *Rembrandt* (37), *Ladies in Retirement* (41), *The Spiral Staircase* (45), *The Inspector-General* (49), *Androcles and the Lion* (53), *Bell, Book and Candle* (57), *Witness for the Prosecution* (57), *Mary Poppins* (64), *Willard* (71), *Murder by Death* (76), *Die Laughing* (80).

## LANDAU, Martin (1933- )

Brooklyn-born Landau was a newspaper cartoonist before gravitating to acting. His movie appearances have often been as a heavy, an example being his mean-eyed villain in *North by Northwest* (59). With his wife Barbara Bain, Landau starred in the TV series *Mission Impossible* and *Space 1999*.
**Selected Films:** *Pork Chop Hill* (59), *North by Northwest* (59), *Cleopatra* (62), *The Greatest Story Ever Told* (65), *Meteor* (79), *Alone in the Dark* (82).

## LANDI, Elissa (1904-1948)

Born Elisabeth-Marie-Christine Kühnelt in Venice, and said to be a granddaughter of the Empress of Austria, whom she closely resembled, Landi by the age of 20 had appeared on the London stage and written the first of her three novels. In 1930 the intelligent and beautiful actress moved to Hollywood, where she was a popular leading lady in films such as *The Sign of the Cross* (32). By the end of the decade her career was in decline.
**Selected Films:** *London* (26), *The Parisian* (30), *Body and Soul* (31), *The Sign of the Cross* (32), *After the Thin Man* (36), *Corregidor* (43).

## LANDIS, Carole (1919-1948)

Born Frances Ridste in Fairchild, Wisconsin, Landis worked as a nightclub singer and hula dancer, before moving to Hollywood. Her main talents were a striking face and 'the best legs in town.' After a few minor roles she appeared in *One Million BC* (40) and became a star. For several years she played in popular if slight films. After a broken romance with Rex Harrison, she died of an overdose of sleeping pills.
**Selected Films:** *A Day at the Races* (37), *One Million BC* (40), *Topper Returns* (41), *Four Jills in a Jeep* (44), *Out of the Blue* (47), *The Brass Monkey* (48).

## LANDIS, Jessie Royce (1904-1972)

Born in Chicago, Landis spent the better part of her career onstage but still appeared occasionally in films. At first playing fluttery young ladies, she aged into character parts as fluttery matrons, as in *To Catch a Thief* (55).
**Selected Films:** *Derelict* (30), *My Foolish Heart* (49), *To Catch a Thief* (55), *My Man Godfrey* (57), *North by Northwest* (59), *Airport* (69).

## LANDON, Michael (1937- )

Born Michael Orowitz in Forest Hills, New York, Landon appeared in occasional films of the 1950s including the title role in *I Was a Teenage Werewolf* (57). He is best known, however, for his roles in the TV series – Little Joe on *Bonanza* and the father on *The Little House on the Prairie*.
**Selected Films:** *I Was a Teenage Werewolf* (57), *God's Little Acre* (58), *The Legend of Tom Dooley* (59).

## LANE, Allan 'Rocky' (1901-1973)

Born in Mishawaka, Indiana, Lane played football at Notre Dame before turning to acting. Making his screen debut in 1929, he played dramatic leads for several years before settling down in Westerns, of which he made dozens. He was also the voice of the talking horse in the TV series *Mr Ed*.
**Selected Films:** *Madam Satan* (30), *Conspiracy* (39), *The Wild Frontier* (46), *Hell Bent for Leather* (60), *Posse from Hell* (61).

*Priscilla, Lola and Rosemary Lane and Gale Page starred in* Four Daughters *(38).*

## LANE, Charles (1899- )

American actor Lane spent nearly half a century in movies playing comic supporting role as disagreeable and/or stingy salesmen, judges, tax collectors, and the like. He was also a regular on the TV series *Petticoat Junction* and later appeared in *Soap*.

**Selected Films:** *The White Sister* (23), *Mr Deeds Goes to Town* (36), *You Can't Take It With You (38), Arsenic and Old Lace* (44), *Teacher's Pet* (58), *The Little Dragons* (80).

## LANE, Diane (1963- )

This fine actress was born in New York City, and began as a stage actress. She received good notices for her work in *The Cherry Orchard, Agamemnon* and *Runaway* on Broadway. Lane started her movie career in the early 1980s.

**Selected Films:** *Touched by Love* (80), *Six Pack* (82), *The Outsiders* (83), *Rumble Fish* (83), *The Cotton Club* (84).

## LANE, Lola (1909-1981)

Born Dorothy Mullican in Macy, Indiana, Lola Lane was one of five daughters of a dentist, three of whom succeeded in movies (her actress sisters were Priscilla and Rosemary). Lola came to the screen first; after minor roles she teamed up with her sisters in several popular Warner comedies from the late 1930s.

**Selected Films:** *Speakeasy* (29), *Four Daughters* (38), *Daughters Courageous* (39), *Four Wives* (39), *Four Mothers* (40), *Zanzibar* (40), *They Made Me a Killer* (46).

## LANE, Lupino (1892-1959)

Born Henry George Lupino in London, into a British family who had been clowns for several generations, the agile Lane took his broad, comic style to Hollywood to make dozens of popular two-reelers in the 1920s. Also appearing in features, he once played 25 parts in one film. With the coming of sound his career declined and Lane returned to Britain to appear in and direct occasional films.

**Selected Films:** *His Cooling Courtship* (15), *The Reporter* (22), *The Deputy Drummer* (35), *Me and My Girl* (39).

## LANE, Priscilla (1917- )

Priscilla Lane was born Priscilla Mullican in Indianola, Iowa, the youngest of five sisters. Their mother sent all the sisters to study voice at Simpson College and four were soon singing professionally; and the whole family changed their names to Lane. Priscilla and her sister Rosemary spent several years singing with Fred Waring. From that point it was a short step to Hollywood, where sister Lola had already gained a foothold. The three Lanes, billed as 'the picture of American girlhood,' made their screen debut as a trio in *Four* Daughters (38). In the wake of that film followed *Daughters Courageous* (39), *Four Wives* (39), and *Four Mothers* (40). Priscilla starred in a number of movies on her own, among them *Brother Rat* (38) and *Arsenic and Old Lace* (44). She retired from the screen in 1948 and later hosted a Boston TV show.

**Selected Films:** *Four Daughters* (38), *Love, Honor, and Behave* (38), *Brother Rat* (38), *Daughters Courageous* (39), *Four Wives* (39), *The Roaring Twenties* (39), *Four Mothers* (40), *Three Cheers for the Irish* (40), *Million Dollar Baby* (41), *Arsenic and Old Lace* (44), *Bodyguard* (48).

## LANE, Richard (1900- )

Lane spent much of his career as a sports announcer, but in a number of movies of the 1930s into the 1950s he played sports announcers, reporters, and other Runyonesque characters.
**Selected Films:** *The Outcasts of Poker Flat* (37), *Meet Boston Blackie* (41), *Take Me Out to the Ball Game* (48), *I Can Get It For You Wholesale* (51).

## LANE, Rosemary (1913-1974)

Another of the movie-star Lane sisters – the others being Priscilla and Lola – Rosemary was perhaps the conventionally prettiest one. Besides appearances with her sisters, Rosemary appeared on her own in supporting roles as a dumb brunette.
**Selected Films:** *Varsity Show* (37), *Four Daughters* (38), *Daughters Courageous* (39), *Four Wives* (39), *Hollywood Hotel* (38), *Four Mothers* (40), *The Return of Dr X* (40), *The Fortune Hunter* (45).

## LANG, June (1915- )

Born Winifred Vlasek in Minneapolis, Minnesota, Lang worked as a dancer before arriving in films in 1931. A beauty but nothing earthshaking as an actress, she was the principal pretty face in a number of minor films of the 1930s and 1940s.
**Selected Films:** *Chandu the Magician* (32), *Bonnie Scotland* (35), *Meet the Girls* (38), *Flesh and Fantasy* (43), *Lighthouse* (48).

## LANGAN, Glenn (1917- )

Born in Denver, Colorado, Langan came to films after extensive stage experience. At first he appeared in major movies including *A Bell for Adano* (45) and *Forever Amber* (47), but was later relegated to leads in low-budget action pictures and thrillers.
**Selected Films:** *The Return of Dr X* (39), *Four Jills in a Jeep* (44), *A Bell for Adano* (45), *Hangover Square* (45), *Forever Amber* (47), *The Treasure of Monte Cristo* (49), *99 River Street* (54), *Mutiny in Outer Space* (65).

## LANGDON, Harry (1884-1944)

Langdon born in Council Bluffs, Iowa, was a comedian who was at the very top for a few years, but whose name and films are now unknown by all but the most dedicated fans of film comedy. After a brief and spectacular success, Langdon plummeted to failure; the reason, most critics said, was that he achieved his success by letting others direct his pictures, and failed when he decided he could be his own director. The character that he created was funny, but Langdon himself could not create a sustained setting for that character. Still, for a time, he was a real star of the likes of Charlie Chaplin, Buster Keaton and Harold Lloyd. Compared to his rivals, Langdon got a late start in the movies. He did not join Mack Sennett until 1923, after a long career in vaudeville. Sennett soon realized that Langdon, although his humor was not of the breakneck, slapstick type that the Sennett studios featured, still had a special talent, and some of the top directors and writers at the studio were assigned to work with him. These men – notably the writers Harry Edwards and Arthur Ripley and the director Frank Capra – built their films around the character suggested by Langdon's makeup, a heavily-powdered face with wide, staring, innocent eyes. It was a baby face on an adult body, and most of the comic situations in Langdon's films got their laughs by showing this helpless, pathetic figure trying to compete in an adult world. Capra called the Langdon character 'the helpless elf whose only ally is God,' and there were such scenes as Langdon trying to fight off a tornoado by throwing pebbles at it (*Tramp, Tramp, Tramp*, 26); Langdon rubbing his chest with what he thinks is camphor but is actually Limberger cheese as he rides on a bus (*The Strong Man*, 26); Langdon trying to kill an inconvenient fiancée but stopping because he sees a sign that says 'No Shooting' (*Long Pants*, 27). These films were made after Langdon had been hired away from Sennett by First National Pictures, who gave him not only a lot of money – $7500 a week – but also complete control over his pictures. When he began to direct his own films, his success ended abruptly. Audiences stopped laughing and Langdon was on a downhill slide. His personal problems (a marriage had broken up), his tendency to spend too much money on his movies, and the coming of sound films speeded the process. A mere five years after Langdon had rocketed to success, he was a has-been. All through the 1930s and well into the 1940s he made a series of low-cost two-reel comedies for various studios. He was still working on these films when he died of a stroke.
**Selected Films:** *Picking Peaches* (23), *Tramp, Tramp, Tramp* (26), *The Strong Man* (26), *Long Pants* (27), *The Chaser* (28), *See America Thirst* (30), *A Soldier's Plaything* (31), *Hallelujah I'm a Bum* (33), *Zenobia* (39), *Spotlight Scandals* (44).

## LANGDON, Sue Ane (1936- )

American actress Langdon has played leads and supporting roles in mostly minor films since the early 1960s, and she appeared in the TV series *Arnie*.
**Selected Films:** *The Outsider* (61), *The Rounders* (65), *A Fine Madness* (66), *A Guide for the Married Man* (67), *The Cheyenne Social Club* (70), *Without Warning* (80), *Zapped!* (82).

## LANGE, Hope (1931- )

Born to a show-business family in Redding Ridge, Connecticut, Lange burst into film with a bang, playing Emma in *Bust Stop* (56) and earning an Oscar nomination for her role in *Peyton Place* (57).

By the 1970s she was most often to be seen in made-for-TV movies like *That Certain Summer* and series like *The Ghost and Mrs Muir*.
**Selected Films:** *Bus Stop* (56), *Peyton Place* (57), *The True Story of Jesse James* (57), *The Young Lions* (58), *Pocketful of Miracles* (61), *Death Wish* (74), *Blue Velvet* (86).

## LANGE, Jessica (1949- )

Most stars begin with hits and deal later with the flops; Jessica Lange did the opposite: her first films would have sunk the careers of anyone less tenacious. Born to the family of a traveling salesman in Cloquet, Minnesota, Lange lived a wandering life during a brief early marriage and ended up studying mime in Paris. She returned to New York to try acting and was spotted by producer Dino De Laurentiis, who cast her in his gargantuan remake of *King Kong* (76). Like the mechanical Kong, the picture was a dud, and Lange had to wait four years for another role. Then, after some forgettable parts, she was a critical success in a critical failure – as the lusty Cora in *The Postman Always Rings Twice* (81). The next year she starred in a project she initiated – *Frances* (82), based on the life of actress Frances Farmer – and again found acclaim in an unsuccessful film. For that tragic and bitter role and for a contrasting one as delicate Julie in *Tootsie* (82), Lange became the first person in decades to be nominated for two Oscars in one year (she won it for *Tootsie*). Having had a child with ballet star Mikhail Baryshnikov, Lange then teamed up personally and professionally with playwright/actor Sam Shepard; she co-produced and together they starred in *Country* (84), a movie she made as a personal statement about the plight of American farmers. In that film Lange clinched her screen transition from a sexy blonde beloved of a big ape, to a serious and determined major actress.
**Selected Films:** *King Kong* (76), *All That Jazz* (79), *The Postman Always Rings Twice* (81), *Frances* (82), *Tootsie* (82), *Country* (84), *Sweet Dreams* (85), *Crimes of the Heart* (86).

## LANGELLA, Frank (1940- )

The actor who was destined, after wide-ranging stage experience, to be typecast as the Dracula of his age, was born in Bayonne, New Jersey, and began acting in childhood. After college drama studies and repertory experience, Langella made his New York debut in 1963 in *The Immoralist*, which gained him the first of three Obies. His movie debut came in *The Twelve Chairs* (70), one of several well-received roles in badly-received movies. Others included *Diary of a Mad Housewife* (70) and *The Wrath of God* (72). Then came the sumptuous 1977 Broadway revival of *Dracula*, in which Langella created a sensation with his elegant, seductive approach to the role. In 1979 he played the Count successfully on screen.
**Selected Films.** *The Twelve Chairs* (70), *Diary of a Mad Housewife* (70), *The Deadly Trap* (71), *The Wrath of God* (72), *Dracula* (77), *Sphinx* (80), *Those Lips, Those Eyes* (81), *Men's Club* (86).

## LANGFORD, Frances (1914- )

Born in Lakeland, Florida, Langford was a popular nightclub and radio singer more than an actress. However, she appeared, singing, in a number of light musical pictures of the 1930s into the 1950s. For some years she was married to actor Jon Hall.
**Selected Films:** *Every Night at Eight* (35), *Swing It, Soldier* (41), *Beat the Band* (46), *The Glenn Miller Story* (54)

## LANSBURY, Angela (1925- )

In a career of playing spiteful or outrageous older women that began when she was relatively young, Angela Lansbury has usually been a rather lovable presence no matter how nasty her characters. Born in London, the daughter of actress Moyna MacGill, Lansbury trained for the stage from her youth, finishing her education in the US when her family fled the Blitz in World War II. At age 18 she sufficiently impressed MGM to gain a long-term contract, beginning her two decades of character roles. Her first screen appearance, as a maid in George Cukor's *Gaslight* (44), earned Lansbury the first of her three supporting-actress Academy Award nominations; the next year she also found acclaim as Sybil Vane in *The Picture of Dorian Gray*. From the beginning, her heavy-lidded eyes and almost cartoonish face landed her in parts beyond her years; she largely played aging harridans and shrews in minor pictures through the 1950s. As spunky in life as in her roles, Lansbury finally rose to stardom at an age when she would have been expected to resign herself to the inevitable, finding resurrection in a series of Broadway roles – as a tartish mother in the 1960 *A Taste of Honey*, as a high-spirited aunt in the musical *Mame*, and as the pieshop owner in *Sweeney Todd*. In the wake of these successes came better screen roles, among them as Laurence Harvey's terrible mother in *The Manchurian Candidate* (62), which earned her another Oscar nomination. In the mystery *Death on the Nile* (78), Lansbury was in fidgety high form as an elderly lady. During the mid-1980s she starred to great effect as a writer and homicide buff in the TV series *Murder, She Wrote* – another of her inimitably quirky-but-lovable roles.
**Selected Films:** *Gaslight* (44), *National Velvet* (44), *The Picture of Dorian Gray* (45), *The Hoodlum Saint* (46), *Till the Clouds Roll By* (47), *State of the Union* (48), *The Three Musketeers* (48), *Samson and Delilah* (49), *The Purple Mask* (55), *The Court Jester* (56), *The Dark at the Top of the Stairs* (60), *Blue Hawaii* (61), *The Manchurian Candidate* (62), *The World of Henry Orient* (64), *The Greatest Story Ever Told* (65), *Bedknobs and Broomsticks* (71), *Death on the Nile* (78), *The Pirates of Penzance* (83).

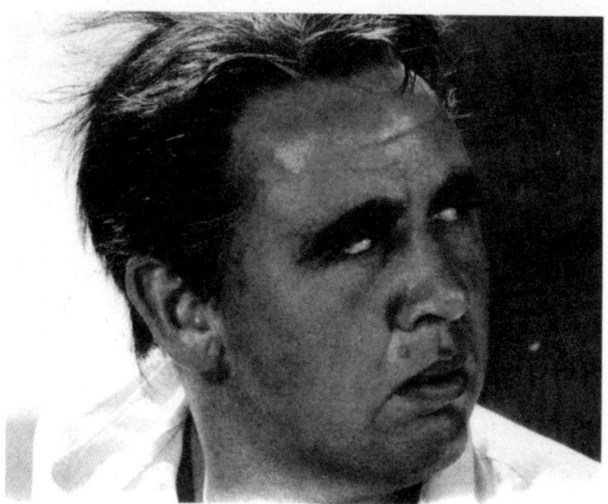

*Charles Laughton in* Mutiny on the Bounty *(35).*

## LANSING, Joi (1928-1972)

Born Joyce Wassmansdorff, blonde American actress Lansing appeared in a number of routine productions such as *The Girl from Jones Beach* (49) and *The Atomic Submarine* (59). She also worked on Robert Cummings' TV series *Love That Bob.*
**Selected Films:** *The Counterfeiters* (48), *The Girl from Jones Beach* (49), *The Atomic Submarine* (59), *A Hole in the Head* (59), *Marriage on the Rocks* (65), *Bigfoot* (71).

## LANSING, Robert (1929-      )

Born Robert H Broom in San Diego, California, Lansing was a robust leading man in a number of action pictures of the late 1950s through the 70s. He also did a good deal of TV work, including the series *The Man Who Never Was.*
**Selected Films:** *The 4-D Man* (59), *A Gathering of Eagles* (63), *Under the Yum Yum Tree* (64), *Wild in the Sky* (72), *False Face* (77).

## LANZA, Mario (1921-1959)

Born Alfredo Cocozza in Philadelphia, this tenor was trained in concert and opera singing before coming to Hollywood. He helped to popularize the operatic style in films, particularly in *The Great Caruso* (51). His inability to overcome a weight problem and his lack of a professional attitude on the set, plus his inability to handle the pressures of movie stardom, eventually led to his loss of popularity and of parts.
**Selected Films:** *That Midnight Kiss* (49), *The Toast of New Orleans* (50), *The Great Caruso* (51), *Because You're Mine* (52), *Serenade* (56), *Seven Hills of Rome* (58), *For the First Time* (58).

## LARSEN, Keith (1925-      )

American actor Keith Larsen was a leading man in a number of workaday films of the early 1950s through 1970s. Among his several TV series was *Northwest Passage.*
**Selected Films:** *Flat Top* (52), *Arrow in the Dust* (54), *Fury River* (61), *Caxambu* (67), *The Trap on Cougar Mountain* (76).

## LASSER, Louise (1939-      )

New York-born Lasser was a Broadway veteran when she made her film debut in Woody Allen's *What's New, Pussycat?* (65). The next year she married Allen and during their marriage co-starred in his movies. Perhaps she was best in the offbeat TV series *Mary Hartman, Mary Hartman.*
**Selected Films:** *What's New, Pussycat?* (65), *Take the Money and Run* (69), *Bananas* (71), *Everything You Always Wanted to Know about Sex (But Were Afraid To Ask)* (72), *Slither* (73), *In God We Trust* (79), *Crimewave* (86).

## LATIMORE, Frank (1925-      )

Born Frank Kline in Darien, Connecticut, Latimore was a romantic leading man in a number of mostly minor films of the 1940s. After spending most of the 1950s making movies in Italy, he returned to Hollywood to play character parts in the 1970s.
**Selected Films:** *In the Meantime, Darling* (44), *The Razor's Edge* (46), *Black Magic* (49), *John Paul Jones* (59), *Patton* (70), *All the President's Men* (76).

## LAUGHTON, Charles (1899-1962)

Born in Scarborough, Yorkshire, Laughton was a brilliant character actor and one of the most popular on screen in the 1930s. He was a perfectionist who had a distinguished stage career and had worked in experimental films before going to Hollywood. Paramount offered both Laughton and his wife, actress Elsa Lanchester, a contract in 1932 and his first American role was in a minor horror classic, *The Old Dark House* (32) which also featured Boris Karloff, and then was a mad scientist in *The Island of Lost Souls* (32). He played mostly villains at first, such as Nero in *The Sign of the Cross* (32) and Captain Bligh in *Mutiny on the Bounty* (35). It was the British-made *The Private Life of Henry VIII* (33) that won him the Academy Award for Best Actor. Worried about being typecast, Laughton returned again to Britain in 1936 to turn in a brilliant performance in the title role in *Rembrandt.* He was to have been the star of the most famous film that was almost made. *I Claudius,* a trouble-plagued epic, was begun in 1937 but never completed. One of his most outstanding acting jobs was as the deformed Quasimodo in *The Hunchback of Notre Dame* (39), in which he was able to communicate the human being behind the grotesque makeup. Although he often appeared in films that were not up to his high standard, and sometimes showed a regrettable tendency to ham it up, he never gave a bad performance and was always worth watching. His last role, as Southern Senator Cooley in *Advise and Consent* (62), was one of his best.

**Selected Films:** *Wolves* (27), *Bluebottles* (28), *Piccadilly* (29), *Down River* (30), *The Old Dark House* (32), *The Island of Lost Souls* (32), *The Sign of the Cross* (32), *The Private Life of Henry VIII* (33), *The Barretts of Wimpole Street* (34), *Ruggles of Red Gap* (35), *Les Misérables* (35), *Mutiny on the Bounty* (35), *Rembrandt* (36), *Jamaica Inn* (39), *The Hunchback of Notre Dame* (39), *They Knew What They Wanted* (40), *The Canterville Ghost* (44), *The Paradine Case* (48), *Young Bess* (53), *Hobson's Choice* (54), *Witness for the Prosecution* (58), *Spartacus* (60), *Advise and Consent* (62).

## LAUREL, Stan, and HARDY, Oliver

Stan Laurel (1890-1965) was born Arthur Stanley Jefferson into a theatrical family in England, and was to become the thin half and chief gag deviser of the Laurel and Hardy team. He joined Fred Karno's troupe which also employed Charlie Chaplin. Laurel toured the Unites States with Chaplin, sometimes understudied him, and later imitated him. He made his first film short in 1915, and made over 50 shorts, mostly for producer Hal Roach, before he teamed up with Hardy in 1926. Oliver Hardy (1892-1957), the fat half of the screen's finest comedy team, noted for his genteel pomposity, tie-twiddle and long-suffering look, was born in Harlem, Georgia, and was making movies as early as 1913. Laurel was the more successful. He had his own series of shorts, whereas Hardy had only small and occasional roles. He, too, was working for Hal Roach. The pair actually appeared together in some 10 short films before Roach decided to team them up permanently. Over the next three years they were turning out one short feature per month. Sound was introduced, but it caused hardly a ripple in their careers, for their best gags didn't rely on dialogue. The archetypical Laurel and Hardy scene is one in which the pair engage in an orgy of mutual destruction with some representative of authority. Several of their films ended with massive pie-throwing sequences. The transition from shorts to full length features was also made smoothly. While Laurel and Hardy worked for a number of different directors, it was always acknowledged that Laurel was the real creative force behind the films. Personally, Laurel and Hardy remained good friends, but Laurel had his disputes with Roach and the team broke up. They worked together again in the 1940s, but were never given creative freedom, so the quality of their work suffered. Neither man became wealthy, and indeed Laurel died in poverty, but he lived long enough to receive a Special Academy Award in 1960 'for his creative pioneering in the field of cinema comedy,' and to see a revival of interest in Laurel and Hardy comedies.

**Selected Films:** *Slipping Wives* (26), *Flying Elephants* (27), *The Battle of the Century* (27), *The Finishing Touch* (28), *You're Darn Tootin'* (28), *Two Tars* (28), *Big Business* (29), *Double Whoopee* (29), *Berth Marks* (29), *Men O'War* (29), *The Perfect Day* (29), *The Rogue Song* (30), *Hog Wild* (30), *Another Fine Mess* (30), *Laughing Gravy* (31), *Come Clean* (31), *Beau Hunks* (31), *Helpmates* (31), *The Music Box* (32), *Towed in a Hole* (33), *Fra Diavolo* (33), *The Midnight Patrol* (33), *Busy Bodies* (33), *Dirty Work* (33), *Sons of the Desert* (33), *Going Bye Bye* (34), *Them Thar Hills* (34), *Babes in Toyland* (34), *Tit for Tat* (35), *Our Relations* (36), *Way Out West* (36), *Blockheads* (38), *The Flying Deuces* (39), *A Chump at Oxford* (40), *Saps at Sea* (40), *Great Guns* (41), *Air Raid Wardens* (43), *The Dancing Masters* (43), *The Bullfighters* (45), *Robinson Crusoeland* (52), *The Golden Age of Comedy* (58), *The Best of Laurel and Hardy* (74).

## LAURIE, Piper (1932- )

Born Rosetta Jacobs in Detroit, Michigan, Laurie came to movies in her teens and during the 1950s was a resident ingenue in Hollywood, a cute face

*Stan Laurel and Oliver Hardy.*

in popular and escapist movies. Finally in 1961 came a meaty role opposite Paul Newman in *The Hustler.* After some years of retirement she returned to the screen as a character actress, earning an Oscar nomination for her role as Sissy Spacek's demented mother in *Carrie.* She was also nominated for her role in *Children of a Lesser God* (86).
**Selected Films:** *Louisa* (50), *Francis Goes to the Races* (51), *Son of Ali Baba* (52), *Ain't Misbehavin'* (55), *The Hustler* (61), *Carrie* (76), *Ruby* (78), *Children of a Lesser God* (86).

## LAUTER, Ed (1940- )

American actor Lauter is one of those faces standing behind the stars in film after film since the early 1970s, familiar but rarely noticed.
**Selected Films:** *The Last American Hero* (73), *The Longest Yard* (75), *King Kong* (76), *Eureka* (83), *The Big Score* (83), *Girls Just Want to Have Fun* (85).

## LAVI, Daliah (1940- )

Born Daliah Levenbuch in Sharei Zion, Lavi came to movies after stage experience in her native Israel. Her exotic beauty graced several international pictures of the 1960s and 1970.
**Selected Films:** *Blazing Sands* (56), *The Return of Dr Mabuse* (61), *Lord Jim* (65), *Catlow* (72).

## LAW, John Phillip (1937- )

Hollywood-born Law worked in repertory theater before his first adult film appearances in Italy. Making his Hollywood debut in *The Russians are Coming, The Russians are Coming* (66), the handsome blond actor went on to roles in international films.
**Selected Films:** *The Magnificent Yankee* (50), *Alta Infedeltà* (65), *The Russians Are Coming, The Russians Are Coming* (66), *Hurry Sundown* (67), *Barbarella* (68), *Skiddoo* (68), *Von Richthofen and Brown* (71), *The Last Movie* (71), *The Cassandra Crossing* (77), *Tarzan the Ape Man* (81), *Tin Man* (82).

## LAWFORD, Peter (1923-1984)

Peter Lawford was born in London, the son of a general, and received an expensive British education. Though he played a small part at age seven in the movie *Poor Old Bill* (30), he did not try film again until 1938, when he appeared in *Lord Jeff.* After his role as a pilot in *Mrs Miniver* (42), Lawford began to appear in mostly romantic leads; he brought his fine-featured looks and his breezily aristocratic manner to dashing-youth parts in movies like *Easter Parade* (48), *Little Women* (49), and *Royal Wedding* (51), Lawford was often in the news for actions other than his acting. He became known as a jet-set playboy, was a member of the 'Rat-Pack' that formed around Frank Sinatra, and for 12 years was married to a sister of John F Kennedy (they divorced in 1966). When his movie roles thinned out in the 1950s, Lawford turned to TV, appearing in the TV series *Dear Phoebe* and *The Thin Man.* He also appeared in several minor films that were more or less in-jokes of the Sinatra gang, including *Ocean's 11* (60), and produced some movies. Lawford's last years were shadowed by alcoholism and depression.
**Selected Films:** *Poor Old Bill* (30), *Lord Jeff* (38), *Mrs Miniver* (42), *The White Cliffs of Dover* (44), *Easter Parade* (48), *Little Women* (49), *Royal Wedding* (51), *Exodus* (60), *Ocean's 11* (60), *The Longest Day* (62), *A Man Called Adam* (66), *The April Fools* (69), *Rosebud* (75), *Body and Soul* (82).

## LAWRENCE, Barbara (1928- )

Born in Carnegie, Oklahoma, Lawrence came to films in the mid-1940s. She was usually cast as one of those strangely specific movie types: the wise-cracking friend of the leading lady.
**Selected Films:** *Diamond Horseshoe* (45), *Margie* (46), *Give My Regards to Broadway* (48), *A Letter to Three Wives* (49), *Oklahoma* (55), *Kronos* (57), *Man in the Shadows* (58).

## LAWRENCE, Florence (1886-1938)

Florence Lawrence was one of the screen's first stars. For the Biograph company she made over a dozen short films in 1908, playing title roles in *Romeo and Juliet, Salome,* and *Antony and Cleopatra.* In those days screen players were not known by name; Lawrence was simply called 'The Biograph Girl.' Later, when Carl Laemmle lured her to his Independent Motion Picture company, she was briefly 'The Imp Girl' before becoming the first film player to be publicized by name. After soaring throughout the teens, Lawrence's career faltered in the 1920s. She committed suicide at the age of 52.
**Selected Films:** *Romeo and Juliet* (08), *Salome* (08), *Antony and Cleopatra* (08), *The Barbarian Ingomar* (08), *All for Love* (12), *A Singular Cynic* (14), *The Satin Girl* (23), *Gambling Wives* (24).

## LAWRENCE, Gertrude (1898-1952)

Born Alexandra Dagmar Lawrence-Klasen, Lawrence spent most of her performing life on the stage in her native Britain and on Broadway, especially noted for her Noel Coward roles. Her film appearances were infrequent during her long career. Julie Andrews played her in *Star!* (68).
**Selected Films:** *The Battle of Paris* (29), *Rembrandt* (36), *Stage Door Canteen* (43), *The Glass Menagerie* (50).

## LAWRENCE, Jody (1930- )

Born in Fort Worth, Texas, Lawrence starred in a number of routine films of the 1950s into the 1960s.
**Selected Films:** *Mask of the Avenger* (51), *Captain John Smith and Pocahontas* (53), *Oklahoma!* (55), *Stagecoach to Dancer's Rock* (62).

## LAWRENCE, Marc (1910- )

Born Max Goldsmith in New York, Lawrence came to films from the stage in 1933. With his rough features and ominous air, he became one of Hollywood's most familiar hoods, appearing in dozens of features for over four decades. In later life he directed some low-budget films.
**Selected Films:** *White Woman* (33), *The Ox-Bow Incident* (43), *Key Largo* (48), *The Kremlin Letter* (70), *Marathon Man* (76), *Swap Meet* (79).

## LAWSON, Wilfrid (1900-1966)

Born Wilfrid Worsnop in Bradford, England, Lawson began acting on the stage in his native Britain and made his film debut in 1936. For some three decades he played character roles, specializing in eccentric or crusty characters like Alfred Doolittle in *Pygmalion* (38) and Black George Seagrim in *Tom Jones* (63).
**Selected Films:** *East Lynne on the Western Front* (31), *Turn of the Tide* (36), *Pastor Hall* (39), *The Great Mr Handel* (42), *The Prisoner* (55), *Room at the top* (59), *The Wrong Box* (66), *The Viking Queen* (67).

## LAWTON, Frank (1904-1969)

Born Frank Lawton Mokeley in London, Lawton played film and stage roles on both sides of the Atlantic during his long career. Among his notable appearances was the title role as the adult *David Copperfield* (34) and *The Mill on the Floss* (37). He was married to actress Evelyn Laye.
**Selected Films:** *Young Woodley* (28), *David Copperfield* (34), *The Mill on the Floss* (37), *The Winslow Boy* (48), *A Night to Remember* (57).

## Le GALLIENNE, Eva (1899- )

Born in London, Le Gallienne came early to Broadway and was one of its leading figures in the first half of the century and the founder of the Civic Repertory Theatre. She appeared in few films.
**Selected Films:** *Prince of Players* (55), *The Devil's Disciple* (59), *Resurrection* (79).

## Le ROY, Baby (1932- )

Born LeRoy Winebrenner in Los Angeles, the child was in movies before he was out of diapers, most notably as the nemesis of W C Fields in *Tillie and Gus* (33) ,and *The Old-Fashioned Way* (34). Le Roy's parents decided he should retire at age 4.
**Selected Films:** *A Bedtime Story* (33), *Tillie and Gus* (33), *Alice in Wonderland* (33), *The Old Fashioned Way* (34), *It's a Great Life* (36).

## LEACHMAN, Cloris (1926- )

Born in Des Moines, Iowa, Leachman was a Miss America runner-up before making her film debut as the glamorous lead in Robert Aldrich's *Kiss Me Deadly* (53). She was relegated to minor roles – and the TV series *Lassie* – until her Oscar-winning supporting role as a lonely housewife in *The Last Picture Show* (71). Leachman thereafter was seen most in a number of TV movies and the TV series *The Mary Tyler Moore Show* and *Phyllis*.
**Selected Films:** *Kiss Me Deadly* (53), *The Chapman Report* (62), *Butch Cassidy and the Sundance Kid* (69), *The Last Picture Show* (71), *Daisy Miller* (74), *History of the World – Part One* (81).

## LEDERER, Francis (1906- )

Born in Prague, Czechoslovakia, Lederer studied drama and in his twenties became a popular romantic lead on the European stage and screen. Arriving in Hollywood in 1932, the suave and strong-featured actor played romantic parts before changing over to character roles.
**Selected Films:** *Pandora's Box* (28), *The Pursuit of Happiness* (34), *Confessions of a Nazi Spy* (39), *The Bridge of San Luis Rey* (44), *The Return of Dracula* (58), *Terror Is a Man* (59).

## LEE, Anna (1914- )

Born Joanna Winnifrith in Ighthem, England, Lee ran away to join a circus at 14 and found her way to an acting career. Coming to the United States in 1939, she starred as Bronwyn in John Ford's *How Green Was My Valley* (41). The petite blonde starred in some two dozen films into the 1960s.
**Selected Films:** *Ebb Tide* (32), *King Solomon's Mines (37)*, *How Green Was My Valley* (41), *Fort Apache* (48), *Gideon's Day* (58), *The Sound of Music* (65), *In Like Flint* (67), *Star!* (68).

## LEE, Belinda (1935-1961)

Born in Budleigh Salterton, Lee first appeared in films in her native England, being groomed as a leading lady. Later appearing in minor European productions, Lee had not out grown the sexy-starlet category when she was killed in a car crash.
**Selected Films:** *The Runaway Bus* (54), *The Belles of St Trinian's* (54), *The Big Money* (56), *Les Drageurs* (59), *Carthage in Flames* (61).

## LEE, Bernard (1908-1981)

Lee was born in London and spent most of his long acting career on the stage in his native Britain, but also appeared in character roles in films, playing a likeable administrator or officer. He is best known as 'M' in several James Bond thrillers.
**Selected Films:** *The River House Mystery* (35), *The Man* (49), *Father Brown* (54), *Dr No* (62), *Thunderball* (65), *Moonraker* (71), *The Spy Who Loved Me* (77).

## LEE, Bruce (1940-1973)

Born Lee Yuen Kam in San Francisco, Lee studied philosophy in college, while training in the martial

arts. Later he opened up Kung Fu training schools on the West Coast and did some minor film and TV acting – the latter including playing Kato in the *Green Hornet* series. In 1973 Lee starred in a low-budget Kung Fu movie called *Fists of Fury*, and the rest is pop history. He made several more flying-extremities pictures before dying under mysterious circumstances at the age of 32. He has been apotheosized into a cult figure, with massive posthumous exploitation (including a movie with three Lee clones).
**Selected Films:** *Marlowe* (69), *Fists of Fury* (73), *The Chinese Connection* (73), *Enter the Dragon* (73), *Return of the Dragon* (73).

## LEE, Canada (1907-1952)

Black American actor Lee first attracted notice onstage in Orson Welles' all-black *Hamlet*. Moving into films, Lee refused to play the shuffling-darky roles that were then all that were available to blacks. In his four film appearances beginning with Hitchcock's *Lifeboat* (44), Lee was one of the first strong black character actors onscreen. That very fact helped get him blacklisted during the McCarthy era; he died shortly therafter.
**Selected Films:** *Lifeboat* (44), *Body and Soul* (47), *Long Boundaries* (49), *Cry, the Beloved Country* (52).

## LEE, Christopher (1922- )

Born in London, England, this gaunt and sinister-looking actor with the ominous voice has probably played more leading horror roles than anyone, including Boris Karloff. Lee made his mark in a series of remakes of classic thrillers produced by Britain's Hammer Studios, and was the leading actor in their spooky stable, often teaming up with Peter Cushing. The film that first brought him attention as a horror star was Hammer's *The Curse of Frankenstein* (57), in which he played the Monster. He is best known for his various portrayals of Dracula, beginning with Hammer's *Horror of Dracula* (58). He has also played the Mummy, Dr Fu Manchu and Sherlock Holmes, as well as assorted Satanists and other evil characters in his more than 100 films. In recent years, he has tried to turn away from strictly horror parts, but he is still identified with the roles that he played for Hammer, particularly Dracula.
**Selected Films:** *Corridor of Mirrors* (47), *Hamlet* (48), *Valley of the Eagles* (51), *The Crimson Pirate* (52), *Moulin Rouge* (53), *Private's Progress* (55), *Moby Dick* (56), *The Curse of Frankenstein* (57), *A Tale of Two Cities* (57), *Horror of Dracula* (58), *Corridors of Blood* (58), *The Hound of the Baskervilles* (59), *The Mummy* (59), *The Hands of Orlac* (60), *Sherlock Holmes and the Deadly Necklace* (62), *The Gorgon* (63), *Dr Terror's House of Horrors* (63), *The Face of Fu Manchu* (65), *The Skull* (65), *Dracula, Prince of Darkness* (65), *Rasputin, the Mad Monk* (65), *Theatre of Death* (66), *Dracula Has Risen from the Grave* (68), *Julius Caesar* (70), *I, Monster* (71), *Dracula AD 1972* (72), *The Three Musketeers* (74), *Killer Force* (75), *Airport 77* (77), *Return to Witch Mountain* (78), *Arabian Adventure* (79), *1941* (79), *The House of Long Shadows* (83), *The Howling II* (85).

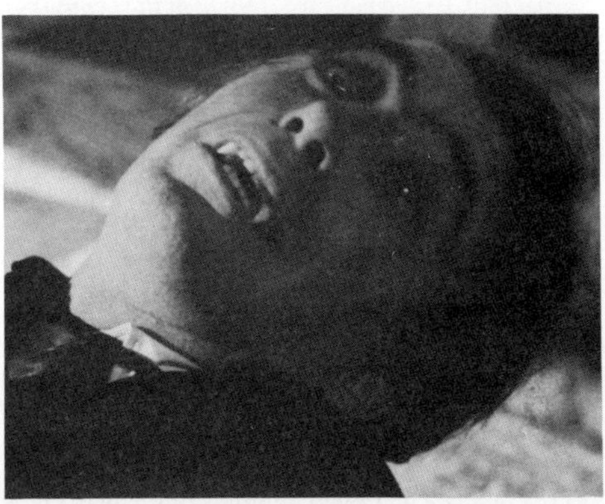

*Christopher Lee in* The Horror of Dracula *(58).*

## LEE, Dixie (1911-1952)

Born Wilma Wyatt, American actress Lee began her film career during the 1920s, appearing in mostly minor productions into the 1930s. She was the first wife of crooner Bing Crosby.
**Selected Films:** *Not for Sale* (24), *The Big Party* (30), *Manhattan Love Song* (34), *Love in Bloom* (35).

## LEE, Dorothy (1911- )

American actress Lee appeared in a number of movies of the 1930s, often teamed with the comedy duo of (Bert) Wheeler and (Robert) Woolsey.
**Selected Films:** *Syncopation* (29), *Cracked Nuts* (31), *Hips, Hips Hooray* (34), *Silly Billies* (36).

## LEE, Gypsy Rose (1914-1970)

Born Rose Louise Hovick in Seattle, Washington, she was a thinking man's striptease dancer, a lively writer, a good actress and a woman of wit and charm. Her mother, Rose Hovick, enrolled Lee and her sister June, who was later to become famous as June Havoc, in dancing school when they were toddlers, and by the time that Lee was six, they were appearing professionally at a Knights of Pythias celebration. At the height of their vaudeville careers as child stars they earned $1250 per week on the Pantages and Keith-Orpheum circuits. At 15 she learned the art of striptease from 'Tessie the Tassel Twirler' and became a featured performer at Minsky's Theater in New York City and assorted other burlesque houses. Lee 'took it off' for a number of causes, among them the Newspaper Guild, the Spanish Loyalists, War Bonds and the Red Cross. In 1937 she went to Hollywood to appear in her first movie, *You Can't Have Everything*, with Alice Faye

and Don Ameche. Lee began writing when newspapermen Walter Winchell asked her to do a guest gossip column. She went on to write several mysteries and her autobiography. In later life, she hosted a television talk show on which she said, 'I've got everything I always had – only it's six inches lower.'
**Selected Films:** *You Can't Have Everything* (37), *Ali Baba Goes to Town* (38), *My Lucky Star* (39), *Belle of the Yukon* (44), *Babes in Bagdad* (52), *Screaming Mimi* (57), *Wind Across the Everglades* (58), *The Stripper* (62), *The Trouble with Angels* (62).

## LEE, Lila (1902-1973)

Born Augusta Apel in Union Hill, New York, Lee appeared in vaudeville at the age of four as 'Cuddles.' She began her film career in the teens and starred with Valentino in *Blood and Sand* (22) and thereafter was a major figure of the silent screen, usually playing demure heroines. Making the transition to talkies, Lee continued leading roles during the 1930s.
**Selected Films:** *The Cruise of the Make-Believe* (18), *Male and Female* (19), *Terror Island* (20), *Blood and Sand* (22), *The Sacred Flame* (29), *False Faces* (32), *Two Wise Maids* (37).

## LEE, Michele (1942-     )

Born Michele Dusiak in Los Angeles, the American actress and singer came to films in the late 1960s. Her most notable movie was the musical *How to Succeed in Business Without Really Trying* (67). Her later TV work has included the movie *Bud and Lou* and the series *Knots Landing*. She is married to actor James Farentino
**Selected Films:** *How to Succeed in Business Without Really Trying* (67), *The Love Bug* (69), *The Comic* (69).

## LEEDS, Andrea (1914-1984)

Born in Butte, Montana, Leeds came to Hollywood to write screenplays, but her lovely features landed her in front of the cameras as a leading lady. In her short career Leeds usually played wholesome roles, but her most noted effort was as a suicidal young actress in *Stage Door* (37). She retired upon her marriage in 1940.
**Selected Films:** *Come and Get It* (36), *Stage Door* (37), *The Goldwyn Follies* (38), *Letter of Introduction* (38), *Swanee River* (39), *Earthbound* (40).

## LEIBER, Fritz (1883-1949)

Born in Chicago, Leiber became a noted Shakespearean on the stage. His movie appearances began with his role as Julius Caesar opposite Theda Bara in *Cleaopatra* (17). He went on to play character roles in films, several of them classics, for over three decades.
**Selected Films:** *Cleopatra* (17), *The Queen of Sheba* (21), *A Tale of Two Cities* (35), *The Hunchback of Notre Dame* (40), *Humoresque* (46), *Devil's Doorway* (50).

## LEIBMAN, Ron (1937-     )

Born in New York, Liebman acted with great success on stage before moving into films as a character actor, sometimes in leads and sometimes in supporting roles. He often plays offbeat characters, like the intense and ironic union organizer in *Norma Rae* (79).
**Selected Films:** *Where's Poppa?* (70), *Slaughterhouse Five* (72), *Won Ton Ton, the Dog Who Saved Hollywood* (76), *Norma Rae* (79), *Up the Academy* (80), *Zorro, the Gay Blade* (81), *Door to Door* (84).

## LEIGH, Janet (1927-     )

Born Jeanette Morrison in Merced, California, she was a California college student with no previous experience when she signed her first movie contract. Leigh was first the typical peaches-and-cream fresh-faced ingénue in such films as *The Romance of Rosy Ridge* (47) and *Little Women* (49). She graduated to playing solid, dependable women who help out their men in pictures like *Houdini* (53) and *Prince Valiant* (54). In *Houdini* she co-starred with her then-husband, Tony Curtis – they had a daughter, Jamie Lee Curtis, who grew up to be a fine actress in her own right. Leigh and Curtis were divorced in 1962. Later in her career, Leigh proved that she had learned her craft by appearing in more demanding roles, such as in *Touch of Evil* (58) and *The Manchurian Candidate* (62). She will always be remembered as the victim in the shower in Alfred Hitchcock's *Psycho* (60).
**Selected Films:** *The Romance of Rosy Ridge* (47), *Words and Music* (48), *Little Women* (49), *That Forsyte Woman* (49), *Angels in the Outfield* (51), *Scaramouche* (52), *Houdini* (53), *Prince Valiant* (54), *The Black Shield of Falworth* (54), *Pete Kelly's Blues* (55), *My Sister Eileen* (55), *Touch of Evil* (58), *The Vikings* (58), *The Perfect Furlough* (58), *Psycho* (60), *The Manchurian Candidate* (62), *Bye Bye Birdie* (62), *Harper* (66), *Grand Slam* (68), *Night of the Lepus* (74), *The Fog* (79).

## LEIGH, Vivien (1913-1967)

Born Vivien Mary Hartley to British parents in Darjeeling, India, she was educated in covent schools in England and on the continent, and made her film debut in *Things Are Looking Up* (34), a British movie. A delicate and graceful woman, Leigh became a talented stage and screen actress, a complex and ambitious performer who won Hollywood's plum role, Scarlett O'Hara, in *Gone with the Wind* (39), after a talent hunt that rivaled a political convention. Although she was British, she played the part of the southern belle to perfection, a feat she achieved again as Blanche du Bois in Tennessee Williams' *A Street Named Desire* (51).

Those two sterling performances alone would qualify her for film immortality, and she won Academy Awards for Best Actress in both of them. Her stage debut occurred in London in 1935. Four months later she appeared in the play *The Mask of Virtue* and became an instant star. Good film offers followed. *Fire Over England* (36), a costume drama, co-starred Laurence Olivier, and their off-screen romance created a stir. Leigh had married a barrister at the beginning of her career and Olivier, too, was married. In 1938 Leigh flew to Hollywood to visit Olivier. *Gone With the Wind* had gone into production without a Scarlett. Legend has it that Leigh was introduced on the set during the filming of the burning of Atlanta, and producer David O Selznick saw at once that he had found his ideal heroine. Not until 1940, when both divorces were sorted out, were she and Olivier free to wed. They were to go on co-starring together. Leigh played Juliet to Olivier's Romeo on Broadway and Emma to his Lord Horatio Nelson in *That Hamilton Woman* (41). She also toured with him in the Old Vic, London's venerable repertory company. They were divorced in 1960. *That Hamilton Woman* proved popular, and Leigh was charming in George Bernard Shaw's *Caesar and Cleopatra* (45) with Claude Rains. But there were complications. Always frail, Leigh saved her limited stamina for her frequent stage appearances. Bouts of physical illness and mental breakdowns also cast a tragic shadow over the brightness of her many achievements. In 1949 Leigh played Blanche du Bois in the London company of *Streetcar* and was cast for the film. Her shimmering interpretation of the character not only won the Oscar but also the British Film Academy Award for Best Actress. One of her finest performances came in her last movie – *Ship of Fools* (65). She died of tuberculosis in 1967.

**Selected Films:** *Things Are Looking Up* (34), *The Village Squire* (35), *Gentleman's Agreement* (35), *Look Up and Laugh* (35), *Fire Over England* (36), *Dark Journey* (37), *Storm in a Teacup* (37), *St Martin's Lane* (38), *Twenty-One Days* (38), *A Yank at Oxford* (38), *Gone With the Wind* (39), *That Hamilton Woman* (41), *Caesar and Cleopatra* (45), *Anna Karenina* (48), *A Streetcar Named Desire* (51), *The Deep Blue Sea* (55), *The Roman Spring of Mrs Stone* (61), *Ship of Fools* (65).

## LEIGHTON, Margaret (1922-1976)

Margaret Leighton was born in Barnet Green, England, and trained for the stage and came to fame with London's Old Vic company under the leadership of Lawrence Olivier and Ralph Richardson. Throughout her career she was most devoted to the stage; among her Broadway roles were Tony-winning performances in *Separate Tables* (56) and *The Night of the Iguana* (62). Her film appearances were occasional, the films variable, but she usually shone in the cast; among her more notable appearances were her debut in *Bonnie Prince Charlie* (48), in *The Sound and the Fury* (58), and *The Go-Between* (70). The latter earned her a supporting-actress Oscar nomination. Leighton tended to be cast as fragile and neurotic women, playing off her tall, distinguished looks. She died of multiple sclerosis, but despite the disease, worked until the end.

**Selected Films:** *Bonnie Prince Charlie* (48), *The Winslow Boy* (48), *Under Capricorn* (49), *The Holly and the Ivy* (54), *The Sound and the Fury* (58), *The Waltz of the Toreadors* (61), *The Loved One* (65), *The Madwoman of Chaillot* (69), *The Go-Between* (70), *Lady Caroline Lamb* (72), *The Nelson Affair* (73), *From Beyond the Grave* (75), *Dirty Night's Work* (76).

## LEMBECK, Harvey (1925-1982)

New York native Lembeck was a character actor in a number of supporting roles from the 1950s into the 1970s. He also appeared on the TV series *The Phil Silvers Show* and *Ensign O'Toole.*

**Selected Films:** *The Frogmen* (51) *Stalag 17* (54), *Sail a Crooked Ship* (62), *Bikini Beach* (65), *There Is No Thirteen* (77).

## LEMMON, Jack (1925- )

Lemmon was born in Boston, Massachusetts, to a well-to-do family and was educated at Phillips Andover Acdemy and Harvard College, where he was the head of that school's Hasty Pudding Club. After a stint in the Navy, he worked as a piano player, a radio actor and in off-Broadway productions. He got most of his steady work in television – over 400 shows in a five-year period. He then went to Broadway where his first breakthrough came in a revival of *Room Service* in 1953. His film debut was in *It Should Happen to You* (54), opposite popular comedienne Judy Holliday. Lemmon's portrayal of Ensign Pulver in the film version of

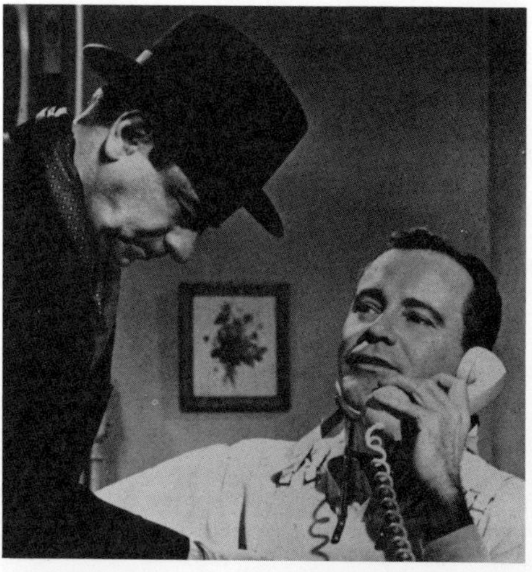

*Walter Matthau and Jack Lemmon in* The Fortune Cookie *(66).*

Mister Roberts (55) won him his first Oscar as Best Supporting Actor. He won another for Best Actor in *Save the Tiger* (73). Lemmon's next big success was in Billy Wilder's *Some Like It Hot* (59), now acknowledged to be one of Hollywood's finest comedies, but at the time that the film was made, it was a risky career move for him, since much of it had to be played in drag. Lemmon was becoming known as the best young comedian in Hollywood, but he proved spectacularly that his talents weren't confined to comedy in *Days of Wine and Roses* (62), a grim and touching story of an alcoholic couple. From then on, he divided his time between comedy and tragedy, and still found time to give bravura stage performances, such as the father in Eugene O'Neill's *Long Days Journey into Night* on Broadway in 1986. Lemmon was married to actress Cynthia Stone from 1950 to 1956. He married actress Felicia Farr in 1962.
**Selected Films:** *It Should Happen to You* (54), *Mister Roberts* (55), *Bell, Book and Candle* (58), *Some Like It Hot* (59), *The Apartment* (60), *Days of Wine and Roses* (62), *Irma La Douce* (63), *The Fortune Cookie* (66), *The Odd Couple* (68), *Save the Tiger* (73), *The Prisoner of Second Avenue* (75), *The Entertainer* (76), *Alex and the Gypsy* (76), *The China Syndrome* (79), *Missing* (82), *Mass Appeal* (84), *That's Life* (86).

## LENYA, Lotte (1899-1981)

Born Caroline Blamauer in Hitzing, Austria, Lenya was a star of the German theater, associated with the remarkable musicals of Bert Brecht and Kurt Weill, who wrote the part of Jenny in *The Three-Penny Opera* for her. She became Weill's wife and greatest interpreter. Lenya's few film appearances began with the German screen version of *The Threepenny Opera* (31).
**Selected Films:** *The Threepenny Opera* (31), *The Roman Spring of Mrs Stone* (61), *From Russia with Love* (63), *Semi-Tough* (77).

## LEONARD, Sheldon (1907- )

Born Sheldon Bershad in New York, Leonard acted on Broadway before getting into films in 1939. He became one of Hollywood's staple hoods in comedies and dramas into the 1960s. Taking up TV producing with considerable success in the 1950s, he largely retired from acting.
**Selected Films:** *Another Thin Man* (39), *To Have and Have Not* (44), *It's a Wonderful Life* (46), *Stop, You're Killing Me* (52), *Guys and Dolls* (55), *Pocketful of Miracles* (61), *The Brink's Job* (78).

## LEONTOVICH, Eugenie (1894- )

Born in Moscow and a stage actress in her native Russia, Leontovich appeared in occasional Hollywood films from the 1940s into the 1960s.
**Selected Films:** *Four Sons* (40), *The Men in Her Life* (41), *Anything Can Happen* (52), *The World in His Arms* (53), *Homicidal* (61).

## LESLIE, Joan (1925- )

Joan Leslie was born Joan Agnes Theresa Sadie Brodel in Detroit, and at 9 was singing and dancing with her sisters as 'The Three Brodels.' She made her film debut at 11, playing Robert Taylor's sister in the Garbo film *Camille* (36). Still as Joan Brodel, she appeared in juvenile roles in movies including *Foreign Correspondent* (40) and, memorably, as Velma in *High Sierra* (41). In the latter she changed her name to Joan Leslie and gradually metamorphosed into a pert and wholesome grownup leading lady in films of the 1940s such as *Yankee Doodle Dandy* (42), *Rhapsody in Blue* (45), and *Cinderella Jones* (46). After leaving Warners in 1946, Leslie was relegated largely to routine action pictures. She retired after *The Revolt of Mamie Stover* (56). She later became a fashion designer.
**Selected Films:** *Camille* (36), *Men with Wings* (38), *Foreign Correspondent* (40), *High Sierra* (41), *Sergeant York* (41), *The Male Animal* (42) *Yankee Doodle Dandy* (42), *This Is the Army* (43), *Hollywood Canteen* (44), *Rhapsody in Blue* (45), *Royal Flush* (46), *Cinderella Jones* (46), *Northwest Stampede* (49), *Born to Be Bad* (51), *Jubilee Trail* (54), *The Revolt of Mamie Stover* (56).

## LESTER, Mark (1958- )

Born into an acting family in Oxford, England, Lester was in films from age six. After several outings, his blond wistfulness and his talent were put to good use in the title role of the musical *Oliver!* (68). Lester continued as a seasoned juvenile player into the 1970s.
**Selected Films:** *The Counterfeit Constable* (64), *Oliver!* (68), *Run Wild Run Free* (69), *Black Beauty* (71), *The Prince and the Pauper* (77).

## LEVANT, Oscar (1906-1972)

Born in Pittsburgh, Pennsylvania, Levant trained to be a concert pianist while playing with dance-bands and writing tunes. In the 1930s he became a protégé of George Gershwin and thereafter was one of the great Gershwin interpreters. After success on radio, Levant appeared in movies of the 1940s and 1950s. He was a striking character in pictures like *Humorosque* (46) and *The Band Wagon* (53). Often, as in the Gershwin biopic *Rhapsody in Blue* (45), Levant played his inimitably neurotic, sharp-tongued self. A self-proclaimed genius, he wrote three autobiographical books before his death.
**Selected Films:** *The Dance of Life* (29), *Kiss the Boys Goodbye* (41), *Rhapsody in Blue* (45), *Humoresque* (46), *An American in Paris* (51), *The Bandwagon* (53), *The Cobweb* (55).

## LEVENE, Sam (1905-1980)

Born in Brooklyn, New York, Levene was one of the great Broadway stars of his time. His film

*Dean Martin and Jerry Lewis.*

career began when he repeated his comedy part in *Three Men on a Horse* on screen in 1936. For some 40 years thereafter, he appeared occasionally onscreen, often as a tough-but-goodhearted Runyonesque character.
**Selected Films:** *Three Men On a Horse* (36), *Crossfire* (47), *The Sweet Smell of Success* (57), *Act One* (63), *And Justice for All* (79).

## LEWIS, Diana (1915- )

American actress Lewis starred in a number of mostly minor films of the 1930s into the 1940s. She retired upon marrying actor William Powell.
**Selected Films:** *It's a Gift* (34), *Forty Little Mothers* (39), *Johnny Eager* (41), *Cry Havoc* (43).

## LEWIS, Jerry (1926- )

For years, moviegoers have either loved Lewis or hated him. Many French critics revere his comedy that reminds them of a reincarnation of Charlie Chaplin, while many American critics feel that their Gallic colleagues are crazy, regarding him as a goonish comedian whose style is a mixture of exaggerated mugging and sticky sentiment. Born Joseph Levitch in Newark, New Jersey, the son of show people, he occasionally joined their act. By the age of 20 he was a seasoned, if not successful, performer. Success came when he teamed up with baritone comedian Dean Martin, and they became the most popular comedy team on stage, television and in night clubs. Films soon followed and the pair made a series of box office winners during the 1950s. They split up with well-publicized bitterness in 1956. Since the breakup, Lewis has had a few successes, the biggest being *The Nutty Professor* (63), but generally the films, many of which Lewis has produced and directed himself, have been panned by critics and avoided by audiences, at least in the United States. His appearance as a television talk-show host in Martin Scorsese's *King of Comedy* (83) gained him the first good US notices he had had in years. For many years, Lewis has campaigned tirelessly to raise money for research funds to fight muscular dystrophy, both on the road and in his annual telethon.
**Selected Films:** *My Friend Irma* (45), *At War with the Army* (51), *That's My Boy* (51), *Sailor Beware* (52), *Jumping Jacks* (52), *Scared Stiff* (53), *Artists and Models* (55), *Hollywood or Bust* (56), *The Delicate Delinquent* (57), *The Geisha Boy* (58), *The Bellboy* (60), *Cinderfella* (60), *The Nutty Professor* (63), *The Disorderly Orderly* (64), *Boeing-Boeing* (65), *Which Way to the Front?* (70), *Hardly Working* (79), *King of Comedy* (83).

## LIGHTNER, Winnie (1901-1971)

Born Winifred Reeves in Greenport, Long Island, Lightner was a popular star of Broadway and vaudeville in the first quarter of the century. She appeared in a few screen musicals of the early sound era.
**Selected Films:** *The Gold Diggers of Broadway* (29), *The Life of the Party* (30), *Manhattan Parade* (32), *I'll Fix It* (34).

## LILLIE, Beatrice (1898- )

Though she was born Constance Munston in Toronto, Lillie became the most famous British stage comedienne of her time, her inimitably sharp features and aggressive wit cracking up audiences for four decades on both sides of the Atlantic. Lillie's few film appearances were rather unsuccessful in containing her. She married Sir Robert Peel and published an autobiography, *Every Other Inch a Lady*.
**Selected Films:** *Exit Smiling* (26), *The Show of Show* (29), *Dr Rhythm* (38), *Around the World in 80 Days* (56), *Thoroughly Modern Millie* (67).

## LINCOLN, Elmo (1889-1952)

Born Otto Elmo Linkenhalter in Rochester, Indiana, Lincoln was one of the screen's early male stars and appeared in two D W Griffith classics, *The Birth of a Nation* (15) and *Intolerance* (16). He is best remembered as the original *Tarzan of the Apes* (18). Lincoln's career faded in the 1920s. In his last years he returned to the screen in small parts.
**Selected Films:** *The Birth of a Nation* (15), *Intolerance* (16), *Tarzan of the Apes* (18), *The Romance of Tarzan* (18), *Elmo the Fearless* (20), *The Right of the Strongest* (24), *Carrie* (52).

## LINDFORS, Viveca (1920- )

Viveca Lindfors was born Elsa Viveca Torstensdötter in Uppsala, Sweden and studied at the Royal Dramatic Theater in Stockholm. After con-

siderable film and stage experience in her native country, she made her Hollywood debut in *Night Unto Night* (47). Thereafter, the dramatically beautiful and highly talented Lindfors appeared in films internationally, though few of them took full advantage of her range, like *The Flying Missile* (51) and *Moonfleet* (55). Her role in the Swiss film *Four in a Jeep* (51) won her an award at the Berlin Film Festival; the same festival honored her for *No Exit* in 1962. Her later work has included character parts in films such as Robert Altman's *A Wedding* (78) and the thriller *Creepshow* (82). Her third husband is playwright/director George Tabori and their son actor Kristoffer Tabori.
**Selected Films:** *Snurriga Familjen* (40), *Night Unto Night* (47), *The Adventures of Don Juan* (48), *The Flying Missile* (50), *Four in a Jeep* (51), *Moonfleet* (55), *The Halliday Brand* (57), *The Story of Ruth* (60), *King of Kings* (61), *No Exit* (62), *Coming Apart* (69), *The Way We Were* (73), *A Wedding* (78), *Voices* (79), *Creepshow* (82).

## LINDSAY, Margaret (1910-1981)

Born Margaret Kies in Dubuque, Iowa, Lindsay made her first impact in movies in the supposedly all-British cast of *Cavalcade* (33). Despite her talent and engaging screen persona, however, Lindsay was largely relegated to supporting roles and B movie leads. She was best known for her supporting role in the Ellery Queen mysteries.
**Selected Films:** *The Fourth Horseman* (32), *Cavalcade* (33), *Dangerous* (35), *Jezebel* (38), *The Spoilers* (42), *Scarlet Street* (46), *The Restless Years* (58), *Please Don't Eat the Daisies* (60), *Tammy and the Doctor* (63).

## LISI, Virna (1937- )

Lisi, a voluptuous and exquisitely beautiful actress, was born Virna Pieralisi in Ancona, Italy. She appeared in Italian melodramas before becoming a glamorous leading lady in international productions, particularly romantic comedies.
**Selected Films:** *La Corda d'Acciaio* (53), *Lost Souls* (58), *Duel of the Titans* (61), *The Black Tulip* (63), *How to Murder Your Wife* (65), *Assault on a Queen* (66), *Not With My Wife You Don't* (66), *The Secret of Santa Vittoria* (69), *Bluebeard* (72), *Cocktails for Three* (78), *Miss Right* (80).

## LITEL, John (1895-1972)

Born in Albany, Wisconsin, Litel started acting after a tour with the French army in World War I. After considerable success on Broadway he entered films in the early sound era. By his death he had played character roles in some 200 movies, most often as bankers, judges, and other solid citizens.
**Selected Films:** *On the Border* (30), *The Life of Emile Zola* (37) *Virginia City* (40), *The Sundowners* (50), *Pocketful of Miracles* (61), *The Sons of Katie Elder* (65), *Nevada Smith* (66).

## LITHGOW, John (1945- )

Born into a theatrical family in Rochester, New York, Lithgow grew up playing child roles in his father's productions. As a Harvard student he was a busy campus actor and director, and on a Fulbright to London polished his skills at the Academy of Music and Dramatic Art. Returning to the United States in the early 1970s to act on Broadway, he won a Tony for his role in *The Changing Room* (73). After a few barely-noticed film roles, Lithgow was cast as a transsexual football player in *The World According to Garp* (82), for which he was nominated for a supporting actor Oscar. It was the first of several engagingly outrageous performances; others include a hysterical plane passenger in *Twilight Zone: The Movie* (83), the fire-and-brimstone preacher in *Footloose* (83), and the beserk Dr Lizardo in *Buckaroo Banzai* (84). Lithgow is also adept at relatively calm characters: a banker in *Terms of Endearment* (83) which earned him his second supporting-actor Oscar nomination, or an astronaut in *2010* (84). Lithgow seems destined for more such roles in the future; he says, 'My days as a romantic lead – even though I've never had them –are behind me.' As a character actor, though, he is one of the best of his generation.
**Selected Films:** *Obsession* (76), *All That Jazz* (79), *Rich Kids* (79), *The World According to Garp* (82), *Dealing* (82), *Blow Out* (83), *Terms of Endearment* (83), *Footloose* (83), *Twilight Zone: The Movie* (83), *Buckaroo Banzai* (84), *2010* (84), *Manhattan Project* (86), *Harry and the Hendersons* (87).

## LITTLE, Cleavon (1939- )

Little was born in Chickasha, Oklahoma and grew up in California. After drama studies in New York, he made a name on Broadway, winning a Tony for his role in *Purlie* (70). His best-known film role has been as the quick-thinking black sheriff in Mel Brooks' *Blazing Saddles* (74).
**Selected Films:** *What's So Bad About Feeling Good?* (68), *Cotton Comes to Harlem* (70), *Blazing Saddles* (74), *Greased Lightning* (77), *High Risk* (81), *Once Bitten* (85).

## LITTLEFIELD, Lucien (1895-1960)

Born in San Antonio, Texas, Littlefield started in movies in 1913. Over the next 40 years he appeared as a supporting actor in hundreds of movies, in a variety of roles.
**Selected Films:** *Rose of the Range* (13), *The Sheik* (22), *Babbitt* (24), *No, No, Nanette* (30), *Tom Sawyer* (30), *Ruggles of Red Gap* (35), *The Little Foxes* (41), *Wink of an Eye* (58).

## LIVESEY, Roger (1906-1976)

Born the son of actor Sam Livesey in Barry, South Wales, Livesey made his stage debut at 11 and his movie debut at 14. He continued both careers until

nearly the end of his life. With his husky voice and roguish air, Livesey was occasionally a leading man but more often a character actor in films. He is best known for his performance as the aging soldier in *The Life and Death of Colonel Blimp* (43). He was married to actress Ursula Jeans.
**Selected Films:** *The Four Feathers* (21), *Rembrandt* (36), *The Life and Death of Colonel Blimp* (43), *I Know Where I'm Going* (45), *The Entertainer* (58), *Of Human Bondage* (64), *Oedipus the King* (68), *Futtock's End* (70).

## LLOYD, Harold (1893-1971)

At one time the most popular of the Hollywood quartet of silent clowns – Charlie Chaplin, Buster Keaton, Harry Langdon and Lloyd – he was a mixture of bold daredevil and ordinary American optimist. Lloyd was usually dressed blandly in everyday clothing and peered at the world through horn-rimmed spectacles. His 'nice-boy' character and his great comedy gifts, especially in hair-raising situations, allowed him to express humor with his whole body, even his teeth. There was nothing subtle about his great gift for stunts, however. His athletic prowess and feats of daring were amazing. Despite an accident in 1920 when a prop bomb turned out to be live and exploded, severing his right thumb and forefinger and leaving his hand partially paralyzed, Lloyd bravely performed incredible stunts and never used a double. In movies such as *Safety Last* (23), when he dangled atop a skyscraper, hanging onto the hand of a clock, he had audiences screaming with laughter and terror. The son of an unsuccessful photographer turned pool hall owner, Lloyd was born in Burchard, Nebraska, but grew up in San Diego, California. He broke into movies as a bit player and an extra in 1912. When his fellow extra Hal Roach set up his own studio that year, Lloyd went to work for him, developing a character named Willie Work, but the one-reel comedy series went nowhere. Roach reorganized under Pathé and, after a stint with Mack Sennett, Lloyd returned to Roach and created a new character, Lonesome Luke. Modeled on Chaplin, Lonesome Luke became popular, but it was the wild chase scenes that made the series a success, and Lloyd was only too glad to dump Luke for a new original persona, the colorless average man who triumphs over life's adversities with inventiveness, pluck and an adventurous spirit. Within a few years, Lloyd was a huge star. He was the idealistic but essentially conventional American in private life, too. In 1923 he married his leading lady, Mildred Davis, and the marriage lasted until his death. He was also active in charitable and service organizations. Lloyd's career declined after the arrival of the talkies, but by then he was a very rich man. In 1952 he received a Special Academy Award for being a 'master comedian and a good citizen.' He issued compilations of scenes from his works in 1962 and 1963. He died of cancer at the age of 77.

*Harold Lloyd in* Safety Last *(23).*

**Selected Films:** *Just Nuts* (15), *Luke's Movie Muddle* (16), *Over the Fence* (17), *Bumping Into Broadway* (19), *Haunted Spooks* (20), *A Sailor-Made Man* (21), *Grandma's Boy* (22), *Safety Last* (23), *Girl Shy* (24), *The Freshman* (25), *For Heaven's Sake* (26), *The Kid Brother* (27), *Speedy* (28), *Welcome Danger* (29), *Feet First* (30), *Movie Crazy* (32), *The Catspaw* (34), *The Milky Way* (36), *Professor Beware* (38), *The Sin of Harold Diddlebock* (47).

## LO BIANCO, Tony ( - )

New York-born Lo Bianco came from the stage to play character roles in films from the early 1970s, among them as one of *The Honeymoon Killers* (70). His TV work includes *Jesus of Nazareth*.
**Selected Films:** *The French Connection* (72), *Demon* (77), *Bloodbrothers* (78), *F.I.S.T* (78), *Separate Ways* (81), *City Heat* (84).

## LOCKE, Sondra (1947- )

Born in Shelbyville, Tennessee, Locke made a striking screen debut in *The Heart is a Lonely Hunter* (68). For the next few years her screen roles were unrewarding. The delicate blonde finally made an impression with Clint Eastwood in *The Gauntlet* (77). They have since co-starred often.
**Selected Films:** *The Heart is a Lonely Hunter* (68), *Willard* (71), *The Gauntlet* (77), *The Outlaw Josey Wales* (77), *Every Which Way But Loose* (80), *Bronco Billy* (80), *Sudden Impact* (83), *Ratboy* (86).

## LOCKHART, Gene (1891-1957)

Eugene Lockhart was born in London, Ontario, and first appeared on Broadway in 1916. He frequently returned to the stage throughout his

60-year show-business career. His pudgy features and crafty air were seen in some 100 film character roles from the 1920s on, in parts ranging from comic to villainous. In 1938 Lockhart won an Oscar nomination for his performance in *Algiers*. He was the husband of actress Kathleen Lockhart and the father of actress June Lockhart.
**Selected Films:** *Smilin' Through* (22), *Star at Midnight* (35), *Algiers* (38), *His Girl Friday* (40), *Going My Way* (44), *Androcles and the Lion* (53), *Carousel* (56), *Jeanne Eagels* (57).

## LOCKHART, June (1925- )

Born to actors Gene and Kathleen Lockhart in New York, June entered the family business at age eight and made her screen debut with her parents in *A Christmas Carol* (38). She grew up to stage roles, wholesome leads in B movies, and supporting parts in major films, but was probably best known for her TV appearances in the series *Lassie* and *Lost in Space*.
**Selected Films:** *A Christmas Carol* (38), *All This and Heaven, Too* (40), *Meet Me in St Louis* (44), *The She-Wolf of London* (46), *The Yearling* (47), *Time Limit* (57).

## LOCKHART, Kathleen (1893-1978)

The American actress was billed as Kathleen Arthur before she married actor Gene Lockhart. Kathleen was a character player in a number of films from the 1930s through the 1950s.
**Selected Films:** *The Devil is a Sissy* (36), *All This and Heaven Too* (41), *Gentlemen's Agreement* (47), *The Glenn Miller Story* (54).

## LOCKWOOD, Gary (1937- )

Born John Yusolfsky in Van Nuys, California, Lockwood got into movies as a stuntman. He graduated to leads and supporting roles in films of the 1960s and 1970s, most notable as the doomed astronaut in *2001: A Space Odyssey* (68). Among his TV work was the series *The Lieutenant. He was married to actress Stephanie Powers.*
**Selected Films:** *Tall Story* (60), *Splendor in the Grass* (61), *2001: A Space Odyssey* (68), *The Model Shop* (69), *Bad Georgia Road* (77).

## LOCKWOOD, Margaret (1916- )

Born to English parents in Karachi, Pakistan, Lockwood appeared on the British stage in her teens. Making her screen debut in *Lorna Doone* (35), the attractive, dark-haired actress spent her early movie career in popular thrillers. Best known for the lead in Hitchcock's classic *The Lady Vanishes* (38), she later turned to character parts.
**Selected Films:** *Lorna Doone* (35), *The Lady Vanishes* (38), *Night Train to Munich* (40), *The Wicked Lady* (45), *Cast a Dark Shadow* (57), *The Slipper and the Rose* (76).

## LODER, John (1898- )

Born John Lowe in London, England, Loder stumbled into films as an extra in his native Britain following World War I service. Before long he had established his screen image as a handsome, suave Englishman, appearing in leads and later supporting roles on both sides of the Atlantic from the 1930s through the 1950s. Among Loder's notable roles were as Ianto in Ford's *How Green Was My Valley* (41). His third wife was Hedy Lamarr.
**Selected Films:** *The First Born* (29), *The Private Life of Henry VIII* (33), *How Green Was My Valley* (41), *Now Voyager* (42), *The Hairy Ape* (44), *Gideon of Scotland Yard* (59), *The Firechasers* (70).

## LOGGIA, Robert (1930- )

Born in New York City, Loggia has played leads and supporting roles in various films since the 1950s, most of them adventures. He also appeared in the TV series *T.H.E. Cat*.
**Selected Films:** *Somebody Up There Likes Me* (56), *Che!* (69), *First Love* (77), *S.O.B.* (81), *An Officer and a Gentleman* (82), *Trail of the Pink Panther* (82), *Scarface* (83), *Jagged Edge* (85), *That's Life* (86), *Over the Top* (87).

## LOLLOBRIGIDA, Gina (1928- )

Born in Subiaco, Italy, the gorgeous and voluptuous Lollobrigida emerged during the great post-World War II boom in Italian film making. A model and beauty contest winner who hoped originally to become a commercial artist, she made her screen debut in *L'aquila nera* in 1946, and by the early 1950s she was a famous European star, affectionately calle 'La Lollo.' *Trapeze* (56) established her as a Hollywood star and she became very popular with American audiences. Hollywood altered her image, coating her natural sexiness with a laquered glamour. In the 1970s Lollobrigida retired from films to become a professional photographer.
**Selected Films:** *L'aquila nera* (46), *Pagliacci* (47), *Fanfan la Tulipe* (51), *Belles de Nuit* (52), *Bread, Love and Dreams* (53), *Beat the Devil* (54), *Trapeze* (56), *Solomon and Sheba* (59), *Come September* (61), *Woman of Straw* (64), *Hotel Paradiso* (66), *Bona Sera, Mrs Campbell* (68), *Bad Man's River* (71), *King, Queen, Knave* (72), *The Lonely Woman* (76).

## LOM, Herbert (1917- )

Born Herbert ze Schluderpacheru in Prague, Czechoslovakia, Lom came to Great Britain in 1939 and soon began his long career as an intense, piercing-eyed actor in mostly supporting roles. His range is large, encompassing a comic crook in *The Ladykillers* (55), the scary lead in *The Phantom of the Opera* (62), and Napoleon in *War and Peace* (56). Lom was also the longsuffering Inspector Dreyfus in several *Pink Panther* movies.

**Selected Films:** *Mein Kampf* (40), *The Seventh Veil* (46), *State Secret* (50), *The Lady Killers* (55), *War and Peace* (56), *The Big Fisherman* (59), *El Cid* (61), *The Phantom of the Opera* (62), *A Shot in the Dark* (65), *Asylum* (72), *The Dead Zone* (83), *King Solomon's Mines* (86), *Memed, My Hawk* 87).

## LOMBARD, Carole (1908-1942)

Born Jane Peters in Fort Wayne, Indiana, Lombard had a spell-binding face, pale blonde hair and a flawless figure. She also had an outrageous sense of humor, often a bit raunchy, and an endless capacity for fun. She was special, and had not only all the beauty and glamor a star should have, but also talents as a brilliant comedienne and a fine actress. Witty, high-spirited, earthy and zany, she was admired throughout Hollywood for her sense of humor and sense of style. She was a smart enough businesswoman to beat the Hollywood studio system, eventually freelancing her way into the big money. She moved to California at the age of six and made her screen debut at 12 in *A Perfect Crime* (21). She had a movie contract while she was still in her teens, but a serious automobile accident cut short this budding career. After much physical pain, she recovered and resumed acting, appearing in a series of Mack Sennett slapstick comedies, beginning with *The Girl From Everywhere* (27). She made the transition to talkies beautifully, appearing with her husband-to-be, William Powell, in *Man of the World* (31). She appeared with Clark Gable, later to be her second husband, in *No Man of Her Own* (32). She proved herself a star and first-rate comedienne in *We're Not Dressing* (34), with Bing Crosby, and in *Twentieth Century* (34), with John Barrymore. Nobody would prove better at screwball comedy. Barrymore described her as 'perhaps the greatest actress I have ever worked with.' *My Man Godfrey* (36), with William Powell; *Nothing Sacred* (37), with Fredric March; and *To Be or Not To Be* (42), with Jack Benny, attested to her ability. She married Clark Gable in 1939. After her marriage she limited her film appearances, and she finished *To Be or Not To Be* just two weeks before her death in a plane crash when she was returning from a war bond drive in the Midwest. Lombard was missed by her fans and critics alike, not only because of her film appearances, but also because of her unique, generous, madcap personality.
**Selected Films:** *A Perfect Crime* (21), *Hearts and Spurs* (25), *The Girl From Everywhere* (27), *Me Gangster* (28), *High Voltage* (29), *Fast and Loose* (30), *It Pays to Advertise* (31), *Man of the World* (31), *Ladies' Man* (31), *No Man of Her Own* (32), *Bolero* (34), *We're Not Dressing* (34), *Twentieth Century* (34), *Now and Forever* (34), *Rhumba* (35), *Hands Across the Table* (35), *Love Before Breakfast* (36), *My Man Godfrey* (36), *The Princess Comes Across* (36), *True Confession* (37), *Nothing Sacred* (37), *Made for Each Other* (38), *They Knew What They Wanted* (40), *Mr and Mrs Smith* (41), *To Be or Not To Be* (42).

## LONDON, Julie (1926- )

Born Julie Peck in Santa Clara, California, London is a singer and actress, having appeared in a number of films of the 1940s into the 1960s in addition to her nightclub and recording career. Despite a sultry persona and competent acting, London never quite clicked in movies. Among her TV work was the series *Emergency*. At one time the wife of actor Jack Webb, she is now married to actor/musician Bobby Troup.
**Selected Films:** *Jungle Woman* (44), *The Fat Man* (51), *Saddle the Wind* (58), *The George Raft Story* (62), *Survival on Charter No. 220* (78).

## LONG, Audrey (1924- )

Born in Orlando, Florida, Long was a model before turning to film. The dark-haired actress was a leading lady in mostly B movies from the mid-1940s to the early 1950s.
**Selected Films:** *A Night of Adventure* (44), Pan Americana (45), *Song of My Heart* (47), *Air Hostess* (49), *Indian Uprising* (52).

## LONG, Richard (1927-1974)

Born in Chicago, Illinois, Long made his movie debut in *The Stranger* (45), and went on to play juvenile roles and then leads in largely minor films. He was best known for his TV work in the 1950s and 1960s, appearing in the series *77 Sunset Strip*, and *The Big Valley*.
**Selected Films:** *The Stranger* (45), *Tomorrow is Forever* (46), *The Egg and I* (47), *Saskatchewan* (54), *Home from the Hills* (59), *Tenderfoot* (64).

## LONG, Shelley (1950- )

Long was born in Fort Wayne, Indiana, and came to TV comedy from Chicago's legendary Second City improvisational troupe. After guest appearances in several series, in 1982 she began her starring role as an intellectual waitress in *Cheers*, for which she won an Emmy in 1983. A sophisticated comedienne, she has made several movies.
**Selected Films:** *A Small Circle of Friends* (80), *Caveman* (81), *Night Shift* (82), *Irreconcilable Differences* (84), *The Money Pit* (86), *Outrageous Fortune* (87).

## LOO, Richard (1903-1983)

Hawaiian-born Loo began acting onstage in the mid-1920s and came to film in the early 1930s. For over 40 years he was one of Hollywood's most familiar Chinese supporting actors, his some 300 roles ranging from yellow-peril villains (especially during World War II) to good guys.
**Selected Films:** *Dirigible* (31), *The Good Earth* (37), *God is My Co-Pilot* (45), *Love is a Many-Splendored Thing* (54), *The Quiet American* (58), *The Sand Pebbles* (66), *One More Time* (71).

## LORD, Jack (1930- )

Born John Joseph Ryan in New York, Lord came to acting after some success as a painter – his work has been shown at the Metropolitan Museum and the Museum of Modern Art. Though he appeared in various films of the 1950s and 1960s, Lord is best known for his starring role in the TV series *Hawaii Five-O*. He has also developed and directed TV shows.

**Selected Films:** *Cry Murder* (50), *The Court-Martial of Billy Mitchell* (55), *God's Little Acre* (58), *Dr No* (62), *Hangman's Tree* (67), *The Counterfeit Killer* (68).

## LORD, Marjorie (1922- )

Born in San Francisco, Lord appeared on Broadway before coming to film in the mid-1930s. For two decades she played leading roles in mostly routine films before finding her greatest fame playing Danny Thomas's wife (the second actress to do so) in the *Make Room for Daddy* TV series from 1957-64.

**Selected Films:** *Border Cafe* (37), *Sherlock Holmes in Washington* (42), *Johnny Come Lately* (43), *Port of Hell* (55), *Boy Did I Get A Wrong Number!* (66).

## LOREN, Sophia (1934- )

The wealth and international fame that Italian actress Loren enjoys today are a far cry from her early years. An illegitimate child, she was born Sophia Scicolone in a charity hospital in Rome, Italy, and grew up in poverty in a Naples slum. In wartime Italy, poverty and breadlines made up her social milieu. She once said, 'Compared to pain, money is never real.' At the age of 15 she won a beauty contest and came to the attention of Italian film producer Carlo Ponti, who changed her professional name and later married her. It was Ponti who guided her spectacular film career from the time that she began appearing as a motion picture extra in 1950. She went to Hollywood in 1958. Loren's talent for both comedy and depressing dramatic roles have provided counterpoint to her talents as a sex symbol. She was hilarious in *Marriage Italian-Style* (64) and *Yesterday, Today and Tomorrow* (63), and electric in *Two Women* (61), for which she won the Academy Award for Best Actress. She still makes an occasional movie, for she says, 'If I stopped working right now, I would feel like my arm was cut off.' But she prefers to spend most of her time with her husband and her sons. Sensual beauty got Loren a boost in the world, but talent, intelligence and good sense have kept her a superstar.

**Selected Films:** *Cuori Sul More* (50), *Aida* (53), *The Sign of Venus* (53), *Tempi Nostri* (54), *Attila* (54), *The Gold of Naples* (54), *Woman of the River* (55), *The Miller's Wife* (55), *Scandal in Sorrento* (55), *The Pride and the Passion* (57), *Boy on a Dolphin* (57), *Desire Under the Elms* (58), *The Key* (58), *Houseboat* (58), *The Black Orchid* (59), *Heller in Pink Tights* (60), *Two Women* (61), *The Millionairess* (61), *El Cid* (61), *Boccaccio* (61), *Yesterday, Today and Tomorrow* (63), *Marriage Italian-Style* (64), *Arabesque* (66), *Lady L* (66), *A Countess from Hong Kong* (66), *Sunflower* (70), *Man of La Mancha* (72), *A Special Day* (77), *Revenge* (79), *Oopsie Poopsie* (81).

## LORNE, Marion (1886-1968)

American comedienne Lorne (born Marion Lorn McDougal) specialized in playing flustered old ladies, and was at her best as Robert Walker's dotty mother in Alfred Hitchcock's *Strangers on a Train* (51). Her TV work included the series *Mr Peepers* and *Bewitched*.

**Selected Films:** *Strangers on a Train* (51), *The Girl Rush* (55), *The Graduate* (68).

## LORRE, Peter (1904-1964)

Born Lazlo Löwenstein in Rosenberg, Hungary, he was trained for the stage in Vienna, Austria. Lorre, with his rolling eyes, timid manner and mysterious personality, who could adapt to either sympathetic or sinister roles, was picked by German director Fritz Lang to play the psychopathic child murderer in *M* (30), a role that gave him an international reputation. A Jew, he left Germany with many other refugees from the Nazis for England. In his first British movie he appeared as a scar-face killer in Hitchcock's *The Man Who Knew Too Much* (34). From there he went to the United States in 1935. Because of his appearance and rather sinister voice, he immediately started playing villains. In 1935 he delivered two memorable performances, as the crazed Doctor Gogol in *Mad Love* and as Raskolnikov in *Crime and Punishment*. Lorre was the Japanese detective in the *Mr Moto* series, but is best remembered for the films he made in the 1940s, often portraying a mysterious, cunning and cowardly villain, such as in *The Maltese Falcon* (41) and *Casablanca* (42). After World War II he went back to Germany to direct and star in a very personal film, *The Lost One* (51),

*Sophia Loren as Aldonza in* Man of La Mancha *(72).*

but returned to Hollywood to appear in large and small character parts. At the end he had become quite fat and appeared mainly as a comic villain.
**Selected Films:** *Frülings Erwachen* (29), *M* (30), *The Man Who Knew Too Much* (34), *Mad Love* (35), *Crime and Punishment* (35), *Secret Agent* (36), *Think Fast, Mr Moto* (37), *Thank You, Mr Moto* (37), *The Face Behind the Mask* (41), *The Maltese Falcon* (41), *Casablanca* (42), *The Mask of Dimitrios* (44), *Arsenic and Old Lace* (44), *The Beast with Five Fingers* (46), *The Lost One* (51), *Beat the Devil* (53), *20,000 Leagues Under the Sea* (54), *Congo Crossing* (56), *The Big Circus* (59), *Tales of Terror* (62), *The Raven* (63), *The Patsy* (64).

## LORRING, Joan (1926- )

Born Magdalen Ellis in Russia, Lorring was evacuated to the United States in 1939 after acting experience in England. She was typecast as a disagreeable teenager in most of her movies. The Cockney adolescent in *The Corn is Green* (45) is typical of the roles she played. Later she worked in theater, radio, and TV.
**Selected Films:** *Girls Under Twenty-One* (41), *The Bridge of San Luis Rey* (44), *The Corn Is Green* (45), *The Verdict* (46), *Stranger on the Prowl* (53).

## LOSCH, Tillie (1901-1975)

Coming to Hollywood after starting a career as a dancer in her native Austria, Losch appeared in several movies of the 1930s and 1940s.
**Selected Films:** *The Garden of Allah* (36), *The Good Earth* (37), *Duel in the Sun* (46).

## LOUISE, Anita (1915-1970)

Born Anita Fremault in New York, Louise was a beautiful child when she began appearing in movies at age eight. She grew up to be one of the most ethereal beauties of the screen. She often played aristocratic ladies in costume dramas such as *Madame Du Barry* (34) and *Marie Antoinette* (38). In *A Midsummer Night's Dream* (35) she played the fairy queen Titania. Later Louise worked on TV, starring in the series *My Friend Flicka*.
**Selected Films:** *The Sixth Commandment* (24), *What a Man* (30), *Madame Du Barry* (34), *A Midsummer Night's Dream* (35), *Anthony Adverse* (36), *Marie Antoinette* (38), *Submarine* (41), *Retreat, Hell!* (52).

## LOUISE, Tina (1934- )

Born Tina Blacker in New York, Louise came to movies from modelling and Broadway musicals. She was cast as a sexpot in various pictures of the 1950s and 1960s. Among her TV roles was in the series *Gilligan's Island*.
**Selected Films:** *Kismet* (55), *God's Little Acre* (58), *Armored Command* (61), *The Wrecking Crew* (68), *The Stepford Wives* (75), *Mean Dog Blues* (78).

## LOVE, Bessie (1898-1986)

Love was born Juanita Horton in Midland, Texas, and made her screen debut in D W Griffith's *Intolerance* (16). She was a vivacious leading lady of the 1920s, but her career spanned the years from silent films to television.
**Selected Films:** *Intolerance* (16), *The Purple Dawn* (20), *Human Wreckage* (23), *The Lost World* (25), *Broadway Melody* (28), *I Live Again* (36), *Journey Together* (45), *Touch and Go* (55), *Isadora* (68), *Sunday, Bloody Sunday* (71), *Ragtime* (80), *Reds* (82).

## LOVE, Montagu (1877-1943)

Born in Portsmouth, England, Love was a veteran stage actor when he moved to the United States in 1913 and became one of the leading villains of silent films. Later, in dozens of talkies, the heavy-set actor played character roles, including Henry VIII in *The Prince and the Pauper* (37).
**Selected Films:** *Hearts in Exile* (15), *Rasputin the Black Monk* (17), *Son of the Sheik* (26), *The Wind* (28), *The Prisoner of Zenda* (37), *The Prince and the Pauper (37)*, *Gunga Din* (39), *Tennessee Johnson* (42), *Devotion* (44).

## LOVEJOY, Frank (1914-1962)

Bronx-born Lovejoy got into acting by way of radio, doing thousands of broadcasts during the 1930s. In movies from the late 1940s, Lovejoy brought his plain, tough face and style largely to roles as cops and military officers.
**Selected Films:** *Black Bart* (48), *The Sound of Fury* (51), *I Was a Communist for the FBI* (51), *House of Wax* (53), *Cole Younger, Gunfighter* (58).

## LOWE, Edmund (1890-1971)

Born in San Jose, California, Lowe came to movies from Broadway in 1919. With his spruce mustache, slicked hair and elegant air, he was often cast a lover, but his most noted role was as crusty Sergeant Quirt in *What Price Glory?* (26).
**Selected Films:** *The Spreading Dawn* (17), *What Price Glory?* (26), *Dinner at Eight* (33), *Dillinger* (45), *The Wings of Eagles* (57), *Heller in Pink Tights* (60).

## LOWE, Rob (1964- )

Lowe was born in Virginina. He started his movie career in the early 1980s, when still a teenager.
**Selected Films:** *The Outsiders* (83), *Class* (83), *The Hotel New Hampshire* (84), *Oxford Blues* (84), *St Elmo's Fire* (85), *About Last Night* (86).

## LOWERY, Robert (1916-1971)

Born Robert Lowery Hanks in Kansas City, Missouri, Lowery came to movies from the stage in the mid-1930s. For some three decades he played leads and supporting roles in minor films as a sort of

low-budget Clark Gable. Today he is best remembered for his title role in the *Batman and Robin* serial of 1949.
**Selected Films:** *Wake Up and Live* (37), *Young Mr Lincoln* (39), *Death Valley* (48), *The Rise and Fall of Legs Diamond* (60), *The Ballad of Josie* (68).

## LOY, Myrna (1905- )

Loy was born Myrna Williams in Raidersburg, Montana, and made more than 60 movies before she became a star. She began her career as a villainous Oriental and then graduated to become the dutiful wife, especially in *The Thin Man* (34) and its sequels, as Nora Charles opposite William Powell's Nick Charles, and as the perfect wife and mother opposite Fredric March in *The Best Years of Our Lives* (46), not to mention the hilarious *Cheaper by the Dozen* (50), opposite Clifton Webb. She was witty, charming and altogether likeable, but of the Golden Age of Hollywood, during which she became the top box office female star, she said, 'When you think of all those years now with all that . . . sweetness and light, you must admit it wasn't that. Quite, quite horrible.' In the mid-1950s she switched from leads to character roles. Offscreen, she always showed an active social conscience. During the McCarthy ere she was one of a handful of actors to protest treatment of actors by the House Committee on Un-American Activities.
**Selected Films:** *Ben-Hur* (25), *The Cave Man* (26), *Don Juan* (26), *The Jazz Singer* (27), *Arrowsmith* (31), *Vanity Fair* (32), *Love Me Tonight* (32), *The Mask of Fu Manchu* (32), *The Animal Kingdom* (32), *When Ladies Meet* (33), *The Thin Man* (34), *Stamboul Quest* (34), *Broadway Bill* (34), *Wife vs Secretary* (36), *The Great Ziegfeld* (36), *Double Wedding* (37), *Test Pilot* (38), *The Rains Came* (39), *The Best Years of Our Lives* (46), *The Bachelor and the Bobby-Soxer* (47), *Mr Blandings Builds His Dream House* (48), *Cheaper by the Dozen* (50), *From the Terrace* (60), *Airport 75* (74), *The End* (79), *Just Tell Me What You Want* (79), *Summer Solstice* (81).

## LUCKINBILL, Laurence (1934- )

Born in Fort Smith, Arkansas, Luckinbill started his screen career in the 1970s with features such as *The Boys in the Band* (70), and *Such Good Friends* (71). Thereafter most of his roles were made-for-TV movies including *Winner Take All,* and *The Lindbergh Kidnapping Case*. He is married to actress Lucie Arnaz.
**Selected Films:** *The Boys in the Band* (70), *Such Good Friends* (71).

## LUGOSI, Bela (1882-1956)

Depending on whom you consult, Lugosi was born Bela Belsko, Bela Balasko or Bela Ferenc Dezso in Lugos, Hungary, and used the stage name of either Ariztid Olt or Aristid Oltz for a while. At any rate, he made his mark playing Dracula on the American stage. When the movie version of the play was being contemplated, Lon Chaney was cast in the role, but when he died of cancer, Lugosi was given the opportunity to recreate his stage role in Tod Browing's film, *Dracula* (30). He was an immediate and overpowering success, and it was the high point of his career. The role typecast him as a horror movie villain, and his heavy accent and highly individualistic acting style made it almost impossible for him to get other types of roles. He appeared in such superior horror movies such as *The Black Cat* (34) and *The Body Snatcher* (45), often playing opposite Boris Karloff. He also appeared in non-horror pictures, notably *Ninotchka* (39) with Greta Garbo. Still, after *Dracula*, his career ran steadily downhill until he wound up working in films with titles such as *Zombies on Broadway* (46) and *Mother Riley Meets the Vampire* (52). When he died he was buried in his Dracula cloak.
**Selected Films:** *A Leopard* (17), *The Silent Command* (23), *The Thirteenth Chair* (29), *Dracula* (30), *The Murders in the Rue Morgue* (32), *White Zombie* (32), *Chandu the Magician* (32), *Island of Lost Souls* (33), *The Black Cat* (34), *Mark of the Vampire* (35), *The Raven* (35), *Son of Frankenstein* (39), *Ninotchka* (39), *The Ghost of Frankenstein* (42), *The Ape Man* (43), *Frankenstein Meets the Wolf Man* (43), *The Body Snatcher* (45), *Zombies on Broadway* (46), *Abbott and Costello Meet Frankenstein* (48), *Mother Riley Meets the Vampire* (52), *Bride of the Monster* (56), *Plan Nine from Outer Space* (56).

*Bela Lugosi in* Dracula *(30).*

## LUKAS, Paul (1894-1971)

Paul Lukas was born Pal Lukàcs in Hungary – on a train, while his mother was traveling to Budapest. After dramatic studies he became a popular stage and screen star all over Central Europe. This attracted the attention of movie mogul Adolph Zukor, who in 1927 brought Lukas to Hollywood to appear opposite Pola Negri in *Loves of an Actress* (28). It was the beginning of a long and highly distinguished film career for Lukas. For a decade or so he was the most visible Continental lover on the America screen, in pictures like *Slightly Scarlet* (30) and *Affairs of a Gentleman* (34). Gradually he took on roles as elegant villains, most notably in Hitchock's *The Lady Vanishes* (38). After several turns as a Nazi, Lukas won a best-actor Academy Award for his playing of an anti-Nazi underground fighter in Lillian Hellman's *Watch on the Rhine* (43), he had previously been praised for the same role on stage. Later, Lukas tended to play sympathetic old men.
**Selected Films:** *Man of the Earth (15), Loves of an Actress* (28), *Three Sinners* (28), *Slightly Scarlet* (30), *Thunder Below* (32), *Little Women* (33), *Affairs of a Gentleman* (34), *The Three Musketeers* (35), *Dodsworth* (36), *The Lady Vanishes* (38), *Confessions of a Nazi Spy* (39), *Watch on the Rhine* (43), *Address Unknown* (44), *Experiment Perilous* (44), *20,000 Leagues Under the Sea* (54), *Tender Is the Night* (61), *Lord Jim* (65), *Sol Madrid* (68).

## LUKE, Keye (1904- )

Luke was born in Canton, China when his parents were there on vacation and educated in the United States, where he got into the film industry as an artist. He made his acting debut in 1934, and played sympathetic Orientals, the best-known of them being Number One Son ('Gee, Pop...') in nine Charlie Chan pictures of the 1930s. He played Kato in Green Hornet serials, was a regular in the Dr Kildare series, and much later played the blind monk Po in the TV series *Kung Fu*.
**Selected Films:** *The Painted Veil* (34), *Charlie Chan in Paris* (35), *The Good Earth* (37), *Across the Pacific* (42), *Dr Gillespie's New Assistant* (42), *Hell's Half Acre* (54), *The Chairman* (69), *Amsterdam Kill* (77).

## LUNA, Barbara (1937- )

Born in New York to a Hungarian-Philippine family, Luna acted onstage as a teenager and got into movies in the late 1950s. In films Luna usually played exotic roles. She was married to actors Doug McClure and Alan Arkin.
**Selected Films:** *Tank Battalion* (58), *The Devil at Four O'Clock* (60), *Ship of Fools* (65), *Woman in the Rain* (76).

## LUND, John (1913- )

Born in Rochester, New York, Lund wrote and acted on Broadway and in radio before turning to films in the mid-1940s. Blond and handsome, he had prominent roles in big films like *A Foreign Affair* (48), and *High Society* (56), before his rather stuffy image demoted him to minor productions.
**Selected Films:** *To Each His Own* (46), *A Foreign Affair* (48), *My Friend Irma* (49), *Chief Crazy Horse* (54), *High Society* (56), *The Wackiest Ship in the Army* (60), *If a Man Answers* (62).

## LUNDIGAN, William (1914-1975)

William Lundigan was born in Syracuse, New York, and started his showbusiness career in radio. In the mid-1930s he moved into films with *Armored Car* (37). In most of his screen appearances, Lundigan played nice-guy leads in second features. Occasionally he showed up as a lead or second lead in features such as *I'd Climb the Highest Mountain* (51). In the 1950s Lundigan worked often on TV, hosting the classic drama series *Climax* and starring in *Men into Space*.
**Selected Films:** *Armored Car* (37), *Three Smart Girls Grow Up* (38), *The Sea Hawk* (40), *Sunday Punch* (42), *What Next, Corporal Hargrove?* (45), *I'd Climb the Highest Mountain* (51), *Down Among the Sheltering Palms* (52), *The White Orchid* (54), *The Way West* (67), *Where Angels Go, Trouble Follows* (68).

## LUNT, Alfred (1892-1977)

Born in Milwaukee, Wisconsin, Lunt teamed with his wife Lynn Fontanne for a long reign as the king and queen of American theater. Lunt's screen roles, some with his wife, were few.
**Selected Films:** *Backbone* (23), *Second Youth* (24), *Sally of the Sawdust* (26), *The Guardsman* (31), *Stage Door Canteen* (43).

## LUPINO, Ida (1918- )

Born in London, England, this tough and talented actress achieved what few women have yet to achieve in films – a career which combines acting, screen writing, directing and producing. The daughter of British comedian Stanley Lupino, she began her film career in England with *Her First Affaire* (33). After going to Hollywood, she appeared in minor films until a strong performance in *The Light That Failed* (40), opposite Ronald Colman, brought her recognition. She frequently played strong ambitious women before turning to directing in the 1950s. It was in the 1950s, too, that she appeared with her husband, actor Howard Duff, in a television series, *Mr Adams and Eve*.
**Selected Films:** *Her First Affaire* (33), *The Gay Desperado* (36), *Artists and Models* (37), *The Light That Failed* (40), *They Drive by Night* (40), *High Sierra* (41), *The Sea Wolf* (41), *Ladies in Retirement* (41), *The Hard Way* (42), *Devotion* (46), *Roadhouse* (48), *On Dangerous Ground* (51), *The Bigamist* (53), *The Big Knife* (55), *Junior Bonner* (72), *The Devil's Rain* (75), *The Food of the Gods* (76).

## LYDON, James (Jimmy) (1923- )

While a student, Lydon, born in Harrington Park, New Jersey, won a contest as 'the typical American boy.' In his acting career he played that boy – on-stage as Tom Sawyer, in movies as the title character in the Henry Aldrich series, and in various other wholesome-juvenile roles. He appeared occasionally into the 1970s.
**Selected Films:** *Back Door to Heaven* (39), *Tom Brown's School Days* (40), *Henry Aldrich for President* (41), *Life with Father* (47), *Island in the Sky* (53), *Brainstorm* (65), *Vigilante Force* (76).

## LYNDE, Paul (1926-1982)

Lynde was born in Mount Vernon, Ohio, and came to movies from Broadway and nightclubs. His toothy grin, ratchety voice, and cynical wit were familiar on screen and TV from the 1950s on, most notably as the father in *Bye Bye Birdie* (63).
**Selected Films:** *New Faces* (54), *Bye Bye Birdie* (63), *Under the Yum Yum Tree* (63), *How Sweet It Is* (68), *Rabbit Test* (78).

## LYNLEY, Carol (1942- )

Born Carolyn Lee in New York, Lynley was a teenage model before starring in films in the late 1950s. Being blonde and irresistably cute, she was cast in fluffy ingenue roles for some years. Later and somewhat surprisingly, Lynley developed into a competent actress in films and TV through the 1970s, and starred in the title role of the made for TV biography *Harlow*.
**Selected Films:** *The Light in the Forest* (58), *Blue Denim* (59), *The Stripper* (62), *Bunny Lake is Missing* (65), *The Shuttered Room* (68), *The Poseidon Adventure* (72), *Vigilante* (83).

## LYNN, Diana (1926-1971)

Born Dolores Loehr in Los Angeles, Lynn was a child prodigy as a pianist. Gravitating to acting after a movie debut in *They Shall have Music* (39) she became a pert and pretty teenager in comedies of the 1940s, including her role as Betty Hutton's sister in *The Miracle of Morgan's Creek* (43). Lynn later worked extensively in TV and theater; she was planning a screen comeback when she died suddenly of a stroke.
**Selected Films:** *They Shall have Music* (39), *The Major and the Minor* (43), *The Miracle of Morgan's Creek* (43), *Our Hearts Were Young and Gay* (44), *My Friend Irma* (49), *The Kentuckian* (55).

## LYNN, Jeffrey (1909- )

Born Ragnar Lind in Auburn, Massachusetts, Lynn was a schoolteacher before taking up acting. In films from the late 1930s, he was typically cast as boyfriends, husbands, and other staunch and amiable characters.
**Selected Films:** *Four Daughters* (38), *A Child is Born* (40), *Four Mothers* (40), *Million Dollar Baby* (41), *Black Bart* (48), *Up Front* (51), *Come Thursday* (64), *Tony Rome* (67).

## LYON, Ben (1901-1979)

Born in Atlanta, Georgia, Lyon started on stage and screen as a teenager and in the 1920s was a popular romantic leading man. Making the transition to sound, he starred in *Hell's Angels* (30), doing his own flying. In the late 1930s Lyon and wife Bebe Daniels became radio personalities in Britain. Later he was talent director for Fox.
**Selected Films:** *Open Your Eyes* (19), *Dance Magic* (27), *Hell's Angels* (30), *I Cover the Waterfront* (33), *Dancing Feet* (36), *This Was Paris* (41), *Life with the Lyons* (54).

## LYON, Sue (1946- )

Born in Davenport, Iowa, Lyon made a splashy movie debut as a teenager, playing the nymphet who bewitches James Mason in Stanley Kubrick's *Lolita* (62). There followed more juvenile-temptress roles, most notably in *Night of the Iguana* (64), before maturity slowed Lyon's career to occasional minor features.
**Selected Films:** *Lolita* (62), *Night of the Iguana* (64), *Seven Women* (65), *The Flim Flam Man* (67), *Evel Knievel* (72), *End of the World* (77), *Towing* (78).

## LYTELL, Bert (1888-1954)

New York-born Lytell was acting on stage from the age of three and came to movies in the teens. Before long he was one of the silent screen's most popular leading men. His roles included Lord Windermere in *Lady Windermere's Fan* (25) and the title role in several Lone Wolf adventures. With the coming of sound Lytell concentrated on stage and radio work.
**Selected Films:** *The Lone Wolf* (17), *Rupert of Hentzau* (23), *Lady Windermere's Fan* (25), *On Trial* (28), *The Single Sin* (31), *Stage Door Canteen* (43).

## MacARTHUR, James (1937- )

Born in Los Angeles, California, and adopted by playwright/director Charles MacArthur and actress Helen Hayes, James appeared onstage at the age of eight. In the late 1950s he began playing youthful leads in movies, several of them Disney pictures. Later he starred in the TV series *Hawaii Five-O*.
**Selected Films:** *The Young Stranger* (57), *The Light in the Forest* (58), *Kidnapped* (60), *The Swiss Family Robinson* (60), *The Truth About Spring* (64), *The Bedford Incident* (65), *Hang 'Em High* (68), *The Angry Breed* (69).

## McAVOY, May (1901-1984)

Born to a wealthy family in New York, McAvoy grew up determined to be an actress. By 1916 she had found her way from modelling to movies, having her first real success in *Sentimental Tommy* (21). For the rest of the decade McAvoy's starry-eyed beauty and her wide acting range made her a major silent star; among her leading roles were in *The Enchanted Cottage* (24) and *Ben-Hur* (27). Finally in 1927 she starred with Al Jolson in the first talkie, *The Jazz Singer*. The coming of sound spelled the end of McAvoy's career, however; she starred in only a few more films.
**Selected Films:** *Hate* (17), *Sentimental Tommy* (21), *Clarence* (22), *The Enchanted Cottage* (24), *Ben-Hur* (25), *Lady Windermere's Fan* (25), *The Jazz Singer* (27), *The Lion and the Mouse* (28), *No Defense* (29).

## McBRIDE, Donald (1894-1957)

Born in Brooklyn, New York, American comic McBride was one of those character actors whose film persona was virtually patented – he was a master blusterer in dozens of roles as cops, executives, and the like. His exasperated hotel manager in *Room Service* (38) was a typical McBride role.
**Selected Films:** *Room Service* (38), *Here Comes Mr Jordan* (41), *Topper Returns* (41), *Good News* (47), *The Seven Year Itch* (55).

## McCALLISTER, Lon (1923- )

Born Herbert Alonso McCallister in Los Angeles, California, McCallister grew up in the theater and stepped naturally into juvenile roles in movies, first finding success as a bashful soldier in *Stage Door Canteen* (43). For a few years he played similar parts before he aged out of juvenile roles. Success and parts eluded him as an adult leading man.
**Selected Films:** *Romeo and Juliet* (36), *Stella Dallas* (37), *Stage Door Canteen* (43), *Home in Indiana* (44), *The Red House* (47), *Combat Squad* (54).

*Sue Lyon as the nymphet,* Lolita *(62).*

## McCALLUM, David (1933- )

Born in Glasgow, Scotland, McCallum studied music as a child before gravitating to acting. He began appearing in films in 1950. Despite supporting roles in a number of movies, the slight blond actor remains best-known as agent Ilya Kuryakin in the TV series *The Man from U.N.C.L.E* and its screen spinoffs. His first wife was Jill Ireland.
**Selected Films:** *The Secret Place* (57), *Freud* (62), *The Great Escape* (63), *The Greatest Story Ever Told* (65), *King Solomon's Treasure* (78), *The Watcher in the Woods* (80), *Terminal Choice* (85).

## McCAMBRIDGE, Mercedes (1918- )

Carlotta Mercedes McCambridge was born in Joliet, Illinois, and began performing on radio before she got out of college. She soon became one of the great stars of the medium when radio was in its heyday; Orson Welles, with whom McCambridge worked in the Ford Theater shows, called her 'the world's greatest living radio actress.' After years of inimitable voice crooning through soap operas, she made her screen debut in *All the King's Men* (49) and for it received a supporting-actress Academy Award. After this auspicious start she appeared in several movies over the next few years. She starred as a vindictive leader of a lynch mob in Nicholas Ray's offbeat Western, *Johnny Guitar* (54), a role typical of her intense, often angry and unsympathetic image. McCambridge's film career slacked off during a long struggle with alcohol. After drying out in the 1960s she resumed active work. Perhaps the best-known of her later roles is a return to her radio days: she was the spin-chilling voice of the demon in *The Exorcist* (73). In the early 1970s she appeared in several TV movies including *Who is the Black Dahlia?*.
**Selected Films:** *All the King's Men* (49) *Inside Straight* (51), *Johnny Guitar* (54), *Giant* (56), *A Farewell to Arms* (57), *Suddenly Last Summer* (59), *Cimarron* (60), *99 Women* (68), *Thieves* (77), *Airport 79: The Concorde* (79).

## McCARTHY, Andrew (1963- )

Born in New York, McCarthy attended New York University. He began his film career in the mid-1980s, making his film debut in *Class* (84).
**Selected Films:** *Class* (84), *Heaven Help Us* (85), *St Elmo's Fire* (85), *Pretty in Pink* (86), *Mannequin* (87).

## McCARTHY, Kevin (1914- )

Born in Seattle, Washington – the brother of writer Mary McCarthy – Kevin began acting at the University of Minnesota and first appeared in New York in the late 1930s. After a decade in the theater he found acclaim on Broadway as Biff in *Death of a Salesman*, and repeated that role to the 1951 screen version. From then on McCarthy was a frequent leading man and supporting actor in

mostly routine films, though there were some first-rate ones as well. Still most famous among his films is the sci-fi classic, *Invasion of the Body Snatchers* (56). In that and his other movies McCarthy made up for a somewhat stolid acting style with a compelling and earnest screen presence: he tended to be someone you believed in. His films in the 1960s included John Huston's *The Misfits* (61) and *If He Hollers Let Him Go* (68); throughout, he has appeared often onstage. In recent years McCarthy has aged into character roles, among them in Robert Altman's amiable Western satire *Buffalo Bill and the Indians* (76) and in the thriller *Twilight Zone: The Movie* (83). Also working frequently on TV, McCarthy starred in the series *Flamingo Road*.
**Selected Films:** *Death of a Salesman* (51), *Drive a Crooked Road* (54), *Stranger on Horseback* (55), *Invasion of the Body Snatchers* (56), *Nightmare* (56), *The Misfits* (61), *A Gathering of Eagles* (63), *The Prize* (63), *Mirage* (65), *A Big Hand for the Little Lady* (66), *To Hell with Heroes* (68), *If He Hollers Let Him Go* (68), *Kansas City Bomber* (72), *Buffalo Bill and the Indians* (76), *The Three Sisters* (77), *The Howling* (81), *Twilight Zone: The Movie* (83).

## MACCHIO, Ralph (1962- )

Long Island-born Macchio began his theatrical career doing TV commercials. Later he was a regular on the TV series *Eight is Enough*. After his screen debut in *Up the Academy* (80), he went on to starring in teen-oriented movies, most successfully in the title role of two *Karate Kid* pictures with Pat Morita.
**Selected Films:** *Up the Academy* (80), *Teachers* (84), *The Karate Kid* (84), *The Karate Kid II* (86).

## McCLURE, Doug (1935- )

Born in Glendale, California, McClure grew up with handsome, stalwart features and a robust figure but no strong presence as an actor. His film roles have been largely in routine thrillers; he is better known in TV series such as *The Virginian*.
**Selected Films:** *The Enemy Below* (57), *Gidget* (59), *Shenandoah* (65), *Beau Geste* (66), *The King's Pirate* (67), *Nobody's Perfect* (68), *Warlords of Atlantis* (77), *Humanoids from the Deep* (80), *The House Where Evil Dwells* (82), *52 Pick-Up* (86).

## McCORMACK, Patty (1945- )

American actress McCormack was an experienced stage and screen actress when at age 11 she caused a sensation playing Rhoda, the evil child in the stage and screen version of *The Bad Seed* (56). Three years later she starred in the TV series *Peck's Bad Girl*, but her roles declined precipitously as she grew up.
**Selected Films:** *Two Gals and a Guy* (51), *The Bad Seed* (56), *Kathy O'* (58), *The Adventures of Huckleberry Finn* (60), *The Explosive Generation* (61), *The Mini-Skirt Mob* (68), *Bug* (75).

## McCORMICK, Myron (1908-1962)

Born in New Albany, Indiana, McCormick spent most of his dramatic career in the theater. He appeared memorably as a character actor in occasional movies from the 1930s to the 1960s.
**Selected Films:** *Winterset* (37), *China Girl* (43), *Not as a Stranger* (55), *No Time for Sergeants* (58), *The Hustler* (61), *A Public Affair* (62).

## McCOWEN, Alec (1925- )

McCowen has spent most of his career on the stage in his native England. He has played occasional leads and supporting roles in movies, most of them British, since the 1950s.
**Selected Films:** *The Cruel Sea* (53), *Town on Trial* (57), *The Loneliness of the Long Distance Runner* (62), *The Agony and the Ecstacy* (65), *The Hawaiians* (70), *Travels With My Aunt* (72), *Stevie* (78), *Never Say Never Again* (83), *The Assam Garden* (86), *Personal Services* (87).

## McCOY, Tim (1891-1978)

One of the big western stars of the 1920s and 1930s, McCoy was not only a real cowboy with a ranch in Wyoming, but also an Army officer, serving in combat in both World Wars. Born in Saginaw, Michigan, McCoy was a leading authority on Indian history. He left fulltime army life as a colonel to enter the movies in 1923 as a technical consultant for the classic silent western, *The Covered Wagon* (23). He was soon starring in westerns and he proved to be one of the kings of the B horse operas. Always immaculately dressed in black, he wore oversized white Stetson hats and carried a pearl-handled gun. When he returned from World War II, all he could get were cameo roles in movies, but he toured with his Wild West Show until his death.
**Selected Films:** *War Paint* (26), *The Indians Are Coming* (30), *The Fighting Fool* (31), *Texas Cyclone* (32), *Whirlwind* (33), *Hell Bent for Love* (34), *Square Shooter* (35), *Requiem for a Gunfighter* (65).

## McCREA, Joel (1905- )

McCrea, who was born in Los Angeles, California, turned out to be one of the most durable actors of all time. He could play anything – drama, comedy, musicals. But it was for his work in westerns that he is most fondly remembered. A wealthy rancher today, he retired some years ago only to come out of retirement for special roles and guest spots in films and on television. He studied acting and got his start in movies as an extra. McCrea worked with dogged determination until he was finally allowed to play a feature role in *The Jazz Age* (29). For the first 15 years of his career, he played in comedies, spy films and adventure pictures as well as westerns. But after that he worked almost exclusively in westerns, reaching the peak of his

*Jeanette McDonald in* The Love Parade *(29).*

popularity in the 1940s and 1950s. He capped his screen career appearing with Randolph Scott, in *Ride the High Country* (62).
**Selected Films:** *The Jazz Age* (29), *Lightnin'* (30), *The Lost Squadron* (32), *Bird of Paradise* (32), *The Most Dangerous Game* (32), *Gambling Lady* (34), *Barbary Coast* (35), *Come and Get It* (36), *Banjo on My Knee* (36), *Wells Fargo* (37), *Dead End* (37), *Union Pacific* (39), *Foreign Correspondent* (40), *Sullivan's Travels* (41), *The More the Merrier* (43), *The Virginian* (46), *The Outriders* (50), *The Tall Stranger* (57), *Ride the High Country* (62), *Mustang Country* (76).

## McDANIEL, Hattie (1895-1952)

Born in Wichita, Kansas, McDaniel grew up to be the personification of the cheerful black mammy – an image unfortunate in the long run, but one that she embodied with an immense flair. McDaniel was the first black woman to sing on radio and the first to win a supporting-actress Oscar, which she received for her immortal performance as Mammy in *Gone With the Wind* (39). She appeared in some 40 other movies, usually playing a servant but still stealing scenes.
**Selected Films:** *The Blonde Venus* (32), *The Story of Temple Drake* (33), *Show Boat* (36), *Gone With the Wind* (39), *The Great Lie* (41), *Song of the South* (47), *Family Honeymoon* (49).

## McDEVITT, Ruth (1895-1976)

Born Ruth Shoecraft, American actress McDevitt appeared in a number of movies and TV shows, most notably in old-lady character parts during the 1960s and 1970s. Among her TV series were *Pistols and Petticoats* and *Kolchak.*
**Selected Films:** *The Parent Trap* (62), *The Birds* (63), *The Out of Towners* (69), *Change of Habit* (72).

## MacDONALD, J Farrell (1875-1952)

Born in Waterbury, Connecticut, MacDonald began his film career as a member of the original IMP company, in 1911 after stage experience and in the early silent years both as a leading man and director. Moving to character parts in the 1920s, he played supporting roles into the 1950s.
**Selected Films:** *The Last Egyptian* (14), *The Heart of Maryland* (15), *Abie's Irish Rose* (28), *The Maltese Falcon* (31), *Topper* (37), *Meet John Doe* (41), *The Miracle of Morgan's Creek* (44), *My Darling Clementine* (46), *Elopement* (51).

## MacDONALD, Jeanette (1903-1965)

MacDonald, born in Philadelphia, Pennsylvania, was a chorus girl who longed to sing in grand opera. Instead she went into Broadway musicals, making her debut in *The Demi-Tasse Revue*, singing and dancing on stage in 1920. The director Ernst Lubitsch cast her opposite Maurice Chevalier on screen in *The Love Parade* (29), in a starring role her first time out. MacDonald was a gifted comedienne, charming and attractive, a star before she appeared with Nelson Eddy, and capable of shining without him, as she proved in *San Francisco* (36) opposite Clark Gable. The first of her eight pictures with baritone Nelson Eddy was *Naughty Marietta* (35), and the mix between the stars and their saccharine romantic stories was a gold mine for MGM. The team broke up after *I Married an Angel* (42), and she went on to an abortive attempt at grand opera, most notably singing Marguerite in *Faust*. Then she returned to Hollywood to make a few more films.
**Selected Films:** *The Love Parade* (29), *The Vagabond King* (30), *One Hour with You* (32), *Love Me Tonight* (32), *Naughty Marietta* (35), *Rose Marie* (36), *San Francisco* (36), *Maytime* (37), *The Firefly* (37), *The Girl of the Golden West* (38), *Sweethearts* (39), *New Moon* (40), *Bitter Sweet* (40), *I Married an Angel* (42), *Cairo* (42), *The Sun Comes Up* (49).

## McDONALD, Marie (1923-1965)

Born Marie Frye in Burgin, Kentucky, McDonald was a model and showgirl before turning to movies in the early 1940s. A vivacious blonde who was dubbed 'The Body,' she appeared in various frothy features over the next decade or so, meanwhile accumulating seven marriages and a good many juicy headlines. Her career fell off in the 1950s and she died from an apparent drug overdose.
**Selected Films:** *It Started With Eve* (41), *Pardon My Sarong* (42), *Getting Gertie's Garter* (46), *Tell It to the Judge* (49), *Geisha Boy* (58), *Promises! Promises!* (63).

## McDOWALL, Roddy (1928- )

McDowall was born in London, England and was acting in British films by the age of eight. He had appeared in more than 30 movies, usually in minor roles, when he and his mother were evacuated to the United States in 1940, during World War II. He was an enormous hit playing young Huw Morgan in *How Green Was My Valley* (41), Darryl F Zanuck's sensitive production about a Welsh mining town. Over the next few years he did his share of growing up to be someone else in his pictures. He grew up to be Tyrone Power in *Son of Fury* (42), Gregory Peck in *The Keys of the Kingdom* (45), and Peter Lawford in *The White Cliffs of Dover* (44). But he did most of his best work at that time as a young friend of animals. *My Friend Flicka* (43) cast him as an American boy who loved a rebellious horse. Audiences accepted MacDowall in the role of a member of a western family despite his accent, and the film led to a sequel, *Thunderhead, Son of Flicka* (45). Meanwhile, moviegoers were also seeing him as a British boy in love with a dog. *Lassie Come Home* (43) started a long series that went on well into the television years. In 1945, when he was moving into what looked like his awkward teenage years, his contract with MGM came to an end. MacDowall got back into movies by acting both on stage and on television, proving that the boy actor had become an adult actor. In the 1960s he had good roles in such pictures as *Cleopatra* (63) and *The Greatest Story Ever Told* (65). He became part of the Walt Disney Stock Company, appearing in several family-oriented comedies including *That Darn Cat* (65) with Hayley Mills and *Bedknobs and Broomsticks* (71) with Angela Lansbury. McDowall also appeared in *Planet of the Apes* (68), which starred Charlton Heston as an American astronaut marooned on a planet where chimpanzees and orangutans ruled. The film was such a success at the box office that a string of four sequels followed. McDowall was in four of the pictures, speaking his lines through an ape mask as Cornelius, who eventually became the hero of the series. A *Planet of the Apes* series came to television with McDowall in a leading role. When the series flopped, he went back to playing humans. He is also a talented semi-professional photographer.

**Selected Films:** *Murder in the Family* (36), *This England* (40), *How Green Was My Valley* (41), *Son of Fury* (42), *My Friend Flicka* (43), *Lassie Come Home* (43), *The White Cliffs of Dover* (44), *The Keys of the Kingdom* (45), *Thunderhead, Son of Flicka* (45), *Macbeth* (50), *The Longest Day* (62), *Cleopatra* (63), *The Loved One* (65), *The Greatest Story Ever Told* (65), *That Darn Cat* (65), *Planet of the Apes* (68), *Escape from the Planet of the Apes* (71), *Bedknobs and Broomsticks* (71), *Conquest of the Planet of the Apes* (72), *The Poseidon Adventure* (72), *The Legend of Hell House* (73), *Battle for the Planet of the Apes* (73), *Funny Lady* (75), *The Cat from Outer Space* (78), *Fright Night* (85), *Dead of Winter* (87).

## McDOWELL, Malcolm (1943- )

Malcolm McDowell was born in Leeds, England, and later said he had planned to try acting 'if all else failed.' In his early years, all else – including working in his father's pub and selling coffee on the road – failed, and he began taking acting classes. After painstakingly shedding his lower-class accent, McDowell got into repertory and Royal Shakespeare Company productions. His first film was *Poor Cow* (67). Director Lindsay Anderson, liking McDowell's air of insolent rebelliousness, cast him as a gun-toting prep-school student in *If...* (69). Two years later he starred as a murderous Beethoven-loving thug in Stanley Kubrick's violent fantasy *A Clockwork Orange* (71). In Anderson's *O Lucky Man* (73), McDowell played a hapless youth for a change; it was the world he lived in that was violently crazy. In the 1970s McDowell's pictures were variable; they included the elegant fantasy *Time after Time* (79) in which he played H G Wells, and the execrable Roman-orgy outing *Caligula* (79). McDowell once observed, 'You could not remain long an actor unless you're content to let yourself become a monster. That's the only way to survive it.' He is married to actress Mary Steenburgen.

**Selected Films:** *Poor Cow* (67), *If...* (69), *The Raging Moon* (71), *A Clockwork Orange* (71), *O Lucky Man* (73), *Royal Flash* (75), *Voyage of the Damned* (76), *Time After Time* (79), *Caligula* (79), *Cat People* (82), *Blue Thunder* (83), *The Caller* (87).

## McENERY, Peter (1940- )

Born in Walsall, England, McEnery came to films in the 1960s, appearing in leading roles in a number of mostly minor films including *I Killed Rasputin* (68) and *Tales that Witness Madness* (73).

**Selected Films:** *Tunes of Glory* (60), *The Moon-spinners* (64), *I Killed Rasputin* (68), *Tales That Witness Madness* (73), *The Cat and the Canary* (78).

## McFARLAND, Spanky (1928- )

Born George Emmett McFarland in Fort Worth, Texas, McFarland entered movies at age three, joining the cast of the *Our Gang* series of shorts and soon becoming the star – he was the immortal fat kid with the beanie. Forcibly retired from movies at age 16 (he had also appeared in some features), McFarland tried unsuccessfully to resume his career.

**Selected Films:** *Day of Reckoning* (33), *O'Shaughnessy's Boy* (35), *Trail of the Lonesome Pine* (36), *Peck's Bad Boy with the Circus* (39), *The Woman in the Window* (44).

## McGAVIN, Darren (1922- )

Born in Spokane, Washington, and trained for the stage at New York's Actors Studio, McGavin has spent his screen career alternating between villains and rather crusty heroes, the former including his dope pusher in *The Man With the Golden Arm* (55). He is best known for his TV roles including *Mike Hammer* and *The Night Stalker*.

**Selected Films:** *Fear* (45), *Queen for a Day* (51), *The Court-Martial of Billy Mitchell* (55), *The Man With the Golden Arm* (55), *Bullet For A Badman* (64), *Airport 77* (77), *Hangar 18* (80), *From the Hip* (87).

## McGILLIS, Kelly (1957- )

The daughter of a physician, McGillis attended both the Juilliard School and the Pacific Conservatory of Performing Arts. She was a waitress before she appeared in the film *Witness* (85).
**Selected Films:** *Reuben, Reuben* (83), *Witness* (85), *Top Gun* (86).

## McGIVER, John (1913-1975)

Born in New York, McGiver studied drama in school but did not get into acting until his 40s. His owlish features and nasal twang were seen in supporting parts in a number of popular films.
**Selected Films:** *Love in the Afternoon* (57), *Breakfast at Tiffany's* (61), *The Manchurian Candidate* (62), *Fitzwilly* (67), *Midnight Cowboy* (69), *The Apple Dumpling Gang* (75).

## McGOOHAN, Patrick (1928- )

Though he is New York-born, McGoohan has lived and worked largely in Britain playing Englishmen. He has been seen in a number of movies since the 1950s and is best known as the star of the TV series *Secret Agent* and *The Prisoner*.
**Selected Films:** *Passage Home* (55), *High Tide at Noon* (56), *Hell Drivers* (57), *Life for Ruth* (62), *Ice Station Zebra* (68), *Mary Queen of Scots* (72), *Silver Streak* (76), *Baby . . . Secret of the Lost Legend* (85).

## McGOVERN, Elizabeth (1961- )

Born in Evanston, Illinois, McGovern studied acting at Juilliard in New York before making her film debut in *Ordinary People* (80). She has since appeared in several major films including *The Bedroom Window* (87).
**Selected Films:** *Ordinary People* (80), *Ragtime* (81), *Lovesick* (83), *Racing With the Moon* (84), *Once Upon a Time in America* (84), *The Bedroom Window* (87), *Native Son* (87).

## McGOWRAN, Jack (1916-1973)

The sharp features of Irish-born McGowran were familiar on the British stage and in films of the 1950s into the 1970s. He usually played quirky character roles.
**Selected Films:** *The Quiet Man* (52), *Darby O'Gill and the Little People* (59), *Tom Jones* (63), *Lord Jim* (65), *Wonderwall (68), The Exorcist* (73).

## MacGRAW, Ali (1938- )

Born Alice MacGraw in Pound Ridge, New York, Ali got a degree in art history from Wellesley but before long was a model in New York. She came to films on the late side for a leading lady, playing her first bit part in *A Lovely Way to Die* (68). The next year MacGraw's role as an archetypal Jewish princess in *Goodbye, Columbus* (69) made her a star overnight. She is best remembered as the dying girl in *Love Story* (71). Her ensuing film career was sporadic, however, as she pursued marriages to producer Robert Evans and then to Steve McQueen, who had been her costar in *Getaway* (73). In the 1980s she appeared mainly in made-for-TV movies including *The Winds of War*.
**Selected Films:** *A Lovely Way to Die* (68), *Goodbye Columbus* (69), *Love Story* (71), *Getaway* (73), *Convoy* (78), *Players* (79), *Just Tell Me What You Want* (79).

## McGRAW, Charles (1914-1980)

New York-born McGraw played tough guys on both sides of the law in films from the 1940s through the 1970s, among them *In Cold Blood* (67) and *Twilight's Last Gleaming* (76).
**Selected Films:** *The Moon is Down* (43), *The Narrow Margin* (50), *The Bridges at Toko-Ri* (51), *Away All Boats* (56), *The Defiant Ones* (58), *Spartacus* (60), *In Cold Blood* (67), *Johnny Got His Gun* (71), *Twilight's Last Gleaming* (76).

## McGUIRE, Dorothy (1919- )

Born in Omaha, Nebraska, Dorothy McGuire appeared onstage in Omaha with Henry Fonda when she was 13. She went on to extensive theater work and by the late 1930s had made it to Broadway. Her lead in the play *Claudia* gained her the attention of producer David O Selznick, who in 1943 brought McGuire to Hollywood to star in the screen version. The next year she played Katie Nolan in *The Enchanted Cottage* and during the rest of the 1940s appeared in several notable pictures including *A Tree Grows in Brooklyn* (44), *The Spiral Staircase* (45), and *Gentleman's Agreement* (47). With her attractive but unglamorous features and intelligently wholesome air, McGuire always appeared in sympathetic parts. From sweet girlfriend roles she moved easily into kindly mothers in films such as Disney's *Old Yeller* (57) and *The Swiss Family Robinson* (60). Stuck in her wholesome image, McGuire saw her films decline in the 1970s; recent appearances have largely been in TV movies such as *Rich Man, Poor Man* and *Ghost Dancing*. She is married to noted photographer John Swope.
**Selected Films:** *Claudia* (43), *A Tree Grows in Brooklyn* (44), *The Enchanted Cottage* (44), *The Spiral Staircase* (45), *Claudia and David* (46), *Till the End of Time* (46), *Gentlemen's Agreement* (47), *Three Coins in the Fountain* (54), *Friendly Persuasion* (56), *Old Yeller* (56), *The Remarkable Mr Pennypacker* (59), *The Swiss Family Robinson* (60), *The Dark at the Top of the Stairs* (60), *Summer Magic* (63), *The Greatest Story Ever Told* (65), *Flight of the Doves* (71).

## McHUGH, Frank (1899-1981)

Born in Homestead, Pennsylvania, McHugh entered movies from vaudeville in the late 1930s. Playing engaging character parts – often with an Irish accent – in some 150 pictures during a career that lasted into the 1960s, he had an infectious laugh and an often surprised air.

**Selected Films:** *If Men Played Cards as Women Do* (28), *The Dawn Patrol* (30), *A Midsummer Night's Dream* (35), *Going My Way* (44), *Mighty Joe Young* (49), *Easy Come, Easy Go* (67).

## McINTIRE, John (1907- )

Born in Spokane, Washington, McIntire entered movies after stage and radio experience. Since the late 1940s he has played stolid, laconic lawmen, politicians, and the like in dozens of films and on TV, including the series *Wagon Train* and *The Virginian*. His wife is actress Jeanette Nolan.

**Selected Films:** *An Act of Murder* (48), *The Asphalt Jungle* (50), *The Far Country* (54), *The Kentuckian* (55), *Psycho* (60), *Summer and Smoke* (62), *Rooster Cogburn* (75).

## MACK, Helen (1913- )

Born Helen McDougall in Rock Island, Illinois, Mack appeared on stage and in minor screen parts as a child. Her starring and supporting roles as an adult were in romantic films of the 1930s and 1940s.

**Selected Films:** *Under the Red Robe* (23), *The Struggle* (31), *Son of Kong* (34), *She* (35), *Last Train from Madrid* (37), *His Girl Friday* (40), *Divorce* (45).

## McKENNA, Siobhan (1923-1986)

Born in Belfast, Northern Ireland, McKenna became a leading star of the Gaelic theater in her native Ireland and joined the famed Abbey Players of Dublin during the 1940s. She later appeared on the British and American stage, specializing in the great Irish dramas. Her film appearances were few and largely in supporting roles. She was married to the Irish actor Denis O'Dea.

**Selected Films:** *Hungry Hill* (47), *The Lost People* (49), *King of Kings* (61), *Playboy of the Western World* (62), *Doctor Zhivago* (65), *Memed, My Hawk* (87).

## McKENNA, Virginia (1931- )

A high-spirited leading lady in often unglamorous parts, McKenna, a native of London, has alternated between stage and movie appearances largely in Britain. She has been married to actors Denholm Elliott and Bill Travers, co-starring with the latter in *Born Free* (66).

**Selected Films:** *The Second Mrs Tanqueray* (52), *The Cruel Sea* (53), *The Horse's Mouth* (53), *A Town Like Alice* (56), *Carve Her Name With Pride* (58), *Born Free* (66), *Waterloo* (70), *Swallows and Amazons* (74), *The Disappearance* (77).

*Victor McLaglen in* The Lost Patrol *(34).*

## McKERN, Leo (1920- )

Born Reginald McKern in Sydney, Australia, McKern has been a commanding presence in dozens of movie character parts since the early 1950s. His notable roles include Thomas Cromwell in *A Man for All Seasons* (66) and Professor Moriarty in *The Adventure of Sherlock Holmes' Smarter Brother* (75).

**Selected Films:** *Murder in the Cathedral* (52), *Time Without Pity* (57), *The Mouse that Roared* (59), *Moll Flanders* (65), *Help!* (65), *A Man for All Seasons* (66), *Ryan's Daughter* (70), *The Adventure of Sherlock Holmes' Smarter Brother* (75), *The Omen* (76), *The French Lieutenant's Woman* (81).

## McLAGLEN, Victor (1883-1959)

Born in Tunbridge Wells, England, McLaglen was a burly, good-humored star of silent films before he went to Hollywood. But before that he had been a miner and a boxer – and he looked it. He usually played a happy-go-lucky tough guy, but his finest performance was as the tortured central character in *The Informer* (35), for which he won the Academy Award for Best Actor.

**Selected Films:** *The Call of the Road* (20), *Beau Geste* (26), *What Price Glory?* (26), *The Lost Patrol* (34), *The Informer* (35), *Under Two Flags* (36), *She Wore a Yellow Ribbon* (49), *Rio Grande* (51), *The Quiet Man* (52), *Sea Fury* (58).

## MACLAINE, Shirley (1934- )

Shirley Maclaine Beaty (she was Warren Beatty's sister) was born in Richmond, Virginia, and began studying ballet when she was two years old. She left for New York after graduating from high school, and her first Broadway musical experience was in the chorus line in *Me and Juliet* (53).Her next Broadway show was *The Pajama Game*, in which she understudied lead dancer Carol Haney. She replaced an injured Haney after the third performance and was spotted by movie producer Hal Wallis, who signed her to a contract. Maclaine made her debut in the delightful Alfred Hitchcock movie, *The Trouble with Harry* (55), and was decorative and funny in several subsequent films. She was finally taken seriously as an actress after her heartbreaking performance as Ginny Moorehead in *Some Came Running* (58), which starred Frank Sinatra. It brought her an Academy Award nomination and many good reviews. Maclaine was hilarious in *Ask Any Girl* (59) and *The Apartment* (59), and both films won her British Film Academy Awards. She claims that she has played prostitutes in 14 movies, including *Irma La Douce* (63) and *Sweet Charity* (68). In the 1970s, Maclaine dropped out of films and opted for politics, working in Senator George McGovern's 1972 campaign. She led the first women's delegation to China and has written some best selling books. Although she fought for and sometimes won stronger and more complex roles, such as in *The Turning Point* (77) and *Being There* (79), she was frequently cast as a soft-hearted female, vaguely Bohemian in life style, but distinctly unpretentious. While waiting to break out of the mold, Maclaine starred in a TV series, *Shirley's World*, in 1971. She also wrote, co-directed and produced a documentary, *The Other Half of the Sky: A China Memoir* (75). Maclaine appeared in cabaret and performed in one-woman shows on Broadway and at the London Palladium. But secure in her Academy Award for Best Actress in *Terms of Endearment* (83), she is considered one of Hollywood's best actresses.

**Selected Films:** *The Trouble with Harry* (55), *Around the World in 80 Days* (56), *Hot Spell* (57), *The Matchmaker* (58), *Some Came Running* (58), *Ask Any Girl* (59), *Can-Can* (59), *The Apartment* (59), *The Children's Hour* (62), *Two for the Seesaw* (62), *Irma La Douce* (63), *What a Way to Go* (64), *Gambit* (66), *Sweet Charity* (68), *The Bliss of Mrs Blossom* (68), *Desperate Characters* (71), *The Turning Point* (77), *Being There* (79), *Loving Couples* (80), *Terms of Endearment* (83).

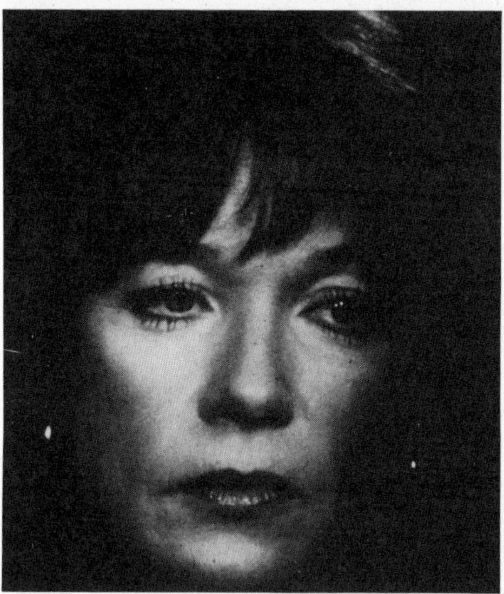

*Shirley Maclaine in* Terms of Endearment *(83).*

## MacLANE, Barton (1902-1969)

MacLane was a burly man who always seemed to play a heavy, and who lost the big fist fight with the hero. He came to movies in the casual way that was the hallmark of bygone Hollywood. Born in Columbia, South Carolina, he was a football player at Wesleyan University in 1924 and ran back a kickoff for a touchdown. Soon he was acting in *The Quarterback* (26), a movie starring Richard Dix. It was only after that that MacLane started to study acting. He appeared in some Broadway plays before returning to Hollywood for a long string of films in which he played the tough guy. One of his more memorable roles was in *The Treasure of the Sierra Madre* (47), in which he played a contractor who gave Humphrey Bogart and Tim Holt construction jobs, cheated them out of their wages and was then beaten up by them in a barroom fight.

**Selected Films:** *The Quarterback* (26), *Tillie and Gus* (33), *Black Fury* (34), *Ceiling Zero* (36), *The Maltese Falcon* (41), *San Quentin* (46), *The Treasure of the Sierra Madre* (47), *Kiss Tomorrow Goodbye* (51), *Captain Scarface* (53), *Backlash* (56), *Geisha Boy* (58), *Law of the Lawless* (63), *Buckskin* (68).

## McLERIE, Allyn (1926- )

Born in Grand Mere, Quebec, dancer and actress McLerie has appeared in occasional films since the late 1940s, but has concentrated on the theater. Also known as Allyn Ann McLerie, she apeared on TV series *The Tony Randall Show*.

**Selected Films:** *Words and Music* (48), *Where's Charley? (52)*, *Battle Cry* (55), *Cinderella Liberty* (74), *All the President's Men* (76).

## MacMAHON, Aline (1899- )

Born in McKeesport, Pennsylvania, MacMahon acted on the stage before beginning her film career in the early 1930s. With her sad eyes and gentle manner, she usually played sad sensitive women, though she was also adept at comedy. MacMahon received a supporting-actress Oscar nomination for her role in *Dragon Seed* (44).

**Selected Films:** *Five Star Final* (31), *Golddiggers of 1933* (33), *Babbitt* (34), *The Lady is Willing* (42), *Dragon Seed* (44), *The Search* (48), *The Eddie Cantor Story* (53), *Cimarron* (60), *All The Way Home* (63).

## MacMAHON, Horace (1907-1971)

Born in South Norwalka, Connecticut, MacMahon made his film debut in the mid-1930s. For some years his craggy face typed him in dozens of movies as a crook. In his own words: 'I was generally a mob boss named Blackie. My pal was always Whitey. If the budget permitted there was a Rocky.' Later, however, in the vagaries of Hollywood typecasting McMahon became a cop. His best-known role in that capacity was Lt Monoghan in the TV series *Naked City*.
**Selected Films:** *Navy Blues* (37), *Rose of Washington Square* (39), *Lady Scarface* (41), *Detective Story* (51), *The Detective* (68).

## MacMURRAY, Fred (1908- )

Born in Kankakee, Illinois, MacMurray began his professional career as a singer and saxophonist in various bands. This durable performer played leads almost from the time he signed a Hollywood contract. Most of the time he played decent, likeable men in comedies, such as *The Egg and I* (47) and *On Our Merry Way* (48). He even did an occasional musical, such as *And the Angels Sing* (44) and *Where Do We Go From Here?* (45). He also proved that he was a fine dramatic actor in such films as *The Trail of the Lonesome Pine* (36), and could star in biopics such as *Captain Eddie* (45), the life story of American flying ace, Eddie Rickenbacker. Once in a while he played a loser and liar, as in *Double Indemnity* (44), and *The Caine Mutiny* (54), roles in which he really shone. In 1954 he married actress June Haver. By the end of his career, a TV series, *My Three Sons*, and wholesome Walt Disney movies kept him on top.
**Selected Films:** *Girls Gone Wild* (29), *Friends of Mr Sweeney* (34), *The Gilded Lily* (35), *The Trail of the Lonesome Pine* (36), *True Confession* (37), *Sing You Sinners* (38), *Men With Wings* (38), *Remember the Night* (40), *Dive Bomber* (41), *And the Angels Sing* (44), *Double Indemnity* (44), *Murder He Says* (44), *Where Do We Go From Here?* (45), *Captain Eddie* (45), *The Egg and I* (47), *On Our Merry Way* (48), *The Caine Mutiny* (54), *The Rains of Ranchipur* (55), *The Shaggy Dog* (59), *The Apartment* (60), *The Absent Minded Professor* (61), *Son of Flubber* (63), *Kisses for My President* (64), *The Happiest Millionaire* (67), *The Swarm* (78).

## McNALLY, Stephen (1913- )

Born Horace McNally in New York, Stephen was a lawyer before turning to films in the early 1940s. For a few years he worked under his own name in various routine films including *Grand Central Murder* (42), *Thirty Seconds Over Tokyo* (44), and *The Harvey Girls* (46). Changing his name to its final form, he scored a major success in 1948, playing a villain in *Johnny Belinda*. From that point McNally was regularly to be seen in leads and supporting roles, sometimes as the hero but more often as the villain. In his films, however, he was mostly underutilized in minor action pictures such as *Black Castle* (53) and *The Fiend Who Walked the West* (58). He also starred in two short-lived TV series, *Target the Corrupters* and *W.E.B.*.
**Selected Films:** *Keeper of the Flame* (42), *Grand Central Murder* (42), *Thirty Seconds Over Tokyo* (44), *Bewitched* (45), *The Harvey Girls* (46), *Rogues' Regiment* (48), *Johnny Belinda* (48), *Sword in the Desert* (49), *Wyoming Mail* (50), *Apache Drums* (51), *Duel at Silver Creek* (52), *Black Castle* (53), *Violent Saturday* (55), *The Fiend Who Walked the West* (58), *Requiem for a Gunfighter* (65), *Black Gunn* (72).

## McNAMARA, Maggie (1928-1978)

New York-born McNamara came to acting from modelling. After appearing on Broadway she made an impressive film debut in *The Moon is Blue* (53), for which she received an Oscar nomination. However, after two more films her career came mysteriously to a virtual halt. She died a suicide.
**Selected Films:** *The Moon is Blue* (53), *Three Coins in the Fountain* (54), *Prince of Players* (55), *The Cardinal* (63).

## McNEAR, Howard (1905-1969)

American comedian McNear appeared in supporting roles in a number of films of the 1950s and 1960s, but was best known for his work in the TV series starring Burns and Allen (as a plumber) and later The Andy Griffith Show (as Floyd, the barber).
**Selected Films:** *The Long Long Trailer* (54), *Voyage to the Bottom of the Sea* (61), *Irma La Douce* (63), *The Fortune Cookie* (66).

## MacNEE, Patrick (1922- )

A veteran of films since the 1940s, British-born actor MacNee is probably best known for his leads in TV series including *The Avengers* and *Empire*.
**Selected Films:** *The Life and Death of Colonel Blimp* (43), *Hamlet* (48), *Les Girls* (58), *Incense of the Damned* (70), *The Howling* (80), *Young Doctors in Love* (82), *A View to A Kill* (85).

## McQUEEN, Butterfly (1911- )

Born Thelma McQueen in Tampa, Florida, McQueen gained her nickname as a youthful dancer in Harlem. After appearing on Broadway she made her all-too-memorable screen debut as the young maid in *Gone with the Wind* (39), squeaking 'Lawsy, Miss Scahlet, Ah don't know nothin' 'bout birthin' babies!' In her occasional later movies and theatrical career McQueen never escaped that stereotype. After a long retirement from the screen she returned in the 1970s in small parts.
**Selected Films:** *Gone With the Wind* (39), *Affectionately Yours* (41), *Cabin in the Sky* (43), *Mildred*

*Pierce* (45), *Duel in the Sun* (47), *Amazing Grace* (74), *The Mosquito Coast* (86).

## McQUEEN, Steve (1930-1980)

He was one of the hottest stars of the 1960s and 1970s, hitting the box office top ten year after year. The heir to Humphrey Bogart, James Cagney and Edward G Robinson, he had a cool self-awareness, ice-blue eyes and a strong sense of independence. He was an anti-hero with heroic traits. Born Terence McQueen in Slater, Missouri, his childhood was anything but pampered. Abandoned by his father, he wound up in reform school, then became a sailor, lumberjack, beachcomber, carnival barker and at last a Marine. The service didn't cure him, and he spent time in the brig for going AWOL and became a drifter after he was discharged. Then he discovered acting, studying at New York's Neighborhood Theater and with Uta Hagen and Herbert Berghof, making his debut in a Yiddish theater on the city's Lower East Side. The Actors' Studio followed and the well-schooled McQueen got his first break when he replaced Ben Gazzara in *A Hatful of Rain* on Broadway in 1955. Moving to Hollywood, McQueen might have been stuck in bit parts and in science-fiction like *The Blob* (58) forever had he not landed the starring role in the TV series, *Wanted: Dead or Alive*, in which he played a western bounty hunter. This role led to his replacing Sammy Davis Jr in Frank Sinatra's *Never So Few* (59). McQueen began his ascent to stardom. In private life a macho type who loved automobile and motorcycle racing, he performed his own stunts in *The Great Escape* (63) with its spectacular motorcycle-chase scene, and became a star. He was good in *The Cincinnati Kid* (65), but Edward G Robinson was much better, and not until *Bullitt* (68), with its pace-setting car chases, did McQueen really carry a film completely on his own. After that he was a superstar. Later came *Papillon* (73) and *Tom Horn* (80), in which he was superb. McQueen's first wife was actress Neile Adams; his second, movie star Ali McGraw. Both marriages ended in divorce. In Hollywood, McQueen had the reputation of being moody, temperamental, and hard to get along with. He was especially hard on directors. At the age of 50 he died of cancer.

**Selected Films:** *Somebody Up There Likes Me* (56), *Never Love a Stranger* (58), *The Blob* (58), *Never So Few* (59), *The Magnificent Seven* (60), *The War Lover* (62), *The Great Escape* (63), *Love with the Proper Stranger* (63), *The Cincinnati Kid* (65), *Nevada Smith* (66), *The Sand Pebbles* (66), *The Thomas Crown Affair* (68), *Bullitt* (68), *The Reivers* (70), *Junior Bonner* (72), *The Getaway* (72), *Papillon* (73), *The Towering Inferno* (74), *An Enemy of the People* (76), *Tom Horn* (80), *The Hunter* (80).

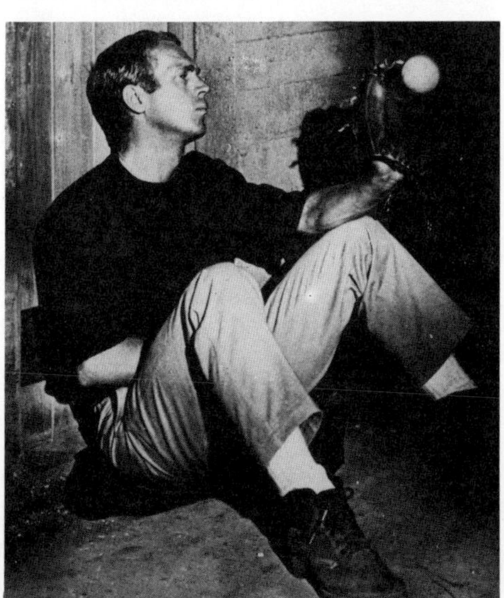

*Steve McQueen in* The Great Escape *(63).*

## MACRAE, Gordon (1921-1986)

Born in East Orange, New Jersey, Macrae was a child stage performer before breaking into movies via radio. He had been the leading baritone on *The Railroad Hour*, a weekly radio program on which standard Broadway musicals were condensed and performed, when Hollywood beckoned. He became a top leading man in filmed musicals in the late 1940s and early 1950s, best remembered for playing the leads in such Rodgers and Hammerstein hits as *Oklahoma!* (55) and *Carousel* (56).

**Selected Films:** *The Big Punch* (48), *Look for the Silver Lining* (49), *Tea for Two* (50), *On Moonlight Bay* (51), *About Face* (52), *By the Light of the Silvery Moon* (53), *The Desert Song* (53), *Oklahoma!* (55), *Carousel* (56), *The Best Things in Life Are Free* (56), *The Pilot* (79).

## MACREADY, George (1909-1973)

Born in Providence, Rhode Island, Macready had a long Broadway career before coming to the screen in the early 1940s. From that point until his death, his scarred features were familiar in villianous roles in some 60 films, among them as Rita Hayworth's nasty spouse in *Gilda* (46), His extensive TV work included the series *Peyton Place*.

**Selected Films:** *The Commandos Strike at Dawn* (42), *I Love a Mystery* (45), *Gilda* (46), *Alias Nick Beal* (49), *Detective Story* (51), *Julius Caesar* (53), *Paths of Glory* (57), *Seven Days in May* (64), *Tora! Tora! Tora!* (70), *The Return of Count Yorga* (71).

## McSHANE, Ian (1942-     )

British-born leading man McShane came to films in the early 1960s, appearing in mostly minor movies and major made-for-TV productions including *Jesus of Nazareth*, *Roots*, and *Grace Kelly*.

**Selected Films:** *The Wild and the Willing* (62), *The*

*Battle of Britain* (68), *Tam Lin* (70), *The Last of Sheila* (73), *Exposed* (83).

## MADISON, Guy (1922- )

Born Robert Mosely in Bakersfield, California, Madison came to movies directly from Navy service in World War II. His small role in *Since You Went Away* (44) made the handsome actor an immediate teen favorite. His acting, however, proved to be on the wooden side. After a decade of indifferent film work he starred in the TV series *Wild Bill Hickok* and thereafter appeared in occasional minor movies, some of them Italian 'spaghetti Westerns,' He was married to actress Gail Russell from 1949 to 1954.
**Selected Films:** *Since You Went Away* (44), *Till the End of Time* (46), *The Charge at Feather River* (53), *The Command* (54), *On the Threshold of Space* (55), *Gunmen of the Rio Grande* (65), *Where's Willie?* (78).

## MADONNA, (1960- )

This singer-actress was born Madonna Louise Ciccone in Bay City, Michigan, where her father was a design engineer for Chrysler Motors. She trained at the University of Michigan and with the Alvin Ailey Dance Company. Before her movie career began, Madonna became a pop singing star and cut many records and made many videos. She married actor Sean Penn in 1986.
**Selected Films:** *Visionquest* (85), *Desperately Seeking Susan* (85), *Shanghai Surprise* (86).

## MAGEE, Patrick (1924-1982)

British-born Patrick Magee came to films from extensive stage experience. His screen appearance were only occasional but often memorable, distinguished by his thin, intense-eyed features and equally thin, intense voice. He was usually cast as a villain or as an outright depraved character. His earlier films include *The Criminal* (60), *Zulu* (64), and *The Masque of the Red Death* (64). In 1967 Magee had one of his rare leads repeating his stage role as a tired and existential Marquis de Sade in the movie version of the play *Marat/Sade*. In Stanley Kubrick's *A Clockwork Orange* (71), Magee played a man crippled and deranged during the rape of his wife who takes revenge on the perpetrator in a particular nasty psychological experiment. Other examples of Magee's tendency to evil roles were in films such as *The Fiend* (71) and *Asylum* (72).
**Selected Films:** *The Criminal* (60), *The Servant* (63), *Zulu* (64), *The Masque of the Red Death* (64), *The Skull* (65), *The Persecution and Assassination of Jean-Paul Marat as performed by the inmates of the Asylum of Charenton under the direction of the Marquis de Sade* (66), *The Birthday Party* (68), *King Lear* (70), *A Clockwork Orange* (71), *You Can't Win 'em All* (71), *The Fiend* (71), *Demons of the Mind* (72), *Asylum* (72), *Rough Cut* (80).

## MAGNANI, Anna (1907-1973)

Magnani was a fiery force, an international star whose unkempt appearance defied convention. She was born in Alexandria, Egypt, and raised in poverty in Rome, Italy. She began her career as a night club singer, then appeared on stage. Her film career was not spectacular until the 1940s when she appeared in Roberto Rossellini's *Open City* (45). Magnani was romantically involved with Rossellini until Ingrid Bergman entered his life. Her Hollywood debut came in *The Rose Tattoo* (55), opposite Burt Lancaster in an adaptation of the Tennessee Williams play. For her work as an earthy, volatile woman who puts aside her husband's memory when a truck driver romances, her, she won the Academy Award for Best Actress. Magnani later returned to Italy, where she was considered a national treasure until her death.
**Selected Films:** *Scampolo* (27), *The Blond Woman of Sorrento* (34), *Tempo Massimo* (36), *Open City* (45), *Angelina* (45), *The Miracle* (50), *Volcano* (53), *The Golden Coach* (54), *Bellissima* (54), *The Rose Tattoo* (55), *Wild Is the Wind* (57), *The Fugitive Kind* (59), *Mamma Roma* (62), *The Secret of Santa Vittoria* (69), *Fellini's Roma* (72).

## MAHARIS, George (1928- )

Born in Astoria, Queens, New York, Maharis studied drama at the Actor's Studio and began working in film and TV in the early 1960s. Though he appeared in occasional movies and made-for-TV productions into the 1980s, he is best known as the star of the TV series *Route 66*.
**Selected Films:** *Exodus* (60), *The Happening* (67), *The Last Day of the War* (69), *The Sword and the Sorcerer* (82).

## MAHONEY, Jock (1919- )

Born Jacques O'Mahoney in Chicago, Illinois, Mahoney came to movies in the 1940s and – being tall, muscular, and not notably expressive as an actor – was cast in various minor adventure movies through the 1970s, including several films as Tarzan. He also starred in the TV series *Yancey Derringer*.
**Selected Films:** *The Fighting Frontiersman* (46), *Away All Boats* (56), *Tarzan the Magnificent* (60), *The Walls of Hell* (66), *The End* (78).

## MAIN, Marjorie (1890-1975)

Born Mary Tomlinson in Acton, Indiana, Main worked in vaudeville and theater before taking her Broadway dramatic role in *Dead End* to the screen in 1937. For some years she played straight parts, but then Hollywood discovered her comic persona as a crusty hayseed: beginning with *The Egg and I* (47) – which won her a supporting-actress Oscar – Main played Ma Kettle opposite Percy Kilbride in the popular and cornball *Ma and Pa Kettle* features

that appeared over the next decade.
**Selected Films:** *A House Divided* (31), *Take a Chance* (33), *Dead End* (37), *The Woman* (39), *Honky Tonk* (41), *Meet Me in St Louis* (44), *The Egg and I* (47), *Ma and Pa Kettle* (49), *Friendly Persuasion* (56).

## MAJORS, Lee (1940-    )

Born in Wyandotte, Michigan, Majors played football in college, getting into TV in the 1960s. Though he has appeared in a few feature films, the rugged actor is best known for his work in TV action series including *The Big Valley* and especially *The Six Million Dollar Man.* For a time he was married to actress Farrah Fawcett.
**Selected Films:** *Will Penny* (67), *The Liberation of L.B. Jones* (70), *The Norseman* (78), *Sharks* (80).

## MAKO, (1933-    )

A character actor of Japanese-American ancestry, Mako has appeared in films since the mid-1960s, among them *Hawaii* (67) and *The Island at the Top of the World* (74). He has also appeared on Broadway and in television.
**Selected Films:** *The Sand Pebbles* (66), *Hawaii* (67), *The Island at the Top of the World* (74), *The Big Brawl* (80), *The Bushido Blade* (80), *Under the Rainbow* (81), *Conan the Barbarian* (82), *Conan the Destroyer* (84).

## MALDEN, Karl (1913-    )

Born Mladen Sekulovich in Gary, Indiana, Malden is a fine actor who made his mark in the theater as early as the 1930s. His congenial homely face and husky build made him a natural for working-class character roles in films, rather than romantic leads, yet often Hollywood has not known what to do with him. Malden can project great innocence and moral strength, infusing his characterizations with complexity, as for example his portrayal of General Omar Bradley against the fiery George C. Scott, who played the title role in *Patton* (69). Malden's gentle character stole almost every scene in which they appeared together. He won an Academy Award for Best Supporting Actor for his work in the screen adaptation of Tennessee Williams' *A Streetcar Named Desire* (52), in which he recreated his Broadway role as Mitch, the suitor of Blanche DuBois (played by Vivien Leigh), and was nominated for the same award for his portrayal of a tough dockside priest on *On the Waterfront* (54).
**Selected Films:** *They Knew What They Wanted* (40), *Winged Victory* (44), *Boomerang* (47), *The Gunfighter* (50), *A Streetcar Named Desire* (52), *Ruby Gentry* (52), *On the Waterfront* (54), *Baby Doll* (56), *The Hanging Tree* (59), *One-Eyed Jacks* (61), *Gypsy* (62), *The Cincinnati Kid* (65), *Hotel* (67), *Patton* (69), *Summertime Killer* (73), *Beyond the Poseidon Adventure* (79), *Twilight Time* (83), *Billy Galvin* (87).

*Karl Malden as General Omar Bradley in* Patton *(69).*

## MALKOVICH, John (1954-    )

Born in Benton, Illinois, he attended Illinois State University, and started the famed Steppenwolf Ensemble with some college friends. He was brilliant in the Broadway revival of *Death of a Salesman*, and received good reviews for his few films.
**Selected Films:** *Places in the Heart* (84), *The Killing Fields* (85), *Eleni* (85), *Making Mr Right* (87), *The Glass Menagerie* (87).

## MALLESON, Miles (1888-1969)

Born in Croydon, England, William Miles Malleson had a remarkable 60-year career in theater and film – as actor, director, playwright and screenwriter. Among the best-known of his numerous screen roles was Canon Chasuble in *The Importance of Being Earnest* (52) and among his screenplays were the classic *The Thief of Bagdad* (40), in which he also played the Sultan.
**Selected Films:** *The Headmaster* (21), *The City of Song* (31), *The Thief of Bagdad* (40), *Major Barbara* (41), *Kind Hearts and Coronets* (49), *The Importance of Being Earnest* (52), *Brothers in Law* (57), *I'm All Right, Jack* (59), *The Magnificent Showman* (64), *Murder Ahoy* (65).

## MALONE, Dorothy (1925-    )

Born Dorothy Maloney in Chicago, Illinois, Malone was discovered by a Hollywood talent scout in a college play. During the 1940s the pretty blonde was cast mostly in ingenue roles, but during the 1950s she appeared in more solid and sultry parts – most notably as a nymphomaniac in *Written on the Wind* (56), which won Malone a supporting-actress Oscar. In the 1960s she worked largely on television, including the series *Peyton Place.*
**Selected Films:** *The Falcon and the Co-eds* (43), *The Big Sleep* (46), *Battle Cry* (55), *Written on the Wind* (56), *Man of a Thousand Faces* (57), *Too Much, Too Soon* (58), *Fate Is the Hunter* (64), *Winter Kills* (79), *Easter Sunday* (80).

## MANDER, Miles (1889-1946)

Born Lionel Mander in Wolverhampton, England, Mander was among other things a farmer, auto racer, novelist, and playwright before he entered films as an actor – and occasional director and screenwriter. After appearing in character roles in various British films including *The Private Life of Henry VIII* (32), he came to Hollywood in 1935 for similar parts. In films until his death, Mander often played political schemers like Disraeli in *Suez* (38).
**Selected Films:** *Once Upon a Time* (18), *The Pleasure Garden* (26), *The Private Life of Henry VIII* (32), *Suez* (38), *Wuthering Heights* (39), *The Three Musketeers* (39), *Farewell My Lovely* (44), *The Walls Came Tumbling Down* (46), *Imperfect Lady* (47).

## MANGANO, Silvana (1930- )

Silvana Mangano was born in Rome and trained to be a dancer. Instead, she modeled and, after winning the Miss Rome beauty contest, started playing bit parts in films. Finally emerging into leads, she made a hit as the sultry star of Giuseppe De Santis' film *Bitter Rice* (49). Meanwhile, Mangano married producer Dino De Laurentiis. Now an international sex star, she appeared in various vehicles including *Anna* (51), *Mambo* (53) and *The Wolves* (56), in the process becoming a substantial actress. However, the arrival on the scene of Gina Lollobrigida and Sophia Loren stole a good deal of Mangano's thunder. Though her film appearances continued, among them *Oedipus Rex* (67) and Luchino Visconti's *Death in Venice* (71), Mangano's later movies were only occasional.
**Selected Films:** *L'Elisir D'Amore* (49), *Bitter Rice* (49), *Anna* (51), *Mambo* (53), *Ulysses* (54), *The Wolves* (56), *The Sea Wall* (57), *Tempest* (59), *Five Branded Women* (61), *Barabbas* (62), *Oedipus Rex* (67), *Theorum* (68), *The Decameron* (70), *Death in Venice* (71), *Conversation Piece* (76), *Dune* (84).

## MANNERS, David (1901- )

Born Rauff de Ryther Duan Acklom in Halifax, Nova Scotia, Manners came to movies from the stage in the early days of sound. He played handsome and debonair leads in many films of the 1930s, ranging from costume pictures like *Kismet* (30) to romantic dramas like *A Bill of Divorcement* (32) with Katherine Hepburn to horror movies like *Dracula* (31) in which he played the role of Jonathan Harker. Manners returned to the theater in the late 1930s and later wrote several novels.
**Selected Films:** *Journey's End* (30), *Kismet* (30), *The Last Flight* (31), *Dracula* (31), *The Mummy* (32), *A Bill of Divorcement* (32), *The Black Cat* (34), *The Mystery of Edwin Drood* (35), *A Woman Rebels* (36).

## MANNING, Irene (1917- )

Born Inez Harvout in Cincinnati, Ohio, Manning came from the operetta stage to movies, at first starring in cheap Westerns. Moving up to leads in first features, she appeared in a number of musicals and dramas of the 1930s and 1940s including *Yankee Doodle Dandy* (42), as Fay Templeton, and *Shine On, Harvest Moon* (44).
**Selected Films:** *Two Wise Maids* (37), *Yankee Doodle Dandy* (42), *The Desert Song* (44), *Shine On, Harvest Moon* (44), *Bonnie Prince Charlie* (48).

## MANSFIELD, Jayne (1933-1967)

Born Vera Jane Palmer in Bryn Mawr, Pennsylvania, this amply-proportioned leading lady was the most flamboyant of the Marilyn Monroe imitators. Mansfield was always good copy for the gossip columns. She had been a beauty queen and a pin-up model before appearing on stage and in films. Her flair for light comedy was rarely shown to good effect, and she appeared in a series of generally dismal films; even when she bared her ample breasts, it didn't seem to help. She was killed in an automobile accident.
**Selected Films:** *Underwater* (54), *Female Jungle* (55), *The Girl Can't Help It* (56), *Will Success Spoil Rock Hunter?* (57), *The Sheriff of Fractured Jaw* (50), *Too Hot to Handle* (60), *A Guide for the Married Man* (67), *Single Room Furnished* (68).

## MARA, Adele (1923- )

Born Adelaida Delgado in Highland Park Michigan, Mara danced and sang with bands before entering films in the early 1940s. She played both nice girls and floozies in B movies like *Alias Boston Blackie* (42) and *Twilight on the Rio Grande* (47).
**Selected Films:** *Navy Blues* (41), *Alias Boston Blackie* (42), *Bells of Rosarita* (45), *Twilight on the Rio Grande* (47), *Sands of Iwo Jima* (50), *Curse of the Faceless Man* (58), *The Big Circus* (59).

## MARAIS, Jean (1913- )

Born Jean Marais Villain, in Cherbourg, France, Marais began acting onstage as a teenager. Turning to films in the 1930s, the strikingly handsome actor proved a bit wooden and for some time was relegated to small roles. Then in the late 1930s he was taken up by the great writer and filmmaker Jean Cocteau, who starred Marais in several of his classics: in *L'Eternal Retour* (43), in a triple role including Beast in *La Belle et la Bête* (46), and in the title role of *Orphée* (50). After Cocteau's death Marais lapsed largely into routine action and costume pictures.
**Selected Films:** *L'Epervier* (33), *L'Eternel Retour* (43), *La Belle et la Bête* (46), *Les Parents Terribles* (48), *Orphée* (50), *Le Testament d'Orphée* (60), *Fantômas* (64), *Peau d'Ane* (70).

## MARCH, Fredric (1897-1975)

March, born Ernest Frederick McIntyre Bickel in Racine, Wisconsin, started out as a banker. Under

*Fredric March in* Dr Jekyll and Mr Hyde *(32).*

the name Fredric March he abandoned himself to his true love, acting, and became a marvelous stage actor who understood subtlety, nuance and characterization. He always projected intelligence and integrity and, at times, was an agreeable comedian, as in *Nothing Sacred* (37), opposite Carole Lombard. In 1926 he married actress Florence Eldridge and they became an important theatrical team. March could play heroes and romantic leading men, and excelled in tragic roles. He won the Academy Award for Best Actor for the dual role of *Dr Jekyll and Mr Hyde* (32), sharing the Oscar with Wallace Beery for *The Champ*, the only time an actor has won the award for a horror film. He won it again for his role as the returning veteran in *The Best Years of Our Lives* (46).
**Selected Films:** *The Dummy* (29), *The Royal Family of Broadway* (30), *Dr Jekyll and Mr Hyde* (32), *The Sign of the Cross* (33), *Death Takes a Holiday* (34), *The Barretts of Wimpole Street* (34), *Les Misérables* (35), *Mary of Scotland* (36), *A Star Is Born* (37), *Nothing Sacred* (37), *The Buccaneer (38)*, *One Foot in Heaven* (41), *I Married a Witch* (42), *Tomorrow the World* (44), *The Adventures of Mark Twain* (44), *The Best Years of Our Lives* (46), *Death of a Salesman* (52), *Executive Suite* (54), *The Desperate Hours* (55), *Alexander the Great* (55), *The Man in the Gray Flannel Suit* (56), *Inherit the Wind* (60), *Seven Days in May* (64), *Hombre* (67), *The Iceman Cometh* (73).

## MARGO, (1918-1985)

Born Maria Marguerita Guadelupe Boldao y Castilla in Mexico City, Margo danced onstage from childhood, and with Xavier Cugat's band caused a sensation in New York by introducing the rhumba. Moving to Broadway and movies in the early 1930s, Margo turned to dramatic roles. Among the exotic-featured actress's notable film appearances were the slum kid in *Winterset* (36) and the young woman who ages magically in *Lost Horizon* (37). Her first husband was actor Francis Lederer, her second Eddie Albert.
**Selected Films:** *Crime Without Passion* (34), *Winterset* (36), *Lost Horizon* (37), *The Leopard Man* (43), *Viva Zapata!* (52), *I'll Cry Tomorrow* (57), *Who's Got the Action?* (63).

## MARGOLIN, Janet (1943- )

New York-born Margolin made her Broadway debut at 18 and the next year made a striking film debut as the disturbed girl in the title role of *David and Lisa* (62). However, that was the peak of Margolin's career; she went on to play ingenue roles in films. By the 1970s she was appearing mostly in TV movies such as *Murder in Peyton Place.*
**Selected Films:** *David and Lisa* (62), *The Greatest Story Ever Told* (65), *Nevada Smith* (66), *Enter Laughing* (70), *Take the Money and Run* (70), *Annie Hall* (77), *Last Embrace* (79).

## MARGOLIN, Stuart (1940- )

American actor Margolin has been seen in character roles since the early 1970s. His movies include the Charles Bronson vehicle *Death Wish* (74), and his TV work the series *Bret Maverick.*
**Selected Films:** *Limbo* (72), *The Stone Killer* (73), *Death Wish* (74), *The Big Bus* (76), *Futureworld* (76), *A Fine Mess* (86).

## MARLEY, John (1916-1984)

American character actor Marley appeared in supporting roles in films from the early 1950s through the 1980s, among them the hits *Love Story* (70) and *The Godfather* (72).
**Selected Films:** *My Six Convicts* (52), *I Want to Live* (58), *Cat Ballou* (65), *Love Story* (70), *The Godfather* (72), *The Car* (77), *Hooper* (78), *Tribute* (80).

## MARLOWE, Hugh (1911-1982)

Born Herbert Hipple in Philadelphia, Pennsylvania, Marlowe came to the screen from radio and theater work in the 1930s. He played character roles in a number of films through the 1960s. His earlier efforts include classics like *Meet Me In St Louis* (44), and *All About Eve* (50); his later ones were mostly thrillers like *Castle of Evil* (66). In the 1970s he starred in the TV soap opera *Another World.*
**Selected Films:** *Married Before Breakfast* (37), *Meet Me in St Louis* (44), *Twelve O'Clock High* (50), *All About Eve* (50), *Castle of Evil* (66).

## MARS, Kenneth (1936- )

American-born comedian Mars has brought his extravagant style to a number of popular pictures

of the 1960s and 1970s including Mel Brooks' *The Producers* (67) and *Young Frankenstein* (74).
**Selected Films:** *The Producers* (67), *What's Up Doc?* (72), *Paper Moon* (73), *The Parallax View* (74), *Young Frankenstein* (74), *The Apple Dumpling Gang Rides Again* (79).

## MARSH, Mae (1895-1968)

Born Mary Marsh in Madrid, New Mexico, Marsh came to films in her teens and was soon taken into D W Griffith's stock company at Biograph. Though the delicate-featured actress starred in a great many films of the silent era, she is largely remembered for her work with Griffith, most notably as 'The Little Sister' in *The Birth of a Nation* (15) and in *Intolerance* (16). Marsh's career declined in the sound era, but she appeared in occasional character roles into the 1960s.
**Selected Films:** *Man's Genesis* (12), *Judith of Bethulia* (13), *The Birth of a Nation* (15), *Intolerance* (16), *Polly of the Circus* (17), *The White Rose* (23), *Over the Hill* (31), *Jane Eyre* (43), *The Robe* (53), *Donovan's Reef* (63), *Arabella (68).*

## MARSHAL, Alan (1909-1961)

Australian-born Marshal came to Hollywood in the mid-1930s after theater experience. He played leads and supporting roles of the dashing variety in films of the 1930s and 1940s. Marshall starred with Garbo in *Conquest* (37) and with Irene Dunne in *The White Cliffs of Dover* (43). He later appeared in occasional character roles.
**Selected Films:** *The Garden of Allah* (36), *Conquest* (37), *Tom, Dick, and Harry* (40), *Lydia* (41), *The White Cliffs of Dover* (43), *The House on Haunted Hill* (59).

## MARSHALL, Brenda (1915- )

Born on Negros Island, in the Philippines, Marshall came to movies from stage bit parts, first appearing opposite Joel McCrea in *Espionage Agent* (39). Over the next decade the dark-haired beauty starred in a number of popular films, notably as Errol Flynn's love in *The Sea Hawk* (40). Marshall retired upon marrying William Holden, from whom she was later divorced.
**Selected Films:** *Espionage Agent* (39), *The Sea Hawk* (40), *Footsteps in the Dark* (41), *The Constant Nymph* (44), *The Tomahawk Trail* (50).

## MARSHALL, E G (1910- )

Everett G Marshall was born in Owatonna, Minnesota, and began on radio in his home state, then pursued theater work and made it to Broadway by the late 1930s. After several years of well-received stage acting, he made his film debut in *The House on 92nd Street* (45). While returning often to the theater, Marshall has brought his imposing and serious features to many film roles over four decades, often playing sympathetic lawyers and other men of integrity. His films have generally been above average; they include *The Caine Mutiny* (54), *Twelve Angry Men* (57) and *Is Paris Burning?* (66). One of his roles in the 1970s was that of an aging patriarch and new groom in Woody Allen's *Interiors* (78). Besides his movie and stage parts, Marshall has starred in two successful TV series, *The Defenders* and *The Bold Ones*; for the former he won two Emmys. He has also appeared in a number of made-for-TV movies such as *A Clear and Present Danger* and *Kennedy*, in which he played Joseph Kennedy.
**Selected Films:** *The House on 92nd Street* (45), *13 Rue Madeleine* (46), *Call Northside 777* (48), *The Bamboo Prison* (54), *The Caine Mutiny* (54), *The Silver Chalice* (54), *Twelve Angry Men* (57), *Compulsion* (59), *Town Without Pity* (61), *Is Paris Burning?* (66), *The Chase* (66), *Tora! Tora! Tora!* (70), *Interiors* (78), *Superman II* (80), *Creepshow* (82), *Power* (86).

## MARSHALL, Herbert (1890-1966)

Marshall's long acting career spanned four decades. Born in London, he lost a leg in World War I, while serving in France. He played smooth, sometimes diffident but always gentlemanly roles. He was a success on stage and screen, reaching his peak in urbane romantic parts in Hollywood movies, making a smooth transition to character roles as he grew older.
**Selected Films:** *Mumsie* (27), *The Letter* (29), *Michael and Mary* (32), *Trouble in Paradise* (32), *The Dark Angel* (35), *Foreign Correspondent* (40), *The Letter* (40), *The Little Foxes* (41), *The Moon and Sixpence* (42), *The Enchanted Cottage* (44), *The Razor's Edge* (46), *Stage Struck* (57), *The Third Day* (65).

## MARSHALL, Tully (1864-1943)

Born William Phillips in Nevada Cidty, California, Marshall came to film in 1914 after years in the theater. From then until his death he played wide-ranging character roles, including Fagin in *Oliver Twist* (16), Louis XI in *The Hunchback of Notre Dame* (23), and Muff Potter in *Tom Sawyer* (30).
**Selected Films:** *The Sable Lorcha* (15), *Intolerance* (16), *Oliver Twist* (16), *The Squaw Man* (18), *The Hunchback of Notre Dame* (23), *The Bridge of San Luis Rey* (29), *Tom Sawyer* (30), *Grand Hotel* (33), *This Gun for Hire* (42), *Hitler's Madmen* (43).

## MARTIN, Chris-Pin (1894-1953)

Born Ysabel Ponciana Chris-Pin Martin Piaz to a Mexican family in Tucson, Arizona, Martin got into films in the early sound era as a comic Mexican. His roly-poly form, extravagant accent, and bemused expression were most familiar as Pancho in the Cisco Kid movies of the 1930s and 1940s.
**Selected Films:** *The Rescue* (29), *The Cisco Kid* (31), *Four Frightened People* (34), *Stagecoach* (39), *The Ox-Bow Incident* (43), *Mexican Hayride* (49), *Ride the Man Down* (52).

## MARTIN, Dean (1917- )

Born Dino Crocetti in Steubenville, Ohio, he began as a singer. This heavy-lidded self-spoofing actor and comedian then teamed with Jerry Lewis and the combination made it big in show business. The two made a series of extremely popular movies in the 1950s, beginning with *My Friend Irma* (49). After the pair had a highly-publicized breakup in 1956, Martin continued to make films, usually comedies or action movies.
**Selected Films:** *My Friend Irma* (49), *At War with the Army* (51), *Scared Stiff* (53), *Living It Up* (54), *Artists and Models* (55), *Ten Thousand Bedrooms* (57), *The Young Lions* (58), *Some Came Running* (58), *Rio Bravo* (59), *Bells Are Ringing* (60), *Ocean's Eleven* (60), *Kiss Me Stupid* (64), *The Silencers* (66), *Bandolero* (68), *Something Big* (71), *The Cannonball Run* (82), *The Cannonball Run II* (82).

## MARTIN, Dewey (1923- )

American-born actor Martin made his screen debut in Nicholas Ray's *Knock On Any Door* (49) and went on to be a stalwart-featured leading man and supporting player. He also appeared in the made-for-TV movie *Wheeler and Murdoch*.
**Selected Films:** *Knock On Any Door* (49), *Kansas Raiders* (50), *The Thing* (52), *The Big Sky* (52), *Land of the Pharaohs* (55), *The Desperate Hours* (55).

## MARTIN, Mary (1913- )

Born in Weatherford, Texas, Martin started in films about the same time that she began her stage career in musical comedy. After several light musicals in the 1940s her screen career never quite took off. Meanwhile, she became one of the great theatrical figures of her time, starring in *South Pacific* and *Peter Pan*, among others. She is the mother of actor Larry Hagman.
**Selected Films:** *The Great Victor Herbert* (39), *Birth of the Blues* (41), *Night and Day* (46), *Main Street to Broadway* (53).

## MARTIN, Strother (1920-1980)

Martin, who most often played a grizzled role in western movies, was actually born in Kokomo, Indiana. A small man, he usually was either a born loser or a con artist in his films. He got his first decent role in *The Asphalt Jungle* (50), and is probably best remembered as the frontier trader who is hoodwinked by Kim Darby in *True Grit* (69). Along the way, he made many guest appearances on western TV series, most notably in *Gunsmoke*.
**Selected Films:** *The Asphalt Jungle* (50), *The Shaggy Dog* (59), *The Man Who Shot Liberty Valance* (62), *The Sons of Katie Elder* (65), *Harper* (66), *Cool Hand Luke* (67), *True Grit* (69), *Butch Cassidy and the Sundance Kid* (69), *The Wild Bunch* (69), *Rooster Cogburn* (75), *Hard Times* (75), *Slap Shot* (77), *Up in Smoke* (78), *The Champ* (79).

## MARTIN, Steve (1945- )

Born in Waco, Texas, Steve Martin was a TV gagwriter for the Smothers Brothers before moving into the spotlight as a standup comedian. In that capacity he developed his unique comic style, playing off his glossy normality with a certain unsettling gooniness. Since the late 1970s Martin has appeared onscreen in starring and supporting roles including the title role in *The Jerk* (79) and the berserk dentist in *Little Shop of Horrors* (86).
**Selected Films:** *The Jerk* (79), *The Muppet Movie* (79), *Pennies from Heaven* (81), *Dead Men Don't Wear Plaid* (82), *Lonely Guy* (84), *All of Me* (84), *Three Amigos* (86), *Little Shop of Horrors* (86).

## MARTIN, Tony (1912- )

Born Alvin Morris in San Francisco, California, Martin became a popular crooner and bandleader in the 1930s. For two decades beginning in 1936 the handsome and genial Martin played romantic leads in a number of light musical films. His first wife was singer/actress Alice Faye, his second dancer/actress Cyd Charisse.
**Selected Films:** *Sing, Baby, Sing* (36), *Ziegfeld Girl* (41), *Casbah*, (48), *Here Come the Girls* (53), *Hit the Deck* (55), *Let's Be Happy* (57).

## MARTINELLI, Elsa (1933- )

Born in Grosselo, Martinelli was a model in her native Italy, before Kirk Douglas signed her up for a role in *The Indian Fighter* (55). A beautiful brunette but no earthshaking actress, she went on to leads in mostly routine pictures through the 1960s, an odd exception being her role in Orson Wells' *The Trial* (63). Since then, most of Martinelli's films have been European.
**Selected Films:** *The Indian Fighter* (55), *The Boatmen* (60), *The Trial* (63), *Marco the Magnificent* (65), *Hatari* (62), *The Tenth Victim* (65), *Woman Times Seven* (67), *Il Garofano Rosso* (76).

## MARVIN, Lee (1924- )

Marvin, who was born in New York City, has often been compared to Humphrey Bogart. While not conveniently good-looking – actually he looks ruthless – he projects a masculinity which can be riveting. Marvin began his film career playing heavies. He was vicious in *The Big Heat* (53). He challenged Marlon Brando as a rival motorcycle gang leader in *The Wild One* (54). And he was so mean in *Bad Day at Black Rock* (55) that when he got his head bashed in audiences felt like cheering. Later he played heroes, although often they were violent ones, as in *Emperor of the North Pole* (73). Marvin also has a fine comic sense, which he displayed to great advantage in a dual role in the western spoof *Cat Ballou* (65), for which he was awarded the Academy Award for Best Actor as well as a British Film Academy Award. He even did a musical, *Paint Your Wagon* (69), where he tried – unsuccessfully – to sing with co-star Clint Eastwood.

**Selected Films:** *You're in the Navy Now* (51), *Eight Iron Men* (52), *The Big Heat* (53), *The Wild One* (54), *The Caine Mutiny* (54), *Bad Day at Black Rock* (55), *Pete Kelly's Blues* (55), *Attack* (56), *Raintree County* (57), *The Man Who Shot Liberty Valance* (62), *The Killers* (64), *Cat Ballou* (65), *Ship of Fools* (65), *The Dirty Dozen* (67), *Point Blank* (67), *Hell in the Pacific* (68), *Paint Your Wagon* (69), *Emperor of the North Pole* (73), *The Big Red One* (79), *Death Hunt* (81), *Gorky Park* (83).

## MARX BROTHERS, The

The Marx Brothers were quite possibly the funniest team that ever appeared on screen. Their films are as fresh and hilarious today as they were half a century ago. The brothers were born in New York city and thrown into vaudeville at an early age by their tough, ambitious mother, Minna, who appeared on stage with them. Starting primarily as musicians and singers (they were called 'The Six Musical Mascots' and Minna was one of the mascots), they gradually introduced humor into their act. 'We played in towns I would refuse to be buried in today,' Groucho once said. Their brand of inspired lunacy caught on – they became Broadway successes and later went to Hollywood. At first there were five Marx Brothers. There was Gummo (born Milton Marx, 1893-1977), who left the act early. There was Zeppo (born Herbert, 1901-1979), who didn't fit in with the craziness and left the act after playing romantic relief in their first five films. But it was the three remaining Marx Brothers whom everyone remembers as *The* Marx Brothers. There was Chico (born Leonard, 1886-1961), who played piano eccentrically and spoke with an impossible Italian accent. There was Harpo (born Adolph but called Arthur, 1888-1964), who was the child-like, girl-chasing mute who also played the harp. And there was Groucho (born Julius, 1890-1977), with his painted moustache, a cigar, a loping walk and most of the wisecracks. They began making films for Paramount in 1929 and their first few films, which grew out of their stage act, were solid, but not overwhelming, successes. By 1933 their film career was in trouble. Ironically, *Duck Soup* (33), released that year, is today considered one of their very best films. The Marxes' contract was picked up by Irving Thalberg of MGM, and he allowed the Marxes to take key sequences from upcoming movies on a road tour, to test the audiences' reaction. Thalberg also insisted that the films have a plot with a love interest and some musical production numbers in which the Marxes were barely involved. The result was almost like two films inexpertly stitched together, but the core remained the humor, and films such as *A Night at the Opera* (35) were enormously popular. After Thalberg's death the quality of the Marx Brothers films declined, and by 1950 they had stopped making films together, although they occasionally appeared as individuals in other films and Groucho went on to a very successful television career. It was Groucho who won a Special Academy Award in 1973 before he died.

*Allan Jones and Harpo, Chico and Groucho Marx in* A Night at the Opera *(35).*

**Selected Films:** *The Cocoanuts* (29), *Animal Crackers* (30), *Monkey Business* (31), *Horse Feathers* (32), *Duck Soup* (33), *A Night at the Opera* (35), *A Day at the Races* (37), *Room Service* (38), *At the Circus* (39), *Go West* (40), *The Big Store* (41), *A Night in Casablanca* (46), *Love Happy* (50), *The Story of Mankind* (57). Groucho Alone: *Copacabana* (47), *Mr Music* (50), *Double Dynamite* (51), *A Girl in Every Port* (52), *Skidoo* (68).

## MASINA, Giulietta (1921- )

Giulietta Masina was born Giulia Anna Masina in Giorgio di Piano, near Bologna, Italy, the daughter of a schoolteacher. She began acting in her teens and in 1942 performed in a radio play written by a student named Federico Fellini. They were married, and she became Fellini's muse and the star of three of both his and the century's greatest films. However, her success in cinema was a time in coming; she retired for some years following her marriage and then, after winning acclaim in the film *Without Pity* (47), was stuck in minor films as a gamine tart. But in 1954 Masina starred in Fellini's *La Strada*; her role as the slow-witted but good-hearted waif who loves oafish Anthony Quinn made Masina in one blow one of the screen's immortals. Three years later she scored another triumph in Fellini's *Nights of Cabiria* (57) for which she won the Best Actress award at the Cannes Festival. From that point Masina's career languished for nearly a decade until she reemerged as an aging woman with perplexing fantasies in another Fellini masterpiece, *Juliet of the Spirits* (65). By then a legendary figure, Masina still appeared only occasionally in films. In the end, it will likely prove to be only her husband who succeeded in shaping her unique and unforgettable talents; this was reconfirmed by her reprise in Fellini's delightful film, *Ginger and Fred* (85).
**Selected Films:** *Paisan* (46), *Without Pity* (47), *Variety Lights* (51), *The White Sheik* (52), *La Strada* (54), *Nights of Cabiria* (57), *And the Wild Wild Women* (58), *Juliet of the Spirits* (65), *The Madwoman of Chaillot* (69), *Ginger and Fred* (85).

## MASON, James (1909-1984)

A polished performer who added luster to every film he was in, suave and handsome Mason played villains and gentlemen with equal ease. Although he never won an Academy Award, the highly acclaimed character actor received Britain's highest film honor, the Golden Seal, in 1977. His contributions to motion pictures spanned five decades. His father was a wool merchant in Huddersfield, England, where Mason was born. Planning on a career in architecture, Mason attended Marlborough College and Cambridge University, but during the Great Depression of the 1930s he came to the unusual decision that he could earn a better living on stage than by designing buildings. He played in repertory in the provinces, appeared with the Old Vic and with the Gate Company in Dublin, Ireland, simultaneously beginning a film career as the leading man in a series of B pictures. Both stage and film roles improved until he had a great success in *The Man in Grey* (43), a Regency melodrama. For a while he made a successful career out of playing nasty, evil men who browbeat sensitive heroines. From 1944 to 1947 he was the top box office draw in Britain. Mason moved to Hollywood in 1946 with his wife of many years, Pamela, and his two children. The couple was divorced shortly afterwards. There was a lot of bad publicity, which irked Mason, who was a very private person, and Hollywood responded by considering him eccentric. He later moved to Switzerland to escape life in a fishbowl, and in 1970 married Clarissa Kay, an Australian actress. Mason broke away from playing villains and cads, but although he hoped to become an internationally recognized leading man, it never happened. His range was simply too great and he was, despite his distinctive voice, always more actor than personality. He left such a mark on many important films, including *The Seventh Veil* (45) and *A Star is Born* (54), that he achieved the kind of stardom most character actors can only dream of.
**Selected Films:** *Late Extra* (35), *Fire Over England* (36), *The Mill on the Floss* (37), *I Met a Murderer* (39), *Hatter's Castle* (42), *The Night Has Eyes* (42), *The Man in Grey* (43), *The Seventh Veil* (45), *Odd Man Out* (46), *The Reckless Moment* (49), *Pandora and the Flying Dutchman* (51), *The Desert Fox* (51), *Five Fingers* (52), *The Desert Rats* (53), *Julius Caesar* (53), *Charade* (53), *20,000 Leagues Under the Sea* (54), *A Star is Born* (54), *Bigger Than Life* (56), *North by Northwest* (59), *Journey to the Center of the Earth* (59), *Lolita* (62), *The Pumpkin Eater* (64), *The Blue Max* (66), *Georgy Girl* (66), *The Deadly Affair* (67), *Child's Play* (72), *The Last of Sheila* (73), *The Mackintosh Man* (73), *Harrowhouse* (74), *Heaven Can Wait* (78), *Murder by Decree* (79), *The Verdict* (82), *The Shooting Party* (85).

## MASON, Marsha (1942- )

Born in St Louis, Missouri, Mason began appearing on the New York stage in the early 1970s and made her first major film role in 1973. She earned best-actress Oscar nominations for her performance as the tart in *Cinderella Liberty* (73) and for the lead in *The Goodbye Girl* (77), in a role written for her by her then husband Neil Simon. Her films since have been occasional.
**Selected Films:** *Hot Rod Hullaballoo* (66), *Blume in Love* (73), *Cinderella Liberty* (73), *The Goodbye Girl* (77), *Audrey Rose* (77), *The Cheap Detective* (78), *Promises in the Dark* (79), *Chapter Two* (79), *Max Dugan Returns* (83), *Heartbreak Ridge* (87).

## MASSEN, Osa (1915- )

Massen, born in Copenhagen, Denmark, came to Hollywood in the 1930s and played starring and

supporting roles in a number of mostly minor productions through the 1950s.
**Selected Films:** *Honeymoon in Bali* (39), *You'll Never Get Rich* (41), *The Cry of the Werewolf* (44), *Tokyo Rose* (45), *Outcasts of the City* (58).

## MASSEY, Daniel (1933- )

Born in London, the son of actor Raymond Massey, Daniel has spent most of his career in the theater. One of his occasional film roles was that of Noel Coward (who happened to be his godfather) in *Star!* (68), for which he received a supporting-actor Oscar nomination.
**Selected Films:** *In Which We Serve* (42), *Girls at Sea* (57), *Moll Flanders* (65), *Star!* (68), *Vault of Horror* (73), *The Incredible Sarah* (76), *Bad Timing* (80), *Victory!* (81), *Love with a Perfect Stranger* (86).

## MASSEY, Ilona (1912-1974)

Born Ilona Hajmassy in Budapest, the Hungarian star was discovered by MGM talent scouts singing opera in Vienna. Brought to Hollywood in the 1930s to be a 'singing Garbo,' the striking blonde ended up starring in routine productions including three Nelson Eddy musicals.
**Selected Films:** *Knox und die Lustigen Vagabunden* (35), *Der Himmel auf Erden* (35), *Rosalie* (37), *Balalaika* (39), *Frankenstein Meets the Wolf Man* (42), *Love Happy* (50), *Jet Over the Atlantic* (59).

## MASSEY, Raymond (1896-1983)

Born in Toronto, Ontario, Canada, and educated at Oxford University, he began his work on the London stage in 1922 and made his film debut in 1931 playing Sherlock Holmes in *The Speckled Band*. Massey became widely respected as a character actor on both sides of the Atlantic, and, oddly enough, this Canadian educated in England became closely identified with the character of Abraham Lincoln, which he played in the stage and screen versions of *Abe Lincoln in Illinois* (the movie was released in 1940), and briefly in *How the West Was Won* (62). Usually he played moralists, evil-doers and fanatics. Massey was wounded in both World Wars in service with the Canadian Army, and he became a United States citizen in 1944. He was married to actress Adrianne Allen. The actor Daniel Massey is their son. On television he is best remembered as Dr Gillespie in the series *Dr Kildare* opposite Richard Chamberlain.
**Selected Films:** *The Speckled Band* (31), *The Old Dark House* (32), *The Scarlet Pimpernel* (35), *Things to Come* (36), *The Prisoner of Zenda* (37), *Abe Lincoln in Illinois* (40), *Desperate Journey* (42), *Action in the North Atlantic* (43), *Arsenic and Old Lace* (44), *Stairway to Heaven* (46), *Mourning Becomes Electra* (47), *The Fountainhead* (49), *Come Fill the Cup* (51), *East of Eden* (55), *Omar Kayyam* (57), *The Naked and the Dead* (58), *How the West Was Won* (62), *Mackenna's Gold* (69).

## MASTRANTONIO, Mary Elizabeth (1958- )

Born in Chicago, Illinois, Mastrantonio came to movies after learning her trade in Broadway plays including *West Side Story* and *Amadeus*. She first gained attention for her film debut as Al Pacino's sister Ginia in *Scarface* (83). She received an Academy Award nomination for her performance in *The Color of Money* (86).
**Selected Films:** *Scarface* (83), *The Color of Money* (86).

## MASTROIANNI, Marcello (1923- )

Born into a peasant family in Fontana Liri, Italy, Mastroianni eventually was to become Italy's most respected and sought-after leading man. He projects a darkly handsome, often cynical, world-weariness on screen, but retains an air of dignity whatever befalls him. He has been an international star since the late 1950s and has appeared opposite some of the most beautiful actresses in Europe, including Sophia Loren, who has co-starred with him in several of his most popular films. He could have become a Hollywood star any time he wished over the past 20 years, a fate he has steadily resisted, and his career has not suffered from this refusal. During World War II he was employed as a draftsman until the Germans sent him to a labor camp. When the war ended, Mastroianni went to Rome, working as a clerk and acting at night. He joined Luchino Visconti's acting company, and appeared on stage in the Italian versions of such plays as Tennessee Williams' *A Streetcar Named Desire* and Arthur Miller's *Death of a Salesman*. He made his debut in films in 1947 in a bit part in the Italian version of *Les Miserables*, called *I Miserabili*. After that he rose steadily both on stage and in pictures until he had a reputation in Italy as a talented, popular actor. International success came to him in *La Dolce Vita* (59), directed by Frederico Fellini, in which Mastroianni was broodingly brilliant as a man trapped by luxury and decadence. Michelangelo Antonioni's *La Notte* (61), Pietro Germi's clever *Divorce Italian Style* (62), which won Mastroianni a British Film Academy Award, and Fellini's *8⅓* (63), solidified the actor's fame. He won another British Film Academy Award for *Yesterday, Today and Tomorrow* (63). In the years that followed, Mastroianni became such a staple ingredient of films by great directors that at times he seemed to personify the modern European male. There have been few actors before him who have so dominated movies.
**Selected Films:** *I Miserabili* (47), *Sunday in August* (49), *Girls of the Spanish Steps* (51), *The Bigamist* (55), *White Nights* (57), *I Soliti Ignoti* (58), *La Dolce Vita* (59), *Il Bell' Antonio* (60), *La Notte* (61), *Divorce Italian Style* (62), *Family Diary* (62), *8½* (63), *Yesterday, Today and Tomorrow* (63), *Marriage – Italian Style* (64), *Casanova 70* (65), *The Tenth Victim* (65),

*Marcello Mastroianni in 8½ (63).*

*Shoot Loud, Louder, I Don't Understand* (66), *The Stranger* (67), *Diamonds for Breakfast* (68), *Sunflower* (70), *Blowout* (73), *The Priest's Wife* (74), *A Special Day* (77), *Traffic Jam* (78), *Macaroni* (85), *Ginger and Fred* (85), *Fever Pitch* (85).

## MATTHAU, Walter (1920- )

Matthau fills the screen with his expansive talent. An ordinary looking man with an elastically expressive face and distinctive voice, Matthau, who was born Walter Matuschanskayasky in New York City, was a poor kid who grew up working at menial jobs until he returned from service in World War II. He built a steady career on stage, in movies and on television until he hit stardom in Neil Simon's Broadway hit, *The Odd Couple,* in which he played Oscar Madison, the slob of a sports writer. Matthau won an Academy Award for Best Supporting Actor for playing the ambulance-chasing lawyer, 'Whiplash' Willy Gingrich, in Billy Wilder's *The Fortune Cookie* (66) and became Hollywood's leading grouch with the heart of gold.
**Selected Films:** *The Kentuckian* (55), *A Face in the Crowd* (57), *Charade* (63), *Mirage* (65), *The Fortune Cookie* (66), *A Guide for the Married Man* (67), *The Odd Couple* (68), *Hello, Dolly!* (69), *Cactus Flower* (69), *A New Leaf* (71), *Plaza Suite* (71), *Pete 'n Tillie* (72), *The Front Page* (75), *The Sunshine Boys* (75), *The Bad News Bears* (76), *Casey's Shadow* (77), *House Calls* (78), *Hopscotch* (80), *First Monday in October* (81), *I Ought to Be in Pictures* (82), *Movers and Shakers* (85), *Pirates* (86).

## MATTHEWS, Jessie (1907-1981)

Billed as 'The Dancing Divinity,' Matthews was born in London and made her first stage appearance at the age of ten, and during her teens she was in the chorus line of London musicals. She was a star of musical revues by the late 1920s and carried her enormous popularity into a string of light screen musicals of the 1930s.
**Selected Films:** *The Beloved Vagabond* (23), *Straws in the Wind* (24), *The Man from Toronto* (32), *The Good Companions* (32), *Friday the Thirteenth* (33), *Evergreen* (34), *First a Girl* (35), *Climbing High* (39), *Candles at Nine* (43), *The Hound of the Baskervilles* (77), *Second to the Right and On till Morning* (80).

## MATURE, Victor (1916- )

Born in Louisville, Kentucky, Mature grew up to be christened 'The Hunk' long before that term for a virile leading man became popular. Critics ridiculed his wooden acting and he never took his career very seriously. Yet he was a symbol of male sex appeal in such pictures as *Samson and Delilah* (49) and a major box office draw during the 1940s and early 1950s. Occasionally he got a part in which he could demonstrate that he could act, such as in *Kiss of Death* (47), and he even showed that he had comic talents, as he did in wonderful self-parody in Peter Sellers' hilarious *After the Fox* (66). He retired in 1972, although he has made a couple of brief screen appearances since.
**Selected Films:** *The Housekeeper's Daughter* (39), *One Million BC* (40), *I Wake Up Screaming* (41), *My Darling Clementine* (46), *Kiss of Death* (47), *Samson and Delilah* (49), *The Robe* (53), *The Egyptian* (54), *After the Fox* (66), *Firepower* (79).

## MAUCH, Billy and Bobby (1925- )

These pleasant-faced identical twins made their debut in the Errol Flynn costume epic *The Prince and the Pauper* (37). They also appeared in several films based on Booth Tarkington's Penrod novels.
**Selected Films:** *The Prince and the Pauper* (37), *Penrod and Sam* (37), *Penrod and His Twin Brother* (38), *Penrod's Double Trouble* (38).

## MAUREY, Nichole (1925- )

Trained as a dancer in her native France, Maury made her film debut in *Les joyeux conscrits* (47), and over the next three decades appeared in British and American productions as well. The best-known of the films she starred in was the science fiction classic, *The Day of the Triffids* (62).
**Selected Films:** *Les joyeux conscrits* (47), *Blondine* (48), *Little Boy Lost* (51), *Secret of the Incas* (54), *Me and the Colonel* (58), *The Day of the Triffids* (62), *The Very Edge* (63), *Gloria* (77).

## MAXWELL, Marilyn (1922-1972)

Marilyn Maxwell, born in Clarinda, Iowa, was christened Marvel. She was dancing on stage at the age of three and was a singer with bands in her teens. After dramatic studies, she landed in films in the early 1940s. Despite her wide-ranging talent, she was cast as a standard voluptuous blonde in various light movies into the 1960s. Perhaps her best role was in *Summer Holiday* (48), a

musical adaptation of O'Neill's comedy *Ah, Wilderness!* Maxwell made many guest appearances on television in her last years; she died of a pulmonary condition.
**Selected Films:** *Stand by for Action* (42), *Presenting Lily Mars* (43), *Summer Holiday* (48), *The Lemon Drop Kid* (51), *Rock-a-By-Baby* (58), *Stage to Thunder Rock* (64), *The Phynx* (70).

## MAY, Elaine (1932-     )

Born Elaine Berlin in Philadelphia, Pennsylvania, the daughter of an actor in the Yiddish theater. May studied drama in her youth. In the 1950s she teamed brilliantly with Mike Nichols to form a satirical duo. When their act broke up, both gravitated to the screen. After a couple of acting roles on film, May began to write and direct as well. She directed *The Heartbreak Kid* (72), a film for which Mays' daughter Jeannie Berlin received an Oscar nomination for her performance.
**Selected Films:** *Luv* (67), *Enter Laughing* (67), *The New Leaf* (71), *California Suite* (78).

## MAYEHOFF, Eddie (1911-     )

American comedian Mayehoff was born in Baltimore, Maryland, and began his show-business career as a band leader. He brought his good-natured image to *That's My Boy* (51) and then starred in a TV series based on the movie.
**Selected Films:** *That's My Boy* (51), *Off Limits* (53), *How to Murder Your Wife* (65).

## MAYNARD, Ken (1895-1973)

Along with Tom Mix, Buck Jones, Tim McCoy and Hoot Gibson, Maynard born in Vevay, Indiana, was one of the Big Five western stars of the 1920s and 1930s who inherited the mantle of William S Hart. Like the others in this group, he was star of B westerns aimed at youngsters. And, like the others, he had a large and devoted following of young fans who idolized this hero in the white hat. Also like the others, he was a real cowboy, a rodeo performer and a trick rider with the circus before entering films. He was the one who taught the young John Wayne about riding and stunting. Unfortunately, Maynard had a drinking problem that hastened the end of his career. He had spent all the money he made as a star, and he ended his life living in a trailer, broke.
**Selected Films:** *The Man Who Won* (23), *Janice Meredith* (24), *Señor Daredevil* (26), *The Red Raiders* (27), *Branded Men* (31), *Texas Gunfighter* (32), *Come On, Tarzan* (32), *Wheels of Destiny* (34), *Heir to Trouble* (34), *Wild Horse Stampede* (45), *Frontier Uprising* (61), *Bigfoot* (69).

## MAYO, Virginia (1920-     )

Born Virginia Jones in St Louis, Missouri, Mayo was a showgirl when she was discovered by Sam Goldwyn. A stunning and slightly earthy blonde of limited dramatic gifts, Mayo was largely cast in decorative roles in musicals and costume spectacles from the 1940s through the 1960s, making a few nostalgic appearances thereafter. Among her few meaty parts were as Dana Andrew's wife in *The Best Years of Our Lives* (46) and co-starring with Danny Kaye in *The Secret Life of Walter Mitty* (47).
**Selected Films:** *Jack London* (43), *Up in Arms* (44), *The Girl from Jones Beach* (49), *The Best Years of Our Lives* (46), *The Secret Life of Walter Mitty* (47), *Captain Horatio Hornblower* (51), *The Silver Chalice* (54), *Young Fury* (65), *Won Ton Ton, the Dog Who Saved Hollywood* (76), *French Quarter* (77).

## MAZURKI, Mike (1909-     )

Born Mikhail Mazurski in Tarnopol, Austria to a Ukrainian family, Mazurki was a football player and professional wrestler before bringing his hefty figure and blunt-instrument features to the screen in the early 1940s. Mazurki has been a familiar face, usually playing dimwitted thugs, in a great many films. He began as an extra.
**Selected Films:** *Black Fury* (35), *The Shanghai Gesture* (41), *Farewell My Lovely* (44), *Blood Alley* (55), *Davy Crockett* (56), *Cheyenne Autumn* (64), *Challenge to Be Free* (76), *The Man With Bogart's Face* (79).

## MEARA, Anne (1929-     )

Born in New York City, this red-headed comedienne seemed to make a career out of being an Irish Catholic. Then she met Jerry Stiller at an opera audition, converted to Judaism and married him in 1954. They formed the Stiller and Meara comedy act to support their acting, and a six show per year contract with the Ed Sullivan television show established them as a comedy team. They also performed together in two of Neil Simon's stage hits – *The Prisoner of Second Avenue* and *The Last of the Red Hot Lovers*. Often they appear singly, however, and Meara has been in several films as well as being a regular on several TV series, most notably on *Archie Bunker's Place* with Carroll O'Connor.
**Selected Films:** *Lovers and Other Strangers* (70), *The Out of Towners* (70), *Nasty Habits* (76), *The Boys from Brazil* (78).

## MEDINA, Patricia (1921-     )

After starring in the theater in her native England, Medina, born in Liverpool, was discovered by Louis B Mayer. A brunette beauty, she was mostly seen in workaday adventure and costume pictures of the 1940s and 1950s. She has been married to actors Richard Greene and Joseph Cotten.
**Selected Films:** *Dinner at the Ritz* (37), *The Day Will Dawn* (42), *The Three Musketeers* (48), *Abbott and Costello in the Foreing Legion* (50), *Phantom of the Rue Morgue* (54), *The Killing of Sister George* (68), *Latitude Zero* (69).

## MEEK, Donald (1880-1946)

Born in Glasgow, Scotland, Meek was a small bald, timid-looking man who spent his film career playing supporting roles that lived up to his name (though sometimes he was so bold as to be waspish). Perhaps the most memorable of his many performances was that of the tremulous liquor salesman in *Stagecoach* (39).
**Selected Films:** *Six Cylinder Love* (23), *The Hole in the Wall* (28), *Captain Blood* (35), *The Adventures of Tom Sawyer* (38), *Stagecoach* (39), *State Fair* (45), *Magic Town* (47).

## MEEKER, Ralph (1920- )

Born Ralph Rathgeber in Minneapolis, Minnesota, Meeker acted in the theater in the 1940s, taking over the role of Stanley Kowalski from Marlon Brando in the Broadway production of *A Streetcar Named Desire*. Rugged of face and form, Meeker has played virile heroes, often with a nasty streak, in films since the 1950s. His best-known role was Mike Hammer in the *film noir* classic *Kiss Me Deadly* (55).
**Selected Films:** *Four in a Jeep* (50), *Teresa* (51), *Kiss Me Deadly* (55), *Paths of Glory* (58), *The Dirty Dozen* (67), *The Anderson Tapes* (71), *Winter Kills* (79), *Without Warning* (80).

## MEIGHAN, Thomas (1879-1936)

Born in Pittsburgh, Pennsylvania, Meighan starred on Broadway before turning to films in 1913. With his stalwart Irish features and air of reliability, he became one of the top stars of the silent era, the peak of his career being the films *The Miracle Man* (19) and *Male and Female* (19). Meighan also found starring roles in the sound era, among them with Jackie Cooper in *Peck's Bad Boy* (34).
**Selected Films:** *The Secret Sin* (15), *The Trail of the Lonesome Pine* (16), *The Miracle Man* (19), *Male and Female* (19), *Manslaughter* (22), *Blind Alleys* (27), *Young Sinners* (31), *Peck's Bad Boy* (34).

## MELCHIOR, Lauritz (1890-1973)

Born in Copehagen, Denmark, Melchior had by the 1930s established himself as one of the greatest operatic tenors of the century, specializing in Wagnerian roles. In the 1940s and 1950s he made a few appearances in minor films. His son is director/screenwriter Ib Melchior.
**Selected Films:** *Thrill of a Romance* (45), *Two Sisters from Boston* (46), *This Time For Keeps* (47), *Luxury Liner* (48), *The Stars Are Singing* (53).

## MELTON, James (1904-1961)

Born in Moultrie, Georgia, Melton was one of several operatic tenors of the century who now and then essayed a film role. He appeared in a few musicals of the 1930s and 1940s, among them *Ziegfeld Follies* (45).
**Selected Films:** *Stars over Broadway* (35), *Sing Me a Love Song* (36), *Melody for Two* (37), *Ziegfeld Follies* (45).

## MENJOU, Adolphe (1890-1963)

Adolphe Menjou was born to a French-American family in Pittsburgh, Pennsylvania, and graduated from Cornell an engineer. Wandering into the movie business in his twenties, he began as an extra around 1912. After many supporting roles in silents, including Louis XIII in *The Three Musketeers* (21), Menjou was cast as the suave star of Chaplin's *A Woman of Paris* (23). From that point on, Menjou's screen image never changed: for the next forty years and 100 or so movies he was the dapper, ironic, and often world-weary man with the waxed mustache. Moving easily into talkies, Menjou received a best-actor Oscar nomination for his performances as Walter Burns, the gritty editor in *The Front Page* (31). He also appeared in a great many comedies of the 1930s, among them *Little Miss Marker* (34). In the 1950s Menjou preserved his screen career by denouncing Communists to the House of Un-American Activities Committee. One of his best roles was in one of his last movies – as a cynical commander in Stanley Kubrick's savage anti-war film *Paths of Glory* (57).
**Selected Films:** *A Parisian Romance* (16), *The Three Musketeers* (21), *A Woman of Paris* (23), *The Sorrows of Satan* (26), *Morocco* (30), *The Front Page* (31), *Little Miss Marker* (34), *A Star is Born* (37), *A Bill of Divorcement* (40), *Roxie Hart* (42), *State of the Union* (48), *Paths of Glory* (57), *Pollyanna* (60).

## MERANDE, Doro (1898-1975)

American-born actress Merande played character roles in films from the early 1940s through the 1960s, specializing in harridans, eccentric old ladies, and similar characters.
**Selected Films:** *Our Town* (40), *Sullivan's Travels* (41), *The Seven Year Itch* (55), *The Cardinal* (63), *The Russians are Coming, The Russians are Coming* (66), *Hurry Sundown* (67).

## MERCER, Beryl (1882-1939)

After learning her craft in the English theater Mercer, born in Seville, Spain, moved to Hollywood in the early 1920s and for the rest of her life was cast mostly in sentimental films as a mother or a maid of the plump and longsuffering variety.
**Selected Films:** *The Christian* (23), *Outward Bound* (30), *Cavalcade* (33), *The Little Minister* (34), *The Hound of the Baskervilles* (39).

## MERCOURI, Melina (1925- )

Born in Athens, Greece, into one of Greece's most distinguished families, she spent a lot of her

privileged youth being thrown out of schools. She also spent a lot of time with writers and politicians who visited her home. Mercouri married at age 17, but soon separated. She enrolled in the National Theater Academy and appeared in numerous plays to critical enthusiasm. Her film career began in 1954 when she starred in the Greek movie, *Stella*. In 1956 she met American film director Jules Dassin, whom she later married, and, despite her years of study of classic drama, became an international star playing a happy hooker in his film, *Never on Sunday* (60). She later starred in another one of his movies, the classic caper *Topkapi* (64). In 1967 she went to star in the Broadway musical version of *Never on Sunday*, which was titled *Ilya, Darling*. Offscreen, she has been active in Greek politics. She was an outspoken critic of the military junta in 1967. After the junta collapsed in 1974, she ran for Parliament and lost by only 92 votes. She was later appointed Minister of Culture for the Greek Government.
**Selected Films:** *Stella* (54), *He Who Must Die* (56), *The Gypsy and the Gentleman* (58), *Never on Sunday* (60), *Phaedra* (61), *The Victors* (63), *Topkapi* (64), *The Player Pianos* (65), *Once Is Not Enough* (75), *Nasty Habits* (76), *A Dream of Passion* (78).

## MEREDITH, Burgess (1908- )

Whether he is underplaying a role or chewing the scenery with his accustomed gusto, Burgess Meredith has been one of the most quirkily memorable character actors of his time on both stage and screen – though Hollywood never quite seemed to know how to handle this creature of the theater. Born George Burgess Meredith in Cleveland, Ohio, Meredith was a boy soprano, before he joined Eva La Gallienne's Student Repertory. In 1933 he became a Broadway star with *She Loves Me Not* and went on to direct as well. In 1936 he repeated his stage success as Mio in the movie version of *Winterset* – his screen debut. He also played the role of George in *Of Mice and Men* (39) on stage and screen. One of his greatest roles – and among his relatively few film leads – was as war journalist Ernie Pyle in William Wellman's classic *The Story of GI Joe* (45). Meredith starred with his then wife Paulette Goddard in *The Diary of a Chambermaid* (46), which he also wrote and co-produced. Despite his wide experience in stage directing, his only directorial effort onscreen was *The Man on the Eiffel Tower* (49). During the next decade, he concentrated on the theater and television. In the 1960s and 1970s Meredith again became a familiar face – also a familiar acid voice – in film appearances ranging from minor productions like *Skiddoo* (68) and the first three of Sylvester Stallone's *Rocky* (76) movies (where Meredith's performance as the boozy trainer shows how he can shine in poor surroundings) to more substantil films like *Advise and Consent* (62) and *The Day of the Locust* (75). Meredith also appeared on the TV series *Batman* as the arch fiend, The Penguin.
**Selected Films:** *Winterset* (36), *There Goes the Groom* (37), *Of Mice and Men* (39), *That Uncertain Feeling* (41), *The Story of GI Joe* (45), *The Diary of a Chambermaid* (46), *Mine Own Executioner* (48), *The Man on the Eiffel Tower* (49), *The Gay Adventure* (53), *Advise and Consent* (62), *The Cardinal* (63), *In Harm's Way* (65), *Hurry Sundown* (67), *Skiddoo* (68), *There Was a Crooked Man* (70), *The Day of the Locust* (75), *Rocky* (76), *The Hindenberg* (76), *Foul Play* (78), *Rocky II* (79), *True Confessions* (81), *Rocky III* (81), *Final Assignment* (82).

## MERIVALE, Philip (1886-1946)

Merivale began acting on the stage in his native Britain, moving to the United States to pursue screen work. His appearances were mostly in minor films of the 1930s and 1940s.
**Selected Films:** *The Passing of the Third Floor Back* (35), *Rage in Heaven* (41), *This Land is Mine* (43), *The Stranger* (45).

## MERIWETHER, Lee (1935- )

Born in San Francisco, California, American actress Meriwether was Miss America of 1955 before turning to acting. She appeared in a number of minor films from the late 1950s – including a repeat of the role of the Catwoman in *Batman*. She also appeared on the long-running TV series, *Barnaby Jones*.
**Selected Films:** *The 4D Man* (59), *Namu the Killer Whale* (66), *Angel in My Pocket* (68), *The Brother's O'Toole* (73).

## MERKEL, Una (1903-1986)

Born in Covington, Kentucky, Merkel entered films in 1920 as a stand-in for Lillian Gish. Within a few years the attractive blonde was playing major roles on her own, most notably as Ann Rutledge in D W Griffith's talkie *Abraham Lincoln* (30). During the 1930s she fell into her most familiar part – as the friend of the leading lady, cracking jokes in a Southern drawl. In a somewhat different mode, Merkel slugged it out in a barroom with Marlene Dietrich in *Destry Rides Again* (39). In later years she played character roles, memorably as Geraldine Page's mother in *Summer and Smoke* (61).
**Selected Films:** *Way Down East* (20), *The Fifth Horseman* (24), *Abraham Lincoln* (30), *Daddy Long Legs* (31), *42nd Street* (33), *Saratoga* (37), *Destry Rides Again* (39), *This Is the Army* (43), *With a Song in My Heart* (52), *Summer and Smoke* (61), *A Tiger Walks* (63), *Spinout* (66).

## MERMAN, Ethel (1908-1984)

Born Agnes Zimmerman in Astoria, Queens, New York, she was a former secretary who, until her death, was able to type 60 words a minute. While she typed during the day, she sang in small clubs at night until she got her first big break at the age of

21. Having changed her name, she appeared in the Gershwins' *Girl Crazy* on Broadway in 1930. In this show, she introduced 'I Got Rhythm,' the song that she used as her signature for more than 50 years. Merman had a quality that can never again spring spontaneously into being. Call it classicalism, call it Olympian simplicity, call it God's pure untainted socko, but call it Merman. The world felt it immediately when she stepped on stage trumpeting 'I Got Rhythm' – holding one note of an entire incredible 16-bar chorus. She never took a singing lesson, but she immortalized more great tunes than anyone else in her 14 Broadway shows. It was said that in 'You're the Top' she gave muscle tone to Cole Porter's sophistication; in 'There's No Business Like Show Business' she gave Himalayan grandeur to Irving Berlin's sentiment; and in 'Everything's Coming Up Roses' she turned *Gypsy*'s hard-driving Rose into the Mother Courage of Broadway. Merman made several movies, beginning with *Follow the Leader* (30), and occasionally was asked to repeat her Broadway role in adaptations of musical comedies, but her style seemed too big for the screen, and Hollywood didn't often use her properly.
**Selected Films:** *Follow the Leader* (30), *We're Not Dressing* (34), *Kid Millions* (34), *Anything Goes* (36), *The Big Broadcast of 1936* (36), *Strike Me Pink* (36), *Happy Landing* (38), *Alexander's Ragtime Band* (38), *Call Me Madam* (53), *There's No Business Like Show Business* (54), *It's a Mad Mad Mad Mad World* (63), *The Art of Love* (63), *Won Ton Ton, the Dog Who Saved Hollywood* (76), *Airplane* (80).

## MERRILL, Dina (1925- )

Born Nedenia Hutton in New York, daughter of the extremely well-to-do Mrs Merriweather Post, Merrill grew up a wealthy blonde socialite who played wealthy blonde socialites on stage, screen, and television. Among her extensive TV work were roles in the series *Checkmate* and *Cannon*. She is married to actor Cliff Robertson.
**Selected Films:** *Desk Set* (57), *The Sundowners* (59), *The Courtship of Eddie's Father* (63), *A Wedding* (78), *Just Tell Me What You Want* (80).

## MERRILL, Gary (1915- )

A native of Hartford, Connecticut, Merrill began acting onstage in the late 1930s and made his film debut in the next decade. In 1950 he played his most memorable role as Bette Davis's husband in *All About Eve*. Soon after, Merrill and Davis began their decade-long marriage. The bulk of the craggy-featured Merrill's roles were in routine action pictures in most of which he was a stolid hero. He also appeared in several TV series including *Young Dr Kildare*.
**Selected Films:** *Winged Victory* (44), *Twelve O'Clock High* (49), *All About Eve* (50), *The Human Jungle* (54), *The Pleasure of His Company* (61), *Destination Inner Space* (66), *Thieves* (77).

## METHOT, Mayo (1904-1950)

American actress Methot played molls and other trampish roles in mostly routine films of the 1930s. She had a troubled marriage with Humphrey Bogart, as his third wife.
**Selected Films:** *Corsair* (31), *Side Streets* (34), *Mr Deeds Goes to Town* (36), *Unexpected Father* (39).

## MIDDLETON, Charles (1874-1949)

A native of Elizabethtown, Kentucky, Middleton performed in the circus and in vaudeville before coming to the screen in the early sound era. For some two decades he largely played baleful-eyed villains, most memorably as Ming the Merciless in the *Flash Gordon* serials.
**Selected Films:** *The Farmer's Daughter* (28), *Duck Soup* (33), *Flash Gordon* (36), *The Grapes of Wrath* (40), *The Last Bandit* (49).

## MIDDLETON, Robert (1911-1977)

Born Samuel Messer in Cincinnati, Ohio, Middleton came to movies by way of stage and radio work. The heavy-set actor was a familiar face, usually as a bad guy, in films of the 1950s into the 1970s. A more sympathetic role was Secretary of War Stanton in *The Lincoln Conspiracy* (77).
**Selected Films:** *The Silver Chalice* (55), *The Desperate Hours* (55), *A Big Hand for the Little Lady* (66), *Which Way to the Front?* (71), *The Lincoln Conspiracy* (77).

## MIDLER, Bette (1945- )

Born in Paterson, New Jersey, she grew up in Hawaii. Her road to stardom began in a Hawaiian pineapple cannery. She landed a bit part in the film *Hawaii* (65) and earned enough money to go to Los Angeles and then New York. After stints at typing and being a salesgirl, she joined the chorus of *Fiddler on the Roof* on Broadway. Three years later, when she left the show, she was playing Tzeitel, one of Tevye's daughters. Her breakthrough into the big time was at the Continental Baths, a New York bathhouse whose toweled clientele was mostly homosexual. With the ingenious arrangements and accompaniments of her then musical director, Barry Manilow, she developed her camp singing style, priding herself on being 'the last of the true tacky women.' Those $50-a-night gigs with her back-up group The Harlettes, at the Continental Baths catapulted her into club dates and a sell-out Philharmonic Hall concert in 1973. Her first big movie role was in *The Rose* (79), a spinoff of the tragic Janis Joplin story in which she delivered a dynamic performance, and she later went on to play comedy, almost burlesquing herself.
**Selected Films:** *Hawaii* (65), *The Rose* (79), *Down and Out in Beverly Hills* (85), *Ruthless People* (86), *Outrageous Fortune* (87).

Toshiro Mifune.

## MIFUNE, Toshiro (1920- )

Mifune, the internationally respected Japanese actor, first came to the attention of the West with *Rashomon* (50), a movie about different perceptions of truth. Set in Japan's fuedal era, it told, from different points of view, of the rape of a nobleman's wife. *Rashomon* won the Venice Grand Prix and the American Academy Award for Best Foreign Language Film. The movie's director, Akira Kurosawa, was recognized as a great artist. Mifune was Kurosawa's favorite leading man and their partnership was legendary. But Mifune, scowling, ferocious, poignantly sensitive, dynamic and versatile, was never merely an interpreter for a director. By the early 1960s he was the most famous Japanese star since Sessue Hayakawa. Born in Tsingtao, China, into a Japanese family with a long medical tradition, he was in the Japanese Army during World War II, then broke into films by winning a studio talent contest. An actor who has appeared in movies with meaning and depth, he is known in the West chiefly through three types of roles. He plays simple ordinary men, modern executives and officers, and samurai, and his samurai incarnation is the most popular. As a medieval warrior – bold, heroic, but often disgusted with cruelty and injustice – Mifune's samurai is more a cross between Douglas Fairbanks, Gary Cooper and Marlon Brando than John Wayne. He brings sanity, sexiness and a world-weary air to historical adventure movies like *Seven Samurai* (54), which was one of the first of its kind to catch on in the West. *The Lower Depths* (57), a Japanese adaptation of Gorki, and *Throne of Blood* (57), a Japanese reworking of *Macbeth*, were also well received. In 1963 Mifune formed his own production company, directing *The Legacy of the Five Hundred Thousand* (63). *Grand Prix* (66) was his first Hollywood film, and by 1975 Mifune had turned his talents to television, playing a samurai. More than any other single actor, Mifune has created an appreciation in the West for Japanese films. He also had the title role in the popular television miniseries, *Shōgun*.

**Selected Films:** *The Drunken Angel* (48), *Rashomon* (50), *Seven Samurai* (54), *The Lower Depths* (57), *Throne of Blood* (57), *The Hidden Fortress* (58), *Yojimbo* (61), *Red Beard* (64), *Grand Prix* (66), *Rebellion* (66), *Red Sun* (71), *Paper Tiger* (75), *Midway* (76), *Winter Kills* (79), *1941* (79), *The Challenge* (82).

## MILES, Sarah (1941- )

Born in Ingatestone, England, the vivacious and intriguing actress made her screen debut in *Term of Trial* (62), playing a schoolgirl who accuses her headmaster, Laurence Olivier, of making advances toward her. In 1967 she married playwright, screen director and screenwriter Robert Bolt. They were divorced in 1976. Miles is the sister of director Christopher Miles.

**Selected Films:** *Term of Trial* (62), *The Servant* (63), *Blow Up* (66), *Ryan's Daughter* (70), *Lady Caroline Lamb* (72), *The Sailor Who Fell from Grace with the Sea* (76), *The Big Sleep* (78), *Steaming* (86).

## MILES, Sylvia (1926- )

Miles studied at the Actors Studio in her native New York and began theater work in the 1950s. She appears onscreen only occasionally in character roles, but is often unforgettable. Perhaps the best-known of her extravagantly brassy types was as the aging woman who beds Jon Voight in *Midnight Cowboy* (69), for which Miles received a supporting-actress Oscar nomination.

**Selected Films:** *Murder, Inc.* (60), *Midnight Cowboy* (69), *The Last Movie* (71), *Heat* (72), *The Sentinel* (77), *Zero to Sixty* (79).

## MILES, Vera (1929- )

Born Vera Ralston in Boise City, Oklahoma, Miles worked extensively in TV in the 1950s before emerging as a mild and pretty leading lady in major films including John Ford's *The Searchers* (56) and Alfred Hitchcock's *The Wrong Man* (57). From the mid-1960s on Miles was largely consigned to minor productions. She was married to actor Gordon Scott. After their divorce in 1959, she married actor Keith Larsen.

**Selected Films:** *For Men Only* (52), *The Searchers* (56), *The Wrong Man* (57), *Psycho* (60), *The Man Who Shot Liberty Valance* (62), *Hell-fighters* (68), *One Little Indian* (75), *Psycho II* (83).

## MILJAN, John (1893-1960)

Born in Lead, South Dakota, Miljan acted onstage in his teens and came to the screen in the mid-

1920s. From then until his death he was one of the screen's more familiar bad guys, usually of the suave and slimy sort.
**Selected Films:** *The Phantom of the Opera* (25), *The Unholy Three* (30), *Double Cross* (41), *Samson and Delilah* (50), *The Pirates of Tripoli* (55), *The Lone Ranger and the Lost City of Gold* (58).

## MILLAND, Ray (1905-1986)

Since Milland made his debut in British films in 1929 under the name of Spike Milland he appeared in literally hundreds of movies as well as on many television programs. Born Reginald Truscott-Jones in Neath, Wales, he was in the Guards before becoming an actor. Charming, attractive and suave, he was merely a light leading man with a ready smile and a happy disposition until he stunned audiences with his portrayal of the desperate alcoholic in *The Lost Weekend* (45). This unsentimental, disturbing film took the audiences through three tortured days in the life of this driven man and won Milland the Academy Award for Best Actor. It also won the Oscar for Best Picture, as did Billy Wilder for Best Director. Following that, Milland played a wide variety of roles, including villains and leads in horror films, and proved himself to be a more than capable screen director.
**Selected Films:** *The Plaything* (29), *Payment Deferred* (32), *The Jungle Princess* (36), *Beau Geste* (39), *The Doctor Takes a Wife* (40), *Skylark* (41), *The Uninvited* (44), *The Lost Weekend* (45), *Kitty* (45), *The Big Clock* (48), *Alias Nick Beal* (49), *Night Into Morning* (51), *Dial M for Murder* (54), *X – The Man With the X-Ray Eyes* (63), *Love Story* (70), *Oliver's Story* (78), *Survival Run* (80).

## MILLER, Ann (1919- )

Long legs and plenty of spunk characterize Ann Miller, the great tap dancer, who added bright moments even to inferior movies and who was one of the best reasons for seeing some of MGM's banner musicals. Born Lucy Ann Collier in Houston, Texas, she was a professional dancer from childhood and broke into movies at the age of 17. Her acting and her dancing brought her early attention, but it wasn't until the late 1940s that her gifts were fully recognized. After her movie career ended, she continued performing in night clubs and in television. Still stunning and a wonderful dancer, she thrilled Broadway audiences when she appeared with Mickey Rooney in *Sugar Babies* in the early 1980s.
**Selected Films:** *New Faces of 1937* (37), *You Can't Take It with You* (38), *Go West, Young Lady* (41), *Reveille with Beverly* (43), *Jam Session* (44), *Eve Knew Her Apples* (45), *Easter Parade* (48), *On the Town* (49), *Two Tickets to Broadway* (51), *Kiss Me Kate* (53), *Small Town Girl* (53), *Deep in My Heart* (54), *Hit the Deck* (55), *The Opposite Sex* (56), *Won Ton Ton, the Dog Who Saved Hollywood* (75).

## MILLER, Marilyn (1898-1936)

Born Mary Ellen Reynolds in Findlay, Ohio, Miller made her stage debut at the age of 5 and in the 1920s became one of the brightest stars on Broadway. She made only three talkies before her early death. Miller was played by Judy Garland in *Till the Clouds Roll By* (46) and by June Haver in *Look for the Silver Lining* (49).
**Selected Films:** *Sally* (30), *Sunny* (31), *Her Majesty Love* (31).

## MILLER, Marvin (1913-1985)

American actor Miller appeared in routine films of the 1940s and 1950s, usually as a heavy. He was best-known as the man who handed out the checks on the TV series *The Millionaire*.
**Selected Films:** *Johnny Angel* (45), *The High Window* (47), *The Shanghai Story* (54).

## MILLER, Patsy Ruth (1905- )

Born in St Louis, Missouri, Miller made her silent screen debut at 16 with Rudolph Valentino and Alla Nazimova in *Camille* (21). Soon she was playing leads, most notably as a delicate Esmeralda opposite Lon Chaney in *The Hunchback of Notre Dame* (23). Her career coasted to a halt with the coming of sound, though she made a brief comeback in *Quebec* (51).
**Selected Films:** *Camille* (21), *The Sheik* (21), *The Hunchback of Notre Dame* (23), *So This is Paris* (26), *Twin Beds* (29), *Lonely Wives* (31), *Québec* (51).

## MILLIGAN, Spike (1918- )

Born in Ahmednagar, India, comic Terence Milligan was a member of the cast of the British *Goon Show* which revolutionized radio, TV, and screen comedy in the 1950s. He appeared in occasional films, mostly in cameo roles.
**Selected Films:** *The Case of the Mukkinese Battlehorn* (56), *Watch Your Stern* (60), *The Magic Christian* (70), *Rentadick* (72), *The Three Musketeers* (74), *The Life of Brian* (79), *Yellowbeard* (83).

## MILLS, Hayley (1946- )

Born in London, England, the daughter of the great British actor, John Mills, and sister of actress Juliet Mills, she began film work while quite young, often appearing in Walt Disney features. She received a Special Academy Award 'for *Pollyanna*, the most outstanding juvenile performance during 1960.' Later Mills made the transition to adult roles via a movie nude scene in the 1960s and a highly publicized affair with producer-director Roy Boulting, which culminated in a six-year marriage.
**Selected Films:** *Tiger Bay* (59), *Pollyanna* (60), *The Parent Trap* (61), *Whistle Down the Wind* (61), *The Chalk Garden* (64), *The Moonspinners* (65), *The Family Way* (66), *The Kingfisher Caper* (75).

## MILLS, John (1908- )

Knighted in 1976 in honor of his illustrious acting career, Mills has presented moviegoers with a fine portfolio of screen portraits. Born in North Elmham, England, he began his show business career as a chorus boy, then appeared in dramas, making his film debut in *The Midshipmaid* (32). During World War II he gained popularity playing stoic heroes. Mills won an Academy Award for Best Supporting Actor in *Ryan's Daughter* (70), in which he played a mute village idiot. Married to the writer Mary Hayley Bell, he is the father of actresses Hayley Mills and Juliet Mills. As a lead or character actor, he always excells. Although his acting style is low-key, he is extremely versatile.
**Selected Films:** *The Midshipmaid* (32), *Those Were the Days* (34), *Goodbye, Mr Chips* (39), *The Young Mr Pitt* (42), *In Which We Serve* (42), *The Way to the Stars* (45), *Great Expectations* (46), *Scott of the Antarctic* (48), *The History of Mr Polly* (49), *Hobson's Choice* (54), *Tiger Bay* (59), *Tunes of Glory* (60), *The Family Way* (66), *The Wrong Box* (66), *Ryan's Daughter* (70), *The Human Factor* (76), *Gandhi* (82).

## MILLS, Juliet (1941- )

Born in London, the daughter of actor John Mills – and older sister of actress Hayley – Juliet has appeared occasionally in movies since the age of 11 weeks, meanwhile concentrating on her work in the theater. She also starred in the TV series *Nanny and the Professor*.
**Selected Films:** *In Which We Serve* (42), *The History of Mr Polly* (49), *No, My Darling Daughter!* (61), *Carry on, Jack* (64), *Oh! What a Lovely War* (69), *Avanti* (72), *Barnaby and Me* (77).

## MILNER, Martin (1927- )

Born in Detroit, Michigan, Milner has been filling in minor roles in movies since his 1947 debut as one of the boys in *Life With Father*. The freckled actor is better-known for his parts in TV series including *The Life of Riley*, *Route 66*, and *Adam 12*.
**Selected Films:** *Life With Father* (47), *Our Very Own* (50), *Pete Kelly's Blues* (55), *Marjorie Morningstar* (58), *Too Much Too Soon* (58), *Valley of the Dolls* (67), *Three Guns for Texas* (68).

## MIMIEUX, Yvette (1939- )

Born in Los Angeles, California, Mimieux made her film debut right out of college in *The Time Machine* (60). A willowy blonde, she was a familiar leading lady of 1960s features but rarely got a substantial role. One exception was her role as a retarded girl in *The Light in the Piazza* (62). In the 1970s Mimieux worked often on television.
**Selected Films:** *The Time Machine* (60), *Where the Boys Are* (61), *The Light in the Piazza* (62), *The Wonderful World of the Brothers Grimm* (63), *Three in the Attic* (68), *The Black Hole* (78), *Mystique* (80).

## MINEO, Sal (1939-1976)

Mineo grew up something of a punk on the streets of the Bronx, New York, a role he was soon to play in movies. After stage experience he entered films in 1955 and that year won an Oscar nomination for his part in *Rebel Without a Cause* as a wide-eyed, trouble kid who tags after James Dean. Over the next 20 years Mineo often played hoods, but also handled a broad variety of supporting parts including an Indian in *Cheyenne Autumn* (64). He died a murder victim.
**Selected Films:** *Six Bridges to Cross* (55), *Rebel Without a Cause* (55), *Giant* (56), *Somebody Up There Likes Me* (57), *Exodus* (60), *Cheyenne Autumn* (64), *Escape from the Planet of the Apes* (71).

## MINNELLI, Liza (1946- )

Minnelli, born in Los Angeles, is the daughter of the legendary star Judy Garland and the genius director Vincente Minnelli. A vibrant talent, she made her show business debut in a bit part at the age of three as the daughter of Garland and Van Johnson in *The Good Old Summertime* (49). She made her Broadway debut when she was 19 in *Flora, the Red Menace*, for which she won a Tony Award. That was in 1965, and she later won another Tony – a Special Tony – in 1974, and still another for *The Act* in 1978. Along the way, she won an Emmy Award for her work in her own TV special, *Liza with a Z*, in 1972. When she made her third film, *The Sterile Cuckoo* (69), she was nominated for an Academy Award for Best Actress. She won the Oscar as Best Actress for her portrayal of the decadent night club singer, Sally Bowles, in *Cabaret* (72). She got her impressive stage and screen career together despite a chaotic youth. During her childhood she attended some 20 schools in California and Europe. During the early 1980s she sought help for drug and alcohol addiction at the Betty Ford Center, after three marriages – to Peter Allen, Jack Haley Jr and her current husband, sculptor Mark Gero.
**Selected Films:** *In the Good Old Summertime* (49), *Charlie Bubbles* (67), *The Sterile Cuckoo* (69), *Tell Me That You Love Me, Junie Moon* (70), *Cabaret* (72), *Lucky Lady* (76), *A Matter of Time* (76), *New York, New York* (77), *Arthur* (81).

## MINTER, Mary Miles (1902-1984)

Born Juliet Reilly in Shreveport, Louisiana, Minter acted in the theater as a child and arrived on screen at age 10, though it was believed she was sixteen. In the next decade she appeared in over 50 films as a delicate and lovely waif in the Mary Pickford vein. Her career terminated abruptly with the murder of her reputed lover, director William Desmond Taylor.
**Selected Films:** *The Nurse* (12), *Barbara Frietchie* (15), *Melissa of the Hills* (17), *Anne of Green Gables* (19), *The Trail of the Lonesome Pine* (23), *The Drums of Fate* (23).

*Liza Minnelli in* Cabaret *(72).*

## MIRANDA, Carmen (1909-1955)

Born Maria do Carmo Miranda da Cunha near Lisbon, Portugal, this dynamic, flamboyant singer enlivened Hollywood musical films of the 1940s. She moved with her parents to Rio de Janeiro, Brazil, when she was a child. She became a local radio and recording star, made a few Brazilian movies, and was imported to Broadway in 1939 to appear in *Streets of Paris*. Billed as 'The Brazilian Bombshell,' she added exotic spice to more than a dozen Hollywood films, often appearing in extravagant costumes and high headgear adorned with tropical fruit. When she died of a heart attack, her body was flown to Brazil, where days of national mourning were declared.
**Selected Films:** *A Voz do Carnival* (33), *Banana da Terra* (39), *Down Argentine Way* (40), *That Night in Rio* (41), *Springtime in the Rockies* (42), *The Gang's All Here* (43), *Doll Face* (46), *Copacabana* (47), *A Date With Judy* (48), *Nancy Goes To Rio* (50), *Scared Stiff* (53).

## MITCHELL, Cameron (1918- )

Born Cameron Mizell, a preacher's son, in Dallastown, Pennsylvania, Mitchell began his acting career in the theater. He first found fame as Happy in the stage and screen versions of *Death of a Salesman* (52); Since then he has most often been cast in routine adventure films including a number of European ones during the 1960s. He has starred in several TV series, most notably *High Chaparral*.
**Selected Films:** *They Were Expendable* (45), *Command Decision* (48), *Death of a Salesman* (52), *Love Me or Leave Me* (55), *The Last of the Vikings* (61), *Hombre* (67), *Viva Knievel!* (77), *Without Warning* (80), *My Favorite Year* (82).

## MITCHELL, Grant (1874-1957)

Born in Columbus, Ohio and educated at Yale and Harvard Law, Mitchell turned to acting and worked in the theater for some three decades before turning to the screen in the 1930s. In films through the late 1940s his mild features were seen in comic roles as bland businessmen, and politicians.
**Selected Films:** *Man to Man* (30), *Dinner at Eight* (33), *The Grapes of Wrath* (40), *The Man Who Came to Dinner* (41), *Arsenic and Old Lace* (44), *It Happened on Fifth Avenue* (47), *Who Killed Doc Robin?* (48).

## MITCHELL, Guy (1925- )

Primarily a singer by trade, Mitchell, born Al Cernick, in Detroit, Michigan, appeared in a few movies of the 1950s and the TV series *Whispering Smith*.
**Selected Films:** *Aaron Slick from Punkin Crick* (52), *Those Redheads from Seattle* (53), *Red Garters* (54).

## MITCHELL, Thomas (1892-1962)

Born in Elizabeth, New Jersey, Mitchell was a theater actor and playwright for many years before entering the movies in the mid-1930s. From then until his death he was one of the most versatile and memorable character actors of the American screen, his over 60 roles ranging from the boozy doctor in *Stagecoach* (39), for which he won an Oscar, to Scarlett's father, Gerald O'Hara, in *Gone With the Wind* (39), Dr Gibbs in *Our Town* (40), and a town elder who nearly gets Gary Cooper killed in *High Noon* (52).
**Selected Films:** *Six-Cylinder Love* (23), *Craig's Wife* (36), *Lost Horizon* (37), *Stagecoach* (39), *Gone With the Wind* (39), *Our Town* (40), *The Black Swan* (42), *Flesh and Fantasy* (43), *It's a Wonderful Life* (46), *High Noon* (52), *While the City Sleeps* (56), *Pocketful of Miracles* (61).

## MITCHUM, James (1938- )

The son of actor Robert Mitchum, James made his screen debut with his father in *Thunder Road* (58). He went on to occasional parts in minor movies.
**Selected Films:** *Thunder Road* (58), *The Young Guns of Texas* (62), *The Victors* (63), *Ambush Bay* (67), *Moonrunners* (75).

## MITCHUM, Robert (1917- )

Sleepy-looking eyes and a lethargic manner are the hallmarks of Mitchum. A strong, durable actor, he was always a forceful on-screen presence, even though in the beginning critics carped that he was no actor at all. Because he was husky and sexy they tended to dismiss him as pure beefcake, yet he was good even in bad films and he played brutal villains better than practically anybody else. Born in Bridgeport, Connecticut, he had a knock-about childhood and a footloose youth, working as a night club bouncer, a promoter for an astrologer and an engine wiper on a freighter. He tried boxing, then married his childhood sweetheart and went to work for Lockheed Aircraft. In 1942 he joined the Long Beach Theater Guild in California and then broke into films as a bit player in a series of Hopalong Cassidy westerns. After that he played supporting roles in comedies, westerns and war films. It was *The Story of GI Joe* (45) which made him a star and earned him an Oscar nomination as a tough but tired Army captain during World War II. Mitchum then joined the real Army. When he returned from service, he was appealingly rugged and casual in lead roles. In 1948 Mitchum was convicted for smoking marijuana, which in those days spelled scandal. It was assumed that his career would be ruined, but his audiences did not desert him. Although it would be quite a while before he would make movies like *Crossfire* (47) and *Out of the Past* (47), *River of No Return* (54), with Marilyn Monroe, made big money, and *Not as a Stranger* (55) was a smash hit. Mitchum was superb as a psychotic killer in *The Night of the Hunter* (55) and as the vicious relentless pursuer in *Cape Fear* (62). He was also well cast as a detective in Raymond Chandler remakes in the 1970. Katharine Hepburn once told him, 'You know you can't act.' He has proven her wrong.

**Selected Films:** *Hoppy Serves a Writ* (43), *When Strangers Marry* (44), *The Story of GI Joe* (45), *The Locket* (46), *Crossfire* (47), *Out of the Past* (47), *Rachel and the Stranger* (48), *Blood on the Moon* (48), *The Big Steal* (49), *Holiday Affair* (49), *The Lusty Men* (52), *Angel Face* (53), *River of No Return* (54), *Not as a Stranger* (55), *The Night of the Hunter* (55), *Heaven Knows, Mr Allison* (57), *Home from the Hills* (60), *The Sundowners* (60), *Cape Fear* (62), *Two for the Seesaw* (62), *The List of Adrian Messenger* (63), *What a Way to Go!* (64), *Villa Rides* (68), *Ryan's Daughter* (71), *Going Home* (71), *Farewell, My Lovely* (75), *The Big Sleep* (78), *That Championship Season* (82).

*Robert Mitchum in* Farewell My Lovely *(75).*

## MIX, Tom (1880-1940)

Universally hailed as 'the greatest cowboy star of them all,' Mix was exactly that. His fame rests not on the quality of his films (they were low-budget movies aimed at juvenile audiences) nor on realistic portrayals of the West (Mix was the original fancy-dress cowboy hero, performing feats of derring-do that defied reality). But at the peak of his fame, Mix was better known than any other cowboy star in history and there was even a daily 15-minute adventure radio show about his fictional adventures. Born in Mix Run, Pennsylvania, he was a champion rodeo rider, a soldier and a cowboy in Oklahoma before breaking into films. Studio publicists invented other wild adventures in his life – fighting in Cuba during the Spanish-American War and also in the Philippines and the Boer War, plus serving as a Texas Ranger – which were false. Mix began in short western films in 1910, with his horse Tony, who would become nearly as famous as he was. He developed a formula of breezy, action-filled westerns that was copied for decades afterward. He did all his own stunts and became 'the idol of every girl and boy in America.' Mix lived in a grandiose style, marrying five times and owning mansions and custom-made cars. When his career began to wane in the 1930s, he earned huge sums touring with his Tom Mix Circus. He died in a car crash, still famous.

**Selected Films:** *The Ranch Life in the Great Southwest* (10), *The Escape of Jim Dolan* (13), *The Way of the Redman* (14), *Western Blood* (18), *North of Hudson Bay* (23), *The Trouble Shooter* (24), *Riders of the Purple Sage* (25), *Dick Turpin* (25), *The Last Trail* (27), *Painted Post* (28), *The Drifter* (29), *Destry Rides Again* (32), *Rustlers' Roundup* (33).

## MONROE, Marilyn (1926-1962)

More than 25 years after her death, the public is still fascinated with Monroe. It seems that everyone but her garbage collector has written a book about her. She was the 1950s favorite blonde, cuddly and vulnerable, whose super-sexy image quickly tarnished, leaving her a frustrated, neurotic and tragic victim of the Hollywood which had created her. The pity was that she had real talent as well as sex appeal. Born Norma Jean Baker in Los Angeles, California, she was an illegitimate child who was abused and neglected in a series of foster homes and was married at age 14. She was without a doubt the last of the great studio movie queens and, for whatever reason, she always got a response from her audience. Her teenage marriage failed, but she had the beauty and drive to break into modeling and from there into the movies. She was pretty much another blonde doing bit parts until she got her first noteworthy role in *The Asphalt Jungle* (50) and, after that, in *All About Eve* (50), and made the audiences sit up and take notice. A born scene-stealer who knew how to flirt with a camera, and a genius at self-promotion, she made it to the top with little help from her studio, 20th Century Fox. The news that Monroe had posed nude for a calendar in 1948 only enhanced her sex symbol status. The ultimate in her sexpot roles came in *Gentlemen Prefer Blondes* (53) and *How to Marry a Millionaire* (53), in CinemaScope, made her one of the top ten box office draws. Her most ethereal, heart-stopping role was in *Bus Stop* (56), and one of her best films was *Some Like It Hot* (59), in which she was a brilliant comedic parody of herself. In 1954 Monroe married famed baseball player Joe DiMaggio and, as far as the public knew, had found her way to happiness. Although *The Seven Year Itch* (55) was a big success, her marriage to DiMaggio didn't last, and despite her hefty salary, she had debts. She fled to New York and the Actors' Studio, but returned to Hollywood. Her 1956 marriage to playwright Arthur Miller was a surprise, although it shouldn't have been. Monroe was never the dumb blonde she played on screen and she fought hard for better roles. She failed in her quest to be taken seriously, never receiving an Academy Award nomination, no matter how good she was in several movies. Monroe's last film, *The Misfits* (61), written by Miller and co-starring Clark Gable, was excellent, but by then things had gone drastically wrong with America's Golden Girl. Divorced from Miller, in and out of psychiatric hospitals, she died of an overdose of barbiturates. It was probably suicide. She had recently told an interviewer from *Life* magazine, 'I never understood it – the sex symbol – I always thought symbols were things you clashed together. That's the trouble, a sex symbol becomes a thing – I just hate to be a thing.' She will always be the image of the beautiful loser, the poor kid who tried, but never really succeeded.

**Selected Films:** *Dangerous Years* (48), *Ladies of the Chorus* (48), *Love Happy* (50), *A Ticket to Tomahawk* (50), *The Asphalt Jungle* (50), *All About Eve* (50), *Let's Make It Legal* (51), *Clash by Night* (52), *Niagara* (52), *Gentlemen Prefer Blondes* (53), *How to Marry a Millionaire* (53), *There's No Business Like Show Business* (54), *The Seven Year Itch* (55), *Bus Stop* (56), *The Prince and the Showgirl* (57), *Some Like It Hot* (59), *Let's Make Love* (60), *The Misfits* (61).

*Marilyn Monroe.*

## MONTALBAN, Ricardo (1920- )

Ricardo Montalban was born in Mexico City and educated in Mexico and Los Angeles – though America did not educate him out of his distinctive Spanish accent. His first dramatic experience was in the theater, including roles on Broadway, and his early films were made in his native country. Hollywood first featured the darkly handsome Montalban in *Fiesta* (47). For the rest of his career he fought, with occasional success, the tendency to cast him as a Latin lover. And during the course of his over three decades in movies, Montalban did escape his image to appear in some fairly good ones, including *Battleground* (49), *Sayonara* (57), *Cheyenne Autumn* (64), and *Sweet Charity* (69). He has worked extensively in television. During the 1950s he appeared in the dramatic series hosted by his sister-in-law Loretta Young. Later he starred in the rather light series *Fantasy Island*. Throughout, Montalban has continued to perform in the theater, often in serious roles that make more use of his range of ability than do his screen and TV work. Among his recent screen appearances was the villain in *Star Trek II: The Wrath of Khan* (82).

**Selected Films:** *El Verdugo de Sevilla* (42), *La Casa de la Zorro* (43), *Pepita Jimenez* (45), *Fiesta* (47), *Battleground* (49), *The Kissing Bandit* (49), *Across the Wide Missouri* (51), *Sombrero* (53), *Latin Lovers* (54), *Sayonara* (57), *Love Is a Ball* (63), *Cheyenne Autumn* (64), *Madame X* (66), *Sol Madrid* (68), *Sweet Charity* (69), *Conquest of the Planet of the Apes* (72), *Joe Panther* (76), *Star Trek II: The Wrath of Khan* (82).

## MONTANA, Bull (1887-1950)

Born Luigi Montagna to an Italian-American family, the husky Montana played dumb thugs in a number of silents.

**Selected Films:** *Brass Buttons* (19), *Painted People* (23), *The Lost World* (24), *Son of the Sheik* (26), *Show of Shows* (29).

## MONTAND, Yves (1921- )

Born Ivo Levi in Monsumagno, Italy, Montand moved to France with his family at an early age. He became a popular French singer in clubs and cabarets, and married the fine French actress Simone Signoret. French chanteuse Edith Piaf got him started in films, and the sexy, handsome Montand starred in French, European and Hollywood movies. He proved that he was a fine actor in *The Wages of Fear* (53), in the non-singing role of a down-and-out truck driver trying to take a load of nitroglycerine over South American mountains to be used to put out an oil well fire. He later gave especially fine performances in the political suspense dramas of director Constantin Costa-Gavras. He has recently been deeply involved in French politics.

**Selected Films:** *Star Without Light* (46), *The Wages of Fear* (53), *The Crucible* (57), *Let's Make Love* (60), *Sanctuary* (61), *Is Paris Burning?* (66), *Grand Prix* (67), *Z* (68), *On a Clear Day You Can See Forever* (69), *The Red Circle* (70), *The Son* (72), *Clair de Femme* (79), *Garçon!* (83).

## MONTEZ, Maria (1920-1951)

Maria Montez was born Maria Africa Vidal de Santo Silas in the Dominican Republic, daughter of a Spanish diplomat. Having grown up to be extravagantly beautiful, she dabbled with acting in Europe, then went to New York as a model until the movies came calling. After some bit parts in films, Montez made a splash in *The Invisible Woman* (41). The next year she played Scheherazade in *Arabian Nights* (42), and that set her firmly in her ensuing roles: with co-stars like Sabu, Turhan Bey, and especially Jon Hall, she appeared in a string of exotic-adventure yarns featuring her exceptional figure plus lavish costuming and singing and dancing, all of which never quite managed to mask the absurdity of the plots. The genre was exquisitely lampooned in Leonard Bernstein's opera *Trouble in Tahiti*. Meanwhile Montez became one of the top pin-ups of the day. She was dubbed 'The Queen of Technicolor,' her typical roles typed as 'Aladdin and His Wonderful Vamp.' In time, however, audience enthusiasm for such films began to wear thin and Montez began to gain weight. With her second husband, French star Jean-Pierre Aumont, Montez went to Europe and appeared in several adventure movies there. She began taking gruelling hot baths to lose weight, and died of a heart attack in one of them. Years later, when the concept of 'hokum' was metamorphosed into 'camp,' Montez's movies were affectionately resurrected.

**Selected Films:** *Boss of Bullion City* (40), *The Invisible Woman* (41), *Arabian Nights* (42), *The Mystery of Marie Roget* (42), *Ali Baba and the Forty Thieves* (44), *Cobra Woman* (44), *Sudan* (45), *Pirates of Monterey* (47), *Siren of Atlantis* (48), *The Thief of Venice* (released – 53).

## MONTGOMERY, Douglass (1907-1966)

Born Robert Douglass Montgomery in Brantford, Ontario, Montgomery began his film career as Kent Douglass in *Paid* (30). Changing his name with *Little Women* (33), he went on to play a pleasant-faced all-purpose leading men in films through the 1940s. He continued to appear on stage till the end of his life.

**Selected Films:** *Paid* (30), *Waterloo Bridge* (31), *Little Women* (33), *The Mystery of Edwin Drood* (35), *The Cat and the Canary* (39). *The Way to the Stars* (45), *Forbidden* (48).

## MONTGOMERY, Elizabeth (1933- )

Born in Hollywood, California, the daughter of actor Robert Montgomery, Elizabeth began appearing occasionally in movies in the mid-1950s. She is best known for her TV work, which includes a number of made-for-TV features like *Belle Starr* and her role as a cute witch in the long-running series *Bewitched*.

**Selected Films:** *The Court Martial of Billy Mitchell* (55), *Who's Been Sleeping in My Bed?* (63), *Johnny Cool* (63).

## MONTGOMERY, George (1916- )

Born George Montgomery Letz, in Brady, Montana, Montgomery was a boxer in college before making his way into Republic westerns in the mid-1930s. Graduating to starring roles, Montgomery was a hero of the stalwart and taciturn sort mostly in westerns, war pictures, and adventures. In the late 1950s he starred in the TV series *Cimarron City* and later directed a few low-budget thrillers. He was married to singer Dinah Shore.

**Selected Films:** *The Singing Vagabond* (35), *The Cisco Kid and the Lady* (39), *Roxie Hart* (42), *Ten Gentlemen from West Point* (42), *Dakota Lil* (50), *Watusi* (59), *Battle of the Bulge* (65), *Huntsville* (67), *The Leo Chronicles* (72).

## MONTGOMERY, Robert (1904-1981)

Born Henry Montgomery in Beacon, New York, he made his screen debut in *So This Is College* (29). Most of the time he was a charming, polished light comedian and romantic leading man. But occasionally he played against type with fine results, as was the case in his chilling performance as a murderer in *Night Must Fall* (37). Montgomery, who only entered acting after failing as a writer, became an innovative director in both films and television. One of his remarkable innovations was seen in *The Lady in the Lake* (46), in which he was both star and director. He played the part of detective Philip Marlowe, but as director he decided to film the picture with a camera placed on his body, so that what the audience saw was what Philip Marlowe saw. Montgomery, the star, was heard, but only seen when he was looking into a mirror.

The father of actress Elizabeth Montgomery, he later forsook the screen for politics, most notably grooming future president Dwight D Eisenhower for his television appearances.
**Selected Films:** *So This Is College* (29), *When Ladies Meet* (33), *Night Must Fall* (37), *Yellow Jack* (38), *The Earl of Chicago* (40), *Here Comes Mr Jordan* (41), *They Were Expendable* (45), *The Lady in the Lake* (46), *Ride the Pink Horse* (47), *The Saxon Charm* (48), *Eye Witness* (50), *The Gallant Hours* (60).

## MOODY, Ron (1924- )

Born Ronald Moodnick in London, the versatile Moody has handled comic roles on stage, screen, and TV since the 1950s. He is best known for his deliciously slimy Fagin in the stage and movie versions of *Oliver!* (68). In 1971 Moody wrote and directed the musical *Saturnalia*.
**Selected Films:** *Make Mine Mink* (59), *The Mouse on the Moon* (63), *Oliver!* (68), *Flight of Doves* (71), *Dominique* (78), *Wrong is Right* (82).

## MOORE, Colleen (1900- )

Born Kathleen Morrison in Port Huron, Michigan and educated in a convent, Moore got into movies in 1947. After a few years of tame roles in minor films, she hit pay dirt when she metamorphosed into the screen's archetypal bobbed-hair, flat-chested, hard-drinking, devil-may-care flapper. During the 1920s Moore was the movie star many girls imitated and nearly every parent feared. After a few talkies Moore retired from film and became a financial analyst. In 1968 she produced an autobiography, *Silent Star*.
**Selected Films:** *The Bad Boy* (17), *The Sky Pilot* (22), *So Big* (25), *Naughty But Nice* (27), *Lilac Time* (28), *Why Be Good?* (29), *The Scarlet Letter* (34).

## MOORE, Constance (1922- )

Moore, born in Souix City, Iowa, was one of a number of band singers who got into movies in the 1930s. She was a pleasant fixture in many minor musicals through the 1940s. Thereafter she occasionally appeared on screen or television.
**Selected Films:** *Prison Break* (38), *Ma, He's Making Eyes at Me* (40), *Show Business* (43), *Atlantic City* (44), *Hats Off to Rhythm.* (47), *Spree* (67).

## MOORE, Demi (1963- )

A delicately pretty brunette, Moore was born Demi Guynes in Roswell, New Mexico. After working as a model and acting on television including a role on the soap *General Hospital*, she made her film debut in *Parasite* (82). Since then Moore has played leading roles in mostly routine films.
**Selected Films:** *Parasite* (82), *Blame It on Rio* (84), *St Elmo's Fire* (85), *About Last Night* (86), *One Crazy Summer* (86), *Wisdom* (87).

## MOORE, Dickie (1925- )

Born John Richard Moore, Jr in Los Angeles, California, he made his screen debut at the age of one in *The Beloved Rogue* (27). A seasoned pro by age five, he was an irresistable blond kid with soulful eyes in many films. He was one of the *Our Gang* troup and had the title role in *Oliver Twist* (33). At 16 Moore shone in *Sergeant York* (41), and in *Miss Annie Rooney* (42) was the first boy to kiss Shirley Temple onscreen – a somewhat epochal event at the time. In the 1950s his screen career coasted to a halt, and he turned to public relations.
**Selected Films:** *The Beloved Rogue* (27), *No Greater Love* (32), *Oliver Twist* (33), *Little Men* (35), *Sergeant York* (41), *Miss Annie Rooney* (42), *Dangerous Years* (47), *The Member of the Wedding* (52).

## MOORE, Dudley (1935- )

A highly talented versatile performer, London-born Moore is an actor, composer, writer, musician and comedian. He has worked closely with comedian Peter Cook and was a member of the famed *Beyond the Fringe* comedy group. Having sparkled on stage, television and cabaret, it remained for Moore to conquer the screen, which he did in *The Wrong Box* (66), playing a young avaricious lecher. *10* (80) gave him a boost, and *Arthur* (82) made him a bigger star yet. Subsequent films have proved to be disasters, in part because Moore, short and not at all the usual leading man, is cast in romantic roles.
**Selected Films:** *The Wrong Box* (66), *Thirty Is a Dangerous Age, Cynthia* (67), *Foul Play* (78), *The Hound of the Baskervilles* (78), *10* (80), *Wholly Moses* (81), *Arthur* (82), *Six Weeks* (82), *Lovesick* (83), *Micki and Maude* (84).

*Dudley Moore and Julie Andrews in* 10 *(80).*

## MOORE, Grace (1901-1947)

Born in the boondocks of Slabtown, Tennessee, Moore grew up to be one of the loveliest – and slenderest – sopranos of the Metropolitan Opera. She graced occasional screen musicals of the 1930s including *One Night of Love* (34) for which she

received an Oscar nomination. A 1953 biopic about Moore, aptly titled *So This is Love*, starred Kathryn Grayson. Moore died in a plane crash.
**Selected Films:** *A Lady's Morals* (30), *New Moon* (30), *One Night of Love* (34), *Love Me Forever* (35), *I'll Take Romance* (37), *Louise* (40).

## MOORE, Kieron (1925- )

Born Kieron O'Hanrahan in Skibbereen, County Cort, Ireland, Moore came to the stage in the early 1940s and to movies soon after. He was a leading man of the staunch and virile sort in features through the 1960s, his more notable roles including Vronsky in *Anna Karenina* (48).
**Selected Films:** *The Voice Within* (44), *Mine Own Executioner* (47), *Anna Karenina* (48), *Darby O'Gill and the Little People* (59), *The Thin Red Line* (64), *Custer of the West* (66).

## MOORE, Mary Tyler (1937- )

Moore was born in Brooklyn, New York and grew up in Los Angeles, California. After several minor television roles, one of them as a detective's secretary on *Richard Diamond*, the series in which every week only her legs were shown, she was signed to play Laura Petrie opposite Dick Van Dyke on *The Dick Van Dyke Show*. Moore returned to New York to play Holly Golightly in the Broadway musical adaptation of Truman Capote's *Breakfast at Tiffany's*. She then made some routine films. But she is best known for her splendid TV series, *The Mary Tyler Moore Show*. Her later film work has been of a much higher quality.
**Selected Films:** *X-15* (61), *Thoroughly Modern Millie* (67), *What's So Bad About Feeling Good?* (68), *Don't Just Stand There* (68), *Change of Habit* (69), *Ordinary People* (80), *Six Weeks* (82), *Just Between Friends* (86).

## MOORE, Roger (1927- )

Born in London, England, this leading man in light comedies hit stardom on the private detective TV series, *The Saint*, playing the title role. Handsome and charming with a debonaire style and a twinkling sense of humor, his screen career boomed when he replaced Sean Connery in the James Bond series of films.
**Selected Films:** *The Fuller Brush Man* (48), *The Last Time I Saw Paris* (54), *The Sins of Rachel Cade* (61), *Crossplot* (69), *The Man Who Haunted Himself* (70), *Live and Let Die* (73), *The Spy Who Loved Me* (77), *Moonraker* (79), *The Sea Wolves* (80), *For Your Eyes Only* (81), *Octopussy* (83), *A View to A Kill* (85).

## MOORE, Terry (1929- )

Born Helen Koford in Los Angeles, California, Moore was a child model before making her screen debut at age 11. She grew up to play sexy roles in a number of films of the 1950s and 1960s; mean-

*Roger Moore as James Bond.*

while, her romantic life garnered as much publicity as her acting. Moore received a supporting-actress Oscar nomination for her part in *Come Back, Little Sheba* (52).
**Selected Films:** *Maryland* (40), *Son of Lassie* (45), *Mighty Joe Young* (50), *Come Back, Little Sheba* (52), *King of the Khyber Rifles* (54), *Peyton Place* (57), *Platinum High School* (60), *Waco (66)*, *Death Dimension* (77).

## MOORE, Victor (1876-1962)

Victor Moore was born in Hammonton, New Jersey, and made his stage debut while still in his teens. After many years in vaudeville and on Broadway, he first appeared in silent films about 1915. Over the next 40 years he alternated between screen and theater, establishing his classic image as the short round guy who was invariably bumbling around with utter helplessness. Moore appeared in dozens of mostly small roles in movies like *Gold Diggers of 1937*, *Louisiana Purchase* (41) and *Duffy's Tavern* (45). One of his last appearances was in *The Seven Year Itch* (55).
**Selected Films:** *Snobs* (15), *The Clown* (16), *Dangerous Dan McGrew* (30), *Gold Diggers of 1937* (36), *Make Way for Tomorrow* (37), *Louisiana Purchase* (41), *It's In the Bag* (45), *Duffy's Tavern* (45), *Ziegfeld Follies* (46), *A Kiss in the Dark* (49), *We're Not Married* (52), *The Seven-Year Itch* (55).

## MOOREHEAD, Agnes (1906-1974)

Born in Clinton, Massachusetts, this sharp-featured American character actress was most often seen in waspish or neurotic roles. One of the best actresses Hollywood ever produced, she

received five Academy Award nominations. A singer, ballet dancer and drama coach as well, her career really took off once she joined the Mercury Players and Orson Welles, most notably in *Citizen Kane* (41). She was also popular as Elizabeth Montgomery's haughty mother, the witch Endora, in the TV series *Bewitched*.
**Selected Films:** *Citizen Kane* (41), *The Magnificent Ambersons* (42), *The Lost Moment* (47), *The Woman in White* (48), *Johnny Belinda* (48), *Show Boat* (51), *The Swan* (56), *Jeanne Eagels* (57), *The Bat* (59), *Pollyanna* (60), *Hush . . . Hush, Sweet Charlotte* (64), *Dear Dead Delilah* (75).

## MORAN, Peggy (1918- )

Born in Clinton, Iowa, Moran grew up to be a pretty brunette leading lady who appeared largely in Universal B movies of the 1940s. She retired upon marrying director Henry Koster.
**Selected Films:** *Girls' School* (39), *The Mummy's Hand* (40), *Horror Island* (41), *Drums of the Congo* (42), *King of the Cowboys* (43).

## MORAN, Polly (1884-1952)

Born in Chicago, Illinois, Moran starred in vaudeville before getting into silent movies, playing Sheriff Nell in the Keystone comedy shorts. She blossomed as a bucktoothed comedienne in talkies of the 1930s, usually teamed to great effect with Marie Dressler.
**Selected Films:** *Skirts* (21), *The Callaghans and The Murphys* (27), *Hollywood Revue* (29), *The Passionate Plumber* (32), *Alice in Wonderland* (33), *Adam's Rib* (49), *The Yellow Cab Man* (50).

## MORANIS, Rick (1954- )

A member of the famed Second City troupe from Chicago, Rick Moranis appeared with the group on the television series *Second City TV* and *SCTV*, where one of his recurring characters was Bob McKenzie, cohost of 'The Great White North,' a Canadian send-up. He made his film debut as McKenzie in *Strange Brew* (83). He also played Sigourney Weaver's wimpy neighbor in *Ghostbusters* (84) and the leading role of the bizarre gardener in *Little Shop of Horrors* (86).
**Selected Films:** *Strange Brew* (83), *Ghostbusters* (84), *Club Paradise* (86), *Head Office* (86), *Little Shop of Horrors* (86).

## MORE, Kenneth (1914-1982)

An amiable image made More one of Britain's most popular stars. Often he played breezy roles, but he was capable of giving powerful performances in such vehicles as *A Night to Remember* (58), in which he played Lt Lightoller, the third officer aboard the *Titanic*. More was born in Gerrard's Cross, England, and made his debut in movies in *Look Up and Laugh* (35). But it wasn't until he returned from naval service after World War II that his career really started to improve. More received a British Film Academy award for his appearance in the comedy *Doctor in the House* (54). As a leading man he played both comic and dramatic roles, later giving compassionate interpretations of middle-aged dreamers. Film makers forsook him after his great successes of the 1950s and he turned to stage and television. The BBC TV series *The Forsyte Saga* won him new admirers.
**Selected Films:** *Look up and Laugh* (35), *Scott of the Antarctic* (48), *Now Barabbas* (49), *No Highway in the Sky* (51), *Appointment with Venus* (51), *Genevieve* (53), *Doctor in the House* (54), *The Deep Blue Sea* (55), *Reach for the Sky* (56), *A Night to Remember* (58), *Sink the Bismark* (60), *The Longest Day* (62), *The Comedy Man* (63), *Oh What a Lovely War* (69), *Leopard in the Snow* (78), *The Spaceman and King Arthur* (79).

## MOREAU, Jeanne (1928- )

It took many years for Moreau to evolve from a sexy, artistically limited French starlet to the great actress that she is today. Born in Paris, she got her training with the Théâtre Nationale Populaire, one of France's most respected repertory companies. Moreau made her film debut in *Last Love* (49), the first of many movies in which she played sexually aware, if not liberated, characters. It was a decade before her film career really began with *Elevator to the Scaffold* (58), in which she worked for director Louis Malle, who recognized her genius. She became extremely popular, a serious actress who was sophisticated and sensual, capable of playing a wide variety of roles. Moreau worked with several great directors. Besides Malle, Michelangelo Antonioni directed her in *La Notte* (61) with Marcello Mastroiani, and she also worked with Françoise Truffaut, whose *Jules et Jim* (61) highlighted Moreau's on-screen charisma. She made her debut as a director with *La Lumière* (76), writing the movie's script and starring in it as well.
**Selected Films:** *Last Love* (49), *Elevator to the Scaffold* (58), *The Lovers* (59), *La Notte* (61), *Jules et Jim* (61), *Diary of a Chambermaid* (65), *Viva Maria* (65), *Chimes at Midnight* (66), *The Bride Wore Black* (67), *Monte Walsh* (70), *La Lumière* (76), *Le débandode* (81).

## MORELAND, Mantan (1902-1973)

Born in Monroe, Louisiana, Moreland came to films in the late 1930s and in the next decades played dozens of stereotyped goggle-eyed, scared-darky roles, among them Charlie Chan's chauffeur. His trademark line was 'Feets, do your stuff!' In later years Moreland found less demeaning roles, among them in an all-black Broadway revival of *Waiting for Godot*.
**Selected Films:** *Spirit of Youth* (38), *Cabin in the Sky* (43), *The Feathered Serpent* (49), *Enter Laughing* (68), *Watermelon Man* (70), *The Young Nurses* (73).

## MORENO, Antonio (1886-1967)

Born Antonio Garride Monteagudo in Madrid, Spain, Moreno acted on the stage before beginning his film career with D W Griffith in 1912. He became one of the favorite Latin Lovers of the screen, starring opposite stars like Greta Garbo and Gloria Swanson. With the coming of sound his thick Spanish accent ended Moreno's starring days, but he appeared in character parts into the 1950s.
**Selected Films:** *Voice of the Million* (12), *The Trail of the Lonesome Pine* (23), *The Temptress* (26), *The Bohemian Girl* (36), *Captain from Castile* (47), *The Searchers* (56).

## MORENO, Rita (1931- )

Rita Moreno was born Rosita Dolores Alverio in Huma, Puerto Rico. She was a professional dancer and singer, and while still in her teens made her Broadway debut at 13 and went to Hollywood the next year for a small part in *A Medal for Benny* (45). She made her major-role debut in *So Young, So Bad* (50); for several years she was cast in musicals and exotic pictures like *Singin' in the Rain (52) and Pagan Love Song* (50). In the course of the 1950s Moreno proved herself an able actress as well, both on screen and in the theater, her movies alternating among musicals, dramas, and adventures; these included *Garden of Evil* (54), *The King and I* (56), and *This Rebel Breed* (60). The role of Anita in *West Side Story* (61) earned Moreno an Academy Award for Best Supporting Actress. Her movie appearances thinned out in the 1960s. She worked extensively on stage, winning a Chicago Critics' Award for her role in a 1969 revival of *The Rose Tattoo*. Moreno also starred in the TV series *Nine to Five*.
**Selected Films:** *A Medal for Benny* (45), *So Young, So Bad* (50), *The Toast of New Orleans* (50), *Pagan Love Song* (50), *Singin' in the Rain* (52), *Fort Vengeance* (53), *The Yellow Tomahawk* (54), *Garden of Evil* (54), *Untamed* (55), *The Lieutenant Wore Skirts* (56), *The King and I* (56), *The Deerslayer* (57), *This Rebel Breed* (60), *Summer and Smoke* (61), *West Side Story* (61), *Popi* (69), *Carnal Knowledge* (71), *The Ritz* (76), *The Four Seasons* (81).

## MORGAN, Dennis (1910- )

Born Stanley Morner in Prentice, Wisconsin, Dennis Morgan arrived in Hollywood via a number of detours. He played several sports in school and after graduating from college worked in his father's lumber business while he studied voice with an eye to an operatic career. He then tried radio, minor stock acting, and semipro baseball for a while. Morgan's assorted ephemeral careers climaxed when he toured in an operatic production and did some singing on radio. Opera star Mary Garden heard him, was impressed, and got him some movie roles at MGM. Making his debut in *I Conquer the Sea* (35) – still as Stanley Morner – he played in several minor roles. Moving to Paramount, he appeared in some routine movies, including *King of Alcatraz* (38) as Richard Stanley. Finally as Dennis Morgan, he gained a good deal of attention for his role in *Kitty Foyle* (40). From that point he was a familiar leading man of the good-natured variety for nearly two decades, his films including *The Desert Song* (43) (where he finally sang onscreen), *My Wild Irish Rose* (47) and *The Gun That Won the West* (55). Morgan also starred in the TV series *21 Beacon Street*.
**Selected Films:** *I Conquer the Sea* (35), *The Great Ziegfeld* (36), *King of Alcatraz* (38), *Kitty Foyle* (40), *Captains of the Clouds* (42), *The Desert Song* (43), *Two Guys from Texas* (46), *My Wild Irish Rose* (47), *The Gun That Won the West* (55). *Uranium Boom* (56), *Won Ton Ton, The Dog Who Saved Hollywood* (70).

## MORGAN, Frank (1890-1949)

Frank Morgan was born Francis Wupperman in New York, one of 11 children of an Angostura-bitters tycoon. After various jobs, Frank followed his actor brother Ralph Morgan onto the stage, making his Broadway debut in 1914. Morgan first appeared in silents in *The Suspect* (16). For over a decade he worked often in films but concentrated on the theater. With the coming of sound, however, Morgan's screen talents became manifest; he moved to Hollywood to become one of the most familiar and beloved character actors in the business. His appearances during the 1930s included parts in *The Affairs of Cellini* (34), *The Great Ziegfeld* (36) and *The Last of Mrs Cheyney* (37). Though it appeared midway in his long career, Morgan's most celebrated role remains his immortal wizard in *The Wizard of Oz* (39). In that and in most of his parts, Morgan was a crackly-voiced, rather befuddled sort with a roguish glint in his eye. He continued appearing in several films a year until the end of his life, later ones including *Tortilla Flat* (42) and (as Willy Grogan) *The Human Comedy* (43). Morgan also wrote thoughtful articles on screen acting. His films finally totalled over a hundred and being a master scene-stealer, he knew what he was talking about.
**Selected Films:** *The Suspect* (16), *A Modern Cinderella* (17), *Bombshell* (33), *The Affairs of Cellini* (34), *Naughty Marietta* (35), *The Great Ziegfeld* (36), *Piccadilly Jim* (36), *The Last of Mrs Cheney* (37), *The Wizard of Oz* (39), *The Vanishing Virginian* (42), *Tortilla Flat* (42), *The Human Comedy* (43), *The Courage of Lassie* (45), *Key to the City* (50).

## MORGAN, Harry (1915- )

Harry Morgan was born Harry Bratsburg in Detroit, Michigan, and attended the University of Chicago. He made his screen debut in *To the Shores of Tripoli* (42), and appeared in dozens of movies over the next four decades. Thin and not particu-

larly striking in features, Morgan tended to play all sorts of roles as more or less average citizens. For those who mainly know Morgan from his extensive TV work, it is surprising how many popular films of the 1950s and 1960s he appeared in; among them *The Teahouse of the August Moon* (56), *Inherit the Wind* (60) and *How the West Was Won* (62). Meanwhile, Morgan was playing supporting roles in TV series almost continually from *December Bride* to *M*A*S*H*. He continued to make occasional movies including *The Shootist* (76).
**Selected Films:** *To the Shores of Tripoli* (42), *The Ox-Bow Incident* (43), *State Fair* (45), *High Noon* (52), *The Glenn Miller Story* (54), *The Teahouse of the August Moon* (56), *Inherit the Wind* (60), *How the West Was Won* (62), *Frankie and Johnny* (66), *Support Your Local Sheriff* (69), *The Apple Dumpling Gang* (75), *The Shootist* (76), *The Apple Dumpling Gang Rides Again* (79).

## MORGAN, Helen (1900-1941)

Born Helen Riggins in Danville, Illinois, Morgan worked her way up to a bigtime Broadway and cabaret career. She is remembered as the first 'torch singer.' In her occasional films she tended to play self-destructive women. Among those roles were Kitty in *Applause* (29) and Julie in *Show Boat* (36), the latter a repeat of her Broadway triumph. Morgan died of alcoholism at 41. Ann Blyth played her in *The Helen Morgan Story* (57).
**Selected Films:** *Applause* (29), *Roadhouse Nights* (30), *You Belong to Me* (34), *Frankie and Johnnie* (36), *Show Boat* (36).

## MORGAN, Michèle (1920- )

Blessed with a delicate classic beauty, Morgan was a leading lady while still in her teens. Born Simone Roussel in Neuilly-sur-Seine, France, she is a star noted for her fascinating on-screen aloofness, sophistication and wonderfully expressive eyes. She made several films under her own name, but it didn't take Morgan long to become France's most popular film actress. She won the Best Actress Award at the Cannes Film Festival for her appearance in *La Symphonie Pastorale* (46). Although she has appeared in Hollywood films, she is at her best in European productions.
**Selected Films:** *Mademoiselle Mozart* (35), *Orage* (36), *Quai des Brumes* (38), *Joan of Paris* (41), *Passage to Marseilles* (44), *La Symphonie Pastorale* (46), *The Fallen Idol* (48), *The Seven Deadly Sins* (51), *Les Grandes Manoeuvres* (55), *Marguerite de la Nuit* (56), *The Mirror Has Two Faces* (60), *Landru* (63), *Lost Command* (66), *Benjamin* (68), *Cat and Mouse* (76), *Seven Steps to Murder* (77), *Robert et Robert* (78).

## MORGAN, Ralph (1882-1956)

Born Raphael Wupperman in New York, brother of actor Frank Morgan, Ralph left the law for the stage. After a few movie appearances he scored a success repeating his stage role in *Strange Interlude* (32) on the screen. For two decades thereafter Morgan was a character actor and occasional lead in dozens of films, most often as a heavy.
**Selected Films:** *The Man Who Found Himself* (25), *Charlie Chan's Chance* (31), *Strange Interlude* (32), *Rasputin and the Empress* (32), *The Power and the Glory* (33), *Little Men* (35), *Forty Little Mothers* (40), *The Monster Maker* (45), *Gold Fever* (52).

## MORGAN, Terence (1921- )

Morgan was born in London and acted on the stage in his native Britain before making his screen debut as Laertes in Laurence Olivier's *Hamlet* (48). The handsome actor went on to leads in a number of films, mostly minor thrillers.
**Selected Films:** *Hamlet* (48), *Mandy* (52), *The Scamp* (56), *The Curse of the Mummy's Tomb* (64), *The Penthouse* (67), *Yesterday's Warriors* (79).

## MORIARTY, Michael (1941- )

Born in Detroit, Michigan, and educated at Dartmouth, Moriarty acted with the New York Shakespeare Festival in his early twenties, meanwhile pursuing a sideline as a jazz pianist. Finding acclaim in *Bang the Drum Slowly* (73), his third screen appearance, he has gone on to intermittent but always strong movie work. He won an Emmy for the TV serial *Holocaust*.
**Selected Films:** *My Old Man's Place* (71), *Bang the Drum Slowly* (73), *The Last Detail* (73), *Who'll stop the Rain?* (78), *The Winged Serpent* (82), *Pale Rider* (85), *The Hanoi Hilton* (87).

## MORISON, Patricia (1915- )

Morison was born in New York to a theatrical family and turned to acting after studies in dance and design. With theater experience the dark-haired beauty received a film contract in 1938, but in the next decade Hollywood consigned her to bland supporting roles. Returning to the theater in 1948, she appeared onscreen again – as George Sand in *Song Without End* (60).
**Selected Films:** *Persons in Hiding* (39), *The Song of Bernadette* (43), *Dressed to Kill* (46), *Walls of Jericho* (48), *Song Without End* (60), *Won Ton Ton, The Dog Who Saved Hollywood* (75).

## MORITA, Noriyuki 'Pat' (1930- )

California-born Morita spent years as an opening-act comic in nightclubs before breaking into television, where he appeared in a number of series including *M*A*S*H* and *Happy Days*. The Japanese-American actor has played character roles in several movies, most recently as the mentor of *The Karate Kid* (84).
**Selected Films:** *Thoroughly Modern Millie* (67), *Midway* (76), *The Karate Kid* (84), *The Karate Kid II* (86).

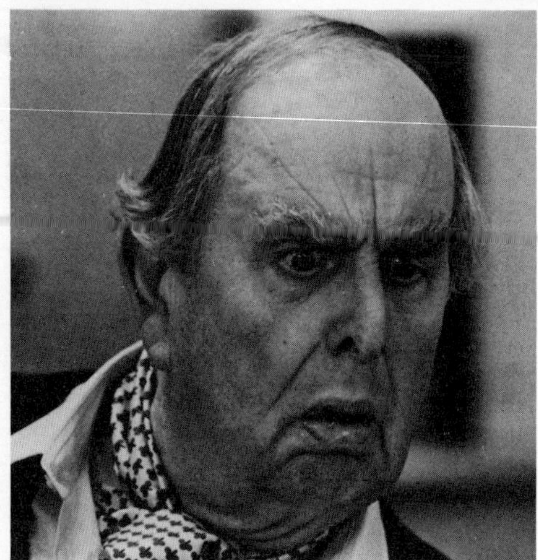

*Robert Morley in* Who Is Killing the Great Chefs of Europe *(78).*

## MORLEY, Robert (1908- )

Portly, rotund, irresistably charming, a master of jolly or pompous comedy roles, Morley is popular on both sides of the Atlantic. An actor and a playwright, he was born in Semley, Wiltshire, England. Morley prepared for a diplomatic career but opted for the stage instead, making his debut in 1929. He later played the title role in *Oscar Wilde* on stage. He made his film debut in Hollywood, playing Louis XVI opposite Norma Shearer in *Marie Antoinette* (38), earning an Oscar nomination. Since then he has had supporting roles in numerous films and is a familiar figure on television, especially for his work on commercials.
**Selected Films:** *Marie Antoinette* (38), *Major Barbara* (40), *The Young Mr Pitt* (42), *I Live in Grosvenor Square* (45), *An Outcast of the Islands* (51), *Gilbert and Sullivan* (53), *Beat the Devil* (53), *The Doctor's Dilemma* (59), *Oscar Wilde* (60), *Murder at the Gallop* (63), *Topkapi* (64), *Theatre of Blood* (73), *Who is Killing the Great Chefs of Europe?* (78), *The Human Factor* (80), *Loophole* (86).

## MORRIS, Chester (1901-1970)

Born John Chester Brooks Morris to a theatrical family in New York, Morris studied drama and made his Broadway debut in 1918, by which time he had already appeared in silent movies. His role as a gangster in *Alibi* (29) made him famous, got him an Oscar nomination, and typed him in crime dramas for the duration. For over 25 years the square-jawed Morris (he looked disconcertingly like Dick Tracy) played roles on both sides of the law, mostly in B movies including the title role of the *Boston Blackie* series. After some 50 movies and years of stage work, Morris started a comeback in *The Great White Hope* (70) but died that year of a barbiturate overdose.
**Selected Films:** *An Amateur Orphan* (17), *Alibi* (29), *The Big House* (30), *Five Came Back* (39), *Meet Boston Blackie* (41), *Blind Spot* (47), *Unchained* (55), *The Great White Hope* (70).

## MORRIS, Wayne (1914-1959)

Born Bert De Wayne Morris in Los Angeles, California, Morris studied drama at the Pasadena Playhouse and made his movie debut in *China Clipper* (36). The next year the blond and wholesome-looking actor was a hit in the title role of *Kid Galahad* (37). For a while thereafter he starred in a number of big Warner's productions. During World War II Morris was a much-decorated flyer; he returned to Hollywood to find himself relegated largely to minor action movies – an exception being a character role in *The Time of Your Life* (48). He died of a heart attack while watching plane maneuvers from an aircraft carrier.
**Selected Films:** *China Clipper* (36), *Kid Galahad* (37), *Brother Rat and a Baby* (39), *Deep Valley* (47), *The Time of Your Life* (48), *The Master Plan* (55), *Paths of Glory* (57), *The Crooked Road* (59).

## MORROW, Jeff (1913- )

New York-born Morrow acted onstage for some years before making his screen debut in the early 1950s. For almost a decade he played leads and supporting parts as a wise older man in films like the sci-fi classic *This Island Earth* (55).
**Selected Films:** *The Robe* (53), *Tanganyika* (54), *This Island Earth* (55), *The Giant Claw* (57), *The Story of Ruth* (60), *Harbor Lights* (63).

## MORROW, Vic (1932-1982)

Born in the Bronx, New York, Morrow made his screen debut in *The Blackboard Jungle* (55) and for a while played young hoods in various movies. He graduated to adult roles as a heavy (as with his Dutch Schultz in *Portrait of a Mobster* [61]) and starred in the TV series *Combat*. In the 1960s and 1970s Morrow directed a few plays and features including *Deathwatch* (66). He was killed in a helicopter accident during the filming of *Twilight Zone: The Movie* (83) in 1982.
**Selected Films:** *The Blackboard Jungle* (55), *Men in War* (57), *God's Little Acre* (58), *Portrait of A Mobster* (61), *The Bad News Bears* (76), *Twilight Zone: The Movie* (83).

## MORSE, Barry (1919- )

British-born Morse emigrated to Canada and in the early 1940s made a name in stage and screen work. His films have been occasional; he is better-known for his TV roles, among them as Lieutenant Gerard in the series *The Fugitive* and Menachem Begin in the TV movie *Sadat*.
**Selected Films:** *The Goose Steps Out* (42), *Daughter of Darkness* (48), *Justine* (69), *The Changeling* (80).

## MORSE, Robert (1931- )

Born in Newton, Masachusetts, Morse worked both on stage and screen before finding his archetypal role as the devious-but-lovable star of the Broadway musical *How to Succeed in Business Without Really Trying*. Morse repeated the role in the screen version (67), but despite that and a few other leads; his screen career never took off.
**Selected Films:** *The Proud and the Profane* (55), *The Matchmaker* (58), *The Loved One* (65), *Oh Dad, Poor Dad, Mama's Hung You in the Closet and I'm Feeling So Sad* (66), *How to Succeed in Business Without Really Trying* (67), *The Boatniks* (70).

## MOSS, Arnold (1910- )

After experience in theater and radio, Moss, born in Brooklyn, New York, made his screen debut in *Temptation* (47) and thereafter played sinister characters in a good many features.
**Selected Films:** *Temptation* (47), *The Black Book* (49), *Viva Zapata!* (52), *Gambit* (66), *Caper of the Golden Bulls* (67).

## MOSTEL, Zero (1915-1977)

Zero Mostel was born to a rabbi's family in Brooklyn, New York. His first interest, to which he returned throughout his life, was painting. During the 1930s he worked for the WPA art project. In the 1940s Mostel made a name for himself as a stand-up comic and that success took him quickly to both stage and screen. His film debut was a dual role in *Du Barry Was a Lady* (43). After a tour in the service during World War II, Mostel resumed his theater and screen work, playing a heavy in the film *Panic in the Streets* (50). For two years his movie roles were frequent, but then disaster struck in the form of the House of Un-American Activities Committee, who accused him of Communist connections. Mostel became one of the victims of that Congressional witch-hunt; it left his acting career in ruins for a decade. However, Mostel finally returned to Broadway with three triumphs in a row – in *Rhinoceros* (61), *A Funny Thing Happened on the Way to the Forum* (63), and as the first and greatest Tevye in *Fiddler on the Roof* (64). His enormous figure and wild comic persona re-emerged in the screen version of *A Funny Thing . . .* (66). During his final decade Mostel appeared in a number of popular movies including Mel Brooks' slapstick classic *The Producers* (67). One of Mostel's last films was *The Front* (76), which was based on screenwriter Walter Bernstein's life on the blacklist. The actor Josh Mostel is his son.
**Selected Films:** *Du Barry Was a Lady* (43), *Panic in the Streets* (50), *The Enforcer* (51), *Mr Belvedere Rings the Bell* (51), *A Funny Thing Happened on the Way to the Forum* (66), *The Producers* (67), *The Great Bank Robbery* (69), *Rhinoceros* (74), *Journey into Fear* (75), *The Front* (76).

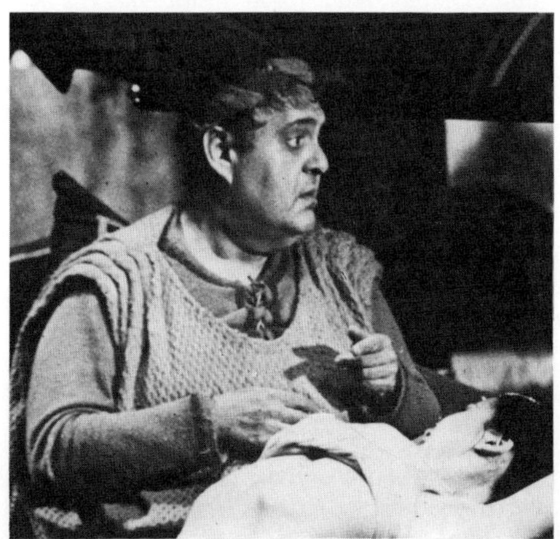

*Zero Mostel in* A Funny Thing Happened on the Way to the Forum *(66).*

## MOWBRAY, Alan (1896-1969)

Born in London, England, Mowbray came to the United States in 1923 and found work in the theater before moving to Hollywood in 1931. From his first notable part as George Washington in *Alexander Hamilton* (31), the strong-featured and suave Mowbray proved a versatile actor. Cast as a butler, general, diplomat, or in similar roles, he appeared in over 200 films.
**Selected Films:** *Alexander Hamilton* (31), *Sherlock Holmes* (32), *My Man Godfrey* (36), *Topper* (37), *Terror by Night* (45), *My Darling Clementine* (46), *The King and I* (56), *A Majority of One* (62).

## MUIR, Gavin (1907-1972)

Muir, born in Chicago, Illinois, began appearing in movies in 1936. For some three decades in dozens of movies he usually played suave bad guys.
**Selected Films:** *Mary of Scotland* (36), *Wee Willie Winkie* (37), *Nightmare* (42), *Abbott and Costello Meet the Invisible Man* (51), *The Sea Chase* (55), *Johnny Trouble* (59), *Night Tide* (63).

## MULDAUR, Diana (1943- )

American actress Muldaur has played various sophisticated but not particularly glamorous roles in films since the late 1960s. She is best known for her TV work, which includes the series *McCloud* and the TV movies *Black Beauty* and *The Word*.
**Selected Films:** *The Swimmer* (68), *The Other* (71), *McQ* (73), *The Chosen Survivors* (74).

## MULHALL, Jack (1888-1979)

Born in Wappingers Falls, New York, Mulhall entered show business as a child and films around 1913. He soon became a handsome leading man in silents, his popularity lasting through the 1920s.

Making the transition to sound, Mulhall appeared in occasional character roles through the 1950s.
**Selected Films:** *The House of Discord* (13), *Dulcy* (23), *Lady Be Good* (28), *Hollywood Boulevard* (36), *Sin Town* (42), *The Atomic Submarine* (56).

## MULHARE, Edward (1923- )

Born in County Cork, Ireland, Mulhare is a fixture of the American stage who now and then takes on a film or TV production. Among his TV appearances have been the series *The Ghost and Mrs Muir*.
**Selected Films:** *Hill 24 Doesn't Answer* (55), *Von Ryan's Express* (65), *Our Man Flint* (65), *Caprice* (67).

## MULLIGAN, Richard (1932- )

Mulligan, a native of New York, has been a character actor in films since the mid-1960s. His occasional TV work includes the series *Soap*.
**Selected Films:** *One Potato, Two Potato* (64), *The Group* (66), *Little Big Man* (70), *The Big Bus* (76), *S.O.B.* (81), *Trail of the Pink Panther* (82), *The Heavenly Kid* (85), *A Fine Mess* (86).

## MUNI, Paul (1896-1967)

Few American actors were as highly respected as was Muni, who was born Muni Weisenfreund in Lemberg, Poland, a member of an Austrian immigrant theatrical family, who got his start with New York's Yiddish Art Theater Company. Conscientious, with a meticulous eye for details of costume, makeup, walk, gestures and other externals, Muni approached his craft in a rigidly controlled way and had a thriving stage and film career. Social dramas and costume epics which celebrated famous people were his mainstay. His movie debut performance in *The Valiant* (28) earned him an Academy Award nomination for Best Actor. In his fourth film, *I Am a Fugitive from a Chain Gang* (32), he gave a sensitive portrayal of a man driven to crime by a ruthless society, and was nominated for the Oscar again. Muni played the title role in *The Story of Louis Pasteur* (36), a biopic of the life of the great French pioneer of science, and this time he won the Best Actor Academy Award. His last nomination as Best Actor came for his work as a cantankerous but kindly Brooklyn physician in *The Last Angry Man* (59).
**Selected Films:** *The Valiant* (28), *Scarface* (32), *I Am a Fugitive from a Chain Gang* (32) *The Story of Louis Pasteur* (36), *The Good Earth* (37), *The Life of Emile Zola* (37), *Juarez* (39), *We Are Not Alone* (39), *Hudson's Bay* (40), *A Song to Remember* (44), *The Last Angry Man* (59).

## MUNRO, Janet (1934-1972)

Born in Blackpool, England to a Scottish family, Munro was a leading lady in films of the 1960s and 1970s including the Disney productions *Darby O'Gill and the Little People* (59), and *The Swiss Family Robinson* (60). She was married to actor Ian Hendry from 1963 to 1971.
**Selected Films:** *Small Hotel* (57), *Third Man on the Mountain* (59), *Darby O'Gill and the Little People* (59), *The Swiss Family Robinson* (60), *The Day the Earth Caught Fire* (62), *Sebastian* (67), *Cry Wolf* (68).

## MUNSHIN, Jules (1915-1970)

New York-born Munshin danced and sang his way from Catskill resorts to stardom in the 1946 Broadway musical *Call Me Mister*. He left the stage occasionally for a movie musical, his best-known role being the tallest and rubberiest of the three sailors who go out *On the Town* (49).
**Selected Films:** *Easter Parade* (48), *Take Me Out to the Ball Game* (48), *On the Town* (49), *Ten Thousand Bedrooms* (56), *Silk Stockings* (57), *Wild and Wonderful* (64), *Monkees, Go Home* (67).

## MUNSON, Ona (1906-1955)

Born Ona Wolcott in Portland, Oregon, Munson started started in vaudeville at age 16 and went on to Broadway. Onscreen from the early 1930s, she usually played 'bad women' leads and supporting roles, most notably as Belle Watling, the tart who comforts Gable in *Gone With the Wind* (39), and Mother Gin Sling in *The Shanghai Gesture* (41). She died a suicide at 49.
**Selected Films:** *Going Wild* (30), *Gone With the Wind* (39), *Drums of the Congo* (40), *The Shanghai Gesture* (41), *The Red House* (47).

## MURPHY, Audie (1924-1971)

A boyish leading man, Murphy was America's most decorated soldier during World War II, and it was this fame that got him a movie contract. He appeared primarily in B westerns, but in a few films, notably *To Hell and Back* (55), based on his autobiography, he displayed real talent. His personal life was marred by violence and financial troubles and he was killed in a plane crash.
**Selected Films:** *Beyond Glory* (48), *The Red Badge of Courage* (51), *Destry* (55), *To Hell and Back* (55), *The Quiet American* (58), *Cast a Long Shadow* (59), *The Quick Gun* (64), *Arizona Raiders* (65), *40 Guns to Apache Pass* (67), *A Time for Dying* (71).

## MURPHY, Eddie (1961- )

Born in Brooklyn, New York, Murphy, the young black comedian, began writing comic routines for himself at the age of 15, and before he was 20 he was a regular cast member of television's popular *Saturday Night Live* program. A superb mimic and impressionist as well as a talented actor, he radiates the kind of star quality which draws audiences in to see movies.
**Selected Films:** *48 Hours* (81), *Trading Places* (83), *Beverly Hills Cop* (84), *The Golden Child* (86), *Beverly Hills Cop II* (87).

## MURPHY, George (1902- )

Born in New Haven, Connecticut, the son of an Olympic track coach, Murphy dropped out of Yale and pursued various jobs before making a name for himself as a song-and-dance man in clubs. By the late 1920s he was a famous Broadway hoofer and a few years later appeared on the screen in a long series of light musicals and comedies including *After the Dance* (35), *Hold that Co-Ed* (38), and *Little Nellie Kelly* (40). While his movie career remained steady through the 1940s, Murphy switched parties to the Republicans and began the interest in politics that would dominate the rest of his life. In the mid-1940s he was president of the Screen Actors Guild trying to defend the industry from accusations during the Red Scare. A year after his last movie, *Talk About a Stranger* (52), Murphy became chairman of the Republican National Convention, allying himself with its conservative wing. Finally, in 1964, Murphy was the first ex-actor to be elected to the US Senate; he lost his bid for re-election. His autobiogrpahy, *Didn't You Used to Be George Murphy?*, appeared in 1970.

**Selected Films:** *Kid Millions* (34), *After the Dance* (35), *Top of the Town* (37), *Hold That Co-Ed* (38), *Two Girls on Broadway* (40), *Little Nelly Kelly* (40), *For Me and My Gal* (42), *Show Business* (44), *Walk East on Beacon* (52), *Talk About a Stranger* (50).

## MURRAY, Bill (1950- )

While it is true that Bill Murray has never successfully played anyone but Bill Murray, he has managed to accumulate an impressive series of TV and screen triumphs with the engagingly sleazy, vaguely whacked-out personality that is his alone. Born in Chicago, Illinois, Murray toyed with careers in medicine and baseball before joining his brother Brian in Chicago's famed Second City improvisational troupe. He accompanied compatriots John Belushi and Harold Ramis into the radio and stage shows of the *National Lampoon* and then, in 1977, joined TV's innovative *Saturday Night Live*. On that show his character emerged: as a critic observed, 'Murray is a master of comic insecurity. He speaks in italics.' His first screen appearance was as an extra in *Next Stop, Greenwich Village* (75). Murray later starred as a loutish but lovable camp counselor in the hit *Meatballs* (79). There followed some major roles in flops – like *Caddyshack* (80) – and a short but memorable turn as Dustin Hoffman's flaky roommate in *Tootsie* (82). *Ghostbusters* (84), starring Murray and co-writers Dan Ayckroyd and Harold Ramis, was a blockbuster. In it the trio played an updated version of the Three Stooges who cleaned the spooks out of New York. Recent efforts have included his first serious role, in *The Razor's Edge* (84).

**Selected Films:** *Next Stop, Greenwich Village* (75), *Meatballs* (79), *Where the Buffalo Roam* (80), *Caddyshack* (80), *Stripes* (81), *Tootsie* (82), *Nothing Lasts Forever* (84), *The Razor's Edge* (84), *Ghostbusters* (85), *Little Shop of Horrors* (86).

*Audie Murphy in* The Red Badge of Courage *(51).*

## MURRAY, Don (1929- )

Born to a theatrical family in Hollywood, California, Murray made his several Broadway debut in 1948 and in the 1950s appeared in several major plays including *The Rose Tattoo*. In 1956 he repeated his stage role as cowboy Bo Decker in the movie version of *Bus Stop*. His co-star was Marilyn Monroe. Murray's later movies increasingly reflected his passionate social concerns, examples being his lead in *The Hoodlum Priest* (61), which he co-wrote, and his directorial debut *The Cross and the Switchblade* (70). For several seasons, he starred in the TV series *Knots Landing*.

**Selected Films:** *Bus Stop* (56), *The Bachelor Party* (57), *The Hoodlum Priest* (61), *Advise and Consent* (62), *The Plainsman* (66), *Kid Rodelo* (66), *Conquest of the Planet of the Apes* (72), *Endless Love* (81), *Peggy Sue Got Married* (86).

## MURRAY, Mae (1885-1965)

Born Marie Adrienne Koenig in Portsmouth, Virginia, Mae Murray began dancing as a child and in 1906 made her Broadway debut with Vernon Castle in *About Town*. The beautiful and graceful platinum blonde went on to appear in the Ziegfeld Follies. Murray's screen debut came with *To Have and to Hold* (16). Before long she was one of the great stars of the silents, her famous pout getting her billed as 'The Girl with the Bee-Stung Lips.' Her co-stars included John Gilbert and Rudolph Valentino. Her films included such wildly-popular and soon-forgotten productions as *The Mormon Maid* (20) and *Circe the Enchantress* (27), but also the Erich von Stroheim classic *The Merry Widow* (25). Murray's life as a star seemed to match the glamorous world of her movies. In 1926 she married her fourth husband, the Georgian Prince David Mdivani, who convinced Murray to

leave her MGM contract. As a result, she made only a few more movies. Her appearances declined in the early 1930s. A decade later she was forgotten except when her personal disasters – divorce, bankruptcy – were noted in the papers. Her 1959 autobiography, *The Self Enchanted*, was largely ignored. At 78 Murray was found wandering the streets of St Louis in a senile daze.
**Selected Films:** *To Have and to Hold* (16), *Her Body in Bond* (18), *The Mormon Maid* (20), *The Gilded Lily* (21), *Fashion Row* (24), *The Merry Widow* (25), *Circe the Enchantress* (27), *Peacock Alley* (31).

## MUSTIN, Burt (1884-1977)

American character comedian Mustin made his screen debut in the early 1950s, when he was 67. He played old men until his death. His films includes *The Big Country* (57) and *Cat Ballou* (65). His TV work includes the series *Phyllis*.
**Selected Films:** *Detective Story* (51), *The Desperate Hours* (55), *The Big Country* (57), *Huckleberry Finn* (61), *Cat Ballou* (65), *Speedway* (68), *Hail Hero* (71), *The Skin Game* (71).

# N

## NADER, George (1921- )

Born in Pasadena, California, Nader was a handsome and stalwart hero in a number of routine Universal action pictures of the 1950s. He continued to appear in films in the United States and abroad, while working in TV series including *Ellery Queen* and *Shannon*. In 1963 Nader produced and directed and appeared in the movie *A Walk by the Sea*.
**Selected Films:** *Memory of Love* (49), *Rustlers on Horseback* (50), *Monsoon* (52), *Lady Godova* (55), *Away All Boats* (56), *Joe Butterfly* (57), *A Walk by the Sea* (63), *The Human Duplicators* (65), *Beyond Atlantis* (73).

## NAGEL, Conrad (1896-1970)

Born in Keokuk, Iowa, Nagel began acting in the theater in 1914 and in films in 1919. Handsome and suave in manner, he became a popular star of drawing-room dramas and comedies. When sound arrived, Nagel proved his continuing value: often heard around Hollywood boardrooms was, 'Get Nagel. He can talk.' Thus he continued his sophisticated ways into films through the 1950s, gradually changing over to character roles. Nagel was a co-founder and president of the Academy of Motion Picture Arts and Sciences and one of the creators of the Academy Awards.
**Selected Films:** *Little Women* (19), *The Exquisite Sinner* (26), *The Jazz Singer* (27), *Bad Sister* (31), *I Want a Divorce* (40), *Stage Struck* (48), *All That Heaven Allows* (55), *The Swan* (56), *The Man Who Understood Women* (59).

## NAISH, J Carrol (1900-1973)

This Irish-American character actor born in New York, got his start on the stage, and made his movie debut in 1926. During his more than four decades before the camera, he played people of every race and nationality except his own – Chinese, Indian, Arab, French, Italian, German and many more – all were his province. He also played Charlie Chan in a TV series (58).
**Selected Films:** *What Price Glory?* (26), *Cheer Up and Smile* (30), *Lives of a Bengal Lancer* (35), *Beau Geste* (39), *Blood and Sand* (41), *Sahara* (43), *A Medal for Benny* (45), *Joan of Arc* (48), *Annie Get Your Gun* (50), *The Young Don't Cry* (57), *The Hanged Man* (64), *The Blood of Frankenstein* (70).

## NAISMITH, Laurence (1908- )

Born Lawrence Johnson in England, Naismith split his career between theater and film acting. He was a staple character actor in movies from the 1940s into the 1970s, his films ranging from Olivier's *Richard III* (56) to adventures like *Sink the Bismarck!* (60) to musicals like *Camelot* (67).
**Selected Films:** *Trouble in the Air* (47), *The Beggar's Opera* (52), *Mogambo* (53), *Richard III* (56), *Sink the Bismarck!* (60), *Jason and the Argonauts* (63), *Camelot* (67), *Diamonds are Forever* (71), *The Amazing Mr Blunden* (72).

## NALDI, Nita (1899-1961)

Naldi, born Anita Donna Dooley in New York City, began in *The Ziegfeld Follies* and then became famous as a silent movie star in the 1920s. She tempted Valentino in *Blood and Sand* (22) and, after her film career faded when sound movies replaced silent pictures, she appeared occasionally on stage and later on television.
**Selected Films:** *Dr Jekyll and Mr Hyde* (20), *Blood and Sand* (22), *Cobra* (25), *The Marriage Whirl* (26), *The Lady Who Lied* (27), *What Price Beauty* (28).

## NAPIER, Alan (1903- )

Born Alan Napier Clavering in Birmingham, England, and later attending the Royal Academy of Dramatic Arts, Napier played servants and aristocrats in dozens of movies from the 1930s through the 1960s, including the Earl of Warwick in *Joan of Arc* (48) and Cicero in *Julius Caesar* (53). The tall, thin actor of dignified mien was also familiar as the butler in the TV series *Batman*.
**Selected Films:** *Caste* (30), *Random Harvest* (42), *The Uninvited* (44), *Joan of Arc* (48), *Julius Caesar* (53), *The Court Jester* (55), *Marnie* (64).

## NATWICK, Mildred (1908- )

Natwick, born in Baltimore, Maryland, made her Broadway debut in 1932 and established herself as a major character actress. In movies occasionally since 1940, the sharp-featured and sharp-voiced Natwick usually plays spunky or eccentric older women, such as Mrs Allshard in *She Wore a Yellow Ribbon* (49), and Miss Gravely in *The Trouble With Harry* (55). In 1967 she received a supporting-actress Oscar nomination for her role in *Barefoot in the Park*.

**Selected Films:** *The Long Voyage Home* (40), *The Enchanted Cottage* (45), *The Late George Apley* (47), *She Wore a Yellow Ribbon* (49), *The Trouble with Harry* (55), *Barefoot in the Park* (67), *Daisy Miller* (74), *Kiss Me Goodbye* (82).

*Alla Nazimova as* Salome *(23).*

## NAZIMOVA, Alla (1879-1945)

Born Alla Nazimoff in Yalta in Russia, Nazimova mastered the violin in her youth before being drawn to the stage and studying with Stanislavsky. She came to the United States in 1905 and established herself on Broadway, where she was known especially for her Ibsen roles, before starting in films in 1916. Her screen image was remote and haunting, her acting highly stylized. The public responded enthusiastically to her performance opposite Valentino in *Camille* (21) and the title role in *Salome* (23). In the sound era Nazimova continued to play occasional character roles.

**Selected Films:** *War Brides* (16), *The Red Lantern* (19), *Camille* (21), *A Doll's House* (22), *Salome* (23), *My Son* (25), *Escape* (40), *The Bridge of San Luis Rey* (44), *Since You Went Away* (46).

## NEAGLE, Anna (1904-1986)

Born Marjorie Robertson in London, Anna Neagle began dancing onstage at an early age. At 14 she came to the attention of producer Herbert Wilcox, who was to become her producer and director and, in good time, her husband. First appearing in films in 1930, Neagle became the most popular British leading lady of the decade, specializing in costumed heroines, such as *Nell Gwyn* (34), Queen Victoria in *Victoria the Great* (37) and *Sixty Glorious Years* (38), and later, as aviatrix Amy Johnson in *They Flew Alone* (42). In 1939 Neagle came to the United States for a few films, among them the title role in *Nurse Edith Cavell* (39) and *No, No, Nanette* (40). Her career slowed in the 1940s and by the 1950s she was appearing only sporadically in movies. After producing three films in the late 1950s, she retired from the screen to concentrate on work in the theater. Neagle was named a Dame of the British Empire in 1969 and published two autobiographies, *It's Been Fun* (49) and *There's Always Tomorrow* (74).

**Selected Films:** *The School for Scandal* (30), *Bitter Sweet* (33), *Nell Gwyn* (34), *Victoria the Great* (37), *Sixty Glorious Years* (38), *Nurse Edith Cavell* (39), *Irene* (40), *No, No, Nanette* (40), *Forever and a Day* (43), *Spring in Park Lane* (48), *They Flew Alone* (42), *Odette* (50), *The Lady with a Lamp* (51), *The Lady is a Square* (58).

## NEAL, Patricia (1926-    )

Born in Packard, Kentucky, Neal, of the well-modulated voice and superb acting talent, made her film debut in a pleasant farce, *John Loves Mary* (49). But it wasn't until she made *Hud* (63), for which she won both an Academy Award and a British Film Academy Award for Best Actress for her portrayal of an earthy woman bruised by men and the drabness of her life, that she found her film niche. She won another British Film Academy Award for her work as a nurse in *In Harm's Way* (64). She was successful on Broadway from the very beginning. After studying drama at Northwestern University, she made her Broadway debut in 1945 in *Seven Mirrors*. The following year she played a leading role in Lillian Hellman's *Another Part of the Forest*, and won a Tony for it. Her Hollywood career was really going nowhere, except for some good reviews for her performance as a nurse in *The Hasty Heart* (50), so in 1952 she returned to Broadway to appear in *The Children's Hour*, and the critics were enraptured. In 1965 she suffered a series of strokes that totally incapacitated and nearly killed her. With the drive and encouragement of her then husband, writer Roald Dahl, she recovered. She returned to the movies and was nominated for another Academy Award for *The Subject Was Roses* (68).

**Selected Films:** *John Loves Mary* (49), *The Fountainhead* (49), *The Hasty Heart* (50), *The Breaking Point* (50), *The Day the Earth Stood Still* (51), *A Face in the Crowd* (57), *Breakfast at Tiffany's* (61), *Hud* (63), *In Harm's Way* (64), *The Subject Was Roses* (68), *The Homecoming* (71), *The Passage* (79).

## NEAL, Tom (1914-1972)

In the early years of his roller-coaster career, Neal, born in Evanston, Illinois, boxed in college, tried and failed on Broadway, and earned a Harvard Law degree in 1938 – the same year that he broke into films. For over a decade he was a staple tough hero of low-budget movies before making the

headlines in 1951, when he beat up Franchot Tone in a brawl over actress Barbara Payton (who then married Tone and Neal in succession). In 1965, after his screen career and a landscaping business had collapsed, Neal was charged with manslaughter for shooting his third wife. He died shortly after his release from prison.
**Selected Films:** *Out West with the Hardys* (39), *The Racket Man* (45), *Navy Bound* (51), *Red Desert* (51).

## NEFF (or KNEF), Hildegarde (1925- )

Born in Ulm, Germany, Hildegard Knef made her first screen appearances in Nazi propaganda films late in the World War II. After the war she found a few roles in German films, among them *The Murderers Are Among Us* (46). This brought the beautiful blonde with the sultry voice to the attention of David O Selznick, who brought Knef to America in 1947. However, the trip produced no parts and Knef returned to Germany for *Film Without a Name* (48). Finally she came to the United States to appear – now as Neff – in *Decision Before Dawn* (51) and *The Snows of Kilimanjaro* (52). Despite a reputation as 'the thinking man's Marlene Dietrich,' her screen career never quite took off; her roles remained occasional in international films through the 1970s, among them in *The Lost Continent* (68). Meanwhile, in 1955 she triumphed on Broadway in the lead in *Silk Stockings*, thereafter developing a second career as a cabaret singer. Knef's frank 1971 narrative of her adventurous life, *The Gift Horse*, was a best-seller; a serious bout with cancer was described in her 1975 book *The Verdict*.
**Selected Films:** *The Murderers Are Among Us* (46), *Film Without a Name* (48), *The Sinner* (50), *Decision Before Dawn* (51), *The Snows of Kilimanjaro* (52), *Henriette* (52), *The Girl from Hamburg* (57), *And So to Bed* (63), *Mozambique* (65), *The Lost Continent* (68), *Fedora* (78), *The Future of Emily* (86).

## NEGRI, Pola (1897-1987)

A successful stage actress who led a colorful life, Negri, born Appolonia Chalupek in Janowa, Poland, became a German film star, at her best when directed by Ernst Lubitsch. Then she went to Hollywood, where she was an exotic attraction on the silent screen. Talkies killed her American career, but she never wholly abandoned pictures.
**Selected Films:** *Die Bestia* (15), *Madame du Barry* (18), *Bella Donna* (23), *Forbidden Paradise* (26), *Madame Bovary* (35), *Hi Diddle Diddle* (43), *The Moonspinners* (64).

## NELLIGAN, Kate (1951- )

An actress who projects both strength and beauty, Nelligan born Patricia Colleen Nelligan in London, Ontario, has been one of the most notable of her generation of stage players. In the British theater, she has played Stella in *A Streetcar Named Desire* and the title role in *Lulu*. Her film appearances have been occasional, among them the starring role in the spy thriller *Eye of the Needle* (80) and the title role in *Eleni* (85).
**Selected Films:** *The Romantic Englishwoman* (75), *Dracula* (79), *Eye of the Needle* (80), *Without a Trace* (82), *Eleni* (85).

*Kate Nelligan in* Eleni *(85).*

## NELSON, Barry (1920- )

Barry Nelson was born Robert Neilson in Oakland, California, and graduated from college right into an MGM contract in 1941, when Hollywood was in the market for actors to replace those going to war. Indeed, the bulk of Nelson's screen work was during World War II. After his debut in *Shadow of the Thin Man* (41), he played in several war movies including *Bataan* (43) and *A Guy Named Joe* (44). After the war Nelson turned to the stage with considerable success – he has starred in Broadway productions including *Winged Victory*, *The Moon is Blue*, *Mary Mary* and *Cactus Flower*. He repeated his lead in the screen versions of two of these plays – *Winged Victory* (44) and *Mary Mary* (63). Otherwise, the amiable, stocky actor is most familiar for his roles in TV productions, among them the TV series *My Favorite Husband* and *Hudson's Bay*.
**Selected Films:** *Shadow of the Thin Man* (41), *Johnny Eager* (41), *Rio Rita* (42), *The Human Comedy* (43), *Bataan* (43), *A Guy Named Joe* (44), *Winged Victory* (44), *The Man with My Face* (51), *The First Travelling Saleslady* (56), *Mary, Mary* (63), *Airport* (69), *Pete 'n Tillie* (72).

## NELSON, Craig T (1946- )

Multi-talented American actor Nelson wrote for television and produced short films about American artists before concentrating on his movie

career. Making his screen debut in *...And Justice for All* (79), he has played sturdy leads and supporting roles in a number of recent popular films including *Poltergeist* (82). His TV work has included appearances in *Charlie's Angels* and *How the West Was Won.*
**Selected Films:** *...And Justice for All* (79), *The Formula* (80), *Private Benjamin* (80), *Poltergeist* (82), *Silkwood* (83), *The Killing Fields* (85), *Poltergeist II* (86).

## NELSON, Gene (1920- )

Born Gene Berg in Seattle, Washington, Nelson returned to films in *I Wonder Who's Kissing Her Now* (47) after an appearance in uniform in *This Is the Army* (43). He went on to sing and dance his way through a number of musicals into the 1960s, the most substantial of them *Oklahoma!* (55). After a serious accident he turned to directing – mostly musicals like *Harum Scarum* (65).
**Selected Films:** *This Is the Army* (43), *I Wonder Who's Kissing Her Now* (47), *Gentleman's Agreement* (48), *Tea for Two* (51), *Lullaby of Broadway* (52), *So This Is Paris* (55), *Oklahoma!* (55), *The Purple Hills* (61), *Thunder Island* (63).

## NELSON, Judd (1959- )

Born in Portland, Maine, Nelson began acting in junior high school. When he arrived at Haverford College, he joined theatrical clubs because of the urging of his lawyer-father and state congressman mother. He left college after two years to study in New York at the Stella Adler Conservatory. His first movie was *Fandango* (85).
**Selected Films:** *Fandango* (85), *St Elmo's Fire* (85), *The Breakfast Club* (85), *Blue City* (86), *From the Hip*, (87).

## NELSON, Ozzie (1906-1975)

Born in Jersey City, New Jersey, Nelson earned a law degree before starting a dance band and marrying his singer Harriet Hilliard in 1935. They developed a following on radio before starting their *Adventures of Ozzie and Harriet* show, which consisted of rather unadventurous stories of suburban life. The show ran over two decades on radio and TV, later co-starring sons David and Ricky. Ozzie's screen appearances were few, mostly in musicals of the 1940s. He directed his son Ricky in *Love and Kisses* (65).
**Selected Films:** *The Letter* (40), *Strictly in the Groove* (42), *Honeymoon Lodge* (43), *Here Come the Nelsons* (52), *The Impossible Years* (68).

## NELSON, Rick (1940-1986)

Born into the family business, the Nelson family TV series, Rick first appeared in *Here Come the Nelsons* (52) and on the series before starting a career as a rock singer, which continued until his death. His few screen appearances, most notably in Hawks' *Rio Bravo* (59), revealed no strong presence as an actor. Nelson died in a plane crash.
**Selected Films:** *Here Come the Nelsons* (52), *Rio Bravo* (59), *The Wackiest Ship in the Army* (60), *Love and Kisses* (65).

## NELSON, Willie (1933- )

One of the best-liked country/western musicians of his time, singer of 'Georgia on My Mind' and other hits, Nelson born in Waco, Texas, occasionally appears in movies as a singing character actor.
**Selected Films:** *The Electric Horseman* (79), *Honeysuckle Rose* (80), *Barbarosa* (82), *Song Writer* (85).

## NERO, Franco (1942- )

Born Franco Spartanero in Italy, Nero has played handsome romantic leads in international films since the 1960s. Perhaps his best-known role was as Lancelot in *Camelot* (67).
**Selected Films:** *Celestina* (64), *The Bible* (66), *Camelot* (67), *Tristana* (70), *Force Ten from Navarone* (78), *Enter the Ninja* (81), *Sweet Country* (87).

## NESBITT, Cathleen (1888-1981)

Beginning her theatrical career in her native Britain in 1910, Nesbitt, born in Cheshire, England, successively acted the full range of roles from beautiful heroines to impossibly old ladies for the next 70 years. Her films were a sideline, most of them character parts in her later years. On television she starred in the series *The Farmer's Daughter* and played the Countess of Southwold in *Upstairs, Downstairs.*
**Selected Films:** *Criminal at Large* (32), *Nicholas Nickleby* (47), *An Affair to Remember* (57), *Staircase* (69), *Family Plot* (76), *Julia* (77).

## NETTLETON, Lois (1929- )

American character actress Nettleton made her film debut in the early 1960s and since then has played supporting roles in mostly minor films. Since the 1970s she has appeared in a number of made-for-TV movies including *Fear on Trial* and *Centennial.*
**Selected Films:** *Period of Adjustment* (62), *Valley of Mystery* (66), *The Honkers* (72), *The Best Little Whorehouse in Texas* (82).

## NEWHART, Bob (1923- )

Born in Oak Park, Illinois, Newhart first made his name as a fashionably cynical stand-up comic with a 'button-down mind.' He has appeared in a few movies since the early 1960s but is best known for his long-running TV series *The Bob Newhart Show* and *Newhart.*
**Selected Films:** *Hell is for Heroes* (62), *Catch 22* (70), *Cold Turkey* (70), *The First Family* (80).

## NEWLEY, Anthony (1931- )

Born the son of a shipping clerk in London, Anthony Newley entered show business at age 14 and soon after became a child star in movies, most notably as the Artful Dodger in *Oliver Twist* (48). Upon his coming of age in the 1950s his movie career fell off somewhat and he began to organize his other talents, which at length led to the smash musical of the London and Broadway stages, *Stop the World – I Want to Get Off*. Newley co-authored, co-composed and directed the show, and his recording of one of its songs, 'What Kind of Fool Am I,' was a hit as well. His next stage production, *The Roar of the Greasepaint, the Smell of the Crowd*, succeeded nearly as well, as giving Newley a great deal more recognition in movies. After appearing with Rex Harrison in the musical film *Dr Doolittle* (67), Newley brought out his own grand screen production – he directed, produced, co-wrote, co-composed, and starred in *Can Heironymus Merkin Ever Forget Mercy Humppe and Find True Happiness?* (69). Despite its epic title, the film was received as a regrettable ego trip. His screen work since has been occasional, though it still displays his versatility: he directed *Summertree* (71) and acted in and wrote the songs for *Mr Quilp* (75). For a time he was married to actress Joan Collins.
**Selected Films:** *The Little Ballerina* (47), *Oliver Twist* (48), *Cockleshell Heroes* (56), *No Time to Die* (58), *Doctor Doolittle* (67), *Can Heironymus Merkin Ever Forget Mercy Humppe and Find True Happiness?* (69), *Mr Quilp* (75), *It Seemed Like a Good Idea at the Time* (76).

## NEWMAN, Nanette (1934- )

Born in Northampton, England, Newman has played leads in mostly British films since the early 1950s, among them Sally Athelney in *Of Human Bondage* (64). One of her few appearances in American movies was in *The Stepford Wives* (75). She is married to writer and director Bryan Forbes.
**Selected Films:** *Personal Affair* (53), *League of Gentlemen* (59), *Of Human Bondage* (64), *The Wrong Box* (66), *The Raging Moon* (70), *The Stepford Wives* (75), *International Velvet* (78).

## NEWMAN, Paul (1925- )

Newman has looks, talent, a successful marriage, a reputation for being a nice guy who gives time and money to worthy causes, a growing salad dressing company and an acting career that merits acclaim. As if this weren't enough, he possesses the bluest pair of eyes ever to look out from a movie screen. He once said, 'I picture my epitaph: "Here lies Paul Newman, who died a failure because his eyes turned brown."' He was born Paul Leonard Newman in Cleveland, Ohio, the son of a sporting goods store owner, and was raised in the affluent suburb of Shaker Heights. Newman entered Kenyon College after serving in World War II. His family expected him to go into business and, as the film deals that he would later negotiate prove, he was more than competent when it came to making money. But he preferred acting to economics, and attended the Yale Drama School and New York's prestigious Actors Studio. His appearance on Broadway in William Inge's *Picnic* led to a movie contract, but his first film, *The Silver Chalice* (54), a costume epic, only served to embarrass him. His career survived, but that of co-star Pier Angeli didn't. Eager to continue his stage career and skeptical of Hollywood, Newman decided to make his home near New York, and he now lives in Westport, Connecticut. He developed a knack for choosing good scripts and many of his movies have been box office blockbusters. He won the Cannes Film Festival Award for Best Actor for *The Long Hot Summer* (58). He has been showered with Oscar nominations – for *Cat on a Hot Tin Roof* (58); *The Hustler* (61), which brought him a British Film Academy Award; *Hud* (63); *Cool Hand Luke* (67), *Absence of Malice* (81); and *The Verdict* (82). He won another British Film Academy Award for the smash hit, *Butch Cassidy and the Sundance* Kid (69), which matched him brilliantly with Robert Redford and allowed Newman's unsuspected gift for comedy and frivolity to shine. Hollywood finally gave him a Special Academy Award in 1985 'in recognition of his many memorable and compelling screen performances and for his personal integrity and dedication to his craft.' He finally won the best Actor Award for *The Color of Money*

*Paul Newman and Geraldine Page in* Sweet Bird of Youth (62).

(86), a sequel of his earlier hit, *The Hustler*. In 1968 Newman made his directing debut with the film *Rachel, Rachel*, starring his second wife, the talented actress Joanne Woodward. He went on to further directing and producing under the aegis of First Productions, a company formed by Newman, Sidney Poitier, Barbra Streisand and other stars during the 1970s. He is still making blockbuster pictures, but his acting time has been cut because of his activities in his food company that markets the Paul Newman brands of salad dressing, spaghetti sauce and popcorn, and his passion for racing his race cars.
**Selected Films:** *The Silver Chalice* (54), *Somebody Up There Likes Me* (56), *The Long Hot Summer* (58), *The Left Handed Gun* (58), *Cat on a Hot Tin Roof* (58), *The Young Philadelphians* (59), *Exodus* (60), *The Hustler* (61), *Sweet Bird of Youth* (62), *Hud* (63), *The Prize* (63), *The Outrage* (64), *Torn Curtain* (66), *Harper* (66), *Hombre* (67), *Cool Hand Luke* (67), *Butch Cassidy and the Sundance Kid* (69), *Judge Roy Bean* (72), *The Sting* (73), *The Towering Inferno* (74), *The Drowning Pool* (75), *Slap Shot* (77), *Absence of Malice* (81), *Fort Apache, the Bronx* (81), *The Verdict* (82), *Harry and Son* (84), *The Color of Money* (86).

## NEWMAR, Julie (1930- )

Born in Los Angeles, California, the tall and leggy Newmar was a decorative sexpot in occasional movies and Broadway musicals of the 1950s and 1960s, an example being her Stupefyin' Jones in *Li'l Abner* (59). She also appeared in the TV series *My Living Doll* and *Batman*.
**Selected Films:** *Seven Brides for Seven Brothers* (55), *The Marriage Go Round* (60), *Mackenna's Gold* (68), *The Maltese Bippy* (69), *Up Your Teddy Bare* (70).

## NEWTON, Robert (1905-1956)

Newton had thunder in his voice and fire in his rolling eyes. He was described as being 'a ham, but a succulent one.' This British actor born in Shaftesbury, was a gripping scene stealer, a top box office star who played villains with panache. His Bill Sikes in *Oliver Twist* (48) and his Long John Silver in *Treasure Island* (50) were bravura performances.
**Selected Films:** *Reunion* (32), *Farewell Again* (37), *Major Barbara* (40), *Hatter's Castle* (41), *This Happy Breed* (44), *Henry V* (45), *Oliver Twist* (48), *Treasure Island* (50), *Tom Brown's Schooldays* (51), *The Beachcomber* (54), *Long John Silver* (55), *Around the World in Eighty Days* (56).

## NEWTON-JOHN, Olivia (1948- )

Singer and sometime actress Olivia Newton-John was born in Cambridge, England, and grew up in Australia. She began singing professionally in England in her teens. By the 1970s the delicate blonde had worked her way up from cabarets and TV to pop music stardom, with a full complement of gold records and Grammys. Newton-John's screen debut was in the hit rock musical *Grease* (78), in which she played a high-school student and the love interest of John Travolta. Newton-John is married to actor Matt Lattanzi.
**Selected Films:** *Grease* (78), *Xanadu* (80), *Two of a Kind* (83).

## NEY, Richard (1917- )

New York-born Ney stumbled into films in the early 1940s, around the time of his brief marriage to actress Greer Garson. Handsome and distinguished-looking, he sporadically played leads and supporting roles in films into the 1960s, including the role of John Apley in *The Late George Apley* (47). He later became a financier and writer of best-selling money books like *The Wall Street Jungle*.
**Selected Films:** *Mrs Miniver* (42), *The Late George Apley* (47), *Joan of Arc* (48), *Babes in Bagdad* (52), *The Premature Burial* (62).

## NICHOLS, Barbara (1929-1976)

Born Barbara Nickerauer in Queens, New York, Nichols was a model and a stripper before turning to acting in the 1950s. She played blonde molls and tarts with more than usual success in several films including *The Sweet Smell of Success* (57), and *The Naked and the Dead* (58).
**Selected Films:** *Miracle in the Rain* (56), *The Sweet Smell of Success* (57), *The King and Four Queens* (57), *The Naked and the Dead* (58), *Where the Boys Are* (63), *The Loved One* (65), *Charley and the Angel* (73).

## NICHOLSON, Jack (1937- )

One of the most charismatic and individualistic of Hollywood stars, Jack Nicholson generally plays

rebels, drifters, outsiders and free spirits. His sarcastic grin and wry bitterness have illuminated some of the finest movies of the 1970s and 1980s. With his talent and idiosyncratic style, he looked like a safe bet for stardom, yet he spent over a decade making cheap horror films. Born in Neptune, New Jersey, Nicholson visited California at the age of 17 and became hooked on motion pictures, finding work as an office boy in M-G-M's cartoon department. He joined the Players Ring Theater and appeared on stage and on television before producer-director Roger Corman cast him in horror and action cheapies, beginning with *The Cry Baby Killer* (58), a film about a juvenile delinquent who panics when he thinks he has committed a murder. Soon Nicholson began writing and producing low-budget films with Corman's protégé, Monte Hellman. He wrote *Head* (68) for the rock group, The Monkees. He must have felt that he would be stranded forever in the netherworld of B movies, but by a stroke of luck he wound up in *Easy Rider* (69), a box office smash and a pace-setter in films geared to the young. He was great as a man who abandoned respectability to join his hippie friends. In many ways a hippie himself, the irreverant Nicholson was in tune with the mood of the 1960s and early 1970s. Audiences sensed this, and *Five Easy Pieces* (70) made him a superstar. Nicholson began collecting Academy Award nominations with some regularity. Although *Chinatown* (74) earned him a New York Film Critics Award, it wasn't until *One Flew Over the Cuckoo's Nest* (76) that he won the Oscar for Best Actor. He gave an eccentric but fascinating performance in Stanely Kubrick's *The Shining* (79), a horror film again, but this time a grade A one. Like other superb movie actors, Nicholson rebounds resiliently from commercial failures, and he has had his share, coming up with the right part at the critical moment to save his career. This was the case with *Terms of Endearment* (83), which won him an Academy Award for Best Supporting Actor as the cynical ex-astronaut with the heart of gold.
**Selected Films:** *The Cry Baby Killer* (58), *Studs Lonigan* (61), *The Little Shop of Horrors* (62), *The Raven* (63), *Ensign Pulver* (65), *Hell's Angels on Wheels* (67), *Easy Rider* (69), *Five Easy Pieces* (70), *Carnal Knowledge* (71), *The Last Detail* (74), *Chinatown* (74), *The Passenger* (75), *One Flew Over the Cuckoo's Nest* (76), *The Shining* (79), *The Postman Always Rings Twice* (82), *Reds* (82), *Terms of Endearment* (83), *Prizzi's Honor* (85), *Heartburn* (86), *The Witches of Eastwick* (87), *Ironweed* (87).

*Jack Nicholson in* One Flew Over the Cuckoo's Nest *(76).*

## NICOL, Alex (1919- )

Born in Ossining, New York, Nicol began acting onstage in 1938 and moved to the screen in 1950. From then into the 1970s he starred mostly in minor action pictures, now and then directing low-budget thrillers like *The Screaming Skull* (58).
**Selected Films:** *The Sleeping City* (50), *Strategic Air Command* (55), *Three Came Back* (60), *Ride and Kill* (63), *Bloody Mama* (69), *Woman in the Rain* (76).

## NIELSEN, Leslie (1925- )

Born in Regina, Saskatchewan, Nielsen came to show business by way of radio in his native Canada. After stage and TV experience he made his film debut in the 1950s. Among his best known films were the sci-fi classic *Forbidden Planet* (56) and *The Plainsman* (66) in which he played Custer. He is more familiar from his roles in several TV series including *The Bold Ones*, and *Police Squad*.
**Selected Films:** *Forbidden Planet* (56), *The Vagabond King* (56), *Tammy and the Bachelor* (57), *The Plainsman* (66), *Beau Geste* (66), *The Poseidon Adventure* (72), *Airplane* (80).

## NILSSON, Anna Q (1889-1974)

Born in Ystad, Nilsson emigrated to the United States from her native Sweden at age 14. After working as an artists' model she made her film debut in 1911. Over the next seventeen years she was a beautiful leading lady in dozens of silents. The advent of sound and a riding accident stopped her career in the late 1920s. She later returned for a few small roles.
**Selected Films:** *Molly Pitcher* (11), *Seven Keys to Baldpate* (17), *The Masked Woman* (25), *The Farmer's Daughter* (47), *Sunset Boulevard* (50).

## NIMOY, Leonard (1931- )

Born in Boston, Massachusetts, this lean-faced character actor is most famous for popularizing the science-fiction genre with his television character, Mr Spock, in the *Star Trek* series. This series was a forum for some of the most intelligent science-fiction film presented during the 1960s, and the intriguing Vulcan provided many an interesting study of psychology and the struggle of emotion versus logic. Nimoy was a drama student at Boston College, then spent several years playing small parts in Hollywood and on television before landing the *Star Trek* role. He has had several poetry books published, including *I Am Not Spock*. Having returned to motion pictures with the current *Star Trek* sequels, some of which he has directed, Nimoy has also appeared in the remake of a science-fiction classic, *The Invasion of the Body Snatchers* (78).

**Selected Films:** *Queen for a Day* (51), *Rhubarb* (51), *The Balcony* (63), *Catlow* (72), *Invasion of the Body Snatchers* (78), *Star Trek – The Movie* (79), *Star Trek II: The Wrath of Khan* (82), *Star Trek III: The Search for Spock* (84), *Star Trek IV: The Voyage Home* (86).

## NIVEN, David (1909-1983)

Debonair and urbane, Niven was a dashing light comedian and an attractive romantic lead. Born James David Graham Niven in Kirriemuir, Scotland, he came from a long line of professional soldiers and attended the Royal Military Academy at Sandhurst, England, then served with the Highland Light Infantry in Malta. But the military life was not for Niven and he began drifting around the world aimlessly, working as a lumberman, a reporter, a promoter and even becoming a small-time crook. When he hit Los Angeles he decided to try his luck as a movie extra. His looks, charm and gentlemanly diction helped him to move quickly into leading and strong supporting roles and he learned his craft as he went along. *Dodsworth* (36) set him on the road to stardom. He was noteworthy in *Bluebeard's Eighth Wife* (38) and *Bachelor Mother* (39). By the start of World War II, Niven was a seasoned professional – competent and reliable – adding a touch of class to many movies. He left Hollywood to join the British Army as a lieutenant and rose to the rank of colonel. After the war, Niven appeared regularly in both British and American pictures, moving comfortably between Hollywood and London, continuing in well-bred roles. He was often far superior to the vehicles he appeared in. In the 1950s he branched out into television and he also starred in the most successful film of his career, *Around the World in Eighty Days* (56), when he played Phileas Fogg in this sweeping costume epic. Niven was long overdue for an Oscar and at last he won an Academy Award for Best Actor and the New York Critics Best Actor Award for his touching performance in *Separate Tables* (58). A gifted author, he wrote a novel and two exceedingly popular autobiographies, *The Moon's a Balloon* and *Bring on the Empty Horses*.

*David Niven in* The Pink Panther *(64).*

**Selected Films:** *Barbary Coast* (35), *Rose Marie* (36), *Thank You Jeeves* (36), *The Charge of the Light Brigade* (36), *Dodsworth* (36), *The Prisoner of Zenda* (37), *Bluebeard's Eighth Wife* (38), *Wuthering Heights* (39), *Bachelor Mother* (39), *Raffles* (40), *The First of the Few* (41), *The Way Ahead* (44), *Stairway to Heaven* (46), *The Other Love* (47), *The Bishop's Wife* (47), *Enchantment* (48), *A Kiss in the Dark* (49), *The Toast of New Orleans* (50), *The Moon Is Blue* (53), *Carrington VC* (55), *Around the World in Eighty Days* (56), *Bonjour Tristesse* (58), *Separate Tables* (58), *Ask Any Girl* (59), *Please Don't Eat the Daisies* (60), *The Guns of Navarone* (61), *The Pink Panther* (64), *Casino Royale* (67), *The Brain* (69), *Paper Tiger* (75), *Murder by Death* (76), *Death on the Nile* (78), *A Nightingale Sang in Berkeley Square* (80), *The Curse of the Pink Panther* (83).

## NOIRET, Philippe (1931- )

Born in Lille, France, Noiret had been a stage actor with the Theatre National Populaire in Paris before making his film debut in *La Pointe Courte* (55). He received great critical acclaim for his performance as the uncle in *Zazie dans le Metro* (60), but is best known for the series of films he made with director Bertrand Tavernier. He has also appeared in a number of American and British thrillers.

**Selected Films:** *La Pointe Courte* (55), *Zazie dans le Metro* (60), *The Night of the Generals* (66), *Topaz* (69), *L'Horloger de Saint-Paul* (73), *La Grande Bouffe* (73), *Dear Detective* (78), *Coup de Torchon* (81), *My New Partner* (84), *Next Summer* (86).

## NOLAN, Jeannette (1911- )

Born in Los Angeles, California, Nolan made a striking debut as Lady Macbeth in Orson Welles' film of *Macbeth* (48). She went on to play character roles in movies through the 1970s and in TV series including *The Richard Boone Show* and *The Virginian* – often starring alongside her husband, actor John McIntire.

**Selected Films:** *Macbeth* (48), *The Big Heat* (53), *April Love* (57), *The Man Who Shot Liberty Valance* (62), *The Winds of Autumn* (76) *Avalanche* (78).

## NOLAN, Lloyd (1902-1985)

A long-time character actor with a plain but nonetheless memorable face, Lloyd Nolan during his long career was adept at everything from comedy to villainy to serious drama. Born in San Francisco, California, he was a seaman before beginning to act onstage around 1927. After a long apprenticeship he made his screen debut in *Stolen Harmony* (35). From that point he spent a decade largely in B action movies, both as heroes and heavies. With *A Tree Grows in Brooklyn* (45) he made himself known as a strong character actor and his pictures became more notable, among them *The House on 92nd Street* (45) and Fred Zinnemann's *A Hatful of Rain* (57). In 1953-54 Nolan played a legendary role as Captain Queeg in the Broadway play *The Caine Mutiny Court Martial*. His films included the disaster thrillers *Earthquake* (74) and *Airport* (69). His valedictory performance, and a striking one, was as a tired old actor in Woody Allen's *Hannah and Her Sisters* (86).

**Selected Films:** *Stolen Harmony* (35), *G-Men* (35), *Michael Shayne, Private Detective* (40), *Bataan* (43), *A Tree Grows in Brooklyn* (45), *The House on 92nd Street* (45), *The Lady in the Lake* (46), *The Last Hunt* (56), *A Hatful of Rain* (57), *Circus World* (64), *Airport* (69), *Earthquake* (69), *The Private Files of J Edgar Hoover* (78), *Hannah and Her Sisters* (86).

## NOLTE, Nick (1940- )

Born in Omaha, Nebraska, Nolte began his screen career in the 1970s and for a few years was mostly seen in leading roles in TV movies including *Rich Man, Poor Man*. After finding popularity but not critical success starring with Jacqueline Bisset in *The Deep* (77), he developed into an able leading man in action movies like *48 Hours* (82).

**Selected Films:** *Return to Macon County* (75), *The Deep* (77), *Who'll Stop the Rain?* (78), *North Dallas Forty* (79), *48 Hours* (82), *Cannery Row* (82), *The Ultimate Solution of Grace Quigley* (85) *Down and Out in Beverly Hills* (85), *Extreme Prejudice* (87).

## NOONAN, Tommy (1921-1968)

Born Thomas Noon in Bellingham, Washington (half brother of actor John Ireland), Noonan came to the screen in the mid-1940s from nightclub entertaining. He was an ebullient presence in mostly comic supporting roles through the 1960s.

**Selected Films:** *George White's Scandals* (45), *Gentlemen Prefer Blondes* (53), *A Star is Born* (54), *The Ambassador's Daughter* (56), *Promises! Promises!* (63), *Cotton Pickin' Chickenpickers* (67).

## NORMAND, Mabel (1894-1930)

Normand, a great comedienne, actress and director, born Mabel Fortesque, in Boston, Massachusetts, was a radiant star in silent films. The daughter of a poor vaudeville pianist, she was a model at the age of 13 and debuted in movies when she was 16. By 1912 she was Mack Sennett's prize female performer. Normand appeared with and even directed Charlie Chaplin. *Tillie's Punctured Romance* (14), starring both of them, was a smash hit and Sennett established the Mabel Normand Feature Film Company. Later Normand signed with Samuel Goldwyn and began living the movie star's life at fever pitch. Scandals over drugs swirled about her and her name was dragged into two sordid murder cases. Normand broke under the strain, making her last major film in 1923, and dying seven years later of pneumonia and tuberculosis.

**Selected Films:** *The Squaw's Love* (11), *Barney Oldfield's Race for Life* (12), *Tillie's Punctured Romance* (14), *Fatty and Mabel Adrift* (15), *Mickey* (17), *Sis Hopkins* (18), *Molly O* (21), *Suzanna* (22), *The Extra Girl* (24), *Raggedy Rose* (26).

## NORRIS, Chuck (1942- )

Born Carlos Ray in Ryan, Oklahoma, Norris studied karate in the army and later became the World Middleweight Karate Champion. Since his film debut in the Bruce Lee vehicle *Enter the Dragon* (73), Norris has inherited the Lee mantle as the main martial-arts movie star.

**Selected Films:** *Enter the Dragon* (73), *A Force of One* (80), *An Eye for an Eye* (81), *Silent Rage* (82), *Forced Vengeance* (82), *Lone Wolf McQuade* (83), *Missing in Action* (84), *Invasion USA* (85), *The Delta Force* (86), *Firewalker* (87).

## NORTH, Sheree (1933- )

Born Dawn Bethel in Hollywood, California, North began dancing onstage at 10. She was married at 15, and had a child at 16. She began playing movie bit parts in the early 1950s, then for a few years was groomed by Fox to be a voluptuous, blonde second-string Marilyn Monroe. Despite her dancing and her growing abilities as an actress, her star never quite rose. After a decade of retirement, North returned to the screen in occasional character roles.

**Selected Films:** *Excuse My Dust* (51), *How to Be Very, Very Popular* (55), *The Best Things in Life are Free* (56), *Mardi Gras* (58), *Charley Varrick* (73), *The Shootist* (76), *Only Once in a Lifetime* (80).

## NORTON, Jack (1889-1958)

In over 200 mostly bit parts in movies, Mortimer Norton, born in Brooklyn, New York, specialized in playing well-dressed, good-natured drunks. With his rubbery features and accomplished stagger, he had run-ins with assorted revolving doors and unstable floors throughout the 1930s and 1940s. An utter teetotaler in real life, he played sober roles in only two movies.
**Selected Films:** *Cockeyed Cavaliers* (34), *The Bank Dick* (40), *Hail the Conquering Hero* (44), *Bringing Up Father* (46), *Variety Time* (47).

## NOVAK, Kim (1933- )

Born Marilyn Novak in Chicago, Illinois, this blonde beauty went to Hollywood, hoping for a break in the movies. She worked in a dime store, ran an elevator and sold refrigerators before she was discovered in a walk-on part in *The French Line* (54). Signed to a contract by Columbia Pictures, she was earning $75 a week when she was given a major part in *Pushover* (54), with Fred MacMurray. Her first big picture, however, was *Picnic* (55), in which she played a small town beauty who succumbed to William Holden. Novak was probably the last screen goddess to emerge from the Hollywood studio system. She was briefly married to actor Richard Johnson.
**Selected Films:** *The French Line* (54), *Pushover* (54), *Five Against the House* (55), *Picnic* (55), *The Man with the Golden Arm* (55), *Jeanne Eagels* (57), *Pal Joey* (57), *Vertigo* (58), *The Notorious Landlady* (62), *The Amorous Adventures of Moll Flanders* (65), *The Legend of Lylah Clare* (68), *The Mirror Crack'd* (80).

## NOVARRO, Ramon (1899-1968)

Destined to be one of the great Latin lovers of the screen, Ramon Novarro was born Ramon Samaniegos in Durango, Mexico. In his mid-teens he found his way to Los Angeles and broke into silents as an extra in 1917. After several years in minor movies, Novarro was picked by producers to star as Rupert of Hentzau in *The Prisoner of Zenda* (22). In that and ensuing romances such as *Scaramouche* (23) he was wildly popular, though never really threatened his rival, Valentino. His most noted performance was the title role in the epic *Ben Hur* (25). Novarro made the transition to sound, more or less, and played opposite Greta Garbo in *Mata Hari* (32). His great days were over, however, and he mainly played character roles in occasional films for the rest of his life, now and then directing Spanish-language versions of films. He was the victim of a brutal murder in 1968.
**Selected Films:** *Joan the Woman* (16), *The Hostage* (17), *The Prisoner of Zenda* (22), *Where the Pavement Ends* (23), *Scaramouche* (23), *The Red Lily* (24), *Ben Hur* (25), *The Student Prince* (27), *The Pagan* (29), *Mata Hari* (32), *The Barbarian* (33), *We Were Strangers* (48), *Heller in Pink Tights* (60).

## NOVELLO, Jay (1905-1982)

Short and wiry American actor Novello played character roles in a great many films from the late 1930s into the 1970s, usually as criminals. He also appeared in the TV series *McHale's Navy*.
**Selected Films:** *Tenth Avenue Kid* (38), *Kiss the Blood Off My Hands* (48), *The Robe* (53), *Pocketful of Miracles* (61), *The Domino Principle* (77).

## NUYEN, France (1939- )

Born France Nguyen Vannga in Marseilles, France, to French and Chinese parents, Nuyen was a model and appeared on Broadway in *The World of Suzie Wong* (58). The beautiful Eurasian appeared in films only occasionally.
**Selected Films:** *In Love and War* (57), *South Pacific* (58), *Satan Never Sleeps* (61), *Diamond Head* (63), *One More Train to Rob* (71), *Battle for the Planet of the Apes* (73).

## OAKIE, Jack (1903-1978)

Born Lewis Offield in Sedalia, Missouri, Oakie came to the screen in the late 1920s after working in vaudeville and on Broadway. Typed from the beginning as a good-natured, pudgy buffoon, he played the eternal freshman in a number of Paramount campus comedies of the 1930s. His finest role was as the Mussoliniesque 'Benzini Napoloni' in Chaplin's *The Great Dictator* (40). Oakie received an Oscar nomination for that performance. With his trademark doubletake – later expanded to a tripletake – Oakie played comic roles into the 1960s.
**Selected Films:** *Finders Keepers* (27), *Paramount on Parade* (30), *College Humor* (33), *The Great Dictator* (40), *Tin Pan Alley* (40), *It Happened Tomorrow* (44), *Around the World in 80 Days* (56), *The Wonderful Country* (59), *Lover Come Back* (62).

## OAKLAND, Simon (1922-1983)

New York-born Oakland was an all-purpose character actor in movies and television from the late 1950s through the 1970s. He played various nationalities, including the Indian Black Kettle in *The Plainsman* (66). His TV work included the series *The Night Stalker*.
**Selected Films:** *The Brothers Karamazov* (58), *Psycho* (60), *The Satan Bug* (65), *The Plainsman* (66), *The Sand Pebbles* (67), *Emperor of the North Pole* (73), *Evening in Byzantium* (78).

## OATES, Warren (1928-1982)

Born in Depoy, Kentucky, Oates came to New York in the mid-1950s to try his hand at acting. After a period of dishwashing he got into TV and then

movies, for some 15 years mostly playing heavies in routine screen and TV Westerns. However, after his performance in *In the Heat of the Night* (67), Oates found belated stardom as a haunted villain in major pictures, including *The Wild Bunch* (69). He played the title role in *Dillinger* (73).
**Selected Films:** *Up Periscope!* (59), *Major Dundee* (65), *In the Heat of the Night* (67), *The Wild Bunch* (69), *The Hired Hand* (71), *Dillinger* (73), *Badlands* (73), *Stripes* (81), *Blue Thunder* (83).

## OBER, Philip (1902-1982)

Born in Fort Payne, Alabama, Ober was a regularly-working supporting actor for 20 years before turning to small roles on screen, during the 1950s and 1960s. He was once married to actress Vivian Vance.
**Selected Films:** *The Secret Fury* (50), *From Here to Eternity* (53), *North by Northwest* (59), *Assignment to Kill* (69).

## OBERON, Merle (1911-1979)

Born Estelle O'Brien Merle Thompson in Tasmania and educated in India, Oberon was an exquisite brunette beauty who generally played rich and glamorous women in British and American films. She went to England in 1928 and worked as a dance hostess until she began to get some bit roles in movies under the name of Estelle Thompson. She was discovered by British film tycoon Alexander Korda, whom she married in 1939. The marriage lasted until 1945. Oberon worked mainly in Hollywood from 1936 on, and is best remembered for costume pictures such as *The Scarlet Pimpernel* (34) and *Wuthering Heights* (39), playing opposite Leslie Howard and Laurence Olivier, respectively. Her private life was almost as glamorous as her on-screen image, and she will be remembered for organizing a scrap drive in New York City during World War II – at the Stork Club. Married four times, she was a glittering international socialite.
**Selected Films:** *Service for Ladies* (32), *The Private Life of Henry VIII* (33), *The Scarlet Pimpernel* (34), *The Dark Angel* (35), *These Three* (36), *The Divorce of Lady X* (38), *The Cowboy and the Lady* (38), *Wuthering Heights* (39), *Lydia* (41), *The Lodger* (44), *Dark Waters* (44), *A Song to Remember* (45), *Desiree* (54), *Hotel* (67), *Interval* (73).

## O'BRIAN, Hugh (1925- )

Born Hugh J Krampe in Rochester, New York, O'Brian was a Marine drill instructor before making his debut on the screen in *Never Fear* (50). After several years of leads in B movies, he starred for six seasons in the popular TV series *Wyatt Earp*. O'Brian left the series to concentrate on his movie career, but it remained sporadic.
**Selected Films:** *Never Fear* (50), *Red Ball Express* (52), *The Fiend Who Walked the West* (58), *In Harm's Way* (65), *Ten Little Indians* (65), *The Shootist* (76).

## O'BRIEN, Dave (Tex) (1912-1969)

Born David Barclay in Big Springs, Texas, O'Brien made his way through a series of jobs in show business as a song-and-dance man, movie bit player in the 1930s, stuntman, a star of B movies and serials. He is best known as the star of the MGM *Pete Smith* comedy shorts of the 1940s. Later he became a gag writer and TV director.
**Selected Films:** *Jennie Gerhardt* (33), *The Little Colonel* (35), *East Side Kids* (39), *Son of the Navy* (40), *Captain Midnight* (42), *Kiss Me Kate* (53), *The Desperadoes Are in Town* (56).

## O'BRIEN, Edmond (1915-1985)

Before he became one of Hollywood's most familiar character actors, Edmond O'Brien spent several years trying to get a shot on the big-time stage in his native New York. After some small roles on Broadway, O'Brien joined Orson Welles' Mercury Theatre in 1937 and began appearing in their stage and radio productions. His film debut came as Pierre Gringoire in *The Hunchback of Notre Dame* (39). For a few years he played mostly heroes and heavies in crime films; then becoming a bit heavy and jowly with age, he began doing character roles, including Casca in *Julius Caesar* (53) and Winston Smith in *1984* (55). In 1954 O'Brien won a Supporting-Actor Oscar for his part as a hustling press agent in *The Barefoot Contessa*; a decade later he received another nomination for his work in *Seven Days in May* (64). He also starred in the TV series *Johnny Midnight* and *Sam Benedict*. Despite illness, O'Brien continued working in movies and TV into the 1970s.
**Selected Films:** *The Hunchback of Notre Dame* (39), *Parachute Battalion* (41), *The Killers* (46), *Another Part of the Forest* (48), *White Heat* (49), *D.O.A.* (00), *Julius Caesar* (53), *The Barefoot Contessa* (54), *1984* (55), *The Third Voice* (59), *The Man Who Shot Liberty Valance* (62), *The Birdman of Alcatraz* (62), *Seven Days in May* (64), *Fantastic Voyage* (66), *The Wild Bunch* (69), *They Only Kill Their Masters* (72), *99 and 44/100% Dead* (74).

## O'BRIEN, George (1900-1985)

Born in San Francisco, California, O'Brien was a champion boxer before getting into movies as a cameraman and stuntman. The beefy actor (later called 'The Chest') got his first lead in John Ford's classic silent *The Iron Horse* (24). For a few years he starred in major films including F W Murnau's *Sunrise* (27). By the 1930s O'Brien was a fixture of Westerns, among his later films were John Ford's *She Wore a Yellow Ribbon* (49) and *Cheyenne Autumn* (64).
**Selected Films:** *White Hands* (22), *The Iron Horse* (24), *Sunrise* (27), *Riders of the Purple Sage* (31), *The Painted Desert* (38), *Fort Apache* (48), *She Wore a Yellow Ribbon* (49), *Gold Raiders* (51), *Cheyenne Autumn* (64).

## O'BRIEN, Margaret (1937- )

In the early 1940s, one of the new child stars to burst upon the screen was a girl named Margaret O'Brien. Reviewing one of her first films, a writer gushed, 'Before we've completely forgotten about the natural charms and talents of Shirley Temple as the wonder-child of the movies, her place is being filled on the screen by another infant prodigy.' That was written in 1944, when O'Brien was only seven years old. Born Angela Maxine O'Brien in San Diego, California, she got her new first name from her first big hit, *Journey for Margaret* (42). She played a little British girl who was evacuated to the United States during World War II, and she immediately captured the hearts of moviegoers. MGM knew a good thing when it came along, and O'Brien was hard at work in no time. She made three films in 1943 and another five in 1945. In one of those movies, *Lost Angel* (43), she played a child prodigy who was being raised by a group of psychology professors and was introduced to the real world by a tough but tender newspaper reporter. 'The tiny tot firmly establishes herself as the marvel of the current cinema,' one reviewer wrote after seeing the picture. She could be funny with Red Skelton (*Thousands Cheer* [43]) or Charles Laughton (*The Canterville Ghost* [44]), be serious with Greer Garson (*Madame Curie* [43]) and even hold her own alongside that masterful actor Orson Welles (*Jane Eyre* [43], in which she played his ballet-dancing French ward). Many critics believed that she did her best work as Judy Garland's kid sister in the classic film musical, *Meet Me in St Louis* (44). Dancing the cakewalk with Garland, giving a convincing portrayal of a child's fear at the possibility of having to leave her beloved home because her father had been offered a new job, she did a memorable piece of work. She was given a Special Academy Award for being the 'outstanding child actress of 1944.' Then her pace slowed down. She made only two films in 1945, in one of them appearing with Edward G Robinson in *Our Vines Have Tender Grapes*, and two in 1946, one of them a typical Wallace Beery Western called *Bad Bascomb*. But adolescence arrived and her fame tailed off. She made a few films, appeared on stage, made some television appearances and married twice.

**Selected Films:** *Babes on Broadway* (41), *Journey for Margaret* (42), *Thousands Cheer* (43) *Lost Angel* (43), *Madame Curie* (43), *Jane Eyre* (43), *The Canterville Ghost* (44), *Meet Me in St Louis* (44), *Music for Millions* (45), *Our Vines Have Tender Grapes* (45), *Bad Bascomb* (46), *Three Wise Fools* (46), *The Unfinished Dance* (47), *Big City* (48), *Little Women* (49), *Her First Romance* (51), *Heller in Pink Tights* (60), *Annabelle Lee* (72), *Amy* (81).

## O'BRIEN, Pat (1899-1983)

Hollywood's future archetypal Irishman was born in Milwaukee, Wisconsin, to, of course, an Irish Catholic family. In military school he met his lifelong pal Spencer Tracy; they went into the Navy together and afterward to drama school. By the late 1920s O'Brien was acting on Broadway. Though he had starred in one silent and appeared in a 1929 talkie, his big break came when he repeated his stage role as Hildy Johnson in the screen version of *The Front Page* (31). For the next two decades he played Irishmen of all stripes, his banty figure and husky voice put to good use as priests, pols, and the like – usually sympathetic but hard-boiled Runyonesque guys in movies like *Angels With Dirty Faces* (38). Among his best-remembered performances was the title role in *Knute Rockne – All American* (40). There followed a string of war movies like *Flight Lieutenant* (42) and *Secret Command* (44). O'Brien's appearances thinned in the 1950s, but he turned up now and then in movies through the 1970s, notably in John Ford's *The Last Hurrah* (58). He also appeared in the TV series *Harrigan and Son*, and in several made-for-TV movies. In 1963 O'Brien published an autobiography, *Wind on My Back*.

**Selected Films:** *Shadows of the West* (21), *Wild* (29), *The Front Page* (31), *Bombshell* (33), *Angels With Dirty Faces* (38), *Boy Meets Girl* (38), *Knute Rockne – All American* (40), *Flight Lieutenant* (42), *The Iron Major* (43), *Secret Command* (44), *Fighting Father Dunne* (48), *The Last Hurrah* (58), *Some Like It Hot* (59), *The End* (78), *Ragtime* (81).

## O'BRIEN, Virginia (1921- )

Born in Los Angeles, California, O'Brien discovered the simple device of singing songs with a straight face. This deadpan characteristic got her dubbed 'Miss Red Hot Frozen Face' and a few years of popularity as a comic. She appeared in some 15 movies of the 1940s, most of them light musicals.

**Selected Films:** *Hullaballo* (40), *The Big Store* (41), *Du Barry was a Lady* (44), *Merton of the Movies* (47) *Francis in the Navy* (55).

## O'CONNELL, Arthur (1908-1981)

New York-born O'Connell acted for years in vaudeville and the theater before coming to films as a character actor in the late 1930s. He usually played gentle and somewhat befuddled, country characters, twice earning supporting-actor Oscar nominations – for his perforances as Howard Bevans in *Picnic* (56) and Parnell McCarthy in *Anatomy of a Murder* (59).

**Selected Films:** *Freshman Year* (38), *The Man in the Gray Flannel Suit* (56), *Picnic* (56), *Bus Stop* (56), *Anatomy of a Murder* (59), *Fantastic Voyage* (66), *Ben* (72), *The Hiding Place* (75).

## O'CONNOR, Carroll (1922- )

Born in the Bronx, New York, O'Connor studied in Ireland and there made his stage debut. Returning

to the United States, he played supporting roles in a number of films before he was cast as bigoted, blustering Archie Bunker in the TV series *All in the Family*.
**Selected Films:** *By Love Possessed* (61), *Cleopatra* (63), *Marlowe* (69), *Law and Disorder* (74).

## O'CONNOR, Donald (1925- )

Born in Chicago, Illinois, the son of former circus performers turned vaudevillians, the engaging O'Connor was a professional entertainer by the time he was 13 and made his screen debut in *Sing You Sinners* (38), in which he and Bing Crosby teamed up in the memorable 'Small Fry' number. He proved himself to be an amusing singer and a very good light comedian, but he was always at his best when he danced. O'Connor graduated from kids' roles to playing juvenile leads in a string of B movies opposite young starlets. He had a talking mule for a companion in a string of *Francis* movies (the mule's voice courtesy of Chill Wills). But his shining hour came in *Singin' in the Rain* (52), when he sang and danced to 'Make 'Em Laugh' – a screen gem. Several other good musicals followed, most notably *Call Me Madam* (53) and *There's No Business Like Show Business* (54), both of them opposite Ethel Merman. His film career declined in the late 1950s because Hollywood stopped making big musicals, but he took his considerable talents to television on *The Donald O'Connor Show*.
**Selected Films:** *Sing You Sinners* (38), *On Your Toes* (39), *Beau Geste* (39), *Mister Big* (43), *Patrick the Great* (45), *Francis* (49), *Singin' in the Rain* (52), *Call Me Madam* (53), *There's No Business Like Show Business* (54), *The Buster Keaton Story* (57), *That Funny Feeling* (65), *That's Entertainment* (74), *Ragtime* (81), *Pandemonium* (82).

## O'CONNOR, Una (1880-1959)

Born Agnes McGlade in Belfast, Ireland, and a member of the Abbey Players in Dublin, O'Connor repeated her London stage role of the maid in Coward's *Cavalcade* in the Hollywood screen version in 1933. She stayed on there to play character roles for 25 years. Plain of face and frail of figure, she usually played comic nattering maids or spinsters, with an occasional serious role, like the mother in *The Informer* (35). O'Connor also cultivated a spine-chilling shriek, which she unleashed to good effect in horror movies.
**Selected Films:** *Dark Red Roses* (29), *Cavalcade* (33), *The Invisible Man* (33), *The Informer* (35), *Bride of Frankenstein* (35), *The Adventures of Robin Hood* (38), *The Bells of St Mary's* (45), *Ivy* (47), *Witness for the Prosecution* (57).

## O'DONNELL, Cathy (1923-1970)

Born Ann Steely in Siluria, Alabama, O'Donnell made an auspicious screen debut as Wilma Cameron, the delicate sweetheart of war-crippled Harold Russell in *The Best Years of Our Lives* (46). Her ensuing movie roles were sporadic. The best known was Tirzah in *Ben Hur* (59).
**Selected Films:** *The Best Years of Our Lives* (46), *They Live by Night* (48), *Detective Story* (51), *The Story of Mankind* (58), *Ben Hur* (59).

## O'DRISCOLL, Martha (1922- )

Born in Tulsa, Oklahoma, O'Driscoll was a child actress in movies of the 1930s and a pretty, leggy leading lady in a number of B movies of the 1940s.
**Selected Films:** *Collegiate*, (35), *The Secret of Dr Kildare* (40), *The Lady Eve* (41), *Ghost Catchers* (44), *House of Dracula* (45), *Criminal Court* (47).

## OGLE, Charles (1865-1940)

A prolific but relatively minor actor of the silent screen, Ogle is remembered in film history as the first man to play the Frankenstein monster on-screen – in a 1909 version of the tale.
**Selected Films:** *The Honour of His Family* (09), *Frankenstein* (09), *Joan the Woman* (17), *The Covered Wagon* (23), *The Flaming Forest* (26).

## O'HANLON, George (1917- )

American-born O'Hanlon played comic supporting parts in movies and on TV from the 1940s through the 1970s. He was perhaps best known as Joe McDoakes in the *Behind the Eight Ball* shorts and several TV series including *The Life of Riley*.
**Selected Films:** *The Great Awakening* (41), *Battle Stations* (55), *Charley and the Angel* (73), *Rocky* (76).

## O'HARA, Maureen (1920- )

Born Maureen Fitzsimmons in Millwall, near Dublin, Ireland, O'Hara was a gloriously beautiful redhead with an engaging personality. An ingénue at the Abbey Theatre in Dublin, she made her British film debut in *My Irish Molly* (38). Her second film was *Jamaica Inn* (39), which was probably one of the few clunkers that Alfred Hitchcock ever directed. But the picture did star Charles Laughton, who took O'Hara under his wing, demanding that she co-star with him as Esmeralda in *The Hunchback of Notre Dame* (39). She could act and her beauty made her a star. O'Hara was beautiful in Technicolor costume pictures, but was at her best in two perky contemporary films, *Miracle on 34th Street* (47) and *Sitting Pretty* (48), in which she played opposite Clifton Webb in the first of the 'Mr Belvedere' films. *The Quiet Man* (52) won director John Ford an Oscar, but her acting performance was one of the reasons he won it.
**Selected Films:** *My Irish Molly* (38), *Jamaica Inn* (39), *The Hunchback of Notre Dame* (39), *A Bill of Divorcement* (40), *How Green Was My Valley* (41), *Miracle on 34th Street* (47), *Sitting Pretty* (48), *The Quiet Man* (52), *Against All Flags* (52), *The Parent Trap* (61), *The Rare Breed* (66), *Big Jake* (71).

*Maureen O'Hara in* Against All Flags *(52).*

## O'HERLIHY, Dan (1919- )

Born in Wexford, Ireland, O'Herlihy studied architecture before acting on the stages of the Abbey and Gate theaters in his native Ireland. After a few British films including *Odd Man Out* (46), he arrived in Hollywood in the late 1940s and played Macduff in Orson Welles' *Macbeth* (48). His considerable talent and offbeat personality were seen to best advantage with his virtual one-man-show in Luis Buñuel's *The Adventures of Robinson Crusoe* (52), for which he earned an Oscar nomination. O'Herlihy went on to play leads and supporting roles in films into the 1980s including FDR in *MacArthur*. He also starred in several TV series including *The Travels of Jaimie McPheeters* and *The Long Hot Summer* .
**Selected Films:** *Odd Man Out* (46), *Macbeth* (48), *The Desert Fox* (51), *The Adventures of Robinson Crusoe* (52), *The Black Shield of Falworth* (54), *Cabinet of Caligari* (61), *Waterloo* (70), *MacArthur* (77), *Halloween III* (82), *The Dead* (87).

## O'KEEFE, Dennis (1908-1968)

Born Edward Flanagan in Fort Madison, Iowa, O'Keefe was a vaudevillian as a child and in his teens wrote scripts for the *Our Gang* shorts. He began appearing in small screen roles – as Bud Flanagan – in the early 1930s. In 1937 Clark Gable helped get Flanagan an MGM contract and he became a leading man as Dennis O'Keefe. After a few years of starring in light romances he played many roles as tough but sympathetic hero in B movies of the 1940s. His career declined in the 1950s.
**Selected Films:** *Cimarron* (31), *La Conga Nights* (40), *Topper Returns* (41), *Up in Mabel's Room* (44), *The Affairs of Susan* (45), *T-Men* (47), *The Diamond Wizard* (54), *All Hands on Deck* (61), *The Naked Flame* (63).

## O'KEEFE, Michael (1955- )

O'Keefe was born in Paulland, New Jersey, and studied at the American Academy of Dramatic Arts. He has worked extensively onstage and his Broadway credits include *Streamers* and *The Fifth of July*. After making his screen debut in *Gray Lady Down* (78), O'Keefe was nominated for a supporting-actor Oscar for his performance as the long-suffering son in *The Great Santini* (80). Recent roles have included a lead in *The Slugger's Wife* (85).
**Selected Films:** *Gray Lady Down* (78), *The Great Santini* (80), *Caddyshack* (80), *Split Image* (82), *Nate and Hayes* (83), *The Slugger's Wife* (85).

## OLAND, Warner (1880-1938)

Born Werner Ohlund in Umea, Sweden, Oland came to the United States at age 10. Moving to films from the theater in 1912, he played both heroes and heavies in a number of silents. After his title role as the villainous *Dr Fu Manchu* (29), the Swedish actor was typecast in Oriental parts. He soon switched sides of the law to play the definitive Chinese detective Charlie Chan in many mysteries of the 1930s.
**Selected Films:** *Jewels of the Madonna* (09), *The Life of John Bunyan* (12), *Don Q, Son of Zorro* (25), *The Jazz Singer* (27), *Dr Fu Manchu* (29), *Charlie Chan Carries On* (31), *Werewolf of London* (35), *Charlie Chan at Monte Carlo* (38).

## OLIVER, Edna May (1883-1942)

Born Edna May Nutter in Boston, Massachusetts, Oliver had a solid career in the theatre before she brought her plain and sharp features to Hollywood in the 1920s. From the 1930s until her death she specialized in gabby, nosey spinsters, including the Nurse in *Romeo and Juliet* (36). The role of Widow McKlennan in *Drums Along the Mohawk* (39) earned Oliver an Oscar nomination.
**Selected Films:** *Icebound* (23), *Fanney Foley Herself* (31), *Little Women* (33), *David Copperfield* (34), *Romeo and Juliet* (36), *Drums Along the Mohawk* (39), *Pride and Prejudice* (40), *Lydia* (41).

## OLIVER, Susan (1937- )

American actress Oliver is best known for her TV work in the 1960s and 1970s, but has occasionally appeared in leads and supporting roles of features.
**Selected Films:** *Green-Eyed Blonde* (57), *The Gene Krupa Story* (60), *Your Cheating Heart* (66), *Change of Mind* (69), *Ginger in the Morning* (75).

## OLIVIER, Laurence (1907- )

Lord Olivier may just be the finest actor of this century. This distinguished, handsome and gifted British stage actor was born in Dorking, England, into a clergyman's family, and made a rather unusual stage debut playing Katharine in a school production of Shakespeare's *The Taming of the Shrew*. In 1926 he joined the Birmingham Repertory, then did a number of plays in London's West End and made his Broadway debut in 1929. His looks and talent did not go unnoticed, but the world did not fall at his feet, and he had to struggle like many other young actors. He made his debut on screen in *Too Many Crooks* (30), and appeared in a few more equally innocuous films. Hired to play opposite Greta Garbo in *Queen Christina* (33), he was replaced, at her request, by John Gilbert. Yet a few years later, he would emerge as an actor whose gifts were unparalleled. Joining the Old Vic in London, he played one great Shakespearean role after another – then *Wuthering Heights* (39), with Merle Oberon, and *Rebecca* (40), with Joan Fontaine, established him as a superb romantic lead in films. In 1944 Olivier was appointed co-director of the Old Vic. He produced, directed and starred in the movie *Henry V* (44), the film version of the Shakespearean play, a magnificent achievement which won him a Special Academy Award. *Hamlet* (48) brought him a step closer to being recognized as a genius. The film won the Academy Award for Best Picture and Olivier won the Oscar for Best Actor. He received a Special Academy Award again at the 1978 ceremonies 'for the full body of his work.' Olivier married actress Jill Esmond in 1930. The couple divorced in 1940 and he married stage and film star Vivien Leigh, and they appeared together on stage frequently. In 1961 Olivier married actress Joan Plowright. Resourceful and entreprenurial, there are few aspects of theater, film or television that Olivier has overlooked. In 1963 he became director of Britain's National Theatre Company. Olivier was knighted in 1947 for his work as a member of the company. In 1970, Sir Laurence became Lord Olivier – a peer of the realm, the only actor to be accorded this honor.

**Selected Films:** *Too Many Crooks* (30), *The Temporary Widow* (30), *Perfect Understanding* (32), *Conquest of the Air* (35), *As You Like It* (36), *Fire Over England* (36), *Q Planes* (39), *Wuthering Heights* (39), *Rebecca* (40), *Pride and Prejudice* (40), *That Hamilton Woman* (41), *Henry V* (44), *Hamlet* (48), *Carrie* (52), *The Beggar's Opera* (52), *Richard III* (53), *The Prince and the Showgirl* (58), *The Devil's Disciple* (59), *Spartacus* (60), *The Entertainer* (60), *Term of Trial* (62), *Bunny Lake Is Missing* (65), *Othello* (65), *Khartoum* (66), *The Shoes of the Fisherman* (68), *Oh! What a Lovely War* (69), *The Three Sisters* (70), *Sleuth* (72), *Marathon Man* (76), *The Seven Percent Solution* (76), *A Bridge Too Far* (77), *The Boys from Brazil* (78), *A Little Romance* (79), *Clash of the Titans* (80), *The Jigsaw Man* (84), *Wild Geese II* (85).

*Laurence Olivier as* Hamlet *(48).*

## OLSEN, Moroni (1889-1954)

Born in Ogden, Utah, Olsen was a leading man of the theater in the 1920s and made his screen debut as Porthos in *The Three Musketeers* (35). From then until his death, the tall, heavy-set actor played character roles as both good guys and bad in some 70 movies.

**Selected Films:** *The Three Musketeers* (35), *Mary of Scotland* (36), *Kidnapped* (38), *The Glass Key* (42), *Samson and Delilah* (49), *Father of the Bride* (50), *The Long Long Trailer* (54).

## OLSEN, Ole (1892-1963)

Born in Wabash, Indiana, comic John Sigurd Olsen worked in vaudeville before teaming (as straight man) with Chic Johnson in 1914 to form one of the most popular comedy acts of the century. In films from the early 1930s, the duo are most remembered for their anarchic stage and screen comedy *Hellzapoppin* (42).

**Selected Films:** *Gold Dust Gertie* (31), *The Country Gentleman* (37), *Hellzapoppin* (42), *Ghost Catchers* (44), *See My Lawyer* (45).

## OLSON, Nancy (1928- )

Born in Milwaukee, Wisconsin, Olson came out of UCLA to a movie contract in the late 1940s. She was a lovely presence in major roles for a few years, notably as the ingenue in *Sunset Boulevard* (50), for which she received a supporting-actress Oscar nomination. After some years of retirement she returned to the screen for occasional character roles. For a time she was married to songwriter Alan Jay Lerner.

**Selected Films:** *Canadian Pacific* (49), *Sunset Boulevard* (50), *Battle Cry* (55), *Pollyanna* (60), *Son of Flubber* (63), *Snowball Express* (73), *Airport 74* (75), *Making Love* (82).

## O'MALLEY, J Pat (1904-1985)

O'Malley was born in Burnley, England, and specialized in playing screen Irishmen from the 1940s through the 1960s. Among his typical roles were as one of Gloria Jean's uncles in *A Little Bit of Heaven* (40) and in *Lassie Come Home* (43). He also did cartoon voices for Disney films.
**Selected Films:** *A Little Bit of Heaven* (40), *Lassie Come Home* (43), *The Long Hot Summer* (58), *The Cabinet of Caligari* (62), *Willard* (70).

## O'MALLEY, Rex (1901-1976)

O'Malley played a dashing young man in the Garbo classic *Camille* (36) and was well received in *Midnight* (39), but thereafter his screen career stalled. He continued to appear on stage.
**Selected Films:** *Camille* (36), *Midnight* (39), *Zaza* (39), *The Thief* (52).

## O'NEAL, Patrick (1927- )

Born in Ocala, Florida, O'Neal acted on stage and later in wide-ranging movie character roles. In the 1970s he appeared in a number of TV productions, including the movies *The Moneychangers* and *The Last Hurrah*, and the series *Kaz*.
**Selected Films:** *The Mad Magician* (54), *King Rat* (65), *Assignment to Kill* (67), *The Kremlin Letter* (69), *The Way We Were* (73), *The Stepford Wives* (75).

## O'NEAL, Ron (1937- )

Born in the black ghetto of Cleveland, Ohio, O'Neal studied drama and acted for years in the theater, winning an Obie in 1970. That same year he made his film debut. In 1972 starred in the blacksploitation hit *Superfly*. He directed, co-wrote and starred in the sequel, *Superfly TNT* (73) and thereafter appeared in occasional films.
**Selected Films:** *Move* (70), *Superfly* (72), *Superfly TNT* (73), *Brothers* (77), *The Final Countdown* (79), *St Helens* (81).

## O'NEAL, Ryan (1941- )

Born Patrick Ryan O'Neal in Los Angeles, California, the boyishly handsome O'Neal, the father of actress Tatum O'Neal, was a lifeguard and amateur boxer. He began his career as a television stunt man, later appearing in the series *Peyton Place*. O'Neal made his screen debut in *The Games* (68), a film about runners in training for the marathon in the Olympics. Then he became the star of several successful films, beginning with *Love Story* (70), and was at his best in *Paper Moon* (73). He also showed a talent for comedy opposite Barbra Streisand in *What's Up Doc?* (72).
**Selected Films:** *The Games* (68), *Love Story* (70), *What's Up Doc?* (72), *Paper Moon* (73), *Barry Lyndon* (73), *Oliver's Story* (79), *Irreconcilable Differences* (84), *Tough Guys Don't Dance* (87).

## O'NEAL, Tatum (1963- )

Born in Los Angeles, California, the daughter of screen star Ryan O'Neal, Tatum won an Oscar (at age nine the youngest ever to do so) for supporting her father as a hard-bitten kid in *Paper Moon* (73). In 1976 she received the highest salary of any child player in history for her role as an ace Little League pitcher in *The Bad News Bears*, that year also starring with Ryan again in *Nickelodeon* (76). Her roles since then have been occasional. She is married to tennis star John McEnroe.
**Selected Films:** *Paper Moon* (73), *The Bad News Bears* (76), *Nickelodeon* (76), *International Velvet* (78), *Circle of Two* (80), *Little Darlings* (80), *Split Image* (82), *Certain Fury* (85).

## O'NEIL, Barbara (1909-1980)

Born in St Louis, Missouri, O'Neil attended Sarah Lawrence and appeared on Broadway before making her first film, *Stella Dallas* (37). Best known for her role as Scarlett O'Hara's mother, in *Gone With the Wind* (39) (which she played at the age of twenty-nine), she received an Academy Award nomination the following year for her performance as the neurotic Duchess in *All This And Heaven Too* (40). She was married to director Joshua Logan in the 1940s.
**Selected Films:** *Stella Dallas* (37), *When Tomorrow Comes* (39), *Gone With the Wind* (39), *All This and Heaven Too* (40), *Shining Victory* (41), *I Remember Mama* (48), *Angel Face* (52), *The Nun's Story* (59).

## O'NEIL, Sally (1913-1968)

Born Virginia Noonan in Bayonne, New Jersey, O'Neil made her silent film debut in *Sally, Irene and Mary* (25), and played waifish roles in light films as a sort of second-string Mary Pickford. Her career trailed off in the 1930s.
**Selected Films:** *Sally, Irene and Mary* (25), *Mike* (25), *Slide, Kelly, Slide* (27), *The Sophomore* (29), *Sixteen Fathoms Deep* (33), *Kathleen* (37).

## O'NEILL, Henry (1891-1961)

Born in Orange, New Jersey, character actor O'Neill came to the screen in the early 1930s after wide theatrical experience. In some 200 movies he played supporting roles as priests and military officers, such as Father Xavier in *Anthony Adverse* (36), Colonel Picquart in *The Life of Emile Zola* (37), and Colonel Dodge in *Dodge City* (39).
**Selected Films:** *I Loved a Woman* (33), *Anthony Adverse* (36), *The Life of Emile Zola* (37), *Jezebel* (38), *Dodge City* (39), *The Virginian* (46), *The Wings of Eagles* (57).

## O'NEILL, Jennifer (1947- )

Born to an American family in Rio de Janeiro, Brazil, O'Neill competed as a horseback rider be-

fore becoming a top model in her teens. The fine-featured brunette made her film debut in 1968 and after big roles in Hawks' *Rio Lobo* (70) and *Summer of '42* (71) seemed headed for major stardom. Instead, her films declined through the 1970s.
**Selected Films:** *For Love of Ivy* (68), *Rio Lobo* (70), *Such Good Friends* (71), *Summer of '42* (71), *The Reincarnation of Peter Proud* (75), *Caravans* (78), *Scanners* (81).

## ONTKEAN, Michael (1950- )

Ontkean was born to a family of actors in Canada and began working in films in the early 1970s. After a few years of appearances in minor films he graduated to major roles in popular films such as *Slap Shot* (77) and *Making Love* (81). He also appeared in the TV series *The Rookies*.
**Selected Films:** *Pickup on 101* (71), *Necromancy* (72), *Slap Shot* (77), *Voices* (79), *Willie and Phil* (80), *Making Love* (81), *Just the Way You Are* (84).

## OPATOSHU, David (1918- )

In his teens Opatoshu began acting in the Yiddish theater in his native New York. Mainly a stage actor since then, he has played varied roles in occasional movies since the late 1940s. His appearances include the aged terrorist in *Exodus* (60).
**Selected Films:** *Naked City* (48), *The Brothers Karamazov* (58), *Exodus* (60), *Guns of Darkness* (63), *Torn Curtain* (66), *Enter Laughing* (67), *Who'll Stop the Rain?* (78).

## OSCARSSON, Per (1927- )

Born in Stockholm, Oscarsson acted on the stage in his native Sweden before coming to the screen in the late 1940s. In 1966 the tall, brooding actor won a Cannes Festival award for his role in *Hunger*; he has since played leads and supporting roles in international films.

**Selected Films:** *The Street* (49), *Barabbas* (53), Hunger (66), *A Dandy in Aspic* (68), *The Last Valley* (71), *The Emigrants* (72), *Endless Night* (72), *Dream City* (76), *Secrets* (78).

## O'SHEA, Michael (1906-1973)

Edward Michael O'Shea, born in Hartford, Connecticut, was a circus and vaudeville performer before getting into movies in the early 1940s. He played good-natured leads in occasional films for about a decade, including the title role in *Jack London* (43) and Hawkeye in *Last of the Redmen* (47), and starred in the TV series *It's a Great Life*. He was married to actress Virginia Mayo.
**Selected Films:** *Jack London* (43), *Lady of Burlesque* (43), *Circumstantial Evidence* (45), *It's a Pleasure* (45), *Last of the Redmen* (47), *The Big Wheel* (49), *The Model and the Marriage Broker* (52), *It Should Happen To You* (55).

## O'SHEA, Milo (1926- )

Character actor O'Shea started his career where most good Irish players do, on the stage of the Abbey Theatre. He has largely acted onstage in comic roles but has appeared in occasional films since the early 1950s, most memorably starring as Leopold Bloom in the screen adaptation of James Joyce's *Ulysses* (67).
**Selected Films:** *You Can't Beat the Irish* (51), *Carry on Cabby* (63), *Ulysses* (67), *Romeo and Juliet* (68), *Barbarella* (68), *Loot* (70), *The Verdict* (82).

## O'SULLIVAN, Maureen (1911- )

Born in Boyle, Ireland but destined to be most familiarly cast as a resident of the jungle, Maureen O'Sullivan was educated in London and Paris, discovered by a Hollywood talent scout at the Dublin Horse Show, and given a screen contract in 1930 with no particular acting experience. Nonetheless, the dark-haired beauty managed to find a great many ingenue starring and supporting roles over the next decade, beginning with *Song o' My Heart* (30). She is most remembered as the favorite Jane of all time, the object of Johnny Weismuller's monosyllabic affections in Tarzan movies from the *Tarzan and His Mate* (34) to *Tarzan's New York Adventure* (42). In fact, O'Sullivan handled a wide range of roles, such as Alisande in *A Connecticut Yankee* (31), Henrietta Barrett in *The Barretts of Wimpole Street* (34), and Jane Bennett in *Pride and Prejudice* (40). In 1936 she married writer/director John Farrow and went into semi-retirement in 1942 to raise their children. She made occasional screen appearances through the 1970s. Her later efforts including the made-for-TV movie *The Great Houdinis*. In 1986 O'Sullivan memorably played her real daughter Mia Farrow's elderly actress mother in Woody Allen's *Hannah and Her Sisters*.
**Selected Films:** *Song o' My Heart* (30), *A Connecticut Yankee* (31), *Strange Interlude* (32), *Tarzan and His Mate* (34), *The Barretts of Wimpole Street* (34), *David Copperfield* (34), *Anna Karenina* (35), *Tarzan Escapes* (36), *A Day at the Races* (37), *A Yank at Oxford* (38), *Pride and Prejudice* (40), *Tarzan's New York Adventure* (42), *Bonzo Goes to College* (52), *Never Too Late* (65), *The Phynx* (70), *The Door Man* (83), *Hannah and Her Sisters* (86), *Peggy Sue Got Married* (86).

## O'TOOLE, Peter (1932- )

When it comes to flamboyance, range and sex appeal, there are few actors as winning as O'Toole. Born in Connemara, Ireland, he began his acting career on stage and on British television. He made his screen debut in the remake of Robert Lewis Stevenson's *Kidnapped* (60), but he almost literally burst into stardom for his performance in the title role of *Lawrence of Arabia* (62) – his fourth movie. He has been delightful in comedies such as *What's New, Pussycat?* (65) and overpowering in such

*Katharine Hepburn and Peter O'Toole in* The Lion in Winter *(68).*

dramas as *The Lion in Winter* (68). O'Toole's career sometimes suffers because of his bouts with alcohol, but he was wonderful in *My Favorite Year* (82), receiving a nomination for the Academy Award for Best Actor.
**Selected Films:** *Kidnapped* (60), *Lawrence of Arabia* (62), *Becket* (64), *Lord Jim* (65), *What's New, Pussycat?* (65), *How to Steal a Million* (66), *The Night of the Generals* (66), *The Lion in Winter* (68), *The Ruling Class* (71), *Zulu Dawn* (79), *My Favorite Year* (82), *Supergirl* (84), *Creator* (85), *Club Paradise* (86).

## OUSPENSKAYA, Maria (1876-1949)

A member of the famed Moscow Art Theater this tiny actress born in Tula, Russia, attained a fine reputation on the European stage before beginning an English language acting career at the age of 50. She appeared in many fine films, but is probably best remembered for her performance as the old gypsy woman, the mother of Bela Lugosi, in *The Wolf Man* (41), a role she repeated in *Frankenstein Meets the Wolf Man* (43).
**Selected Films:** *Dodsworth* (36), *Love Affair* (39), *The Rains Came* (39), *Waterloo Bridge* (40), *The Wolf Man* (41), *Frankenstein Meets the Wolf Man* (43), *A Kiss in the Dark* (49).

## OVERMAN, Lynne (1887-1943)

Overman, born in Naryville, Missouri, came to the screen in a series of shorts in the early 1930s after vaudeville experience. In some 50 movies during the last decade of his life he played supporting parts and occasional leads, most often in cynical but sympathetic comic roles.
**Selected Films:** *Little Miss Marker* (34), *The Jungle Princess* (36), *Her Jungle Love* (38), *Death of a Champion* (39), *Roxie Hart* (42), *The Desert Song* (43).

## OWEN, Reginald (1887-1972)

Born in Wheathampstead, Hertfordshire, England, Owen made his London theater debut in 1905 and his Broadway debut in 1925. In movies from the early talkie era, he played an immense variety of character roles in over 100 films, among them Sherlock Holmes in *A Study in Scarlet* (33), Talleyrand in *Conquest* (37), Scrooge in *A Christmas Carol* (38), and Louis XV in *Monsieur Beaucaire* (46).
**Selected Films:** *The Letter* (29), *Queen Christine* (33), *A Study in Scarlet* (33), *A Tale of Two Cities* (36), *Trouble for Two* (36), *Conquest* (37), *A Christmas Carol* (38), *Mrs Miniver* (42), *Random Harvest* (42), *Lassie Come Home* (43), *Kitty* (45), *Monsieur Beaucaire* (46), *Red Garters* (54), *Mary Poppins* (64), *Bedknobs and Broomsticks* (71).

## OWENS, Patricia (1925- )

Canadian-born Owens starred in a number of British and American films from the early 1940s to the late 1960s, most of them minor but including the horror classic *The Fly* (58).
**Selected Films:** *Miss London Ltd* (43), *The Good Die Young* (54), *Sayonara* (57), *No Down Payment* (57), *The Fly* (58), *Seven Women From Hell* (61), *Black Spurs* (65), *The Destructors* (68).

# P

## PACINO, Al (1939- )

Born Alfredo Pacino into a working class Sicilian-American family in New York City, this serious actor gives both intensity and depth to his every performance. Pacino attended the High School of Performing Arts in New York, dropping out and doing odd jobs to earn the money to study at Herbert Berghof's acting school and at the Actors' Studio. He appeared in off-Broadway and Broadway productions, earning critical praise and receiving awards. With only two films behind him, he was chosen to play Michael Corleone, a difficult and complex character, in *The Godfather* (72). The movie was a blockbuster and Pacino became a star. He often plays tough but intelligent and sensitive anti-heroes on screen, frequently accepting challenging and controversial roles. He has been nominated for Academy Awards several times: for *The Godfather*, for *Serpico* (73), for *The Godfather, Part II* (74), for *Dog Day Afternoon* (75) and for *. . . And Justice for All* (79). However, the theater has remained his first love.
**Selected Films:** *Me, Natalie* (687), *The Panic in Needle Park* (71), *The Godfather* (72), *Serpico* (73), *The Godfather, Part II* (74), *Dog Day Afternoon* (75), *Bobby Deerfield* (77), *. . . And Justice for All* (79), *Cruising* (80), *Author! Author!* (82), *Scarface* (83), *Revolution* (85).

## PAGE, Gale (1911-1983)

Born Sally Rutter in Spokane, Washington, Page was a singer and radio actress before rocketing to stardom alongside the three Lane sisters in *Four Daughters* (38) and its sequels. After a decade of roles as a wholesome female, her appearances fell off in the 1950s.

**Selected Films:** *Four Daughters* (38), *Crime School* (38), *Daughters Courageous* (39), *Four Wives* (40), *Knute Rockne – All American* (40), *Four Mothers* (41), *The Time of Your Life* (48), *About Mrs Leslie* (54).

## PAGE, Geraldine (1924-1987)

An actress unconventional in her career, her style, and her roles, Geraldine Page was nonetheless a familiar and popular star of stage and screen from the 1950s. Born in Kirksville, Missouri she began acting in stock as a teenager and by the early 1950s was working on and off Broadway, winning New York Drama Critics awards for her roles in two Tennessee Williams plays, *Summer and Smoke* and *Sweet Bird of Youth*, she repeated both roles on the screen, respectively in 1961 and 1962, and for both was nominated for best-actress Oscars. After an early screen appearance in *Out of the Night* (47), Page was nominated for a supporting-actress Oscar for her performance as the spinster in *Hondo* (53) and likewise for roles in *You're a Big Boy Now* (67) and *Pete 'n' Tillie* (72). The next best-actress nomination came for another of her eccentric performances as the mother in Woody Allen's *Interiors* (78). At long last, Page secured an Academy Award as best actress for her lead in *The Trip to Bountiful* (85). Her two husbands have been violinist Alexander Schneider and actor Rip Torn.

**Selected Films:** *Out of the Night* (47), *Hondo* (53), *Taxi* (53), *Summer and Smoke* (61), *Sweet Bird of Youth* (62), *Toys in the Attic* (63), *Dear Heart* (64), *You're a Big Boy Now* (67), *Pete 'n' Tillie* (72), *The Day of the Locust* (75), *Interiors* (78), *I'm Dancing as Fast as I Can* (82), *The Trip to Bountiful* (85), *Native Son* (86).

## PAGET, Debra (1933- )

Born Debralee Griffin in Denver, Colorado, Paget got into movies in her teens. Her role in *Broken Arrow* (50) was the first of several performances as American Indians. Otherwise she was a staple semi-sexy second lead of costume and Biblical epics like *Demetrius and the Gladiators* (54) and *The Ten Commandments* (56). Paget played the object of Elvis's affections in his first film, *Love Me Tender* (56). She was once married to director Budd Boetticher for three weeks.

**Selected Films:** *Cry of the City* (48), *Broken Arrow* (50), *Les Miserables* (52), *Demetrius and the Gladiators* (54), *Prince Valiant* (54), *The Ten Commandments* (56), *Love Me Tender* (56), *Tales of Terror* (62), *The Haunted Palace* (64).

## PAIGE, Janis (1922- )

This actress/singer in light musicals planned a career on the operatic stage. Born Donna Mae Tjaden in Tacoma, Washington, Janis Paige studied voice in her youth. Discovered by a movie talent scout while waitressing at the Hollywood Canteen, she got into movies in the mid-1940s and for the next decade was seen, often with Jack Carson, in second leads of both dramas and musicals; these included *Hollywood Canteen* (44), *Of Human Bondage* (46), and *Two Gals and a Guy* (51). In 1954 came her finest role, as co-star of the Broadway hit *Pajama Game*. After that, she returned to Hollywood for a few more years of major screen roles in pictures like *Silk Stockings* (57) and *Please Don't Eat the Daisies* (60), meanwhile starring briefly in the TV series *It's Always Jan*. Paige's movie career trailed off during the 1960s, though she kept working in theater and in nightclubs. In the 1970s she appeared in made-for-TV movies including *Lanigan's Rabbi*.

**Selected Films:** *Hollywood Canteen* (44), *The Time the Place and the Girl* (46), *Of Human Bondage* (46), *Romance on the High Seas* (48), *Two Gals and a Guy* (51), *Mr Universe* (51), *Silk Stockings* (57), *Please Don't Eat the Daisies* (60), *Follow the Boys* (63), *Welcome to Hard Times* (67).

## PAIGE, Mabel (1879-1954)

Born in New York and onstage from her early childhood, Paige appeared in movie comedy shorts in the teens. She is best remembered, however, for a number of old-lady character roles in her last decade, most notably the lead in *Someone to Remember* (43).

**Selected Films:** *Mixed Flats* (15), *Lucky Jordan* (43), *Someone to Remember* (43), *Johnny Belinda* (48), *Houdini* (53).

## PAIGE, Robert (1910- )

Born John Arthur Paige in Indianapolis, Indiana, Paige came to movies from radio in the mid-1930s and played romantic leads under the name David Carlyle. Changing his name to Robert Paige in 1938, he began a career that lasted over two decades, as the lead in mostly minor films ranging from thrillers to musicals and comedies. He was later a TV quiz-show host, and appeared on the series *Run Buddy Run*.

**Selected Films:** *Annapolis Farewell* (35), *Hellzapoppin* (41), *Son of Dracula* (43), *Tangier* (46), *Abbott and Costello Go to Mars* (53), *Bye Bye Birdie* (63).

## PAIVA, Nestor (1905-1966)

Paiva was born in Fresno, California, and came to the screen in the late 1930s with a hulking presence and a gift for dialect. For the next thirty years he played small roles, usually as foreigners of one nationality or another. For eleven years, he also

appeared in the Los Angeles company of *The Drunkard*. In later years he performed in horror movies like *The Creature from the Black Lagoon* (54).
**Selected Films:** *Ride a Crooked Mile* (38), *The Song of Bernadette* (43), *Mighty Joe Young* (49), *The Creature from the Black Lagoon* (54), *The Mole People* (56), *The Spirit Is Willing* (66).

## PALANCE, Jack (1920- )

Born Walter Palanuik in Lattimer, Pennsylvania, Palance was burned severely in a bomber crash during World War II. Plastic surgery gave his face a taut, almost skull-like, appearance. With a sinister voice to match, he has frequently appeared as a villain in Hollywood films, and more recently in international movies. He has also been a frequent performer on television, and his most memorable role was in that medium – as the over-the-hill prize fighter in Rod Serling's *Requiem for a Heavyweight*.
**Selected Films:** *Panic in the Streets* (50), *Shane* (53), *Sign of the Pagan* (54), *The Big Knife* (55), *I Died a Thousand Times* (55), *Che!* (69), *Oklahoma Crude* (73), *Alone in the Dark* (82), *Ladyfingers* (80).

*Jack Palance in* Shane *(53).*

## PALIN, Michael (1943- )

One of the principals of Britain's legendary Monty Python comedy troupe, Palin was educated at Oxford and has had the busiest post-Python acting career of the lot, starring in *The Missionary* (82) and playing a major role in ex-Python Terry Jones's *Brazil* (85).
**Selected Films:** *Monty Python and the Holy Grail* (75), *Jabberwocky* (77), *The Life of Brian* (79), *The Missionary* (82), *Monty Python's the Meaning of Life* (83), *Brazil* (85), *A Private Function* (85).

## PALLETTE, Eugene (1889-1954)

Born in Winfield, Kansas, Pallette started in silent film in the teens as a lithe leading man, with Douglas Fairbanks as one of *The Three Musketeers* (21). By the time sound arrived, however, Pallette had expanded to 275 pounds. For the rest of his screen career he was a heavy character actor with a foghorn voice, best known as the definitive Friar Tuck in *The Adventures of Robin Hood* (38).
**Selected Films:** *The Tattooed Arm* (13), *Intolerance* (16), The Three Musketeers (21), *The Ten Commandments* (23), *My Man Godfrey* (36), *The Adventures of Robin Hood* (38), *The Lady Eve* (41), *Lake Placid Serenade* (45), *Silver River* (48).

## PALMER, Betsy (1929- )

Born Patricia Brumek in East Chicago, Indiana, Palmer was a sweet-faced presence in several films of the 1950s. She is best-known as a TV quiz-show panelist, and one of the *Today Show* girls.
**Selected Films:** *The Long Gray Line* (55), *Queen Bee* (55), *The Tin Star* (57), *The Last Angry Man* (59), *It Happened to Jane* (59).

## PALMER, Lilli (1914-1986)

Palmer was born Lilli Peiser in Posen, Germany, to an Austrian family. She made her stage debut in Berlin, but left after the Nazis rise to power. She made her film debut in London in *Crime Unlimited* (34). Palmer appeared regularly in British movies until she came to the United States with her then husband, actor Rex Harrison. Hollywood movies and Broadway plays followed. She continued her stage career in Europe, and also wrote two novels and her autobiography, *Change Lobsters and Dance*.
**Selected Films:** *Crime Unlimited* (34), *Secret Agent* (36), *Thunder Rock* (42), *The Rake's Progress* (45), *My Girl Tisa* (47), *The Fourposter* (52), *But Not for Me* (58), *The Pleasure of his Company* (61), *Sebastian* (67), *De Sade* (69), *Night Hair Child* (71), *The Boys From Brazil* (78).

## PANGBORN, Franklin (1894-1958)

Born in Newark, New Jersey, Pangborn was a straight stage actor for years before coming to the screen in the mid-1920s. For three decades he played over 100 comic roles as flustered, fidgety, harrassed hotel clerks and similar parts.
**Selected Films:** *Exit Smiling* (26), *Getting Gertie's Garter* (27), *My Man Godfrey* (36), *A Star is Born* (37), *The Bank Dick* (40), *Hail the Conquering Hero* (44), *The Story of Mankind* (57).

## PAPAS, Irene (1926- )

An intense actress of striking but unconventional dark-haired beauty, Irene Papas has played a wide variety of roles in her three-decade screen career, but perhaps will best be remembered for her masterful work in the classical dramas of her native Greece. Born Irene Lelekou in Chiliomodion, Greece, Papas sang and danced in variety shows in her teens, meanwhile studying classical theater in Athens. She began appearing in Greek movies in 1950 and during the next decade worked in Italy and the United States as well. Her films of the 1950s include potboilers like the Italian *Attila* (54) and the American production *Tribute to a Bad Man* (56). From that point Papas moved easily between popular action films including *The Guns of* Navarone (61) and more serious parts, like the title role of the classical *Electra* (62). Perhaps her best-known role is as a doomed widow in *Zorba the Greek* (64). Over the next years she played Yves Montand's wife in Z (69) and Catharine of Aragon in *Anne of the Thousand Days* (70). Among Papas' classical roles were a memorable Helen of Troy in *The Trojan Women* (71) and Clytemnestra in *Iphgenia* (77).
**Selected Films:** *Necropolitia* (51), *Attila the Hun* (54), *Tribute to a Bad Man* (56), *The Guns of Navarone* (61), *Electra* (62), *The Moon-Spinners* (64), *Beyond the Mountains* (66), *Zorba the Greek* (69), *Z* (69), *Anne of the Thousand Days* (71), *The Trojan Women* (71), *Moses* (76), *Iphigenia* (77), *Bloodline* (79), *Sweet Country* (87).

## PARIS, Jerry (1925-1986)

Born in San Francisco, California, Paris began acting onscreen in 1950 and played supporting roles in several major films. As an actor he is best known as the neighbor on *The Dick Van Dyke Show*. After directing several episodes of that show, Paris went on to direct several TV series including *Happy Days* and movies including *Viva Max!* (69).
**Selected Films:** *Cyrano de Bergerac* (50), *The Caine Mutiny* (54), *Marty* (55), *The Naked and the Dead* (58), *The Great Imposter* (61).

## PARKER, Cecil (1897-1971)

Born Cecil Schwabe in Hastings, England, Parker made his stage debut in 1922 and his film debut in 1929. For forty years thereafter he was one of the screen's classic stiff-lipped, British aristocrats, in leads and supporting roles, both in straight plays and comedies. He played Britannus in *Caesar and Cleopatra* (45) and one of the crooks in *The Ladykillers* (55).
**Selected Films:** *The Woman in White* (29), *The Lady Vanishes* (38), *Caesar and Cleopatra* (45), *The Chiltern Hundreds* (49), *The Court Jester* (55), *The Ladykillers* (55), *Moll Flanders* (65), *Oh! What a Lovely War* (69).

## PARKER, Cecilia (1905- )

Born in Fort William, Ontario, Parker studied voice before arriving in Hollywood in the early 1930s. She played leads in minor movies and supporting roles in major ones before, at 32, beginning her tenure as the teenage sister of Mickey Rooney in the Andy Hardy movies.
**Selected Films:** *Young as You Feel* (31), *The Painted Veil* (34), *A Family Affair* (37), *Seven Sweethearts* (42), *Andy Hardy Comes Home* (58).

## PARKER, Eleanor (1922- )

Born in Cedarville, Ohio, Parker appeared briefly on the stage before she was given a Hollywood contract. She was a stunning redhead who kept getting better and better roles, although she made her debut as an extra in *They Died with Their Boots On* (41), until she became a leading lady in the 1950s. Never typecast, she played a wide variety of characters and was nominated for an Academy Award three times – for *Caged* (50), a prison film; for *Detective Story* (51), as the ignored wife of detective Kirk Douglas; and for *Interrupted Melody* (55), in which she played the part of Marjorie Lawrence, the Australian opera star, who made a comeback after being crippled by polio. Later she shifted to supporting roles.
**Selected Films:** *Buses Roar* (42), *Mission to Moscow* (43), *Pride of the Marines* (45), *Of Human Bondage* (46), *The Voice of the Turtle* (47), *Caged* (50), *Detective Story* (51), *Scaramouche* (52), *The Naked Jungle* (54), *Interrupted Melody* (55), *The Sound of Music* (65), *Eye of the Cat* (69), *Sunburn* (79).

## PARKER, Fess (1925- )

Parker, born in Fort Worth, Texas, grew up rangy and rugged and gravitated naturally to frontiersman roles in movies. Onscreen from the early 1950s he is best remembered for the popular screen and TV versions of Disney's *Davy Crockett* and as *Daniel Boone* in the TV series. He also starred in several other Disney features.
**Selected Films:** *Untamed Frontier* (52), *Davy Crockett – King of the Wild Frontier* (54), *Old Yeller* (57), *The Jayhawkers* (59), *Hell is for Heroes!* (62), *Smoky* (66).

## PARKER, Jean (1912- )

Born Lois Mae Greene in Butte, Montana, Parker was spotted in a high school photograph by MGM and given a term contract. For some years she played pretty ingenue roles, including Beth in *Little Women* (33). In the 1940s she was mostly consigned to second-feature action movies and by the 1950s was playing hard-boiled dames.
**Selected Films:** *Divorce in the Family* (32), *Little Women* (33), *Sequoia* (34), *The Ghost Goes West* (36), *Power Dive* (41), *A Lawless Street* (55), *Apache Uprising* (66) *Stigma* (72).

## PARKER, Suzy (1932- )

Born in San Antonio, Texas, Parker became one of the top fashion models of the 1950s. Accompanied by much publicity, she was cast with Cary Grant in *Kiss Them for Me* (57) and with Gary Cooper in *Ten North Frederick* (58), but finally demonstrated little gift for acting onscreen.
**Selected Films:** *Kiss Them for Me* (57), *Ten North Frederick* (58), *The Best of Everything* (59), *Circle of Deception* (61), *Chamber of Horrors* (66).

## PARKS, Larry (1914-1975)

Samuel Lawrence Kleusman Parks was born in Olathe, Kansas, and began his film career in the early 1940s and seemed settled in B movies when he rocketed to fame in the title role of *The Jolson Story* (46). After the sequel, *Jolson Sings Again* (49), Parks was briefly a star, but his career was interrupted by the Red Scare of the 1950s and he made only sporadic appearances onstage and in film. He was married to actress Betty Garrett.
**Selected Films:** *Mystery Ship* (41), *The Jolson Story* (46), *The Gallant Blade* (48), *Jolson Sings Again* (49), *The Light Fantastic* (51), *Freud* (63).

## PARKS, Michael (1938- )

Born in Corona, California, Parks was cast early in his career as Adam in John Huston's *The Bible* (66). He went on to play occasional screen roles – including Robert Kennedy in *The Private Files of J Edgar Hoover* (77) – and TV productions including the series *Then Came Bronson* and *The Young Lawyers*.
**Selected Films:** *Wild Seed* (65), *The Bible* (66), *The Happening* (67), *The Private Files of J Edgar Hoover* (77), *The Evictors* (79), *Savannah Smiles* (82).

## PARRISH, Helen (1922-1959)

Born in Columbus, Georgia, Parrish first appeared onscreen at age five. She played child roles in full length films and appeared in some *Our Gang* shorts. Parrish then graduated to leads and supporting roles in mostly B movies. She was the sister of director Robert Parrish and was once married to screenwriter Charles Lang.
**Selected Films:** *Babe Comes Home* (27), *The Big Trail* (31), *A Dog of Flanders* (34), *Too Many Blondes* (41), *They Live in Fear* (44), *The Wolf Hunters* (50).

## PARSONS, Estelle (1927- )

Born in Lynn, Massachusetts, Parsons got her law degree and was a TV writer and producer before settling into acting on stage and screen. In movies from the early 1960s she has played striking supporting parts, winning an Oscar for her performance as Blanche Barrow in *Bonnie and Clyde* (67) and receiving a nomination the next year for her role in *Rachel, Rachel*.
**Selected Films:** *Ladybug, Ladybug* (63), *Bonnie and Clyde* (67), *Rachel, Rachel* (68), *Don't Drink the Water* (69), *I Never Sang for My Father* (70), *For Pete's Sake* (74), *Foreplay* (75).

## PARTON, Dolly (1946- )

Born Dolly Rebecca Parton in Locust Ridge, Sevier County, Tennessee, she was the fourth of 12 children raised in a two-room shack. Parton began writing songs at the age of five, and at eight she received her first guitar. After high school, she headed for Nashville, existing for three weeks on hot dog relish and mustard. Parton got her first big break when country and western singer Porter Wagonner asked her to join his road show and helped her land a recording contract with RCA. She soon was one of the most prominent country and western singers in the country, and decided to try her hand at movies. She has become quite an adept comedienne.
**Selected Films:** *9 to 5* (80), *The Best Little Whorehouse in Texas* (82), *Rhinestone* (84).

## PATRICK, Gail (1911-1980)

Born Margaret Fitzpatrick in Birmingham, Alabama, Patrick studied law before being discovered by Paramount. Appearing in films of the 1930s and 1940s, the dark-haired actress usually played leads and second leads as cold career woman or often unsympathetic 'other women.' She later produced the TV series *Perry Mason*.
**Selected Films:** *If I Had a Million* (32), *The Phantom Broadcast* (32), *My Man Godfrey* (36), *Artists and Models* (37), *My Favorite Wife* (40), *The Plainsman and the Lady* (46), *The Inside Story* (48).

## PATRICK, Lee (1906-1982)

New York-born Patrick acted on Broadway in her teens and made her screen debut in 1929. In some 60 films she usually played character roles as hard-bitten blondes. In later years she was cast in prickly old lady roles. She also played Henrietta, the wife on the TV series *Topper*.
**Selected Films:** *Strange Cargo* (29), *The Maltese Falcon* (41), *Now Voyager* (42), *Vertigo* (58), *Wives and Lovers* (63), *The Black Bird* (75).

## PATRICK, Nigel (1913-1981)

Born Nigel Wemyss in London, England, Patrick made his stage debut in 1932 and his screen debut in *Mrs Pym of Scotland Yard* (39). He played suave Englishmen, often with a cynical streak, in leads and supporting roles into the 1970s. He continued his acting stage career and directed two films including *How to Marry a Rich Uncle* (57).
**Selected Films:** *Mrs Pym of Scotland Yard* (39), *Spring in Park Lane* (47), *The Pickwick Papers* (53), *The League of Gentlemen* (60), *The Mackintosh Man* (73), *Silver Bears* (77).

## PATTEN, Luana (1938- )

American-born Patten made her film debut as a child, in Disney's *Song of the South* (46). She went on to play teenage roles in films of the 1950s, among them Disney's *Johnny Tremain* (57). Although she appeared occasionally in the 1960s, an adult career never materialized.
**Selected Films:** *Song of the South* (46), *So Dear to My Heart* (48), *Johnny Tremain* (57), *The Little Shepherd of Kingdom Come* (61), *Follow Me, Boys* (66).

## PATTERSON, Elizabeth (1876-1966)

Born in Savannah, Tennessee, the gaunt-featured Patterson spent her long career on stage and screen mostly playing mothers and aunts both sympathetic and catty. Her film appearances finally numbered over a hundred.
**Selected Films:** *The Book of Charms* (26), *The Boy Friend* (27), *Daddy Long Legs* (30), *A Bill of Divorcement* (32), *The Cat and the Canary* (39), *Tobacco Road* (41), *Intruder in the Dust* (48), *Little Women* (49), *Bright Leaf* (50), *Pal Joey* (57), *The Oregon Trail* (59) *Tall Story* (60).

## PATTERSON, Neva (1925- )

Born in Nevada, Iowa, Patterson has played character roles on TV and in movies since the mid-1950s. Among her TV work have been appearances on the series *The Governor and JJ* and *Nichols*.
**Selected Films:** *Desk Set* (57), *Too Much Too Soon* (58), *The Domino Principle* (77).

## PAVAN, Marisa (1932- )

Born Marisa Pierangeli in Cagliari, Sardinia – the sister of actress Pier Angeli – Pavan made her American screen debut in *What Price Glory?* (52). The dark-haired beauty went on to major roles through the 1950s, winning a supporting-actress Oscar nomination for her performance in *The Rose Tattoo* (55). She is married to actor Jean-Pierre Aumont.
**Selected Films:** *What Price Glory?* (52), *Drum Beat* (54), *The Man in the Gray Flannel Suit* (56), *Solomon and Sheba* (59), *A Slightly Pregnant Man* (73).

## PAXINOU, Katina (1900-1973)

Born Katina Constantinopolous in Piraeus, the distinguished Greek actress came to the United States during World War II to tour in *Hedda Gabler*. For her first American screen role as the gypsy Pilar in *For Whom the Bell Tolls* (43), she received a supporting-actress Academy Award. Despite ensuing movie roles, including Christine Mannon in *Mourning Becomes Electra* (47), Paxinou was never really established in Hollywood. Finally she returned to Greece to help found the Royal Theater, with her husband, actor Alexis Minotis, and appeared occasionally in European films.
**Selected Films:** *For Whom the Bell Tolls* (43), *Confidential Agent* (44), *Mourneing Becomes Electra* (47), *Mr Arkadin* (55), *Rocco and His Brothers* (60), *Zita* (68) *Un Eté Sauvage* (72).

## PAYNE, John (1912- )

Beginning his movie career as a handsome leading man, John Payne ended up toting a gun in minor westerns and action pictures. Born in Roanoke, Virginia, he studied drama at Columbia. After theater experience, Payne made his film debut in *Dodsworth* (36). Over the next 15 years he mostly starred – singing occasionally – in light pictures, often teamed with Betty Grable, Sonja Henie or Alice Faye; these included *Tin Pan Alley* (40), *Sun Valley Serenade* (41), and *Hello, Frisco, Hello* (43). Later Payne was seen in routine films like *Raiders of the Seven Seas* (53) and *Hell's Island* (55). He produced, co-wrote, and acted in *The Boss* (56). He left the screen to star in the TV series *The Restless Gun*. In 1974 he and old co-star Alice Faye starred in a revival of the stage musical *Good News*. Payne's wives have included actresses Anne Shirley and Gloria De Haven.
**Selected Films:** *Dodsworth* (36), *College Swing* (38), *Kid Nightingale* (39), *Tin Pan Alley* (40), *Sun Valley Serenade* (41), *The Great American Broadcast* (41), *Hello, Frisco, Hello* (43), The Dolly Sisters (45), *Miracle on 34th Street* (47), *Raiders of the Seven Seas* (53), *Rails into Laramie* (54), *Hell's Island* (55), *The Boss* (56), *Gift of the Nile* (68), *The Savage Wild* (70).

## PAYTON, Barbara (1927-1967)

Born in Cloquet, Minnesota, Payton was a sexy, leading lady of second features in the 1950s. She was best known as a generator of headlines – when actors Franchot Tone and Tom Neal brawled over her in 1951, after which she briefly married Tone and then returned to Neal.
**Selected Films:** *Trapped* (49), *Bride of the Gorilla* (51), *Bad Blonde* (53), *Murder is My Beat* (55).

## PEARCE, Alice (1913-1966)

A New York-born character actress, Pearce first found screen success sneezing chronically in *On the Town* (49). She went on to lively comic roles in movies and was a staple of the TV series *Bewitched*.
**Selected Films:** *On the Town* (49), *The Opposite Sex* (56), *Tammy and the Doctor* (63), *Kiss Me Stupid* (64), *The Glass Bottom Boat* (66).

## PEARY, Harold (1909-1985)

Born in Portugal, comedian Peary played the windbaggy character of The Great Gildersleeve on radio and in a few films of the 1940s.
**Selected Films:** *Comin' Round the Mountain* (40), *Seven Days Leave* (42), *The Great Gildersleeve* (43), *Wetbacks* (56), *Clambake* (67).

*Gregory Peck in* The Omen *(76).*

## PECK, Gregory (1916- )

Peck is a leading man who projects strength, sincerity, moral fiber, intelligence, kindness and conviction, rather than flashy heroics. He also conveys all this virtue in a likeable way, a rare achievement. Dark and broodingly handsome, he is also a sex symbol – but the kind who would make a good son-in-law. Peck was one of the first of the post-World War II actors to take advantage of the crumbling Hollywood studio system, working out financially rewarding deals for himself, and working only in the pictures he chose. His steady, stoic style was sometimes called wooden by critics, but when he had good material, he was an easy-to-love blockbuster star. Born Eldred Gregory Peck in La Jolla, California, he attended San Diego State College, then enrolled in New York's Neighborhood Playhouse, making his debut on Broadway in *The Morning Star*, by Emlyn Williams, in 1942. A spinal injury prevented him from seeing any military service in World War II, and in those war years, when leading men were at a premium in Hollywood, he was given a contract. His first film was *Days of Glory* (43) – a war movie. Peck proved strong on classy sex appeal and was a hit in many kinds of pictures. He starred in *Spellbound* (45), Alfred Hitchcock's famous psychological thriller that also starred Ingrid Bergman; *Gentleman's Agreement* (47), an Oscar-winning movie about anti-Semitism; and *The Gunfighter* (50), an innovative and mature Western. He fell in love with Audrey Hepburn in *Roman Holiday* (53), was Captain Ahab in *Moby Dick* (56) and won an Academy Award for Best Actor playing a liberal Southern lawyer in *To Kill a Mockingbird* (63). Peck's career went on the downswing as he grew older and there were rumors that he was through, especially when he took the lead in *The Omen* (76). The film made more money than anything he had ever done, and he came bouncing back, this time as a Nazi doctor in *The Boys from Brazil* (78). Active in many charities, Peck was the recipient of the Medal of Freedom Award and the Academy of Motion Picture Arts and Sciences Jean Hersholt Humanitarian Award.
**Selected Films:** *Days of Glory* (43), *The Keys of the Kingdom* (44), *The Valley of Decision* (44), *Spellbound* (45), *The Yearling* (46), *Duel in the Sun* (46), *The Macomber Affair* (47), *Gentleman's Agreement* (47), *The Paradine Case* (47), *Twelve O'Clock High* (49), *The Gunfighter* (50) *Captain Horatio Hornblower* (51), *The Snows of Kilimanjaro* (52), *Roman Holiday* (53), *The Man in the Gray Flannel Suit* (56), *Moby Dick* (56), *The Big Country* (58), *On the Beach* (59), *The Guns of Navarone* (61), *Cape Fear* (62), *To Kill a Mockingbird* (63), *Captain Newman, MD* (63), *Arabesque* (66), *The Stalking Moon* (68), *The Omen* (76), *The Boys from Brazil* (78), *Sea Wolves* (80).

## PEGGY, Baby (1917- )

Born Peggy Montgomery in Rock Island, Illinois, Peggy made her screen debut at age three and appeared in a number of silent comedy shorts and features as a kid and some B movies in her teens. Much later she published an book about child stars called *Hollywood Children*.
**Selected Films:** *Peggy Behave* (22), *The Law Forbids* (24), *Arizona Days* (28), *Eight Girls in a Boat* (34).

## PENDLETON, Nat (1895-1967)

Born near Davenport, Iowa, Pendleton was an Olympic and professional wrestler before starting in movies in the mid-1920s. For 25 years he played mostly supporting roles as big dumb characters, like the ambulance driver in the *Dr Kildare* series.
**Selected Films:** *The Hoosier Schoolmaster* (24), *The Thin Man* (34), *At the Circus* (39), *Jail House Blues* (42), *Death Valley* (49).

## PENN, Sean (1960- )

Penn was born to a theatrical family in Santa Monica, California and served a theater apprenticeship in Los Angeles. After some TV experience he made his screen debut in *Taps* (81) and then shot to stardom in the teen movie *Fast Times at Ridgemont High* (82). Penn has been the most visible of the Hollywood 'brat pack'; his fast-and-furious lifestyle and aversion to publicity have assured him featured places in the headlines. In 1985, Penn was married to the rock star Madonna.
**Selected Films:** *Taps* (81), *Fast Times at Ridgemont High* (82), *Bad Boys* (83), *Crackers* (84), *Racing with the Moon* (84), *The Falcon and the Snowman* (85), *Shanghai Surprise* (86), *At Close Range* (86).

## PEPPARD, George (1928- )

Born in Detroit, Michigan, Peppard is a good-looking leading man who tends to play tough heroes. He began his career on Broadway and has a few golden moments in films, such as in *The Blue Max* (64), in which he played an arrogant and ambitious German fighter pilot during World War I. But often the vehicles he appears in are not up to his talents. Peppard has achieved some of his greatest success on television in the series *Banacek* and *The A-Team*.
**Selected Films:** *The Strange One* (57), *Home from the Hill* (60), *Breakfast at Tiffany's* (61), *How the West Was Won* (62), *The Victors* (63), *The Carpetbaggers* (64), *The Blue Max* (66), *Rough Night in Jericho* (67), *Newman's Law* (74), *Battle Beyond the Stars* (80), *Five Days From Home* (80).

## PEPPER, Barbara (1912-1969)

Pepper was one of those actresses in mostly second features of the 1930s and 1940s who specialized in playing loose ladies. She appeared occasionally onscreen into the 1960s.
**Selected Films:** *Our Daily Bread* (33), *Lady in the Morgue* (38), *Brewster's Millions* (45), *The D I* (57), *Kiss Me Stupid* (64).

## PERKINS, Anthony (1932- )

Born in New York City, the son of actor Osgood Perkins, he has been both a leading man and fine supporting actor. Tall, slightly-built and boyishly charming, Perkins first film was *The Actress* (53), based on actress Ruth Gordon's remembrances of her life in the 1920s. He made quite an impression in *Friendly Persuasion* (56), a film about a Quaker family in Indiana during the Civil War, in which he played the son who, in spite of his pacifist beliefs, decides to join the Union Army. Perkins is, of course, most famous for his role as Norman Bates, the homicidal proprietor of the Bates Motel, in Alfred Hitchcock's spine-chiller, *Psycho* (60).
**Selected Films:** *The Actress* (53), *Friendly Persuasion* (56), *Desire Under the Elms* (57), *Fear Strikes Out* (57), *This Angry Age* (58), *Green Mansions* (58), *On the Beach* (59), *Tall Story* (60), *Psycho* (60), *Is Paris Burning?* (65), *Catch 22* (70), *Murder on the Orient Express* (74), *Winter Kills* (79), *Psycho II* (83), *Crimes of Passion* (84), *Psycho III* (86).

## PERKINS, Millie (1939- )

A native of Passaic, New Jersey, Perkins came from drama school to make her screen debut in the title role of *The Diary of Anne Frank* (59). She played ingenue roles in the 1960s and appeared occasionally thereafter, but her career never truly took off.
**Selected Films:** *The Diary of Anne Frank* (59), *Wild in the Country* (61), *Wild in the Streets* (68), *The Witch Who Came from the Sea* (76), *Table for Five* (83), *Jake Speed* (86), *At Close Range* (86).

## PERKINS, Osgood (1892-1937)

American character actor Perkins spent most of his career on the stage but did appear in occasional films of the 1920s and 1930s. He was the father of actor Anthony Perkins.
**Selected Films:** *The Cradle Buster* (22), *Knockout Reilly* (27), *Scarface* (32), *I Dream Too Much* (35).

## PERREAU, Gigi (1941- )

Born Ghislaine Perreau-Saussine to a French family in Los Angeles, California, Perreau got into movies at age six. For several years she was a charming, apple-cheeked child star, but failed to make the successful change to adult roles.
**Selected Films:** *Madame Curie* (43), *Green Dolphin Street* (47), *My Foolish Heart* (49), *The Man in the Gray Flannel Suit* (56), *Tammy Tell Me True* (61), *Follow the Sun* (69).

## PERRINE, Valerie (1944- )

Born in Galveston, Texas, Perrine was a college dropout and topless dancer before making her movie debut in *Slaughterhouse Five* (72). Her appearances have been mostly decorative, though her role as Lenny Bruce's wife in *Lenny* (74) proved Perrine could handle a serious part and earned her an Oscar nomination.
**Selected Films:** *Slaughterhouse Five* (72), *The Last American Hero* (73), *Lenny* (74), *WC Fields and Me* (76), *The Electric Horseman* (79), *Superman II* (80), *The Border* (82).

## PERSOFF, Nehemiah (1920- )

A native of Jerusalem, Israel, Persoff emigrated to the United States and studied drama at New York's Actor's Studio. After stage experience he made his movie debut in 1948. Since then he has played a great many character roles in major films.
**Selected Films:** *The Naked City* (48), *On the Waterfront* (54), *This Angry Age* (57), *Some Like It Hot* (59), *The Comancheros* (62), *Fate is the Hunter* (64), *Psychic Killer* (75), *Yentl* (83).

## PETERS, Bernadette (1948- )

The future perennial about-to-be-superstar was born Bernadette Lazzara in Queens, New York. Peters made her professional debut at age five and in her teens, already an accomplished musical-comedy performer, was part of a road show of *The Most Happy Fella*. In the mid-1960s she began her long string of well-received roles in mediocre productions, with occasional equivocal successes; including the musicals *George M!* (68) and *Dames at Sea* (68). After several small movie parts and a number of TV guest appearances, Peters co-starred in Norman Lear's TV series *All's Fair* (76). Teaming up personally and professionally with comic Steve Martin, she was the femal lead in his *The Jerk* (79)

and *Pennies from Heaven* (81). In her next film, *Heartbeeps* (81), she and Andy Kaufman played robots in love. Peters returned to the musical stage to star in two moderately successful productions, *Sunday in the Park with George* (84) and *Song and Dance* (86).
**Selected Films:** *Ace Eli and Rodger of the Skies* (73), *WC Fields and Me* (76), *Silent Movie* (76), *The Jerk* (79), *Pennies from Heaven* (81), *Heartbeeps* (81), *Annie* (82).

## PETERS, Brock (1927- )

New York-born Peters established himself on-stage in the 1950s with his rich voice and powerful acting. Making his film debut in 1954, the black actor has proved adept both as villains, including Crown in *Porgy and Bess* (59), and sympathetic roles.
**Selected Films:** *Carmen Jones* (54), *Porgy and Bess* (59), *To Kill a Mockingbird* (62), *Heavens Above* (63), *Major Dundee* (65), *The McMasters* (70), *Two-Minute Warning* (76).

## PETERS, Jean (1926- )

Born in Canton, Ohio, Elizabeth Jean Peters won a 1946 beauty contest in her native state and for a prize won a trip to Hollywood. A year later the wholesomely pretty brunette made her movie debut starring with Tyrone Power in *Captain from Castile* (47). Over the next eight years she starred in a number of major films, among them with Brando in *Viva Zapata!* (52). In 1955 Peters abruptly vanished from the screen, marrying billionaire Howard Hughes and following him into seclusion. She divorced Hughes in 1971 and returned to occasional roles on television.
**Selected Films:** *Captain from Castile* (47), *Deep Waters* (48), *As Young as You Feel* (51), *Viva Zapata!* (52), *Three Coins in the Fountain* (54), *A Man Called Peter* (55).

## PETERS, Susan (1921-1952)

Born Suzanne Carnahan in Spokane, Washington, Peters began appearing in movies (at first under her real name) in her teens. For several years she played roles as a sweet kid, receiving a supporting-actress Oscar nomination for *Random Harvest* (42). After being partially paralyzed in a hunting accident, she gamely returned to occasional stage and screen roles in a wheelchair before her early death. She was married to actor/director Richard Quine from 1943 to 1948.
**Selected Films:** *Sockaroo* (39), *Santa Fe Trail* (40), *Random Harvest* (42), *Assignment in Brittany* (43), *Song of Russia* (43), *Keep Your Powder Dry* (45), *The Sign of the Ram* (48).

## PETROVA, Olga (1886-1977)

Born Muriel Harding in Britain (though later studio publicity had it she was a Russian aristocrat born in Poland), Petrova began her film career in 1914 and for several years was a leading *femme fatale* of the silent screen. She later wrote for and acted on the stage and in 1942 published an autobiography, *Butter with My Bread*.
**Selected Films:** *The Tigress* (14), *The Vampire* (15), *The Undying Flame* (17), *Panther Woman* (18).

## PFEIFFER, Michelle (1957- )

This exquisitely beautiful actress was born in Santa Ana, California. She began her film career at the age of 25, playing a teenager in *Grease II* (82), and has since graduated to more complex characters.
**Selected Films:** *Grease II* (82), *Scarface* (83), *Into the Night* (85), *Ladyhawke* (85), *Sweet Liberty* (86), *The Witches of Eastwick* (87).

## PHILBIN, Mary (1903- )

A native of Chicago, Illinois, Philbin was a beauty-contest winner before arriving in movies in the early 1920s. She became a popular star of the late silent era, best-known today as the love object of Lon Chaney in *The Phantom of the Opera* (25). Her career did not survive the coming of sound.
**Selected Films:** *The Blazing Trail* (21), *The Temple of Venus* (23), *The Phantom of the Opera* (25), *The Man Who Laughs* (27), *The Shannons of Broadway* (29).

## PHILIPE, Gérard (1922-1959)

Gérard Philipe had all the ingredients of a legendary screen star: stunningly handsome, his style a mixture of insouciance and soulfulness, and dying at an early age, he was a sort of French version of James Dean. He also happened to be a well-trained and superlative actor. Philipe was born in Cannes, France, and switched from medical studies to acting in the early 1940s. Soon he was appearing on screen and stage, the latter including classical roles in Corneille and Racine. His breakthrough into international stardom came with his performances as a teenager who has a hopeless crush on a married woman in *Le Diable au Corps* (47). From that point Philipe appeared in several films a year through the 1950s, becoming one of the most popular French actors of all time. His notable performances included Faust in the comedy *Beauty and the Devil* (50), the title role in the swashbuckler *Fanfan la Tulipe* (51) and as the painter *Modigliani of Montparnasse* (58). In his later years Philipe wrote screenplays and directed, doing both in *Les Aventures de Till l'Espiègle* (56). He died suddenly at 37 of a heart attack, while working on Luis Buñuel's *Republic of Sin*.
**Selected Films:** *Les Petites du Quai aux Fleurs* (44), *The Idiot* (46), *Le Diable au Corps* (47), *Riptide* (49), *Beauty and the Devil* (50), *La Ronde* (50), *Fanfan la Tulipe* (51), *Pot-Bouille* (57), *Modigliani of Montparnasse* (58), *Les Liaisons dangereuses* (59).

## PHILLIPS, MacKenzie (1960- )

The daughter of singer John Phillips of The Mamas and the Papas, Phillips, born in Alexandria, Virginia, made her screen debut at 13, playing a teenybopper in *American Graffiti* (73). She has since done occasional screen and TV work including the TV movie *Eleanor and Franklin*.
**Selected Films:** *American Graffiti* (73)

## PICERNI, Paul (1922- )

Born in New York, Picerni began his film career in 1950 and for a decade starred and supported mostly in thrillers and adventures including *House of Wax* (53) and *To Hell and Back* (55). He also appeared on the TV series *The Untouchables*. His occasional screen appearances continued into the 1970s.
**Selected Films:** *Saddle Tramp* (50), *Maru Maru* (52), *House of Wax* (53), *To Hell and Back* (55), *Miracle in the Rain* (56), *Marjorie Morningstar* (58), *Che!* (69), *Kotch* (71).

## PICKENS, Slim (1919-1983)

Born Louis Lindley, Jr in Kingsberg, California, Pickens was a rodeo clown before making his screen debut in the early 1950s. He played drawling sidekicks mostly in minor Westerns until Stanley Kubrick, in an inspired bit of casting, put Pickens in the role of a bomber pilot who rodeo-rides an H-bomb into Russia in *Dr Strangelove* (64). Thereafter Pickens was a much-loved comic figure in a number of films including *Blazing Saddles* (74) and *Pat Garrett and Billy the Kid* (73).
**Selected Films:** *Rocky Mountain* (50), *The Great Locomotive Chase* (56), *One-Eyed Jacks* (59), *Dr Strangelove* (64), *Major Dundee* (65), *The Cowboys* (72), *Pat Garrett and Billy the Kid* (73), *Blazing Saddles* (74), *Honeysuckle Rose* (80), *The Howling* (81), *Pink Motel* (82).

## PICKFORD, Jack (1896-1933)

Born Jack Smith in Toronto, Ontario, Pickford began acting on stage as a child with his sister Gladys, who became silent superstar Mary Pickford and helped pave Jack's way into movies. He became a popular light romantic leading man, later doing occasional producing and co-directing, but his career ended with the sound era. Among his wives were actresses Olive Thomas and Marilyn Miller.
**Selected Films:** *The Kid* (10), *Tom Sawyer* (17), *Just Out of College* (21), *The Goose Woman* (25), *Brown of Harvard* (26), *Gang War* (28).

## PICKFORD, Mary (1893-1979)

She was 'America's Sweetheart' and, later on 'The World's Sweetheart' – a bigger box office draw than any other of her peers, including Charlie

*Mary Pickford in* The Little American *(17).*

Chaplin. She caught the fancy of millions of film goers from 1912 to 1928. People loved her for her blonde curls, her baby face and her air of virginity and innocence. Although she tried a wide variety of roles, Pickford's audiences preferred her as the plucky, innocent young girl, rich only in spirit, for whom a happy ending waits. For almost 25 years she may have been the most famous female on earth, a star known almost everywhere, as long as movies were shown there. Then she made a mistake. She grew up, and it finished her movie career. Born Gladys Smith in Toronto, Ontario, Canada, she became a child actress at the age of five after her father's death. Touring as 'Baby Gladys,' she was the chief source of income for her family, although eventually her sister Lottie and her brother Jack also went into acting. At age 14 she was on Broadway and at age 16 she became a Biograph player, working with director D W Griffith. Like the other players, her name wasn't listed in the movie credits, but her blonde ringlets won her the nickname 'the girl with the golden curls,' and, as such, she became very popular. She became a superstar in the motion picture *A Poor Little Rich Girl* (17), in which she played a child, although she was 24. Her personal wardrobe consisted of mature, stylish clothes to be worn at home, and girlish frills for public appearances. Pickford moved from film company to film company, negotiating the best deals she could get. Her salary was soon astronomical and she remained fabulously wealthy all her life. Accused of having 'a mind like a cash register,' she actually fought hard for artistic control. In 1919, she joined Charlie Chaplin, D W Griffith and husband-to-be Douglas Fairbanks in forming United Artists, so that the stars could produce, release and distribute their own films and the movies of others. Fairbanks and Pickford were Hollywood's royal couple, living in a palace called 'Pickfair.' It was the second marriage for each, and less rosy than the fan magazines painted it. Besides, a career crisis loomed for Pickford. She had played an ingenue in *Pollyanna* (19) and continued doing Cinderella roles into her thirties. By 1928, when she was 34,

she was sick of ringlets and appeared in her first talkie, *Coquette* (29), all grown up with her hair cut short. She won an Academy Award for her performance, but the movie didn't catch on with the public. She retired from films in the early 1930s, although she appeared frequently on radio. In 1936 she divorced Fairbanks and married Charles 'Buddy' Rogers. In 1975 she received a Special Academy Award 'in recognition of her unique contributions to the film industry and the development of film as an artistic medium.'
**Selected Films:** *Her First Biscuits* (09), *The Violin Maker of Cremona* (10), *The Paris Hat* (13), *Madame Butterfly* (15), *Less Than the Dust* (16), *A Poor Little Rich Girl* (17), *The Little American* (17), *The Little Princess* (17), *Rebecca of Sunnybrook Farm* (17), *Stella Maris* (18), *Pollyanna* (19), *Suds* (20), *Little Lord Fauntleroy* (21), *The Love Light* (21), *Tess of the Storm Country* (22), *Rosita* (23), *Dorothy Vernon of Haddon Hall* (24), *Little Annie Rooney* (25), *My Best Girl* (27), *The Taming of the Shrew* (29), *Coquette* (29), *Kiki* (31), *Secrets* (33).

## PICON, Molly (1898- )

Born in New York, Picon, a member of the Yiddish Theater has worked onstage for most of her acting career. She also appeared in occasional movies of the 1960s and 1970s.
**Selected Films:** *Come Blow Your Horn* (63), *Fiddler on the Roof* (71), *For Pete's Sake* (74).

## PIDGEON, Walter (1897-1984)

Pidgeon was strong without being threatening, reassuring without being insipid, a comfortable benign leading man, especially appealing during World War II when audiences dreamed of peaceful domesticity. He was born in East St John, New Brunswick, Canada, and went to the New England Conservatory of Music. His 50-year career in films began in 1925, when he appeared in *Mannequin*. Pidgeon starred as a supporting actor, then sang in early musicals, such as *Kiss Me Again* (30), when sound came in. During the 1940s he appeared in a number of important movies and was especially effective opposite Greer Garson. He switched to character roles in the 1950s and was effective in such disparate roles as a semi-mad scientist in the impressive science-fiction classic *Forbidden Planet* (56) and as a prominent senator in *Advise and Consent* (62).
**Selected Films:** *Mannequin* (25), *The Thirteenth Juror* (27), *Kiss Me Again* (30), *Saratoga* (37), *The Girl of the Golden West* (38), *Society Lawyer* (39), *Dark Command* (40), *Man Hunt* (41), *Blossoms in the Dust* (41), *How Green Was My Valley* (41), *Mrs Miniver* (42), *White Cargo* (42), *Madame Curie* (43), *Cass Timberlain* (47), *That Forsyte Woman* (49), *The Miniver Story* (50), *The Bad and the Beautiful* (52), *Executive Suite* (54), *Forbidden Planet* (56), *Voyage to the Bottom of the Sea* (61), *Advise and Consent* (62), *Funny Girl* (68), *Rascal* (69), *Sextette* (78).

## PISCOPO, Joe (1951- )

Born in Passaic, New Jersey, Piscopo worked in standup comedy, improvisational theater, and regional theater before getting his break in 1980 as a regular on TV's *Saturday Night Live*. Blessed with an intense comic presence behind his working-class Italian appearance, Piscopo retired from SNL in 1984 to pursue other projects including a career in film.
**Selected Films:** *Johnny Dangerously* (84), *Wise Guys* (86).

## PITT, Ingrid (1944- )

Born Ingrid Petrov in Poland Pitt had an estblished career in Berlin before she 'literally came over the wall.' She has appeared in a number of productions since the late 1960s, among them horror films like *The Vampire Lovers* (70) and *The House that Dripped Blood* (71), and the TV mini-series *Smiley's People*.
**Selected Films:** *Where Eagles Dare* (69), *The Vampire Lovers* (70), *The House That Dripped Blood* (71), *Countess Dracula* (71), *The Wicker Man* (73), *Who Dares Wins* (82).

## PITTS, ZaSu (1898-1963)

Born in Parsons, Kansas, Pitts came to the screen at 19 and in 1924 gave a magnificent performance in the lead of Von Stroheim's *Greed*. However, after several humorous roles, producers found that audiences were laughing at her death scene in *All Quiet on the Western Front* (30) and she was replaced in the sound version of the film. From that point on, Pitts was cast as a fluttery, featherbrained, reedy-voiced comedienne in movies until her death, among them a popular series of shorts with Thelma Todd in the 1930s. She was familiar to TV audiences from her role in the series *Oh Susanna*.
**Selected Films:** *The Little Princess* (17), Better Times (19), *Patsy* (21), *Greed* (24), *The Wedding March* (28), *All Quiet on the Western Front* (30), *Ruggles of Red Gap* (35), *Life with Father* (47), *It's a Mad Mad Mad Mad World* (63).

## PLATT, Edward (1916-1974)

Born in Staten Island, New York, Platt was a singer before arriving in movies in the mid-1950s. He usually played generals, and other bosses. He is most familiar as the Chief in the TV series *Get Smart*.
**Selected Films:** *Rebel Without a Cause* (55), *Designing Woman* (57), *North by Northwest* (59), *Bullet for a Badman* (64), *The Man from Button Willow* (65).

## PLEASANCE, Donald (1919- )

Rather roly-poly of figure and with a certain crazed eagerness in his cold blue eyes, Donald Pleasance

has played off his looks to portray quirkily sympathetic parts and rather elfin psychopaths in character roles for three decades, in films from the distinguished to the downright sleazy. Born in Worksop, England, Pleasance was an experience stage performer when he came to the screen in the mid-1950s. His first big part in a typical Pleasance mode was the title role in *Dr Crippen* (64). There followed a series of horror movies which included *Halloween* (78), in which he investigated the gore rather than perpetrated it. Pleasance won critical acclaim in the film of Harold Pinter's *The Caretaker* (64). Other of his staring-eyed villains included Pontius Pilate in *The Passover Plot* (76) and Heinrich Himmler in *The Eagle Has Landed* (76). Now and then Pleasance has played eccentric nice guys, among them his role as an old man in an inhuman world in George Lucas's *THX 1138* (71).
**Selected Films:** *The Beachcomber* (54), *Look Back in Anger* (59), *The Great Escape* (63), *Dr Crippen* (64), *The Caretaker* (64), *Fantastic Voyage* (66), *Soldier Blue* (70), *THX 1138* (71), *The Passover Plot* (76), *The Eagle Has Landed* (76), *Oh, God!* (77), *Halloween* (78), *Halloween II* (81).

## PLESHETTE, Suzanne (1937- )

New York-born Pleshette made her screen debut in *The Geisha Boy* (58). During the 1960s she played leads and supporting roles in many popular films, but never quite became a major star. By the 1970s she was mostly working in TV movies such as *Flesh and Blood*, and was a regular on *The Bob Newhart Show*.
**Selected Films:** *The Geisha Boy* (58), *The Birds* (63), *Youngblood Hawke* (64), *If It's Tuesday This Must Be Belgium* (69), *Return of the Pink Panther* (75), *Oh God!, Book Two* (80).

## PLUMMER, Christopher (1929- )

Born in Toronto, Ontario, Canada, Plummer had a formidable stage reputation in his native country before going to Broadway and then to Hollywood, making his film debut in *Stage Struck* (58), a film that told the story of a Broadway-bound actress (Susan Strasberg) and wasted the talents, not only of Plummer, but also of Henry Fonda, Joan Greenwood and Herbert Marshall. His most popular role was as Baron von Trapp, the patriarch in *The Sound of Music* (65), although his singing was dubbed by Bill Lee. Plummer was also effective as Sherlock Holmes in *Murder by Decree* (78), in which James Mason played Dr Watson. Plummer has appeared frequently on television, often in Shakespeare. He is the father of talented actress Amanda Plummer.
**Selected Films:** *Stage Struck* (58), *The Fall of the Roman Empire* (64), *The Sound of Music* (65), *Inside Daisy Clover* (66), *Oedipus the King* (68), *The Return of the Pink Panther* (75), *The Man Who Would Be King* (75), *The Disappearance* (77), *Murder by Decree* (78), *International Velvet* (78), *Somewhere in Time* (81), *The Amateur* (82), *The Boy in Blue* (86).

## POITIER, Sidney (1927- )

Poitier, a handsome black actor, broke many racial barriers and thus made it easier for other blacks to achieve commercial success in films. Poitier was born in Miami, Florida, and raised in the Bahamas. Although sometimes cast as a symbol rather than a character, he was still able to turn out magnetic performances in movies like *The Blackboard Jungle* (55), in which he was one of a class full of high school delinquents who terrorized teacher Glenn Ford. In 1958 he appeared with Tony Curtis in *The Defiant Ones*, a film about two escaped convicts, one black, the other white, chained together but divided by racial bigotry and hatred. Both Poitier and Curtis were nominated for the Best Actor Academy Award. *Lilies of the Field* (63), in which he played a Southern GI who helped five refugee nuns build a chapel and start a new life, won him the Academy Award for Best Actor – the first black ever to win this Oscar. He starred with Spencer Tracy and Katharine Hepburn in *Guess Who's Coming to Dinner* (67), a blockbuster hit dealing with the then touchy subject of black/white romance. He also directs movies, such as *A Piece of the Action* (77), in which he starred with Bill Cosby and James Earl Jones.
**Selected Films:** *No Way Out* (50), *The Blackboard Jungle* (55), *The Defiant Ones* (58), *Lilies of the Field* (63), *In the Heat of the Night* (67), *To Sir with Love* (67), *Guess Who's Coming to Dinner* (67), *Brother John* (71), *A Piece of the Action* (77).

*Sidney Poitier and Rod Steiger in* In the Heat of the Night *(67).*

## POLLARD, Michael J (1939- )

Noted for playing a collection of spaced-out little goofs, Passaic, New Jersey-born Pollard came to the screen after appearing in the 1961 Broadway musical *Bye Bye Birdie*. His supporting part as runny-nosed C W Moss in *Bonnie and Clyde* (67) won Pollard an Oscar nomination and several ensuing leads, among them in *Little Fauss and Big Halsy* (70). Roles for his weird personality remained slim, however, and faded in the 1980s.
**Selected Films:** *The Stripper* (63), *The Russians Are Coming, The Russians Are Coming* (66) *Bonnie and Clyde* (67), *Little Fauss and Big Halsey* (71), *Dirty Little Billy* (72), *Melvin and Howard* (79).

## POLLARD, Snub (1886-1962)

Born Harold Frazer in Melbourne, Australia, Pollard came to America in the teens and ended up in Hal Roach short comedies. Over the next years he supported Harold Lloyd for a while and then starred, with his trademark drooping mustache, in slapstick one and two-reelers. In the sound era he appeared in occasional small roles up to *Pocketful of Miracles* (61).
**Selected Films:** *Lonesome Luke – Gangster* (15), *Hook, Line and Sinker* (22), *The Perils of Pauline* (47), *Pocketful of Miracles* (61).

## POOLE, Ray (1924-1986)

California-born Poole came to the theater after service in World War II and was active on Broadway in musicals and plays including *1776* and *St Joan*.
**Selected Films:** *Up the Down Staircase* (67), *1776* (72), *Mandingo* (75), *Network* (76).

## PORTER, Don (1912- )

Born in Miami, Oklahoma, Porter starred in a number of second features of the 1940s and 1950s and pursued character roles into the 1970s. He is best known as a likable supporting player in the TV series *Private Secretary*.
**Selected Films:** *Top Sergeant* (42), *Our Miss Brooks* (56), *Youngblood Hawke* (64), *The Candidate* (72), *White Line Fever* (75).

## PORTER, Eric (1928- )

London-born Porter began acting on the British stage in 1945 and has worked extensively with the Royal Shakespeare Company. He has played stalwart parts and occasional leads in movies since the mid-1960s, but is best-known for the role of Soames in the TV dramatization of *The Forsythe Saga*. He also appeared in the TV series *The Jewel in the Crown*.
**Selected Films:** *The Pumpkin Eater* (64), *Nicholas and Alexandra* (71), *Hennessy* (75), *The 39 Steps* (78).

## PORTMAN, Eric (1903-1969)

Yorkshire-born Portman came from the Shakespearean stage to the screen with *The Girl From Maxim's* (33). After some years of playing gentlemen leads, he graduated to villains and other character roles.
**Selected Films:** *The Girl From Maxim's* (33), *The Prince and the Pauper* (37), *49th Parallel* (41), *Millions Like Us* (43), *The Colditz Story* (54), *Wanted for Murder* (46), *The Deep Blue Sea* (55), *Assignment to Kill* (67), *Deadfall* (68).

## POSTON, Tom (1927- )

Born in Columbus, Ohio, Poston came to fame as part of the troupe in Steve Allen's TV comedy show. He has largely worked on TV since, most recently in the series *Newhart*, but has appeared in occasional movies.
**Selected Films:** *The City that Never Sleeps* (53), *Zotz!* (62), *The Happy Hooker* (75), *Rabbit Test* (78), *Up the Academy* (80).

## POWELL, Dick (1904-1963)

Born in Mountain View, Arkansas, Powell began his career as a singer and instrumentalist and had several hit records. He started his movie work in the early 1930s and became a premier juvenile lead

*Dick Powell in* Gold Diggers of 1935 *(35).*

in Warner Bros. backstage musicals, including *42nd Street* (33), *Gold Diggers of 1933* (33) and *Footlight Parade* (33). After his career in musicals ended, he made an amazing role-reversal, becoming a tough guy type, often playing private eyes such as detective Philip Marlowe. A veteran survivor, Powell pulled off another coup when he became a competent director, for films like *The Enemy Below* (57), and an ambitious producer – one of the founders of Four Star Television. He was married twice, first to actress Joan Blondell and then to actress/singer June Allyson.
**Selected Films:** *Blessed Event* (32), *42nd Street* (33), *Gold Diggers of 1933* (33), *Footlight Parade* (33), *Dames* (34), *Wonder Bar* (34), *Flirtation Walk* (34), *A Midsummer Night's Dream* (35), *On the Avenue* (37), *Christmas in July* (40), *Model Wife* (41), *It Happened Tomorrow* (44), *Murder My Sweet* (44), *Cornered* (45), *Johnny O'Clock* (47), *Pitfall* (48), *The Reformer and the Redhead* (50), *Cry Danger* (51), *The Bad and the Beautiful* (52), *Susan Slept Here* (54).

## POWELL, Eleanor (1910-1982)

Born in Springfield, Massachusetts, Powell was crowned the world's greatest female tap dancer by the Dancing Masters of America in 1937 – the same year that she was appearing on screen in *Broadway Melody of 1938*. She had been carefully groomed for her screen career. At the age of 13, she had been discovered on an Atlantic City beach. She appeared on Broadway for several years and then was signed for a film contract by MGM. Voice teachers, orthodontists and other beautifiers prepared her for her film debut in *George White's Scandals* (35). At her peak she earned $125,000 per movie and cut several records tapping out dance routines to musical accompaniment. In 1943 she married actor Glenn Ford and retired when she became pregnant. But in 1961, her son Peter encouraged her to end her retirement and she put together a successful night club act.
**Selected Films:** *George White's Scandals* (35), *Broadway Melody of 1936* (35), *Born to Dance* (36), *Broadway Melody of 1938* (37), *Rosalie* (38), *Honolulu* (39), *Broadway Melody of 1940* (40), *Lady Be Good* (41), *Ship Ahoy* (42), *Thousands Cheer* (43), *Sensations of 1945* (44), *The Duchess of Idaho* (50).

## POWELL, Jane (1928-     )

Powell was born Suzanne Burce in Portland, Oregon. Her small size allowed her to play adolescent parts long after she had ceased to be an adolescent. Indeed, she was 21 when she made *Nancy Goes to Rio* (50). But she matured into a fine actress with a melodious singing voice and was outstanding in such musicals as *Royal Wedding* (51) and *Seven Brides for Seven Brothers* (54).
**Selected Films:** *Song of the Open Road* (44), *Holiday in Mexico* (46), *A Date with Judy* (48), *Nancy Goes to Rio* (50), *Royal Wedding* (51), *Small Town Girl* (53), *Three Sailors and a Girl* (53), *Three Sailors and a Girl* (53), *Seven Brides for Seven Brothers* (54), *Hit the Deck* (55), *The Female Animal* (58), *The Girl Most Likely* (57), *Enchanted Island* (58).

## POWELL, William (1892-1984)

For more than 30 years, Powell was one of the most suave leading men in Hollywood, and perhaps the best dressed. He began as a cowboy villain in Westerns, but soon switched to comedy, and is probably best remembered for his roles opposite Myrna Loy, especially in the *Thin Man* series. Born in Pittsburgh, Pennsylvania, he began his stage career in 1912, and a decade later he was in silent films. With the coming of sound he became a leading man, although often a cynical one, starting with a series of light mysteries in which he was detective Philo Vance. From 1931 to 1933 he was married to actress Carole Lombard and was engaged to Jean Harlow when she died. Later he starred in mature character roles, such as the patriarch with the will of iron in *Life with Father* (47) and the ship's doctor in *Mister Roberts* (55).
**Selected Films:** *Sherlock Holmes* (22), *Romola* (24), *Beau Geste* (26), *The Canary Murder Case* (29), *Street of Chance* (30), *One Way Passage* (320, *Manhattan Melodrama* (34), *The Thin Man* (34), *The Great Ziegfeld* (36), *My Man Godfrey* (36), *Another Thin Man* (39), *Life with Father* (47), *Mister Roberts* (55).

## POWER, Tyrone Sr (1869-1931)

Born in London, the grandson of a stage star and later the father of a movie star – all three named Tyrone Power – Power Sr began acting onstage in his teens and by the end of the century was a Broadway matinee idol. He appeared in many silent films and one talkie – *The Big Trail* (30) with young John Wayne.

**Selected Films:** *Aristocracy* (14), *Dream Street* (21), *The Lone Wolf* (24), *Bride of the Storm* (26), *The Big Trail* (30).

## POWER, Tyrone (1913-1958)

A member of a famous Irish acting family, Power was born in Cincinnati, Ohio. His stage and silent-movie actor father, also named Tyrone Power, encouraged him to seek a theatrical career, and his first picture was *Tom Brown of Culver* (32), in which he played a cadet at a military school in Indiana. Power was extraordinarily good looking, with soft, velvety eyes, and he quickly developed into one of Hollywood's leading romantic stars, although he was effective in swashbucklers, too. During World War II he served with the United States Marines, but when he came back from the service he was once again pulling audiences into theaters in *The Razor's Edge* (46). Power was sometimes taken to be nothing more than a pretty face, but he was a fine actor when given the right material, as in *Nightmare Alley* (47) and *Witness for the Prosecution* (57). He died in his forties of a heart attack.
**Selected Films:** *Tom Brown of Culver* (32), *Lloyds of London* (37), *In Old Chicago* (38), *Alexander's Ragtime Band* (38), *Rose of Washington Square* (39), *Jesse James* (39), *Johnny Apollo* (40), *The Mask of Zorro* (40), *Blood and Sand* (41), *The Razor's Edge* (46), *Nightmare Alley* (47), *The Eddie Duchin Story* (56), *The Sun Also Rises* (57), *Witness for the Prosecution* (57).

## POWERS, Mala (1931- )

Born Mary Ellen Powers in San Francisco, California, Powers came to the screen in the early 1940s after stage and radio experience. She played leads in a number of films of the 1950s, most notably as Roxanne to Jose Ferrer's *Cyrano de Bergerac* (50).
**Selected Films:** *Tough as They Come* (41), *Cyrano de Bergerac* (50), *City Beneath the Sea* (53), *Tammy and the Bachelor* (57), *Daddy's Gone A-Hunting* (69), *Six Tickets to Hell* (75).

## POWERS, Stephanie (1942- )

Born Stephania Federkiewicz in Hollywood and first appearing in movie bit parts as Taffy Paul, lithe brunette Powers made her debut using her new name as Lee Remick's sister in *Experiment in Terror* (62). She went on to starring in minor films of the 1960s and then leads in TV series, most recently *Hart to Hart*.
**Selected Films:** *Tammy Tell Me True* (61), *Experiment in Terror* (62), *The Interns* (620, *Fanatic* (65), *Herbie Rides Again* (74), *Escape to Athena* (79).

## PREISSER, June (1921-1984)

Onstage from the age of two, New Orleans, Louisiana-born Preisser was an ebullient singing and dancing star of a number of light films and musicals of the 1940s including *Babes in Arms* (39) and *Babes on Swing Street* (44).
**Selected Films:** *Babes in Arms* (39), *Strike Up the Band* (40), *Henry Aldrich for President* (41), *The Fleet's In* (41), *Babes on Swing Street* (44), *High School Hero* (46), *Music Man* (48).

## PREMINGER, Otto (1905-1986)

Preminger, born in Vienna, was an actor and assistant to Max Rheinhardt before directing his first film *Die Grosse Liebe* (31). He became one of Europe's best-known producer-directors before leaving Austria during the Nazi rise to power. After a year in New York, Preminger went to Hollywood briefly to direct two films and quarrel with Darryl F Zanuck. During the war, he returned to Hollywood and directed the screen version of his successful Broadway production *Margin for Error* (41) which he also appeared in. While at 20th Century Fox he also directed the mysterious thriller *Laura* (44) and *Daisy Kenyon* (47) which starred Joan Crawford. He became an independent producer in 1953, the year he directed the film version of his successful stage play *The Moon Is Blue*, one of the first movies to challenge the contemporary morality and the censorship code of that era. Another was Preminger's production of one of the first films about drug addiction, *The Man With the Golden Arm* (55), starring Frank Sinatra. A martinet in direction, Preminger also kept an eye on all facets of the production, an attitude which enabled him to produce his movies as he wished and keep them underbudget. His later films include *Anatomy of a Murder* (59), *Exodus* (60), *Advise and Consent* (61), and two all-black musicals *Carmen Jones* (54), and *Porgy and Bess* (59). Preminger also appeared in four films ironically, always as a Nazi.
**Selected Films:** *The Pied Piper* (42), *Margin for Error* (43), *They Got Me Covered* (43), *Stalag 17* (53).

## PRENTISS, Paula (1939- )

Born Paula Ragusa in San Antonio, Texas, Prentiss came out of college into her screen debut in *Where the Boys Are* (61). The lanky dark-haired actress soon proved herself an adept and effortlessly sexy comedienne in mostly light movies. She starred with her husband Richard Benjamin in the unsuccessful TV series *He and She*.
**Selected Films:** *Where the Boys Are* (61), *Man's Favorite Sport?* (64), *What's New, Pussycat?* (65), *Catch-22* (69), *The Parallax View* (74), *The Stepford Wives* (74), *Buddy Buddy* (81).

## PRESLEY, Elvis (1935-1977)

Presley was born in Tupelo, Mississippi, and was to become a sensation, especially with teenagers. His fans still call him the king of rock 'n' roll. With his mellow, crooning singing, his guitar playing and his sinuous and suggestive movements while

on stage, he was a sensation – either loved or hated. His film career was different from that of practically any other movie star. All of his pictures were predictable, tailor-made vehicles which gave him a chance to sing. Although sometimes he had good co-stars, the scripts were mediocre or worse. Critics hated Presley films and most ordinary film-goers avoided them, but the pictures were not made for the ordinary moviegoer. They were made for his fans, and there were millions of them, enough to make him one of the top box office draws from the mid-1950s through the mid-1960s. After 1967 both the quality and popularity of the Presley films declined, and he appeared only in documentaries after 1969. His sudden death, however, spawned a large Presley cult, and his movies are now popular on TV and video cassettes.
**Selected Films:** *Love Me Tender* (56), *Loving You* (56), *Jailhouse Rock* (57), *King Creole* (58), *GI Blues* (60), *Blue Hawaii* (61), *Wild in the Country* (61), *Kid Galahad* (62), *Roustabout* (64), *Viva Las Vegas* (64), *Girl Happy* (65), *Frankie and Johnny* (66), *Double Trouble* (67), *Stay Away Joe* (68), *Change of Habit* (69), *Elvis on Tour* (70).

## PRESNELL, Harve (1933- )

A tall and handsome star of stage musicals, Presnell, born in Modesto, California, sang in a few screen musicals of the 1960s.
**Selected Films:** *The Unsinkable Molly Brown* (64), *The Glory Guys* (65), *Where the Boys Meet the Girls* (66), *Paint Your Wagon* (69).

## PRESTON, Robert (1918-1987)

Born Robert Preston Meservey in Newton, Massachusetts, Preston began his screen career in *King of Alcatraz* (38), and did quite well for many years, usually playing villains or second leads who often died in the last reel. A vigorous actor with a melodious voice, he didn't really become a star for almost 20 years. In 1957 came the premiere of Meredith Willson's *The Music Man* on Broadway, and it told of a con artist who arrives in River City, Iowa, to organize a boys' band, and, incidentally, to sell instruments and uniforms to all the kids. He is reformed by the town librarian. Preston starred as the mountebank, Professor Harold Hill, and this was his first musical. But he sang as if he had been doing it all his life and he had dance steps that would have won first place in an old-fashioned dance contest. He was superb, giving a lusty, vibrant, virtuoso performance, and making one of the most sensational comebacks in theater history. The film version of *The Music Man* (62) also starred Preston, and it was every bit as good as he had been on the stage version. Suddenly the world found out how good he was. His touching performance as the small town father involved in tragedy in *All the Way Home* (63) proved that he was a fine dramatic actor. When he played an impudent homosexual entertainer who takes Julie Andrews under his wing in *Victor/Victoria* (82), he established himself as a master screen comedian.
**Selected Films:** *King of Alcatraz* (38), *Union Pacific* (39), *Beau Geste* (39), *Northwest Mounted Police* (40), *Reap the Wild Wind* (42), *This Gun for Hire* (42), *Wake Island* (42), *The Macomber Affair* (47), *Tulsa* (49), *The Dark at the Top of the Stairs* (60), *The Music Man* (62), *All the Way Home* (63), *Mame* (73), *S.O.B.* (81), *Victor/, Victoria* (82).

## PRÉVOST, Marie (1898-1937)

Born Mary Dunn in Ontario, Canada, Prévost was a chorus girl before becoming one of Mack Sennett's Bathing Beauties onscreen. In the early 1920s she rose to stardom in a number of popular light romances, notably three by Lubitsch in 1924-5 – *The Marriage Circle, Three Women*, and *Kiss Me Again*. Surviving the transition to talkies, she began to struggle with a weight problem; compulsive dieting led to her death of malnutrition at 38.
**Selected Films:** *Her Nature Dance* (17), *The Beautiful and the Damned* (22), *The Marriage Circle* (24), *Three Women* (25), *Kiss Me Again* (25), *Up in Mabel's Room* (26), *Getting Gertie's Garter* (27), *Sporting Blood* (31), *Tango* (36).

## PRICE, Dennis (1915-1973)

Dennis Price was one of those actors who successfully aged from leading roles into even more successful character parts. Born Dennistoun Franklyn John Rose-Price in Twyford, England to the family of a military officer, Price studied at Oxford and made his British stage debut in 1937. His first film role was in *A Canterbury Tale* (44). For the next decade or so he played urbane light leading men in a number of films, including the title role in *The Bad Lord Byron* (49). His most memorable film was in the black comedy *Kind Hearts and Coronets* (49) in which Price played the heir who kills off the members of his family who stand between him and a title (all eight vicitims being played by Alec Guinness). Price continued in character parts until the year of his death, including a scheming publisher in *The Naked Truth* (58) and another supporting role with Guinness in *Tunes of Glory* (60).
**Selected Films:** *A Canterbury Tale* (44), *Good Time Girl* (48), *The Bad Lord Byron* (49), *Kind Hearts and Coronets* (49), *Lady Godiva Rides Again* (51), *Private's Progress* (55), *The Naked Truth* (58), *I'm All Right Jack* (59), *Tunes of Glory* (60), *Victim* (61), *Ten Little Indians* (65), *Theatre of Blood* (72).

## PRICE, Vincent (1911- )

Price was born in St Louis, Missouri, and was educated as an art historian at Yale University, but he got his start in acting on the London stage playing Prince Albert, the husband of Queen Victoria, in *Victoria Regina*. The play was brought

*Vincent Price in* The Raven *(63).*

to New York as a vehicle for Helen Hayes, and Price came along with it, making a hit with the critics and public alike. All this when he was but 23 years old. Hollywood beckoned and he made his screen debut in *Service de Luxe* (38). In the beginning he was cast mainly in costume dramas, and went from playing a fop, a cad and a villain to becoming the king of horror films in the 1950s and 1960s. Price often returned to the stage, scoring in such vehicles as *Outward Bound, Angel Street, Don Juan in Hell* and *The Lady's Not for Burning*. In films, after he gave masterful performances in such movies as *Laura* (44) and many others, he found himself playing a mad sculptor in *House of Wax* (53), and hit his stride in the horror film genre. Price then went on to star in a number of films loosely based on Edgar Allan Poe stories made by Roger Corman. Many of them were hammy and a few were hilariously funny, but Price was always in command. He is married to the actress Coral Browne.
**Selected Films:** *Service de Luxe* (38), *Tower of London* (39), *The Invisible Man Returns* (40), *The House of the Seven Gables* (40), *The Song of Bernadette* (43), *Laura* (44), *Dragonwyck* (46), *The Three Musketeers* (48), *House of Wax* (53), *The Fly* (58), *The House of Usher* (60), *The Pit and the Pendulum* (61), *The Raven* (63), *The Masque of the Red Death* (64), *The Tomb of Ligeia* (64), *Witchfinder General* (68), *The Abominable Dr Phibes* (71), *Theatre of Blood* (73), *Romance in the Jugular Vein* (80), *The Whales of August* (87).

## PRINCE, William (1913- )

Born in Nichols, New York, Prince began acting in the theater in the mid-1930s. Since the mid-1940s he has occasionally played leads and supporting roles in movies, among them Christian in *Cyrano de Bergerac* (50).
**Selected Films:** *Destination Tokyo* (44), *Carnegie Hall* (48), *Cyrano de Bergerac* (50), *The Heartbreak Kid* (72), *Family Plot* (76).

## PRINE, Andrew (1936- )

American actor Prine has appeared in leads and supporting roles of films since the early 1960s, among them *The Miracle Worker* (62) and *Grizzly* (76). He also starred in the TV series *The Wide Country*.
**Selected Films:** *The Miracle Worker* (62), *Company of Cowards* (64), *Bandolero* (68), *One Little Indian* (73), *Grizzly* (76).

## PRINGLE, Aileen (1895- )

Born Aileen Bisbee to a wealthy family in San Francisco, California, Pringle made her stage debut in Britain and came to the American screen from Broadway in 1919. She became a major star when she was chosen by Elinor Glyn to appear in two films of 1924 that were based on her novels which were considered quite steamy for the time – *Three Weeks*, with Conrad Nagel, and *His Hour*, with John Gilbert. She continued into the sound era but at length was relegated to minor features.
**Selected Films:** *Redhead* (19), *Three Weeks* (24), *Wife of a Centaur* (24), *His Hour* (24), *Adam and Evil* (27), *Jane Eyre* (33), *The Girl from Nowhere* (39), *Happy Land* (43).

## PROUTY, Jed (1879-1956)

Born in Boston, Massachusetts, Prouty got into acting in his teens and played small roles in a great many silents of the 1930s. He moved to light character roles in talkies and found his greatest fame in the 1930s as the bespectacled, comfortable father of a dozen or so *Jones Family* comedies.
**Selected Films:** *The Conquest of Canaan* (21), *The Broadway Melody* (29), *The Jones Family* (35), *Mug Town* (43), *Guilty Bystander* (50).

## PROVINE, Dorothy (1937- )

Born in Deadwood, South Dakota, Provine began singing and dancing at an early age. In her first year in movies she was a hit in the title role of *The Bonnie Parker Story* (58) and followed that success to her best-known turn, as Pinky Pinkham in the TV series *The Roaring Twenties*. Thereafter Provine appeared in occasional films of the 1960s, among them as a barroom singer in *The Great Race* (65).
**Selected Films:** *The Bonnie Parker Story* (58), *It's a Mad Mad Mad Mad World* (63), *That Darn Cat* (65), *The Great Race* (65), *Who's Minding the Mint?* (67), *Never a Dull Moment* (68).

## PROWSE, Juliet (1937- )

Born in Bombay, India and reared in South Africa, leggy dancer/actress Prowse came to Hollywood in

the 1950s and starred in several musicals and occasional dramas through the 1960s.
**Selected Films:** *Gentlemen Marry Brunettes* (55), *Can-Can* (59), *GI Blues* (60), *The Second Time Around* (61), *Who Killed Teddy Bear?* (65), *Spree* (67).

## PRYCE, Jonathan (1947- )

Pryce has been active in the theater for years, appearing in his native Britain with the Royal Shakespeare Company and winning a Tony in 1977 for his leading role in the Broadway company of *Comedians.* Wiry, and often with an air of earnest desperation, Pryce played supporting roles in forgettable films before co-starring in *Something Wicked This Way Comes* (83) and finding acclaim as the hapless Sam in the black comedy *Brazil* (85).
**Selected Films:** *Voyage of the Damned* (77), *Breaking Glass* (80), *Something Wicked This Way Comes* (83), *The Doctor and the Devils* (85), *BraZil* (85), *Haunted Honeymoon* (86), *Jumpin' Jack Flash* (86).

## PRYOR, Richard (1940- )

Born in Peoria, Illinois, to poor parents, Pryor held menial jobs until he broke into show business. This undeniable comic genius and potential fine actor was á bitter, foul-mouthed comic in night clubs and on stage, and appeared on the screen mostly in minor roles or weak vehicles. His experience of setting himself on fire when freebasing cocaine, and his near death and months of forced rehabilitation, seemed to change his character. He is no longer afraid to show his emotions and has become a gentle comedian. Still, only in his films of his stage performance, such as *Richard Pryor – Live in Concert* (79), has he been able to display the full force of his extraordinary talent.
**Selected Films:** *Wild in the Streets* (68), *The Phynx* (70), *Lady Sings the Blues* (71), *Some Call It Loving* (73), *Uptown Saturday Night* (74), *The Bingo Long Traveling All-Stars and Motor Kings* (76), *Silver Streak* (76), *Richard Pryor – Live in Concert* (79), *Stir Crazy* (80), *Bustin' Loose* (81), *Richard Pryor Live on the Sunset Strip* (82), *The Toy* (82), *Superman III* (83), *Brewster's Millions* (85), *JoJo Dancer, Your Life is Calling* (86), *Critical Condition* (87).

## PRYOR, Roger (1901-1974)

Born the son of a bandleader in New York, Pryor began acting onstage in his teens and made his Broadway debut in 1925. In the 1930s and 1940s he starred in second features before turning to radio, bandleading, and finally business. For a time he was married to actress Ann Sothern.
**Selected Films:** *Moonlight and Pretzels* (33), *Fugitive From Justice* (40), *Scared Stiff* (45).

## PULVER, Lilo (or Liselotte) (1929- )

A native of Berne, Switzerland, Pulver came from the stage to star in European movies, among them *The Confessions of Felix Krull* (57) and *Buddenbrooks* (59). She appeared in a few American films including *A Time to Live and a Time to Die* (59) and *One, Two, Three* (61).
**Selected Films:** *Four Days' Leave* (49), *Hanussen* (55), *The Confessions of Felix Krull* (57), *Buddenbrooks* (59), *A Time to Live and a Time to Die* (59), *One, Two, Three* (61), *Lafayette* (62), *A Global Affair* (64), *La Religieuse* (65) *Pistol Jenny* (69), *Brot and Steine* (79).

## PURCELL, Dick (1908-1944)

During his short life, Purcell, born in Greenwich, Connecticut, appeared in B movies with titles like *Air Devils* (38) and *King of the Zombies* (41). He usually played a tough-guy hero, occasionally a villain.
**Selected Films:** *Ceiling Zero* (35), *King of Hockey* (36), *Nancy Drew – Detective* (38), *Air Devils* (38), *The Bank Dick* (40), *King of the Zombies* (41), *Captain America* (44).

## PURDOM, Edmund (1924- )

Born in Welwyn Garden City, England, Purdom came from the Shakespearean stage in his native Britain and a career on Broadway to a Hollywood contract with the accompaniment of full star publicity. For a few years he played major roles in costume epics, among them Strato in *Julius Caesar* (53) and the title role in *The Prodigal* (55). However, Hollywood seemed soon to tire of his chiselled features. By the 1960s he was largely appearing in cheap Italian costume pictures and only occasionally returned to American and British films.
**Selected Films:** *Titanic* (53), *Julius Caesar* (53), *The Student Prince* (54), *The Egyptian* (54), *The Prodigal* (55), *The Cossacks* (60), *The Yellow Rolls-Royce* (64), *Mr Scarface* (76), *Absurd* (81).

*Richard Pryor in* Silver Streak *(76).*

## PURVIANCE, Edna (1894-1958)

A native of Lovelock, Nevada, Purviance was a secretary with no acting experience or ambitions when she met Charlie Chaplin at a party in San Francisco. She became his lover and his co-star, appearing as the goldenhaired girl in most of his comedies from 1915 to 1923 and in his drama *A Woman of Paris* (23). After a stormy romance and a scandal resulting from a shooting in her home, Chaplin retired Purviance in 1924 but paid her a salary for the next 30 years. She later appeared in Josef von Sternberg's unreleased film *A Woman of the Sea* (26). In two of his later films Chaplin used Purviance as an extra.
**Selected Films:** *A Night Out* (15), *The Floorwalker* (16), *Easy Street* (17), *Shoulder Arms* (18), *The Kid* (21), *A Woman of Paris* (23), *Monsieur Verdoux* (47), *Limelight* (52).

## PYLE, Denver (1920- )

Born in Bethune, Colorado, Pyle began appearing in movies in the late 1940s and since has held down character roles in a number of major films. He played the sheriff in *Bonnie and Clyde* (67). He has also worked much on television, including the series *Wyatt Earp*, *The Doris Day Show*, and *The Dukes of Hazzard*.
**Selected Films:** *The Man from Colorado* (48), *To Hell and Back* (55), *The Man Who Shot Liberty Valance* (62), *Bonnie and Clyde* (67), *Buffalo Bill and the Indians* (76), *Welcome to L.A.* (77).

## QUAID, Randy (1953- )

Randy Quaid was a college drama major in his native Houston, Texas when director Peter Bogdanovich picked him for a small role in *The Last Picture Show* (71). From that point on, Quaid has appeared regularly in movies, most often in supporting roles as awkward or troubled characters. In *The Last Detail* (73) he played a baby-faced sailor whom Jack Nicholson escorts to a long term in the brig, a role which earned Quaid an Academy Award nomination. His films and roles since have ranged widely, including the violent story of Americans in a Turkish prison, *Midnight Express* (78), a light comedy about teenagers called *Foxes* (80) and the western *The Long Riders* (80).
**Selected Films:** *The Last Picture Show* (71), *What's Up, Doc?* (72), *The Last Detail* (73), *Lolly-Madonna XXX* (73), *Paper Moon* (73), *The Apprenticeship of Duddy Kravitz* (75), *The Missouri Breaks* (76), *Bound for Glory* (76), *The Choirboys* (77), *Midnight Express* (78), *Foxes* (80), *The Long Riders* (80), *Heartbeeps* (81), *National Lampoon's Vacation* (83), *Wraith* (86), *Sweet Country* (87).

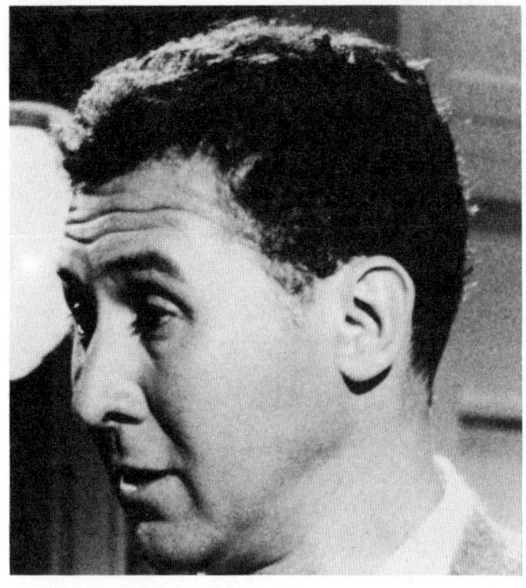

*Anthony Quayle in* The Wrong Man *(57).*

## QUAYLE, Anthony (1913- )

Starting his stage career in vaudeville, Anthony Quayle soon proved himself a distinguished theatrical actor and director. Though movies have been a sideline, he has still graced a good many supporting roles and occasional leads in films since the late 1940s. Born in Ainsdale, England, Quayle joined the Old Vic in 1932. After playing Marcellus in Laurence Olivier's screen version of *Hamlet* (48), he began regular movie work in the mid-1950s, appearing in Alfred Hitchcock's *The Wrong Man* (57), David Lean's *Lawrence of Arabia* (62), and as Cardinal Wolsey in *Anne of the Thousand Days* (69) – for the latter he received an Oscar nomination. Meanwhile remaining busy in the theater, Quayle managed the Shakespearean company at Stratford-on-Avon from 1948 to 1956 and starred in a long-running Broadway production of *Sleuth* in the early 1970s. Recently he played character roles in the made-for-TV movies *Masada* and *The Last Days of Pompeii*.
**Selected Films:** *Hamlet* (48), *Pursuit of the Graf Spee* (56), *The Wrong Man* (57), *The Guns of Navarone* (61), *Lawrence of Arabia* (62), *Mackenna's Gold* (69), *Anne of the Thousand Days* (69), *The Tamarind Seed* (74), *The Eagle Has Landed* (76), *Murder By Decree* (78), *The Antagonists* (80).

## QUILLAN, Eddie (1907- )

Born in Philadelphia, Pennsylvania, Quillan played in vaudeville as a child and became a wide-eyed and energetic screen comic in the mid-1920s. For the next 50 years he mostly played comic roles but ably handled dramatic parts, as with his performances as Ellison in *Mutiny on the Bounty* (35) and Connie Rivers in *The Grapes of Wrath* (40).
**Selected Films:** *A Love Sundae* (26), *Big Money* (30),

*Mutiny on the Bounty* (35), *Young Mr Lincoln* (39), *The Grapes of Wrath* (40), *Flying Blind* (41), *Brigadoon* (54), *The Ghost and Mr Chicken* (66), *The Strongest Man in the World* (75).

## QUINE, Richard (1920- )

Born in Detroit, Michigan, Quine was a child player in vaudeville and a screen actor from age 12. After juvenile roles he grew into a pleasant-faced supporting actor in films of the 1940s. By 1950 he had begun directing and over the next three decades made a good many respected films including *The Solid Gold Cadillac* (56) and *Oh Dad, Poor Dad, Mama's Hung You in the Closet and I'm Feeling So Sad* (66).
**Selected Films:** *The World Changes* (33), *Jane Eyre* (34), *My Sister Eileen* (42), *No Sad Songs for Me* (50).

## QUINLAN, Kathleen (1954- )

Born in Pasadena, California, Quinlan began playing bit parts in films while still in high school. After appearing in several TV movies, she emerged into major screen roles with *Lifeguard* (76). She is probably best known for her performance as a mental patient in *I Never Promised You a Rose Garden* (77).
**Selected Films:** *Lifeguard* (76), *I Never Promised You a Rose Garden* (77), *Airport 77* (77), *The Promise* (79), *The Runner Stumbles* (79), *Hanky Panky* (82), *Twilight Zone* (83), *Independence Day* (83).

## QUINN, Aidan (1959- )

Quinn was working in Chicago as a hot tar roofer in 1980, and then graduated to performing in a production of *Hamlet* in Chicago's Wisdom Bridge Theatre, followed by a part in an off-Broadway show, *Fool for Love*.
**Selected Films:** *Reckless* (84), *Desperately Seeking Susan* (85), *The Mission* (86).

## QUINN, Anthony (1915- )

Quinn, that forceful and engaging actor most noted for his full-blooded performances, was born in Chihuahua, Mexico, to Irish and Mexican parents. This international star grew up in the United States and began appearing in films in 1936. Despite his marriage to Katherine de Mille, the daughter of producer-director Cecil B de Mille, he made stardom on his own after playing bit and supporting roles as tough guys or American Indians. Success on Broadway gave his career a boost, as did winning Academy Awards for Best Supporting Actor in *Viva Zapata!* (52), with Marlon Brando, and *Lust for Life* (56), in which he played the French painter Paul Gauguin opposite Kirk Douglas as the Dutch painter Vincent Van Gogh. After that he switched to even more virile leads and is especially famous for his role in *Zorba the Greek* (64).
**Selected Films:** *Parole!* (36), *The Plainsman* (37), *Last Train from Madrid* (37), *Union Pacific* (39), *Blood and Sand* (41), *The Ox-Bow Incident* (43), *Tycoon* (48), *The Brave Bulls* (51), *Viva Zapata!* (52), *La Strada* (54), *Attila the Hun* (54), *Ulysses* (55), *Lust for Life* (56), *The Hunchback of Notre Dame* (56), *Last Train from Gun Hill* (58), *Warlock* (59), *The Guns of Navarone* (61), *Lawrence of Arabia* (62), *Barabbas* (62), *Requiem for a Heavyweight* (63), *The Visit* (63), *Zorba the Greek* (64), *A High Wind in Jamaica* (65), *The Shoes of the Fisherman* (68), *The Secret of Santa Vittoria* (69), *Mohammed* (76), *The Destructors* (74), *Valentina* (83).

# R

## RADFORD, Basil (1897-1952)

Radford was born in Chester, and began acting on the stage in his native Britain in the early 1920s, making his screen debut in *Barnum Was Right* (29) which was one of his few American films. He was memorable as one of the two cricket fans who refuse to be bothered by all the shooting in *The Lady Vanishes* (38) and went on to be a popular character comedian in movies into the 1950s.
**Selected Films:** *Barnum Was Right* (29),*Broken Blossoms* (36), *The Lady Vanishes* (38), *Dead of Night* (45), *The Winslow Boy* (48), *Whiskey Galore* (48), *The Galloping Major* (51).

## RAFFERTY, Chips (1909-1971)

Born John Goffage, the tall and skinny Rafferty made his movie debut in his native Australia in 1938 and became the screen's archetypal Aussie. With a series of slaptstick roles as a rustic named Dinkum he became a major star in Australia. Later he played character parts, several of them in American movies like *The Sundowners* (60).
**Selected Films:** *Ants in his Pants* (38), *Forty Thousand Horsemen* (41), *The Overlanders* (46), *Eureka Stockade* (47), *Kangaroo* (52), *The Wackiest Ship in the Army* (60), *The Sundowners* (60), *Mutiny on the Bounty* (62), *Skullduggery* (70), *Outback* (71).

## RAFFERTY, Frances (1922- )

Born in Sioux City, Iowa, Rafferty arrived at MGM in 1942 and for a few years played ingenues, among them Mickey Rooney's date in *Girl Crazy* (43). In *Demon Seed* (44) she had a serious part as a murder victim. Her movie career declined and she turned to TV, appearing on *December Bride*.
**Selected Films:** *Seven Sweethearts* (42), *Girl Crazy* (43), *Demon Seed* (44), *Lady at Midnight* (48), *Rodeo* (52), *Wings of Chance* (61).

## RAFT, George (1895-1980)

Born George Raft in New York City, Raft had been a prizefighter and a gigolo and was reputed to be the world's fastest Charleston dancer. He was, for a

time, a gambler, too, and never denied his close association with mobsters. The role of a gangster was the one he always played best. This smooth, rather sinister leading man came to Hollywood in the late 1920s, first appearing in *Queen of the Night Clubs* (29), and was briefly heralded as a second Rudolph Valentino, but it was his role as the coin-flipping gangster, Guido Rinaldo, in *Scarface* (32) that made him a major star, and he remained one for over a decade. Fights with the studios, a remarkably poor choice of scripts and his own limited acting talents threw his career into permanent decline. Raft was, however, instrumental in creating two screen legends. In 1932 he invited an old girl friend from vaudeville days, Mae West, to appear with him in *Night After Night*. He later turned down roles in *Dead End* (37), *The Maltese Falcon* (41), *High Sierra* (41) and *Casablanca* (42), all of which were played by Humphrey Bogart.
**Selected Films:** *Queen of the Night Clubs* (29), *Scarface* (32), *Night After Night* (32), *The Eagle and the Hawk* (33), *The Glass Key* (35), *Souls at Sea* (37), *Spawn of the North* (38), *The Lady from Kentucky* (39), *Background to Danger* (43), *Rogue Cop* (54), *Black Widow* (54), *Some Like It Hot* (59), *Hammersmith Is Out* (72), *The Man with Bogart's Face* (80).

## RAGLAND, Rags (1905-1946)

Born John Morgan Ragland in Louisville, Kentucky, Ragland was a boxer and burlesque slapstick comedian before arriving on Broadway in 1938 and then in movies in 1941. In the last five years of his life he played some two dozen comic roles for MGM.
**Selected Films:** *Ringside Maisie* (41), *Whistling in the Dark* (41), *Panama Hattie* (42), *Girl Crazy* (43), *Anchors Aweigh* (45), *Abott and Costello Go to Hollywood* (45), *The Hoodlum Saint* (46).

## RAIMU (1883-1946)

The great French character actor and comedian Raimu was born Jules Muraire in Toulon. Starting his career as a music hall extra, he worked his way up to revues and cafes and finally the legitimate theater. Raimu was onscreen from the early teens, though for some time he was better-known for his stage work. Perhaps the summit of his career came in a trilogy of films by Marcel Pagnol, in which he created his immortal role of pudgy, mustachioed cafe owner César – *Marius* (31), *Fanny* (32), and *César* (34). Later, Pagnol's *La Femme du Boulanger* (38) made Raimu an international star. He continued his characteristic blend of humor and pathos in memorable roles to the end of his life.
**Selected Films:** *L'Homme Nu* (12), *Marius* (31), *Fanny* (32), *César* (34), *Les Jumeaux de Brighton* (36), *Gribouille* (37), *Un Carnet de Bal* (37), *La Femme du Boulanger* (38) *Les Inconnus dans la Maison* (42), *Monsieur la Souris* (42), *L'Arlésiènne* (42), *L'Homme au Chapeau Rond* (46).

## RAINER, Luise (1909- )

Born in Vienna, Austria, Luise Rainer began acting onstage in her childhood and studied with the great theatrical director Max Reinhardt. In the early 1930s she appeared in a few German films and then arrived in Hollywood, where MGM publicity proclaimed the dark-haired, liquid-eyed beauty another Garbo. For exactly three years Rainer fit her billing. After her American debut with William Powell in *Escapade* (35), she starred as Anna Held in *The Great Ziegfeld* (36), her sensational telephone scene helping her win a best-actress Academy Award. Then in 1937 she and Paul Muni played the poor Chinese couple in the sentimental *The Good Earth*. For that role Rainer won a second best-actress Oscar in a row, an unprecedented feat. From that point, however, her fall in Hollywood was as meteoric as her rise; following a few appearances in routine films, she retired from the screen after *Hostages* (43). Both MGM and her husband at the time, playwright Clifford Odets, have been blamed for her fall. After divorcing Odets in 1940, Rainer married publisher Robert Knittel and settled with him in London.
**Selected Films:** *Ja der Himmel über Wien* (30), *Senhsucht 202* (32), *Heute kommt's drauf an* (33), *Escapade* (35), *The Great Ziegfeld* (36), *The Good Earth* (37), *The Emperor's Candlesticks* (37), *Big City* (37), *The Toy Wife* (38), *The Great Waltz* (38), *Dramatic School* (38), *Hostages* (43).

## RAINS, Claude (1889-1967)

Although his face appeared only briefly, this British-born actor had the title role in his first film, *The Invisible Man* (33), and his London stage-trained voice dominated the picture. Born in South London, he had been in the British theater since he was 11 years old. Rains often played a villain, as he did in *The Adventures of Robin Hood* (38). He was often a cynic, as he was in *Casablanca* (42). He was often kindly, as he was playing the aging emperor taking the young queen under his wing in George Bernard Shaw's *Caesar and Cleopatra* (45). But he was always one of Hollywood's consummate character actors.
**Selected Films:** *The Invisible Man* (33), *Crime without Passion* (34), *The Mystery of Edwin Drood* (35), *Anthony Adverse* (36), *The Prince and the Pauper* (37), *The Adventures of Robin Hood* (38), *Mr Smith Goes to Washington* (39), *Here Comes Mr Jordan* (41), *King's Row* (41), *Casablanca* (42), *The Phantom of the Opera* (43), *Mr Skeffington* (44), *Caesar and Cleopatra* (45), *Notorious* (46), *Lawrence of Arabia* (62), *The Greatest Story Ever Told* (65).

## RAINES, Ella (1921- )

Born Ella Raubes in Snoqualmie Falls, Washington, Raines was discovered by Howard Hawks, who cast her in *Corvette K-225* (43). The pretty brunette went on to starring roles largely in

Universal thrillers and melodramas, among them *Phantom Lady* (44). In the 1950s her career declined to Republic B movies.
**Selected Films:** *Corvette K-225* (43), *Cry Havoc* (43), *Hail the Conquering Hero* (43), *Phantom Lady* (44), *Brute Force* (47), *Ride the Man Down* (53).

## RALPH, Jessie (1864-1944)

Born Jessie Ralph Chambers in Gloucester, Massachusetts, Ralph had a long Broadway career before making her talkie debut in her mid-sixties (she had appeared briefly in silents). Throughout the 1930s she was one of the screen's greatest old ladies, memorable as Nurse Pegotty in *David Copperfield* (35) and Nanine in *Camille* (37).
**Selected Films:** *Such a Little Queen* (21), *Elmer the Great* (33), *The Affairs of Cellini* (34), *Jalna* (35), *David Copperfield* (35), *Captain Blood* (35), *San Francisco* (36), *Camille* (37), *The Blue Bird* (40), *The Bank Dick* (40), *They Met in Bombay* (41).

## RALSTON, Vera Hruba (1921- )

Born Vera Helena Hruba in Prague, Czechoslovakia, Ralston gained the spotlight as a skater, finishing second to Sonia Henie in the 1936 Olympics. Following Henie to Hollywood, Ralston was a leading lady in some of Republic's more expensive films of the 1940s and 1950s. In 1952 she married the head of the studio, Herbert Yates.
**Selected Films:** *Ice Capades* (41), *Lake Placid Serenade* (44), *Wyoming* (47), *Fair Wind to Java* (53), *The Man Who Died Twice* (58).

## RAMBEAU, Marjorie (1889-1970)

Born in San Francisco, California, Rambeau began her long acting career at age 12 and became a beautiful leading leady of the theater. Coming to silent films in the mid-teens, she entered talkies as a character actress and into the 1950s played a succession of often tattered old ladies, like the lead in *Tugboat Annie Sails Again* (40) and Bessie Lester in *Tobacco Road* (41).
**Selected Films:** *The Dazzling Miss Davison* (16), *Min and Bill* (30), *Tugboat Annie Sails Again* (40), *Tobacco Road* (41), *In Old Oklahoma* (43), *The Man of a Thousand Faces* (57).

## RAMIS, Harold (1944- )

Chicago-born Ramis is a triple-threat in films, having involved himself as writer, director and/or actor in some of the more popular movies of the late 1970s and 1980s. A member of Chicago's Second City troupe in the early 1970s he moved to Hollywood, where he has: co-written *Animal House* (78), co-written and directed *Caddyshack* (80), co-written and acted in *Stripes* (81), and co-written and acted in *Ghostbusters* (84).
**Selected Films:** *Stripes* (81), *Ghostbusters* (84).

## RAMPLING, Charlotte (1945- )

Born in Sturmer, England, Rampling arrived on the screen in the mid-1960s as a leading lady who blended intelligence and intensity with sizzling and somewhat kinky sensuality. Her roles in European and American films have been as hard to place as she is. They include *The Night Porter* (74) and straight dramatic leads like that opposite Paul Newman in *The Verdict* (82).
**Selected Films:** *The Knack . . . And How to Get It* (65), *Georgy Girl* (66), *The Damned* (69), *Zardoz* (73), *The Night Porter* (74), *Farewell My Lovely* (75), *Stardust Memories* (80), *The Verdict* (82), *Angel Heart* (87).

## RAND, Sally (1904-1979)

Born Helen Gould Beck in Hickory, Missouri, Rand left home in her teens and made her way to Hollywood, where she appeared in a few racy films of the 1920s such as *Man Bait* (26) and *Getting Gertie's Garter* (27). Jobless with the coming of sound, she signed on as a dancer at the 1933 Chicago World's Fair. Her fan dance became the last word in naughtiness for a generation, and Rand kept dancing to the end of her life.
**Selected Films:** *The Texas Bearcat* (25), *Man Bait* (26), *Gigolo* (26), *The King of Kings* (27), *Getting Gertie's Garter* (37), *Bolero* (34).

## RANDALL, Tony (1920- )

Tony Randall, one of America's favorite players of comic nervous urbanites, was born Leonard Rosenberg in Tulsa, Oklahoma, and was bitten by the acting bug upon seeing his first play at the age of 12. He studied drama at Northwestern University and then headed for New York and more training at the Neighborhood Playhouse. After breaking into professional life as an actor on radio soap operas, Randall began finding stage roles. His big break came when he took the part of Harvey Weskitt in Wally Cox's classic TV series *Mr Peepers*. Randall thus began his fame on TV, where he was at length destined to settle, but from his screen debut in *Oh Men! Oh Women!* (57) through the 1960s he appeared often in movies. Throughout his career Randall has largely specialized in playing leads and supporting roles as the sort of harried urbanites whose greatest exponent is Jack Lemmon. In the Jayne Mansfield film *Will Success Spoil Rock Hunter?* (57), for example, Randall played an advertising executive. In *Pillow Talk* (59) he lost Doris Day to Rock Hudson. Among his films of the 1960s were *The Seven Faces of Dr Lao* (64), in which he played multiple roles, and *The Alphabet Murders* (66), in which he was miscast as detective Hercule Poirot. During the 1970s Randall concentrated on television, beginning with his memorable run as the fastidious and likeable Felix Unger in the series *The Odd Couple*. Later he starred in *The Tony Randall Show*, meanwhile

becoming a familiar – and virtually ageless – figure on talk shows, on anything to with his passion for the opera, and in occasional movies. Most recently Randall has starred in the TV series *Love, Sidney* and appeared in a few films including Scorsese's *The King of Comedy* (83). Never really a powerful screen personality, Randall has succeeded over the long run by being an amiable man and a consummate actor.
**Selected Films:** *Oh Men! Oh Women!* (57), *Will Success Spoil Rock Hunter?* (57), *No Down Payment* (58), *The Mating Game* (59), *Pillow Talk* (59), *The Adventures of Huckleberry Finn* (60), *Lover Come Back* (61), *Boys Night Out* (62), *The Seven Faces of Dr Lao* (64), *Send Me No Flowers* (64), *Fluffy* (65), *Our Man in Marrakesh* (66), *The Alphabet Murder* (66), *Scavenger Hunt* (79), *Foolin' Around* (80), *The King of Comedy* (83), *Sunday Drive* (87).

## RANDELL, Ron (1918- )

Born in Sydney, Randell got his start on stage and screen in his native Australia. Coming to Hollywood in the mid-1940s, he proved himself an able leading man in a wide variety of films. He played the title role in *Bulldog Drummond at Bay* (47) and Cole Porter in *Kiss Me Kate* (53).
**Selected Films:** *Pacific Adventure* (46), *Bulldog Drummond at Bay* (47), *It Had to Be You* (47), *Kiss Me Kate* (53), *I Am a Camera* (55), *The Longest Day* (62), *The Seven Minutes* (71), *Exposed* (83).

## RATHBONE, Basil (1892-1967)

Rathbone will probably be best remembered as Sherlock Holmes in a series of films made during the 1940s based on the Arthur Conan Doyle stories, and frequently reshown on television. But in most of his films he played a villain, everything from Pontius Pilate to Nazi spies, and he was usually superb. He was born in Johannesburg, South Africa, and educated in England. He began appearing on stage in Shakespearean roles in 1913, often taking such parts as Iago and Cassius – the sharp-featured actor did indeed have a lean and hungry look. After service in World War I, he began making films in England, starting with *Innocent* (21), and in the mid-1920s he went to Hollywood, where his career did not prosper at first. It was an American movie, *David Copperfield* (35), in which he played an absolutely loathsome Mr Murdstone, that set him up for a long series of wonderful roles as the heavy, although he wasn't quite a villain in one of his most famous pictures, *Son of Frankenstein* (39). He played the over-curious, but basically decent son of the original monster maker. Rathbone frequently returned to the stage, most notably in Archibald MacLeish's poetry-drama, *J.B.*, in the mid-1950s. Unfortunately, by the end of his career, the quality of his films had deteriorated badly.
**Selected Films:** *Innocent* (21), *The Last of Mrs Cheyney* (29), *Captain Blood* (35), *David Copperfield* (35), *Anna Karenina* (35), *The Garden of Allah* (36), *The Adventures of Robin Hood* (38), *The Adventures of Marco Polo* (38), *Son of Frankenstein* (39), *Tower of London* (39), *The Hound of the Baskervilles* (39), *The Adventures of Sherlock Holmes* (40), *The Mark of Zorro* (40), *Sherlock Holmes and the Spider Woman* (44), *The Secret Claw* (45), *We're No Angels* (55), *The Last Hurrah* (58), *The Comedy of Terrors* (63), *Hillbillies in a Haunted House* (68).

*Basil Rathbone, with Greta Garbo and Freddie Bartholomew in* Anna Karenina *(35).*

## RATOFF, Gregory (1897-1960)

Born in St Petersburg, Russia, Ratoff fought for the Tsar and acted with the Moscow Art Theatre before coming to the United States in the 1920s. After establishing himself as a Broadway actor and director he went on to to the same in films. For 30 years Ratoff was one of the screen's staple Slavs, usually playing an extravagant impresario in films including *I'm No Angel* (33) and *All About Eve* (50). He began directing in the mid-1930s; outstanding among his many productions was *Intermezzo* (36), which introduced Ingrid Bergman to America.
**Selected Films:** *Symphony of Six Million* (32), *I'm No Angel* (33), *Cafe Metropole* (37), *The Corsican Brothers* (41), *All About Eve* (50), *The Sun Also Rises* (57), *Exodus* (60), *The Big Gamble* (61).

## RAY, Aldo (1926- )

Born Aldo de Re in Pen Argyl, Pennsylvania, this beefy character actor with a voice like a foghorn specialized in playing brawny but lovable tough guys. He was in politics and casting agents spotted him when he ran for sheriff in a California town. He proved adept at comedy in *We're No Angels* (55), and he was sterling in adventure movies such as *The Naked and the Dead* (58).
**Selected Films:** *The Marrying Kind* (51), *Pat and Mike* (52), *We're No Angels* (55), *The Naked and the Dead* (58), *Johnny Nobody* (61), *The Bad Bunch* (76), *Human Experiments* (80).

## RAYMOND, Gene (1908- )

Born Raymond Guion in Brooklyn, New York, Raymond made his first stage appearance at the

age of five and starred on Broadway in the 1920s. Making his film debut in *Personal Maid* (31), he spent the 1930s as a handsome blonde leading man mostly in romantic second features. He was married to Jeanette MacDonald, and he appeared with her in *Smilin' Through* (41). Raymond acted onscreen occasionally into the 1960s.
**Selected Films:** *Personal Maid* (31), *Zoo in Budapest* (33), *Seven Keys to Baldpate* (34), *Smilin' Through* (41), *The Locket* (46), *Hit the Deck* (550, *I'd Rather Be Rich* (64).

## RAYMOND, Paula (1923- )

Born Paula Ramona Wright in San Francisco, California, Raymond was a model before making her acting debut. In the late 1940s she moved to the screen. She was a dark-haired leading lady of a number of B movies of the 1940s and 1950s and appeared now and then through the 1960s.
**Selected Films:** *Rusty Leads the Way* (48), *The Beast from 20,000 Fathoms* (53), *The Gun that Won the West* (55), *Blood of Dracula's Castle* (70).

## REAGAN, Ronald (1911- )

Born in Tampico, Illinois, he graduated from Eureka College in 1932 and worked for five years as a sports announcer in Des Moines, Iowa, specializing in broadcasting the games of the Chicago Cubs. He began his successful career in the movies with *Love Is on the Air* (37), in which he starred as a brash headline-making radio personality who goes after corrupt city officials. Reagan appeared in some 50 movies, often as a romantic lead, but equally often as the second lead who doesn't get the girl. Most of these pictures were forgettable but on the few occasions when he was offered a meaty part, Reagan performed admirably. He was excellent as the young man who lost both legs in an accident in *King's Row* (41). And, although it has become a cliché, he was memorable asking Coach Rockne to tell the Notre Dame football team to 'win one for the Gipper,' when he played the legendary athlete George Gipp opposite Pat O'Brien in *Knute Rockne – All American* (40). Reagan was also outstanding as the American patient in the British front line hospital in *The Hasty Heart* (50). And he was always able to demonstrate his gift for comedy in a host of films. He served as a captain in the United States Army Air Corps during World War II. His declining movie career was revived by television, especially on the series *Death Valley Days*. He served as president of the screen actors guild and became increasingly involved in politics. In 1960 he was elected governor of California for the first of two terms, and in 1980 he was elected President of the United States and re-elected in 1984. Reagan's first wife was Academy Award-winner Jane Wyman, and he is married to former actress Nancy Davis.
**Selected Films:** *Love Is on the Air* (37), *Dark Victory* (39), *Hell's Kitchen* (39), *Santa Fe Trail* (40), *Knute Rockne – All American* (40), *International Squadron* (41), *King's Row* (41), *Desperate Journey* (42), *This Is the Army* (43), *Stallion Road* (47), *That Hagen Girl* (47), *The Voice of the Turtle* (47), *Night Unto Night* (48), *John Loves Mary* (49), *The Hasty Heart* (49), *Bedtime for Bonzo* (51), *Hong Kong* (52), *Prisoner of War* (54), *Hellcats of the Navy* (57), *The Killers* (64).

## REASON, Rex (1928- )

Reason began his acting career in California with the Pasadena Playhouse. During the 1950s he was a stalwart leading man in a number of B movies (for a while working under the name Bart Roberts) and the TV series *The Roaring Twenties*.
**Selected Films:** *Storm over Tibet* (52), *This Island Earth* (55), *The Creature Walks Among Us* (56), *The Rawhide Trail* (58), *The Sad Horse* (59).

## REASON, Rhodes (1928- )

The twin of actor Rex Reason, Rhodes followed his brother into B movies of the 1950s and also appeared in the TV series *White Hunter*.
**Selected Films:** *Crime Against Joe* (56), *Jungle Heat* (57), *Yellowstone Kelly* (59), *King Kong Escapes* (68).

## REDFIELD, William (1927-1976)

Born in New York, Redfield was a child performer onstage and made his screen debut at age 12. In his relatively short life he played literally hundreds of theater, radio, and occasional film productions.
**Selected Films:** *Back Door to Heaven* (39), *I Married a Woman* (58), *Fantastic Voyage* (66), *Death Wish* (74), *One Flew Over the Cuckoo's Nest* (76), *Mr Billion* (77).

## REDFORD, Robert (1936- )

Assuredly his striking blond good looks helped make Redford a star, but he has turned out to be far more than just another Hollywood sex object or conventional leading man. Born Charles Redford in Santa Monica, California, he was a high school athlete who attended the University of Colorado on a baseball scholarship. Wanting to be an artist, he dropped out of college and traveled in Europe. He returned to study art at the Pratt Institute in Brooklyn, New York. When he continued to get nowhere as a painter, he began to study acting at the American Academy of Dramatic Arts. Television followed, as well as stage acting. It was in *Barefoot in the Park* on Broadway in 1963 that he scored his biggest success up to that time. Redford began appearing in movies as early as 1961, in *War Hunt*. But oddly enough, his looks were something of a handicap at first. He was in danger of being typecast as an attractive but bland executive type, and he fought for a wide range of roles and won. The film *Butch Cassidy and the Sundance Kid* (69) made Redford a blockbuster superstar. He and Paul Newman were fantastic together and they

*Robert Redford in* Out of Africa *(85).*

never looked better. They were great together again in the charming film *The Sting* (73). Women fell in love with Redford in droves and by 1974 he was the number-one box office star in America. He has won an Academy Award as Best Director for the film *Ordinary People* (80), his directing debut. Redford, a strong athlete off screen, and an agile performer of stunts on screen, proved popular with men, too, especially in adventure movies. In private life Redford is a serious conservationist who owns a huge tract of land in Utah. An active supporter of liberal causes, he produced and starred in *All the President's Men* (76), about the Watergate Investigation. Redford is not a compulsive performer, and after staying away from the screen after *Brubaker* (79), pundits wondered whether he still had the golden touch. *Out of Africa* (85) with Meryl Streep was a major success, proving that Redford still has that special charisma.
**Selected Films:** *War Hunt* (61), *Inside Daisy Clover* (65), *The Chase* (66), *Barefoot in the Park* (67), *Tell Them Willie Boy Is Here* (69), *Butch Cassidy and the Sundance Kid* (69), *Downhill Racer* (69), *Little Fauss and Big Halsy* (70), *Jeremiah Johnson* (72), *The Candidate* (72), *The Way We Were* (73), *The Sting* (73), *The Great Gatsby* (74), *The Great Waldo Pepper* (75), *Three Days of the Condor* (75), *All the President's Men* (76), *The Electric Horseman* (79), *Brubaker* (79), *The Natural* (84), *Out of Africa* (85), *Legal Eagles* (86).

## REDGRAVE, Lynn (1943- )

The London-born daughter of actor Michael Redgrave and his wife actress Rachel Kempson and sister of actress Vanessa Redgrave, she is especially good at comedy. Beginning her film career in *Tom Jones* (63), she proved affecting and touching in *Georgy Girl* (66), playing an ugly duckling. She has continued her movie career, but along the way, has scored successes on Broadway, especially in *My Fat Friend* (opposite George Rose), and *Black Comedy* and on television, where she costarred on the comedy series, *House Calls.*
**Selected Films:** *Tom Jones* (63), *Girl With Green Eyes* (64), *Georgy Girl* (66), *The Deadly Affair* (67), *Blood Kin* (69), *Every Little Crook and Nanny* (72), *The Happy Hooker* (75), *The Big Bus* (76), *Sunday Lovers,* (80), *Morgan Stewart's Coming Home* (87).

## REDGRAVE, Michael (1908-1985)

Sir Michael Redgrave was an eminent British actor, born in Bristol, the son of an early screen actor Roy Redgrave. He was also a director, producer and playwright who was knighted for services to the theater in 1959. Redgrave was educated at Cambridge University, and was a journalist and teacher before becoming an actor. Versatility and intelligence marked him as a consummate performer from the start – witness his performance in Alfred Hitchcock's *The Lady Vanishes* (38). And he gave one of the most electrifying performances in a horror film, playing the music hall ventriloquist whose dummy takes over his soul in one segment of *Dead of Night* (45). Redgrave was a man who preferred challenging roles, and had a distinguished stage and screen career. Married to Rachel Kempson, he was the father of actresses Lynn and Vanessa Redgrave.
**Selected Films:** *Secret Agent* (36), *The Lady Vanishes* (38), *The Stars Look Down* (39), *Kipps* (41), *Thunder Rock* (42), *The Way to the Stars* (45), *Dead of Night* (45), *Fame Is the Spur* (47), *Mourning Becomes Electra* (47), *The Browning Version* (50), *The Importance of Being Ernest* (52), *The Quiet American* (58), *The Loneliness of the Long Distance Runner* (63), *The Go-Between* (71).

## REDGRAVE, Vanessa (1937- )

Born in London, England, Redgrave is a powerful and celebrated actress, the daughter of Sir Michael Redgrave and Rachel Kempson and the sister of Lynn Redgrave. She is also a colorful and controversial presence off-screen, known for her support of left-wing causes. Indeed, she is as well known for her political espousals as her acting. Redgrave attended London's Central School of Music and Drama. A stint with the Royal Shakespeare Company enhanced her budding reputation in the theater, and with movies like *Morgan* (66) and *Blow Up* (66) to her credit, she became an important film actress. *Julia* (77), won her an Academy Award for Best Supporting Actress, for her portrayal of an anti-Nazi activist. She has also made several stinging made-for-television movies, such as *Playing for Time,* in which she was a Jewish violinist who was trying to save herself in a German concentration camp by playing in the orchestra.
**Selected Films:** *Behind the Mask* (58), *Morgan* (66), *Blow Up* (66), *Camelot* (67), *The Charge of the Light Brigade* (68), *Isadora* (68), *The Seagull* (69), *The Trojan Women* (71), *Murder on the Orient Express* (74), *The Seven Per Cent Solution* (76), *Julia* (77), *Agatha* (79), *Yanks* (79), *Bear Island* (79), *The Bostonians* (84), *Weatherby* (85), *Steaming* (86).

## REDMOND, Liam (1913- )

Redmond came to films from the celebrated stage of the Abbey Theatre in his native Ireland and from the mid-1940s through the 1960s played Irish characters in films on both sides of the Atlantic.
**Selected Films:** *I See a Dark Stranger* (45), *High Treason* (51), *Night of the Demon* (57), *The Ghost and Mr Chicken* (65), *The Last Safari* (67).

## REED, Alan (1908-1977)

Born Teddy Bergman in New York, Reed worked on radio in the 1930s and from the mid 1940s held down a number of character roles in films. He was probably most familiar, however, as the voice of Fred Flintstone in the TV cartoon series.
**Selected Films:** *Days of Glory* (44), *The Postman Always Rings Twice* (46), *Viva Zapata!* (52), *Breakfast at Tiffany's* (61), *A Dream of Kings* (69).

## REED, Donna (1921-1986)

Born Donna Belle Mullenger in Denison, Iowa, Reed in her teens won beauty contests and acted in school plays before securing an MGM screen test in 1941. For a decade after her movie debut that year in *The Getaway*, she played wholesome, pretty young ladies in productions including *The Human Comedy* (43) and *It's a Wonderful Life* (46). Then in 1951 she signed with Columbia, who cast Reed against type as prostitute Alma in *From Here to Eternity* (53). The role won her a supporting-actress Academy Award. For some reason, though, her ensuing movies were minor, and in 1959 she turned to television, beginning the long-running series *The Donna Reed Show*. In the 1970s she appeared occasionally in productions including the TV movie *The Best Place to Be*.
**Selected Films:** *The Getaway* (41), *The Courtship of Andy Hardy* (42), *The Human Comedy* (43), *See Here, Private Hargrove* (44), *The Picture of Dorian Gray* (44), *Its a Wonderful Life* (46), *Green Dolphin Street* (47), *From Here to Eternity* (53), *The Last Time I Saw Paris* (55), *The Benny Goodman Story* (56), *Pepe* (60), *The Yellow Headed Summer* (74).

## REED, Oliver (1938- )

Burly and scowling, and in his off-screen life a bit of a bar room fighter, Reed makes a super villain, but he is also a good actor in general. The nephew of British director Sir Carol Reed, he was born in London, dropped out of school in his teens and worked as a bouncer, a boxer and a taxi driver. In 1960 Reed began playing bit roles in British films, beginning in *The Rebel* (60), and landed the lead in the Hammer Studios production of the classic horror movie, *The Curse of the Werewolf* (62), in which he gave a moving performance as a man trapped by a horrible force he could not control. Stardom came when he played the vicious Bill Sikes in the movie musical *Oliver!* (68), based on the Charles Dickens novel *Oliver Twist*. Reed comes across as forcefully masculine on screen.
**Selected Films:** *The Rebel* (60), *The Curse of the Werewolf* (62), *The Damned* (62), *Paranoic* (63), *The System* (64), *The Trap* (66), *The Shuttered Room* (66), *The Jokers* (66), *Oliver!* (68), *Women in Love* (69), *The Devils* (71), *Sitting Target* (72), *The Three Musketeers* (73), *The Four Musketeers* (74), *Burnt Offerings* (76), *The Brood* (79), *The Sting II* (83), *Captive* (87).

## REEVE, Christopher (1952- )

Born in New York City, Reeve caught the acting bug while he was in high school, and worked in a summer theater. He went on to study acting under John Houseman at the Julliard School. His first big time appearance was with Katharine Hepburn in the Broadway play, *A Matter of Gravity*, in 1976, although from 1974 to 1976 he had been a regular on the television soap opera *Love of Life*. He became one of those Hollywood 'overnight successes' when he starred in the title role of *Superman: The Movie* (78). This film had taken two years to make, and the producers had wanted Robert Redford to play the role, but he wanted more money and a finished script. Others turning down the role were Paul Newman, Clint Eastwood, Steve McQueen, Charles Bronson, Ryan O'Neal, Sylvester Stallone, Burt Reynolds, Nick Nolte, Jan Michael Vincent, David Soul, Kris Kristofferson and Robert Wagner. Reeve turned out to be the ideal choice. He was handsome, had done stage work, was not typecast and was willing to work out in a fitness program. With his movie career so successfully launched, he surprised many people by returning to his first love – the Broadway stage – to appeare in *Fifth of July* in 1980 and *The Marriage of Figaro* in 1985. Despite his appearances in three *Superman* films, Reeve refuses to be typecast. He has been a movie priest, in *Monsignor* (82), a psychotic in *Deathtrap* (82) and on stage a crippled Vietnam War veteran in *Fifth of July*.
**Selected Films:** *Gray Lady Down* (78), *Superman: The Movie* (78), *Somewhere in Time* (80), *Superman II* (80), *Deathtrap* (82), *Monsignor* (82), *Superman III* (83), *The Bostonians* (84), *The Aviator* (84), *Street Smart* (87).

## REEVES, George (1914-1959)

Born George Besselo in Woodstock, Iowa, Reeves made his screen debut as Brent Tarleton in *Gone With the Wind* (39), and went on to play leading roles in minor films and minor roles in major films into the 1950s. He found his greatest success as the star of the TV series *Superman*. Unfortunately, after being typed as the Man of Steel and unable to find work, Reeves died a suicide.
**Selected Films:** *Gone With the Wind* (39), *Strawberry Blonde* (41), *Blood and Sand* (42), *Jungle Jim* (49), *Samson and Delilah* (50), *From Here to Eternity* (53), *Westward Ho the Wagons* (57).

## REEVES, Steve (1926- )

Born in Glasgow, Montana, Reeves worked his way up through the various bodybuilding titles from, Mr America to Mr World to Mr Universe before parlaying his muscles into movie stardom. He flexed his way through roles as mythic heroes in a string of successful cheap Italian films.
**Selected Films:** *Athena* (54), *Hercules Unchained* (58), *The Last Days of Pompeii* (59), *Son of Spartacus* (62), *A Long Ride From Hell* (68).

## REID, Beryl (1918- )

Reid, born in Hereford, spent the better part of two decades as a music hall and revue comedienne in her native Britain before she came to movies in the mid-1950s. She has played a number of memorable character roles since, not all of them comic – she shone in the title role of an old lesbian actress in *The Killing of Sister George* (68).
**Selected Films:** *The Belles of St Trinians* (54), *Star!* (68), *The Killing of Sister George* (68), *Joseph Andrews* (76), *Yellowbeard* (83).

## REID, Carl Benton (1894-1973)

Born in Lansing, Michigan, Reid was a traveling stage actor for some 20 years before making his screen debut in the early 1940s. Among his character roles over the next 25 years were Oscar Hubbard in *The Little Foxes* (41), Sir Ensor Doone in *Lorna Doone* (51), and Clem Rogers in *The Story of Will Rogers* (52). He also appeared on the TV series *Burke's Law*.
**Selected Films:** *The Little Foxes* (41), *North Star* (43), *Lorna Doone* (510, *The Great Caruso* (51), *The Story of Will Rogers* (52), *The Egyptian* (54), *The Gallant Hours* (60), *The Ugly American* (63), *Madame X* (66).

## REID, Kate (1930- )

Canadian-born Reid appeared in occasional supporting film roles of the 1960s and 1970s and in TV productions including the series *The Whiteoaks of Jalna* and the TV movie *Death Among Friends*.
**Selected Films:** *This Property is Condemned* (66), *The Andromeda Strain* (71), *Fire With Fire* (86).

## REID, Wallace (1890-1923)

Born in St Louis, Missouri, Reid acted on the stage before turning to silent films around 1910. Over the next dozen years he starred in and directed dozens of films, becoming one of the great movie idols of the time. After a train accident in 1919, Reid was given morphine and became addicted, beginning a downhill slide to his death at 32. He was married to actress Dorothy Davenport.
**Selected Films:** *The Phoenix* (10), *The Deerslayer* (11), *The Birth of a Nation* (15), *To Have and to Hold* (16), *Forever* (21), *The Dictator* (22).

## REINER, Carl (1922- )

Multi-talented Reiner, who has succeeded as a comedian, TV comedy writer, screen writer and director, was born in the Bronx, New York, and appeared on Broadway after World War II. He came to fame as a comedian and writer on the classic Sid Caesar TV series of the 1950s. Since then Reiner has written a novel, *Enter Laughing*, which he turned into a play and a 1967 movie which he directed and acted. He has directed and written several popular screen comedies including *Where's Poppa?* (70), *Oh God!* (77), and *The Jerk* (79), has been straight man to Mel Brooks' 2000-year-old man, and has occasionally acted in movies. He is the father of actor/director Rob Reiner.
**Selected Films:** *The Gazebo* (59), *It's a Mad Mad Mad Mad World* (63), *The Russians Are Coming! The Russians are Coming!* (66), *The End* (78).

## REINER, Rob (1945- )

The son of director/writer/comic Carl Reiner, Rob got into acting by way of regional theater and improvisational comedy. In 1971 he began his long run as Mike 'Meathead' Stivic on the TV series *All in the Family*. In 1984 Reiner inaugurated a promising career as a director with the offbeat pseudo-rock-documentary *This Is Spinal Tap*, in which he also appeared. Recent directorial efforts are *The Sure Thing* (85) and *Stand By Me* (86).
**Selected Films:** *This Is Spinal Tap* (84).

## REINHOLD, Judge (1956- )

Born in Wilmington, Delaware, he attended Mary Washington College and the North Carolina School of Arts. Reinhold has done much television work, and he made his film debut in the late 1970s.
**Selected Films:** *Running Scared* (79), *Stripes* (81), *Thursday the Twelfth* (81), *Fast Times at Ridgemont High* (82), *Gremlins* (84), *Beverly Hills Cop* (84), *Roadhouse* (85), *Ruthless People* (86).

## REMICK, Lee (1935- )

Born in Boston, Massachusetts, Remick acted and danced on stage and on television before making her film debut in *A Face in the Crowd* (57), in which she was magnificent. Flirtatious and energetic in her early movies, she matured into an actress of depth and skill. Icy as the supposedly raped wife in *Anatomy of a Murder* (59), poignant as the alcoholic wife in *Days of Wine and Roses* (62), terrified as the mother of the devil in *The Omen* (76), she has never given a bad performance. She also played Jennie Jerome, the mother of Winston Churchill, in the British TV mini-series *Jennie*.
**Selected Films:** *A Face in the Crowd* (57), *The Long Hot Summer* (58), *Anatomy of a Murder* (59), *Days of Wine and Roses* (62), *The Hallelujah Trail* (65), *A Severed Head* (70), *A Delicate Balance* (73), *The Omen* (76), *The Europeans* (79), *Tribute* (80).

## RENALDO, Duncan (1904?-1980)

A foundling who knew neither when nor in what country he was born, Renaldo worked at menial jobs before his arrival in Hollywood in the 1920s. Onscreen from 1928, he appeared in some big MGM adventure films like *Trader Horn* (30) but then settled largely into routine serials and Westerns including the 'Three Mesquiteers' series. In 1945 he began his best-known role, as the Cisco Kid in 12 features and a TV series.
**Selected Films:** *The Naughty Duchess* (28), *Trader Horn* (30), *The Bridge of San Luis Rey* (31), *Rose of the Rio Grande* (38), *For Whom the Bell Tolls* (43), *The Gay Amigo* (49), *Zorro Rides Again* (59).

## RENNIE, Michael (1909-1971)

Tall, thin, almost gaunt, Rennie was born in Bradford, and began as an extra in British films. He moved on to substantial roles in Hollywood movies, particularly during the 1950s. Probably his most memorable performance was as Klaatu, the alien, in Robert Wise's *The Day the Earth Stood Still* (52). He also gained popularity in the TV series *The Third Man*.
**Selected Films:** *Secret Agent* (36), *Dangerous Moonlight* (40), *The Wicked Lady* (45), *The Black Rose* (50), *Les Miserables* (52), *The Day the Earth Stood Still* (52), *The Robe* (53), *Desiree* (54), *The Rains of Ranchipur* (55), *The Lost World* (60), *The Devil's Brigade* (68), *The Battle of El Alamein* (68), *Subterfuge* (69), *The Last Generation* (71).

## RETTIG, Tommy (1941- )

Born in Jackson Heights, New York, Rettig acted onstage from age six and made his movie debut at nine. After several films including *The 5000 Fingers of Dr T* (53), he spent four years co-starring with a dog, as Jeff in the TV series *Lassie*. Unable to find adult roles, Rettig retired.
**Selected Films:** *Panic in the Streets* (50), *Elopement* (51), *The 5000 Fingers of Dr T* (53), *The Egyptian* (54), *The Cobweb* (55), *At Gunpoint* (57).

## REVERE, Ann (1923- )

During the 1930s New York-born Revere established herself as a major character actress of the American stage. In the 1940s she concentrated on film, usually playing old maids and schoolteachers and winning a supporting-actress Oscar for her role as Elizabeth Taylor's mother in *National Velvet* (44). She also received Oscar nominations for *The Song of Bernadette* (44) and *Gentleman's Agreement* (47). Blacklisted during the Red Scare, Revere returned to the stage. In the 1970s she appeared in occasional films.
**Selected Films:** *Double Door* (34) *The Song of Bernadette* (44), *The Keys of the Kingdom* (44) *National Velvet* (44), *Gentleman's Agreement* (47), *A Place in the Sun* (51), *Birch Interval* (76).

## REVILL, Clive (1930- )

New Zealand-born Revill has played mostly comic character roles in British and American movies of the 1960s and 1970s. He has also worked on Broadway including as Fagin in *Oliver!*.
**Selected Films:** *The Headless Ghost* (59), *Bunny Lake is Missing* (65), *The Shoes of the Fisherman* (68), *Avanti!* (72), *Galileo* (75), *Matilda* (78).

## REY, Alejandro (1930-1987)

Born in Buenos Aires, Argentina, Rey appeared in a number of minor American thrillers and TV shows in the early 1970s. His film appearances include two Charles Bronson pictures *Mr Majestyk* (74) and *Breakout* (75).
**Selected Films:** *The Wild Pack* (72), *The Stepmother* (73), *Mr Majestyk* (74), *Breakout* (75), *High Velocity* (76), *The Swarm* (78), *The Ninth Configuration* (80), *Moscow on the Hudson* (84).

## REY, Fernando (1915- )

Born Fernando Arambillet in La Coruña, Spain, Rey was an architecture student before getting into Spanish film by way of being an extra and dubbing English movies. By the mid-1940s he was acting in major roles, usually as a distinguished character, like King Philip I in *The Mad Queen* (48). In 1949, while on location in Mexico, Rey met the surrealist filmmaker Luis Buñuel, who perhaps noticed a certain tincture of craziness behind Rey's dignified, bearded facade. At any event, Buñuel was to star Rey in a number of his best pictures over the next decades. These include *Viridiana* (62) and *The Discreet Charm of the Bourgeoisie* (72). Meanwhile, Rey had become an international star in a remarkable variety of roles, appearing as Worcester in Orson Welles's *Chimes at Midnight* (66), as the archcriminal of *The French Connection* (71), and as a concentration camp victim in Lina Wertmuller's *Seven Beauties* (76). In Buñuel's last film, *That Obscure Object of Desire* (77), Rey was in top form as a frustrated older lover of an elusive and mysterious girl.
**Selected Films:** *Tierra Sedienta* (45), *Don Quixote* (47), *The Mad Queen* (48), *Don Juan* (56), *Viridiana* (62), *Chimes at Midnight* (66), *The Return of the Seven* (66), *The French Connection* (71), *The Discreet Charm of the Bourgeoisie* (72), *The French Connection II* (75), *Seven Beauties* (76), *That Obscure Object of Desire* (77), *Saving Grace* (86), *Padre Nuestro* (87).

## REYNOLDS, Burt (1936- )

A good sense of humor and easy-going charm are two reasons why this handsome star is so popular. Reynolds made it to the top the modern way via television and mass-media publicity. But critics seldom take him seriously, which is a shame because he is talented and has shown wit and sparkle in many light comedies. Reynolds was born in

*Burt Reynolds in* Hustle *(75).*

Waycross, Georgia. His paternal grandmother was a Cherokee Indian and later Reynolds was frequently cast as an Indian on television. He grew up in Palm Beach, Florida, the son of the town's police chief, and he was a wild youngster who ran away from home at 14, but returned and won a football scholarship to Florida State University. A knee injury and an automobile accident put an end to his promising athletic career and he shifted to acting, moving to New York. Despite the move, Reynolds remained deeply attached to the South. Things did not go easily for him at first, but eventually he appeared in several television series beginning with *Riverboat*. He played Quint Asper, Dodge City's blacksmith in *Gunsmoke*, and had the title roles on *Hawk* and *Dan August*. He broke into films as a stuntman. Appearances on television talk shows, where he proved an amusing guest, a much-publicized romance with singer Dinah Shore, and the fuss raised over his becoming the first nude male centerfold in the April 1972 issue of *Cosmopolitan* magazine brought the fans in to see his movies. *Deliverance* (72), a terrifying but excellent film, gave him superstar status. One of Hollywood's foremost male sex symbols, Reynolds fascinated gossip columnists. In 1963, before he became famous, he married television's *Laugh-In* 'sock it to me' comedienne, British actress Judy Carne. Later his name was linked with tennis champion Chris Evert and actress Sally Field. Although *Smokey and the Bandit* (77) and *The Cannonball Run* (81) made huge sums of money, Reynolds is at his best in the exciting *The Longest Yard* (74), the off-beat *The End* (78) and opposite Goldie Hawn in *Best Friends* (82). It would be interesting to see what Reynolds could do with a demanding dramatic role which called upon him to be more versatile.

**Selected Films:** *Angel Baby* (61), *Navajo Joe* (67), *Shark!* (68), *Deliverance* (72), *White Lightning* (73), *The Longest Yard* (74), *Gator* (76), *Smokey and the Bandit* (77), *Semi-Tough* (77), *The End* (78), *Hooper* (78), *Starting Over* (79), *Smokey and the Bandit II* (80), *The Cannonball Run* (81), *Best Friends* (82), *The Best Little Whorehouse in Texas* (82), *City Heat* (84), *Stick* (85), *Heat* (87), *Malone* (87).

## REYNOLDS, Debbie (1932- )

Reynolds was a cute, perky little teenager when she started in films, beginning with *June Bride* (48), and she became a popular star of musicals and light comedies, the image of the girl next door. But she seemed to be eternally typecast as the wholesome All-American girl and it nearly finished her career. Born Mary Frances Reynolds in El Paso, Texas, and raised in California, she won the Miss Burbank title and got a screen test from Warner Bros. After a few bit parts, she transferred to MGM and appeared in *Three Little Words* (50) as the 'boop boop a doop' girl. Her best role was in *Singin' in the Rain* (52). Reynolds considerable comic skills emerged in *The Tender Trap* (55). She played a straight dramatic role in *The Catered Affair* (56) with skill, but returned to cute roles in *Bundle of Joy* (56) with her then-husband, singer Eddie Fisher. Reynolds again played an adorable ingenue in *Tammy and the Bachelor* (57). *It Started with a Kiss* (59) had humor with more bite. *The Rat Race* (60) was no humor, all bite, and a dramatic departure for her. Fans sided with her when Fisher left her for Elizabeth Taylor in 1959. Reynolds' most memorable film in the 1960s was *The Unsinkable Molly Brown* (64). In 1973 she scored a triumph on Broadway in a revival of the musical *Irene*.

**Selected Films:** *June Bride* (48), *The Daughter of Rosie O'Grady* (50), *Three Little Words* (50), *Singin' in the Rain* (52), *Susan Slept Here* (54), *Hit the Deck* (55), *The Tender Trap* (55), *The Catered Affair* (56), *Bundle of Joy* (56), *Tammy and the Bachelor* (57), *The Mating Game* (59), *The Gazebo* (59), *The Pleasure of His Company* (61), *The Unsinkable Molly Brown* (64), *The Singing Nun* (66), *What's the Matter with Helen?* (71), *That's Entertainment* (74).

## REYNOLDS, Gene (1925- )

As a teenager, American-born Reynolds appeared in many productions of the 1930s and 1940s. After a few adult roles he moved successful to TV producing, including the series *M*A*S*H*.

**Selected Films:** *Thank You Jeeves* (36), *In Old Chicago* (38), *The Blue Bird* (40), *Eagle Squadron* (44), *The Country Girl* (54), *Diane* (55).

## REYNOLDS, Marjorie (1921- )

Born Marjorie Goodspeed in Buhl, Idaho, Reynolds was a child actress in silents and made a few talkies as Marjorie Moore. Changing her name to Reynolds in 1937, she became a wholesome and pretty dancer and actress in popular films of the 1940s including *Holiday Inn* (42) with Fred Astaire. She also appeared in Fritz Lang's drama *Ministry of Fear* (43). In the 1950s Reynolds played William Bendix's wife Peg in the TV series *Life of Riley*.

**Selected Films:** *Scaramouche* (23), *Holiday Inn* (42), *Star Spangled Rhythm* (43), *Ministry of Fear* (43), *Heaven Only Knows* (47), *Models, Inc* (52), *The Silent Witness* (64).

## RHODES, Erik (1916- )

A native of El Reno, Oklahoma, Rhodes played comic character roles in radio and on Broadway before turning to the screen in the 1930s. Of his many roles as effete clerks and the like, the man with the little mustache is best remembered playing a hysterical Italian in two Astaire/Rogers films, *The Gay Divorcee* (34) and *Top Hat* (35).
**Selected Films:** *The Gay Divorcee* (34), *Top Hat* (35), *A Night at the Ritz* (35), *One Rainy Afternoon* (36), *On Your Toes* (39).

## RHUE, Madlyn (1934- )

Born Madeleine Roche, American actress Rhue was seen in supporting roles of films in the 1960s and 1970s, meanwhile appearing in the TV series *Bracken's World* and *Executive Suite*.
**Selected Films:** *Operation Petticoat* (59), *It's a Mad Mad Mad Mad World* (63), *He Rides Tall* (64), *Stand Up and Be Counted* (72).

## RICE, Florence (1907-1974)

Born in Cleveland, the daughter of sportswriter Grantland Rice, Florence played wholesome girlfriends and such in a great many films of the late 1930s and early 1940s, most of them for MGM.
**Selected Films:** *The Best Man Wins* (34), *Sweethearts* (39), *At the Circus* (39), *The Ghost and the Guest* (43).

## RICH, Irene (1891- )

Born Irene Luther in Buffalo, New York, Rich came from the real estate business to movie bit parts in 1918. By the 1920s she was a star, usually playing wicked women. In talkies she moved to character roles, among them as Will Rogers' henpecking wife in three films. During the 1930s Rich starred in a popular radio show, 'Dear John,' then returned to the screen in occasional small parts.
**Selected Films:** *Stella Maris* (18), *Beau Brummell* (24), *Lady Windermere's Fan* (25), *Craig's Wife* (28), *So This is London* (30), *Joan of Arc* (48).

## RICHARDS, Addison (1887-1964)

Like many players, Richards, born in Zanesville, Ohio, came to movies by way of the Pasadena Playhouse. From 1933 to his death he played numerous supporting roles as authority figures – officers, executives and lawyers. He also appeared in several TV series including *Rawhide*.
**Selected Films:** *Riot Squad* (33), *My Favorite Blonde* (42), *The Mummy's Curse* (46), *The Oregon Trail* (59), *For Those Who Think Young* (64).

## RICHARDSON, Ralph (1902-1983)

Sir Ralph Richardson was one of Britain's greatest actors, admired around the world. He appeared in movies chiefly in character roles, partly because he lacked his colleague Laurence Olivier's good looks, a prime requisite for a romantic lead in those days. Especially good on screen playing basically ordinary well-bred types or intellectuals, he projected integrity, blunt intelligence and an underlying vulnerability. His characterizations were always unique, often eccentric and usually memorable. Theater was his true love, not film, and it was on stage that he was most brilliant. Born in Cheltenham, Gloucester, England, Richardson began working as an office boy in an insurance company. A small legacy freed him to study acting. He toured for a while, and then joined the Birmingham Rep and went to the Old Vic in 1930. Richardson was to return to the Old Vic several times, becoming one of its mainstays, playing many important Shakespearean roles, including Petruchio, Henry V, Iago, Brutus and Sir Toby Belch. He also appeared frequently on Broadway. Richardson made his film debut in *The Ghoul* (33). He was a villain in *Bulldog Jack* (34), and delightful in *The Man Who Could Work Miracles* (36). Some think his finest screen role was the squire in *South Riding* (38). He had smaller parts than Laurence Olivier in *The Divorce of Lady X* (38) and Robert Donat in *The Citadel* (38), but he was a match for them. During the 1940s he married actress Meriel Forbes and was knighted in 1947. His dedication to the stage at this point made it difficult for him to accept film roles, but he made *Anna Karenina* (48) with Vivien Leigh and was so good in Graham Greene's *The Fallen Idol* (48) that Greene considered his performance the finest interpretation of any of his character ever. *The Heiress* (49) brought Richardson an Academy Award nomination and *Breaking the Sound Barrier* (52) won him the British Best Actor Award.
**Selected Films:** *The Ghoul* (33), *The Return of Bulldog Drummond* (34), *Bulldog Jack* (34), *Things to Come* (36), *The Man Who Could Work Miracles* (36), *South Riding* (38), *The Divorce of Lady X* (38), *The Citadel* (38), *Q Planes* (39), *The Four Feathers* (39), *The Silver Fleet* (43), *Anna Karenina* (48), *The Fallen Idol* (48), *The Heiress* (49), *Outcast of the Islands* (51), *Breaking the Sound Barrier* (52), *Richard III* (56), *Our Man in Havana* (59), *Long Day's Journey Into Night* (62), *Woman of Straw* (64), *Doctor Zhivago* (65), *The Wrong Box* (66), *Khartoum* (67), *Lady Caroline Lamb* (72), *A Doll's House* (73), *O Lucky Man!* (73), *Charlie Muffin* (79), *Dragonslayer* (81), *Time Bandits* (81), *Tarzan of the Apes* (84).

## RICHMOND, Kane (1906-1973)

Born Frederick Bowditch, in Minneapolis, Minnesota, Richmond distributed movies before he began starring in them. Starting with the 1930 serial *The Leather Pushers*, he was a handsome square-jawed hero in many B features and serials through the 1940s.
**Selected Films:** *Politics* (31), *The Adventures of Rex and Rinty* (35), *Mars Attacks the World* (38), *Spy Smasher* (42), *Brick Bradford* (47), *Stage Struck* (48).

## RICKLES, Don (1926- )

American comic Rickles, born in New York, is best known as a standup insult artist in nightclubs and on television. However, he also played supporting roles in occasional films of the 1950s and 1960s, among them Carl Reiner's *Enter Laughing* (67).
**Selected Films:** *Run Silent, Run Deep* (58), *The Rabbit Trap* (59), *Enter Laughing* (67), *The Money Jungle* (68), *Kelly's Heroes* (70).

## RIGG, Diana (1938- )

Born in Doncaster, England, Rigg first made a name for herself as a Shakespearean actress on the British stage, and among her first screen roles was Helena in *A Midsummer Night's Dream* (68). By that point, however, she had typed herself in a rather contrasting direction, becoming virtually a cult figure as karate-chopping agent Emma Peel in the TV series *The Avengers*. Rigg's movie assignment thereafter included thrillers capitalizing on her *Avengers* image like *The Assassination Bureau* (68). She also played Portia in *Julius Caesar* (70) and starred in Paddy Chayevsky's cynical study of the medical world in *The Hospital* (71), and the horror sendup *Theatre of Blood* (73). In all those roles Rigg was a lithe, dark-haired beauty whose vaguly kinky image never quite obscured her basic intelligence as an actress. In 1973 she starred in the short-running TV series *Diana*.
**Selected Films:** *A Midsummer Night's Dream* (68), *The Assassination Bureau* (68), *On Her Majesty's Secret Service* (69), *Julius Caesar* (70), *The Hospital* (71), *Theatre of Blood* (73), *A Little Night Music* (77), *Evil Under the Sun* (81).

## RINGWALD, Molly (1968- )

A native of Los Angeles, Ringwald sang with her father's band as a toddler and made her community theater debut at age five. In her early teens she appeared in the TV series *The Fact of Life*, and arrived onscreen playing John Cassavetes' daughter in *Tempest* (82). Then came three starring roles for director John Hughes, in which the redhead became the personification of the modern suburban teenager.
**Selected Films:** *Tempest* (82), *Sixteen Candles* (84), *The Breakfast Club* (85), *Pretty in Pink* (86).

## RISDON, Elizabeth (1887-1958)

Born Elizabeth Evans in London, England, Risdon starred in British silents before moving to Hollywood, where she played character parts from the mid-1930s to the mid-1950s. Among her many roles as matrons were Raskolnikov's mother in *Crime and Punishment* (35) and the Widow Douglas in *Huckleberry Fin* (39).
**Selected Films:** *Maria Marten* (13), *Crime and Punishment* (35), *Dead End* (37), *Huckleberry Finn* (39), *Abe Lincoln in Illinois* (40), *High Sierra* (41), *The Egg and I* (47), *Scaramouche* (52).

## RITCHARD, Cyril (1896-1977)

Though born in Sydney, Australia, Ritchard was a star of the British musical stage. His lively style and acid voice appeared only occasionally onscreen. In the Disney cartoon feature *Peter Pan* (53), Ritchard was the voice of Captain Hook.
**Selected Films:** *Piccadilly* (29), *Blackmail* (30), *I See Ice* (38), *Half a Sixpence* (67).

## RITTER, Tex (1907-1974)

Born Woodward Maurice Ritter in Murvaul, Texas, he was popular both as a Western singer and recording artist and the star of innumerable Western films. He was often labeled 'America's most beloved cowboy' and may be best remembered for singing the title song in the Cary Cooper classic *High Noon* (52). He was the father of actor/comedian John Ritter.
**Selected Films:** *Song of the Gringo* (36), *Sing Cowboy Sing* (37), *Rainbow Over the Range* (40), *Deep in the Heart of Texas* (42), *The Old Chisholm Trail* (42), *Marshal of Gunsmoke* (44), *The Girl from Tobacco Row* (66).

## RITTER, Thelma (1905-1969)

Born in Brooklyn, New York, Ritter began acting onstage in her youth and came out of retirement to appear in movies in 1947. For the next two decades she played a succession of cynical servants who commented on the shenanigans of the principals. The first of her six supporting-actress Oscar nominations came for her unforgettable role as Bette Davis's dresser in *All About Eve* (50).
**Selected Films:** *Miracle on 34th Street* (47), *All About Eve* (50), *The Model and the Marriage Broker* (51), *Rear Window* (54), *A Hole in the Head* (59), *The Misfits* (61), *Birdman of Alcatraz* (62), *What's So Bad About Feeling Good?* (68).

## RITZ BROTHERS, The (Al, 1901-1965; Jim, 1903-1985; Harry, 1906-1986)

The comedy trio whose hyperbolic style defined the word *zany* were born Al, Jim, and Harry Joachim in Newark, New Jersey, and grew up in Brooklyn. In their youth all three brothers got into vaudeville separately. In 1925 they joined up at a Coney Island show and stayed together, reportedly taking their new name from a laundry sign seen from an agent's office. By the 1930s their mugging, screaming, and generally outlandish patter had brought them stardom: subtle they were not, but they were a popular feature of vaudeville, nightclubs, musicals, and between the girlie panoramas in *Earl Carroll's Vanities*. The Ritz's movie debut came with *Sing Baby Sing* (36). For the next decade they fractured screen musicals and comedies as a sort of low-budget Marx

Brothers, perhaps their most memorable romp being in the unlikely roles of *The Three Musketeers* (39). After Al's death Harry and Jim made guest appearances in some films.
**Selected Films:** *Sing Baby Sing* (36), *On the Avenue* (37), *The Goldwyn Follies* (38), *The Gorilla* (39), *The Three Musketeers* (39), *Hi Ya, Chum* (43). Harry and Jim – *Won Ton Ton, the Dog Who Saved Hollywood* (76). Harry only – *Silent Movie* (76).

## RIVERA, Chita (1933- )

As a dancer and singer, Rivera, born in Washington, DC, has been a staple musical comedy performer on the American stage since the 1950s. Among her few screen films has been the musical *Sweet Charity* (69).
**Selected Films:** *Sweet Charity* (69).

## ROBARDS, Jason Jr (1922- )

Born in Chicago, Illinois, the son of the famed stage actor Jason Robards, he first gained attention for his performances in the plays of Eugene O'Neill. Television and movie stardom followed. He began making pictures in the late 1950s. In 1976 he won the Academy Award for Best Supporting Actor for his work as *Washington Post* editor Benjamin Bradlee in *All the President's Men*. Bradlee had been a pivotal figure in the exposure of the Watergate scandal that ultimately led to the resignation of President Richard M Nixon. The following year, Robards won the Oscar again for his portrayal of the writer Dashiell Hammett in *Julia* (77). He was nominated for Best Supporting Actor a third time for his role as billionaire Howard Hughes in *Melvin and Howard* (80). Robards' third wife was the legendary Lauren Bacall.
**Selected Films:** *The Journey* (58) *Tender is the Night* (61), *Long Day's Journey into Night* (62), *The Hour of the Gun* (67), *All the President's Men* (76), *Julia* (77), *Comes a Horseman* (78), *Melvin and Howard* (79), *Max Dugan Returns* (83), *Square Dance* (87).

## ROBERTI, Lyda (1910-1938)

Born in Warsaw, Poland, Roberti was a performer in European circuses as a child and grew up to be a cabaret singer. Emigrating to the United States in the 1920s, the platinum blonde worked on Broadway before coming to the screen in 1932. Until her sudden death of a heart attack, she appeared in a number of popular movie musicals.
**Selected Films:** *Million Dollar Legs* (32), *The Big Broadcast of 1936* (35), *George White's Scandals* (35), *Wide Open Faces* (37).

## ROBERTS, Eric (1956- )

Roberts was born to an actor's family in Biloxi, Mississippi and began appearing onstage in childhood. After studies at the Royal Academy of Dramatic Art in London and the American Academy of Dramatic Arts in New York, he appeared in the Broadway production of *Mass Appeal*. His screen debut came in *King of the Gypsies* (78). Since then Roberts has been outstanding as sleazy killer Paul Snider in *Star 80* (83) and has played leads in *The Coca-Cola Kid* (85) and *Runaway Train* (85), for which he received an Academy Award nomination.
**Selected Films:** *King of the Gypsies* (78), *Raggedy Man* (81), *Star 80* (83), *The Pope of Greenwich Village* (84), *The Coca-Cola Kid* (85), *Runaway Train* (85), *Nobody's Fool* (86).

## ROBERTS, Pernell (1930- )

A native of Waycross, Georgia, Roberts appeared in a few movies of the 1950s and 1960s but is best known for his TV roles as one of the brothers in the series *Bonanza* and as the star of *Trapper John, MD*.
**Selected Films:** *Ride Lonesome* (58), *The Magic of Lassie* (78).

## ROBERTS, Rachel (1927-1980)

Born in Llanelly, Wales, Rachel Roberts trained for the stage and spent most of her career acting in the theater, with occasional and memorable forays into a wide variety of films. After a few movies in the 1950s including *Our Man in Havana* (59), she appeared in Karel Reisz's offbeat drama *Saturday Night and Sunday Morning* (60) and for it won a British Film Academy Award. She received another and a best-actress Oscar nomination came for her performance as a widow in Lindsay Anderson's bleak drama *This Sporting Life* (63). A decade later she worked with Anderson again, playing three parts in his black comedy *Oh Lucky Man!* (73). Other notable films of that decade were *Picnic at Hanging Rock* (76) and *Yanks* (79); for the latter she won another BFA award. During the 1960s Roberts was married to actor Rex Harrison.
**Selected Films:** *Valley of Song* (52), *Our Man in Havana* (59), *Saturday Night and Sunday Morning* (60), *This Sporting Life* (63), *A Flea in Her Ear* (68), *Oh Lucky Man!* (73), *Murder on the Orient Express* (74), *Picnic at Hanging Rock* (76), *Foul Play* (78), *Yanks* (79), *When a Stranger Calls* (79), *The Wall* (81).

## ROBERTS, Tanya (1955- )

Bronx-born Roberts acted off-Broadway before joining the other pretty ladies in the cast of the TV series *Charlie's Angels*. Her early films have included the jungle-girl yarn *Sheena* (84).
**Selected Films:** *The Beastmaster* (82), *Sheena* (84), *A View To A Kill* (85).

## ROBERTS, Tony (1939- )

This genial actor was born in New York City, and appeared often on the stage before making his film

debut. He is often seen in Woody Allen pictures, playing Allen's best friend and confident.
**Selected Films:** *The Beach Girls and the Monster* (70), *Star Spangled Girl* (71), *Play It Again, Sam* (72), *Serpico* (73), *Annie Hall* (77), *Just Tell Me What You Want* (80), *A Midsummer's Night's Sex Comedy* (82), *Amityville 3D* (83), *Radio Days* (87).

## ROBERTSON, Cliff (1925- )

Born in La Jolla, California, Robertson spent years on the stage before making his first picture, *Picnic* (55). Even today he spends his time between movies by acting in summer stock. This hard working actor has been in countless films, including the masterpiece, *Charly* (68), for which he won the Academy Award as Best Actor, but is probably remembered best for his portrayal of John F Kennedy in *PT 109* (63). Robertson was married to actress Cynthia Stone from 1957 to 1959, and is currently married to actress Dina Merrill, whom he married in 1966. He refers to himself as being 'the last old-fashioned Presbyterian' because of his work ethic. He also directs.
**Selected Films:** *Picnic* (55), *Autumn Leaves* (56), *The Naked and the Dead* (58), *Battle of the Coral Sea* (59), *PT 109* (63), *Sunday in New York* (64), *The Best Man* (64), *Charly* (68), *Man on a Swing* (74), *Three Days of the Condor* (76), *The Pilot* (79), *Brainstorm* (83), *Skater Run* (85), *Malone* (87).

## ROBERTSON, Dale (1923- )

Born in Oklahoma City, Oklahoma, Robertson was a boxer before making his screen debut as Jesse James in *Fighting Man of the Plains* (49). For the next two decades he was a likeable and rugged leading man of routine westerns, but is better known for TV series including *Tales of Wells Fargo*.
**Selected Films:** *Fighting Man of the Plains* (49), *Sitting Bull* (54), *Blood on the Arrow* (65), *One-Eyed Soldiers* (67), *Melvin Purvis: G-Man* (74).

## ROBESON, Paul (1898-1976)

Born in Princeton, New Jersey, Robeson, a powerful black man with an equally powerful bass voice, was an All-American football player at Rutgers. He began his show business career in the mid-1920s and appeared in his first picture in 1924 – *Body and Soul*. His most famous film role was that of Joe, a slave, in *Show Boat* (36), in which he left audiences thunderstruck with his singing of 'Ol' Man River.' In the late 1940s he was stunning theater audiences with his portrayal of Shakespeare's *Othello*, which also starred Uta Hagen as Desdemona and Jose Ferrer as Iago. His career fell apart after that because of his espousal of Communist causes.
**Selected Films:** *Body and Soul* (24), *The Emperor Jones* (33), *Sanders of the River* (35), *Show Boat* (36), *Song of Freedom* (37), *Jericho* (38), *King Solomon's Mines* (38), *The Proud Valley* (39), *Native Land* (42), *Il Canto dei Grandi Fiumi* (55).

## ROBINSON, Bill (1878-1949)

This black tap dancer, nicknamed 'Bojangles,' had attained nearly legendary status and Broadway stardom before he was brought to Hollywood. Audiences took him to their hearts in four Shirley Temple movies, but he also appeared in other films, such as *Stormy Weather* (43), with Lena Horne. He was probably most famous for his celebrated dancing with Temple.
**Selected Films:** *Dixiana* (30), *The Little Colonel* (35), *In Old Kentucky* (36), *Rebecca of Sunnybrook Farm* (38), *Stormy Weather* (43).

## ROBINSON, Edward G (1893-1973)

Robinson was the quintessential tough guy actor. To this day there is a bit of Robinson in many gangster characterizations in films and on television. But he was skillful in other roles as well. Born Emmanuel Goldenberg in Bucharest, Romania, he came to America at the age of 10. After years on Broadway he went to Hollywood, making his debut in *The Bright Shawl* (23). He became a star when he played the title role in Mervyn LeRoy's gangster film *Little Caesar* (30). The tough, stocky little man with the unique way of drawling out his 'Yeah,' Robinson could never have the sheer physical appeal of his contemporaries such as James Cagney and Humphrey Bogart. For one thing, he wasn't handsome. But his kind of attraction came from the sheer power he radiated. When he came on the screen as a hired gun in *Little Caesar*, audiences knew that he was going to fight his way to the top, no matter whom he had to rub out. When he was shot down and gasped out his famous last words, 'Mother of God, is this the end of Rico?' the audiences felt that only bullets could stop this insatiable drive for power. Many actors would have stayed in the successful rut of the kind that Robinson abandoned. But he was truly versatile, playing federal agents, scientists, Biblical characters, business men, religious brothers, bank clerks, and he even went on to turn in gangster performances that poked fun of his former persona. Attacks by the House of Un-American Activities Committee during the 1950s led to career problems and financial difficulties. Family and personal problems plagued him as well, but he continued to act. In 1972 he received a Special Academy Award.
**Selected Films:** *The Bright Shawl* (23), *Little Caesar* (30), *Five Star Deal* (31), *The Whole Town's Talking* (34), *Barbary Coast* (35), *Bullets or Ballots* (36), *Kid Galahad* (37), *A Slight Case of Murder* (38), *The Amazing Dr Clitterhouse* (38), *Confessions of a Nazi Spy* (39), *Dr Ehrlich's Magic Bullet* (40), *Brother Orchid* (40), *The Sea Wolf* (41), *Double Indemnity* (44), *Scarlet Street* (45), *All My Sons* (48), *Key Largo* (48), *House of Strangers* (49), *A Bullet for Joey* (55), *The Ten Commandments* (56), *Two Weeks in Another Town* (62), *Cheyenne Autumn* (64), *The Cincinnati Kid* (65), *Soylent Green* (73).

## ROBSON, Flora (1902-1984)

Born in South Shields, England, this distinguished character actress of stage and screen graduated from the Royal Academy of Dramatic Art. She debuted on stage in the 1920s and on screen in *Dance Pretty Lady* (31). She was made a Dame of the British Empire in 1960.
**Selected Films:** *Dance Pretty Lady* (31), *Fire Over England* (36), *Wuthering Heights* (39), *Saratoga Trunk* (43), *Caesar and Cleopatra* (45), *Black Narcissus* (46), *Innocent Sinners* (57), *Murder at the Gallop* (63), *Seven Women* (65), *Dominique* (78), *A Man Called Intrepid* (79).

## ROBSON, May (1858-1942)

Born Mary Robison in Melbourne, Australia, Robson came to the United States in her teens and made her stage debut in 1883. She appeared in a few silent moves but came into her own in talkies, where she was one of the great old ladies of the screen in turns as sharp-tongued but sympathetic matrons; among her many roles were as Apple Annie in *Lady for a Day* (33) and Aunt Polly in *The Adventures of Tom Sawyer* (38).
**Selected Films:** *How Molly Made Good* (15), *King of Kings* (27), *If I Had a Million* (32), *Lady for a Day* (33), *A Star is Born* (37), *Bringing Up Baby* (38), *The Adventures of Tom Sawyer* (38), *Four Daughters* (38), *Granny Get Your Gun* (40), *Joan of Paris* (42).

## ROC, Patricia (1918- )

Born Felicia Riese in London, Roc acted briefly onstage before becoming a leading lady in British films of the late 1930s. The attractive blonde appeared in two American movies, the second of them *The Man on the Eiffel Tower* (50).
**Selected Films:** *The Rebel Son* (38), *Let the People Sing* (42), *Madonna of the Seven Moons* (44), *The Brothers* (47), *The Man on the Eiffel Tower* (50), *Something Money Can't Buy* (53), *Bluebeard's Ten Honeymoons* (60).

## ROGERS, Charles 'Buddy' (1904- )

Born in Olathe, Kansas, Buddy Rogers got into silent films in the mid-1920s and in 1927 was one of the leads in the aviation spectacular *Wings*. By then he had already been a hit in *Fascinating Youth* (26). When talkies arrived, the wavy-haired and handsome Rogers became known as 'America's Boy Friend,' one of the most popular light leading men of the day. In 1937 America's Boy Friend married America's Sweetheart – Mary Pickford, 11 years his senior, who had just divorced Douglas Fairbanks. Pickford and Rogers had co-starred in *My Best Girl* (27). Rogers' popularity lasted through the 1930s in films like *This Reckless Age* (32), *Old Man Rhythm* (35), and *Let's Make a Night of It* (38). After military service in World War II he returned to occasional movie appearances.
**Selected Films:** *Fascinating Youth* (26), *Wings* (27), *My Best Girl* (27), *Abie's Irish Rose* (29), *Paramount on Parade* (30), *Young Eagles* (31), *This Reckless Age* (32), *Old Man Rhythm* (35), *One in a Million* (36), *Let's Make a Night of It* (38), *Golden Hooves* (41), *Mexican Spitfire's Baby* (43), *Don't Trust Your Husband* (48), *The Parson and the Outlaw* (57).

## ROGERS, Ginger (1911- )

Rogers, sassy and sexy with a tart tongue, was a clever wisecracking comedienne who longed for dramatic roles, but who was swept into movie immortality in the arms of Fred Astaire instead. The films they danced in during the 1930s were the best musicals that Hollywood ever made. She was born Virginia McMath in Independence, Missouri. Although her mother had hoped that Rogers would become a painter, she changed her mind when Rogers, at the age 14, debuted professionally with Eddie Foy's vaudeville troupe. A year later she won the Texas State Charleston Contest, and her mother quit her jobs to become her manager. In 1928, Rogers appeared with her first husband, Jack Pepper, playing half of the 'Ginger and Pepper' team. Later she sang with a band, appeared in film shorts and found some success in Broadway musicals. Her first film after she went to Hollywood was *Young Man of Manhattan* (30). She was a bright addition to movie musicals such as *Gold Diggers of 1933* (33) and *42nd Street* (33). Even in such early films, Rogers projected toughness, calculating shrewdness and self-sufficiency with engaging charm. There was no top billing for her or Fred Astaire for *Flying Down to Rio* (33), but they stole the picture dancing 'The Carioca.' From then on they were top box office stars. Rogers made other films on her own during her years with Astaire, and afterwards tackled a variety of roles, winning an Academy Award for Best Actress for her work in the title role in *Kitty Foyle* (40). She was delicious posing as a child in *The Major and the Minor* (43), opposite Ray Milland. In 1945, she was the highest paid performer in Hollywood and had the eighth highest individual income in the United States. Although Rogers continued in films through the 1950s and even into the 1960s, she devoted more and more of her time to the stage, pulling in crowds after taking over the lead in *Hello, Dolly!* on Broadway and *Mame* in London. She has been married several times, and her second husband was actor Lew Ayres.
**Selected Films:** *Young Man of Manhattan* (30), *Gold Diggers of 1933* (33), *42nd Street* (33), *Flying Down to Rio* (33), *The Gay Divorcee* (34), *Roberta* (35), *Top Hat* (35), *Follow the Fleet* (36), *Swingtime* (36), *Shall We Dance?* (37), *Stage Door* (38), *Carefree* (38), *The Story of Vernon and Irene Castle* (39), *Bachelor Mother* (39), *Kitty Foyle* (40), *Roxie Hart* (42), *The Major and the Minor* (43), *Lady in the Dark* (43), *I'll Be Seeing You* (44), *The Barkleys of Broadway* (48), *We're Not Married* (52), *Dream Boat* (52), *Black Widow* (54), *Harlow* (65).

## ROGERS, Roy (1912- )

Born Leonard Slye in Cincinnati, Ohio, Rogers became one of the most famous Western stars of all time – in movies, television and personal appearances. He was billed by Republic Studios and himself as 'King of the Cowboys' when Gene Autry, the number one B western star, enlisted in the Army during World War II. Republic built a huge publicity campaign around Rogers, who didn't go into the service. He went on to fame and fortune, marrying Dale Evans, the co-star of many of his films. Rogers had copied the Autry 'singing cowboy' formula in the late 1930s, and his pleasant voice and personality enabled him to go with it. He had been a radio singer with a Western Band using the name of Dick Weston. The name of the band was Bob Nolan and his Tumblin' Tumbleweeds – later known as the Sons of the Pioneers. He played some bit parts in a couple of Autry films and some other B westerns. When he hit it big as the wartime replacement for Autry, he wore even more outlandish costumes, looking like a Liberace of the plains and became the idol of millions of children. He was equally successful in his television show of the 1950s.
**Selected Films:** *Tumblin' Tumbleweeds* (35), *Under Western Skies* (38), *Red River Valley* (41), *Robin Hood of the Pecos* (42), *The Man from Music Mountain* (44), *Roll On, Texas Moon* (47), *Son of Paleface* (52), *Pals of the Golden West* (53), *Mackintosh and TJ* (75).

## ROGERS, Will (1879-1939)

Born in Oologah, Indian Territory, now Oklahoma, he began his show business career as a trick rider and rope twirler in wild west shows. Rogers then gradually introduced bits of humor and homespun philosophy into his act. This rustic comedian with the crackerbarrel philosophy went on to star in the Ziegfeld Follies and in vaudeville. Sound movies helped his career and by the time he was killed in an airplane crash, he had become the voice of the common man in the United States – a national hero whose newspaper column was read by millions.
**Selected Films:** *Laughing Bill Hyde* (18), *Jubilo* (19), *The Ropin' Fool* (22), *Don't Park There* (24), *The Cowboy Sheik* (24), *They Had to See Paris* (29), *Young As You Feel* (31), *State Fair* (33), *David Harum* (34), *Handy Andy* (34), *Judge Priest* (34), *Life Begins at Forty* (35), *Steamboat 'Round the Bend* (35).

## ROLAND, Gilbert (1905- )

Born Luis Antonio Damaso de Alonso in Juarez, Mexico, he first trained as a bullfighter – his father's profession. He made his film debut in *The Plastic Age* (25), and often starred as a dashing Latin lover in silents. He matured into a durable character actor in a number of films.
**Selected Films:** *The Plastic Age* (25), *Camille* (27), *Men of the North* (29), *She Done Him Wrong* (33), *Last Train from Madrid* (37), *Juarez* (39), *The Sea Hawk* (40), *Captain Kidd* (45), *We Were Strangers* (49), *The Bullfighter and the Lady* (51), *Beyond the Twelve Mile Reef* (53), *The Big Circus* (59), *Islands in the Stream* (77), *The Black Pearl* (77), *Barbarosa* (81).

## ROLAND, Ruth (1893-1937)

As a child, Roland, born in San Francisco, California, worked onstage as 'Baby Ruth.' Making her screen debut in 1911, she developed into one of the great stars of serial cliffhangers and the main rival of Pearl White. She also played leads in occasional features before sound finished her career.
**Selected Films:** *Arizona Bill* (11), *Hands Up* (18), *The Masked Woman* (26), *From Nine to Nine* (36).

## ROMAN, Ruth (1924- )

Born in Boston, Massachusetts, Ruth Roman attended the Bishop Lee Dramatic School before beginning her acting career in the theater. She made her screen debut in the early 1940s, appearing in a number of popular pictures including *Stage Door Canteen* (43), the Marx Brothers' *A Night in Casablanca* (45), and *The Window* (49). Today Roman is best remembered for her starring role opposite Farley Granger in Alfred Hitchcock's great thriller *Strangers on a Train* (51). In that film Roman played her most familiar role, an outwardly chilly and inwardly melting lady. During the rest of the 1950s she appeared largely in routine films such as *Maru, Maru* (52) and *Five Steps to Danger* (57). Roman worked often on TV, including the series *The Long Hot Summer* and the TV movie *Go Ask Alice.*
**Selected Films:** *Stage Door Canteen* (43), *Ladies Courageous* (44), *A Night in Casablanca* (45), *The Window* (49), *Three Secrets* (50), *Strangers on a Train* (51), *Maru, Maru* (52), *Down Three Dark Streets* (54), *Joe Macbeth* (56), *Five Steps to Danger* (57), *Desert Desperadoes* (59), *Love Has Many Faces* (65), *Day of the Animals* (77), *Echoes* (80).

## ROMERO, Caesar (1907- )

Born in New York City, Romero nevertheless became one of Hollywood's chief Latin lovers of the 1930s, 1940s and 1950s. His film career began with *The Shadow Laughs* (33), and he went on to play in countless movies. Romero later moved into character roles. He was *The Cisco Kid* in early installments of that film series, and on television, he was the star of *Passport to Danger*, a series that aired in 1956, but also played the part of the villainous 'The Joker' on the popular *Batman* series.
**Selected Films:** *The Shadow Laughs* (33), *The Thin Man* (34), *The Devil Is a Woman* (35), *Wee Willie Winkie* (37), *Ride On, Vaquero* (42), *Springtime in the Rockies* (42), *Captain from Castile* (48), *Vera Cruz* (54), *Marriage on the Rocks* (65), *Batman* (66), *Madigan's Millions* (68), *The Spectre of Edgar Allan Poe* (73), *The Strongest Man in the World* (74).

## ROONEY, Mickey (1920- )

Known for his small size, his energy and versatility, his numerous marriages and his ability to bounce back from adversity, Rooney made his film debut at the age of six. Born Joe Yule, Jr to a vaudeville family in Brooklyn, New York, before he was two years old, he had crawled out on a stage during a performance and was in his parents' act after that. In 1926 a Hollywood studio announced that it was holding auditions for a series of short features based on a character named Mickey McGuire, who was in the popular comic strip 'Toonerville Folks.' In the strip, McGuire had black hair. Young Joe was a blonde, but his stage-savvy mother used shoe polish to darken it and tugged him off to the audition. He got the role, and carried the Mickey McGuire series for six years. For a while his parents thought of changing his name to Mickey McGuire. Instead, they chose Mickey Rooney. It was a good idea, because the McGuire shorts were just the beginning. At an age when some child star's careers were ending, Rooney was moving on to bigger things. Before he was a teenager, he was starring in big-budget films. Among his odder roles was that of Puck, a blithe spirit, in the film version of Shakespeare's *A Midsummer Night's Dream* (35). In 1937 MGM had the idea of using Rooney in a film version of a domestic play about a typical American family named Hardy. Rooney played Andy Hardy, who was an almost painfully typical teenager. In the first film, *A Family Affair* (37), Lionel Barrymore played Andy's father, Judge Hardy, and Spring Byington was his mother. For the rest of the Andy Hardy series the parents were played by Lewis Stone and Fay Holden. The series went through a total of 17 films in 20 years, earned $25 million for MGM, and featured, along the way, such talents as Judy Garland, Lana Turner, Esther Williams and Susan Peters. At the same time, Rooney appeared in other pictures. He won a Special Academy Award in 1938 for playing a tough kid in *Boys' Town*; he had the title role in *Young Tom Edison* (40); he was impressive in the film version of William Saroyan's novel *The Human Comedy* (43); he made musicals with Judy Garland, and much, much more. At the ripe old age of 28 Rooney left off being a young actor and began just being an actor. His acting career as an adult continues to this day. His private life hasn't always been smooth, but he has bounded through life with endless energy, appearing in everything from tired comedies (*Francis in the Haunted House*, a 1956 film featuring a talking mule) to serious drama (*The Bold and the Brave*, another 1956 film for which he was nominated for an Academy Award). His adult credits also include a stint on Broadway in *Sugar Babies* and his Emmy Award-winning performance in the television movie, *Bill*. In 1982 he received another Special Academy Award 'in recognition of his 60 years of versatility in a variety of memorable film performances.' His first wife was Ava Gardner.

**Selected Films:** *Orchids and Ermine* (27), *My Pal the King* (32), *A Midsummer Night's Dream* (35), *Ah, Wilderness* (35), *Captains Courageous* (37), *A Family Affair* (37), *Boys' Town* (38), *Love Finds Andy Hardy* (38), *The Adventures of Huckleberry Finn* (39), *Babes in Arms* (39), *Young Tom Edison* (40), *Strike Up the Band* (40), *Babes on Broadway* (41), *The Human Comedy* (43), *Girl Crazy* (43), *National Velvet* (44), *Words and Music* (48), *The Bold and the Brave* (56), *Francis in the Haunted House* (56), *Baby Face Nelson* (58), *Breakfast at Tiffany's* (61), *It's a Mad Mad Mad Mad World* (63), *The Comic* (69), *The Black Stallion* (79), *Find the Lady* (80).

## ROSE, George (1920- )

Born in Bicester, England, Rose came from the stage to the screen in the early 1950s and has since played character roles in a number of mostly British features.

**Selected Films:** *Pickwick Papers* (52), *The Sea Shall Not Have Them* (54), *Brothers in Law* (57), *Hawaii* (66), *The Pirates of Penzance* (83).

## ROSENBLOOM, 'Slapsie Maxie' (1906-1976)

New York-born Max Rosenbloom came out of reform school to the boxing ring, winning the light-heavyweight title in the early 1930s. It was Damon Runyon himself who dubbed Rosenbloom 'Slapsie Maxie,' and in movies from the mid-1930s to the mid-1960s he played punchy Runyonesque mugs. In the end his injuries caught up with him.

**Selected Films:** *Mr Broadway* (33), *Nothing Sacred* (37), *The Kid Comes Back* (38), *Irish Eyes Are Smiling* (44), *Abbott and Costello Meet the Keystone Kops* (55), *The Beat Generation* (59), *Don't Worry, We'll Think of a Title* (66).

## ROSS, Diana (1944- )

Destined for unequivocal stardom as a pop singer and somewhat elusive stardom in movies, Detroit, Michigan-born Diana Ross began like many black vocalists by singing in church. In the 1960s she teamed up with Florence Ballard and Mary Wilson to form The Supremes. With their slinky dresses, steel-helmet hair, and irresistable drive, they became the headliners of the Motown Label and one of the most popular singing groups of the day, their hits including 'Baby Love' and 'Stop, in the Name of Love.' Having led The Supremes for several years, Ross broke away on her own in 1970. Her movie debut in *Lady Sings the Blues* (72) was anticipated with dubiousness (she had no acting experience), but Ross triumphed in the leading role of tragic singer Billie Holiday, redeeming an otherwise pedestrian movie and earning a best-actress Academy Award nomination. After that a film critic wrote that Ross 'should be the biggest movie superstar to come along since Barbra Streisand,' but Hollywood seemed unready for a

black leading lady; she did not appear onscreen again for three years. Her next film was *Mahogany* (75), a full-scale superstar treatment in which she played a model who rises from the ghetto to become a famous fashion designer. Despite the presence of considerable talent in the movie, including Billy Dee Williams, Anthony Perkins, and Jean-Pierre Aumont, *Mahogany* was a major bomb. Ross's latest project, as a rather mature Dorothy in the all-black musical *The Wiz* (78), fared little better. Since then Ross has appeared occasionally as a solo singer.
**Selected Films:** *Lady Sings the Blues* (72), *Mahogany* (75), *The Wiz* (78).

## ROSS, Katherine (1942- )

Born in Los Angeles, California, Ross studied drama before she appeared on television and made her screen debut in *Shenandoah* (65). After several unrewarding parts she was launched into stardom as Dustin Hoffman's sweetly sensual love in *The Graduate* (67). In 1969 she played the female lead in the hit *Butch Cassidy and the Sundance Kid,* but since then her films have been middling.
**Selected Films:** *Shenandoah* (65), *The Singing Nun* (66), *The Graduate* (67), *Tell Them Willie Boy is Here* (69), *Butch Cassidy and the Sundance Kid* (69), *The Stepford Wives* (75), *The Final Countdown* (80), *Wrong is Right* (82).

## ROSS, Shirley (1909-1975)

Born Bernice Gaunt in Omaha, Nebraska, Ross was a pianist and band singer before she began playing movie bit parts in the mid-1930s. She graduated to occasional leads, several times opposite Bob Hope, including *Thanks for the Memory* (38).
**Selected Films:** *Bombshell* (33), *The Age of Indiscretion* (35), *San Francisco* (36), *The Big Broadcast of 1938* (37), *Thanks for the Memory* (38), *A Song for Miss Julie* (45).

## ROSSELLINI, Isabella (1952- )

Born in Rome, the daughter of actress Ingrid Bergman and director Roberto Rossellini, she attended Rome's Academy of Fashion and Costume and worked for her father in the film studio costume department. She also worked on Italian television as an interviewer and an actress, became a model and appears in films. Rossellini has been married to director Martin Scorsese and Jon Widemann, by whom she had a daughter.
**Selected Films:** *Il Pirata* (78), *White Nights* (85), *Blue Velvet* (86), *Tough Guys Don't Dance* (87).

## ROTH, Lillian (1910-1980)

Born Lillian Rutstein in Boston, Massachusetts, Roth was a stage and screen actress as a child and a vaudeville star in her teens. After glittering success on Broadway, she returned to films in 1929 as a sexy young woman. However, within four years she was out of movies. Not until the 1950s did Roth reveal her alcoholic decline. In 1954 her best-selling autobiography, *I'll Cry Tomorrow*, was made into a biopic starring Susan Hayward. In the 1970s Roth found a few stage and TV roles and appeared in the film *Communion* (77).
**Selected Films:** *Pershing's Crusaders* (18), *The Love Parade* (29), *The Vagabond King* (30), *Animal Crackers* (30), *Paramount on Parade* (30), *Madame Satan* (30), *Take a Chance* (33), *Communion* (77).

## ROUNDTREE, Richard (1942- )

Born in New Rochelle, New York, Roundtree was a janitor, salesman, and model while studying to be an actor. After appearing with the Negro Ensemble Company in the 1960s, he broke into film and became a major black star in three films (and a short-lived TV series) as macho detective Shaft.
**Selected Films:** *What Do You Say to a Naked Lady?* (70), *Shaft* (71), *Embassy* (72), *Shaft's Big Score* (72), *Shaft in Africa* (73), *Earthquake* (74), *The Winged Serpent* (82), *The Big Score* (83), *City Heat* (84).

## ROURKE, Mickey (1956- )

Born in Schenectady, New York, Rourke studied drama in New York and made his film debut with a small part in *1941* (80). Since gaining notice as an arsonist in *Body Heat* (81), he has worked regularly, tending to play unstable and sometimes violent young men, like the con artist in *The Pope of Greenwich Village* (84).
**Selected Films:** *1941* (80), *Heaven's Gate* (80), *Body Heat* (81), *Diner* (82), *Rumble Fish* (83), *The Pope of Greenwich Village* (84), *Year of the Dragon* (85), *9½ Weeks* (85), *Angel Heart* (87), *Barfly* (87).

## ROWLANDS, Gena (1934- )

Born Virginia Rowlands in Cambria, Wisconsin, Rowlands began acting onstage in the 1940s and arrived on Broadway in 1952. Since the late 1950s she has appeared in occasional films, notably those of her actor/director husband John Cassavetes. These include *A Woman Under the Influence* (74), which earned Rowlands an Oscar nomination.
**Selected Films:** *The High Cost of Loving* (58), *Faces* (68), *Minnie and Moskowitz* (71), *A Woman Under the Influence* (74), *Two Minute Warning* (76), *Opening Night* (77), *Gloria* (80), *Light of Day* (87).

## ROYLE, Selena (1904-1983)

New York-born Royle was an established character actress in the theater when she came to the screen in the early 1930s. In a number of films into the 1950s she usually played mothers.
**Selected Films:** *The Misleading Lady* (32), *Thirty Seconds Over Tokyo* (44), *Joan of Arc* (48), *Robot Monster* (53), *Murder is My Beat* (55).

## RUDLEY, Herbert (1911- )

American actor Rudley played supporting roles onscreen from the late 1930s through the 1950s, among them Ira Gershwin in *Rhapsody in Blue* (45). Later he appeared in several TV series including *The Californians*, and *The Mothers-in-Law*.
**Selected Films:** *Abe Lincoln in Illinois* (39), *The Seventh Cross* (44), *Rhapsody in Blue* (45), *A Walk in the Sun* (46), *Joan of Arc* (48), *The Silver Chalice* (55), *Beloved Infidel* (59).

## RUGGLES, Charles (1886-1970)

This American character actor, born in Los Angeles, California, began his career in *Peer Gynt* (15) and played in occasional films while he was pursuing his stage career. In 1928 he began devoting his full time to the screen. He was the brother of actor and director Wesley Ruggles, and in his inimitably diffident manner, became a Hollywood favorite, especially as a hen-pecked husband opposite Mary Boland. Audiences loved his wistful timidity, and he was in nearly 100 films.
**Selected Films:** *Peer Gynt* (15), *The Lady Lies* (29), *Charley's Aunt* (30), *Trouble in Paradise* (32), *Ruggles and Red Gap* (35), *Bringing Up Baby* (38), *A Stolen Life* (46), *The Pleasure of His Company* (61), *The Ugly Dachshund* (66).

## RULE, Janice (1931- )

Born in Norwood, Ohio, Rule was a leading lady in the theater and on the screen from the early 1950s, and continued in character roles into the 1980s, while she pursued a second career as a psychotherapist. She was married to actor Ben Gazzara from 1961 to 1979.
**Selected Films:** *Goodbye, My Fancy* (51), *Bell, Book and Candle* (58), *The Chase* (66), *Kid Blue* (73), *Three Women* (77), *Missing* (82).

## RUMAN, Sig (1884-1967)

Born Sigfried Rumann in Hamburg Germany, Ruman came to the United States in the 1920s and moved to Hollywood in 1929. In films for nearly 40 years, he usually played comic character roles as a pop-eyed, blustering German or middle European, like the Soviet emissary in *Ninotchka* (39). He also shone as Schultz in *Stalag 17* (53).
**Selected Films:** *The Royal Box* (29), *A Night at the Opera* (35), *A Day at the Races* (37), *Ninotchka* (39), *To Be or Not To Be* (42), *A Night in Casablanca* (45), *Stalag 17* (53), *The Wings of Eagles* (57), *The Fortune Cookie* (66).

## RUSH, Barbara (1927- )

Born in Denver, Colorado, Rush acted at the Pasadena Playhouse before turning to Hollywood in the early 1950s. For over a decade she was a pretty face in mild leading roles of popular films, and was married for a time to teen idol Jeffrey Hunter. Rush appeared onscreen occasionally into the 1980s and starred in the TV series *Flamingo Road*.
**Selected Films:** *Molly* (50), *When Worlds Collide* (51), *It Came From Outer Space* (53), *Magnificent Obsession* (54), *The Young Philadelphians* (59), *Come Blow Your Horn* (63), *Superdad* (74), *Summer Lovers* (80).

## RUSSELL, Gail (1924-1961)

Russell, born in Chicago, Illinois, was discovered by a Hollywood talent scout while a student at Santa Monica High. After training and star buildup from Paramount she made her screen debut in *Henry Aldrich Gets Glamour* (43) and through the 1950s played leading roles as lovely, shy, delicate ladies. Among her notable films was the thriller *Night Has a Thousand Eyes* (48). However, Hollywood was too much for Russell. After some busted romances (among them John Wayne), a divorce from actor Guy Madison, several drunken-driving arrests, and a declining screen career, she was found dead at 36 in her Los Angeles apartment.
**Selected Films:** *Henry Aldrich Gets Glamour* (43), *Lady in the Dark* (43), *The Uninvited* (44), *The Unseen* (45), *Night Has a Thousand Eyes* (48), *Wake of the Red Witch* (49), *Air Cadet* (51), *The Tattered Dress* (57), *The Silent Call* (61).

## RUSSELL, Harold (1914- )

Born in Sydney, Nova Scotia and reared in Boston, Russell went off to fight in World War II and lost his hands in a grenade explosion. After appearing in an Army documentary about rehabilitation, he was given the role of a handicapped veteran in Wyler's *The Best Years of Our Lives* (46). For it, Russell won a supporting-actor Oscar and a special Oscar for his courage – the only time two Oscars have been given for the same role. He was later a businessman and President of the Disabled American Veterans.
**Selected Films:** *The Best Years of Our Lives* (46), *Inside Moves* (80).

## RUSSELL, Jane (1921- )

Born in Bemidji, Minnesota, Russell got her first big break in show business when an agent sent her photograph to multimillionaire film maker Howard Hughes. He cast her in the lead in his picture *The Outlaw* (40), and the big buildup began. Studio flacks emphasized her physical attributes, concentrating on her bustline. She wore low cut dresses in the film and she did climb in bed with her co-star, Jack Buetel, but only to keep him warm when he was under the weather. Nevertheless, the movie was not released for three years because of censor trouble. This bosomy brunette sex symbol later proved that she was more than a passing fad when she co-starred in comedies with

*Margaret Rutherford in* Murder Most Foul *(63).*

Bob Hope and in musicals with Marilyn Monroe. Russell later went on to appear on Broadway.
**Selected Films:** *The Outlaw* (40), *The Paleface* (48), *Son of Paleface* (52), *Gentlemen Prefer Blondes* (53), *The Tall Men* (56), *Fate Is the Hunter* (64), *Darker Than Amber* (70), *The Jackass Trail* (81).

## RUSSELL, John (1921- )

Born in Los Angeles, California, Russell came to the screen in 1937 and for the next 40 years – except service during World War II – was a hardy perennial in second leads of Westerns and action features. In the late 1950s he played Marshal Dan Troop in the TV series *Lawman.*
**Selected Films:** *The Duke Comes Back* (37), *Jesse James* (39), *The Bluebird* (40), *Forever Amber* (47), *The Last Command* (55), *Rio Bravo* (59), *Six Tickets to Hell* (76), *Uncle Sam* (81).

## RUSSELL, Kurt (1951- )

Russell, born in Springfield, Massachusetts, began his acting career as a cute blonde kid in movies of the 1960s, including several for the Disney studios like *Superdad* (74). He grew up to play macho characters, a number of them in John Carpenter films, including the title role in the TV movie *Elvis* and a killer in leather and eyepatch in *Escape from New York* (81).
**Selected Films:** *The Absent-Minded Professor* (60), *Charley and the Angel* (73), *Superdad* (74), *Escape from New York* (81), *The Thing* (82), *Silkwood* (83), *Swing Shift* (84), *Big Trouble in Little China* (86).

## RUSSELL, Rosalind (1908-1976)

Wit, elegance and class were her strong points. Russell was excellent playing bold, independent working women who tossed quips at the men in their lives. But she was never too tough to be a lady and there was no hard edge to the romance in her films. Born into a wealthy family in Waterbury, Connecticut (her father was a lawyer and her mother was a fashion editor), she made her stage debut in the 1920s, and her screen debut in *Evelyn Prentice* (34). She never won the Academy Award that her strong performances deserved, but she was nominated four times: for her role as the brainy sister in *My Sister Eileen* (42); for her portrayal of *Sister Kenny* (46), an idealized film biography of the nurse who developed a controversial method of treating polio victims; for her performance in *Mourning Becomes Electra* (47); and her larger than life portrayal in *Auntie Mame* (58), in which she played the lively and Bohemian lady with the big zest for life. Oddly enough, she was not nominated for what most critics think was her finest achievement – *Picnic* (56). She did, however, receive the Academy's Jean Hersholt Humanitarian Award in 1972.
**Selected Films:** *Evelyn Prentice* (34), *China Seas* (35), *Craig's Wife* (36), *Night Must Fall* (37), *The Citadel* (38), *The Women* (39), *His Girl Friday* (40), *Design for Scandal* (41), *My Sister Eileen* (42), *Sister Kenny* (46), *Mourning Becomes Electra* (48), *Picnic* (56), *Auntie Mame* (58), *Gypsy* (62), *Rosie* (68), *Mrs Pollifax – Spy* (70).

## RUTHERFORD, Ann (1917- )

Born in Toronto, Ontario, Canada, the daughter of an actress and an operatic tenor, Rutherford began acting and singing in California as a child and in the 1930s was discovered by Hollywood. After a few years of leads in routine Westerns, the pretty brunette played Mickey Rooney's sweetheart, Polly Benedict in eleven Andy Hardy movies. Meanwhile many other leads and supporting roles, including Careen O'Hara in *Gone With the Wind* (39), came her way. She retired in 1950, returning once in *They Only Kill Their Masters* (72).
**Selected Films:** *The Fighting Marines* (35), *Love Finds Andy Hardy* (38), *Gone With the Wind* (39), *Pride and Prejudice* (40), *The Secret Life of Walter Mitty* (47), *The Adventures of Don Juan* (48), *Operation Haylift* (50), *They Only Kill Their Masters* (72).

## RUTHERFORD, Margaret (1892-1972)

Dame Margaret Rutherford was an inimitable, garrulous, shapeless, endearing British comedy actress who usually seemed to be playing someone's dotty old aunt. Born in London, she specialized in eccentric characters like the medium, Madam Arcati, in Noel Coward's *Blith Spirit* (45) and the elderly detective Miss Marple in *Murder She Said* (62). This veteran of stage and screen won the Academy Award for Best Supporting Actress for her role as a querulous airplane passenger in *The VIPs* (63), with Elizabeth Taylor and Richard Burton. Married to actor Stringer Davis, she was created a Dame in 1967.
**Selected Films:** *Talk of the Devil* (36), *The Demi Paradise* (43), *Blithe Spirit* (45), *Miranda* (47), *The Happiest Days of Your Life* (50), *The Importance of Being Earnest* (42), *Murder She Said* (62), *Murder Most Foul* (63), *The VIPs* (63), *Arabella* (68).

## RUYSDAEL, Basil (1888-1960)

Born in America to a Russian family, Ruysdael came to the screen in the late 1920s and for the next three decades played character roles, usually as executives, grandfathers, and other elderly parts.
**Selected Films:** *Cocoanuts* (29), *Come to the Stable* (49), *Broken Arrow* (50), *The Blackboard Jungle* (56), *The Last Hurrah* (58).

## RYAN, Irene (1903-1973)

Born Irene Riordan in El Paso, Texas, Ryan came from radio and vaudeville to play comic character roles in films from the early 1940s. She was best known as Granny Clampett on the TV series *The Beverly Hillbillies.*
**Selected Films:** *Melody for Three* (41), *The Diary of a Chambermaid* (46), *Blackbeard the Pirate* (52), *Spring Reunion* (57), *Don't Worry, We'll Think of a Title* (66).

## RYAN, Peggy (1924- )

Born Margaret Ryan in Long Beach, California, Peggy played in vaudeville as a child and arrived onscreen in the mid-1930s. Over the next 15 years she sang and danced her way through light leads mostly in routine musicals, several of them with Donald O'Connor. In the 1970s she occasionally showed up as Jack Lord's secretary on the TV series *Hawaii Five-O.*
**Selected Films:** *Top of the Town* (37), *Top Man* (43), *Bowery to Broadway* (44), *All Ashore* (52).

## RYAN, Robert (1909-1973)

This strong-featured versatile leading man and character actor never seemed to get the parts he deserved. Ryan was a college athlete who tried boxing and modeling before becoming an actor. His first film was *Golden Gloves* (40). Consistently good in films of all kinds and a success on stage, the modest and low-keyed Ryan never became as famous as less talented but flashier stars, although he was nominated for an Academy Award for Best Supporting Actor in *Crossfire* (47).
**Selected Films:** *Golden Gloves* (40), *Gangway for Tomorrow* (43), *Crossfire* (47), *The Set-Up* (49), *The Racket* (51), *Clash by Night* (52), *Bad Day at Black Rock* (55), *God's Little Acre* (58), *Odds Against Tomorrow* (59), *Billy Budd* (62), *The Dirty Dozen* (67), *The Outfit* (74).

# S

## SABU, (1924-1963)

Born Sabu Dastagir in Mysore, India, he had been a young stable hand when he was discovered by documentary director Robert Flaherty. His first film, *Elephant Boy* (37), in which he played a carefree youth who had a way with pachyderms, made him an international star. He moved to England and later to Hollywood, where he usually played an Indian or an Oriental.
**Selected Films:** *Elephant Boy* (37), *The Drum* (38), *The Thief of Baghdad* (40), *The Jungle Book* (42), *Arabian Nights* (42), *Cobra Woman* (44), *Black Narcissus* (46), *Song of India* (49), *A Tiger Walks* (63).

## SAHL, Mort (1927- )

Sahl was born in Montreal, Quebec, Canada, but made his name in show business in the United States. He became one of the most unusual stand-up comedians on the night club circuit. His speciality was political satire, and his patter changed constantly, since it was based on the current events of the day. He did make a few films, but Hollywood never seemed to know what to do with his brand of humor.
**Selected Films:** *In Love and War* (58), *All the Young Men* (60), *Doctor, You've Got to Be Kidding* (68).

## SAINT, Eva Marie (1924- )

Born in Newark, New Jersey, this blonde, cool, intelligent actress began her career on Broadway and later went to Hollywood, where she made an astonishing debut opposite Marlon Brando in *On the Waterfront* (54) and won the Academy Award for Best Supporting Actress. Although primarily a dramatic actress, she proved effective in thrillers, such as Alfred Hitchcock's *North by Northwest* (59), and in comedies, such as *The Russians Are Coming! The Russians Are Coming!* (66).
**Selected Films:** *On the Waterfront* (54), *That Certain Feeling* (56), *A Hatful of Rain* (57), *Raintree County* (57), *North by Northwest* (59), *Exodus* (60), *The Sandpiper* (65), *The Russians Are Coming! The Russians Are Coming!* (66), *Grand Prix* (66), *Cancel My Reservation* (72), *Nothing in Common* (86).

## ST JACQUES, Raymond (1930- )

This elegant black actor was born James Johnson in Hartford, Connecticut. His early experience included not only acting at the American Shakespeare Theater in Stratford, Connecticut, but also serving as an assistant director and fencing director there. He appeared in several off-Broadway plays, and made his film debut in *Black Like Me* (64). He made his film directorial debut with *Book of Numbers* (73). St Jacques has also appeared on television in serious roles and comedy parts.
**Selected Films:** *Black Like Me* (64), *The Pawnbroker* (65), *The Comedians* (67), *Madigan* (68), *The Green Berets* (68), *Cotton Comes to Harlem* (70), *Book of Numbers* (73), *Lost in the Stars* (74), *Born Again* (78).

## SAINT JAMES, Susan (1946- )

Born Susan Miller in Los Angeles, California, Saint James seems to specialize in playing slightly kooky but determined young women, especially in her

television roles. After she graduated from Connecticut College for Woman, she worked as a model for six years, then made her film debut in *What's So Bad About Being Good?* (65). She has starred in television series, such as *The Name of the Game, McMillan and Wife* and *Kate and Allie.*
**Selected Films:** *What's So Bad About Feeling Good?* (65), *P.J.* (67), *Where Angels Go . . . Trouble Follows* (68), *Love at First Bite* (79), *How to Beat the High Cost of Living* (80), *Carbon Copy* (81).

## ST JOHN, Al 'Fuzzy' (1893-1963)

Born in Santa Ana, California, this character comedian made his film debut in the early teens. He appeared in hundreds of B western films, usually as the grizzled sidekick of the hero.
**Selected Films:** *Mabel's Strange Predicament* (13), *Special Delivery* (27), *Dance of Life* (29), *Wanderer of the Wasteland* (35), *Call of the Yukon* (37), *Arizona Terrors* (42), *Frontier Revenge* (49).

## ST JOHN, Betta (1903- )

Born Betty Streidler in Hawthorne, California, she made her Broadway debut in Rodgers and Hammerstein's *Carousel,* and later appeared in their *South Pacific* on Broadway and in London. She made her Hollywood debut in *Dream Wife* (53), a comedy that starred Cary Grant.
**Selected Films:** *Dream Wife* (53), *All the Brothers Were Valiant* (53), *The Robe* (53), *The Student Prince* (54), *The Naked Dawn* (56), *Tarzan and the Lost Safari* (57), *Horror Hotel* (60), *Corridors of Blood* (62).

## ST JOHN, Howard (1905-1974)

St John usually played a father, an executive or a military leader. In short, he was the perfect elderly character actor. Born in Chicago, he began his show business career in 1925 on the stage, and went to Hollywood in 1948.
**Selected Films:** *Born Yesterday* (50), *David Harding, Counterspy* (50), *The Tender Trap* (55), *Lil Abner* (59), *Straitjacket* (63), *Sex and the Single Girl* (64), *Strange Bedfellows* (65), *Don't Drink the Water* (69).

## ST JOHN, Jill (1940- )

She was born Jill Oppenheim in Los Angeles, California, and her parents were restauranteurs. St John broke into show business at the age of five, and was soon heard on the network radio series *One Man's Family.* At the age of 16 she married Neil Dublin. After their divorce, she married Lance Reventlow, the scion of the Revlon cosmetics fortune, who later died in a racing car accident.
**Selected Films:** *Summer Love* (57), *Holiday for Lovers* (59), *The Lost World* (60), *The Roman Spring of Mrs Stone* (61), *Tender Is the Night* (62), *Come Blow Your Horn* (63), *Who's Been Sleeping in My Bed?* (63), *The Liquidator* (66), *Tony Rome* (67), *Diamonds Are Forever* (71), *The Concrete Jungle* (82).

## SAKALL, S Z (1884-1955)

Sakall was born Eugene Gero Szakall in Budapest, Hungary. He started his career in vaudeville and on the stage in his native land, then began making movies in Europe in 1916. He went to Hollywood in 1939 and, because of his chubbiness and likeability, this comic supporting actor became known as 'Cuddles.'
**Selected Films:** *Suszterherceg* (16), *It's a Date* (40), *Ball of Fire* (41), *Casablanca* (42), *Thank Your Lucky Stars* (43), *Wonder Man* (45), *Cinderella Jones* (46), *Whiplash* (48), *In the Good Old Summertime* (49), *Tea for Two* (50), *The Student Prince* (54).

## SALMI, Albert (1928- )

This chunky American character actor, born in Brooklyn, is famous mainly for his stage work, most notably in the cast of William Inge's *Bus Stop,* in which he played the lovesick cowboy. But he has given memorable performances on screen, particularly in *The Brothers Karamazov* (58). He was married to former child actress Peggy Ann Garner.
**Selected Films:** *The Brothers Karamazov* (58), *Wild River* (60), *The Ambushers* (67), *The Deserter* (70), *Lawman* (71), *The Take* (74), *Empire of the Ants* (77), *Viva Knievel* (77), *Brubaker* (80), *St Helens* (81), *Born American* (86).

## SAN JUAN, Olga (1927- )

Although she was born in Brooklyn, she often played a Latin bombshell. But she was a talented dancer and comedienne. San Juan got her start on radio and went to Hollywood in the mid-1940s.
**Selected Films:** *Rainbow Island* (44), *Blue Skies* (46), *The Beautiful Blonde from Bashful Bend* (49), *The Countess of Monte Cristo* (49), *The Third Voice* (60).

## SANDA, Dominique (1948- )

Sanda was born Dominique Varaigne in Paris, France. She had a strict Catholic upbringing, and her parents even refused to let her attend art school. She was a model for a while and then began to make movies in the 1970s. She has a child by the actor/director Christian Marquand.
**Selected Films:** *Une Femme Douce* (70), *The Garden of the Finzi-Continis* (71), *The Conformist* (71), *The Mackintosh Man* (73), *Steppenwolf* (74), *1900* (76), *Damnation Alley* (77), *A Room in Town* (82).

## SANDERS, George (1906-1972)

Before ending his life with an overdose of sleeping pills, Sanders wrote a note mentioning boredom as the main reason for his suicide. It seemed perfectly in keeping with the cynical, world-weary character he had played so often on the screen. The brother of actor Tom Conway, Sanders was born of British parents in St Petersburg, Russia. The family returned to England during the Russian

Revolution. Sanders tried business, but became an actor in the early 1930s, moving to Hollywood in 1936. From then on he made most of his films in the United States. This suave actor usually played villains, cads, scoundrels and crooks. He also played the lead in 'The Saint' series and 'The Falcon.' When given a meaty part, such as that of the cynical theater critic in *All About Eve* (50), Sanders could excell. That role won him an Academy Award for Best Supporting Actor.
**Selected Films:** *Find the Lady* (36), *Dishonor Bright* (36), *Lloyds of London* (37), *The Saint Strikes Back* (39), *Rebecca* (40), *Foreign Correspondent* (40), *The Gay Falcon* (41), *The Moon and Sixpence* (42), *The Ghost and Mrs Muir* (47), *All About Eve* (50), *Ivanhoe* (52), *Call Me Madam* (53), *That Certain Feeling* (56), *Village of the Damned* (50), *Psychomania* (72).

## SANDS, Tommy (1937- )

Born in Chicago, Sands began his career as a rock 'n' roll singer, and was soon making films in Hollywood – most often cast as a rock 'n' roll singer. Later he graduated to more mature parts.
**Selected Films:** *Sing, Boy, Sing* (58), *Love in a Goldfish Bowl* (59), *Babes in Toyland* (60), *The Longest Day* (62), *Ensign Pulver* (64), *None But the Brave* (65), *The Violent Ones* (67).

## SANTSCHI, Tom (1878-1931)

Born in Kokomo, Indiana, this rugged silent screen star began his film career in 1909. His specialties were melodramas and action films, in which he played brutish heroes or ruthless villains.
**Selected Films:** *On the Border* (09), *Davy Crockett* (10), *The Spoilers* (14), *The Garden of Allah* (17), *Thundering Dawn* (23), *The Primrose* Path (25), *Isle of Lost Men* (28), *In Old Arizona* (29), *The Last Ride* (31).

## SARA, Mia (1968- )

Born in Brooklyn, New York, Sara's father was a commercial photographer who helped her get television commercial bookings when she was very young. At the age of 14, she spent a summer in the cast of the television soap opera, *All My Children*. At 16 she appeared in her first picture – *Legend* (84) – with Tom Cruise.
**Selected Films:** *Legend* (84), *Ferris Bueller's Day Off* (86).

## SARANDON, Chris (1942- )

This fine character actor was born in Beckley, West Virginia. After attending West Virginia University, he worked in television. He was a sensation as the male lover of the would-be bank robber (Al Pacino) who wants a sex change operation in *Dog Day Afternoon* (75).
**Selected Films:** *Dog Day Afternoon* (75), *Lipstick* (76), *Cuba* (79), *Atlantic City* (81), *Protocol* (84), *Fright Night* (85).

## SARANDON, Susan (1946- )

Born Susan Tomaling in New York City to Armenian-American parents, she attended Catholic University and the University of Washington, but did not take acting lessons. She broke into show business in television, playing in *A World Apart* and several other soap operas. Her first big movie part was in *Joe* (70), and she was nominated for an Academy Award for her performance in *Atlantic City* (81). Sarandon is the former wife of actor Chris Sarandon.
**Selected Films:** *Joe* (70), *The Front Page* (74), *The Great Waldo Pepper* (75), *The Rocky Horror Picture Show* (75), *King of the Gypsies* (78), *Pretty Baby* (78), *Atlantic City* (81), *Tempest* (82), *The Hunger* (83), *Compromising Positions* (85), *The Witches of Eastwick* (87).

## SARGENT, Dick (1933- )

Born in Carmel, California, this gangling actor began in films when he was in his twenties. He is best known for playing opposite Elizabeth Montgomery in the television comedy, *Bewitched*.
**Selected Films:** *Bernardine* (57), *Operation Petticoat* (59), *That Touch of Mink* (62), *The Ghost and Mr Chicken* (66), *The Private Navy of Sergeant O'Farrell* (68), *Hardcore* (79).

## SARRAZIN, Michael (1940- )

Born Jacques Michel André Sarrazin in Quebec City, Quebec, Canada, this leading man is usually cast in the role of a young innocent. He broke into show business on the Canadian Broadcasting Corporation's television network at the age of 17. Sarrazin began making Hollywood films in the mid-1960s.
**Selected Films:** *Gunfight in Abilene* (67), *The Flim Flam Man* (67), *A Man Called Gannon* (68), *They Shoot Horses Don't They?* (69), *In Search of Gregory* (70), *The Pursuit of Happiness* (71), *For Pete's Sake* (74), *The Gumball Rally* (76), *Caravans* (78), *Double Negative* (80), *Fighting Back* (82), *Joshua, Then and Now* (85).

## SAVALAS, Telly (1924- )

Savalas was born Aristotle Savalas in Garden City, New York. This bald character actor had a modest film career primarily playing heavies from Genghis Khan to Al Capone. It was as the shaven-headed detective *Kojak* in the popular television series of that name that he became a real star.
**Selected Films:** *The Young Savages* (61), *Cape Fear* (62), *Birdman of Alcatraz* (62), *The Man from the Diners Club* (63), *Battle of the Bulge* (65), *The Greatest Story Ever Told* (65), *Beau Geste* (66), *The Dirty Dozen* (67), *On Her Majesty's Secret Service* (69), *Kelly's Heroes* (70), *Horror Express* (74), *Killer Force* (75), *Capricorn One* (78), *Beyond the Poseidon Adventure* (79).

## SAWYER, Joseph (1901-1982)

Born Joseph Sauer, he had a long career in films. Sawyer was often seen in B pictures cast as a tough policeman or an army sergeant. He was probably best known for his supporting role in the TV series *Rin Tin Tin*.
**Selected Films:** *College Humor* (33), *The Marines Have Landed* (36), *The Roaring Twenties* (40), *Sergeant York* (41), *About Face* (42), *Fall In* (44), *It Came From Outer Space* (53), *The Killing* (56), *How the West Was Won* (62).

## SAXON, John (1935- )

Born Carmen Orrico in Brooklyn, New York, he was a male model before turning to acting. He made his debut in *Running Wild* (55), and had his moments in *The Reluctant Debutante* (58), as Sandra Dee's love interest. Saxon was also a regular on the television series *The Bold Ones*.
**Selected Films:** *Running Wild* (55), *The Reluctant Debutante* (58), *War Hunt* (62), *The Cardinal* (63), *The Appaloosa* (66), *Joe Kidd* (72), *Blazing Magnum* (76), *The Bees* (78), *The Electric Horseman* (79).

## SCALA, Gia (1934-1972)

She was born Giovanna Sgoglio in London, England, to an Irish mother and an Italian father. She was raised in Rome from the time she was three and came to the United States in 1951 to study with Stella Adler in New York. She made a few American films before her death from an accidental overdose of drugs and alcohol.
**Selected Films:** *The Price of Fear* (56), *Don't Go Near the Water* (56), *The Garment Jungle* (57), *The Guns of Navarone* (61), *Operation Delilah* (66).

## SCHAFER, Natalie (1912- )

Schafer was born in New York City and began her show business career on the stage. She made her screen debut in *Marriage Is a Private Affair* (44), and went on to appear in many more films, usually playing rich bubble-headed women. She is most famous for her role as the wife of the wealthy banker (played by Jim Backus) in the TV series *Gilligan's Island*.
**Selected Films:** *Marriage Is a Private Affair* (44), *Wonder Man* (45), *The Snake Pit* (48), *Payment on Demand* (51), *Anastasia* (56), *40 Carats* (73), *The Day of the Locust* (75).

## SCHEIDER, Roy (1934- )

Some actors always give solid performances but don't project star quality even when they are leading men. This is the case with Scheider. He is thin and ordinary-looking, and his large nose is the result of a punch when he was a Golden Gloves boxer in high school. But he has been an important addition to several Oscar-nominated films. Born in Orange, New Jersey, he made his professional stage debut in 1961 playing Mercutio in the New York Shakespeare Festival production of *Romeo and Juliet*. He continued to appear in classic roles on stage, and made his film debut in *The Curse of the Living Corpse* (64), a terrible Grade Z horror picture. He came into his own in the 1970s and became a major movie lead and character actor.
**Selected Films:** *The Curse of the Living Corpse* (64), *Klute* (71), *The French Connection* (71), *Jaws* (75), *Marathon Man* (76), *Jaws II* (79), *All That Jazz* (79), *Still of the Night* (82), *Blue Thunder* (83), *2010* (84), *52 Pick-Up* (86), *The Men's Club* (86).

## SCHELL, Maria (1926- )

Schell is the sister of actor Maximilian Schell, and she was born in Vienna, Austria. In 1942 she made her screen debut in Switzerland in *Steibruch*, under the name of Gritli Schell. In 1954 she won the Cannes Film Festival Award for Best Actress for *Die letzte Brücke/The Last Bridge*, and in 1956 she received the Venice Festival Prize for her work in *Gervaise*. Schell retired from movies in 1963 but came back in 1968 to play character roles.
**Selected Films:** *Steibruch* (42), *The Last Bridge* (54), *Gervaise* (56), *White Nights* (57), *The Brothers Karamazov* (58), *Cimarron* (61), *Women* (69), *The Odessa File* (74), *Voyage of the Damned* (76), *Superman* (78), *Just a Gigolo* (79), *Nineteen Nineteen* (86).

## SCHELL, Maximilian (1930- )

Born in Vienna, Austria, this younger brother of Maria Schell made his film debut in a German film, *Kinder, Mütter und ein General* (55). When he was eight years old, he and his family fled from Austria to Switzerland after the Anschluss, and he attended the universities of Zurich, Basel and Munich. After appearing on stage in New York, he played his initial role in a Hollywood movie in *The Young Lions* (58). He then won an Academy Award for Best Actor for his role as an enigmatic defense attorney in *Judgement at Nuremberg* (61). He also received Oscar nominations for his performances in *The Man in the Glass Booth* (75) and *Julia* (77). In the 1960s, in addition to acting, he turned to directing, producing and screen writing. *The Pedestrian* (74), which he wrote, produced, directed and starred in, was nominated for the Academy Award for Best Foreign Film. In 1986 he also produced a documentary on the career of Marlene Dietrich.
**Selected Films:** *Kinder, Mütter und ein General* (55), *The Young Lions* (58), *Judgement at Nuremberg* (61), *Five Finger Exercise* (62), *Topkapi* (64), *The Pedestrian* (74), *The Odessa File* (74), *The Man in the Glass Booth* (75), *Julia* (77), *The Black Hole* (79).

## SCHILDKRAUT, Joseph (1895-1964)

Born in Vienna, Austria, the son of actor Rudolph Schildkraut, he trained for the stage under character actor Albert Basserman, who was a rival of his father. Accompanying his father on a tour of the United States, he enrolled in the American Academy of Dramatic Arts. In 1920 he settled in the United States and became a Broadway star appearing in such dramas as *Liliom*, opposite Eva Le Gallienne. His first film in the United States was *Orphans of the Storm* (22), and he won an Academy Award for Best Supporting Actor for his performance of Major Alfred Dreyfus in *The Life of Emile Zola* (37).

**Selected Films:** *Schlemiel* (15), *Orphans of the Storm* (22), *The Song of Love* (24), *The King of Kings* (27), *Show Boat* (29), *Viva Villa!* (34), *The Garden of Allah* (36), *The Life of Emile Zola* (37), *Idiot's Delight* (39), *Flame of the Barbary Coast* (45), *The Diary of Anne Frank* (59), *The Greatest Story Ever Told* (65).

## SCHNEIDER, Romy (1938-1982)

She was born Rosemarie Albach-Retty in Vienna, Austria. Schneider became a movie star in her teens in a series of films about the Austrian imperial family. Because of her work with directors Luchino Visconti (*Boccaccio '70* [62]) and Orson Welles (*The Trial* [62]), she became an international star.

**Selected Films:** *Wenn der weisse Flieder wieder blüht* (53), *Mädchen in Uniform* (58), *Boccaccio '70* (62), *The Trial* (62), *The Cardinal* (63), *Good Neighbor Sam* (64), *What's New, Pussycat?* (65), *The Assassination of Trotsky* (72), *The Infernal Trio* (74), *Lover on a String* (75), *The Old Gun* (76), *Sidney Sheldon's Bloodline* (79).

## SCHWARZENEGGER, Arnold (1947- )

Born in Graz, Austria, Schwarzenegger became a body-builder, being named Mr Olympia seven times. He was discovered on *The Merv Griffin Show* by Lucille Ball, who cast him in one of her television shows. In his second film, *Stay Hungry* (76), he won the Golden Globe Award for Best New Actor. Schwarzenegger married Maria Shriver of the Kennedy clan in 1986.

**Selected Films:** *Hercules in New York* (70), *Stay Hungry* (76), *The Villain* (79), *Conan the Barbarian* (82), *Conan the Destroyer* (84), *The Terminator* (84), *Commando* (85), *Red Sonja* (85), *Raw Deal* (86).

## SCOFIELD, Paul (1922- )

Although he won the Academy Award as well as the British Film Academy Award for Best Actor for his work as Sir Thomas More in *A Man for All Seasons* (66), a repeat of his stage success, his films have been infrequent. Scofield was born in Hurstpierpoint, England, and was on the British stage from the time he was 14 years old.

**Selected Films:** *That Lady* (55), *Carve Her Name with Pride* (58), *The Train* (64), *A Man for All Seasons* (66), *King Lear* (69), *Bartleby* (71), *Scorpio* (73), *A Delicate Balance* (73), *Nineteen Nineteen* (86).

*George C Scott in* The Hustler *(61).*

## SCOTT, George C (1927- )

Impressive and magnetic, Scott is a shrewd, aggressive actor and a cranky individualist off screen. Born George Campbell Scott in Wise, West Virginia, he attended the University of Missouri. Scott served four years in the Marines, then was a teacher and aspiring writer before he tried acting. His performances on off-Broadway, Broadway and television brought him acclaim. Despite his great success in movies, he is openly contemptuous of Hollywood and returns to the stage periodically. He refused to accept an Academy Award for Best Actor for his performance in the title role in *Patton* (70), referring to the Academy Awards as 'a meaningless, self-serving meat parade.' Shortly after this he won an Emmy for his work in Arthur Miller's 'The Price' on television. He did not accept this prize, either. Formerly married to actress Colleen Dewhurst, he is presently married to actress Trish Van Devere. Scott has also directed.

**Selected Films:** *Anatomy of a Murder* (59), *The Hustler* (61), *The List of Adrian Messenger* (63), *Dr Strangelove* (63), *The Bible* (66), *Patton* (70), *They Might Be Giants* (71), *The Hospital* (72), *The New Centurions* (72), *The Prince and the Pauper* (77), *Islands in the Stream* (77), *Movie Movie* (78), *Hardcore* (79), *The Changeling* (79), *Taps* (82).

## SCOTT, Gordon (1927- )

Born Gordon M Wershkul in Portland, Oregon, Scott was educated at the University of Oregon. He was a soldier, a cowboy, a fireman and a lifeguard before making films. He is best remembered for a series of Tarzan movies and some Italian muscle epics. He was married to actress Vera Miles.

**Selected Films:** *Tarzan's Hidden Jungle* (55), *Tarzan and the Lost Safari* (57), *Tarzan's Fight for Life* (58), *Tarzan's Greatest Adventure* (59), *Tarzan the Magnificent* (60), *Samson and the Seven Miracles of the World* (61), *Gladiator of Rome* (62), *The Lion of St Mark* (64), *The Tramplers* (66).

## SCOTT, Lizabeth (1922- )

This alluring, sexy-voiced star of the decade following World War II was born Emma Matzo in Scranton, Pennsylvania. She was educated at Marywood College and the Alvienne School of Drama in New York. Scott went into stock and became the understudy to Tallulah Bankhead in *The Skin of Our Teeth* on Broadway in 1942. Her work as a model won her a screen test, and she went to Hollywood as a rival to Lauren Bacall and Veronica Lake.

**Selected Films:** *You Came Along* (45), *The Strange Love of Martha Ivers* (46), *Dead Reckoning* (47), *Pitfall* (48), *Too Late for Tears* (49), *Dark City* (50), *The Racket* (51), *Red Mountain* (52), *Scared Stiff* (53), *Bad for Each Other* (54), *The Weapon* (56), *Loving You* (57), *Pulp* (72).

## SCOTT, Martha (1914- )

Born in Jamesport, Missouri, and educated at the University of Michigan, she went into stock and then scored a triumph in her first Broadway play, acting the lead role, Emily Webb, in *Our Town* (38). She was nominated for an Academy Award for the screen version of the play in 1940. Later in her career she specialized in character roles.

**Selected Films:** *Our Town* (40), *Cheers for Miss Bishop* (41), *One Foot in Heaven* (41), *In Old Oklahoma* (43), *So Well Remembered* (47), *Strange Bargain* (49), *When I Grow Up* (51), *The Desperate Hours* (55), *The Ten Commandments* (56), *Sayonara* (57), *Ben Hur* (59), *Airport 1975* (74), *The Turning Point* (77).

## SCOTT, Randolph (1903-1987)

Scott always looked like the quintessential Western hero, with his rugged face, athletic build and soft-spoken manner. In his long career, he became one of the most familiar and best-liked Western stars in high-quality productions, although he had appeared in more than his fair share of B westerns. He contributed greatly to the genre with his solid, realistic portrayals of cowboys in scores of films, but he also was excellent in outdoor adventure, detective and comedy movies. At the height of his career, in the 1950s, he was among the top box office stars in Hollywood, making superior pictures which withstood the competition of television. Born Randolph Crane in Orange County, Virginia, the scion of an old Southern family, he managed to lie his way into the Army at the age of 14 and saw combat service in World War I. Educated at Georgia Tech and the University of North Carolina, he emerged with an engineering degree, but went into acting instead, getting into films accidentally after meeting eccentric producer and billionaire Howard Hughes on the golf course. Scott began his career in romantic comedies and soon switched almost exclusively to Westerns. Working with John Wayne, Henry Fonda, Errol Flynn and others, he gained tremendous respect in Hollywood. His last film was his best, the classic *Ride the High Country* (62), made with his friend Joel McCrea. Scott retired after that film, and became one of the richest retired actors.

**Selected Films:** *The Far Call* (29), *Hot Saturday* (32), *The Lone Cowboy* (33), *Murders in the Zoo* (33), *She* (35), *Roberta* (35), *The Last of the Mohicans* (36), *Rebecca of Sunnybrook Farm* (38), *Western Union* (41), *The Shores of Tripoli* (42), *Home, Sweet Homicide* (46), *Return of the Badman* (48), *Sugarfoot* (51), *Man in the Saddle* (51), *The Man Behind the Gun* (53), *The Bounty Hunter* (54), *Seven Men from Now* (56), *The Tall T* (57), *Ride Lonesome* (59), *Comanche Station* (60), *Ride the High Country* (62).

## SCOTT, Zachary (1914-1965)

Scott was born in Austin, Texas. He dropped out of the University of Texas after his freshman year and sailed to England, where he began his acting career in the provinces. He returned to Texas and the university, graduated, and started playing in stock companies. After he signed a contract with Warner Bros., his debut was in *The Mask of Dimitrios* (44), as a ruthless scoundrel. He followed this up with a powerful performance as a sharecropper in *The Southerner* (45). Unfortunately, he became typecast as a sleek, charming villain for most of his career. He died of a brain tumor, and was survived by his wife, the actress Ruth Ford.

**Selected Films:** *The Mask of Dimitrios* (44), *The Southerner* (45), *Mildred Pierce* (45), *Stallion Road* (47), *Cass Timberlane* (47), *Ruthless* (48), *Flamingo Road* (49), *Pretty Baby* (50), *The Secret of Convict Lake* (52), *Shotgun* (55), *Bandido* (56), *Man in the Shadow* (60), *It's Only Money* (62).

## SCOURBY, Alexander (1913-1985)

Scourby was born in New York City and attended West Virginia University. His resonant voice was ideal for the stage and for television commercials, and he did make a few movies. He was probably most noted for the narration of the TV series, *Victory at Sea*. Scourby was married to television soap opera actress Lori March.

**Selected Films:** *With These Hands* (50), *Because of You* (52), *The Glory Brigade* (53), *Sign of the Pagan* (54), *The Silver Chalice* (55), *Giant* (56), *The Big Fisherman* (59), *Man on a String* (60), *The Devil at 4 O'Clock* (61), *The Executioner* (70).

## SEAGULL, Barbara: See HERSHEY, Barbara

## SEARLE, Jackie (1920- )

Searle (who also went by the name of Searl) was born in Anaheim, California, and began as a radio performer at the age of three. In films of the 1930s

he often played brats, most notably as Tom's cousin Sid, in *Tom Sawyer* (30). In the 1940s he played adult supporting roles and became a character actor on television.
**Selected Films:** *Daughters of Desire* (29), *Tom Sawyer* (30), *Skippy* (31), *Huckleberry Finn* (31), *Alice in Wonderland* (33), *No Greater Glory* (34), *Peck's Bad Boy* (34), *Ginger* (35), *Little Lord Fauntleroy* (36), *Angels Wash Their Faces* (39), *My Little Chickadee* (40), *Glamour Boy* (41), *The Fabulous Dorseys* (47), *The Paleface* (48).

## SEARS, Heather (1935- )

This pleasant leading lady of the British stage, television and films was born in London, England. She trained at the Central School of Speech and Drama, making her stage debut in 1955 and her film debut in *Dry Rot* (56).
**Selected Films:** *Dry Rot* (56), *The Story of Esther Costello* (57), *Room at the Top* (58), *Sons and Lovers* (60), *The Phantom of the Opera* (62), *The Black Torment* (64).

## SEBERG, Jean (1938-1979)

Born in Marshalltown, Iowa, she was a freshman at the University of Iowa when she was selected for the title role in Otto Preminger's *Saint Joan* (57) when she was a mere 17 years old. She did not become a Hollywood star despite a massive publicity campaign, and the movie flopped. She was better in Preminger's next film, *Bonjour Tristesse* (58), but she still seemed washed up in show business. But then she moved to France and found new audiences and new respect in Jean-Luc Godard's *Breathless* (60). She went on to become an international star and for a time was married to French novelist, diplomat and film director Romain Gary. Still, she was a tragic figure, and personal difficulties coupled with the harassment by the FBI because of her left-wing activism were the reasons given for her suicide.
**Selected Films:** *Saint Joan* (57), *Bonjour Tristesse* (58), *The Mouse that Roared* (59), *Breathless* (60), *In the French Style* (63), *Lilith* (64), *Pendulum* (69), *Airport* (70), *The Wild Duck* (76).

## SECOMBE, Harry (1921- )

This burly comedian, born in Wales, was a partner of Peter Sellers and Spike Milligan on the BBC's *The Goon Show* on radio. His fine tenor voice is more fitted to the stage than the movies, although he has made a few films.
**Selected Films:** *Davy* (57), *Oliver!* (68), *Song of Norway* (70), *The Magnificent Seven Deadly Sins* (71), *Sunstruck* (73).

## SEGAL, George (1934- )

Segal was born in New York City and attended Columbia University. He worked as a janitor, an usher and a jazz musician while breaking into show business in New York clubs and in off-Broadway plays. His first film was *The Young Doctors* (61), and he went on to excell as an intellectual leading man in both dramas and light comedies. He was nominated for an Academy Award for Best Supporting Actor for his work in *Who's Afraid of Virginia Woolf?* (66).
**Selected Films:** *The Young Doctors* (61), *Act One* (63), *Ship of Fools* (65), *King Rat* (65), *Who's Afraid of Virginia Woolf?* (66), *The Owl and the Pussycat* (70), *Where's Poppa?* (73), *A Touch of Class* (73), *Fun with Dick and Jane* (77), *Rollercoaster* (77), *Who Is Killing the Great Chefs of Europe?* (78), *The Last Married Couple in America* (79), *Carbon Copy* (81), *Stick* (86).

## SEGAL, Vivienne (1897- )

A singer and actress, Segal was born in Philadelphia, Pennsylvania, and became a star of operettas and Broadway musicals from the age of 16. She was the star of such notable musical comedies as *The Desert Song* (26) and *Pal Joey* (40) on Broadway, and made very few movies.
**Selected Films:** *Song of the West* (31), *Bride of the Regiment* (31), *Golden Dawn* (31), *Viennese Nights* (31), *The Cat and the Fiddle* (34).

## SELLARS, Elizabeth (1923- )

Born in Glasgow, Scotland, she began performing on the British stage at the age of 15. She has played leads and supporting roles on television and in movies.
**Selected Films:** *Floodtide* (48), *Madaleine* (51), *The Barefoot Contessa* (54), *Desiree* (54), *Prince of Players* (55), *Law and Disorder* (58), *55 Days at Peking* (63), *The Chalk Garden* (64), *The Mummy's Shroud* (67), *The Hireling* (73).

## SELLECK, Tom (1945- )

Selleck is really a creation of television, having

*George Segal in* King Rat *(65).*

starred for many years in the adventure series, *Magnum PI.* Born in Detroit, Michigan, he moved with his family to Sherman Oaks, California, when he was five years old. He won an athletic scholarship to the University of Southern California and majored in business administration. A drama coach, however, suggested that he become an actor and he made his debut in *Myra Breckinridge* (70), playing a 'stud' in that tasteless film. He was in the cast of the television soap opera, *The Young and the Restless*, and appeared occasionally in *The Rockford Files.* Then came *Magnum PI.* After the tremendous success of this series, Selleck began to make the occasional film.
**Selected Films:** *Myra Breckinridge* (70), *Seven Minutes* (71), *Daughters of Satan* (72), *Midway* (76), *Coma* (78), *High Road to China* (83), *Lassiter* (84), *The Aviator* (84), *Runaway* (86).

## SELLERS, Peter (1925-1980)

Sellers, a masterful mimic, was a brilliantly original comic with an instinct for satire who often combined pathos with humor, the mark of a great clown. He described himself as a man without personality, a vacuum waiting to be filled by a character. Whether this was true or not, the characters that he created were extraordinarily real and complete. Born in Southsea, England, into a family of music hall performers, Sellers began his acting career as a child and at age 17 he joined the RAF where he was a camp entertainer. Beginning in 1949, Sellers appeared on BBC radio on *The Goon Show* with Harry Secombe and Spike Milligan. He also did television and made short films. His first feature film, *Penny Points to Paradise* (51) also featured Secombe and Milligan. *The Ladykillers* (55), starring Alec Guinness, gave Sellers' career a big boost. He played three characters in *The Mouse That Roared* (59), which was especially popular in the United States. *I'm All Right, Jack* (59), was a massive hit in Britain, winning Sellers the British Film Academy Award for Best Actor. Sellers' wonderful interpretation of the bumbling but dignified detective, Inspector Clouseau, was first seen in *The Pink Panther* (63), and it launched a blockbuster series. When director Stanley Kubrick cast Sellers as the ex-Nazi scientist in *Dr Strangelove* (63), Sellers made screen history. He also played President Muffley of the United States and an RAF officer in the film. Kubrick wanted Sellers to play even more roles because nobody else could match his talent and versatility. Sellers had arrived as an international star. His private life was different. Besides marrying four times, he was a compulsive worker who was barely slowed down by heart attacks, driven at fever pitch right to the moment of his untimely death. One of Sellers' final films, *Being There* (79), featured one of his best performances, and the one of which he was most proud. He received a nomination for an Academy Award for Best Actor for it, and it is comforting to remember this when one contemplates the patched-together butchered version of the Pink Panther series released after his death.

*Peter Sellers in* Being There *(79).*

**Selected Films:** *Penny Points to Paradise* (51), *The Ladykillers* (55), *The Naked Truth* (58), *The Mouse That Roared* (59), *I'm All Right, Jack* (59), *The Battle of the Sexes* (60), *Two-Way Stretch* (60), *Only Two Can Play* (62), *Lolita* (62), *The Wrong Arm of the Law* (63), *The Pink Panther* (63), *Dr Strangelove* (63), *The World of Henry Orient* (64), *What's New, Pussycat?* (66), *I Love You Alice B Toklas* (68), *The Return of the Pink Panther* (75), *Murder by Death* (76), *Being There* (79), *The Fiendish Plot of Dr Fu Manchu* (79).

## SERNAS, Jacques (1925- )

This leading man, later a character actor, was born in Kaunas, Lithuania. He was educated in Paris, and joined the French Resistance during World War II, was captured by the Germans and spent a year in the Buchenwald concentration camp. After the war, he made his screen debut, and was elevated to international stardom when he was chosen to play Paris in *Helen of Troy* (56). He was memorable as a fading matinee idol in *La Dolce Vita* (60).
**Selected Films:** *Miroir* (47), *Golden Salamander* (50), *Bluebeard* (51), *Jump Into Hell* (55), *Helen of Troy* (56), *La Dolce Vita* (60), *Midas Run* (69), *Hornet's Nest* (70), *Children of Rage* (75).

## SERRATO, Massimo (1917- )

Usually seen in swashbucklers, this virile leading man was born Giuseppi Segato in Italy. He began in films in 1941, and has been a popular actor ever since.
**Selected Films:** *Man of the Sea* (41), *Outcry* (46), *La Traviata* (47), *The Thief of Venice* (52), *The Man from Cairo* (53), *The Naked Maja* (59), *David and Goliath* (59), *El Cid* (61), *55 Days at Peking* (62), *The Tenth Victim* (65), *Don't Look Now* (73).

## SERVAIS, Jean (1910-1976)

This leading man of the French stage and screen was born in Angers, Belgium. He later changed to

character roles, using his excellent voice and melancholy intelligent face to perfection. He was married to actress Dominique Blanchar.
**Selected Films:** *Criminel* (32), *La Valse Eternelle* (36), *La Danse de Morte* (47), *Riptide* (49), *House of Pleasure* (52), *Rififi* (55), *He Who Must Die* (57), *The Liars* (61), *That Man From Rio* (64), *Lost Command* (66), *Black Jesus* (68), *The Devil's Nightmare* (73).

## SEYMOUR, Anne (1909- )

Seymour was born in New York City, and had a great deal of stage experience before she went to Hollywood. This fine character actress also was seen in the television series *Empire*.
**Selected Films:** *All the King's Men* (49), *Whistle at Eaton Falls* (51), *Man on Fire* (57), *Desire Under the Elms* (58), *Pollyanna* (60), *Good Neighbor Sam* (64), *How to Succeed in Business Without Really Trying* (67), *So Long Blue Boy* (73), *Gemini Affair* (75), *Never Never Land* (81).

## SEYMOUR, Dan (1915-1982)

Born in Chicago, Illinois, this burly character actor was the scowling menace of countless films. He was also often on television playing menacing villainous roles. He broke into films after working as a burlesque and night club performer.
**Selected Films:** *The Road to Morocco* (42), *Casablanca* (42), *To Have and Have Not* (44), *Intrigue* (47), *Key Largo* (48), *Johnny Belinda* (48), *The Blue Veil* (51), *Rancho Notorious* (52), *Abbott and Costello Meet the Mummy* (55), *The Buster Keaton Story* (57), *Watusi* (59), *The Return of the Fly* (59), *Escape to Witch Mountain* (75).

## SEYMOUR, Jane (1951- )

Born Joyce Frankenberg in Hillingdon, England, Seymour trained as a dancer and appeared with the London Festival Ballet at age 31. Since the early 1970s she has played leading roles in occasional and mostly minor films, meanwhile appearing on Broadway and in a number of TV mini-series.
**Selected Films:** *Oh, What a Lovely War* (70), *Young Winston* (72), *Somewhere in Time* (79), *Lassiter* (84), *Head Office* (86).

## SHANNON, Harry (1890-1964)

This versatile player in Hollywood movies in the 1940s and 1950s was born in Saginaw, Michigan. He made his screen debut in the 1930s after many years as a Broadway actor. He first played a strong, dependable type, and later became a character actor, often as a sympathetic father or a rustic.
**Selected Films:** *Heads Up* (31), *Young Tom Edison* (40), *Citizen Kane* (41), *This Gun for Hire* (42), *The Eve of St Mark* (44), *Captain Eddie* (45), *The Farmer's Daughter* (47), *Champion* (49), *Three Little Words* (50), *High Noon* (52), *Executive Suite* (54), *Written on the Wind* (57), *The Buccaneer* (58), *Gypsy* (62).

## SHARIF, Omar (1932- )

Born Michael Shalhoub in Alexandria, Egypt, Sharif entered acting over the objections of his wealthy family. His good looks and the influence of some of his friends got him a lead opposite the popular Egyptian actress Faten Hamama, whom he later married. The couple has since divorced. Sharif made a large number of Egyptian films, few of which were seen outside of the Arab world. He became an international star when he was chosen to play Sherif Ali ibn Kharish in the epic *Lawrence of Arabia* (62). United States and European producers decided that Sharif looked 'foreign,' but it didn't matter what nationality. He has played everything from a Spanish priest to the Mongol conqueror Genghis Khan. He has been a Nazi and a Jew; Prince Rudolf of Austria and Che Guevara. His greatest success came in the title role of *Doctor Zhivago* (65), in which he played the Russian poet/doctor. Sharif has often expressed his boredom with acting, and insists that he far prefers bridge, at which he is an international champion.
**Selected Films:** *The Struggle for the Valley* (53), *Goha* (57), *The Agony of Love* (60), *Lawrence of Arabia* (62), *The Fall of the Roman Empire* (64), *Behold a Pale Horse* (64), *The Yellow Rolls Royce* (64), *Genghis Khan* (65), *Doctor Zhivago* (65), *The Night of the Generals* (67), *Funny Girl* (67), *Mayerling* (68), *Mackenna's Gold* (69), *Che!* (69), *The Tamarind Seed* (74), *Bloodline* (79), *Top Secret* (84).

## SHATNER, William (1931- )

Popular among science-fiction fans as Captain Kirk of the *Enterprise* in *Star Trek* on television and in the movies, Shatner was born in Montreal, Quebec, Canada, and studied at McGill University there, appearing in a great many youth theater productions in his early acting years. He has an extensive Shakespearean background and has played roles in several of the Stratford (Ontario, Canada) Shakespeare Festivals. An actor with Broadway experience as well, Shatner appeared in numerous films and made-for-television movies.
**Selected Films:** *The Brothers Karamazov* (58), *Judgement at Nuremberg* (61), *The Outrage* (64), *The Devil's Rain* (75), *Star Trek: The Motion Picture* (79), *Star Trek II: The Wrath of Khan* (82), *Visiting Hours* (82), *Star Trek III: The Search for Spock* (83), *Star Trek IV: The Voyage Home* (86).

## SHAUGHNESSY, Mickey (1920-1985)

This tough-looking comic character actor often played a dumb prizefighter or a small time hoodlum. After stage experience, he made his Hollywood debut in *The Last of the Comanches* (52).
**Selected Films:** *The Last of the Comanches* (52), *From Here to Eternity* (53), *Don't Go Near the Water* (57), *Don't Give Up the Ship* (59), *How the West Was Won* (62), *A House Is Not a Home* (64), *Never a Dull Moment* (68), *The Boatniks* (70).

*Omar Sharif and Barbra Streisand in* Funny Girl *(67).*

## SHAW, Robert (1927-1979)

Born in Westhoughton, England, Shaw was raised in both Scotland and in Cornwall. After training at the Royal Academy of Dramatic Art, he made his stage debut at the Shakespeare Memorial Theatre at Stratford-on-Avon and went on to films in the 1950s. For a long time he was seen mainly in character roles and as nasty villains. But he became a star in his late fifties when he appeared in such films as *The Sting* (73), *Jaws* (75) and *The Deep* (77). Shaw was nominated for a Best Supporting Academy Award for his portrayal of King Henry VIII in *A Man for All Seasons* (66). He was also the author of several novels, the most famous being the harrowing *The Man in the Glass Booth*, which he adapted into a play that was a tremendous success in London and on Broadway and later made into a film in 1975. He died of a heart attack. Shaw's second wife was actress Mary Ure.
**Selected Films:** *The Dam Busters* (54), *A Hill in Korea* (56), *Sea Fury* (59), *From Russia with Love* (63), *A Man for All Seasons* (66), *The Sting* (73), *The Taking of Pelham One-Two-Three* (74), *Jaws* (75), *The Deep* (77), *Black Sunday* (77), *Force 10 from Navarone* (78), *Avalanche Express* (79).

## SHAW, Sebastian (1905- )

This handsome British leading man of the 1930s was born in Holt, England. He made his stage debut when he was nine years old. Later in his film career he switched to character roles.
**Selected Films:** *Caste* (30), *Taxi to Paradise* (33), *Men Are Not Gods* (36), *The Spy in Black* (39), *East of Piccadilly* (41), *The Glass Mountain* (48), *It Happened Here* (64), *A Midsummer Night's Dream* (68).

## SHAWN, Dick (1929-1987)

A zany comedian, Shawn was born Richard Schulefand in Buffalo, New York, After studying at the University of Miami, he began appearing with his comedy act in night clubs and on television. He also appeared in a few movies.
**Selected Films:** *The Opposite Sex* (56), *Wake Me When It's Over* (60), *It's a Mad Mad Mad Mad World* (63), *What Did You Do in the War, Daddy?* (66), *The Producers* (68), *The Happy Ending* (69), *Looking Up* (77), *Love at First Bite* (79), *Maid to Order* (87).

## SHEARER, Moira (1926- )

Shearer was born Moira King in Dunfermline, Scotland, and was a ballet dancer from the age of six. She made her professional debut with the International Ballet at the age of 15 and the next year she joined England's Sadler's Wells ballet company. She came to films as a dancer, starring in *The Red Shoes* (48) and *Tales of Hoffman* (51). Shearer later got non-dancing parts. She married news analyst and novelist Ludovic Kennedy and retired for a time, but returned to the London stage in 1974 in the drama *Man and Wife*.
**Selected Films:** *The Red Shoes* (48), *Tales of Hoffman* (51), *The Story of Three Loves* (53), *The Man Who Loved Redheads* (55), *Black Tights* (60).

## SHEARER, Norma (1900-1983)

MGM billed Shearer as 'The First Lady of the Screen.' Her elegance and style won her a wide public following and critical praise. Born Edith Norma Shearer in Montreal, Quebec, Canada, she trained for the theater from childhood. Shearer got no farther than featured parts in films until she met and later married Irving Thalberg, supervisor of production at MGM. From then on she had her pick of roles, co-stars and directors. Frequently nominated for an Oscar, she won the Academy Award for Best Actress for *The Divorcee* (30). When Thalberg died in 1936 her career declined, in part because of poor script choices – she turned down the starring roles in *Gone With the Wind* (39), and *Mrs Miniver* (42). She retired from the movies in 1942. Her brother Douglas was, for many years, the head of the MGM Sound Department.
**Selected Films:** *The Flapper* (20), *He Who Gets Slapped* (24), *The Trial of Mary Dugan* (29), *The Divorcee* (30), *A Free Soul* (31), *Strange Interlude* (32), *Smilin' Through* (32), *The Barretts of Wimpole Street* (340, *Romeo and Juliet* (36), *Marie Antoinette* (38), *Idiot's Delight* (39), *The Women* (39), *Escape* (40), *Her Cardboard Lover* (42).

## SHEEDY, Ally (1962- )

Born in New York City, by the age of seven she had appeared with the American Ballet Theater, and by the age of 12 she had written a book, *She Was Nice to Mice*. Her first movie was *Bad Boys* (83) in which she played the victim of a rape. For a time she combined her film-making with classes at the University of Southern California.
**Selected Films:** *Bad Boys* (83), *War Games* (84), *The Breakfast Club* (85), *St Elmo's Fire* (85), *Blue City* (86), *Short Circuit* (86), *Maid to Order* (87).

## SHEEN, Charlie (1966- )

Born Charles Estevez in Santa Monica, California, the son of actor Martin Sheen and the brother of actors Emilio and Ramon Estevez, Sheen made his first appearance on television at the age of nine. He had a ten-second closeup in his father's made-for-TV feature, *The Execution of Private Slovik.* His first film was *Grizzly II – The Predator* (84).
**Selected Films:** *Grizzly II – The Predator* (84), *Red Dawn* (84), *The Boys Next Door* (85), *Wraith* (85), *Lucas* (86), *Platoon* (86), *Three for the Road* (87).

## SHEEN, Martin (1940- )

Sheen was born Ramon Estevez in Dayton, Ohio, to a Spanish immigrant father and an Irish mother. As soon as he graduated from high school, he headed for New York and enrolled in the off-off-Broadway Living Theater. While he was working there, he was also supporting himself by being a janitor, a soda jerk, a car washer and a messenger. Finally he had a success as the star of the Broadway production of *The Subject Was Roses.* Sheen made his screen debut in *The Incident* (67), as a punk who terrorizes the passengers on a New York subway train. The next year he repeated his role in the screen version of *The Subject Was Roses* (68). He was sensational as the youth on a killing spree in *Badlands* (73), and was probably the best thing about the forgettable *Apocalypse Now* (79), during the filming of which he suffered a heart attack. He has also been splendid on television, most notably in *The Execution of Private Slovik.*
**Selected Films:** *The Incident* (67), *The Subject Was Roses* (68), *Catch 22* (70), *Pickup on 101* (72), *Badlands* (73), *The Cassandra Crossing* (77), *Apocalypse Now* (79), *The Final Countdown* (79), *Gandhi* (82), *The Dead Zone* (83), *Loophole* (86).

## SHEFFIELD, Johnny (1931- )

Born in Pasadena, California, he appeared in the original cast of *On Borrowed Time* on Broadway when he was seven years old. MGM chose him to play Tarzan's foundling son in the jungle films of the 1970s, and when he grew too old for that, he appeared in his own series, *Bomba, the Jungle Boy.*
**Selected Films:** *Tarzan Finds a Son* (39), *Babes in Arms* (39), *Lucky Cisco Kid* (40), *Tarzan's Secret Treasure* (41), *Tarzan's New York Adventure* (42), *Tarzan Triumphs* (43), *Tarzan and the Huntress* (47), *Bomba, the Jungle Boy* (49), *The Lost Volcano* (50), *The Lion Hunters* (51), *Bomba and the Jungle Girl* (52), *Safari Drums* (53), *The Golden Idol* (54), *Lord of the Jungle* (55).

## SHELLEY, Barbara (1933- )

Shelley was born in London, England, where she began her professional career as a model. She began her movie career in Italy in 1953, but beginning in the late 1950s she returned to Britain, starring in a huge number of horror movies.
**Selected Films:** *Cat Girl* (57), *Blood of the Vampire* (58), *Village of the Damned* (60), *The Shadow of the Cat* (61), *Death Trap* (62), *The Gorgon* (64), *Dracula – Prince of Darkness* (66), *Five Million Years to Earth* (67), *Ghost Story* (74).

## SHEPARD, Sam (1943- )

Born Samuel Shepard Rogers in Illinois, Shepard was drawn to the theater and began writing plays at an early age. By his mid-twenties he had won the first of several Obies for *Icarus' Mother.* In 1978 his drama *Buried Child* won both an Obie and the Pulitzer Prize. Acting has been a sideline for the rangy and craggily handsome Shepard, but he has brought great power to his screen roles, most notably as Chuck Yeager in *The Right Stuff* (83).
**Selected Films:** *Days of Heaven* (78), *Resurrection* (80), *Raggedy Man* (81), *Frances* (82), *The Right Stuff* (83), *Country* (84), *Fool for Love* (85), *Crimes of the Heart* (86).

## SHEPHERD, Cybill (1949- )

Shepherd, the beautiful and glamorous screen and television star, was born in Memphis, Tennessee, and was elected Miss Teenage Memphis. She soon became a model, and at the tender age of 20, was cast by director Peter Bogdanovich (after he had spotted her face on the cover of *Glamour* magazine) as the lead in *The Last Picture Show,* which was released in 1971. She and Bogdanovich had an affair, but her career went downhill. Despite creditable performances in *Taxi Driver* (76) and *The Heartbreak Kid* (72), she received an almost unbroken succession of floggings by the critics. Shepherd returned to Memphis, married an auto-parts dealer, had a baby and a divorce, and returned to Hollywood, where she was told she wasn't marketable. In 1985, she was cast as Maddie, the female lead in the television series, *Moonlighting,* and her career was off and running again.
**Selected Films:** *The Last Picture Show* (71), *The Heartbreak Kid* (72), *Daisy Miller* (74), *At Long Last Love* (75), *Taxi Driver* (76), *Special Delivery* (76).

## SHEPPERD, John (1907-1983)

Born Shepperd Strudwick in Hillsboro, North Carolina, he was usually the cultivated, gentlemanly leading man or character actor. He began his stage work in 1928, belonged to the Actors Studio and made his film debut in *Congo Maisie* (40). He changed his professional name to John Shepperd in 1941 and back to Shepperd Strudwick in 1948.
**Selected Films:** *Congo Maisie* (40), *Belle Starr* (41), *The Loves of Edgar Allan Poe* (42), *Chetniks* (43), *Joan of Arc* (48), *All the King's Men* (49), *A Place in the Sun* (51), *The Eddie Duchin Story* (56), *The Sad Sack* (57), *Daring Game* (68), *Slaves* (69), *Cops and Robbers* (73).

## SHERIDAN, Ann (1915-1967)

Expressive eyes, warmth, sexiness, a sense of humor and down-to-earth charm made her a star. Born Clara Lou Sheridan in Denton, Texas, Sheridan planned to be a teacher and headed for Hollywood only because she had won a 'Search for Beauty' contest in 1933, which gave her a bit part in a Paramount film. She was signed to a starlet's contract and in less than two years she had appeared in bit parts in 20 forgettable movies. She switched to Warner Bros. in 1936 and her career improved. Sheridan made her way to the top with the help of a publicity campaign billing her as the 'Oomph Girl.' She appeared as a wise, open-hearted girl in several social-crime melodramas, but it wasn't until *King's Row* (41) that she was permitted to show that she could act. She went on to score in comedies, dramas, and even exhibited a warm contralto voice in a couple of musicals. When her film career began to slip, she turned to television, and was starring in a situation comedy, *Pistols and Petticoats* at the time of her death from cancer. She was married three times, and all of her husbands were actors – Edward Norris, George Brent and Scott McKay.
**Selected Films:** *College Rhythm* (34), *Fighting Youth* (35), *San Quentin* (37), *Angels with Dirty Faces* (38), *They Made Me a Criminal* (39), *They Drive by Night* (40), *King's Row* (41), *The Man Who Came to Dinner* (41), *Edge of Darkness* (43), *Shine on Harvest Moon* (44), *The Unfaithful* (47), *I Was a Male War Bride* (49), *Woman on the Run* (50), *Come Next Spring* (56), *The Woman and the Hunter* (57).

## SHIELDS, Arthur (1896-1970)

The younger brother of character actor Barry Fitzgerald, Shields was born in Dublin, Ireland, and settled in Hollywood after a stellar career with Dublin's Abbey Players. He was never to gain the fame that his brother had, but he was a highly respected actor who often played priests, missionaries or fanatics.
**Selected Films:** *The Plough and the Stars* (37), *Drums Along the Mohawk* (39), *The Long Voyage Home* (40), *How Green Was My Valley* (41), *Lassie Come Home* (43), *The White Cliffs of Dover* (44), *National Velvet* (44), *The Keys of the Kingdom* (45), *The Corn Is Green* (45), *She Wore a Yellow Ribbon* (49), *The Quiet Man* (52), *Night of the Quarter Moon* (59), *The Pigeon That Took Rome* (62).

## SHIELDS, Brooke (1965- )

Born in New York City, Shields was a professional model before she was one year old, becoming the 'Ivory Snow Baby,' and was featured in advertisements for many other popular products. She made her first film when she was 11, and two years later had a major role in the controversial film *Pretty Baby* (78). At times her face seems to be everywhere, but as to whether Shields is an actress or just a very beautiful celebrity, only time will tell. She did prove her dedication when she took time out from her movie career to attend and graduate from Princeton University.
**Selected Films:** *Holy Terror* (78), *Pretty Baby* (78), *King of the Gypsies* (78), *Tilt* (79), *Wanda Nevada* (79), *Just You and Me, Kid* (79), *The Blue Lagoon* (80), *Endless Love* (81), *Sahara* (84).

## SHIGETA, James (1933- )

Born in Hawaii, Shigeta often plays Japanese men in his films. He has been a leading man and a supporting actor, and is probably best known for his leading role in *Flower Drum Song* (61).
**Selected Films:** *The Crimson Kimono* (59), *Walk Like a Dragon* (60), *Flower Drum Song* (61), *Paradise, Hawaiian Style* (66), *Nobody's Perfect* (68), *Lost Horizon* (73), *The Yakuza* (75), *Midway* (76).

## SHIMURA, Takashi (1905-1982)

This former stage actor was born in Hyogo, Japan, and became one of the leading actors in Japanese movies, appearing at his best in the films of director Akira Kurosawa. Shimura is probably best remembered for his roles as the woodcutter in *Rashomon* (50) and as the Samurai leader in *The Seven Samurai* (54).
**Selected Films:** *The Last Days of Edo* (41), *The Quiet Duel* (49), *Rashomon* (50), *Living* (52), *The Seven Samurai* (54), *I Live in Fear* (55), *Samurai Saga* (59), *Yojimbo* (61), *Sanjuro* (62), *Red Beard* (65), *The Day the Sun Rose* (68), *Oginsaga* (79).

## SHIRE, Talia (1947- )

The younger sister of director Francis Ford Coppola, she was born Talia Coppola in Lake Success, New York. After she attended the Yale School of Drama, she appeared in a few Roger Corman movies before getting her first big break in *The Godfather* (72), which her brother directed. In *The Godfather, Part II* (74), she repeated her role as Connie Corleone, Al Pacino's sister, and was nominated for an Academy Award for Best Supporting Actress and won the New York Film Critics Award. She gave another series of memorable performances as the wife of Sylvester Stallone in the *Rocky* pictures. She is married to David Shire, a talented Hollywood composer.
**Selected Films:** *The Wild Racers* (68), *The Dunwich Horror* (70), *The Godfather* (72), *The Godfather, Part II* (74), *Rocky* (76), *Old Boyfriends* (79), *Rocky II* (79), *Prophesy* (79), *Windows* (80), *Rocky III* (83), *The Butcher* (83), *Rocky IV* (85).

## SHIRLEY, Anne (1918- )

Shirley was born Dawn Eveleen Paris in New York City, and started making Hollywood pictures at the age of five, billed as Dawn O'Day. Her first big break came when she was assigned the lead role in

*Anne of Green Gables* (34), and she changed her name to Anne Shirley. She was nominated for the Academy Award as Best Supporting Actress for her work in *Stella Dallas* (37). She retired in 1945. Her first husband was actor John Payne, her second was producer Adrian Scott, and her third was screenwriter Charles Lederer, who became one of the Hollywood Ten during the Red scare of the 1950s.
**Selected Films:** *Moonshine Valley* (22), *Riders of the Purple Sage* (25), *Liliom* (30), *So Big* (32), *Anne of Green Gables* (34), *Steamboat 'Round the Bend* (35), *Stella Dallas* (37), *Mother Carey's Chickens* (38), *Saturday's Children* (40), *All That Money Can Buy* (41), *The Powers Girl* (42), *Government Girl* (43), *Murder My Sweet* (44).

## SHORE, Dinah (1917- )

Shore is one of those improbable people whom nobody seems to hate, a reputation she manages with charm and wit. Born Frances Rose Shore in Winchester, Tennessee, she contracted polio at the age of two, and it crippled her right leg and foot. Her strength was restored by swimming, tennis and massage. At Vanderbilt University, Shore was president of her sorority and head of the women's government. After graduation, she went to New York and adopted her first name from the popular song, 'Dinah.' Shore, along with Frank Sinatra, was a singer on Martin Block's WNEW radio program, and later got her big break as the singer with the Leo Reisman Orchestra. After being named the 'New Star of Radio' in 1940, she went to Hollywood, debuting in a small part in the movie revue *Thank Your Lucky Stars* (43). She appeared in several films and her best role was opposite Danny Kaye in *Up in Arms* (44). She then switched to television, where *The Dinah Shore Show* ran for 12 years. She was married to actor George Montgomery from 1943 to 1962.
**Selected Films:** *Thank Your Lucky Stars* (43), *Up in Arms* (44), *Follow the Boys* (44), *Belle of the Yukon* (44), *Till the Clouds Roll By* (46), *Fun and Fancy Free* (47), *Aaron Slick from Punkin Crick* (52), *Oh God!* (77), *Health* (79).

## SIDNEY, Sylvia (1910- )

She was born Sophie Kosow in The Bronx, New York, and trained for the stage at the Theatre Guild School. She made her first Broadway appearance at the age of 17 and almost immediately was a leading lady. She played a screaming witness in the film *Thru Different Eyes* (29), and two years later she was a Hollywood star, usually cast as a proud but poor girl of the working class. Tired of her type-casting, she retired from the movies in the 1950s, and concentrated on the theater. She did appear in *Summer Wishes, Winter Dreams* (73), for which she was nominated for an Oscar. And she was magnificent as the dying wife of Robert Preston in *Finnigan, Begin Again*, a made-for-television movie in 1985. Her first husband was publisher Bennett Cerf and her second was actor Luther Adler.
**Selected Films:** *Thru Different Eyes* (29), *Street Scene* (31), *Accent on Youth* (35), *The Trail of the Lonesome Pine* (36), *Dead End* (37), *The Searching Wind* (46), *Love from a Stranger* (47), *Violent Saturday* (55), *Summer Wishes, Winter Dreams* (73), *God Told Me So* (76), *I Never Promised You a Rose Garden* (77), *Damien: Omen II* (78), *Hammett* (80).

## SIGNORET, Simone (1921-1985)

Born Simone Kaminker in Wiesbaden (in what is now West Germany), where her Jewish father was a soldier in the French army of occupation, she grew up in the well-to-do Paris suburb of Neuilly-sur-Seine. Signoret began to act during World War II and, as a precaution, used her mother's maiden name because it was not recognizably Jewish. During the war, her father escaped to London to join Charles De Gaulle's Free French Army, but she and her brothers remained in France, where she quit school to support her family, marrying movie director Yves Allegret, who cast her in her first leading role in *Les Démons de l'Aube* (45). She played a prostitute in *Dédée d'Anvers* (48), the movie which first brought her significant attention. The combination of strength and vulnerability she projected was unique. She would often play prostitutes and lovesick women, ultimately maturing into more complex and interesting roles. In 1951 Signoret, now divorced, married singer and actor Yves Montand, with whom she lived until her death. *La Ronde* (50) made her an international star and she won a British Film Academy Best Foreign Actress Award for *Casque d'Or* (52), another for *Les Sorcières de Salem* (57), the French version of Arthur Miller's play *The Crucible*, and a third for *Room at the Top* (58), which also brought her a Cannes Film Festival Award and an American Academy Award as Best Actress. *Les Diaboliques* (54) was not only one of the best horror suspense films ever made, but it was also one of the first foreign language films to get wide distribution in Britain and America. Signoret refused all offers to go to Hollywood until *Ship of Fools* (65), which brought her an Oscar nomination. Unlike many actresses, she allowed herself to gain weight and grow older without a battle, switching comfortably to character roles, winning fresh acclaim for *Le Chat* (72), with Jean Gabin, and *Madame Rosa* (78), which earned her a Cesar, the French equivalent of an Oscar.
**Selected Films:** *Les Démons de l'Aube* (45), *Macadam* (45), *Against the Wind* (47), *Dédée d'Anvers* (48), *Managès* (49), *La Ronde* (50), *Casque d'Or* (52), *Therèse Racquin* (53), *Les Diaboliques* (54), *Les Sorcières de Salem* (57), *Room at the Top* (58), *Term of Trial* (62), *The Day and the Hour* (63), *Ship of Fools* (65), *The Sleeping Car Murders* (65), *The Deadly Affair* (67), *The Seagull* (68), *Le Chat* (72), *Madame Rosa* (78), *L'Etoile du Nord* (80).

## SILLS, Milton (1882-1930)

Sills was born in Chicago, Illinois, and became involved in drama while he was a student at the University of Chicago. After graduation, he joined stock companies, making his Broadway debut in 1908. His first film was *The Pit* (14), and he soon was a star. Sills was a tall, rugged, versatile actor and played leads in swashbucklers, westerns, comedies and melodramas. He made a triumphant shift to talkies, especially in *The Sea Wolf* (30), but died that year of a heart attack.
**Selected Films:** *The Pit* (14), *The Rack* (15), *Souls Adrift* (17), *Shadows* (19), *The Weekend* (20), *Burning Sands* (22), *Adam's Rib* (23), *Madonna of the Streets* (24), *Paradise* (26), *The Valley of the Giants* (27), *His Captive Woman* (29), *The Sea Wolf* (30).

## SILVA, Henry (1928- )

He was born in Brooklyn, New York and earned a living as a delivery boy and a longshoreman before he tried acting with Group Theatre and at the Actors Studio. Because he was beady-eyed and had high cheekbones, he often played Indians, Mexicans or Orientals in films, and then became typecast as a sadistic villain.
**Selected Films:** *Viva Zapata!* (52), *A Hatful of Rain* (57), *Green Mansions* (59), *Cinderfella* (60), *The Manchurian Candidate* (62), *Johnny Cool* (63), *The Reward* (65), *Never a Dull Moment* (68), *Sharkey's Machine* (81), *Wrong is Right* (82), *Code of Silence* (85), *Allan Quartermain and the Lost City of Gold* (87).

## SILVERA, Frank (1914-1970)

Silvera was born in Kingston, Jamaica and was educated at Northeastern Law School. He was a stage veteran, and began in films in the 1950s, most notably in *Viva Zapata!* (52). Silvera was often cast as a Mexican, Indian or Oriental villain, and he starred in the television series *The High Chaparral.*
**Selected Films:** *Viva Zapata!* (52), *Crowded Paradise* (56), *Key Witness* (60), *Mutiny on the Bounty* (62), *Toys in the Attic* (63), *The Greatest Story Ever Told* (65), *The Appaloosa* (66), *Hombre* (67), *Che!* (69), *Valdez Is Coming!* (71).

## SILVERHEELS, Jay (1919-1980)

Silverheels was born Harold J Smith on the Six Nations Indian Reservation in Ontario, Canada. He was the son of a Mohawk chief, and was an outstanding lacrosse player and amateur boxer before he began his film career. His specialty was character parts, and he gained fame on television as Tonto, The Lone Ranger's faithful Indian companion. He retired from show business in 1974 and started a new career as a harness racing driver.
**Selected Films:** *Key Largo* (49), *Broken Arrow* (50), *The Lone Ranger* (56), *Alias Jesse James* (59), *Indian Paint* (65), *The Man Who Loved Cat Dancing* (73), *Santee* (73).

## SILVERS, Phil (1912-1985)

Silvers, who was born Philip Silver in Brooklyn, New York, was appearing in vaudeville by the age of 13 – as a boy singer. He was in a few two-reel musicals before he joined Minsky's burlesque troope in 1934, where he became a comedian. His first feature film was *Hit Parade of 1941* (40), and he went on to make more light comedies and musicals, usually playing the hero's friend. He also starred on television as the scheming Sergeant Ernie Bilko in *The Phil Silvers Show* (also called *You'll Never Get Rich*) for which he won an Emmy Award.
**Selected Films:** *Hit Parade of 1941* (40), *Tom, Dick and Harry* (41), *Lady Be Good* (41), *Roxie Hart* (42), *Coney Island* (43), *Cover Girl* (44), *Summer Stock* (50), *Top Banana* (54), *It's a Mad Mad Mad Mad World* (63), *A Funny Thing Happened on the Way to the Forum* (66), *The Boatniks* (70), *Won Ton Ton, The Dog Who Saved Hollywood* (76), *The Cheap Detective* (78) *Racquet* (79), *There Goes the Bride* (80).

## SIM, Alastair (1900-1976)

Sim's face and voice were utterly unique, and he created an unmatched gallery of eccentric and usually hilarious characters. He was born in Edinburgh, Scotland, and was a professor of elocution before making his stage debut at the age of 30. He is best remembered for his role as Scrooge in *A Christmans Carol* (51), revived on television every Christmas, and in the dual role of the dotty headmistress and her bookie brother in *The Belles of St Trinians* (54). He also appeared on the London stage in plays which he produced or directed.
**Selected Films:** *Riverside Murder* (35), *The Terror* (38), *Alf's Button Afloat* (38), *This Man Is News* (38), *Inspector Hornleigh* (39), *Cottage to Let* (41), *Let the People Sing* (42), *Green for Danger* (46), *London Belongs to Me* (48), *The Happiest Days of Your Life* (49), *Laughter in Paradise* (51), *A Christmas Carol* (51), *An Inspector Calls* (54), *The Belles of St Trinians* (54), *Wee Geordie* (55), *The Green Man* (56), *Blue Murder at St Trinians* (57), *School for Scoundrels* (60), *Royal Flash* (75), *Escape from the Dark* (76).

## SIMMONS, Jean (1929- )

Delicately beautiful, Simmons became a professional actress in her early teens, blossoming into a leading lady. Born in London, England, she was only 14 when she was chosen from among a group of dance students to play Margaret Lockwood's sister in *Give Us the Moon* (44). She gained popularity as the spoiled young Estella in *Great Expectations* (46). Simmons hit stardom when she was picked by Laurence Olivier to play opposite him as Ophelia in *Hamlet* (48), which won her an Academy Award nomination and the Best Actress Prize at the Venice Film Festival. In 1950 she married actor Stewart Granger and went with him to Hollywood. She divorced Granger in 1960 and

married director Richard Brooks, who directed her in *Elmer Gantry* (60). She was nominated again for an Oscar for *The Happy Ending* (69), and semi-retired from movies in the early 1970s, but was to be seen often on television.
**Selected Films:** *Give Us the Moon* (44), *Caesar and Cleopatra* (45), *Great Expectations* (46), *Black Narcissus* (47), *Hamlet* (48), *The Blue Lagoon* (49), *Young Bess* (53), *The Robe* (53), *Desiree* (54), *Guys and Dolls* (55), *The Big Country* (58), *Home Before Dark* (58), *Elmer Gantry* (60), *Spartacus* (60), *All the Way Home* (63), *Mister Buddwing* (66), *The Happy Ending* (69), *Mr Sycamore* (75), *Dominique* (79).

## SIMON, Simone (1911- )

She was born in Béthune, France, but grew up in Marseilles. In 1930 she became a fashion designer and a model in Paris, making her film debut in 1931. Hollywood beckoned in 1936, and she was given a studio buildup that even told moviegoers how to pronounce her name – SEE-moan SEE-moan. She made some impressive films, most notably *All That Money Can Buy* (41) and *Cat People* (42), and returned to France after World War II.
**Selected Films:** *Mam'zelle Nitouche* (31), *Le Lac aux Dames* (34), *Girls' Dormitory* (36), *Seventh Heaven* (37), *All That Money Can Buy* (41), *Cat People* (42), *The Curse of the Cat People* (44), *Mademoiselle Fifi* (44), *Temptation Harbor* (47), *La Ronde* (50), *House of Pleasure* (52), *The Extra Day* (56).

## SIMPSON, O J (1947- )

Born Orenthal James Simpson in San Francisco, California, he became famous as a great running back on the University of Southern California football team, winning the Heisman Trophy as the outstanding college football player in the country in 1968. He went on to play professional football with the Buffalo Bills, and then went into show business as a sports commentator and actor.
**Selected Films:** *The Towering Inferno* (74), *The Cassandra Crossing* (77), *Capricorn One* (78), *Firepower* (79).

## SIMPSON, Russell (1878-1959)

This gaunt American actor was in scores of films, beginning in the silent era and appearing until the year of his death. He specialized in kindly older men, especially in westerns.
**Selected Films:** *Billy the Kid* (31), *Way Down East* (36), *Ramona* (37), *Dodge City* (39), *The Grapes of Wrath* (40), *My Darling Clementine* (46), *Seven Brides for Seven Brothers* (54), *Friendly Persuasion* (56), *The Horse Soldiers* (59).

## SINATRA, Frank (1915- )

Sinatra was the singing idol of the bobby soxers of the 1940s. Then, just when his career seemed finished, he rescued it with his surprisingly fine acting. He was born in Hoboken, New Jersey, and began his career as a band singer. His popularity soared during the post-World War II era and he appeared in a number of musicals, most notably with Gene Kelly in *Anchors Aweigh* (45), often in secondary roles. In 1952 his vocal chords hemorrhaged and he was dropped by his record company. Sinatra begged Columbia Pictures to give him a dramatic role in *From Here to Eternity* (53), for which he was paid a paltry $8000. His performance as the tragic Maggio was superb and won him an Oscar for Best Supporting Actor. His voice recovered, and he has risen to legendary status as 'The Chairman of the Board [of Show Business]' or merely as 'Old Blue Eyes.' Although Sinatra's performances in films such as *The Man with the Golden Arm* (55) and *The Detective* (68), have been excellent, he has often relied on his image, not his acting. Since 1970 he has rarely appeared in movies.

*Frank Sinatra in* Anchors Aweigh *(45).*

**Selected Films:** *Las Vegas Nights* (41), *Higher and Higher* (43), *Anchors Aweigh* (45), *It Happened in Brooklyn* (47), *Take Me Out to the Ball Game* (49), *From Here to Eternity* (53), *Guys and Dolls* (55), *The Tender Trap* (55), *The Man with the Golden Arm* (55), *High Society* (56), *The Joker Is Wild* (57), *Pal Joey* (57), *Some Came Running* (59), *Ocean's Eleven* (60), *The Manchurian Candidate* (62), *Von Ryan's Express* (65), *Assault on a Queen* (66), *Tony Rome* (67), *The Detective* (68), *Dirty Dingus Magee* (70), *The First Deadly Sin* (80).

## SINDEN, Donald (1923- )

Born in Plymouth, England, Sinden began his stage career in the early 1940s and his film career in the early 1950s. In the 1960s he shifted to character roles after 20 years as a leading man.
**Selected Films:** *The Cruel Sea* (53), *Mogambo* (53), *The Beachcomber* (54), *The Captain's Table* (58), *Villain* (71), *The Day of the Jackal* (73), *That Lucky Touch* (75).

## SINGLETON, Penny (1908- )

Most famous for her portrayal of a comic strip character in the *Blondie* films, Singleton was born Mariana Dorothy McNulty in Philadelphia, Penn-

sylvania. Educated at Barnard College, she made her stage debut in 1927 as a singer and acrobat in the Broadway musical *Good News* and went to Hollywood to appear in the screen version of the play in 1930. She played in various comedies, changing her name to Singleton after she married a man by that name in 1938. The *Blondie* series ran from 1938 to 1950, and then she appeared in night clubs and in 1971 replaced by Ruby Keeler on Broadway in *No, No, Nanette*. Singleton was prominent in the American Guild of Variety Artists for years, serving as vice president and executive secretary.
**Selected Films:** *Good News* (30), *After the Thin Man* (36), *Vogues of 1938* (37), *The Mad Miss Manton* (38), *Blondie* (38), *Young Widow* (46), *The Best Man* (64).

## SKELTON, Red (1913- )

Born Richard Bernard Skelton in Vincennes, Indiana, he was raised in poverty by his cleaning-woman mother, since his circus clown father had died before he was born. At the age of seven, he was singing for pennies in the streets of Vincennes, and he quit school at ten to join a medicine show. Until he was in his teens, he was working in circuses, burlesque, vaudeville, and on show boats. Until the 1930s he was doing one-night stands as a comic and was finally booked at the Paramount Theater in New York. Success on radio followed and in 1938 he made his screen debut in *Having a Wonderful Time*. In the 1940s and 1950s he was one of MGM's comedians. He capped his screen success with a long run on television's *The Red Skelton Show*.
**Selected Films:** *Having a Wonderful Time* (38), *Whistling in the Dark* (41), *Lady Be Good* (41), *Panama Hattie* (42), *Du Barry Was a Lady* (43), *Bathing Beauty* (44), *Ziegfeld Follies* (46), *The Fuller Brush Man* (48), *Neptune's Daughter* (49), *Three Little Words* (50), *Lovely to Look At* (52), *Public Pigeon No. 1* (57), *Those Magnificent Men in Their Flying Machines* (65).

## SKINNER, Cornelia Otis (1903-1979)

Born in Chicago, Illinois, she was the daughter of the great stage actor, Otis Skinner. Primarily a stage actress, she made few movies, but her semi-autobiographical book, *Our Hearts Were Young and Gay* (co-written with Emily Kimbrough), was made into a movie in 1944.
**Selected Films:** *The Uninvited* (44), *The Girl in the Red Velvet Swing* (55), *The Swimmer* (67).

## SKIPWORTH, Alison (1863-1952)

Skipworth was born Alison Groom in London, England, and when she was young she was a real beauty. She married a poor artist and went on to the London stage at the age of 31 to help supplement his meager income. Then in 1895 she made her Broadway debut and began concentrating on the American stage, first as a leading lady, then as a supporting actress. Her first film was *Handcuffs or Kisses* (21), and she waited until 1930 to make her next. For the next several years, she made many movies, usually playing lofty matrons, most memorably opposite W C Fields.
**Selected Films:** *Handcuffs or Kisses* (21), *Raffles* (30), *Devotion* (31), *If I Had a Million* (32), *Tillie and Gus* (33), *Alice in Wonderland* (33), *The Captain Hates the Sea* (34), *Becky Sharp* (35), *The Gorgeous Hussy* (36), *Two Wise Maids* (37), *Ladies in Distress* (38).

## SLATER, Helen (1965- )

Slater was born in Massapequa, New York. She studied acting at the High School of the Performing Arts in New York City, where she also studied piano and flute. She broke into show business in television commercials, and made her screen debut in *Supergirl* (84).
**Selected Films:** *Supergirl* (84), *The Legend of Billie Jean* (85), *Ruthless People* (86), *Secret of My Success* (87).

## SLEZAK, Walter (1902-1983)

Slezak was the son of the operatic tenor Leo Slezak. Born in Vienna, Austria, he had studied medicine and worked as a bank clerk when he was discovered by director Michael Kertesz (who later changed his last name to Curtiz) in 1922. He played romantic roles in German films, but he kept gaining weight and was forced into character parts. He made his Broadway debut in 1931 and began making movies in Hollywood in 1942.
**Selected Films:** *Queen of Sin and the Spectacle of Sodom and Gomorra* (22), *Chained* (24), *Die Lorelei* (27), *Once Upon a Honeymoon* (42), *Lifeboat* (44), *The Princess and the Pirate* (45), *The Pirate* (48), *The Inspector General* (49), *Call Me Madam* (53), *The Miracle* (59), *Emil and the Detectives* (64), *The Caper of the Golden Bulls* (67), *Treasure Island* (72), *The Mysterious House of Dr C* (76).

## SLOANE, Everett (1909-1965)

Sloane was born in New York City and educated at the University of Pennsylvania. He lost his job as a Wall Street runner in the Stock Market Crash of 1929, and became an actor, appearing both on the stage and on the radio. Joining Orson Welles' Mercury Theatre, he appeared with Welles on Broadway and then went with him to Hollywood, where he made his screen debut as Bernstein in Welles' *Citizen Kane* (41). Sloane went on to become a formidable supporting actor.
**Selected Films:** *Citizen Kane* (41), *Journey into Fear* (42), *The Lady from Shanghai* (48), *The Men* (50), *Sirocco* (51), *The Desert Fox* (51), *The Big Knife* (55), *Patterns* (56), *Somebody Up There Likes Me* (56), *Lust for Life* (56), *Marjorie Morningstar* (58), *Home from the Hill* (60), *By Love Possessed* (61), *The Patsy* (64), *The Disorderly Orderly* (64).

## SMITH, Alexis (1921- )

She was born Gladys Smith in Penticton, British Columbia, Canada, and had some acting experience in Canadian summer stock before attending Los Angeles City College in California, where she was discovered by a talent scout in a school play. For the next ten years she played charming, resourceful, cool and calculating leading ladies. She retired from films in the late 1950s and made a smashing Broadway debut as the star of the musical *Follies,* returning to the screen in triumph after 15 years' absence. She has been married to actor Craig Stevens for more than 40 years.
**Selected Films:** *The Lady with Red Hair* (40), *Dive Bomber* (41), *Gentleman Jim* (42), *The Constant Nymph* (43), *The Doughgirls* (44), *Rhapsody in Blue* (45), *Night and Day* (46), *The Woman in White* (48), *Any Number Can Play* (49), *Montana* (50), *The Turning Point* (52), *Split Second* (53), *The Eternal Sea* (55), *Beau James* (57), *The Young Philadelphians* (59), *Jacqueline Susann's Once Is Not Enough* (75), *Casey's Shadow* (78), *Tough Guys* (86).

## SMITH, C Aubrey (1863-1948)

He was born Charles Aubrey Smith in London, England, and, to a generation of American moviegoers, Sir C Aubrey Smith, the bushy-browed character actor, was the image of the crusty English gentleman. Educated at Cambridge University, Smith had been a member of England's national cricket team before making his stage debut at the age of 30. He appeared in a huge number of silent and sound films in both Britain and America. He was knighted in 1944.
**Selected Films:** *Builder of Bridges* (15), *The Witching Hour* (16), *Trader Horn* (31), *Bachelor Father* (31), *Tarzan the Ape Man* (32), *Love Me Tonight* (32), *Trouble in Paradise* (32), *Morning Glory* (33), *Queen Christiana* (33), *Cleopatra* (34), *Lives of a Bengal Lancer* (35), *The Prisoner of Zenda* (37), *The Four Feathers* (39), *Another Thin Man* (39), *Rebecca* (40), *Dr Jekyll and Mr Hyde* (41), *The White Cliffs of Dover* (44), *And Then There Were None* (45), *An Ideal Husband* (47), *Little Women* (49).

## SMITH, Kent (1907-1985)

Smith was born in New York City and educated at Harvard College. A reliable actor on Broadway he went to Hollywood in the late 1930s, playing leading men effectively despite his lack of sex appeal. In the late 1950s he shifted to character roles. Smith was married to actress Edith Atwater.
**Selected Films:** *The Garden Murder Case* (36), *Cat People* (42), *Hitler's Children* (43), *The Curse of the Cat People* (44), *The Spiral Staircase* (46), *The Voice of the Turtle* (47), *The Fountainhead* (49), *The Damned Don't Cry* (50), *Comanche* (56), *Sayonara* (57), *Susan Slade* (61), *The Balcony* (63), *Youngblood Hawke* (64), *The Trouble With Angels* (66), *Games* (67), *Death of a Gunfighter* (69), *Pete 'n' Tillie* (72).

## SMITH, Maggie (1934- )

Born in Ilford, England, this supremely gifted light comedienne and dramatic actress trained at the Oxford Playhouse School. She made her London stage debut in a revue in 1952, and her first Broadway appearance in *New Faces* in 1956. Rave reviews have followed her throughout her career. Chiefly a stage actress, her screen appearances have also been notable. She won an Academy Award for Best Actress for *The Prime of Miss Jean Brodie* (69), and an Academy Award for Best Supporting Actress for *California Suite* (78). She was also nominated for an Oscar for *Othello* (65), *Travels with My Aunt* (72) and *Room With a View* (86). Her first husband was actor Robert Stephens.
**Selected Films:** *Nowhere to Go* (58), *Go to Blazes* (62), *The VIPs* (63), *The Pumpkin Eater* (64), *Othello* (66), *The Prime of Miss Jean Brodie* (69), *Travels with My Aunt* (72), *California Suite* (78), *Death on the Nile* (78), *Evil Under the Sun* (82), *A Private Function* (84), *Room With a View* (86).

## SNODGRASS, Carrie (1945- )

She was born in Park Ridge, Illinois and educated at Northern Illinois University and also worked at Chicago's Goodman Theater. Snodgrass, the talented leading lady of stage, screen and television, after earning an Academy Award nomination for *Diary of a Mad Housewife* (70), retired from the screen for several years, setting up house with rock star Neil Young and giving birth to their son, Zeke.
**Selected Films:** *Diary of a Mad Housewife* (70), *Rabbit Run* (70), *The Fury* (78), *A Night in Heaven* (83), *Murphy's Law* (86).

## SOKOLOFF, Vladimir (1889-1962)

This fine character actor was a veteran of the Moscow Art Theatre. Born in Moscow, he left Russia in 1923, continuing his acting in Berlin and Paris, on stage and in films. He arrived in Hollywood in 1937, and appeared in scores of movies, usually playing old Slavic men, although he also played people of almost every European nationality.
**Selected Films:** *Uneasy Money* (26), *Napoléon* (27), *The Threepenny Opera* (31), *Song of the Street* (33), *Mayerling* (36), *The Life of Emile Zola* (37), *Blockade* (38), *Juarez* (39), *Comrade X* (40), *For Whom the Bell Tolls* (43), *Song of Russia* (44), *Scarlet Street* (46), *Macao* (52), *While the City Sleeps* (56), *Twilight for the Gods* (58), *The Magnificent Seven* (60), *Mr Sardonicus* (61), *Taras Bulba* (62).

## SOMMER, Elke (1940- )

This sexy blonde leading lady of American and international movies was born Elke Schletz in Berlin, Germany. The daughter of a Lutheran minister, she went to a German university and

planned to become a diplomatic interpreter, but she could make more money by modeling, and then her screen career took off. She is married to writer Joe Hyams.
**Selected Films:** *Das Totenschiff* (59), *Love, Italian Style* (60), *Don't Bother to Knock* (61), *The Prize* (63), *A Shot in the Dark* (64), *The Oscar* (66), *The Wrecking Crew* (69), *Zeppelin* (71), *Ten Little Indians* (75), *The Swiss Conspiracy* (77), *The Prisoner of Zenda* (79), *Exit Sunset Boulevard* (80).

## SONDERGAARD, Gale (1899-1985)

Despite her many roles as an exotic villainess, Sondergaard was born Edith Holm Sondergaard in Litchfield, Minnesota – a professor's daughter. After graduating from the University of Minnesota, she began playing in stock companies, getting to Broadway in the late 1920s. She went to Hollywood and had her first movie role in *Anthony Adverse* (36), winning the Academy Award for Best Supporting Actress for her performance. By the late 1940s she was Hollywood's premier evil woman, but her career was sabotaged by her blacklisting during the Red Scare of the 1950s. She returned to films in 1969.
**Selected Films:** *Anthony Adverse* (36), *Seventh Heaven* (37), *The Life of Emile Zola* (37), *Juarez* (39), *The Cat and the Canary* (39), *The Mark of Zorro* (40), *The Letter* (40), *The Black Cat* (41), *My Favorite Blonde* (42), *A Night to Remember* (43), *Sherlock Holmes and the Spider Woman* (44), *Anna and the King of Siam* (46), *The Road to Rio* (47), *Slaves* (69), *The Return of a Man Called Horse* (76), *Echoes* (80).

## SORDI, Alberto (1919- )

This Italian leading man and comic actor was born in Rome, and when he was 13 he won a contest for imitating Oliver Hardy. He later became a comedian in music halls and on the Italian stage. Sordi made his screen debut in *La Principessa Tarakanova* (38), and by the 1950s he was one of the most beloved movie personalities in Italy. He often writes and directs his own films.
**Selected Films:** *La Principessa Tarakanova* (38), *La Signorina* (42), *I Vitelloni* (53), *The Sign of Venus* (55), *A Farewell to Arms* (57), *The Best of Enemies* (60), *To Bed or Not to Bed* (63), *Those Magnificent Men in Their Flying Machines* (65), *The Witches* (67), *To Love, Perhaps to Die* (75), *Le Temoin* (78).

## SORVINO, Paul (1939- )

This tall, chubby character actor, born in New York City, most often plays comedy roles, but he has been seen in drama, and sometimes as a leading man. His film appearances are infrequent.
**Selected Films:** *Where's Poppa?* (70), *The Panic in Needle Park* (71), *A Touch of Class* (73), *The Day of the Dolphin* (73), *The Gambler* (74), *Oh God!* (77), *Bloodbrothers* (78), *Lost and Found* (79), *Cruising* (80), *Reds* (81), *The Stuff* (85), *A Fine Mess* (86).

## SOTHERN, Ann (1909- )

Born Harriette Lake in Valley City, North Dakota, she was trained as a singer by her mother, and made her screen debut at the age of 20 in a bit part of an early Warner Bros. sound musical, *The Show of Shows* (29). After a few walk-on parts, she headed for Broadway, where she quickly began getting leads. It was back to Hollywood in 1933, where she changed her name to Ann Sothern and became a lighthearted heroine of B pictures for Columbia and RKO. When she moved to MGM in 1939, she became the heroine of the *Maisie* series of movies – and there were ten of them. She later was starred in musicals, and she proved that she could act in such films as *Cry Havoc* (43). In the early 1950s she switched to television with *Private Secretary* and *The Ann Sothern Show*, and toured with stage plays. She was married to actor Roger Pryor from 1936 to 1942, and to actor Robert Sterling from 1943 to 1949.
**Selected Films:** *The Show of Shows* (29), *Let's Fall in Love* (33), *Kid Millions* (34), *The Girl Friend* (35), *My American Wife* (36), *There Goes the Groom* (37), *Maisie* (39), *Lady Be Good* (41), *Panama Hattie* (42), *Cry Havoc* (43), *April Showers* (49), *A Letter to Three Wives* (49), *Shadow on the Wall* (50), *The Best Man* (64), *The Killing Mind* (73), *Crazy Mama* (75), *The Little Dragons* (80).

## SPAAK, Catherine (1945- )

This daughter of Belgian screenwriter Charles Spaak was born in Paris, France, and grew up among movie people. By the 1960s she was appearing as a leading lady in French, Italian and international films.
**Selected Films:** *The Night Watch* (60), *The Empty Canvas* (64), *Weekend at Dunkirk* (64), *Hotel* (67), *The Libertine* (69), *The Cat o' Nine Tails* (71), *Sebbre d'a Cavallo* (77), *Per Vivere Meglio* (79).

## SPACEK, Sissy (1949- )

Born in Quitman, Texas, Mary Elizabeth Spacek, was once considered an oddity who specialized in creepy teen-age parts. She has since shown herself to be one of the most accomplished of the modern screen actresses, with a potential for true greatness. She originally wanted to be a country-rock singer, but six months studying acting at the Lee Strasberg Theater Institute in New York changed her mind, although, because of her role as Loretta Lynn, the country singer, in *Coal Miner's Daughter* (79), she won a gold record for her singing and guitar playing on the sound track and her election as the American Guild of Variety Artists Entertainer of the Year for 1981. While she was in New York, she would play her guitar and sing in Washington Square or at hootenannies at The Bitter End for $10 a night. She worked as an extra for Andy Warhol and tried modeling. Then she went to Hollywood. Although her first film, a sex,

blood and gore film called *Prime Cut* (72), was a disaster, critics noticed the uniqueness of the tiny, freckle-faced girl with the froggy voice. Then came *Badlands* (73), an underrated movie with Martin Sheen based on the Charles Starkweather murders. Although she was in her mid-twenties, she could convincingly play teenagers, as she did when she played a tormented high school girl with murderous powers in *Carrie* (76) and received her first Oscar nomination. She won the Best Actress Oscar in 1979 for *Coal Miner's Daughter*. She has been nominated since for Best Actress for her role opposite Jack Lemmon in *Missing* (82), for her work as the farm wife in *The River* (84) and for her performance as the youngest sister in *Crimes of the Heart* (86). Spacek is married to movie director Jack Fisk, and they have a daughter, Schuyler.
**Selected Films:** *Prime Cut* (71), *Badlands* (73), *Carrie* (76), *Welcome to LA* (77), *Heartbeat* (79), *Coal Miner's Daughter* (79), *Raggedy Man* (81), *Missing* (82), *The River* (84), *Marie* (85), *Violets Are Blue* (86), *Crimes of the Heart* (86), *'night, Mother* (86).

## SPARKS, Ned (1883-1957)

This hard-boiled, cigar-chewing character actor was often seen as a grouchy reporter or an agent in movies of the 1930s. Born Edward A Sparkman in Ontario, Canada, he had a long career on stage before moving to Hollywood, where his raspy voice and countenance devoid of a smile made him a comedy favorite.
**Selected Films:** *A Wide-Open Town* (22), *Seven Keys to Baldpate* (25), *Alias the Lone Wolf* (27), *Nothing But the Truth* (29), *Iron Man* (31), *42nd Street* (43), *Gold Diggers of 1933* (33), *Imitation of Life* (34), *Sweet Adeline* (35), *Wake Up and Live* (37), *The Star Maker* (39), *For Beauty's Sake* (41), *Stage Door Canteen* (43), *Magic Town* (47).

## SPARV, Camilla (1943-      )

Born in Sweden, Sparv came to the United States in the 1960s and appeared as a leading lady in several films.
**Selected Films:** *The Trouble with Angels* (66), *Murderers' Row* (66), *Dead Heat on a Merry-Go-Round* (66), *Department K* (67), *Mackenna's Gold* (68), *Downhill Racer* (69), *The Italian Job* (69).

## STACK, Robert (1919-      )

Born Robert Modini in Los Angeles, California, he was educated at the University of Southern California. When he was 20 years old, his film career began with a splash when he was cast as 'the first boy to kiss Deanna Durbin' in *First Love* (39). For a while he played the usual youthful romantic leads, and came back from the Navy after World War II to do more of the same. His first good part was the lead in *The Bullfighter and the Lady* (51), in which he played an American who goes to Mexico to learn the art of bullfighting. He was excellent as a pilot in *The High and the Mighty* (54) but, of course, the movie was stolen by John Wayne. Stack received an Academy Award nomination for Best Supporting Actor for his work as an irresponsible playboy-millionaire in *Written on the Wind* (56). But American audiences remember him best for his portrayal of T-Man Eliot Ness in the television series, *The Untouchables*.
**Selected Films:** *First Love* (39), *The Mortal Storm* (40), *Eagle Squadron* (42), *A Date with Judy* (48), *The Bullfighter and the Lady* (51), *The High and the Mighty* (54), *House of Bamboo* (55), *Written on the Wind* (57), *John Paul Jones* (59), *The Last Voyage* (60), *The Caretakers* (63), *Is Paris Burning?* (66), *A Second Wind* (78), *1941* (79), *Airplane!* (80), *Big Trouble* (86).

## STALLONE, Sylvester (1946-      )

Stallone was a down and nearly out actor when he wrote a screenplay about a down and nearly out boxer who triumphs over the odds. Stallone sold the script on the provision that he play Rocky Balboa – the lead character. The film *Rocky* (76) was a huge hit, and it propelled Stallone from obscurity to stardom. His road to success had not been easy. He was born into poverty in New York City and grew up in the rough Hell's Kitchen neighborhood, then in Silver Spring, Maryland, then in a sleazy section of Philadelphia, spending several years in the homes of foster parents. Because of his muscular physique he was able to attend the American College in Switzerland on an athletic scholarship, and he briefly studied drama at the University of Miami. In New York, he worked as an usher in a theater and got some off-Broadway parts and a few film roles. Nearly broke, he wrote the first draft of *Rocky* in three days. Because of his business sense, he became a star. The film won Academy Awards for Best Picture and Best Director (John Avildsen) and earned a nomination for Best Actor and Best Screenplay for Stallone.
**Selected Films:** *Bananas* (71), *The Lords of Flatbush* (74), *The Prisoner of Second Avenue* (75), *Capone* (75), *Farewell My Lovely* (75), *Rocky* (76), *No Place to Hide* (77), *F.I.S.T.* (78), *Paradise Alley* (78), *Rocky II* (79), *Rocky III* (82), *Rhinestone* (84), *Rocky IV* (85), *Cobra* (86), *Over the Top* (87).

## STAMP, Terence (1940-      )

Born in London, England, Stamp became a prominent juvenile lead in British movies of the 1960s after having some stage experience. He was nominated for an Academy Award for Best Supporting Actor for his first film, in which he played the title role – *Billy Budd* (62). He won the Best Actor Award at the Cannes Film Festival for *The Collector* (65).
**Selected Films:** *Billy Budd* (62), *Term of Trial* (62), *The Collector* (65), *Modesty Blaise* (66), *Far From the Madding Crowd* (67), *Poor Cow* (67), *The Mind of Mr Soames* (70), *Superman* (78), *The Thief of Baghdad* (79), *Superman II* (80), *Legal Eagles* (86).

## STANDER, Lionel (1908- )

Born in New York City and educated at the University of North Carolina, this gravel-voiced character actor began his stage work at the age of 19. In 1932 he started making film shorts and then came movie features in 1935, excelling in eccentric comedy roles. His career was interrupted in the early 1950s when he refused to cooperate with the House Un-American Activities Committee, and he was blacklisted. He worked in summer stock, then as a Wall Street broker, returned to films in the late 1960s while he was living in Rome making 'Spaghetti Westerns.' He was also successful in the television series *Hart to Hart.*

**Selected Films:** *The Scoundrel* (35), *Mr Deeds Goes to Town* (36), *A Star is Born* (37), *Guadalcanal Diary* (43), *The Kid from Brooklyn* (46), *Call Northside 777* (51), *The Loved One* (65), *A Dandy in Aspic* (68), *The Gang That Couldn't Shoot Straight* (71), *The Black Bird* (75), *New York, New York* (77), *Matilda* (78).

## STANDING, Guy (1873-1937)

This prominent actor on the British and American stage was born in London, England. In the 1930s he went to Hollywood, where he played character parts. Knighted for his theatrical achievements, he was also the father of actress Kay Hammond.

**Selected Films:** *The Story of Temple Drake* (33), *The Eagle and the Hawk* (33), *Death Takes a Holiday* (34), *The Lives of a Bengal Lancer* (35), *Lloyds of London* (36), *Bulldog Drummond Escapes* (37).

## STANDING, John (1934- )

Born John Leon in England, he is the son of actress Kay Hammond and the grandson of actor Sir Guy Standing. Standing is a successful character actor, both on stage and on the screen.

**Selected Films:** *The Wild and the Willing* (62), *King Rat* (65), *Walk, Don't Run* (66), *Torture Garden* (67), *Zee and Co.* (71), *The Eagle Has Landed* (77).

## STANLEY, Kim (1925- )

Stanley was born Patricia Kimberley Reid in Tularosa, New Mexico, and was educated at the University of New Mexico. She began acting on stage in college and later went into stock. She worked as a model in New York while training at the Actors Studio under Elia Kazan and Lee Strasberg. Stanley won rave reviews as a 'Method' actress both on the Broadway and the London stage. She has made few films, but her work was memorable, and she received an Academy Award nomination for Best Actress for her performance in *Seance on a Wet Afternoon* (64). She suffered from a breakdown soon after that and began teaching drama at the College of Santa Fe, New Mexico.

**Selected Films:** *The Goddess* (58), *Seance on a Wet Afternoon* (64), *The Three Sisters* (77), *The Right Stuff* (83).

## STANTON, Harry Dean (1926- )

Lean and leathery, with a face dominated by hollowed cheeks and deep-set eyes, Stanton has long played tough guys, psychopaths and criminals. He appeared in some 50 films before he played Travis in *Paris, Texas* (83), his first role as a leading man. He was born in West Irvine, Kentucky, and after service in the Navy during World War II in which he served on an LST in the Pacific; he enrolled at the University of Kentucky, majoring in drama, but dropping out before graduation. He studied at the Pasadena Playhouse in California and later went into movie work, billing himself at first as Dean Stanton.

**Selected Films:** *The Proud Rebel* (58), *The Hostage* (67), *Cool Hand Luke* (67), *Day of the Evil Gun* (68), *Pat Garrett and Billy the Kid* (73), *The Godfather, Part II* (74), *The Missouri Breaks* (76), *Alien* (79), *Repo Man* (83), *Paris, Texas* (83), *Fool for Love* (84), *Pretty in Pink* (86), *Slam Dance* (87).

## STANWYCK, Barbara (1907- )

The tough, aggressive women that Stanwyck portrayed were played with a conviction that came from experience. Born Ruby Stevens in Brooklyn, New York, she was orphaned at the age of four and was raised by her older sister and assorted relatives. She began as a dancer in speakeasies and by the age of 15 she was a Ziegfeld chorus girl. Stage roles followed, as did minor parts in silent films. Her debut was in *Broadway Nights* (27). Her hard-bitten, sensuous appearance made her typecasting inevitable in such films as *Ten Cents a Dance* (31) and *Illicit* (31), but directors admired her professionalism, lack of temperament and enthusiastic love of her profession. She had arrived in Hollywood with her then-husband, the comedian Frank Fay. By 1932 and *So Big*, she was a critic's delight and a big box office draw. By the late 1930s she was a durable leading lady. In 1937 she made *Stella Dallas*, a tear jerker and classic 'woman's movie.' Stanwyck was equally good at comedy in *The Mad Miss Minton* (38). But her peak performance was in *Double Indemnity* (44), for which she was nominated for an Academy Award as Best Actress. She was also nominated for *Stella Dallas* (37), *Ball of Fire* (41) and *Sorry, Wrong Number* (48). In 1981 she won a Special Academy Award 'for superlative creativity and unique contribution to the art of screen acting.' Later she went to television, winning an Emmy Award for the series, *The Big Valley*. Her second husband was actor Robert Taylor.

**Selected Films:** *Broadway Nights* (27), *Ten Cents a Dance* (31), *Illicit* (31), *So Big* (32), *Baby Face* (33), *Annie Oakley* (35), *Stella Dallas* (37), *The Mad Miss Minton* (38), *Golden Boy* (39), *The Lady Eve* (41), *Ball of Fire* (41), *Meet John Doe* (41), *Double Indemnity* (44), *The Strange Love of Martha Ivers* (46), *Sorry, Wrong Number* (48), *The Lady Gambles* (49), *Clash by Night* (52), *Executive Suite* (54), *Roustabout* (64), *The Night Walker* (65).

## STAPLETON, Jean (1923- )

This delightful comedienne of great experience on stage, screen and television was born Jeanne Murray in New York City. Educated at Hunter College, she was once a secretary, then began her show business career singing with the Robert Shaw Chorale. Her stage debut came in stock in 1941, and she made it to Broadway in the mid-1950s, when she appared in musicals such as *Damn Yankees* and *Bells Are Ringing*. Her first two films were these musicals, in which she repeated her Broadway roles. She is best remembered as Edith Bunker, on the TV series *All In the Family*.
**Selected Films:** *Damn Yankees* (58), *Bells Are Ringing* (60), *Something Wild* (61), *Up the Down Staircase* (67), *Cold Turkey* (71), *Klute* (71).

## STAPLETON, Maureen (1925- )

A native of Troy, New York, she went to New York City in 1943 and worked as a model and waitress while attending classes at the Herbert Berghof Acting School. She first appeared on Broadway in 1946 and was a hit in 1951 in Tennessee Williams' *The Rose Tattoo*. An excellent performer, she was in many Broadway plays, including several by Williams, and was able to be vital, world-weary, vulnerable and strong – seemingly all at the same time. She was nominated for the Academy Award for Best Supporting Actress in her first film, *Lonelyhearts* (59), and again for *Interiors* (78). She finally won for her performance as Emma Goldman in Warren Beatty's *Reds* (81).
**Selected Films:** *Lonelyhearts* (59), *The Fugitive Kind* (60), *A View from the Bridge* (62), *Bye Bye Birdie* (63), *Airport* (70), *Plaza Suite* (71), *Interiors* (78), *Reds* (81), *Johnny Dangerously* (84), *Cocoon* (85), *Heartburn* (86), *Sweet Lorraine* (87).

## STARRETT, Charles (1904-1986)

Starrett was born in Athol, Massachusetts, and began his film career as an extra while he was attending Dartmouth College. He went on to star in numerous cowboy B pictures, retiring in 1952.
**Selected Films:** *The Quarterback* (26), *Sky Bride* (32), *Green Eyes* (34), *Blazing Six Shooters* (40), *Gunning for Vengeance* (46), *Texas Dynamo* (50), *The Kid from Broken Gun* (52).

## STEEL, Anthony (1920- )

This tall, robust leading man was born in London, England, and educated at Cambridge University. Steel made his screen debut in *Saraband* (48), in a small role. He was the first husband of actress Anita Ekberg.
**Selected Films:** *Saraband* (48), *The Mudlark* (50), *Laughter in Paradise* (51), *The Master of Ballantrae* (53), (54), *Storm over the Nile* (55), *A Matter of Choice* (63), *Anzio* (68), *The Story of O* (75), *The World Is Full of Married Men* (79), *The Mirror Crack'd* (80).

## STEELE, Barbara (1938- )

She was born in Trenton, England. Steele trained as a painter, but started acting in repertory in 1957. She began her film career in 1958 and became famous in Italian horror films, such as *Black Sunday* (60), and *The Pit and the Pendulum* (61). One of the few actresses ever to specialize in horror films, she has become a cult figure.
**Selected Films:** *Bachelor of Hearts* (58), *Black Sunday* (60), *The Pit and the Pendulum* (61), *Castle of Blood* (64), *Nightmare Castle* (65), *Caged Heat* (74), *I Never Promised You a Rose Garden* (77), *Pretty Baby* (78), *The Silent Scream* (79).

## STEELE, Bob (1906- )

The son of Robert North Bradbury, a prolific director of silent action films, Steele was born Robert North Bradbury Jr in Pendleton, Oregon. He began working with his father and his twin brother Bill in a series of nature shorts called *The Adventures of Bob and Bill* (20). He went on to play juvenile parts in his father's feature Westerns, as Bob Bradbury Jr, and began his career as a cowboy star in 1927. He starred in Westerns through the mid-1940s, and was popular as one of the 'Three Mesquiteers.' His most notable role, however, was as Curly, the rancher whose hand is crushed by the simple-minded Lennie in *Of Mice and Men* (40) – a non-western. He went on to play character parts.
**Selected Films:** *Davy Crockett at the Fall of the Alamo* (26), *Driftin' Sands* (28), *Hunted Men* (30), *Hidden Valley* (32), *Powdersmoke Range* (35), *Desert Patrol* (38), *Of Mice and Men* (40), *Westward Ho!* (42), *The Big Sleep* (46), *Killer McCoy* (47), *The Enforcer* (51), *Rio Bravo* (59), *The Comancheros* (61), *Requiem for a Gunfighter* (65), *Hang 'Em High* (68), *Rio Lobo* (70), *Something Big* (71)

## STEELE, Tommy (1936- )

This actor and singer was born Thomas Hicks in London, England. After service as a merchant seaman, he became popular in the mid-1950s as a pop singer, later developing into an all-round entertainer – especially in cockney roles. His biggest hit was *Half a Sixpence*, a musical that he starred in on the London and Broadway stages. He also made some movies.
**Selected Films:** *Rock Around the World* (57), *The Duke Wore Jeans* (58), *Tommy the Toreador* (59), *Light Up the Sky* (60), *The Dream Maker* (63), *The Happiest Millionaire* (67), *Half a Sixpence* (67), *Finian's Rainbow* (67), *Where's Jack?* (69).

## STEENBURGEN, Mary (1953- )

Born in Newport, Arizona, this talented leading actress studied drama at Hendrix College. While she was learning her acting craft, she worked in a Doubleday book shop in New York City. Steenburgen broke into films in 1978 in *Goin' South*, a

comedy Western in which she played a spinster who marries Jack Nicholson to save him from a lynch mob. She is married to actor Malcolm McDowell.
**Selected Films:** *Goin' South* (78), *Time After Time* (79), *Melvin and Howard* (80), *Ragtime* (81), *A Midsummer Night's Sex Comedy* (82), *Cross Creek* (83), *Dead of Winter* (87).

## STEIGER, Rod (1925- )

Born Rodney Stephen Steiger in Westhampton, New York, he quit high school at age 16 and joined the Navy, and served for the duration of World War II on a destroyer in the Pacific. He stayed on as a civilian clerk and began acting in amateur productions. Then it was on to New York City and serious theater studies, including a stint with the prestigious Actors Studio. Steiger, burly and imposing, emerged as one of the foremost method actors in the 1950s. His early work was in television, most notably in the title role of the television drama *Marty*. His first role in films was in a small part in *Teresa* (51), and then he exploded on the screen playing Marlon Brando's older brother in *On the Waterfront* (54). It earned him an Academy Award nomination for Best Supporting Actor. He received another Oscar nomination for *The Pawnbroker* (65), and finally won the Academy Award for *In the Heat of the Night* (67), playing the part of a bigoted Southern sheriff, a role that also won him the British Film Academy Award. Steiger's second wife was actress Claire Bloom.
**Selected Films:** *Teresa* (51), *On the Waterfront* (54), *The Big Knife* (54), *The Harder They Fall* (56), *Al Capone* (58), *Cry Terror* (58), *The Mark* (61), *The Pawnbroker* (65), *Doctor Zhivago* (65), *In the Heat of the Night* (67), *No Way to Treat a Lady* (68), *The Amityville Horror* (79), *The Chosen* (82), *The Kindred* (86), *American Gothic* (87).

## STEN, Anna (1908- )

She was born Annel (Anjuschka) Stenskaja Sudakevich in Kiev, Russia, the daughter of a Russian ballet master and a Swedish mother. After working as a waitress, she studied at the Moscow Art Theatre under Stanislavsky. She appeared in some Soviet films before moving to Germany, where her performance in the movie, *The Murderer Dmitri Karamazov* (31), caught the eye of Sam Goldwyn, who brought her to Hollywood. After several failed films, Goldwyn conceded she was no threat to Garbo or Dietrich and ended her contract. She continued to appear in some films, but her career was really over.
**Selected Films:** *When Moscow Laughs* (27), *Storm Over Asia* (28), *The Murderer Dmitri Karamazov* (31), *Tempest* (32), *Nana* (34), *The Wedding Night* (35), *Two Who Dared* (36), *Nile Express* (39), *The Man I Married* (40), *So Ends Our Night* (41), *Chetniks* (43), *Three Russian Girls* (44), *Let's Live a Little* (48), *Runaway Girls* (56), *The Nun and the Sergeant* (62).

## STEPHENS, Martin (1949- )

Born in England, Stephens was appearing in movies by the time he was 12 years old. His specialty was playing eerily obsessed or possessed children.
**Selected Films:** *The Hellfire Club* (61), *Village of the Damned* (62), *The Innocents* (62), *The Battle of the Villa Fiorita* (65), *The Witches* (66).

## STEPHENS, Robert (1931- )

Born in Bristol, England, this leading man and supporting player was trained at the Northern Theatre School in Bradford, and spent his first six professional years in repertory. He became the associate director of the National Theatre in 1967 and his second wife was actress Maggie Smith.
**Selected Films:** *A Taste of Honey* (61), *Cleopatra* (63), *Morgan!* (66), *Romeo and Juliet* (68), *The Prime of Miss Jean Brodie* (69), *The Private Life of Sherlock Holmes* (70), *Travels with My Aunt* (72), *The Duellists* (77), *Luther* (73), *The Shout* (78).

## STEPHENSON, Henry (1871-1956)

This veteran of the London and New York stage was born Henry S Garroway in Granada, British West Indies. He was sent to England to be educated at Rugby. Generally a character actor, he usually played kindly old gentlemen.
**Selected Films:** *The Spreading Dawn* (17), *Men and Women* (25), *Cynara* (32), *Little Women* (33), *Mutiny on the Bounty* (35), *Captain Blood* (35), *The Charge of the Light Brigade* (36), *The Prince and the Pauper* (37), *Suez* (38), *The Adventures of Sherlock Holmes* (39), *The Private Lives of Elizabeth and Essex* (39), *This Avove All* (42), *Mr Lucky* (43), *Night and Day* (46), *Oliver Twist* (48), *Challenge to Lassie* (49).

## STERLING, Ford (1883-1939)

This silent film clown was born George Ford Stitch in LaCrosse, Wisconsin, and he ran away from home to join the circus, appearing as Keno, the Boy Clown. He went on to vaudeville and the legitimate stage before joining Mack Sennett's company at Biograph in 1911, following him to Keystone in 1912 to star in many Keystone comedies. He was often a villain, but best remembered as Captain Teheezal of the Keystone Kops. Sterling later left Sennett to appear in feature films.
**Selected Films:** *Abe Gets Even with Father* (11), *A Bear Escape* (12), *Safe in Jail* (13), *The Hunt* (15), *His Wild Oats* (16), *Her Screen Idol* (18), *An Unhappy Finish* (21), *The Spoilers* (23), *The Show-Off* (26), *Gentlemen Prefer Blondes* (28), *Sally* (29), *Kismet* (30), *Alice in Wonderland* (33), *The Black Sheep* (35).

## STERLING, Jan (1923- )

Born Jane Sterling Adriance in New York City, she trained at Fay Compton's School in England,

making her Broadway debut in 1938 at the age of 15. Ten years later she was in the cast of the film *Johnny Belinda* (48). Sterling often played high class floozies in movies, and she was nominated for an Academy Award for Best Supporting Actress in *The High and the Mighty* (54), playing just that type of role. She was married to actor Paul Douglas.
**Selected Films:** *Johnny Belinda* (48), *Caged* (50), *Rhubarb* (51), *Flesh and Fury* (52), *Pony Express* (53), *The High and the Mighty* (54), *1984* (56), *Slaughter on Tenth Avenue* (57), *Love in a Goldfish Bowl* (61), *The Incident* (67), *The Minx* (69), *Sammy Somebody* (76).

## STERLING, Robert (1917- )

He was a second-string leading man of Hollywood features in the 1940s. Sterling was born William John Hart in New Castle, Pennsylvania, the son of Walter S Hart, a catcher for the Chicago Cubs baseball team. He was a clothing salesman before he broke into movies in *Only Angels Have Wings* (39). Although he was in scores of pictures, he is probably best remembered for his portrayal of George Kerby, one of the ghosts on the TV series *Topper*, playing opposite his second wife, Anne Jeffreys. His first wife was actress Ann Sothern.
**Selected Films:** *Only Angels Have Wings* (39), *Yesterday's Heroes* (40), *Johnny Eager* (42), *The Secret Heart* (46), *The Sundowners* (50), *Show Boat* (51), *Return to Peyton Place* (61), *Voyage to the Bottom of the Sea* (61), *A Global Affair* (64).

## STEVENS, Connie (1938- )

This perky, spunky actress-singer was born Concetta Ann Ingolia in Brooklyn, New York, and was winning talent contests at an early age. While in her teens, she started making teenage-oriented films in 1957. Meanwhile she was making recordings. She later became a leading actress on television (in the series *Hawaiian Eye*) and on Broadway (in *The Star Spangled Girl*). She was married to actor James Stacy and singer Eddie Fisher.
**Selected Films:** *Young and Dangerous* (57), *Rock-a-Bye Baby* (58), *The Party Crashers* (58), *Parrish* (61), *Susan Slade* (61), *Palm Springs Weekend* (63), *Never Too Late* (65), *Way . . . Way Out* (66), *The Grissom Gang* (71), *Scorchy* (76), *Back to the Beach* (87).

## STEVENS, Craig (1918- )

This native of Liberty, Missouri, was born Gail Shikles Jr, a schoolteacher's son. He became interested in acting while he was in pre-dental studies at the University of Kansas. Trained at Paramount's acting school and at the Pasadena Playhouse, he went on to stock. In 1941 he began his film career in leads in second features and supporting parts in major movies. He is best remembered for playing the title role on the TV detective series *Peter Gunn*. Stevens has been married to actress Alexis Smith for more than 40 years.
**Selected Films:** *Affectionately Yours* (41), *Spy Ship* (42), *The Doughgirls* (44), *Since You Went Away* (44), *Roughly Speaking* (45), *Humoresque* (46), *The Man I Love* (47), *Night Unto Night* (49), *Where the Sidewalk Ends* (50), *Murder Without Tears* (53), *The French Line* (54), *The Deadly Mantis* (57), *Gunn* (67), *The Limbo Line* (68), *S.O.B.* (81).

## STEVENS, Inger (1934-1970)

The product of a broken home, she was born Inger Stensland in Stockholm, Sweden, and came to the United States at the age of 13 with her father, who was on a Fullbright Scholarship to Harvard University. When he remarried and moved to Manhattan, Kansas, she ran away from home, making her show business debut in a Kansas City burlesque house at the age of 16. Stevens went to New York two years later, working in the garment district and as a chorus girl in the Latin Quarter while studying at the Actors Studio. She got work in television commercials and TV plays. In 1957 she broke into films with *Man on Fire* and gradually became a star, especially after her hit television situation comedy *The Farmer's Daughter.* Her personal life was not so bright. She went through a divorce after being married but four months; she had unhappy romances with prominent personalities, including Bing Crosby before he married for the last time. Stevens attempted suicide in 1959, and in 1970 died of an overdose of barbiturates.
**Selected Films:** *Man on Fire* (57), *Cry Terror* (58), *The Buccaneer* (58), *The World, the Flesh and the Devil* (59), *The New Interns* (64), *A Guide for the Married Man* (67), *Madigan* (68), *Hang 'Em High* (68), *House of Cards* (69), *A Dream of Kings* (69).

## STEVENS, K T (1919- )

The daughter of director Sam Wood, she was born Gloria Wood in Hollywood, California, and educated at the University of Southern California. She began in plays and movies as a child, billing herself as Katherine Stevens. In the 1940s and 1950s she played leading and supporting roles in films, turning to character parts later. For a time she was married to actor Hugh Marlow, with whom she had toured in John Van Druten's hit play, *The Voice of the Turtle.*
**Selected Films:** *Peck's Bad Boy* (34), *Kitty Foyle* (40), *The Great Man's Lady* (42), *Address Unknown* (44), *Port of New York* (49), *Harriet Craig* (50), *Vice Squad* (53), *Missile to the Moon* (58), *Bob & Carol & Ted & Alice* (69), *Pets* (74).

## STEVENS, Mark (1915- )

Born Richard Stevens in Cleveland, Ohio, he has, at various times, billed himself as Mark Stevens, Stephen Richards and Paul Mark Stevens, the latter probably to avoid being mistaken for Mark (or Marc) Stevens, a star of porno movies. After

studying painting, he appeared on stage and in radio in Canada, and became a radio announcer. His film career began in the early 1940s.
**Selected Films:** *Passage to Marseilles* (44), *Objective Burma* (45), *Pride of the Marines* (45), *The Snake Pit* (48), *Dancing in the Dark* (49), *Target Unknown* (51), *Torpedo Alley* (52), *Cry Vengeance* (54), *September Storm* (60), *Fate Is the Hunter* (64), *Frozen Alive* (66).

## STEVENS, Onslow (1902-1977)

Born Onslow Ford Stevens in Los Angeles, California, he was the son of character actor Houseley Stevenson. He made his acting debut at the Pasadena Community Playhouse in 1926 and later divided his time between Broadway and Hollywood, often playing heavies and character parts.
**Selected Films:** *Heroes of the West* (32), *The Three Musketeers* (36), *Under Two Flags* (36), *When Tomorrow Comes* (39), *House of Dracula* (45), *O.S.S.* (46), *The Night Has a Thousand Eyes* (48), *State Penitentiary* (50), *Them* (54), *All the Fine Young Cannibals* (60), *Geronimo's Revenge* (63).

## STEVENS, Rïse (1913- )

This all-American operatic mezzo-soprano was born in New York City. She had a brilliant career at the Metropolitan Opera and later became an opera administrator. She was beautiful, and made a fine contribution to the few films that she was in.
**Selected Films:** *The Chocolate Soldier* (41), *Going My Way* (44), *Carnegie Hall* (47).

## STEVENS, Stella (1936- )

This delectable blonde actress was born Estelle Egglestone in Hot Coffee, Mississippi, and educated at Memphis State University. After being a sensation as a *Playboy* magazine centerfold, she first gained motion picture attention as the vamp, Appasionata von Climax, in the film version of *Li'l Abner* (59), and went on to become a respected actress.
**Selected Films:** *Li'l Abner* (59), *Say One for Me* (59), *The Courtship of Eddie's Father* (63), *The Nutty Professor* (63), *Synanon* (65), *The Mad Room* (69), *The Ballad of Cable Hogue* (70), *The Poseidon Adventure* (72), *Arnold* (73), *Nickelodeon* (76), *The Manitou* (78).

## STEWART, Elaine (1929- )

Born Elsa Steinberg in Montclair, New Jersey, this striking leading lady got her start in show business as an usherette and cashier in a Montclair movie theater. She became a model and broke into films in the early 1950s.
**Selected Films:** *Sailor Beware* (51), *The Bad and the Beautiful* (52), *Young Bess* (53), *Take the High Ground* (53), *Brigadoon* (54), *Night Passage* (57), *Escort West* (59), *The Rise and Fall of Legs Diamond* (60), *The Most Dangerous Man Alive* (61).

*James Stewart in* The Shop Around the Corner *(39).*

## STEWART, James (1908- )

This leading actor with his inimitable slow drawl and gangly walk has been playing honest heroes for over 50 years. He is appealingly shy, the gawky nice fellow with the nasal voice who epitomizes the best of American small town values, the on-screen embodiment of good sense, modesty and decencey. Yet the unassuming characters that he creates are never maudlin, dull or foolishly sentimental, and they never strike a false note. Born in Indiana, Pennsylvania, a small town which loves him and which he loves, Stewart first acted in a Boy Scout play and became an amateur magician and accordionist. He attended Princeton University, appearing in college productions and taking a degree in architecture. He was persuaded to follow his true love, the theater, and joined an acting group which included Henry Fonda and Margaret Sullavan. He and Fonda became close friends although political differences later came between them, as Fonda was a supporter of liberal causes and Stewart became a strong conservative. Sullavan had Stewart cast in many of her films once she reached Hollywood. Although at first an unusual leading man and hero, Stewart's sincerity and his air of being slightly embarrassed at all times caught on with the public. He was simply great in *You Can't Take It With You* (38), *Mr Smith Goes to Washington* (39) and *The Philadelphia Story* (40), which brought him an Academy Award. During World War II he became a bomber pilot and achieved the rank of full colonel. He was a brigadier general in the Air Force Reserve until retiring in 1968, the highest-ranking Hollywood entertainer in the United States military. Stewart moved smoothly into a wider variety of roles after the war, dazzling critics and fans alike with his wonderful performance in the gentle *Harvey* (50), in which he played the mild-mannered alcoholic, Elwood P Dowd – the only one who can see the giant rabbit after whom the movie was named. He also played detectives, western heroes and had the lead in Alfred Hitchcock blockbusters. Despite his position as one of Hollywood's top personalities, he has kept his private life private, and has been

married to the same woman since 1941.
**Selected Films:** *Murder Man* (35), *Next Time We Love* (36), *Rose Marie* (36), *Wife Versus Sectretary* (36), *The Gorgeous Hussy* (36), *Born to Dance* (36), *Seventh Heaven* (37), *Navy Blue and Gold* (37), *Of Human Hearts* (38), *Vivacious Lady* (38), *You Can't Take It With You* (38), *It's a Wonderful World* (39), *Mr Smith Goes to Washington* (39), *Destry Rides Again* (39), *The Shop Around the Corner* (39), *The Mortal Storm* (40), *No Time for Comedy* (40), *The Philadelphia Story* (40), *It's a Wonderful Life* (46), *Magic Town* (47), *Call Northside 777* (47), *Rope* (48), *The Stratton Story* (49), *Winchester 73* (50), *Broken Arrow* (50), *Harvey* (50), *No Highway in the Sky* (50), *The Greatest Show on Earth* (51), *Carbine Williams* (52), *The Glenn Miller Story* (53), *Rear Window* (54), *Strategic Air Command* (55), *The Man from Laramie* (55), *The Man Who Knew Too Much* (56), *The Spirit of St Louis* (57), *Vertigo* (58), *Bell, Book and Candle* (58), *Anatomy of a Murder* (59), *The Man Who Shot Liberty Valance* (62), *Mr Hobbs Takes a Vacation* (62), *How the West Was Won* (62), *Take Her, She's Mine* (63), *Cheyenne Autumn* (64), *Shenandoah* (65), *The Flight of the Phoenix* (65), *The Rare Breed* (66), *The Cheyenne Social Club* (70), *The Shootist* (76), *The Magic of Lassie* (78), *The Green Horizon* (81).

## STEWART, Paul (1908-1986)

Born in New York City, Stewart made his film debut in Orson Welles' *Citizen Kane* (41), and went on to appear in some 50 films, usually cast as the villain. He married Peg LaCentra, a singer with Artie Shaw's band, in 1939, and they often appeared on radio dramas together.
**Selected Films:** *Citizen Kane,* (41), *Johnny Eager* (42), *Champion* (49), *The Bad and the Beautiful* (52), *In Cold Blood* (67), *The Day of the Locust* (75), *Tempest* (82).

## STING, (1951- )

Sting was born George Sumner in Newcastle, England, and came into prominence as a member of a rock group, Police. He began his film career in the 1980s as an actor, rather than a singer.
**Selected Films:** *Dune* (84), *Plenty* (84), *The Bride* (85).

## STOCKWELL, Dean (1936- )

When he broke into films it was as a curly-headed child star in *The Valley of Decision* (45), but he grew up into a sensitive and intense leading man. Born in Hollywood, California, he made his acting debut at the age of seven in *The Innocent Voyage* on Broadway. He grew up successfully in his films, but as an adult had better roles on television than in movies. Stockwell was formerly married to actress Millie Perkins, and is the brother of actor Guy Stockwell.
**Selected Films:** *Valley of Decision* (45), *Anchors Aweigh* (45), *The Green Years* (46), *Gentleman's Agreement* (47), *The Boy With Green Hair* (48), *The Secret Garden* (49), *Kim* (50) *The Careless Years* (57), *Compulsion* (59), *Sons and Lovers* (60), *Long Day's Journey into Night* (62), *Psych-Out* (68), *The Dunwich Horror* (70), *The Loners* (72), *Win, Place or Steal* (75), *Tracks* (77), *Wrong is Right* (82), *Dune* (84), *Blue Velvet* (86), *Gardens of Stone* (87).

## STOCKWELL, Guy (1938- )

Born in Hollywood, California, the younger brother of actor Dean Stockwell, he made his acting debut on Broadway with his brother in *The Innocent Voyage* when he was five years old. Stockwell later became a respected leading actor.
**Selected Films:** *The War Lord* (65), *Blindfold* (65), *And Now Miguel* (66), *Beau Geste* (66), *The Plainsman* (66), *Tobruk* (66), *In Enemy Country* (68), *The Gatling Gun* (72), *Airport 75* (74), *It's Alive!* (76).

## STONE, George E (1903-1967)

George E 'Georgie' Stone was born George Stein in Lodz, Poland, but grew up in the United States. He started in show business as a child, doing song-and-dance in vaudeville and made many movies while he was still in his teens. His first adult role was as the Sewer Rat in *Seventh Heaven* (27) and he went on to play character roles in almost 200 movies, often as a comic gangster. He also played 'The Runt,' Boston Blackie's pal, in several films.
**Selected Films:** *Children of the Feud* (16), *Jackie* (21), *Seventh Heaven* (27), *Melody Lane* (29), *Little Caesar* (31), *The Front Page* (31), *The Last Mile* (32), *42nd Street* (33), *Bullets or Ballots* (36), *Mr Moto's Gamble* (38), *Northwest Mounted Police* (40), *Confessions of Boston Blackie* (41), *Abie's Irish Rose* (46), *Guys and Dolls* (55), *The Man with the Golden Arm* (55), *Some Like It Hot* (59), *Pocketful of Miracles* (61).

## STONE, Lewis (1879-1953)

Stone was born in Worcester, Massachusetts, and as a young man became a matinee idol on Broadway. After his movie debut in *The Man Who Found Out* (15) and a few other films, he served as a major in World War I. After the war, he became a popular leading man in such films as *The Prisoner of Zenda* (22), and was nominated for an Academy Award for Best Actor for *The Patriot* (28). After sound came, he continued playing leads and then shifted to character parts, most notably as the kindly Judge Hardy in the *Andy Hardy* series.
**Selected Films:** *The Man Who Found Out* (15), *The River's End* (20), *The Prisoner of Zenda* (22), *Scaramouche* (23), *The Lost World* (25), *The Patriot* (28), *Madame X* (29), *The Big House* (30), *The Sin of Madelon Claudet* (31), *Mata Hari* (31), *Grand Hotel* (32), *Queen Christina* (33), *Treasure Island* (34), *David Copperfield* (35), *You're Only Young Once* (37), *Yellow Jack* (38), *The Hoodlum Saint* (46), *State of the Union* (48), *Any Number Can Play* (49), *It's a Big Country* (52), *All the Brothers Were Valiant* (53).

## STONE, Milburn (1904-1980)

Born in Burton, Kansas, he toured with repertory companies for ten years before making his screen debut in *The Milky Way* (36), and went on to play leads of low-budget action features and supporting actors in more expensive films. Later he became a villainous supporting character actor, and ended his career as the gruff Doc Adams on the TV series *Gunsmoke*, for which he won an Emmy in 1968.

**Selected Films:** *The Milky Way* (36), *China Clipper* (36), *Crime School* (38), *Young Mr Lincoln* (39), *Reap the Wild Wind* (42), *Gung Ho!* (43), *Jungle Woman* (44), *The Spider Woman Strikes Back* (46), *Calamity Jane and Sam Bass* (49), *Branded* (51), *Pickup on South Street* (53), *Black Tuesday* (55), *The Long Gray Line* (55), *Drango* (57).

## STOOGES, The Three

This comedy team specializing in violent, and sometimes vulgar, slapstick started out with but two members. The team was formed in vaudeville in 1923 by two brothers, Moe Howard (1897-1975, from Brooklyn, New York) and his brother Shemp (1900-1955, born Samuel Howard, also in Brooklyn). The two played second bananas to comedian Ted Healy (1886-1937) in an act called 'Ted Healy and His Stooges.' Five years later the two became three, with the addition of Larry Fine (1911-1974, from Philadelphia, Pennsylvania). They were brought to Hollywood by Healy as supporting players in *Soup to Nuts* (30), where they called themselves 'The Racketeers.' Then Shemp saw an opportunity to strike out on his own, and Moe and Larry were joined by another Howard brother, Curly (1906-1952, born Jerome Howard in Brooklyn). These Three Stooges occasionally appeared in feature films and in 1934 began making two-reel comedies – the longest-running series in the history of Hollywood. About 200 shorts were made between 1934 and 1958, with the boys hitting each other, gouging each other's eyes, kicking each other, and dousing each other. Curly left the team after having a stroke in 1946 and was replaced by his brother Shemp. After Shemp died, he was replaced by Joe Besser (1900-1972), and Besser was replaced by Joe De Rita – 'Curly Joe' – in 1959, when the team began making feature films because of their new-found popularity among the young caused by the release of their old comedies to television.

**Selected Films:** *Soup to Nuts* (30), *Dancing Lady* (33), *The Captain Hates the Sea* (34), *Start Cheering* (38), *My Sister Eileen* (42), *Swing Parade of 1946* (46), *Have Rocket, Will Travel* (59), *Stop, Look and Laugh* (60), *Snow White and the Three Stooges* (61), *The Three Stooges in Orbit* (62), *It's a Mad Mad Mad Mad World* (63), *Four for Texas* (63), *The Outlaws Is Coming* (65).

## STORM, Gale (1922- )

Born Josephine Owaissa Cottle in Bloomington, Texas, this wholesome little girl won a radio 'Gateway to Hollywood' contest while she was still in high school. After a rather lack-luster film career, she became a star on television in *My Little Margie* and *The Gale Storm Show* – both of them situation comedies.

**Selected Films:** *Tom Brown's School Days* (40), *Foreign Agent (42)*, *Revenge of the Zombies* (43), *Forever Yours* (45), *It Happened on Fifth Avenue* (47), *The Dude Goes West* (48), *Stampede* (49), *The Texas Rangers* (51), *Women of the North Country* (52).

## STOSSEL, Ludwig (1883-1973)

Stossel, who was born in Lockenhaus, Austria, began acting on the stage when he was 17 years old. He left Austria in the 1930s, went to London, and arrived in Hollywood in 1940. Stossel went on to play character parts in numerous movies, usually as kindly middle-European types. He was excellent playing Gary Cooper's father in *The Pride of the Yankees* (42) – a biopic of the life of Lou Gehrig. Stossel was also memorable in a long series of television commercials as 'The Little Old Winemaker.'

**Selected Films:** *Bockbierfest* (30), *O Schwarzwald! O Heimat!* (36), *Four Sons* (40), *Woman of the Year* (42), *The Pride of the Yankees* (42), *Casablanca* (43), *Dillinger* (45), *The Beginning or the End* (47), *The Merry Widow* (52), *Me and the Colonel* (58), *The Blue Angel* (59), *GI Blues* (60).

## STRAIGHT, Beatrice (1918- )

Straight was born in Old Westbury, New York, and had a fine career on the stage before entering films, appearing in such Broadway plays as *A Streetcar Named Desire*, *The Heiress*, *Ghosts*, *The Lion in the Winter*, and winning a Tony Award in *The Crucible*. She won the Academy Award for Best

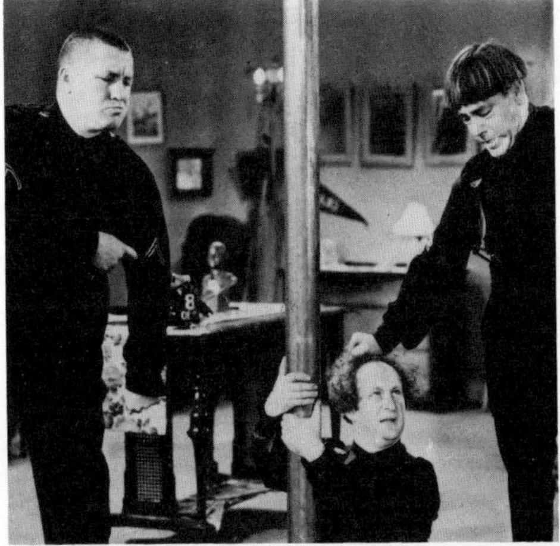

*The Three Stooges.*

Supporting Actress for *Network* (76), in which she played a deserted wife. She also has done television work.
**Selected Films:** *Phone Call from a Stranger* (52), *Patterns* (56), *The Nun's Story* (59), *Network* (76), *The Promise* (78), *The Formula* (80), *Endless Love* (81), *Poltergeist* (82).

## STRANGE, Glenn (1899-1973)

Born in Weed, New Mexico, of Irish-Cherokee Indian parentage, he worked as a rancher, a deputy sheriff and a rodeo performer before entering show business as a member of the Arizona Wranglers radio singing group. Entering films in the mid-1930s, he played supporting roles in scores of B western films – often as the villain. He went on to play the Frankenstein Monster, and ended his career as Sam, the bartender of the Long Branch Saloon, in the TV series *Gunsmoke*.
**Selected Films:** *The New Frontier* (35), *Arizona Days* (37), *Range War* (39), *The Mad Monster* (42), *Action in the North Atlantic* (43), *House of Frankenstein* (45), *House of Dracula* (45), *Abbott and Costello Meet Frankenstein* (48), *Red River* (48), *The Red Badge of Courage* (51), *The Vanishing American* (55), *Quantrill's Raiders* (58).

## STRASBERG, Lee (1901-1982)

He was born in Budzanow, Austria, but was raised in the United States from the age of nine. He trained at the American Laboratory Theatre and made his stage debut in 1925. One of the founders of the Group Theatre in New York City in 1930, he became the artistic director of the Actors Studio in 1948, and he established the Lee Strasberg Institute of the Theatre in New York and Los Angeles, California in 1969. After helping countless stars to make a name for themselves, he finally made his screen debut in 1974, at the age of 73, as the mobster Hyman Roth in *The Godfather, Part II*, for which he received a nomination for an Academy Award for Best Supporting Actor. He was the father of actress Susan Strasberg.
**Selected Films:** *The Godfather, Part II* (74), *The Cassandra Crossing* (77), *Boardwalk* (79), *And Justice for All* (79), *Going in Style* (79).

## STRASBERG, Susan (1938- )

Strasberg was born in New York City to Lee and Paula Strasberg, the founders of the Actors Studio. Although she was raised in the limelight of the stage, she did not go to her parent's school, making her stage debut off-Broadway at the age of 14. She won plaudits for her performance as the Jewish girl in *The Diary of Anne Frank* on Broadway. She has since played gentle leads in the movies.
**Selected Films:** *The Cobweb* (55), *Picnic* (56), *Hemingway's Adventures of a Young Man* (62), *The Brotherhood* (68), *Sweet Hunters* (69), *Sammy Somebody* (76), *In Praise of Older Women* (78).

## STRAUSS, Peter (1947- )

Strauss was born in Croton-on-Hudson, New York, and was educated at Northwestern University. He made his film debut in *Hail Hero* (69), and is most famous for his performance in the television mini-series *Rich Man, Poor Man*.
**Selected Films:** *Hail Hero* (69), *Soldier Blue* (70), *The Last Tycoon* (76), *The Man Without a Country* (73), *A Whale for the Killing* (81).

## STRAUSS, Robert (1913-1975)

This burly character actor of the stage and screen was born in New York City, and his father was a theater costume designer. Before he broke into acting, Strauss worked as a busboy, a salesman and a singing waiter. He was outstanding in the role of 'Animal' in the Broadway production of *Stalag 17*, and when he recreated the role in the film version of 1953, he was nominated for an Academy Award for Best Supporting Actor.
**Selected Films:** *Sailor Beware* (52), *Jumping Jacks* (52), *Stalag 17* (53), *The Bridges of Toko-Ri* (55), *The Seven Year Itch* (55), *The Man With the Golden Arm* (55), *Li'l Abner* (59), *Wake Me When It's Over* (60), *The Thrill of It All* (63), *Harlow* (65), *Fort Utah* (67), *Dagmar's Hot Pants* (71).

## STREEP, Meryl (1951- )

Blonde and delicately beautiful, Streep is one of the brightest stars to appear in years, a winner of numerous awards and much critical acclaim. Born in Basking Ridge, New Jersey, she began to take voice lessons at the age of 12, aiming at a career as an opera singer. But her appearances in high school plays made her decide to become an actress. She majored in drama at Vassar College, and then attended the Yale University School of Drama. After playing leads in several productions of the Yale Repertory Theater she went to New York and appeared successfully in a number of Broadway plays, among them *27 Wagons Full of Cotton*, by Tennessee Williams, for which she was nominated for a Tony Award. In 1976 she joined the New York Shakespearean Festival, and in the following year she made her screen debut in *Julia* (77), rising to the top in films almost instantly. She was nominated for an Academy Award as Best Supporting Actress for *The Deer Hunter* (78) and won the National Society of Film Critics Award for her role. She also won an Emmy Award for her performance in the television drama *Holocaust*. She later won an Academy Award for Best Supporting Actress for *Kramer vs Kramer* (79), and an Oscar for Best Actress for *Sophie's Choice* (82).
**Selected Films:** *Julia* (77), *The Deer Hunter* (78), *Manhattan* (79), *The Seduction of Joe Tynan* (79), *Kramer vs Kramer* (79), *The French Lieutenant's Woman* (81), *Sophie's Choice* (82), *Still of the Night* (82), *Silkwood* (83), *Falling in Love* (84), *Out of Africa* (85), *Plenty* (85), *Heartburn* (86), *Tina* (87).

*Meryl Streep and Kevin Kline in* Sophie's Choice *(82).*

## STREISAND, Barbra (1942- )

Born in Brooklyn, New York, this self-confident charismatic presence with a voice of glorious brass made her own way to the top of her profession. After she graduated from high school she worked as a switchboard operator while trying to become an actress. Her first big break came at the age of 18 when she won a talent contest in 1960 at The Lion, a Greenwich Village, New York, night club. She went on to have some modest success in night clubs and appeared in an off-Broadway review before making a big impression playing Miss Marmelstein in the 1962 Broadway musical *I Can Get It For You Wholesale*. She won the New York Critics Award for her performance opposite Elliott Gould, whom she married in 1963 and divorced in 1971. Superstardom seemed to come almost overnight. She was a sensation playing Fanny Brice in the Broadway musical hit *Funny Girl*; she gained the notice of the nation appearing on television with Judy Garland; she continued to play supper clubs. In her first film, again as Fanny Brice in the movie version of *Funny Girl* (68), she was good enough to win an Academy Award as best actress. In 1970, proving that Broadway had not forgotten her, she received a special Tony Award for being the best actress of the decade. During her career she has had her ups and downs on screen. She has been able to mesmerize audiences as Fanny Brice or Dolly Levi in *Hello Dolly!* (69), and her performance with Robert Redford in *The Way We Were* (73) helped to make that motion picture become a great romantic classic. But she has also embarrassed her fans by donning boxing gloves and sparring with Ryan O'Neal in *The Main Event* (79). She wrote, produced, directed and starred in *Yentl* (83). When she made the popular *A Star Is Born* (76), a resetting of the classic Judy Garland film of 1954, invidious comparisons were made between her and Garland, but she won another Academy Award for composing the song 'Evergreen' for the picture. Along the way, she has picked up five Emmys and seven Grammys.
**Selected Films:** *Funny Girl* (68), *Hello Dolly!* (69), *On a Clear Day You Can See Forever* (70), *The Owl and the Pussycat* (70), *What's Up, Doc?* (72), *Up the Sandbox* (72), *The Way We Were* (73), *For Pete's Sake* (74), *Funny Lady* (75), *A Star Is Born* (76), *The Main Event* (79), *All Night Long* (81), *Yentl* (83).

## STRITCH, Elaine (1926- )

Stritch is a character comedienne of stage, screen and television. Born in Detroit, Michigan, she studies with Erwin Piscator at the Dramatic Workshop of the New School in New York City. She made her debut on Broadway in 1946, and became a star of the stage. Her movie appearances have been few, but she has distinguished herself. She married an English actor, John Bay, in 1973, and moved to London, where she has appeared as the star of the British TV series, *Two's Company*.
**Selected Films:** *The Scarlet Hour* (56), *A Farewell to Arms* (57), *The Perfect Furlough* (59), *Who Killed Teddy Bear?* (65), *Pigeons* (70), *The Spiral Staircase* (75), *Providence* (77).

## STRODE, Woody (1914- )

Woodrow Strode was born in Los Angeles, California, and educated at the University of California at Los Angeles. A star end in the Canadian Football League, and later a professional wrestler, he made his film debut in *Sundown* (41). It wasn't until 1960 that he was given a decent role on screen – in the title role of John Ford's *Sergeant Rutledge*, in which he played a black cavalryman accused of rape and murder. He has been given meatier roles ever since.
**Selected Films:** *Sundown* (41), *The Gambler from Natchez* (54), *The Ten Commandments* (56), *Pork Chop Hill* (59), *Sergeant Rutledge* (60), *Spartacus* (60), *The Sins of Rachel Cade* (61), *The Man Who Shot Liberty Valance* (62), *Genghis Khan* (65), *Black Jesus* (68), *Shalako* (68), *Che!* (69), *The Last Rebel* (71), *The Gatling Gun* (73), *Winter Hawk* (75), *Kingdom of the Spiders* (77), *Key West Crossing* (79), *The Black Stallion Returns* (83).

## STROUD, Don (1937- )

Born in Hawaii, he made his screen debut in *Games* (67), and has developed into a solid leading man. Stroud is usually seen in tough, gutsy roles.
**Selected Films:** *Games* (67), *Madigan* (68), *Coogan's Bluff* (68), *Bloody Mama* (70), *The Killer Inside Me* (78), *Sudden Death* (77), *The Choirboys* (77), *Search and Destroy* (78), *The Buddy Holly Story* (78), *The Amityville Horror* (79).

## STRUDWICK, Shepperd: See SHEPPERD, John

## STUART, Gloria (1910- )

This glamorous blonde leading lady of Hollywood films of the 1930s was born Gloria Stuart Finch in Santa Monica, California, and was educated at the University of Californa, Berkeley. After some stage work, she made her film debut in 1932. Stuart retired from acting in the mid-1940s, and took up painting. She was talented enough to have a one-woman show in New York in 1961.

**Selected Films:** *The Old Dark House* (32), *Back Street* (32), *The Invisible Man* (33), *Roman Scandals* (33), *Here Comes the Navy* (34), *The Prisoner of Shark Island* (36), *Rebbecca of Sunnybrook Farm* (38), *The Three Musketeers* (39), *The Whistler* (44), *She Wrote the Book* (46), *My Favorite Year* (82).

## SULLAVAN, Margaret (1911-1960)

Sullavan was born Margaret Brooke in Norfolk, Virginia. She studied dance and drama from the time she was a child and made her professional debut at the age of 17 with the University Players, along with other young actors, including Henry Fonda and James Stewart. She first appeared on Broadway in 1931 and Universal Pictures signed her to a contract in 1933. She was good at both drama and sophisticated comedy, but her clashes with her studio often sent her back to Broadway. Hollywood often cast her in women's pictures, and she won the New York Film Critics Award for playing Robert Taylor's tubercular wife in *Three Comrades* (38). She also won the New York Drama Critics Award for her role on Broadway in *The Voice of the Turtle* (43). She retired from the screen in 1943, returning only to appear in *No Sad Songs for Me* (50), when she was almost completely deaf. She died of suicide at age 49 by an overdose of barbiturates. The first three of her four husbands were actor Henry Fonda, director William Wyler and producer-agent Leland Hayward.

**Selected Films:** *Only Yesterday* (33), *So Red the Rose* (35), *Next Time We Love* (36), *Three Comrades* (38), *The Shopworn Angel* (38), *The Shop Around the Corner* (40), *The Mortal Storm* (40), *Back Street* (41), *Cry Havoc* (43), *No Sad Songs for Me* (50).

## SULLIVAN, Barry (1912- )

Sullivan was born Patrick Barry in New York City, and was educated at Temple University. Before he made his Broadway debut in 1936 he worked as a theater usher and a buyer for a department store. After arriving in Hollywood in the early 1940s he became a dependable leading man, often appearing in thrillers and gangster movies.

**Selected Films:** *Woman of the Town* (43), *Lady in the Dark* (44), *Framed* (47), *The Great Gatsby* (49), *Payment on Demand* (51), *Jeopardy* (53), *Forty Guns* (57), *The Light in the Piazza* (62), *A Gathering of Eagles* (63), *Harlow* (65), *Buckskin* (68), *This Savage Land* (69), *Tell Them Willie Boy Is Here* (70), *Earthquake* (74), *Oh God!* (77), *Caravans* (78), *Casino* (79).

## SULLIVAN, Francis L (1903-1956)

This heavyweight character actor of stage and screen was born in London, England. He first appeared on stage in 1921, and made his film debut in *The Missing Rembrandt* (33). For more than 20 years Sullivan appeared in movies, often as a villain or a barrister.

**Selected Films:** *The Missing Rembrandt* (33), *Great Expectations* (34), *The Mystery of Edwin Drood* (35), *The Citadel* (38), *The Avengers* (42), *Caesar and Cleopatra* (45), *Great Expectations* (46), *Oliver Twist* (48), *Joan of Arc* (48), *The Winslow Boy* (48), *The Red Danube* (49), *My Favorite Spy* (51), *Drums of Tahiti* (54), *The Prodigal* (55), *Hell's Island* (55).

## SUMMERVILLE, Slim (1892-1946)

The lanky, naive-looking character actor was born George J Sommerville in Albuquerque, New Mexico. Raised in Canada and Oklahoma, Summerville joined the Mack Sennett troupe in 1913, becoming a member of the Keystone Kops and part-time gag writer. Moving on to the Sunshine Comedy studios at Fox, he became a director of comedy shorts in the early 1920s. In the late 1920s he switched back to acting, and made a series of feature comedies with ZaSu Pitts. Summerville's most memorable role was as the German private, Tjaden, in *All Quiet on the Western Front* (30).

**Selected Films:** *The Knockout* (14), *Tillie's Punctured Romance* (14), *The Three Slims* (16), *Skirts* (21), *The Chinese Parrot* (27), *Tiger Rose* (29), *All Quiet on the Western Front* (30), *The King of Jazz* (31), *The Spoilers* (31), *The Front Page* (31), *Tom Brown of Culver* (31), *Love Birds* (34), *The Farmer Takes a Wife* (35), *Pepper* (36), *The Road Back* (37), *Rebecca of Sunnybrook Farm* (38), *Jesse James* (39), *Western Union* (41), *Tobacco Road* (41), *The Hoodlum Saint* (46).

## SUTHERLAND, Donald (1934- )

Born in St John, New Brunswick, Canada and educated at the University of Toronto, he began acting during his college days. In 1956 he went England to study at the London Academy of Music and Dramatic Art, making several appearances on the London stage before making his screen debut in 1964, playing a dual role in an Italian horror picture, *Castle of the Living Dead*. Tall, talented and imposing, he played low-key supporting parts until he soared to stardom as Captain Benjamin Franklin 'Hawkeye' Pierce, the irreverent Army surgeon, in *M*A*S*H* (70). He has since remained a most popular actor in pictures, at his best in off-beat movies.

**Selected Films:** *Castle of the Living Dead* (64), *The Dirty Dozen* (67), *M*A*S*H* (70), *Klute* (71), *Don't Look Now* (73), *The Day of the Locust* (75), *1900* (76), *Casanova* (76), *Invasion of the Body Snatchers* (78), *Murder by Decree* (79), *Ordinary People* (80), *Eye of the Needle* (81), *Revolution* (85).

## SUTTON, Grady (1908- )

Born in Chattanooga, Tennessee, he went to Hollywood when he was 16, and grew up to play slow-witted rural yokels or small-town business men in many pictures. This flabby character comedian was at his best as the foil of W C Fields.
**Selected Films:** *This Reckless Age* (32), *College Humor* (33), *Alice Adams* (36), *My Man Godfrey* (36), *Stage Door* (37), *Alexander's Ragtime Band* (38), *You Can't Cheat an Honest Man* (39), *It's a Wonderful World* (30), *The Bank Dick* (40), *A Lady Takes a Chance* (43), *Since You went Away* (44), *A Bell for Adano* (45), *Anchors Aweigh* (45), *My Wild Irish Rose* (47), *A Star is Born* (54), *White Christmas* (54), *Jumbo* (62), *My Fair Lady* (64), *Myra Breckinridge* (70), *Support Your Local Gunfighter* (71).

## SUTTON, John (1908-1963)

Sutton was born to British parents in Rawalpindi, India, and as a young man spent 10 years in various British colonies as a hunter, rancher and plantation manager. Hollywood used him as a technical advisor in the mid-1930s on films with a British Empire setting. He began his career as a handsome leading man in *Bulldog Drummond Comes Back* (37), and went on to carve out a fine reputation in adventure films, especially swashbucklers.
**Selected Films:** *Bulldog Drummond Comes Back* (37), *Tower of London* (39), *The Invisible Man Returns* (40), *Hudson's Bay* (41), *A Yank in the RAF* (41), *My Gal Sal* (42), *Tonight We Raid Calais* (43), *Jane Eyre* (44), *Captain from Castile* (48), *The Three Musketeers* (48), *David and Bathsheba* (51), *My Cousin Rachel* (52), *Sangaree* (53), *Beloved Infidel* (59), *The Canadians* (61), *Of Human Bondage* (64).

## SVENSON, Bo (1941- )

Born in Sweden, he came to the United States in 1958. Educated at the University of California, Los Angeles, he began his film career in *The Great Waldo Pepper* (74), and went on to become the lead in several action pictures. He had previously served with the United States Marine Corps and had been a professional hockey player, a race car driver and a judo champion.
**Selected Films:** *The Great Waldo Pepper* (74), *Part II: Walking Tall* (75), *The Breaking Point* (75), *Final Chapter Walking Tall* (76), *Son of the Sheik* (78), *The Snow Beast* (78), *North Dallas Forty* (79), *Counterfeit Commandos* (81), *Choke Canyon* (86), *Heartbreak Ridge* (87).

## SWANSON, Gloria (1897-1983)

This silent film star had glamour and she was Hollywood's leading box office draw from 1918 to 1926. Swanson was born Josephine Swensen in Chicago, Illinois, and appeared in her first movie, *The Meal Ticket* (15) at the age of 18. A genius at self-promotion, she caused fans to go mad over her high-fashion clothes, her marriage to a genuine marquis and her exceptional sultry beauty. Swanson married Wallace Beery in 1916 and made romantic comedies for Mack Sennett, starting as a Mack Sennett bathing beauty. Dramas and suggestive comedies were her forte and it was director Cecil B de Mille who made her a star in such films as *Male and Female* (19). She formed her own production company and starred in the phenomenally successful *Sadie Thompson* (28). But she lost most of her money producing *Queen Kelly* (28), which was not released in the United States in her lifetime. Swanson continued to appear, although less frequently, in films in the 1930s and 1940s, and then had a triumph as the aging silent film star and recluse in *Sunset Boulevard* (50), in which Cecil B de Mille had a small part as himself. It was her best picture, and her performance as an ebbing, insane film star was universally applauded and earned her her third Academy Award nomination. She had previously been nominated for *Sadie Thompson* and *The Trespasser* (30).
**Selected Films:** *The Meal Ticket* (15), *Teddy at the Throttle* (17), *Shifting Sands* (18), *Don't Change Your Husband* (18), *Male and Female* (19), *Why Change Your Wife?* (19), *The Affairs of Anatol* (21), *Adam's Rib* (23), *Madame Sans Gene* (25), *Untamed Lady* (26), *Sadie Thompson* (28), *Queen Kelly* (28), *The Trespasser* (30), *Indiscreet* (31), *Perfect Understanding* (33), *Music in the Air* (34), *Father Takes a Wife* (41), *Sunset Boulevard* (50), *Three for the Bedroom* (52), *Nero's Mistress* (56), *Airport 75* (74).

## SWARTHOUT, Gladys (1904-1969)

Swarthout, born in Deepwater, Missouri, was an opera star before she began making movies. She started singing in church choirs when she was 12, and went on to study music at the Bush Conservatory in Chicago, making her professional debut with the Chicago Civic Opera Company in 1924, and joined New York's Metropolitan Opera Company in 1929, lending her lustrous mezzo-soprano voice to *Carmen*, *Lakme* and *Norma*. Hollywood called this beautiful and talented singer in the mid-1930s, and Paramount set her up as a rival to MGM's Jeanette MacDonald and Columbia's Grace Moore.
**Selected Films:** *Rose of the Rancho* (36), *Give Us This Night* (36), *Champagne Waltz* (37), *Romance in the Dark* (38), *Ambush* (39).

## SWEET, Blanche (1895-1986)

Born in Chicago, Sweet began her career at the age of four, dancing on stage. In films she played determined heroines, making 124 motion pictures for such producers as D W Griffith and Thomas Edison, leaving Hollywood for Broadway in 1930.
**Selected Films:** *The Man With Three Wives* (09), *Judith of Bethulia* (13), *Anna Christie* (23), *The Silver Horde* (30).

## SWIT, Loretta (1947- )

Most famous for playing the Army nurse, Major Margaret 'Hot Lips' Hoolihan, on the hit TV series *M*A*S*H*, Swit was born in Passaic, New Jersey. She was a student at the American Academy of Dramatic Arts and a member of the Gene Frankel Repertoire Theatre in New York City. After stage appearances on Broadway, she made a few pictures in Hollywood.
**Selected Films:** *Stand Up and Be Counted* (72), *Freebie and the Bean* (74), *Race with the Devil* (75), *S.O.B.* (80), *Beer* (85).

## SWITZER, Carl 'Alfalfa' (1926-1959)

Born in Paris, Illinois, he became the freckled, squeaky-voiced, pomaded-hair member of the Our Gang troupe, joining the comedy short series in 1935 and remaining until 1942. He had started off in show business as a child singer, and had a well-trained voice, which he had to hide behind the off-key singing required in the role of Alfalfa. Later he appeared in feature films, but as his career declined he became a hunting and fishing guide in northern California, just to eke out a living. He ended up as a bartender and was shot to death in a drunken brawl over a $50 debt.
**Selected Films:** *General Spanky* (36), *Wild and Woolly* (37), *I Love You Again* (40), *The Human Comedy* (43), *Going My Way* (44), *State of the Union* (48), *A Letter to Three Wives* (49), *Pat and Mike* (52), *The High and the Mighty* (54), *The Defiant Ones* (58).

## SYDNEY, Basil (1894-1968)

Sydney was born Basil Sydney Nugent in St Osyth, England, and started his stage career at the age of 15. He came to the United States in 1920 and made his screen debut in the Hollywood version of his London stage play *Romance* (20). For the next ten years he toured the United States in stage plays and then returned to England where he continued to act in movies and on the stage, returning to Hollywood only sporadically.
**Selected Films:** *Roman* (20), *Transatlantic Tunnel* (35), *Ships with Wings* (41), *Caesar and Cleopatra* (45), *Hamlet* (48), *Treasure Island* (50), *Ivanhoe* (52), *Salome* (53), *The Dam Busters* (54), *Sea Wife* (57), *The Devil's Disciple* (59), *The Hands of Orlac* (61).

## SYKES, Eric (1924- )

Sykes was born in Oldham, England, and early in his career he was an actor and screenwriter. He later became a stalwart of the BBC as a comedian and actor. He made occasional movies.
**Selected Films:** *Orders are Orders* (54), *Charley Moon* (59), *Invasion Quartet* (61), *Kill or Cure* (63), *Heavens Above* (63), *Those Magnificent Men in Their Flying Machines* (65), *Rotten to the Core* (65), *The Spy with a Cold Nose* (67), *Shalako* (68), *Rhubarb* (70), *Theatre of Blood* (73), *The Boys in Blue* (83).

## SYMS, Silvia (1934- )

Born in London, England, she was educated at the Royal Academy of Dramatic Art. This blonde leading lady is primarily known for her work in British films and television, although she was a stage actress early in her career.
**Selected Films:** *My Teenage Daughter* (56), *Expresso Bongo* (59), *The World of Suzie Wong* (60), *Victim* (61), *The Quare Fellow* (62), *East of Sudan* (64), *Operation Crossbow* (65), *The Desperados* (69), *Born to Win* (71), *Asylum* (72), *There Goes the Bride* (79).

# T

## TALBOT, Lyle (1904- )

Born Lisle Henderson in Pittsburgh, Pennsylvania, Talbot acted on the road as a child and appeared in the first of his 150 movies in 1932. For the next three decades he usually played heroes in B movies and both sides of the law in major films. During the 1950s and 1960s he was a regular on several TV series including *The Adventures of Ozzie and Harriet* and *The Bob Cummings Show*.
**Selected Films:** *Love is a Racket* (32), *Mexican Spitfire's Elephant* (42), *There's No Business Like Show Business* (54), *Sunrise at Campobello* (60).

## TALBOT, Nita (1930 )

Born in New York, Talbot started her acting career in the mid-1950s. She has since played wry roles onscreen and in several TV series including *Hot off the Wire* and *Here We Go Again*.
**Selected Films:** *Bundle of Joy* (56), *A Very Special Favor* (65), *Buck and the Preacher* (71), *The Day of the Locust* (75), *Night Shift* (82).

## TALMADGE, Constance (1898-1973)

Born in Brooklyn, New York, the sister of actresses Norma and Natalie, Constance arrived onscreen in 1914 and soon displayed her talent as a comedienne. A notable example of her talent was the Mountain Girl in Griffith's *Intolerance* (16). During the 1920s, Constance's sophisticated comedies were nearly as popular as her sister Norma's dramas. Constance retired without attempting a sound movie.
**Selected Films:** *Buddy's First Call* (14), *Intolerance* (16), *Matrimaniac* (16), *The Honeymoon* (17), *Happiness a la Mode* (19), *Lessons in Love* (21), *Her Sister From Paris* (25), *Venus* (29).

## TALMADGE, Norma (1897-1957)

Born in Brooklyn, New York, to a stage mother determined to see screen stardom for her three daughters Norma, Constance and Natalie, Norma was the first to break into movies. She played her first roles at age 13. The next year she starred in *A Tale of Two Cities* (11). For several years she was a

popular leading lady in silents, but her marriage to producer Joseph Schenck took her to superstardom. Supported as much by the machinery of studio publicity as by real dramatic ability, she played leads in a series of popular dramas including *The New Moon* (19) and *Camille* (27). The arrival of sound revealed Talmadge's limitations. She starred in a few talkies and then retired after the unsuccessful *DuBarry, Woman of Passion* (30). After divorcing Schenck, Talmadge was married for a time to entertainer George Jessel.
**Selected Films:** *Love of Chrysanthemum* (10), *Uncle Tom's Cabin* (10), *The Dixie Mother* (11), *A Tale of Two Cities* (11), *Battle Cry of Peace* (14), *Forbidden City* (18), *The New Moon* (19), *The Sign on the Door* (21), *Kiki* (26), *Camille* (27), *New York Nights* (30), *DuBarry, Woman of Passion* (30).

## TALMAN, William (1915-1968)

Onscreen mainly in minor productions from the late 1940s through the 1960s, American character actor Talman was best-known as the long-suffering DA in the TV series Perry Mason.
**Selected Films:** *Red Hot and Blue* (49), *The Armored Car Robbery* (50), *The Hitch Hiker* (52), *Two-Gun Lady* (59), *The Ballad of Josie* (67).

## TAMBLYN, Russ (1934- )

Born in Los Angeles, California, Tamblyn danced onstage as a kid and onscreen as a teenager. He usually played supporting roles enlivened by his vivacious and acrobatic dancing style, in notable films like *Seven Brides for Seven Brothers* (54) and *West Side Story* (61). He was nominated for a supporting-actor Oscar for *Peyton Place* (57).
**Selected Films:** *The Boy With Green Hair* (48), *Seven Brides for Seven Brothers* (54), *Hit the Deck* (55), *Peyton Place* (57), *tom thumb* (58), *West Side Story* (61), *The Wonderful World of the Brothers Grimm* (63), *The Haunting* (63), *Win, Place, or Steal* (75), *Human Highway* (82).

## TAMIROFF, Akim (1899-1972)

Born in Baku, Russia, Tamiroff came to the United States in the 1920s and acted in the theater. His screen debut came in *Queen Christina* (33). For the next 35 years he was a very familiar face, playing a great variety of character roles in some 100 movies. He was usually a villain, occasionally an eccentric or even tragic lead, often in comic roles in his later years. He played the title role in *The General Died at Dawn* (36), two different characters named Pablo in *Tortilla Flat* (42) and *For Whom the Bell Tolls* (43), and Wu Lien in *Dragon Seed* (44).
**Selected Films:** *Queen Christina* (33), *Lives of a Bengal Lancer* (35), *The General Died at Dawn* (36), *The Great McGinty* (40), *Tortilla Flat* (42), *For Whom the Bell Tolls* (43), *The Bridge of San Luis Rey* (44), *Dragon Seed* (44), *Confidential Report* (55), *Alphaville* (65), *Sabra* (70).

## TANDY, Jessica (1909- )

London-born Jessica Tandy made her British stage debut at 16 and her New York debut at 21. Within a few years she had risen to stardom, a position she has since maintained (often working with her husband since 1942, Hume Cronyn). Tandy was the original Blanche du Bois in Tennessee Williams' *A Streetcar Named Desire* (48), winning a Tony for that performance and another much later, for *The Gin Game* (78). Since her first screen appearance in *The Indiscretions of Eve* (32), Tandy has been a solid presence in occasional films including *Forever Amber* (48).
**Selected Films:** *The Indiscretions of Eve* (32), *Murder in the Family* (38), *The Seventh Cross* (44), *Dragonwyck* (46), *Forever Amber* (48), *A Woman's Vengeance* (48), *The Desert Fox* (51), *The Light in the Forest* (58), *Hemingway's Adventures of a Young Man* (62), *The Birds* (63), *Butley* (74), *The World According to Garp* (82), *Best Friends* (82), *Cocoon* (85).

## TANI, Yoko (1932- )

Japanese actress Tani played leads in several American films of the 1950s and 1960s, among them Nicholas Ray's *The Savage Innocents* (59), in which she played an Eskimo.
**Selected Films:** *The Wind Cannot Read* (57), *The Savage Innocents* (59), *Marco Polo* (61), *Who's Been Sleeping in My Bed?* (63), *Invasion* (66).

## TANNER, Tony (1932- )

British review player Tanner appeared in occasional films of the 1960s including *Stop the World, I Want to Get Off* (66).
**Selected Films:** *Strictly for the Birds* (64), *A Home of Your Own* (65), *The Pleasure Girls* (65), *Stop the World, I Want to Get Off* (66).

## TASHMAN, Lilyan (1899-1934)

Born in Brooklyn, New York, Tashman was a Ziegfeld Girl before making her screen debut in 1921. She became a silent star and then moved into talkies, usually as a sophisticated, sharp-tongued blonde with a throaty voice. Before her early death, she was a popular hostess in Hollywood.
**Selected Films:** *Experience* (21), *Manhandled* (24), *New York Nights* (29), *Murder by the Clock* (31), *Frankie and Johnny* (33), *Riptide* (34).

## TATE, Sharon (1943-1969)

In the 1960s Sharon Tate was a Hollywood starlet, playing decorative roles in films. She was married to Roman Polanski, who directed her in *The Fearless Vampire Killers* (67). In 1969 she was murdered by the Charles Manson gang.
**Selected Films:** *Eye of the Devil* (67), *Valley of the Dolls* (67), *The Fearless Vampire Killers* (67), *Wrecking Crew* (67).

## TATI, Jacques (1908-1982)

Born Jacques Tatischeff in Le Pecq, France, this actor/director was the grandson of the Tsar's former ambassador to Paris. He trained to be an artist, but then he found sports, especially rugby, which he played with the Racing Club team. He became a cabaret and music hall entertainer in the early 1930s, and several of his routines were turned into short films. After World War II, he hit his prime, appearing in movies that emphasized visual humor. His comic masterpiece was *Mr Hulot's Holiday* (53), a fond throwback to silent screen comedy.
**Selected Films:** *Oscar, Champion de Tennis* (32), *Mr Hulot's Holiday* (53), *My Uncle* (58), *Playtime* (68), *Traffic* (71).

## TAYBACK, Vic (1929- )

A native of New York, Tayback largely played tough guys in supporting roles of films from the late 1960s through the 1970s.
**Selected Films:** *Bullitt* (68), *With Six You Get Egg Roll* (68), *Lepke* (73), *Alice Doesn't Live Here Anymore* (75), *Thunderbolt and Lightfoot* (75), *The Choirboys* (77).

## TAYLOR, Don (1920- )

Beginning in the early 1940s, Taylor, born in Freeport, Pennsylvania, played light leads and supporting roles in films including *The Naked City* (48), and *Stalag 17* (53). In the 1960s he turned to directing and has since made a number of lowbrow films including *Escape from the Planet of the Apes* (71).
**Selected Films:** *Winged Victory* (44), *The Naked City* (48), *Father of the Bride* (50), *Submarine Command* (51), *Stalag 17* (53), *I'll Cry Tomorrow* (57), *The Savage Guns* (62), *Tom Sawyer* (73), *The Final Countdown* (79).

## TAYLOR, Elizabeth (1932- )

Taylor has been the subject of more press coverage than almost any Hollywood star – most of it nasty. But she is just plain unsinkable and demonstrates that living well is the best revenge. As she put it, 'Success is a great deodorant.' She typifies what most people mean when they say 'movie star.' Born in London, England, to American parents, her family was evacuated to the United States in 1939, at the beginning of World War II. Already a beauty, she was groomed by her mother to be an actress. She began her film career at the age of ten in a bit part in *There's One Born Every Minute* (42). *National Velvet* (44) may still rank as her finest film. Early on she matured into a radiant woman, capable of playing romantic roles well beyond her years, famous for her dark hair, violet eyes and ripe figure. Taylor played Amy in *Little Women* (49) and, at 18, played her first romantic lead in *Conspirator* (49), opposite Robert Taylor. *The Harvard Lampoon*, echoing popular sentiment, gave her an award 'for so gallantly persisting in her career despite a total inability to act.' She was courted by the industrialist billionaire Howard Hughes before she married the heir to the Hilton Hotel chain, Nicky Hilton, while still in her teens. The marriage lasted only long enough to make *Father of the Bride* (50) a hit movie. Taylor began taking her acting seriously with *A Place in the Sun* (51), also starring Montgomery Clift and Shelley Winters. By then she was secure in her position as a top box office superstar, one of the most well-publicized women in the world. Her exciting private life and many marriages continued fueling public interest. In 1952 Taylor married British actor Michael Wilding. In the late 1950s she married show business impresario Michael Todd. After he died in a plane crash she married singer Eddie Fisher. Fans painted her as the wicked temptress who lured Fisher away from his wholesome wife Debbie Reynolds. Taylor won back the sympathy of her fans when she almost died of pneumonia, and then by winning the Academy Award for Best Actress for *Butterfield 8* (60). Her romance with Richard Burton on the set of *Cleopatra* (62) fed gossip columns. Taylor and Burton married, divorced, remarried and redivorced. One of the films they made together, *Who's Afraid of Virginia Woolf?* (66) brought her another Oscar for Best Actress which she certainly deserved. When their movie appeal faltered, the Burtons appeared on stage together quite successfully. Taylor also fared well on Broadway on her own. Over the years she has emerged as a magnificent character and a survivor of the Hollywood studio system at its most vicious.
**Selected Films:** *There's One Born Every Minute* (42), *Lassie Come Home* (43), *Jane Eyre* (43), *The White Cliffs of Dover* (44), *National Velvet* (44), *Cynthia* (47), *Life With Father* (47), *A Date with Judy* (48), *Julia Misbehaves* (48), *Little Women* (49), *Conspirator* (49), *Father of the Bride* (50), *Father's Little Dividend* (51), *Quo Vadis* (51), *A Place in the Sun* (51), *Ivanhoe* (52), *Elephant Walk* (54), *Giant* (56), *Raintree County* (57), *Cat on a Hot Tin Roof* (58), *Suddenly Last Summer* (60), *Butterfield 8* (60), *Cleopatra* (62), *The VIPs* (63), *The Sandpiper* (65), *Who's Afraid of Virginia Woolf?* (66), *The Taming of the Shrew* (67), *The Comedians* (67), *Reflections in a Golden Eye* (67), *Secret Ceremony* (68), *Under Milk Wood* (71), *Hammersmith Is Out* (72), *Ash Wednesday* (73), *The Blue Bird* (76), *The Mirror Crack'd* (80).

## TAYLOR, Kent (1907-1987)

Among those actors, handsome and stalwart in looks and a bit wooden in action, who alternated leads in Bs and supporting parts in As, Kent Taylor, born Louis Weiss, in Nashua, Iowa, was one of the handsomest and most long-lived – his 50 or so films stretched from the early 1930s into the 1970s. In the early 1950s he starred in the TV series

*Boston Blackie.*
**Selected Films:** *Road to Reno* (31) *Death Takes a Holiday* (34), *Two Fisted* (35), *Bombers Moon* (43), *Slightly Scarlet* (56), *Satan's Sadists* (69), *Girls for Rent* (74).

## TAYLOR, Robert (1911-1969)

Taylor was born Spangler Arlington Brugh in Filley, Nebraska, the son of a country doctor. Educated at Doane College, he majored in music, specializing in the cello. When his cello professor went to Pomona College, Taylor followed him to California. His performance in a campus stage production won him a contract with MGM, and he he was one of their principal players for 30 years. He made his debut in *Handy Andy* (34), and really hit his stride in *Magnificent Obsession* (35) opposite Irene Dunne. During World War II he was a flight instructor with the Navy's Air Transport, returning from service to regain his star status. He was a hard-working professional, who, if he rarely soared, rarely crashed. Blessed with very good looks, he rivaled Clark Gable as a romantic lead. He gradually got rid of the glamorous image and developed into a mature actor of solid character. Taylor was married twice, to Barbara Stanwyck from 1939 to 1951 and to Ursula Theiss from 1954 until his death from lung cancer.
**Selected Films:** *Handy Andy* (34), *Broadway Melody of 1936* (35), *Magnificent Obsession* (36), *His Brother's Wife* (36), *The Gorgeous Hussy* (36), *Camille* (37), *A Yank at Oxford* (38), *Waterloo Bridge* (40), *Billy the Kid* (41), *Johnny Eager* (42), *Bataan* (43), *Undercurrent* (46), *Conspirator* (50), *Quo Vadis* (51), *Ivanhoe* (52), *Knights of the Round Table* (53), *Saddle the Wind* (58), *Party Girl* (58), *The Glass Sphynx* (68), *Where Angels Go, Trouble Follows* (68).

## TAYLOR, Rod (1929- )

Taylor, born in Sydney, began acting on stage and screen in his native Australia before coming to Hollywood in 1955. Being both handsome and robust, he naturally gravitated to leads and supporting roles in adventure and action pictures, among them *The Hell With Heroes* (68) and *Trader Horn* (73). However, Taylor also worked often in comedies and offbeat films; the latter include his lead in Hitchcock's *The Birds* (63). By the late 1960s he was largely seen in routine films.
**Selected Films:** *Long John Silver* (54), *Giant* (56), *Raintree County* (57), *The Time Machine* (60), *The Birds* (63), *Thirty-Six Hours* (64), *Zabriskie Point* (70), *Trader Horn* (73), *On the Run* (82).

## TAYLOR-YOUNG, Leigh (1944- )

Born in Washington DC, Taylor-Young was one of the crop of pretty, fresh-faced leading ladies who arrived onscreen in the late 1960s. She appeared in several trendy pictures of the era including *I Love You, Alice B Toklas* (68). For a time she was married to actor Ryan O'Neal.
**Selected Films:** *I Love You, Alice B Toklas* (68), *The Big Bounce* (68), *The Adventurers* (69), *The Horsemen* (71), *The Gang That Couldn't Shoot Straight* (72), *Can't Stop the Music* (80), *Looker* (81).

## TEARLE, Conway (1878-1938)

Born Frederick Levy in New York, Tearle grew up in England with his half brother Godfrey Tearle. After success onstage in England and on Broadway, Conway arrived in films in the mid-teens and played stalwart men of the world in a great many silents and talkies. The latter included *Vanity Fair (32) and Romeo and Juliet* (36).
**Selected Films:** *The Nightingale* (14), *Stella Maris* (18), *Lilies of the Field* (24), *The Gold Diggers of Broadway* (29), *Vanity Fair* (32), *Klondike Annie* (36), *Romeo and Juliet* (36).

## TEARLE, Godfrey (1884-1953)

Born in New York, the half brother of actor Conway Tearle, Godfrey moved early to London, where he acted onstage as a child. Growing up to be a distinguished theater actor, he appeared now and then in films, most notably as the spy with a missing finger in Hitchcock's *The Thirty-Nine Steps* (35) and the aviator lead in *One of Our Aircraft is Missing* (42).
**Selected Films:** *Romeo and Juliet* (08), *Sinless Sinner* (19), *Infatuation* (30), *The Thirty-Nine Steps* (35), *One of Our Aircraft is Missing* (42), *The Titfield Thunderbolt* (53).

## TEASDALE, Verree (1904- )

Born in Spokane, Washington, Teasdale was one of several Hollywood actresses of the 1930s who pursued roles as the wisecracking friend of the heroine and similar second leads. Among the striking blonde's less typical roles were as Hippolyta in *A Midsummer Night's Dream* (35). She was married to actor Adolphe Menjou.
**Selected Films:** *Syncopation* (29), *Roman Scandals* (33), *Madame Du Barry* (34), *A Midsummer Night's Dream* (35), *Topper Takes a Trip* (38), *Love Thy Neighbor* (40), *Come Live With Me* (41).

## TEMPLE, Shirley (1928- )

In the 1930s, Hollywood was in the heyday of one of its Golden Eras – awash with some of the greatest personalities in its history. But sitting atop the heap – the biggest box-office draw on earth – was Shirley Temple, a curly-haired little girl who was less than four feet tall and had never taken an acting lesson in her life. She was born in Santa Monica, California, the daughter of a bank manager. At the age of three, she went to dancing school for lessons. Before she was four years old she was discovered at the dancing school by Charles Lamont, a director at a second-line studio called

Educational Pictures, and Temple was put in a series called *The Baby Burlesques*. They were one-reelers in which she imitated such stars as Marlene Dietrich. Then she moved into another series called *Frolics of Youth*. Her first notable feature film was *Stand Up and Cheer* (34), in which she was an immediate hit and was signed to a seven-year contract by Fox Productions at a salary that seemed immense – $150 per week. Temple made nine films in 1934, four in 1935, four in 1936 and two in 1937. She received a Special Academy Award in 1934 'in grateful recognition of her outstanding contribution to screen entertainment' and 'for bringing more happiness to millions of children and millions of grownups than any child of her years in the history of Hollywood.' Her salary was up to $300,000 a picture by 1939 and she was the center of a remarkable cult. There were Shirley Temple dolls, dresses, plates and dishes and even a Shirley Temple cocktail – non-alcoholic, of course. In her films she was often either an orphan who found a happy home with a new family or the child of a single parent who found a new mate for her father or mother. There was always a pause for a few songs and a dance or two with such stars as Bill Robinson, Buddy Ebsen, James Dunn or George Murphy. Even though the studio tried to keep her looking young by having her wear false front teeth when her baby ones fell out, eventually she did grow up. Her contract with 20th Century-Fox ran out in 1940, and she was cut loose by the studio; moving to MGM, she made just one movie. Then she signed with David O Selznick and was successful in several films as a teenager. At the age of 17 she married John Agar, who had starred with her in *Fort Apache* (48), but the marriage ended in divorce in 1949. The next year she married Charles A Black. As Shirley Temple Black she had a remarkable career in politics and diplomacy. She lost in an effort to be elected to the House of Representatives as a Republican in California, but she was named Ambassador to Ghana in 1974 (after serving in the United States Delegation to the United Nations), and in 1976 she was given the post of Chief of Protocol under President Gerald Ford – the first woman to hold that post. In 1977 she was given the Life Achievement Award of the American Center of Films for Children.
**Selected Films:** *The Red-Haired Alibi* (32), *To the Last Man* (33), *Stand Up and Cheer* (34), *Little Miss Marker* (34), *Baby Take a Bow* (34), *Bright Eyes* (34), *The Little Colonel* (35), *Curly Top* (35), *The Littlest Rebel* (35), *Captain January* (36), *Poor Little Rich Girl* (36), *Dimples* (36), *Wee Willie Winkie* (37), *Heidi* (37), *Rebecca of Sunnybrook Farm* (38), *Little Miss Broadway* (38), *The Little Princess* (39), *Susannah of the Mounties* (39), *The Blue Bird* (40), *Young People* (40), *Kathleen* (41), *Miss Annie Rooney* (42), *Since You Went Away* (44), *I'll Be Seeing You* (44), *Kiss and Tell* (45), *The Bachelor and the Bobby Soxer* (47), *That Hagen Girl* (47), *Fort Apache* (48), *Mr Belvedere Goes to College* (49), *A Kiss for Corliss* (49), *Adventure in Baltimore* (49), *The Story of Seabiscuit* (49).

## **TERHUNE, Max** (1890-1973)

A native of Franklin, Indiana, Terhune was a vaudevillian before coming to the screen in the mid-1930s. For years he was a fixture of low-budget westerns, first in the 'Three Mesquiteers' series, then the 'Range Busters' series, and finally as a sidekick to Ken Maynard and Johnny Mack Brown. In the 1950s he played small roles in major features.
**Selected Films:** *Ride, Ranger Ride* (36) *Along the Oregon Trail* (47), *Jim Thorpe – All American* (51), *Giant* (56).

## **TERRY, Don** (1902- )

Born Donald Locher in Natick, Massachusetts, Terry attended Harvard and boxed in the Olympics before starting in movies in the early sound era. For two decades he played tough leading men in low-budget action features and serials.
**Selected Films:** *Me, Gangster* (28), *Whistlin' Dan* (32), *The Secret of Treasure Island* (38), *White Savage* (43), *Grand Canyon Trail* (48).

## **TERRY, Philip** (1909- )

American actor Terry was largely a B-movie leading man, with occasional forays into first features, from the mid-1930s through the 1960s. He was married to Joan Crawford from 1942 to 1946.
**Selected Films:** *Navy Blue and Gold* (37), *The Parson of Panamint* (41), *Bataan* (43), *The Lost Weekend* (45), *Born to Kill* (47), *The Navy vs the Night Monsters* (66).

## **TERRY-THOMAS** (1911- )

Born Thomas Terry Hoar-Stevens to an upper class family in London, Terry-Thomas fought in World War II and acted onstage before arriving in films in *Helter Skelter* (49). It was some years before his inimitable comic persona made its mark with his commanding officer in *Private's Progress* (56). From that point he became a staple supporting actor on both sides of the Atlantic, his gap-toothed grin and twitty manner typing him as one of the screen's great silly Englishmen. Notable among his films were the classic *I'm All Right, Jack* (60), *Those Magnificent Men in Their Flying Machines* (65), and *How to Murder Your Wife* (65). In the 1970s Terry-Thomas' career declined to roles in *Dr Phibes* movies and similar features.
**Selected Films:** *Helter Skelter* (49), *Private's Progress* (56), *Blue Murder at St Trinians* (57), *Carleton Browne of the FO* (58), *I'm All Right Jack* (60), *The Wonderful World of the Brothers Grimm* (63), *It's a Mad Mad Mad Mad World* (63), *The Mouse on the Moon* (63), *Those Magnificent Men in Their Flying Machines* (65), *How to Murder Your Wife* (65), *Don't Look Now* (68), *The Abominable Dr Phibes* (71), *The Bawdy Adventures of Tom Jones* (76), *The Last Remake of Beau Geste* (77), *The Tempest* (79).

## THATCHER, Torin (1905-1981)

Thatcher established himself onstage in Britain before beginning his screen career in the mid-1930s. The solidly-built actor played tough characters in a good many films on both sides of the Atlantic. Among his roles were Bentley Drummle in *Great Expectations* (46), and Ulysses in *Helen of Troy* (56).
**Selected Films:** *General John Regan* (34), *Major Barbara* (40), *Great Expectations* (46), *The Robe* (53), *Helen of Troy* (56), *The Sandpiper* (65), *Hawaii* (66), *The King's Pirate* (67).

## THAXTER, Phyllis (1921- )

Born in Portland, Maine, Thaxter came to the screen in the mid-1940s after stage experience. From her debut as Van Johnson's wife in *Thirty Seconds Over Tokyo* (44), she tended to play long-suffering spouses. For many years she was married to CBS TV chief James Aubrey.
**Selected Films:** *Thirty Seconds Over Tokyo* (44), *Blood on the Moon* (48), *Springfield Rifle* (53), *The World of Henry Orient* (64), *Superman* (78).

## THESIGER, Ernest (1879-1961)

This British actor, London-born, appeared in both British and American films, usually in a character part. He was most famous in his role as the mad scientist Dr Praetorius in *Bride of Frankenstein* (35).
**Selected Films:** *Nelson* (18), *West End Wives* (29), *The Old Dark House* (32), *The Ghoul* (33), *Bride of Frankenstein* (35), *The Man Who Could Work Miracles* (36), *They Drive by Night* (38), *Caesar and Cleopatra* (45), *The Man in the White Suit* (52), *Father Brown* (54), *The Roman Spring of Mrs Stone* (61).

## THIESS, Ursula (1929- )

An attractive actress from Hamburg, Germany, Thiess played leads in a few routine American films of the mid-1950s. She is the widow of actor Robert Taylor.
**Selected Films:** *Monsoon* (52), *The Iron Glove* (54), *Bengal Brigade* (55), *Bandido* (56).

## THINNES, Roy (1938- )

American actor Thinnes is best known for starring in TV movies and series including *The Long Hot Summer*, *The Invaders* and *From Here to Eternity*. He has appeared in a few films.
**Selected Films:** *Journey to the Far Side of the Sun* (69), *Charlie One Eye* (72), *Airport 75* (74), *The Hindenberg* (75).

## THOMAS, Danny (1914- )

Born Amos Jacobs to a Lebanese Catholic family in Deerfield, Michigan, Thomas went from success as a stand-up comedian and MC to the screen. After a few film roles, among them as Gus Kahn in *I'll See You in My Dreams* (51), he moved to TV for a seven-year run in his own series. He is the father of actress Marlo Thomas.
**Selected Films:** *The Unfinished Dance* (47), *Big City* (48), *Call Me Mister* (51), *I'll See You in My Dreams* (51), *The Jazz Singer* (53).

## THOMAS, Richard (1951- )

Thomas, born in New York, began playing juvenile roles in films in the late 1960s and made occasional appearances through the 1970s. He is best-known for his role as John-Boy in the long-running TV series *The Waltons*.
**Selected Films:** *Winning* (69), *Last Summer* (70), *Red Sky at Morning* (71), *Battle Beyond the Stars* (80).

## THOMPSON, Jack (1940- )

Born John Payne in Australia, Thompson changed his name because it was already spoken for. He has been one of the main figures in the industry in his native country, starring in several important pictures including *Breaker Morant* (79).
**Selected Films:** *Outback* (70), *Wake in Fright* (71), *Sunday Too Far Away* (75), *Mad Dog Morgan* (76), *The Chant of Jimmie Blacksmith* (78), *Breaker Morant* (79), *Merry Christmas, Mr Lawrence* (83), *Flesh and Blood* (84).

## THOMPSON, Lea (1962- )

Born in Minneapolis, Minnesota, she studied ballet for 11 years. After working as a waitress, she got her first break in movies in an appearance in *Jaws 3-D* (83).
**Selected Films:** *Jaws 3-D* (83), *All the Right Moves* (84), *Back to the Future* (85), *Space Camp* (86), *Howard the Duck* (86).

## THOMPSON, Marshall (1925- )

Born James Marshall Thompson in Peoria, Illinois, Thompson arrived in films in his late teens and for some years played wholesome youths. After several low-budget sci-fi and horror films in the 1950s, he starred in *Clarence, the Cross-Eyed Lion* (65). This led to a number of animal films including the TV series *Daktari*.
**Selected Films:** *Reckless Age* (44), *Homecoming* (48), *My Six Convicts* (52), *It! The Terror From Beyond Space* (58), *Clarence, the Cross-Eyed Lion* (65), *The Turning Point* (77), *Bog* (78).

## THOMPSON, Sada (1929- )

Thompson, born in Des Moines, Iowa, has usually played sympathetic mothers on screen and on TV, a role she played to perfection in the TV series *Family*. Most of her work has been on stage.
**Selected Films:** *The Pursuit of Happiness* (70), *Desperate Characters* (71).

## THORNDIKE, Sybil (1882-1976)

Thorndike, born in Gainsborough, England, first trained as a concert pianist. After a hand injury she turned to the stage, finding acclaim in plays such as George Bernard Shaw's *Saint Joan*, which was said to have been written for her. She appeared onscreen only occasionally, most often as regal old ladies. Among her several memorable performances were as Mrs Squeers in *Nicholas Nickleby* (47), Queen Victoria in *Melba* (53), and the Grand Duchess in *The Prince and the Showgirl* (57). She was made a Dame in 1931.
**Selected Films:** *Moth and Rust* (21), *Dawn* (29), *Tudor Rose* (36), *Major Barbara* (40), *Nicholas Nickleby (47)*, *Stage Fright* (50), *Melba* (53), *The Prince and the Showgirl* (57), *Alive and Kicking* (58), *Uncle Vanya* (63).

## THREE STOOGES, The: See STOOGES, The Three

## THULIN, Ingrid (1929- )

Following ballet training, Thulin, born in Sollefta, gravitated to dramatic studies in her native Sweden and made her screen debut in 1948. Beginning with *Wild Strawberries* (58), the blonde actress with the forbidding features was one of Ingmar Bergman's regulars, playing major roles in several of his greatest films; among them were the mousy mistress of a minister in *Winter Light* (62) and a vindictive wife in *Cries and Whispers* (72). Like most of Bergman's stars, she has only occasionally been seen in good films by other directors; among those are Alain Resnais' fine *La Guerre est Finie* (66).
**Selected Films:** *Where the Winds Blow* (48), *Foreign Intrigue* (56), *Wild Strawberries* (58), *The Magician* (58), *Winter Light* (62), *The Silence* (63), *Night Games* (66), *La Guerre est Finie* (66), *The Damned* (69), *Cries and Whispers* (72), *Moses* (76), *The Cassandra Crossing* (77), *One Plus One* (78).

## TIBBETT, Lawrence (1896-1960)

One of the great baritones of his time and for decades a star of the Metropolitan Opera, Tibbett, born in Bakersfield, California, starred in a number of screen musicals in the early sound era. For his first, *The Rogue Song* (30), he was nominated for a best-actor Oscar.
**Selected Films:** *The Rogue Song* (30), *New Moon* (30), *The Prodigal* (31), *Cuban Love Song* (32), *Metropolitan* (36), *Under Your Spell* (37).

## TIERNEY, Gene (1920- )

Gene Tierney was born to a prosperous family in Brooklyn, New York. When the exquisitely beautiful young lady expressed interest in acting, her father formed a company to promote her, and before long she found herself on Broadway. Picked up by Fox, Tierney first appeared onscreen in 1940 and next year had an uncharacteristic role as poor-white Ellie May in *Tobacco Road*. Directly after, she played in the title role of *Belle Starr* (41). Somewhat on the wooden side as an actress, Tierney had a career largely in routine first features, but a few were notable – she was the mysterious object of obsession in *Laura* (44) and the bitchy villainess of *Leave Her to Heaven* (45). Tierney's men figured large in headlines and in her life. After playing the field (including dating a young Navy man named John F Kennedy), she married fashion designer Oleg Cassini, divorced him and picked up Aly Khan after his divorce from Rita Hayworth, and finally married the ex-husband of Hedy Lamarr; meanwhile, she had a couple of nervous breakdowns. (Her troubles were frankly dealt with in her 1979 book *Self Portrait*). Tierney's final screen efforts were a few appearances in the 1960s.
**Selected Films:** *The Return of Jesse James* (40), *Tobacco Road* (41), *Belle Starr* (41), *Son of Fury* (42), *Laura* (44), *A Bell for Adano* (45), *Leave Her to Heaven* (45), *Dragonwyck* (46), *The Razor's Edge* (46), *Close to My Heart* (51), *The Egyptian* (54), *The Left Hand of God* (54), *Advise and Consent* (62), *Toys in the Attic* (63), *The Pleasure Seekers* (64).

## TIERNEY, Lawrence (1919- )

Born in Brooklyn, New York, and the older brother of actor Scott Brady, Tierney arrived onscreen in 1943 and two years later played his most famous role, as the title gangster in *Dillinger* (45). From that point he largely played tough-guy parts into the 1980s, meanwhile gaining a similar reputation offscreen in a number of public brawls.
**Selected Films:** *The Ghost Ship* (43), *Dillinger* (45), *San Quentin* (47), *The Greatest Show on Earth* (52), *Custer of the West* (68), *Such Good Friends* (71), *Midnight* (82).

## TIFFIN, Pamela (1942- )

A model in her teens, Tiffin, born Pamela Wonso in Oklahoma City, Oklahoma, came to the screen in 1961 and for a decade played cute young things in major productions. After her star declined in Hollywood, she appeared in cheap Italian movies.
**Selected Films:** *Summer and Smoke* (61), *State Fair* (62), *Come Fly With Me* (63), *The Lively Set* (64), *Harper* (66), *Viva Max!* (69), *Deaf Smith and Johnny Ears* (73), *Evil Fingers* (74).

## TOBEY, Kenneth (1919- )

American actor Tobey played likeable character roles in films from the late 1940s through the 1970s and also starred in the TV series *Whirlybirds*.
**Selected Films:** *Kiss Tomorrow Goodbye* (49), *About Face* (51), *The Thing* (52), *The Man in the Grey Flannel Suit* (56), *Billy Jack* (73), *W.C. Fields and Me* (76), *MacArthur* (77).

## TOBIAS, George (1901-1980)

A theater veteran, born in New York, Tobias came to the screen in the late 1930s and over the next three decades played a wide variety of supporting roles as good guys and bad, in dozens of films.
**Selected Films:** *Ninotchka* (39), *Sergeant York* (41), *Yankee Doodle Dandy* (42), *Mildred Pierce* (45), *The Glenn Miller Story* (53), *The Glass Bottom Boat* (66), *The Phynx* (69).

## TOBIN, Dan (1909-1982)

American character actor Tobin appeared in films from the late 1930s into the 1970s, usually playing small roles as fussbudgets. He also appeared in the long-running TV series *Perry Mason*.
**Selected Films:** *The Stadium Murders* (38), *Woman of the Year* (41), *The Velvet Touch* (49), *The Last Angry Man* (59), *The Love Bug Rides Again* (73).

## TOBIN, Genevieve (1901-1975)

New York-born Tobin began acting onstage as a child and spent most of her career in the theater until the sound era. During the 1930s the vivacious blonde played flirts and similar roles in a number of popular films. She was married to director William Keighley.
**Selected Films:** *No Mother to Guide Her* (23), *The Lady Surrenders* (31), *Easy to Wed* (34), *The Petrified Forest* (36), *Zaza* (39), *No Time for Comedy* (40), *Queen of Crime* (41).

## TODD, Ann (1909- )

Ann Todd Mayfield, born in Hartford, England, began acting onstage in her native Britain in the late 1920s and shortly thereafter began her long screen career. After 15 years of largely routine leads and supporting roles, Todd's breakthrough came with *The Seventh Veil* (45), in which she played a concert pianist torn between her guardian and her psychiatrist, played by James Mason and Herbert Lom. In 1949 Todd married David Lean, who directed her in several films including *The Passionate Friends* (48) and *Madeleine* (49). While appearing in a few European films in the 1960s, Todd wrote, produced, and directed several documentaries.
**Selected Films:** *Keepers of Youth* (31), *The Return of Bulldog Drummond* (34), *Things to Come* (36), *South Riding* (38), *The Seventh Veil* (45), *The Paradine Case* (48), *The Passionate Friends* (48), *Madeleine* (49), *The Sound Barrier* (52), *Son of Captain Blood* (62), *Ninety Degrees in the Shade* (65), *The Human Factor* (79).

## TODD, Richard (1919- )

Born Richard Palethorpe-Todd in Dublin, Todd acted in the Irish theater and fought in World War II before starting his screen career in the late 1940s. He was a stolid leading man through the 1960s.

*Richard Todd in* The Hasty Heart *(50).*

After being nominated for a best-actor Oscar for his performance as the dying soldier in *The Hasty Heart* (50), he went on to star in several swashbucklers, including the title roles in *The Story of Robin Hood* (52) and *Rob Roy – The Highland Rogue* (53).
**Selected Films:** *For Them That Trespass* (48), *The Hasty Heart* (50), *The Story of Robin Hood* (52), *Rob Roy – The Highland Rogue* (53), *A Man Called Peter* (55), *The Longest Day* (62), *The Big Sleep* (78), *House of the Long Shadows* (83).

## TODD, Thelma (1905-1935)

A native of Lawrence, Massachusetts, Todd came to the screen after modelling and schoolteaching and played vamps in silents. Moving easily into talkies, the perky blonde enlivened a number of comedies, including the Marx Brothers classics *Monkey Business* (31) and *Horse Feathers* (32). She also played ably in dramas. In 1935 Todd was murdered. The case was never solved.
**Selected Films:** *Fascinating Youth* (26), *Vamping Venus* (28), *Aloha* (30), *Monkey Business* (31), *The Maltese Falcon* (31), *Horse Feathers* (32), *Hips Hips Hooray* (34), *The Bohemian Girl* (35).

## TOGNAZZI, Ugo (1922- )

Born in Cremona, Italy, Ugo Tognazzi was an accountant who wandered into films in the 1950s by way of amateur theater. A decade later he was a staple leading man and occasional director of Italian films. With the French fantasy *Barbarella* (68), Tognazzi began to appear in films elsewhere in Europe. He is best known for his warm and memorable comic role as an aging drag queen in *La Cage aux Folles* (79), and its sequel. Tognazzi made his American screen debut as an old flirt in Gene Wilder's *Sunday Lovers* (80).
**Selected Films:** *I Cadetti di Guascogna* (50), *Quelle Joie de Vivre* (60), *The Conjugal Bed* (63), *The Magnificent Cuckold* (64), *A Question of Honour* (66), *Barbarella* (68), *Blowout* (73), *Viva Italia* (77), *La Cage aux Folles* (79), *La Cage aux Folles II* (80), *Sunday Lovers* (80), *La Cage aux Folles III* (86).

## TOLER, Sidney (1874-1947)

Born in Warrensburg, Missouri, Toler was a veteran of the stage when he entered the movies in the late 1920s. After a decade of general character parts including Daniel Webster in *The Gorgeous Hussy* (36), he took over the role of Charlie Chan upon the death of Warner Oland and played the philosophical Chinese detective in 25 movies.
**Selected Films:** *Madame X* (29), *Spitfire* (35), *The Gorgeous Hussy* (36), *Charlie Chan in Honolulu* (38), *The Scarlet Clue* (45), *The Trap* (47)

## TOMLIN, Lily (1939- )

Born Mary Jean Tomlin in Detroit, Michigan, she started working at the age of 14 in a dime store. Later she dropped out of her pre-med studies at Wayne State University to work in a Detroit cabaret. In 1966 she went to New York, performing skits on the coffee-house circuit and landing a job on *The Garry Moore show* on television. Three years later she joined the regular cast of the *Laugh-In* television show. It was on this program that she established herself as a masterful entertainer with an ability to capture detailed characterizations. Her debut as a dramatic actress in *Nashville* (75) earned her an Academy Award nomination as Best Supporting Actress. In the film she played a gospel singer and won the New York Film Critics Award for Best Supporting Actress.
**Selected Films:** *Nashville* (75), *The Late Show* (77), *9 to 5* (80), *All of Me* (84), *Pete 'n' Tillie* (84), *Lily Tomlin – The Film Behind the Show* (87).

## TONE, Franchot (1905-1968)

A future player of sophisticated heroes, Franchot Tone was born Stanislaus Pascal Franchot Tone into a wealthy family in Niagara Falls, New York, and began acting at Cornell University. After Broadway experience he made his film debut in *The Wiser Sex* (32) and was seen in drawing-room comedies. Then Tone was a hit in two supporting roles – as the colonel's son in *Lives of a Bengal Lancer* (35) and as Roger Byam in *Mutiny on the Bounty* (35); for the latter he was nominated for an Oscar. For several years Tone was one of the top box-office stars in Hollywood, but in the 1940s his films declined – with the exception of the strong thrillers *Five Graves to Cairo* (43), and *Phantom Lady* (44). Unhappy with his movie roles, Tone concentrated on the stage during the 1950s. In the 1960s he appeared in a few films and the TV series *Ben Casey*. His four wives were all actresses, the first two being Joan Crawford and Jean Wallace.
**Selected Films:** *The Wiser Sex* (32), *Moulin Rouge* (34), *Lives of a Bengal Lancer* (35), *Mutiny on the Bounty* (35), *They Gave Him a Gun* (37), *Five Graves to Cairo* (43), *Phantom Lady* (44), *I Love Trouble* (48), *The Man on the Eiffel Tower* (50), *Advise and Consent* (62), *The High Commissioner* (68).

## TOOMEY, Regis (1902- )

Born in Pittsburgh, Pennsylvania, Toomey came to the screen in the early sound era. For some four decades he largely inhabited the grainy world of B movies, playing cops and crooks in some 150 crime dramas. Later he worked on TV, including the series *Richard Diamond*, *Burke's Law* and *Petticoat Junction*.
**Selected Films:** *Framed* (29), *G-Men* (35), *The Big Sleep* (46), *Guys and Dolls* (55), *Peter Gunn* (67), *The Carey Treatment* (72), *C.H.O.M.P.S.* (79).

## TOREN, Marta (1926-1957)

Born in Stockholm, Toren was discovered in drama school in her native Sweden and sent to Hollywood, where she largely wasted in routine films beginning with *Casbah* (48). Finally she returned to Europe to make a few films before her early death.
**Selected Films:** *Casbah* (48), *Rogue's Regiment* (49), *Panthers' Moon* (51), *Sirocco* (51), *Maddalena* (54), *La Puerta Abierta* (57).

## TORMÉ, Mel (1923- )

A perennially popular American singer and songwriter (*The Christmas Song:* 'Chestnuts roasting on an open fire'), Tormé, born in Chicago, Illinois, has appeared in movies from the early 1940s.
**Selected Films:** *Higher and Higher* (43), *Junior Miss* (45), *Duchess of Idaho* (50), *The Patsy* (64), *A Man Called Adam* (66).

## TORN, Rip (1931- )

Born Elmore Torn in Temple, Texas, he began acting to try and get enough money to buy a ranch. That led to New York's Actors Studio and dance study with Martha Graham, and then award-winning roles on the New York stage. Since his film debut in *Baby Doll* (56), Torn has appeared fitfully but memorably in films. Among his TV roles in the 1970s was Nixon in *Blind Ambition*. He is married to actress Geraldine Page.
**Selected Films:** *Baby Doll* (56), *Cat on a Hot Tin Roof* (58), *The Cincinnati Kid* (65), *Payday* (73), *The Man Who Fell to Earth* (76), *Heartland* (80), *City Heat* (84), *Beer* (85), *Extreme Prejudice* (87).

## TORRENCE, Ernest (1878-1933)

Torrence, born in Edinburgh, Scotland, was a light opera singer before arriving onscreen in silents. After success in *Tol'able David* (21), the formidable-looking actor went on to superlative supporting roles as villains and occasionally as good guys into the sound era.
**Selected Films:** *Tol'able David* (21), *The Hunchback of Notre Dame* (23), *The Trail of the Lonesome Pine* (23), *The Covered Wagon* (23), *The Bridge of San Luis Rey* (29), *Sherlock Holmes* (33).

## TORRES, Raquel (1908- )

Born Paula Marie Osterman in Hermosillo, Mexico and educated in Los Angeles, Torres was a hit in *White Shadows of the South Seas* (28) and went on to play fiery senoritas in films of the 1930s, among them the Marx Brothers' classic *Duck Soup* (33).
**Selected Films:** *White Shadows in the South Seas* (28), *The Bridge of San Luis Rey* (29), *The Woman I Stole* (33), *Duck Soup* (33), *The Red Wagon* (36).

## TOTTER, Audrey (1918- )

Totter, born in Joliet, Illinois, came to the screen by way of radio. From the late 1940s she appeared in films usually as a hard-bitten blonde or gun moll. Later she played in several TV series including *Cimmaron City* and *Medical Center.*
**Selected Films:** *Main Street After Dark* (44), *The Postman Always Rings Twice* (45), *The Lady in the Lake* (46), *Women's Prison* (54), *The Carpetbaggers* (64), *The Apple Dumpling Gang Rides Again* (79).

## TRACY, Lee (1898-1968)

After stage and screen experience, William Lee Tracy, born in Atlanta, Georgia, played newsman Hildy Johnson in *The Front Page*. From then on he was the screen's archetypal fast-talking journalist, though he played other character roles as well. Late in life he was nominated for a supporting-actor Oscar for *The Best Man* (64).
**Selected Films:** *Big Time* (29), *Liliom* (30), *Doctor X* (32), *The Half Naked Truth* (32), *Dinner at Eight* (33), *Bombshell* (33), *Behind the Headlines* (37), *The Payoff* (43), *Power of the Press* (43), *I'll Tell the World* (45), *The Best Man* (64).

## TRACY, Spencer (1900-1967)

Actors from Humphrey Bogart to Laurence Olivier admired Tracy. Unlike actors who, if they are around long enough, generally need at least one or two strong come-back films, Tracy's popularity rose steadily. In his extraordinary movie career he rarely received a bad review. His low-key style and his ability to react to other actors in a completely natural way have never been bettered. His uneven features gained him gangster roles to begin with, then he switched to priests and friends of the hero, then he was in comedies. But his chief mature image was that of a tough, humorous fellow who was also a pillar of integrity. Born in Milwaukee, Wisconsin, he was educated at a Jesuit Preparatory School and originally planned to become a priest. In 1917 he joined the Navy, then went to Ripon College where he discovered acting. Although he had changed his life goals, he remained a devout Catholic. In 1923 he married actress Louise Treadwell and they never divorced even though Tracy's name was later linked romantically with screen star Loretta Young and his long-standing intimate relationship with Katharine Hepburn was a Hollywood legend. Tracy studied acting in New York, eventually appearing on Broadway in 1922. On stage he had the reputation of being solidly dependable and disciplined during performances. But off stage he was moody, quarrelsome, short-tempered and had a drinking problem. These characteristics carried over to his film career. Tracy's craggy, rugged appearance let him play a wide variety of screen roles, yet he was never a typical leading man. He received many Oscar nominations, and he won two in succession for *Captains Courageous* (37), in which he played a Portuguese fisherman, and *Boys' Town* (38), in which he played a priest – Father Flanagan, the founder of that orphan boys' home. He and Hepburn were wonderful together in a series of films, such as *Adam's Rib* (49) and *Pat and Mike* (52). They teamed again for *Guess Who's Coming to Dinner* (67), Tracy's last film. He won a British Film Academy Award for that picture, and audiences went to see the film in droves to pay posthumous homage to the man whose humor, masculinity, sincerity and dignified unpretentiousness on screen had brought so much pleasure to so many of them.
**Selected Films:** *Up the River* (30), *Quick Millions* (31), *Sky Devils* (32), *Twenty Thousand Years in Sing Sing* (32), *The Power and the Glory* (33), *A Man's Castle* (33), *Marie Galante* (34), *Dante's Inferno* (35), *Fury* (36), *San Francisco* (36), *Libeled Lady* (36), *Captains Courageous* (37), *Test Pilot* (38), *Boys' Town* (38), *Stanley and Livingstone* (39), *Northwest Passage* (40), *Edison the Man* (40), *Boom Town* (40), *Dr Jekyll and Mr Hyde* (41), *Woman of the Year* (42), *A Guy Named Joe* (43), *The Seventh Cross* (44), *Thirty Seconds Over Tokyo* (44), *Without Love* (45), *Sea of Grass* (46), *Cass Timberlane* (47), *State of the Union* (48), *Edward My Son* (49), *Adam's Rib* (49), *Father of the Bride* (50), *Father's Little Dividend* (51), *Pat and Mike* (52), *Bad Day at Black Rock* (55), *The Desk Set* (57), *The Old Man and the Sea* (58), *The Last Hurrah* (58), *Inherit the Wind* (60), *Judgment at Nuremberg* (61), *It's a Mad Mad Mad Mad World* (63), *Guess Who's Coming to Dinner* (67).

## TRACY, William (1917-1967)

Born in Pittsburgh, Pennsylvania, Tracy went from the American Academy of Dramatic Arts to extensive theater experience and repeated his stage role in *Brother Rat* in the 1938 screen version. Over the next years he was typecast as a simple minded character, an example being his Dude Lester in *Tobacco Road* (41).
**Selected Films:** *Brother Rat* (38), *Strike Up the Band* (40), *Tobacco Road* (41), *The Walls of Jericho* (49), *The Wings of Eagles* (56).

## TRAVERS, Bill (1922- )

Coming to the screen in the early 1950s, British actor William Lindon-Travers, a native of Newcastle-on-Tyne, was a handsome and rugged

player in a number of films of the 1950s. His roles included Benvolio in *Romeo and Juliet* (54) and Robert Browning in *The Barretts of Wimpole Street* (57). He starred with his wife Virginia MacKenna in *Born Free* (64). Other animal films followed.
**Selected Films:** *Conspirator* (49), *The Wooden Horse* (50), *Romeo and Juliet* (54), *Wee Geordie* (55), *The Smallest Show on Earth* (57), *The Barretts of Wimpole Street* (57), *Born Free* (64), *An Elephant Called Slowly* (70), *Christian the Lion* (76).

## TRAVERS, Henry (1874-1965)

Born Travers Haegerty in Ireland, Travers came after long stage experience to the screen in the early 1930s. For some two decades he played supporting roles as sympathetic elderly gentlemen in a good many films, several of them classics. He is best remembered as Clarence the angel in *It's a Wonderful Life* (46). Travers was nominated for an Oscar for *Mrs Miniver* (42).
**Selected Films:** *Reunion in Vienna* (32), *Seven Keys to Baldpate* (35), *Dark Victory* (39), *Ball of Fire* (41), *High Sierra* (41), *Mrs Miniver* (42), *The Moon is Down* (43), *It's a Wonderful Life* (46), *Beyond Glory* (48), *The Girl from Jones Beach* (49).

## TRAVIS, Richard (1913- )

Travis was born in Carlsbad, New Mexico, and came from radio to film, appearing mostly as tough leads in B movies and occasionally in first-feature supporting roles, during the 1940s and 1950s.
**Selected Films:** *The Man Who Came to Dinner* (41), *Buses Roar* (43), *Operation Haylift* (48), *Mask of the Dragon* (51), *Missile to the Moon* (58).

## TRAVOLTA, John (1954- )

Born in Englewood, New Jersey, he dropped out of high school to act in summer stock. He later did commercials and appeared in off-Broadway plays. Travolta moved to California and won a part in the touring company of the stage musical *Grease*, eventually winding up in the Broadway cast. His big break came when he joined the cast of the television situation comedy *Welcome Back, Kotter* in 1975, playing the part of the dim-witted high school student Vinnie Barbarino. His role of Tony Manero, the king of the Brooklyn disco scene, in the film *Saturday Night Fever* (77) made him a star, and he was also good in the movie version of *Grease* (78).
**Selected Films:** *The Devil's Rain* (75), *Carrie* (75), *Saturday Night Fever* (77), *Grease* (78), *Moment by Moment* (78), *Urban Cowboy* (80), *Blow Out* (82), *Staying Alive* (83).

## TREACHER, Arthur (1894-1975)

Born in Brighton, England, Treacher acted in the theater before coming to the screen in the early 1930s. Before long he was cast as the comic butler in the title role of *Thank You, Jeeves* (36), and for the rest of his career, as Jeeves and otherwise, he was Hollywood's favorite butler – long of face, impassive of mein, with just the right tone of polished sarcasm. Occasionally Treacher got other roles, and later efforts included lending his name to a fast-food restaurant chain.
**Selected Films:** *Battle of Paris* (29), *David Copperfield* (34), *Madame Du Barry* (34), *Thank You, Jeeves* (36), *Step Lively, Jeeves* (37), *The Little Princess* (39), *National Velvet* (44), *Love That Brute* (50), *Mary Poppins* (64).

## TREVOR, Claire (1909- )

Born Claire Wemlinger in New York City, Trevor was a highly gifted actress who projected vulnerability so well that she wound up typecast as the tramp with the heart of gold or the gangster's moll in B pictures. Yet she was superb when she was given the occasional chance to act in a good film. *Dead End* (37), *Stagecoach* (39) and *The High and the Mighty* (54) brought her the recognition she deserved. *Key Largo* (48) did even more and brought her an Oscar for Best Supporting Actress.
**Selected Films:** *The Mad Game* (33), *Black Sheep* (35), *Dead End* (37), *The Amazing Dr Clitterhouse* (38), *Stagecoach* (39), *Honky Tonk* (41), *Murder My Sweet* (44), *Crack Up* (46), *Key Largo* (48), *Hard, Fast and Beautiful* (51), *The High and the Mighty* (54), *Lucy Gallant* (55), *Marjorie Morningstar* (58), *Two Weeks in Another Town* (62), *The Stripper* (63), *How to Murder Your Wife* (65), *The Cape Town Affair* (67), *Kiss Me Goodbye* (82).

## TRINTIGNANT, Jean-Louis (1930- )

Born in Piolenc, France, Trintignant gave up the study of law to become an actor, and attended the Dullin Balachova Drama School. He starred with Brigitte Bardot in *And God Created Woman* (56), but is best known for appearing opposite Anouk Aimée in *A Man and a Woman* (66). He also won a French Academy Award for Z (69). Recently he has also tried directing.
**Selected Films:** *Si Tous les Gars du Monde* (55), *And God Created Woman* (56), *Les Liasons Dangereuses* (59), *A Man and a Woman* (66), *Is Paris Burning?* (66), *Z* (69), *Ma Nuit Chez Maud* (69), *The Conformist* (70), *Une Journée Bien Remplie* (73), *La Nuit de Varennes* (82), *Vivement Dimanche* (83), *A Man and a Woman: 20 Years Later* (86).

## TROWBRIDGE, Charles (1882-1967)

American actor Trowbridge was in films from the 1940s to the 1950s, usually playing supporting roles as professors, fathers, and other patriarchal characters.
**Selected Films:** *I Take This Woman* (31), *The Thirteenth Chair* (36), *Confessions of a Nazi Spy* (39), *The Mummy's Hand* (40), *Mildred Pierce* (45), *The Wings of Eagles* (57).

## TRUEX, Ernest (1890-1973)

Born in Kansas City, Missouri, Truex acted onstage before coming to film in the mid-teens. After playing some silent leads, in talkies Truex settled into character roles that suited his diminutive size – often as henpecked husbands. His extensive TV work included the series *Mr Peepers.*
**Selected Films:** *Caprice* (13), *Whistling in the Dark* (33), *His Girl Friday* (40), *The Leather Saint* (56), *Fluffy* (65).

## TRUFFAUT, Françoise (1932-1984)

Born in Paris, Truffaut began as a film critic before becoming a director. His first film, *Les Mistons* (57) about the attraction of an older woman to a group of young boys, was followed by *The 400 Blows* (59), a perceptive study, based on Truffaut's own childhood, of a misunderstood youth. Truffaut used the main character, Antoine Doinel in subsequent films. Considered one of the major New Wave talents, Truffaut also wrote and directed *Shoot the Piano Player* (60), *Jules and Jim* (61), *La Peau Douce* (64) and *Fahrenheit 451* (66). He appeared in and directed the semi-documentary *L'Enfant Sauvage* (70), and a number of other films including *Day for Night* (73) which won the Academy Award for Best Foreign Film. He also appeared in Stephen Spielberg's *Close Encounters of the Third Kind* (77) and several documentaries.
**Selected Films:** *L'Enfant Sauvage* (70), *Day for Night* (73), *Close Encounters of the Third Kind* (77), *La Chambre Verte* (78).

## TRYON, Tom (1919- )

Before he started acting, Tryon, born in Hartford, Connecticut, attended Yale, was a sailor in World War II, studied painting, and was a TV production assistant. Onscreen from the mid-1950s, he played some tough leads in action films and the title role in *The Cardinal* (63). He then began a successful career as a writer. His supernatural novel *The Other* was filmed in 1972.
**Selected Films:** *The Scarlet Hour* (55), *I Married a Monster from Outer Space* (57), *The Cardinal* (63), *In Harm's Way* (65), *Johnny Got His Gun* (71).

## TUCKER, Forrest (1919-1986)

Born in Plainffeld, Indiana, Tucker worked in burlesque before landing roles in films with *The Westerner* (40), the first of his many westerns. After years of mostly low-budget starring roles, the rangy and rugged actor began playing character parts in the 1970s, among them in the comedy *The Night They Raided Minsky's* (68). He also appeared as Sgt O'Rourke in the TV series *F Troop*.
**Selected Films:** *The Westerner* (40), *The Yearling* (46), *Sands of Iwo Jima* (50), *The Abominable Snowman* (57), *The Night They Raided Minsky's* (68), *Final Chapter – Walking Tall* (77), *Carnauba* (81).

## TUCKER, Sophie (1884-1966)

Born Sonia Kalish in Russia, she first saw the light of day when her mother was 'on the road' – traveling to join her husband in America where he had fled to avoid military service. Meanwhile, the husband, fearful of being apprehended by Russian authorities, had taken the identity of a deceased Italian friend, so Tucker grew up as Sophia Abuza. Tucker's father owned a restaurant in Hartford, Connecticut, where she would sing from time to time. But her parents didn't want her in show business, so she ran away from home, landing in New York in 1906. She won a part in an amateur show and had to wear blackface because the manager thought her 'too big and ugly.' She sang between the acts of a *Ziegfeld Follies* production, but was fired because the stars resented her popularity, so Tucker joined the Morris vaudeville circuit. Her nickname, 'The Last of the Red Hot Mamas,' stemmed from her choice of off-color songs dealing with sex, she said, not vice. During World War I she popularized the song 'Mother (The Word That Means the World to Me).' She was a favorite all over Europe, too. Her films were not successful because they did not capture the essential Tucker. But when she sang 'Some of These Days,' she was in her prime.
**Selected Films:** *Honky Tonk* (29), *Gay Love* (34), *Broadway Melody of 1937* (37), *Thoroughbreds Don't Cry* (37), *Atlantic City* (44), *Follow the Boys* (44), *Sensations of 1945* (44).

## TUFTS, Sonny (1912-1970)

Born Bowen Tufts III in Boston, Massachusetts, Tufts attended Yale and tried opera before landing parts in Broadway musicals. He came to screen leads in the mid-1940s and for a few years, riding a flood of studio publicity, he was a beefy, amiable leading man in films like *So Proudly We Hail* (43). By the 1950s, however, his career had declined to films like *Cat Women of the Moon* (53). He died after a few comeback attempts.
**Selected Films:** *Ambush* (39), *So Proudly We Hail* (43), *I Love a Soldier* (44), *Duffy's Tavern* (45), *Cat Women of the Moon* (53), *The Seven Year Itch* (55), *Cottonpickin' Chickenpickers* (67).

## TULLY, Tom (1896-1982)

A native of Durango, Colorado, Tully worked his way through the Navy, radio, and the stage before arriving onscreen in the mid-1940s. He tended to play tough, streetwise, but likeable characters; that also applied to his TV series *The Lineup* (54-59). Tully was nominated for a supporting-actor Oscar for his performance as Captain De Vreiss in *The Caine Mutiny* (54).
**Selected Films:** *Northern Pursuit* (43), *Destination Tokyo* (44), *Where the Sidewalk Ends* (50), *The Caine Mutiny* (54), *The Wackiest Ship in the Army* (61), *Charley Varrick* (73).

Left: *Jack Nicholson, Kathleen Turner and Anjelica Huston starred in* Prizzi's Honor *(85), directed by John Huston.*

Above: *Lana Turner and Fernando Lamas in* The Merry Widow *(62).*

## TURNER, Kathleen (1956- )

Kathleen Turner has been called 'perhaps the movies' first authentically mysterious presence since Garbo.' This captures some of the reason for Turner's elusive quality and her resounding success; in practice, however, she lacks the haunting face of Garbo but has handled a wider range of roles. Turner was born to a diplomat's family in Springfield, Missouri (she is evasive about the exact year) and began studying drama while in high school in London. After college and professional stage experience, in 1978 she landed a part in the TV soap *The Doctors*. Three years later she secured her first screen role, starring as the steamy Matty in *Body Heat* (81). Her next films were Steve Martin's comedy *The Man With Two Brains* (83) and *Romancing the Stone* (84). In the latter, Turner played a drab writer who ends up in a Perils-of-Pauline-style jungle adventure; it was her first smash hit. Her roles since have continued ranging widely: she was a sleazy streetwalker in *Crimes of Passion* (84), a beautiful Mafia killer in *Prizzi's Honor* (85), an adventuress again in *Jewel of the Nile* (85) (a sequel to *Romancing the Stone*). For her performance as a housewife who magically returns to her youth in *Peggy Sue Got Married* (86), Turner was nominated for the Best Actress Oscar.
**Selected Films:** *Body Heat* (81), *The Man with Two Brains* (83), *Romancing the Stone* (84), *Crimes of Passion* (84), *Prizzi's Honor* (85), *Jewel of the Nile* (85), *Peggy Sue Got Married* (86).

## TURNER, Lana (1920- )

As a teen-aged blonde starlet, she became Hollywood's 'Sweater Girl,' then matured into a glamorous star. Born Julia Turner in Wallace, Idaho, she went with her mother to California after her father was robbed and murdered. At the age of 15 she was discovered by a Hollywood talent scout in a drug store across the street from her high school. Turner was taken to director Mervyn LeRoy who signed her for a small but memorable part in *They Won't Forget* (37). After her appearance in *We Who Are Young* (40), she was taken seriously as an actress, at least seriously enough to put her in major productions. *Ziegfeld Girl* (41), *Dr Jekyll and Mr Hyde* (41) and *The Postman Always Rings Twice* (45) were some of her best films of the 1940s. Married numerous times, including to band leader Artie Shaw and ex-Tarzan Lex Barker, she was the center of a well-publicized scandal when in 1958 her daughter, Cheryl Crane, stabbed Turner's gangster lover Johnny Stompanato to death. Turner has remained a glittering celebrity.
**Selected Films:** *They Won't Forget* (37), *Love Finds Andy Hardy* (39), *Ziegfeld Girl* (41), *Dr Jekyll and Mr Hyde* (41), *Honky Tonk* (41), *Somewhere I'll Find You* (42), *The Postman Always Rings Twice* (45), *Green Dolphin Street* (46), *Cass Timberlane* (47), *The Three Musketeers* (48), *The Merry Widow* (52), *The Bad and the Beautiful* (52), *Peyton Place* (57), *Imitation of Life* (59), *Portrait in Black* (60), *Bittersweet Love* (76).

## TURPIN, Ben (1874-1940)

Turpin was born in New Orleans and began his long film career in Essanay short comedies. Most of his humor came from his severely crossed eyes and his gift for slapstick humor. He appeared in some early Charlie Chaplin shorts, but he worked mainly for Mack Sennett. During the sound era, Turpin played cameo roles in occasional films.
**Selected Films:** *Mr Flip* (09), *His New Job* (15), *Uncle Tom's Cabin* (19), *A Small Town Idol* (21), *The Prodigal Bridegroom* (26), *Show of Shows* (29), *The Love Parade* (30), *Make Me a Star* (32), *Hollywood Cavalcade* (39), *Saps at Sea* (40).

## TUSHINGHAM, Rita (1940- )

After brief stage experience, Tushingham, born in Liverpool, England, made a much-heralded screen debut in *A Taste of Honey* (61). For a few years the

actress with big eyes and plain features appeared in fashionably offbeat films like *The Knack* (65) as well as major ones like *Doctor Zhivago* (65).
**Selected Films:** *A Taste of Honey* (61), *The Leather Boys* (63), *Girl with Green Eyes* (64), *The Knack* (65), *Doctor Zhivago* (65), *The Trap* (66), *The Guru* (69), *The Human Factor* (75), *Mysteries* (78), *The Housekeeper* (87).

## TWELVETREES, Helen (1908-1958)

Born Helen Jurgens in Brooklyn, New York, Twelvetrees acted onstage before beginning a meteoric career in films with *The Ghost Talks* (29). During the 1930s she starred in a number of popular melodramas before her career sank as abruptly as it rose. She died a suicide.
**Selected Films:** *The Ghost Talks* (29), *The Cat Creeps* (30), *The Painted Desert* (31), *Times Square Lady* (35), *Hollywood Roundup* (38), *Unmarried* (39).

## TWIGGY, (1949- )

Born Lesley Hornby in London, England, Twiggy was regarded as the world's leading fashion model by the time that she was 17 years old. A thin, seemingly very shy girl, she soon appeared in West End shows and then was a success in movies, beginning with *The Boy Friend* (71). In 1983 she became the toast of Broadway in *My One and Only*, costarring Tommy Tune.
**Selected Films:** *The Boy Friend* (71), *'W'* (74), *There Goes the Bride* (79), *The Blues Brothers* (80), *The Doctor and the Devils* (85), *Club Paradise* (86).

## TYLER, Beverly (1924- )

American actress Tyler was a familiar leading lady of routine films during the 1940s.
**Selected Films:** *Best Foot Forward* (43), *The Beginning or the End* (47), *Chicago Confidential* (47), *Cimarron Kid* (51)

## TYLER, Tom (1904-1954)

Born Vincent Markowski in Port Henry, New York, Tyler was a coal miner, seaman, lumberjack, prize fighter and weightlifter before beginning his film career in 1924 as a stunt man and extra. He became a star of B Westerns in the 1920s and was still a star into the 1940s. He died of a heart attack at the age of 50 after suffering for years with a crippling rheumatic condition.
**Selected Films:** *Galloping Gallagher* (24), *The Cowboy Cop* (26), *The Sorcerer* (29), *Riding the Lonesome Trail* (34), *Pinto Rustlers* (38), *Roamin' Wild* (39), *The Mummy's Hand* (40), *Valley of the Sun* (42), *San Antonio* (45), *Cow Country* (53).

## TYSON, Cicely (1932- )

Tyson was born in New York City and made her screen debut in the 1950s. She had previously been the first black actress to have a continuing role in a television series – *East Side/West Side*, which starred George C Scott. Her first important film role was in *Twelve Angry Men* (57). She won an Academy Award nomination and rapturous reviews for her leading role in *Sounder* (72) and an Emmy for her starring role in *The Autobiography of Miss Jane Pittman*, a 1974 television special.
**Selected Films:** *Twelve Angry Men* (57), *A Man Called Adam* (66), *The Comedians* (67), *Sounder* (72), *The River Niger* (76), *A Hero Ain't Nothin' but a Sandwich* (77), *Airport '79 Concorde* (79).

# U

## ULLMANN, Liv (1939- )

Ullmann, a great dramatic actress and an earthy natural beauty, has appeared in numerous Swedish and international films. Born in Tokyo, Japan, to Norwegian parents, she went with her family to Canada at the outbreak of the hostilities in the Pacific during World War II, and later to New York. After her father's death she moved to Norway, achieving prominence on the stage in Oslo and in Norwegian movies. She had worked closely with Swedish film director Ingmar Bergman, starring in some of his greatest pictures. They also lived together for several years and are the parents of a daughter. She was twice nominated for an Academy Award for Best Actress – in *The Emigrants* (72) and *Face to Face* (76).
**Selected Films:** *The Wayward Girl* (59), *Persona* (66), *Hours of the Wolf* (67), *Shame* (68), *A Passion* (70), *The Emigrants* (72), *Cries and Whispers* (72), *Scenes from a Marriage* (73), *Lost Horizon* (73), *Forty Carats* (73), *The New Land* (73), *Face to Face* (76), *A Bridge Too Far* (77), *The Serpent's Egg* (77), *Autumn Sonata* (78), *The Gates of the Forest* (80).

## UMEKI, Miyoshi (1929- )

Umeki was born in Otaru, Hokkaido, Japan and when she was in her teens she became a radio and night club vocalist. She came to the United States in the 1950s and appeared on television. These appearances led to a part in the film *Sayonara* (57), in which she played opposite Red Buttons. They were a pair of doomed lovers who eventually would have to part, and both of them won Academy Awards for their supporting roles. Later she appeared on Broadway in *Flower Drum Song*, repeating her role in the film version in 1961.
**Selected Films:** *Sayonara* (57), *Cry for Happy* (61), *Flower Drum Song* (61), *The Horizontal Lieutenant* (62), *A Girl Named Tamiko* (63).

## URE, Mary (1933-1975)

Born in Glasgow, Scotland, Ure was better known as a stage actress than a movie star, but she gave some telling performances on the screen. Possibly her best role was in *Sons and Lovers* (60), and she

was nominated for an Academy Award for Best Supporting Actress for her performance. Once married to playwright John Osborne, she later married actor/writer Robert Shaw. Ure died of an accidental mixture of alcohol and barbiturates.
**Selected Films:** *Storm Over the Nile* (55), *Windom's Way* (58), *Look Back in Anger* (59), *Sons and Lovers* (60), *The Mind Benders* (63), *The Luck of Ginger Coffey* (64), *Custer of the West* (68), *Where Eagles Dare* (69), *A Reflection of Fear* (73).

## USTINOV, Peter (1921- )

Ustinov, the talented actor, screenwriter, director, playwright and novelist, was born in London, England, to a Russian father and a French mother. He trained for the stage at the London Theater Studio and made his acting debut at the age of 17. He soon emerged as one of the most versatile talents of the British and American stage and screen. He won Academy Awards for Best Supporting Actor for *Spartacus* (60), as a Roman slave-holder, and for *Topkapi* (64), as a sly and clumsy rogue in this caper film. He was also nominated for Best Supporting Actor for his role as Nero in *Quo Vadis* (51). In addition, he won an Emmy Award for his portrayal of Dr Johnson in *The Life of Samuel Johnson* on television.
**Selected Films:** *Hullo Fame* (40), *One of Our Aircraft Is Missing* (42), *Private Angelo* (49), *Hotel Sahara* (51), *Quo Vadis* (51), *Beau Brummel* (54), *The Egyptian* (54), *We're No Angels* (55), *The Sundowners* (60), *Spartacus* (60), *Romanoff and Juliet* (61), *Topkapi* (64), *Viva Max!* (69), *Logan's Run* (76), *Ashanti* (78), *Death on the Nile* (78), *Evil Under the Sun* (82), *Memed My Hawk* (87).

# V

## VALENTINO, Rudolph (1895-1926)

No one ever had more star quality than Rodolpho Alfonzo Raffaele Pierre Philibert Guglielmi of Castellaneta, Italy, otherwise known as Rudolph Valentino. He was the great Italian-American leading man who was typecast in the 1920s as a passionate Arab or Latin. His animal magnetism, flashing dark eyes, elegant taste in clothes and aura of mystery and wickedness made him the great idol and male sex symbol of the silent-movie era, although excerpts from his diary published after his death indicate that the screen's great lover might have been homosexual. His early life is a record of failure. This Italian Navy dropout was begging on the streets of Paris in 1912. In 1913 he was in New York, where he was booked several times by the police on suspicion of petty theft and blackmail. He found work as a taxi dancer, moved into the nightclub class, toured with a show and wound up in Hollywood. He began in films playing gigolos, villains and seductive dancers. While still a bit player he married actress Jean Acker, who

*Rudolph Valentino in* The Four Horsemen of the Apocalypse *(21).*

later divorced him, claiming the marriage was never consummated. Contacts and luck brought him the lead in *The Four Horsemen of the Apocalypse* (21), a record-breaking smash hit. *The Sheik* (21) made women swoon and started an Arabian fad in interior decorating. Valentino's second wife was Natasha Rambova (born Winifred Shaunessy), and, until they separated, she managed his career. Valentino was arrested for bigamy after marrying her because their wedding took place before his divorce from Acker was made final. Rambova and Valentino went on an extensive dance tour and he published a popular book of poetry called *Day Dreams*. If women loved Valentino, men despised him. In 1926 *The Chicago Tribune* attacked him for being a 'Pink Powder Puff,' a 'painted pansy.' Valentino did appear in some of his films in elaborate and highly decorative costumes, but he often appeared in very little, which seemed to be the way his female fans liked him best. In 1926 he was rushed to a New York hospital, suffering from a perforated ulcer. When newspapers reported that he had died, many American women became hysterical. His sudden death caused several suicides and his funeral was a national event. Rioting broke out in the crowd waiting to file past his casket and more than one hundred police reinforcements were required to calm things down. Valentino's fan clubs developed into cults and the reaction to his death did not go unnoticed on Wall Street. Thanks to Valentino, movies became regarded as a business.
**Selected Films:** *My Official Wife* (14), *Patria* (16), *Alimony* (18), *The Delicious Little Devil* (19), *The Married Virgin* (20), *The Cheater* (20), *Passion's Playground* (20), *One to Every Woman* (20), *The Four Horsemen of the Apocalypse* (21), *Unchained Seas* (21), *Camilla* (21), *The Sheik* (21), *The Young Rajah* (22), *Blood and Sand* (22), *Monsieur Beaucaire* (24), *Cobra* (24), *The Eagle* (25), *Son of the Sheik* (26).

## VALLEE, Rudy (1901-1986)

Born Hubert Prior Vallee in Iron Pond, Vermont, Vallee soon moved with his family to Westbrook, Maine, where he attended high school while teaching himself to play the clarinet. Switching to the saxophone, he worked his way through college at the University of Maine and later Yale University, by playing in dance bands. In 1928 he opened at the Heigh Ho Club in New York with his own band, the Connecticut Yankees. His twangy crooning style, aided by a handheld megaphone, made him a singing idol of the 1930s and 1940s. In 1929 he and his orchestra were called to Hollywood to make *The Vagabond Lover* for RKO, a film named for one of Vallee's biggest hit songs. He made a series of unmemorable motion pictures in the 1930s and joined the Coast Guard during World War II, conducting the 11th Naval District Coast Guard Band. After the war, he continued to play club dates and appear in films. His big Hollywood hit came in 1967, when he re-created his Broadway role of J B Biggley, the wicked tycoon, in *How to Succeed in Business Without Really Trying.*

**Selected Films:** *The Vagabond Lover* (29), *Sweet Music* (34), *Gold Diggers in Paris* (38), *Second Fiddle* (39), *Too Many Blondes* (41), *The Palm Beach Story* (42), *The Bachelor and the Bobby Soxer* (47), *Unfaithfully Yours* (48), *The Beautiful Blonde from Bashful Bend* (49), *Ricochet Romance* (54), *Gentlemen Marry Brunettes* (55), *The Helen Morgan Story* (57), *How to Succeed in Business Without Really Trying* (67), *Live a Little, Love a Little* (68), *Won Ton Ton, The Dog Who Saved Hollywood* (76).

## VALLI, Alida (1921- )

Born Alida Maria Altenburger in Pola, Italy, Valli studied screen acting in her youth and arrived in films at age 15. Within a few years the dark-haired beauty was one of Italy's favorite leading ladies, starring in a series of light romances and comedies during the 1930s. By *Piccolo Mondo Antico* (41), Valli had developed into an actress of considerable range; her role in the film won the Venice Film Festival award. After the war she was brought to the United States by producer David O Selznick, but in her two American films, *The Paradine Case* (46) and *The Miracle of the Bells* (46), she made no great impact. Her next film, made in England, made her an international star: she was the woman that Joseph Cotten failed to get in *The Third Man* (50). Thereafter Valli (often working under her last name only) played starring roles in films all over Europe and America. In 1954 her acting career was put on hold for a couple of years when she was implicated in a drug-and-murder scandal in Italy.

**Selected Films:** *I Due Sergenti* (36), *Manon Lescaut* (39), *Piccolo Mondo Antico* (41), *I Pagliacci* (42), *Eugenie Grandet* (46), *The Paradine Case* (46), *The Miracle of the Bells* (46), *Walk Softly, Stranger* (50), *The Third Man* (50), *Senso* (53), *Ophelia* (61), *The Cassandra Crossing* (77), *Aspern* (82), *Inferno* (86).

## VALLONE, RAF (1916- )

For someone who began his screen career playing peasants in Italian neorealist movies, Vallone had quite a literate background. Born in Tropea, Italy, he played professional soccer after university studies and then was a sports reporter, music critic, and film critic before arriving onscreen as a virile laborer in *Bitter Rice* (48). He had leads in Italian films through the 1950s, including Giuseppe Garibaldi in *Anita Garibaldi* (52) and the title role of *Andrea Chenier* (55). In 1961 he played a supporting role in the Italian/American epic *El Cid.* His first English-speaking part was in the film of Arthur Miller's *A View From the Bridge* (62), which Vallone had starred in and directed in American and French stage productions. He continued to appear in films internationally through the 1970s.

**Selected Films:** *Bitter Rice* (48), *Vendetta* (49), *Anita Garibaldi* (52), *Andrea Chenier* (55), *Two Women* (60), *El Cid* (61), *A View from the Bridge* (62), *The Cardinal* (63), *Harlow* (65), *Nevada Smith* (66), *The Kremlin Letter* (70), *The Other Side of Midnight* (77), *Omar Mukhtar – Lion of the Desert* (80).

## VAN, Bobby (1930-1980)

Born Robert King in New York, Van was an experienced song-and-dance man in cabarets, musicals, and TV when he came to the screen in the early 1950s. After several movies, notably *Kiss Me Kate* (53), his career declined in the 1960s. He came back in the hit revival of *No No Nanette* (71) and the flop remake of *Lost Horizon* (73).

**Selected Films:** *Because You're Mine* (52), *Small Town Girl* (52), *Kiss Me Kate* (53), *The Navy vs the Night Monsters* (66), *Lost Horizon* (73).

## VANCE, Vivian (1911-1979)

Born in Cherryvale, Kansas, Vance appeared in a few films of the 1950s and 1960s but was best known as Ethel, the neighbor of the Ricardos in the classic TV sitcom *I Love Lucy.*

**Selected Films:** *The Secret Fury* (50), *The Blue Veil* (51), *The Great Race* (65).

## VAN CLEEF, Lee (1925- )

Born in Somerville, New Jersey, Van Cleef returned from naval service during World War II, joined a little theatre group, and went straight on to films. His sharp features and narrow steely eyes made him ideal as a villain, and he was typecast as a cruel evil-doer in many Hollywood Westerns. He finally achieved stardom as the savage hero of several 'Spaghetti Westerns.'

**Selected Films:** *High Noon* (52), *The Man Who Shot Liberty Valance* (62), *For a Few Dollars More* (65), *The Good, the Bad and the Ugly* (66), *Captain Apache* (71), *Take a Hard Ride* (75), *Killers* (77), *The Hard Way* (79), *The Octagon* (80), *The Squeeze* (82).

## VAN DEVERE, Trish (1944- )

Born in Tenafly, New Jersey, Van Devere came to the screen in 1970 and while making *Where's*

*Poppa?* (70) met actor George C Scott, whom she married and with whom she co-starred in *Day of the Dolphins* (73). While giving most of her time to the theater, she appeared in occasional films.
**Selected Films:** *Where's Poppa?* (70), *The Landlord* (70), *The Last Run* (71), *One is a Lonely Number* (72), *Day of the Dolphins* (73), *Movie Movie* (78), *The Changeling* (80).

## VAN DOREN, Mamie (1933- )

Born Joan Olander in Rowena, South Dakota, Van Doren studied drama and made a straight stage debut before arriving in films in the mid-1950s. A platinum blonde of steamy effect onscreen, she had a few years of roles in major features like *Teacher's Pet* (58), before being relegated to the status of B movie sexpot.
**Selected Films:** *Forbidden* (54), *The Second Greatest Sex* (55), *High School Confidential* (58), *Teacher's Pet* (58), *College Confidential* (60), *The Candidate* (64), *You Got to Be Smart* (67).

## VAN DYKE, Dick (1925- )

Born in West Plains, Missouri, Van Dyke worked in nightclubs and on television before finding success on Broadway starring in *Bye Bye Birdie* and making his screen debut in the 1963 film of the musical. Meanwhile he had begun his classic long-running TV comedy series *The Dick Van Dyke Show*. During the 1960s the affable and agile Van Dyke appeared in some successful films, notably opposite Julie Andrews in *Mary Poppins* (64), but was more often found in disappointing ones. In the 1970s his career languished because of his drinking problem. Since his recovery he has appeared occasionally on film and in TV movies.
**Selected Films:** *Bye Bye Birdie* (63), *Mary Poppins* (64), *Lt Robin Crusoe* (65), *Divorce, American Style* (67), *Fitzwilly* (67), *Chitty Chitty Bang Bang* (68), *The Comic* (69), *The Runner Stumbles* (79).

## VAN EYCK, Peter (1911-1969)

Born Götz von Eyck in Germany, Van Eyck came to the United States in the 1930s and worked as a pianist and arranger before his blonde Teutonic looks got him into films playing Nazis in the early 1940s. He played Gestapo agents as often as not in movies over the next two decades, appearing in both American and European films, including the classic thriller *The Wages of Fear* (53).
**Selected Films:** *The Moon is Down* (42), *Five Graves to Cairo* (43), *The Desert Fox* (51), *The Wages of Fear* (53), *The 1000 Eyes of Dr Mabuse* (60), *The Spy Who Came in from the Cold* (65), *Assignment to Kill* (69).

## VAN FLEET, Jo (1919- )

Van Fleet, born in Oakland, California, starred on Broadway for years before making her screen debut as James Dean's slatternly mother in *East of Eden* (55), the role which won her a supporting actress Oscar. While concentrating on the theater, she appeared occasionally in films through the 1970s, usually playing unsympathetic ladies older than her real age.
**Selected Films:** *East of Eden* (55), *The Rose Tattoo* (55), *I'll Cry Tomorrow* (55), *Wild River* (60), *Cool Hand Luke* (67), *The Tenant* (76).

## VAN PATTEN, Dick (1928- )

Born in Kew Gardens, New York, the older brother of actress Joyce Van Patten, Dick began performing professionally as a child and made his screen debut with Joyce at age 12. From the mid-1960s on he appeared occasionally onscreen, usually in comic character roles, several for Mel Brooks. He is best known for his TV series *Eight is Enough*.
**Selected Films:** *Reg'lar Fellers* (41), *Psychomania* (64), *Charly* (68), *Superdad* (74), *High Anxiety* (77), *Spaceballs* (87).

## VAN PATTEN, Joyce (1934- )

Along with her brother Dick, New York-born Joyce began acting in childhood. She has been in films since the early 1950s but is best known for her roles on TV series, including *The Danny Kaye Show* and *The Good Guys*. For a time she was married to actor Martin Balsam.
**Selected Films:** *Reg'lar Fellers* (41), *14 Hours* (51), *The Goddess* (58), *I Love You, Alice B Toklas* (68), *Making It* (71), *Mame* (74), *The Bad News Bears* (76), *Billy Galvin* (87).

## VAN ROOTEN, Luis (1906-1973)

Born to an American family in Mexico City, Van Rooten acted onstage and in radio before making his screen debut as Himmler in *The Hitler Gang* (44). After nearly two decades of playing mostly down-at-heels villains, he played Himmler again in his last film, *Operation Eichmann* (61).
**Selected Films:** *The Hitler Gang* (44), *Two Years Before the Mast* (44), *Champion* (49), *Detective Story* (51), *The Sea Chase* (55), *Operation Eichmann* (61).

## VAN SLOAN, Edward (1882-1964)

Van Sloan was born in San Francisco, California. He began as a commercial artist and then switched to acting, making his mark as character actor in numerous Hollywood films of the 1930s and 1940s. He usually played doctors, professors and other intellectuals and is best remembered for being the fearless vampire hunter, Dr Van Helsing, in *Dracula* (30).
**Selected Films:** *Dracula* (30), *Frankenstein* (31), *The Last Mile* (32), *The Mummy* (32), *The Scarlet Empress* (34), *The Last Days of Pompeii* (35), *The Story of Louis Pasteur* (36), *Dracula's Daughter* (36), *Before I Hang* (40), *Mission to Moscow* (43), *Betty Co-Ed* (47), *A Foreign Affair* (48).

## VAN ZANDT, Philip (1904-1958)

Born in Amsterdam, Holland, Van Zandt came to the United States in his teens and acted in a great many plays before making his screen debut in *Those High Gray Walls* (39). Though perhaps his best-known role is as the head newsman in the screening-room scene of *Citizen Kane* (41), he spent most of his career playing bad guys. He died a suicide.

**Selected Films:** *Those High Gray Walls* (39), *Citizen Kane* (41), *Wake Island* (42), *House of Frankenstein* (45), *Viva Zapata!* (52), *Knock on Wood* (54), *Man of a Thousand Faces* (57).

## VARSI, Diane (1938- )

After a troubled and wandering early life, Varsi, born in San Francisco, California, was nominated for an Oscar for her first film role, as Lana Turner's pretty but unhappy daughter in *Peyton Place* (57). Then, after starring in major films including *Ten North Frederick* (58), she had a nervous breakdown and walked out on a Fox contract. In the mid-1960s Varsi began appearing in occasional films again, but never regained major roles.

**Selected Films:** *Peyton Place* (57), *Ten North Frederick* (58), *Compulsion* (59), *Sweet Love, Bitter* (66), *Wild in the Streets* (68), *Bloody Mama* (70), *I Never Promised You a Rose Garden* (77).

## VAUGHN, Robert (1932- )

Vaughn was born in New York and grew up in Minneapolis. While working toward a doctorate in political science he pursued an acting career and made his screen debut in *Hell's Crossroads* (57). He has since played strong supporting roles in *The Young Philadelphians* (59), which earned him an Oscar nomination, and *The Magnificent Seven* (60), among others. He remains best-known for his tongue-in-cheek spy Napoleon Solo in the TV series *The Man From U.N.C.L.E.* Active in liberal political causes, Vaughn wrote a book on the Hollywood Red Scare called *Only Victims.*

**Selected Films:** *Hell's Crossroads* (57), *Teenage Caveman* (58), *The Young Philadelphians* (59), *The Magnificent Seven* (60), *Bullitt* (68), *The Towering Inferno* (74), *Brass Target* (78), *Superman III* (83), *Black Moon Rising* (86).

## VEIDT, Conrad (1893-1943)

Veidt was born in Potsdam, Germany, and first appeared on stage in Max Reinhardt's theater in Berlin. He started making German movies in 1917. His gaunt figure and expressive face led him to be cast in tormented or demonic roles, notably as Cesare, the murderous sleepwalker in *The Cabinet of Dr Caligari* (19). He was also in *The Student of Prague* (26) and *The Hands of Orlac* (26) – two other fine horror movies. Veidt was unpopular with the Nazis, especially because he had a Jewish wife, and when they rose to power he moved to England. When he returned to Germany briefly to make a film, the Nazi Government created an international incident by refusing to let him leave. The Germans finally relented after his film studio, Gaumont British, sent its own physicians to prove that he was not ill, as the Nazis had claimed. In 1939, Veidt became a British citizen. When Veidt went to Hollywood, he ironically specialized in playing Nazis, most memorably in *Casablanca* (42).

**Selected Films:** *Der Spion* (16), *The Cabinet of Dr Caligari* (19), *Waxworks* (24), *Lucrezia Borgia* (25), *The Student of Prague* (26), *The Hands of Orlac* (26), *The Man Who Laughs* (27), *The Congress Dances* (31), *Rome Express* (32), *The Wandering Jew* (33), *The Passing of the Third Floor Back* (35), *Under the Red Robe* (36), *Dark Journey* (37), *The Spy in Black* (39), *The Thief of Baghdad* (49), *Nazi Agent* (42), *Casablanca* (42), *Above Suspicion* (43).

## VELEZ, Lupe (1908-1944)

Born Maria Guadalupe Velez de Villalobos in Mexico and educated in Texas, Velez got into silents in 1926 and had her first hit as a Latin firebrand opposite Douglas Fairbanks in *The Gaucho* (27). She played that role onscreen and off for the rest of her life, her movie career finally ending up in the *Mexican Spitfire* comedies with Leon Errol. She was married to Johnny Weissmuller from 1933 to 1938.

**Selected Films:** *The Gaucho* (27), *The Squaw Man* (31), *The Girl from Mexico* (38), *Mexican Spitfire* (39), *Mexican Spitfire's Elephant* (42), *Mexican Spitfire's Blessed Event* (43), *Nana* (44).

## VENABLE, Evelyn (1913- )

Born in Cincinnati, Ohio, Venable acted briefly in the theater before being discovered by Paramount in the early 1930s. For a while she played mostly demure types in major films, but after several years of unrewarded outings she retired in 1943.

**Selected Films:** *Cradle Song* (33), *Mrs Wiggs of the Cabbage Patch* (34), *Alice Adams* (35), *Female Fugitive* (38), *He Hired the Boss* (43).

## VERA-ELLEN (1926-1981)

Born Vera-Ellen Westmeyr Rohe in Cincinnati, Ohio, she studied dancing from the age of ten. She was a Radio City Music Hall Rockette and appeared in night clubs and in Broadway musicals before making her film debut in *Wonder Man* (45), which starred Danny Kaye. This petite energetic blonde became one of Hollywood's most accomplished and versatile dancers, especially with Gene Kelly and Fred Astaire. She retired from movies in the late 1950s.

**Selected Films:** *Wonder Man* (45), *The Kid from Brooklyn* (46), *Words and Music* (48), *On the Town* (49), *Three Little Words* (50), *Call Me Madam* (53), *White Christmas* (54), *Let's Be Happy* (57).

## VERDON, Gwen (1925- )

Born in Culver City, California, the vivacious dancer and actress rose to stardom on the Broadway musical stage in the 1950s, starring in *Can-Can* and *New Girl in Town* among others. Of her occasional film roles, best-known is her Lola in *Damn Yankees* (58), which she originated on the stage. For a time she was married to director/choreographer Bob Fosse.
**Selected Films:** *On the Riviera* (51), *David and Bathsheba* (51), *The Farmer Takes a Wife* (53), *Damn Yankees* (58), *Cocoon* (85).

## VERDUGO, Elena (1926- )

Born to a Spanish family in Hollywood, California, Verdugo made her debut in the early 1940s and for some years had a middling career playing leads in B movies and supporting roles in major films. She is best known for her role in the TV series *Marcus Welby*.
**Selected Films:** *Down Argentine Way* (40), *Belle Starr* (41), *The Moon and Sixpence* (42), *House of Frankenstein* (45), *Cyrano de Bergerac* (50), *How Sweet It Is!* (68), *Angel in My Pocket* (69).

## VERNON, Wally (1904-1970)

American comedian Vernon played eccentric supporting roles in a good many films of the later 1930s into the 1960s.
**Selected Films:** *Mountain Music* (37), *Alexander's Ragtime Band* (38), *Always Leave Them Laughing* (49), *What Price Glory?* (52), *What a Way to Go* (64).

## VICKERS, Martha (1925-1971)

Born Martha MacVicar in Ann Arbor, Michigan, Vickers arrived in films at age 18 and for several years acted under her real name. Changing names in 1946 to play Lauren Bacall's kid sister in *The Big Sleep*, she seemed headed for major roles, but her ensuing films were mostly minor. For two years she was married to Mickey Rooney.
**Selected Films:** *Frankenstein Meets the Wolf Man* (43), *The Falcon in Mexico* (44), *The Big Sleep* (46), *The Man I Love* (47), *Bad Boy* (49), *Alimony* (55), *The Burglar* (57), *Four Fast Guns* (60).

## VIDOR, Florence (1895-1977)

Born Florence Cobb in Houston, Texas, Florence came to Hollywood in 1915 with her new husband, soon-to-be-director King Vidor. By the 1920s she was a popular silent star. Her parts included the title roles in *Alice Adams* (23) and *Barbara Frietchie* (24). She retired after one talkie. Following divorce from Vidor, she was married for years to violinist Jascha Heifetz.
**Selected Films:** *The Yellow Girl* (15), *Alice Adams* (23), *Barbara Frietchie* (24), *The Grand Duchess and the Waiter* (26), *Chinatown Nights* (29).

## VINCENT, June (1919- )

Blonde American actress Vincent played leads in several second features of the 1940s.
**Selected Films:** *Ladies Courageous* (44), *Can't Help Singing* (44), *Here Come the Co-eds* (45), *Black Angel* (46), *Shed No Tears* (48).

## VINSON, Helen (1907- )

Born Helen Rulfs in Beaumont, Texas, Vinson arrived in films in the early 1930s. She played cool, aristocratic leads and supporting roles in a number of popular movies into the 1940s, including the gritty classic *I Am a Fugitive from a Chain Gang* (32).
**Selected Films:** *Jewel Robbery* (31), *I Am a Fugitive from a Chain Gang* (32), *The Power and the Glory* (33), *Torrid Zone* (40), *The Lady and the Doctor* (46).

## VITTI, Monica (1933- )

Born Maria Ceciarelli in Rome, Italy, Vitti studied drama in her teens and made her screen debut in 1955. A soulful beauty, she seemed destined for minor films until she was discovered by director Michelangelo Antonioni, who starred her in four of his classics: in *L'Avventura* (60), *La Notte* (61), *L'Eclisse* (62), and *Red Desert* (64) she played troubled women who were a mouthpiece for the director. Since then Vitti has starred to good effect in both comedies and dramas internationally, but her work has never come up to the level of that with Antonioni.
**Selected Films:** *Ridere Ridere Ridere* (55), *L'Avventura* (60), *La Notte* (61), *L'Eclisse* (62), *Red Desert* (64), *Modesty Blaise* (65), *An Almost Perfect Affair* (79), *The Mystery of Oberwald* (80).

## VOIGHT, Jon (1938- )

Voight was born the son of a golf pro in Yonkers, New York. He began acting in high school plays and at Catholic University, from which he graduated in 1960. After work at the Neighborhood Playhouse in New York, he got a part in the stage musical *The Sound of Music*. He went on to off-Broadway, stock and television work before making his first film of 1967. He rocketed to stardom by his portrayal of Joe Buck, the pathetic hustler, in *Midnight Cowboy* (69), winning both the New York Film Critics Award for Best Actor and a nomination for the Academy Award. He scored another success in *Deliverance* (72). In 1978 he was named Best Actor at the Cannes Film Festival and was awarded the Oscar for Best Actor for his portrayal of the paraplegic Vietnam War veteran in *Coming Home*. He received another nomination for *Runaway Train* (85).
**Selected Films:** *Hour of the Gun* (67), *Midnight Cowboy* (69), *Catch 22* (70), *Deliverance* (72), *The Odessa File* (74), *Coming Home* (78), *The Champ* (79), *Table for Five* (83), *Runaway Train,* (85), *Desert Bloom* (86).

## VON SEYFFERTITZ, Gustav (1863-1943)

A native of Vienna, Austria, Von Seyffertitz had long acted onstage in Germany and America before he came to the silent screen in the mid-teens. For over two decades he was one of the screen's best villains, his roles including a number of venomous Germans. Among his best-known roles was that of *Moriarty* (22).
**Selected Films:** *The Devil Stone* (17), *Old Wives for New* (18), *Moriarty* (22), *Docks of New York* (28), *Queen Christiana* (33), *She* (35), *In Old Chicago* (38), *Nurse Edith Cavell* (39).

## VON STROHEIM, Erich (1885-1957)

Contrary to popular myth, often spread by von Stroheim himself, he was not the descendant of Prussian aristocracy, but rather Erich Oswald Stroheim, the son of a Jewish hatter, born in Vienna, Austria. Although he served briefly in the Austro-Hungarian Army, most of his youth was spent managing his father's hat factory. Stroheim came to the United States about 1906 and wound up in Hollywood as part of D W Griffith's company. During World War I he was billed as 'The Man You Love to Hate,' often playing a cruel Prussian officer with a sarcastic monocled gaze. After the war he began directing films and established a reputation as a perfectionist, a genius and a profligate spender. His epic *Greed* (23) ran seven hours and was released only in a severely cut form. The original is said to be a masterpiece, but it lost a fortune and he was given few additional opportunities to direct. Stroheim went back to acting, usually in his 'The Man You Love to Hate' character, and during World War II he was back to playing cruel Prussian officers. He co-starred with Gloria Swanson in *Sunset Boulevard* (50), playing the butler who had once been Norma Desmond's director and husband.
**Selected Films:** *The Heart of Humanity* (18), *Blind Husbands* (19), *Foolish Wives* (21), *Three Faces East* (30), *The Lost Squadron* (32), *The Crime of Dr Crespi* (35), *La Grande Illusion* (37), *Five Graves to Cairo* (43), *North Star* (43), *Storm over Lisbon* (44), *Sunset Boulevard* (50), *Napoleon* (54).

## VON SYDOW, Max (1929- )

Strikingly gaunt, tall, blonde and impressive, von Sydow is a great international film star who was frequently cast in the movies of Swedish director Ingmar Bergman. Born Carl Adolf von Sydow in Lund, Sweden, his family was a middle class one, his father being a university professor. Von Sydow attended Stockholm's Royal Dramatic Theater School and made his film debut in *Only a Mother* (49). His forte was playing a modern man at his most tortured. His brooding intensity, rich voice and imposing screen presence impressed

*Erich von Stroheim in* Five Graves to Cairo *(43).*

audiences world-wide, leading to his portrayal of Jesus Christ in *The Greatest Story Ever Told* (65) and the embattled priest in *The Exorcist* (73).
**Selected Films:** *Only a Mother* (49), *Miss Julie* (51), *The Seventh Seal* (56), *Wild Strawberries* (57), *The Face* (59), *The Virgin Spring* (60), *Through a Glass Darkly* (61), *Winter Light* (62), *The Mistress* (62), *The Greatest Story Ever Told* (65), *Hawaii* (66), *Hour of the Wolf* (67), *The Emigrants* (72), *The Exorcist* (73), *The New Land* (75), *Three Days of the Condor* (76), *The Hurricane* (79), *Flash Gordon* (80), *Victory* (81), *Dune* (83), *Hannah and Her Sisters* (86), *Duet for One* (87), *The Second Victory* (87).

## VOSKOVEC, George (1905-1981)

Voskovec began acting onstage in his native Czechoslovakia and came to the American screen in the early 1950s. Among his roles were as a German-American juror in *Twelve Angry Men* (57).
**Selected Films:** *Anything Can Happen* (52), *Twelve Angry Men* (57), *The Spy Who Came in from the Cold* (65), *The Boston Strangler* (68).

## VYE, Murvyn (1913-1976)

Born in Quincy, Massachusetts, Vye acted on Broadway before coming to films in the later 1940s. Heavyset of form, he usually played heavies onscreen, though he also did light roles and worked on the TV series *The Bob Cummings Show*.
**Selected Films:** *Golden Earrings* (48), *A Connecticut Yankee in King Arthur's Court* (49), *Road to Bali* (52), *Al Capone* (58), *Andy* (65).

## WAGNER, Lindsay (1949- )

Wagner was born in Los Angeles, California, and educated at the University of Oregon. She became a model and worked with a rock group before starting her acting career. Wagner is best remembered for the TV series *The Bionic Woman*.
**Selected Films:** *Two People* (73), *The Paper Chase* (73), *Second Wind* (75), *Nighthawks* (81).

## WAGNER, Robert (1930- )

Born into a wealthy family, the son of a steel executive in Detroit, Michigan, Wagner expected to go into business. His good looks and pleasant personality made him a teenage movie idol early in his acting career. He made his debut in *Halls of Montezuma* (50), a grim, good war picture about the Marines. Wagner eventually matured into a solid leading man and a popular television star in the *It Takes a Thief*, *Switch* and *Hart to Hart* adventure series. He married, divorced and remarried actress Natalie Wood. In between he was married to actress Marion Marshall.
**Selected Films:** *Halls of Montezuma* (50), *The Happy Years* (50), *With a Song in My Heart* (52), *A Kiss Before Dying* (56), *The War Lover* (62), *The Pink Panther* (64), *Harper* (66), *Winning* (69), *The Towering Inferno* (74), *I Am the Cheese* (83).

## WAITE, Ralph (1929- )

Waite was born in White Plains, New York. He began his film work in the 1960s as a general purpose actor. It was not until he appeared as the father in the enormously successful television series *The Waltons* that audiences realized how well that he could act.
**Selected Films:** *Cool Hand Luke* (67), *Last Summer* (69), *Five Easy Pieces* (70), *The Grissom Gang* (71), *Kid Blue* (72), *The Stone Killer* (73), *Red Alert* (84).

## WALBROOK, Anton (1900-1967)

This distinguished actor was born Adolf Anton Wilhelm Wohlbrück in Vienna, Austria, a descendant of ten generations of circus clowns. After appearing on stage in Austria and Germany, he made his screen debut in *Mater Dolorosa* (22). It took him until the early 1930s to become a star. In 1937 he went to Hollywood to star in *Michael Strogoff*, then settled in Britain, starring in many films as a charming, aristocratic leading man.
**Selected Films:** *Mater Dolorosa* (22), *Trapeze* (31), *Viktor und Viktoria* (33), *Masquerade in Vienna* (34), *Der Student von Prag* (35), *Michael Strogoff* (37), *Victoria the Great* (37), *Gaslight* (40), *The Life and Death of Colonel Blimp* (43), *The Red Shoes* (48), *La Ronde* (50), *Lola Montes* (55), *I Accuse!* (58).

## WALBURN, Raymond (1887-1969)

Born in Plymouth, Indiana, this character actor played comic roles and cowardly villains in films for more than 25 years. Before he went to Hollywood, he had had many years of stock and Broadway experience.
**Selected Films:** *The Laughing Lady* (29), *The Count of Monte Cristo* (34), *Mr Deeds Goes to Town* (36), *Professor Beware* (38), *Louisiana Purchase* (41), *Dixie* (43), *And the Angels Sing* (44), *Hail the Conquering Hero* (44), *The Plainsman and the Lady* (46), *State of the Union* (48), *Red Hot and Blue* (49), *Riding High* (50), *Excuse My Dust* (51), *The Spoilers* (55).

## WALKEN, Christopher (1943- )

This sensitive, youthful-looking lead and supporting actor was born in Astoria, Queens, New York. He was educated at Hofstra University. He won an Obie Award for his off-Broadway work in *Kid Champion* and a Theater World Award for his performance in the New York City Center revival of *The Rose Tattoo*. He has appeared in 84 different plays in New York. Walken began his film work with a bit part in *Me and My Brother* (68), and won both the New York Film Critics Award and an Academy Award for Best Supporting Actor for his performance in *The Deer Hunter* (78).
**Selected Films:** *Me and My Brother* (69), *The Anderson Tapes* (71), *The Happiness Cage* (72), *Next Stop, Greenwich Village* (76), *Annie Hall* (77), *The Deer Hunter* (78), *Last Embrace* (79), *The Dogs of War* (80), *Pennies from Heaven* (82), *The Dead Zone* (83), *View to a Kill* (85), *At Close Range* (86).

## WALKER, Clint (1927- )

This muscular leading man was born in Hartford, Illinois. He joined the Merchant Marine, then became a sheet metal worker, a carpenter, a deputy sheriff and an oil prospector before becoming an actor. Although most famous for his TV series *Cheyenne* and *Kodiak*, he has made several movies.
**Selected Films:** *The Ten Commandments* (56), *Fort Dobbs* (58), *Yellowstone Kelly* (59), *Gold of the Seven Saints* (61), *Send Me No Flowers* (64), *None But the Brave* (65), *The Night of the Grizzly* (66), *The Dirty Dozen* (67), *Pancho Villa* (74), *Baker's Hawk* (76), *The White Buffalo* (77).

## WALKER, Helen (1920-1968)

She was born in Worchester, Massachusetts, and appeared on stage before going to Hollywood, where she became a leading lady in movies of the 1940s and early 1950s. After Walker had a serious automobile accident in 1946, she never really made it back, and retired in 1955.
**Selected Films:** *Lucky Jordan* (42), *The Man in Half Moon Street* (44), *Brewster's Millions* (45), *Cluny Brown* (46), *Nightmare Alley* (47), *Call Northside 777* (48), *My True Story* (51), *The Big Combo* (55).

## WALKER, Nancy (1921- )

This pint-sized character actress-comedienne-singer has done it all. Born Ann Myrtle Swoyer Barto in Philadelphia, Pennsylvania, she was an immediate smash in *Best Foot Forward* (41), *On the Town* (44) and many more Broadway musicals. She went on to appear in films, but is probably best remembered for playing Mrs Morgenstern on *The Mary Tyler Moore Show* on television, and for all those commercials as Rosie, the owner of the diner, selling paper towels.
**Selected Films:** *Stand Up and Be Counted* (72), *Forty Carats* (73), *The World's Greatest Athlete* (73), *Murder by Death* (76), *Won Ton Ton, The Dog Who Saved Hollywood* (76).

## WALKER, Robert (1918-1951)

Born in Salt Lake City, Utah, he attended the San Diego Army and Naval Academy, where he appeared in school plays. Walker went to New York and enrolled in the Academy of Dramatic Arts in 1938. In 1939 he married a fellow student named Phyllis Isley, who was later to be known as Jennifer Jones. The two left for Hollywood, but they had to be satisfied with bit parts. After they returned to New York, Walker landed a part in a radio series. They went back to Hollywood in 1942, both of them having studio contracts. Walker did well as a slight, modest-looking actor – a sort of boy-next-door leading man. After his divorce, he had several breakdowns and took to drinking. His marriage to John Ford's daughter Barbara lasted but six weeks. After he was released from institutionalization for another breakdown, he returned to films, scoring a tour de force as a villain in Alfred Hitchcock's *Strangers on a Train* (51). Walker died suddenly in 1951, in the middle of the shooting of *My Son John*, a victim of over-sedation.
**Selected Films:** *Winter Carnival* (39), *Bataan* (43), *Madame Curie* (43), *See Here, Private Hargrove* (44), *Since You Went Away* (44), *Thirty Seconds Over Tokyo* (44), *What Next, Corporal Hargrove?* (45), *The Clock* (45), *Till the Clouds Roll By* (46), *The Sea of Grass* (47), *Song of Love* (47), *One Touch of Venus* (48), *Please Believe Me* (50), *Strangers on a Train* (51), *My Son John* (52).

## WALKER, Robert Jr (1940- )

Born in New York City, the son of actors Robert Walker and Jennifer Jones, he started his show business career playing bongo drums in European cafes before appearing in movies in the early 1960s. Walker looks so much like his father that he seems to have been type-cast in youthful parts.
**Selected Films:** *The Hook* (63), *Ensign Pulver* (64), *The Happening* (67), *The War Wagon* (67), *Easy Rider* (69), *Road to Salina* (70), *Beware – The Blob* (72), *The Spectre of Edgar Allan Poe* (73), *Gone with the West* (75), *The Passover Plot* (76), *God Bless Dr Shagetz* (77), *A Touch of Sin* (83)

## WALLACE, Jean (1923- )

This blonde leading lady was born Jean Wallasek in Chicago, Illinois, and she made her screen debut in *Louisiana Purchase* (41). She married actor Franchot Tone in 1941. They were divorced in 1948 and in 1951 she married actor-director Cornell Wilde and has starred in some of his independent productions.
**Selected Films:** *Louisiana Purchase* (41), *You Can't Ration Love* (44), *When My Baby Smiles at Me* (48), *Jigsaw* (49), *The Man on the Eiffel Tower* (50), *The Good Humor Man* (50), *Native Son* (51), *Storm Fear* (56), *Maracaibo* (58), *Beach Red* (67), *No Blade of Grass* (70).

## WALLACH, Eli (1915- )

Wallach is a distinguished American 'Method' actor, noted for his range and versatility, whose career spans stage, films and television. He was born in Brooklyn, New York, and graduated from the University of Texas and earned a master's degree from the City College of New York, planning to become a teacher. But since his first appearance on stage in amateur theater at the age of 15, he had really dreamed of becoming an actor. He trained at New York's Neighborhood Playhouse and after military service in World War II he made his Broadway debut in 1945. His screen debut came in 1956, in *Baby Doll*, an enormous hit. He often plays villains and tough guys in movies, and his favorite co-star is his wife, Anne Jackson.
**Selected Films:** *Baby Doll* (56), *The Magnificent Seven* (60), *The Misfits* (61), *Act One* (63), *The Moon-Spinners* (64), *The Good, the Bad and the Ugly* (67), *The Tiger Makes Out* (67), *The Angel Levine* (70), *Crazy Joe* (73), *Cinderella Liberty* (74), *Nasty Habits* (77), *Movie Movie* (78), *Winter Kills* (79), *The Wall* (81), *Tough Guys* (86).

*Eli Wallach in* Ace High *(68).*

## WALSH, Kay (1914- )

A former dancer, Walsh was born in London, England. She was trained in West End revues in her native city, and then went on to play leads in many British movies before switching to character parts in the early 1960s.
**Selected Films:** *How's Chances?* (34), *The Luck of the Irish* (35), *The Last Adventurers* (37), *In Which We Serve* (44), *This Happy Breed* (44), *Oliver Twist* (48), *Stage Fright* (50), *The Magic Box* (51), *Young Bess* (53), *Cast a Dark Shadow* (55), *The Horse's Mouth* (58), *Tunes of Glory* (60), *The L-Shaped Room* (62), *Circus World* (64), *The Virgin and the Gypsy* (70), *Scrooge* (71), *The Ruling Class* (72).

## WALSTON, Ray (1918- )

This veteran comedian was born in New Orleans, Louisiana, and went on to appear in movies, on stage and on television. He won a Tony Award as the devil (Mr Applegate) in the stage musical comedy *Damn Yankees* and repeated the role in the 1958 film version. Walston is probably best remembered for his work in the television series *My Favorite Martian*.
**Selected Films:** *Kiss Them for Me* (57), *South Pacific* (58), *Damn Yankees* (58), *Tall Story* (60), *The Apartment* (60), *Who's Minding the Store?* (63), *Kiss Me Stupid* (64), *Paint Your Wagon* (69), *The Sting* (73), *Silver Streak* (76), *The Happy Hooker Goes to Washington* (77), *Popeye* (81), *Fast Times at Ridgmont High* (82).

*Ken Clark and Ray Walston in* South Pacific *(59).*

## WALTER, Jessica (1940- )

This Hollywood leading lady was born in Brooklyn, New York, and trained for the stage at the Bucks County Playhouse in Pennsylvania and at the Neighborhood Playhouse in New York City. She made her Broadway debut in the early 1960s and later went into motion pictures.
**Selected Films:** *Lilith* (64), *The Group* (66), *Grand Prix* (66), *Bye Bye, Braverman* (68), *Number One* (69), *Play Misty for Me* (71), *Goldengirl* (79).

## WALTHALL, Henry B (1878-1936)

This venerable actor, born in Shelby City, Alabama, had a screen career that stretched over 27 years. After studying law he went to Broadway and became an actor. Walthall joined D W Griffith's Biograph troupe in 1909, often playing leads opposite Mary Pickford. His first big part was that of the Little Colonel in *The Birth of a Nation* (15). He left Griffith after that picture. Later he switched to character roles in sound films, and was quite effective. He died during the filming of his last movie, *China Clipper* (36).
**Selected Films:** *In Old Kentucky* (09), *Ramona* (10), *The Informer* (12), *The Wedding Gown* (13), *Home Sweet Home* (14), *The Birth of a Nation* (15), *The Great Love* (18), *Flower of the North* (21), *One Clear Call* (22), *The Face on the Barroom Floor* (23), *The Plastic Age* (25), *The Scarlet Letter* (26), *Wings* (27), *London After Midnight* (27), *The Bridge of San Luis Rey* (29), *Abraham Lincoln* (30), *Tol'able David* (30), *Strange Interlude* (32), *Cabin in the Cotton* (32), *42nd Street* (33), *Viva Villa!* (34), *A Tale of Two Cities* (35), *China Clipper* (36).

## WANAMAKER, Sam (1919- )

Actor-director Wanamaker was born in Chicago, Illinois, and attended Drake University. He trained for the stage at Chicago's Goodman Theater, making his debut at the age of 17. He went on to play in stock companies, then graduated to Broadway. When he returned from service after World War II he made his film debut in *My Girl Tisa* (48), and promptly moved to England, where he appeared in several British movies. Blacklisted during the Red Scare of the 1950s, he turned to directing, and then back to acting in the 1960s.
**Selected Films:** *My Girl Tisa* (48), *Give Us This Day* (49), *Mr Denning Drives North* (51), *The Secret* (55), *The Concrete Jungle* (60), *Taras Bulba* (62), *Those Magnificent Men in Their Flying Machines* (65), *The Spy Who Came in From the Cold* (65), *Warning Shot* (67), *Voyage of the Damned* (76), *Death on the Nile* (78), *Private Benjamin* (80), *The Aviator* (84), *Raw Deal* (86).

## WARD, Rachel (1958- )

Born in England, the niece of the Earl of Dudley, Ward grew up on an 1800-acre estate. She left

school at 16 to become a model. Her first movie was *Sharky's Machine* (81) with Burt Reynolds. Her first big break came when she starred in the television mini-series, *The Thorn Birds*, and it was on the set of that production that she met her husband, actor Bryan Brown.
**Selected Films:** *Sharky's Machine* (81), *Dead Men Don't Wear Plaid* (82), *Against All Odds* (84), *Hotel Colonia* (87), *The Good Wife* (87).

## WARD, Simon (1941- )

This British leading actor of the 1970s was born in London, England, and has had prominent parts on television in the United Kingdom. His film career began in *If* (68).
**Selected Films:** *If* (68), *Frankenstein Must Be Destroyed* (69), *I Start Counting* (71), *Young Winston* (72), *Hitler – The Last Ten Days* (73), *The Three Musketeers* (74), *The Four Musketeers* (75), *All Creatures Great and Small* (75), *Aces High* (76), *Children of Rage* (77), *Zulu Dawn* (79), *Supergirl* (84).

## WARDEN, Jack (1920- )

A former prizefighter, he was born in Newark, New Jersey. After returning from service as a paratrooper during World War II, he became a stage actor in repertory in Dallas, Texas. His film career began in the early 1950s, and he usually plays tough characters. He also has been a regular on several TV series. Warden was nominated for the Academy Award for Best Supporting Actor twice – for *Shampoo* (75) and *Heaven Can Wait* (78).
**Selected Films:** *You're in the Navy Now* (51), *Red Ball Express* (52), *From Here to Eternity* (53), *12 Angry Men* (57), *That Kind of Woman* (59), *Wake Me When It's Over* (60), *Donovan's Reef* (63), *Blindfold* (66), *Summertree* (71), *The Man Who Loved Cat Dancing* (73), *The Apprenticeship of Duddy Kravitz* (74), *Shampoo* (75), *All the President's Men* (76), *Heaven Can Wait* (78), *Death on the Nile* (78), *The Champ* (79), *Being There* (79), *The Verdict* (82), *The Aviator* (84).

## WARNER, David (1941- )

Born in Manchester, England, and primarily a stage actor, Warner was the Royal Shakespeare Company's youngest *Hamlet*. He made his screen debut in *Tom Jones* (63).
**Selected Films:** *Tom Jones* (63), *Morgan* (66), *A Midsummer Night's Dream* (68), *The Bofors Gun* (68), *The Fixer* (68), *The Ballad of Cable Hogue* (70), *Straw Dogs* (71), *A Doll's House* (73), *The Omen* (76), *Providence* (77), *Time After Time* (79), *Time Bandits* (81), *Tron* (82), *The Man With Two Brains* (83).

## WARNER, H B (1876-1958)

Warner was born Henry Byron Warner-Lickford in London, England. His father, Charles Warner, was a famous British stage actor. Although Warner debuted at his father's theater at age seven, he later studied medicine at London's University College until opting for acting. Success on stage led to a prolific Hollywood film career. He played Jesus Christ in Cecil B De Mille's *The King of Kings* (27) and he received an Academy Award nomination for Best Supporting Actor for his performance as the lama, Chang, in *Lost Horizon* (37).
**Selected Films:** *The Lost Paradise* (14), *The Pagan God* (19), *Zaza* (23), *Whispering Smith* (26), *The King of Kings* (27), *The Trial of Mary Dugan* (29), *The Crusader* (32), *Christopher Bean* (33), *A Tale of Two Cities* (55), *Mr Deeds Goes to Town* (36), *Lost Horizon* (37), *Victoria the Great* (37), *Topper Returns* (41), *Sunset Boulevard* (50), *The Ten Commandments* (56), *Darby's Rangers* (57).

## WARREN, Leslie Ann (1946- )

New York-born Warren studied at the Actors Studio before making her screen debut at age 20 in *The Happiest Millionaire* (66). She is a striking brunette who often projects sensitivity behind her sultriness, and her screen appearances have been occasional but often outstanding: she was nominated for a supporting-actress Oscar for her performance in *Victor/Victoria* (82) and made a fine brassy-but-vulnerable Eve in *Choose Me* (83).
**Selected Films:** *The Happiest Millionaire* (66), *Race to the Yankee Zephyr* (82), *Victor/Victoria* (82), *Songwriter* (83), *Choose Me* (83), *A Night in Heaven* (83), *Clue* (85), *Apology* (86), *Burglar* (87).

## WARRICK, Ruth (1915- )

A former radio singer, this brunette leading lady of movies of the 1940s was born in St Louis, Missouri. Educated at the University of Missouri, she made her screen debut in *Citizen Kane* (41), playing Orson Welles' first wife. She is still active on stage and in night clubs and has starred in soap operas on television.
**Selected Films:** *Citizen Kane* (41), *The Corsican Brothers* (41), *Journey Into Fear* (42), *Secret Command* (44), *China Sky* (45), *Song of the South* (46), *Daisy Kenyon* (47), *Let's Dance* (50), *Ride Beyond Vengeance* (66), *The Great Bank Robbery* (69), *The Returning* (83).

## WARWICK, Robert (1878-1964)

Born Robert Taylor Bien in Sacramento, California, he was a boy soprano in church choirs. He went to Paris to study music, intending to become an opera singer, but he later became a star on Broadway in leading roles. Warwick made his film debut in 1914 and played romantic leads through the 1920s, with time out when he served as an army captain during World War I. When sound movies came in, he switched to character roles, usually playing dignified middle-aged men.
**Selected Films:** *Across the Pacific* (14), *Alias Jimmy Valentine* (15), *The Mad Lover* (17), *Secret Service*

(19), *The City of Masks* (20), *The Spitfire* (24), *The Royal Bed* (31), *So Big* (32), *I Am a Fugitive From a Chain Gang* (32), *Cleopatra* (34), *A Tale of Two Cities* (35), *Mary of Scotland* (36), *Romeo and Juliet* (36), *The Prince and the Pauper* (37), *The Life of Emile Zola* (37), *The Awful Truth* (37), *The Adventures of Robin Hood* (38), *Juarez* (39), *The Private Lives of Elizabeth and Essex* (39), *The Sea Hawk* (40), *Sullivan's Travels* (41), *I Married a Witch* (42), *Francis* (50), *Salome* (53), *While the City Sleeps* (56), *The Buccaneer* (59).

## WATERS, Ethel (1896-1977)

This singer and actress was born in Chester, Pennsylvania, in abject poverty. She married at 12 years old and worked as a scrubwoman, a laundress and a chambermaid before she began appearing in night clubs as 'Sweet Mama Stringbean' at the age of 17. Her blues singing was legendary, and she was the first black woman to achieve star billing on the stage and screen, playing both in musicals and in straight drama. Waters was nominated for an Academy Award for Best Supporting Actress for her role in *Pinky* (49).
**Selected Films:** *On With the Show* (29), *Gift of Gab* (34), *Tales of Manhattan* (42), *Cabin in the Sky* (43), *Pinky* (49), *The Member of the Wedding* (52), *The Heart Is a Rebel* (56), *The Sound and the Fury* (59).

## WATERSTON, Sam (1940- )

This intelligent general purpose actor on stage and screen was born in Cambridge, Massachusetts, and educated at Yale University. Waterston won the Drama Desk Award as Best Actor for his work in Joseph Papp's Broadway production of *Much Ado About Nothing* in the early 1970s. He made his screen debut in 1967. Waterston was nominated for Best Actor for his performance in *The Killing Fields* (84).
**Selected Films:** *Fitzwilly* (67), *Generation* (69), *Savages* (72), *The Great Gatsby* (74), *Rancho Deluxe* (75), *Journey Into Fear* (75), *Coup de Foudre* (77), *Interiors* (78), *Eagle's Wing* (79), *Heaven's Gate* (79), *The Killing Fields* (84), *Just Between Friends* (87).

## WATSON, Bobs (1930- )

Born in Hollywood, California, into a show business family, he appeared in short subjects while he was still in diapers. As a child actor, he was famous for his ability to cry at the drop of a hat, most memorably as Pee Wee in *Boys' Town* (38). He retired from films in the early 1940s, but occasionally appeared in character parts after that. In 1968 he was ordained a minister of the United Methodist Church.
**Selected Films:** *In Old Chicago* (38), *Boys' Town* (38), *Kentucky* (38), *The Story of Alexander Graham Bell* (39), *On Borrowed Time* (39), *Dr Kildare's Crisis* (40), *Men of Boys' Town* (41), *The Bold and the Brave* (56), *What Ever Happened to Baby Jane?* (62), *First to Fight* (67).

## WATSON, Lucile (1879-1962)

Watson was born in Quebec, Canada, and was educated in a convent. She went to New York to train at the American Academy of Dramatic Arts and played Broadway leads at the turn of the century. Watson went to Hollywood and made her screen debut in *What Every Woman Knows* (34), and was soon established as a leading character actress in movies. Typecast in matronly roles, she was nominated for an Academy Award for Best Supporting Actress for her work as Bette Davis' mother in *Watch on the Rhine* (43).
**Selected Films:** *What Every Woman Knows* (34), *The Garden of Allah* (36), *Sweethearts* (38), *The Women* (39), *Waterloo Bridge* (40), *Rage in Heaven* (41), *Watch on the Rhine* (43), *Till We Meet Again* (44), *The Razor's Edge* (46), *Ivy* (47), *The Emperor Waltz* (48), *Little Women* (49), *Harriet Craig* (50), *My Forbidden Past* (51).

## WAYNE, David (1914- )

This wiry character actor was born Wayne McMeekan in Traverse City, Michigan, and was educated at Western Michigan University. After college, he was a statistician, but switched to acting, making his stage debut in 1936. Wayne became a star in such Broadway plays as *Finian's Rainbow* and *Mister Roberts*, and he was the original Sakini in *The Teahouse of the August Moon*. He began his film career in the late 1940s, and was highly praised in both comedies and dramas.
**Selected Films:** *Adam's Rib* (49), *My Blue Heaven* (50), *M* (51), *With a Song in My Heart* (52), *How to Marry a Millionaire* (53), *Hell and High Water* (54), *The Tender Trap* (55), *The Naked Hills* (56), *The Three Faces of Eve* (57), *The Last Angry Man* (59), *The Big Gamble* (61), *The Andromeda Strain* (71), *Huckleberry Finn* (74), *The Front Page* (74), *The Apple Dumpling Gang* (75), *Lassie: The New Beginning* (79), *House Calls* (80).

## WAYNE, John (1907-1979)

He was more than a movie star. To millions throughout the world he was the symbol of rugged masculinity. Although even his most fervent admirers would admit that the only part that he could ever really play was himself, that didn't make any difference. This tall, tough, genial, generally inimitable American leading man became the biggest moneymaker in movie history. Wayne was born Marion Michael Morrison in Winterset, Iowa. Later the family moved to Glendale, California, a suburb of Los Angeles, where he picked up his nickname, 'Duke.' He had a dog named Duke, and everybody knew the dog's name. Wayne earned a football scholarship to the University of Southern California and spent summers lugging props around a movie studio. Since he was big and looked good in a cowboy hat, he got bit parts, mainly in westerns. After an

*Randolph Scott, John Wayne and Marlene Dietrich in* The Spoilers *(42).*

injury cost him his scholarship, he went into acting full time and made a huge number of B or worse westerns. He even became the screen's first singing cowboy, although his singing voice was dubbed. Wayne's breakthrough film was *Stagecoach* (39), directed by John Ford. The movie was a huge financial and critical success; it changed the image of the western from a Saturday afternoon entertainment for kids to a vehicle capable of carrying a real story with first-rate performances. When World War II broke out, Wayne tried to enlist, but his age (he was 34) and his old football injury kept him out of the Army but not off the screen. From a cowboy hero he became a war hero. After the war it was back in the saddle again for some of his best westerns, including *Red River* (48). His most successful non-western was *The Quiet Man* (52), about an Irish-American boxer who returns to the old country. Although the film had no shoot-out, its most memorable scene was a long brawl between Wayne and Victor McLaglen. The off-screen Wayne was very much like the characters he played – a tough, hard-drinking, brawling 'man's man' who seemed to prefer the company of his drinking buddies to the sustained company of women. He had three not terribly successful marriages and his divorce from Mexican actress Chata in 1953 was accompanied by charges of drunkenness and violence. Wayne was outspoken about his hawkish, right-wing politics. He even financed a couple of movies to promote his point of view; however, they were not commercially successful. He was stricken with lung cancer in 1964, but after a serious operation he went right back to making movies, including *True Grit* (69), for which he received his only Oscar. Although he never really recovered his health, he continued making motion pictures almost to the end.

**Selected Films:** *Hangman's House* (28), *Mother Machree* (28), *Salute* (29), *The Big Trail* (30), *Range Feud* (31), *Two Fisted Law* (32), *The Sagebrush Trail* (33), *Riders of Destiny* (33), *The Man from Utah* (34), *The Dawn Rider* (35), *The Lonely Trail* (36), *Pals of the Saddle* (37), *Red River Range* (38), *Stagecoach* (39), *Allegheny Uprising* (39), *The Long Voyage Home* (40), *Seven Sinners* (40), *The Shepherd of the Hills* (41), *Reap the Wild Wind* (42), *The Spoilers* (42), *Flying Tigers* (42), *Pittsburgh* (42), *In Old Oklahoma* (43), *The Fighting Seabees* (44), *Back to Bataan* (44), *Flame of the Barbary Coast* (45), *They Were Expendable* (45), *Fort Apache* (48), *Red River* (48), *Wake of the Red Witch* (48), *She Wore a Yellow Ribbon* (49), *Sands of Iwo Jima* (49), *Flying Leathernecks* (51), *The Quiet Man* (52), *Hondo* (53), *The High and the Mighty* (54), *The Conqueror* (55), *The Searchers* (56), *Rio Bravo* (59), *The Alamo* (60), *The Comancheros* (61), *The Man Who Shot Liberty Valance* (62), *The Longest Day* (63), *How the West Was Won* (63), *McLintock!* (63), *Circus World* (64), *The Sons of Katie Elder* (65), *In Harm's Way* (65), *The Green Berets* (68), *True Grit* (69), *Rio Lobo* (70), *The Cowboys* (72), *Cahill: United States Marshal* (73), *McQ* (74), *Rooster Cogburn* (75), *The Shootist* (76).

*Harry Dean Stanton, Ian Holm, John Hurt, Veronica Cartwright, Tom Skerrit, Sigourney Weaver and Yaphet Kotto in* Alien *(79).*

## WAYNE, Naunton (1901-1970)

Born Henry Wayne Davies in Llanwonno, Glamorgan, Wales, he was a stage star, playing mostly light comedy parts, until 1931, when he turned to films, making his debut in *The First Mrs Fraser*. Wayne became well known when he co-starred with Basil Radford playing Englishmen abroad.

**Selected Films:** *The First Mrs Fraser* (31), *Going Gay* (33), *For Love of You* (34), *The Lady Vanishes* (38), *Night Train to Munich* (40), *Crooks' Tour* (41), *Next of Kin* (42), *Dead of Night* (45), *It's Not Cricket* (48), *Quartet* (48), *Passport to Pimlico* (48), *Obsession* (49), *The Titfield Thunderbolt* (53), *You Know What Sailors Are* (53), *Nothing Barred* (61), *Double Bunk* (64).

## WAYNE, Patrick (1939- )

The son of actor John Wayne, he was born in Los Angeles, California, and educated at Loyola University of Los Angeles. He began acting at the age of 16 in John Ford movies. In the late 1950s and early 1960s he was in several of his father's pictures, and later became a leading man on his own.

**Selected Films:** *The Long Gray Line* (55), *Mister Roberts* (55) *The Searchers* (56), *The Alamo* (60), *The Comancheros* (61), *Donovan's Reef* (63), *McLintock! (63)*, *Cheyenne Autumn* (64), *Shenandoah* (65), *An Eye for an Eye* (66), *The Green Berets* (68), *Big Jake* (71), *The Gatling Gun* (73), *Mustang Country* (76), *The People That Time Forgot* (77).

## WEAVER, Dennis (1924- )

Probably best known for his portrayal of the limping Chester Goode on the TV series *Gunsmoke*, Weaver is a fine actor. Born in Joplin, Missouri, he attended the University of Oklahoma, where he was a track star. He later served as a Navy pilot, and began making films in the early 1950s. He has starred in many made-for-TV movies and the series *McCloud*.

**Selected Films:** *The Lawless Breed* (52), *The Mississippi Gambler* (53), *Dangerous Mission* (54), *The Bridges at Toko-Ri* (55), *Storm Fear* (55), *Touch of Evil* (58), *The Gallant Hours* (60), *Way Way Out* (66), *Gentle Giant* (67), *A Man Called Sledge* (71), *What's the Matter with Helen?* (71).

## WEAVER, Fritz (1926- )

This leading man and character player was born in Pittsburgh, Pennsylvania. Weaver is mainly known for his stage work, but he has made a few films and is often seen on television.

**Selected Films:** *Fail Safe* (64), *To Trap a Spy* (66), *The Maltese Bippy* (69), *A Walk in the Spring Rain* (70), *The Day of the Dolphin* (73), *Marathon Man* (76), *Black Sunday* (77), *The Big Fix* (78), *The Martian Chronicles* (79).

## WEAVER, Marjorie (1913- )

Born in Grossville, Tennessee, and educated at the University of Kentucky and Indiana University, she started her show business career as a band singer. She was also a model and had some stock experience. In the 1930s she began making movies, usually starring in second features, many of them mysteries.

**Selected Films:** *Transatlantic Merry-Go-Round* (34), *China Clipper* (36), *This Is My Affair* (37), *Sally, Irene and Mary* (38), *Young Mr Lincoln* (39), *Charlie Chan's Murder Cruise* (40), *Michael Shayne, Private Detective* (40), *Man at Large* (41), *Let's Face It* (43), *Fashion Model* (45), *We're Not Married* (52).

## WEAVER, Sigourney (1949- )

Born in Los Angeles, California, the daughter of television executive Sylvester 'Pat' Weaver, she graduated from Stanford and the Yale School of Drama. This tall, cameo-featured woman has played a variety of parts, from astronaut to embassy attaché to television reporter. She received an Academy Award nomination for her performance in *Aliens* (86).
**Selected Films:** *Alien* (79), *Eyewitness* (81), *The Year of Living Dangerously* (83), *Ghostbusters* (84), *Aliens* (86), *One Woman or Two* (86), *Half Moon Street* (86).

## WEBB, Clifton (1891-1966)

Webb was born Webb Parmallee Hollenbeck in Indianapolis, Indiana, and he trained as a dancer and and an actor from childhood. A seasoned actor by the time he was ten years old, he left school at 13 to study painting and music and at 17 he was singing with the Boston Opera Company. Webb became a leading ballroom dancer in New York night clubs at the age of 19, and was a star in Broadway musical comedies beginning in 1917. In the 1920s he switched to dramatic roles on Broadway, in London's West End and in occasional silent movies. After 20 years' absence, he returned to the screen in 1944 as the elegant villain, Waldo Lydecker in *Laura* (44), for which he was nominated for an Academy Award for Best Supporting Actor. He was later nominated for the same award for his work in *The Razor's Edge* (46). Perhaps his most memorable role, however, was the pompous baby-sitter, Mr Belvedere, in *Sitting Pretty* (48), and its sequels.
**Selected Films:** *Polly With a Past* (20), *The Heart of a Siren* (25), *Laura* (44), *The Razor's Edge* (46), *Sitting Pretty* (48), *Mr Belvedere Goes to College* (49), *Cheaper by the Dozen* (50), *Stars and Stripes Forever* (52), *Titanic* (53), *Three Coins in the Fountain* (54), *The Man Who Never Was* (56), *Boy on a Dolphin* (57), *The Remarkable Mr Pennypacker* (59), *Satan Never Sleeps* (62)

## WEBB, Jack (1920-1982)

This actor-director-producer was born in Santa Monica, California. Discharged from the Air Force after World War II, he became a radio announcer in San Francisco. By 1946 he was starring in his own radio series and in 1949 he launched the *Dragnet* show on radio. This was later turned into a long-running television series with Webb as the star. Webb also appeared in a few movies. His first wife was actress-singer Julie London.
**Selected Films:** *He Walked by Night* (48), *The Men* (50), *Sunset Boulevard* (50), *The Halls of Montezuma* (51), *Dragnet* (54), *Pete Kelly's Blues* (55), *The D.I.* (57), *The Last Time I Saw Archie* (61).

## WEBBER, Robert (1924- )

Born in Santa Ana, California, he started appearing on stage in the early 1940s. After his discharge from the Marines at the end of World War II, he appeared on Broadway, and later was seen on numberless television shows. Webber began his screen career in 1951.
**Selected Films:** *Highway 301* (51), *12 Angry Men* (57), *The Stripper* (63), *The Sandpiper* (65), *Harper* (66), *The Dirty Dozen* (67), *The Great White Hope* (70), *$* (71), *Midway* (76), *The Choirboys* (77), *Revenge of the Pink Panther* (78), *Private Benjamin* (80), *S.O.B.* (80), *Wrong Is Right* (82).

## WEGENER, Paul (1874-1948)

Born in Bischdorf, East Prussia, Wegener went on the stage when he was 21, but then went back to school to study law. In 1906 he returned to the stage at Max Reinhardt's Deutches Theater in Berlin. Wegener was a classic actor and he developed into a giant of German theater. His first film was *The Student of Prague* (13), and he continued in the movies until his death. During the Hitler regime, he made propaganda pictures and was named Actor of the State. One of his five wives was the actress Lyda Salmonova, with whom he had made several movies.
**Selected Films:** *The Student of Prague* (13), *The Golem* (14), *The Pied Piper of Hamlin* (16), *The Yogi* (16), *Medea* (20), *One Arabian Night* (20), *The Lost Shadow* (21), *Loves of Pharaoh* (21), *The Magician* (26), *Svengali* (27), *The Living Dead* (32), *Horst Wessel* (33), *Stronger Than Love* (38), *Der grosse Mandarin* (49).

## WEIDLER, Virginia (1927-1968)

This child star of the 1930s and 1940s was born in Eagle Rock, California, and she began her movie career at the age of three. Weidler specialized in mischievous but lovable little girls. She found it difficult to find roles when she matured, and tried stage and night club jobs to no avail. She retired in 1945 and died at the age of 40 of a heart attack.
**Selected Films:** *Surrender* (31), *Mrs Wiggs of the Cabbage Patch* (34), *Freckles* (35), *Trouble for Two* (36), *Souls at Sea* (37), *Mother Carey's Chickens* (38), *The Women* (39), *Young Tom Edison* (40), *The Philadelphia Story* (40), *Barnacle Bill* (41), *Babes on Broadway* (42), *Best Foot Forward* (43).

## WEISSMULLER, Johnny (1904-1984)

Born Peter John Weissmuller in Windber, Pennsylvania, he was educated at the University of Chicago. He won five gold medals for his swim-

ming at the Olympic Games in Amsterdam in 1928 and began appearing in swimming extravaganzas before he was hired by MGM to play Tarzan in a series of films. Weissmuller was an ideal king of the jungle in 12 of these productions, and when audiences began to lose interest in Tarzan, he went to Columbia Pictures and appeared in the *Jungle Jim* series of films. Later he formed a swimming pool company. Weissmuller's third wife was actress Lupe Velez, and the couple was constantly making headlines because of their frequent quarrels.
**Selected Films:** *Glorifying the American Girl* (29), *Tarzan the Ape Man* (32), *Tarzan and His Mate* (34), *Tarzan Escapes* (36), *Tarzan Finds a Son* (39), *Tarzan's Secret Treasure* (41), *Tarzan's New York Adventure* (42), *Tarzan's Desert Mystery* (43), *Swamp Fire* (46), *Jungle Jim* (48), *The Lost Tribe* (49), *Captive Girl* (50), *Jungle Manhunt* (51), *Jungle Jim in the Forbidden Land* (52), *The Killer Ape* (53), *Cannibal Attack* (54), *Devil Goddess* (55), *The Phynx* (70), *Won Ton Ton, The Dog Who Saved Hollywood* (76).

## **WELCH, Raquel** (1940- )

Born Raquel Tejada in Chicago, Illinois, to a Bolivian-born engineer and a mother of English stock, Welch moved with her family to California where she took ballet lessons as a child and began winning beauty contests at age 14. When she was 18 she married James Welch, her high school sweetheart; they had two children and separated in 1961. She took drama at San Diego State College and did some amateur stage work. Welch moved to Dallas, Texas, after her divorce. There she became a model and cocktail waitress and had her nose fixed. She went to Hollywood and after two bit parts, she met press agent Patrick Curtis, who decided to merchandise Welch's voluptuous body and sensual face. He got her a movie contract, a few parts on television, and took her on a publicity tour of Europe. She became a major international star before she had appeared in a single decent movie. She was now the major sex goddess of the 1960s and one of the top money-earners in Hollywood. She was expected to fade with the first wrinkle, but she has proved to be a tough and talented survivor.
**Selected Films:** *A House Is Not a Home* (64), *Fantastic Voyage* (66), *One Million Years BC* (66), *Myra Breckinridge* (70), *Fuzz* (72), *The Last of Sheila* (73), *The Three Musketeers* (74), *The Four Musketeers* (75), *Mother, Jugs and Speed* (77), *The Prince and the Pauper* (77), *Restless* (79), *The Swindle* (81).

## **WELD, Tuesday** (1943- )

She was born Susan Ker Weld in New York City, and she began working as a child model at the age of three. By the time she was nine she had had her first nervous breakdown. At ten she was a problem drinker, and at 12 she attempted suicide. Weld made her screen debut in *Rock, Rock, Rock* (56), making the first of her many appearances as an innocent-looking nymphet. It was downhill after that until the mid-1960s, when people began to notice that she could act, and she became the center of a cult following. Weld was briefly married to actor Dudley Moore.
**Selected Films:** *Rock, Rock, Rock* (56), *Rally Round the Flag, Boys!* (58), *The Five Pennies* (59), *Sex Kittens Go to College* (60), *Wild in the Country* (61), *Bachelor Flat* (61), *Soldier in the Rain* (63), *The Cincinnati Kid* (65), *Pretty Poison* (68), *Play It As It Lays* (72), *Looking for Mr Goodbar* (77), *Who'll Stop the Rain?* (78), *The Serial* (79), *Author! Author!* (82).

## **WELLES, Orson** (1915-1986)

He was an actor, director, producer and screenwriter. He was also an egotist, a flamboyant character and a genius, a man who fought for artistic integrity throughout his career, and who appeared in poor films from time to time simply to earn money to finance his own serious projects. He had admirers and detractors. To some he was a self-indulgent charlatan who usurped other people's ideas, and who was moody and difficult to deal with. To others he was simply an artist who failed to live up to his enormous early potential. His admirers point to his originality and flair, his magnificent speaking voice and to his great film triumph, the masterpiece *Citizen Kane* (41). Born in Kenosha, Wisconsin, into a wealthy family, Welles was a genuine prodigy with an audacious streak who talked his way into a leading role at Dublin's respected Gate Theatre when he was only 16. He directed the Negro People's Theatre production of

*Joan Fontaine and Orson Welles in* Jane Eyre *(43).*

Shakespeare's *Macbeth* with an all-black cast in 1936, when he was 21. By then he had also appeared on Broadway. In 1937 he founded the Mercury Theater with John Houseman, and dramatized H G Wells' *The War of the Worlds* so effectively on radio on Halloween 1938 that listeners panicked and fled their homes. Welles then went to Hollywood, creating a stir with *Citizen Kane*. With its thinly disguised critical depiction of newspaper mogul William Randolph Hearst, the movie brought down the wrath of the Hearst newspapers on Welles' head, seriously affecting the film's commercial success and making it difficult for Welles to continue working in Hollywood. When he directed *The Magnificent Ambersons* (42), based on the novel by Booth Tarkington, a gem, the studio cut it brutally. Welles was imposing as Rochester in *Jane Eyre* (43), and as Claudette Colbert's crippled husband in *Tomorrow Is Forever* (44). *The Lady from Shanghai* (47) co-starred wife-of-that-time Rita Hayworth, and his conception of *Macbeth* (48), although boldly unconventional, was hampered by a low budget. Welles went to Europe, creating a memorable screen role in *The Third Man* (49). His daring *Othello* (51), his acting and directing in *Touch of Evil* (58) and his performance in *The Long Hot Summer* (58) are all worthy of note. He won a special Academy Award in 1970 'for supreme artistry and versatility in the creation of motion pictures,' and the American Film Institute's Life Achievement Award in 1975.
**Selected Films:** *Citizen Kane* (41), *Journey into Fear* (42), *Jane Eyre* (43), *Tomorrow Is Forever* (44), *The Stranger* (45), *The Lady from Shanghai* (47), *Black Magic* (47), *Macbeth* (48), *Prince of Foxes* (49), *The Third Man* (49), *Othello* (51), *Trouble in the Glen* (53), *Mr Arkadin* (55), *Moby Dick* (56), *Touch of Evil* (58), *The Long Hot Summer* (58), *Roots of Heaven* (58), *Compulsion* (59), *The Trial* (62), *The VIPs* (63), *Is Paris Burning?* (66), *A Man for All Seasons* (66), *Marco the Magnificent* (66), *Casino Royale* (67), *Catch 22* (70), *Treasure Island* (72), *Voyage of the Damned* (76), *The Muppet Movie* (78), *The Man Who Saw Tomorrow* (82), *Butterfly* (82).

## WERNER, Oskar (1922-1984)

Born Oskar Josef Schleissmayer in Vienna, Austria, he played bit parts in movies while still in secondary school. In the early 1940s he studied at the Burgtheatre in Vienna. Following his discharge from the army he began playing leading men in motion pictures while remaining basically a classical stage actor. Following his portrayal of Jules in *Jules and Jim* (61) he became an international star, and was nominated for an Academy Award for Best Actor in *Ship of Fools* (65).
**Selected Films:** *Angel with a Trumpet* (48), *Eroica* (49), *Decision Before Dawn* (51), *The Sins of Lola Montes* (55), *Jules and Jim* (61), *Ship of Fools* (65), *The Spy Who Came in From the Cold* (65), *Fahrenheit 451* (66), *The Shoes of the Fisherman* (68), *Voyage of the Damned* (76).

*Mae West and W C Fields in* My Little Chickadee *(39).*

## WEST, Adam (1928- )

West was born William Anderson in Walla Walla, Washington. Educated at Whitman College, he became a leading man on television and in movies, but he is most famous for his appearance in the title role of the TV series *Batman*.
**Selected Films:** *The Young Philadelphians* (59), *Geronimo* (62), *Soldier in the Rain* (63), *Robinson Crusoe on Mars* (64), *Batman* (66), *The Girl Who Knew Too Much* (69), *The Marriage of a Young Stockbroker* (71), *Hell River* (74), *The Specialist* (75), *Hooper* (78).

## WEST, Mae (1892-1980)

West, of the half-mast eyelids, come-hither voice and no-nonsense seductiveness, was a living American institution. Her aggressive sexuality and comic genius established her as a diamond-studded star. She was the archetypal sex symbol, splendidly vulgar, mocking, overdressed and endearing. She owed a lot to sex and sex probably owes a lot to her. She was a gifted blonde comedienne and egomaniac with plenty of brains – a one-of-a-kind original, ahead of her time when it came to notions of sexual freedom for women, able to turn those notions into a vastly lucrative stage and film career. Just before her death she remarked, 'I was the first liberated woman, y'know. No guy was gonna get the best of me; that's what I wrote all my scripts about.' Born in Brooklyn, New York, West never bothered much with school because she was too busy performing, first as an amateur and later in burlesque, billed as 'The Baby Vamp.' At 14 she began appearing in vaudeville and in Broadway revues – it was West who introduced the shimmy on stage. She was also a male impersonator. This, plus her tough, 'macho,' guilt-free attitude to sex eventually led to a rumor that she was actually a man in disguise. West's countless lovers put the lie to that one. In 1926 she wrote a play called *Sex*, which led to her being jailed for eight days on charges of obscenity. Some of her lines were deliciously lacking in subtlety, such as 'Are you packin' a rod or are you just glad to see me?' In 1927 she wrote a play about homosexuality called *Drag* which was never performed on Broadway. Her best writing was a play in which she also starred – *Diamond Lil* – that opened in Brooklyn in 1928. It was an enormous hit, since she could make the telephone directory sound like a proposition. By now she was a theatrical star, a 1920s celebrity, admired by Cole Porter and other luminaries, but still incorruptably unrespectable, boldly advertising her habit of picking up virile prize fighters. She arrived in Hollywood in 1932 and appeared with George Raft in *Night After Night*, stealing, as he said, 'everything but the cameras.' She became a great film star, breaking box office records. Lines like 'Come up and see me' passed into common usage. She made Cary Grant a star with *She Done Him Wrong* (33) and vied with W C Fields in *My Little Chickadee* (39), but by then the American puritanism was on the upswing and censorship ended her movie career. She went back on stage and at age 62 started a nightclub act, surrounding herself with male bodybuilders. By then she was a legend and a cult figure, a high priestess of sex in a white gown, white furs and a diamond necklace, telling the hypocrites where to get off and showing everyone a good time.

**Selected Films:** *Night After Night* (32), *She Done Him Wrong* (33), *I'm No Angel* (33), *Going to Town* (34), *Belle of the Nineties* (34), *Klondike Annie* (36), *Go West Young Man* (37), *Every Day's a Holiday* (37), *My Little Chickadee* (39), *The Heat's On* (43), *Myra Breckinridge* (70), *Sextette* (77).

## WESTCOTT, Helen (1928- )

A native of Hollywood, California, she was born Myrthas Helen Hickman. As a child she was a stage actress, and appeared in only one picture – in a small part in *A Midsummer Night's Dream* (35). As an adult, she returned to films in the late 1940s to play standard female roles in many routine productions.

**Selected Films:** *A Midsummer Night's Dream* (35), *Adventures of Don Juan* (48), *Flaxy Martin* (49), *The Gunfighter* (50), *Take Care of My Little Girl* (51), *With a Song in My Heart* (52), *Abbott and Costello Meet Dr Jekyll and Mr Hyde* (53), *Hot Blood* (56), *The Last Hurrah* (58), *Studs Lonigan* (60), *Bourbon Street Shadows* (62), *I Love My Wife* (70).

## WESTLY, Helen (1875-1942)

This Hollywood character actress was born Henrietta Meserole Manney in Brooklyn, New York. After graduating from the American Academy of Dramatic Arts, she was a Broadway actress at the turn of the century, then went into vaudeville and stock. In 1915 she was one of the founders of the Greenwich Square Players in New York City, and was also one of the founders of the Theatre Guild in 1918. She moved to Hollywood in 1934 to play crusty and sometime domineering matrons.

**Selected Films:** *Death Takes a Holiday* (34), *Anne of Green Gables* (34), *Roberta* (35), *Show Boat* (36), *Heidi* (37), *Rebecca of Sunnybrook Farm* (38), *Alexander's Ragtime Band* (38), *Zaza* (39), *Lillian Russell* (40), *Adam Had Four Sons* (41), *My Favorite Spy* (42).

## WESTMAN, Nydia (1902-1970)

She was born in New York City into a show business family; her father was actor-composer Theodore Westman and her mother was actress-playwright Lily Wren Westman. She appeared in her parent's stage act when she was a child, and from the age of 16 she played in many Broadway and stock productions. Westman started her Hollywood career in *Strange Justice* (32) and continued playing fluttery, nervous character roles until her death.

**Selected Films:** *Strange Justice* (32), *Little Women* (33), *One Night of Love* (34), *Craig's Wife* (36), *The Goldwyn Follies* (38), *The Cat and the Canary* (39), *Forty Little Mothers* (40), *The Chocolate Soldier* (41), *Princess O'Rourke* (43), *The Late George Apley* (47), *The Velvet Touch* (48), *The Swinger* (66), *The Horse in the Gray Flannel Suit* (68), *Rabbit Run* (70).

## WESTON, Jack (1925- )

This roly-poly comic character actor was born Jack Weinstein in Cleveland, Ohio. When he was ten years old, he began his theatrical training at the Cleveland Playhouse, dropping out of public school at 15, after his father died in an accident. He was a theater usher and an actor for a while, and after his discharge from the service at the end of World War II, he went to New York to study at the American Theatre Wing. While he was there, he supported himself and his wife, the actress Marge Redmond, by working as a dish washer, an elevator operator and a postal clerk. By 1950 he was getting work in featured roles on Broadway and in the infant television industry, making his film debut in 1958 in *Stage Struck*. But it wasn't until the mid-1970s that audiences began to notice him when he appeared on Broadway in Neil Simon's *California Suite* and on screen in the movie version of the play *The Ritz* (76).

**Selected Films:** *Stage Struck* (58), *Please Don't Eat the Daisies* (60), *It's Only Money* (62), *Palm Springs Weekend* (63), *The Incredible Mr Limpet* (64), *The Cincinnati Kid* (65), *Wait Until Dark* (67), *The Thomas Crown Affair* (68), *Cactus Flower* (69), *A New Leaf* (71), *Fuzz* (72), *Marco* (73), *The Ritz* (76), *Cuba* (79), *The Four Seasons* (81), *High Road to China* (83), *The Longshot* (86), *Ishtar* (87).

*Robert Woolsey, Eddie Quillan, Kitty Kelly, Dorothy Lee, Mitzi Green and Bert Wheeler in* Girl Crazy *(32).*

## WHEELER, Bert (1895-1968)

Born Albert Jerome Wheeler in Paterson, New Jersey, he was on the stage when he was a boy. By the time he was in his early 20s, he was a vaudeville comedy star, and he and his wife Betty starred in *The Ziegfeld Follies* in 1923. Ziegfeld teamed Wheeler with Robert Woolsey in his Broadway musical, *Rio Rita*, and the two of them went to Hollywood to do the film version in 1929. They were a favorite comedy team in movies until Woolsey's death in 1938. Wheeler went back to his stage work, then appearing in a few pictures as a solo act.
**Selected Films** (alone): *Captain Fly-By-Night* (22), *Too Many Cooks* (31), *Cowboy Quarterback* (39), *Las Vegas Nights* (41).
(With Woolsey): *Rio Rita* (29), *The Cuckoos* (30), *Cracked Nuts* (31), *Girl Crazy* (32), *Diplomaniacs* (33), *Kentucky Kernels* (34), *The Nitwits* (35), *Mummy's Boys* (36), *High Flyers* (37).

## WHELAN, Arlene (1916- )

This pretty, red-headed leading lady of the 1940s was born in Salt Lake City, Utah. Whelan had been a beauty salon manicurist before she was tapped by Hollywood. When her popularity began to wane in the mid-1950s, she retired.
**Selected Films:** *Kidnapped* (38), *Young Mr Lincoln* (39), *Sabotage* (39), *Charley's Aunt* (41), *The Senator Was Indiscreet* (47), *That Wonderful Urge* (48), *Dear Wife* (50), *The Sun Shines Bright* (53), *Raiders of Old California* (57).

## WHITE, Jesse (1919- )

Born Jesse Wiedenfeld in Buffalo, New York, he was raised in Akron, Ohio. When he was 15 he made his first appearance on a stage in an amateur performance. White had a variety of occupations before he made it to the professional stage in the early 1940s. He hit Broadway in 1943 after appearing in vaudeville, burlesque and stock. One of Hollywood's most reliable comedic character actors, he has also done a great deal of television work. Probably his most memorable role was as the asylum orderly in *Harvey* (50) – his first film role.
**Selected Films:** *Harvey* (50), *Death of a Salesman* (51), *Million Dollar Mermaid* (520, *The Bad Seed* (56), *Designing Woman* (57), *Marjorie Morningstar* (58), *It's a Mad Mad Mad Mad World* (63), *A House Is Not a Home* (64), *Bless the Beasts and Children* (71), *Return to Campus* (75), *New Girl in Town* (77), *The Cat From Outer Space* (78).

## WHITE, Pearl (1889-1938)

Born a farmer's daughter in Green Ridge, Missouri, she made her amateur stage debut at the age of six, playing Little Eva in *Uncle Tom's Cabin*. By the age of 13 she was a circus equestrienne, but a spinal injury she sustained when she fell off a horse forced her to quit the circus. She was working as a secretary at a film company when her good looks won her a role in a Western film, *The Life of Buffalo Bill* (10). She did most of her own stunts, but required a double at times because of her back injury. White was most famous for playing the heroine in the most successful movie serial ever made, *The Perils of Pauline* (14). She was, for a time, the most popular female star in the movies, outdistancing even Mary Pickford. Later in her career she attempted dramatic roles, but did not succeed, and she retired to France.
**Selected Films:** *The Life of Buffalo Bill* (10), *The Perils of Pauline* (14), *The Exploits of Elaine* (15), *The White Moll* (20), *Know Your Men* (21), *A Virgin Paradise* (21), *Plunder* (23), *Perils of Paris* (24).

## WHITELAW, Billie (1932- )

She is primarily known for her stage work, which she began in 1950. Born in Coventry, England, she first entered show business as an assistant stage manager. She became a star in 1960s, winning the British Film Award for *Charlie Bubbles* (68).

**Selected Films:** *Bobbikins* (59), *Make Mine Mink* (60), *No Love for Johnny* (61), *Charlie Bubbles* (68), *The Adding Machine* (69), *Start the Revolution Without Me* (70), *Eagle in a Cage* (71), *Frenzy* (72), *Night Watch* (73), *The Omen* (76), *The Water Babies* (79), *An Unsuitable Job for a Woman* (81).

## WHITMAN, Stuart (1926- )

Born in San Francisco, California, he was in the Army Corps of Engineers during World War II, and he also competed as a light heavyweight boxer. After his discharge, he majored in drama at the Los Angeles City College. Whitman started out in bit parts in films in 1951, and gradually became a featured player and then a lead. He was nominated for an Academy Award for Best Actor for his role as a repentant child molester in *The Mark* (61).

**Selected Films:** *When Worlds Collide* (51), *Rhapsody* (54), *War Drums* (57), *Ten North Frederick* (58), *The Sound and the Fury* (59), *The Story of Ruth* (60), *The Mark* (61), *The Comancheros* (61), *The Longest Day* (62), *Those Magnificent Men in Their Flying Machines* (65), *Night of the Lepus* (72), *Crazy Mama* (75), *The White Buffalo* (77), *Run for the Roses* (78), *Delta Fox* (79), *Hostages* (80), *Butterfly* (82).

## WHITMORE, James (1921- )

This craggy character actor was born in White Plains, New York, and educated at Yale University, where he was a member of the Yale Drama School Players. He was in the Marines during World War II, and after his discharge went into stock. He made his Broadway debut in 1947 as a non-commissioned officer in *Command Decision*. Whitmore went to Hollywood in 1949, where he played important supporting roles, and was nominated for an Academy Award for Best Supporting Actor for his performance in *Battleground* (49) – only his second movie. He was nominated as Best Actor for his work in a one-man movie about President Truman, *Give 'Em Hell, Harry* (75).

**Selected Films:** *The Undercover Man* (49), *Battleground* (49), *The Asphalt Jungle* (50), *It's a Big Country* (52), *Kiss Me Kate* (53), *Them* (54), *Battle Cry* (55), *Oklahoma!* (55), *The Eddie Duchin Story* (56), *Black Like Me* (64), *Madigan* (68), *Tora! Tora! Tora!* (70), *Give 'Em Hell, Harry* (75), *The Serpent's Egg* (77), *Bully* (78), *The First Deadly Sin* (80).

## WHITTY, May (1865-1948)

Born in Liverpool, England, she made her debut in ballet at 16 and was on the London stage at 17. By the turn of the century she was a respected actress on both sides of the Atlantic. She was created Dame Commander of the British Empire in 1918 for her services to her country during World War I. She made her first film, *Enoch Arden*, in 1915, and in her first sound film she played the terrified old lady in *Night Must Fall* (37), for which she received an Academy Award nomination for Best Supporting Actress. She was nominated for the same award for her work in *Mrs Miniver* (42). She was married to the stage actor Ben Webster and was the mother of actress/director/producer/playwright Margaret Webster.

**Selected Films:** *Enoch Arden* (15), *Night Must Fall* (37), *The Lady Vanishes* (38), *Mrs Miniver* (42), *My Name Is Julia Ross* (45), *The Return of October* (48).

## WHORF, Richard (1906-1966)

This sullen-looking actor-director was born in Winthrop, Massachusetts. At the age of 15 he quit school to try his hand at the stage in Boston, later becoming a director and set designer. Whorf first appeared in Broadway in 1927 and appeared often with Alfred Lunt and Lynne Fontanne in the late 1930s. His first film was *Midnight* (34), but he didn't return to Hollywood until 1940. In 1944 he turned director and specialized in comedies, switching almost completely to television direction in the late 1950s.

**Selected Films:** *Midnight* (34), *Blues in the Night* (41), *Yankee Doodle Dandy* (42), *The Cross of Lorraine* (43), *Chain Lightning* (50).

## WICKES, Mary (1916- )

A lanky, gawky character comedienne, she was born Mary Isabelle Wickenhauser in St Louis, Missouri. Educated at Washington University in St Louis, she went into stock and then to Broadway. Possibly her most memorable movie role was that of the terrified, intimidated nurse in *The Man Who Came to Dinner* (42).

**Selected Films:** *The Man Who Came to Dinner* (42), *Higher and Higher* (43), *June Bride* (48), *On Moonlight Bay* (51), *The Actress* (53), *White Christmas* (54), *Don't Go Near the Water* (57), *It Happened to Jane* (59), *The Music Man* (62), *The Trouble with Angels* (66), *Snowball Express* (72), *Touched By Love* (80).

## WIDMARK, Richard (1914- )

Widmark was so brilliant playing villains at the start of his film career that he had to do battle against typecasting. He evolved into a solid, durable star, even though as a hero he tends to be a tough loner. Born in Sunrise, Minnesota, he was educated at Lake Forest College in Lake Forest, Illinois, where he later taught. At the college, he discovered football and acting, and acting won. Radio dramas gave him a start and Broadway came next. His screen debut was as Tommy Udo, a psychopathic killer whose chilling laugh terrified audiences, in *Kiss of Death* (47), and no one could

forget the scene in which, laughing all the way, he pushed a little old lady, in her wheelchair, down a long flight of stairs. He received an Academy Award nomination as Best Supporting Actor for the role. Eventually he formed his own movie production company and also appeared on television.
**Selected Films:** *Kiss of Death* (47), *Slattery's Hurricane* (49), *Panic in the Streets* (50), *The Cobweb* (55), *Saint Joan* (57), *Judgment at Nuremberg* (61), *The Bedford Incident* (65), *Madigan* (68), *Murder on the Orient Express* (74), *Rollercoaster* (77), *Bear Island* (79), *Hanky Panky* (82), *Against All Odds* (84).

## WIEST, Dianne (ca 1955- )

Born in Kansas City, Missouri, Wiest studied ballet and then turned to acting, working much in the theater before making her screen debut in *I'm Dancing as Fast as I Can* (82). A character actress, Wiest has come to fame with strong supporting roles, usually as a neurotic character in several Woody Allen films. She won the Academy Award for Best Supporting Actress for her performance in *Hannah and Her Sisters* (86).
**Selected Films:** *Independence Day* (82), *Footloose* (84), *The Purple Rose of Cairo* (85), *Hannah and Her Sisters* (86), *Radio Days* (87).

## WILCOXON, Henry (1905-1984)

Born Harry Wilcoxon to British parents in Dominica, West Indies, he first appeared on the London stage. After seven years of theater work, he made his first movie *The Perfect Lady* (31). Cecil B De Mille brought this handsome leading man to Hollywood to play Marc Antony to Claudette Colbert's Cleopatra in *Cleopatra* (34). From then on, his best roles were for De Mille, and he was often cast in other films as a supporting actor. Toward the end of his career he became an executive for De Mille, acting as associate producer and producer. He was once married to actress Joan Woodbury.
**Selected Films:** *The Perfect Lady* (31), *Lord of the Manor* (33), *Cleopatra* (34), *The Crusades* (35), *The Last of the Mohicans* (36), *Souls at Sea* (37), *If I Were King* (38), *Mystery Sea Raider* (40), *That Hamilton Woman* (41), *Mrs Miniver* (42), *A Connecticut Yankee in King Arthur's Court* (49), *Samson and Delilah* (49), *The Greatest Show on Earth* (52), *The Ten Commandments* (56), *The War Lord* (65), *Man in the Wilderness* (71), F.I.S.T. (78), *Sweet Sixteen* (81).

## WILDE, Cornel (1915- )

This actor-director-producer was born Cornelius Louis Wilde in New York City. Much of his youth was spent in Europe with his father, who traveled for a New York firm, and he became fluent in several languages. The family settled permanently in the United States in 1932, and Wilde entered a pre-med program at the City College of New York, working his way through school as a toy salesman, commercial artist and advertising salesman. He won a scholarship to Columbia University's College of Physicians and Surgeons, but acting beckoned, and he went into stock and then to Broadway. Along the way he passed up an invitation to be on the United States fencing team at the 1936 Berlin Olympics. His acting career improved when he was hired as a fencing instructor and featured player (as Tybalt) in the Laurence Olivier-Vivien Leigh production of *Romeo and Juliet* on Broadway. He began his movie career in small roles, usually as heavies, and he became a star playing Frederic Chopin in *A Song to Remember* (45), for which he was nominated for an Academy Award for Best Actor. For a while he starred in A pictures, but was sent to the Bs in the early 1950s, often playing in swashbucklers. In 1955 he formed his own company and produced and directed his own pictures, most notably *The Naked Prey* (66).
**Selected Films:** *The Lady with Red Hair* (40), *High Sierra* (410, *Wintertime* (43), *A Song to Remember* (45), *Leave Her to Heaven* (45), *Centennial Summer* (46), *Forever Amber* (47), *Road House* (48), *Two Flags West* (50), *The Greatest Show on Earth* (52), *Treasure of the Golden Condor* (53), *Star of India* (56), *Edge of Eternity* (59), *The Naked Prey* (66), *The Comic* (69), *Shark's Treasure* (75), *The Fifth Musketeer* (79).

## WILDER, Gene (1935- )

Wilder, a protégé of Mel Brooks, specializes in nervous or embarrassed comic characters. Born Jerry Silberman in Milwaukee, Wisconsin, he took drama classes at the University of Iowa and after graduation studied at the Old Vic Theatre School of Bristol, England. He returned to the United States and joined the Actors Studio and appeared in several Broadway productions. His film debut was a small but notable part in *Bonnie and Clyde* (67), in which he was the frustrated owner of one of the cars that the bank robbers stole. His real success, however, came in Mel Brooks' films, particularly *Young Frankenstein* (74). Wilder's career slipped a bit when he started writing and directing his own films, but he has been redeemed somewhat with the success of *The Woman in Red* (84). He is married to actress/comedienne Gilda Radner.
**Selected Films:** *Bonnie and Clyde* (67), *The Producers* (68), *Willie Wonka and the Chocolate Factory* (71), *Everything You Always Wanted to Know About Sex* (72), *The Little Prince* (73), *Blazing Saddles* (74), *Young Frankenstein* (74), *The Adventures of Sherlock Holmes' Smarter Brother* (75), *Silver Streak* (76), *The Frisco Kid* (79), *The Woman in Red* (84), *Haunted Honeymoon* (86).

## WILDING, Michael (1912-1979)

Wilding was born in Westcliff-on-Sea, England, and began as a painter and worked in the art department of a British film studio. He then switched to acting and became a polished leading

man. He is probably best remembered for being the second husband of Elizabeth Taylor and the father of two of her children. He was also married to actress Margaret Leighton.
**Selected Films:** *Pastorale* (33), *The Wedding Group* (35), *In Which We Serve* (42), *English Without Tears* (44), *An Ideal Husband* (47), *Under Capricorn* (49), *Stage Fright* (50), *The Egyptian* (54), *The Glass Slipper* (55), *The World of Suzie Wong* (60), *The Naked Edge* (61), *The Sweet Ride* (67), *Waterloo* (70), *Lady Caroline Lamb* (72).

## WILLIAM, Warren (1895-1948)

This suave leading man was born Warren Krech in Aitkin, Minnesota, and he started out as a newspaper reporter. He served in the Armed Forces in Europe during World War I, and after his discharge he trained at the American Academy of Dramatic Arts in New York City, then played in stock and a few silent movies, including a serial, *Plunder* (23), opposite Pearl White. After becoming a leading man on Broadway in the mid-1920s, he went to Hollywood, often playing detectives, reporters and adventurers in B pictures. One exception was his role as Julius Caesar in Cecil B De Mille's *Cleopatra* (34).
**Selected Films:** *The Town That Forgot God* (22), *Plunder (23), Twelve Miles Out* (27), Horror of the Family (31), *Gold Diggers of 1933* (33), *Cleopatra* (34), *The Dragon Murder Case* (34), *The Case of the Howling Dog* (34), *Imitation of Life* (34), *Go West, Young Man* (36), *The Firefly* (37), *Madame X* (37), *Arsene Lupin Returns* (38), *The Lone Wolf Spy Hunt* (39), *The Man in the Iron Mask* (39), *Lillian Russell* (40), *The Wolf Man* (41), *Passport to Suez* (43), *Fear* (46), *The Private Affairs of Bel Ami* (47).

## WILLIAMS, Bill (1916- )

Born Herman Katt in Brooklyn, New York, and educated at Pratt Institute, Williams had been a professional swimmer and a singer before beginning his acting career in stock and vaudeville. Following World War II military service, he started making motion pictures. He is married to actress Barbara Hale.
**Selected Films:** *Murder in the Blue Room* (44), *Thirty Seconds Over Tokyo* (44), *West of the Pecos* (45), *Till the End of Time* (46), *The Stratton Story* (49), *Son of Paleface* (52), *Apache Ambush* (55), *Legion of the Doomed* (58), *Oklahoma Territory* (60), *Law of the Lawless* (64), *Rio Lobo* (70), *The Giant Spider Invasion* (75), *69 Minutes* (77).

## WILLIAMS, Billy Dee (1937- )

Born in New York City, this leading man was raised in Harlem. He made his stage debut at seven, and later trained at Sidney Poitier's acting workshop. At one time he preferred painting to acting, and he won a scholarship the National Academy of Fine Arts and Design. When he was nine, he had appeared on Broadway in *The Firebrand of Florence*, and he returned to Broadway as an adult. Williams appeared in occasional films beginning in the late 1950s, but he didn't become a star until he played the male lead in *Lady Sings the Blues* (72), although he had been exceptionally good as the black football star, Gayle Sayers, in the made-for-television movie, *Brian's Song*. He also played Lando Calrissian in *The Empire Strikes Back* (80) and *Return of the Jedi* (83).
**Selected Films:** *The Last Angry Man* (59), *The Out-of-Towners* (70), *Lady Sings the Blues* (72), *Hit!* (73), *The Take* (74), *Mahogany* (75), *The Bingo Long Traveling All-Stars and Motor Kings* (76), *Scott Joplin* (77), *The Empire Strikes Back* (80), *Nighthawks* (81), *Return of the Jedi* (83).

## WILLIAMS, Cara (1925- )

This comedienne of radio, television and motion pictures was born Bernice Kamiat in Brooklyn, New York. She started acting as a child and went to Hollywood in her teens, where she attended the Hollywood Professional School and often provided voice-overs for movie cartoon characters. Williams graduated to supporting parts in films, with an occasional lead thrown in, in both comedies and dramas. She was nominated for an Academy Award for Best Supporting Actress for her work in *The Defiant Ones* (58). Williams was married for seven years to actor John Barrymore Jr.
**Selected Films:** *Happy Land* (43), *Something for the Boys* (44), *Boomerang* (47), *Sitting Pretty* (48), *Knock on Any Door* (49), *Meet Me in Las Vegas* (46), *The Defiant Ones* (58), *The Man From the Diners' Club* (63), *Doctors' Wives* (71), *The White Buffalo* (77).

## WILLIAMS, Cindy (1947- )

Born in Van Nuys, California, she majored in drama at the Los Angeles City College, and worked as a waitress for a time before she began getting small parts on television and in the movies. She received good notices for her role in *American Graffiti* (73), but her real fame came as Shirley Feeney on the TV series *Laverne and Shirley*.
**Selected Films:** *Gas-s-s-s* (70), *Drive, He Said* (71), *Travels with My Aunt* (72), *American Graffiti* (73), *The Conversation* (74), *Mr Rico* (75), *The First Nudie Musical* (76), *More American Graffiti* (79), *Uforia* (85).

## WILLIAMS, Emlyn (1905- )

This actor-playwright-screen writer-director was born George Emlyn Williams in Mostyn, Wales. Although he was raised in a poor coal mining community, he was saved from the mines by an understanding school teacher, and won scholarships in Switzerland and to Oxford University, later rising to stardom on the English and American stage. The best known of his many plays is *The Corn Is Green*, an autobiographical drama about

his own boyhood. Williams began his movie work as an actor in 1932.
**Selected Films:** *The Case of the Frightened Lady* (32), *The Man Who Knew Too Much* (34), *Broken Blossoms* (36), *The Citadel* (38), *The Stars Look Down* (39), *Major Barbara* (41), *Three Husbands* (50), *Ivanhoe* (52), *The Deep Blue Sea* (56), *I Accuse!* (57), *The L-Shaped Room* (62), *The Walking Stick* (70).

## WILLIAMS, Esther (1923- )

Born in Los Angeles, she was a swimming champion at the age of 15, and later was a part-time model at a department store. She was a student at Los Angeles City College when she dropped out to become a swimmer in the Billy Rose's Aquacade show at the San Francisco World Aquacade show at the San Francisco World's Fair in 1939. She was spotted by an M-G-M scout and she made her film debut in *Andy Hardy's Double Life* (42) opposite Mickey Rooney. Then the Hollywood moguls reasoned that this swimmer might be a rival for skater Sonja Henie, and her first big film was *Bathing Beauty* (44), the first of a long string of lavish musical comedies featuring Williams and her swimming scenes. In the 1950s her career faded when she shifted to dramatic parts, although she was good in such films as *The Unguarded Moment* (56) in which she played a school teacher who is almost raped by a student. She retired in the early 1960s and invested in business ventures, most notably Esther Williams swimming pools. Her third husband was actor Fernando Lamas, and she is the mother of actor Lorenzo Lamas.
**Selected Films:** *Andy Hardy's Double Life* (42), *A Guy Named Joe* (43), *Bathing Beauty* (44), *Thrill of a Romance* (45), *Ziegfeld Follies* (46), *This Time for Keeps* (47), *On an Island with You* (48), *Take Me Out to the Ball Game* (49), *Neptune's Daughter* (49), *Pagan Love Song* (50), *Texas Carnival* (51), *Skirts Ahoy!* (52), *Million Dollar Mermaid* (52), *Dangerous When Wet* (53), *Easy to Love* (53), *Jupiter's Darling* (55), *The Unguarded Moment* (56), *Raw Wind in Eden* (58), *The Big Show* (61).

## WILLIAMS, Guinn (1899-1962)

Guinn 'Big Boy' Williams, the amiably tough character actor, was born in Decatur, Texas, and began his movie work as an extra in 1919. The son of a Untied States congressman, he had played some semi-professional football before he began getting some bit parts. In the early 1920s he starred in many westerns, then shifted to character parts, most notably in Will Rogers pictures. It was Rogers who nicknamed him 'Big Boy.' After another fling as a western star in the 1930s, he became a character actor again, often as a dim-witted cowhand.
**Selected Films:** *Almost a Husband* (19), *The Cowboy King* (22), *Big Stunt* (25), *Babe Comes Home* (27), *Noah's Ark* (29), *Liliom* (30), *You Said a Mouthful* (32), *Flirtation Walk* (34), *The Littlest Rebel;* (35), *A Star Is Born* (37), *Dodge City* (39), *Santa Fe Trail* (40), *Billy the Kid* (41), *Swamp Water* (41), *The Desperadoes* (43), *Belle of the Yukon* (45), *Brimstone* (49), *Springfield Rifle* (52), *Southwest Passage* (54), *The Alamo* (60), *The Comancheros* (62).

## WILLIAMS, JoBeth (1953- )

Born in Houston, Texas, she was educated at Brown University. She appeared in repertory companies in Rhode Island, Philadelphia, Boston and Washington, DC, and played in soap operas on television for two years. Williams began her film career in the late 1970s.
**Selected Films:** *Kramer vs, Kramer* (79), *Stir Crazy* (80), *The Dogs of War* (80), *Poltergeist* (82), *Endangered Species* (82), *The Big Chill* (83), *Teachers* (84), *Desert Bloom* (86), *Poltergeist II* (86).

## WILLIAMS, John (1903-1983)

This suave, polished character actor who often was seen in comedies was born in Chalfont St Giles, England, and was educated at Lancing College. He was performing on the British Stage at the age of 13, and on the Broadway stage when he was 21. Williams began his film career in England in the mid-1930s, and started making Hollywood movies in the late 1940s. His most memorable role was that of Inspector Hubbard in the stage, screen and television versions of *Dial M for Murder* – the film was released in 1954 and was directed by Alfred Hitchcock.
**Selected Films:** *Emil and the Detectives* (35), *Somewhere in France* (42), *A Woman's Vengeance* (48), *Kind Lady* (51), *Dial M for Murder* (54), *Sabrina* (54), *To Catch a Thief* (55), *The Solid Gold Cadillac* (56), *Will Success Spoil Rock Hunter?* (57), *Witness for the Prosecution* (58), *Midnight Lace* (60), *Harlow* (65), *Double Trouble* (67), *Lost in the Stars* (74), *Hot Lead and Cold Feet* (78).

*John Williams in* Dial M for Murder *(54).*

## WILLIAMS, Rhys (1897-1969)

Born in Wales, Williams was brought to Hollywood as a technical advisor and dialect coach for the making of *How Green Was My Valley* (41), and was given the role of Dai Bando, the boxer who teaches young Roddy McDowall to fight the bullies. He stayed on in Hollywood to make countless films as a supporting actor.
**Selected Films:** *How Green Was My Valley* (41), *Mrs Miniver* (42), *Random Harvest* (42), *The Corn is Green* (45), *The Bells of St Mary's* (45), *The Spiral Staircase* (46), *The Farmer's Daughter* (47), *Hills of Home* (48), *The Inspector General* (49), *Lightning Strikes Twice* (51), *Les Miserables* (52), *Johnny Guitar* (54), *The Kentuckian* (55), *Raintree County* (57), *Merry Andrew* (58), *Midnight Lace* (60), *The Sons of Katie Elder* (65), *Our Man Flint* (66), *Skullduggery* (70).

## WILLIAMS, Robin (1952- )

Williams was born in Chicago, Illinois, and as a child would memorize the recording of comedian Jonathan Winters. He began to let go when the family moved to Tiburon, California, in laid-back Marin County. When he was 18 he discovered his vast talent for comic improvization. Moving to New York, he studied drama with John Houseman at the Juilliard School, and then moved back to California, where he performed in comedy clubs. He won the part of an alien in an episode of the TV sitcom *Happy Days*, and the notion of another sitcom, *Mork and Mindy*, was born. After the run of this zany series, Williams was off and running, playing everything from a comic book character to a defecting Russian to the introspective Garp.
**Selected Films:** *Popeye* (80), *The World According to Garp* (82), *Moscow on the Hudson* (84), *Club Paradise* (86).

## WILLIAMS, Treat (1948- )

This handsome young actor was born in Rowayton, Connecticut. He got his start on stage with the Fulton Repertory Company in Pennsylvania during college vacations – doing Shakespeare. Later he was the understudy for the character Danny Zuko, the hero of *Grease*, on Broadway. He began his film career in *The Ritz* (76).
**Selected Films:** *The Ritz* (76), *The Eagle Has Landed* (76), *Hair* (79), *Why Should I Lie* (80), *Prince of the City* (81), *The Pursuit of D B Cooper* (81), *The Men's Club* (86), *Smooth Talk* (86), *Sweet Lies* (87).

## WILLIAMSON, Fred (1938- )

This black action hero was born in Gary, Indiana, and educated at Northwestern University. A professional football player for ten years, he began his film career in *M*A*S*H* (70), as Spearchucker, the Army surgeon. Williamson began directing, producing and writing some of his own movies in the mid-1970s.
**Selected Films:** *M*A*S*H* (70), *Tell Me That You Love Me, Junie Moon* (70), *Hammer* (72), *Black Caesar* (73), *Black Eye* (74), *Boss Nigger* (75), *No Way Back* (76), *Mr Mean* (77), *Vigilante* (83).

## WILLIAMSON, Nicol (1938- )

This imposing leading man was born in Hamilton, Scotland. Williamson made his screen debut in *Six Sided Triangle* in 1964. In 1966 he was nominated for a Tony Award for his performance in *Inadmissible Evidence* on Broadway, and he later played *Hamlet* and was invited to do a one-man show at the White House. Williamson was formerly married to actress Jill Townsend.
**Selected Films:** *Six Sided Triangle* (64), *Inadmissible Evidence* (68), *The Bofors Gun* (68), *Hamlet* (69), *The Jerusalem File* (72), *The Wilby Conspiracy* (75), *Robin and Marian* (76), *The Seven-Per-Cent Solution* (76), *The Goodbye Girl* (77), *The Cheap Detective* (78), *Venom* (81), *Black Widow* (87).

## WILLS, Chill (1903-1978)

This Western character actor was born in Seagoville, Texas, and was in show business since his early childhood, appearing in tent shows, vaudeville and stock in the Southwest. He formed a singing group, Chill Wills and the Avalon Boys, in the 1930s, and began his film career in a Hopalong Cassidy movie, *Bar 20 Rides Again* (35). In his more than 40 years in films he played in countless movies, most of them Westerns, and he also provided the voice of the mule in the *Francis* comedy series. Wills was nominated for Best Supporting Actor for his work in *The Alamo* (60).
**Selected Films:** *Bar 20 Rides Again* (35), *Way Out West* (37), *Allegheny Uprising* (39), *Boom Town* (40), *The Westerner* (40), *Belle Starr* (41), *Best Foot Forward* (43), *Meet Me in St Louis* (44), *The Yearling* (46), *Red Canyon* (49), *Rio Grande* (50), *The Man From the Alamo* (53), *Giant* (56), *The Alamo* (60), *The Cardinal* (63), *The Rounders* (65), *Pat Garrett and Billy the Kid* (73), *Mr Billion* (77).

## WILSON, Dooley (1894-1953)

This black actor-musician was born Arthur Wilson in Tyler, Texas, and became a minstrel performer at the age of 12. He went on to vaudeville and stock and led his own band in Paris and London night clubs in the 1920s. Wilson returned to the United States in the 1930s and appeared in Federal Theater productions of Orson Welles and John Houseman and in the Broadway musical *Cabin in the Sky*. He began his film career in 1942, and is best remembered as Sam in *Casablanca*, the man who played 'As Time Goes By.' But Wilson was a drummer, and the piano playing had to be dubbed.
**Selected Films:** *My Favorite Blonde* (42), *Cairo* (42), *Casablanca* (43), *Stormy Weather* (43), *Seven Days Ashore* (44), *Triple Threat* (48), *Come to the Stable* (49), *Passage West* (51).

## WILSON, Marie (1916-1972)

One of the best of all Hollywood stars cast in 'dumb blonde' roles, she was born Katharine Elizabeth Wilson in Anaheim, California. Wilson began her film career in 1934, and was most famous for her radio, television and screen versions of *My Friend Irma.*
**Selected Films:** *Babes in Toyland* (34), *China Clipper* (36), *Boy Meets Girl* (38), *Virginia* (41), *Shine on Harvest Moon* (44), *Young Widow* (46), *My Friend Irma* (49), *My Friend Irma Goes West* (50), *Never Wave at a WAC* (53), *Mr Hobbs Takes a Vacation* (62).

## WINDOM, William (1923- )

Windom, the fine character actor, was born in New York City, and was educated at Williams College, The Citadel, Antioch College, the University of Kentucky, Biarritz American University, Fordham University and Columbia University. He trained at the American Repertory Theatre, and was on stage for years. After service with the 508th Parachute Infantry Division during World War II, he made his movie debut in the early 1960s. Windom has often appeared on television, as the star of two situation comedies – *The Farmer's Daughter* and *My World and Welcome to It.* He also won an Emmy for his work on the latter program.
**Selected Films:** *To Kill a Mockingbird* (62), *For Love or Money* (63), *Cattle King* (63), *One Man's Way* (64), *The Americanization of Emily* (64), *Hour of the Gun* (67), *The Detective* (68), *The Angry Breed* (69), *The Gypsy Moths* (69), *Brewster McCloud* (70), *Echoes of Summer* (74), *Mean Dog Blues* (78).

## WINDSOR, Marie (1922- )

This former Miss Utah was born Emily Marie Bertelson in Marysville, Utah, was educated at Brigham Young University, and studied under Maria Ouspenskaya. After a few years as a telephone operator, appearances on the stage and radio, she began playing in movies in the 1940s. At times she played the domineering hussy and at times she was a respectable leading lady.
**Selected Films:** *All-American Co-Ed* (41), *Force of Evil* (48), *The Fighting Kentuckian* (49), *Little Big Horn* (51), *The Jungle* (52), *Trouble Along the Way* (53), *No Man's Woman* (55), *The Killing* (56), *Day of the Bad Man* (58), *Paradise Alley* (62), *Critic's Choice* (63), *Bedtime Story* (64), *Support Your Local Gunfighter* (71), *The Outfit* (74), *Freaky Friday* (77).

## WINFIELD, Paul (1941- )

This black leading man was born Paul Edward Winfield in Los Angeles, California, and was educated at the University of Portland, Stanford University, Los Angeles City College, The University of California, Los Angeles, The University of Hawaii and the University of California, Santa Barbara. He began his Hollywood career in the 1960s, and has often been seen on television, being nominated for an Emmy Award for *King* (78) and *Roots II* (80). He also was nominated for an Academy Award for his work in *Sounder* (72).
**Selected Films:** *The Lost Man* (69), *RPM* (70), *Brother John* (71), *Sounder* (72), *Gordon's War* (73), *Conrack* (74), *Huckleberry Finn* (74), *Hustle* (75), *Damnation Alley* (77), *Twilight's Last Gleaming* (77), *A Hero Ain't Nothin' But a Sandwich* (78), *Carbon Copy* (81), *Star Trek II: The Wrath of Khan* (82), *On the Run* (82), *Death Before Dishonor* (87).

## WINGER, Debra (1955- )

Winger was born in Cleveland, Ohio, but moved to California when she was six. After graduating from high school, she moved to Israel for a time, but returned home. In 1973, an auto accident left her partially paralyzed and blind, and when she recovered, she pursued an acting career, becoming one of the hottest young stars of the 1980s. Her first big break came when she appeared opposite John Travolta in *Urban Cowboy* (80), in which she was vulnerable and appealing. She then replaced Raquel Welch in *Cannery Row* (82). Her next triumph was the immensely successful *An Officer and a Gentleman* (82), and she was nominated for an Academy Award for her role in *Terms of Endearment* (83). She married actor Timothy Hutton in 1986.
**Selected Films:** *Urban Cowboy* (80), *Cannery Row* (82), *An Officer and a Gentleman* (82), *Terms of Endearment* (83), *Legal Eagles* (86), *Black Widow* (87).

*Debra Winger in* An Officer and A Gentleman *(82).*

## WINKLER, Henry (1945- )

Born in New York City, he was the son of a lumber company executive and was educated at Emerson College and the Yale Drama School. He started his show business career in stock and on the New York stage. In the 1970s he started on television, and became a star as The Fonz in the TV series *Happy Days*. Winkler has also made a few movies.
**Selected Films:** *Crazy Joe* (74), *The Lords of Flatbush* (74), *The One and Only* (78), *Night Shift* (82).

## WINNINGER, Charles (1884-1969)

This chubby, lovable character actor was born Karl Winninger in Athens, Wisconsin, the son of show people. At nine he dropped out of school to join the family act in vaudeville. He played stock and repertory, and made it to Broadway in 1912. His movie career started in short comedies in 1915 and by the 1920s he was in feature pictures. He was the original Cap'n Andy in *Show Boat* on Broadway in 1927. In 1930 he settled in Hollywood, and for the rest of his career was a genial character actor.
**Selected Films:** *Pied Piper Malone* (24), *Summer Bachelors* (26), *Soup to Nuts* (30), *The Sin of Madelon Claudet* (31), *Show Boat* (36), *Three Smart Girls* (36), *Nothing Sacred* (37), *Babes in Arms* (39), *Destry Rides Again* (39), *Ziegfeld Girl* (41), *Coney Island* (43), *State Fair* (45), *Give My Regards to Broadway* (48), *Father Is a Bachelor* (50), *The Sun Shines Bright* (53), *Raymie* (60), *The Miracle of Santa's White Reindeer* (63).

## WINSLOW, George 'Foghorn' (1946- )

This throaty popular child actor was born George Wentzlaff in Los Angeles, California. His only asset was his unusual bullfrog voice. Winslow was introduced on Art Linkletter's radio show *People Are Funny*, and he was a hit in small roles in a few films before retiring at the age of 12.
**Selected Films:** *Room for One More* (52), *My Pal Gus* (52), *Gentlemen Prefer Blondes* (53), *Mr Scoutmaster* (53), *The Rocketman* (54), *Artists and Models* (56), *An Affair to Remember* (57), *Wild Heritage* (58).

## WINTERS, Jonathan (1925- )

This chubby, oval-faced comedian was born in Dayton, Ohio, and educated at Kenyon College. His off-the-wall repertoire includes mimicry, characterizations and madcap impersonations. He began his show business career on radio, then was extremely popular on television in variety spots and talk shows. He also has made a few movies.
**Selected Films:** *It's a Mad Mad Mad Mad World* (63), *The Loved One* (65), *The Russians Are Coming! The Russians Are Coming!* (66), *Penelope* (66), *Oh Dad, Poor Dad – Mama's Hung You in the Closet and I'm Feeling So Sad* (67), *Eight on the Lam* (67), *Viva Max!* (69), *The Fish That Saved Pittsburgh* (79).

## WINTERS, Roland (1904- )

Born in Boston, Massachusetts, this heavily-built character actor started out on stage and radio. He was brought to Hollywood to become the third interpreter of the character of Charlie Chan, the Chinese detective, in six movies, and he went on to play in many other films.
**Selected Films:** *The Chinese Ring* (47), *Cry of the City* (48), *The Feathered Serpent* (49), *Captain Carey, USA* (50), *So Big* (53), *Bigger Than Life* (56), *Top Secret Affair* (57), *Never Steal Anything Small* (59), *Cash McCall* (60), *Blue Hawaii* (61), *Loving* (70).

## WINTERS, Shelley (1922- )

Winters today is heavy, dynamic, colorful and exciting. When she started in films she was thin, dynamic, colorful and exciting – one of the sexiest actresses in Hollywood. Born Shirley Schrift in St Louis, Missouri, she grew up in Brooklyn, New York. Her first important Broadway plays were *The Night Before Christmas* and *Rosalinda*, and because of them she got a contract from Columbia Pictures, appearing in her first film, *What a Woman!* in 1943. Winters was usually cast as a tawdry, stupid victim of men. Her finest variation of this theme was when she bravely shed her glamor to appear in *A Place in the Sun* (51), for which she was nominated for an Oscar. She won Academy Awards for Best Supporting Actress for *The Diary of Anne Frank* (59) and *A Patch of Blue* (65). Today the mercurial outspoken Winters plays matronly roles with zest.

*Shelley Long and Henry Winkler in* Night Shift *(82).*

Two of her husbands were actors – Vittorio Gassman and Anthony Franciosa.
**Selected Films:** *What a Woman!* (43), *Knickerbocker Holiday* (44), *Cover Girl* (44), *A Double Life* (48), *A Place in the Sun* (51), *The Big Knife* (55), *The Night of the Hunter* (55), *The Diary of Anne Frank* (59), *Lolita* (62), *A Patch of Blue* (65), *Alfie* (66), *Harper* (66), *What's the Matter With Helen?* (70), *The Poseidon Adventure* (72), *Pete's Dragon* (77), *S.O.B.* (81).

*Shelley Winters in* A Place in the Sun *(51).*

## WINWOOD, Estelle (1883-1984)

This character actress, so famous for her eccentric fluttery roles, was born Estelle Goodwin in Lee, England. She was a 75-year veteran of show business, on stage and on screen.
**Selected Films:** *The House of Trent* (33), *Quality Street* (37), *The Glass Slipper* (55), *The Swan* (56), *This Happy Feeling* (58), *Alive and Kicking* (59), *The Misfits* (61), *The Notorious Landlady* (62), *Dead Ringer* (64), *Camelot* (67), *The Producers* (68), *Jenny* (70), *Murder by Death* (76).

## WISEMAN, Joseph (1918- )

Primarily a stage actor, Wiseman was born in Montreal, Quebec, and made his stage debut in the United States in the mid-1930s. He made his film debut in *With These Hands* (50), and is often cast as a villain, most notably as the cerebral evildoer in the first James Bond movie, *Dr No* (62).
**Selected Films:** *With These Hands* (50), *Detective Story* (51), *Viva Zapata!* (52), *The Silver Chalice* (54), *The Garment Jungle* (57), *Dr No* (62), *The Night They Raided Minsky's* (68), *Lawman* (71), *Journey into Fear* (75), *The Betsy* (78), *Jaguar Lives* (79).

## WITHERS, Googie (1917- )

Born Georgette Lizette Withers in Karachi, India, she was convent-educated in England. Withers first appeared on the British stage in 1929, eventually becoming a leading lady. She switched to the screen in 1934, debuting in *Girl in the Crowd*. In the 1950s she moved to Australia with her husband John McCallum.
**Selected Films:** *Girl in the Crowd* (34), *Accused* (36), *The Lady Vanishes* (38), *Bulldog Sees It Through* (40), *Jeannie* (41), *One of Our Aircraft Is Missing* (42), *On Approval* (44), *Dead of Night* (45), *Miranda* (48), *Once Upon a Dream* (49), *Night and the City* (50), *White Corridors* (51), *Devil on Horseback* (54), *Port of Escape* (56), *The Nickel Queeen* (70).

## WITHERS, Grant (1904-1959)

Born Granville G Withers in Pueblo, Colorado, he became a fine general purpose actor on over 200 movies, beginning in mid-1920s. He had been a salesman and a newspaper reporter before turning to acting, and in the mid-1940s he was generally seen in low-budget pictures and some serials. In 1930s he eloped to Yuma, Arizona, with the 17-year-old Loretta Young, but the marriage was annulled the next year. Withers committed suicide by taking an overdose of sleeping pills.
**Selected Films:** *The Gentle Cyclone* (26), *Bringing Up Father* (28), *Saturday's Children* (29), *Swanee River* (31), *Secrets of Wu Sin* (33), *Hold 'Em Yale* (35), *Paradise Express* (37), *Navy Secrets* (39), *Billy the Kid* (41), *In Old Oklahoma* (43), *The Fighting Seabees* (44), *My Darling Clementine* (46), *Fort Apache* (48), *Rio Grande* (50), *Run for Cover* (55), *I, Mobster* (58).

## WITHERS, Jane (1926- )

This mischievous child star of the 1930s was born in Atlanta, Georgia, and was performing on radio and in vaudeville by the time she was four. She debuted on screen when she was six, in *Handle With Care* (32), becoming one of Hollywood's top child stars. Her career went downhill when she became a teenager and she retired from films in 1947. Occasionally seen in character parts, she is best known today for the commercials in which she played Josephine the Plumber.

**Selected Films:** *Handle With Care* (32), *Bright Eyes* (34), *The Farmer Takes a Wife* (35), *Pepper* (36), *The Holy Terror* (37), *Rascals* (38), *Boy Friend* (39), *The Girl from Avenue A* (40), *Her First Beau* (41), *The Mad Martindales* (42), *The North Star* (43), *My Best Gal* (44), *Danger Street* (47), *Giant* (56), *The Right Approach* (61), *Captain Newman, MD* (64).

## WITHERSPOON, Cora (1890-1957)

This character comedienne, often seen as a shrewish wife, was born in New Orleans, Louisiana. She began her stage career in 1910 and her screen career in the early 1930s. Witherspoon's most memorable role was as the domineering wife of W C Fields in *The Bank Dick* (40).

**Selected Films:** *Night Angel* (31), *Midnight* (34), *Libeled Lady* (36), *Madame X* (37), *Marie Antoinette* (38), *Dark Victory* (39), *The Women* (39), *The Bank Dick* (40), *I've Always Loved You* (46), *The Mating Season* (51), *Just for You* (52).

## WOLFE, Ian (1896- )

Wolfe was born in Canton, Illinois, and appeared in many plays before debuting in movies in the 1930s. Usually he was cast as a coward or a greedy human being.

**Selected Films:** *The Barretts of Wimpole Street* (34), *Mutiny on the Bounty* (35), *On Borrowed Time* (39), *Saboteur* (42), *The Moon Is Down* (43), *Confidential Agent* (45), *Bedlam* (46), *Johnny Belinda* (48), *A Place in the Sun* (51), *Julius Caesar* (53), *Seven Brides for Seven Brothers* (54), *Rebel Without a Cause* (55), *Witness for the Prosecution* (58), *The Lost World* (60), *Games* (67), *The Fortune* (75), *Reds* (81).

## WOLFIT, Donald (1902-1968)

Born in Newark-on-Trent, England, he began his distinguished stage career in 1920. Wolfit was knighted in 1957 for his missionary work in bringing Shakespearean plays to the provinces during his innumerable tours with his own acting troupe. This towering actor did make a few movies, most notably in the title role of *Svengali* (54).

**Selected Films:** *Death at Broadcasting House* (34), *Drake of England* (35), *The Pickwick Papers* (53), *Svengali* (54), *Guilty* (56), *I Accuse!* (58), *Room at the Top* (59), *Lawrence of Arabia* (62), *Becket* (64), *Life at the Top* (65), *The Charge of the Light Brigade* (68).

## WOLHEIM, Louis (1880-1931)

Wolheim, who seemed to specialize in brutish roles, was born in New York City, and earned an engineering degree from Cornell University, where he stayed on for six years as a mathematics instructor. He then went to New York to appear on the stage, and made his screen debut in a couple of serials. His first feature film was *Dr Jekyll and Mr Hyde* (20), which starred John Barrymore. Wolheim's most memorable role was as a German soldier, Katczinsky, in *All Quiet on the Western Front* (30).

**Selected Films:** *Dr Jekyll and Mr Hyde* (20), *Orphans of the Storm* (21), *Little Old New York* (23), *America* (24), *Sorrell and Son* (27), *Two Arabian Knights* (27), *Tempest* (28), *Condemned* (29), *All Quiet on the Western Front* (30), *The Sin Ship* (31).

## WONG, Anna May (1907-1961)

One of the first stars of Chinese descent, she was born Wong Liu Tsong in California, in the Chinatown section of Los Angeles. At the age of 12 she was in movies working as an extra, working her way up into featured roles. Her big break came in *The Thief of Bagdad* (24), in which she played a slave girl. She became a star in the late 1920s, playing mysterious Oriental seductresses. In 1929 she went to Europe, where she lectured and starred in British and German pictures and appeared on stage with Laurence Olivier in *Circle of Chalk*. She semi-retired in 1942 after her career had gone downhill.

**Selected Films:** *Red Lantern* (19), *Shame* (21), *Drifting* (23), *The Thief of Bagdad* (24), *A Trip to Chinatown* (26), *Mr Wu* (27), *The Crimson City* (28), *The Flame of Love* (30), *Daughter of the Dragon* (31), *Shanghai Express* (32), *Tiger Bay* (33), *Limehouse Blues* (34), *King of Chinatown* (39), *Lady from Chungking* (42), *Impact* (49), *Portrait in Black* (60).

## WOOD, John (1930- )

Wood is best known for his work onstage in his native Britain (with the Old Vic among others) and on Broadway (where he won a Tony for his performance in*Travesties*). He has played supporting roles, usually as thoughtful men or academics in occasional films since the early 1970s.

**Selected Films:** *Nicholas and Alexandra* (72), *Slaughterhouse Five* (72), *Somebody Killed Her Husband* (77), *War Games* (83), *The Purple Rose of Cairo* (85), *Ladyhawke* (85), *Lady Jane* (86), *Jumpin' Jack Flash* (86).

## WOOD, Natalie (1938-1981)

Everyone remembers little Natalie Wood, the sulky-sweet child star of *Miracle on 34th Street* (47). Unlike many other child stars, Wood grew up, playing the stripper Gypsy Rose Lee in *Gypsy* (62). She was born Natasha Gurdin in San Francisco,

*Natalie Wood and James Dean in* Rebel Without a Cause *(55).*

California, a daughter of Russian immigrants. Her mother was a ballerina, and both mother and daughter got bit parts in *Happy Land* (43), when she was four years old. Then she threatened to upstage co-star Orson Welles in *Tomorrow is Forever* (46), when she was only eight. She made many movies in the 1940s and 1950s, and finally broke into adult roles in *Rebel Without a Cause* (55), opposite the legendary James Dean. Wood married, divorced and remarried actor Robert Wagner, and her tragic death from drowning was front-page news.
**Selected Films:** *Happy Land* (43), *Tomorrow Is Forever* (46), *Miracle on 34th Street* (47), *Rebel Without a Cause* (55), *Marjorie Morningstar* (58), *Splendor in the Grass* (61), *West Side Story* (61), *Love with the Proper Stranger* (64), *Inside Daisy Clover* (66), *Bob & Carol & Ted & Alice* (69), *Meteor* (79), *Brainstorm* (83).

## WOOD, Peggy (1892-1978)

This distinguished character actress was born in Brooklyn, New York. When she was eight years old she began taking singing lessons, and by the time she was 18 she was in the chorus of *Naughty Marietta* on Broadway. She became a tremendously versatile actress, playing in musicals and in Shakespeare. She began her screen career in *Almost a Husband* (19), and was nominated for an Academy Award for Best Supporting Actress for her role as the Mother Abbess in *The Sound of Music* (65). Wood was also on television, playing the title role in the *Mama* series.
**Selected Films:** *Almost a Husband* (19), *Wonder of Women* (29), *Handy Andy* (34), *Jalna* (35), *A Star Is Born* (37), *The Magnificent Doll* (46), *Dream Girl* (48), *The Story of Ruth* (60), *The Sound of Music* (65).

## WOODS, Donald (1904- )

Born Ralph L Zink in Brandon, Canada, he first appeared on the stage and then went to Hollywood in the early 1930s. Woods was the lead in many B pictures and second leads in more ambitious films. In the 1950s he turned more and more to the stage and television, and also became a real estate broker.
**Selected Films:** *As the Earth Turns* (34), *Sweet Adeline* (35), *A Tale of Two Cities* (35), *The Story of Louis Pasteur* (36), *The Black Doll* (38), *Mexican Spitfire* (40), *Watch on the Rhine* (43), *The Bridge of San Luis Rey* (44), *Wonder Man* (45), *Night and Day* (46), *Barbary Pirate* (49), *The Beast from 20,000 Fathoms* (53), *True Grit* (69).

## WOODS, James (1947- )

Woods was born in Vernal, Utah, and attended the Massachusetts Institute of Technology, although he left college to pursue an acting career. He began off-Broadway, where he appeared in such fine plays as *Borstal Boy*, *Conduct Unbecoming*, *The Trial of the Catonsville Nine* and *Moonchildren*. In addition to his many screen appearances, he has been in several television movies. He received a nomination for Best Actor for his performance as the venal reporter in *Salvador* (86).
**Selected Films:** *Visitors* (71), *The Way We Were* (73), *Alex and the Gypsy* (76), *The Choirboys* (78), *The Black Marble* (80), *Eyewitness* (81), *Fast Walking* (81), *Videodrome* (82), *Against All Odds* (84), *Once Upon a Time in America* (84), *Joshua, Then and Now* (85), *Salvador* (86).

## WOODWARD, Edward (1930- )

Woodward was born in Croydon, Surrey, England, and studied at the Royal Academy of Dramatic Art, later appearing in the Farnham Repertory. Before his acting career began, he was a worker in the office of a sanitary engineer. In pictures he is most often cast in supporting roles, and he is most effective in thrillers. Woodward also sings. He has cut eleven LP records and has received one gold record. A prolific television performer, he currently appears in the series *The Equalizer*.
**Selected Films:** *Where There's a Will* (55), *Becket* (64), *The File of the Golden Goose* (69), *Sitting Target* (72), *The Wicker Man* (73), *Stand Up Virgin Soldiers* (77), *Breaker Morant* (80), *Who Dares Wins* (82).

## WOODWARD, Joanne (1930- )

Woodward is far more than simply the wife of superstar Paul Newman. She is an outstanding talent, magnificent in dramas, clever in comedy, with an eye for off-beat roles. She is also politically active in liberal causes. Born in Thomasville, Georgia, she attended Lousiana State University and studied acting in New York at the Actors Studio. Her first job on Broadway was as an understudy in *Picnic* (53), where she met Newman. She made her screen debut in *Count Three and Pray* (55), in which she played a strong-willed orphan

girl in post-Civil War days. Her first big Hollywood splash came in *The Three Faces of Eve* (57), for which she won the Academy Award for Best Actress. Curiously, after *From the Terrace* (60), she didn't get a really good part until *A Fine Madness* (66). Her finest film performance, under her husband's direction, was *Rachel, Rachel* (68), for which she won the New York Film Critics' Award. Newman also directed her – and their daughter – in *The Effect of Gamma Rays on Man-in-the-Moon Marigolds* (72), for which she won the Cannes Film Festival Award for Best Actress. Woodward also won an Emmy for Best Actress for her performance in the television movie *See How She Runs*.
**Selected Films:** *Count Three and Pray* (55), *A Kiss Before Dying* (56), *The Three Faces of Eve* (57), *No Down Payment* (57), *The Long Hot Summer* (58), *The Sound and the Fury* (59), *From the Terrace* (60), *The Stripper* (63), *A Big Hand for the Little Lady* (66), *A Fine Madness* (66), *Rachel, Rachel* (68), *They Might Be Giants* (71), *The Effect of Gamma Rays on Man-in-the-Moon Marigolds* (72), *The Drowning Pool* (75), *The End* (78), *The Glass Menagerie* (87).

## WOOLLEY, Monte (1888-1963)

Born Edgar Montillion Woolley in New York City, he studied at both Yale University and Harvard College and returned to Yale to become an English instructor and drama coach. He gave up the college life in 1936 to take up acting on Broadway and made his screen debut in 1937. Most often cast as an irascible character, he was most famous for his portrayal of Sheridan Whiteside, both on stage and on screen, in *The Man Who Came to Dinner*. Woolley was nominated for an Academy Award for Best Actor for *The Pied Piper* (42), and for Best Supporting Actor for *Since You Went Away* (44).
**Selected Films:** *Live, Love and Learn* (37), *Nothing Sacred* (37), *Three Comrades* (38), *Midnight* (39), *The Man Who Came to Dinner* (42), *The Pied Piper* (42), *Holy Matrimony* (43), *Since You Went Away* (44), *Molly and Me* (45), *Night and Day* (46), *The Bishop's Wife* (47), *As Young As You Feel* (51), *Kismet* (55).

## WOOLSEY, Robert (1889-1938)

Woolsey was born in Oakland, California, and his first important job was as a jockey. Forced to retire early because of injuries sustained when he was thrown by a horse, he tried odd jobs and eventually turned to the theater, later reaching Broadway. In 1927 this comedian was teamed up with Burt Wheeler by Florenz Ziegfeld, and the funny duo starred in the Ziegfeld musical *Rio Rita*. The two went to Hollywood to appear in the 1929 screen version of the play, stayed together, and starred in vaudeville and several comedy movies.
**Selected Films** (alone): *Everything's Rosie* (31).
(With Wheeler): *Rio Rita* (29), *The Cuckoos* (30), *Cracked Nuts* (31), *Girl Crazy* (32), *Diplomaniacs* (33), *Kentucky Kernels* (34), *The Nitwits* (35), *Mummy's Boys* (36), *High Flyers* (37).

## WORTH, Irene (1916- )

Primarily a stage actress, she was born in Nebraska and educated at the University of California, Los Angeles. She made her Broadway debut in *The Two Mrs Carrolls* (43), and later went to England where she appeared with the Old Vic Company. In the 1960s she was a member of the Royal Shakespeare Company. Worth has appeared in scores of British plays, on television, and in a few movies. She won the British Film Award for her work in *Orders to Kill* (58).
**Selected Films:** *One Night with You* (48), *Secret People* (51), *Orders to Kill* (58), *Seven Seas to Calais* (63), *King Lear* (69), *Nicholas and Alexandra* (71), *Rich Kids* (79), *Deathtrap* (82).

## WRAY, Fay (1907- )

Born in Alberta, Canada, and raised in Los Angeles, California, She landed occasional parts in movies, beginning with *Gasoline Love* (23), and achieved stardom when Erich von Stroheim cast her as the lead in his *The Wedding March* (28). She went on to star in many films, opposite the likes of Gary Cooper, Ronald Colman, Fredric March, William Powell and Richard Arlen. Unfortunately, she will be forever remembered as the frail girl clutched in the hand of the giant gorilla in *King Kong* (33). She retired from the screen after her marriage to screen writer Robert Riskin in 1942, and after his death she made a comeback in the 1950s playing character parts.
**Selected Films:** *Gasoline Love* (23), *The Wedding March* (28), *Legion of the Condemned* (28), *The Four Feathers* (29), *The Texan* (30), *Dr X* (32), *The Most Dangerous Game* (32), *The Mystery of the Wax Museum* (33), *Vampire Bat* (33), *King Kong* (33), *Below the Sea* (33), *The Captain Hates the Sea* (34), *Murder in Greenwich Village* (37), *Wildcat Bus* (40), *The Cobweb* (55), *Crime of Passion* (57), *Dragstrip Riot* (58).

## WRIGHT, Teresa (1918- )

Born Muriel Teresa Wright in New York City, she was an apprentice at the Wharf Theater in Provincetown, Massachusetts. She arrived on Broadway in 1938 and became Martha Scott's understudy in *Our Town*, and the following year she was the ingenue in *Life With Father*, the role in which Samuel Goldwyn saw her and signed her to a contract. Wright was nominated for an Academy Award for Best Supporting Actress for her work in her very first film, *The Little Foxes* (41). In 1942 she received two nominations: for Best Actress in *The Pride of the Yankees* and for Best Supporting Actress for *Mrs Miniver*. Wright was married to novelist Niven Busch from 1942 to 1952, and semi-retired from the screen after marrying playwright Robert Anderson. Later she did some character roles in movies, but was best known for her stage work, appearing on Broadway in 1962 in *Mary,*

*Fay Wray in* King Kong *(33).*

*Mary* and acting brilliantly in the 1975 Broadway revival of *Death of a Salesman.*
**Selected Films:** *The Little Foxes* (41), *Mrs Miniver* (42), *The Pride of the Yankees* (42), *Shadow of a Doubt* (43), *The Best Years of Our Lives* (46), *Pursued* (47), *The Men* (50), *The Steel Trap* (52), *The Actress* (53), *Track of the Cat* (54), *The Restless Years* (58), *Roseland* (77), *Somewhere in Time* (79).

## WYATT, Jane (1911- )

This leading lady of the 1930s and 1940s was born in Campgaw, New Jersey, and educated at Barnard College. At the age of 19 she made her stage debut as an understudy, going on to play ingenues and leading ladies in several plays on Broadway. She arrived in Hollywood in 1934 and appeared in 30 pictures during the next 30 years, often cast as an understanding wife. During that time she continued acting in the occasional play. Most of her movies were rather routine, but she was outstanding in such better films as *Lost Horizon* (37), and *Boomerang* (47). She is probably best known for her work as Margaret Anderson, the wife in the TV series *Father Knows Best*, for which she won Emmy Awards in three successive years.
**Selected Films:** *One More River* (34), *Great Expectations* (35), *Lost Horizon* (37), *Weekend for Three* (41), *None But the Lonely Heart* (44), *Boomerang* (47), *Gentleman's Agreement* (47), *Task Force* (49), *My Blue Heaven* (50), *The Man Who Cheated Himself* (51), *Interlude* (57), *Never Too Late* (65), *Treasure of Matecumbe* (76), *Star Trek IV: The Voyage Home* (86).

## WYCHERLY, Margaret (1881-1956)

Born in London, England, this character actress was raised in the United States. For a time, beginning when she was in her teens, she played leads in Broadway plays before switching to character parts, most notably in *Tobacco Road* (33). She began her film career in 1929 in *The 13th Chair*, and was nominated for an Academy Award for Best Supporting Actress for *Sergeant York* (41).
**Selected Films:** *The 13th Chair* (29), *Midnight* (34), *Victory* (40), *Sergeant York* (41), *Random Harvest* (42), *Keeper of the Flame* (42), *The Moon Is Down* (43), *The Yearling* (46), *Forever Amber* (47), *White Heat* (49), *The President's Lady* (53).

## WYMAN, Jane (1914- )

Born Sarah Jane Fulks in St Joseph, Missouri, she and her mother spent several months in Hollywood trying to get her a job as a child actress. After they gave up, Wyman returned to school, ending up at the University of Missouri. In 1935 she became a radio singer, billing herself as Jane Durrell. The following year she signed her first studio contract with Warner Bros. and began in bit parts and in chorus lines. Then for ten years she played dumb blondes in comedies until at last her dramatic talent was recognized. The turning point was in *The Lost Weekend* (45), playing the girl friend of an alcoholic. She was nominated for an Academy Award for her work in *The Yearling* (46), and in 1948 won the Oscar for Best Actress for *Johnny Belinda*, playing a deaf-mute rape victim. She received two additional Oscar nominations: for *The Blue Veil* (52) and *Magnificent Obsession* (54). The second of her four husbands was Ronald Reagan. Wyman went on to a highly successful career in television, most notably in *Falcon Crest.*
**Selected Films:** *My Man Godfrey* (36), *Slim* (37), *Brother Rat* (38), *Tugboat Annie Sails Again* (40), *My Favorite Spy* (42), *Princess O'Rourke* (43), *The Lost Weekend* (45), *The Yearling* (46), *Johnny Belinda* (48), *The Blue Veil* (52), *Magnificent Obsession* (54), *All That Heaven Allows* (55), *Miracle in the Rain* (56), *Pollyanna* (60), *How to Commit Marriage* (69).

## WYMORE, Patrice (1926- )

Born in Miltonvale, Kansas, the daughter of a film exhibitor, she began her show business career as a child actress in tent shows, county fairs and vaudeville, in a song-and-dance act. Later she modeled, sang in night clubs and appeared in stock and on Broadway. She began her movie career in 1950, the year that she married Errol Flynn. Wymore retired from pictures in 1953. After Flynn's death in 1959, she returned to the movies for a brief time.
**Selected Films:** *Tea for Two* (50), *I'll See You in My Dreams* (51), *The Big Trees* (52), *She's Back on Broadway* (53), *The Sad Horse* (59), *Ocean's Eleven* (60), *Chamber of Horrors* (66).

## WYNN, Ed (1886-1966)

Born Isaiah Edwin Leopold in Philadelphia, Pennsylvania, he ran away from home at 15 and joined a traveling stage company as a utility boy, eventually becoming an actor. The company folded and he returned home, where he sold hats for a time. Then it was off to New York and vaudeville, where he became a successful comic before he was 18. Billed as The Perfect Fool, he appeared in several *Ziegfeld Follies*. In the 1930s he began a new career on radio, billed as The Texaco Fire Chief, but at the end of that decade he suffered several financial crises and had a nervous collapse. It seemed as if he were through, but in the 1940s he returned to Broadway and in 1949 won the first Emmy Award for Best Actor in a television series. More hard times followed in the early 1950s, but he made another comeback because of the encouragement of his son, actor Keenan Wynn, and became a dramatic character actor. He was nominated for an Academy Award for Best Supporting Actor for *The Diary of Anne Frank* (59).
**Selected Films:** *Rubber Heels* (27), *Follow the Leader* (30), *The Chief* (33), *Stage Door Canteen* (43), *The Great Man* (57), *Marjorie Morningstar* (58), *The Diary of Anne Frank* (59), *Cinderfella* (60), *The Absent-Minded Professor* (61), *Mary Poppins* (64), *That Darn Cat* (65), *The Gnome-Mobile* (67).

## WYNN, Keenan (1916-1986)

Born Francis Xavier Aloysius James Jeremiah Keenan Wynn in New York City, he made his first stage appearance when he was a few months old, when his father, the legendary comedian, Ed Wynn, interrupted a comedy routine at the Winter Garden Theater, dashed to the wings and returned to center stage carrying a blanketed bundle. 'You might as well start now,' he told the audience, 'because you'll see a lot of him from here on.' Wynn didn't really start acting until 1935, but his stage work was based on the fact that he was Ed Wynn's son, and it was years before he became one of the world's most respected character actors on screen and in television. He attended St John's Military Academy and got his early acting experience on stage at the Lakewood Summer Theater in Skowhegan, Maine, and a part in the Broadway production of *Room Service*. Then he went to radio before signing an MGM contract in the early 1940s. In Hollywood, he entered the old studio system and landed a part in *For Me and My Gal* (42). He went on to appear in more than 200 movies and 250 television shows, and was probably best remembered for playing a clowning thug in *Kiss Me Kate* (53) and as the crazed paratrooper officer who shot a Coca-Cola machine in *Dr Strangelove* (64). His only appearance with his father occurred in the classic television production of *Requiem for a Heavyweight*, in which he played the greedy fight handler for Jack Palance as the boxer, and Ed Wynn played the elderly trainer.
**Selected Films:** *For Me and My Gal* (42), *See Here, Private Hargrove* (44), *Under the Clock* (45), *The Hucksters* (47), *Annie Get Your Gun* (50), *Kiss Me Kate* (53), *A Hole in the Head* (59), *Dr Strangelove* (64), *The Americanization of Emily* (65), *The Great Race* (65), *Herbie Rides Again* (73), *Nashville* (75), *The Devil's Rain* (76), *Best Friends* (86), *Prime Risk* (86).

## WYNN, May (1930- )

She was born Donna Lee Hickey in New York City, and before she appeared in movies she was a model, a chorus girl and a singer. Her first role was as a girl named May Wynn in *The Caine Mutiny*, and she adopted the name as her own.
**Selected Films:** *The Caine Mutiny* (54), *They Rode West* (54), *Violent Men* (55).

## WYNTER, Dana (1930- )

Wynter was born Dagmar Spencer-Marcus in London, England, the daughter of a surgeon. While she was in her teens, the family moved to Rhodesia, where she enrolled as a pre-med student. But she enjoyed her work in amateur theater, and when the family returned to England in the early 1950s, she began appearing on the stage and in occasional movies. Wynter went to Hollywood in the mid-1950s and became an elegant leading lady of American pictures.
**Selected Films:** *White Corridors* (51), *The View from Pompey's Head* (55), *Invasion of the Body Snatchers* (56), *Something of Value* (57), *Fraulein* (58), *Shake Hands with the Devil* (59), *Sink the Bismark!* (60), *The List of Adrian Messenger* (63), *If He Hollers Let Him Go!* (68), *Airport* (70), *Lovers Like Us* (75).

## WYNYARD, Diana (1906-1964)

This distinguished leading lady of the British stage was born Dorothy Isobel Cox in London, England. After appearing in London's West End, she made her Broadway debut in *The Devil Passes* (32), and was given a Hollywood contract. Wynyard was nominated for an Academy Award for Best Actress for *Cavalcade* (33), and then she returned to the London stage, appearing in the occasional motion picture. Her second husband was director Carol Reed.
**Selected Films:** *Rasputin and the Empress* (33), *Cavalcade* (33), *Reunion in Vienna* (33), *One More River* (34), *The Fugitive* (39), *Gaslight* (40), *Kipps* (41), *Tom Brown's Schooldays* (51), *The Feminine Touch* (56), *Island in the Sun* (57).

## YORK, Dick (1928- )

Born Richard Allen York in Ft Wayne, Indiana, he was educated at the drama school at DePauw University. He began his show buiness career on

*Michael York in* The Last Remake of Beau Geste *(77).*

radio shows and in commercials, and appeared on stage in *Tea and Sympathy* and *Bus Stop*. York has made a few movies, but is probably most famous for playing Elizabeth Montgomery's husband on the television situation comedy, *Bewitched*.
**Selected Films:** *Three Stripes in the Sun* (55), *My Sister Eileen* (55), *Cowboy* (57), *They Came to Cordura* (59), *Inherit the Wind* (60).

## YORK, Michael (1942- )

York was born in Fulmer, England, and educated at Oxford University. The Oxford University Dramatic Society and the Dundee Repertory gave him acting experience and in the late 1960s he began appearing in films. York rose quickly to the status of leading man, at his best opposite Liza Minnelli in *Cabaret* (72).
**Selected Films:** *Accident* (67), *Romeo and Juliet* (68), *Zeppelin* (71), *Cabaret* (72), *England Made Me* (72), *Lost Horizon* (73), *The Three Musketeers* (73), *The Four Musketeers* (74), *Murder on the Orient Express* (74), *Conduct Unbecoming* (75), *The Last Remake of Beau Geste* (77), *The Riddle of the Sands* (79).

## YORK, Susannah (1941- )

Born Susannah Yolande Fletcher in London, England, she was raised in a remote Scottish village. She graduated from The Royal Academy of Dramatic Art in London and began her acting career in repertory in the provinces. York made her screen debut in 1960, playing small roles. Her first big role was in John Huston's *Freud* (62), and she achieved stardom in *Tom Jones* (63). She was nominated for an Academy Award for Best Supporting Actress for *They Shoot Horses, Don't They?* (69), and won the Best Actress Award at the Cannes Film Festival for *Images* (72).
**Selected Films:** *Tunes of Glory* (60), *The Greengage Summer* (61), *Freud* (62), *Tom Jones* (63), *A Man for All Seasons* (66), *The Killing of Sister George* (68), *They Shoot Horses, Don't They?* (69), *Zee & Co.* (71), *Images* (72), *Superman* (78), *The Awakening* (80), *Loophole* (86), *Pretty Kill* (87).

## YOUNG, Alan (1919- )

Young was born Angus Young in North Shields, England, but was raised in Canada. At the age of 13 he was on stage as a comedy monologist. Later he became a commercial artist and cartoonist while appearing on radio in Canada and the United States. After wartime service with the Canadian Navy he made his film debut in 1946 in *Margie*. He was outstanding as Androcles in *Androcles and the Lion* (53), but became most successful on television as the star of both *The Alan Young Show* and *Mr Ed*. After several years as the head of the film and broadcasting department of the Christian Science Church, he returned to the screen in the mid-1970s.
**Selected Films:** *Margie* (46), *Mr Belvedere Goes to College* (49), *Aaron Slick from Punkin Crick* (52), *Androcles and the Lion* (53), *Gentlemen Marry Brunettes* (55), *tom thumb* (58), *The Time Machine* (60), *Baker's Hawk* (76), *The Cat from Outer Space* (78).

## YOUNG, Burt (1940- )

Born in New York City, he was a boxer, a trucker and held several other jobs before turning to acting. Young had joined the Actors Studio and was in off-Broadway plays, and that led to his Hollywood career.
**Selected Films:** *Cinderella Liberty* (73), *The Gambler* (74), *Chinatown* (74), *The Killer Elite* (75), *Rocky* (76), *Twilight's Last Gleaming* (77), *The Choirboys* (77), *Convoy* (78), *Uncle Joe Shannon* (78), *All the Marbles* (81), *Rocky II* (82), *Amityville II: The Possession* (82), *Over the Brooklyn Bridge* (84), *Once Upon a Time in America* (84), *The Pope of Greenwich Village* (84), *Rocky IV* (85), *Back to School* (86).

*Susannah York in* Tom Jones *(63).*

## YOUNG, Clara Kimball (1890-1960)

This popular movie heroine of the silent screen was born Clara Kimball in Chicago, Illinois, and took the last name of Young after her marriage to director-actor James Young, whom she had met in a Salt Lake City stock company. Young made her stage debut at the age of three and began making movies with Vitagraph in 1909. By 1914 she was voted the most popular screen actress by a fan magazine. Sometimes she played comedy, but she was usually cast in dramas in mature, worldly roles. Her career took a downturn in the early 1920s when her second husband, Harry Garson, took control of her films as her producer-director. She left Hollywood for vaudeville, and returned to motion pictures in the early 1930s, playing in low-budget films as a character actress. She retired permanently in 1942.
**Selected Films:** *A Midsummer Night's Dream* (09), *Uncle Tom's Cabin* (10), *Cardinal Wolsey* (12), *Beau Brummel* (13), *Camille* (15), *Trilby* (15), *Magda* (17), *The Claw* (18), *Mid-Channel* (20), *What No Man Knows* (21), *The Worldly Madonna* (22), *Lying Wives* (25), *Kept Husbands* (31), *Probation* (32), *The Return of Chandu* (34), *His Night Out* (35), *The Frontiersman* (38), *The Roundup* (41), *Mr Celebrity* (42).

## YOUNG, Gig (1913-1978)

Young was born Byron Elsworth Barr in St Cloud, Minnesota, and raised in Washington, DC. He was offered a scholarship to the Pasadena Playhouse in California and his work there earned him a Warner Bros. contract. His first featured role was as a character, Gig Young, in *The Gay Sisters* (42), and he stopped billing himself as Byron Barr or Byron Fleming. He served with the Coast Guard in World War II, returned to Hollywood, and became type-cast as a second lead – usually in sophisticated comedies. Finally the studios found out that he could act, and he was nominated for Academy Awards for Best Supporting Actor for *Come Fill the Cup* (51) and *Teacher's Pet* (58), finally winning the Oscar for *They Shoot Horses, Don't They?* (69), in which he played the sleazy master of ceremonies for a marathon dance contest. Young's third wife was actress Elizabeth Montgomery. He died tragically, apparently shooting his fifth wife, a 31-year-old German-born actress, and then himself. Ironically, his last film was *The Game of Death* (79).
**Selected Films:** *Misbehaving Husbands* (40), *The Gay Sisters* (42), *The Woman in White* (48), *The Three Musketeers* (48), *Come Fill the Cup* (51), *The City That Never Sleeps* (53), *Teacher's Pet* (58), *The Tunnel of Love* (58), *That Touch of Mink* (62), *The Shuttered Room* (68), *They Shoot Horses, Don't They?* (69), *The Killer Elite* (75), *The Game of Death* (79).

*Gig Young in* The Tunnel of Love *(58).*

## YOUNG, Loretta (1913- )

Born Gretchen Young in Salt Lake City, Utah, Young and her two sisters grew up in Hollywood, when, in 1918, their mother opened a boarding house there. All three of the girls began working as child extras in films. When Young turned up for a bit role slated for her older sister, Polly Ann, she won the part and a contract. She was 15 years old and made her debut in *Laugh Clown Laugh* (28). By the mid-1930s she was a major star. She was ethereally, sweetly beautiful, and graceful elegance and glamorous costumes added to her allure. From 1927 to 1953, she acted in more than 90 films under such directors as Frank Capra, Orson Welles, William Wellman and John Ford, and co-starred with almost all the leading men of Hollywood's Golden Era. She married actor Grant Withers in 1930 and had the marriage annulled the following year. Rumors of love affairs with Clark Gable and Spencer Tracy aroused fan interest. Then she married advertising executive Tom Lewis in 1940. Young won the Academy Award for Best Actress for *The Farmer's Daughter* (47) and became a popular television star on *The Loretta Young Show* before retiring from acting.
**Selected Films:** *Laugh Clown Laugh* (28), *Loose Ankles* (29), *Kismet* (30), *The Devil to Pay* (30), *Life Begins* (32), *Zoo in Budapest* (33), *A Man's Castle* (33), *The House of Rothschild* (34), *The Crusaders* (35), *Clive of India* (35), *Call of the Wild* (35), *Ramona* (36), *Suez* (38), *Kentucky* (38), *The Story of Alexander Graham Bell* (39), *The Doctor Takes A Wife* (39), *A Night to Remember* (42), *Along Came Jones* (46), *The Farmer's Daughter* (47), *The Bishop's Wife* (48), *Rachel and the Stranger* (48), *Come to the Stable* (49), *Half Angel* (51), *It Happens Every Thursday* (53).

## YOUNG, Robert (1907- )

Born in Chicago, Illinois, and raised in California, Young was soothing, wholesome and kind – a debonair romantic lead at first, later an engaging on-screen husband, and finally television's favorite dad and doctor on *Father Knows Best* and

*Charles Laughton and Robert Young in* The Canterville Ghost *(44).*

*Marcus Welby, MD*. He was one of Hollywood's most durable and prolific performers, starring in over 100 movies opposite leading ladies such as Joan Crawford, Claudette Colbert, Greer Garson and, most delightfully, Dorothy McGuire. His warmth and charm brought him success even in television commercials, despite rumors of problems with alcohol and depression.
**Selected Films:** *The Sin of Madelon Claudet* (31), *Strange Interlude* (31), *The House of Rothschild* (34), *Spitfire* (34), *Secret Agent* (36), *H M Pulham, Esquire* (41), *Journey for Margaret* (42), *Claudia* (43), *The Canterville Ghost* (44), *The Enchanted Cottage* (44), *Claudia and David* (46), *Crossfire* (47), *Sitting Pretty* (48), *That Forsyte Woman* (49), *Goodbye My Fancy* (51), *The Secret of the Incas* (54).

## YOUNG, Roland (1887-1953)

This character actor was born in London, England, and educated at Sherborne College and London University, training for the stage at the Royal Academy of Dramatic Art. He made his London stage debut in 1908 and was on Broadway in 1912. Young decided to stay in the United States and served with the US Army during World War I. He made a few movies in the early 1920s, but he became a real screen personality in the 1930s and 1940s, when he often played a whimsical or ineffective character. He was nominated for an Academy Award for Best Supporting Actor for his role as the bumbling, lovable banker, Cosmo Topper, who was haunted by the Kerby ghosts in *Topper* (37).
**Selected Films:** *Sherlock Holmes* (22), *Grit* (24), *The Bishop Murder Case* (30), *New Moon* (31), *One Hour With You* (31), *Pleasure Cruise* (33), *David Copperfield* (35), *Ruggles of Red Gap* (35), *The Man Who Could Work Miracles* (36), *Topper* (37), *The Young in Heart* (38), *The Philadelphia Story* (40), *Tales of Manhattan* (42), *And Then There Were None* (45), *Bond Street* (47), *The Great Lover* (49), *Let's Dance* (50), *That Man from Tangier* (53).

## YURKA, Blanche (1887-1974)

Born Blanche Jurka in Czechoslovakia, her family moved to the United States while she was still a baby, and she was raised in St Paul, Minnesota. The family moved to New York City when she was 11, and when she was 15 she was given a scholarship to the Metropolitan Opera's school. After singing with the Met in a production of *Parsifal*, she made her Broadway debut in 1907. In the 1920s she appeared in *Hamlet* (22) opposite John Barrymore, and Ibsen's *The Wild Duck* (25). After a tremendous career on the Broadway stage, she turned to films when she was nearly 50, usually in character parts. During the 1920s she was married to actor Ian Keith.
**Selected Films:** *A Tale of Two Cities* (35), *Escape* (40), *A Night to Remember* (42), *Keeper of the Flame* (42), *The Song of Bernadette* (43), *The Bridge of San Luis Rey* (44), *The Southerner* (45), *13 Rue Madeleine* (47), *The Furies* (50), *At Sword's Point* (52), *Thunder in the Sun* (59).

# Z

## ZERBE, Anthony ( - )

Born in Long Beach, California, Zerbe attended Pomona College and then studied at the Stella Adler Theater Studio in New York City. A veteran of the United States Air Force, he appeared in many regional theaters and then was seen on Broadway in such plays as the 1981 revival of *The Little Foxes*. He was also the recipient of an Emmy for his work on the television series, *Harry-O*. Zerbe has made a few movies.
**Selected Films:** *Cool Hand Luke* (67), *Will Penny* (67), *The Omega Man* (70), *Farewell, My Lovely* (75), *The Turning Point* (77), *Who'll Stop the Rain?* (78), *The First Deadly Sin* (80), *The Dead Zone* (83).

## ZETTERLING, Mai (1925- )

This capable leading lady was born in Vasteras, Sweden, and was trained at Stockholm's Royal Dramatic Theater School. At the age of 16 she made her stage and screen debuts and her first big film role was in Alf Sjöberg's *Torment* (44), with its script by Ingmar Bergman. In 1946 she moved to England to appear in British films, and she also made some American pictures. In the 1960s she switched to being a highly-praised director.
**Selected Films:** *Lasse-Maja* (41), *Torment* (44), *Sunshine Follows Rain* (46), *Night is My Future* (48), *The Girl in the Painting* (48), *The Lost People* (49), *The Frightened Bride* (52), *Desperate Moment* (53), *Knock on Wood* (54), *Abandon Ship!* (57), *The Truth About Women* (58), *Offbeat* (61), *The Vine Bridge* (65).

## ZIMBALIST, Efrem Jr (1923- )

The son of concert violinist Efrem Zimbalist and opera singer Alma Gluck, he was born in New York City and educated at Yale University. He trained for the stage at New York's Neighborhood Playhouse, and after returning from World War II with a Purple Heart, he appeared in many plays, making his movie debut in *House of Strangers* (49). He gave up acting for a time, but returned in the late 1950s and became a star on television in the series *The FBI*.
**Selected Films:** *House of Strangers* (49), *Band of Angels* (57), *Home Before Dark* (58), *By Loved Possessed* (61), *The Chapman Report* (62), *Wait Until Dark* (67), *Airport 75* (74), *Terror Out of the Sky* (79).

## ZORINA, Vera (1917- )

This talented ballet dancer and actress was born Eva Brigitta Hartwig in Berlin, Germany, to Norwegian parents. She was a professional dancer from the age of seven, and at the age of 12 she got good notices as the first elf in the Max Reinhardt's Berlin Production of *A Midsummer Night's Dream*, in 1929. Joining the Ballet Russe in 1930, she toured England and the United States. In 1937 she was the star of the London production of the musical comedy *On Your Toes*, where Sam Goldwyn signed her to appear in the Gershwin film *The Goldwyn Follies* (38). Also in 1938 she made her Broadway debut in *I Married an Angel*, and did, indeed, get married, to George Balanchine, the legendary choreographer. After they were divorced, she married the president of Columbia Records, Goddard Lieberson. Her career went downhill in the late 1940s, and since that time she has been an opera director and music consultant.
**Selected Films:** *The Goldwyn Follies* (38), *On Your Toes* (39), *I Was an Adventuress* (40), *Louisiana Purchase* (41), *Star Spangled Rhythm* (42), *Follow the Boys* (44), *Lover Come Back* (46).

## ZUCCO, George (1886-1960)

Zucco was born in Manchester, England, and made his acting debut in Canada in 1908. He then went into vaudeville in the United States, graduating to the Broadway and London stage. He began his film career in the early 1930s and most often was cast as a master criminal, a mad scientist and an assortment of other arch-villains.
**Selected Films:** *The Dreyfuss Case* (31), *Autumn Crocus* (34), *The Man Who Could Work Miracles* (36), *Saratoga* (37), *Suez* (38), *The Adventures of Sherlock Holmes* (39), *The Mummy's Hand* (40), *The Monster and the Girl* (41), *The Mummy's Tomb* (42), *The Mad Ghoul* (43), *The Voodoo Man* (44), *House of Frankenstein* (45), *Moss Rose* (47), *The First Legion* (51).

*Eddie Albert and Vera Zorina in* On Your Toes *(39).*

# Acknowledgements

The authors and publisher would like to thank the following people who have helped in the preparation of this book: Mike Rose, who designed it, Jean Chiaramonte Martin who did the picture research and Elizabeth Miles Montgomery who edited it.

# Picture Credits

All illustrations are from the Bison Picture Library, except the following:
The Museum of Modern Art/Film Stills Archive: 13, 16, 27, 41, 57, 70, 74, 75, 76, 99 bottom, 100, 118 top, 134, 145, 154 right, 161, 164, 176, 187, 191, 192, 217, 228, 234, 239, 252, 265, 270, 314, 338, 410 right, 424, 429, 446.

National Film Archive, London: 25, 55, 79, 97, 229, 347, 441.

Phototeque: 139, 140, 141, 181, 443 bottom.